CORNELL STUDIES IN ENGLISH

VOLUME XXIII
EDITED BY
LANE COOPER

CORNELL STUDIES IN ENGLISH
XXIII

THE GREEK ANTHOLOGY IN ITALY TO THE YEAR 1800

BY

JAMES HUTTON

ASSISTANT PROFESSOR OF CLASSICS
IN CORNELL UNIVERSITY

ITHACA · NEW YORK
CORNELL UNIVERSITY PRESS
LONDON: HUMPHREY MILFORD
OXFORD UNIVERSITY PRESS
1935

The expense of publishing this volume was in part borne by a grant from the Charles Edwin Bennett Fund for Research in the Classical Languages.

TO MY MOTHER

PREFACE

The effect of Greek and Roman literature upon the modern literatures of Europe is no new theme. It is, in fact, a theme that must be endlessly worked out by those who profess to make the modern literatures the object of serious study. The purpose of the present volume is to fulfil a portion of that task.

Ten years ago I began to assemble materials on the Anthology in English literature, and became aware that the subject could not be clarified save by a study of Continental intermediaries. The modern Latin poets in particular, I saw, had been the middlemen, by whom such Greek motives as those of the epigrams had been passed on to vernacular writers, including the English. It seemed best to make substantial studies of the Anthology in Italy and France before returning to my original subject. Those studies formed in 1927 a doctoral dissertation. Since then materials have accumulated until I feel justified in publishing the present collection for Italy. Well knowing that it cannot be exhaustive, I yet think it contains enough of the existing material to be useful.

The Introduction and the Register are partly planned with a view to the ultimate publication of my collections for France and England.

In the body of the work the biographical notices that precede most of the articles are drawn from various sources, but a general reference may here be made to the works of Quadrio, Mazzuchelli, and Tiraboschi, to the *Biographie Universelle* and the *Nouvelle Biographie Générale*, and to the regional bio-bibliographies so far as these have been obtainable. I could not have done without Legrand's *Bibliographie Hellénique* nor De Nolhac's *Bibliothèque de Fulvio Orsini*. I have tried to use my authorities with caution, and hope that the inevitable margin of error may not be large.

The generous assistance rendered me from time to time by a number of friends deserves my best thanks. The book owes more than I can express to the kindness of Professor Walter L. Bullock of the University of Chicago, who has not only lent me many volumes from his valuable sixteenth-century library, but has allowed me incessantly to draw upon his learning by correspondence, and has latterly, by reading the work in manuscript or in proof, purged it of numerous errors and obscurities. Professor Harry Caplan of Cornell University has read the manuscript; and Mr. Andrew Bongiorno of Oberlin College the proofs. To the following I am indebted for aid in my difficult search for books: Professor W. S. Howell of Dartmouth College, Monsignor George Lacombe of Paris, Dr. Walter MacKellar of New York University, Professor William F. McDonald of the Ohio State University, the late Wilfred P. Mustard of Johns Hopkins, and the keepers of the Union Catalogue in the Library of Congress. From Professor James F. Mountford, formerly at Cornell, now at the University of Liverpool, I received valuable suggestions in the early stages of my work. This study was begun under the direction of Professor Lane Cooper, with his encouragement it has been carried through, and as an editor of the series in which the book appears he has devoted precious hours to the details of its publication.

Finally I desire to acknowledge the grant of three hundred dollars made to me in 1929 by the American Council of Learned Societies to aid me in making one of my journeys abroad in search of materials.

JAMES HUTTON

CONTENTS

	PAGE
PREFACE	ix
INTRODUCTION	1
1. Epigrams of the Anthology in other Greek Books. . .	2
2. The Greek Epigrams in Latin Literature	10
3. Manuscripts of the Anthology	29
4. Knowledge of the Epigrams before the *Editio Princeps* .	35
5. Editions of the Anthology; Selections	37
6. Neo-Latin Writers and the Anthology	39
7. Vernacular Writers and the Anthology	45
8. The Epigram. Observations	55
PART I. LATIN WRITERS OF THE RENAISSANCE TO *c.* 1650 .	81
APPENDIX TO PART I	273
PART II. VERNACULAR WRITERS OF THE SIXTEENTH CENTURY	291
PART III. THE SEVENTEENTH AND EIGHTEENTH CENTURIES .	345
REGISTER	443
INDEX	651

THE GREEK ANTHOLOGY IN ITALY

INTRODUCTION

The Greek epigrams have come down to us in two principal collections, the Palatine Anthology, so called from its single manuscript, *Palatinus* 23, at Heidelberg, and the Planudean Anthology, made by Maximus Planudes in 1301. Together they provide some 4150 epigrams. The two collections are ultimately derived from the same sources, and in their principal contents coincide, though the Palatine Anthology contains about 1200 epigrams not in the Planudean, and the latter about 400 not in the Palatine.

Throughout most of the period embraced by the present study only the Planudean Anthology was read. The Palatine manuscript was discovered by Salmasius in 1606/7, but was not committed to the press till near the end of the eighteenth century. While the new material it contained was well known to many scholars from manuscript *apographa*, for the ordinary reader of Greek the Anthology continued from the fifteenth to the end of the eighteenth century to mean the Planudean collection. The Palatine arrangement was finally adopted only in Friedrich Jacobs' edition of 1813-4; since then the Planudean Anthology has been disused. In a sense, therefore, we are here concerned with the whole life of the Planudean collection.[1]

For many of the epigrams contained in the Anthology, the Anthology is not the only source. Epigrams are freely quoted by Greek writers of every period, beginning with Herodotus, and, being short, are commonly quoted entire. A study of the influence of the Greek epigrams must attempt to control these subsidiary sources, and such an attempt is made in the following pages. Further, a sketch of the influence of the Greek epigrams on Latin literature has been added, since it is often a Roman copy, not the Greek original, that forms the immediate source of a modern imitation. This indispensable background I have tried to complete by as full an enumeration as I am at present able to make of the existing manuscripts of the epigrams.

[1] See below, pp. 9-10. Since we now read only the Palatine Anthology, my references are to it (*A.P.*), in the edition of Dübner, 2 vols. Paris (Didot), 1888, or in the Loeb edition with translation by W. R. Paton, 5 vols. London, 1916-20. I do not take account of the numerous Greek epigrams that happen not to be included in the Anthologies.

1. Epigrams of the Anthology in other Greek Books[1]

The influence of the Greek epigrams is properly to be observed first within the Anthology itself. A single theme would be handled by successive epigrammatists, perhaps century after century, and all the resulting versions gathered into the collections. Nothing is more characteristic of the Greek epigram. The difficulty of determining which of these versions a modern imitator may have had in mind is at times insurmountable; the Register (below, p. 443), therefore, provides cross-references between epigrams of similar content. See, for example, under *A.P.* 6.13 and 9.56.[2]

The epitaph on the Spartans who fell at Thermopylae is better known from Herodotus than as a part of the Anthology. Herodotus has 34 other pieces in common with this collection—mostly oracles.[3] The famous jest—the Chians are bad, not some bad and some good, but all bad, except Proclus, and Proclus is a Chian (*A.P.* 11.235)—is applied to the Lerians, perhaps in parody, by Phocylides as quoted by Strabo. *A.P.* 9.110 is like some verses of Archilochus; four epigrams (*A.P.* 9.50, 118; 10.36, 40) are among the *Theognidea*; two of the Homeric epigrams are in the Anthology.[4] *A.P.* 10.110 comes from Aristophanes (*Frogs* 1431).[5] Thucydides quotes *A.P.* 6.197.

Plato quotes and criticizes *A.P.* 7.153 in the *Phaedrus*; the

---

[1] References are given in the Register. I have tried to record every instance in which the epigram is reasonably complete. Notice is not taken of the few epigrams that survive in papyri, nor of fragmentary quotations like those in the *Etymologicon Magnum* and most of those in Suidas; nor are variant readings noticed, however considerable. Imitations by the epigrammatists of thoughts and phrases in other writers are not listed unless they are likely to cause difficulty in determining a modern writer's source. Most of the quotations have already been observed in Jacobs', Dübner's, or Stadtmüller's editions of the Anthology, or in Preger's *Inscriptiones Graecae Metricae*. Similarly the details of Section 2 have mainly been noted before by editors of the Anthology and of the Roman writers in question. Credit can hardly be assigned for the discovery of these parallels; the notices have in many cases descended from editor to editor since the Renaissance.

[2] Among the numerous Greek epigrams that have not come into the Anthology, four are close enough to epigrams there included to be mentioned here. They may be found in Cougny's Appendix to the Didot Anthology through references given below in the Register under *A.P.* 7.617; 9.363, 366; and 12.235.

[3] *A.P.* 6.6–8, 341, 343; 7.248, 249, 677; 9.509, 527, 703; 14.69, 78–99, 112. *Ed. pr.*, Venice, 1502, but see below, p. 99.

[4] *A.P.* 7.153 and 9.448; in the *ed. pr.* of Homer, Florence, 1488.

[5] Certain fragments of long poems are known only from the Anthology: *A.P.* 9.50 (Mimnermus), 129 (Nestor of Laranda); 10.107 (Euripides); and 11.438 (Menander). *A.P.* 10.30 and 11.62 have parallels in Euripides.

proverb, Many are the thyrsus-bearers (*A.P.* 10.106), is in the *Phaedo;* and *A.P.* 10.108 in the *Second Alcibiades.* A fragment of Antiphanes in Stobaeus resembles *A.P.* 9.127. Demosthenes quotes *A.P.* 6.197 and 9.786; Isocrates and Philemon have the sentiment of *A.P.* 11.193; Lycurgus quotes *A.P.* 7.249. The theme on which *A.P.* 9.359 closes—that the best thing is not to be born, next best to die soon—is an old one in Greek; it is what Silenus revealed to Midas (Plut., *Moral.* 115, from Aristotle, *Eudemus, frg.* 40 Rose);[1] Theognis has it (425-8); the Chorus in Sophocles' *Oedipus Coloneus* (1225) repeats it; the comic poet Alexis (*frg.* 141) gives it; and it is in the *Contest of Homer and Hesiod* (315). The epigram, with its companion-piece, *A.P.* 9.360, suited the moralizing vein of the Renaissance, and found numerous translators. Aristotle made a brief anthology of epigrams on the heroes who fell at Troy, calling it a *Peplus;* the surviving *Peplus,* whether his or not, contains *A.P.* 7.145 and 322. The first two lines of *A.P.* 11.286 are among the fragments of Menander. Theophrastus recalls *A.P.* 9.120 in one of his *Characters.*

The epigrams of Callimachus and Theocritus are fairly numerous in the Anthology, and have also been commonly printed (and translated and imitated) with their other works. Most of those of Callimachus have no other MS. authority, and were first transferred to his works by Stephanus in 1577. Many of the epigrams of Theocritus, however, appear in his MSS.; 24 of them are our concern.[2] Thirty epigrams are ascribed to Lucian in the Anthology, but being of doubtful authorship are rarely printed with his works. Those attributed to Sappho and Anacreon, however, usually accompany their other poems.

The *Amor Fugitivus,* ascribed to Moschus, occurs in the MSS. of the bucolic poets and also in the Anthology (*A.P.* 9.440). As this poem has enjoyed an immense popularity apart from the Anthology, its influence is seldom touched on in the present study. It has been the subject of several extensive papers.[3]

---

[1] Cf. Cicero, *Tusc.* 1.114.

[2] *A.P.* 6.177, 336-40; 7.262, 658-64; 9.338, 432, 433, 435-7, 598-600; 13.3. *A.P.* 9.205 and 434 occur in MSS. of Theocritus; and early editions also have *A.P.* 15.21. The first edition of Theocritus to contain many of the epigrams was that of Callierges, Rome, 1516, which has 19. The third line of *A.P.* 5.247 is adapted from Theoc. 6.17.

[3] By Mustard, *Amer. Journ. of Philol.* 30.245; by the present writer, *ibid.* 49.105; by Fucilla, *ibid.* 50.190 and in *Class. Philol.* 26.135. To the imitations before noted add: (1) Battista Guarini, son of Guarino da Verona [Barotti, *Mem. Istor. Lett. Ferrar.*

Near the beginning of the Christian era we find quotations from the epigrams in Strabo[1] and Diodorus Siculus.[2] One of the more important transmitters of the epigrams is Plutarch, who quotes them freely both in his ever popular *Lives* and in the *Moralia*. The *Moralia* first appeared in print at Venice in 1509, and the *Lives* at Florence in 1517, but translations of both had long been in circulation.[3] Dio of Prusa (*c*. 100 A. D.) quotes seven of the epigrams.[4] Aelian's *Varia Historia* contains *A.P.* 7.94; *De Natura Animalium* has the anecdotes of *A.P.* 9.10, 268, and 272.[5] *A.P.* 9.402 is in Appian's *Civil War*.[6] The orator Aristides quotes three epigrams;[7] his contemporary, Pausanias, five.[8] Dio Cassius has *A.P.* 7.704. Julius Pollux quotes *A.P.* 7.304. 1–2; the *Chrestomathia* of Proclus, which may belong to the second century, has three epigrams.[9] The *Contest of Homer and Hesiod*, in its present form dating, it seems, from the same period, makes use of seven.[10] The proverb that appears so often in Renaissance books—as vain as to try to wash an Ethiop white—is sometimes derived from *A.P.* 11.428, ascribed by Planudes to Lucian, but more often from Lucian's *Adv. Indoctum* 28: Αἰθίοπα σμήχειν ἐπιχειρῶ,[11] or from Aesop, *Fab*. 13. Aelius

---

(1793) 2.55]; (2) V. Vasolli (below, p. 208), *Virid*., f. 23ʳᵒ; Isabella Andreini, *Rime*, Milan, 1601, p. 161 (2 madrigals); (4) Fr. Cappone, *Liriche Parafrase*, Venice, 1670, p. 265; (5) G. B. Marino—besides a madrigal (*La Lira*, 1602, 2.17), Marino tastelessly modeled on these verses a poem called *Christo Smarrito* (*Lira*, 1630, pt. 3, p. 488). Cf. also the first canto of *Adone*; (6) Fr. Bracciolini, *Scherno degli Dei*, Florence, 1618, 2.54; (7) Alessandro Talenti, *Affetti Poetici*, Bergamo, 1609, p. 62; (8) Giovan-Agostino Pollinari in Gobbi's *Rime d'Alcuni ill. Aut. Viventi*, pt. 4, Venice, 1727, p. 381.

[1] *A.P.* 7.249; 9.509; 11.235; 16.27, 82. *Ed. pr.* Venice, 1516. Strabo also relates the anecdote on which *A.P.* 6.54 is founded.

[2] *A.P.* 6.343; 7.248, 249, 296, 322; 14.69; 16.27. *Ed. pr.* Basel, 1539 (Books 16–20), Geneva, 1559 (Books 1–5, 11–16). *A.P.* 6.130; 14.76, 78–9, 83, are in the *Excerpta Vaticana*, published by Mai, 1825–38.

[3] *Lives*: *A.P.* 6.50, 130; 7.247, 306, 313, 320.3–4; 10.110; 14.150; 16.26**. *Moralia*: 6.50, 197, 215; 7.39.3–4, 119, 229, 250, 347, 433, 709; 9.700; 16.120, 292, 296.

[4] *A.P.* 7.53, 153, 304.1–2, 325, 347; 14.88.1–2; 16.28.1. *Ed. pr.* Milan, 1476; but Latin translations had already been printed—see Fabricius, *Bibl. Graec. A.P.* 7.53, 304, and 347 are in the *Corinth.*, not by Dio.

[5] *Ed. pr. V.H.*, Rome, 1545; *N.A.*, Zürich, 1556.

[6] *Ed. pr.* Paris, 1551; a Latin translation was published in 1472.

[7] *A.P.* 7.248, 250, and 296. He also gives the anecdote related in *A.P.* 9.296.

[8] *A.P.* 6.130; 7.54; 9.700; 14.65; 16.26*. Pausanias gives 7.54 when describing the alleged discovery of Hesiod's bones at Orchomenos (9.38), saying that it was inscribed on the tomb. *Ed. pr.* Venice, 1516.

[9] *A.P.* 7.53; 9.448; 14.65.

[10] *A.P.* 7.3, 53, 54, 153 (with differences); 9.448; 14.88, 147. Cf. also 9.359.9–10 and *Contest* 315. *Ed. pr.* Paris, 1573.

[11] In the epigram it is not an Ethiopian, but an Indian. With *A.P.* 11.141 may be compared Lucian, *Rhet. Praec.* 18; and with *A.P.* 9.74 cf. *Nigrinus* 26.

Theon, a second-century writer on rhetoric, alludes to the sentiment of *A.P.* 10.27. *A.P.* 7.471 is quoted by Sextus Empiricus.

In the third century we meet another of the chief authorities, outside the Anthology, for the epigrams. Diogenes Laertius, before composing his *Lives of the Philosophers*, had made a great number of epigrams on eminent men, calling his collection *Pammetros*. Many of these, together with others that seemed appropriate, he later inserted in the *Lives*. The *Lives of the Philosophers* contains 82 epigrams in common with the Anthology, including many of those best known, in particular a number of the supposed compositions of Plato.[1] Down at least to the nineteenth century Diogenes was a popular classic; after the Homer of Pilatus, Traversari's Laertius was the first complete translation of a pagan Greek author to be made in Italy. Fifteen epigrams find a place in Athenaeus' *Banquet of the Sophists*.[2] Clement of Alexandria gives the anecdote of *A.P.* 6.54, and refers to *A.P.* 9.497. Philostratus, in his life of Apollonius, quotes *A.P.* 7.256; his *Amatory Epistles* recall the amatory parts of the Anthology at many points.[3] From Philostratus rather than from *A.P.* 5.91, 143, or 261, is drawn Ben Jonson's song *To Celia*. The *Heroicus* of Philostratus 'the Lemnian' contains the anecdote of *A.P.* 9.177, and alludes to *A.P.* 9.455. A description of Lysippus' statue of *Time* forms the sixth *Imago* of his imitator Callistratus; it must be compared with *A.P.* 16.275.

In the fourth and fifth centuries the epigrams are little quoted by Greek writers. Eusebius has *A.P.* 14.66 and 68; Dionysius Byzantinus *A.P.* 7.169; the orator Themistius *A.P.* 14.69. Quintus Smyrnaeus has a reminiscence of *A.P.* 7.385. There are two quotations from Heliodorus' *Aethiopica* in the Anthology (*A.P.* 9.485, 490). Julian quotes the verses that appear as *A.P.* 7.704. St John Chrysostom gives the substance of *A.P.* 7.676 in a homily on the Acts of the Apostles. Synesius alludes to the point of *A.P.* 9.455, and quotes 9.577 and 16.79. Zosimus quotes *A.P.* 7.747. Tryphon, if he is the author of the Περὶ τρόπων, quotes a part of *A.P.* 14.40. Cyril of Alexandria

---

[1] Diogenes quotes *A.P.* 5.78–80; 7.57, 60–62, 80, 83–130, 133, 153, 217, 259, 326, 508, 615–20, 669, 670, 706, 744; 9.39, 44, 496, 497, 540, 569, 596; 11.296; 14.101; 16.334. References are to Cobet's ed. Paris (Didot), 1862.

[2] *A.P.* 6.49; 7.119, 217 (with differences), 306, 345, 348, 454, 708; 10.38; 13.29; 14.40, 64; 16.19*, 27, 204. *Ed. pr.* Venice, 1514.

[3] Cf. in particular under *A.P.* 5.91, 143, 226, 261.

gives *A.P.* 7.746. The *Anthologion* of Orion contains *A.P.* 10.108.

By the end of the fourth century the poems known to us as the *Anacreontea* were probably in circulation. These little compositions, in their characteristic metre, about 60 in number, are written on themes of conviviality, and have attracted attention ever since they were first published by Stephanus in 1554. They have usually been associated with the Greek epigrams; our principal collection of them being preserved in the same MS. as the Palatine Anthology. Imitation of them has given rise to what amounts to a separate type in modern literature. Two of the *Anacreontea* (4 and 8) appear, with changes, in the Anthology (*A.P.* 11.48 and 11.47). Others sufficiently resemble certain epigrams: *A.P.* 11.54 is very like *Anac.* 7; *A.P.* 5.237 resembles *Anac.* 10; while the metamorphoses of *Anac.* 22 are further examples of those in *A.P.* 5.83, 84, and 15.35—'Would I were a rose, that you might pluck and wear me,' etc.[1] Finally, *Anac.* 6 is found only in the Anthology (*A.P.* 16.388).

At the beginning of the sixth century an anthology of a different, but very ancient, kind was put together by Joannes Stobaeus out of quotations from the philosophers and poets; he includes seven of our epigrams.[2] Aristaenetus has a passage resembling *A.P.* 5.261. Achilles Tatius quotes *A.P.* 14.34. *A.P.* 10.120 is an excerpt from Nonnos, who elsewhere has a passage resembling *A.P.* 9.136. There are epigrams in the works of Stephanus Byzantinus,[3] Joannes Lydus,[4] Hesychius of Miletus,[5] and Choeroboschus,[6] and in the *History* of Agathias, who was one of the collectors of our Anthology.[7] Choricius of Gaza quotes one epigram (*A.P.* 16.117), makes prose paraphrases of two (*A.P.* 9.394 and 730), and alludes to others (*A.P.* 9.160 and 16.135–40).

The various biographies are rich in epigrams; ten pieces that

---

[1] *A.P.* 5.83, 84 and 15.35 form one epigram in the Planudean Anthol. References to the *Anacreontea* are to the ed. of Preisendanz, Leipzig (Teubner), 1912.

[2] *A.P.* 5.5.3–4; 7.704; 9.54, 118, 359, 491; 14.101. Cf. also under *A.P.* 9.127 and 11.381. But old edd. have many others inserted, e.g., at the end of *Flor.* 10 (περὶ ἀδικίας) the following: *A.P.* 9.45; 11.165–73, 264, 289, 294, 309, 313, 325, 366, 387, 389, 391, 397, 413; 16.18.

[3] *A.P.* 7.325; 11.437; 14.65, 115.

[4] *A.P.* 10.107; 11.238, 270.

[5] *A.P.* 7.106, 115, 127, 128, 169; 9.540; 16.66.

[6] *A.P.* 14.40 in a poor prose version.

[7] *A.P.* 9.498.

appear in the Anthology are also in the several lives of Homer;[1] Tzetzes' life of Hesiod has *A.P.* 7.54; Marinus' life of Proclus, *A.P.* 7.341; Porphyry's life of Pythagoras, *A.P.* 7.746; a life of Pindar, *A.P.* 16.305; the lives of Euripides, *A.P.* 7.45 and 9.450; a life of Thucydides, *A.P.* 2.372; the lives of Plato, *A.P.* 7.313, 316.1–2; a life of Aratus, *A.P.* 9.507; and a life of Oppian, *A.P.* 16.311.

The later Byzantine writers paid much attention to the epigrams. St. Maximus (†662) quotes *A.P.* 10.58 and a version of 10.73 in his *Loci Communes*. Photius quotes *A.P.* 14.73; Constantine Porphyrogenitus five epigrams (*A.P.* 7.169; 9.641; 11.237, 238; 16.82); Codinus three (*A.P.* 7.169; 14.115; 16.66); Cedrenus *A.P.* 7.95 and 16.82. The Lexicon of Suidas gives portions of some 450 epigrams; but only 19 are quoted entire.[2] Suidas was much consulted by the early humanists. Zonares,[3] Constantine Manasses,[4] and Tzetzes,[5] all show that they used the Anthology. Eumathius Macrembolites gives *A.P.* 7.311 among his *Enigmas*. The twelfth-century romance of Nicetas Eugenianus, *Drosilla and Charicles*, contains long passages that are no more than transcriptions from the Anthology into Nicetas' cramped verses.[6] A passage from Theodore Prodromus, given in Boissonade's *Anecdota*, alludes to *A.P.* 11.430.[7] Elsewhere he quotes 11.186. Prodromus was himself a voluminous epigrammatist on sacred subjects. The *Florilegium Monacense*, printed in Meineke's Stobaeus, contains *A.P.* 9.653 and 10.120.[8]

---

[1] *A.P.* 7.3, 53, 153; 9.448; 11.442; 14.65, 66, 88; 16.292, 296. The ancient *vitae* were first printed at various times; dates of the *edd. pr.* are given in the *Praef.* of Westermann's collection, Braunschweig, 1845. My references are to this edition.

[2] *A.P.* 6.197, 239, 248.1–6, 257, 261; 7.3, 116, 120, 126, 239, 248, 249, 259, 620, 704; 9.75, 497; 14.73, 148; 16.334. *Ed. pr.* Milan, 1499.

[3] *A.P.* 7.116; 9.641, 657.

[4] *A.P.* 11.237.

[5] *A.P.* 6.213; 7.3, 54, 77, 433; 9.448; 11.442; 14.64; 16.92, 115, 120.3–4.

[6] As Nicetas was unknown to Renaissance writers, and was not printed till 1819 (J. B. Boissonade, *Nicetae Eug. Narratio Amatoria et Constantini Manassis Fragmenta*, 2 vols, Leyden), his borrowings could have little effect on European literature up to that time. I have nevertheless listed his principal debts in the Register under *A.P.* 5.3, 59, 67, 69, 83, 123, 224, 225, 229, 237, 246, 252, 253, 257, 258, 259, 273; 12.65; 16.388.

[7] An anonymous writer in the same collection expresses the thought of *A.P.* 10.73 partly in the same words.

[8] The *Violaria*, professing to be by the Empress Eudocia, but in reality a sixteenth-century compilation, contains *A.P.* 7.90, 155.1–2, 304; 9.524; 16.27, 334.

The writers of *scholia* often had recourse to the Anthology.[1]
The commentaries of David and Ammonius on Porphyry's
Isagoge contain epigrams (the former *A.P.* 7.471; 9.137, the
latter *A.P.* 7.471); and the commentary of Elias on Porphyry
and on the *Categories* of Aristotle has *A.P.* 7.741 and 9.358.

The anecdotal epigrams occasionally make use of stories that
have wide currency in other forms. Since these epigrams usually
express a moral judgment, it is difficult to separate them from
the versified fable. Very naturally, therefore modern fabulists
have on occasion gone to the epigrams for material. Their
source can only be fixed by noting verbal reminiscences or some
peculiar detail. Bianor, an epigrammatist of the Augustan
period, favored animal subjects; he has versified the fable of the
Crow and the Pitcher (*A.P.* 9.272). Plutarch, *On the Sagacity of
Animals*, tells the same story; so does Aelian, *N.A.* 2.48; a similar anecdote is related by Pliny, *H.N.* 10.60; and it forms the
twenty-seventh fable of Avianus.[2] The fables of Aesop have
eight stories in common with the Anthology;[3] Babrius has four.[4]

As with fables, so also with proverbs. If point and brevity
are essential to the epigram, then the proverb is an epigram.
It will be seen how useful Erasmus found the Greek epigrams
for his *Adagia*. The second part of the tenth book of the Palatine Anthology is almost a book of proverbs—two of its epigrams are simply well-known aphorisms (*A.P.* 10.32 and 106),
which naturally appear elsewhere in Greek.[5] Zenobius (*Prov.*

---

[1] Olympiodorus on Plato has *A.P.* 6.1; Eustathius on the *Iliad: A.P.* 7.145, 311;
9.190; 10.43; 11.437, and, on Dionysius Perieg., *A.P.* 9.509. Demetrius Triclinius on
Sophocles: *A.P.* 7.311; Melampus on Dionysius Thrax: *A.P.* 15.21.1-2; Xiphilinus on
Dio: *A.P.* 9.402. The *Schol. Venet.* on the *Iliad* contain *A.P.* 9.387; *schol.* on Pindar:
A.P. 6.214; on Euripides: *A.P.* 14.64, 67; on Aristophanes: *A.P.* 9.75 and 16.27; on
Plato: *A.P.* 9.700; on Theocritus: *A.P.* 14.73; on Aristides' *Panath.: A.P.* 7.150, 253,
257, 296; 16.6*; on Aristides' *Milt. A.P.* 7.77. The *Schol. Vat.* on Dionysius Thrax transmit *A.P.* 6.6; 7.471; 9.684; 11.442; *schol.* on Hermogenes: *A.P.* 7.259; on Tzetzes'
Chil.: A.P. 9.387; on Dio of Prusa: *A.P.* 5.83 and 84. *A.P.* 14.64 (riddle of the Sphinx)
occurs in mss. of Sophocles; *A.P.* 9.357, 358, and 366 in mss. of Plato; and similarly
others in various mss. Proclus on Plato, *Resp.*, has *A.P.* 10.108.
[2] It was carried on by Avianus' imitators—the author of the *Novus Avianus* (*c.*
1100 A.D.), and the two metrical epitomizers, described by Hervieux, *Les Fabulistes
Latins*, Paris, 1894, 2.443, 486, and 497.
[3] *A.P.* 9.19, 44, 47, 75, and 87 (cf. Dio of Prusa 12.7; 72.14), 431; 11.428; 16.187. I
refer to Halm's edition, Leipzig, 1884. Aesop, *Fab.* 29 in old edd. (De Furia, 1810, p. 15)
puts *A.P.* 11.348 into prose (Didot Anthol. 2.388).
[4] *A.P.* 9.3, 19, 75; 16.187. References are to Crusius' ed., Leipzig, 1897.
[5] 'There's many a slip 'twixt the cup and the lip.' 'Many are the thyrsus-bearers, but
few the initiated.' The occurrences of these two proverbs are listed by Leutsch and
Schneidewin, *Paroemiographi Graeci* 1.148 (*A.P.* 10.32) and 1.151 (*A.P.* 10.106).

6.22) has *A.P.* 13.29. *A.P.* 11.381 is likewise an old saying, ascribed to Hipponax. The collectors of proverbs, Apostolios and Arsenios, though Greeks, already belong to the Italian Renaissance, and are mentioned below among the Italians.[1]

What we know as the Greek Anthology is a product of Constantinople. The foundation was laid by Meleager, a Syrian Greek, who gathered his *Garland* (Στέφανος), probably at Cos, in the early part of the first century before Christ. A new collection appeared about a hundred years later in the *Garland* of Philippus of Thessalonica. A third Anthology ('Ανθολόγιον), so-called for the first time, was made in the time of Hadrian by the grammarian Diogenian. These, had they survived, would present an appearance quite unlike our Anthology; for they were arranged not by subject or type, in several books, but alphabetically, the epigrams being grouped by the first letter of the first word. A little later than Diogenian, Strato of Sardis put together his Μοῦσα Παιδική. Finally Agathias of Myrina, a well-known literary man of Justinian's time, provided a new anthology in his *Cycle* (Κύκλος), including his own and his friends' epigrams as well as earlier work, and arranging it on the familiar division by subjects.

All these collections persisted in some form, probably less than complete, until the end of the ninth century A.D. At that time Constantine Cephalas, following the scheme of Agathias, digested the contents of all, together with other epigrammatic material,[2] into one great Anthology, divided into at least four books—amatory epigrams, votive epigrams, epitaphs, and descriptive epigrams. Other smaller selections were made both before and after the great *corpus* of Cephalas, some of them

---

[1] A number of our epigrams have been preserved on the monuments. Though this circumstance played little part in their later influence, a list of them follows for the sake of completeness; certain of them have but a few letters remaining, and have only been identified by the clever work of scholars. *A.P.* 6.138 = Kaibel 758; 6.144 = Geffcken 63; 6.343 = Kaibel 748; 7.164 = Kaibel 248; 7.245 = Kaibel 27; 7.344 cf. *C.I.G.* 2168; 7.451 cf. *C.I.G.* 6276 (7–8); 7.740 is imitated in Kaibel 298; 9.524 (1–3, 5, 15) = *C.I.G.* 38; 9.704 = Kaibel 889b; 10.111 = Kaibel 1116; 11.8 resembles Geffcken 209; 11.38 (5–6) = *C.I.G.* 7298 (on a gem); 13.16 = Geffcken 129; 16.340 = Kaibel 935. See also Kaibel's Index vii. *A.P.* 7.15 is said to have been seen on a stone at Pergamum by Jucundus (= *C.I.G.* 3555).
For Greek epigrams inscribed in Italy and Gaul see below, p. 13, n. 3.

[2] Besides what he had from the anthologies, he probably used separate collections for several writers not included in them, as Leonidas of Alexandria, Rufinus, Palladas, and others. He also added pieces from Plutarch, Diogenes Laertius, and the like, though he probably found them already excerpted by others. We know he added some newly-collected inscriptions. (Cf. Waltz, *Anth. Gr.* 1.xxviii.)

probably for the use of schools.[1] About 980 A.D. there was put
together our Palatine Anthology, which is, as Waltz says, a
'revised and augmented edition' of Cephalas.[2]

In somewhat varied forms the Anthology of Cephalas seems
to have served for about three centuries. In 1301 a new edition
of the epigrams was prepared by Maximus Planudes. He appears to have employed good MSS. of the collection of Cephalas,
but not our Palatine MS. It was the Anthology of Planudes that
was in vogue among the Greeks who came to Italy about a
hundred years later, and this collection, therefore, was first
committed to the press (1494). It was called Ἀνθολογία διαφόρων
ἐπιγραμμάτων παλαιῶν, in Latin *Florilegium diversorum epigrammatum veterum*.[3]

2. The Greek Epigrams in Latin Literature

Many of the Greek epigrammatists lived in Rome; their
themes are drawn from the common Graeco-Roman life; while
Greek epigrams passed for current coin in Roman conversation,
Romans decorated their houses with scenes from the Anthology,
and borrowed its epitaphs for their tombs. In literature the
first that can be shown to have employed our epigrams as
models are the poets of the generation just before Cicero—the
circle of Q. Lutatius Catulus.[4] The few remaining epigrams of
Aedituus, Catulus, and Licinus are almost all preserved in one
page of Gellius (*N.A.* 19.9.14). At a birthday feast were sung
some verses of 'Anacreon,' known to us from the Anthology

---

[1] See below, p. 32.

[2] It contains fifteen books, to which Jacobs added a sixteenth consisting of epi-
grams from the Planudean Anthology not found in the Palatine. The contents of the
Anthologia Palatina are: Book 1, Christian epigrams; Book 2, Description of the statues
in the public gymnasium called Zeuxippus; Book 3, Inscriptions from Cyzicus; Book
4, The Proems of Meleager, Philippus, and Agathias; Book 5, Amatory epigrams;
Book 6, Votive epigrams; Book 7, Epitaphs; Book 8, Epigrams by St. Gregory the
Theologian; Book 9, Epideictic epigrams; Book 10, Hortatory epigrams; Book 11,
Convivial and satirical epigrams; Book 12, Strato's Μοῦσα Παιδική; Book 13, Epigrams
in various metres; Book 14, Riddles and oracles; Book 15, Miscellanea; [Book 16, The
Planudean Appendix.]

[3] The *Anthologia Planudea* is arranged in seven books: 1, Descriptive and epideictic
epigrams; 2, Satirical epigrams; 3, Epitaphs; 4, Epigrams on works of art; 5, Description of the Zeuxippus, and inscriptions from the Hippodrome in Constantinople; 6,
Votive epigrams; 7, Amatory epigrams. Planudes subdivided his seven books into chapters of varying length; he professedly omitted much that seemed indecent, and even
altered many of the poems that he retained. He has, in all, only about 2500 pieces,
while the Palatine collection has some 3700.

[4] Their epigrams are discussed by Büttner, *Porcius Licinus und der Litterarische
Kreis des Q. Lutatius Catulus*, Leipzig, 1893, cap. 9.

(*A.P.* 11.48); and a question was raised as to the relative merits of the Greek and Latin amatory lyric. Thereupon one of the guests chanted four old Latin epigrams which he thought superior to the Greek. Yet every one of them depends on a Greek reminiscence. The first, an epigram by Aedituus, recalls the φαίνεταί μοι of Sappho; the second, also by Aedituus, employs the conceit of an epigram by Callimachus (*A.P.* 9.15)—an epigram that may also be the original of the third set of verses sung, those of Licinus.[1] The last epigram quoted, by Catulus, has behind it another epigram of Callimachus (*A.P.* 12.73) which in turn rests on the well-known Platonic epigram *A.P.* 5.78.

From Cicero (*Pro Arch.* 3.6) we learn that Catulus was a friend of the epigrammatist Archias; and in *De Orat.* 3.194 the same Catulus is addressed as having been at least acquainted with Antipater of Sidon, one of the greater epigrammatists of the Anthology. From the time of Cicero to the close of the principate of Tiberius there have been counted fourteen poets of the Anthology whose lives were in part at least passed in Rome.[2] Only four, however, belong to the Republic—Archias, Philodemus the friend of Piso, Thyillus who was with Cicero in 67 (*Ad Att.* 1.9.2),[3] and Tullius Laureas, said to have been Cicero's freedman (Pliny, *N.H.* 31.7). Indeed Cicero's literary circle seems to have been a chief centre of epigram-writing in this period.

Three epigrams have gained currency through Cicero's use of them. In the *Tusculans* (1.84) he refers to *A.P.* 7.471: 'Callimachi quidem epigramma in Ambraciotam Cleombrotum est, quem ait, cum ei nihil accidisset adversi, e muro se in mare abiecisse lecto Platonis libro' (the *Phaedo*). A little farther on (101) he translates the epitaph on the Spartans (*A.P.* 7.249):

> Dic, hospes, Spartae nos te hic vidisse iacentes,
> Dum sanctis patriae legibus obsequimur.

---

[1] Cf. also *A.P.* 16.209. These parallels and those to be mentioned may be traced through the Register.

[2] Hillscher, 'Hominum Litteratorum Graecorum ante Tiberii Mortem in Urbe Roma Commoratorum Historia Critica' (*Jahrb. f. Class. Philol.*, suppl. 8, 1892, pp. 353–444). Perhaps Alcaeus of Messene was the Epicurean philosopher driven out of Rome with Philiscus in 173 or 155 B.C. (Aelian, *V.H.* 9.12). Catulus need not have known Antipater in Rome.

[3] The identification of the epigrammatist with Cicero's friend is not certain.

And in the same treatise (5.101) he translates the epitaph of
Sardanapalus (*A.P.* 7.325):[1]

> Haec habeo, quae edi, quaeque exsaturata libido
> Hausit; at illa iacent multa et praeclara relicta.

The relations of Catullus to the Alexandrian poets have more
than once been studied, and the general resemblances of sub-
ject-matter and technique have been demonstrated; it does not,
however, seem possible to designate any substantial borrowing
by him from the poets of the Anthology.[2]

Lucretius 4.181–2 may be compared with *A.P.* 7.713.8–9, by
Antipater of Sidon:

> Parvus ut est cygni melior canor, ille gruum quam
> Clamor in aetheriis dispersus nubibus austri.
>
> Λωΐτερος κύκνου μικρὸς θρόος ἠὲ κολοιῶν
> κρωγμὸς ἐν εἰαριναῖς κιδνάμενος νεφέλαις.

The *Imagines* of M. Terentius Varro doubtless owed something
to the Greek epigrams; Varro was in any case acquainted with
them (below, p. 22). Nepos (*Paus.* 1) gives a prose version of
A.P. 6.197.

Among the Greek epigrammatists in Rome in the period of
the early Empire, the most distinguished were Antipater of
Thessalonica, and Crinagoras. This Antipater found a patron
in L. Calpurnius Piso, who, as proconsul of Macedonia, made
the poet governor of Thessalonica. Crinagoras was attached to
the court of Augustus, and has epigrams addressed to the Emperor (*A.P.* 9.224), to the young Marcellus (*A.P.* 6.161; 9.545),
to Tiberius (*A.P.* 16.61), and to Germanicus (*A.P.* 9.283).
Other epigrammatists seem to have been members of the circle
surrounding the elder Seneca. Also at Rome at this time were

---

[1] He refers to it again in *De Fin.* 2.32. 106, taking it from Aristotle. In all, Cicero
refers to *A.P.* 7.128 (*Ad Att.* 16.11.1), 249 (*Tusc.* 1.101), 325 (*Tusc.* 5.101 and *De Fin.* 2.
106), 471 (*Tusc.* 1.84), 704 (*De Fin.* 3.64). Compare also *De Off.* 3.90 with *A.P.* 9.269
and *Tusc.* 1.114 with *A.P.* 9.359. 10. The proverbial trimeter, *A.P.* 11.176.5, is quoted
in *Ad. Fam.* 9.7.
[2] See Kroll's edition of Catullus (2nd ed., 1929), Lafaye, *Catulle et ses Modèles*,
Paris, 1894, and Hezel, *Catull und das griechische Epigramm*, Stuttgart, 1932. Some of
the closer parallels may here be mentioned: the poems on the *passer*, especially 3, may
be compared with certain epitaphs on pet animals; cf. 3.11–2 with Simias (4th cent.
B.C.) on a dead partridge (*A.P.* 7.203): Passer mortuus . . . Qui nunc it per iter tene-
bricosum Illuc, unde negant redire quemquam: ᾤχεο γὰρ πυμάταν εἰς Ἀχέροντος ὁδόν.
Cat. 70 is compared by Lafaye with *A.P.* 5.6, and lines 3–4 of that poem give a Latin
version of the proverb contained in *A.P.* 5.8.4–5. Cf. Cat. 97 and *A.P.* 11.241, 242, and
415.

Philippus, who composed the second *Garland*, Automedon, Apollonides, Boethus of Tarsus, Evenus, Thallus of Miletus, Pompeius Junior, and Alpheius of Mytilene. Antiphanes, Parmenion, Antigonus, and Diodorus of Sardis may also have been there. An amusing anecdote concerning Augustus and a Greek epigrammatist is preserved by Macrobius (*Sat.* 2.4).

Striking evidence of the popularity of the Greek epigrams in Italy before the year 79 is the discovery of the vestiges of three of those now in the Anthology on the walls of a *cubiculum* in a Pompeian house, each illustrated by a painting.[1] The first was *A.P.* 6.13, the frequently-imitated votive epigram of Leonidas of Tarentum on the offerings made to Pan by three brothers. The second was *A.P.* 9.448—the riddle put to Homer by the fishermen. The picture represents an old man sunk in thought.[2] The third epigram is *A.P.* 9.75, by Evenus:

Κἤν με φάγῃς ἐπὶ ῥίζαν, ὅμως ἔτι καρποφορήσω
ὅσσον ἐπισπεῖσαί σοι, τράγε, θυομένῳ.

[Even though you eat me to the root, billy-goat, I will yet bear grapes enough to furnish a libation for you when you are sacrificed.] In the right-hand side of the picture a goat is seen nibbling at a vine; on the left side the same goat is being dragged towards an altar while a man squeezes a cluster of grapes over its head.[3]

Several passages in the poems of Virgil recall the Greek epigrams, none, however, directly, unless it be a line in the ninth Eclogue (52) that with some probability has been referred to a famous epigram of Callimachus (*A.P.* 7.80).[4]

---

[1] Dilthey, *Epigrammatum Pompeis repertorum trias* (Programm) Zürich, 1876.

[2] The anecdote is in Valerius Maximus 9.12.3.

[3] Here may be conveniently gathered the epigrams of the Anthology that appear as inscriptions in Italy or Gaul. The tomb of a son of Q. Sulpicius Maximus bears two Greek epigrams, one of which contains an imitation of *A.P.* 7.80 (Kaibel 618a). On the walls of a house on the Esquiline were found vestiges of *A.P.* 12.118 (Kaibel 1111). To the second century possibly belongs a herm found near the Porta Trigemina, and showing, with other verses, *A.P.* 7.6 (Kaibel 1084a). *A.P.*11.8 is found on the tomb of Cerellia Fortunata (Kaibel 646b); another epitaph takes its thought from *A.P.* 7.670 (Kaibel 568). Besides the three epigrams mentioned above, two others appear at Pompeii—*A.P.* 11.269.1 (Kaibel 1138) and 16.387** (Kaibel 1124). *A.P.* 10.43, doubtless composed for a sundial, was found on a sundial at Herculaneum (Kaibel 1122). An imitation of *A.P.* 9.610 was discovered at Monte Cassino (Kaibel 1118). At Lyons in 1825 *A.P.* 11.193 (Kaibel 1115) was discovered on the tomb of Lucretia Valeria and her husband Sex. Avius Hermeros. At Bordeaux is an epitaph ending with a verse like *A.P.* 7.465.7–8 (Kaibel 675).

[4] Saepe ego longos Cantando puerum memini me condere soles: ἐμνήσθην δ'ὁσσάκις ἀμφότεροι ἥλιον ἐν λέσχῃ κατεδύσαμεν. Compare also *Aen.* 7.598: Nam mihi parta

A similarity of spirit between many of the Odes of Horace and certain Greek epigrams must strike any reader; in the Satires one is arrested by verbal reminiscences. *Carm.* 1.38 has been compared with Philodemus in *A.P.* 11.34; and *Carm.* 1.30 with *A.P.* 12.131, by Posidippus.[1] In *Serm.* 1.2.92 *O crus, o bracchia,* has been referred to an epigram of Philodemus (*A.P.* 5.132): Ὦ ποδός, ὦ κνήμης, and probably the Philodemus mentioned in line 121 is the epigrammatist. Lines 105–8 of this Satire Horace translated from Callimachus (*A.P.* 12.102). I give Horace's lines and then the Greek with corresponding Latin phrases:[2]

'Leporem venator ut alta
In nive sectetur, positum sic tangere nolit,'
Cantat et apponit: 'Meus est amor huic similis, nam
Transvolat in medio posita et fugientia captat.'

Ὠγρευτής, Ἐπίκυδες, ἐν οὔρεσι πάντα λαγωόν
venator   leporem

διφᾷ, καὶ πάσης ἴχνια δορκαλίδος,
sectetur

στίβῃ καὶ νιφετῷ κεχρημένος. ἢν δέ τις εἴπῃ·
alta in nive

'Τῆ, τόδε βέβληται θηρίον,' οὐκ ἔλαβεν.
positum   sic tangere nolit.

quies, omnisque in limine portus, with *A.P.* 9.49 (below, p. 27). Hecker (Didot Anthol. 1.509) suggested that *Catal.* 11 depends on *A.P.* 7.725 by Callimachus. *Geor.* 1.437 is a version of a line of Parthenius also adapted by 'Lucian' in *A.P.* 6.164—Glauco et Panopeae et Inoo Melicertae: Γλαύκῳ καὶ Νηρῆι καὶ Ἰνώῳ Μελικέρτῃ *A.P.* 6.164, and so Parth. *ap.* Macrob. *Sat.* 5.17; Gellius reads: εἰναλίῳ Μελικ. Likewise *Ecl.* 7.4: Arcades ambo, and *A.P.* 6.96: Ἀρκάδες ἀμφότεροι, had a common source. E. Reitzenstein (*Rh. Mus.* 79 (1930) 65) sees in *Catal.* 1 an imitation of *A.P.* 12.26–7 and in *Catal.* 2 an imitation of *A.P.* 16.19*. See also Norden, *Aeneis, Buch vi,* 2nd ed., 1916, Commentary, *passim.*

A fragment of the poet Rabirius (Seneca, *Benef.* 6.31)—Hoc habeo, quodcumque dedi—probably is a parody of Cicero's translation of the epitaph of Sardanapalus (*A.P.* 7.325). Likewise a fragmentary Pompeian inscription (*C.I.L.* 4.1941) may be an imitation of *A.P.* 16.209: Tu qui lucernam cogitas accendere: οὗτος ὁ τὸν δαλὸν φυσῶν, ἵνα λύχνον ἀνάψῃς,

[1] R. Reitzenstein in *Neue Jahrb.* N.F. 21.90; Reitzenstein also compares *Carm.* 3.9.5–8 with *A.P.* 9.63. See further Hendrickson. *Amer. Journ. Philol.* 39.27, and F. A. Wright, *ibid.* 42.168. The following I have not seen: Z. K. Vysoky, 'Horace et l'épigramme de l'époque hellénistique,' *Listy Filologicke* 1925, pp. 193, 328.

Comparison may also be made between *Carm.* 1.4 and *A.P.* 9.363; between *Carm.* 1.11 and *A.P.* 11.62; and between *Carm.* 4.10 and *A.P.* 12.28–33 and *A.P.* 6.1. *Carm.* 2.4 resembles *A.P.* 5.18, and *Carm.* 3.16 has the same theme as *A.P.* 5.217, but here the two Greek epigrams are later than Horace. *Ars. Poet.* 63 has been compared with *A.P.* 10.105.2, ascribed to Simonides: Debemur morti nos nostraque: θανάτῳ πάντες ὀφειλόμεθα.

[2] Ariosto (*Or. Fur.* 10.7) takes the figuref rom Horace.

χοὐμὸς ἔρως τοιόσδε· τὰ μὲν φεύγοντα διώκειν
meus est amor huic similis fugientia captat

οἶδε, τὰ δ'ἐν μέσσῳ κείμενα παρπέταται.
in medio posita transvolat.

Though *A.P.* 9.74 is later than the time of Horace, yet, for a possible relation in the sources, it deserves to be compared with *Serm.* 2.2.133–5:

'Αγρὸς 'Αχαιμενίδου γενόμην ποτέ, νῦν δὲ Μενίππου·
καὶ πάλιν ἐξ ἑτέρου βήσομαι εἰς ἕτερον. κ.τ.λ.

Nunc ager Umbreni sub nomine, nuper Ofelli
Dictus, erit nulli proprius, sed cedet in usum
Nunc mihi, nunc alii.

Two of the *Priapea* have close parallels among the Greek epigrams. These are *Priap.* 10, with which cf. *A.P.* 16.86, and *Priap.* 23, which must have been formed on *A.P.* 16.236. The second follows:

Hic me custodem fecundi villicus horti
    Mandati curam iussit habere loci.
Fur habeas poenam, licet indignere 'feram' que
    'Propter olus' dicas 'hoc ego?' Propter olus.

Αὐτοῦ ἐφ' αἱμασιαῖσι τὸν ἀγρυπνοῦντα Πρίηπον
    ἔστησεν λαχάνων Δεινομένης φύλακα.
ἀλλ' ὡς ἐντέταμαι, φώρ ἔμβλεπε, 'τοῦτο δ',' ἐρωτᾷς,
    'τῶν ὀλίγων λαχάνων εἵνεκα;' τῶν ὀλίγων.

In Greek and Latin literature a sharp distinction is at times hard to draw between elegy in general and a species of it, the epigram. In Latin the earlier erotic poets favored the short form; after Gallus they more commonly attempted longer flights. Yet even to the later poets the Greek epigrams would seem a natural source to draw upon.[1] Tibullus perhaps never directly imitates any poem preserved in our Anthology, but his terminology, his figures, and his themes are evidently drawn from the same stock, and many happy illustrations can be

---

[1] The Latin elegists were always conscious of the inscriptional uses of their verse. Martial, of course, writing epigrams, often pretends to be making a real inscription; but so also does Propertius—the twenty-first poem of his first book is an epitaph, the elegy on Cornelia (4.11) is best so regarded, and the poem on Vertumnus is a long inscription. To be noticed also is the convention of Latin elegy whereby epitaphs and dedicatory inscriptions are introduced into a longer poem (Propert. 2.13.35–6; 2.14.27–8. Tibul. 1.3.55–6; 1.9.83–4; Lygd. 2.29–30). Through Latin elegy it passed to the Italian sonnet (cf. Gaspara Stampa's sonnet beginning: *Piangete, donne, e con voi pianga Amore*).

found for them in the epigrams.[1] Propertius and Ovid, for their part, were evidently familiar with many of our poems.

Propertius' substantial debt to the Anthology is at once acknowledged in his translation of an epigram by Leonidas of Tarentum (*A.P.* 9.337):

> Et leporem, quicumque venis, venaberis, hospes,
> Et si forte meo tramite quaeris avem:
> Et me Pana tibi comitem de rupe vocato,
> Sive petes calamo praemia sive cane.
>
> (Propert. 3.13.43–6)

The Greek follows with the corresponding Latin words subjoined:

> Εὔαγρει, λαγόθηρα, καὶ εἰ πετεεινὰ διώκων
> [venaberis] leporem et si avem quaeris
>
> ἰξευτὴς ἥκεις τοῦθ' ὑπὸ δισσὸν ὄρος,
> quicumque venis meo tramite
>
> κἀμὲ τὸν ὑληωρὸν ἀπὸ κρημνοῖο βόασον
> et me   de rupe vocato
>
> Πᾶνα· συναγρεύω καὶ κυσὶ καὶ καλάμοις.
> Pana comitem sive cane sive calamo.

When, therefore, we read the beginning of the sixth elegy of Book 2,

> Non ita complebant Ephyreae Laidos aedis,
> Ad cuius iacuit Graecia tota fores,

we properly think of the Platonic epigram (*A.P.* 6.1) beginning:

> Ἡ σοβαρὸν γελάσασα καθ' Ἑλλάδος, ἥ ποτ' ἐραστῶν
> ἑσμὸν ἐπὶ προθύροις Λαῒς ἔχουσα νέων.

These and other like passages are details. Two of Propertius' poems call for special regard from a student of the Anthology; these are 2.12 and 3.7.[2] The first is a description of Love, quite in the Alexandrian style; and imitations of it are easily confused with imitations of the Ἔρως Δραπέτης of Moschus (*A.P.* 9.440), in the knowledge of which it must have been written.

---

[1] Parallels to Tibullus may be seen in the following (see Register): *A.P.* 5.6, 10, 30, 97, 133, 186, 228 (Paulus Sil.), 234 (*id.*), 260 (*id.*); 6.283; 7.735; 12.44, 147. Correspondences between Latin poets and Greek epigrammatists who lived later than they, are worth noticing. The Byzantine poets may have read the Latin poets (cf. Veniero, *Paolo Silenziario, passim*); but possibly they had common sources in Alexandrian poems since lost.

[2] With these should be noticed 1.2, with which *A.P.* 5.270 (Paulus Silentiarius) may be compared.

A.P. 5.176 and 179, by Meleager, may also have lingered in Propertius' mind as he wrote. Among the sepulchral epigrams of the Anthology the number and the reality of the epitaphs on persons lost at sea have always drawn the attention of readers. When Propertius has to treat such a theme he cannot fail to recall these epigrams. Thus the elegy on Paetus (3.7) eminently deserves to be described as an 'extended epigram'; it reminds one of the demonstrable expansion of a Greek epigram on a similar theme that we find in the poems of André Chénier (*La Jeune Tarentine*). The whole elegy is contained in an epigram by Leonidas of Tarentum (*A.P.* 7.652),[1] whose poems we know Propertius admired. The similarities between the elegy and the Greek epigrams may be tested by the following parallel passages:

> Sed tua nunc volucres astant super ossa marinae,
>   Nunc tibi pro tumulo Carpathium omne mare est.
>   (11–12)

> Οὐ κόνις οὐδ' ὀλίγον πέτρης βάρος, ἀλλ' Ἐρασίππου
>   ἦν ἐσορᾷς αὕτη πᾶσα θάλασσα τάφος·
> ὤλετο γὰρ σὺν νηΐ· τὰ δ' ὀστέα ποῦ ποτ' ἐκείνου
>   πύθεται, αἰθυίαις γνωστὰ μόναις ἐνέπειν.
>   (*A.P.* 7.285)

> Et quotiens Paeti transibit nauta sepulcrum,
>   Dicat, 'et audaci tu timor esse potes.'
>   (27–8)

> Εἴη ποντοπόρῳ πλόος οὔριος· ὃν δ' ἄρ' ἀήτης,
>   ὡς ἐμὲ τοῖς Ἀΐδεω προσπελάσῃ λιμέσιν,
> μεμφθέσθω μὴ λαῖτμα κακόξενον, ἀλλ' ἔο τόλμαν,
>   ὅστις ἀφ' ἡμετέρου πείσματ' ἔλυσε τάφου.
>   (*A.P.* 7.264)

Notice must be taken in passing of a possible relation between the abusive elegy on the *lena* (Propert. 4.5 and Ovid, *Am.* 1.8) and the Greek epigram; especially since the subject is handled by Propertius in a form reminiscent of the Greek epitaph, and particularly the abusive epitaph. The Latin poets of the Renaissance have caught the theme from the ancient Latin poets. Precisely this theme is not treated in the Anthology, but it is close enough to become confused with another common theme, the

---

[1] There are similarities to this elegy also in *A.P.* 7.264, 269, 271–274, 285, 292, 395, 404, 495, 532, 586; of these, 292, 395, and 586 are later than Propertius.

abuse of the aged courtesan, treated by countless writers after Meleager (*A.P.* 5.204).[1]

No one will be surprised to find Ovid repeating in his elegies all the themes, by this time well-worn, of amatory verse. As with Petrarchan themes in the later Italian sonneteers, they are so worn that the character of their ultimate source has faded almost beyond recognition. The following lines in the *Ars Amatoria* are entirely made up of such commonplaces (3.65–70):

> Utendumst aetate: cito pede labitur aetas
> Nec bona tam sequitur, quam bona prima fuit.
> Hos ego, qui canent, frutices violaria vidi,
> Hac mihi de spina grata corona datast.
> Tempus erit, quo tu, quae nunc excludis amantes,
> Frigida deserta nocte iacebis anus.

With the first line editors compare *A.P.* 11.51: τῆς ὥρας ἀπό-λαυε· παρακμάζει ταχὺ πάντα· ἐν θέρος ἐξ ἐρίφου τρηχὺν ἔθηκε τράγον —obviously but a mere analogue; with the second couplet they similarly compare *A.P.* 11.53. The third couplet recalls an epigram of Callimachus (*A.P.* 5.23); and the comparison implied in the last four lines is the greatest commonplace of amatory verse.

Yet Ovid had really read the Greek epigrams. In the first book of the *Fasti* he explains the origin of animal-sacrifice; it was, he says, the revenge of Ceres upon a greedy sow that rooted up the crops, and upon the he-goat that failed to learn from the example:

> Sus dederat poenas; exemplo territus huius
> Palmite debueras abstinuisse, caper.
> Quem spectans aliquis dentes in vite prementem
> Talia non tacito dicta dolore dedit:
> 'Rode, caper, vitem! tamen hinc, cum stabis ad aram,
> Ad tua quod spargi cornua possit, erit.'
> Verba fides sequitur: noxae tibi deditus hostis
> Spargitur adfuso cornua, Bacche, mero.

The third couplet is a literal translation of *A.P.* 9.75; and it

---

[1] Similarities have been seen between Propert. 4.5 and *A.P.* 7.315, 320, 353, 455, 536 (Karl Prinz, *Martial und die Griechische Epigrammatik*, Leipzig, 1911, p. 44).

Parallels to the following epigrams are to be found in Propertius; for references see the Register. The first group (A) comprises epigrams from which Propertius seems to have borrowed, the second (B) those that may have been influenced by him.

(A) *A.P.* 5.4, 8, 23, 25, 77, 98, 131, 145, 212; 6.1; 7.264, 285, 320, 324, 353, 652 9.102, 337, 440, 713; 12.43, 45, 46, 101. (B) *A.P.* 5.69, 74, 94, 255, 257, 267, 268, 270 275, 301; 7.403, 586.

would not be hard to believe that Ovid had seen the Pompeian wall-painting already referred to, or another copy of it. He refers to the anecdote again in *Met.* 15.114.

It is still possible to think that Ovid wrote the elegy *Nux*.[1] At all events, as is well known, it is an expansion into 182 lines of a Greek epigram (*A.P.* 9.3) ascribed variously to Plato and to Antipater of Thessalonica, Ovid's contemporary.[2]

From the time of Tiberius to the end of Hadrian's reign Greek epigrammatists swarmed in Rome, among them Antiphilus of Byzantium, Leonidas of Alexandria, Julius Polyaenus, and probably Lucilius. From Suidas we learn that Tiberius was himself an epigrammatist, and the imitator of Rhianus and Euphorion (Suet. *Tib.* 70) would not ignore the Alexandrian epigram. From Suidas, again, it is known that *A.P.* 7.704 pleased him. His nephew and adopted son, Germanicus, appears as an epigrammatist both in the Latin and in the Greek Anthology. In the Greek Anthology verses ascribed to him are *A.P.* 7.73, 74 (wrongly), and 9.17-8; *A.P.* 9.387 is ascribed to him or to Hadrian, but, since it is the same epigram that appears in Latin under the name of Germanicus (Baehr. *PLM* 4.102), his claim may be thought the better. A second Latin epigram by Germanicus has its Greek form in *A.P.* 7.542 under the name of Flaccus or in *A.P.* 9.56 by Antipater of Thessalonica.[3]

A.P. 7.704, an epigram that had pleased Tiberius, according to Suetonius caused the burning of Rome (*Nero* 38): 'Nec populo aut moenibus patriae pepercit Nero. Dicente quodam in sermone communi: Ἐμοῦ θανόντος γαῖα μιχθήτω πυρί! Immo, inquit, ἐμοῦ ζῶντος! planeque ita fecit; nam quasi offensus deformitate veterum aedificiorum . . . incendit urbem.'[4]

The epigram translated by Ovid and represented on a house-wall at Pompeii (*A.P.* 9.75) once struck terror into the timid heart of Domitian (Suet. *Dom.* 14): 'Minimis etiam suspitionibus praeter modum commovebatur. Ut edicti de excidendis

---

[1] Cf. Carl Ganzenmüller, *Die Elegie Nux und ihr Verfasser.* Tübingen, 1910.

[2] Parallels between the poems of Ovid and the Anthology may be found under *A.P.* 5.3, 26, 57, 83, 129, 132, 145, 248, 275; 6.1; 7.8, 80, 100, 185, 188, 285; 9.3, 64, 75, 277, 497; 11.4, 30; 12.5, 102, 118, 194, 208, 235. Compare also *Pont.* 4.1.34: Ut similis verae Vacca Myronis erat, with *A.P.* 9.713 ff.

[3] See below, p. 29. Hadrian also appears as a Greek epigrammatist in *A.P.* 9.137.

[4] Seneca (*De Clem.* 2.2) refers to this verse, in which he says one 'se mortuo terram misceri ignibus iubet.' *De Clem.* is addressed to Nero. *A.P.* 7.704 seems to be a fragment from a tragedy; it is the ancient equivalent of *Après moi le déluge.*

vineis propositi gratiam faceret non alia magis re compulsus creditur, quam quod sparsi libelli cum his versibus erant' (he quotes the epigram).[1]

The study of rhetoric had its effect in polishing the points not only of the prose written in this period but also of the verse. We can see its reflection not only in Martial but also in the Greek epigrams contemporary with him. It is perhaps significant that Quintilian mentions with approval among the 'conjectural cases' given to pupils for practice in his youth certain themes that recall the Anthology (*Inst. Orat.* 2.4.26): 'Solebant praeceptores mei neque inutili et nobis etiam iucundo genere exercitationis praeparare nos coniecturalibus causis, cum quaerere atque exsequi iuberent "Cur armata apud Lacedaemonios Venus" [cf. *A.P.* 9.320, 321; 16.171, 173-7] et "Quid ita crederetur Cupido puer atque volucer et sagitto ac face armatus" [cf. *A.P.* 5.180; 9.440; 16.201] et similia.'

The elder Pliny, though he quotes none of the epigrams, plainly consulted them. When he writes of a sculptor, 'qui Satyrum in phiala gravatum somno conlocavisse verius quam caelasse dictus est,' (*N.H.* 33.156), he undoubtedly had in mind *A.P.* 16.248: τόν Σάτυρον Διόδωρος ἐκοίμισεν, οὐκ ἐτόρευσεν. We may understand him to say that the epigrams on Myron's *Heifer* (*A.P.* 9.713ff) were at least as famous as the statue itself: 'Myronem . . . bucula maxime nobilitavit celebratis versibus laudata, quando alieno plerique ingenio magis quam suo commendantur' (*N.H.* 34.57).[2] Similarly he alludes to *A.P.* 16.178 ff. (*N.H.* 35.91).

Petronius occasionally recalls a Greek epigram.[3] A line of Persius (5.41) goes back by way of Virgil to an epigram of Callimachus (*A.P.* 7.80). An epigram in the Latin Anthology under the name of the younger Pliny, on the united power of Bacchus and Cupid, has parallels among the Greek epigrams

[1] Above, p. 13. In the second line Politian here read: ἐπισπεῖσαι Καίσαρι θυομένῳ.
[2] The statement (*ibid.*), 'Myronem . . . fecisse et cicadae monumentum ac locustae carminibus suis Erinna significat,' almost certainly points to *A.P.* 7.190; but if so, as Hardouin observed, Pliny has confused the girl Myro with the sculptor. In the mention of works of art Pliny and the Anthology several times illustrate each other; cf. *N.H.* 35.98 with *A.P.* 7.623; *N.H.* 34.178 with *A.P.* 7.709; *N.H.* 35.136 with *A.P.* 16.83, 135-40, 143, 128; *N.H.* 36.23 with *A.P.* 9.756. Pliny speaks of the epigrammatist Tullius Laureas (*N.H.* 31.7), and mentions a fever that annually attacked Antipater of Sidon on his birthday (*N.H.* 7.172). *N.H.* 10.43 may be compared with *A.P.* 9.272.
[3] *A.P.* 5.78; 10.35; 12.20; cf. below, p. 26.

(compare *PLM* 4.103 and *A.P.* 12.119).[1]

It would be of interest to determine how far Martial is merely a Roman practitioner of a Greek art, and wherein his epigrams differ from the Greek and are Latin and his own. Here, however, we must be content merely to show certain substantial correspondences between Martial and the Greek epigrams such as might occasion ambiguity in determining the later influence of either.[2]

The themes of Martial's epigrams are very often those of the Greek epigrammatists—that was to be expected from the conditions of ancient life; but in certain cases there is an identity of subject that can come only from conscious borrowing, and the Latin poet is probably the borrower. This identity exists between a number of Martial's epigrams and those of Lucilius, a Greek epigrammatist who lived, probably, in Rome in the time of Nero. Lucilius has an epigram ridiculing advocates who filled their speeches in court with historical allusions, no matter how inappropriate these were to the case in hand:[3]

> Χοιρίδιον καὶ βοῦν ἀπολώλεκα, καὶ μίαν αἶγα,
> ὧν χάριν εἴληφας μισθάριον, Μενέκλεις·
> οὔτε δέ μοι κοινόν τι πρὸς 'Οθρυάδαν γεγένηται,
> οὔτ' ἀπάγω κλέπτας τοὺς ἀπὸ Θερμοπυλῶν·
> ἀλλὰ πρὸς Εὐτυχίδην ἔχομεν κρίσιν· ὥστε τί ποιεῖ
> ἐνθάδε μοι Ξέρξης καὶ Λακεδαιμόνιοι;
> πλὴν κἀμοῦ μνήσθητι νόμου χάριν, ἢ μέγα κράξω·
> "Ἄλλα λέγει Μενέκλης, ἄλλα τὸ χοιρίδιον.'

It would be difficult to believe that Martial was not adapting Lucilius when he wrote (6.19):

> Non de vi neque caede nec veneno,
> Sed lis est mihi de tribus capellis:

[1] The divided flame, said to have arisen from the pyre of Eteocles and Polyneices (Lucan, *Ph.* 1.551; Statius, *Th.* 12.439; Dante, *Inf.* 26.52), forms the theme of *A.P.* 7.396 and 399. It seems, however, to have been a regular accompaniment of the Theban story. Ovid (*Tr.* 5.5.33) refers to it, seemingly on the authority of Callimachus; cf. Pausanias 9.18.3.

[2] The parallels between Martial and the Anthology have mostly been noted by editors, especially by Jacobs. I have not been able to add materially to those gathered into Friedländer's Martial (2 vols., Leipzig, 1886). The unfinished work of Karl Prinz mentioned above, p. 81, n., without adding new parallels, presents a good discussion of the question mainly in relation to the satirical epigrams.

[3] *A.P.* 11.141. 'A little pig and a cow have I lost, and one she-goat; and it is on their account Menecles, that you received your fee. I never had anything in common with Othryades, nor do I prosecute for theft the heroes of Thermopylae: I am suing Eutychides. What good, then, do Xerxes, and the Spartans do me here? Pray, make mention of me too, just for form's sake, or else I will shout: "Menecles says one thing, my little pig another."'

Vicini queror has abesse furto.
Hoc iudex sibi postulat probari:
Tu Cannas Mithridaticumque bellum
Et periuria Punici furoris
Et Sullas Mariosque Muciosque
Magna voce sonas manuque tota.
Iam dic, Postume, de tribus capellis.

This theme has often been imitated in the modern languages. A second example of Martial's borrowing from Lucilius shows him employing his model somewhat more freely (Mart. 5.53).[1]

Colchida quid scribis, quid scribis, amice, Thyesten?
Quo tibi vel Nioben, Basse, vel Andromachen?
Materia est, mihi crede, tuis aptissima chartis
Deucalion vel, si non placet hic, Phaethon.

Lucilius wrote (*A.P.* 11.214):

Γράψας Δευκαλίωνα, Μενέστρατε, καὶ Φαέθοντα,
ζητεῖς τίς τούτων ἄξιός ἐστι τίνος.
τοῖς ἰδίοις αὐτοὺς τιμήσομεν· ἄξιος ὄντως
ἐστὶ πυρὸς Φαέθων, Δευκαλίων δ'ὕδατος.

Besides the Anacreontic (*A.P.* 11.48), introduced by Gellius in rivalry with the old Latin epigrammatists, other notices of the Greek epigrams are to be found in the *Noctes Atticae*. The proverb, *A.P.* 10.32, has its Latin equivalent in *N.A.* 13.17; Gellius refers to *A.P.* 7.53 on the authority of Varro (*N.A.* 3.11); *A.P.* 16.297 is alluded to in the same passage.[2] An entire chapter (19.11) is devoted to the Platonic epigram, *A.P.* 5.78, which, as Gellius says, had always been a popular one He quotes the Greek, and adds a free Latin imitation of it by a young friend of his:[3]

Τὴν ψυχὴν 'Αγάθωνα φιλῶν ἐπὶ χείλεσιν ἔσχον·
ἦλθε γὰρ ἡ τλήμων ὡς διαβησομένη.

Dum semihiulco savio
Meum puellum savior,
Dulcemque florem spiritus

---

[1] The more important correspondences between Martial and the Greek Anthology are noted under *A.P.* 5.42; 6.307; 7.461, 660, 743; 9.56, 58, 268 (cf. 311), 562, 687; 10.102; 11.11, 39, 66, 67, 68, 110, 141, 153, 155, 171, 176, 191, 214, 226, 239, 249, 257 (cf. 118), 310, 371, 403, 408, 420; 12.67, 175, 191, 16.238.

[2] Inferior mss. here give a Greek version, not exactly *A.P.* 16.297; below, p. 83. Some mss. at *N.A.* 2.18 have had *A.P.* 7.676 inserted.

[3] Marcus Aurelius, writing to Fronto, alludes to the Platonic epigram: 'At ego ubi animus meus sit, nescio; nisi hoc scio illo nescio quo ad te profectum eum esse' (*Front. Epist.*, ed. by Naber, p. 4).

Duco ex aperto tramite,
Anima <male> aegra et saucia
Cucurrit ad labeas mihi.
Rictumque in oris pervium
Et labra pueri mollia
Rimata itineri transitus
Ut transiliret nititur.
Tum si morae quid plusculae
Fuisset in coetu osculi
Amoris ignis percita
Transisset, et me linqueret.
Et mira prorsum res foret
Ut ad me fierem mortuus,
Ad puerum intus viverem.

At an early point in the *Apologia* of Apuleius (cc. 9–11) the author disposes of the charge made against him of writing verses in a strain unworthy of a philosopher. Among other precedents he cites Plato, some of whose amatory epigrams he seizes the occasion to quote. According to the best manuscripts he gives only *A.P.* 7.670, 7.100, and the last line of 7.99; but Renaissance manuscripts insert *A.P.* 7.669, and make up the last couplet of 7.99. These manuscripts also present Latin renderings of the four quotations—Renaissance translations, it seems —which appear in the early editions, and have had, therefore, a peculiar bearing on the popularity of these epigrams.[1]

Third-century Latin writers, apparently, took no interest in the Greek epigrams; but the revival of pagan letters that marks the fourth century brings with it the most considerable imitator of the Anthology among Latin authors—Ausonius. He imitates about 50 epigrams—or about 75, if all those given to him in early editions could be regarded as his. The following, one of his certainly genuine pieces, is slightly expanded from *A.P.* 9.44:[2]

Qui laqueum collo nectebat, repperit aurum
Thesaurique loco deposuit laqueum.
At qui condiderat, postquam non repperit aurum,
Aptavit collo quem reperit laqueum.

Poor as it is, this translation has been known everywhere. A second example is from *A.P.* 6.1:[3]

[1] See the ed. of the *Apologia* by Butler and Owen (Oxford, 1914), p. 29 (Com.). In the Register these translations have been recorded under the name of Apuleius.
[2] Quoted below, p. 315.
[3] Ἡ σοβαρὸν γελάσασα καθ᾽ Ἑλλάδος ,ἥ ποτ᾽ ἐραστῶν

Lais anus Veneri speculum dico: dignum habeat se
Aeterna aeternum forma ministerium.
At mihi nullus in hoc usus, quia cernere talem,
Qualis sum, nolo, qualis eram, nequeo.

The translations now regarded with suspicion first appeared
among the works of Ausonius in 1496 and 1499, and with one
exception have been assigned by Peiper to Giorgio Merula.[1] If
they are Renaissance work, still, despite certain blemishes noticed by Peiper, they are mostly worthy of Ausonius. Throughout the period here in view they were not, of course, regarded
as spurious, but enjoyed in full measure the authority of
Ausonius' name.[2]

If any of the epigrams appearing in the Anthology under the
name Claudianus are the work of the Latin poet, he is the
latest of the writers like Tullius Laureas and Germanicus who
are known as Latin poets and Greek epigrammatists.[3] At all
events, Claudian has two Latin epigrams (16 and 17) that represent *A.P.* 5.50, the first literally. He seems to echo *A.P.* 10.122
(*Carm. Min.* 5.38); refers to *A.P.* 9.125 (*In Ruf.* 2.112); and,
finally, alludes to *A.P.* 6.1 in the following lines (*In Eutrop.*
1.90):

Haud aliter iuvenum flammis Ephyreia Lais
Et gemino ditata mari, cum serta refudit
Canities, iam turba procax noctisque recedit
Ambitus et raro pulsatur ianua tactu
Seque reformidat speculo damnante senectus.

ἐσμὸν ἐπὶ προθύροις Λαῒς ἔχουσα νέων,
τῇ Παφίῃ τὸ κάτοπτρον· ἐπεὶ τοίη μὲν ὁρᾶσθαι
οὐκ ἐθέλω, οἵη δ᾿ἦν πάρος οὐ δύναμαι.

The following translations appear among Ausonius' genuine works: *A.P.* 5.21, 42,
68, 88, 158; 6.1; 7.64, 66, 139, 144, 145, 228, 229, 670; 9.18, 44, 145, 159, 357, 359, 366,
489, 506 (cf. 571), 713, 721, 726, 730, 731, 734, 783; 10.30 (2 versions); 11.113, 114, 145
(2 versions; cf. 149, 151), 163, 225, 254; 16.92, 129, 162, 174, 263, 275, 317, 318 (2
versions), 333. His epigrams on Myron's *Heifer*, while suggested by the Greek (*A.P.*
9.713ff), cannot always be assigned to a certain model. He has, besides, an exercise in
Greek based on 9.759–60, another with a line adapted from 7.670, and a reference to
the riddle of the Sphinx (14.64). References are to *Opuscula*, ed. by Peiper, Leipzig
(Teubner), 1886.

[1] See below, p. 102. The epigrams here concerned are translations or echoes of *A.P.*
5.95; 7.224, 311, 396, 670; 9.12 (2 versions), 44, 145, 168, 366, 715, 721, 730; 10.26;
11.104, 254, 255, 266, 279; 16. 135–7, 151, 174, 178. A version of *A.P.* 9.366 Peiper assigns to Taddeo Ugoleto, editor of the 1499 Ausonius.

[2] Specimens of these translations may be seen below, p. 105.

[3] Ascribed to Claudianus are *A.P.* 1.19, 20; 5.86; 9.139, 140, 753, 754. Perhaps 1.19,
20; 9.139 and 140 are the work of a Byzantine; but others are in a vein adopted by the
Latin poet; 9.753 in particular is very like a series of Claudian's Latin epigrams (31–7
in Jeep's ed.).

In the fifth century, Greek studies were definitely on the wane. St. Jerome, however, quotes a translation of *A.P.* 11.193:

> Iustius invidia nihil est, quae protinus ipsum
> Auctorem rodit excruciatque animum.

Macrobius quotes two epigrams (*A.P.* 7.676 and 11.437). In a commentary on Psalm 125 St. Augustine alludes to the famous epigrams on the blind man and the lame man (*A.P.* 9.11–13); his theme is almsgiving: 'Iste non potest ambulare; qui potest ambulare, pedes suos accommodat claudo; qui videt, oculos suos accommodat caeco; . . . portat illum,' etc. Chalcidius in the sixth century, in translating some lines of Empedocles, hit upon *A.P.* 9.569.1–2.

The Latin Anthology is a modern compilation, the nucleus of which, however, the Salmasian MS., was put together about the middle of the sixth century. Apart from the verses of Germanicus and the younger Pliny already mentioned, little of what is genuinely antique in the Latin Anthology betrays any substantial debt to the Greek epigrams, though many pieces show the Latin writer doing the same sort of thing that we see done in the Greek Anthology in the way of *technopaegnia*.[1] Some lines of Regianus (Baehr. *PLM* 4.359) may, however, be compared with *A.P.* 9.626. The so-called *Epitaphium Senecae* (Riese 667), begins, like several real epitaphs, with a variation of *A.P.* 9.49:

> Cura, labor, meritum, sumpti pro munere honores,
> Ite, alias posthac sollicitate animas.

We have noticed the Renaissance translations of Greek epigrams that have crept into early editions of Apuleius and Ausonius. The Latin Anthology was particularly open to similar

---

[1] References are to Baehrens' *Poetae Latini Minores*. 6 vols. Leipzig, 1878–86. Verses that can be read backwards may be seen in *PLM* 4.268–9, 3.169, and 6.365 and in *A.P.* 9.53; verses that contain all the letters of the alphabet are *PLM* 3.169 and *A.P.* 9.538–9. The nine Muses with their attributes are listed by Florus (*PLM* 4.279) and in a piece ascribed to Cato (*PLM* 3.243): compare *A.P.* 9.504–5. Similarly the months are described in Latin verse (*PLM* 1.206ff; 4.290; 5.214, 354–5, 379) and in Greek (*A.P.* 9.383–4, 580). The names and the aphorisms of the Seven Sages are the subject of like exercises; compare Luxorius (*PLM* 4.414) and the anonymous verses of *PLM* 3.159 with *A.P.* 9.366. Virgilian centos form a large section of the minor Latin poems (*PLM* 4.191ff); compare *A.P.* 9.212. *Periochae* of the books of the *Aeneid* (*PLM* 4.173–8) have their counterpart in *A.P.* 9.385 where the *Iliad* is similarly treated. Riddles are naturally versified in all languages, and there is little in those of Symphosius to remind one of the fourteenth book of the Palatine Anthology, unless it be the one on sleep (99), which does bear a certain resemblance to *A.P.* 14.110.

frauds; and, once an imitation of the Greek had got itself into
that collection, it was in a favorable position for gaining the
attention of modern writers. Burmann had the following from
a collection of metrical inscriptions made by an anonymous
Englishman; it is a fair version of *A.P.* 6.189:[1]

> Nymphae fonticolae, Nymphae, quae gurgitis huius
>   Aeternum roseo tunditis ima pede,
> Lysimachum servate! sub alta maxima pinu
>   Numinibus posuit qui simulacra tuis.

Best-known of these false antiques is a version of Meleager's
epigram on Bacchus (*A.P.* 9.331).[2] It was edited in 1585 by
Binet in Dousa's Petronius, but had been printed in 1555
among Fracastoro's poems as 'vetus epigramma' (below, p.
192):

> Infantem Nymphae Bacchum quo tempore ab igne
>   Prodiit, inventum sub cinere abluerant.
> Ex illo Nymphis cum Baccho gratia multa est,
>   Seiunctus quod sit ignis et urat adhuc.

Other epigrams no longer regarded as antique are imitations of
A.P. 7.15 (below, p. 94); 9.249 (Burmann 5.216), 826 (Burmann 1.81); 11.249 (Burmann 3.56), and 371 (Baehrens 5.390).

Possibly modern also is the imitation of *A.P.* 9.627 edited by
Baehrens (*PLM* 4.438) from a fifteenth-century MS. Baehrens
was unaware that the verses had been printed once in the sixteenth, and again in the eighteenth century, as the work of
Niccolò d'Arco (below, p. 211). Baehrens' MS. (*Riccard.* 2939)
admittedly is made up largely of neo-Latin verse. It will be
recalled that the last two sonnets of Shakespeare ultimately
come from this same Greek epigram.

> Baiarum dum forte capit sub mollibus umbris
>   Fessus Amor somnum murmure captus aquae,
> Ipsa facem accurrens gelida celavit in unda,
>   Ut veteres flammas vindicet, alma Venus.
> Quam primum liquor ille aeternos concipit ignes,
>   Igne novo (quisnam crederet?) arsit aqua.
> Flammivomis igitur fumant haec balnea lymphis,
>   Quod facula una omnes vincit Amoris aquas.

Several of our Greek epigrams appear on stones found in

---

[1] Burmann 5.215; Didot Anthol. 1.243.
[2] *Anth. Lat.*, ed by Riese, 891; Baehrens 5.406.

Italy or Gaul. It is but natural, then, to find the influence of
the Anthology in certain Latin inscriptions. Indeed the custom
of making permanent inscriptions was generally assimilated in
Rome to the Greek fashion.

A.P. 9.49 has caught the attention of epitaph-makers both
ancient and modern; and is itself probably a shortened and perfected form of an older epitaph containing the same striking
phrases:

> Ἐλπὶς καὶ σύ, Τύχη, μέγα χαίρετε· τὸν λιμέν' εὗρον·
> οὐδὲν ἐμοὶ χ'ὑμῖν· παίζετε τοὺς μετ' ἐμέ.

[To Hope and to thee, O Fortune, a long farewell! I have found
the haven. You and I have no more to do with each other; make
sport of those who come after me.][1] A second epigram in the
Anthology (9.134) employs the same first line, and develops the
thought through eleven hexameters. Palladas, many of whose
epigrams are variations of old proverbs, uses this one (*A.P.*
9.172) to express his freedom as a poor man from the cares of
wealth. In much the same way it was employed some thirteen
centuries later by Le Sage in *Gil Blas*. No trace of these formulas appears in any extant Greek inscription; but in Latin inscriptions we have five echoes of the epigram. On the tomb of a
ten-year-old boy we read (Buecheler, *Carm. Epig.* 434.13):

> Effugi tumidam vitam. Spes, forma valete:
> Nil mihi vobiscum est, alios deludite quaeso.
> Haec domus aeterna est; hic sum situs, hic ero semper.

On another tomb (Buecheler-Lommatzsch 2139):

> Ha, evasi, effugi. Spes et Fortuna valete:
> Nil mihi vobiscum est; ludificate alios.

It appears on the tomb of a young soldier (Buecheler 409.8) and
in the *Epitaphium Senecae* already quoted. The sentiment is not
out of place on the tomb of a Christian (De Rossi 2.267, 20):

> Gloria, divitiae, fundi, domus ampla, valete;
> Olim vos, olim pondera vestra tuli:
> Me praesens tumulus cognato caespite claudit;
> Vos ite et dominos ludificate novos.

---

[1] See Register for a list of imitations. The phrases of the inevitable Latin translation, given by William Lily, became better known than the original:
> Inveni portum, Spes et Fortuna valete.
> Nil mihi vobiscum, ludite nunc alios.

See below, p. 165.

Other metrical inscriptions resemble *A.P.* 7.325, 346, 461,
464, 603; 10.112;[1] and 11.294. The sentiments, of course, of
many Greek and Latin epitaphs are similar, as the situations
are alike. Certain formulas were used by both, e.g. Sit tibi terra
levis: Εἴη σοι . . . κούφη κόνις (*A.P.* 11.226), and the sentiment
expressed in several epitaphs for Plato, as *A.P.* 7.61:

> Γαῖα μὲν ἐν κόλποις κρύπτει τόδε σῶμα Πλάτωνος,
> ψυχὴ δ'ἀθάνατον τάξιν ἔχει μακάρων.

Cf. the epitaph of a Christian (De Rossi 2.137):

> Corpus habet tellus, animam caelestia regna.

One puzzling exception breaks the general ignorance of the
Greek epigrams in the Western Middle Ages.[2] This occurs in a
poem by Paulus Diaconus, whose life falls within the years
720–800.[3] Paul was invited, perhaps in 783, by Charlemagne to
give instruction in Greek to the clerics who were to accompany
the princess Rothrud to Constantinople. The invitation came
in the form of a poem from the hand of Peter of Pisa, in which
no praises of Paul's linguistic knowledge were spared. Paul replied in verse, modestly saying that if the clerics went to Constantinople with no more knowledge of Greek than he could
give them, they would be derided for silent statues. Yet, lest it
be thought he was totally ignorant of languages, he adds a few
verses taught to him as a child; the rest has escaped him in his
advancing years:

> Sed omnino ne linguarum dicar esse nescius,
> Pauca, mihi quae fuerunt tradita puerulo,
> Dicam; cetera fugerunt iam gravante senio.

DE PUERO QUI IN GLACIE EXTINCTUS EST

> Trax puer adstricto glacie dum ludit in Hebro,
> Frigore concretas pondere rupit aquas;

----

[1]
> Balnea, vina, Venus corrumpunt corpora nostra;
> Set vitam faciunt b.v.V.

This couplet (Buecheler 1499), the antiquity of which has been suspected, was quoted
by Soter (below, p. 274) in 1525 as an illustration of *A.P.* 10.112. Similar is *C.I.L.* 3.12274c
(Engstrom 148): Balnea vina Venus faciunt properantia fata; this is nearer the Greek.

[2] Honainus (Ishaq ibn Honain, who died *c.*910) translated *A.P.* 7.60 and 16.31 in
his Life of Plato (Preger, *Inscr. Graec. Met.*, p. 10, from Roper, *Lectiones Abulphara-
gianae*, Danzig, 1844, 2.13).

[3] Manitius, *Gesch. d. Lat. Lit. d. Mittelalt.* 1.257–72; Karl Neff, *Die Gedichte des
Paulus Diaconus*, Munich, 1908 (Traube's *Quell. u. Untersuch.* 3.4); cf. Rubensohn in
Neue Jahrb. 147 (1893). 764.

Dumque imae partes rapido traherentur ab amni,
    Praesecuit tenerum lubrica testa caput.
Orba quod inventum mater dum conderet urna,
    'Hoc peperi flammis, cetera,' dixit, 'aquis.'

This is an imitation of *A.P.* 7.542 (cf. 9.56), and is, with slight variations, the imitation that appears in the Latin Anthology under the name of Germanicus, save that it wants the last couplet.[1] This omission only brings the Latin closer to the Greek. We may suppose that Paulus had learned the Greek poem, and the Latin version as a sort of gloss. He may himself have taught Greek in that way (Neff, p. 58). The possibility exists that he really added the Greek version here, and it proved too much for later copyists.[2]

3. Manuscripts of the Anthology

The idea of the Greek epigrams, and of an Anthology, that was entertained by the earliest humanists was necessarily that of their teachers, the latest Byzantines. The name Anthology did not come into use until after the publication of the *editio princeps* (1494), and not generally till somewhat later; even Lascaris, the first editor—like Suidas—speaks only of 'the epigrams.' The Planudean Anthology alone bears the title now universal.[3] 'The epigrams' is a less precise designation; and doubtless many Byzantine scholars had but a vague notion of the extent of the collection, knowing it rather from small selections. Manuscripts of such selections are fairly numerous, and in many cases are older than the Anthology of Planudes. In the following pages an attempt is made to name the MSS. of the

---

[1] *PLM* 4.103; the missing couplet is:
    Me miserum! plus amnis habet solumque reliquit,
      Quo nati mater nosceret interitum.
The original is as follows:
    Ἕβρου χειμερίοις ἀταλὸς κρυμοῖσι δεθέντος
      κοῦρος ὀλισθηροῖς ποσσὶν ἔθραυσε πάγον,
    τοῦ παρασυρομένοιο περιρραγὲς αὐχέν' ἔκοψεν
      θηγαλέον ποταμοῦ Βιστονίοιο τρύφος,
    καὶ τὸ μὲν ἡρπάσθη δίναις μέρος· ἡ δὲ τεκοῦσα
      λειφθὲν ὑπερθε τάφῳ μοῦνον ἔθηκε κάρα.
    μυρομένη δὲ τάλαινα, 'Τέκος, τέκος,' εἶπε, 'τὸ μέν σου
      πυρκαϊή, τὸ δέ σου πικρὸν ἔθαψεν ὕδωρ.'

[2] Our text comes from a MS. of the late 9th century (Neff, p. xix).

[3] The Palatine MS. is entitled: ἡ βίβλος τῶν ἐπιγραμμάτων.

Greek epigrams which were in Italy, or may have been there, in the fifteenth and sixteenth centuries.[1]

Complete MSS. of the Planudean Anthology are not numerous. Obviously the first in importance is the autograph of Planudes himself, which is preserved in St. Mark's Library at Venice (*Marc.* 481).[2] This MS., no doubt brought to Italy for Cardinal Bessarion, was part of his bequest to the Venetian library. All other MSS. of the Planudean collection must have been derived from it. In the same collection, but not from Bessarion, is a MS. (*Marc.* 621) written by Demetrius Triboles of Sparta in 1472.[3] At Padua in 1466 Demetrius Chalcondyles, with Joannes Laurentius, went through and corrected a MS. of the Anthology which was subsequently taken to Florence, and is now in the Laurentian Library (*Laur.* 31, 28). At Rome the Vatican Library possesses two fifteenth-century MSS. (*Vat. Graec.* 63 and *Vat. Pal. Graec.* 130), a sixteenth-century MS. (*Vat. Graec.* 1372) once owned by Fulvio Orsini; and, in the Barberini collection, a MS. No. 123, of the fourteenth and sixteenth centuries. Two fifteenth-century MSS. are in the Ambrosian Library at Milan—*Amb.* 39 (A 114 suppl.) and 57 (A 161 suppl. olim N 139).[4]

A great number of Greek MSS. now in Paris came thither from Italy in the sixteenth century. In particular the acquisition, *c.* 1550, by Pietro Strozzi, Marshal of France, of the library of Cardinal Ridolfi, took from Rome many valuable MSS. now in the Bibliothèque Nationale.[5] They passed from Strozzi to Catherine de' Medici. Three of the five MSS. of the *Planudea* in Paris are from this library of Catherine's—*Paris.* 2740 [15 cent.]; 2863 [15–16 cent.]; and 2891 [15–16 cent.]. The other two are *Paris.* 2739 [15 cent. from the library at Fontainebleau] and 2741 [16 cent.]. Of these, *Paris.* 2891 is of interest

---

[1] These notices I have collected from the available printed catalogues.

[2] Described by Zanetti and Bongiovanni, *Graeca D. Marci Bibliotheca Codicum* MSS. Venice, 1740, pp. 252–3. The epigrams are followed by an epic paraphrase of the Gospel of St. John, and it is the paraphrase that Planudes says he finished copying in September 1301. Special value was not attached to *Marc.* 481 by the early editors, though it was used for the first Aldine edition; it seems first to have been recognized as Planudes' autograph by Philippe D'Orville (*c.* 1729), but his note did not see the light until the nineteenth century.

[3] Cf. Vogel and Gardthausen, *Griech. Schreiber*, p. 105.

[4] Described by Martini and Bassi, *Catalogus Codicum Graecorum Bibl. Ambrosianae*, Milan, 1906. The first MS. contains some childish scribbling, the second the inscription: 'Iste liber est mey'—nothing further.

[5] One source of Ridolfi's collection was the library of Janus Lascaris (below, p. 119).

because it was copied by Janus Lascaris (below, p. 119), and 2739 because it was made by Michael Apostolios, and possibly was the original from which Lascaris copied his.[1]

In Germany Schneidewin notices a MS. of the fifteenth or sixteenth century, now at Hamburg, having been given to the library in 1652; and a second, of the fourteenth century, *Cod. Gudianus* 77 (Wolfenbüttel).[2]

The chief MS. of the Anthology, the basis of all modern editions, *Palatinus* 23 at Heidelberg, was, as aforesaid, discovered at Heidelberg by Salmasius in 1606/7. How it came thither has never been satisfactorily explained. It may have been previously in Italy, but, if so, had no effect on the knowledge of the Greek epigrams there. Cf., however, below, p. 333, n. 3. What evidence we have on its early history has been set forth by Preisendanz, and need not here be detailed.[3] Possibly John Clement, the protégé of Sir Thomas More, brought it from Italy about 1525; it was from a MS. of his that Stephanus says he got several enigmas (*A.P.* 14.52, 56–8, 60, 62) for his Anthology of 1566; and Stephanus' MS. of the *Anacreontea*, now at Leyden, probably comes somehow from the *Palatinus*. On the other hand, a letter of J. J. Scaliger, to Gruter, dated Feb. 20, 1607, says that the newly discovered MS. is doubtless that 'complete MS. of the Anthology' which Francesco Porto had more than once told him he had seen in the hands of Nicolaus Sophianus. This Nicolaus was father or uncle of the better-known Michael Sophianus, a scholar who died at Ferrara in 1565, who may have inherited the MS. Pierre Herbert (Jovy, *Pierre Herbert et ses Travaux inédits*, p. 178) suggests that the MS. came into the hands of Francesco Porto himself, since he was teaching at Ferrara about this time, and passed to his son Emilio, who lived as student and professor at Heidelberg from 1593 to 1610. This is the less likely because Scaliger doubtless knew Francesco between 1572 and 1574 while they were both at Geneva, at which time, according to Herbert, Porto himself had the MS.! Nor, if Emilio had ever possessed the MS., would he have remained silent when Salmasius proclaimed its discovery almost in his own presence at Heidelberg.

[1] Apostolios' MS. was at Fontainebleau in 1550, since it appears as No. 184 in the Catalogue of that year (Omont, *Catalogues des Manuscrits Grecs de Fontainebleau sous François I et Henri II*, Paris, 1889).

[2] Schneidewin, *Progymnasmata ad Anth. Graec.*, p. 4.

A fourteenth-century MS. of the *Planudea* exists in the library of the Monastery of the Holy Sepulchre at Jerusalem, described by A. Papadopoulos-Kerameos, Ἱεροσολυμιτικὴ Βιβλιοθήκη (Petrograd, 1891–99) 1.144–5. See also below, p. 35, n. 1.

In Lambros' *Catalogue of the Greek MSS. on Mt. Athos* (Cambridge, 1895, 1900), No. 645, 6 [17 cent.] contains epigrams, so also Nos. 3816, 57 and 3816, 80 [16 cent.]. A complete MS. of the *Planudea* is No. 1396 (K 109), 14, in Spyridon and Eustraliades, *Catalogue of the Greek MSS. in the Library of the Laura on Mt. Athos* (Cambridge, Mass., 1925).

[3] Karl Preisendanz, Preface to Sijthoff's phototype edition, *Anthologia Palatina* (Leyden, 1911), 1.ii-vii, cxlv-cxlvii. See also his *Anacreontea*, Leipzig (Teubner), 1912. On a new suggestion by Sabbadini, see below, p. 86, n. 1.

The Anthology is not in Sylburg's catalogue of the Heidelberg MSS., made in 1584. It may have been acquired between 1584 and 1596, the date of Sylburg's death, or Sylburg may have had it in his private collection, since his copy of the second Aldine, till recently in the Heidelberg library but now lost, is said to have contained in his hand a partial collation of the *Palatinus*.

For the later history of the Palatine MS., see below, pp. 263 and 392.

Manuscripts containing extracts from the Anthology fall into two classes: (1) Those that are virtually small independent collections, perhaps antedating Planudes, and existing usually in more than one MS. They have a textual authority comparable to that of the *Planudea* or the *Palatina*, and are known as *syllogae minores*. (2) Extracts made from a Planudean MS. merely for the occasional use of some student. These exist only in single MSS., and have little textual value. Five or six *syllogae minores* have been recognized; while MSS. of the second kind are almost numberless.

The so-called *Sylloge Euphemiana* is older than the work of Cephalas, going back to the ninth century; it contains 82 epigrams.[1] In two MSS. (*Flor.* and *Paris.* 1773) the *Euphemiana* is preceded by a larger collection of 121 epigrams (*Sylloge Σ*), thought to have been made in the thirteenth or fourteenth century. Both MSS. were written by Bartolommeo Comparini, who lived in Florence towards the end of the fifteenth century.[2] A third *sylloge*, the *Crameriana*, contains 114 epigrams; its two MSS. are of the thirteenth and fourteenth centuries, but the age of the collection is unknown.[3] The fourth collection is the *Appendix Barberino-Vaticana*, extant in two sixteenth-century MSS., but put together probably in the fifteenth century. It contains 54 erotic epigrams, 47 of which are not in the Planudean Anthology. Its MSS. are *Vaticanus* 240 and a part of *Barberinus* 123 (above, p. 30).[4] This part of the Barberini MS. seems to

[1] Extant in three MSS., *Florentinus* 57, 29; *Paris.* 1773; *Paris.* 2720. It was made in the reign of the Emperor Leo (886–912), and is dedicated to a certain Euphemios. On it see Schneidewin, *Progymn. ad Anth. Graec.* Göttingen, 1885. Of epigrams not in *Plan.* it contains *A.P.* 6.330 (No. 4); 9.361 (No. 45), 364 (No. 66); 11.108 (No. 39); 14. 71 (No. 71), 72 (No. 72). It also contains several pieces neither in *Plan.* nor in *Pal.*

[2] For contents see Stadtmüller in *Neue Jahrb.* 139 (1889). 770. Only epp. 64 and 65 (*A.P.* 9.205 and 434) are unknown to *Plan.*

[3] Published by Cramer in *Anecdota Graeca Paris.*, Oxford, 1841, 4.366–88, from *Paris. suppl.* 352; noted by Dilthey in *Paris.* 1630 [14 cent.]. It has the following epigrams absent from Planudes: *A.P.* 12.18, 21, 28, 58, 118, 181, 185, 196, 209, 214, 224, 241; 14.17, 71.

[4] Published by Sternbach, *Anthologiae Planudeae Appendix Barberino-Vaticana.* Leipzig, 1890. Epigrams not in *Plan.* are: *A.P.* 5.18, 31, 37, 41, 50, 60, 71, 77, 96, 128,

have been made by Fulvio Orsini from a copy in the library of Angelo Colocci. A fifth *sylloge minor* (Σ^π) is attached to the Palatine MS. Perhaps *Marcianus* 11,1, by Planudes, should be reckoned as a sixth.[1]

The small MSS. of our second class are mainly excerpts from the Planudean collection. Some of them contain interlinear glosses that suggest their having been employed in school-instruction; others are copies made by humanists for their own purposes. In the Vatican Library there are at least 25 partial MSS. of the epigrams; of which *Vat. Graec.* 1373 is notable as having been made for himself by Politian.[2] Martini's catalogue notices for the *Biblioteca Vallicellana* in Rome two MSS. containing epigrams, which were once owned by the archaeologist Achilles Statius, and three once owned by Leone Allacci.[3] There are eight small MSS. in the Laurentian Library at Florence, of

---

135, 158, 172, 186, 242, 243, 244, 246, 252, 255, 259, 272, 275, 285, 289, 294; 9.361, 381; 11.108; 12. 1, 2, 4, 17, 20, 59, 60 (with ταύτην for Θήρωνα), 65, 69, 75, 76, 77, 79, 86, 173, 196, 237.

[1] A further collection may be recognized in the following MSS., the contents of which are nearly identical: *Vat. Graec.* 20 [14 cent.]; *Vat. Graec.* 98, 4 [13 cent.]; *Vat. Graec.* 100, 8 [14 cent.]; *Vat. Urb. Graec.* 152, f 175vo [14 cent.]; *Ambros. Graec.* 295 (E 81 suppl.) [14–15 cent.]. It is a collection of some 71 of the best-known epigrams; the contents may be seen in the printed Catalogue of the Vatican MSS. under, e.g., *Vat. Graec.* 20. This MS. and No. 98 contain an interlinear gloss and notes. There may be a connection between these MSS. and *Marc.* 11,1 (cf. Finsler, *Krit. Untersuch. zur Geschichte der Gr. Anth.*, Zürich, 1876, p. 70). Compare also *Laur.* 59, 44 and *Vat. Graec.* 87 and 123.

[2] This list is mainly compiled from the printed Catalogue not yet completed Besides *Vat. Graec.* 240 mentioned above, and the four MSS. mentioned in note 1 above, I note: *Vat. Graec.* 29 [*an.* 1292, 11 epp.]; 62 [15 cent. A large selection from *Plan.*]; 87 [15 cent., 55 epp.]; 114 [13–14 cent., 3 epp.]; 123 [15 cent., 30 epp.]; 743 [Sternbach, *op. cit.*, p. xviii]; 1347 [Pesenti, *Boll. di Filol. Class.* 26 (1920). 140]; 1373 [15 cent. Politian]; 1386 [15 cent. Cf. below, p. 153, n. 2]; *Vat. Pal. Graec.* 128 [15 cent., 13 epp.]; *Vat. Urb. Graec.* 125.ff. 197vo, 203vo, 303vo, 307vo [14 cent.? In all about 33 epp.]; *Urb. Graec.* 95.f. 83vo [*A.P.* 9.47]; 123.f.1 [14 cent. *A.P.* 7.325-6]; 110ff. 142–54 [end of 14 cent. A large section of *Plan.*]; *Vat. Ottobon. Graec.* 194. A fifteenth-century MS. of *Iliad* A–H, once in the private library of Pius II, begins with an epigram on Hercules (cf. *AP.* 16.92) and four epigrams on Homer: *A.P.* 7.3, 7, 6, 4 (Stevenson, *Codices Reginae Suecorum et Pii PP. II Graeci*, No. 38). In the Queen of Sweden's collection No. 142 [16 cent.] contains (ff. 1–26) more than 190 epigrams of the Anthology; it came from the library of Alexander Petavius in Paris (Stevenson, *op. cit.*, p. 98); in the same collection *Cod.* 166 [14–15 cent.] contains *A.P.* 16.233-4. The Barberini Library, now part of the Vatican, besides *Barb.* 123, already mentioned, has three MSS.—Nos. 50, 69, and 185 in the summary cat. by Seymour de Ricci (*Rev. des Biblioth.* 17 (1907). 81ff.) The last, however, is a recent excerpt from the *Palatinus*. No. 50 contains notes by Leone Allacci. A second apograph of Pal. (17th cent.) is No. 11 of the Bibliotheca Corsiniana (Pierleoni in *Stud. Ital. Filol.* Class. 9.473).

[3] Emidio Martini, *Catalogo di manoscritti Greci esistenti nelle biblioteche Italiane* (Milan, 1893–1902) 2.37, 137 (MSS. B 99 and F 14) for Statius; *ibid.* 2.216 (MSS. xciv, cxvi, cxxxii) for Allacci.

which *Laur.* 32, 16 belonged to Filelfo.[1] The Catalogue of the Ambrosian Library in Milan, besides two complete MSS., notices some 20 MSS. containing small groups of epigrams; several of these entered the Ambrosian from the libraries of well-known humanists like Merula and Bonamico.[2] At Venice, St. Mark's has two minor MSS., one of which was formerly possessed by Cardinal Bessarion, founder of the collection.[3] The National Library at Naples has two MSS. containing epigrams. One of them, containing five plays of Euripides, begins with 27 folios of epigrams from the Anthology; this part seems to belong to the fifteenth century.[4] The second MS. contains nothing but epigrams; no date is assigned to it.[5] The *Biblioteca Governativa* in Cremona has a fifteenth-century MS. containing epigrams.[6]

Constantine Lascaris made a large selection from the Planudean Anthology at Milan in 1464. His manuscript is now in the National Library in Madrid (*Matrit.* 24; below, p. 108).[7]

---

[1] Besides *Laur.* 57, 29 (above, p. 32, n. 1) and 32, 16 [13 cent.? See below, p. 95] these are: *Laur.* 33, 50 [16 cent.]; 59, 44 [age unknown]; 74, 13 [15 cent.]; 91, suppl. 8 [15 cent. In a printed Theocritus of (?) 1497]; *Magliabec.* cl. viii, n. 1425 [15 cent. Belonged to 'Jacobus Franciscus de Segnis.' See Olivieri in *Stud. Ital. Filol. Class.* 5.408]; and *Conv. Sopr.* 440 [16 cent., with Latin transl. See Rostagno, *Stud. Ital. Fil. Class.* 6.149]. Several other MSS. contain a few epigrams each, e.g., *Abb. Fior.* 2762, written in 1291 (Rostagno and Festa in *Stud. Ital.* 1.158) and *Riccard. Graec.* 89, written by Lorenzo Giacomini in 1565 (Vitelli in *Stud. Ital.* 2.530).

[2] Martini and Bassi, *Catalogus. Cod.* 218 (D 15 suppl.) [15 cent. From the Pinelli Library]; 247 (D 71 suppl.) [15 cent.]; 277 (E 26 suppl.) [16 cent.]; 295 (E 81 suppl.) [14–5 cent. 'Est Georgii Merlani Alexandrini et amicorum.']; 426 (H 22 suppl.) [?15 cent. Contains first two books of *Plan.*; formerly in Pinelli Library]; 450 (I 4 suppl.) [? 13 cent. In an *Iliad* that belonged to Francesco da Castiglione in 1452, later to Pinelli]; 597 (O 122 suppl.) [In the hand of Lazarus Bonamico; with notes on the epp.; dated 1519]; 705 (Q 123 suppl.) [16 cent.]; 886 (C 222 inf.), f 360vo [13–4 cent. Belonged to G. Merula]. The following contain a very few epigrams each: *Cod.* 15 (A 78 suppl.); 18, f.142 (A 81 suppl.).; 40, f. 505 (A 115 suppl.); 52, f.213 (A 155 suppl.); 92, f.58vo (B 52 suppl.); 119 (B 97 suppl.); 164 (C 4 suppl.); 216 (D 12 suppl.) [Belonged to G. Merula]; 268 (E 6 suppl.) [Brought from Chios in 1606]; 569 (N 234 suppl.); 973 (D 430 inf.) [written by Laz. Bonamico].

[3] For Bessarion's MS. see below, p. 98, n. 1. The second (*Marc.* 11, 1) is mentioned by Finsler (above p. 33, n. 1), who calls it an autograph of Planudes.

[4] Salvator Cyrillus, *Catalogus*, Naples, 1826–32, 2.186. *Cod. Graec.* 198 (II.F.41).

[5] *Cod. Graec.* 201 (II.F.44); Cyrillus 2.190.

[6] Martini, *Catalogo*, vol. 1, pt. 2, p. 302 (cf. p. 271). A MS. of the *Iliad* in the Biblioteca Regia at Parma contains three epigrams (Martini, vol. 1, pt. 1, p. 171); an *Odyssey* in the Bibl. Malatestiana at Cesena, written in 1311, contains *A.P.* 7.3 and 15 (*Mélanges d'Archéol.* 2 (1882). 224). But such isolated epigrams cannot be enumerated.

A paper MS., 'Graeca quaedam veterum epigrammata,' belonging to one Nicolaus Trivisanus at Padua in 1639, was reported by G. F. Tomasini, *Bibliothecae Patavinae Manuscriptae Publicae et Privatae*, Udine, 1639, p. 115.

Cod. Graec. 63 (15–16 cent.) of the Bibl. Estense at Modena contains a small group of epigrams (Puntoni in *Stud. Ital. Filol. Class.* 4.427).

[7] In the Escurial is a MS. (Ѵ–iv–1) containing a few epigrams (Emmanuel Miller, *Catalogue*, Paris, 1848, p. 439). It once belonged to Joannes Syncleticus of Cyprus.

Besides complete MSS. of the Anthology, and seventeenth- and eighteenth-century excerpts from the *Palatinus*, which do not here concern us, there are in Paris 19 small MSS. of epigrams, most of which were at one time in Italy.[1]

4. Knowledge of the Epigrams before the *Editio Princeps*

The Anthology probably was not known in Italy till after 1460. Certain epigrams were known before that; from a source we cannot trace even Boccacio knew two of them. Early in the fifteenth century Ambrogio Traversari, Filelfo, and others had a good notion of Greek epigrams from Diogenes Laertius. Meanwhile Ciriaco d'Ancona had begun his travels in search of inscriptions, and seems to have picked up several of our epigrams, perhaps from MSS., in the Orient; these he communicated to Filelfo and other scholars. Most of the epigrams known, however, were read in Diogenes, Strabo, Plutarch, and Herodotus.[2]

Miller published from a MS. in the Escurial the Catalogue of the library of Cardinal Sirleto, in which No. 12 under 'Rhetoric and Poetry' (Miller, p. 328) was a paper MS. of the Anthology. Sirleto's library came ultimately from Alberto Pio of Carpi. On MSS. of *scholia* in Madrid see below, pp. 156–7.

[1] From Omont's *Inventaire Sommaire*, Paris, 1886–98. *Paris.* 1773, 2720 [from the Medici Library; copied in part by Scipione Carteromaco], 1630, and 352 suppl. have already been mentioned. The others are: *Paris.* 1739, f.271vo [15 cent. Medici]; 2276, f.139–47 [16 cent. Fontainebleau]; 2562, f.97–111 [14–5 cent.]; 2722, f.33 [14–5 cent.]; 2744, f.16–33 [13 cent.]; 2864 [15 cent. Colbert]; 2865, f.1–3 [16 cent. 9 epp. From library of Kings of Naples]; 3019, *passim* [15 cent]; 3027, f. 70–4 [16–7 cent.]. *Paris.* *Suppl.* 455 [15 cent.]; 565, ff.275, 292vo; 1164, f.4–22 [14 cent.]; 1199 [14 and 16 cent.]. *Paris. Coislin.* 341, f.381 [copied in 1318 by Callinichos], 352 [17 cent.]. *Paris.* 2511 2633, 2824, and 2847 contain one or two epigrams each. A part of the Palatine MS. (pp. 615–709) remains at Paris (*Suppl. Graec.* 384).

There is a copy of epigrams from the Anthology in the University Library at Upsala, perhaps of the 16 cent. (Graux and Martin in *Archives des Missions*, Ser. 3, vol. 15). Harles, Fabricius, *Bibl. Graec.* 4.437, mentions a 14th-cent. MS. belonging to B.N. Krohn of Hamburg in 1793 (cf. Jacobs and Ukert, *Beiträge zur ältern Litteratur*, Leipzig, 1835, 1.205).

Selections from *Plan.* in eighteenth-century MSS. can be of little interest; they have probably been made from printed copies. I note, however, the following: at Bucharest, No. 716, 19 in C. Litzica's *Catalogul Manuscriptelor Grecesti* (Bucharest, 1909); at Athens, in I. and A. Sakkelion's Κατάλογος of the National Library (Athens, 1892), Nos. 1076, 1120 (17 cent.), and 1183; and at Jerusalem, in the catalogue by Papadopoulos-Kerameos mentioned above, Nos. 394, 453, 458, 476, 480, 486. These excerpts seem mainly to be from the first book of *Plan.*, probably for use in school-instruction.

[2] The Erizzi palace in Venice is reported to have possessed in the seventeenth century a stone, brought from Greece in the Renaissance, bearing *A.P.* 9.599 (Theocritus) and another, 'in the courtyard, at the *piscina* of St. Moses,' on which was cut the figure of a seated dog, with *A.P.* 7.64 for the inscription. These were shown to Spon by the abate Gradenigo in 1675 (Jacob Spon and George Wheler, *Voyage d'Italie, de Dalmatie, de Grèce, et du Levant, fait aux années 1675 et 1676*, The Hague, 1724, 1.45). Finally, Spon also reported seeing *A.P.* 16.103 in the same palace inscribed on a statue of Hercules (*Misc. Erud. Antiq.*, Lyons, 1685, p. 50).

We first catch sight of the Anthology in the hands of the exiled Greeks who are about to transmit it to their Italian pupils. Bessarion possessed MSS. of the epigrams. Constantine Lascaris copied a large part of the Anthology at Milan in 1464. Demetrius Chalcondyles and Joannes Laurentius were at work on a MS. at Padua in 1466. Chalcondyles taught there from *c.* 1463 to 1471, when he went to Florence to succeed Argyropulos. Among his pupils at Padua was Janus (then Joannes) Lascaris, who was to be editor of the first printed Anthology, and was destined to play a great rôle in the spread of humanism through Europe. Toward the end of 1472 Lascaris followed Chalcondyles to Florence; and for more than twenty years both were connected with the Medici. That Chalcondyles continued to be interested in the Greek epigrams is suggested by the fact that Politian, one of his Florentine pupils, wrote Greek epigrams in his honor. Lascaris made the Anthology the basis of his lectures during a part of one year. His 'opening lecture' is preserved, in which he speaks of having commented on Sophocles and Thucydides in the year preceding, and promises to 'interpret' Demosthenes and the Greek Epigrams in the year then beginning. Unluckily which years these were cannot be determined; probably the lecture belongs to the beginning of 1493. In it Lascaris made a noble introduction of the Anthology to the West, and sketched the channels in which its influence was to run. 'From no other book,' he said, 'can we gain so much, whether respecting language and learning, or respecting judgment on human actions, or the constitution of manners and life. So great is the variety in it, such a supply of names and matter, such exquisite judgments on almost everything that falls within the realm of human action, together with such brevity and elegance, such grace and charm, that you might think the genius and judgment of all the wisest of men, rivaling and vying with one another, had been brought together into this single volume. Let each one, therefore, translate these pieces, delight in them, imitate them; among them let him practise, who wishes, besides other advantages, to attempt any like poem and to succeed.'

If this lecture was delivered in 1493, the activity it outlines was already under way. Politian's imitations of the Greek epigrams went back to his boyhood, perhaps to 1470, though the highest pitch of his interest in them was reached almost precisely in 1493. Lascaris has himself left some translations of the epigrams into Latin; as has also another Greek resident in Florence, his friend Marullus. Alessandra Scala, who became Marullus' wife, was a pupil of Lascaris; she composed Greek epigrams in honor of Politian; while her father Bartolommeo, Gonfaloniere of the Republic, imitated the Anthology in Latin. Outside of Florence, it is just possible that Guarino da Verona had used the Greek epigrams as a schoolbook at Ferrara. At all events, his pupils Joannes Pannonius, Tito Strozzi, and Antonio Costanzi were among the first to translate them; and his son and successor, Giovanni Battista, was the teacher of Urceo Codro, the younger Costanzi, L. G. Giraldi, and Calcagnini, all of whom show an interest in the Anthology. Merula, as we know, had manuscripts of the epigrams at Milan. In an academic lecture on Homer, dated April 1, 1486, an anonymous scholar quotes *A.P.* 16.296, giving a Latin translation. The place is unknown.[1] At Naples, Pontano, Del Tuppo, Sannazaro, and Gravina probably read the Anthology before the first edition was printed. Indeed the Anthology already stood in the full light of the Renaissance; Politian had only to tell his friend Urceo Codro at Bologna that his own Greek epigrams were intended to rival the Anthology, and Codro could without difficulty turn to the original to compare them.

5. Editions of the Anthology; Selections

The first edition of the Planudean Anthology was published by Lascaris in August 1494, at the press of Alopa in Florence. It is a beautiful volume, and, to judge from the numbers of copies still extant, was issued in a fairly large edition. Its beauty, of course, tended to preserve it. Nine years later followed the first Aldine, enriched from the Marcian MS. The Juntine edition appeared at Florence in 1519; the second Aldine at Venice in 1521; the edition of the Nicolini at Venice in 1550; followed in 1551 by the third Aldine. The French editions of Badius Ascensius, Paris, 1531; of Jean Brodeau, Basel, 1549;

[1] Gollob, 'Die Griechische Lit. in den HSS. der Rossiana in Wien,' *Sitsungsb. d. K. Akad. d. Wiss. in Wien* 164 (1910).3.110 (No. 44, f. 65). The MS. (16 cent.) came from the library of Canon Rossi and Commendatore Torquato Rossi in Rome in the nineteenth century. The lecture is headed: 'Kalendis Aprilis 1486 in scholis publicis.' An eighteenth-century MS. in the same collection (Gollob 45) contains *A.P.* 11.365.

and of Stephanus, Paris, 1566; and the Wechel edition, Frankfort, 1600, also sent copies into Italy. The same is true of the
edition with complete prose-translation by Eilhardus Lubinus,
Heidelberg, 1603–4, and the corpus of *Poetae Graeci Veteres*,
Cologne, 1614, in which Lubinus' version was reprinted. Among
the greater Greek classics only Homer and Isocrates were in
print before the Anthology; and during the sixteenth century
few of the classics were more often re-edited. After 1614, however, no other edition of the Anthology appeared for a century
and a half; the reason being that all expected some scholar—
first Salmasius, then Grotius, Le Clerc, and D'Orville—to get
out an edition from the Palatine MS. This expectation was only
partially fulfilled by the *Carmina Sepulcralia* (Leipzig, 1745)
of J. H. Leich, and by Reiske in Vol. 9 of the *Miscellanea
Lipsiensia* (1752) and in his *Anthologiae . . . libri tres* (Leipzig,
1754)—the latter republished by Thomas Warton, Oxford,
1766; it was not completely fulfilled until the *Analecta* of
Brunck appeared (Strassburg, 1772–6) followed by the monu-
mental *Anthologia Graeca* of Jacobs (Leipzig, 1794–1814). The
Planudean collection, with additions from Brunck, had meanwhile been reprinted by Carcani (Naples, 1788–96) and by De
Bosch (Utrecht, 1795–1822).[1]

Probably more effective in spreading the knowledge of the
epigrams were the numerous editions of selections, especially
those with translations, and schoolbooks. Of all these selections
none enjoyed a wider popularity than the *Epigrammata Graeca*
of Joannes Soter, first published at Cologne in 1525, and again,
with additions, in 1528; appropriated by Cornarius in 1529;
made over by the Jesuits in 1608; and finally passing into the
large collection of translations published by Rivinus in 1651.[2]
It served as model and source for Stephanus' book of translations (1570), and for numerous schoolbooks. Lubinus published
the first book of Planudes with verse-translation at Rostock in

---

[1] The Μοῦσα Παιδική (*A.P.* Book 12) was edited by Klotz in 1764. Besides editions'
separate commentaries were also printed, and had their influence (cf. Obsopoeus, below, p. 286). Portions of the *Anthologia inedita*, as the *Palatinus* was called, began to
circulate among scholars immediately after its discovery by Salmasius. Libraries in
France, Germany, and England are burdened with these often useless *apographa*. A
few epigrams from these came into print: Heinsius published several in his *Poemata
Graeca* (1640); Vavasseur a part of the Proems in *De Epigrammate* (1669); Joannes
Jensius a selection in *Lucubrationes Hesychianae* (1742); and D'Orville in his *Chariton*
(1750).
[2] Below, p. 274.

1600; and Jerome Megiser made a book of selections like Soter's (*Anthologia seu Florilegium Graecolatinum*. Frankfort, 1602). Copies of these are still to be found in Italian libraries.

Ever since the lectures of Lascaris, and probably before, the Anthology has had its place in school instruction, usually in a selection such as those just mentioned. The Jesuits especially found a place for it. Many a writer who speaks easily of the Anthology relies on the memory of his school days. 'L'Antologia greca ha fatto la delizia dei miei studi giovenili,' said Cardinal Quirini, who had studied with the Jesuits at Brescia (*c.* 1695). An *Anthologia Nova*, Greek text only, is said to have been published at Rome in 1597; I have not seen it.[1] The reworking of Soter in 1608 has been mentioned. A schoolbook issued by Simeone Occhi at Venice in 1746 contains a selection of Greek epigrams. Zenobetti's *Anthologia Selecta* (1753) was arranged, as were certain English school selections, with epigrams in distich first, then those in four lines, and so advancing. It was intended to be an easy and delightful introduction to Greek poetry, inspired, says Zenobetti, by a love of the Greek epigrams that had been awakened in him by the teaching of Giovan Andrea Giulianelli at Florence.

6. Neo-Latin Writers and the Anthology

Politian died in September, 1494, hardly a month after the Anthology was printed; Chalcondyles had already departed from Florence for Milan; and Lascaris, quietly getting the dedication to Piero de' Medici removed from the remaining copies of his Anthology, followed the victorious Charles VIII to France. Florence for a time lost the intellectual leadership. In the next generation only Crinitus and Dazzi show an interest in the Anthology. Later, about the time of the Juntine edition, some use was made of the epigrams by Benedetto Accolti; and, in the succeeding generation, by the circle of Fabio Segni and Benedetto Varchi.

At Venice the Academy of Aldus was occupied with the Anthology. The Greeks, Arsenios and Musurus, of course, knew it well. Scipione Fortiguerri (Carteromaco) composed Greek epigrams, and a letter by him was printed in the first Aldine edition. The Anthology claimed the centre of attention when

---

[1] *Bibliotheca Heberiana*, London, 1809, 1.15.

the edition was preparing in 1503. Janus Lascaris was then in
Venice as ambassador of the French king, and must on occasion
have been consulted by Aldus. A little later Erasmus visited
Venice, and learned to know and esteem Lascaris, with whom,
as with Thomas More, he doubtless had many conversations
about the epigrams which occupy so conspicuous a place in the
works of all three scholars. Venetian Latin poets, nevertheless,
show little interest in the Anthology—Bembo, for example,
none. Navagero is virtually alone in imitating it; but his imitations are almost the best we have. He had been a pupil of Lascaris. About the middle of the sixteenth century the Venetian
Natale Conti, a professor at Padua, inserted numerous versions
of the epigrams into his work on mythology.

At Ferrara the first-fruits of humanism are represented by
Tito Strozzi, followed by Calcagnini, Ariosto, and Lilio Gregorio Giraldi. Ariosto in his youth was a true neo-Latin poet; he
has his *epigrammata*, and among them eight translations from
the Anthology. Calcagnini is a typical Renaissance figure,
soldier, Latin poet, and scholar with a passion for Greek. He
has more than 30 versions from the Anthology. Giraldi translates epigrams on numerous pages of his philological works.
Later in the sixteenth century, translations were still being
made by Giraldi Cintio, G. B. Pigna, and Elio Crotti.

Besides Urceo Codro at Bologna, the elder Beroaldo is able to
quote the epigrams, but only from a Latin version of Laertius.
His pupil Giambattista Pio, however, knew the Anthology.
Alciati studied at Bologna, and later taught there. His *Emblemata*, for which the Anthology is the chief source, has been one
of the most popular books of modern times, so that those epigrams which he imitated have been widely known.

Hints from the Anthology had been developed by Sannazaro
with a delightful freedom; Pontano had known the collection;
Gravina had made translations from it. Later Neapolitan Latin
poets still went to it for material, among them Pomponio
Gaurico, Giano Anisio, Girolamo Angeriano, Berardino Rota,
and Scipione Capece. Gaurico, in his Commentary on the *Ars
Poetica* of Horace, lists the Greek poets of various kinds that a
modern poet should imitate; for the epigram he names more
than fifty poets of the Anthology. His own epigrams include
nine translated from the Greek.

Though the new learning had been encouraged in Rome about the middle of the fifteenth century, it had declined by the time the Anthology was beginning to be known; and hence it is only with the age of Leo X that Roman poets begin to show its influence. An exception may be seen in Volaterranus, who earlier in the century employed a few epigrams in his *Urban Commentaries* (1506). Lascaris came to Rome at the beginning of Leo's pontificate. Valeriano Bolzani, a pupil of Lascaris in Venice, was tutor to Leo's nephews. He is the first considerable translator of the epigrams. The most considerable of all early Italian translators is Fausto Sabeo, at this time custodian of the Vatican Library; the greater part of his large volume of verse is given up to translations from the Anthology. Though the work of his youth, Bolzani's translations did not appear till the year 1550, while Sabeo's, also early works, were only published in 1556. Francesco Maria Molza, Francesco Franchini, Benedetto Accolti, secretary to Clement VII, often turn to the epigrams; Marcantonio Casanova, 'prince of epigrammatists,' and Marcantonio Flaminio less often. Paolo Manuzio resided in Rome from 1561 to 1570, and there perhaps made his prose version of the Anthology, never printed. Fulvio Orsini and his friend Lorenzo Gambara paid some attention to the Anthology. Orsini's library contained five copies of the first Aldine; his interest in MSS. has already been noticed. Angelo Colocci, Bishop of Nocera, owned a MS. of the Anthology.

Attention was paid to the Anthology at the university of Padua where Chalcondyles, J. Lascaris, and Musurus had taught. Musurus lectured on the Anthology there in 1506. At Milan after the time of Merula, Constantine Lascaris, and Chalcondyles, there is little to indicate much interest in the epigrams. Alciati began his *Emblemata* at Milan; but most of his life was spent elsewhere. Among the other Milanese who show the influence of the Anthology, G. M. Toscano spent his life in Paris, and Francesco Spinula lived in Venice. Cruceius and Scaphenatus, on the other hand, seem to have spent their lives in Milan. Vasolli and, later, Cardano may be reckoned for Pavia. Parma gives Anselmo; Fano the two Costanzi and Ippolito Capilupi. Toward the end of the sixteenth century Genoa gives us Pinelli, and Trieste Rapitius. Others lived beyond the Alps; among them, Tagliacarne (Teocreno) of

Genoa, who became tutor to the children of Francis I and
Bishop of Grasse, G. M. Toscano, Julius Caesar Scaliger, and
Matteo Toscano whose book entitled *Anthologia* appeared at
Bordeaux in 1620.

For neo-Latin writers the liveliest interest in the Anthology
falls within a period extending from 1475 to 1550; after 1550
names are scarcer. In fact the period of supreme interest virtually coincides with the active life of Janus Lascaris; after his
death (1535) began the decline of Greek studies. As we shall
see, however, this was about the time when the vernacular
writers began to make common use of themes from the epigrams. At the end of the century the study of Greek a little revived with the establishment of the Jesuit schools. The adapta-
tion of the Anthology to their needs could not better be shown
than by the *Selecta Epigrammata Graeca* (1608), already mentioned. Little more, so far as the epigrams are concerned, than a
reprint of the book of Joannes Soter, it is made fit for orthodox
schoolboys by the suppression of the names of all heretical
translators—for example, Sleidan—while their work is retained.
Orthodox translators are left in possession of their own. The
editor may have been Bandino Gualfreducci, secretary to the
General of the Order.

From the beginning the Greek epigrams were turned to a
variety of uses. They were quoted as evidence for the usages
of antiquity; they were commented on, as by Politian in his
Miscellanea; they were imitated in Greek verse; and they were
translated into Latin.

The practice of writing Greek epigrams, of which Politian
boasts himself the inaugurator in the West, has been the elegant
amusement of countless scholars since his time. Relatively few
have published their verses in separate collections.[1] In the early
Renaissance such verses commonly were produced for a single
purpose—as complimentary epigrams for the books of one's
friends, a practice that may go back to antiquity. So far as
Greek is concerned, Lascaris' Anthology itself is the first
printed book to bear such an epigram. In the same year (1494)
Aldus issued his Musaeus, perhaps his first work, at the front
of which are two epigrams by Marcus Musurus, and one (*A.P.*
7.615) from the Anthology. At first Janus Lascaris, Musurus,

---

[1] E.g., Cottunius, Joseph Scaliger, Daniel Heinsius, Gilles Ménage.

and Scipione Carteromaco appear most often as authors of these commendatory pieces. Presently they are the vogue. In France, Dorat, the 'father' of the Pléïade, turned out hundreds of such Greek epigrams. For these exercises the epigrams of the Anthology obviously were models. Later, the more or less extempore composition of Greek epigrams was practised by scholars in their informal gatherings, much as the Alexandrian epigrammatists practised it in their day. Thus we hear of such exercises at the house of Francesco Porto in Modena about the middle of the sixteenth century:[1] 'E in ciascuna cena era proposto alcuno esercizio ingegnoso, come che ciascuno dovesse comporre Epigramma Greco, o Latino, o Sonetto, o Madrigale, sopra alcuna, o alcune vivande recate in tavola.' These exercises were still later caught up from the humanists by the Jesuits, and by them formalized for the schools.

Latin epigrams had been written in Italy fairly continuously since the time of Ennius. No doubt they began to be written in imitation of the Greek; and Greek epigrams were the models down to the time of Ausonius. Such was hardly again the case until the fifteenth century, when it probably holds true of Marullus, for example, and Politian. Still the fifteenth-century humanist was an irascible being, and the general run of Latin epigrams then written savor more of Martial than of the Anthology. With the age of Leo X we pass into a more urbane atmosphere. Now, Martial was everywhere dispraised (Tiraboschi, *Stor.* 2.93); and the Anthology became the chief model of the epigrammatists who abounded in Italy. 'Under Leo X Latin epigrams were like daily bread.'[2] Even writers who do not acknowledge their allegiance by translations, do so by a new grace and ease of style, and by a bent for votive epigrams and the like, that must go to the Anthology for models. And for the Latin poets of this period, one learns to expect, in turning the pages of their pretty volumes, to come upon the superscription *e Graeco*, which generally means the Anthology.

Soter and Cornarius had published their select translations with the avowed purpose of setting examples to the young. Frequently the translators, like Bolzani and Alciati, assert that in their versions from the Anthology they have been prevailed

[1] Castelvetro quoted by Tiraboschi, *Bibl. Mod.* 1.5.
[2] Burckhardt, *Culture of the Renaissance*, Eng. trans. (1878) 1.378.

upon to print the exercises of their youth. Evidently for exercise, they often turn the same epigram in several ways, a practice already used by Calcagnini and carried further by Sabeo, who has twelve versions of *A.P.* 7.545. This feat, however, was nothing to the ingenuity later displayed by Henri Estienne and John Stockwood.

The Jesuits, again, are responsible for a new lease of life taken by the Latin epigram in the seventeenth century. The composition of Latin epigrams was a regular exercise in their schools, borrowed by them from the humanists, and passed on to their imitators. Many a famous man of letters first distinguished himself at school in such compositions. The renewed interest in Greek on the part of the Jesuits joins with this practice, and *e Graeco* reappears in their books. The writing of Latin verse was an exercise of the Rhetoric classes, the upper division of the Jesuit grammar school. The *Ratio Studiorum* suggests that, while the master is correcting papers, his pupils may spend the time in imitating a passage from a poet or an orator, in varying the same sentence in many ways, in turning one kind of poem into another, or in writing epigrams, inscriptions, and epitaphs.[1] In his Greek prelections the master may once a week introduce a few epigrams.[2] On vacation days his prelection, instead of being a historian or poet, may be something more abstruse as Hieroglyphics or Emblems, or else a discussion of the poetic art: of the Epigram, Epitaph, Ode, Elegy, etc.[3] Ample provision is made for honoring the successful writer of verse; for example, the best poems are to be exhibited on the school wall nearly every second month and on special occasions. Successful efforts often saw the light later among the published epigrams of their authors. Such perhaps are the translations and imitations of the Anthology made by Gualfreducci, Finotti, Matteo Toscano, the younger Aleander, Bargiocchi, Urban VIII, Vincenzo Guinisi, and Pietro Alois. Not all these writers were trained by the Jesuits; but the Jesuit training was universally imitated. These Latin poems were read, yet were taken for the academic exercises that they were. The serious spirit of literature had some time since passed to the vernacular.

---

[1] *Ratio atque Institutio Studiorum Societatis Jesu*, Antwerp, 1635, p. 122.
[2] *Ibid.*, p. 126.
[3] *Ibid.* On treatises *De Epigrammate*, often written by Jesuit schoolmasters, see below, pp. 60–73.

Works of scholarship continued to be written in Latin; and in these, from the time of Politian onward, the Greek epigrams were frequently quoted. When so quoting them, a scholar felt bound to supply a metrical translation, and, if unprovided with any of his own, usually resorted to the collection of Soter. Among treatises adorned with metrical versions may be mentioned those of G. B. Pio (1496), Volaterranus (1506), L. G. Giraldi (various dates), Costanzo Landi (1559), Minturno (1559), Alsario (1595), Marescotti (1610), the younger Aleander (1616), Tomasini (1639), Allacci (1640), and Argoli (1642). After the middle of the seventeenth century there is little point in discussing any Latin writings apart from the Italian.

7. Vernacular Writers and the Anthology

Italian vernacular literature, awakened by the troubadours of Provence, had sprung into wonderful life in the days of Dante, and had gone on with vigor through the fourteenth century. Yet even before the death of Boccaccio it met with a check. Petrarch from the first and Boccaccio in his later years felt the superiority of Latin to Italian; both had been entranced with a vision of the ancient world, and gave the authority of their influence and example to the revival of antiquity. For the next hundred years all the best intelligence of the peninsula was humanist. At times men toyed with the vernacular, but a distinguished Italian poem can hardly be found between the time of Boccaccio and the youth of Politian. The humanism of the fifteenth century was not exclusively Latin; Greek, because of its novelty, was the centre of attention. The new Latin and Greek literature that the humanists were producing inevitably chose models among the ancient classics; its peculiar character was that it depended on those models.

Towards the end of the century Italian literature again raised its head in Florence, Ferrara, and Naples. We naturally look to see whether the recent attention to classical models has had an effect on the revived vernacular, and find that apparently it has not. Italian literature had its traditions, its own themes, its own forms, inherited from the Middle Ages. Even though the new poets were commonly also humanists—Politian, Ariosto, Sannazaro, Bembo—when they wrote in the vernacular they employed the themes and forms of the vernacular tradition, when they wrote in Latin they employed the themes and forms of the ancient classics. Yet the change was there; Bembo was in search, not of a 'sweet new style,' but of models, which he found in the vernacular tradition. The next generation, taking the inevitable step, mixed the two traditions; and for three centuries a main literary problem in every country of Europe has been the modification of mediaeval types by the imitation of the Greek and Latin classics.

A difficulty that confronts every tracer of literary influences lies in the independent expression of similar ideas by various writers. In the present study this question becomes important chiefly for the amatory epigrams. The terms of a dedication, an epitaph, an anecdote, or a jest, can rarely be borrowed without carrying hints of their origin; but the language of love tends to be everywhere the same.

Few conceits of Petrarch were more widely imitated by later poets than that of Sonnet 156:

> Passa la nave mia colma d'oblio
> Per aspro mare, a mezza notte il verno,
> Enfra Scilla e Caribdi, et al governo
> Siede 'l signore anzi 'l nemico mio:
> A ciascun remo, un penser pronto e rio
> Che la tempesta e 'l fin par ch' abbi' a scherno;
> La vela rompe un vento umido, eterno,
> Di sospir, di speranze, e di desio. . . .
> Morta fra l'onde è la ragion e l'arte,
> Tal ch' i' 'ncomincio a desperar del porto.

This theme is as much a commonplace in the Anthology; compare Meleager (*A.P.* 5.190):[1] 'O bitter wave of Love, and unresting gales of Jealousy, and wintry sea of revelries, whither am I borne? The rudders of my reason are completely carried away. Shall we ever look again on tender Scylla?'

Another commonplace of amatory poetry is the theme, Love has sculptured—or painted—my lady's image in my heart.[2] Meleager has it for the whole thought of an epigram (*A.P.*

---

[1] Again *A.P.* 12.157, also by Meleager.
[2] Even the troubadour Piere Vidal (†1192) has something like it (*Poésies*, ed. by Anglada, Paris, 1913, p. 49):

> Vers, vai t' en ves Montoliu
> E di m' a las tres serors,
> Que tan mi platz lor amors,
> Qu' ins en mon cor las escriu.

5.155); centuries later it still serves Paul the Silentiary (*A.P.* 5.274). Petrarch has this conceit at least twice (*Canz.* 13.35 and *Son.* 75.5–6). Boiardo has it:[1]

> Ma quella dolce angelica sembianza
> Che sempre fu scolpita nel mio core.

Ariosto more than once employs it; Bembo uses it (*Rime*,1808, p. 160); and, in a word, it is the common property of all sonneteers in every language.

There are many other themes common to the Greek epigrammatists and to the mediaeval vernacular poets. For example: Beauty blooms like a flower, and like a flower it fades (*A.P.* 5.74; 12.235); Love like a fowler spreads his nets (*A.P.* 5.100; 12.132); the courtesan's old age (*A.P.* 5.204); the lover's dream (*A.P.* 5.2, 243); the beloved both makes the wound and heals it (*A.P.* 5.225); the lady's golden locks are her lover's chains (*A.P.* 5.230); the lover has no room left for more of Love's darts (*A.P.* 5.98). These and other conceits may on occasion be drawn from the Anthology, but are usually taken from the common stock of amatory ideas gathered by the mediaeval vernacular poets. Doubtless much of this stock goes back to the older reservoir of Graeco-Roman literary themes to which the Greek epigrams themselves belong. The verses of Serafino and Tebaldeo are often a tissue of these commonplaces.[2]

Coincidence between the themes of Italian poetry at the end of the fifteenth century and the themes of the Anthology stands, then, upon the basis just indicated. One might think of Meleager in reading the following *rispetto* by Politian, but Politian was almost certainly thinking of Petrarch:[3]

> Io son la sventurata navicella
> In alto mar tra l'onda irata e bruna,
> Tra le secche e gli scogli, meschinella,
> Combattuta da' venti e da fortuna,
> Senza àlbore o timon; nè veggio istella,
> E il ciel suo isforzo contro mi rauna:
> Pure il cammin da tal nocchier m' è scorto,
> Ch' i' spero salvo pervenire in porto.

---

[1] *Poesie Volgari e Latine*, ed. by Solerti, p. 78.
[2] For example, compare Tebaldeo's sonnet, Non più saetti amor, non ce più horma Loco nel corpo mio (*Opere d'Amore*, Venice, 1550, Son. 152) with *A.P.* 5.98: ἐγὼ γὰρ ἔχω τραύματος οὐδὲ τόπον.
[3] *Le Stanze, l'Orfeo, e le Rime*, ed. by Carducci, Bologna, 1912, p. 586.

Politian's *Stanze* on the tournament of Giuliano de' Medici are a piece of mediaeval paganism, and might have been written by Boccaccio. A fine stanza of this poem (1.101) describes Venus rising from the sea; and may have given the hint to Botticelli for his more famous picture:[1]

> Giurar potresti che dell' onde uscisse
> La dea premendo con la destra il crino,
> Con l'altra il dolce pomo ricoprisse;
> E, stampata dal piè sacro e divino,
> D' erbe e di fior la rena si vestisse;
> Poi con sembiante lieto e peregrino
> Dalle tre ninfe in grembo fusse accolta,
> E di stellato vestimento involta.

With the second line Carducci compares Ausonius' version of *A.P.* 16.178 (complexa manu madidos salis aequore crines); and it is noteworthy that some time later Politian chose this Greek epigram, or *A.P.* 16.180, which is similar, as model for a Greek epigram of his own.[2] *A.P.* 16.178 is on the Aphrodite Anadyomene of Apelles, and is by Antipater of Sidon: 'Behold the labor of Apelles' brush—Cypris rising but now from the sea, her mother; how with her hand she grasps her hair dripping with water, and wrings the foam from her wet locks,' etc.[2]

With Sannazaro the tendency to pass material from Greek and Latin originals into the vernacular begins somewhat to grow. His *Arcadia* owes much to the classics; but while the action takes place in classical landscapes reminiscent of Virgil and Theocritus, no use is made of the mass of suitable material that might have been drawn from the Anthology. Yet Sannazaro imitated the Greek epigrams in his Latin verse.[3]

The *Libro di Natura d'Amore* of Mario Equicola occupies an odd position between neo-Latin and vernacular literature. The author first wrote it in Latin, but published it in Italian. It is equally devoted to vernacular and to classical lore on its subject; and towards the end contains catalogues of what all the

---

[1] Cf. A. Streeter, *Botticelli*, London, 1907, p. 98.

[2] Cf. below, p. 136. Carducci (*op. cit.*, p. 75) names the Anthology among the Greek and Latin sources which, he says, provided the 'elementary lines' of this part of the *Stanze*, where the palace of Venus is described. His sole justification seems to be the comparison noticed above.

[3] In one passage Scherillo thought he detected an echo of Meleager's poem on Spring (*Arcadia*, ed. by Scherillo, Turin, 1888, p. 11); but the two passages are similar only in commonplaces which occur as well in countless other descriptions of Spring.

poets known to Equicola have had to say on love. The Greek epigrammatists are not ignored, as is evident from Equicola's amazing summary given on a later page. The *Natura d'Amore* was in process of writing from 1496 to 1525.

Extensive borrowing from the Greek could hardly be expected as long as the forms of Italian poetry remained mediaeval; but when, about 1515, the forms of classical poetry began to be imitated in the vernacular, the floodgates of 'plagiarism' were opened. We shall speak again of the rise of the Italian epigram; enough here to observe that Luigi Alamanni, its first regular practitioner, out of 114 epigrams has 35 imitations of the Greek. Some Greek epigrams had already reached Italian in the *strambotti* of Bernardo Accolti (1513) and in the *Versi et Regole* of Claudio Tolomei and his friends (1539). Tolomei and his Academy carried the notion of imitating classical forms to the degree of imitating classical metres, an experiment in which they were to find followers in all the languages of Europe. Epigrams were about of a length to suit such an experiment, and the *Versi et Regole* contains numbers of them. These epigrams are mainly translations from the neo-Latin epigrammatists; and so it happens that a few themes from the Anthology indirectly reach the *Versi et Regole*. Alamanni was writing epigrams about 1545; after him the epigram took a respectable place in Italian literature, but the influence of the Anthology on it was felt more in form than in materials. Still, later epigrammatists, like Bernardino Baldi at the end of the century, on occasion turn to the Greek for matter.

As the Anthology played its greatest rôle in neo-Latin verse during the first half of the sixteenth century, so in vernacular verse the period of its greatest influence falls within the limits of 1550 and 1610. This influence was, I believe, in most cases not direct. The poets of the late sixteenth and early seventeenth century were, with some exceptions, men of moderate learning. They had some Greek, but they read Latin. They read and pillaged the neo-Latin poets who preceded them. This practice, it will be remembered, Du Bellay in France specifically recommended; we have seen it already in use by Tolomei and his circle. Between many an Italian poem and its original in the Anthology will be found a modern Latin intermediary.

For the influence of the Anthology possibly more important

than the formation of an Italian epigram was what may be
termed the doctrine of equivalence of forms, whereby it was
asserted that the sonnet (sometimes the madrigal) takes in
Italian the place of the epigram in Greek (below, p. 56). A
sonnet on the theme of *A.P.* 16.200 by Molza was printed by
Domenichi in 1545. Thereafter the practice was extended by
Molza's friend Rainerio (1553), and carried on by Riccio
(1552), by Beccuti (before 1553), by Berardino Rota (1560),
by Lodovico Paterno (1560), and by Orlandini (1571), Luigi
Groto (1587), Tasso, Celso Cittadini, Marino, G. B. Manso,
and Giuseppe Battista.

The sixteenth-century madrigal appears to have been developed with the epigram for model. Luigi Cassola, perhaps the
first to publish an entire volume of madrigals (Venice, 1544),
owes nothing to the Anthology; but already in the elder
Giovan Battista Strozzi, before 1571, the form becomes more
epigrammatic, and he has a madrigal on the theme of *A.P.*
9.346. Minturno declares the madrigal rather than the sonnet
to be the modern equivalent of the epigram, and himself makes
a number of madrigals from themes found in the Anthology.
Tasso has at least one; his friend Filippo Alberti four madrigals
based on Greek epigrams; Girolamo Casone one, and other
poets one or more. The Anthology was fairly ransacked for
madrigals by Luigi Groto, a popular writer well-known throughout Europe as 'Il Cieco d'Hadria.' Even better known was
Stefano Guazzo, who introduces several translations into his
Civil Conversazione and his *Dialoghi*, but more, in the form
of madrigals, into his *Ghirlanda*. A 'garden' of madrigals was
published by Maurizio Moro in 1593, increased to three 'gardens'
in 1602; a dozen of his madrigals are transplanted from the
Anthology. These fanciful titles for madrigal-collections—
Ghirlanda and *Giardini*—irresistibly remind one of the 'wreath'
of Meleager and of the Anthology or *Florilegium*, titles under
which the Greek collection goes.[1] The first years of the seventeenth century saw the rage for madrigals at its height. Gaspare
Murtola takes nineteen of his from the Anthology; his rival
Marino has ten from the same source. Alessandro Guarini has
one; Tommaso Stigliani four. In 1611 there was published a

They are also reminiscent of the titles sometimes affected by the neo-Latin poets,
e.g. *Pratum, Viridarium* (cf. below, p. 209).

thick anthology of madrigals *Il Gareggiamento Poetico*; twenty-four pieces by various writers are from the Greek epigrams. In some cases these madrigals from the Anthology were set to music, for example, Tasso's version of *A.P.* 7.669.

Miscellanies of minor poetry, such as the *Gareggiamento*, must often be made with the Anthology in mind. In an early and highly valued one, the *Fiori delle Rime de' Poeti Illustri* (Venice, 1558), the editor, Girolamo Ruscelli, distinctly claims it as his model. Poets themselves in arranging their *rime* by subject sometimes think of the Planudean arrangement; an example of this is Stigliani. Later, with the rise of literary periodicals, a casual allusion to the Greek Anthology may at times be intended in the recurring use of *Antologia*, *Nuova Antologia*, and the like for titles. The *Antologia Romana* for Feb., 1796, even contains a (modern) Greek epigram.

Translations from the epigrams easily find a place as quotations in dialogues and essays such as Possevino's *Dialogo dell' Honore* (1553), Ridolfi's *Aretefila* (1560), and Guazzo's dialogues already mentioned. The Anthology is a less obvious source for novels; yet Giraldi Cintio manages in his *Hecatommithi* to hold the reader's interest with a manipulation of *A.P.* 9.44. Somewhat similarly Lodovico Guicciardini drew materials from the Anthology for his book of anecdotes. A natural place for the epigrams is found in Germano's proverbs. In works of erudition the epigrams are plainly useful as illustrative material. Cartari alludes to one in his *Imagini* (1556); Costanzo Landi quotes them in his Italian as well as in his Latin works; Tasso uses one in his criticism of a sonnet by Della Casa. Above all, the commentaries of Castelvetro on Petrarch (1582) and Mazzoni on Dante (1587) both draw heavily on the Greek epigrams.

As we advance into the seventeenth century, the draft of the lyric poets upon the Anthology quickly thins out. In the matter of style Loredano and perhaps Chiabrera owe something to the Greek epigrams. Brignole Sale openly professes to imitate them, but never employs a theme from the Anthology. Giuseppe Battista alone (1665) has as many as eleven versions; but he, the literary executor of Manso, is a belated Marinist. Towards the end of the century translations are ascribed to M. A. Torcigliano and to Carlo Maria Maggi; these unfortunately I have failed to find. The reaction against Marinism and all that the Marinisti favored was a prime cause of this decline. The poets of Marino's day had read the neo-Latin poets of the sixteenth century, and from them had picked up themes derived from the Anthology. These Latin poets were now comparatively neglected.

Though the Palatine MS. was brought to Rome in 1623, and remained there for the better part of two centuries, almost nothing was done with it by Italians. A beginning was made by Leone Allacci, to whom the pope had entrusted the transfer of the Palatine collection from Heidelberg; but he had no successor. Northern scholars laboring with their meagre *apographa* should have been a reproach to Italy. The epigrams, however, were more and more used as illustrative matter for the kind of scholarship that was pursued. Some Latin treatises of the first half of the century have already been mentioned. Writers on the epigram, as Cottunius, Patavinus, and Gallus, of necessity quote Greek epigrams. A translation of Theophrastus' *Characters* by Ansaldo Cebà (1620) is illustrated from them. The department of literary history, set in motion by L. G. Giraldi, and carried forward by Patrizi, flourished in the seventeenth century. In Giraldi's *Dialogues* due attention had been paid to the Greek epigrammatists; Patrizi's *Poetica* (Ferrara, 1586) amazingly omits all mention of them both in the historical and in the theoretical parts of the book. The *Proginnasmi Poetici* of Benedetto Fioretti, first published in 1620, again makes full use of the Anthology. Lorenzo Crasso's *History of the Greek Poets* (1678) is filled with Greek epigrams. Milton's friend Carlo Dati quotes ten in his *Lives of the Ancient Painters* (1667), of which he translates three. Francesco Redi draws upon the Anthology in his commentary on his own dithyramb (1685). Giuseppe Barberio's *De Miseria Poetarum Graecorum* (1685) contains eleven translations.

Very notable is a series of 86 dissertations (in Latin) delivered in 1676–7 at the University of Pisa by the professor of Greek Literature, Benedetto Averani, and later published in his works (1717). He does not advance beyond the average Italian scholarship of his time—he seems never to have heard of the Palatine collection; but shows again how the Anthology, with its unparalleled variety, may be made to illuminate numerous departments of Greek life. He adorns his lectures with 36 verse-translations. Averani was a great teacher; enthusiasm was his power; and to him can largely be traced the revival of Hellenism at Florence in the succeeding generation, centring in his distinguished pupil A. M. Salvini. The twenty-first lecture of Averani's course may well be compared with the opening lecture of Lascaris, delivered at Florence nearly two hundred years before.

The illustrative use of the epigrams continued throughout the eighteenth century. Salvini seems always to have had the Anthology at his side when he sat down to annotate the Italian poets. Biscioni on Lippi's *Malmantile* translates *A.P.* 11.78. Gravina quotes and translates *A.P.* 9.26 in his *Ragion Poetica*. Such works as Banduri's *Imperium Orientale* and Bonada's *Carmina ex Antiquis Lapidibus* naturally made free use of the Greek epigrams. Quadrio gives a fair account of the Anthology. Pasquale Carcani illustrates the *Antichità di Ercolano* with some 55 epigrams, which he translates. Attention of a sort was even given to the Palatine MS. by Cardinal Quirini, by Zenobetti, and by Spalletti, more as scribes, however, than as scholars.

In Italy, as in the rest of Europe, the eighteenth century was an age of translations. No one can say how much they contributed to the renewal of taste that marks the end of the period. A thin stream of translation, in Latin and Italian, from the Anthology runs down through the seventeenth century; Dati, Bartolommeo Beverini (1674), Maggi, Averani, Cappellari (1697), Carlo d'Aquino (1701), Zappi, and Francesco Forzoni Accolti made occasional versions. But about 1720 translation became every scholar's business. Salvini is said to have left in manuscript almost a complete translation of the Anthology. The first considerable translation to be published since the middle of the sixteenth century occurs in one of the little books that in Italy are put out in honor of the marriage of a friend. This volume is by Antonio Bongiovanni and Girolamo Zanetti, and was published in Venice for the wedding of Tommaso Mocenigo-Soranzo and Elena Contarini, September 6, 1752. It contains versions of 130 epigrams. Later in the century Bettinelli produced translations on similar occasions. Giovanni Ricolvi translates 55 epigrams in his *Dissertazione sull'Antologia*, published in 1762 but written before 1748. Luigi

Subleyras devoted himself to translating the epigrams (1759).
The most extensive Latin verse-translation made from the
Anthology by an Italian since the time of Sabeo is that of
Raimondo Cunich (1771), containing about 500 epigrams.
These were virtually all turned from Cunich's Latin freely into
Italian verse by the poet Passeroni (1789). Averardo de' Medici
translated 50 epigrams into both Latin and Italian, his first collection being issued in 1772, a second in 1780, a third in 1790. In
1781 Girolamo Pompei put 100 of the epigrams very pleasingly
into Italian verse in his *Raccolta Greca*. The abate Carlo Felici
published 145 in *Epigrammi tratti dal Greco* in 1787, and followed these with 50 more under the same title in 1795. The second selection was dedicated to the Cardinal Duke of York. In
the following year (1796) an amazing Dane of Spanish descent,
Count Vargas, in his *Saggio dell' Epigramma Greco*, published at
Siena, translated about 100 pieces from the Anthology. In this
year was completed the edition of the Anthology by Gaetano
Carcani containing a translation into *versi sciolti* of the entire
collection—the first complete translation to be made into any
modern language. Finally, at the very end of the century, Luca
Antonio Pagnini published some 432 translations into Italian
verse. To these must be added the translators of Theocritus,
who always deal with about 24 of our epigrams—Salvini (1717),
Regolotti (1729), Della Torre (1775), Vicini (1781), and Pagnini (1786).

The Italian epigram had been created in the sixteenth century by Alamanni and others, largely in imitation of the neo-
Latin epigram and the Greek Anthology; it was renewed, and
it flourished, in the eighteenth century mainly in imitation of
the French. Still the Greek epigrams had a part in the revival.
The translations just enumerated spread its influence. Epigrammatists like Bertòla, Vannetti, Cerretti, Mariani, and Pananti
sometimes included an imitation of the Greek among their
original epigrams. Roncalli has 41 such pieces, going back to the
Anthology mostly through Cunich's Latin versions. Finally,
theorists of the epigram, like Count Vargas and Bettinelli,
advocated a revival of the Greek type. Here may be asked
what part the Anthology had received in the theory of the
epigram since the Renaissance, and what had been its formal
influence.

8. The Epigram

The Greek epigram was the result of several origins, and showed its multiple beginnings to the end.[1] As the word implies, the epigram was first of all an inscription; it became attached to Ionic elegy, and the epigram of the best period has been well described as simply a brief elegy. It has the metre, usually the dialect, and the themes of elegy, with the brevity of an inscription. Reitzenstein has attempted to show how it was affected by the practice of reciting epigrams at banquets.

The ancients have left no extended theory of the epigram. Two writers in the Anthology, Parmenion and Cyrillus, both belonging to a late age, have epigrams on the epigram (*A.P.* 9.342, 369); they merely insist on its brevity. Martial, in pronouncing upon the form, likewise is mainly concerned with brevity, and with defending his own jocose style.[2] If all periods are taken together, the Greek epigram does not admit of definition, in the sense in which tragedy and the epic poem do. Its only *differentia* is brevity. Point, in the rhetorical sense, is relatively rare in the Greek epigram of the best periods; its place is taken in the Alexandrian epigram by what we should call 'conceits.' Point, however, is not long separable from brevity, and the proper form of the epigram came naturally to be thought of as not only brief but pointed. Point, again—such was human nature in the Roman period—inevitably tended to be satirical. The epigram reached its full development as a brief, pointed, and mainly satirical poem. It reached this stage, at which it rested, long after the Greek spirit had passed its zenith. The epigram, in its ultimate form, was best written by a Roman. We preferably think of the Greek epigram as the comparatively unstable, but nobler, form, the brief elegy, written before and during the Alexandrian age.

The practice of Martial established the form for the Western Middle Ages. Brevity and point were everything. 'Quod ad epigrammata spectat,' writes Sidonius Apollinaris (*Epist.* 8.9), 'non copia sed acumine placent.' In this mold all Latin epigrams

---

[1] Much still remains obscure in the history of the Greek epigram; see, however, Reitzenstein, *Epigramm und Skolion* (Giessen, 1893), the same scholar's article 'Epigramm' in Pauly-Wissowa, *Real-Encycl.*, Wilamowitz, *Sappho und Simonides* (Berlin, 1913), and Geffcken, 'Studien zum Griechischen Epigramm' in *Neue Jahrb.* 39 (1917). 88–117.

[2] *Epig.* 1.1–5; 2.1, 77, 86; 3.69; 4.23, 29.

were cast, at least up to the beginning of the sixteenth century.
J. A. Campanus (†1477) so describes them:[1] 'Poscunt collectam
et rotundam brevitatem epigrammata, et tunc probantur
maxime, cum exacuuntur spiculis et sale.' Yet in the vigorous
growth of epigram-writing that took place in the time of
Leo X, Martial, as aforesaid, was largely deserted, and the
classical Greek epigram exalted to the place of model. The
origin of the modern Latin epigram is therefore sufficiently evident. The origin of the vernacular epigram is more difficult to
seize.

The Italians and French had several small verse-forms, more
or less 'lyrical' in character, well-accepted in the vernacular
tradition—*strambotti, rispetti, dizains, madrigali, ballati,* and
above all the sonnet. These were often in many respects the
equivalents of the Greek epigram. Writers of these forms in the
Renaissance became conscious of the similarity, and their consciousness led to formal modification as well as to substantial
borrowing. The madrigal, as developed by Strozzi, Tasso, and
Guarini, is crisper and more pointed than the verses of Petrarch
to which the same name is given, while the equivalence of the
sonnet and the ancient epigram is constantly asserted.

This assertion I have been unable to trace earlier than the
Art Poétique of Sebillet, published in 1548:[2] 'Sonnet n'est autre
chose que le parfait épigramme de l'italien comme le dizain du
françois.' Nothing like this statement occurs in Bembo's *Volgar
Lingua* (1525), in Daniello (1536), or in Trissino (1529, 1563);
but it became a commonplace about 1550. Pigna (1554) chooses
to compare the madrigal with the epigram of the Greeks and
Romans, and refers the sonnet now to the epigram and now to
the lyric poem.[3] The assertion is introduced as a commonplace
in Varchi's *Ercolano* (*c.* 1560): '*Cesare:* Quanto agli epigrammi?
Varchi: I Greci furono in questa sorte di poesia felicissimi; i
Latini antichi, da quelli di Catullo, della Priapea, e pochi altri
in fuora, si può dire che ne mancassero; ma i moderni hanno in
questa parte larghissimamente sopperito. Per la qual cosa, se il
sonetto corrisponde all' epigramma, noi vinciamo di grandis-
sima lunga; se il madriale, o mandriale, non perdiamo.' He then

---

[1] *Epistolae et Poemata,* ed. by Menckenius, Leipzig, 1707, p. 179.
[2] Ed. by Gaiffe, Paris, 1910, p. 115. No Italian source has been found for Sebillet's
chapters on the epigram and sonnet.
[3] *I Romanzi,* Venice, 1554, p. 62.

speaks of Alamanni's epigrams.[1] To Minturno in 1564 it is surely a commonplace: '*Bernardino Rota:* Adunque voi non assomigliate il sonetto a quel, che i Greci e li Latini chiamano epigramma? *Minturno:* Anzi credo, che da lui sia molto differente; perciocchè l'epigramma è particella dell' epica poesia, il sonetto della melica,' etc.[2] Tasso has the statement;[3] and it continued to figure in nearly all discussions of the sonnet.[4]

This doctrine of equivalence was not without a certain foundation in reality. The Italian sonnet, for example, would readily submit to the classification given to the epigram in the Anthology: amatory, dedicatory, sepulchral (and laudatory), moral, anecdotal, satirical sonnets, and sonnets on works of art. But whether the example of the Greek and of the neo-Latin epigram, together with the conscious theory of equivalence, played a decisive or even an important part in keeping the sonnet open to these various uses, is not easily determined without a detailed comparison of the sixteenth-century sonnet and the sonnet of earlier centuries. That cannot here be undertaken. My impression is that the effect of the epigram was greater than is generally recognized. Certainly the dedicatory or votive sonnet, so common in the sixteenth century, cannot but be the offspring of the Greek dedicatory epigram, or rather descended from it through neo-Latin imitations.

To end the sonnet with a striking 'point,' though this was far from being a new feature, became a somewhat more conscious aim on the part of certain sixteenth-century sonneteers. Writers on the sonnet found that they could draw on the epigram-treatises. Tasso, for instance, treats of the place of *acume* in the sonnet: it was often held—but Tasso dissents—that the place for the most striking point was in the final couplet.[5] The ending in a crisp couplet favored by Shakespeare may be regarded as an extreme form of this epigrammatic tendency.[6] In this care

[1] *L'Ercolano*, Milan, 1804, 2.268. Varchi was a friend of Alamanni. Observe the omission of Martial from Varchi's list of Latin epigrammatists.

[2] *L'Arte Poetica*, Naples, 1725, p. 240.

[3] *Prose Diverse*, ed. by Guasti, 2.123, and *Dialoghi*, ed. by the same, 3.110.

[4] Cf. Fioretti (below, p. 362); Meninni, *Rit. del Son.*, pp. 7-14; Becelli, *Della Novella Poesia*, Verona, 1732, p. 40; Quadrio (below, p. 395); Ireneo Affò, *Dizionario Precettivo*, Milan, 1824, p. 229.

[5] *Dialoghi*, ed. by Guasti, 3.74-5.

[6] Cf. *Son.* 21, ending:

Let them say more that like of hearsay well;
I will not praise that purpose not to sell.

for 'points' again there may be seen a certain influence from the epigram, especially in those circles where the equivalence of the sonnet and epigram was a commonplace of literary talk.[1]

Despite such similarities, a sonnet was not after all an epigram; and admirers of classical literature desired to possess in their own language the thing itself. Possibly the suggestion that sonnet and epigram were equivalent arose from the discussions attendant on the creation of the Italian form. The vernacular epigram originated at almost the same time in French and in Italian literature, but independently. In France, Marot undertook to modify the old *dizains* and the like by importing into them the substance and movement of Martial and the neo-Latin epigram. His *Épigrammes*, published in 1538, are the first in any modern language really to deserve the name. Yet they represented the form still not quite disengaged from the mediaeval small-forms; they were *quatrains*, *huitains*, or more commonly *dizains*, and among these without distinction were mingled fourteen-line sonnets. Indeed, save that Marot calls his verses epigrams (which is important), they advance only a little on the way to the classical epigram beyond the *strambotti* of Bernardo Accolti (1513). In Italy the vernacular epigram came into existence just following the bloom of the Latin epigram under Leo X, and found its models preferably among the Latin epigrammatists of that age. It appears not to have grown out of a modification of the *strambotti* or *rispetti*, but was an immediate imitation of the Latin and Greek form. Claudio Tolomei and his friends attempted a vernacular epigram in the exact image of their Latin models; their book (1539) contains probably the first instance of the Italian word *epigramma* (in pl. *epigrammi*) meaning an Italian poem equivalent in every respect to the Greek and Latin type. Their metrical

---

But see an article by Walter L. Bullock in *Mod. Lang. Notes* 39 (1924). 477–8 for a list of Italian sonnets written before 1400, and ending in the rhymed couplet.

[1] Modern writers of Latin, having occasion to mention the sonnet, generally translate *sonetto* by *epigramma*. In Marino's first pastoral idyl, as noticed by Mennini (*Rit.*, p. 9), this usage is carried into the vernacular (but cf. Register under *A.P.* 5.210):

> Vedi questo fra gli altri? appunto questo
> Grazioso *Epigramma*
> Fu dettato a miei prieghi
> Con *arguzie vivaci*
> Odi come comincia:
> Nera sì; ma sei bella, o di Natura.

experiment, however, went too far.[1] Certainly the first epigrams in Italian to be widely known, and influential, were those of Alamanni, completed before 1546. Alamanni wrote them in France, but there is no evidence that he learned anything from Marot; instead he modeled himself directly on the Greek and Latin writers without reference to mediaeval forms. Undoubtedly he knew Tolomei's work. His epigrams are composed in a verse-form intended to suggest, but not to reproduce, the Greek and Latin distich.[2] His object in founding the Italian epigram was that it should be as inclusive a form as the Greek, many examples of which he translates—historical, mythological, sepulchral, and descriptive epigrams, but seldom the satirical type. Here again is reflected the taste of the age of Leo.

The form set by Alamanni was closely followed by Girolamo Pensa (1570), by Bernardino Baldi, and by others. Side by side with this regular epigram went the more 'popular' quatrain, commonly resorted to for satirical verses—for example, by Machiavelli and Il Lasca. The two forms only coalesced in the seventeenth century. In the eighteenth century both in Italy and in France, the epigram enjoyed an immense vogue, doubtless in large measure prompted by the attention paid to it in Jesuit colleges. Since the vernacular form was supposed to be the exact counterpart of the Latin and Greek epigram, the laws of the epigram as laid down in the treatises *De Epigrammate* were equally understood to apply to it. These treatises, as we have noticed, were studied in the Jesuit schools.

The want of any specific theory of the epigram coming down from antiquity has been amply made up by modern writers. As we review some of their treatises, the theory will be seen to become more definite and elaborate until Scaliger is reached; then, among the schoolmasters, the principles, mainly formed on Scaliger, pass from one to another almost unchanged; only

---

[1] An earlier use of the word *epigrammi* for vernacular poems, but not for epigrams in any usual sense, occurs in a letter of Pietro Summonte to Angelo Colocci, the reference being to Italian translations from Provençal; the letter is dated July 20, 1515 (quoted by Pércopo, *Rime di Benedetto Gareth detto il Chariteo*, Naples, 1892, p. ccxiv). The *strammotti* of Chariteo are essentially epigrams, a fact of which the writer, a friend of Sannazaro, must have been fully conscious.

[2] Hauvette, *Luigi Alamanni*, p. 258. The rhyme-scheme is usually *aabb*, intended to give the effect of the distich; and, though all the lines are hendecasyllables, they were written and printed with every second line indented, again to give the appearance of the distich. Hauvette observes that the two-line epigram in Italian has continued to be so indented, but not longer ones.

towards the close of the eighteenth century are these rules and
divisions discarded in Germany by Lessing and in Italy by
Bettinelli.[1]

Writers on the epigram commonly quote the following lines
by Calcagnini:

> Malim elegos, malim sylvas contexere longo
> 　Carmine, quam ductu cultum epigramma brevi.
> Quippe illic fas est spatioso excurrere campo:
> 　Hic agilem angusto limite flectis equum.
> Illa sat est plane, satis est dixisse latine,
> 　Hic lepor et brevitas mixta lepore decet.
> Ni lectum legisse iuvet, ni pruriat auris,
> 　Iudice me carmen non epigramma voces.

These lines were well-known; they express the ideal of the Latin
epigram in the early sixteenth century; and they are a paraphrase of the Greek epigrams on the epigram given in the Anthology. The prime qualities of the form, be it observed, are
lepor and *brevitas*, not *aculeus*.

L. G. Giraldi's *Dialogues* appeared in 1545. For the epigram
the author sees three uses:[2] (1) as an inscription, (2) in verse of
praise or blame, (3) in making an acute observation on anything that befalls by chance or appears marvelous. It is not to
be written in affected or strained language, but with the supreme art of simplicity and candor. Some, he says, have likened
the epigram to an animal without head and feet—nothing but
body, while others have compared it with the scorpion, which,
while it threatens with all its parts, bears an effective venom in
its tail.[3]

The first elaborate theory of the epigram was the work of

---

[1] Some of the more notable writers on the epigram are: L. G. Giraldi, Sebillet, Ro-
bortello, Minturno, J. C. Scaliger, Vauquelin de la Fresnaye, Corréa, Pontanus (Span-
müller), Gallo, Possevino, Patavinus, Cottunius, Alexander Donatus, Antonio Rubio,
Nicole, Vavasseur, Mercier, G. J. Voss, Colletet, Grotius (*Epist. de Epig.*), Edward
Phillips, Ménage, Balzac, Renaldini, Crescimbeni, F. J. Freire, Batteux, Rapin, Boileau,
Quadrio, Thomas Pope Blount, Le Brun, De Senecé, Saint-Mard, Voltaire (*Dict. Phil.*),
Joseph Trapp, V. Comaschi, Bettinelli, Vargas, Lessing. Indeed most writers on the
poetic art consider this form. Epigrammatists commonly have epigrams on the epi-
gram: Calcagnini, Opitz, De Cailly, John Owen, Roncalli, J. B. Rousseau, Gombauld,
Le Brun.

[2] *De Poetis* 10, in *Opera*, Basel, 1580, 2.364.

[3] Cf. the following couplet, of unknown origin. It is here quoted from an anonymous
article on the Epigram in the *Quarterly Review* 117 (1865). 206.

> Omne epigramma sit instar apis; sit aculeus illi;
> 　Sint sua mella; sit et corporis exigui.

Robortello (1548).[1] So far as possible he treats the epigram on principles drawn from the *Poetics* of Aristotle. His plan is (1) to discover to what form of poetry the epigram belongs, then (2) to set forth what its proper materials are, and (3) to say what is to be sought for or avoided in its composition.

1. The epigram is a species of a larger form of poetry. As many epigrams are drawn from a portion of a comedy or a tragedy, so the epigram may be regarded as a part of comedy, tragedy, or some other poem (p. 35). Does the epigram involve 'imitation'? Some do, Robortello finds, while others have only 'simple narration.' Catullus' *Acmen Septimius* is built on imitation; his *Chommoda dicebat* is not. The epigram originated in inscriptions on shields, on ships, and on tombs; he instances *A.P.* 6.130, taking it from Pausanias.

2. The materials of comedy are the ridiculous, those of tragedy the serious, whereas the epigram, being a particle of various types, has no specific materials, but treats now those of comedy, now those proper to tragedy or to the epic poem (p. 36). [Robortello's concern with proper materials seemingly comes from Daniello's *Poetica*.] Yet in practice the epigram leans more to the materials of comedy. In ridiculing the vices of others there is need of *lepor* and *sal*, as may be seen from the want of these qualities in the numerous 'recent writers who cram the libraries with the volumes of their epigrams' (p. 37). [Robortello evidently cares more for point than did the recent neo-Latin poets.] Both 'Old' and 'New Comedy' provide materials for epigrams; and to be reckoned as comic matter are amatory themes. From epic poetry the epigram derives themes in praise of heroes. Many Greek epigrams, he observes, are written on heroes—on Eteocles [cf. *A.P.* 7.396, 399], Polynices [the same], Protesilaus [*A.P.* 7.141, 385], Hector [*A.P.* 7.137–40], Achilles [e.g., *A.P.* 7.142], Ajax [*A.P.* 7.145–52], Priam [*A.P.* 7.136]. Fables of the gods also find their way from epic poetry to the epigram. Since Catullus and Martial avoid making gods speak *in propria persona*, Robortello slightly deprecates the practice among his contemporaries, but admits that they have a model for it in the Anthology; he cites *A.P.* 7.145 (p. 39).

---

[1] After his commentary on Aristotle's *Poetics* (*In Librum Aristotelis De Arte Poetica Explicationes*, Florence, 1548): *Eorum omnium quae ad Methodum et Artificium scribendi Epigrammatis spectant Explicatio, ex Aristotelis libro de Poetica magna ex parte desumpta.*

3. Among things to be sought by the epigrammatist are propriety of language (Catullus and Martial are the models), *suavitas* (this resides in 'things,' as 'running streams,' 'kisses,' 'green trees'), a proper use of apostrophe, and finally 'sharp sayings' (he instances *A.P.* 9.13 as translated by Ausonius). Paronomasia was effectively employed by the Greeks (he cites *A.P.* 9.113). Among things to be avoided are the intermixture of too many Greek words, and such devices as acrostics. So much for rules; the rest must be learned from reading the ancient poets and from exercise in writing (p. 40).

The pronouncements of Calcagnini, Giraldi, and Robortello were addressed to the modern writer of Latin. Sebillet appears to be the first to give a theory of a vernacular epigram (1548); he draws it from the practice of Marot. The French epigram should not exceed twelve lines; eight- and ten-syllable lines are best, but Alexandrines are permissible. The epigram is to be as 'fluid' as possible, and the last two lines must be pointed (*aigus*). He asserts that the French epigram is founded on the Latin.

Ten years after Robortello's book appeared, epigrammatic theory was further elaborated by Minturno.[1] He follows Robortello, and goes beyond him in applying the principles of Aristotle's *Poetics*. His interest in the Greek Anthology, as is clear from other evidence, was greater than that of his predecessor, and strongly colors his theory:

The epigram is the oldest form of literary composition, as is clear from its inscriptional uses, an example of which is the epitaph of Midas [*A.P.* 7.153].[2] Later it was turned to various purposes. Whatever can be elegantly, acutely, and briefly expressed, whether concerning persons or things, and whether in praise or blame, the serious as well as the jocose, comes within its limits. These materials are supplied by history, tragedy, comedy, and epic poetry. Examples of all these kinds of arguments are furnished by Simonides, Alcaeus, Archias, Athenaeus, Agathias, Antipater, Palladas, Philippus, Antiphilus, Lucian, Bianor, Lucilius, and countless other Greek epigrammatists whose verses are still read, and among the Latins by Catullus, Martial, and Ausonius who translated many of the Greek epigrams.

The function of the epigram is not to surprise and delight only, but also to instruct. Sepulchral and honorary epigrams inspire the reader to imitate the virtues of the illustrious dead. Epigrams that employ

[1] *De Poeta ad Hectorem Pignatellum . . . libri sex.* Venice, 1559. The epigram is discussed in Book 5 (pp. 411–5) after elegy.

[2] Minturno usually gives Latin verse-translations of the Greek epigrams he quotes.

materials calling forth pity and fear thereby purge those passions. 'The epigram is a poem in which is briefly and wittily expressed whatever is thought worthy of remark, but the expression has not always the same manner.' It may be cast in the form of 'simple narration,' of '*allocutio*,' of '*imitatio per conformationem*,' of 'colloquy,' or in a 'mixed manner of narration.' Brevity is the 'soul' of the epigram, and is rightly insisted on by Cyrillus [*A.P.* 9.369] and Parmenion [*A.P.* 9.342]. The Latin epigrammatist is advised to seek models of brevity and wit among the Greek poets rather than among the Romans (p. 413).

The diction is to be 'suitable.' While avoiding the harsh and the obsolete, an epigrammatist is free to invent words, make compounds, employ old or foreign words, etc. The metre preferred for epigrams is the elegiac distich, but other forms are not excluded. The epigram, finally, is a division of epic poetry, since 'every poem is epic in which music and spectacle have no part.'

De Poeta was intended for modern Latin poets. For the vernacular poet, Minturno in 1563 issued an Italian form of his work.[1] Certain changes had, of course, to be made, but often the Italian *Poetica* is simply a translation of the *De Poeta;* the theory of the epigram remains almost the same. The comparison of sonnet and epigram, already quoted, is of course peculiar to the Italian form of Minturno's work. As to verse, the eleven-syllable line is recommended in the Italian epigram, either simple or alternating with seven-syllable lines, rimed or unrimed. It is of interest to see the advice to imitate the Greek epigrammatists turned from the Latin writer to the Italian.[2] As Alamanni in practice, so Minturno in theory seeks to form the Italian epigram firmly on the Greek.

In the epigram, however, as in other branches of poetry, the great lawgiver was Julius Caesar Scaliger. His *Poetics* was published in 1561, three years after his death. He owes much to Robortello, but, unlike him and Minturno, goes to the *Rhetoric* rather than to the *Poetics* of Aristotle for principles on which to base a theory of the epigram. This theory is set forth in the third book of his *Poetics*.[3]

---

[1] References are to the Naples edition of *L'Arte Poetica*, 1725.

[2] *De Poet.*, p. 413: Tu vero in eo veteres, Graecosque potius quam nostros velim imitere. Nam et leporem et, quae in hoc praecipue requiruntur, argutias perdit operis longitudo. *L'Art. Poet.*, p. 280: Ma, perciocchè non una volta par, che' Latini abbiano i termini di questa composizione trapassati, vorrei, che' nostri in lei ad imitare i Greci più tosto che' Romani si dessero; perciocchè la lunghezza dell' opera perde la leggiadria, e la piacevolezza, e l'arguzia, che questa Poesia richiede.

[3] Virtually nothing is said of the epigram in the historical part of the treatise. My references are to the fourth ed., *Poetices libri septem*, [Heidelberg], 1607.

After a word on inscriptions, Scaliger defines the epigram as follows: 'Epigramma igitur est poema breve cum simplici cuiuspiam rei, vel personae, vel facti indicatione, aut ex propositis aliquid deducens.' The definition then yields the following classification of epigrams: (1) those making a simple indication of the thing in question, as in dedications [he instances *A.P.* 9.647 and the beginning of 11.235]; (2) epigrams deducing something new from what is laid down in the first lines; these he calls 'composite.' 'Deduction' is to proceed by the rhetorical categories of 'more and less,' etc. Epigrams employ all kinds of verse, all kinds of diction, even barbarisms, and all kinds of materials. Brevity is the *proprium* of the epigram; wit or subtlety (*argutia*) its 'soul' or form. The epigram is not [as Robortello believed] a species of a large poem.

There are as many kinds of epigram as there are kinds of oratory—judicial, deliberative (*suasoria*), and demonstrative (based on praise and blame). [This application of the divisions of Aristotelian Rhetoric to the epigram seems to originate with Scaliger, and was much used by his followers. It obviously applies mainly to the 'composite' type of epigram.] To the demonstrative type belong *epitaphia* and *elogia*. Amatory epigrams are in general 'deliberative'; they should have the following character: *candida, culta, tersa, mollia, affectuum plena, interdum arguta in fine, interdum deficientia et mutila* (this last to show passion). He warns against puns in laudatory epigrams, but advises their use in satirical pieces. He observes that the Greeks do not succeed so well as the Latins in the latter type. The 'echo' he regards as an interesting device.[1]

Scaliger adds an appendix on the style of epigrams. Beyond the three ordinary styles—lofty, low, and middle—they have the following peculiarities: the relaxed style of Catullus and the mordant style of Martial. The first he designates by the word *mel*. The second has four subdivisions: one obscene, to be avoided, another characterized by *fel*, another by *acetum*, a fourth by *sal*. Several composite styles are also possible.

Scaliger, himself an epigrammatist, is interested in the type, giving it rather more space than he gives, for example, to satire or to lyric poems. His interest, however, is almost wholly Latin, and, while he pays his respects to the Greek epigrams, he is

---

[1] On the 'echo' see below, p. 77.

mainly thinking of only two styles—that of Catullus and that of Martial. Possibly, had Minturno been heard, the influence of the Anthology on the modern epigram would have been greater. The Latin Scaliger caught the attention of the world north of the Alps, and the attention of the Jesuit schoolmasters.

The first separate treatise on the epigram seems to be that of Tommaso Corréa, a Portuguese who taught rhetoric at Palermo, Rome, and Bologna. His book appeared eight years after Scaliger's *Poetics*, upon which it is evidently based.[1]

Corréa's definition is virtually Scaliger's: 'Epigramma . . . nihil est aliud quam breve poema cum simplici rei cuiuspiam indicatione, vel personae, vel facti; seu est contestatio deducta ex propositis in commendationem rei alicuius, seu detestationem' (p. 15). The 'soul' of the epigram is *argutia;* and this calls for brevity. 'Argutia enim animum excitat et capit, brevitate haeret memoria, et reficit' (chap. 7). The epigram is superior to other kinds of poetry in that every word has to be important. Finally, one learns to write epigrams 'by imitation and by judgment'; and as for imitation, here as elsewhere, Corréa advises, make the Greeks your models. Yet he quotes no Greek epigrams. Corréa lays his theory out in the following chapters: Preface; 1. On the word epigram [inscription]; 2. The definition; 3. On the simple and composite types; 4. Kinds of verse [any kind that fits the subject]; 5. Diction [pure, choice, sincere, elegant]; 6. Use of the epigram [as inscription]; 7. The form and power of the epigram [*argutia* and *brevitas*]; 8. On certain virtues of the epigram [*venustas, suavitas, energia*]; 9. Relation of epigrams to the several kinds of oratory; 10. On the conclusion [All epigrammatic virtues must be concentrated in the last line]; 11. The several styles; first, the 'sweet'; 12. The 'bitter'; 13. Pointed; 14. Urbane; 15. Cumulative; 16. Noble; 17. Amatory; 18. The Echo; 19. The Epitaph; 20. The Lament; 21. The Epicedium; 22. The Monodia; 23. The Threnus; 24. The Elogium; 25. On picture-poems; 26. The Palinode; 27. By what the epigram may be perfected [*Imitatio* and *iudicium*]; 28. That the epigram must be polished with care; 29. Examples of polish from the Latin epigrammatists; 30. How to set forth your material whether new or borrowed [from Horace's *Ars Poet.*].

A more influential book than Corréa's appeared in 1594 at Ingolstadt in Germany. This was the *Poeticae Institutiones* of Jacobus Pontanus or Spanmüller. It was produced as a Jesuit schoolbook, and for many years widely employed in their colleges; numerous editions were issued in various parts of Europe.[2]

---

[1] *De Toto eo Poematis Genere, quod Epigramma Dicitur,* Venice, 1569; again, with the title, *De Epigrammate,* Bologna, 1590. I use the latter.

[2] My references are to the edition of M. G. Büchler, Amsterdam, 1672.

Spanmüller's remarks on the epigram begin with Chapter 49 of his book. The treatment is based on Corréa, as the subjects of the chapters will show: 49. The word epigram; use of the epigram; 50. Definition of the epigram; its divisions; 51. The epigram in dialogue form; 52. The echo; 53. The emblem; 54. The prime virtues of an epigram—*argutia* and *brevitas;* 55. On *suavitas* and other ornaments of the epigram; on the witty conclusion; 56. On epitaphs; 57. On variety of verses.

But Spanmüller gives Scaliger's definition word for word, without the slight verbal changes of Corréa. With Robortello he divides the epigram into a 'tragic' and a 'comic' type. He follows Scaliger and Corréa in treating the epigram according to the kinds of oratory.

His examples at least are his own. He takes four translations of Greek epigrams from Soter—*A.P.* 7.542 (Germanicus, p. 50); 9.52 (Velius, p. 50), 61 (Marullus, p. 51); 11.391 (More, p. 64). The first three illustrate Chapter 50; and the last Chapter 55.[1]

A brief theory of the epigram is presented by the well-known Jesuit writer Antonio Possevino in Chapter 19 of his *Tractatio de Po"si et Pictura* (Lyons, 1595). He recognizes two main parts in an epigram—*expositio* and *clausula* or *conclusio*—with several minor distinctions. Epigrams he divides into three kinds —narrative, dramatic, and mixed (as the poet himself speaks, lets imaginary persons speak, or both). The style may be simple, grave and noble, tempered and elegant (*concinnum*), or light and lively (*tenue ac festivum*). He procedes to a criticism of the Greek epigrams (below, p. 252).

The German Jesuit, Matthaeus Raderus, composed a disser-

Spanmüll er (1542–1626)—called Pontanus from his birthplace, Brugg in Bohemia— was educated in Germany, and joined the Jesuits. His busy life was spent as a professor of rhetoric in his Order, and in writing schoolbooks, until ill-health forced him to retire from teaching to the quieter services of a translator. His books, says the *Biographie Universelle,* being employed for above a hundred years in the greater number of the colleges of Europe, formed a great many distinguished pupils. He died at Augsburg.

Not only was Pontanus' work used in the colleges of Europe. The celebrated Spanish Jesuit Antonio Rubio (1568–1615) adapted it for the use of Mexicans: *Poeticarum institutionum liber . . . ad usum studiosae iuventutis. Per Congregationem B. M. V. Annuntiatae in Societatis Iesu Collegii Mexicani gymnasiis auctoritate apostolica institutam.* Mexico City (H. Martinez), 1605. Instruction on the epigram, emblem, and epitaph occupies pp. 280–373. I give Rubio's chapter-heads: 1. Epigramma quid sit et quotuplex; 2. Quae et quotuplex materia epigrammatis; 3. Quae servanda in epigrammate; 4. De brevitate; 5. De suavitate; 6. De argutia; 7. De aucta et scita epigrammatis conclusione; 8. Epigrammatis exempla; 9. De artificioso epigrammate; 10. De dialogico epigrammate; 11. De epigrammate echico; 12. De anagrammate; 13. De artificii genere alio; 14. De hieroglyphico symbolo, emblemate, schemate, stemmate, [etc.]; 15. De aenigmate. The epitaph follows: 1. Epitaphium quid sit; 2. Epitaphii exempla; 3. De epicedio, naenia, monodia. Among the examples of epigrams (p. 301) is Germanicus' version of *A.P.* 7.542; among the epitaphs a version of *A.P.* 7. 308.

[1] That these translations came from Soter is shown by the quotation in Chap. 51 of a versified version of a dialogue of Lucian that appears only in Soter's book.

tation on the epigram as Chapter 4 of the Introduction to his edition of Martial, published at Ingolstadt in 1602 (2nd ed. *ibid.*, 1609). He adds nothing to Scaliger, but quotes a large number of Greek epigrams, with translations.[1] As his was an important edition, Raderus' version of the epigrammatic theory gained considerable attention.

A widely-used book on the epigram was that of Vincenzo Gallo, first published at Milan in 1626, and reaching a fifth edition in 1641.[2] Gallo declares that he has returned to Pliny for his definition of the epigram: 'Epigramma ita Plinius definivit—est carmen argutum et breve.' He agrees with Scaliger that the epigram is an independent literary form: 'Epigramma per se poema est, non elegiae, vel epopeiae, vel tragediae, vel comoediae pars, ut quidam [Robortello and Minturno] putarunt.' He teaches more by example than by precept, the bulk of his book (305 pages) being made up of epigrams, mostly from Martial. His theory is wholly based on Scaliger; but he deserves credit for the way in which, taking *argutia* to be the 'soul' of the epigram, he endeavors to show how in particular it is secured by each kind of epigram and each device he describes.

Gallo's chapters are divided as follows. 1. The word 'epigram'; the definition; 2. Materials; metres; 3. Quantitative parts of the epigram. [It does not have *exordium, narratio,* and *epilogus*—only *narratio* and *conclusio*]; 4. *Epigramma simplex et multiplex;* 5. *Epigramma simplex* [Among examples are 'Ausonius's' imitations of *A.P.* 9.13 and 145]; 6. Sepulchral epigrams—epitaphs, etc.; 7. Examples of the *Epigramma multiplex* [among them Germanicus' version of *A.P.* 7.542]; 8. The *Epigramma compositum;* 9. *Epigramma ex generibus causarum;* 10. On wit (*argutia*); 11. *Argutia* in 'words'; 12. *Argutia* in 'things'; 13. *Argutia* depending on figures of speech; 14. *Argutia* arising when more is deduced than the situation makes one expect [e.g., Ausonius' version of *A.P.* 11.104]; 15. *Argutia* arising when less is deduced; a third type, to which enigmas belong, in which things are put differently from what they are. [In 11–15 he follows Scaliger's hint on the category of 'more and less.']; 16. *Argutia* arising from the artifice of the verses— the 'echo,' dialogue, and figure-poem; 17. The emblem; 18. The symbol; 19. The fable; 20. Brevity [does not reside so much in keeping to

---

[1] About 70 in the whole work, including the Commentary.

[2] At first it was issued as part of Gallo's treatise *De Lyrico Poemate.* My references are to the fourth edition: *Opusculum, in quo Epigrammata . . . Veterum Scriptorum Exemplis Traduntur. Accessere . . . complurima exempla nobilissima.* Milan, 1632. Gallo was a native of Cremona; and he belonged to the religious order of St. Paul. He probably taught rhetoric in his order.

a certain number of verses as in having nothing superfluous]; 21. On diction; 22. On the *lemma* [to be a short summary of the poem].

In 1632 Joannes Cottunius (below, p. 268) published a book on the epigram: *De Conficiendo Epigrammate* (Bologna). He takes something from nearly every one of his predecessors. Following Minturno, but also because he himself was a Greek, he pays good attention to the Anthology. He combats the statement in Gellius that Latin epigrams have more *suavitas* than the Greek;[1] and his illustrations from the Anthology are unusually numerous. His definition of the epigram is verbatim from Scaliger; and his divisions are the conventional ones:

1. De nomine et veteri usu ep. Inscriptio; 2. De ep. antiquitate [After Minturno he gives a translation of *A.P.* 7.153]; 3. Explicatur definitio ep.; tum huius partitio in simplex et compositum [Scaliger]; 4. De epigrammate composito; 5. Partitio ep. [into the three kinds of oratory]; 6. [Examples of the demonstrative type; 7. of the deliberative; 8. of the judicial]; 9. Divisio ep. juxta varia poematum genera. [Rests on Aristotle]; 10. De ep. dictione. [Elaborates Minturno; from Aristotle]; 11. De dictionibus peregrinis, tum distortis, etc. [Instances Palladas, *A.P.* 9.502]; 12. De ideis seu formis orationis; 13. De proprietatibus dictionis; 14. De generibus dicendi; 15. De ep. brevitate; 16. De suavitate; 17. De argutia; 18. De conclusione; 19. De epigrammatibus quae peculiari quodam artificio terminantur; 20. Quomodo narrandum sit in ep.; 21. Quonam versuum genere. 22. De passionibus [Cf. Minturno]; 23. De acrostichis; 24. [An acrostic on Urban VIII]; 25. De echone; 26. De epp. correlativis et concordantibus; [e. g., *A.P.* 9.108]; 27. De epp. antistrophis [Instances *A.P.* 9.53 and 16.387*]; 28. De epp. declinatis et coniugatis [in which a noun is declined or a verb conjugated from line to line].

A similar handbook appeared at Cologne in 1651: *De Arte Epigrammatica sive de Ratione Epigrammatis rite Conficiendi libellus.* The author's name is given as Carolus Aconitanus a S. Antonio Patavino, whence he is usually referred to as Patavinus. He sets out from Scaliger's definition, and takes up the usual topics. Some interest attaches to his arrangement, as he digests everything under *narratio* and *conclusio* (or *argutia*). Like other writers for the schools, he mainly depends on Latin examples, giving Greek epigrams only in translations marked *e Graeco*.[2]

[1] Above, p. 11. *De Confic.*, p. 60.
[2] His table of contents follows: 1. Epigramma quid sit et quotuplex; 2. Epigrammatum materia quae sit et quot sint genera, et quot partes; 3. De narratione, prima epi-

Nicolas Mercier (Mercurius) published his *De Conscribendo Epigrammate* at Paris in 1653. It is divided into two parts—(1) Precepts, (2) Examples. The precepts are but slightly modified from those of his predecessors. His definition is that given by Gallo. He once quotes Cottunius; gives Gallo's treatment of *argutia;* uses Scaliger's *mel, fel, sal;* and at the end quotes his definition.

In the same year appeared *Épigrammes . . . avec un Discours de l'Épigramme,* by Guillaume Colletet. The *Discours* contains many of the familiar divisions; as authorities are quoted Minturno, Scaliger, Raderus, and Patavinus. The definition is mainly Scaliger's: 'Tout poème succinct, qui designe et qui marque naïfvement, ou une personne, ou une action, ou une parole notable; ou qui insère agréablement une chose surprenante de quelque proposition advancée, soit extraordinaire ou commune.' Colletet finds the Greek epigrams insipid, and prefers Martial.

A great number of persons in France and England received their idea of the epigram from the Jansenist *Epigrammatum Delectus,* published for the school of Port-Royal in 1659. The selection, it seems, was made by Claude Lancelot, while the introductory essay was the composition of Nicole.[1] In England the book was adopted by the authorities of Eton College, and went through many editions in the service of that school.[2]

The *Dissertatio* begins with some general principles on which the epigrams had been selected. They were required to be smooth and agreeable in sound; harshness, says Nicole, is the

grammatis parte, eiusque virtutibus; 4. De locis, seu modis aliquot, quibus narratio in epigrammate comparatur. Et haec decem loca, tamquam insigniora, connotantur et illustrantur exemplis: a. repetitio, b. similitudo seu comparatio, c. correlatio, d. contrapositio, e. hyperbole, f. allegoria, g. anagramma, h. congeries, i. descriptio, j. dialogus; 5. De argutia, altera epigrammatis parte, eiusque virtutibus; 6. De locis, seu modis aliquot, quibus argutia in epigrammate comparatur. Et haec decem loca, tamquam insigniora, connotantur et illustrantur exemplis: a. verbum diversum, idem pene litteris, b. irrisio, c. hyperbole, d. sententia, e. etymologia, f. enumeratio nominum praepositorum, g. allegoria, h. allusio, i. ambiguitas, j. inexpectata conclusio; 7. De toto epigrammate—quanam ratione epigramma optimum conficiatur, subjectis exemplis.

[1] *Epigrammatum delectus ex omnibus tum veteribus, tum recentioribus poetis accurate decerptus cum Dissertatione de vera pulchritudine et adumbrata.* I use the 12th ed., *in usum Scholae Etonensis,* London, 1752. A French translation of the *Dissertatio,* by Brugière de Barante, was inserted in the *Recueil des plus belles épigrammes,* Paris, 1698, and reprinted by Martinière in his *Nouveau recueil,* Amsterdam, 1720. On the *Delectus* see Sainte-Beuve, *Port-Royal* (1878) 3.506, 529-31, 625.

[2] Though the selection is entirely Latin, a small section *Ex Anthologia* is included, consisting of six Latin translations from the Greek; several others appear among the epigrams of Ausonius, Sannazaro, and Gaurico.

special fault of Latin translations from the Greek Anthology and the compositions of German poets. Their diction must be suited to the thought. They must not suffer from excess of metaphors. They must be true; not built on equivoques; nor hyperbolical—a fault Nicole finds characteristic of the Greek epigrams, as a bad example of which he cites Ausonius' version of *A.P.* 11.104; nor must they leave the reader in doubt as to truth or falsehood. They should be penetrating, not concerned with mere accidents like *A.P.* 7.542, which is quoted in the translation of Germanicus. Nicole rejects obscene and offensive epigrams; also those that make sport of faults of body and calamities of fortune; and those that are garrulous, trite, or based on mere word-play.

In the second place the special nature of the epigram is examined. First, *Epigrammatis nomen unde ductum, eius definitio, forma, leges.* Nicole begins with Scaliger, like him speaking of inscriptions, and gives his definition in part—'poema breve, cum simplici cuiusdam rei vel personae vel facti indicatione.' He argues that an epigram need not end with a pointed or weighty sentiment. Then, *Epigrammatum materia; inde divisio in varia genera.* Its materials are all things. Its division into types means to Nicole merely a division into the lofty, middle, and low styles. Finally: 'Of all the virtues of the epigram none is more difficult to attain . . . than . . . the proper unfolding of the argument so that there may be nothing redundant, nothing lacking, nothing absurd or obscure, no impediment in the words, nor anything too sudden and ill-prepared for.'

Nicole's Essay delighted the poet Chapelain; but ten years later (1669) it underwent a detailed censure in five chapters of the *De Epigrammate* by the Jesuit François Vavasseur, a man of learning far beyond anything Nicole could pretend to. Vavasseur finds the entire *Delectus* little better than the work of a clever pupil. Nearly every point of Nicole's Essay is objected to—the notion of 'truth,' the rejection of equivoques, the requirement of beauty. He complains that Catullus and, above all, the Greek Anthology are slighted in the Selections. A summary of Vavasseur's own theory follows:[1]

The making of poetry is the task of ingenious writers, and the construction of a good epigram the work of the most ingenious. Epigrams

[1] References are to his second edition: *De Epigrammate liber, et Epigrammatum libri tres, editio auctior*, Paris, 1672.

were originally inscriptions. The epigram is a brief and charming or witty poem (*breve, venustum, acutum*), indicating and setting forth a single subject, and coming to its wittiest at the end. The forms of the epigram are two—simple and composite; its parts are two—exposition and conclusion; its 'virtues' three—brevity, charm, and point. Vavasseur proceeds to discuss each of these.

The 'simple' form was favored by the Greeks and by Catullus, the composite by Martial and his followers. Brevity is required in both kinds; point only in the second; while charm is more characteristic of the first or simple form, though all epigrams must be smooth in sound. Point is traced to the study of rhetoric. It arises from 'words' and 'things.' It may be secured (1) by the rhetorical topics of 'more and less,' etc., or (2) from figures of speech, (3) from jests, (4) by keeping back the explanation of the situation envisaged in the first part of the epigram and letting it appear suddenly in the last line, (5) from ambiguities, (6) most effectively of all by letting one thing be expected and then saying another, or finally, (7) point may be derived from putting a sharp saying in sententious form [he cites Martial 2.68].

In treating of the divisions of the epigram, Vavasseur says he has mainly to refute the opinions of his predecessors. Scaliger's division into judicial, deliberative, and demonstrative types might be as well applied to any kind of poetry.[1] Equally absurd is his classification by styles—lofty, middle, and low; while his *mel, fel, sal,* and *acetum* do not exhaust the list of condiments he might with equal propriety have mentioned. Actually there are but two types of epigram: 1. that in which the point is given at the beginning, and pleasure arises from seeing it completed, and 2. that in which the point is held in suspense till the end.

Materials of all kinds may be treated in epigrams. Obscenity and personal abuse are to be avoided, but the epigrammatist (*pace* Nicole) will make sport of bodily defects and the like, for which practice Vavasseur finds authority in the Greek epigrams.

In the 'exposition' must be sown hints out of which the 'conclusion' may spontaneously arise. The epigram must have point. If in a long poem Homer may sometimes nod, that privilege never is granted to the epigrammatist. His diction must be pure whether he writes in Greek, Latin, or the vernacular, and as elegant as the subject permits. Finally the young epigrammatist will make Catullus and Martial his models.[2]

Vavasseur evidently owes more to his predecessors, Scaliger in particular, than he is inclined to admit.

[1] Vavasseur might have observed that it actually had been applied by Scaliger and others to elegy and to the lyric poem. His objection is not well taken.

[2] The remainder of Vavasseur's treatise is taken up with a discussion of the ancient Latin epigrammatists, of the Anthology, and of the shortcomings of the Port-Royal *Delectus*.

To return to the Italians.[1] Crescimbeni, in his *Volgar Poesia* (1698), does little more than quote from Minturno on the epigram. He makes it clear that the Italian epigram is not a mediaeval type, but is directly modeled on the Greek and Latin form; yet notes that the Italians had a sort of epigram in their *deche*. Quadrio (below, p. 395) is somewhat fuller; he once more directs the Italian epigrammatist to the Anthology for models.

The ideas of Bettinelli's rambling volume, *Lettere a Lesbia Cidonia sopra gli Epigrammi* (below, p. 415), are mainly impressionistic, and mainly exist to exhibit his translations. 'Chi diede mai leggi e precetti alle grazie, ai risi, agli amorini, se non fu un barbaro?' (*Lett.* 15). He performed a certain service in turning the attention of his countrymen to the contemporary French school of epigrammatists. The Greek epigram also he professes to admire, and he would keep the Italian type broad enough to include it.

The 'laws and precepts' scorned by Bettinelli were held in higher esteem by others even at the end of the eighteenth century.[2] The *Saggio dell' Epigramma Greco* (1796) of Count Vargas is chiefly made up of translations arranged according to the principles of Scaliger and his followers, albeit somewhat simplified—'senza pretendere di avervi comprese tutte le distinzioni di questo genere di poesia' (p. 91). Again, Italian epigrammatists are counseled to imitate the Greek: 'Chi vuole imitare i Greci lasci . . . le allusioni locali e personali, e si attenga in preferenza ai modelli, che piacciono e rapiscono anche dopo mille e mille anni. Si attacchi ai semplici sentimenti della natura, alla storia degli eroi, e degli uomini grandi, ai nobili affetti del cuore, alla riconoscenza, alla pietà figliale, all' amicizia, al virtuoso amore' (p. 107).

The value of this advice to an epigrammatist may be doubted.

---

[1] The *Ritratto del Sonetto* (1677) of Federigo Meninni owes so much to the treatises on the epigram that it must almost be reckoned as one of them. Meninni discusses the similarity of the sonnet and the epigram, refers freely to writers on the epigram, treats of *arguzie*, and has chapters on *il dialogo, l'eco, la repetizione, la correlazione, la congerie, la retrogradazione, la descrizione, la comparazione, la contraposizione, l'allegoria, l'argomento a maiori*, etc.—in a word, on all the topics of the epigram-treatises (compare the chapter-headings of Patavinus, above, p. 68, n. 2).

[2] Somewhat earlier Francisco Jose Freire, known as a restorer of taste in Portugal, in his *Arte Poetica* (Lisbon, 1748, p. 388), has the conventional divisions and the definition made by Scaliger. He mentions the equivalence of the sonnet and epigram; and (p. 393) gives a sketch of the history of the Greek Anthology down to the time of Planudes.

The Greek epigram, as aforesaid, was hardly a unified form; those who wrote it had different impulses and aims which could only be brought together under the rather superficial character of 'brevity.' When this unstable type was carried over from Greek, Latin, and neo-Latin writers into the vernacular by Alamanni and others in the sixteenth century, it encountered a goodly number of small forms already established, which satisfied the desire of brevity and neatness, and took up many of the impulses that were expressed in Greek and Latin through the epigrammatic form. The epigram could not drive them out, but the effect of the encounter was felt on both sides. On the one hand, the smaller vernacular forms, *rispetti*, *strambotti*, and the like, that most nearly resembled the epigram, were largely assimilated to it; and it becomes for the most part a matter of indifference whether a late writer calls his verses epigrams or madrigals. The sonnet to some extent conceded its less serious materials to the epigram. For its part, the epigram was forced into a narrowed territory of its own, but too far in. The modern epigram rightly does not attempt to rival the delicate sentiments of Asclepiades or Meleager, but has lost by becoming too often exclusively satirical. There is room for a form of verse embodying, as the theorists have said, 'acute observations on all matters.' The proper form of the modern type is well described by Lessing, who expressly discards the distinctions of Scaliger and Vavasseur; the epigram, he says, first puts the reader into a state of expectancy with regard to some unusual subject, and then satisfies that expectation by an unforeseen conclusion.[1]

In modern times the epigram has flourished especially among the neo-Latin poets of the Renaissance, and among the French and Italians of the seventeenth and eighteenth centuries; possibly the English of the Jacobean period should be added. The neo-Latin poets commonly modeled their epigrams on the Anthology; yet even they as a rule took care to make their 'points' discernible. Their influence was felt by writers of the sonnet, the madrigal, and the vernacular epigram in the second half of the sixteenth century. In France, however, after the example of Marot, the satirical epigram came more and more to

[1] *Anmerkungen über das Epigramm* (1771). Reitzenstein (*Ep. u. Skol.*, p. 103) justly observes that Lessing's celebrated theory of the epigram misses the mark so far as the Anthology and Martial are concerned. Still it provides a good ideal for the narrowed modern form.

be regarded as the norm; in the seventeenth century there arose
in France a proverbial expression applied to anything insipid—
soupe à la Grecque—the reference being precisely to the Greek
Anthology. The heyday of epigram-writing, long prepared for
by the instructions of Jesuit and other schoolmasters, came with
the decaying society of the eighteenth century. The prevailing
character of this later modern epigram, both in Italy and in
France, is generalized satire.

To illustrate the course of the epigram in Italy a few examples must suffice.[1] The life of the humanist epigram at the
end of the fifteenth century was personal abuse; a quotable instance is Sannazaro's couplet on Caesar Borgia:

> Aut nihil aut Caesar vult dici Borgia: quid ni?
> Cum simul et Caesar possit et esse nihil.

The influence of the Anthology on the Latin epigram in the
time of Leo X may be seen in a characteristic piece by M. A.
Flaminio (cf. *A.P.* 5.83):

> Hos tibi purpureos in serta nitentia flores,
>   Dum Sol exoritur, Thestyli cara, lego,
> Dumque lego, crebra ingeminans suspiria dico,
>   O utinam fieri vos, mea dona, queam!

Presently more point was required. The following lines by
Girolamo Amalteo (†1574) are described by Joseph Warton as
'the most justly celebrated of modern epigrams':[2]

> Lumine Acon dextro, capta est Leonilla sinistro;
>   Et potis est forma vincere uterque deos.
> Blande puer, lumen, quod habes, concede sorori:
>   Sic tu caecus Amor, sic erit illa Venus.

A specimen of the small vernacular form, an epigram in
everything but name, may be found in the following quatrain
ascribed to Machiavelli:

> La notte che morì Pier Soderini
> L'alma n'andò dell' Inferno alla bocca;
> E Pluto le gridò: Anima sciocca,
> Che Inferno? Va' nel Limbo de' bambini.

---

[1] Epigrams of every period are given by L. De-Mauri (Ernesto Sarasíno), *L'Epigramma Italiano dal Resorgimento delle Lettere ai Tempi Moderni*, Milan, 1918.
[2] *An Essay on the Genius and Writings of Pope*, London, 1772, 1.298. Throughout
the seventeenth and eighteenth centuries this epigram, which was quoted in scores of
books, was commonly but erroneously said to be translated from the Anthology.

The earliest Italian epigrams so-called, those of Tolomei's *Versi et Regole* and of Alamanni, were, in different degrees, replicas of the Greek and Latin form. Thus Alamanni:

> Sendo detto a Caton quando morìo:
> Tu non devi temer, Cesare è pio;
> Rispose: Io che romano e Caton sono,
> Non fuggo l'ira sua, fuggo il perdóno.

The attempt to suggest the movement of the elegiac distich is evident. This strictly classical form has found few imitators since Alamanni. Epigrammatists of the seventeenth and eighteenth centuries returned by preference to the quatrain and other free lyrical metres. Still, in their choice of subjects, and particularly in their liking for generalized satire, they show the effect of the ancient epigram and the long schooling of the epigrammatic theorists. The following lines by Filippo Pananti are characteristic enough; they turn on a conceit similar to that of *A.P.* 11.80:

> Dal fodero la spada
> Fuora traendo il capitan Tempesta,
> Non v'è spada, dicea, nella contrada,
> Sì buona come questa.—
> Buona davvero, replicò qualcuno,
> Perchè non fece mai male a nessuno.

To present some notion of the influence of the Greek epigrams, both in substance and as a poetic form, has been the object of the preceding pages. A few observations remain to be made.

The amatory epigrams (*A.P.* 5; *Plan.* 7), while a general influence of their style and a certain infiltration of their conceits can often be detected, are not the part of the Anthology most often translated or directly imitated, at any rate down to the beginning of the nineteenth century. One observes that Meleager of Gadara, who to-day in the minds of many stands as the typical amatory epigrammatist, was hardly distinguished as a personality before the end of the eighteenth century. In many lists of the Greek epigrammatists his name does not appear.[1]

---

[1] E.g., the lists of Gaurico and Minturno; Equicola, however, does not forget him. Much of Meleager's importance for us depends on our knowing him to be the first collector of the Anthology.

The dedicatory epigram (*A.P.* 6; *Plan.* 6) played a great part in the neo-Latin verse of the early sixteenth century, and passed therefrom to the sonnet and madrigal of the second half of the century.

Epitaphs and *Encomia* (*A.P.* 7; *Plan.* 3) form the largest section of the Anthology. Literary epitaphs were composed in Italy throughout the Middle Ages; after the Anthology became known they were often written, particularly by the neo-Latin poets, with Greek models in mind. *Encomia* (often taking the form of the epitaph) were much practised by the modern Latin writers—for example by Paolo Giovio (*Elogia*) and by J. C. Scaliger (*Heroes*)—and became a common school-exercise. The model for these was probably as often the Anthology as the similar exercises of Ausonius.

Epigrams founded on anecdotes (*A.P.* 9; *Plan.* 1) form the part of the Anthology most imitated by modern writers; and not merely because they occupy the first place in Planudes' collection, though that circumstance played its part. The amatory, dedicatory, and sepulchral epigrams often presuppose moral or religious views with which a modern imitator may have but little sympathy; but no limitation of time or place interferes with the effect of the 'demonstrative' epigrams, and hence they are best adapted to please all and always. One has only to turn to the tables drawn up in the following pages for various translators and imitators of the Anthology: Book 9 regularly occupies the largest place. The 'epideictic' (demonstrative) epigrams please the eighteenth-century Jesuit (e.g., Cunich) as much as they do the sixteenth-century humanist (Sabeo). A similar remark applies to the moral epigrams which are included by Planudes in the same book (but *A.P.* 10).

The satirical epigram (*A.P.* 11; *Plan.* 2) coincides with the prevalent modern conception of the form, and consequently, where the point does not depend on social customs peculiar to antiquity, has found favor with translators and imitators. Its themes—misers, ugly persons, bad poets, bad singers, and the like—are the themes of the modern epigrammatist. He often writes in consciousness of this, but rarely adopts the precise substance of any given Greek epigram.

The composition of epigrams on works of art (*A.P.* 16; *Plan.* 4) has been learned by modern writers from the Greek. Aphrodite rising from the sea, Aphrodite admiring her own image made by Praxiteles, Aphrodite in armor, Niobe turned to stone by the gods and from stone to a living woman by Praxiteles, the realism of Timomachus' *Medea*, Love turned ploughboy, the *Heifer* of Myron—these and other themes like them have many imitators. The type was early applied to modern works of art. Calcagnini' even makes *A.P.* 16.32 serve for several epigrams on certain works of Dossi. Possibly a famous epigram on Michel Angelo's *Night* was suggested by the Anthology. On the other hand, with the doubtful exception of Botticelli's *Venus*, no statue or painting produced by the Italian masters seems to have been influenced directly or indirectly by our epigrams.

Some minor technical devices have come into modern verse partly or wholly from the Anthology. The figure-poems (*A.P.* 15) have had their imitators, for example, G. B. Pigna and Baldassarre Bonifacio.[1] The modern Latin poets on occasion have amused themselves with *reciproca*—couplets that can be read backwards (cf. *A.P.* 6.314–20; 9.53). Another *techno-paegnion* is the 'echo'—verses in which Echo is made to answer the poet's questions. Politian first amused himself with this toy, taking a hint from *A.P.* 16.152, an epigram that he later discussed in his *Miscellanea*. It enjoyed a vogue among the neo-Latin poets, and quickly passed to the vernacular (indeed Politian's 'echo' was in Italian), where the existence of rhyme gave it the more point. A truly charming use was made of it by Guarini in the fourth act of his *Pastor Fido*. Politian and the Anthology certainly had a part in creating this vogue, though a greater part was doubtless taken by Ovid (*Met.* 3.379–92).[2]

According to the Register at the end of this volume, there are thirteen epigrams that have been translated or otherwise used twenty times or more each by writers in Italy; these are: *A.P.* 16.129; 7.669; 9.346; 16.200; 6.1; 9.39; 9.56; 16.14; 5.78; 9.108; 9.61; 9.163; and 16.174. Allowance, however, must be made for multiple translations by the same hand.[3] *A.P.* 16.129, on the

---

[1] Bonifacio's *Musarum libri xxv* (Venice, 1628) is wholly made up of figure-poems —poems in the shape of wheels, wings, altars, etc.

[2] 'Echoes' in six languages were collected by Theodore Dousa and published at Utrecht in 1638.

[3] The following figures were obtained by disregarding all notices of ancient quotations or allusions, and of translations by German, French, English, or Spanish writers that enter the Register from the book of Soter, the 1621 Commentary on Alciati's *Emblemata*, and the like sources.

Niobe of Praxiteles, leads with 38 entries; but these include 11 translations by Sabeo alone. The Platonic epigram, Aster contemplating the stars (*A.P.* 7.669), is next with 36 entries; its companion-piece (*A.P.* 7.670) has only 19. The epigram on a swallow nesting on Medea's picture (*A.P.* 9.346) has been translated or imitated 31 times; *A.P.* 16.200, Eros turned ploughboy, has 29 entries; Lais' dedication of her mirror to Venus (*A.P.* 6.1) has served 28 writers. *A.P.* 9.39, an altercation between Venus and the Muses, is echoed 25 times; and the same number goes for *A.P.* 9.56 (or 7.542), the Thracian boy's death in the river Hebrus; and for *A.P.* 16.14, on a statue of Eros placed beside a fountain. The theme of the Thracian boy's death, however, is treated 13 times by Sabeo alone. The Platonic epigram *A.P.* 5.78 (Kissing Agathon) also has 25 notices. *A.P.* 9.108, a sharp reply of Eros to Zeus, has 25; *A.P.* 16.174, Venus in armor, has 22; *A.P.* 9.61, the Spartan mother slaying her coward son, and *A.P.* 9.163, on Aeneas rescuing Anchises, have 20 entries each.

Some interest may be derived from noticing the epigrams employed from ten to nineteen times each. There are seventy-four of these. *A.P.* 5.95 (four are the Graces) and 7.670 are echoed 19 times; *A.P.* 9.357 and 10.30 have 18 entries; *A.P.* 5.94 and 9.12 have 17. Seven epigrams are noticed 16 times;[1] eight epigrams 14 times;[2] five epigrams 13 times;[3] ten epigrams 12 times;[4] fourteen epigrams 11 times;[5] and twenty-four epigrams 10 times.[6]

This enumeration fails to indicate the popularity of certain themes treated in more than one epigram. The common theme of *A.P.* 9.11–13, for example, is, altogether, used by 38 Italian writers; the theme of *A.P.* 9.30–1, 33, 35, 105, 131, and 376 (on a pine-tree used in building a ship) has 24 notices; Venus in armor (*A.P.* 9.320–1; 16.171–7) is the subject of 56 imitations.

The popularity of a given epigram does not necessarily spring from the merit of the lines themselves. Men are apt to see through the eyes of others; a Greek poem used by a well-known

---

[1] *A.P.* 7.617 (7 tr. by Sabeo); 9.44, 47, 126, 497; 11.193; 16.171.
[2] *A.P.* 7.308, 9.13.1–2, 48, 130, 148, 391; 11.76; 16.207.
[3] *A.P.* 6.77; 9.221, 331, 647; 11.430.
[4] *A.P.* 5.74, 83; 7.217 (7 tr. by Sabeo), 311; 9.110, 162, 721; 16.107, 275, 297.
[5] *A.P.* 7.15, 348; 9.49, 74, 146, 166, 231, 369, 515, 530; 11.408, 431; 16.1, 223.
[6] *A.P.* 5.168; 6.336; 7.229, 313, 534; 9.18, 66, 72, 111, 133, 369, 394, 577; 10.27, 43, 74, 108, 112; 11.53, 294, 381; 16.151, 178, 185.

writer thereby has the eyes of many directed upon it. Modern attention to *A.P.* 16.129 and 174, for instance, is largely due to the translations by Ausonius. Again, the first epigram of the first book of the Planudean Anthology (*A.P.* 9.357), merely because of its position, has found more translators than it deserves. The makers of selections, from the *syllogae minores* to the most recent schoolbook, have played a decisive part in creating a taste for certain pieces; their choices may often be detected behind the choices of translators.

The Anthology is only one of the literary remains of Greek antiquity, and can hardly claim to be the best-known. All the more significant therefore is the record of its permeating influence in Italian literature. More than 275 writers are mentioned in this volume; but no count can be made of the thousands of cultivated persons to whom, as to Cardinal Quirini, the Anthology has been a delight in youth—perhaps also in later life—but whose impressions have never been conveyed to the public in print.

PART I

LATIN WRITERS OF THE RENAISSANCE
(TO *c.* 1650)

GIOVANNI BOCCACCIO
(1313–1375)

Petrarch had finally settled in Italy, at Milan, in 1353. Boccaccio paid him a visit in 1359, and doubtless from their conversations at this time was induced to begin the study of Greek. There was then in northern Italy a Calabrian—though he affected to be from Thessaly—named Leontius Pilatus; him Boccaccio succeeded in attracting to Florence in the winter of that year, secured him the place of teacher of Greek in the *Studio*, and made him a member of his own household. Pilatus remained in Florence till October, 1362, and produced—with the help of his pupils, for he had little Latin—a translation of the whole of Homer. The greater part of the Greek learning that appears in Boccaccio's later works, the *Comento sopra Dante* and the *Genealogia Deorum Gentilium*, was gleaned from him.

Yet Boccaccio may have known something of two Greek epigrams even earlier than this. These are *A.P.* 9.448 and 16.297, both on Homer.[1] In the *Comento* there is a long account of Homer in illustration of *Inf.* 4.88, beginning:[2] 'Dell' origine della vita, e degli studii d'Omero, secondochè diceva Leon Tessalo, scrive un valente uomo Greco, chiamato Callimaco, più

---

[1] The anecdote concerning Homer and the fishermen, which is the subject of *A.P.* 9.448, was well-known in the Middle Ages; the point of the present notice is that Boccaccio knew the Greek. The story is told by Valerius Maximus (9.12.3). John of Salisbury (*Polycraticus*, ed. by Webb, 1.141), Vincent of Beauvais (*Spec. Hist.* 3.87), and Walter Burley (*De Vit. et Mor. Philos.* 14) have an account almost word-for-word the same. They all differ from Boccaccio.

[2] Boccaccio, *Opere Volgari*, Florence, 1831, 10.245–51.

pienamente che alcun altro.'[1] Among the facts said to have been derived from Callimachus are the following:

È il vero che . . . sette nobili città di Grecia . . . ebber quistione della sua origine . . . Samos, Smirne, Chios, Colofon, Philos, Argos, Atene. . . . Della morte sua, secondochè scrive Callimaco, fu uno strano accidente cagione; perciocchè essendo egli in Arcadia, ed andando solo su per lo lito del mare, sentì pescatori, li quali sopra uno scoglio si stavano, forse tendendo o racconciando loro reti: li quali esso domandò se preso avessero, intendendo seco medesimo de' pesci. Costoro risposero, che quelli che presi aveano avean perduti, e quelli che presi non aveano se ne portavano. (Era stata fortuna in mare, e però non avendo i pescatori potuto pescare, come loro usanza è, s'erano stati al sole, e i vestimenti loro aveano cerchi, e purgati di que' vermini che in essi nascono: e quegli che nel cercar trovati e presi aveano, gli aveano uccisi, e quegli che presi non aveano, essendosi ne' vestimenti rimasi, ne portavan seco.) Omero udita la risposta de' pescatori, ed essendogli oscura, mentre al doverla intendere andava sospeso, per caso percosse in una pietra, per la qual cosa cadde, e fieramente nel cader percosse, e di quella percossa il terzo dì appresso si morì. Alcuni voglion dire, che non potendo intender la risposta fattagli da' pescatori, entrò in tanta maninconia che una febbre il prese, della quale in pochi dì si morì, e poveramente in Arcadia fu seppellito.

The account of the seven contending cities was also employed by Boccaccio in the *Genealogia* (14.19), into which it may have been introduced before it was used in the *Comento*:[2] 'Quod ego etiam testari vetustissimo greco carmine, satis inter eruditos vulgato, legisse memini, sic aiente: ἑπτά διεῥίζουσιν πόλεις διὰ ῥίζης ὁμήρου. σάμος, σμύρνη, χῖος, κολοφών, πῖλος, ἀργος, ἀϑῆναι.[3] On the lower margin of the page in the Laurentian MS. of the *Genealogia* is this translation:[4]

[1] The *Comento* was written about 1374. That Callimachus wrote a life of Homer is true, but certainly Pilatus could not have read it; nor is it likely that any of the existing lives of Homer went under the name of Callimachus in Byzantium. At all events, no one of them contains all the information given to Boccaccio on the authority of 'Callimachus.'

[2] The *Genealogia* was in process of writing for at least thirty years, and the precise date of its final revision is uncertain, though near the end of the author's life. See Charles G. Osgood, *Boccaccio on Poetry*, Princeton, 1930, p. xiii, note 2.

Boccaccio's knowledge of these two epigrams is discussed by Henri Hauvette in *Mélanges d'Archéologie et d'Histoire* (École fr. de Rome) 14 (1894). 95–100; by Oskar Hecker, *Boccaccio-Funde*, Braunschweig, 1902, pp. 153–157; and previously by Attilio Hortis, *Studj sulle Opere latine del Boccaccio*, Trieste, 1879, p. 340.

[3] The text of Hecker, *op. cit.*, p. 252, from the Laurentian MS. 52, 9, f. 152.

[4] The *Genealogia* was translated into Italian by Giuseppe Betussi of Bassano, Venice, 1547, who gives the following curious version of the epigram (f. 245 in the ed. of 1581): 'Sette cittadi litigan d'Homero Samo, con Smirne, Colophone e Chio. Indi Pilo, con Argo, e con Athene.'

Septem litigant civitates de radice omeri
Samos, smirne. chios. colophon, pilos. argos athine.

As a matter of fact, Boccaccio's Greek is identical with none of the versions that have come down to us. The first is *A.P.* 16.297:

'Επτὰ ἐριδμαίνουσι πόλεις διὰ ῥίζαν 'Ομήρου·
Κύμη, Σμύρνα, Χίος, Κολοφὼν, Πύλος, "Αργος, 'Αθῆναι.

A second is preserved in MSS. of Gellius (3.11):

'Επτὰ πόλεις διερίζουσιν περὶ ῥίζαν 'Ομήρου·
Σμύρνα, 'Ρόδος, Κολοφών, Σαλαμίν, "Ιος, "Αργος, 'Αθῆναι.

The third (*A.P.* 16.298) is quite different:

'Επτὰ πόλεις μάρναντο σοφὴν διὰ ῥίζαν 'Ομήρου·
Σμύρνα, Χίος, Κολοφών 'Ιθάκη, Πύλος, "Αργος, 'Αθῆναι.

Boccaccio's version is most like the first, save that διερίζουσιν seems to come from the second. Samos, as one of the seven cities, is unknown to any of them. Boccaccio's Greek lines are metrically awry.

Before his death Boccaccio turned his library over to Fra Martino da Signa, a monk of Santo Spirito in Florence, who in turn was to deposit the books in the convent of Santo Spirito. Time has dispersed most of them; but what are left are in the Laurentian Library. Among these is Boccaccio's MS. of Terence, copied by his own hand. On the *verso* of the last folio appears the following:[1]

Homerus poeta egregius dum quadam die secus mare solus in-cederet, quosdam piscatores interrogavit, num quid aliquid cepissent. Qui responderunt: quos ceperant perdiderant, quos non ceperant portabant. Habuerant quidem tempus adversum et ideo non pis-catierant, sed potius vestes suas ab immundis verminibus prout potuerant mundaverant. Et hoc est quod dicunt, scilicet quod quos ceperant scilicet vermes perdiderant, etc. Quod quidem cum Homerus non posset intelligere, secum diu dicta revolvens tedio affectus inde infirmatus et post modum mortuus est ut creditur. Interrogatio vero Homeri et piscatorum responsio in subsequentibus duobus metris Graecis continetur.

hoīes de archadia piscatores habetisne   Interrogatio
Andres aparchadias alijtores ire comenti

---

[1] Known for Boccaccio's since the time of Mehus (1759), and often discussed. The subject is well dealt with by Hauvette and Hecker, who both give photographic repro-ductions of this page of the MS.

quos accepimus perdidimus quos non   accepimus portamus Responsio
os   elomen   lipomesta. os   uche elomen   feromesta.

De predicto homero unde .s. fuerit non habetur aput presentes et
idcirco plures grecie civitates illum ex se ortum fuisse contendunt ut
in sequentibus duobus carminibus continetur.

  septem litigant civitates de radice homeri .s.
  Epta erimenusi polis dyarison homiru
  ci. ci. ci. ci. ci. ci. ci.
  Chimi smirni chios colophon pylos argos athyne

  ἄνδρες ἀπ' ἀρκαδίας, ἀλῖεις, ἔχομέν τί
  ὅσσ' ἔχομεν λειπόμεθα, ὅσσοὐκ ἔχομεν φερόμεθα.

  ἑπτά διερίζουσιν πόλεις διὰ ῥίζης ὁμήρου
  σάμος, σμύρνη, χῖος, κολοφών πῖλος, ἄργος, ἀθῆναι.

It is plain that these last Greek lines (in Greek letters) are
the same version of *A.P.* 16.297 as that given in the *Genealogia*
and in the *Comento*; Samos, unknown to other versions, is in
all three of these. Moreover, the interlinear translation to the
Greek in Latin letters is identical with that in the margin of the
Genealogia ms. Probably, then, this note on the Terence ms. is
the basis of the passages in the finished *Comento* and *Genealogia*.[1]

The lines in Greek script appear to have been written later,
and to have been derived, with some curious errors, from those
in Latin script. In both epigrams the Latin form is more correct.
In the first (line 1) the metre of the Greek is defective because
the writer was unable to transform 'alijtores ire comenti' correctly into ἀλιήτορες ἢ ῥ'ἔχομέν τι. In the second epigram διερίζουσιν is substituted for 'erimenusi' (= ἐριδμαίνουσι), seemingly
from a vague memory of the epigram in Gellius; while 'Σάμος'
is a rash substitute for 'Chimi' (= Κύμη).

That Boccaccio had the Latin version before he had the
Greek is further proved by this: that, whereas in *Genealogia* and
Comento he has 'Samos,' in the *Vita di Dante*, written earlier,
he has 'Chimi.'[2]

Hauvette concludes that the Greek version was made by
Pilatus from the Latin, and copied into the Terence ms. by

---

[1] In the *Comento*, as Hauvette observes, two accounts of Homer's death are given,
one of which—that Homer, ruminating on the riddle, stumbled, fell, and injured himself—does not appear in the Terence ms. Hauvette (*op. cit.*, p. 97, note 2) regards this
incident as an elaboration by the author of the *Decameron*. It occurs, however, in the
life of Homer given by Proclus (Westermann 3.40): καὶ οὕτως ὀλισθέντα περιπταῖσαι λίθῳ
καὶ τριταῖον τελευτῆσαι. Cf. *Com.*: 'percosse in una pietra ... e ... il terzo dì appresso si morì.'

[2] Hecker, p. 154 note. Bocc., *Op. Volg.* 15.40.

Boccaccio. Hecker, in a careful argument, makes it probable that the Greek script in the Terence MS. itself was written by Pilatus.[1]

Whence, then, did Boccaccio derive the version written in Latin script of these two epigrams, neither of them surely, in Italy at that day, 'satis inter eruditos vulgatum'?[2] To this question there seems to be no satisfactory answer. Since, however, Greek phrases were commonly thus written in Latin letters in Latin MSS., it may be supposed that Boccaccio found his epigrams in some such place.

There is no question here of so much as an idea of the type 'Greek epigram,' to say nothing of a conception of the Anthology; Boccaccio calls the verses *carmina* or *metra*. As the discoverer of Ausonius, of whose works he made a copy, he could, of course, know the themes of a number of Greek epigrams.

TRAVERSARI'S *LAERTIUS*

After the death of Boccaccio, Greek studies made little or no progress in Italy until the arrival of Chrysoloras, who may be credited with the chief rôle in finally bringing Greek back to the West. It was now the duty of the first Italians who mastered the language to put their new knowledge at their countrymen's service by Latin translations. Most distinguished in this activity were Lionardo Bruni and Ambrogio Traversari. The first, in translating several of the works of Plutarch, occasionally had an epigram to translate; but can hardly be said to have contributed to a knowledge of the Anthology (cf. below, p. 142). Traversari, however, translated Diogenes Laertius, whose book, as we have seen, contains a very large number of epigrams. The treatment accorded to these epigrams in Traversari's version deserves our attention, inasmuch as the verse-translations appearing in the printed editions of it became widely known through Soter's book of selections from the Anthology, in which they were reprinted.

Ambrogio Traversari (1386–1439) was born at Portico in Romagna. In 1400 he entered the Camaldolese convent of Santa Maria degli Angioli at Florence, and probably at that time learned Greek from Chrysoloras. Pope Eugene IV noticed him, and made use of his learning at the Councils of Basel, Ferrara, and Florence. In 1431

---

[1] *Op. cit.*, pp. 154–156. The proof rests on the shape of the letter ς in the Terence MS. and in the Laurentian *Genealogia*, on similar errors in accents, and on the fact that the accent and a diæresis, placed just before the second ι in διερίζουσιν, in the Terence MS., have come to be over the ρ in the *Genealogia* MS. In other words, Boccaccio in the *Genealogia* MS. was painfully tracing what his teacher wrote for him in the MS. of Terence.

[2] Petrarch refers to the anecdote concerning the death of Homer in *Remed.* 1.64, and to both anecdotes in *Fam.Epist.* 24.12; but neither reference throws any light on the present question. Coluccio Salutati, writing on Sept. 29, 1392, has 'litigant civitates Chimis, Smyrna,' etc., perhaps from the Terence MS. (*Epist.*, ed. by Novati, 2.399).

Traversari became General of his Order. The journal of his travels in Italy, on visits to religious houses, which goes under the name of *Hodoeporicon*, contains accounts of the conditions he found prevailing in those institutions. The book was published in 1680 at Florence. He was in correspondence with the leading men of Italy, and his letters form a most valuable source of information on the times; they were edited, with an elaborate life of Traversari, by Lorenzo Mehus (2 vols. fol., Florence, 1759).[1]

The translation of Laertius was made at the request of Cosimo de' Medici, about 1433. A number of manuscript copies of it still lie in European libraries. It was first printed in 1475; and between that date and 1878, when it was included in the Didot edition, it was printed more than twenty-seven times. In fact, several editions of the Latin, and an Italian abstract made from it, had appeared before Froben issued the *editio princeps* of the Greek at Basel in 1533.[2]

Traversari, however, made no translations of the epigrams into verse, and seems to have omitted them altogether when they chanced not to be necessary to the argument. The manu-

---

[1] Attention has been called by Sabbadini (*Boll. di Filol. Class.* 35.99) to a letter from Aurispa to Traversari (Mehus 2.1023), beginning, as Sabbadini quotes it: 'Mitto ad te illa Ἐπιγράμματα, ut inde excerpas "ad evangelium" quod cupiebas.' Sabbadini believes that this refers to the Palatine MS., and that 'ad evangelium' points to *A.P.* 1.44, entitled: Εἰς τὸν εὐαγγελισμόν. It must, however, be observed that εὐαγγελισμός means 'the Annunciation,' and not 'the Gospel.' Moreover in Mehus—I have been unable to consult the letter in Martène and Durand 3.710—the words are: 'id evangelicum.' We cannot know, therefore, without more light, what the ἐπιγράμματα lent to Traversari by Aurispa may have been.

[2] Some of the printings of Traversari's version are: Venice, ed. by Brugnolo (Jenson), 1475; Brescia (Britannicus), 1485; Venice (Locatelli), 1490; *ibid.* (Pasquale), 1493; Bologna (Ragazzoni), 1495; Venice (Pinzi), 1497; Paris (Enguilbert and Marnef), *c.* 1500; Basel, ed. by Curio (Curio), 1524; Lyons, 1541; *ibid.* (Gryphe), 1546; *ibid.* 1551; 1559; Paris, 1560; Lyons, ed. by Boulierus, 1561; Antwerp, ed. by Sambucus, 1585; Lyons, 1592; Geneva (H. Estienne), 1593; Lyons (Chouet), 1595; Cologne, 1595; Leyden (Plantin), 1596; Cologne, 1616; Amsterdam, ed. by Meibomius, 1692; Hof in Bavaria, ed. by Longolius, 1739; Leipzig, ed. by Huebner, 1828.

A new Latin translation by Tommaso Aldobrandini (*c.* 1525–1572) was published by his nephew, Cardinal Pietro Aldobrandini, Rome, 1594 (reprinted, Cologne, 1615; London, 1664; Rome, 1794). The epigrams, however, are given only in a prose translation.

The Italian abstract referred to above must not be called a translation: *Il Libro dela Vita de Philosophi . . . extracto da D. Lahertio et da altri antiquissimi auctori.* Venice, 1480 (Florence, 1488; Bologna, 1494; etc.). It contains translations of none of the verses. The reported translation: *Diogene Laertio delle Vite*, Venice, 1535, may be only an error for B. and P. Rossettini da Prato Alboino, *Le Vite degli Illustri Filosofi.* Venice, 1545. I have not seen this, nor the version of Giovan Felice Astolfi, Venice, 1598; 1602; 1606; etc. For A. M. Salvini's translation of the sixth book, see below, p. 383. I reserve the mention of French and English translations until I come to treat of the Greek epigrams in those countries. Ordinarily I have not noticed translations of single biographies; yet a translation of the *Vita Platonis* would contain versions of some important epigrams.

scripts of his translation are without verses. Yet he had not intended it to be so. He had applied to Filelfo—who owed him
much—to supply him with the verse-translations. At first he
received promises, and in the end insults. At the close of a
letter to Ambrogio, dated Florence, May 30, 1430, Filelfo makes
the promise:[1] 'De Diogenis Laertii versibus, quorum me iubes
interpretem, obtemperabo tuae benevolentissimae voluntati.'
Again, three years later, in a letter dated Florence, May, 2,
1433, he writes:[2] 'De Diogenis autem Laertii versibus, quod
perurbane expostulas, ne mihi succenseas rogo. Nam partim
occupationibus meis, partim animi molestia ob continuas in-
vidiorum in me insidias, factum est, ut versus illos Latinos
facere, ut iusseras, distulerim in hanc diem. Sed geram profecto
morem voluntati tuae, idque propediem.' With these protesta-
tions the following lines written by Filelfo in a satire addressed
to Manetti form a very curious contrast. He complains of
Traversari's importunity in demanding these translations from
him, and adds:[3]

> Si reddere quaeque Latina
> Nititur Ambrosius, cur non quoque versibus ornat
> Scripta suis? Nescit metrum.

In the end Ambrogio had to send his translation to Cosimo
without the verses; but he makes the best of it in his dedicatory
epistle:[4] 'Sane quoniam versus plurimos et diversos, tum alienos,
tum suos, auctor interserit (quod abhorrere videtur a gravitate
historiae) illos traducere consulto [!] omisi: ita tamen ut nihil
deesse ex sensu necessario sim passus.'

Nevertheless the first printed edition of Traversari's translation contains verse-translations of the epigrams. The book was
edited by Benedetto Brugnolo at Venice in 1475, and was
printed by Nicolas Jenson. It is not certain from the editor's
Preface that he made the verse-translations himself; he says:[5]
'Quod ad me attinuit, pro suscepti muneris officio illud arbitror
me consecutum esse, ut non aliter a fratre Ambrosio, qui e

---

[1] Rosmini, *Vita di Filelfo* 1.117.
[2] Filelfo, *Epistolae*, Florence, 1743, 1.88.
[3] *Satyrae*, Venice, 1502, p. 48.
[4] Mehus 2.290; cf. the first epistle to Cosimo, *ibid.* 2.330.
[5] This letter (here quoted from the 1475 edition) is reprinted in Henri Estienne's
1593 edition of Diogenes, and in the *Bibliotheca Smithiana* (Venice, 1755) 2.cxxxiv.
Rivinus, in his *Florilegium* (1651), puts these translations under Brugnolo's name.

Graeco in Latinum eum vertit (hoc enim maxime quaesitum est) traductus fuerit, quam magistro Nicolao a me traditus fuit imprimendus, exceptis tantummodo epigrammatibus et versibus quibusdam, quos ab illo praetermissos, componendos curavimus eique addendos.'

Benedetto Brugnolo (1427–1502), who thus becomes responsible for some of the earliest translations of the Greek epigrams to be made in Italy, was born at Legnago near Verona. Later he lived at Verona, where, according to the testimony of Julius Caesar Scaliger, he was the preceptor of Benedetto Scaliger, the father of Julius.[1] Most of Brugnolo's life was passed at Venice, where he taught for more than forty years. Sabellico praises him. He died at Venice, and was buried in the Church of the Frari, where, at least in Mazzuchelli's time, his epitaph might still be read. Brugnolo edited a number of classics besides Traversari's Laertius: Valla's Herodotus (Venice, 1474), a Priscian (*ibid.*, 1485), Cicero's *De Officiis* (*ibid.*, 1520); and produced a commentary on Cicero's *Paradoxa*, published at Venice in 1506.

Where Brugnolo found an epigram already translated by Traversari into prose, he did not remove the translation, but merely added a metrical version after it; for example, in Book 3, his edition reads thus (the epigram is *A.P.* 7.670): 'Iam dudum lucebat viventibus matutinum; nunc Hesperus fulges, vita functus, mortuis.

> Iam dudum vivis fulgebas lucifer, at nunc
> Defunctis luces Hesperus exanimis.'

Twenty-seven of Laertius' epigrams, common to him and the Anthology, are still without translations in Brugnolo's edition.[2] As further examples of Brugnolo's translations we may take the following, the first from *A.P.* 7.153, the other from 5.80:

> Aenea virgo Midae celebri sum nixa sepulchro,
> Alluit unda flumen, et plurima germinat arbos,
> Phoebus at exoriens et splendida luna refulget,
> Flumina labuntur, placidae de montibus undae
> Littora commiscent, deflecto hic marmore multum
> Flucta, Midam moneo, qui praeterit, esse sepultum.

---

[1] Scaliger's poem in Brugnolo's honor is the final piece in his *Heroes* (*Poemata*, 1600, 1.314).

[2] A list of the epigrams common to Laertius and the Anthology has been given above, p. 5, n. 1. Of these Brugnolo has no translations of: *A.P.* 7.93, 94, 95, 98, 99, 101, 103, 104, 107, 113, 117–20, 326, 618, 706, 744; 9.499, 569; 16.334. For *A.P.* 5.78 he (and later Bentinus) used the version of Gaza (below, p. 97). The remaining 54 epigrams are referred to in my Register by the 1475 edition; but, as this has no folio- or signature-numbers, references are given by Book and Chapter of Laertius.

Malum ego, me mittit, qui te succenditur unus,
Annue, Xanthippe: linquit utrunque decor.

The versions from Brugnolo's edition of Traversari enter the stream of the Anthology's influence through Joannes Soter, who included many of them in his *Epigrammata Graeca*, under the name, 'Laertii Interpres' (below, p. 276).

As we have seen, Brugnolo had not supplied all the verses lacking in Traversari; nor were his translations always satisfactory. Valentine Curio, therefore, in producing an edition of Traversari's version at Basel in 1524, filled the gaps, and had virtually a new set of verse-translations made. His translator was Michael Bentinus; and the versions made by this young scholar remained, with some modification, in all editions down to that of Cobet in the Didot Classics (1878). Often, to be sure, the new translations were little more than a reworking of the old ones printed by Brugnolo.[1]

Michael Bentinus (*c.* 1495–1527) was born in Flanders. He may have attended the University of Paris, and there met Guillaume Farel.[2] He was correcting for Froben in 1520; and is addressed in a poem by Ursinus Velius in the latter's *Poemata*, published at Basel by Froben in 1522. He seems to have been in Flanders in March, 1524, but soon returned to Basel, where he began to correct for Curio. He married in the autumn of this year. The Diogenes (September 1, 1524) must have been one of his earliest works for Curio. He edited several classics, and is said to have been a good critic. In 1527, November perhaps, the plague wiped out his entire family—himself, his wife, and their child.

Curio prints the Greek text along with the Latin translations of the epigrams—the first pieces of Laertius' original to be edited. The following passages from his Preface bear on the matter of the epigrams:[3]

Quae [epigrammata] in hoc Graece apprimenda curavimus, quod

---

[1] The *Bibl. Graec.* of Fabricius (Harles) 5.570 ascribes the verse-translations in this edition to Conrad Heresbach: 'In qua editione Conradus Heresbachius collato codice graeco Matthaei Aurogalli quaedam correxit, praecipue epigrammata, et versus quosdam, ab Ambrosio et Brognolo etiam omissos, latine vertit, et graece itidem adscripsit.' This must rest on a misunderstanding of Curio's preface. For his part, Curio seems to ascribe the translations to himself; but I venture to follow Soter in assigning them to Bentinus.

[2] Herminjard, *Correspondence des Réformateurs* (1866) 1.224; here Bentinus is mentioned in a letter to Farel from Le Fèvre d'Étaples; see also a letter from Bentinus to Oecolampadius (1525), *ibid.*, p. 398; and Allen, *Erasmi Epistolae* 5.423.

[3] Curio's Preface (here quoted from the 1524 edition) is reprinted in Meibomius' edition (1692) 2.568.

scirem carminis venustatem et argutiam peregrina lingua non posse
reddi, et gratum fore studiosis sperebam, si exhiberem gustum Laer-
tianae phrasis, quoniam adhuc apud nos nihil illius Graece excusum
novimus . . . Neque hic mihi probandus videtur interpres [Ambro-
sius], qui in praefatione quam huic operi praefixit, fatetur se versus
plurimos et diversos . . . consulto omisisse, quod id a gravitate historiae abhorrere videretur [Cf. above, p. 87]. Quod ipsum non solum
abhorrere a gravitate historiae puto, verum etiam multum derogare
historiae veritati . . . si quid omittatur, quod ad sententiae integrita-
tem faciat. Sed hoc non tam in causa fuit, ut ipse videtur innuere, cur
non reddiderit versus versibus, quam rei difficultas. Itaque quales
quales sunt, et quales ex tali exemplari haberi potuerunt, Graece
addidimus, *et Latine, ut potuimus, reddidimus;* ex quibus aliquot qui
prosae orationi affiniores erant, et ut ingenue fatear nobis ignoti,
intactos reliquimus, servata duntaxat sententia. [Here he expresses a
suspicion that the Latin Laertius is not the work of Traversari; then
a second time thanks Aurogallus for the loan of his ms.]. . . . Non nihil
et Michaeli Bentino debetur, qui nobis in labore adfuit.

From the words I put in italics it would appear that Curio
himself made the verse-translations. Nevertheless I ascribe
them to Bentinus. These versions also enter the stream of the
Anthology's influence by being largely represented in Soter's
Epigrammata Graeca. In his first edition (1525), published only
a few months after Curio's Laertius, Soter assigns them to
Curio; but in his second edition (1528), near following on Bentinus' death, he changes Curio's name throughout to Bentinus.
He must have had good reason for so doing.

Bentinus' translations of *A.P.* 7.153 and 5.80 may be compared with their predecessors given above:[1]

> Aenea sum virgo, Midae quae incumbo sepulchro.
> Dum fluit unda levis, sublimis nascitur arbor,
> Dum sol exoriens, et splendida luna relucet,
> Dum fluvii labuntur, inundant littora fluctus,
> Hic constanter ago, lachrymisque in littore tincto
> Fixa, Midam moneo hic tumulatum, chare viator.

> Malum ego, me iaculatur, amat qui te: annue, quaeso,
>   Xanthippe, tibi mox nam et mihi forma perit.

---

[1] In the Register Bentinus' translations are referred to Curio's edition (1524);
many of them may be found in Soter (below, p. 276). Caution must be exercised in
quoting as by Bentinus the verse-translations in later editions of Laertius, since subsequent editors touched them up. From the full tale of Laertius' epigrams Bentinus still
lacks eleven: *A.P.* 7.94, 95, 98, 104, 107, 113, 117, 618, 706, 744; 9.497. Translations
of these are supplied in later editions, but I have not thought it necessary to trace out
their first appearance.

It was therefore the fortune of Traversari's Latin Laertius, though it left Traversari's hands without verse-translations, nevertheless to provide in the end two sets of metrical versions of the epigrams. These both joined the stream of the Anthology's influence when Soter included a great number of them in his very popular selection of Greek epigrams—the old translations, provided by Brugnolo, under the name 'Laertii Interpres,' and the new, from Curio's edition, under the name of Bentinus.

GUARINO DA VERONA
(1370–1460)
GREGORIO TIFERNAS
(*c.* 1415–1466)

Nicholas V is usually said to have commissioned both Guarino and Tifernas to make translations of Strabo. Why he should have done so cannot now be ascertained; on the other hand, there is no evidence to prove that he did not. Certainly translations were completed by both scholars. Guarino's appears to have been finished at Ferrara, July 13, 1458, some three years after the death of Nicholas.[1] When Tifernas finished his version is not known.

Guarino, believed to have been the first Italian to give public lectures on Greek, was a native of Verona. He first studied with John of Ravenna, the teacher also of Vittorino and Poggio, and then, desiring to learn Greek, went to Constantinople, where for five years he lived and studied with Manuel Chrysoloras, a relation, it seems, of the well-known scholar of the same name. Returning to Italy about the beginning of the fifteenth century, Guarino taught successively at Florence, Venice, Verona, and finally at Ferrara, where his school was one of the first great seminaries of the new learning. Among his pupils were Angelo Decembrio, Tito Vespasiano Strozzi, Janus Pannonius, Robert Fleming, John Free, and William Grey. The three Englishmen became respectively Dean of Lincoln, Bishop of Bath and Wells, and Bishop of Ely. Giovan Battista, one of Guarino's six sons, succeeded him as professor of Greek at Ferrara.

Tifernas was born at Città di Castello (Tifernum) in the Papal States. His teacher in Greek is not known. He gave instruction in the language first in his native place, then at Naples, then at Milan; and

---

[1] Rosmini, *Vita e Disciplina di Guarino* (Brescia, 1805–6) 2.134–6, reports a MS., said to be in the hand of Guarino, containing the note: 'absolutus est . . . 1458 tertio Idus Julias Ferrariae'; and a second MS., not in the hand of Guarino, dated: 'anno Christi 1436 tertio Idus Julias Ferrariae.' That 1458 is the right year follows from a statement, also quoted by Rosmini, of Vespasiano da Bisticci, a contemporary of Guarino, to the effect that Nicholas V, who had commanded the transaltion, died before it was finished.

was welcomed in Rome by Pope Nicholas, probably at the time of the latter's election. His translation of Strabo was presumably done at this time. On the death of Nicholas in 1455 he went to Paris, and later returned to teach in Venice, where he died. Among his pupils are numbered Giorgio Merula, Battista Mantovano, and Pontano. Besides Strabo he translated Dio Chrysostom; he composed some Latin poems printed at the end of the Ausonius that appeared at Venice in 1472.

When Giovan Andrea di Bussi, Bishop of Aleria, came to publish a Latin Strabo at the press of Sweynheym and Pannartz in Rome about 1469,[1] he had before him these two translations. He published a part of each—the first ten books of Guarino's version, and the last seven of Tifernas'.[2] He also, with the help of his friends—Theodore Gaza for one—filled some *lacunae*. This composite translation of Strabo remained the only one until Xylander's (1571).

The following translation of the Spartans' epitaph in Book 9 must be by Guarino (*A.P.* 7.249):

> Dic Lacedaemoniis hac hospes parte iacere,
> Dum illorum rigidis legibus obsequimur.

A.P. 9.509, also in Book 9 of Strabo, must be likewise in Guarino's translation; while the following version of Sardanapalus' epitaph (*A.P.* 16.27), from Book 14, will be by Tifernas; but lines 4–5 are taken from Cicero (above, p. 12):

> Cum te mortalem noris, praesentibus exple
> Deliciis animum—post mortem nulla voluptas.
> Namque ego sum pulvis, qui nuper tanta tenebam:
> Haec habeo quae edi, quaeque exaturata libido
> Hausit; at illa manent multa et praeclara relicta.
> Hoc sapiens vitae mortalibus et documentum.

Soter (below, p. 278) ascribes to Guarino translations of *A.P.* 7.3, 60, 61, 669, 670; 16.292, 296.[3] Of these the translation of *A.P.* 16.292 was often quoted in the sixteenth century:

---

[1] The date is not certain.

[2] 'Quorum [the translations of Guarino and Tifernas] ego in manibus sumptis exemplaribus, ex Gregorii archetypis Asiam atque Africam describi feci, Guarini autem Europa perlecta'—from his Preface in the edition of A. Mancinellus, Venice (Rubeus), 1494. An Italian translation by Alfonso Buonacciolli was published in two parts, Venice, 1562, and Ferrara, 1565.

[3] Here I have not succeeded in tracing Soter's sources. Every one of these epigrams was probably known to Guarino from other books than the Anthology. *A.P.* 7.3 is in Suidas; 7.60, 61, and 669 are in Diogenes Laertius; and 16.292 and 296 are in Plutarch. Guarino possessed a MS. of Diogenes and one of Suidas (H. Omont, 'Les MSS. grecs de Guarino de Vérone' in *Rev. des Bibliothèques* 2.78–81); and also of Plutarch, of whom he

Nate Milete, decus Graiorum ac splendor, Homere,
  Nobilitas patriam qui Colophona tuam.
Divina geminas genuisti mente puellas
  Semideum scribens inclyta gesta virum;
Altera multivagi reditum cantavit Ulyssis,
Altera Graiugenas Dardaniosque duces.

CIRIACO PIZZICOLLI D'ANCONA
(1391–c. 1455)

While other enthusiasts for antiquity ransacked monastic libraries
in search of manuscripts, Ciriaco made the collecting of inscriptions
his province. These collections he shared with various scholars in
Italy, and copies of many of them are still extant. His life was spent
in travel, beginning with his ninth year, when he accompanied his
maternal grandfather, a merchant, on a journey through Italy.
Outside of Italy in the course of his life he visited Egypt, the Aegean
Islands, Asia Minor, Cyprus, Sicily, Dalmatia, Constantinople, Chios,
Rhodes, Syria, Thrace, Delos, Adrianople, the Thracian Bosphorus,
the Propontis, Samothrace, Mt. Athos, Aenos, Crete, Samos, Ephesus,
Lesbos, and perhaps Spain; several of these places he visited more
than once. His last years are not well known; there is a report that
Mahomet II, while laying siege to Constantinople, passed the time by
having Diogenes Laertius and other Greek and Latin authors read to
him by Ciriaco d'Ancona and another Italian. Ciriaco died about 1455
at Cremona, and was there buried.[1]

Only in one instance can Ciriaco's own words be construed to
mean that he had found an epigram, known to us in the Anthology, actually on a stone. This is *A.P.* 7.53—the dedication of
Hesiod's tripod to the Muses. Ciriaco notices that Gellius
speaks of the verses appearing on the tripod on Mt. Helicon,
and goes on to say that they may be seen on a marble at
Thessalonica, written in the Attic alphabet. He gives a Latin
translation.[2]

Ciriaco had better sources for knowing the epigrams of the
Anthology than most other Italian scholars of the time.[3] In 1448

was a notable translator. The version of *A.P.* 16.296 is ascribed to Guarino also by
Urceo Codro (below, p. 123). Müllner, in *Wiener Studien* 19 (1897).128, quotes from
Cod. Ambros. G 44 *suppl.* verses by Guarino on the Seven Sages, with which may be
compared *A.P.* 9.366.

[1] The best account of Ciriaco is given by De Rossi, *Inscr. Christ.* 2.356ff.

[2] *Cod. Parm.* f. 60 in De Rossi, *op. cit.* 2.381. The translation occurs in Alciati's
collection of inscriptions, f.78, according to Mommsen (*C.I.L.* 3.xix). A curiously
similar claim concerning this epigram was made by Urceo Codro (below, p. 123, n. 2).

[3] De Rossi has vindicated him from the charge of pretending to have seen the epigrams here in question on stones, when he must actually have received them from manuscript sources (*op. cit.* 2.381); yet see Preger, *Inscr. Graec. Met.*, p. 130, on *A.P.* 16.334.

he sent to Filelfo a copy of *A.P.* 7.5. Filelfo was interested in its testimony as to the birthplace of Homer; he replied from Milan, Nov. 20, 1448: 'Eulogium Homeri sepulcro insculptum subdens id satis esse argumento Homerum non Smyrnaeum extitisse sed Chium.'[1] Ciriaco could have had his verses only from a MS. The same is true of *A.P.* 7.15, on Sappho, which has been taken into the *Corpus* of Greek inscriptions (*C.I.G.* 3555) on the authority of MSS. that go back to Ciriaco.[2] It is accompanied by a Latin translation that has passed for an antique:[3]

> Tantum ego carminibus superavi Sappho puellas,
> Maeonides quantum vicerat ante viros.

This translation has also been copied into the Marcian MS. of the Anthology, where it is accompanied by the following half-finished imitation:[4]

> Blandus Amor docuit numeros, probavit Apollo;
> Nomen erat Sappho, patria Lesbos erat;
> Ut cantu Maeonides nemini concessit Homerus,
> Sic Sappho Lesbiadas devici carmine nymphas.

It is probably only a coincidence that on the cover of the same MS. of the Anthology are copied some half-dozen inscriptions, including *A.P.* 7.15, all of which are derived from Ciriaco's notebooks.[5]

Ciriaco himself composed several literary works in Latin and others in Greek, among them, apparently, Greek and Latin epigrams; but these seem not to have survived. In a poem addressed to Ciriaco, his contemporary Carlo Marsuppini writes:[6]

> Eloquio Graio dictas epigrammata saepe,
> Saepe etiam nostro carmina multa facis.

[1] De Rossi 2.376. *Cod. Laur.* 80, 22, ff. 325–8 (14 epigrams) is, De Rossi says, a collection sent to Filelfo by Ciriaco. What is known of Ciriaco's relations with Filelfo is outlined by Calderini in the article cited below, p. 95, n. 1.

[2] See Mommsen, *C.I.L.* 3.32*. The epigram appears in a MS. of Michael Fabricius Ferrarinus, who died between 1488 and 1493 as a Carmelite Prior (*C.I.L.* 3.xxv), and also in a MS. of Joannes Jucundus of Verona (*c.* 1492). Jucundus is supposed to have seen it at Pergamum on a stone (Didot Anthol. 1.419). The same epigram (*A.* P.7.15) and *A.P.* 16.120.2–4 occur in a fifteenth-century MS. of Ovid now in the Bodleian Library (Lat. class. d.5); they are accompanied by a prose-translation. (Robinson Ellis in *Journ. of Philol.* 24.161).

[3] See above, p. 26. This translation occurs in Alciati's collection of inscriptions, was taken therefrom by Moroni, and from Moroni's MS. by Heinsius, and was received into the Latin Anthology by Burmann (*Anthol. Lat.* 2.210).

[4] Stadtmüller at *A.P.* 7.15.

[5] Carl Radinger in *Rhein. Mus.* 58.302.

[6] *Carmina Illust. Poet. Ital.* 6.277 (lines 5–6). Filelfo congratulates Ciriaco on his Greek style (*Griechischen briefe des Fr. Philelphus*, ed. by Klette, Greifswald, 1890, p. 104). His Latin style is not distinguished by its elegance: 'Quare Cyriacana scripta

FRANCESCO FILELFO
(1398–1481)

Filelfo was born of an obscure family at Tolentino in the March of Ancona. He studied rhetoric, law, and philosophy at Padua, where at the age of eighteen he began teaching rhetoric. Called to Venice in 1417, he lectured there with considerable success, and was chosen to go as secretary to the Venetian legation to Constantinople in 1420. There he remained to learn Greek, studying with Joannes Chrysoloras, a brother of Guarino's teacher, and with Manuel Chrysococceus (*Epist. Fam.*, Deventer, 1488, 6.35). The Emperor, John Paleologus, sent him on an embassy to the Emperor Sigismund at Budapest (1423). On returning to Constantinople he married Chrysoloras' daughter, Theodora; and, accompanied by her, came back to Venice late in 1427 to teach Greek. At this point in his life his fascinating letters begin. The plague drove him from Venice, war drove him from Bologna, and he made his way to Florence, where his lectures, three daily, were thronged. Having made enemies of the Medici, he was compelled to withdraw from Florence. To pass over his quarrels and most of his wanderings, he was at length received with honor at Milan, and later went to Naples at the invitation of King Alfonso. When the Turks took Constantinople, Filelfo secured from the Sultan the liberation of his mother-in-law and sisters-in-law. At the end of his life he was allowed by Lorenzo to return to Florence to teach; but had been only a few days in the city when he died.

Filelfo's promise to Traversari to translate the epigrams in Laertius has already been mentioned. A closer connection between him and the Anthology exists in *Cod. Laur.* 32, 16, a manuscript once in his possession, and containing, with much other matter, two groups of epigrams.[1] The first (ff. 3ro–6vo) consists of 104 selections, mostly from the amatory, sepulchral, and epideictic epigrams; the second (ff. 381vo–383vo) consists of 61 epigrams from the dedicatory section of the Anthology, from the oracles and enigmas, and from the epigrams now known as the Planudean Appendix. Neither group follows the order of *Pal.* or *Plan.*[2] On f. 8vo Filelfo's name is twice written in Greek

et fragmenta singularis cuiusdam et hybridae dictionis indicio facillime agnoscuntur' (De Rossi 2.357). Yet Aurispa could write of him (*Carm. Illust. Poet. Ital.* 1.493):

> Cyriace, orantem Ciceronem vincere solus
> Tu potes et solus carmine Virgilium;
> Nec minus hoc vincis Graece Demosthenis orans,
> Nilque minus Graece Scionis Iliada.

[1] On Filelfo's Greek studies in general see Aristide Calderini, 'Ricerche intorno alla Biblioteca e alla Coltura Greca di Francesco Filelfo' in *Stud. Ital. di Filol. Class.* 20 (1913) .298ff.; on *Laur.* 32, 16, see Alberto Chiari in *Raccolta di Scritti in Onore di Felice Ramorino*, pp. 568–74.

[2] A list of the epigrams is given by Chiari, pp. 568, 572.

and Latin, with the note: 'Emptus Constantinopoli ἀπὸ τῆς γυναικός viri clarissimi Johannis Chrysolorae sub anno MCCCCXXIII pd. Nonas Januarias.' At the end his name again appears in his own hand.[1]

There is no evidence that Filelfo ever came to know the whole Planudean collection. In a letter, written April 15, 1433, to Niccolò Luna, he quotes *A.P.* 11.193, ascribing it to Aristotle; in a letter to Cicco Simonetta, Feb. 24, 1461, he again quotes it, and provides a translation: 'Invidia est quod pessimum, sed habet quiddam in se bonum, nam oculos corque invidorum facit intabescere.'[2] This epigram is in *Laur.* 32, 16, f. 3ᵛᵒ. In 1448, as noticed above (p. 94), he was glad to receive from Ciriaco a copy of *A.P.* 7.5. Such of his original Latin epigrams as are in print show no traces from the Anthology.[3]

When forced to quit Florence, Filelfo was at work on a translation of Plutarch's *Apophthegmata*, which he finished at Siena, Oct. 1, 1454. The two epigrams quoted in that work—*A.P.* 7.229 and 433—he put into verse, the first as follows:[4]

> Exanimus Pitanen clypeo Thrasybulus in acri
>   Confossus septem vulneribus rediit,
> Passus ab Argivis, quae tergo nulla gerebat.
>   Tynnichus hunc igni cum daret, haec loquitur:
> 'Flere decet timidos, oculis te, nate, sepulchro
>   Condo meum siccis ac Lacedaemonium.'

THEODORE GAZA

(*c.* 1400–1475)

Gaza was born in Thessalonica, and came to Italy when his native place fell to the Turks in 1430; little is known of his life before that date. For many years he taught Greek at Siena and Ferrara; in 1451 he went, at the invitation of Nicholas V, to Rome. Later he was under the protection of King Alfonso at Naples (1455–1458), retired

---

[1] Chiari, p. 574.

[2] *Epist. Fam.*, Deventer, 1488; Calderini, pp. 275–6.

[3] His immense book of epigrams, *De Jocis et Seriis*, has never been printed. It has been studied by Cesare Picci in *Il 'De Jocis et Seriis' di Francesco Filelfo*, Varallo, 1911. Picci remarks that, with a considerable interest in Martial, Filelfo nevertheless had no real notion of an epigram, a judgment that is borne out by the pieces he quotes.

[4] The translation was published with other miscellaneous pieces at Milan in 1481. I use the edition of Amerbach, *Orationes*, etc., Basel, (?) 1495. The versions of the two epigrams were introduced by Soter into his *Epig. Graec.*, and were borrowed by Raffaello Regio (†1520) for his translation of the *Apoph.* (in *Plut. Opuscula Quaedam*, Mainz, 1522, p. 160). Filelfo himself quotes his version of *A.P.* 7.433 near the end of his *Orat. Funeb. iii* (*Orat.*, sig. I vi).

to a monastery on the Lucanian coast where he passed the years 1458–1464, then reappeared at Rome under Paul II (1464–1472), and finally returned to his Lucanian monastery where he died. Gaza was a good Latin scholar, having studied with Vittorino, and has left translations of Aristotle's *Mechanical Problems* and *History of Animals*, and of St. John Chrysostom, *On the Incomprehensible Nature of God*. He is best known for his Greek Grammar.

During Gaza's second period in Rome he assisted Giovan Andrea di Bussi, Bishop of Aleria, especially in Greek matters, in several of the works edited by Di Bussi for the press of Sweynheym and Pannartz.[1] In the Dedicatory Epistle to his Gellius (Rome, 1469) Di Bussi acknowledges Gaza's help:[2] 'Theodoro . . . opitulante, multa, ut arbitror, latina feci veriora, et ut graeca latine legerentur consequutus sum.' Indeed, every Greek word in Gellius is carefully glossed in Di Bussi's edition, while the metrical passages are mostly rendered into verse. As the editor employed what are now counted as inferior MSS. of Gellius, we have from Gaza translations not only of *A.P.* 5.78 and 11.48, but also of the interpolated epigrams, *A.P.* 7.676 and 16.297.[3] Gaza's translations of *A.P.* 5.78; 7.676; and 16.297 gained currency, and were frequently quoted by later writers:[4]

> Savia dans Agathoni animam ipse in labra tenebam;
> Aegra etenim properans tanquam abitura fuit.
> (*A.P.* 5.78)

> Servus Epictetus fueram, qui corpore mancus,
> Pauperie pressus, carus eram superis.
> (*A.P.* 7.676)

> Septem urbes certant de stirpe insignis Homeri:
> Smyrna, Rhodos, Colophon, Salamin, Ius, Argos, Athenae.
> (*A.P.* 16.297)

CARDINAL BESSARION
(1403–1472)

Bessarion, a native of Trebizond, studied in Constantinople, where at one time he was a fellow student of Filelfo in the school of

---

[1] Cf. above, p. 91.
[2] Quoted by Legrand, *Bibl. Hell.* I. xlix. I otherwise use the edition of Di Bussi's Gellius published by Bernardino di Chori and Simone di Luere, Venice, August 13, 1489, from which the Epistle was omitted.
[3] Above, p. 22, n. 2.
[4] *A.P.* 11.48 was not translated into verse.

Manuel Chrysococceus. About 1425 he joined the order of St. Basil; and soon after went to Sparta to study with Gemistos Plethon. He rose rapidly in his Church, and was a natural choice to be sent to the Council of Florence (1438–9). He served with Ambrogio Traversari on the committee that drafted the final decree of Union between the Eastern and the Western Church. The Union being badly received in Constantinople, Bessarion, already cardinal, returned to Italy for good in 1450. Thereafter he resided mainly in Rome, where he died. Though himself a scholar and translator, his best service to the Italian Renaissance was in assembling the third great library of the peninsula, and, through his position, in protecting young Greek scholars who had followed him to the West. Of the persons we are concerned with, Constantine Lascaris, Gaza, Chalcondyles, and Janus Lascaris owed much to his patronage.

The Marcian manuscript of the Anthology, so important for the early history of the Greek epigrams in the Occident, was among the books bequeathed by Bessarion to Venice. These books, to which St. Mark's Library owes its real foundation, began to be transported from Bessarion's palace in Rome to the Ducal Palace (where the library was first housed) in 1469. An Aristotle in the same collection also contains a group of epigrams.[1] There is nothing, however, to show that Bessarion took any special interest in the Anthology. His own works are scarcely of a kind to show any such interest. Only in his defence of Plato he quotes, from Diogenes Laertius, the first couplet of *A.P.* 7.109 as a sample of 'the epigrams filled with all praise' which Diogenes composed in Plato's honor. The Latin translation of this treatise, conceivably by Bessarion himself, gives the following version of these lines:[2]

> Sol genuit terris Asclepion atque Platona,
> Scilicet hic animam, corpus ut ille regat.

LORENZO VALLA

(1407–1457)

Valla's family belonged to Piacenza, but at the time of his birth his parents were living in Rome. He early lost his father; but his future was assured by his mother's fortune, and by the care of an uncle who was

---

[1] The Planudean autograph (*Marc.* 481) seems to be No. 456 in the catalogue published by Omont in *Rev. des Bibl.* 4 (1894). 168: 'Liber Epigrammatum in pergameno.' The MS. of Aristotle's *Moralia* is No. 373 (=*Marc.* 213?).

[2] *In Calumniatorem Platonis* (4.2.15), ed. by Ludwig Mohler as vol. 2 of his *Kardinal Bessarion*, Paderborn, 1927, p. 493.

Apostolic Secretary. On completing his studies he became professor of eloquence at Pavia; and presently was plunged in the disputes that were to occupy the greater part of his life. His quarrel with Poggio was the most bitter of them, and must indeed have passed beyond all bounds of decency, since even Filelfo says so. Valla taught at Milan, Genoa, and Florence, and was finally attracted to the court of Alfonso at Naples. Although he returned to Rome in 1443, the storm raised by his work on the false donation presently drove him back to Alfonso. The rest of his life was spent partly at Naples and partly at Rome, amid endless disputes. He died at Rome. His best works are the *Declamatio de Falso Credita et Ementita Constantini Donatione* and *Elegantiarum libri sex;* in each he touches the heart of what was then a lively issue.

At the time of Valla's death he was engaged in making a Latin translation of Herodotus; apparently having it almost finished, since it was printed entirely as his at the press of Rubeus, Venice, 1474.[1] We need not hesitate, therefore to accept as Valla's the metrical translations therein contained. Valla's translation had been twice printed before the *editio princeps* of Herodotus in Greek. His version of *A.P.* 7.249 will serve as a specimen.[2]

> Nos Lacedaemoniis refer hic, peregrine, iacentes,
> Exhibito illorum vocibus obsequio.

TITO VESPASIANO STROZZI

(*c.* 1422–1505)

Strozzi belonged to that branch of the great Florentine house which had taken refuge in Ferrara from the political feuds of Florence. He was educated by Guarino da Verona. Borso d'Este and his successor Ercole I took him into their favor; the second in particular employing him in many honorable capacities. In 1485 Ercole raised him to the

---

[1] Reprinted by Pannartz, Rome, 1475; Venice, 1494; Paris (Petit), [1510]; Cologne, 1526; and often down to the nineteenth century. My references are to the 1474 edition This is without folio- or signature-numbers, but, as early owners have often supplied the folio-enumeration, I have ventured to give this in the Register, from a copy in the Harvard College Library. Without this, one must search through the book of Herodotus in which a given epigram occurs, for the 1474 translation is also without chapter-numbers. Finding the epigram is made doubly difficult by the circumstance of the verse being printed as prose. At the end of the volume, after the announcement of the translator's identity, there is a letter to Nicolaus Donatus, a noble Venetian, by Benedetto Brugnolo. Valla's translation is accessible in the Valckenaer-Wesseling edition of Herodotus (Amsterdam, 1763), but the verse-translations have there been remodeled.

[2] Translations of all the epigrams in Herodotus as listed above, p. 2, n. 3 are given by Valla with one exception; this (*A.P.* 14.81) occurs in a section of the *Histories* (1.141–178) that is missing in his translation.

highest office in the State next his own, as Judge of the Twelve Sages. The incumbent of this office had to bear the brunt of popular disfavor in a time when many demands were being made upon the people to support the magnificence of their prince. As Strozzi advanced in years he spent more and more of his time at one or another of his country places; he died, more than eighty years old, at his estate called *Racano*. He was one of the very good Latin poets of the second half of the fifteenth century, though surpassed in ease and grace by his son Ercole. Tito Vespasiano was an uncle of the poet Boiardo.

The poems of the elder and the younger Strozzi were published in 1513 at Venice by Aldus, who had been a friend of the father and schoolmate of the son: *Strozii Poetae Pater et Filius* [*:Poemata*].[1] The verse of the elder consists of six books of *Amores*, three of *Æolosticha* (miscellaneous pieces), three of *Satyrae*, three of *Epigrammata* and *Epitaphia*, and an unfinished epic poem on Borso d'Este called the *Borsiad*. Conjointly they make a typical book of humanist verse. The typical humanist regularly includes one or two translations from the Greek Anthology; Strozzi has one (*A.P.* 9.738):

> Naturam atque Artem in vacca petiisse Myronis
> Partem aiunt: morem gessit utrique Myro.
> Qui vaccam spectat, 'Natura hanc protulit,' inquit;
> At si contigerit, dixerat: 'Artis opus.'

Ercole Strozzi shows no knowledge of the Greek epigrams.

DEMETRIUS CHALCONDYLES

(1424–1511)

Chalcondyles, originally Chalcocondyles, was by birth an Athenian. He came to Italy in 1447, settling first in Rome, and later, about 1450, in Perugia, where he taught Greek. He was at Padua from 1463 to 1471, and from there went to Florence, where the best part of his life was passed. Politian attended his lectures; and with Politian Chalcondyles was in some way associated as tutor to Lorenzo's children. Giovio's account of a quarrel between the two scholars appears to be without foundation; yet it is not known for what reason the Greek removed in 1491 or 1492 from Florence to Milan. In his later years at Florence he had many distinguished pupils, among them Trissino, Linacre, Grocyn, and Latimer. There also he published the first printed edition of Homer (1488). Of his ten children, all born

---

[1] I have not seen the ed. of the elder Strozzi's poems, collated with the MSS., by Anita della Guardia, Modena, 1916.

between 1485 and 1501, one, his son Basilius, finds a place in the present study (below, p. 165).

Chalcondyles' name is intimately associated with the introduction of the Anthology, in its corporate form and no longer in scattered epigrams, to the scholars of the West. As already noticed (above, p. 30), he had, with Joannes Laurentius, reviewed (and perhaps copied) a MS. of the Planudean Anthology while at Padua, finishing his work in 1466. This MS. either preceded or accompanied him to Florence, where it now is. At the end he wrote the following words:[1] τέλος τοῦ ἑβδόμου τμήματος τῆς Ἀνθολογίας τῶν ἐμπεριεχομένων διαφόρων ἐπιγραμμάτων, ἃ δὴ διήλθομέν τε καὶ διωρθώσαμεν, ὡς ἐνῆν, ἐγώ τε Δημήτριας ὁ Χαλκοκανδύλης καὶ Ἰωάννης ὁ τοῦ Λαυρεντίου, ἔτει τῷ ἀπὸ τῆς κυριακῆς γεννήσεως χιλιοστῷ τετρακοσιοστῷ ἑξηκοστῷ ἑκτῷ.

Probably Janus Lascaris owed some of his interest in the Anthology to Chalcondyles. Politian's interest in the Greek epigrams, possibly first excited by Argyropulos, was at least fostered by Chalcondyles, to whom several of his own Greek epigrams are addressed. One of these is modeled after the Platonic epigram on Aristophanes:[2]

Εἰς τοὺς Σπουδαίους περὶ τοῦ Δημητρίου.

Φεύγετε Πιερίδων ἀδινοὶ θεράποντες ἄρουραν,
πᾶς Ἑλικωνιάδων ἦλθε πόλινδε χορός.

---

[1] Bandini, *Cat. Codd. Mss. Graec. Bibl. Laur.* 2.103; Legrand, *Bibl. Hell.* 1.xcvi. The relations of this MS. to others might prove interesting. Calderini has studied the *scholia* it contains.

The identity of Joannes Laurentius has been rediscovered by Pierre de Nolhac (*Mélanges d'Archéol. et d'Hist.* 8.3–18). He was a Venetian of obscure parentage, born about 1440. His work with Chalcondyles on the Anthology belongs to the end of his student years at Padua. His friendship with the Greek scholar continued to the end of his life. Gaza also appears to have been his teacher. After 1472 he lived at Rome in the protection of Marco Barbo, Cardinal of St. Mark, whose secretary he became in 1476. In 1484 he was made secretary to Innocent VIII, and a year later his librarian. Ecclesiastical honors followed. Under Alexander VI he lost his post as librarian, though not apparently that of secretary. He died, according to Valeriano, by poison, probably in 1501. The next story is that after his death his brother, finding among his papers some written in Greek against the Borgias, translated them into Latin, and sent them to Venice to be printed. The agents of the Borgias got wind of this; the brother was arrested; and when the Venetian ambassador intervened, he was told that the prisoner had already been judged, strangled, and thrown into the Tiber. Laurentius was admired as a scholar, cultivated by men of learning, especially the Greeks, and took an interest in affairs. His letters (*Vat.* 5641), Nolhac believes, deserve the attention of historians.

[2] This famous epigram, unfortunately omitted from the Anthology, occurs in the Life of Plato by Olympiodorus:

Αἱ Χάριτες τέμενός τι λαβεῖν ὅπερ οὐχὶ πεσεῖται
ζητοῦσαι, ψυχὴν ηὗρον Ἀριστοφάνους.

Politian's verses are in his *Prose Volgari*, ed. by Del Lungo, p. 192.

εἰ δέ τις αὖ κείνου θαλάμους καὶ δώματ' ἐρευνᾷ,
Χαλκεοκονδύλου στήθεα ναιετάει.

Chalcondyles was himself an epigrammatist; yet few of his poems have seen the light. The following epitaph for Theodore Gaza is printed by Iriarte from a Madrid MS.:[1]

Εἰς Θεοδῶρον Γάζην

Ἡ ἀτρεκὴς σοφίη δηρὸν χθονίους προλιποῦσα,
νοῦν Θεοδώρου δεῦρ' ἤλυθεν εὑραμένη·
αὐτὴν τῷ Μοῦσαι δόσαν Ἑλλάδα τ' Αὐσονίην τε,
ὡς σοφίης μεταδῷ ἀμφοτέρῳ γένεϊ.
νῦν δὲ θανὼν φεῦ ἤπιος ὢν λίπεν ἄλγεα πᾶσι,
ψυχὴ δ' ἐς μακάρων ᾤχετ' ἀποπταμένη.

[True learning having long left mankind, came hither again, finding the mind of Theodore; and to him the Muses gave Greece herself and Italy, that he might impart to both nations a share of learning. Now he is dead, alas! and since he was gentle has left grief to all; but his soul hath winged her way to the abode of the Blest.]

The first distich of this epitaph recalls the same Platonic epigram that Politian imitates in complimenting Chalcondyles himself. The last distich echoes the Platonic epigram on Aster (*A.P.* 7.670):[2]

Ἀστὴρ πρὶν μὲν ἔλαμπες ἐνὶ ζωοῖσιν Ἑῷος·
νῦν δὲ θανὼν λάμπεις Ἕσπερος ἐν φθιμένοις.

GIORGIO MERULA
(*c.* 1424–1494)

Merula's teachers in Greek were Filelfo and Tifernas, with whom he studied in his native city of Milan. He himself became a teacher at Milan, and then, from 1464 to 1482, in Venice. In the latter year Lodovico Sforza recalled him to Milan to write the history of the city, a task which Merula fulfilled. He was the first editor of Martial (Venice or Rome, *c.* 1471), and had an important part in the Ausonius published at Milan in 1490.[3] Merula was a tireless collector of MSS. and a fearless controversialist. He died at Milan in March, 1494.

That Merula was acquainted with the Greek epigrams is perhaps evident from a controversy between him and Politian,

[1] *Regiae Bibliothecae Matritensis Codices Graeci MSS.*, Madrid, 1769, p. 257. I give the text of Legrand, *op. cit.*, I.xli.

[2] Aster (Star), once you shone among the living as the Morning Star; but now having died you shine as the Evening Star among the dead.

[3] It is to be noticed that none of the spurious epigrams had yet made their appearance in this edition.

involving *A.P.* 9.517 or 266, to which we shall have occasion to
return.[1] Moreover three small MSS. now in the Ambrosian
Library, but formerly in Merula's possession, contain selections
from the Anthology—namely *Ambros. Graec.* 295, 886, and 216.[2]

In speaking of Ausonius (above, pp. 24–5), we have already
found it needful to mention the conjecture, first advanced by
Peiper, that the new epigrams given to this poet in the editions
of 1496 and 1499 are in reality the compositions of Merula.[3] A
few words must here be added. If the translations in question
are not by Ausonius but by Merula, the substitution was, as
Peiper remarks, probably done in complete innocence on the
part of all concerned. Merula died in 1494, and his papers were
turned over to the Secretary of State of Milan, Bartholomaeus
Chalcus; by some confusion certain compositions of Merula's
may have been taken for copies of an ancient MS.

The eighteen epigrams added to the edition of 1496, eleven
of them translated from the Anthology, were there said to have
been recently (*superioribus annis*) discovered in Milan by the
poet Franciscus Nurcisius of Verona, private secretary to
Queen Caterina Cornaro, and by him turned over to Bartolommeo Merula of Mantua for publication. The epigrams
translated in this group are: *A.P.* 7.670; 9.12 (2 versions), 45,
168(?), 515; 10.26; 11.279; 16.151; 174, 178.

Further additions were made by Taddeo Ugoleto, editor of
the 1499 Ausonius. These consist (1) of nine new epigrams, six
of them translated from the Anthology, printed at the end of
the volume with those that had been added in 1496. All these
twenty-seven pieces are preceded by the words: *Epigrammata
Ausonii quae feruntur emanasse e bibliotheca Georgii Alexandrini*
[i.e. Giorgio Merula] *viri de lingua latina benemerenti.* The six
new translations from the Anthology are from *A.P.* 7.396;
11.104, 266; 16.135, 136, 137. Further, (2) Ugoleto inserted into
the body of Ausonius' genuine epigrams eight new pieces; six of
these again being translated from the Anthology—*A.P.* 7.224,
311; 9.715, 721, 730; 11.255. Finally, (3) Ugoleto completed the

---

[1] Below, p. 126.
[2] Above, p. 34, n. 2.
[3] Rudolf Peiper, 'Die handschriftliche Ueberlieferung des Ausonius' in *Jahrb. f.
Class. Philol.*, suppl. 11 (1880). 226–56; also Peiper's edition of Ausonius (1886), *Praef.*
In the Register I have referred these epigrams to 'Ausonius?' There is, of course, still a
possibility that they are by Ausonius.

translations of *A.P.* 7.224 and 9.145, partial versions of both being found among Ausonius' genuine epigrams.

In Peiper's opinion all these additional epigrams (except the supplementary lines just mentioned) are the work of Merula, exercises done by him some time after the first edition of Ausonius (Venice, 1472) had taught him the trick of imitating the Greek Anthology.[1] So near did he come to equaling his model in this practice that, after his death, others, finding these translations among his MSS., took them for genuine productions of Ausonius, and printed them as such. Peiper makes a detailed examination of a number of these translations, and points out faults which perhaps only a Renaissance versifier would commit.[2] He is able to compare with them a translation from the Anthology, almost certainly done by Merula, and appearing in his Commentary on Juvenal (*Sat.* 8); it is a version of *A.P.* 9.357.[3]

Quattuor exercet certamina Graecia sacra,
 Mortali duo sunt et duo sacra deo.
Sunt Jovis et Phoebi atque Palaemonis Archemorique,
 Pinum, oleam, atque apium, malaque victor habet.

The translations added to Ausonius in 1496 and 1499, whether made by Ausonius, Merula, or another, appear to differ from the certain translations by Ausonius in a stricter adherence to the letter of their originals; but, a few doubtful expressions aside, they are by no means inferior to them in grace. In two cases, *A.P.* 7.670 and 16.174, the supposed imitator and Ausonius have translated the same epigram.[4] In the translation of *A.P.* 16.174 the suspected epigram appears to have the better of it; I give the original, then the version of Ausonius, and then the version supposed to be by Merula.

Παλλὰς τὰν Κυθέρειαν ἔνοπλον ἔειπεν ἰδοῦσα·
 'Κύπρι, θέλεις οὕτως ἐς κρίσιν ἐρχόμεθα ;'
ἡ δ'ἁπαλὸν γελάσασα· 'Τί μοι σάκος ἀντίον αἴρειν ;
 εἰ γυμνὴ νικῶ, πῶς ὅταν ὅπλα λάβω ;'

---

[1] The original of no one of these 23 epigrams happens to occur in any of the MSS. of Greek epigrams mentioned above as belonging to Merula.

[2] *Jahrb.*, pp. 240–248.

[3] I quote it from Peiper's article, p. 250; he had not himself seen the *Comm. in Juv.*, but takes the translation from Rivinus' *Florilegium*, Gotha, 1651.

[4] Possibly also in *A.P.* 9.44, where I follow Peiper in referring the 'Renaissance' version to 9.45.

Armatam vidit Venerem Lacedaemone Pallas;
 'Nunc certemus, ait, iudice vel Paride.'
Cui Venus: 'Armatam tu me temeraria temnis,
 Quae, quo te vici tempore, nuda fui?'

Armatam Pallas Venerem Lacedaemone visens,
 'Vis nunc iudicium sic ineamus!' ait.
Cui Venus arridens: 'Quid me, galeata, lacessis?
 Vincere si possum nuda, quid arma gerens?'

Particularly well-known among these translations possibly by
Merula are the versions of *A.P.* 9.12, 45; 11.104; and that of
16.174 just quoted.

Ambulat insidens caeco pede captus utroque
 Atque alterna subit munia debilitas;
Nam caecus claudo pedes commodat, ille vicissim
 Mutua dat caeco lumina pro pedibus.
                    (*A.P.* 9.12)[1]

Thesauro invento qui limina mortis inibat,
 Liquit ovans laqueum, quo periturus erat;
At qui, quod terrae abdiderat, non repperit aurum,
 Quem laqueum invenit, nexuit ac periit.
                    (*A.P.* 9.45)

Faustulus insidens formicae ut magno elephanto
 Decidit et terrae terga supina dedit.
Moxque idem ad mortem est mulcatus calcibus eius,
 Perditus ut posset vix retinere animam.
Vix tamen est fatus: 'Quid rides, improbe livor?
 Quod cecidi: cecidit non aliter Phaëthon.'
                    (*A.P.* 11.104)

ALAMANNO RINUCCINI
(1426–1504)

Rinuccini was a Florentine, and held a number of honorable offices
in the government of his city. Landino (*Camal. Disp.*, Ded. Epist.)
mentions his favor with Lorenzo. He translated into Latin several of
the *Lives* of Plutarch, and the *Life of Apollonius of Tyana* by Philostratus. The latter, completed in 1473, was not printed until 1501,
when it was set up by Aldus; even so, it seems not to have been issued
until 1504: *Philostrati de Vita Apollonii Tyanei libri octo. Iidem libri*

---

[1] This is the second of the two versions of this epigram.

latini interprete Alemano Rinuccino Florentino. Eusebius contra Hiero-
clem . . . interprete Zenobio Acciolo.[1]

The *Life of Apollonius* contains *A.P.* 7.256, and this Rinuccini rendered into verse:[2]

> Qui quondam Aegaei ruimus salis aere profundum,
>   Ecbatanum hoc campo contegimur medio.
> · Patria clara olim vale, Eretria, vos et Athenae
>   Vicinae Euboees, ponteque amice, vale!

The original, among the finest of the epigrams ascribed to Plato,
is for the Eretrians settled by Darius in the heart of Persia
(Herod. 6.119).

GIOVANNI PONTANO

(1426–1503)

Pontano's birthplace was Cerreto in Umbria. His father, a man or
good family, was killed in a rising of the people; and the young
Pontano was taken by his mother to Perugia to be educated. When
his education was completed, failing in an attempt to regain his
father's property, he joined the army of King Alfonso, whom he followed to Naples. There Panormita befriended him, and after Panormita's death he became head of the Academy founded by the elder
scholar, but henceforth known as the Academy of Pontano. Under
Ferdinand I he had a leading part in diplomatic missions to every
part of Italy; but when Charles VIII of France occupied Naples, Pontano hastened to welcome him. This was doubtless an act of prudence;
but naturally, on the re-entry of Ferdinand II, he was deprived of
his offices. The enforced leisure that followed he spent in perfecting
his Latin works. His poems were first published in two volumes at
Venice, 1505, 1508.

Pontano's sources of inspiration are mainly Latin. He has,
however, among his Latin poems, an imitation of Moschus'
Amor Fugitivus (*A.P.* 9.440), a poem *De Venere et Amore* that
recalls *A.P.* 9.15, and the following epigram in imitation of
A.P. 7.670:[3]

---

[1] Renouard, *Annales des Aldes* (1803) 1.58. The date at the end of the Greek text
is March, 1501; the Preface of the Latin is dated May, 1504; and at the end of the Latin
is the date February, 1502. The reason for delay seems to be given by Aldus himself,
who says he took a distaste to the work because of the triviality of the subject, and
could hardly bring himself to finish it.

[2] Here quoted from Soter's *Epigrammata* of 1528 (below, p. 277); Soter gives it
under the name 'Philostrati Interpres.'

[3] All three are in his book of amatory epigrams entitled *Eridanus*. In the above order
they are in the 1518 Aldine edition of his poems on ff. 105, 112, and 107; in the Basel
Opera Omnia of 1556, in vol. 4, pp. 3557, 2572, and 3562.

DE STELLA

Nostra die quod Stella nitet, quod nocte refulget,
  Solem Stella die, sidera nocte refert.
Nocte eadem surgente nitet, cedente refulget,
  Phosphoron hic, illic Hesperon ipsa refert.
Ergo eadem mihi sol, eadem mihi sidus, et una
  Lucifer est, eadem vesper et una mihi.

GIOVAN ELISIO CALENZIO (CALENTIUS)

(†c. 1503)

Calenzio, a native of Anfratta in Apulia, was a member of Pontano's Academy in Naples, and a close friend of Altilio and Sannazaro. He is said to have been tutor to Federigo III in his youth. Calenzio's Latin poems were published at Rome in the year, probably, of the author's death.[1] His elegies were addressed to Colocci, perhaps at the time when the future Bishop of Nocera was living in semi-exile at Naples, and was a member of the Academy. The Hieracus of the *Epistolae* is King Federigo. Calenzio's love-poems are amply described by Ellinger, and need not detain us.[2]

Only one poem contains a reminiscence of the Anthology—and that probably very indirect (*A.P.* 5.94):

Foelix qui teneros tuos ocellos
Et labellula laeta basiabit,
Aurimpiola tantulum tenella
Quantulum puto flosculus iacinti
Aut albi folium novum ligustri;
Sed foelix magis, et deus profecto
Ille est, qui thalamos tuos, puella,
Intrabit gelidus, thoroque in uno
Haerebit lateri cubans tenello. . . .

CONSTANTINE LASCARIS

(1434–1501)

How closely Constantine was related to Janus Lascaris is not known. He was born at Constantinople, and studied there with Joannes Argyropulos. He was made captive by the Turks, but seems

---

[1] *Opuscula* [*Elegiarum Aurimpiae ad Colotium libri iii; Epigrammaton libellus; Epistolarum ad Hieracum libri iii; Hectoris horrenda Apparitio; De Bello Ranarum libri iii; Satyra contra Poetas; Satyra ad Longum; Carmen Nuptiale; Nova Fabula*] Rome, 1503.

[2] Georg Ellinger, *Italien und der Deutsche Humanismus in der Neulateinischen Lyrik* (being vol. 1 of a *Geschichte der Neulateinischen Literatur Deutschlands im sechzehnten Jahrundert*), Berlin, 1929, pp. 65–7. I shall cite this book hereafter as 'Ellinger.' It is unfortunately without any bibliographical information on the authors it discusses, but is otherwise good.

soon to have been liberated. Nothing certain is known of his fortunes between 1453 and 1460; probably he joined his relations in Corfu, perhaps he was already in Italy during that period. In 1560, at all events, he was teaching Greek in Milan, where he had for pupil Hippolita, daughter of Francesco Sforza. On her marriage in 1465 to Ferdinand I of Naples, Lascaris was invited to that city to occupy the chair of Greek; but, soon finding Naples intolerable, he was glad to be appointed by Bessarion to one of the chairs of Greek founded by the Senate of Messina in connection with the Sicilian Order of St. Basil. His fame attracted many pupils to Messina, among them the young Pietro Bembo from Venice. He is last seen dictating his will from the window of a house where he had been confined on suspicion of the plague. His *Grammar* was the first book to be printed in Greek (Milan, 1476).

Before Lascaris' death he had given his rich collection of manuscripts to the city of Messina, where it remained till 1679. It was then transferred by the Count of Santo Stefano to Palermo; and was later taken to Spain, where it now is (76 MSS.) in the National Library. Two years before Chalcondyles worked on his copy of the Planudean Anthology, Lascaris had made a large selection of the epigrams in a MS. written in his own hand and dated 1464; he was then in Milan. This MS. is now *Matrit.* xxiv, and was fully described in 1769 by Iriarte.[1] The epigrams are mingled with other selections drawn from Laertius, the verses of Solon, etc., and are disposed in an order quite different, for the most part, from that of Planudes.[2] So far as they coincide with the Anthology they are 460 in number, largely drawn from the sepulchral epigrams.[3] The readings of the MS. that differ from those of the printed Anthologies are supposed to be Lascaris' conjectures; but, as a matter of fact, they are mainly found in the *lemmata*, and do not concern the text of the epigrams. The few marginal notes are without interest.

The only one of Lascaris' printed works to contain a reference to the Greek epigrams seems to be his *Prolegomena* to the Orphic *Argonautica*, in which he quotes *A.P.* 7.617.[4]

[1] *Reg. Biblioth. Matrit. Codd. Gr. MSS.*, Madrid, 1769, pp. 89ff. Cf. Stadtmüller' *Anthol. Graec.* 2.lxiv. Waltz probably says truly (*Anthol. Grec.* 1.lvii) that scholars have given this MS. an importance it does not deserve; yet it would be worth knowing from what source Lascaris took his epigrams. Waltz appears to confuse Constantine with Janus.

[2] Before the epigrams, at the end of the first part of the MS. which contains other matter, is written: κτῆμα Κωνσταντίνου Λασκάρεως ἐν Μεδιολάνῳ ὑπ' αὐτοῦ ἐκγραφέν.

[3] The collection contains about 490 epigrams in all.

[4] The *Prolegomena* was printed, with a Latin translation, by Rivautella and Ricolvi in their *Marmora Taurinensia*, Turin, 1743, 1.93–104; the epigram is on p. 96.

CRISTOFORO LANDINO

(1434–1504)

Landino was admired in his time as a student of philosophy and of Greek, as a Latin poet, and as a cultivator of the vernacular literature. He first studied with Angiolo da Todi at Volterra; and, though destined by his father to a legal career, the favor of the Medici returned him to his chosen studies. He taught literature at the *Studio* in Florence, became a close friend of Politian and Ficino, and was a member of the Platonic Academy. He also became Secretary to the Signoria, but in 1497 withdrew from all official duties. Of his numerous works in prose and verse several remain unprinted; his Commentaries on Dante, Virgil, Horace, and the *Symposium* of Plato, his Orations, and his Dialogues on the nobility of the soul, have, on the other hand, often been printed, and have enjoyed their portion of fame.

A.P. 7.617 is quoted with the following translation by Landino in his Commentary on Horace (Florence, 1482). He is illustrating *Carm.* 1.12.7.

> Orphea chrysolyram Musae hoc posuere sepulchro,
> Fulmine quem stravit Iuppiter alta videns.

LORENZO LIPPI

(*fl.* 1478)

Lippi was a native of Colle di Val d'Elsa near Florence, and made his home either there or, more probably, in Florence itself. Hardly anything is known of his life. The Laurentian Library possesses manuscript translations by him of several Greek works, including the *Nicocles* of Isocrates; his translation of Oppian, *De Piscatu et de Venatione*, was printed by the Aldine Press in 1517 and reprinted by Morel, Paris, 1555.

Lippi is best known as a writer of Latin epigrams in distich. These *Disticha* were dedicated to Lorenzo de' Medici, and printed at Colle, September 12, 1478.[1] They are mainly written on objects of nature—fruits and vegetables, birds and beasts, fishes, precious stones, etc. There are a few exceptions, one of which is a translation of *A.P.* 9.48:

> Fit cycnus, taurus, satyrus, fit Iuppiter aurum,
> Pro Leda, Europaque, Antiopa, Danaë.

---

[1] I use Pictorius (Bigi), *Sacra et Satyrica Epigrammata* (Basel, 1518), where Lippi's distichs appear on pp. 60–72. The two here quoted may also be found in *Carm. Illust. Poet. Ital.* 6.132.

A second is an imitation of this:

> Gradivus, Bacchus, Leneus, Vulcanus amavit
> Asteropen, Cressam, Nyctiopen, Venerem.

MARSILIO FICINO
(1433–1499)

Ficino's father, a native of Figline near Florence, was a favorite physician of Cosimo de' Medici. The son was born at Figline, but early taken to Florence, where he learned grammar from Luca da San Gemignano and Comando di Simone Comandi. From 1449 to 1451 he studied at Pisa; and then for five years, in Florence again, he studied philosophy with Tignosi da Foligno. At this time he began to be attracted to Plato, though he probably knew no Greek, and extracted what he could from the Latin Platonists. In 1458 his father sent him to Bologna to get a medical training; but these studies were soon interrupted. On the occasion of a visit at home he had been presented by his father to Cosimo, who, struck by the young man's enthusiasm for Plato, conceived the plan of making him the founder of the Platonic Academy he had long desired to establish in Florence. With Cosimo's protection Ficino set his face wholly towards Plato. He now gained a knowledge of Greek, possibly from Platina, of which the first fruits were a translation of the Orphic Hymns (1462). Cosimo presented him with a country house at Careggi, and provided him with manuscripts of Plato and Plotinus. Ficino translated the *Pimander* of Hermes Trismegistus in 1463 (pub. Treviso, 1471), and began to translate Plato. His great work was completed in 1468, but not perfected till 1482 (pub. Florence, 1484). Cosimo's care for Ficino was continued by Piero, who induced the philosopher to take part in public instruction, and by Lorenzo, who had been Ficino's pupil. After 1469 he began to interest himself in Christian theology, and finally at the age of forty-one took orders, receiving a benefice and relinquishing his patrimony to his brothers. But he was a Platonist still; his sermons are Platonic discourses. His *De Christiana Religione* appeared in 1475, his *Theologia Platonica* in 1482. Other works of importance in his later period are his *Liber de Vita* (pub. 1489), his translation of Plotinus, with commentary (1492), *De Sole* (1493), and *Epistolarum libri xii* (1495). After the death of Lorenzo, in the troubled years succeeding, the Platonic Academy naturally suffered; but Ficino labored on for seven years until his death at Careggi, October 1, 1499.[1]

There is no evidence that Ficino knew the Anthology as a collection; but from Plato, Herodotus, and Diogenes Laertius a few epigrams inevitably found their way into his works. In his Plato he necessarily translates *A.P.* 7.153; 10.106, and 108,

---

[1] Arnaldo della Torre, *Storia dell' Accademia Platonica*, Florence, 1902.

all three in prose.[1] In a letter to Giovanni Cavalcanti he gives
a verse-translation of the oracle in Herodotus concerning Lycurgus (= *A.P.* 14.69).[2] In his well-known letter to Francesco
Bandini *De Vita Platonis* (1477), he gives in prose the substance
of *A.P.* 7.60, 61, and 108, which he read in Laertius.[3] And in the
first part of his *Liber de Vita* (*c.* 7) he makes use of *A.P.* 9.39,
presumably also from Laertius. Among the 'monsters' that be-
set the path of a literary man who would lead a healthy life,
he says, are lust, gluttony, and late hours. The first he finds to
be ruinous to the intellect; he commends antiquity for ascribing
the character of chastity to Minerva and the Muses:

> Huc Platonicum illud spectat: cum Venus Musis minitaretur, nisi
> sacra venerea colerent, se contra illas suum filium armaturam, re-
> sponderunt Musae: 'Marti, o Venus, Marti talia minitare; tuus enim
> inter nos Cupido non volat.'

ANTONIO COSTANZI (CONSTANTIUS)
(1436–1490)

With Costanzi, a pupil of Guarino at Ferrara, the Anthology takes
its place as one of the regular sources of neo-Latin verse. Costanzi, on
finishing his studies, appears to have returned to his native Fano,
there to spend the remainder of his life in teaching. His poems, edited
after his death by his son Giacomo, are entitled: *Epigrammatum
Libellus, Odae* [etc.], Fano, 1502; at the end are Giacomo's own *Epigrammata* (below, p. 147).[4]

Among the epigrams of the elder Costanzi are scattered 23
translations from the Anthology; his source is always acknowledged. These translations are rarely made from epigrams of
more than two lines in length, a fact which, taken with a certain roughness in them, suggests that they may have been
school-exercises; or Costanzi may have taken to heart the statement of *A.P.* 9.369, which he translates:

> Perpulchrum est epigramma, vocant quod distichum; adde
> Tantundem: historiam non epigramma canis.

In all, he has Latin versions of *A.P.* 7.46, 136, 150, 282, 669; 9.8,

---

[1] References are to Emm. Bekker's ed. of Plato (1816–18), where Ficino's translation is printed from the first ed. and the Venice ed. of 1491.
[2] *Opera*, Basel, 1561, 1.631.
[3] *Op.* 1.770.
[4] There is a notice of Antonio Costanzi in Mercati's *Cronologia della Vita e degli
Scritti di Niccolò Perotti* in *Studi e Testi* 44 (1925).141.

48, 55, 66, 166, 369, 515; 10.27, 28, 39, 58, 65, 112; 11.50, 193, 307; 16.14, 98. Here follow his versions of *A.P.* 7.46, 669, and 11.307, in that order:

> Euripides, tua non sunt haec monumenta, sed horum
> Tu, redimit nomen nam monumenta tuum.

> Stella meus stellas dum suspicit, ipsum ego caelum
> Esse velim, ut multo hunc lumine despiciam.

> Est uxor Cytherea tibi natusque Cupido:
> Iure, faber, curvo nunc pede carpis iter.

NICCOLÒ LEONICENO
(1428–1524)

Leoniceno, a native of Lunigo near Vicenza, was known as a physician, 'philosopher,' and 'orator'; he taught medicine at Padua, and later at Ferrara, for more than sixty years. He is said to have made many Latin translations from the Greek— for one, the first book of Aristotle's *De Partibus Animalium;* and among several things translated by him into Italian are the Dialogues of Lucian. He is associated with Musurus and Carteromaco in a set of Latin translations from the Greek epigrams, now in a MS. at Basel.[1] Musurus and Carteromaco were with him at Padua.

MICHAEL TARCHANIOTA MARULLUS
(c. 1450–1500)

Marullus was a Greek, born at Constantinople, but was only a small child when the Turks took the city and he was brought to Ancona by his parents. Hence he received a Latin education, and was perhaps the best master of Latin among the expatriate Greeks; he studied Latin at Naples and, some say, philosophy at Padua. After some experience in arms under the Greek Rallis, he repaired to Florence, where he was well received by Lorenzo. There he won the hand of the beautiful and learned Alessandra Scala, and gained the enmity of Politian who had been his rival. We shall see how this affair exploded in epigrams.[2] Marullus married in 1493, and continued to live in Florence. In 1500, when returning one day from a visit to Raffaelle Maffei at Volterra, he was swallowed up in the quicksands of the Cecina. The scholarly world at first could not believe that so awful a

---

[1] Below, p. 156.
[2] Below, p. 127.

fate had befallen him, but, as the report became confirmed, honored his memory with multitudes of sepulchral epigrams.[1]

While wanting somewhat of the spontaneity of Politian and Sannazaro, Marullus wrote Latin verse superior to that of most of the Italians of his time. His poems consist of Epigrams in four books, Hymns in four books, and an incomplete *De Principium Institutione*. The epigrams were published at Rome in 1493,[2] and again with the hymns in 1497 at Florence. These were reprinted posthumously (with his longer poems and certain *naenia* on his death) at Fano in 1515; then followed *Epigrammata et Hymni*, Brescia, 1531; and this book again was printed at Paris, edited by G. Crispus, in 1561.[3]

As a member of the Florentine group, Marullus was certain to know the Anthology; he has imitations of some seventeen epigrams: *A.P.* 5.78; 7.161, 617, 670; 9.61, 108, 146, 163, 346, 456, 506; 11.307; 16.151, 200, 275, 295.[4] *A.P.* 9.346 is a well-known epigram on a bird nesting on a picture of Medea; this Marullus interprets as follows:

> Quid vaga tot terras urbesque emensa, volucris,
>   Colchidos in saevo nidificas gremio?
> Pignoribusque tuis credis male sana fidelem,
>   Ipsa suos partus quae laniavit atrox?
> Ni foetus exosa tuos, Pandione nata,
>   Phasiaca quaeris perdere saevitia.

Almost as well known have become the verses on Aeneas rescuing his father (*A.P.* 9.163); we shall find many later versions to compare with this of Marullus:

> Cum ferret medios proles Cytheraea per hostes
>   Impositi collo languida membra patris:
> 'Parcite, ait, Danaï, levis est sene gloria rapto,
>   At non erepto gloria patre levis.'

Marullus has left no translation of *A.P.* 16.129; yet, according to a remark of his reported by Crinitus (below, p. 146), he esteemed no epigram more highly.

---

[1] See Ariosto's elegy on the death of Marullus, addressed to Ercole Strozzi, in Pigna's *Carmina*, p. 284. On Marullus' life and poems see the article by P. L. Ciceri in *Giorn. Stor.* 64 (1914). 289–357.

[2] Perhaps previously at Florence in 1490.

[3] It is to the Paris edition that I refer to as *Epig.* in the Register.

[4] Some of these versions are not found in Marullus' *Epigrammata* of 1561, and are here ascribed to him on the authority of Soter, namely versions of *A.P.* 5.78; 7.617, 670; 16.200, and 275. The Commentary of the 1521 Alciati (below, p. 206) ascribes to Marullus a translation of *A.P.* 7.161 which seems not to be in the *Epig.*

JANUS LASCARIS

(1445-1535)

Janus Lascaris was probably born at Constantinople, and the epithet Rhyndacenus, which often accompanies his name, points to the original home of his family, Rhyndacus in Asia Minor.[1] His was the imperial family of the Lascarids, of which Constantine Lascaris also was a member. Janus was barely eight years old when his native city was captured by the Turks, and his father, Theodore, carried him for safety to the Peloponnesus. Thence he seems to have been taken to Crete, and finally, at the invitation of Bessarion, to Venice. The Cardinal of Nicaea became his virtual guardian, and sent him to Padua to be educated. There, as already noticed, he studied under Demetrius Chalcondyles.

Cardinal Bessarion died near the end of 1472, and Lascaris was forced to seek another protector. Chalcondyles had already found a haven in Florence. Probably through his offices Lascaris too was favorably received in that city by the Medici. If he came to Florence about 1473, it must be confessed that we know nothing of his life there for almost twenty years.[2] He may have been connected with Lorenzo's library from the beginning. At all events, it is certain that he made two journeys on Lorenzo's behalf to Greece and to Asia Minor in search of Greek MSS. for the library. Of the first journey we have little detailed knowledge; he was gone for two years, and had only been in Florence again for three months when he set out on his second journey, about the beginning of May, 1491.[3] He visited among other places

---

[1] Lascaris' name was originally Joannes—so given at the end of the dedicatory Epistle to his Anthology. The life of Lascaris, which is very important not only in the history of the Greek Anthology but in general for the spread of Greek learning in Europe, is best given by Legrand, *Bibl. Hell.* 1.cxxxi–clxii, who supersedes Henri Vast, *De vita et operibus Jani Lascaris*, Paris, 1878; but Humphrey Hody's *De Graecis illustribus*, London, 1742, contains matter that is still not easily accessible elsewhere. Indispensable are K. K. Müller's article in the *Centralblatt für Bibliothekswesen* 1 (1884). 333–412, Pierre de Nolhac's 'Inventaire des manuscrits grecs de Jean Lascaris' in *Mélanges d'Arch. et d'Hist.* 6 (1886).251–274, the same scholar's *Fulvio Orsini*, Paris, 1887, and his *Correspondents d'Alde Manuce*, Paris, 1888, and Müllner's publication of Lascaris' oration in *Wiener Studien* 21 (1899). 128–143. See also Abel Lefranc, *Histoire du Collège de France*, Paris, 1893, L.-G. Pélissier in *Mémoires présentés à l'Académie des Inscr. et Belles-lettres* 11 (1901). 177–218, Léon Dorez in *Rev. des Bibliothèques* 2 (1892). 280 and 5 (1895). 325–9, and L. Delaruelle in *Rev. du Seizième Siècle* 13 (1926). 95–111.

[2] Apparently Lascaris gave no lectures in the Florentine *Studio*, at least until 1492; he is not mentioned before that time in Prezziner's *Storia del Pubblico Studio di Firenze* (2 vols, Florence, 1810). A document dated Oct. 2, 1492 reads (*Stor.* 1.176): 'Joannem Georgii Lascherum Graecum ad legendum in Studio Florentino lectiones duas graece in philosophia et poetica facultate cum salario florenorum 168.' As Janus' father's name was almost certainly Theodore, 'Georgii' is hard to explain. Could the person here in question be another Joannes Lascaris, the one distinguished by Dorez in *Rev. des Bibl.* 5.325? This Joannes would then be a relation of Janus, and not, as Dorez supposes, a homonymous brother. For the present, however, I assume the person named in the notation to be Janus Lascaris himself.

[3] Legrand, *loc. cit.*, and especially K. K. Müller's article in *Centralblatt;* also E. G. Vogel, *Serapeum* 15 (1854). 154. It may be noticed that Politian, on May 7, 1491, copied a portion of a MS., lent to him by Lascaris, which he probably returned before

Corfu, Thessalonica, Mount Athos, and Constantinople, where he is
said to have interviewed the Sultan. He returned for a month or so to
Florence, but had gone back to Crete to conclude negotiations for
certain of the MSS. when he received word of the death of Lorenzo
(April 8, 1492).

Were it proper to call *Cod. Vat. Graec.* 1412, as Nolhac does,
'the notebook of Lascaris' travels,'[1] we might suppose that the
excerpts from the Anthology contained in it were made from
MSS. seen by Lascaris in the East; but since it contains also an
inventory of Lorenzo's Greek MSS. and a copy of Alessandra
Scala's verses on Politian (below, p. 128), this assumption
would be unsafe; the epigrams may have been copied from a
MS. at Florence. On folios 11–12 are some Latin translations by
Lascaris from the Anthology:[2]

> Parvula ne temnas, parvis nam gratia iuncta est:
>   Et puer est Veneris parvulus ales Amor.
> <div align="center">(<i>A.P.</i> 9.784)</div>

> Praedicit Nemesis cubito frenoque cometo;
>   Hoc sine nil facias; hoc sine parce loqui.
> <div align="center">(<i>A.P.</i> 16.223)</div>

> En cubitum Nemesis teneo: cur, forte requiris;
>   Admoneo cunctos: Hoc praeterire nephas.
> <div align="center">(<i>A.P.</i> 16.224)</div>

Though Lorenzo was dead, Lascaris returned to Florence,
and continued to work at the library. At this juncture probably,
but by no means certainly, he was appointed professor of Greek
literature and moral philosophy at the *Studio*. We have an
'opening lecture' delivered by him at the beginning of the second year of his tenure.[3] We can only conjecture the date to be
1493. Besides the probability that he is the Joannes Lascherus
appointed to lecture at the *Studio*, Oct. 2, 1492 (above, p. 114,

the owner left Florence: *Paris. Graec.* 3069, f. 243vo: 'Excripsi vii. die maii 1491, ego
Angelus Politianus, ex libro, quem mihi Joannes Lascaris Graecus commodaverat';
and f. 250vo: 'Absolvi ego Politianus, die maii vii, 1491. exemplar autem habui a Joanne
Lascari Graeco' (Henri Omont, 'Manuscrits grecs datés de la Bibl. Nat.' in *Rev. des
Bibliothèques* 2 (1892). 27. Further information on Lascaris' second journey is con-
tained in a letter from him to Sergius Stissus, dated Florence, Sept. 3, 1492, printed by
Legrand in *Cent-dix Lettres Grecques de Filelfe*, Paris, 1892, p. 361.

[1] Nolhac, *Fulvio Orsini*, p. 155; below, p. 245.

[2] Müller, *Centralbl.* Several original epigrams by Lascaris are in the same MS. In
Lascaris' *Epigrammata* (Paris, 1544) the second line of the first epigram printed above
is improved to read: 'Parvulus et Paphiae filius ales Amor.' *A.P.* 9.784 is on a small
bath.

[3] Müllner in *Wiener Studien*, as above.

note 2), the fact that the lecture we have concerns the Greek
Anthology suggests 1493, since it is likely he would be specially
interested in the Anthology at the time when he was getting
ready to edit it. The lecture in question tells us that his course
in the year preceding had dealt with Sophocles and Thucydides;
it makes a general defence of Greek studies, and announces that
his lectures for the ensuing year are to be on Demosthenes and
the Greek Anthology. The lecture is a mosaic of classical allusions, and the Anthology is several times quoted.[1] At the end,
in announcing his coming lectures, he makes a striking judgment on the Anthology:[2]

De epigrammatis . . . hoc unum satis in praesentia fuerit: A nullo
nos libro tantam utilitatem posse consequi aut ad linguam et erudi-
tionem aut ad iudicium circa humanas actiones et ad morum et vitae
compositionem. Tanta est in eo varietas, tanta copia et nominum et
rerum, tam exquisita iudicia de rebus fere omnibus, quae in humanis
actionibus possunt incidere, cum tanta brevitate et elegantia, tanto
lepore et venere, ut sapientissimorum omnium ingenium et iudicium
non sine φιλοτιμίᾳ et concertatione quadam in unum hunc librum
collatum esse existimes. Haec itaque transferat unusquisque, in his se
oblectet, haec imitetur, in his se exerceat qui praeter alias utilitates
tale quid etiam et tentare cupit et perficere. Quin et in soluta oratione
haud quaquam rhythmum et concinnitatem et numerum deprehen-
dere aut deligere et constituere poteris, nisi prius carminibus saltem
luseris et modulis.

In 1491 Lascaris and Politian were still on good terms, lend-
ing books to each other; but soon after Lascaris' return from
Greece their relations became less friendly. Probably Lascaris'
friendship with Marullus had something to do with this (below,
p. 127); no doubt Politian was hard to conciliate. In his later
years he affected a Roman disdain for the Greeks. The quarrel
broke out over a Greek epigram. Politian had translated into
Greek the fourteenth-century Latin epigram of Pulex on Hermaphroditus.[3] This performance Lascaris presumed to rival,
and added an epigram alluding to Politian's boast of having
written Greek epigrams in his sixteenth year; he said that
Politian's learning was still as remarkably advanced in his for-
tieth year as in his sixteenth—and no farther.[4]

---

[1] *A.P.* 7.429.10; 9.540.3–4; the phrase καὶ σπάνις εἰν Ἀίδῃ from 9.53; Σωκρατικοῖς
ἀδροῖς from 9.358; Ἀριστόξεινον ἀγητόν from 11.352; the second line of 11.275.
[2] Translated in part above, p. 36.
[3] Both Greek and Latin are in Del Lungo's edition of Politian cited below, p. 127.
[4] No doubt Lascaris was piqued by Politian's slighting remarks on the Greek

Lascaris meantime was preparing his edition of the Anthology, which appeared from the press of Lorenzo d'Alopa on August 11, 1494.[1] The first edition of the Greek Anthology is justly famous as one of the most beautiful of fifteenth-century printed books. It was the first of five works published by Lascaris at Alopa's press, and printed in small Greek capitals with accents.[2] The volume is a quarto of 238 unnumbered folios—signatures A-Ω and AA-KK—with 7 folios at the end without signatures. These last seven folios contain an eighteen-line Greek epigram by Lascaris, and a long epistle of dedication to Piero de' Medici. Most copies, however, are without the last seven folios.[3] A reasonable explanation of their absence was given by Roscoe in 1816, and is as follows: The Anthology was published on August 11, 1494. In September Charles VIII entered Florence, and Piero de' Medici was forced to flee from the city. Some copies of the book with its laudatory dedication to Piero had already gone out; but the editor—who may already have intended to accept the patronage of Charles—quickly suppressed the last folios in the remaining copies.

The Greek epigram by Lascaris is merely a flourish on the wonders of printing. The Epistle, while it contains precious information on the Laurentian library, has little to say about the Anthology, being mostly devoted to remarks on the forms of the Greek letters.[4] Only in the last paragraph Lascaris excuses himself from making the expected remarks on the epigrams, as they will sufficiently recommend themselves to the learned. He does wish it to be known that the Anthology—here so-called—was the work of Agathias (he knew nothing of Cephalas), and not of Planudes, who merely 'mutilated' it.

With the publication of Lascaris' edition the influence of the

epigrams written by Greeks in recent times; see below, p. 135. Legrand, *op. cit.*, 1.cxxxvii–cxxxix, gives an account of the quarrel, and quotes the epigrams in question. His date for these events in 1493.

[1] ΑΝΘΟΛΟΓΙΑ ΔΙΑΦΟΡΩΝ ΕΠΙΓΡΑΜΜΑΤΩΝ, ΑΡΧΑΙΟΙΣ ΣΤΝ ΤΕΘΕΙΜΕΝΩΝ ΣΟΦΟΙΣ, ΕΠΙ ΔΙΑΦΟΡΟΙΣ ΤΠΟΘΕΣΕΣΙΝ ΕΡΜΗΝΕΙΑΣ ΕΧΟΝΤΩΝ ΕΠΙΔΕΙΞΙΝ ΚΑΙ ΠΡΑΓΜΑΤΩΝ Η ΓΕΝΟΜΕΝΩΝ, Η ΩΣ ΓΕΝΟΜΕΝΩΝ ΑΦΗΓΗΣΙΝ. ΔΙΗΡΗΜΕΝΟΤ Δ'ΕΙΣ ΕΠΤΑ ΤΜΗΜΑΤΑ ΤΟΤ ΒΙΒΛΙΟΤ, ΚΑΙ ΤΟΤΤΩΝ ΕΙΣ ΚΕΦΑΛΑΙΑ ΚΑΤΑ ΣΤΟΙΧΕΙΟΝ ΔΙΕΚΤΕΘΕΙΜΕΝΩΝ, ΤΑΔΕ ΠΕΡΙΕΧΕΙ ΤΟ ΠΡΩΤΟΝ· κ. τ. λ.

[2] It seems probable that the first edition reproduced the ms. that Lascaris himself had prepared, now *Paris.* 2891 (below, p. 119).

[3] The several copies still in existence which were at one time in the possession of Lascaris himself, and which contain notes in his hand, are without these folios.

[4] The Epistle is reproduced by Maittaire, *Ann. Typ.* 1.272–283, by Bandini, *Bibl. Laur. Codd. Graec.* 2.105ff, and by Legrand, *Bibl. Hell.* 1.30–38.

Anthology really begins. Hitherto a limited number of scholars could study the few complete MSS. or make excerpts from them for themselves; henceforth it was open to hundreds.[1]

The expedition of Charles VIII into Italy had vast intentions of one kind, and immeasurable results of another. Doubtless Charles aimed to enroll himself with Alexander and Caesar among the conquerors of the world; after Italy he intended to reduce the Orient to his power. Lascaris, who had always at heart a dream of liberating Greece from the Turk, gladly followed the promise he thought he saw in the French king. These hopes faded away, but the Italian expedition hastened the French Renaissance at a thousand points; and it brought Lascaris to Paris. This was probably early in 1496. Charles died in 1498 in his twenty-eighth year.

After the death of Charles, Lascaris enjoyed the favor of Louis XII, and followed his Court in its swift migrations. He gained the friendship of many French scholars, and in particular helped Budé improve himself in Greek. In 1503 he was in Venice from June till near the end of the year as a special agent of the French king. He must have taken an interest in the first Aldine edition of the Anthology which was going through the press that summer, and appeared in November (below, p. 148). After a brief return to France he was made ambassador of Louis XII at Venice, a post which he held from 1504 to 1509, when the League of Cambrai put an end to his mission. In Venice he lived in constant intercourse with the scholars who flocked to that city, and was associated with the Academy of Aldus. He lent assistance to Erasmus, who published an augmented edition of his *Adagia* with Aldus in September, 1508. Perhaps Lascaris, whose aid Erasmus acknowledges, is in part responsible for the considerable use made of the Greek epigrams in the *Adagia*.[2]

For a time Lascaris appears to have served the French king in some official capacity at Milan. In 1513, on the elevation of Lorenzo's son to the papal throne as Leo X, he repaired to Rome, where Leo received him with open arms. Together they set about founding a college for young Greeks on the Quirinal. The Greek college lasted until about 1520, at which time we find Lascaris trying to get it established at Milan by Francis I. This attempt failed, and in 1522 he returned to Rome.

After the battle of Pavia Clement VII sent him to persuade Charles V to deal generously with King Francis; this was in Lascaris' eightieth year. A year later (1526) he was in Paris now trying to get the Greek College founded there; again he failed, and returned to Rome in 1529. At Rome he lived in honor with the scholarly world, but in some poverty as it seems, and conscious that Greek studies had declined in

---

[1] The number of copies printed in the first edition would be hard to estimate. There must still be scores in existence; most European libraries of any size contain one, and some of them more than one.

[2] Erasmus, *Opera Omnia* (ed. by Clericus, Leyden, 1703) 2.403 B-D.

Italy as they had vanished from Greece. He probably died in 1535.
He is buried in Sant' Agata.[1]

The death of Lascaris was mourned by the scholarly world in in-
numerable sepulchral epigrams. Few volumes of Latin poetry, printed
about the middle of the century in Italy or France, will be found to be
without verses in Greek or Latin addressed to Lascaris or in his
memory: 'Nulla est virtuti terra aliena suae,' says the epitaph written
for him by Colocci, for once almost with truth.[2] Nothing more clearly
demonstrates his importance as a sort of ambassador of learning on
both sides of the Alps.

Despite a life of frequent removals Lascaris kept a respectable library about him till near the time of his death. In 1527,
it seems, a Roman banker, Alano Cibo, who had lent money to
him, attached his books for the debt; but Cardinal Ridolfi had
also lent Lascaris money, and the Camera awarded the library
to him.[3] Immediately after Lascaris' death an inventory of his
MSS. was made by his secretary, Michael Davaris, one of the
young Greeks educated at the Greek College. In this list No. 88
is:[4] 'τὰ παλαιὰ ἐπιγράμματα' in the hand of Lascaris. As it happened, Davaris became librarian to Cardinal Ridolfi. When,
therefore, together with Nicholas Sophianus, he drew up a catalogue of that library, he marked the books that had belonged to
Lascaris. The library of Ridolfi eventually went to Catherine
de' Medici in France, and, thanks to Davaris, we can point to
Paris. 2891 in the National Library as the manuscript of the

---

[1] Of Lascaris' marriage there seems to be no record; a son Angelo was a man of some
note. On Lascaris' last visit to Paris, see a letter of Brixius to Erasmus (Aug. 11, 1526)
in Allen, *Eras. Epist.*, No. 1734.
[2] Among the *Encomia Illustrium Virorum* of John Leland (†1552) is an epigram on
Lascaris (*Collectanea*, London, 1771, 5.177). The 'epitaph' composed for Lascaris by
Antonio Tebaldeo—though suggested by the facts—may owe something to *A.P.* 7.311
(on Niobe according to *Plan.*, Lot's wife according to *Pal.*):
    Lascaris hic, Graium specimen; ne crede cadaver
    Illius esse sub hoc marmore sed statuam.
    Altera quippe fuit Niobe, dolor impius illam
    Natorum, hunc podagrae transtulit in lapidem.
              (*Carm. Illus. Poet. Ital.* 9.249)
[3] This is the sense of a document published by Léon Dorez (*Rev. des Bibl.* 2.280);
but the date of the act, Feb. 7, 1527, and references to Lascaris as no longer living, apparently defy explanation. The date 1535 for Lascaris' death is only traditional. That
he was alive, however, though ailing, in 1532, seems to be proved by a letter of Pierre
Bunel to Emilio Perotti, June 12, 1532. Bunel describes a visit recently paid by him to
the aged humanist in Rome (*Epistolae P. Bunelli*, etc., ed. by Grauff, Bern, 1837,
p. 33; Legrand, *op. cit.* 1.clvi).
[4] The inventory was published from *Vat. Graec.* 1414 by Nolhac in 1886 (above, p.
114, n. 1). At the same time Nolhac published an inventory in the hand of Lascaris
of an unknown Roman library, later than 1523. Among the books there listed are three
unbound copies of an Anthology—probably of the first edition (*Mélanges* 6.265).

Anthology made by Lascaris himself, doubtless when preparing the first printed edition.[1]

Not all Lascaris' library went to Ridolfi, who perhaps took only manuscripts. Davaris himself seems to have acquired a considerable portion of the printed books, and possibly through him several of them entered the collection of Fulvio Orsini.[2] Of these, three are copies of the 1494 Anthology, with manuscript notes in the editor's own hand.[3] All three are without his Greek epigram and his Epistle to Piero de' Medici. Lascaris apparently kept about him a number of copies of the first book he edited, and made notes in any one that came under his hand. Besides the three that Orsini owned, a fourth is reported as having belonged at the end of the eighteenth century to Christoph von Murr, also from Lascaris' library.[4]

Lascaris was himself an epigrammatist, of equal facility in Greek and in Latin.[5] Perhaps his success in neither was very considerable. One easily subscribes to the view of Ménage that Politian's version of the epigram on Hermaphroditus is really better than that of his rival, and to that of Daniel Heinsius, who, after searching long for a copy of Lascaris' epigrams, found them hardly capable of sustaining the fame of their author.[6]

Among his Greek epigrams are two on Homer which imply a knowledge of *A.P.* 9.24 and 16.297–8, one on Myron's *Heifer*, that already by Soter (1525) is placed with *A.P.* 9.738, and a fourth on the alabaster pipe-organ belonging to Isabella d'Este

[1] Omont, *Inventaire Sommaire*. It is a paper MS. of 234 ff. Some additional epigrams appear at the beginning and end of the Anthology, and after those at the end are the verses of Theognis (f. 206) and sententious lines from other poets.

[2] Nolhac, *Fulvio Orsini*, p. 157.

[3] Nolhac (*Fulvio Orsini*, p. 158) has identified these volumes as *Inc.* 813b, 813c, and 813d of the Vatican Library. The first, he says, is completely filled with notes and with additions to the epigrams of the 1494 edition. Sixteen interfoliations at the end are filled with Greek notes and additional epigrams. What are these additional epigrams, and what is their source? *Inc.* 813d is partly annotated in a second hand, seemingly that of one Francesco Giustiniani. Lascaris also possessed and annotated a copy of Chalcondyles' Suidas (Milan, 1499), which may have interested him because of the epigrams (now *Vat. inc.* 1025).

[4] Fr. Jacobs, *Anthol. Graec.* Prolog., p. xciii, from the testimony of Von Murr himself.

[5] His *Epigrammata* were first published by Ascensius, Paris, 1527 (Legrand 1.195); (2) Basel (Cratander), 1533; (3) with excerpts from Polybius, Basel (Oporinus), 1537; (4) Paris, 1542; (5) Paris (Jac. Bogardus), 1544. It is this last that I refer to by the abbreviation *Epig.* A Vatican MS. (*Cod. Graec.* 1352) contains a commentary on Lascaris' epigrams by a pupil of his at the Greek College, Christopher Contoleone (Nolhac, *op. cit.*, p. 161).

[6] Heinsius, *Poemata Graeca*, Leyden, 1640, p. 7. Ménage's judgment is quoted by Legrand.

at Mantua, which may have been written with an epigram by
the Emperor Julian (*A.P.* 9.365) in mind.[1] On Myron's *Heifer*
Lascaris wrote:

Σεῖο Μύρων δάμαλιν θηεύμενος ἔννεπε Μῶμος·
στεῦτ' ἀνάθημα Μύρων, θῦμα δ'ἔνεικε θεοῖς.
ἁπτόμενος δ', ἀνάθημ' ὁπότ' ᾔσθετο γ'αὖθις ἔειπε·
θῦμα μὲν οὐ, δακρύων δ'ἄμμι τάδε πρόφασις.

For Latin verses, too, as we have already observed, Lascaris
sometimes has recourse to translation from the Anthology. His
versions of three epigrams have already been given; in all, he
translates *A.P.* 9.784; 11.395; 16.14, 223, and 224.[2] Here follows
his version of 16.14:

Quis puerum Veneris statuit prope fluminis haustus?
Providus, hanc flammam scilicet unda premit.

BARTOLOMMEO COMPARINI
(*fl.* 1484)

Bartolommeo Comparini of Prato was living in Florence
about 1484. He is known only as a copyist of Greek MSS.; and
three of the MSS. he is known to have copied are selections
from the Anthology—*Vat. Ottob.* 388; *Laur.* 57, 29; and *Paris.*
1773.[3]

FRANCESCO DEL TUPPO
(1445–?)

Del Tuppo, a native of Naples, and a doctor of laws of its
University, held an office of some importance in the government of Ferdinand I. In 1471, when Sixtus Reissinger brought a
printing-press to Naples, Del Tuppo joined him. For the most
part, both before and after Reissinger left Naples (1479), the
productions of the press were legal commentaries and the like,

---

[1] References to all these epigrams are given in the Register. Calcagnini (Pigna,
Carm., p. 217) has an epigram on the same alabaster organ. This instrument was presented to Isabella by Castiglione in 1522. Cf. Julia Cartwright (Mrs. Ady), *Isabella
d'Este*, London, 1903, 2.207.
[2] The last two are not in Lascaris' *Epig.*, but were published by Müller in *Centralblatt* (as above, p. 114, n. 1).
[3] See above, p. 32. Vogel-Gardthausen, *Griech. Schreiber*, p. 50, refer to Cianfogni,
Memorie Istoriche dell' Ambrosiana R. Basilica di S. Lorenzo, Florence, 1804, p. 280. He
also copied a part of *Cod.* 1235 in the Bibliothèque Mazarine (Omont, *Invent. Som. des
Manuscrits grecs conservés dans les Bibl. Pub. de Paris autres que la B. Nat.*, Paris, 1883,
p. 5.

so that Del Tuppo's Italian Fables of Aesop, *Fabulae Aesopicae*, 1485, is now the only book he printed that is much sought after by collectors.[1] The work consists of sixty-six fables in Italian, each followed by an illustrative anecdote from recent Italian events, or from literature or mythology; accompanying these there are eighty-seven wood-engravings; and the whole is preceded by the Life of Aesop in Latin and Italian after Planudes.

At the end of the *Confirmatio Exemplaris* of Fable 34—*De Musco et Calvo*—Del Tuppo adds the following epigram translated into Latin from *A.P.* 9.86. It will be noticed that he involves the theme in circumstances unknown to the original:[2]

> Ostrea servabat clausa piscator in archa
> Quae madidus paulo traxerat ante mari.
> Mus subit, ostrumque [*sic*] videns is pandere callum
> Mordet ad unde petit, fit cibus ille, cibum.
> Nanque caput strictis abscisum faucibus intus
> Mansit, et exterius caetera muris erant.
> Cumque comesturus piscator poneret igni,
> Ostrea clausa patent, miraque praeda caput.
> Contigit hoc alios cuicumque offendere mens est
> Saepius offensa deperit ille sua.

ANTONIO CODRO URCEO
(1446–1500)

Antonio Urceo was one of the striking personalities among the scholars of the fifteenth century. He knew every one; we shall find Politian seeking his opinion on Greek epigrams (below, p. 135); he was a friend of Giovan Battista Pio (below, p. 144); Copernicus studied Greek under him.[3] Urceo was born at Rubiera, and was educated at Ferrara under Battista Guarini and Luca Riva. About 1469 the tyrant Pino Ordelaffi took him to Forlì as tutor to his natural son Sinibaldo. After Pino's death arose a war for the succession; and Sinibaldo dying in the midst of it, Urceo withdrew to Bologna (1480), where he professed grammar, rhetoric, and poetry until his death.

In Urceo's Latin poetry—*Sylvarum libri duo et Epigrammata* —there is no trace of the Anthology; but he occasionally quotes

---

[1] Del Tuppo's *Fabulae* were reprinted at Aquila in 1493, and at Venice in 1492, 1495, and 1553. I have seen only the edition of 1493.

[2] I give a literal translation of *A.P.* 9.86: 'An omnivorous mouse, dainty in eating, creeping through the house, spied an oyster with its lips open and nipped the seeming flesh of its moist beard. At once the house of shell clapped together and was closed tight because of the pain; and the mouse, caught in a prison it could not escape from, got for itself a death-dealing tomb.'

[3] There is a good study of Urceo by Carlo Malagola, *Della Vita e delle Opere di Antonio Urceo detto Codro*, Bologna, 1878.

from it in his prose works.[1] Thus in *Sermo xi*, a discourse on Hesiod, he quotes and translates *A.P.* 7.54:

Hesiodum tuli Ascra ferax, sed lumine cassi
Plexippi tellus ossa sepulta tenet,
Plurima quem totum decantat fama per orbem,
Spectatosque super tollit in astra viros.

In most instances he gives no translation, once he gives a paraphrase in prose, once he uses a translation by the elder Guarino, and on another occasion a translation by Gaza, so that the version of *A.P.* 7.54 given above seems to be Urceo's only attempt at verse-translation from the Greek epigrams.[2]

GIAMBATTISTA CANTALICIO (CANTALYCIUS)

(†1514)

Cantalicio, who in 1503 became Bishop of Altri and Penna, published his epigrams at Venice in 1495: *Epigrammata Cantalycii et aliquorum Discipulorum eius*. In the twelve books of these epigrams, to which are added two books of *disticha*, no trace of the Anthology appears, unless, as seems probable, the following is a conscious reversal of the theme of *A.P.* 9.455:[3]

DE MATARATIO
Quidquid grandiloquo loquitur Mataratius ore,
Excipit et tabulis mandat Apollo suis.

A MS. at Rome (*Casenat.* 1209) contains *A.P.* 9.39, with a Latin translation by Cantalicio.[4]

---

[1] My references are to *Opera*, Basel, 1540.

[2] In all, he employs *A.P.* 7.3 (*Op.* p. 177 without trans.), 53 (p. 207, prose-trans.), 54 (p. 207 verse, as above); 9.448(p. 177, without trans.); 11.442 (p. 177, without trans.); 16. 296 (p. 176, trans. by Guarino), 297 (p. 176, trans. by 'Gellius,' i.e., Gaza). Of *A.P.* 7.53 Urceo says: 'Huius epigrammatis mentio ab Varrone libro de Imaginibus facta est a Gellio repetita. Verum in nullo codice Gelliano epigramma ipsum legitur. Ego autem e Graecorum antiquissimis penetralibus litteris Thessalicis scriptum reperi, et repertum Latinis litteris et studiosis viris edidi ac divulgavi.' He translates: 'Hesiodus Musis Heliconiadibus hunc tripodem dedicavit, hymno cum vicisset in Chalcide divinum Homerum.' See above, p. 93.

In the Catalogue of the library of Fulvio Orsini, as given by Nolhac, appears the following item: 'Epigrammatario con scholij de Ant. Codro Urceo, ligato alla greca in corame berettino, in-8°, d'Aldo.' This copy of the 1503 Aldine Anthology is identified by Nolhac as Vat. A. 18 in-8°. Obviously, as Urceo died in 1500, he could not have owned this book. According to Nolhac it is filled with marginal notes in Greek (*Ful. Ors.*, p. 175).

[3] In the Greek, Apollo is made to say: 'I it was who made the song, but divine Homer wrote it down.' On Matarazzo see Tiraboschi, *Stor.* 6.3.5.60 n.

[4] Bancalari in *Stud. Ital. Filol. Class.* 2.186.

ANGELO AMBROGINI POLIZIANO
(1454–1494)

Born at Montepulciano, Politian was sent at the age of ten to Florence, where the rest of his life was mainly passed. Here he studied under the most famous teachers of the time—Ficino, Argyropulos, Andronicus Callistos, Landino, and Chalcondyles.[1] He became professor of Greek and Latin literature in the *Studio* (1480), and as tutor to the children of Lorenzo lived in close intimacy with the Medici. His life was filled with his duties as teacher, with the usual humanist controversies, with philological investigations, and with the production of admirable verses in Latin, Greek, and Italian.

Politian died on September 24, 1494, hardly more than a month after the publication, at Florence, of the first printed edition of the Anthology. Doubtless before he died he held in his hands a copy of the printed book; but any influence the Greek epigrams had upon his writings must have come out of manuscripts. As it happens, there exists in the Vatican Library a brief manuscript (*Cod. Graec.* 1373) of Greek epigrams, copied out by Politian for his own use perhaps as early as 1472, and revised by him at a later date.[2]

Joannes Argyropulos read Aristotle in the Florentine *Studio* from 1456 to 1471, and was succeeded by Chalcondyles. Chalcondyles had recently been at work on a MS. of the Anthology, and from him Politian may well have first learned to imitate the Greek epigrams. Politian's earliest Greek epigram is dated 1471. Yet in 1473 he wrote three Greek epigrams in honor of Argyropulos. His own MS. of a part of the Anthology, if it goes back to 1472, should, however, probably be connected with Chalcondyles.[3] At all events his interest in the Anthology began early.

---

[1] In a letter to Lorenzo de' Medici (*Epistole Inedite*, ed. by D'Amore, Naples, 1909, p. 13) Politian names Agryropulos, Callistos, and Chalcondyles as his chief masters in Greek.

[2] The MS. came to the Vatican from the library of Fulvio Orsini (Nolhac, *Fulvio Orsini*, p. 208). It has been studied by G. Pesenti in *Boll. di Filol. Class.* 26 (1920). 140, who finds the variant readings introduced into the MS on its revision to be identical with readings of Lascaris' *ed. pr.* As he says, Politian may either have seen the MS. from which the edition was made, or he may have used the printed text. Nolhac, Pesenti says, was wrong in believing that *Vat.* 1373 contains epigrams of Politian's own composition. At Florence, *Laur.* 66,31 may have been written by Politian; it contains *A.P.* 7.153 (Rostagno, in *Stud. Ital. Filol. Class.* 6.157).

[3] Carteromaco, a pupil of Politian, seems to connect the latter's writing of Greek epigrams with Argyropulos, for he has in mind the composition of epigrams when he says, in a lecture noticed below, p. 152; 'Nostra quoque tempestate non defuere qui Graece scriberent, ut praeceptor noster Politianus, quem et Joanni quoque Argyropulo, Graeco homini, saepe admirationi fuisse vidimus.' Argyropulos, however, was mainly Politian's instructor in Greek philosophy.

When, however, we examine Politian's Greek verses, arranged
by him in chronological order, we discover that those in which
he has imitated the substance of particular epigrams in the Anthology all appear to belong to the last three years of his life;
and we may guess that the presence of Janus Lascaris in Florence, his lectures on the Anthology, and his preparations to edit
it, had some part in renewing Politian's interest, or rather gave
it a new turn, for Politian's *Miscellanea* and parts of his Latin
poems suggest a lifelong interest in the Anthology.

Politian's fame as a scholar in the strict sense now largely
rests on his *Miscellanea*, a set of papers on various subjects in
ancient literature. In this short but significant book, first published at Florence in 1489, epigrams from the Anthology several
times come under discussion.[1] For example, Chapter 22 deals
with the device called the 'Echo.' The form is described, and
mention is made of Politian's own vernacular 'echo':[2] 'I have
myself composed similar verses in Italian, which, recommended
by the music of Enrico,[3] are now popular with the musicians.
Some ten years ago I sent them to Piero Contareno, a noble and
cultivated Venetian, who was marvelously bent on getting
them, and likewise to several other admirers of literature. But
there exist also some in Greek by an ancient poet named
Gauradas, which I subjoin.' Here he quotes *A.P.* 16.152. The
vernacular poem referred to is Politian's *Pan e Eco:*

> Che fai tu, Eco, mentr' io ti chiamo?—Amo.
> Ami tu dua o pur un solo?—Un solo.
> Et io te sola e non altri amo—Altri amo.
> Dunque non ami tu un solo?—Un solo.
> Questo è un dirmi: Io non t'amo—Io non t'amo.
> Quel che tu ami amil tu solo?—Solo.
> Chi t'ha levata dal mio amore?—Amore.
> Che fa quello a chi porti amore?—Ah more!

In Chapter 26 is discussed the relation of Ovid, *Fasti* 1.357,
to the epigram of Evenus (*A.P.* 9.75) from which that passage

---

Something might be learned by comparing the original text of *Vat. Graec.* 1373 with
that of *Laur. Graec.* 31, 28 (Chalcondyles' MS.).

[1] My references are to Politian's *Opera*, Lyons (Gryphe), 1550; the *Miscellaneorum
centuria prima* occupies pp. 457–648.

[2] *Le Stanze*, etc., ed. by Carducci, Bologna, 1912, p. 563.

[3] This musician may possibly be identified with the Enricho sacristano mentioned
by Eitner (*Quellen-Lexikon* 3.341) as in the lists of singers at the ducal chapel in Milan,
March 30 and December 4, 1475.

comes. Politian allows the Greek a certain charm, lost in the Latin version, but in general, true to his usual prejudice, asserts that what Latin lacks is less the copiousness of Greek than the wantonness. He gives the anecdote from Suetonius concerning *A.P.* 9.75.[1] Chapter 49 is entitled *Contentio Epigrammatum Graeci Posidippi et Latini Ausonii super Occasionis Imagine* (*A.P.* 16.275 and Ausonius 19.33). He points out in detail the differences between the two descriptions of Occasion, and remarks on the superior qualities of the Greek poem, the Latin in this case being but a copy. He is concerned with showing that Lysippus and not Phidias (as in Ausonius) was the sculptor.

Before turning to Politian's Latin and Greek poems, we must pause to connect the Anthology with one or two events in his life in which it somewhat accidentally figures. Controversy was then an expected phase of the scholarly life; but Politian's quarrels were not merely the altercations of a scholar, nor do they all shed glory on his character. We are obliged first to notice his dispute with Merula, then his rivalry with Marullus, and finally his quarrel with Bartolommeo Scala.

Though fairly important among Politian's disputes, that with Merula (1494) need not detain us.[2] Incidental mention of the Greek epigrams enters into a letter written by Politian to Merula, when he suggests that Merula would not have made certain statements but for ignorance of the epigrams in question: 'Nam de Rinthone,' he says in one place, 'bis peccas, et quod rusticos authores hic quoque contaminas, et quod vilissimum fuisse nugatorem falso credis, cuius etiam graeco epigrammate poemata celebrantur.'[3] The epigram referred to is *A.P.* 7.414, by Nossis. Again in the same letter: 'Glaphyram vero, qui tamen est apud te Glaphyrus, nunquam profecto comoedum citharoedumve credidisses, si graeca teneres Antipatri epigrammata et Philippi' (*A.P.* 9.517 and 266). As Merula's original remarks seem not to be available, the point of this remains somewhat obscure. The form 'Glaphyrus' is now known to be correct.[4]

---

[1] Above, p. 19.

[2] It arose from the publication of Politian's *Miscellanea*, some of the notions of which book Merula censured, while others he claimed as his own.

[3] *Illustrium Virorum Epistolae ab Angelo Politiano partim scriptae partim collectae*, Paris, 1523, 11.10. The *Epistolae* first appeared at Paris, without date, but probably in 1500.

[4] Merula, an editor of Martial, doubtless had that writer in mind (*Epig.* 4.5).

Alessandra Scala was the eldest daughter of Bartolommeo Scala, Secretary of the Florentine Republic; she was probably born in 1475. She was well-versed in Greek, her teachers being Lascaris and Chalcondyles. About 1492, as it seems, Politian and the Greek Michael Marullus found themselves in the position of rivals for the hand of Alessandra.[1] Whether Marullus addressed Greek epigrams to her is doubtful; she appears to be the Neaera of his Latin poems. Politian, however, has six Greek epigrams in her praise. As these show a modern writer bringing his composition of Greek epigrams out of the study to play a part in daily life, we may look at one of them:[2]

> Εὕρηχ' εὕρηχ' ἦν θέλον, ἦν ἐξήτεον αἰεί,
> ἦν ἤτουν τὸν Ἔρωθ', ἦν καὶ ὀνειροπόλουν·
> παρθενικήν, ἦς κάλλος ἀκήρατον, ἦς ὅγε κόσμος
> οὐκ εἴη τέχνης ἀλλ' ἀφελοῦς φύσεως·
> παρθενικήν, γλώττησιν ἐπ' ἀμφοτέρῃσι κομῶσαν,
> ἔξοχον ἔν τε χοροῖς, ἔξοχον ἔν τε λύρῃ.
> ἦς περὶ σωφροσύνης τ' εἴη Χαρίτεσσι θ' ἀμίλλα,
> τῇ καὶ τῇ ταύτην ἀντιμεθελκομέναις·
> εὕρηχ'—οὐδ' ὄφελος· καὶ γὰρ μόλις εἰς ἐνιαυτόν
> οἰστροῦντι φλογερῶς ἔστιν ἅπαξ ἰδέειν.

This was written in 1493. The writer was nearly forty, Alessandra probably eighteen. Marullus was about forty-three. The poetess's reply, in the same learned language, easily surpasses her admirer's effusion in recondite allusion. Was Alessandra, then, a student of the Anthology too, and an imitator of its

The Planudean mss. have the form Γλαφύρῳ in *A.P.* 9.266 and Γλαφύρα in 517, but Lascaris' edition has the form from Γλαφύρας in both places. Here perhaps is evidence that Politian did use the ms. from which that edition was made.

[1] The best account of Alessandra Scala is that of Pesenti in *Giorn. Stor.* 85 (1925). 241–67. The assumption of a rivalry between Politian and Marullus rests on the conjectures of Brouckhusius and Menckenius (*Historia Vitae . . . Angeli Politiani*, by F. O. Menckenius, Leipzig, 1736, p. 381). It depends on the identification of Marullus with the Mabilius of Politian's Latin epigrams, and of Politian with the Ecnomus of Marullus', and on the tone of Politian's Greek epigrams addressed to Alessandra. The Latin poems of Landino, six mss. of which exist in the Laurentian Library (*Laur.* 33, 23ff), are entitled *Xandra*, and have often been said to be addressed to Alessandra Scala, but Pesenti denies it. A selection from them is printed in the *Carm. Illust. Poet. Ital.*, vol. 5.

[2] Politian, *Prose Volgari Inedite e Poesie Latine e Greche Edite e Inedite . . .* raccolta e illustrata da Isidoro del Lungo, Florence, 1867, p. 200. Hereafter I shall refer to this book as 'Del Lungo.' A translation of the epigram follows: 'I have found! I have found the one I wanted, the one I ever looked for, the one I sought from Love, the one I dreamed of—a maiden whose immortal beauty could not be the effect of art but only of simple nature, a maiden versed in both Greek and Latin, distinguished for her dancing and for playing the lyre. Concerning her modesty the Graces might strive with each other, drawing her now this way now that. I have found her—but it avails me not, since scarcely once a year for all my fiery passion am I permitted to behold her.'

forms? Possibly, but I think her teacher Lascaris wrote this poem for her, though we need not deny her its sentiments.[1]

Οὐδὲν ἄρ' ἦν αἴνοιο παρ' ἐμφρονὸς ἀνδρὸς ἄμεινον,
κἀκ σέθεν αἶνος ἐμοὶ γ'οἷον ἄειρε κλέος.
πολλοὶ θριοβόλοι, παῦροι δέ τε μάντιές εἰσιν.
εὗρες; ἄρ' οὐχ εὗρες, οὐδ' ὄναρ ἠντίασας.
φῆ γὰρ ὁ θεῖος ἀοιδός· Ἄγει θεὸς ἐς τὸν ὁμοῖον.
οὐδὲν Ἀλεξάνδρη σοῦ δ' ἀνομοιότερον.
ὡς σύ γ' ὁποῖα Δανούβιος, ἐκ ζόφου μέσον ἦμαρ
καῦθις ἐπ' ἀντολίην, αἰπὰ ῥέεθρα χέεις.
φωναῖς δ'ἐν πλείσταις σόν τοι κλέος ἠέρ' ἐλαστρεῖ,
Ἑλλάδι, Ῥωμαϊκῇ, Ἑβραϊκῇ, Λυδίη.
ἄστρα, φύσις, δ'ἀριθμοί, ποιήματα, κύρβις, ἰατροί
Ἀλκείδην καλέει σ'ἀντιμεθελκόμενα.
τἀμὰ δὲ παρθενικῆς σπουδάσματα, παίγνια φασί,
Βόκχορις ἐξείποι, ἄνθεα καὶ δρόσος ὥς.
τοὶ γὰρ μὴδ' ἐλέφαντος ἐναντία βόμβον ἀείρω·
αἴλουρον Παλλὰς καὶ σύ γ' ὑπερφρονέεις.

Alessandra's third line is modeled on the proverb known to us in *A.P.* 10.106:

Πολλοί τοι ναρθηκοφόροι, παῦροι δέ τε βάκχοι.

The proverb in the last line but one was presently to come to Politian's mind with respect to Alessandra's father.

Alessandra married Marullus. Politian's dislike of his successful rival now burst forth, again into epigrams; and he was answered in kind by Marullus and by Marullus' Neapolitan friends, Sannazaro in particular.[2] These epigrams, however, were written in the language of Martial, not that of Meleager.

About the same time Politian had further reason for bitter-

---

[1] The epigram follows that of Politian in Del Lungo's edition. It is far too learned not to excite suspicion, and it resembles Lascaris'style of expression; in addition we have a very telling circumstance in the presence of a copy of it in Lascaris' manuscript note-book of just this time—*Vat. Graec.* 1412 (above, p. 115). A similar suspicion of Lascaris' hand in Alessandra's epigram had occurred, I find, to Pesenti (*Giorn. Stor.* 85.259).

The sense of the epigram is: 'Surely nought is better than praise from a prudent man; and what glory has your praise evoked for me! Many are the soothsayers, but the true seers are few. You have found? No, you have not found, nor have you even dreamed. For the divine bard has said: "God bringeth like to like." And there is nothing less like to Alessandra than you. Like the Danube, from west to south and again to the eastward, your deep current rolls, and in many tongues your fame dispels the mists—in Greek, Latin, Hebrew, and Tuscan. The heavenly bodies, nature, numbers, poems, laws, and physicians, give you the name of Hercules, pulling you this way and that. But mine are the studies of a girl, bagatelles they call them—King Boccharis would say, like flowers and dew. No, I shall not raise up a gnat against an elephant; and you and Athena alike despise a cat.' [The last phrase refers to the proverb, Ἀθηνᾷ τὸν αἴλουρον, meaning 'a bad companion.']

[2] Sannazaro, *Epigram.* 1.61–2.

ness against the family of Alessandra, and again it is a question of Greek epigrams. He quarreled with her father.

Bartolommeo Scala was sprung from an obscure family of Colle di Val d'Elsa in Tuscany, where he was born in 1430. Coming to Florence to study law, he attracted attention by his merits, gained the good will of the Medici, and by their favor became Secretary to the Republic. After acting as ambassador to Innocent VIII on his elevation to the Holy See, Scala was made Gonfaloniere. His literary works include *Historiae Florentinorum libri v* (printed, together with his Life of Vitalianus Borrhomaeus, in Graevius' *Thesaurus Antiquitatum et Historiarum Italiae*, vol. 8, pt. 1); a dialogue *De Consolatione*, and a number of poems. The dialogue, which has never been printed, exists in a MS. at Florence (*Laur. Lat.* 54, 10) which also contains *Collectiones Cosmiae*, a number of poetical praises of Cosimo de' Medici from various hands, put together by Scala and presented to Lorenzo. Four of Scala's shorter poems are in the *Carm. Illust. Poet. Ital.* 8.489–91; a number of letters by him are in Politian's collection. He died in 1497.

Among Scala's small pieces was an epigram on a gnat. This he sent to Politian, who discovered that the writer had had taken the word *culex* to be feminine, whereupon he, perhaps needlessly, composed an epigram of his own on Scala's epigram, and sent it to him. Scala came back with another epigram, after which Politian addressed to him the following letter:[1]

Egi tecum liberius (ita enim soleo) qui quoniam tu culicem muliebri genere, quod contra virili decuit, usurpaveras in epigrammate, luserim sic ex tempore culicis verbis:

> Non sum foemina, Scala, nec Latinis
> Nec Graecis: ideo placet puella.

Quos tu meos versiculos aliis eiusdem generis remuneratus es bellis mehercules et facetis, sed in syllaba tamen una et altera neglegentibus, ut in quibus hoc sit: *Congressum petis sic meae puellae;* rursusque: *Sed tu ni caveris, scio iacebis.* Possis enim in priore (sicuti veteres illi solebant, cum fluerent adhuc lutulentiores) elidere s litteram; quod hendecasyllabis tamen puto non licet, sicuti nec hexametris iam liquidioribus, nisi tu grammaticis credis parum docte putantibus ita legendum est apud Maronem: *Inter se coiisse viros et decernere ferro.* Sed et illa videntur ἄκυρα: *Citare somnum, Bonam cutem ferire,* sicuti ὑποσόλοικον, *Pasce meas carnes,* pro illo, *Vescere meis potius carnibus.* Caeterum quoniam tu versiculos ais istos ad imitationem te fecisse Graeci cuiusdam Epigrammatis, libuit etiam mihi nunc epigrammate Graeco tueri causam culicum. [Politian subjoins his own epigram in Greek in defence of the gnats.]

[1] *Epist.* 12.9.

Scala's poem is not extant, or at least never has been printed; but we can tell a good deal about it from Politian's letter: it was in hendecasyllables, its subject was The Gnat and the Girl, it was modeled on a Greek epigram, and it contained the following expressions (which are here arranged in at least a reasonable succession):

[stridaculum, clangacem][1]
Congressum petis sic meae puellae.
. . . . citare somnum
. . . . . bonam cutem ferire.
Carnes pasce meas [?] . . . .
Sed tu ni caveris, scio iacebis. . . .

O gnat [that utterest] a shrill-voiced, noisy sound, that dost thus seek to visit my girl . . . to disturb her sleep[2] . . . to smite her excellent skin[3] . . . feed rather on my flesh. . . . But if thou dost not take heed, thou wilt be laid low, I ween. . . .

These fragments are enough to show that Scala was imitating the following epigram by Meleager:[4]

Ὀξυβόαι κώνωπες, ἀναιδέες, αἵματος ἀνδρῶν
σίφωνες, νυκτὸς κνώδαλα διπτέρυγα,
βαιὸν Ζηνοφίλαν, λίτομαι, πάρεθ' ἥσυχον ὕπνον
εὕδειν τὰμὰ δ' ἰδοὺ σαρκοφαγεῖτε μέλη.
καίτοι πρὸς τί μάτην αὐδῶ; καὶ θῆρες ἀτεγκτοι
τέρπονται τρυφερῷ χρωτὶ χλιαινόμενοι.
ἀλλ' ἔτι νῦν προλέγω, κακὰ θρέμματα, λήγετε τόλμης,
ἢ γνώσεσθε χερῶν ζηλυτύπων δύναμιν.

Scala had said his original was a Greek epigram, and another reference makes it virtually certain that this was the epigram he copied. In supporting a criticism directed at Politian in a later letter, he quotes a phrase from this very epigram: 'At Graecus excellentissimus poeta telluris animal appellat, γαίης κνώδαλα διπτέρυγα.'[5] Finally, as Scala probably showed in a letter not in our collection, his feminine *culex* could find her sisters

---

[1] These two words are from *Epist.* 12.12.
[2] Scala consents (*Epist.* 12.11) to change *citare* to *fugare*.
[3] Politian (*Epist.* 12.12) would prefer *nitidam, teneram,* or *bene curatam* to *bonam*.
[4] *A.P.* 5.151. 'O shrill-voiced gnats, without shame, who suck the blood of men, Night's winged beasts of prey, I entreat you, let Zenophila sleep peacefully a while, and, look you, devour these my limbs. Yet why in vain do I speak? Even hard-hearted wild beasts enjoy warming themselves with her tender skin. But even now I forewarn you, evil creatures, cease your boldness, or you will know the power of jealous hands.'
[5] *Epist.* 12.16. I can find nothing like this phrase in any other author than Meleager as above; but γαίης seems not to be a variant of νυκτός in any known MS. Scala's not naming his author is perhaps suspicious. Is it possible that, observing Politian's failure to recognize the original of his poem, he ventured to quote a little freely from it?

in the first line of Meleager's epigram. Oddly enough, Politian, who knew the Anthology so well, seems never to recognize Scala's original. Yet possibly he refuses to mention it, because the gender of κώνωπες is against him.

To Politian's first letter Scala returned a polite note of thanks. Then in a longer epistle he defends himself, and criticizes Politian's Greek epigram:[1] 'The Greek epigram you have sent me I can hardly, in such poverty of Greek, get the verbal sense of, to say nothing of perceiving any beauty of verse, but I suppose it is yours.'[2] This maddening ambiguity Politian gravely turns against the writer:[3] 'I come now to my epigram, the beauty of which—such is your modesty—you say you cannot perceive for want of the Greek language; nevertheless you say you believe it is my composition; in what sense I am to take that remark I do not see.' And after some further defence of his poem: 'But enough of this . . . lest our gnat turn into an elephant.'[4] This is moderation itself. Scala's next letter strikes a different note; it begins:[5] 'I can scarcely believe that this last letter which you have sent me on the Gnat is yours; it is too slight, too cantankerous, suspicious, and vain.' Politian takes the same level in his reply:[6] 'If you would know what I think about your epigram—it is exceedingly like your other things, and, to use the common expression, entirely cast in the same mold (eiusdem farinae).'

We need not follow in detail a quarrel that grew ever more bitter. Obviously there was more behind it than a dispute about Latin quantities; one thing that rankled with Scala was his knowledge that Lorenzo had turned some of his official letters over to Politian for correction before sending them out.[7] Once Scala attempted a reconciliation, evoking the memory of their common friend Lorenzo, now only a year in his tomb; but

[1] *Epist.* 12.11.

[2] 'Graecum epigramma, quod ad me misisti, tanta inopia linguae est Graecae, vix verbis interpretor, nedum elegantiam perspicere possim carminis, sed puto tuum est.' By way of postscript he adds a page of criticism. These strictures, I am convinced, were lent to Scala by Lascaris, who probably also drew the attention of Scala to *A.P.* 5.151 in the first place.

[3] *Epist.* 12.12. 'Venio nunc ad epigramma, cuius elegantiam perspicere te negas (ut homo es modestus) ob inopiam Graecae linguae; sed putare tamen ais esse meum, quod in utram partem mihi sit accipiendum, non video.'

[4] Cf. the proverb quoted by Alessandra Scala above.

[5] *Epist.* 12.13.

[6] *Epist.* 12.14.

[7] So at least Politian says, *Epist.* 12.18.

matters had gone too far, and at last Politian refused to answer any more letters.

On all this the scenes were soon to close, and on the brilliance of Florentine humanism. In another year Politian was dead, and Florence dominated by Charles VIII; Scala died in 1497; in 1500 occurred the tragic death of Marullus; while Alessandra, who had acted with applause in the plays of Sophocles, and had sought to be the Sappho of her age, spent her last years, and in 1506 died, in the convent of San Pier Maggiore. Meanwhile scholars throughout the world were still mourning her husband and his rival—some in Latin epigrams, and some in Greek.

We may now turn to Politian's Latin poems. Many of these cannot be dated except approximately.[1] Certain of them were the work of his youth, as, for example, his translation of the *Amor Fugitivus* of Moschus, which he says he made *paene puer;* but his youthful poems were preferably in Italian, as the *Orfeo* and the *Stanze*. His chief Latin poems belong to the decade before his death. The epigrams were presumably done at various times, but we suspect that most of those taken from the Anthology belong to his last years, as do his Greek epigrams presently to be discussed.

Yet, from the time of Politian's early studies, the Anthology had been one of the books which thoroughly laid hold of his mind. The following couplet on the poetess Cecca da Siena, written about 1479, is evidently taken from *A.P.* 9.66:[2]

> Mnemosyne audito Senensis carmine Cicchae:
> Quando, inquit, decima est nata puella mihi?

A number of passages in Politian's *Sylvae* are probably to be referred to the Anthology. For example, in his *Manto*, or introductory poem to Virgil's *Bucolica*, he makes use of the well-worn epigrams on Homer's birthplace (*Manto* 199: *A.P.* 16.297–8). In the *Nutricia*, on poetry and poets, written in 1486, and the finest of his Latin poems, some eleven passages

---

[1] My references are to Del Lungo. The *Sylvae* appeared at Florence as they were composed: *Manto* (1482), *Rusticus* (1483), *Ambra* (1485), *Nutricia* (1491). Virtually everything else was printed only after the author's death, in the *Opera Omnia* published by Aldus in 1498. See Del Lungo, pp. xxii–xxxv.

[2]
> Μναμοσύναν ἕλε θάμβρος, ὅτ' ἔκλυε τᾶς μελιφώνου
> Σαπφοῦς, μὴ δεκάταν Μοῦσαν ἔχουσι βροτοί.

Dread seized Mnemosyne, when she heard sweet-voiced Sappho, lest men had now a tenth Muse.

very likely come from the Anthology, though, it must be allowed, several of these may rest upon other originals.[1] His account of the female poets, however, is not only certainly, but somewhat remarkably, drawn from *A.P.* 9.26:

> Non illi [Sappho] Praxilla suos praedoctaque Nossis
> Contulerint Myrtisque modos, non dulcis Agacles,
> Non Anyte, non quae versus Erinna trecentos
> Castalio ceu melle rigat, non candida Myro,
> Nec Thelesilla ferox, non quae canit aegida saevae
> Pallados effusum crinem vittata Corinna.

The original is by Antipater of Thessalonica:

> Τάσδε θεογλώσσους Ἑλικὼν ἔθρεψε γυναῖκας
>   ὕμνοις, καὶ Μακεδὼν Πιερίας σκόπελος,
> Πρήξιλλαν, Μοιρώ, Ἀνύτης στόμα, θῆλυν Ὅμηρον,
>   Λεσβιάδων Σαπφὼ κόσμον ἐϋπλοκάμων,
> Ἤρινναν, Τελέσιλλαν ἀγακλέα, καὶ σέ, Κόριννα,
>   θοῦριν Ἀθηναίης ἀσπίδα μελψαμέναν,
> Νοσσίδα θηλύγλωσσον, ἰδὲ γλυκυαχέα Μύρτιν,
>   πάσας ἀενάων ἐργάτιδας σελίδων.
> ἐννέα μὲν Μούσας μέγας Οὐρανός, ἐννέα δ᾽αὐτὰς
>   Γαῖα τέκεν, θνατοῖς ἄφθιτον εὐφροσύναν.

Antipater, be it observed, makes a great point of there being nine poetesses as there are nine Muses. But Politian has ten! And the intruder, Agacles, has a masculine name. His ghostly existence plainly is owing to the epithet given to Telesilla—ἀγακλέα, 'renowned'— in the fifth line of the Greek.[2]

When we come to Politian's direct translations from the Anthology, we find little to excite enthusiasm. His versions are correct and faithful to their originals. Yet they are not remarkably superior to similar exercises by Politian's contemporaries; and, if the suspected translations that go under the name of Ausonius should prove to be Renaissance work, Politian will several times have to yield the palm to them, and thus possibly to Merula.[3]

---

[1] *Nut.* 339: *A.P.* 9.24; *Nut.* 345: *A.P.* 9.455; *Nut.* 382f.: *A.P.* 9.64 (and Hesiod, *Theog.* 22f.); Nut. 388: *A.P.* 7.53 (and *Cont. of Hom. and Hes.* 322); *Nut.* 395: *A.P.* 7.54.2 (and *Cont.* 325); *Nut.* 558f.: *A.P.* 16.305 or 7.34; *Nut.* 585f.: *A.P.* 16.307, 309, and 7.31; *Nut.* 615f.: *A.P.* 7.714, 745; *Nut.* 618: *A.P.* 9.571; *Nut.* 633: *A.P.* 9.26, and cf. 9.190 for Erinna; *Nut.* 637f.: *A.P.* 9.506; 7.14; 9.66.

[2] Politian's strange error was pointed out at the end of the next century by Sanchez in his Notes on the *Nutricia* (in his *Opera*, Geneva, 1766, 2.485). L. G. Giraldi meantime had included *Agacles* in his history of the ancient poets (below, p. 183). Politian himself, in his letter to Cassandra Fedele (*Epist.* 3.17), about 1490, mentions most of these poetesses, but drops Agacles.

[3] Politian translates *A.P.* 6.331; 7.217, 311, 489; 9.124, 130, 146, 346, 391, 440

Though yielding to none in his knowledge of Greek, Politian often chose to assume the rôle of an ancient Roman, and to express something like contempt for the *Graeculi* not only of his own day. In the economy of his version of *A.P.* 9.346 there is a tacit rebuke to Leonidas of Alexandria who composed the original. Yet the parsimony of Politian's version may still not please some so well as the grace of the version of this same epigram by his rival Marullus (above, p. 113).

LEONIDAS

Αἶαν ὅλην νήσους τε διϊπταμένη σύ, χελιδών,
    Μηδείης γραπτῇ πυκτίδι νοσσοτροφεῖς·
ἕλπῃ δ' ὀρταλίχων πίστιν σέο τήνδε φυλάξειν
    Κολχίδα μηδ' ἰδίων φεισαμένην τεκέων ;

POLITIAN

Medeae statua est, misella hirundo,
Sub qua nidificas. Tuosne credas
Huic natos, rogo, quae suos necavit?

The next is Politian's version of *A.P.* 7.311 (on Niobe, in *Plan.*):

Hoc est sepulchrum intus cadaver non habens,
Hoc est cadaver et sepulchrum non habens,
Sed est idem cadaver et sepulchrum sibi.

Compare it with the version ascribed to Ausonius. If such trifles can be weighed, Politian's is here the better translation. Ausonius:

Habet sepulchrum non id intus mortuum,
Habet nec ipse mortuus bustum super,
Sibi sed est ipse hic sepulchrum et mortuus.

Politian's manner more favorably impresses us in his version of *A.P.* 16.200—the well-known epigram on Love as Ploughboy, which has been ascribed to Moschus:

Peram humeris habilem, posito nunc induit arcu,
    Et posita baculum lampade sumpsit Amor:
Subque iugum missos stimulo citat ecce iuvencos
    Improbus, et cultae semina mandat humo.
Suspiciensque polos, 'Imple, inquit, Iupiter arva,
    Ne cogam Europae te iuga ferre bovem.'

(*Amor Fugit.*), 529, 654; 16.200, 278, 304. In the first edition, these translations were dispersed among his original epigrams without notice of their source. The verses *In Chrysocomum* (Del Lungo, p. 145) contain an echo of *A.P.* 5.236.

We have seen that Politian practised the composition of
Greek epigrams from his sixteenth year onwards, and have noticed that he arranged his pieces in chronological order so as to
display the progress of his skill. This arrangement was made
with a view to publication, and was one of the last acts of his
life.[1] Confident of success he announced himself not as the imitator but the rival of the ancient epigrammatists. Early in the
summer of 1494 he wrote as follows to Antonio Urceo Codro:[2]

I have composed nearly a book of Greek epigrams, which my friends
often urge me to publish; and they say—for so they flatter me—that
it will be not only to the glory of the Latins, but altogether to the
glory of the age, if I, a Latin, arouse the Grecian Muses that have been
sleeping now so long. In fact, not a poem is to be found, written by a
Greek these six hundred years, that can be read with patience. To-
day, however, one or two persons are said to make something of an
attempt, though nothing yet appears. For the purpose, therefore, of
either calling forth or stirring up these same persons, I thought to publish some such book as this of mine—unless you advise me against it.
. . . Meantime I am sending you certain of these epigrams—not selected, but chance specimens—no, that is not true, selected specimens
rather, since, as a matter of fact, I am sending those in which particularly I have sought to rival the ancient Greeks—if that is not too
shameless! Do you compare them, anyhow, and wherever I displease
you, fancy that some which might have pleased you have been left

[1] They were not published until after Politian's death; yet, apparently before that
event, Lascaris had seen them in the chronological arrangement (above, p. 116).

[2] *Epist.* 5.9. Angelus Politianus Antonio Urceo Codro S.D. Composui propemodum
libellum Graecorum epigrammatum, quem saepe ut edam, familiares mei me rogant,
et pertinere dicunt (ita enim mihi palpantur) non ad Latinorum modo sed omnino
ad saeculi gloriam, si Latinus homo tamdiu iam dormienteis excitem Graecas musas.
Non enim poema reperitur ullum citra sexcentos annos a Graecis conditum, quod
patienter legas. Sunt hodie tamen unus et alter, qui nonnihil dicuntur conari, quanquam adhuc non appareat. Ut igitur hos ipsos vel evocem vel irritem, cogitabam
libellum qualemcunque hunc nostrum publicare: modo tu non dissentias. . . . Mitto
interim quaedam tibi ex ipsis, non delecta sed fortuita, mentior, immo delecta potius,
siquidem illa potissimum, quibus cum veteribus Graecis, nisi tamen hoc nimis improbum,
certavi. Tu confer tamen, et utrunque displicuero, praerepta crede quibus poteram
placere. Lege vero primum, quod in Apelleam Venerem post tot antiquorum composui.
[The epigrams I give in the text.] . . . Sed et id armatam Venerem tandiu post alios ita
lusi: . . . In matrem quoque Lacaenam, trito Graecis argumento, ad hunc modum:
. . . Nec reveritus Iulianum principem sum, cuius heroicis versibus de organo musico
meos elegos et quidem pauciores opposui, quos et ipsos ascribam: . . . Extant etiam
nobilissima duo epigrammata in puerum super Hebri glacie ludentem, sicuti Latinum
quoque non invenustius, quod Augusto tribuitur. Sed cum Graecis illis ita quidem Graece
contendimus. . . . Sed nimis tibi sum fortasse molestus, itaque iam desinam. Prius tamen
illud testabor, me non ideo certasse cum tam praeclaris ingeniis, quae diu comprobavit
antiquitas, praesertim in herena ipsorum, quod inde mihi victoriam vel sperarem vel
quaererem, sed quod hoc magis videbar illa cognituṛus quo minus in experiundo con-
sequerer. Tu tamen qualiacunque sint ludicra haec mea velim diligenter explores, agni-
turus et in ceteris eiusdem generis, quae vel iam scripsi vel adhuc scripturio prorsus eundem gustum. Vale.

out. And read first of all what I have written, following the example of so many of the ancients, on the Venus of Apelles:[1]

Κύπριν Ἀπελλείας ἔργον, χερὸς ὡς ἴδον, ἔσταν
δαρὸν θαμβαλέος, τὰν ἀναδυομέναν.
τᾶς ἅτε παρθενικᾶς ἅτε καὶ φιλοπαίγμονος, αἰδώς
τὰν ὄψιν μίγδαν ἔλλαχεν ἠδὲ γέλως.
καὶ τᾷ μὲν ῥαθάμιγγας ἁλιβρέκτοιο καράνου
δεξιτερᾷ θλίβεν, καὶ κελάρυζεν ἀφρός,
ἦν δ' ἄρα τᾶς νοτίδος τὶς ἐμοὶ φόβος· ἀδέ γε λαιᾷ
ἔσκεπε τὰν ἄβαν τὰν ἔθ' ὑποβρύχιον,
καὶ γὰρ ἕως λαγόνων ὕφαλος πέλε, καί τις ἔτι φρὶξ
ματρὸς ἀπ' ὠδίνων ὄμφακα μαστὸν ἔλεν.
εἰ τοίαν πόκ' Ἄρης ἔχε δέσμιος, οὐκ ἀποδοῦναι
οὐ δ' Ἀφαιστείας ἤθελ' ἀλυκτοπέδας.

But on the theme 'Venus in Armor,' following others, I have amused myself thus:[2]

Ἐς τί σάκος κρατέεις, Παφία, λόγχαν τε τινάσσεις,
καὶ θώρακ' ἐνέδυς καὶ κόρυν ἀμφίφαλον;
μέμνασ' ὄττ' οὐ σοὶ δέδοται πολεμήϊα ἔργα
τᾷ τρυφερᾷ, διέπεις δ' ἱμερόεντα γάμον.—
ἀλλ' οὐκ ἐς δᾶριν θωρήσσομαι· ὅπλα δ' Ἄρηος
ἐνδύομ', ὡς κ' Ἄρης ἐκλελάθοιτο μάχας.

[1] Cf. *A.P.* 16 178–182, especially 180:

Κύπρις ὅτε σταλάουσα κόμας ἁλιμυρέος ἀφροῦ
γυμνὴ πορφυρέου κύματος ἐξανέδυ,
οὕτω που κατὰ λευκὰ παρήϊα χερσὶν ἑλοῦσα
βόστρυχον, Αἰγαίην ἐξεπίεζεν ἅλα,
στέρνα μόνον φαίνουσα, τὰ καὶ θέμις· εἰ δὲ τοιήδε
κείνη, συγχείσθω θυμὸς Ἐνυαλίου.

Politian's epigram may be thus translated: 'When I saw Venus the work of Apelles' hand, I stood long in astonishment—I mean the Venus Anadyomene. Mingled modesty and laughter possessed her countenance, which was that of a maiden and also one fond of sporting; and with her right hand she pressed the drops from her sea-drenched hair, and there was a spattering of foam, while I felt a certain dread of that spray. With her left hand she concealed her secret parts which the water still covered, for the sea still rose to her sides; and her unripe breast was still trembling from the birth-pangs of her mother. If she had been like this of old when Mars, in bonds, possessed her, he would not have cared to escape from the shackles of Vulcan.'

As this epigram was composed about 1490, it can have no direct connection with Politian's use of the theme in his *Stanze* written many years before (above, p. 48), nor with Botticelli's picture.

[2] Cf. *A.P.* 16.171:

Ἄρεος ἔντεα ταῦτα τίνος χάριν, ὦ Κυθέρεια,
ἐνδέδυσαι, κενεὸν τοῦτο φέρουσα βάρος;
αὐτὸν Ἄρη γυμνὴ γὰρ ἀφώπλισας· εἰ δὲ λέλειπται
καὶ θεός, ἀνθρώποις ὅπλα μάτην ἐπάγεις.

The translation of Politian's epigram is: 'Why, O Paphian Goddess, do you hold a shield and brandish a lance, why are you dressed in a corselet and a crested helmet? Bethink you, deeds of war are not your province, but love—the joys of marriage are in your care.'—'But I am not arming for war; these are Ares' arms I am putting on so that he may forget battle; for finding both arms and love in me alone, he will never depart from my bed.'

ἐν γὰρ ἐμοὶ μώνᾳ καὶ τεύχεα καὶ Κύπριν εὑρών,
οὔ ποκ' ἐμῶν θαλάμων ἔσσετ' ἀπαυλόσυνος.

On the 'Spartan Mother,' a well-worn theme among the Greeks, I write thus:[1]

Ἐκπροφυγόντα μάχας τὸν ἐὸν παῖδ' ὡς ἐνόησεν
Σπαρτιάτις μάτηρ, φασγάνῳ ἀντίασεν,
καὶ κτάνε τὸν δύστανον, ὃν ἔτρεψεν ὃν τέκεν αὐτά.
ταῦτα δ' ἐκερτόμεεν, λοξ' ἐπιδερκομένα·
εἰ τοῖον σ' ἐδόκουν, οὐκ ἂν τέκον· ἔρρε Λακαίνας
ὡς πάϊς, οὐκ ἐθέλων ὡς Λακεδαιμόνιος.

I have not even respected the Emperor Julian, to whose hexameters I have opposed my elegiacs—and fewer than his lines, too, in number. I shall quote them also.[2]

Χάλκειον δονάκων ὁρόω στίχον· ἀλλὰ τίς αὐτῷ
τεχνᾶται κρύβδην τὸν πολύθρουν κέλαδον;—
οὗτος ὁ τοῖς πλαγτῆρσιν εὔτροχα δάκτυλα παλμοῖς
δινεύων, τρομεράς τ' ἀμφισοβῶν σελίδας.—
ἀλλὰ πολυσπερέων πόθεν οἱ τόσος ἐσμὸς ἀητῶν;—
οὐκ ἀθρεῖς ἀσκοὺς διχθαδίους ὄπιθεν;

There are also extant two very well-known epigrams on a boy playing on the ice of the river Hebrus; as there is also on the same subject a no less graceful epigram in Latin ascribed to Augustus. This is the manner in which I vie in Greek with those Greek poems:[3]

[1] Cf. *A.P.* 7.230, 433, 531; 9.61, 397, 447 (7.531 could not be known to Politian). I give *A.P.* 9.61:

Γυμνὸν ἰδοῦσα Λάκαινα παλίντροπον ἐκ πολέμοιο
παῖδ' ἐὸν ἐς πάτραν ὠκὺν ἰέντα πόδα,
ἀντίη ἀΐξασα δι' ἥπατος ἤλασε λόγχαν,
ἄρρενα ῥηξαμένα φθόγγον ἐπὶ κταμένῳ·
Ἀλλότριον Σπάρτας, εἶπεν, γένος, ἔρρε πρὸς ᾅδαν,
ἔρρ', ἐπεὶ ἐψεύσω πατρίδα καὶ γενέταν.

A translation of Politian's epigram follows: 'When a Spartan mother saw her son fleeing from the battle, she assailed him with a sword, and slew the unhappy man whom she had borne and nursed; and looking at him askance she taunted him thus: Had I thought you would be like this, I would not have borne you. Die then, as the son of a Spartan woman, since you would not die as a Spartan man.'

[2] Julian's lines are *A.P.* 9.365:

Ἀλλοίην ὁρόω δονάκων φύσιν. Ἦπου ἀπ' ἄλλης
χαλκείης τάχα μᾶλλον ἀνεβλάστησαν ἀρούρης,
ἄγριοι οὐδ' ἀνέμοισιν ὑφ' ἡμετέροις δονέονται·
ἀλλ' ἀπὸ ταυρείης προθορῶν σπήλυγγος ἀήτης
νέρθεν ἐϋτρήτων καλάμων ὑπὸ ῥίζαν ὁδεύει·
καί τις ἀνὴρ ἀγέρωχος ἔχων θοὰ δάκτυλα χειρῶν,
ἵσταται ἀμφαφόων κανόνας συμφράδμονας αὐλῶν·
οἱ δ' ἁπαλὸν σκιρτῶντες ἀποθλίβουσιν ἀοιδήν.

Politian's epigram: 'I see a row of brazen reeds; but who is making therein, unseen, the mighty sound?—He who, with wandering strokes, is moving his nimble fingers and agitating the trembling keys all about him.—But whence so great a swarm of scattering winds?—Do you not see the double bellows behind?'

[3] Cf. *A.P.* 7.542 and 9.56; the first of these is quoted above, p. 29n. Politian's version of the theme may be rendered as follows: 'A little child in play leaped on the ice of the

Παῖς Ἕβρῳ ἐπέθρωσκε πεπηγότι τυτθὸς ἀθύρων·
κρυστάλλου δ'ἐάγη μαρμαρόεν δάπεδον,
χ'ὸ μὲν ὀλισθαίνων πέσεν εἰς βυθόν. ἀλλ' ἀδιάντου
κρατὸς ἔκερσε δέρην ὀστρακόεις παγετός·
σκῆνος ἄρ' ἐνδόμυχον ῥοθίου ταχὺς ἔσπασεν ὁλκός·
τῷ πυρὶ δ'ἡ μήτηρ μοῦνον ἔδωκε κάρη.
εἶπε δ'ἐπιστενάχουσα· τί δύσμορος υἱὸν ἔτεξα ;
ἄρ' ὡς στοιχείοιν βρῶμα γένοιτο δυοῖν.

[At this point Politian gives the Greek epigram which he has made
from the well-known Latin epigram on Hermaphroditus; see above,
p. 116.] But possibly I weary you too much, and so I make an end.
Yet I assure you of this: I have sought to rival those glorious geniuses,
so long admired by antiquity, and especially in their own field, not
because I either hoped or desired to gain a victory over them, but because I thought I should learn to know them the better the less I
succeeded in my attempt. Nevertheless I should like you carefully to
examine what may be the character of these trifles of mine, as you will
discover precisely the same flavor in other things of this kind which I
have written or still desire to write.

This letter was delivered to Urceo at Bologna on a hot day
at the beginning of July—*in magnis Iulii caloribus;* his reply
is dated from that city, July 5, 1494. Politian's letter, it was
easy to see, was less a request for criticism than for praise. The
tone of Urceo's response may be judged from the following excerpt:[1] [He has praised the other epigrams in detail.] 'But in
what words shall I praise the sentiment which you employ at
the end of your *Venus Anadyomene:* "If Mars, being bound,
had possessed Venus as she is here, he never would have
wished to escape from Vulcan's chains." My dear Angelo, my
esteemed friend—I do not flatter you, but from my heart I
speak—in the others you are not inferior to the Greeks, in this
one, in my opinion, you even surpass them. I do not, therefore,
merely urge you to publish what you have written, but beg
and entreat you to do so. Publish, publish as quickly as possi-

---

frozen Hebrus, the marble floor of glass was broken, and slipping he fell into the depths.
But his head was not wetted, for the shell-like ice severed it at the neck; whereas the
swift current of the stream carried off the trunk unseen. The head alone his mother
consigned to the flames, and moaning said: Why did I bear a son to my sorrow? Surely
it was that he might become the food of two elements.'

[1] Politian, *Epist.* 5.10. Sed quibus verbis laudabo illam sententiam, qua in fine
Veneris Anadyomenes usus es, ubi scripsisti: Si Mars ligatus talem habuisset Venerem,
noluisset unquam vinculis Vulcaniis dissolvi? Angele mi observande, non tibi blandior,
sed ex animo loquor: in aliis quidem non es Graecis inferior, in hoc vero etiam es, ut
sentio, superior. Quare non te tantum hortor ut edas quae scripsisti, sed rogo et ob-
testor. Ede, ede quam celerrime. . . . Vale, et memento nos Epigrammaton Graecorum
volumen integrum expectare.

ble. . . . Farewell, and remember I am expecting the complete
volume of your Greek epigrams.'

This volume Urceo was not destined to receive from the hand
of Politian, who died some two months later without realizing his plan. About a year after this, his young friend Zenobio
Acciaiuoli prepared the Greek epigrams for the press (Dec. 1,
1495), but the call of Savonarola presently drawing Acciaiuoli
into the religious life, he left them unprinted. They appeared in
Politian's *Opera Omnia* of 1498. Politian's intention had been to
publish them together with his Latin epigrams.[1] There are more
imitations of the Anthology than those he sent to Urceo; out
of his 57 Greek epigrams 9 are direct imitations of this sort. He
takes the themes of *A.P.* 9.13, 56, 61, 137, 357, 365, 476; 16.171,
180.[2] Besides these, his epigram on the Gnats is related to *A.P.*
5.151 through Scala's imitation of that epigram; an epigram on
a book belonging to the Duke of Urbino begins with an echo of
A.P. 9.192; while another, addressed to Giovanni Pico della
Mirandola, suggests the theme of *A.P.* 16.251—Eros and An-
teros—and borrows a phrase from it.[3] Oddly enough, Epigram
26 (Del Lungo, p. 196) recalls *A.P.* 12.69, which, however,
could hardly have been known to Politian. Epigram 19 (*ibid.*,
p. 192) on Chalcondyles is modeled upon the epigram of Plato
in praise of Aristophanes (above, p. 101). And in general as a
writer of Greek epigrams Politian keeps his eye on the poets of
the Anthology, and supposes himself picking up where they left
off. The refashioning of old themes, as we know, was in itself
an ancient practice.

If subjected to a rigorous grammatical criticism, Politian's
Greek epigrams would not come forth unscathed.[4] Yet they do
him honor, and doubtless served his purpose of making himself
feel the finer points of the ancient epigrams. We have recorded
(p. 116) Lascaris' opinion of Politian's performance. In the
middle of the seventeenth century Daniel Heinsius, in publishing his own book of Greek epigrams, declared that only the

---

[1] Cf. the (undated) letter of Politian to Antonio Zeno sending him his translation
of *Amor Fugitivus* and his *Elegia de Violis* (*Epist.* 7.14): 'Epigrammata tibi non mitto,
quod ea simul cum Graecis publicare statim cogito.'

[2] Assignments to *A.P.* 9.56, 61, and 16.180 are not absolute; the same themes are
treated elsewhere in the Anthology; see Register.

[3] Politian: καὶ πυρὶ φλέξε τὸ πῦρ; *Anthol.*: φλέξει τις πυρὶ πῦρ.

[4] A certain number of false quantities, pointed out by Salvini, are duly recorded in
Del Lungo's notes.

Venus Anadyomene and *Venus Armata* were tolerable. It is hard to dissent wholly from this judgment; the *Venus Armata* is surely the best of Politian's attempts. For the most part his points, which seemed to Politian himself, and apparently to Urceo, to be so well taken, fall somewhat coldly on a modern ear. Judged simply as landmarks in the resurgence of ancient studies they are notable achievements. Politian shows that he can write correctly both in the ordinary dialect of the epigrammatic poets, and also, when his models suggest it, in Doric. His vocabulary is mostly simple and unexceptionable. We may notice that in his *Venus Armata* the last word, ἀπαυλόσυνος (away from the αὐλή or courtyard), must have been taken from *A.P.* 6.221, since it occurs nowhere else.[1] This at least shows how thoroughly Politian had ransacked the Anthology. In his verses on the organ, ἀμφισοβῶν is a compound of his own forming. The word ὀστρακόεις in the epigram on the boy killed by the ice, is quoted only for *A.P.* 9.86 and Suidas (*s.v.* Στυφελισμός); the chances are that Politian took it from the epigram.

The Anthology has left few obvious marks on Politian's vernacular works; elsewhere with this wonderful and typical man it is in full play. Several persons in Italy before him had used the Greek epigrams in this way or that; Politian uses them in almost every way—he emulates them in Greek verse, translates them into Latin, weaves materials from them into the fabric of his original poems, he imitates their form when writing billets-doux to a blue-stocking, and discusses them and evokes them as authorities in his dissertations and learned epistles. If later scholars employed the epigrams to better effect in any of these ways, it was Politian who had shown them how; in particular his imitations of the Anthology, both in Greek and in Latin, became widely known, and were themselves frequently translated.[2]

---

[1] The word is suspected by Lobeck.

[2] On Politian's Italian poems see above, pp. 47–8. Two items may be added to our account of his use of the epigrams. In a letter to King Matthew of Pannonia (*Epist.* 9.1) he quotes a Greek proverb that he probably got from *A.P.* 11.176—πολλοὶ μαθηταὶ κρείττονες διδασκάλων. In his *Praefatio in Homerum* (*Opera*, Lyons, 1537, 3.66) he quotes *A.P.* 16.296, adding without comment the translation assigned above, p. 93, to Guarino da Verona on the authority of Urceo, who was a pupil of Guarino's son (cf. Del Lungo, p. 544).

The Latin prose translation of Politian's Greek epigrams made by Jacobus Thussanus (Paris, 1519) usually accompanies the text. Soter (below, p. 274) has a number of Politian's pieces.

JACOPO SANNAZARO (ACTIUS SYNCERUS)
(1458–1530)

Sannazaro was born at Naples on July 28, 1458; his family was of Lombard origin. He early lost his father. In Latin and Greek his teacher was Giuniano Maggio, and by him Sannazaro was presented to Pontano, who recognized his abilities and brought him into the Neapolitan Academy under the name of Actius Syncerus. In his youth, whether from unrequited love, or from a desire to see the world, or for both reasons, he spent some years in travel, perhaps visiting the Orient. In this period also the *Arcadia*, his chief vernacular work, was composed. Unlike Pontano, Sannazaro, when he became a member of the Neapolitan Court, remained faithful to the king; and when Federigo III in 1501 had to retire to France, the poet went with him, and only returned after Federigo's death in 1504. Thereafter he led a private life until his own death in 1530.

Sannazaro is one of the few neo-Latin poets whose verses still, when examined, show some signs of life; he is better in his shorter pieces than in his ambitious *De Partu Virginis*. In particular his Eclogues, in which, perhaps borrowing a hint from Theocritus, he removes the scene from the pasture and the hill to the seashore, deserve their great success; the 'piscatory eclogue' is virtually his invention. His success was no less marked in the epigram; and the reward accorded to him by the Venetian Republic for his epigram on their city has become a commonplace of literary history. The Latin poems were published together at Naples in 1526.

In Sannazaro's Latin poems there are echoes or imitations of six Greek epigrams: *A.P.* 5.95 (twice); 9.108, 440; 16.171, 174, 297.[1] Sannazaro was not capable of making mere translations; what Politian did in his Greek epigrams, he does in Latin, only he goes further; he takes only a hint from a Greek epigram, and develops it into something new. This is his *Venus Armata* (*A.P.* 16.171):

> Induerat thoraca humeris, galeamque decoro
>   Aptarat capiti Marte iubente Venus.
> 'Nil opus his,' Sol, 'Diva,' inquit; 'sumenda fuerunt,
>   Cum vos ferratae circuiere plagae.'

He elaborates the setting but retains the point of *A.P.* 9.108:

> De Veneris nato questa est Dictynna Tonanti,
>   Quod nimis ille puer promptus ad arma foret.
> Tum pater accito ostendens grave fulmen Amori,
>   'Hoc tibi, saeve puer, spicula franget,' ait.
> Cui lascivus Amor motis haec reddidit alis:
>   'Quid si iterum posito fulmine cycnus eris?'

---

[1] In the Register '*Poem.*' refers to *Sannazarii Poemata, accessit eiusdem Vita J. A. Vulpio auctore*, Padua, 1731. On Sannazaro's vernacular works see above, p. 48.

RAFFAELLE MAFFEI (VOLATERRANUS)

(1451–1522)

Maffei takes the name Volaterranus, by which he is best known, from his birthplace, Volterra. He is said to have studied under Politian, though three years that scholar's senior; in any case, there exists among Politian's epistles a letter to Maffei congratulating him on his speedy acquisition of the Greek language. The letter is in Greek.[1] Maffei was also a friend of Marullus (above, p. 112). His later years, at least after 1500, seem to have been spent in Rome; and there he completed his huge encyclopedia: *Commentariorum Urbanorum Libri xxxviii* (3 vols., Rome, 1506).[2] This work is divided into three parts: (1) *Geographia*, a description of the world and its peoples; (2) *Anthropologia*, on famous men of all ages and nations; (3) *Philologia*, on the arts.

An associate of the Florentine humanists could not ignore the Anthology. In the second part of Maffei's *Commentaries*, there is a notice of the miraculous effect produced by the tomb of Timon: 'Sed et mortuo mirum contigit, ut sepulchrum eius, quod erat in littore, mare quasi perosum, exundatione ab se absterruerit, longeque expulerit. In quo hoc erat epigramma.' He then quotes *A.P.* 7.313, with the following translation, which, however, seems to be by Lionardo Bruni:[3]

> Hic sum post vitam miseramque inopemque sepultus.
> Nomen non quaeras: Di lector, te male perdant.

In speaking of Epictetus he quotes *A.P.* 7.676 (from Macrobius), and gives his own translation:

> Servus Epictetus genitus sum, corpora claudus,
> Paupertate Irus, Dis at amicus eram.

His version of *A.P.* 9.357 occurs in the third part of his book:[4]

---

[1] Politian, *Epist.* 12.20, apparently written about 1493. The priest who stabbed Lorenzo in the tumult of the Pazzi Conspiracy (April 26, 1478), and who three days later was mutilated and hanged by the Florentine mob, was Antonio Maffei, a brother of Raffaelle. The latter, some days after, was the recipient of a kind letter, couched in elegant Latin, from the hand of the philosophic Lorenzo. Maffei himself is the authority for this anecdote (Roscoe, *Lorenzo*, London, 1846, p. 418).

[2] I use the edition in one volume printed by Froben, Basel, 1559.

[3] At all events, Giraldi, in quoting the same translation (below, p. 185), assigns it to 'Aretinus.' The epigram is given by Plutarch, several of whose works Bruni translated.

[4] In all, Volaterranus provides translations of the following: *A.P.* 7.313 (Bruni), 348, 676; 9.357, 577; 10.43; 13.29.1–2. The version of *A.P.* 9.577 I have failed to find in *Comm.*; it is given by Soter. In *Comm.*, p. 382 Volaterranus quotes *A.P.* 7.616 in the translation given by Brugnolo, and on p. 341 quotes *A.P.* 11.437 (from Macrobius) without translation. Baillet's judgment on him (quoted in *Nouv. Biog. Gén.*) is too severe: 'Cet homme, nonobstant sa reputation, n'était fort habile en quoique ce fût;

Graecia concelebrat duo bis certamina sacra,
Quorum hominum duo sunt, caetera coelicolum.
Sacra Iovis Phoebique, Palaemonis Archemorique,
Dona oleaster erunt, mala, selina, pinus.

FILIPPO BEROALDO THE ELDER

(1453–1505)

Beroaldo was born at Bologna, lived in Parma, Milan, and Paris, and finally returned to his birthplace, where he taught eloquence and literature until his death. He was accounted one of the great teachers of his time, and owes much of his reputation to his numerous and distinguished pupils.

Though a Latin poet of a certain merit, Beroaldo never employs the Greek epigrams for his verses.[1] He does, however, make use of several incidentally in his *Orationes* and *Varia Opuscula*.[2] From the manner in which he introduces translations of them, the reader might suppose Beroaldo himself the translator; they are, however, mainly taken by him from the Traversari-Brugnolo translation of Diogenes Laertius. Most of his quotations are in his essays on the ancient philosophers, where he is always largely dependent on Laertius.[3]

PIETRO GRAVINA

(1453–1527)

Gravina was born at Palermo into a noble family of Norman descent, formerly resident in the Kingdom of Naples. After studying with Aurelio Bienati, he repaired to Nola and thence to Rome, but settled in Naples. Here apparently he was received at Court, and certainly was received into the Neapolitan Academy, his closest friends being Pontano, Sannazaro, Gaurico, and Antonio Capece. The great Gonsalvo was his protector; and, after Gonsalvo left Italy in 1507, he enjoyed the patronage of Prospero and Vespasiano Colonna. In 1527, the plague visiting Naples, he took refuge in the Castello di Conca (Terra di Lavoro); and there died. His death is said to have

---

mais il était pitoyable en traduction, parcequ' il ne savait pas le grec.' All Volaterranus' translations from the Anthology are in Soter's *Epigrammata*. For his account of Planudes in *Comm.* 2, see below, p. 347 n.

[1] *Epigrammata ac Ludicra quaedam Facilioris Musae Carmina*, Paris, 1508.

[2] *Varia Opuscula*, Paris, 1508; *Orationes, Praelectiones, Symbolae Pythagorae, ibid.*, 1515.

[3] The epigrams are: *A.P.* 5.78 (*Orat.* f. vi); 7.85 (*Var. Op.* f. xii^vo), 86 (*Var. Op.* f. xii^ro), 87 (*ibid.*), 88 (*Var. Op.* f. xii^vo), 90 (*ibid.*), 91 (*ibid.*), 619 (*ibid.*), 620 (*ibid.*). These are all from the Traversari-Brugnolo Laertius. *A.P.* 16.27, the epitaph of Sardanapalus, is given in *Var. Op.* (sig. Aiii) in the version of Tifernas (above, p. 92).

been caused by an infection following a stab from a bur as he reclined beneath a chestnut-tree.[1]

The literary product of Gravina consists of Latin epistles, orations, and poems. These last, like those of several other poets in Pontano's Academy, are occasionally reminiscent of the Anthology. They were published after Gravina's death.[2] Among the epigrams are imitations of *A.P.* 5.151 and 236, and a translation of *A.P.* 9.222. The last follows:[3]

SUMPTUM EX GRAECO

Humanum mediis fluitare cadaver in undis
Ut vidit delphin, in vada sicca tulit.
Vique sua eiectus longeque in littora pulsus,
'Pro meritis, inquit, mors mihi munus erit,
Heu pietas! sortem quid permutavimus? Unda
Te mea submersit, me tua terra rapit.'

GIAMBATTISTA PIO
(*c.* 1460 – *c.* 1540)

By birth Pio belonged to Bologna, where he studied with Filippo Beroaldo, and later opened a school of his own (1494). From Bologna he went to Milan and Bergamo; in 1509 he was invited to Rome to be Reader to Leo X. The year 1524 found him again in Bologna teaching literature. Presently he seems to be in Lucca. In 1534 he was appointed professor of eloquence in Paul III's College of Wisdom. In Rome he formed a close friendship with M. A. Flaminio. Giovio, with his love of the unusual, relates that one day after dinner Pio opened Galen at the place where are enumerated the symptoms of approaching death, and, having recognized one of these signs in the spots on his finger-nails, hastily made his final dispositions, and in a few moments expired. Bernardo Tasso was one of Pio's pupils.[4]

As Soter included a number of Pio's metrical versions from the Anthology in his *Epigrammata Graeca*, they have gained a wide circulation. For the most part they first appeared as occasional translations in Pio's *Adnotationes*, first published with Beroaldo's book of the same name and with Politian's

---

[1] On Gravina see Giovanni Verro, *Pietro Gravina e le sue Opere* (36 pp.), Corleone, 1898.

[2] *Poematum Liber: Epigrammatum Liber, Sylvarum et Elegiarum Liber, Carmen Epicum ad Illust. Joannem Franciscum de Capua Palenensium Comitem.* Naples, 1532.

[3] Verro, *op. cit.*, p. 20, detects the style of the Anthology in the following couplet, which might be compared with *A.P.* 16.211 (also on Cupid unarmed and asleep):
Ne dubita, non bella movet sopitus, inermis;
Tunc fuge cum vigil est et pharetratus Amor.

[4] The best account of Pio is that by Giovanni Fantuzzi, *Notizie degli Scrittori Bolognesi*, Bologna, 1789, 7.31–41.

Miscellanea at Brescia in 1496.[1] In the *Adnotationes*, besides being used for illustrative purposes, the epigrams are sometimes themselves the object of comment. Thus Pio quotes *A.P.* 9.357, and observes:[2] 'Comprehendunt haec carmina et amplectuntur blandiloquenti et suavissimo sermone certamina, quae per Graeciam celebrantur, frequenter et ferventer conficiebantur. Inibique *athla*, hoc est praemia agonica, quae per diverticula et minutias a paucis Latinis visuntur enarrata collectim; nos otium nacti, etenim satius est (ut inquit ille) otiosum esse quam nihil agere, intulimus in Latinum idioma, atque maluimus interpres esse quam metaphrastes. Audi, laetaberis:

> Quatuor insignis certamina conficit Hellas;
>   Sunt duo quippe hominum, sunt superumque duo:
> Archemori, Iovis, et Phoebi, atque Palaemonis, ipsa
>   Pinus, olivaster praemia, poma, apium.'

His observations can scarcely be described as searching; the translation may be compared with that of Maffei (above, p. 143).[3]

Pio's Latin poems, published under the title *Elegidiae*, Bologna 1500 and 1509, have no echoes of the Anthology.[4] Yet he seems to have made a serious business of translating the epigrams, and Fantuzzi (*Scritt. Bologn.* 7.40) reports an unprinted set of versions by him, contained in a MS. in the Vatican (*Vat. Lat.* 2851): *Joannis Baptistae Pii Bononiensis Vetera Graecorum Epigrammata in Latinum translata, ad Paulum III.* It is in Pio's autograph.

PIETRO RICCIO (CRINITUS)
(*c.* 1465–*c.* 1505)

Crinitus—for Riccio is best known under his Latin name—was a Florentine and a pupil of Politian. He became tutor to the children

---

[1] My quotations from the *Adnot.* are from the edition in Gruter's *Lampas sive Fax Artium Liberalium*, Frankfort, 1602, 1.353–583. Pio edited a great number of classical authors, and seems frequently to have drawn on the Anthology for illustrations; doubtless it was from one or another of these editions, not seen by me, that Soter, Cornarius, and Henri Estienne drew the translations for which I have had to depend on them.

[2] *Lamp.* 1.384.

[3] Nine translations by Pio are listed in the Register: *A.P.* 2.92; 6.331; 9.125, 357, 489 (from Cornarius), 502, 561 (H. Estienne, *Epig. Sel.*, 1570, p. 4), 567; 11.239 (Soter). Unless otherwise stated, these are in *Adnot.*; likewise in *Adnot.* he quotes without translation: *A.P.* 9.383 (*Lamp.* 1.473), 503 (*ibid.*, p. 442); 16.214 (*ibid.*, p. 539), and 315 (*ibid.*, p. 455). In his *C. Valerii Flaci Commentarii* (Rome?, 1519), f. xiiii, he quotes, in illustration of *Arg.* 1.25, *A.P.* 9.346, and gives a prose version.

[4] I have not seen the edition under the name *Poemata*, Geneva, 1608, said to be more complete.

of several prominent citizens; and his premature death is said to have been the result of an accident that occurred while he was playing with some of his pupils. His three books, always printed together, passed through at least seven editions; they are: *De Honesta Disciplina libri xxv*, *De Poetis Latinis libri v*, and *Poematon libri ii*. These were first printed at Florence in 1500.[1]

A pupil of Politian should be well acquainted with the Anthology. Though Crinitus' *Poemata* contains no translations, the epigrams duly appear in his other works. In the *Honesta Disciplina* his verses *ad Neaeram ex epigrammate Platonis* are a paraphrase of *A.P.* 5.78. He need not have gone to the Anthology for this nor for an exercise on the theme of *A.P.* 7.229, as the one appears in Diogenes Laertius, the other in Plutarch. Verses entitled *De Tarchonte et Statua Ultrice Hostis* may be an imitation of *A.P.* 9.67, and are so given by Soter. A translation of *A.P.* 16.388 must have been made from the Anthology, since this anacreontic appears nowhere else:

> Dum sacrum Paphiae deae
> Sertis cum roseis paro,
> Et inter violas simul
> Nectuntur candida lilia,
> Raptim cum tremula face
> Atrox Idaliae puer
> In me saevius insilit,
> Et in praecordia, vaeh mihi!
> Illapsus fremit et procax
> Me flammis agitat suis,
> Quo semper Glycerem bonam
> Vesanis ignibus ardeam.

In *De Honesta Disciplina* 11.4 Crinitus quotes *A.P.* 16.129 together with the translation of Ausonius, and *ibid.* 19.6, *A.P.* 16.263 again with Ausonius' Latin.[2] In the case of 16.129—the well-known epigram on the Niobe of Praxiteles[3]—he adds the opinion of Marullus to his own: 'Quo carmine nihil utique legi potest cultius, limatius, doctius; adeo ut Marullus noster Byzantius, vir eleganter doctus, atque in examinandis carminibus gravis censor, aperte affirmarit, nihil se usquam legisse, aut etiam audisse, elegantius, melius, absolutius.'[4]

---

[1] I use the Lyons edition (Gryphe) of 1543.
[2] *Ed. cit.*, pp. 175 and 293.
[3]   Ἐκ ζωῆς με θεοὶ τεῦξαν λίθον· ἐκ δὲ λίθοιο
         ζωὴν Πραξιτέλης ἔμπαλιν εἰργάσατο.
[4] In the collection of Politian's *Epistolae* (12.22) there is a letter from Crinitus to

Crinitus further shows his acquaintance with the Anthology in his remarks on Tullius Laureas (above, p. 11), in his *De Poetis Latinis:* 'Leguntur et apud Graecos Epigrammata Laureae in quibus par elegantia atque eruditio habetur. Mihi non satis constat an idem fuit, qui fuerit M. Tulli libertus.'

GIACOMO COSTANZI (CONSTANTIUS)

(*fl.* 1502)

Giacomo Costanzi is as little known as his father Antonio (above, p. 111). Like the father, the son appears to have passed his life at Fano, where he probably taught. Giacomo was the editor of his father's poems, and published his own with them. He says, in the Epistle, addressed to Agostino Villa of Ferrara, that it was on Villa's advice that he had undertaken the publication of his father's poems; and he recalls how he had made the acquaintance of Villa while studying at Ferrara under Battista Guarini, Paniciatus, and Luca Riva.[1] Apparently the task of editing his father's verses suggested the addition of his own.[2]

The younger Costanzi has about 100 epigrams, of which 25 are from the Anthology. Several other examples could be cited of an interest in the Greek epigrams passing from father to son —most notable being the case of Henri and Paul Estienne. The reader will also think of John Addington Symonds, the elder and younger.

At the head of his translations Costanzi puts this legend: *Sequuntur epigrammata quaedam quae Latina civitate donavimus.* He follows his father even in a preference for two-line epigrams. The following may be compared with Antonio's version of the same epigram (*A.P.* 9.369):

> Scribere me brevibus numeris epigrammata culpas?
> Vis epigramma canam, Zoile, an historiam?

Unlike his father he does not eschew amatory themes, as *A.P.* 5.94:

Alexander Sartius, who was collecting Politian's works. Among other matters Crinitus touches on the *Aitia* of Callimachus, mentioning that the poem is alluded to in several Greek epigrams, and particularly in *A.P.* 11.275 which he quotes.

[1] He has a poem *Ad Baptistam Guarinum praeceptorem.*

[2] *Epigrammata quaedam; eiusdem Epicidion in Thadaeam Matrem* is the title of Giacomo's poems in his father's *Epigrammatum Libellus*, Fano, 1502. Community of interests between father and son is evinced by the following fact. Among the elder's works printed with his epigrams, is a dissertation proving that Ovid addressed his *Fasti* to Germanicus, not to Tiberius; the son, in turn, published in 1508 at Fano a *Collectanea* consisting of papers on this poet.

Iuno oculos, Thetis alma pedes, Cytherea papillas,
Atque manus Pallas cessit, amica, tibi;
Qui videt is felix, qui te audit ter magis, heros
Quisquis amat, tecum cui licet esse deus.

In all, Giacomo translates: *A.P.* 5.20, 42, 59, 94; 9.9.5–6, 118, 133, 167, 357, 369, 394, 648, 654, 751, 773; 10.29, 30, 67, 80, 119; 11.5, 273, 381; 16.9, 194.

ALDO MANUZIO (ALDUS MANUTIUS)

(1449–1515)

Aldus was born at Sermonetta, a village in the Papal States near Velletri. He was educated first at Rome, and then at Ferrara under Battista Guarini, where he had for fellow students Ercole Strozzi and Giovanni Pico. In 1482, on the approach of the Venetian army to Ferrara, he accepted the invitation of Pico to withdraw with him to Mirandola. Pico helped him to make the acquaintance of Politian; and about the same time (1485) put him in charge of the education of the young lord of Carpi, Alberto Pio, Pico's nephew. Between 1490 and 1495 Aldus, with the pecuniary aid of the house of Carpi, established his press at Venice. He had married a daughter of Andrea Torresano d' Asola, who had taken over the press of Nicolas Jenson (above, p. 87). The first publication of Aldus appears to have been his Musaeus of 1494/95—a brief trial-piece. Thereafter the history of Aldus is the history of his publications, except for the founding in 1500 of his Academy.[1] In 1506 his work was interrupted by the war that followed the League of Blois, and again in 1510–11 by the war of the League of Cambrai. With these two intervals the press of Aldus continued until his death, and long after, to issue the neat, correct, and inexpensive volumes which have become a necessary part of our idea of the Italian Renaissance.

Lascaris' edition of the Anthology may have been exhausted by 1503; it must always have been an expensive book. Aldus issued his edition in the small octavo to which he owes his success;[2] hence the point made by Carteromaco in his epistle printed at the end of the volume (below, p. 152). The first Aldine Anthology was printed in November, 1503. It was set up from a copy of Lascaris' edition now in the Bibliothèque Nationale at Paris and formerly the property of Renouard, the historian of the Aldine Press. He describes the volume as

---

[1] Besides Aldus, the persons connected with the Academy, who show an interest in the Anthology, are: J. Lascaris, Chalcondyles, Navagero, Aleander, Musurus, Erasmus and Carteromaco.

[2] Signatures A-NN.

follows:[1] [J'ai] 'en ma possession [un exemplaire] de l'Anthologie grecque, édition de Florence, 1494, in-4°, entièrement annoté par Alde, qui même a copié de sa main les 45 dernières pages manquant à cet exemplaire. Ce volume, qui porte sur le premier feuillet le nom d'Alde, avec l'ancre figurée à la main, est évidemment celui qui a servi de copie aux ouvriers compositeurs pour l'édition aldine de 1503; ce qu'on reconnoît aux corrections marginales, introduites dans le texte de 1503, aux petits mandats ou avis écrits par le maître aux ouvriers, sur les feuilles de copie, et enfin aux marques usitées par les compositeurs pour indiquer sur leur copie la progression de leur travail et la division des feuilles de leur nouvelle impression.' The same copy possibly served Francesco d'Asola for the second Aldine edition.[2]

As set up, then, the first Aldine is virtually nothing more than a reproduction in cursive type of the edition of Lascaris.[3] At the end, however, Aldus added the following matter not in the edition of 1494: two epigrams by Lascaris;[4] the poem of Paulus Silentiarius on the *Thermae;* a versified problem of Euclid; an epigram by Theon on the planets; verses by 'Hermes Trismegistus' or 'Orpheus' on Earthquakes and the Zodiac; 21 pages of variant readings together with 19 new epigrams to be inserted in the text at the points indicated; and finally the Greek letter of Carteromaco, already mentioned, on behalf of the book. The Latin title of the Anthology, *Florilegium,* so long in use, was invented by Aldus for this edition— it is said, from Ovid, *Met.* 15.366: *Florilegae nascuntur apes.*[5]

Of the variants and the additional epigrams, printed under the heading 'Επιδιόρθωσις, Aldus merely says they were found 'in other copies.'[6] This probably means no more than the Marcian MS.[7] The new epigrams are, in this order:

---

[1] *Annales de l'Imprimerie des Aldes* (1803) 2.156.

[2] See below, p. 172, n. 1, where the quotation from Renouard is continued.

[3] 'Ανθολογία Διαφόρων 'Επιγραμμάτων ἀρχαίοις συντεθειμένων σοφοῖς . . . εἰς ἑπτὰ τμήματα . . . *Florilegium Diversorum Epigrammatum in septem libros.* At the end: *Venetiis in aedibus Aldi mense Novembri* M.DIII.

[4] Herbert, *Trav. Inéd.,* p. 105, suggests that these were included as an honor to the ambassador (Lascaris); if so, the honor was of a private nature, since they were printed as anonymous.

[5] Waltz, *Anth.* 1.lxxi, note 8.

[6] 'Επιδιόρθωσις τουτωνὶ τῶν ἐπιγραμμάτων καὶ διαφοραί τινες ἀμάτε, προσθήκη τινῶν ἐπιγραμμάτων καὶ στίχων ἄτινα ἐν ἄλλοις εὕρομεν ἀντιγράφοις.

[7] Thus in *A.P.* 9.1 (*Plan.* 1.33.1) the 1494 ed. has θηλύν in line 3, the 'Επιδ. of Aldine[1] has θηλήν as has *Marc.* 481 (but in the same epigram, line 2, εἰδοῦσα of the

A.P. 9.53;[1] 11.98; 11.41; 7.540; 7.297; 7.76; 16.44; 16.73; 16.74; 9.604; 16.30; 16.202; 16.212; 16.240; 16.266; 9.627; 9.660; 9.189; 9.784. Lascaris had in some degree made a false start in printing the Planudean Anthology from a secondary MS.; Aldus's Ἐπιδιόρθωσις brought the text back into line with the autograph of Planudes. Nothing better could be done till the Palatine MS. was discovered.[2]

ARISTOBOULOS APOSTOLIOS (ARSENIOS)

(1465–1535)

Arsenios was a Cretan, son of Michael Apostolios. Much of his life was spent in Crete, but for a time he corrected for Aldus. A quarrel ended this engagement. Not long after, however, he was appointed Bishop of Monembasia by the pope, an appointment which gave rise to many contentions that we need not here review. Arsenios was subsequently director of Leo X's Greek College in Rome. He died in Venice.[3]

As a friend of Lascaris, Arsenios may have received as a gift a copy of the first edition of the Anthology now in the Bibliothèque Nationale at Paris.[4] Into this volume he copied an extract from the *scholia* of Musurus. From Arsenios the book passed to the brother-in-law of Aldus, Giovan Francesco Torresano d'Asola, whose name, as in all his books, is written on the lower margin of fol. 2 recto.[5] A second copy of the 1494

1494 ed. is not corrected to οἰδοῦσα of *Marc.* 481). In *A.P.* 9.375 (*Plan.* 1.2.2) the 1494 ed. reads χαμαδὶς βάλεν where *Marc.* 481 has the superior ἀπό μιν βάλεν, and this is reported in ᾽Επιδ. (As is well known, the Marcian MS. consists of two parts. This epigram appears in both parts, in the second with the reading χαμαδὶς). In *A.P.* 9.12 (*Plan.* 1.4.2) the name of the epigrammatist, ΛΕΩΝΙΔΟΥ, is added in ᾽Επιδ. from *Marc.* 481. Again, in *A.P.* 9.266.2 (*Plan.* 1.11.1.2), where the 1494 ed. has Γλαφύρα, the ᾽Επιδ. of Aldine[1] has Γλαφύρῳ—cf. above, p. 126. These relations may be examined in Stadt-müller's ed., where full use is made of the early edd.

[1] In the reverse form, which *Marc.* 481 alone gives.

[2] The first Aldine is not, comparatively speaking, a very rare book. It is of interest to note that the British Museum has a copy bearing the autograph of Ulrich von Hutten.

In the Musaeus of 1494, already mentioned, Aldus quotes *A.P.* 7.615 with a prose translation (reprinted in *Musaei Opuscula*, 1517). After the Preface of the *ed. pr.* of Aristophanes (1498) is given *A.P.* 9.186, and similarly *A.P.* 9.213 is printed in the *ed. pr.* of Discocorides and Nicander (1499). See Botfield, *Prefaces to the First Editions*, London, 1861.

[3] An account of Arsenios may be found in Legrand, *Bibl. Hell.* 1.clxv ff.

[4] Rés. Y 503. See Legrand, *op. cit.* 1.clxxiii.

[5] Legrand, *loc. cit.* Cf. Delisle, *Le Cabinet des Manuscrits de la Bibl. Nat.* 1. 158. About 70 MSS. bearing the signature of D'Asola were brought from Italy to Fontainebleau in the last years of Francis I (died 1547), and were bound early in the reign of Henry II. The Anthology here in question still bears the arms of that monarch, and,

Anthology, at Troyes, is also said to have notes by Musurus in the hand of Arsenios (below, p. 157).

Arsenios' father had, at the suggestion of Gaspar Zacchi, Bishop of Osimo (near Ancona), made a great collection of Greek proverbs, which he called Ἰωνιά, in Latin *Violetum;* but had died before he could put it into final shape. Lascaris suggested to the son that he complete the work. This he did, dedicating the result to Leo X; but he published only a portion of it.[1] His autograph MS., which must have been completed at the very beginning of the sixteenth century, is at Paris (*Paris. Graec.* 3058). The first edition of the *Violetum* was that of Christian Waltz (Stuttgart, 1832).[2]

The elder Apostolios, of course, knew the Anthology, and makes one or two references to it.[3] Arsenios, however, perhaps through the influence of Lascaris, goes out of his way to introduce Greek epigrams into his work. From the Anthology he quotes:[4] *A.P.* 6.197; 7.86, 89, 104, 229, 249, 296, 669, 670; 9.48, 54; 10.34, 58, 95; 14.73, 91; 16.223, 224. There is nothing to distinguish the text of Arsenios from that of Lascaris' edition, save in a few details that can be easily explained.

Though the work of Arsenios hardly circulated widely enough to be read by many persons, it had the fortune to be employed by the man most capable of using it. Erasmus arrived in Venice (1508) too late to make the acquaintance of Arsenios; but he received a copy of the *Violetum* from Girolamo Aleandro, and made use of it for his *Adagia.*[5]

SCIPIONE FORTIGUERRI (CARTEROMACO)
(1466–1515)

Fortiguerri assumed the Greek form of his name, probably, when he became a member of the Aldine Academy. He was born at Pistoia

though a printed book, probably came to France with the MSS. According to a note of Legrand (*op. cit.* 1.30), this volume also contains manuscript notes by Constantine Calopar. See also Herbert, *Trav. Inéd.*, p. 109.

[1] *Praeclara Dicta Philosophorum, Imperatorum et Poetarum.* Rome, 1519.

[2] Leutsch (*Paroemiographi Graeci*, vol. 2, Göttingen, 1851) published the proverbs from the Paris MS., separating the work of Arsenios from that of Apostolios. The earlier edition of Waltz is not so complete for the proverbs, but contains the *Apophthegmata.*

[3] *A.P.* 7.225 (Ap. 16.44); 9.366 (see Leutsch's Index), 685 (Ap. 11.49); and 11.251 (Ap. 6.39).

[4] In the Register *Viol.* refers to the ed. of Waltz, *Paroem.* to that of Leutsch.

[5] Erasmus himself supplies this information in *Adag.* 2.1.1 (*Festina lente*) in *Op. Om.*, ed. by Clericus, 2.405D.

into a poor but prominent family, and received his early schooling at his native place. In 1478 the *Studio* of Pisa was removed to Pistoia to escape the plague, and Lorenzo de' Medici for the same reason sent a part of his family thither. With them came Politian, and the child Fortiguerri is supposed to have heard lectures from the young scholar at this time. Certainly he studied with Politian at one time or another. He likewise visited the professors of Rome, Bologna, and Padua. At Rome he made the acquaintance of Aldus, who later, when establishing his press, invited Fortiguerri to join him in Venice. Many of Aldus' books are adorned with Greek epistles or epigrams by 'Carteromaco.' In 1506, when scholarship at Venice was interrupted by war, Carteromaco went to Rome under the protection of Cardinal Franciotti; and soon after, on the Cardinal's death, retired to Pistoia. Again he returned to Rome to live with Angelo Colocci. The last two years of his life were passed in Florence, whither Leo X had induced him to accompany Giulio de' Medici.[1]

While at Venice Carteromaco held a sort of professorship of Greek in Aldus' Academy; his inaugural oration is preserved.[2] In this oration he touches on the writing of Greek epigrams by Romans—Germanicus ('whose verses are still read'), Tiberius, and Hadrian; and finally mentions Politian's success in this kind.[3] Most of Carteromaco's own Greek epigrams were produced as inscriptions for his friends' books;[4] but he composed others as well which have not been printed. In 1556 Fulvio Orsini addressed a letter to Michele Fortiguerri, Scipione's nephew, requesting a copy of the uncle's Greek epigrams for a miscellany he intended to publish; but the project was not carried out.[5] A letter of Carteromaco to Politian, dated April 27, 1493, has at the end an epigram in Latin and one in Greek by the writer. The last four lines of the sixteen-line Latin poem are reminiscent of *A.P.* 16.296:[6]

> De patria magni certatum est semper Homeri,
> Vindicet ut tantum hunc urbs sibi quaeque virum.
> Tu maioris eris certaminis, Angele, causa,
> Terra etenim ac caelum te volet esse suum.

The Greek letter from Carteromaco to Aldus printed in the first Aldine Anthology may be rendered as follows:[7]

[1] The best account of Carteromaco is that of Sebastiano Ciampi, *Memorie di Scipione Carteromaco*, Pisa, 1811.
[2] Printed at the front of Stephanus' Greek *Thesaurus*.
[3] Above, p. 124, n. 3.
[4] A list of these is given by Ciampi, *op. cit.*, pp. 52–4, and several of them are reproduced, *ibid.*, pp. 85–94.
[5] Nolhac, *Fulvio Orsini*, p. 81.
[6] Politian, *Epist.* 12.25.
[7] The original is reproduced in Bandini's Catalogue of the Laurentian Library 2.104.

The smaller valuable things are, the more most persons are pleased by them; for, as the epigram [*A.P.* 9.784] says: 'Charm goeth with little things.'[1] Accordingly, since the manuscript book of epigrams is of all poetry the most valuable, by putting it into the smallest possible compass in print you have made it most pleasing to all. No one but will be mad about it in this shape; for the charm of the contents will not be so attractive as the portable form. Thus, having greatly assisted lovers of the beautiful to the possession of books, you have now also given thought to the manner in which they may be helped to the use of them; so that no one, being burdened by affairs, may fail of leisure for the exercise of the mind in reading.

Carteromaco naturally received from Aldus one of the fine copies of the Anthology printed on parchment. This, filled with the owner's marginalia, remained in Carteromaco's library, which was kept intact by his heirs at Pistoia until 1565. In that year poverty induced them to sell the autographed volumes to Fulvio Orsini, who was making a collection of books once owned by the great humanists. The Anthology is No. 50 in Orsini's Inventory: 'Epigrammatario, in carta pergama, tocco dal Carteromacho, legato alla greca in corame versicolore, d'Aldo.' It seems since to have disappeared.[2]

Carteromaco's reputation has suffered from the fact that though the friend of the greatest of printers, his own works were never given to the press. About the time when the Aldine Anthology was published, he, Musurus, and Leoniceno made some Latin translations from the epigrams. These remain in a ms. at Basel.[3] An interesting essay on rabies in dogs, addressed by Carteromaco to Colocci, was only printed by Ciampi in 1811. Near the end of the piece an epigram from the Anthology is introduced in the following manner:[4]

Firmin-Didot (*Alde Manuce*, p. 531) prints a version of this epistle among unpublished Greek letters. These had come to him from Renouard who had brought them from Venice. Didot, though he owned Grolier's copy of the first Aldine, seemingly was unaware that this letter was printed therein and elsewhere. However, his version considerably differs from the one Aldus printed, and probably is an earlier draft. As the difference is mainly verbal, I translate the version that appeared in the 1503 Anthology.
    [1] The epigram was an inscription for a little bath—translated by Lascaris, above, p. 115.
    [2] Nolhac, *Fulvio Orsini*, p. 354 and p. 181, note 6. Carteromaco probably possessed a copy of the *ed. pr.* (cf. below, p. 167). Orsini had also a manuscript miscellany, containing Greek epigrams, that came to him from Carteromaco—now *Vat. Graec.* 1386 (Nolhac, pp. 181 and 344); Nolhac says the annotations it contains are of little interest. A ms. at Paris (*Paris.* 2720), containing some of the Anthology, was copied in part by Carteromaco.
    [3] Below, p. 156. This work escaped the notice of Ciampi.
    [4] Ciampi, pp. 108-10.

But, dear Colocci, inasmuch as I am aware of your exceeding fond-
ness for Greek epigrams (being yourself one who in Latin often delight in that style of composition, succeeding in it too, not only from
nature and ability but also by study and practice), it appeared to me
not beside the point, in passing, to bring some facts borrowed from the
Greeks into connection with the well-known epigram in the seventh
book in which mention is made of the mad dog. These facts will considerably explain the sense of the epigram, and serve as a sort of
corollary to what I have said above. The Greek epigram is as follows.
[He quotes *A.P.* 5.266]. This I have translated literally into Latin for
the sake of those who do not know Greek:

> Percussum rabiente canis, fert fama, veneno
> Cernere belvinam iam effigiem sed in aquis.
> In me forsan amor dentes impressit amaros,
> Sicque furore animum, dum rabit, eripuit.
> Namque mihi e ponto pergrata occurrit imago
> Et Bacchi patera et vorticibus fluvium.

The epigram is then illustrated by quotations from Galen on
the effects of a mad dog's bite. The second line probably would
have been mended, if Carteromaco had himself published his
work.

NICCOLÒ LEONICO TOMEO

(1456–1531)

Leonico was born in Venice of Albanian parentage. He
studied Greek with Chalcondyles at Florence; and is credited
with having 'opened a new era in the scholarly study of Aristotle.'[1] There is an irony, therefore, in the discovery by Cardinal
Mai that a MS. of Aristides, once owned by Leonico and now in
the Vatican Library, contains under the Aristides a tenth-
century *Politics* of Aristotle.[2] Among the books belonging to
Leonico, which, like the MS. just mentioned, passed through the
hands of Fulvio Orsini into the Vatican collection, is an Aldine
Anthology of 1503 'legato alla Greca in corame rosso.' It bears
annotations by Leonico, and is, according to Nolhac, 'orna-
mented with two curious miniatures.'[3]

---

[1] Sandys, *Hist. of Classical Scholarship*, 2.110.
[2] Nolhac, *Fulvio Orsini*, p. 172.
[3] Now Vat. A. 18 in-8°.

MARCUS MUSURUS

(*c*. 1470–1517)

A native of Retimo in Crete, Musurus migrated to Italy when about fifteen years old, and studied with Janus Lascaris in Florence.[1] About 1491 he returned to Crete on a visit to his family, but the year 1494 found him in Venice; and thereafter he was more or less continuously associated with Aldus. He was the editor of the nine comedies of Aristophanes issued in 1498 (above, p. 150, n. 2). In 1499 he appears to have been a member of the household of Alberto Pio of Carpi. Four years later he was made Censor of Greek books to the Venetian Republic; and in 1505 Professor of Greek at Padua. The war following the League of Cambrai caused him to retire to Venice, where in 1513 he edited the Platonic Dialogues, with his celebrated Hymn to Plato. On the death of Aldus (1515), Musurus accepted an invitation of Leo X to join Lascaris in establishing the college for young Greeks in Rome. None of the expatriate Greeks had more to do than Musurus in the publication of important classical authors; he took part in the editing of Aristophanes, Plato, the *Etymologicon Magnum*, Euripides, Hesychius, Pausanias, Theocritus, and, in a word, most of the Greek books printed by Aldus.

While Professor of Greek at Padua, in 1506, Musurus lectured on the Greek Anthology. His Greek notes prepared for this course were probably the first *scholia* of any importance written on the epigrams.[2] Little that may be called *scholia* can be found in the Palatine MS.; the Laurentian MS. contains a few meagre notes; Stephanus in 1566 printed a few from an unknown source. Otherwise, it seems, all the so-called *scholia* go back to Musurus. Such at least remains the probability.[3] These notes, it seems, were widely spread abroad in manuscript during the sixteenth century, not only being multiplied in complete or fragmentary copies, but also being transcribed into copies of the early printed editions of the Anthology. They were published in a mutilated form in the Wechel Anthology of 1600.[4]

---

[1] Legrand, *Bibl. Hell.* i.cviii and 79.

[2] Among his hearers was Aldus' brother-in-law, Francesco d'Asola, who, after a note written in the margin of his copy of the 1494 Anthology, has added: 'Hoc audivi a Marco Musuro, viro optimo, Patavi, 1506.' Cf. below, p. 172.

[3] Calderini, in the first of his articles summarized below, hints that the *scholia* in *Cod. Vat. Urb.* 152 may differ from the rest.

[4] The editors give the following account of the provenience of their *scholia:* 'Graeci commentarioli in aliquot epigrammata unicum exemplar habebamus a Cl. viro Fr. Pithoeo, quum ecce aliud prodiit ab amplissimo et humaniss. viro P. Petavio Regio Senatore, illi paene par, nisi quod paucula quaedam huic interdum, interdum illi deerant. Utrumque diligenter inter se comparatum et expressum damus fideliter.' Probably they received from Pithou and Petau copies of the 1494 edition, into the

These notes are rhetorical, etymological, and grammatical—such as the professor may well have given to his pupils. The brief note on *Plan.* 1.2.1 (*A.P.* 9.561) will serve as an example. The epigram (an address to a wild grape-vine) begins with the words: τίς σε πάγος δυσέρημος . . . ἐξέθρεψεν; The note is: 'κατ' ἀποστροφίην σχῆμα.' In the second line the word ἄμπελον (vine) is explained: 'ἄμπελος, ἀπὸ τοῦ ἄνω καὶ τοῦ π έ λ ε ι ν.' In line 5 the form ἐγείναο is noticed: 'ἀπὸ τοῦ γείνω, ὁ μέλλων, γενῶ, ἀόριστος ἔγεινα, ὁ μέσος ἐγεινάμην, ἐγείναο.'

In the Public Library at Basel, according to Haenel, there is a MS. containing Greek epigrams with Latin translations by Musurus, Leoniceno, and Carteromaco:[1] Epigrammata Graeca, per plerosque libros in Latinum sermonem ab aliquot interpretibus M. a Musuro Cretensi, Nicolao Leoniceno, Scipione Carteromacho S. deducta, scripta Venetiis. 4°.

ADDITIONAL NOTE ON THE *Scholia*

A good start was made by Aristide Calderini in 1912 on a study of the *scholia* of the Planudean Anthology; apparently he abandoned the task. As a matter of fact the probable recentness of these notes, and their want of intrinsic value, make them of little importance except to a study of the present kind. Calderini's principal article is: 'Scolî Greci all' Antologia Planudea' in *Memorie del R. Istituto Lombardo di Scienze e Lettere*, Classe di Lettere e Scienze morali e storiche, Vol. 22 (13 of Ser. III), fasc. 8. Milan, 1912. The copies of *scholia* listed by Calderini are as follows:

1. *Schol. Ambros.* [*Cod. Amb.* 333 (= F 30 suppl.), f. 1–102]. 15th cent.
2. *Schol. Monacens.* [*Cod. Monac. Gr.* 130, f. 191–302]. 16th cent. Brought by Stephen Gerlach to Tübingen from Constantinople in 1568.
3. *Schol. Nat. Matrit.* [*Cod. Nat. Matrit.* O.37 (No. 10 in *Cat.*)]. Ann. 1552.
4. *Schol. Escur.* I [*Cod. Escur.* R-III-26 (Miller 56), f. 1–187]. Copied by Andreas Darmarios for Basguno Scolastico, a Spanish nobleman, and finished at Madrid, June, 18, 1577.

Calderini notes as *Schol. Escur.* II, *scholia* contained in a MS. apparently lost in the fire of 1671 [*Cod. Escur.* X-1-16 (Miller 303)]; from a surviving description of the contents of the MS. the *scholia* are judged to have been the same as *Schol. Nat. Matrit.* (No. 3).

margins of which parts of the *scholia* had been written. At all events Pierre Herbert pointed out a copy of that edition, in the Library at Troyes, that contains the *scholia* and that formerly belonged to Pithou.

[1] G. Haenel, *Catalogi Librorum Manuscriptorum*, etc., Leipzig, 1830.

5. *Schol. Reg. Matrit.* [*Cod. Reg. Matrit.* 39]. Also copied by Darmarios, and finished July 24, 1577.
6. *Schol. Laur.* Some notes in *Laur.* 31, 28 (above, p. 101).
7. *Schol. Vat.* I [*Vat. Urb.* 152] (above, p. 33, n. 1).
8. *Schol. Vat.* II [*Vat. Graec.* 1416] 'ἐκ τῶν Μουσούρου καὶ ἄλλων εἰς τὴν τῶν ἐπιγραμμάτων ἀνθολογίαν.' This formerly belonged to Fulvio Orsini, and seems to be written in his hand; its entry in his Inventory reads: 'Libro di varie emendationi del Musuro sopra l' Epigrammi Greci et alcuni epigrammi di più.' (See Nolhac, *Ful. Ors.*, pp. 151, 349 and Sternbach, *Appendix Barb.-Vat.*, p. vi.)
9. *Schol. Paris.* [*Paris. Graec. Suppl.* 316]. Wrongly ascribed to Tzetzes; written in 1579 by Darmarios.

The next four are written in the margins of printed Anthologies:
10. *Schol. edit. Bern.* [Inc. III. 87]. A copy of the 1494 ed.; see Stadtmüller, *Anth. Graec.* 2. xxxii.
11. *Schol. edit. Paris.* [Rés. Y 503]. Also the 1494 ed.; *scholia* are in the hand of Arsenios Apostolios, *q. v.*
12. *Schol. edit. Aug. Tricass.* [above, p. 151]. 'Cum scholiis mss. Marci Musuri, manu Arsenii.'
13. *Schol. edit. Lips.* A copy of the 1494 ed. in the University Library, Leipzig [? the copy mentioned by Jacobs (*Anth. Graec. Comment.* 1. cxxiv) as belonging to Von Murr of Nürnberg, and originally to Lascaris].

Calderini tentatively divides these *scholia* into three groups:
I. *Schol. Ambros.—Schol. Nat. Matrit.* (mostly)—[*Schol. Escur.* II]—*Schol. Reg. Matrit.—Schol. edit. Bern.—Schol. edit. Paris.—Schol. edit. Aug. Tricass.—Schol. edit. Lips.*—[*Schol. Pithoei*]—[*Schol. Petav.*]—*Schol. Wechel.*[1]
II. *Schol. Nat. Matrit.* (in margin)—*Schol. Escur.* I—*Schol. Paris.*
III. *Schol. Monacens.*

Schol. Laur.—Schol. Vat. I—*Schol. Vat.* II—and the few Greek notes printed by Stephanus (1566) and Brunck (1776) in their editions are without known relationships.

The first group embraces the more extensive sets of *scholia*, and the *scholia* that were written in copies of the *ed. pr.* These may well go back to Musurus, as several of them profess to. In his article Calderini makes a detailed comparison only between the *Schol. Ambros.* and the printed *scholia* of the Wechel Anthology, showing that they are substantially the same. The *Schol. Bern.* (10), already studied by Stadtmüller, are like them.

The second group evidently belong together, being all contained in MSS. of similar content copied by Darmarios in 1577 and 1579. They have yet to be studied.

The third group and the remainder are *scholia* that seem not likely to fit into the first or second group. Calderini studied *Schol.*

---

[1] The last three, not among the 13 enumerated above, are, of course, the *scholia* printed in the Wechel Anthology of 1600; above, p. 155, n. 4.

Laur. and the notes printed by Stephanus, in *Classici e Neolatini* 8 (1912). 261–271. The *Schol. Laur.*, he says, seem to have been written by the copyist of the MS. (above, p. 101), but are in two inks, red and black; those in black may have been written at the time when the epigrams were copying, those in red appear to be subsequent additions. Calderini finds these *scholia*—they number only 36—independent of his first group. The 26 brief notes printed by Stephanus are likewise not of the first group, nor have they anything in common with *Schol. Laur.* Calderini believes that Stephanus selected them from a larger body of *scholia* that he had before him.

These brief *scholia* last mentioned evidently have no relation to Musurus; we remain in suspense as to the relations of Group II; but nothing has appeared to cast doubt on the tradition that the most extensive Greek notes on the Anthology are the composition of Musurus.[1]

[To the 13 MSS. of *scholia* listed by Calderini may be added: (1) a MS. in the Bibliotheca Nazionale of Turin (C-VI-11), 16th cent., written by Darmarios at Toledo (Mazzatinti-Sorbelli, *Inventari* 28.42: No. 357); (2) *Vat. Incun.* 813b (above, p. 120, n. 3); (3) a copy of the 1503 Aldine in the Vatican (Vat. A. 18 in-8°)—above, p. 123, n.2; (4) in the Bodleian Library, MS. D'Orville 260 (seemingly a copy of *Cod. Reg. Matrit.* 39).]

FILIPPO BEROALDO THE YOUNGER

(1472–1518)

The younger Beroaldo belonged to the same noble Bolognese family as the elder, though their precise relationship is not known. The younger scholar was a favorite pupil of the elder. He became professor of literature at the age of twenty-six. About the end of the century he removed to Rome, where in 1514 he became president of the Roman Academy. Among his closest friends were Bembo, Bibbiena, Molza, and Flaminio. Cardinal Giovanni de' Medici had attached Beroaldo to himself as secretary, and after becoming pope, as Leo X, took the first opportunity to make him librarian of the Vatican (1516). Beroaldo's literary works are few, but his scholarship is said to have been second to that of none of his contemporaries. He published *C. Taciti Annalium libri v priores* (Rome, 1515); his *Carminum libri tres et Epigrammaton liber* appeared some time after his death (Rome, 1530).

Beroaldo's three books of *Carmina* are almost entirely inspired by Horace; his *Epigrammata* owe most to Catullus, but something as well to the Greek Anthology. In particular he

---

[1] Yet one may ask why, if these notes were only written about 1506, they seem always to be transcribed into copies of the 1494 edition and never into copies of the Aldine ed. of 1503.

translates *A.P.* 7.524; 9.130, and 391; and has echoes of *A.P.*
5.91; 9.346; and 11.164. The following is his version of *A.P.*
7.524:

Sexte, quid est infra?—Tenebrae.—Num scansio ad astra est?—
  Nulla.—Quid est Pluto?—Fabula vana hominum.—
Cerberus estne istic, Proserpina, Thesiphoneque?—
  Non mage quam Pluto quamque ager Elysius.—
Quae natura animae?—Quae corporis. Illa perinde
  Interit ut corpus, nec magis illa viget.
Proinde tibi indulge, dum vivis; dum licet uti,
  Utere deliciis. Omnia mors adimit.

LODOVICO ARIOSTO

(1474–1533)

'When Lodovico Ariosto came to years of adolescence, Tito Strozzi
was the poet of Ferrara, but in the shadow of the father's glory was
growing up the son, Ercole Strozzi, four years Lodovico's senior;
Battista Guarini and Luca Riva continued to spread the work of the
Renaissance, by their school, their commentaries, and their translations, among a generation now fully steeped in classical poetry to such
a degree as to sing to music the Latin odes of Lodovico Carbone in
praise of Ercole I.' In these terms Carducci sums up his description
of the literary surroundings of the young Ariosto, whose youth, he
says, perhaps too absolutely, was 'all Latin.'[1] Ariosto, to be sure, did
not attend the lectures of the younger Guarini or of Luca Riva, but,
with the young Alberto Pio of Carpi, received instruction from the no
less excellent Gregorio da Spoleto. He began the serious writing of
Latin verse when about twenty years of age, and for at least ten years
thereafter regarded himself as a Latin poet, possibly destined to rival
the Strozzi.

Although Gregorio da Spoleto was an excellent Greek scholar,
Ariosto, as he himself relates, never gained a knowledge of the
language.[2] Yet he was not without Greek culture; in him the
Latin translations made by fifteenth-century humanists bore
good fruit; and in particular he appears to be familiar with
Homer and the dramatists. Among his Latin poems are eight
epigrams from the Anthology—*A.P.* 5.81 (2 versions), 95; 9.47,
130, 231; 16.171, 176.[3] All are treated with more freedom than

---

[1] Giosuè Carducci, *La Gioventù di Ludovico Ariosto e la Poesia Latina in Ferrara*
(*Opere*, vol. 15, Bologna, 1905, p. 131).
[2] *Satira* VII, especially lines 166–183; Carducci, *op. cit.*, p. 37.
[3] Ariosto's Latin poems were not printed until 1553, when G. B. Pigna published
them with his own verse and that of Calcagnini (below, p. 247). They are more

Ariosto might have allowed himself had he been translating directly from the Greek. It is useless, however, to speculate on how he may have come by them. He had several friends who could have supplied him with prose versions on which to base his verse—Gregorio da Spoleto, Tito Strozzi, Musurus, or even Janus Lascaris. One thing seems certain—he did not copy any verse-translations made by his predecessors.[1]

Ariosto's eight translations follow—first his two versions of *A.P.* 5.81:[2]

[AD PUELLAM VENDENTEM ROSAS]

Hasne rosas, an te vendes, an utrumque, puella,
    Quae rosa es, atque inquis vendere velle rosas?

DE EADEM

Vendere velle rosas inquis. Cum sis rosa, quaero,
    Tene rosasne velis, virgo, an utrumque dare?

The following is somewhat freely modeled on *A.P.* 5.95:[3]

DE IULIA

O rarum formae decus, o lepidissima verba,
    O bene deductum pollice et ore melos!
An Charitum quarta? an Venus altera, an addita Musis
    Est decima? an simul haec Gratia, Musa, Venus?
Iulia quin sola est, qua cantu Musa, lepore
    Gratia, qua longe est victa decore Venus.

The next is closer to its original—*A.P.* 9.47—but contains a development of Ariosto's own in the second line.[4]

completely given by Polidori in his edition of Ariosto's *Opere Minori*, 2 vols, Florence, 1857. When Carducci wrote his essay above referred to, he was not aware that the eight epigrams here in question were from the Greek. The defect was only in part repaired in a communication from Stefano Grosso printed by Carducci in his second edition (*op. cit.*, pp. 253–260).

[1] *A.P.* 5.95 and 16.171 had been used by Sannazaro, and *A.P.* 9.130 and 16.171 by Politian, but Aristo's versions owe nothing whatever to theirs.

[2] Pigna, p. 295; Polidori 1.356. Titles given in square brackets are those of the autograph MS. at Ferrara, as reported by Carducci, *op. cit.*, pp. 13–26; those not in brackets are from Pigna.

[3] Pigna, p. 294; Polidori 1.354. The original:

Τέσσαρες αἱ Χάριτες, Παφίαι δύο, καὶ δέκα Μοῦσαι,
    Δερκυλὶς ἐν πάσαις Μοῦσα, Χάρις, Παφίη.

[4] Pigna, p. 296; Polidori 1.356. The original:

Τὸν λύκον ἐξ ἰδίων μαζῶν τρέφω οὐκ ἐθέλουσα
    ἀλλά μ' ἀναγκάζει ποιμένος ἀφροσύνη.
αὐξηθεὶς δ'ὑπ' ἐμοῦ, κατ' ἐμοῦ πάλι θηρίον ἔσται·
    ἡ χάρις ἀλλάξαι τὴν φύσιν οὐ δύναται.

In the last line Ariosto originally wrote: *Vertit nam ingenium gratia nulla malum.*

DE LUPO ET OVE

Foetum invita lupae sed iussu nutrit herili,
  Et sua lacte suo pignora fraudat ovis.
Scilicet ut meritam bene de se perdat adultus,
  Mutare ingenium gratia nulla potest.

A.P. 9.130, again, is treated with greater freedom.[1] This composition, if indeed it is not a later work than Carducci supposes, was recollected by the poet long after it was written, and repeated to his son Virginio, who thus reports it:[2] 'Io mi ricordo che mi recitò il principio dell' infrascritto epigramma, la sentenza del quale era, che mentre l' ortolano stava chino a piantar l'erbe, sentì un movimento, al quale rivolgendosi sentì un olivo che incominciò a parlare in questa forma:[3]

Hicne rosas inter Veneris bulbosque Priapi
  Et Bacchi vites, Palladis arbor ero?
Immeritoque obscoena et adultera et ebria dicar,
  Sobria quae semper casta pudensque fui?
Hinc me auferte, aut me ferro succidite, quaeso,
  Ne mihi dent turpem probra aliena notam.'

Plainly the introductory lines recalled by Virginio were never written down.

De Populo et Vite, on a somewhat similar theme, is more literal, but the point is slighted. The original is *A.P.* 9.231:[4]

Arida sum, vireoque aliena populus umbra,
  Sumque racemiferis undique operta comis,
Gratae vitis opus, quae cum moritura iaceret,
  Munere surrexit laeta feraxque meo.
Nunc nostri memor officii, docet unde referri
  Magna etiam possit gratia post obitum.

In the next we have Ariosto's version of *Venus Armata*

---

[1] Pigna, p. 293; Polidori 1.352. The Greek:
  Παλλάδος εἰμὶ φυτόν· Βρομίου τί με θλίβετε κλῶνες;
    ἄρατε τοὺς βότρυας· παρθένος οὐ μεθύω.
[2] Giannandrea Barotti, *Memorie Istoriche di Letterati Ferraresi*, Ferrara, 1792, 1.224; Carducci, *op. cit.*, p. 245.
[3] Entitled *Oliva* in the editions.
[4] Pigna, p. 293; Polidori 1.352. The Greek:
  Αὕην με πλατάνιστον ἐφερπύζουσα καλύπτει
    ἄμπελος· ὀθνείη δ' ἀμφιτέθηλα κόμῃ,
  ἡ πρὶν ἐμοῖς θαλέθουσιν ἐνιθρέψας' ὁροδάμνοις
    βότρυας, ἡ ταύτης οὐκ ἀπετηλοτέρη.
  τοίην μέντοι ἔπειτα τιθηνείσθω τις ἑταίρην,
    ἥτις ἀμείψασθαι καὶ νέκυν οἶδε μόνη.

(*A.P.* 16.171); the reader may compare it with other versions of the theme given in this book:[1]

[IN VENEREM ARMATAM LACEDAEMONE]

Arma, Venus, Martis sunt haec. Quid inutile pondus,
    Mortali bellum si meditare subis?
Nil opus est ferro, ferri cum nuda potentem
    Exueris spoliis omnibus ipsa deum.

Ariosto is one of the few translators of *A.P.* 16.176:[2]

DE SPARTANIS

Arma Deo sua sunt; hospes, ne fallere; Sparta est
    Haec, ubi de patrio sunt data more mihi.
Meque decent saevo in fluctu quae sanguine nata;
    Quae sum Martis amor, quae Lacedaemoniae.

It will be obligatory in the present study to take account of translations and imitations inferior to these; yet some of them certainly bear out the judgment rendered on all Ariosto's Latin verse by his countryman Giraldi—they are a trifle harsh.[3]

Carducci, a little arbitrarily, dates all these—and several other—epigrams within the years 1500–1503, at the very close of Ariosto's Latin period.[4] This may be right; but it is impossible to be sure when they were written. Ariosto knew the elder Strozzi well and was a companion of the younger; he also knew and esteemed Marullus and Musurus.[5]

The Anthology has left, so far as I know, no distinct mark on Ariosto's vernacular works.[6]

---

[1] Pigna, p. 296; Polidori 1.356. *A.P.* 16.171 is given above, p. 136, n. 2. In line 2, Ariosto first wrote: *si meditare paras;* in line 4, *deum* is for an earlier *Jovem.*

[2] Pigna, p. 294; Polidori 1.352. The Greek:

Καὶ Κύπρις Σπάρτας· οὐκ ἄστεσιν οἷά τ' ἐν ἄλλοις
    ἵδρυται, μαλακὰς ἐσσαμένα στολίδας·
ἀλλὰ κατὰ κρατὸς μὲν ἔχει κόρυν ἀντὶ καλύπτρας,
    ἀντὶ δὲ χρυσείων ἀκρεμόνων κάμακα.
οὐ γὰρ χρὴ τευχέων εἶναι δίχα τὰν παράκοιτιν
    Θρᾳκὸς Ἐνναλίου καὶ Λακεδαιμονίαν.

[3] Ingeniosa sed duriuscula (*Poet. Nost. Temp. i* in *Op.* (1580) 2.395).

[4] Carducci, *op. cit.*, pp. 198, 211–2.

[5] Cf. above, p. 113, n. 1. Musurus is joined with Lascaris and Navagero in the famous catalogue in Canto 46 of the *Orlando*. In all some seventeen persons named in that list are mentioned in the present study as influenced by the Anthology—evidence enough of the degree to which the Greek epigrams had penetrated the literary circles of the early sixteenth century.

[6] Cf., however, above, p. 14, n. 2. The Latin poems of Lodovico's brother Gabriele show no knowledge of the Greek epigrams.

ANDREA DAZZI (DACTIUS)
(1475–1548)

Dazzi was a Florentine. He early lost his father, and his education was interrupted by numerous hardships. After 1502 he taught Greek and Latin in Florence, and not even the total loss of his sight, which overtook him in his later years, could make him lay aside his career. His only published work seems to be his *Poemata*, published at Florence in the year following his death, by his son Giovanni. The poems consist of *Aeluromachiae libri iii*, *Sylvae octo*, and *Epicedia et Poemata Varia*. They are of a miscellaneous nature, but on the whole reflect the taste of the last years of the fifteenth century. Some epistles and a few verses by Dazzi remain unprinted in the Laurentian Library.[1]

In the men of Dazzi's generation, pupils of Politian, Aldus, and Lascaris, Greek studies bore fruit in the form of imitations; their pupils again—Vettori studied with Dazzi—turned more to interpretation and text-criticism. Dazzi has many original Greek poems—more than Politian; one (*Poem.*, p. 111) is a Greek epitaph for Alessandra Scala. His translations from the Anthology are fairly numerous; they are mingled with his own inventions, but the source is always indicated. The satirical strain is strong in Dazzi, and he shows a preference for the satirical parts of the Anthology.[2] The following, his version of *A.P.* 11.214, is neat, and gains some additional interest from being imitated in Italian by Marino (below, p. 352):

E GRAECO

Deucaliona meus pinxit Liger et Phaëtonta,
Et quo sit pretio dignus uterque rogat.
'Da sua cuique, Liger,' dictant oracula,—'dignus
Igne suo Phaëton, aequore Deucalion.'

MARCANTONIO CASANOVA
(1476–1527)

While one of the more celebrated neo-Latin poets, Casanova has never been accorded a separate edition of his verse; his poems, mainly epigrams, were printed in Ubaldini's *Carmina Poetarum Nobilium* (Milan, 1563) and may also be read in the third volume of the *Carmina Illustr. Poetarum Ital.* His unhappy life—he was a Roman,

---

[1] On Dazzi's poems see Ellinger 1.185, and W. Rüdiger, *Andreas Dactius aus Florenz* (Studien zur humanistischen Litteratur Italiens, Heft 2), Halle, 1897.

[2] He translates *A.P.* 6.163; 7.308; 9.138, 231; 11.19, 77, 131, 159, 166, 169, 186, 187, 198, 214, 406; 12.60; 16.19.

and perished from hunger or the plague following the sack of Rome—is sketched by Ellinger (1.258).

Casanova has two echoes of the Anthology, neither very close; one of *A.P.* 9.61 and one of 16.297. The first is:

DE SPARTANA MATRE FILIUM INTERFICIENTE

Dum se et dum patria indignum Spartana necaret,
Quaerenti dixit: 'Nunc ego mater ero—
Plus pariet mihi ventre manus: facit ista parentem,
Quae mihi, quae patriae non peritura parit.'

ZENOBIO ACCIAIUOLI
(1461–1519)

Acciaiuoli was a Florentine, and in his youth a close friend of Politian and Ficino. We have already noticed his unfulfilled intention of publishing Politian's Greek epigrams (above, p. 139). He joined the Dominican Order, weathered the stormy years that followed the expulsion of Piero de' Medici, and at last found a haven with Leo X, who made him prefect of the Vatican Library. To him are due a number of translations from the Greek—parts of Eusebius, Olympiodorus, Theodoretus, and the like. He is mentioned here because a copy of the 1494 edition of the Anthology, recorded by Jacobs (*Anth. Graec.* Comment. 1.cxxiv), is reported to contain the *scholia* ascribed to Musurus written in Acciaiuoli's hand. Jacobs had his information from Wilhelm Uhden, who had examined the volume in the library of Cardinal Zelada in Rome.

FRANCESCO PUCCI
(1462–1512)

Of Francesco Pucci nothing is known save what appears in his epitaph, and even his epitaph seems to exist only in a transcription.[1] It was copied from Pucci's tomb in the Church of S. Onofrio in Rome by Alveri for his *Roma in Ogni Stato* (Rome, 1664) as follows (as the writer mentioned in the footnote says, the first letter is an obvious misprint):

---

[1] I have not gone beyond the careful researches of a writer in *Notes and Queries* 10.9.324 who signed himself V.H.I.L.I.C.I.V. He made several unsuccessful attempts to have the tomb of Pucci discovered in S. Onofrio.

ΙΝΩΘΙ ΣΑΥΤΟΝ

Francisco Puccio Patria & Canon. Florentino Archidiacono Legionen.
Card. de Aragonia a secretis fide-
lissimorum gravitate ingenioque
praestanti SS. utriusque linguae
multiplicisque doctrinae Professori
qui plerisque Regibus Aragon. e-
gregiam operam navavit cuique
importuna mors maioresque honores ti-
tulosq; praeripuit vix. ann. xlix.
mens. xi. d. xxi. obijt die xxiv.
Aug. Ann. MDXII amici flen-
tes posuere.
Inveni portū spes et fortuna valete
Nil mihi vobiscū ludite nūc alios.

The verse at the end is a translation of *A.P.* 9.49 (above, p.
27); and the translation is that of Janus Pannonius (below,
p. 284)—but also, as it happens, the version hit upon by
William Lily.[1]

JOANNES PETRUS FERETRIUS

(*fl.* 1500)

Feretrius was a native of Ravenna, and a doctor of civil and
canon law at the University of Siena. He has verses that echo
A.P. 9.66:[2]

Myrteolis flores legerent cum forte canistris,
Orchomeni ad ripas, Charitum Libethrides agmen,
Audito obstupuit Franciscae carmine Scottae
Mnemosyne et dixit: 'Decima est mihi nata puella.'

BASILIUS CHALCONDYLES

(1490–1514)

Basilius Chalcondyles, son of Demetrius, in a letter to Janus
Parrhasius, dated Rome, August 31, but without indication of
the year, urges Parrhasius to hasten to the city to occupy the
chair of Eloquence presented to him by Leo X, and incidentally

---

[1] The translation does not appear in Pannonius' works until the ed. of 1569, but as
it does appear in the ed. of 1784, which was based on an examination of Pannonius'
MSS., the writer in *N. & Q.* seems to be right in believing it authentic. Lily's version
was first printed in 1518.

[2] Quoted by Del Lungo, *op. cit.*, p. 126 n., from *Sena Vetus, per Io. Petrum Feretrium
. . . Carmine Illustrata*, Siena (Simeone Rubeo), 1513 (vs. 378–81).

draws an argument from *A.P.* 9.221. Since Parrhasius' removal from Cosenza to Rome is well known to have taken place in 1514 (Tiraboschi, *Storia* 7.3.8), the letter certainly belongs to that year. Chalcondyles' letter is a reply to one from Parrhasius, hastily written on August 25, in which he related two domestic misfortunes that were likely to delay his coming.[1] In the first place, the widow of one of his brothers had remarried, and it was necessary to return her dowry. The second calamity was more serious, and concerned the family of another brother. One of this brother's daughters had been married to a certain Niccolò Bombino; she died; and some time later Bombino was discovered to have seduced a sister of his dead wife. As this was designated incest, both, it seems, were liable to the death penalty, unless they could secure from the pope a dispensation allowing them to marry. Parrhasius desired Chalcondyles to get the dispensation. It was granted, and Chalcondyles' reply is designed to be wholly reassuring in its lightness of tone. I quote only the passage that relates to the epigram:

Abrumpendae tibi sunt omnes tricae atque domesticae necessitates, neque te vincant illecebrae semperque viris exitiosae muliebres lachrymae. Nosti puto argumentum epigrammatis de Cupidine, in quo tantulus infans fortissimi leonis tergo eques insidet, altera manu flagellum, quo verbera intendit, altera habenas continens. Cave ne te talem mulierculis γυναίοις exhibeas, tametsi illis parum obnoxium atque obtemperantem te sciebam.

ANGELO COLOCCI

(1467–1549)

Colocci came of a noble and wealthy family of Iesi in the March of Ancona. Political troubles exiled them to Naples, where Angelo allied himself with the circle of Pontano. Honorably recalled to Iesi, he was entrusted in 1498 with an embassy to Alexander VI. He resolved to remain in Rome, and there his wealth and the ecclesiastical offices that later came to him enabled him to become one of the great patrons of the age. In his famous gardens he received the Roman Academy,

---

[1] Both letters are in the following volume: *Marquardi Gudii . . . Epistolae, quibus accedunt ex Bibliotheca Gudiana Clariss. et Doctiss. Virorum . . . Epistolae*, ed. by Peter Burmann, Utrecht, 1697, pp. 137–9. Joannes Basilius Romulus Chalcondyles was born at Florence in 1490; his sister, Theodora, was Parrhasius' wife. It is pleasant to find Janus Lascaris protecting the children of his old teacher; in the present letter the younger Chalcondyles refers to him as 'patronus et fautor noster' (whose authority with the pope is second to none—'cuius unius perlonge maxima est authoritas'). Basilius was a pupil of Lascaris. He must have died soon after writing this letter, if, as Valeriano says (*De Infelic.*), he was twenty-four when he died. The date of his birth is fixed by his father's records, which are still preserved (Legrand, *Bibl. Hell.* 2.305–6).

homeless since the death of Pomponio Leto. Colocci was twice married. After the death of his second wife he took orders, became Secretary to Leo X, and received the reversion of the bishopric of Nocera. Clement VII increased his honors, and used him in the negotiations that allied the papacy with Francis I, and led to the sack of Rome in 1527. In that disaster Colocci's house was burned, his collections destroyed, and himself made to pay a ransom for his liberty. In 1537 he received the bishopric of Nocera, which he resigned in 1546 in favor of a nephew. He died at Rome three years later.

Apparently Colocci was totally ignorant of Greek.[1] Yet he took an interest in Greek literature through translations, some of them specially made for him by his friends. He also collected Greek books.

Colocci was an early protector of Fulvio Orsini, who thus became familiar with the library formed by Colocci after his first was pillaged. According to Harles (Fabricius, *Bibl. Graec.* 4.430), Orsini wrote in his own MS. of the Planudean Anthology (?*Vat. Graec.* 1372), at the end of Planudes' note on his omissions: 'ἀλλὰ καὶ ταῦτα ἐν παλαιῷ εἰσι παρ' Ἀγγέλου τοῦ Κολλωτίου.' Harles and others have imagined that this might mean that Colocci possessed our Palatine MS.; but the work of Sternbach allows us only to suppose it was a brief Appendix.[2]

Colocci had also a copy of the 1494 Anthology with a few, naturally unimportant, notes in his own hand. It may have come to him from Carteromaco.[3]

Possibly the following Latin epigram by Colocci is based on *A.P.* 6.236, which he could have known through one of his friends, as Carteromaco or Lascaris:[4]

> Cum ratis Antoni pelago pugnavit aperto,
>   Quae non sustinuit Caesaris arma Dei,
> In Latium translata Forum est, inque aere tridenti
>   Caerea tecta sibi daedala fecit apis.
> Fatale hoc rostris fuit, ut Ciceronis adempti
>   Pro dulci eloquio dulcia mella forent.

---

[1] See the evidence of De Nolhac in *Mélanges d'Archéol. et d'Hist.* 6 (1886). 270. Cf. the words of Carteromaco to Colocci, above, p. 154.

[2] Above, p. 32. Several brief appendices to the *Planudea* were made in the sixteenth century—one by Lascaris (above, p. 120) and another in Orsini's library, described in his Inventory (Nolhac, p. 355) as : 'Epigrammatario d'Aldo [1503], con un quinterno d'Epigrammi non impressi.'

[3] Nolhac, *Fulvio Orsini*, pp. 158 n. 4 and 182.

[4] Colocci's Latin poems are highly praised; cf. Ellinger 1.220-2 and above, p. 154. Orsini intended to publish them, but they remained for the most part unprinted till edited with Colocci's Italian verse by G. F. Lancelotti, Rome, 1772. I have seen only the selection in *Carm. Illust. Poet. Ital.*, vol. 3.

The point is different from that of the Greek, which merely
states that Caesar has made the arms of his enemy bear the
fruits of peace.

LUDOVICUS CAELIUS RHODIGINUS (RICCHIERI)

(*c.* 1460—*c.* 1525)

Ricchieri, generally called Rhodiginus from the name of his native
place, Rovigo (*Lat.* Rhodigium), studied philosophy under Niccolò
Leoniceno at Ferrara, and law at Padua. After some years spent in
France, he returned in 1491 to Rovigo, and attained a public chair as
professor (1497). For reasons unknown he lost his place and was
banished in 1505. Thereafter his life was a series of vicissitudes. He
opened a school that had some success, at Vicenza. Called to Ferrara
in 1508 by Alfonso I, he had soon to leave because of the wars, and
lived for a time wretchedly at Padua. In 1512 he was living at Reggio.
In 1515 Francis I appointed him to the chair Chalcondyles had held
at Milan; and there he remained till the waning of the French authority made it prudent for him to withdraw again to Padua (1521).
Finally the influence of his foreign friends sufficed to get him recalled
to Rovigo (1523), where he died, his death being hastened, it is said,
by the news of Francis' capture at Pavia. Rhodiginus' chief work is
his *Antiquae Lectiones,* of which sixteen books appeared at Venice in
1516 (Paris, 1517), and the remaining fourteen after his death in an
edition got out by a nephew, Camillo Ricchieri, at Basel in 1550.[1]
It consists of a series of chapters on all manner of subjects connected
with antiquity.

In Rhodiginus' vast encyclopedia the Anthology could not
fail to come several times into play. An epigram illustrative of a
given point is commonly quoted with the addition of a prose
translation or paraphrase; and in this way Rhodiginus employs
A.P. 6.309.1–2; 7.348; 9.133, 190.7–8, 320, 540; 10.84, 112;
11.50, 436; and 13.29. For example, *A.P.* 9.190 is quoted in a
chapter (14.1) on 'Mulieres in doctrinis celebres,' in which he
speaks particularly of Corinna and Erinna. Most of what he
says about Erinna comes from the epigram, though he quotes
only the last two lines. Once in passing he makes a perfunctory
reference to the epigrammatists in general (7.4): 'Epigrammato-
graphi. . . . In hoc genere Simonides inclaruit antiquior, cuius
commeminit Herodotus; junior Alcaeus, Vespasiani tempestate ac Titi; Atheniensis Proclus, Palladas, Agathias, innumeri
alii.'

---

[1] My references are to the Wechel edition of 1599 in one volume: *Lectionum Anti-*
quarum libri triginta.

ANGELO BARBATO

(*fl.* 1517)

Angelo Barbato, otherwise unknown, was the author of a translation of Plutarch's *De Exilio*, published in 1517 at Paris.[1] In it he necessarily translated *A.P.* 7.709 on Alcman, which he put into verse as follows:

> Sardiaci patres vestro sub culmine tecti,
>   Auratis celsas vestibus aut macelas,
> Concava discinctus pulsarem tympana, qui nunc
>   Spartanis Alcman civibus annumeror,
> Vatibus et Graiis: me dulcis Musa tyrannos
>   Dascyleon supra sustulit et Gygeon.

THE EDITION OF THE GIUNTI

(1519)

The third printed edition of the Anthology was put out by the heirs of Filippo Giunta—his sons Bernardo and Benedetto —at Florence in 1519: Ἀνθολογία Διαφόρων Ἐπιγραμμάτων. *Florilegium Diversorum Epigrammatum in septem libros.* At the end: *Impressum Florentiae per heredes Philippi Juntae Florentini.*(8ᵛᵒ.) It is said to be only an incorrect reprint of the first Aldine. Although it promises corrections and additions, these turn out to be merely those made by Aldus in 1503.[2]

GIROLAMO ANGERIANO

(*fl.* 1520)

No details of the life of Angeriano seem to be known. From his books we can only learn that he was originally from Naples, but was

---

[1] It is included in Stephanus' Plutarch of 1572, from which I quote.

[2] Jacobs, *Anth. Graec.* Proleg. p. xcvii. I have not myself examined this edition. Renouard notices (*Ann. des Alde*, 1.68) that it was in the Juntine edition that a curious error, perpetuated in the edition of Badius Ascensius and even in that of Stephanus, was first made. Brunck, who had not seen the Juntine ed., notices it first in Ascensius. This was in the poem of Paulus Silentiarius on the *Thermae*, introduced into the Anthology by Aldus from the Marcian ms. Aldus printed it on four pages, two columns to a page, but in such a way that one is not to read down the column, but across the page from column to column. The Juntine editors in each case, not having read the poem, set the second column on the end of the first, so that down to line 27 the lines 1, 3, 5, 7, etc., follow each other, then after 27, the lines 2, 4, 6, and so on. Stephanus too failed to try to read the poem he was printing. The Aldine editions, since they followed that of 1503, never fell into the error; but that was mere luck; the editors mechanically set up the pages as they were in the first ed., and doubtless thought as did the Juntine editors that the columns were to be read downwards. The error was first pointed out by Huet.

connected with the literary men of Rome at the beginning of the sixteenth century. His Latin poems, however, were very well known in
the sixteenth century, for all that they seem to have escaped the notice
of Giraldi; at least four editions were called for. They were first
printed at Naples in 1520: 'Ερωτοπαίγνιον, *Eclogae*, *De Obitu Lydae*,
De Vero Poeta, *De Parthenope*.[1] They were evidently read in England,
as the *Erotopaegnion* has been shown to form one of the two principal
sources of Giles Fletcher's *Licia*.[2] In France Angeriano was admired
and imitated by Ronsard and his group.

Angeriano is a typical 'anacreontic' poet, and he evidently
acquired his manner largely from a study of the Greek epigrams. His similarity to the Greeks was noticed by Scaliger,
who says of him:[3] 'Angerianus fecit arguta multa epigrammata,
sed parum argute. Neque enim satis est, sententias pedibus
conclusisse. Romanis, dico, nam Graeci modo dicant, quo
dicant modo, nihil pensi habent. Graece igitur ea si essent
scripta, pro divinis haberentur. Nunc autem Latina puritas
alias leges postulat.' As a matter of fact, thirty of Angeriano's
poems are more or less direct translations from the Anthology.[4]

Unlike most of his contemporaries, but true to his own vein,
Angeriano favors the amatory epigrams. The following represents *A.P.* 5.15:

> Nunc ubi Praxiteles? ubi Scopas? priscaque virtus
>   Illorum artificum? cuncta sepulta iacent.
> Heu doleo, nostrae quis marmore scalpet in albo
>   Pectora? quis fulgens lumen et ora deae?
> Erigere huic statuam, et templum aedificare decebat,
>   Oblatas caperet pro Iove ut una preces.

At times he takes great liberties with his originals. Venus in
Armor (*A.P.* 16.171) supplies him with the following theme:

DE CAELIA ET AMORE

> Ibat venatum in silvas, telumque gerebat
>   Caelia, et alipedi maxima stabat equo.
> Obvius it volucris puer illi telaque vibrans

---

[1] My references are to this edition. There was an edition at Venice (Sabienses),
1535; another (with the poems of Marullus and Joannes Secundus), Paris, 1542; and
another, Paris, 1582. Angeriano was also the author of *De Miseria Principum*, Florence
(Giunti), 1522.

[2] *Les Sonnets Élizabéthains* by Miss Janet G. Scott, Paris, 1929, p. 105.

[3] *Poetics*, Book 6.

[4] *A.P.* 5.15, 70, 74, 80, 92, 95, 97 (2 versions), 98, 144, 145, 155 (2 imitations), 168,
268 (?); 9.48, 65, 440, 497, 515, 627 (2 imitations); 10.84, 85; 11.3, 53; 16.160 (2 imitations), 171, 211 (?).

'Certemus, fatur, dum geris arma, simul.'
Caelia sed tenerum ridens ait: 'Arma gerentem
Stulte petis? Non te vici ego inermis? Abi.'

THE SECOND ALDINE ANTHOLOGY

(1521)

After the death of the elder Aldus (1515) and during the minority of his sons, the Aldine Press was conducted by Aldus' father-in-law, Andrea Torresano d'Asola and the latter's sons Giovan Francesco and Federico. This arrangement lasted until 1529; then after an interval Paolo Manuzio, the son of Aldus, succeeded to the control (below, p. 230).

In January, 1521, two years after the appearance of the Juntine edition, the Asolani brought out the second Aldine Anthology: *Florilegium Diversorum Epigrammatum in septem libros, Solerti nuper repurgatum cura . . .* [Greek title] *Nunc exit castigatius quam alias umquam, pristinis elustratum erroribus multisque adauctum epigrammatibus.*[1]

It has been said that the fault of the Aldine editions produced under Andrea d'Asola and his sons is that the publishers depended wholly on their own scholarship for their texts. Probably the *solertus* of the title-page was Giovanni Francesco, as we have evidence that he was interested in the epigrams.

The second Aldine was set up from a copy of the first; and most of the improvements in the text consist in the insertion, at the proper points, of the material placed in the Ἐπιδιόρθωσις of the first edition (above, p. 149). The last phrase of the title—*multisque adauctum epigrammatibus*—is not justified. The editor, by numbering the folios and the chapters of the Anthology, has made a more useful book than his predecessors.

There are said to be some few corrections in this edition which go beyond the Ἐπιδ. of 1503; and these have been supposed to come from the copy of the 1494 edition in which Aldus made his notes, and which also bears notes in the hand of Francesco d'Asola.[2] I cannot find, however, that anything at all

---

[1] A copy of the second Aldine, now in the British Museum, was owned and annotated by Richard Bentley.

[2] Pierre Herbert (*Trav. Inéd.*, p. 110) emphatically states that this is so, but gives no evidence. I have not been able to make a complete collation of the two editions, but in a brief comparison of them have found nothing new in the text of 1521 that is not already in the Ἐπιδ. of 1503.

significant is printed for the first time in the second Aldine. Possibly Renouard's book was used by Aldus for a collation of the Marcian MS.; the variants found were noted in the margin of the book; and—it being too late to introduce them into the text of the 1503 edition—they were gathered into the Ἐπιδιόρθωσις. The volume was then saved and employed for the second Aldine, the corrections being more easily introduced into the text from it than from the Ἐπιδ. of 1503. There are notes in it also by Francesco d'Asola. The printers' marks noticed by Renouard may be those made at the printing of the second edition.[1]

The notes added to this copy of the 1494 edition by Asolano were in part derived from Marcus Musurus. Thus, as already noticed above, p. 155, after some remarks in the margin of the seventh book he writes: 'Hoc audivi a Marco Musuro, viro optimo, Patavii, 1506'; and again in the margin of Book 3 are the initials 'M.M.'[2] In a second copy of the 1494 edition, which had come to Asolano from Arsenios, there is further evidence that he had heard or studied the notes of Musurus.[3]

The beautiful Parallel Lives of Plutarch, published by the Aldine Press in 1519, was edited by Giovan Francesco and dedicated to Bembo.[4] After the table of Contents is printed *A.P.* 16.331 with the following translation (? by the editor):

> Hanc statuam posuere tibi, Plutarche, decoram
> Usque adeo Ausonium martia corda genus:
> Inclyta Graiugenum quia confers gesta Latinis,
> Graecaque Romanis nomina principibus.
> At tamen ipse tibi nequeas componere quemquam,
> Quod similem non sit, nec reperire parem.

---

[1] Renouard's remarks quoted above (p. 149) thus continue: 'On y trouve en outre d'autres corrections, les unes de la main d'Alde, les autres de celle de F. d'Asola, dont j'ai confronté l'écriture avec celle d'un Homère de 1488, rempli de notes manuscrites, existant à la Bibliothèque Nationale. Cet exemplaire de l'Anthologie aura été conservé avec soin, d'abord par Alde et ensuite par ses successeurs, avec l'intention d'en faire usage dans la plus prochaine réimpression. C'est ce qui a été depuis effectué en 1521, l'édition de cette année ayant toutes celles des corrections portées sur cet exemplaire qui ne sont pas encore dans l'édition précédente.'

[2] Pierre Herbert, *Trav. Inéd.*, p. 109.

[3] Above, p. 150.

[4] *Plutarchi quae vocantur Parallela*, etc. Venice, fol., 1519.

GIORGIO ANSELMO (GEORGIUS ANSELMUS NEPOS)

(*c.* 1470–1525)

Anselmo belonged to a noble family of Parma, and spent his life in that city, practising medicine, and perhaps teaching in the university. He was on friendly terms with the great Latin poets of his day— Marullus, Navagero, and Pontano. In addition to his poems, which are mainly amatory verses, we have from Anselmo a commentary on Plautus (Parma, 1509; Venice, 1518) and a life of the famous romancer Caviceo (in the latter's *Libro del Peregrino*, in the second edition, Parma, 1513, and subsequently). Anselmo's poems appeared post-humously: *Epigrammaton libri septem*, Parma, 1526.[1]

Anselmo's renderings from the Anthology, numbering twenty-eight, are firm and true, and this style marks him as belonging to the good age of modern Latin poetry. He appears to have served at one time in the wars (Ellinger, p. 118), a fact that lends point to the title under which his version of *A.P.* 7.233 is printed—*De se ipso:*

> Quem non hostiles debellavere phalanges,
>   Nunc intestino languidus hoste premor.
> Quin eat in pectus prius hoc Aedapsius ensis,
>   Hoste velut, pulsa Febre, perire iuvat.

More in Anselmo's vein is *A.P.* 5.14:

> Suavia mi Ina nimis tua suavia summa madescunt
>   Vel mea vix blandis si labia in labiis.
> At labia actutum si quid per summa morantur,
>   Eximis ex imis unguibus, Ina, animam.

Most of Anselmo's love-poems are addressed to 'Furnia,' as is the following version of *A.P.* 5.225:

> Plaga Amor est misero; fluit alto a vulnere tabes;
>   Heu! numquam sicco a vulnere inops lacrima.
> Deficit auxilii mens indiga—nulla Machaon
>   Sollicitus spargis pharmaca semianimi.
> Telephus ah! perii, nisi tu, fera Furnia, Achilles:
>   Forma salus eadem est unica, quae pupugit.

He translates *A.P.* 9.515 also for Furnia:

> Gratiae erant quondam tres; sed nunc addita quarta es,
>   Furnia: Gratiae enim gratiam et inde petunt.

---

[1] My references are to the 1526 edition; a second was published at Venice in 1528. On Anselmo's poetry see Ellinger 1.117–20.

In Amorem Ligatum is a version of *A.P.* 16.198:

> Funde diu vinctus gemitum, deus improbe, et exlex
>   Funde diu tepidas ex oculis lacrimas;
> Praedo pudicitiae et rationis, mentis abactor,
>   Caecum vulnus, edax cura, protervus Amor.
> Absolvunt homines gravidis tua vincula curis:
>   Tu modo da rapidis irrita verba Notis.
> Nam quem accendisti miseris in mentibus ignem,
>   Extinctum lacrimis nunc quoque cerne tuis.

Anselmo's epigrams include translations of the following: *A.P.* 5.14, 74, 78, 95, 225; 6.334; 7.1, 233, 666; 9.61, 146, 163, 192, 293, 321, 323, 447, 515, 737; 11.76, 266, 273, 278, 431; 12.60; 16.1, 107, 198.

GIANO ANISIO (ANYSIUS)
(1472–*c.* 1536)

In Anisio we have one more Latin poet of Pontano's Academy who gave his attention to the Greek epigrams. He was young enough to form a link between Pontano's generation and that of Minturno. It was his generation that admired Vittoria Colonna, to whom he himself addressed the following somewhat harsh version of *A.P.* 9.515:

> Tres Charites sunt, sed Victoria, quae tribus una,
>   Sit nata, ipsam habeant ut Charites charita.

These lines give the principal character of Anisio's verse—contemporary allusion and personal details mingled with literary reminiscences.[1] His verse is usually smoother.

At times he treats the borrowed theme with some freedom, as when *A.P.* 6.1 becomes:

> Qua non in Latio forma praestantior ulla,
>   Aut fuit, aut reliqua in tempora forsan erit,
> Suspendit speculum tibi Myrtis pulchra, Dione,
>   Amplius haud rugas passa videre suas.

In honor of Virgil he combines two epigrams on Homer (*A.P.* 9.455 and 575):

> Aureus aurata cithara cantabat Apollo,
>   Excepit vates carmina Virgilius,

---

[1] *Varia Poemata et Satyrae ad Pompeium Columnam Card.* Naples, 1531. See Ellinger's estimate of Anisio, *op. cit.* 1.67–9.

Luminaque extingui poterunt prius aurea Phoebi,
Et mundi immensi sydera deficere,
Quam tanti vatis deleri nomen honorque
Quem celebrat fama, et charta sacravit anus.

'*Charta anus*' is from Catullus (68.46). At other times Anisio is simply literal, as when he translates *A.P.* 16.14:

Heus tu qui ad fontem flammatum pingis Amorem,
Falleris, haud ignem extinguit Amoris aqua.

In all, Anisio makes use of *A.P.* 5.74, 78, 237; 6.1; 7.153; 9.39, 108, 157, 158, 166, 258, 455, 497, 515, 549, 575, 593; 10.41; 11.52, 381; 16.14.

GIAMPIETRO VALERIANO BOLZANI (JOANNES PIERIUS VALERIANUS)
(1477–1558)

Valeriano is the earliest of the really considerable translators from the Anthology. He was born at Belluno of a noble family; yet they were too impoverished to give him an education. On the death of his father, an uncle, Urbano Bolzani, remembered as a Franciscan traveller, took him to Venice. There he studied under Benedetto Brugnolo, Giorgio Valla, Janus Lascaris, and Sabellico. In 1512, after some years that we cannot make out, but spent between Venice and Rome, he found an asylum in the house of Cardinal Giovanni de' Medici. When the Cardinal became Leo X (1513), Valeriano was made tutor to his nephews. Under Clement VII his fortunes rose still higher, and he held several offices of honor about the pope. He followed the young Medici to Florence, fled from Florence with them in 1527, and returned with them in 1530. After the death of Ippolito (1535) and the murder of Alessandro (1537), he retired to his studies at Padua. Valeriano produced several works of great learning, among which may be mentioned his *Hieroglyphica, sive de Sacris Aegyptiorum aliarumque Gentium Litteris Commentariorum libri lviii* (Basel, 1556); but the work by which he will be remembered is his brief and entertaining collection of anecdotes: *De Literatorum Infelicitate*, into which is gathered a certain amount of valuable information on the literary men of the period. It was not published till long after the writer's death. His *Poemata* were published at Basel in 1538; *Amorum libri v et alia Poemata*, Venice, 1549, and *Hexametri, Odae, et Epigrammata*, Venice, 1550.[1] A good account of Valeriano is given by Roscoe, *Leo X* (1846) 2.302–304.

---

[1] I use the volume: *Pro Sacerdotum Barbis . . . Declamatio . . . accesserunt Varia Poemata dimidia parte auctiora.* Frankfort on Main (Erasmus Kämpffer), 1613 (referred to in the Register as '*Poem.*'). All Valeriano's translations from the Anthology may also be found in the *Carm. Illust. Poet. Ital.*, vol. 10.

One entire section of Valeriano's Latin poems, consisting of 54 epigrams, is translated from the Anthology. These translations are addressed to a certain Giovan Cornelio Fantini, who appears to have asked for a copy of them. Valeriano insists that they were the exercises of his boyhood: at that time he had made many translations from the epigrams, sometimes in prose, sometimes in verse, and sometimes he had composed replies to his Greek original. They were first published with the *Hexametri* of 1550.[1]

> Ad Joann. Cornelium Fantini Clariss. F. Epigrammata Graeca, olim a me Latina facta, deposcentem.
>
> Quid me, Iane, iubes studium puerile tot annos
>   Posthabitum immemorem nunc renovare senem?
> Scilicet antiquos tibi vis me promere lusus,
>   Et data Atheneae Romula plectra lyrae.
> Haec etenim tibi erant cordi memini et mihi cordi
>   Illud idem, noram quod placuisse tibi;
> Multa quidem tunc versa mihi pede libera ab omni,
>   Multa etiam iniectis undique compedibus,
> Nec satis interdum Graecis insistere verbis,
>   Saepe etiam contra ludere lusus erat.
> Sed iuveni illa quidem vix allatura decorem,
>   Nunc forte opprobrio, si repetantur, erunt.
> Quid, rogo, quae surgit nunc aetas aurea dicet?
>   Nam nostra argento vix numeranda fuit.
> Vestra quid in veras Flammata Academia laudes,
>   Quae patrocinio nunc viget aucta tuo?
> Cum nos vilia quaedam et inepta parasse videbunt
>   Ipsi auro, gemmis, murice conspicui.
> Verum olim haec, olim perierunt ludicra nobis,
>   Scilicet aetati nunc magis apta tuae.
> Esto datum vetulis equitare in arundine Graiis,
>   Censura tamen hoc non licet Ausonia:
> Sed puerum esse mihi tam grandi aetate vetat quis,
>   Ante annos partes si senis ipse rapis?
> Quare age, quod tanto studio me poscis, habeto:
>   Insanire licet vindice amicitia.

Valeriano's taste in Greek epigrams—formed probably by Janus Lascaris—is in harmony with that of the Renaissance in general; he prefers the declamatory and moral epigrams of Books 9 and 10. *A.P.* 9.163, an epigram that attracted many translators, thus appears in his version:

[1] *Poem.*, p. 112.

Igne ex Iliaco telisque hostilibus heros
 Aeneas referens pondera cara patrem,
Argivis, 'Miserescite, ait: sene praeda retracto
 Parva erit, at nato maxima ut extulerit.'

He is among the first to turn the Greek epigrams to the purposes of contemporary allusion.[1] Thus *A.P.* 9.184, when translated, is inscribed: *In laudem Jo. Aurelii Augurelli, De novem Lyricis; A.P.* 5.80: *Philodemi ad Xanthippen, nos vero ad Flaviam; A.P.* 7.109; *Ad illud Antipatri de Platone, nos de marmoreo eius capite apud Bellinos Venetiis.* The last-mentioned reads as follows:

Produxit Aesculapium mortalibus
Apollo, corpus ut foveret languidum:
Dehinc Platonem protulit sanctissimum,
Animum ut foveret, et beatum redderet;
Qui mox peractis lege nuptiis sua
Adscendit urbem quam sibi construxerat,
Et collocarat in pavimento Iovis;
Nobis relicta, quam vides, imagine.

Valeriano is perhaps the first to write replies to some of the epigrams, a practice in which he had many followers. He has answers to *A.P.* 9.375 and 16.14, first, of course, translating the epigram in question. Here follows *A.P.* 16.14:

ZENODOTI

Exculptum ad fontes quis consecravit Amorem,
 Ignem hunc forte ratus posse perire in aquis?

ZENODOTO RESPONDET

Propter aquas, flammae dominum non fixit Amorem,
 Extingui hos ignes quod putet ullus aquis:
Sed quia, visceribus succensis, unda ab ocellis
 Liquitur, estque simul flammae et aquae dominus.

These translations were somewhat widely read, and were taken into various books where versions of the Greek epigrams were wanted—for example, into the Commentary of the 1621 edition of Alciati's *Emblemata*. Valeriano translates *A.P.* 5.80, 81; 7.109, 309, 669 (2 versions), 670; 9.10, 13, 31, 50, 54, 74, 94, 126, 163, 184, 199, 331, 375 (with a reply), 394 (with supplementary verses), 410, 489 (with explanatory verses), 497, 515 (with a free imitation); 10.28, 37, 43, 95, 108, 110, 116, 124;

---

[1] Cf. above, p. 174 and below, p. 200.

11.51, 77, 117, 151, 167, 235 (with a version of Phocylides), 254, 307, 381 (2 versions), 414, 431; 16.14 (with reply), 223, 388.

BENEDETTO LAMPRIDIO

(†1540)

Lampridio was born at Cremona; he taught at Padua, and was later tutor in the household of Francesco Gonzaga. Among his Latin poems he has a version of *Amor Fugitivus* (*A.P.* 9.440) with traits from *A.P.* 5.177.[1]

CELIO CALCAGNINI

(1479–1541)

Calcagnini was a natural son of an Apostolic Notary at Ferrara. He studied under Pietro Pomponazzo, and had L. G. Giraldi for a fellow student. On the completion of his studies he entered upon a career of arms, serving in the forces of Maximilian and of Julius II in Germany and Poland. Eventually he returned to Ferrara, took orders, and was granted ecclesiastical offices under the protection of the Estensi. Several of the Plautine comedies presented before the Court are said to have been translated by him (Gardner, *King of Court Poets*, p. 239). He naturally was on a friendly footing with a great number of the well-known persons of the day, and has Latin verses addressed to Tito Strozzi, Ariosto, Rhodiginus, Lampridio, Aleander, Raphael, Camillo Capilupi, and G. B. Giraldi. He died Canon of the cathedral and Professor of literature at the *Studio*. In Ariosto's description of the fountain of noble women (*Orlando* 42.90) Calcagnini is represented with another Latin poet, Marco Cavallo, supporting Diana d'Este:

> Il dotto Celio Calcagnin lontana
> Farà la gloria e 'l bel nome di quella
> Nel regno di Monese, in quel di Iuba,
> In India e Spagna udir con chiara tuba.

Perhaps Calcagnini's closest friends were Valeriano Bolzani and L. G. Giraldi. The latter, in his first dialogue *On the Poets of Our Time*, praises the learning of his friend, noticing, however, its obtrusion upon his poetry. Calcagnini's Latin verse, *Carminum libri iii*, was first published by Pigna with his own poems and those of Ariosto at Venice in 1553; my references are to this volume (below, p. 247). Calcagnini's *Opera* appeared at Basel in 1544.

The Anthology was a favorite source with Calcagnini; he is not a voluminous poet, yet in more than thirty-five instances

---

[1] *Carmina* (with those of J. B. Amaltheus), Venice, 1550; the poem is printed in part in *Amer. Journ. of Philol.* 49 (1928).113.

his poems betray its influence. He treats his borrowed themes
with some freedom, yet is more a translator than an imitator.
For example, he merely puts the name of Nero in place of that
of Orestes in his version of *A.P.* 9.126. Even where he does not
directly employ the Greek epigrams, his style shows that he has
studied them. And his theory of the epigram is drawn from the
Anthology (above, p. 60). The second couplet of his epigram
on the epigram repeats the figure used by Parmenion (*A.P.*
9.342), and the last line is from Cyrillus (*A.P.* 9.369).

Here follows Calcagnini's version of *A.P.* 9.331:[1]

> Ardentis Semeles audens puer excidit alvo,
>   Ardebatque uno mater et ille rogo.
> Et spes nulla super miserae succurrere matri,
>   At puer in flammis non tamen ustus erat,
> Ogygis occurrit, sed non prius attigit illum,
>   Succubuit multae quam Iovis ignis aquae.
> Ignis abit, sed non abiit vis ignea prorsus
>   Quique cuti summae parcit in ima furit.
> Nympha igitur procul o puerum ne tangito clamat
>   Quisquis es: ignis enim est ni prius imbre laves.

The following versions of *A.P.* 16.32 illustrate two ways in
which the Greek epigrams have often been employed—first, for
the display of skill in multiple variations, secondly, the application of Greek themes to modern instances. Here the original
is an epigram by Leontius Scholasticus on Gabriel, Prefect of
Constantinople:[2]

> Καὶ Φαέθων γραφίδεσσιν ἔχει τύπον· ἀλλὰ χαράσσει
>   ἠέλιον τέχνη, κρυπτομένων φαέων.
> Καὶ σέ, σοφὲ πτολίαρχε, γράφει, Γαβριήλιε, τέχνη
>   ἐκτὸς σῶν ἀρετῶν, ἐκτὸς ὅλων καμάτων.

This epigram Calcagnini applies to a portrait of Ercole II of
Ferrara by Dosso Dossi.[3] The portrait is now lost.

> Exprimit in tabula Phaethontem Cous Apelles,
>   Sed lucem et radios non potis exprimere.
> Sic tua, mi princeps, Dossus forte exprimit ora,
>   Virtutem et mores non potis exprimere.

---

[1] In the Commentary of the 1621 edition of Alciati's *Emblemata*, p. 144, this translation is erroneously ascribed to Caelius Rhodiginus.

[2] 'Even Phaethon [the sun] has his likeness in paintings; but art paints the sun with
his rays concealed. So thee too, wise ruler of the city, O Gabriel, art doth paint without thy virtues, without all thy deeds.'

[3] See E. G. Gardner, *The Painters of the School of Ferrara*, p. 165.

In his second version he leaves Dossi out, applying this exercise
to a sculpture; he changes his mind on the painter who painted
the sun—not specified in the Greek:

> Parrasii arte potest pingi Phaethontius ardor,
> Non facile radii vel nitor ille potest.
> Sic facile exculpi possunt ora Herculis auro,
> Non facile virtus ingeniumque potest.

The epigram evidently loses in the attempt to make it refer to a
statue. A third version, however, at least clears away the weak
antithesis between what cannot be done for the sun in painting
and what cannot be done for the hero in sculpture;

> Exprimere arte potes sacros Hyperionis ignes,
> Splendorem, et radios non potes exprimere.
> Exprimere Alcidem potes et producere in auro,
> Virtutem ac mores non potes exprimere.

Calcagnini makes use of *A.P.* 5.143; 7.24, 217, 275; 9.13, 27,
108, 126, 162 (2 versions), 331, 342, 369, 647 (2 versions), 713,
721, 723, 726, 728, 730, 732, 735, 738, 740; 16.14 (2 versions),
32 (3 versions), 103 (cf. 211 and 203), 129 (2 versions), 155, 223,
224.[1]

LAZZARO BONAMICO

(1479–1552)

Bonamico was born at Bassano. He studied at Padua with Janus
Lascaris and Musurus, and afterwards taught for a time at Rome and
studied the antiquities of the city. Thence he went to Bologna to act
as tutor in the family of Cardinal Alessandro Campegio. Apparently
he returned to Rome, for he laments the loss of his entire library in the
sack of the city in 1527. His last years were spent in Padua, teaching
in the university. Among those addressed in his verses are Calcagnini,
Lampridio, Paolo Manuzio, Cardinal Pole, and Caspar Ursinus Velius
(below, p. 277). His Latin poems remained scattered in the collections
of Ubaldini, Toscano, Gruter, and Bottari, until 1770, in which year
they were collected and printed with a biography by Verci: *Carmina
et Epistolae, una cum Vita a J. B. Verci conscripta, quibus adduntur
Carmina nonnulla Faustini Amici et Andreae Navarini.* Venice, 1770
[*Carm.*].

Bonamico is no great poet, but has some pleasing verses.[2] If
the tables of Greek epigrams imitated by each of the Renais-

---

[1] Ten of these, from 9.713 to 740, are epigrams on Myron's *Heifer.* The verses inspired by *A.P.* 7.24 are quoted by Giraldi (below, p. 185), and are in the *Carm. Illust.
Poet. Ital.* 3.105, but not in Pigna.

[2] See the criticism of Bonamico by Ellinger, *op. cit.* 1.257ff.

sance writers we have thus far examined are reviewed, it will be seen that up to this time little attention seems to have been paid to the epigrams of the sixth book—the dedicatory epigrams. With the poets of Bonamico's generation they begin to be very popular. Calcagnini has a number of votary epigrams, imitating the style, but never the substance, of the Greek poems. Bonamico, too, favors the dedicatory epigram, and is plainly conscious of the Anthology as his model. Yet his only translation from the sixth book is from *A.P.* 6.1:

> Jam domita ingratae canes, rugisque senectae
> Illa olim innumeris Lais amata viris,
> Ante tuos, Venus alma, pedes repetita iuventae
> Dona ferens, speculum, talia dicta dedit:
> Qualis eram quia non licet hoc me cernere, qualis
> Sum vero nunc odi, hoc tibi, Cypris, habe.

He also translates *A.P.* 7.669 and 9.577, the second as follows:

> Mortalem me nosco breves superesse per annos,
> Cui datur afflicto semper et esse animo.
> Sed quum contemplor caelum, superosque moventes
> Astriferi aeterno tempore signa poli,
> Tunc humili videor longe tellure remotus
> Cum Iove depasci nectar et ambrosiam.

A ms. in the Ambrosian Library (*Cod.* 597), written by Bonamico, contains notes on various authors and (ff. 136–222) on the Anthology, with the text of the epigrams commented on. It is dated 1519. A second ms. in the same library, containing two or three epigrams, was also his (above, p. 34, n. 2).

BENEDETTO TAGLIACARNE (THEOCRENUS)

(*c.* 1480–1536)

Tagliacarne, a native of Sarzana in Liguria, was at one time secretary to the city of Genoa. In 1522, having lost his possessions in the sack of that city by the imperial forces, he retired to France under the protection of Fregoso. He became tutor to the children of Francis I (1524), remaining with them while they were hostages in Spain (1528–29). Despite some incidents of displeasure, the king's favor to him continued until in 1535 he made him Bishop of Grasse; but Tagliacarne did not long survive to enjoy his new dignity. He was on terms of intimacy with many of the literary men then prominent in France, especially with Salmon Macrin. He is known as Teocreno.

Tagliacarne's Latin poems were published at Poitiers in the year of his death (1536): *Poemata quae Juvenis admodum Lusit.* If these were mostly written in his youth, his several translations from the Anthology, contained among them, are perhaps exceptions, since they appear to have been made while he was a member of the French Court. An allusion to *A.P.* 9.56, for instance, is accompanied by some lines on King Francis' translation of that epigram. Other Latin versions from the epigrams are preceded, in Tagliacarne's *Poemata*, by the rival versions of Vido Baldus and Jacques Colin. On Baldus I have no information; Colin, however, was secretary to the king, and died in 1547; he is remembered as a translator.[1]

Tagliacarne has translations or imitations of *A.P.* 7.741; 9.47, 56, 231, 322. Baldus translates 7.741 and 9.322; and Colin 7.741; 9.231, and 322.[2] Here follow their translations of *A.P.* 7.741:

TAGLIACARNE

Othryadem, Spartae rarum decus, et Cynegyron
    Naumachon, atque alios Marte ubique bonos,
Anteit Ausonius miles, qui vulnere multo
    Dum iacet ad Rheni iam moribundus aquas,
Charae ubi raptam aquilam prospexit ab hoste cohorti,
    Colligit extremae relliquias animae,
Irruit, obtruncat raptorem, signa reportat:
    Invictae titulos mortis et unus habet.

VIDO BALDUS

Semianimis miles transfixus undique telis
    Italus, ad Rheni magna fluenta iacens,
Vicit et Othryadem Spartae decus et Cynegirum
    Naumachon, et veterum fortia facta virum.
Nam quum aquila ordinibus charis raperetur ab hoste,
    En iterum e mediis caedibus erigitur;
Abstulit hosti animam signumque recepit amicis,
    Invictae solus mortis honore cadens.

---

[1] See V.-L. Bourrilly, *Jacques Colin, Abbé de Saint-Ambroise*, Paris, 1905, (*Bibliothèque d'Hist. Mod.* 1.4), especially pp. 55–8. On Tagliacarne see also Pierre Jourda, 'Un Humaniste Italien en France: Théocrenus, 1480–1536,' in *Revue du 16e Siècle* 16 (1929).40; and Jean Plattard, 'L'Humaniste Théocrenus en Espagne, 1526–1530,' *ibid.*, p. 68. There is a letter from Tagliacarne to Paolo Giovio in the *Epistolae* of Gudius (above, p. 166, n. 1).

[2] Henri Estienne drew upon Tagliacarne's translations for his *Epigrammata Graeca Selecta* (Paris, 1570); and reprinted the lines on King Francis' version of *A.P.* 9.56 in Beza's *Poemata*, [Geneva], 1569.

JACQUES COLIN

Obrutus innumera Latialis arundine miles
    Martis et ad Rheni semiperemptus aquas,
Ut raptam sociis aquilam conspexit ab hoste,
    Prosilit e mediis ecce cadaveribus:
Et raptore suis caeso servavit ademptam,
    Solus ab invicta morte ferens titulum.
I nunc, Othryadem patrium decus obiice Sparta,
    Et siquid bello Graecia maius habet.

LILIO GREGORIO GIRALDI

(1479–1552)

Giraldi, a native of Ferrara, and a pupil of Battista Guarini, was one of the very learned men of the Italian Renaissance, and numbered among his friends most of the well-known scholars of his day. He visited the principal Italian centres of learning, and lived long in Rome, where he was Protonotarius Apostolicus. A considerable number of literary works came from his pen, among which the most deserving of remembrance are his *Historia de Diis* (Strassburg, 1512), his *Historiae Poetarum tam Graecorum quam Latinorum Dialogi decem* (Basel, 1545), and his two dialogues *De Poetis Nostrorum Temporum* (Florence, 1551). This last work will always be important as a first-hand document on the literary life of the age of Leo X; the first dialogue was written early in Leo's pontificate, the second in 1548. The best editions of Giraldi's *Opera* are those of 1580 and 1696.[1] His *Poemata* appeared at Lyons (Gryphe), in 1536.

The Greek epigrams find a place on many a page of Giraldi; he quotes them mainly in illustration of historical points, sometimes translating them, sometimes giving translations by others, and sometimes merely paraphrasing.

In the *Historia Poetarum* he lists among the Greek lyric poetesses 'Agacle'—feminine, to be sure, but as unreal as Politian's Agacles, whence she is derived.[2] In Dialogue 3 he deals with the Greek epigrammatists. Typical references are: 'Philodemus: Leguntur adhuc quaedam Graeca in quasdam mulieres epigrammata';[3] and: 'Christodorus: ex Copto, Aegyptia civitate, duxit originem, tametsi Planudes in Graecorum

---

[1] My references are to the 1580 edition: *Opera quae extant Omnia*, 2 vols, Basel (Guarinus). The 1696 edition was prepared by Jean Faes and Paul Colomies, and published at Leyden. There is a modern edition of the *De Poet. Nost. Temp.*, by Karl Wotke (Berlin, 1894) in Herrmann's *Lateinische Litteraturdenkmäler des xv und xvi Jahrhunderts*.

[2] Giraldi, *Op.* (1580) 2.124; see above, p. 133.

[3] *Op.* (1580) 2.133.

epigrammatum scholiis Thebanum putavit.'[1] After an extended enumeration of the epigrammatists he closes his history with a recommendation of the Anthology: 'Graecorum epigrammaton volumina, quae propter eorum varietatem assidue vobis terenda sunt.'

Giraldi's *Historia de Diis* provides a good example of his use of the epigrams to illustrate a subject he is discussing:

Occasionem Latini deam fecere, sicut Graeci deum καιρόν. . . . Quare cum Posidippus Καιρὸν pulchre Graece descripserit, et ab eo Ausonius Gallus Latine Occasionem, visum est mihi utriusque descriptionem hac nostri libri parte apponere, ut qui eorum imagines habere voluerint, habeant unde facile excerpere possint. Intellego enim illustres quosdam principes his diebus id meditari. Hoc est ergo Posidippi epigramma, quod post Th. Morum et Erasmum, viros summe doctos, ideo est a me ita conversum vel concinnatum potius, quod Erasmus quidem quatuor addiderat versus, Thomas duo dempserat. Graecum si cupis, in 4 Epigrammatum leges, quod ita est a me refectum [*A.P.* 16.275]:

> Unde hic est plastes? Sicionius.—Ede age nomen.
> Lysippus.—Tu quis? Caerus ego, omne domans.—
> Cur summis instas pedibus? Semper rotor.—Alas
> Cur plantis gestas? Ut levis aura feror.—
> Dextrae est cur inserta novacula? Signum homini hoc est,
> Vis conferri acie quod mihi nulla potest.—
> Cur coma fronte iacet? Venientem ut prendere possis.—
> Parte est cur calvum posteriore caput?
> Quod postquam levibus praeceps effugero pennis,
> Ne valeat tergo qui revocare velit.
> Talem vos propter me plastes finxerat, hospes,
> Pro foribus positus qui documenta darem.

He then gives Ausonius' version. Evidently he had read Politian's discussion of this subject (above, p. 126). Of the intention of certain princes to erect statues to Opportunity I know nothing further; Giraldi's statement may be ironical.

In all, Giraldi has, scattered through his prose works, verse-translations of the following: *A.P.* 5.83+4; 6.130; 7.3, 9.5–6, 45, 53, 54, 80, 348, 615, 616, 617, 674; 9.190.7–8, 231.5–6, 383, 402, 434, 504, 569; 10.43; 11.331; 14.40, 65, 66.1–6, 90, 101; 15.35; 16.173.5–6, 221.9–10, 223, 275 (with Ausonius). Of the following he quotes the Greek, and, usually, gives a prose version or paraphrase:[2] *A.P.* 6.340 (1.374); 7.345 (2.125), 9.198 (2.214), 448

---

[1] *Op.* (1580) 2.193.
[2] References in parentheses are to the edition of 1580.

(2.448), 497 (2.255), 525 (1.242); 11.437 (2.115). Without giving versions of his own, and mostly without the Greek, he quotes translations of *A.P.* 7.24 (2.341 Calcagnini), 313 (2.97 Aretinus),[1] 745 (2.342 Aegidius), 677 (2.335 [Valla]); 9.56 (2.195 Germanicus), 527 (2.459 [Valla]); 10.30 (2.533 Ausonius); 14.64 (2.449 Erasmus, Ausonius); 16.174 (1.377 Ausonius), 185 (1.324 Alciati), 251 (1.395 Alciati), 263 (1.447 Ausonius). He refers without quotation or translation to *A.P.* 7.714–15 (2.341); 9.26 (2.123), 248 (2.168), 478; 16.265–6 (1.44), 306–7 (2.340).[2]

In the second of the dialogues *De Poetis Nostrorum Temporum* (*Op.* 2.405) Giraldi speaks of the translations made by More and Lily in their *Progymnasmata*. Probably he also knew Cornarius' *Selecta Epigrammata* (below, p. 283).

GIROLAMO ALEANDRO

(1480–1540)

Aleander, a native of Motta in Friuli, was sent at the age of thirteen to study in Venice. There, besides Latin and Greek, he acquired a knowledge of Hebrew. Already esteemed a prodigy of learning in 1501, he was sent by the Papal Legate at Venice on a mission to Hungary. Aldus gave him his friendship, and through Aldus he met Erasmus, whom he assisted in the Venetian edition of that scholar's *Adagia*. In 1508 he settled in Paris, becoming the first regular teacher of Greek there, and, in 1512, Rector of the University. Leaving Paris to escape an epidemic, he became chancellor to the Prince-Bishop of Liège, Érard de la Marck, by whom in 1517 he was sent on a mission to Rome. Leo X determined to keep him in Rome, made him librarian of the Vatican (1519), and in 1520 sent him to combat the heresy of Luther at the Diet of Worms. Aleander's zeal on this mission brought upon him the censures of his former friend Erasmus. As apostolic nuncio he accompanied Francis I at Pavia, where he was captured by the Spaniards, but released through the efforts of influential friends. He was in Rome when it was sacked by the Imperial troops in 1527, and from the ramparts of Sant' Angelo witnessed the pillage of his own house. Mainly in recognition of his services against the Lutheran heresy, he was created Cardinal of San Chrysogono by Paul III in 1538, two years before his death, which occurred shortly after his return from a last mission to Germany.

Although the few poems of Aleander's that remain show no

---

[1] Cf. above, p. 142.

[2] The reference to *A.P.* 9.478 seems not to be in the 1580 edition, but is in the 1696 edition 1.738.

traces of the Anthology, there is evidence that he knew the epigrams. He had made the acquaintance of Lascaris in Venice. Possibly it is not merely by chance that in a letter written by him to Paolo Emilio, in which he praises Lascaris, he quotes from one of the epigrams (*A.P.* 9.24). The letter is dated Paris, June 5, 1510; it is an invitation to Emilio to share the writer's house:[1]

Proinde si venire vis, non tanquam hospes apud nos, aut quilibet e contubernalibus, sed contubernii dominus eris. Interim ἐγώ μου δεσπότης εὔχομαι εἶναι, sed dum ipse abes, nam exorto sole ἀμαυροῦνται ἱερὰ κύκλα σελήνης. Omissis iocis, gaudeo te incolumem.

In 1525 Joannes Soter (below, p. 275) printed as the work of Aleander the following version of *A.P.* 9.44 or 45, but the source he drew it from escapes me:[2]

Aurum qui reperit, laqueum proiecit, at aurum
Qui mersit, nexit quem reperit laqueum.

POMPONIO GAURICO

(*c.* 1482–*c.* 1530)

Pomponio was a younger brother of the famous astronomer Luca Gaurico; their native place was Giffoni in the province of Salerno. Pomponio was educated at Padua, and became professor in the University of Naples and tutor to Ferrante Sanseverino, prince of Salerno. He is chiefly known for his treatise *De Sculptura*, but in the sixteenth century his Latin poems were widely read and quoted. He also composed a commentary on the *Ars Poetica* of Horace, and several shorter treatises. Much of his work remained unpublished probably because of his untimely death. The mystery that surrounded this event has never been cleared up. It appears that, while riding once from Salerno to Castellamare, he wandered from the way, and, as he never returned, his friends concluded that he had been done to death and his body thrown into the sea. Pércopo thinks he may have fallen into the hands of some soldiers of Lautrec's army (*Pomponio Gaurico, Umanista Napoletano*, Naples, 1894, p. 230). The year of his death would then have to be 1528.

---

[1] The source of Aleander's quotation is pointed out by Paquier, *Lettres Familières de Jérome Aléandre*, Paris, 1909, p. 9. *A.P.* 9.24 is by Leonidas of Tarentum in praise of Homer; the first couplet is:

Ἄστρα μὲν ἠμαύρωσε καὶ ἱερὰ κύκλα σελήνης
ἄξονα δινήσας ἔμπυρος ἠέλιος.

[2] A MS. of Aleander's (*Vat. Lat.* 3922; Paquier, *Jérome Aleandre*, Paris, 1900, p. xxxiv) is inscribed by him: ΑΝΘΟΛΟΓΙΑ—FLORILEGIUM. Since, however, it comprises a collection of notes for the most part on subjects connected with ecclesiastical history, the title was probably taken from Stobaeus and not from the collection of epigrams.

At the end of his commentary *Super Arte Poetica Horatii*
(Rome, 1541) Gaurico lists the Greek poets in several kinds
of verse—*epicedia, monodiae, threni,* and *epitaphia*—that are
worthy of imitation. For *epitaphia* his catalogue is evidently
drawn from the Anthology: when we review the distinctions
of the dead on the tomb itself, that is an epitaph—

Sed epigrammata quoque dicta, quae clarissimorum virorum statuis
inscriberentur. Mox ad vivos describendos adducta. Horum autem
scriptores propemodum innumerabiles; praecipui tamen fuere Simo-
nides maior cuius meminit Herodotus, Antipater Sidonius, Antipater
Thesssalus, Archias, Agathias, Addaeus, Alcaeus, Alphaeus, Antistius,
Arabius, Bassus, Bianor, Boethus, Crates Cinicus, Callimachus,
Cerealius, Cirillus, Diotimus, Dioscorides, Ericius, Egesippus, Eveni
Parii duo qui et elegias scripsere, Euodus, Ermiodorus, Epigonus,
Germanicus Caesar, Getulicus, Gersus [?Glaucus], Io, Leonides Taren-
tinus, Lollius, Lucilius, Macedonius Consul, Maecius, Metrodorus,
Menecrates, Mirinus, Musiccius, Honestus, Plato Minor, Pancratius,
Paetus, Proclus, Posidippus, Philo, Philodemus, Ruffus, Ruffinus,
Sarapio, Statillius Flaccus, Satirus, Simmias, Tullius Geminus, Ti-
berius Caesar, Tiberius Illus., Zosimus Thasius, et caetera quam tu
optime nosti multitudo.

Gaurico's Latin poems were published, probably at Naples,
in 1526: *Elegiae xxix, Eclogae iv, Sylvae iii, Epigrammata.* In
all, he has ten translations from the Anthology:[1] *A.P.* 7.471;
9.110, 145, 359; 10.30 (2 versions), 105; 16.135, 151, 275.

Gaurico is one of the few translators who have rendered *A.P.*
9.359 without its companion piece 9.360:[2]

> Quis queat humanae tot vitae incommoda ferre?
>   Humanae vitae quis mala ferre queat?
> Si vitam statuas urbanam, iam tibi praebet
>   Mille domus curas, iurgia mille forum.
> Sin tua rura colas, circumstant mille labores;
>   Et pelago tecum mors comitata venit.
> Nulli gratus, inops; admota uxore quietem
>   Nil speres, viduo nec potes esse thoro;
> Orbus eris sine prole, graves in prole labores,
>   Mente labat iuvenis, debilitate senex;
> Nil quoniam superest, quod me vixisse iuvabit,
>   Optandum misero sit mihi posse mori.

---

[1] The version of *A.P.* 7.471 is not in Gaurico's *Epigrammata*, but is taken from
Bocchi's *Symbolicae Quaestiones* (below, p. 222); likewise the version of 16.135 is
from Soter; while that of 16.275 is in Gaurico's *Dialogus de Tempore* printed at the end
of his Commentary on the *Ars Poetica* as well as in his *Epigrammata*.

[2] This is printed with other poems of Gaurico in the *Carm. Illust. Poet. Ital.*, but
with several changes from the text of 1526 as given above—1. *ferre incommoda vitae;*
3. *Si vitam vivas;* 12. *Optandum misero nil, nisi posse mori.*

Gaurico's translation of *A.P.* 16.135, on the *Medea* of Timo-machus, is particularly well done. The *Medea* was, however, a painting.

DE STATUA MEDEAE

Quod natos feritura ferox Medea moratur,
    Praestitit hoc magni dextera Timomachi.
Tardat amor facinus: strictum dolor incitat ensem;
    Vult, non vult, natos perdere et ipsa suos.

His translation of *A.P.* 16.275 may be compared with that of Giraldi given above, p. 184.

Cuius opus?—Quondam Lysippi.—Dic mihi, quis tu?—
    Tempus.—Quidnam operae sit tibi?—Cuncta domo.—
Cur tam summa tenes?—Propero super omnia velox.—
    Cur celeres plantae?—Me levis aura vehit.—
Cur tenuem tua dextra tenet tonsoria falcem?—
    Omnia nostra secans radit acuta manus.—
Cur tibi tam longi pendent a fronte capilli?—
    Fronte quidem facilis sum bene posse capi.—
Cur tibi posterior pars est a vertice calva?—
    Me quia posterior prendere nemo potest;
Talem me finxit quondam Sicionius, hospes,
    Et monitorem hoc me vestibulo posuit.
Pulchrum opus artificem laudat; proh Iuppiter, o quam
    Debuit hoc pigros sollicitare viros.

ANTONIO TELESIO (THYLESIUS)

(*c.* 1482–*c.* 1534)

Telesio was born at Cosenza, and there studied either with Thydeus Actianus or Acciarinus Picenus. Several years of his youth were spent in travel. About 1517 he was summoned to teach Greek at Milan; and in 1523 went to Rome where he lectured on the Roman poets. There he made the friendship of Giovio and Vida and of his countryman Francesco Franchini. Following the sack of Rome he retired to Venice, and published a treatise *De Coloribus* and a tragedy *Imber Aureus*. In 1531 he left Venice for Naples, but the death of Pompeo Colonna dis-appointing his hopes of patronage, he returned in the next year to his native place. He died there in 1533 or 1534, and was buried in the cathedral church.

The Latin poems of Telesio were published at Rome in 1524. In 1762 at Naples an edition of his *Opera* was published by Francesco Daniele; and in 1808 also at Naples was published a supplement to this: *Carmina et Epistolae, quae ab editione*

Neapolitana exulant, with a portrait of Telesio and a sketch of his life by Daniele. This last publication contains the following version by Telesio of *A.P.* 16.204:[1]

> Praxiteles, quem passus erat, bene finxit Amorem,
>   Ex proprio formam concipiens animo;
> Meque mei pretium Phrinae dedit: amplius arcu
> Non utor: qui me conspicit, ille furit.

ANDREA NAVAGERO (NAUGERIUS)
(1483–1529)

Navagero was a Venetian. His education was begun under Sabellico, and continued, for Greek, under Pietro Pomponazzi and under Musurus at Padua. Some years of his early life were spent in editing classics for the Aldine press—Cicero's *Orations* of 1519, for example, had a Preface by him. He gained further fame by his funeral orations —for the General Alviano, in whose patronage he had been, for the Doge Leonardo Loredano (1521), and for Caterina Cornaro, Queen of Cyprus. He was expected to succeed Sabellico as librarian of St. Mark's. In 1523 he was appointed ambassador of Venice to Charles V, and spent four years in Spain, during which period he is traditionally said to have taught the Spanish poets how to write sonnets. On his return to Venice he was appointed ambassador to the Court of Francis I; but he died at Blois very shortly after his arrival. Before his death he burned some portion of his works, including an incomplete History of Venice; and the remainder were published at Venice in 1530.[2] Navagero was widely acquainted among the literary men of his day, and was most closely allied, perhaps, with Bembo, Fracastoro, Contarini, Ramusio, and with Raimondo and Giambattista della Torre (Tiraboschi's list). Navagero is probably the purest in style of the neo-Latin poets.

With him we enter the best period of Italian neo-Latin poetry, a period that corresponds roughly with the pontificates of Leo X and Clement VII. The epigram now flourished as it had once flourished at Alexandria, once at Rome, and once at Constantinople. The general character of the epigrams written in the early sixteenth century is not satirical. Martial was not highly esteemed in this great age of the epigram.[3] Catullus was

---

[1] Originally printed by Morelli in his *Bibliotheca Manuscripta Marciana* (1802) 1.457.

[2] The best edition of Navagero's *Opera* is that by J. A. Volpi, Padua, 1718.

[3] Cf. Tiraboschi, *Stor.* 2.1.2.28: 'Io rifletterò solamente che nel secolo XVI, quando a comun parere regnava in Italia il buon gusto, poco conto facevasi di Marziale, e appena giudicavasi degno di venire a paragon con Catullo.' He cites the story about Navagero and also the judgment of Martial given by Giraldi, *De Poet.*, Dial. x.

admired, but I do not hesitate to affirm that the real model of these epigrammatists was the Greek Anthology. The poets of the age of Leo were precisely the pupils of the great humanists of the close of the fifteenth century; then as never before or since in Italy the literary world was steeped in Greek. In Italy alone four editions of the Anthology were called for in the twenty-five years between 1494 and 1521. Paolo Giovio relates of Navagero that annually on a stated day he cursed a number of volumes of Martial and devoted them to Vulcan; and in the same sentence he characterizes the epigrams of Navagero as 'ending not in witty and pointed lines, but with a tender and very sweetly primitive grace' (*praedulci prisca suavitate*). Navagero's method seems to have consisted in trying to reproduce in himself the spirit of the Greek epigrammatists, and then in that spirit to write something of his own. The results are admirable; and in their turn Navagero's verses have found imitators among the Italian and French vernacular poets.

In particular the dedicatory epigram seemed to Navagero and his contemporaries to be typically Greek. It became one of their favorite forms. The most admired poem in this type is Du Bellay's *Vœu d'un Vanneur de Blé aux Vents*. This was inspired by a *votum* of Navagero's, which itself is founded on a Greek epigram ascribed to Bacchylides (*A.P.* 6.53). Here we may look at Navagero's poem and its original:[1]

---

[1] Navagero's Latin poems are not numerous; they were most widely read in the following volume (referred to hereafter as *C.P.Q.*): *Carmina Quinque Illustrium Poetarum*, Florence (Torrentinus), 1553. Du Bellay may have used this book; his poem first appeared in his *Jeux Rustiques* in 1558.

In Navagero's *Opera Omnia*, Padua, 1817, p. 281, the following translation of his Latin is ascribed to Pietro Angelio of Barga (below, p. 240). It was found written in Angelio's hand (according to Apostolo Zeno) in a copy of the 1534 edition of Navagero's works.

> Aure, che tra le frondi mormorate,
> Questo bel vaso pieno
> Di crochi, e d'amaranti,
> Di narcisi, e crisanti,
> Alcon vi sparge al ciel caldo sereno.
> Voi temprate l'ardor volando intorno,
> Mentr' egli pallia il grano a mezzo il giorno.

An Italian sonnet was made from Navagero's poem by Lodovico Paterno (below, p. 314); see also below, p. 354, n. 2. Possibly Agostino Beazzano—himself a Latin poet and admirer of Navagero, on whom he wrote an epitaph—caught something from this epigram for the first lines of a poem of his:

> Vaghe aure, c'hor con l'ale preste, hor lente,
> Per i campi de l'aer spirando andate, etc.

(*Rime Volgari e Latine*, Venice, 1551, sig. Bvi^vo). His, however, is a political poem.
Among writers of *vota* must be mentioned Bernardino Parthenio (De' Frances

Aurae, quae levibus percurritis aëra pennis,
  Et strepitis blando per nemora alta sono:
Serta dat haec vobis, vobis haec rusticus Idmon
  Spargit odorato plena canistra croco.
Vos lenite aestum, et paleas seiungite inanes:
  Dum medio fruges ventilat ille die.

Εὔδημος τὸν νηὸν ἐπ' ἀγροῦ τόνδ' ἀνέθηκεν
  τῷ πάντων ἀνέμων πιοτάτῳ Ζεφύρῳ·
εὐξαμένῳ γάρ οἱ ἦλθε βοαθόος, ὄφρα τάχιστα
  λικμήσῃ πεπόνων καρπὸν ἀπ' ἀσταχύων.

In the poem just quoted Navagero is playing freely with the
theme of an epigram that can be definitely identified as his
original; in the following inscription for a cool fountain—perhaps his best-known poem—he is still more freely writing something similar to what the Greeks wrote. There are a number of
epigrams in the Anthology that he might have had in mind;
perhaps *A.P.* 9.374 is most similar:[1]

Et gelidus fons est, et nulla salubrior unda,
  Et molli circum gramine terra viret,
Et ramis arcent soles frondentibus alni,
  Et levis in nullo gratior aura loco est,
Et medio Titan nunc ardentissimus axe est,
  Exustusque gravi sidere ferunt ager.
Siste, viator, iter, nimio iam torridus aestu es.
  Iam nequeunt lassi longius ire pedes,
Accubitu languorem, aestum aura umbraque virenti
  Perspicuo poteris fonte levare sitim.

Probably, before Navagero could develop his skill in writing
epigrams in the Greek manner, he had translated many of them
in a fairly literal form. If he did so, these *pastiches* are lost, destroyed doubtless by their author. An exercise on the theme of
A.P. 16.177—Venus in Armor—comes nearer than any other
verses of Navagero to being that sort of thing:

chini) of Spilimbergo in Friuli (†1589); he also has a dedication to the Zephyrs (*Carm.
Illust. Poet. Ital.* 7.98):
          Luteolam hanc caltham hosque immortales amarantos
            Collapsos pleno Chloridos e gremio
          Servat Acon vobis, Zephyri, texitque coronam;
            Conveniunt vestris mollia serta comis. . . .
  [1] I give a translation of *A.P.* 9.374: 'I am the pure fountain, ever flowing, that the
neighboring grove pours forth for passing travelers; all about I am beautifully en-
circled with plane-trees and softly blooming laurels, and I refresh the shady bower.
Therefore, do not in summer pass me by, but, assuaging thy thirst, rest from toil also
beside me in peace.'
  Navagero's poem was put into Italian verse by Tolomei, Tansillo, and Marchetti,
and Tansillo's version was turned into French by Desportes.

Quid magis adversum bello est bellique tumultu
  Quam Venus? Ad teneros aptior illa iocos.
Et tamen armatam hanc magni pinxere Lacones
  Imbellique data est bellica parma Deae.
Quippe erat id signum forti Lacedaemone natum
  Saepe et foemineum bella decere genus.
'Sic quoque non quod sim pugna versatus in ulla
  Haec humeris pictor induit arma meis,
Verum hoc quod bello, hoc patriae quod tempore iniquo,
  Ferre vel imbellem quemlibet arma decet.'

The epigrams from which Navagero probably took direct hints are: *A.P.* 5.4; 6.48, 53, 57, 158; 9.374 (?); 16.177, 325.

GIROLAMO FRACASTORO

(1478–1553)

Fracastoro, born at Verona, studied and taught at Padua and later, under the patronage of Alviano, at Pordenone in Friuli. Here he met Navagero, and in his society developed his own talent as a Latin poet. When Alviano was taken prisoner in the battle of Agnadello, Fracastoro retired to Verona, where he remained, practising medicine and perfecting his literary works, until his death, except that in 1545–7 he attended the Council of Trent at the command of Paul III. He is best known for his long poem: *Syphilidis sive de Morbo Gallico libri tres* (Verona, 1530).

Fracastoro's connection with the Anthology is slight and ambiguous. In his *Opera Omnia*, published at Venice in 1555, two years after his death, there appears (p. 234) a translation of *A.P.* 9.331 under the heading *Vetus Epigramma*.[1] It may be seen on p. 26, above. Possibly it is Fracastoro's composition; certainly it is not an ancient Latin one. The question becomes more interesting from the fact that a MS. in the Vatican Library (*Cod. Vat. Lat.* 9948, f. 175ᵛᵒ), contains a poem by Fracastoro, and also what, from the printed Catalogue, I judge to be a translation of *A.P.* 9.331, beginning: *Quem Nymphae e flammis*. The translation printed in the *Opera* of 1555 begins: *Infantem Nymphae Bacchum, quo tempore ab igne*. It is printed at the end of Fracastoro's *De Vini Temperatura*.

---

[1] This heading might easily be misunderstand. Cf. Valeriano, ed. of 1550, f. 123: *Io. Pierii Valeriani Bolzanii Epigrammata Vetera*—his own compositions.

JULIUS CAESAR SCALIGER

(1484–1558)

Scaliger was born, he believed, at Riva on the Lago di Garda; he spent the first forty-two years of his life in Italy. He claimed descent from the Della Scala, lords of Verona, and asserted that his father was the celebrated captain, Benedetto della Scala, and that his early instruction was received from the famous Fra Giocondo. Others have tried to prove that he was the son of the miniaturist Benedetto Bordoni, was born in Padua, and was taught by Caelius Rhodiginus. Scaliger was an able physician as well as scholar, and it was in the former capacity that he accompanied the Bishop of Agen to France in 1525. He became naturalized in 1528. His defense of Ciceronianism against Erasmus first made him known; but his fame was more securely established by numerous translations and by his works on the Latin language. Most of all, his *Poetics* (1561) took first place as the handbook of the poetic art during two centuries. Scaliger married Andiette de Roques-Lobejac, and had a numerous family. His *Poemata* were first collected at Geneva in 1574.

When one considers the Latin verse composed by Scaliger, keeping in mind the extent of his whole scholarly activity, its bulk at least is truly amazing. Verse-epistles, satires, epigrams of all kinds, epitaphs, anacreontics, laments, enigmas, hymns, crowd more than a thousand pages.[1] Their quality has never been highly esteemed, though the verse obviously is competent. Few would care to reject the opinion of Ménage, who says (*Menagiana* 4.96): 'Il n'y a guère de plus méchant livre; à peine y trouve-t-on quatre ou cinq épigrammes qui puissent passer à la montre.' This does not prevent the book from being most interesting from a different point of view; Scaliger is an interesting man, if not a poet, and his book of Latin verses is an excellent index to his mind and character—not the least so perhaps when in his epitaphs for the great (*Heroes* in *Poem.* 1.313) he follows one on Cicero by two on himself.

The mainly Latin bias of Scaliger's interests is evident in his *Poemata*, and is the more noticeable in the 1600 edition in which the last part of the volume is occupied by the poems of Joseph Scaliger, for these are almost wholly from the Greek or in Greek. Yet a few imitations of the Anthology are scattered through the elder scholar's poems, namely imitations or translations of *A.P.* 5.78; 7.137, 238, 311; 9.110, 567, 717, 718; 11.47, 171(?), 237; 16.129 (2 versions), 174 (*responsio*), 223, 326.

Scaliger, like Politian—perhaps in imitation of him—regards himself as rival rather than as imitator of his ancient models.

---

[1] I use the edition of Commelinus: *Poemata omnia in duas partes divisa*, etc. [Heidelberg], 1600 (referred to as *Poem.*).

Thus the following Latin epigram is introduced by the words: *Certat cum Antipatro—*

> Quae segmentatis pressisset parvula cunis
>   Mollia purpureis stragula picta notis:
> Cuius tabificis lumen quod spirat ocellis
>   Mollitia superant quae bona somnus habet:
> Lenta trahens liquido illa, atque osse carentia duro
>   Brachia (nam Pholoe lactea tota fuit)
> Millia tela suis hebetavit lusibus. Hoc est:
>   Sola adimit Marti fortia tela Venus.

The modern poet has attempted to generalize the theme of his model, by leaving out all that is local and particular in it. The original, ascribed to Antipater of Sidon, is *A.P.* 9.567:[1]

> Ἡ καὶ ἔτ' ἐκ βρέφεος κοιμωμένη Ἀντιοδημὶς
>   πορφυρέων, Παφίης νοσσίς, ἐπὶ κροκύδων,
> ἡ τακεραῖς λεύσσουσα κόραις μαλακώτερον ὕπνου,
>   Λύσιδος ἀλκυονίς, τερπνὸν ἄθυρμα Μέθης,
> ὑδατίνους φορέουσα βραχίονας, ἢ μόνη ὀστοῦν
>   οὐ λάχεν (ἦν γὰρ ὅλη τοὶν ταλάροισι γάλα),
> Ἰταλίην ἤμειψεν, ἵνα πτολέμοιο καὶ αἰχμῆς
>   ἀμπαύσῃ Ῥώμην μαλθακίνῃ χάριτι.

Possibly Scaliger does better to vie with a Latin poet. Thus he quotes Ausonius' version of *A.P.* 16.174 (given above, p. 105), ignoring the Greek, and adds the following *Responsio* of his own:

> Imbelli imbellis placuisti, et inermis inermi.
>   Quid mirum, simili si favet ille sibi?
> Sunt onus, haud honor haec, sumptis es nudior armis.
>   Nudam esse, et tua sunt arma, valere nihil.

The last line is brief to the point of obscurity.

Scaliger's theory of the epigram, as expressed in his *Poetics*, has received attention above.[2] He incidentally quotes *A.P.* 9.647 (*Poet.* 3.125), and refers to 11.235 (*ibid.*). Scaliger did not, one gathers, really care much for the Greek epigrams; his judgment of the poems of Angeriano, which he finds to be too much in the Greek manner, shows this clearly enough (above, p. 170).

---

[1] 'She who from infancy slept on purple cloth, Antiodemis, the Paphian's nursling, she who with her melting eyes casts glances softer than sleep, the halcyon of Lysis, the delightful plaything of Methé [Drink], with arms that flow like water, even she who alone has no bones (for she is milk just turning to cheese), has gone to Italy, that by her softening grace she may make Rome give over war and arms.'

[2] Pp. 63–5.

ALVISE PRIULI (ALOYSIUS PRIULUS)

Priuli's Latin poems seem to have been printed for the first time in Toscano's *Carmina Illustrium Poetarum*, Paris, 1577. Priuli was a Venetian, possibly the poet who published *Rime* in 1533 (cf. Sanuto, *Diar.* 54.324). Two of his poems are addressed to Galeazzo Florimonte. Among his verses there is a votive epigram that plainly shows him to have been a student of the Anthology. As so often happens with these dedicatory pieces, it is not quite possible to assign the poem to one certain model; it most resembles *A.P.* 6.30 or 38. In form it is a close imitation of the Greek—the dedication, the description of the dedicant's life, the prayer at the end. The presentation of the implements of a fisherman's trade to the god of the sea comes directly from the Greek epigrams.

VOTA LYCONIS NEPTUNO

Haec, Neptune, tibi contrito retia lino,
　　Hos calathos atque haec ferrea tela Lycon
Dedicat, inque altas supplex en porricit undas
　　Iam senior tremula lacque merumque manu.
Dum licuit validis scrutatus viribus aequor,
　　His large eduxit seque suamque domum.
Nunc senio gravis exiguos vix litore pisces
　　Considens calamis captat arundineis.
Tu vero vasti cui parent aequora ponti,
　　Et quicquid magni continet unda maris,
Fac vacuus redeat nunquam sub vespere praeda
　　Ille domum—parva haec munera parva petunt.

ANDREA ALCIATI

(1492–1550)

Alciati takes his name from his birthplace, Alzate, a village near Como. When still very young he was taken to Milan, and began his studies there under Janus Parrhasius. Possibly at one time he received lessons from Janus Lascaris.[1] Among his early friends were Francesco Calvi and Aurelio Albuzzi (Albucius); the former became a learned bookseller in Rome, the latter like Alciati himself became a jurist. He also knew the Latin poet Bartolommeo Simonetta (below, p. 208). After Milan, Padua and Bologna were the scenes of Alciati's student years. At Padua he is said to have known Pomponio Gaurico. At Bologna he received the doctorate and completed his first book. He

---

[1] Ernst von Moeller, *Andreas Alciat*, Breslau, 1907, p. 11.

then returned to Milan (1514), and for four years practised law in that city.

Early in 1518 Alciati left Milan to become professor of jurisprudence at Avignon. There he taught in great honor until the spring of 1521, when, perhaps because his salary had not been regularly paid, he returned to Milan. A period of busy leisure followed. He courted the Visconti; on occasion practised his profession; and found time to compose several literary works. The idea of his *Emblemata* was conceived at the beginning of this period. Yet it was a time of turmoil in Milan; and Alciati himself appears to have had his house burnt in the tumults of 1523.

Again in 1529 the clouds were black over Italy. Alciati was glad to find in his knowledge of jurisprudence a source of welcome in France. His friend Albucius, who had already made his home there, probably in Bourges, urged Alciati to join him; the invitation was couched in the form of an epigram, which Alciati later included in his own *Emblemata*.[1] He began teaching at Bourges in April, 1529, and remained there till 1533. It was in this period that his Latin poems were published. His fame was now reaching its height. He had many famous pupils, among whom may be mentioned for his connection with the Anthology the Latin poet Joannes Secundus.

Finally in 1533 Alciati realized his lifelong desire to secure a chair in one of the Italian universities. He was called to Pavia. He then taught successively at Bologna (1537–41), again at Pavia (1541–3), and at Ferrara (1543–7); and his third period at Pavia closed with his death.

Alciati was undoubtedly a great jurist; but he enjoyed also a popular success, which to-day alone keeps his name alive, from his little book of verses and pictures. Doubtless during his younger years he had amused his leisure with the composition of Latin verses, many of which would be translations from the Anthology. A collection of these seems to have been presented to Ambrogio Visconti; but little appeared in print until the publication of Cornarius' *Selecta Epigrammata* in 1529, followed by the first *Emblemata* in 1531.[2] These we proceed to consider in turn.

I.

About 1520, while Alciati was still at Avignon, he allowed Boniface Amerbach, who was then with him, to excerpt from

---

[1] *Emb.* 143: *Albutii ad D. Alciatum suadentis, ut de tumultibus Italicis se subducat, et in Gallia profiteatur.* On Albucius see Mazzuchelli.

[2] Alciati's epigrams mostly remain unprinted. His MS. *Epigrammatum libri v*, is mentioned by Argelati (*Bibl. Med.*) and by Mazzuchelli as existing in their time in the library of the marchesi Visconti at Milan. Presumably this MS. was the source from which Amerbach, as mentioned below, drew Alciati's translations of the Greek epigrams. Cf. also below, p. 208.

his manuscripts a great number of verse-translations of the
Greek epigrams, and to carry them with him to Basel. The
Epigrammata Graeca of Joannes Soter, which appeared in 1525,
contained eleven translations by Alciati; but these were taken
from his previously published works.[1] In 1529, however, the
whole of Amerbach's excerpts were printed by Janus Cornarius
in a book founded on Soter's, but increased several times in
bulk by these translations of Alciati's and by many others from
the hand of Luscinius and of Cornarius himself. The *Selecta
Epigrammata* will occupy us again on a later page; here we need
notice only Alciati's part in it and his feelings about its publication.[2]

Cornarius' *Selecta Epigrammata* was published at Basel by
Bebellius in August, 1529. Alciati had just settled at Bourges.
Amerbach, who had copied the translations of Alciati, had
turned them over to Bebellius; his manuscript copy is still in
the University Library at Basel.[3] Bebellius had determined to
print them with the work of a number of German translators
in a new edition of Soter. This apparently was not pleasing to
Alciati, and he complained to Amerbach, who replied as follows in a letter dated January 1, 1529, seven months before the
book appeared:[4] 'I understand your finding some translations
of the epigrams not to be good. We have translated them in-
discriminately—those of us who are learned and those who are
not. More than a few are found among us, so uneasy with the
itch of conceit that in bringing to birth the offspring of their
wit they mostly miscarry.' Alciati propably had no intention
of obstructing the publication of the book.[5] Again, however,
after the book was published, he was inclined to be ashamed of

---

[1] Below, p. 206. The epigrams are: *A.P.* 7.357, 704; 9.357; 11.70, 233, 244, 256;
16.3, 32*, 68, 247. Two more (*A.P.* 7.152 and 16.275) were added in the third (1544)
edition of Soter. Rubensohn (*Griechische Epigramme und andere kleinere Dichtungen in
deutschen Uebersetzungen des xvi und xvii Jahrhunderts*, Weimar, 1897, p. lvi) implies
that all 13 were in the 1525 edition, and specially remarks that two of them are among
Alciati's *Emblemata* ('und das ist von Interesse'). These are precisely the last two mentioned above as appearing neither in the 1525 nor in the 1528 edition of Soter; they
could have reached the 1544 edition from the *Emblemata* by that time published or
from Cornarius. Hence no special interest attaches to them.
[2] The full title of the book with other details is given below, p. 283.
[3] Was, at least, in 1894, according to Th. Burckhardt-Biedermann, *Bonifacius Amerbach und die Reformation*, Basel, 1894, p. 215 n.
[4] Burckhardt-Biedermann, *op. cit.*, p. 214.
[5] It is curious to note that Cornarius' book contains no translations by Amerbach.

his company. In a letter to Calvi at Rome he writes (January 21, 1531):[1]

Scribis te cum non paucis eruditis admirari, cur permiserim carmina nostra Teutonicis illis ineptiis immisceri. Dicam tibi, quid in re sit. Quo tempore operam mihi Bonifacius Amorbacchius Avenione dabat —agitur, opinor, octavus annus—excerpserat ex autographis meis illa omnia, quae deinde ut Bebellii officinam adiuvaret, ei imprimenda communicavit idque me inconsulto. Tuli id non satis aequo animo; quod pleraque in eis erant a me tum puero edita, quae famae nocere potuissent, nisi legali doctrina hosce omnes naevos discussissem. Cogor itaque ferre aequius, postquam quod factum est fieri infectum non potest. Poteris tu una opera et huic malo mederi, et studiosis plurimum utilitatis adferre, si huius argumenti academicas translationes collegeris, invulgaverisque, adhibito tamen et in nostris quoque delectu, quorum plurima sunt ipsi mihi auctori displicentia.

If the date assigned to the letter of Amerbach, quoted above, is right, Alciati's 'me inconsulto' is here disingenuous; so too, perhaps, is the modest reason he gives for his displeasure.

Cornarius boasts that his book of selections contains more than 500 new translations. Of these, 300 are by Cornarius himself, 90 by Luscinius, and 154 by Alciati.[2] The versions of Alciati are on the whole the best, but their superiority is hardly enough to warrant any complaint of the 'German ineptitudes.' The following will serve as an example of the various styles, and will show how Cornarius' (and Soter's) book is arranged. First comes the text—here of *A.P.* 11.428—then follow the several translations.

ΛΟΥΚΙΑΝΟΥ

Εἰς τί μάτην νίπτεις δέμας Ἰνδικόν; ἴσχεο τέχνης·
οὐ δύνασαι δνοφερὴν νύκτα καθηλιάσαι.

ALCIATUS

Abluis Aethiopem quid frustra? ah desine, noctis
Illustrare nigrae nemo potest tenebras.

---

[1] *Marquardi Gudii Epistolae*, Utrecht, 1697, p. 110; also quoted by Rubensohn, *op. cit.*, p. lvii, who has corrected the date from 1530. Another letter to Calvi, written some months before, September 3, 1530, tells of his having sent Bebellius a collection of Greek epigrams, presumably Greek epigrams of his own composition, to print. Seemingly they never appeared. This letter is also in Gudius' collection, p. 108: 'Admirareris, si scires quam religiose me impressorum magistri plerique non sine muneribus adeant. . . . Cratandro recognita auctaque Paradoxa tradidi, quae nunc ille sub praelo habet, Bebellio Epigrammatum Graecorum Farraginem, quam ad te mittendam curabo, Frobeniis aliud.'

[2] There are 165 translations by Alciati in the book, but 11 of them had already appeared in Soter.

CORNARIUS

Aethiopem quid, stulte, lavas? Desistito ab arte:
In noctem nunquam lumina Solis ages.

LUSCINIUS

Indi parce lavare cutem, si proficis arte,
Phoebeum tentem nocte referre iubar.

IO. SLEIDANUS

Aethiopem quid, stulte, lavas? Nam splendida nunquam
Nox fuerit, lumen sole negante suum.[1]

Most of Alciati's translations are literal. Occasionally, however, he works up a hint from the Anthology into a composition
of his own. For example, Cornarius prints the following set of 28
verses as 'Alciati Imitatio fere omnium huius tituli [*Anth. Plan.*
2.13] Epigrammatum':[2]

Quis statuam erexit?—Dinoglyphus.—Eia age nomen
Ipse tuum?—Dicor Gryphus.—Id unde venit?—
Incurvo quod sum naso, hoc me nomine mordax
Zoilus et critici doctaque turba vocat.—
Cur facies nigra est fuligine?—Vana loquebar
Pro rostris, voci rhetoris obstrepitans.
Quum me chalcotypi crasso manus unguine tinxit,
Amplius haud potuit tergier ille color.—
Lumina tetra Merops tibi dic cur vellicet?—Odi
Patrem, ast ipsa patri est officiosa suo.—
Cur corpus maculis pallens distinguitur atris?
Anne cutem usserunt ferrea caela tuam?—
Ignea caela nihil, scabies sed Gallica, scorti
Contactu hic dudum me male morbus habet.—
Fallor an in facie tibi pyramis eminet? Eia
Dic sibi quid vultus pyramis illa velit?—
Falleris, in facie mihi nulla est pyramis, ingens
Sed nasus pilae more sedet Phariae.—
Dic, agedum, tanti quae nam sint commoda nasi,
Hispida quem sepes intus adacta premit?—
Si placuit fodisse, bidens; si caedere, falx est;
Si sterto, dices protinus esse tubam;

[1] Cornarius, p. 144. It will be noticed how easily three out of the four translators substitute 'Ethiop' for 'Indian.' Alciati's version of this epigram was employed by him, with an appropriate picture, for an emblem (No. 59), under the motto: '*Impossibile.*' 'To wash an Ethiop' became a common proverb in the sixteenth century; and doubtless Alciati's Emblem shared with an Adage of Erasmus much of the responsibility for its spread, both going back to the Anthology (cf. above, p. 4). The device in the 1531 *Emblemata* is crude—the patient is not even an Ethiop. It is bettered in 1534; but the best picture is in the Lyons edition of 1547; after that it declines.
[2] Cornarius, p. 169. Compare, e.g., *A.P.* 11.203.

Radere si villos mens est, tot colligo setas,
  Possit ut udones texere mille, cylix.
Si libuit piscari, instar mihi harundinis, aere
  Squammigenum flexo guttura fixa trahit.
Delphicus hic agitur gladius? puto. Sed tamen et vas
  Pandorae, clausum quum bene tegmen erat.

Several of Alciati's translations obtain a special interest by
his applying them to personal or at least modern purposes.
Thus an epigram of Crinagoras, glorifying Germanicus, (*A.P.*
9.291) is turned by Alciati to the praise of the Emperor Charles
V (Cornarius, p. 10). Again, the epigrammatist Agathias—also
a jurist in his time—composed a love-poem in nine books called
the *Daphniaca,* and on his work wrote the following epigram
(*A.P.* 6.80):

Δαφνιακῶν βίβλων 'Αγαθία ἡ ἐννεάς εἰμι·
  ἀλλά μ' ὁ τεκτήνας ἄνθετο σοί, Παφίη·
οὐ γὰρ Πιερίδεσσι τόσον μέλω, ὅσσον Ἔρωτι,
  ὄργια τοσσατίων ἀμφιέπουσα πόθων.
αἰτεῖ δ' ἀντὶ πόνων, ἵνα οἱ διὰ σεῖο παρείη
  ἤ τινα μὴ φιλέειν, ἤ ταχὺ πειθομένην.

[I am the nine books of Agathias' *Daphniaca:* he who made me
dedicates me to thee, O Paphian. I am less beloved of the Muses than
of Eros, since I discourse of the mysteries of so many loves. He asks, in
return for his toil, that through thee it may befall him either not to
love any one, or else one who quickly consents.]

Alciati's friend, the jurist Albucius, also wrote love-poems,
though they were of a somewhat serious cast.[1] Alciati therefore
imitates for him the verses of Agathias:

IMITATIO IN ALBUTII LIBELLOS

Deliciae hic vatis, flavique leguntur amores,
  Haec addicta tibi suscipe scripta, Venus.
Non hunc Pierides tantum fecere poetam,
  Sed puer et tristi mitis Amor pharetra.
Tu diva Aureolo concede haec praemia, nullam
  Ardeat, aut captum da cito posse frui.

---

[1] I cannot be sure whether Alciati refers to any of Albucius' published poems. His
verse is mainly religious. Even his *Heroidum Epistolarum libri iv* (Milan, 1542), which
may be what Alciati has in mind, is introduced by the same Alciati in the following
manner:
  Tempora nostra suas, ut habent, viden Heroinas?
    Quae superis homines insinuare student.
  Crimen amor veterum, laus est et gloria nostris,
    Et merito, illae homines, hae coluere Deos.

Again, *A.P.* 7.73 is an epitaph for Themistocles, in which all Greece is declared not to be too great a tomb for him—'Aντὶ τάφου λιτοῖο ϑὲς 'Ελλάδα, κ.τ.λ. Alciati uses this to pay a tribute to Gian Galeazzo Visconti, Duke of Milan—'Pro tumulo pone Italiam,' etc.[1]

Such was the nature of the translations excerpted by Amerbach and published by Cornarius in 1529.[2] As will already have been understood, some of them were later to be employed by Alciati for his great book, the *Emblemata*. To be precise, 28 of the translations printed in Cornarius' book appeared almost without changes among the 104 emblems published by Alciati in 1531; two others were added later.[3] This brings us to consider the *Emblemata*.

2.

As a matter of fact, Alciati had conceived the idea of his *Emblemata* some years previously, and had consecrated these epigrams to that use. It is necessary to return again to the year 1521. He had come back to Milan from Avignon, and was living on terms of familiarity with the Visconti, to whom he was possibly related by marriage. The Emblems were invented as a Christmas gift for Ambrogio Visconti. Alciati explains his conception to Calvi in a letter of December 9:[4] 'His Saturnalibus, ut illustri Ambrosio Vicecomiti morem gererem, libellum composui epigrammaton, cui titulum feci *Emblemata;* singulis enim epigrammatibus aliquid describo, quod ex historia vel ex rebus naturalibus aliquid elegans significet, unde pictores, aurifices, fusores id genus conficere possint, quae scuta appellamus et

---

[1] This later became *Emb.* 133.

[2] In Cornarius' book the following are translated by Alciati: *A.P.* 5.69, 70, 94, 127, 222, 302; 6.77, 80, 158, 283, 303, 309; 7.73, 89, 145, 152, 161, 172, 216, 233–4, 266, 288, 335, *357*, 383, 396, 433, 574, *704*;

9. 11–13B, 15, 16, 26, 31, 39, 42, 47, 52, 74, 86, 94, 95, 111, 115, 117, 118, 122, 132, 133, 141, 146 (2 versions), 148, 150, |158, 162, 165–7, 173, 221, 222, 223, 248, 259, 279, 291, 308, 339, *357*, 379, 391, 394, 410, 420, 441, 444, 456, 497, 515, 523, 548, 557, 664, 713–717, 720, 729, 730;

10.26, 27, 43, 48, 58, 67, 84, 88, 93, 98; 11.47, 50, *70*, 76, 107, 120, 153, 171, 198, 200, 203, 226, *233*, *244*, 251. *256*, 268, 272, 273, 278, 294, 369, 376, 381, 391, 395, 403, 404, 405, 406, 410, 413, 418, 421, 428, 431;

16.3, 4, 19, *32**, 60, *68*, 107, 108, 115+116, 129, 145, 146, 152, 171, 197, 201, 207, 209, 224, *247*, 250, 251, 275.

[3] The 30 epigrams reprinted as emblems are the versions of *A.P.* 7.145, 152, 161, 172, 216; 9.12, 42, 47, 86, 95, 115, 122, 146, 148, 158, 221, 291, 308, 339, 548; 10.98; 11.428; 16.4, 107, 115+116, 201, 207, 250, 251, 275. See below, p. 204.

[4] *Gudii Epist.*, p. 96. The letter is printed as of 1522; I agree with Rubensohn (*op. cit.*, p. liv) that it must have been written twelve months earlier.

petasis figimus, vel pro insignibus gestamus, qualis anchora
Aldi, columba Frobenii, et Calvi elephas tam diu parturiens,
nihil pariens.'

In this letter we assist at the birth of an artistic species, one
that flourished in a manner that is surprising, when its hybrid
nature is considered. The very germ of his notion Alciati does
not give us; the idea of this union of *pictura* and *poesis* might
have come from the Anthology in which there are many epigrams that may well have served some such purpose, or it may
have come from Varro's *Imagines*. In a way the epigram is only
an expansion of the motto that regularly accompanies the heral-
dic device; for it would seem that at first Alciati conceived of
little more in the way of pictures than such things as the anchor
of Aldus. In his emblems, as finally printed, however, there is a
motto as well as an epigram.[1] Alciati does not mention the
moral purpose which always informs the emblem; that was implied in the very word. The emblems suited the taste of the
Renaissance, and soon became a popular type; great artists—
Titian, Michelangelo, and Dürer—drew the devices for them.
Emblems became one of the larger departments of modern
literature.[2]

Although his first collection was made in 1521, Alciati did not
publish any Emblems until 1531, while he was teaching at
Bourges, and two years after his translations from the Anthology had been published by Bebellius. He then issued a collection of 104 Emblems from the press of Steyner at Augsburg.
Nine more were added in the Paris (Wechel) edition of 1534. A
collection of 86 new Emblems was printed at the Aldine Press in
1546. A combined edition of 198 Emblems appeared at Lyons
in 1547; and finally the Lyons edition of 1550—the year of
Alciati's death—has the full 211.[3]

---

[1] The word *emblema* properly refers only to the picture; it is derived from ἐμβάλλειν,
'to insert,' and was used in antiquity in reference to mosaic and tesselated work, and
to raised ornaments; cf. Cicero, *In Verr.* 2.4.17.22: 'scaphia cum emblematis Lily-
baei'.

[2] We still lack the bibliography of emblem-books proposed by Henry Green
(*Andrea Alciati and his Book of Emblems*, London, 1872, p. viii). Green says he had
himself formed an index of them, in which the titles numbered upwards of 3000 and
the authors above 1300.

[3] Green has noted about 180 editions. My references, unless otherwise specified,
are to the Paduan edition (by J. Thuilius), 1621.

The influence of Alciati's emblems is nearly as extensive a subject as the influence
of the Greek Anthology. I have therefore not attempted to record the Italian, French,
and English translations of each of Alciati's borrowings from the Greek epigrams. The

In imagining this amusement for Visconti, Alciati wasted no time in an attempt to concoct suitable epigrams; he drew on the accumulated manuscripts of his youth—the same manuscripts that he had recently put at the disposal of Amerbach. The result was, as already noticed, that a good many of his Emblems are translations from the Anthology. We have already suggested that some of the Greek epigrams may themselves originally have served a similar purpose; *A.P.* 16.207 by Palladas almost irresistibly requires this. Alciati has it as his 107th Emblem:[1]

POTENTIA AMORIS

Nudus Amor viden' ut ridet, placidumque tuetur?
 Nec faculas, nec quae cornua flectat, habet:
Altera sed manuum flores gerit, altera piscem,
 Scilicet ut terrae iura det atque mari.

chief translations were, according to Green, the following: Italian translations were made by (1) Giovanni Marquale (Lyons, 1549, 1551), (2) Paolo Emilio Cadamosto (Padua, 1626), and (3) Aurelio Amalteo (MS. about 1670–80, Green, p. 266). The French translators are: (1) Jacques le Fèvre (Paris, 1536, etc.), (2) Barthélémy Aneau (Lyons, 1549), and (3) Claude Mignault (Paris, 1583, 1587). Whitney's English versions (1586) I mean to describe in another place.

[1] The device, here reproduced from Green's *Andreae Alciati Emblematum fontes quatuor* (London, 1870), is that of the Wechel edition of 1534, the first edition to have Alciati's full approval. Though the actual designer is unknown, Wechel's devices are

Out of the 104 Emblems published in the first edition, 40 are translations from the Anthology. In subsequent editions the number of Emblems was more than doubled, but only 10 of the additions are from the Greek epigrams. Perhaps it is fair to infer that Alciati's interest in the Anthology was greatest in his early years. Yet among the 211 Emblems that make up what Green calls 'the full stream,' the 50 that are drawn from the Anthology are conspicuous, and probably give the character to the whole. Further, as Alciati's *Emblemata* assumed a place as one of the greatly popular books of modern times, we cannot easily overestimate its importance in making the themes of these epigrams generally known.[1]

Alciati's *Emblemata* was promptly subjected to learned comment; and the commentators were quick to point out material taken from the Anthology. There are two principal commentaries: (1) that of Francesco Sanchez, published at Lyons in 1573, and (2) that of Claude Mignault, published at Antwerp by Plantin in 1574.

Francisco Sanchez de Brozas (Sanctius) was one of the great Spanish humanists (1523–1601); he was professor of rhetoric and Greek in the University of Salamanca.[2] Sanchez leaves no doubt of the important part played by the Anthology in Alciati's Emblems. He quotes in the course of his commentary 56 epigrams, giving the translations of Thomas More, Ursinus, Alciati himself, and others—evidently drawing on the *Selecta Epigrammata* of Cornarius; some, however, he took from Erasmus' *Adagia*; and 21 he translated himself. His own are translations of *A.P.* 7.73, 146, 216; 9.88, 115, 116, 221,

---

said to have originated at Basel under the influence of Holbein; so G. Duplessis, *Les Emblèmes d'Alciat* (Paris, 1884), pp. 2, 13. This notion was unknown to Green, and Duplessis offers no proof of it. Perhaps he had in mind the strking similarity between the device for the emblem *In fertilitatem sibi ipsi damnosam* (Wechel, p. 43) and the printer's mark of the London printer Reginald Wolfe, said to have been designed by Holbein about 1543. This device may be seen in Woltmann's *Holbein and his Times*, Eng. tr., London, 1872, p. 381.

[1] Here follows a list of the Greek epigrams translated in the 'full stream' of the Emblems. In parentheses is given (from Green, pp. 318–25) the signature-number of the leaf on which each epigram appears in the first (1531) edition. When an epigram did not appear in the first edition, reference is made to the edition in which it first occurs. In the Register references are to the number of the Emblem in the 1621 edition.

A.P. 5.234 (D6), 237 (1546 leaf 40); 6.1 (B3^{vo}), 54 (1534, p. 114); 7.69 (1546 leaf 47), 73 (F3), 145 (A5^{vo}), 152 (1534, p. 119), 161 (E2), 172 (E2^{vo}), 216 (D7^{vo}), 225 (1546 leaf 1), 311 (1546 leaf 34vo); 9.3 (B8^{vo}), 12 (B2^{vo}), 42 (C2^{vo}), 47 (E5^{vo}), 86 (E3^{vo}), 95 (C3), 115 (B8), 122 (E8^{vo}), 130 (C5^{vo}), 146 (A6^{vo}), 148 (E7), 158 (C4^{vo}), 163 (D5), 221 (A4^{vo}), 231 (A6), 285 (E), 291 (C8), 308 (A6), 331 (D4), 339 (D7), 346 (E8^{vo}), 366 (1546 leaf 32), 548 (E4^{vo}); 10.50 (1546 leaf 10vo), 98 (A3); 11.397 (C6), 428 (E3); 16.4 (C8^{vo}), 107 (C7), 115+116 (1546 leaf 16), 183 (1534, p. cxiiii), 185 (1546, leaf 3), 201 (E5), 207 (D8), 223 (A7), 250 (D7), 251 (D6^{vo}), 275 (A8).

[2] Life in *Opera Omnia*, 4 vols., Geneva, 1766. The Commentary on Alciati's *Emblemata* is in vol. 3.

231, 366, 483, 584; 10.42, 98; 11.397; 13.29; 16.107, 129, 183, 207, 275, 276.¹ He thus translates 16.129, on the *Niobe* of Praxiteles:

> Vivebam: fecere Dii me marmora; marmor
> Sed rursum vivit munere Praxitelis.

Two epigrams (*A.P.* 7.172 and two versions of 9.95) are translated by Francesco's brother Fernando Sanchez; and 9.95 is also rendered by his friend Alphonsus Nunius of Medellin.

Claude Mignault, or Claudius Minos, (1536–1606), born at Dijon, was an *avocat du roi* at Étampes (Seine). It was on his journeys between Paris and Étampes that he rendered the Emblems into French verse (above, p. 202, n. 3). His commentary was not published until that of Sanchez had already been a year before the public, but is said to have been completed in 1571. Mignault was urged to compose his comments by Legier Bontemps, a monk of Dijon.

Like Sanchez, Mignault not only notices most (not all) of the Greek epigrams on which the Emblems are founded, but also many others that illustrate the theme in question, however remotely. These do not, however, by any means all appear in the earlier editions of his work. Those that do appear in the earlier editions are supplied with metrical translations borrowed, without acknowledgment, from Soter's *Epigrammata Graeca*, and sometimes with prose versions by Mignault.

In his later editions Mignault quotes 70 epigrams, and supplies most of them with an (unacknowledged) translation from Soter, and with a prose version and a second metrical version which are his own.² He thus has metrical versions of the following:³ *A.P.* 5.176, 234; 7.62, 71, 73, 142, 145, 152, 161, 172, 216, 225; 9.12, 13, 13B, 39, 42, 47 (2 versions), 86, 95, 115, 116, 122, 130, 158, 163, 221 (2 versions), 231, 285, 291, 302, 308, 331, 339, 346, 375, 548, 584; 10.50, 98, 110; 11.49 (2 versions), 397; 16.93, 107, 183, 201, 207, 223, 224, 250, 251, 275. I give Mignault's translation of *A.P.* 9.308:

> Praecipitem e navi citharoedum aliquando latrones
> In vastum pelagi forte dedere fretum;

---

¹ Included in the Register, where references are to the number of the Emblem of Alciati under which Sanchez' translation appears in his edition; if the 1621 edition is used, add 1 to each number above 80.

In Sanchez' Notes on Politian's *Nutricia* he translates *A.P.* 6.314; 7.54; 9.26, 184; and in his *Vida de Epicteto, A.P.* 7.676.

² In adding his own to the version of *A.P.* 16.183 taken from Soter in illustration of *Emb.* 23, Mignault explains his purpose in the following words: 'Nos eundem hunc dialogismum duplici interpretatione expressimus, quam hic, lector optime, repraesentamus, ut etiam aliorum Epigrammatum Graecorum, quorum non pauca sibi sumpsit Alciatus ad sua cudenda Emblemata, non ut putes nos cum artifici nobili Alciato certamen suscepisse, sed ut intellegas libera esse studia, et non parvae laudi fore vel in minimis aemulari meliores. Hoc genus versionis multos annos recondidi, ea mente, ne unquam foras evolaret; sed ex amicis nostris plerique vim mihi iniecerunt, et putaverunt esse satius edere quam perdere, ad excitandam saltem, quod aiunt, "studiosorum industriam." Hic igitur animum, non carmina iacto, quae fieri multo meliora possunt. Sed quocunque res abeat, id contentionis genus si tibi probatur, aut non prorsus improbatur, nullum mihi palmarium deposco liberalius.'

³ These translations are referred to in the Register by the numbers of Alciati's Emblems in the 1608 (Plantin) edition; for the 1621 edition, add 1 to emblems above 80.

Protinus in mediis delphin apparuit undis,
  Illicio gratae dulcisonaeque chelys.
Sessoremque isthmum devexit adusque Corinthi,
  Fluctibus et mediis reddidit incolumem.
Hinc patet indomito meliores aequore nasci
  Pisces, quam tellus gignat alumna viros.

The commentaries of Sanchez and Mignault flowed into the 'monster commentary' of a Breisgau professor, Joannes Thuilius, which was printed at Padua in 1621. Thuilius adds some translations from the Anthology to those previously made, but I have not thought it to the purpose to extract them. Besides his own translations he adds a few from Sabeo, others from Cornarius, and some from various sources. His book is the last word in commentaries, containing 1003 large pages printed in double columns.

3.

We have noticed that before Cornarius' Epigrams came out Soter was able to find eleven of Alciati's translations in previous publications.[1] Five of them were from Alciati's first book, published at Bologna in 1513, *Annotationes in tres posteriores Codicis libros*, in which eight epigrams are quoted.[2] His *Annotationes in Tacitum* (1517) contains *A.P.* 10.44 and 16.68; his *Dispunctiones* (c. 1517), *A.P.* 16.32*; his *Praetermissa* (1518), *A.P.* 7.357; 11.233, 244; and 16.60. In the treatise *De Singulari Certamine* (1529) he uses *A.P.* 9.39 and 391; and in *De Verborum Significatione* (1529) he quotes a line from *A.P.* 11.355. But his most considerable use of the epigrams in this incidental way occurs in his *Parerga Juris* (1536, 1543, 1551), where he quotes twenty-one of them.[3] His Commentaries on the Pandects (publ. 1560) naturally gave less scope for such quotation, and the Anthology there comes into play only a few times.[4] There are also a few scraps in minor posthumous works—references to *A.P.* 9.8 and 10.50 in his comments on the metres and diction of Plautus;[5] in his History of Milan he

---

[1] The source from which Soter drew Alciati's translation of *A.P.* 11.256 still eludes me.

[2] *A.P.* 6.42.4, 179.1–2; 7.704; 9.357; 11.70; 16.3, 247, 387.1–2, all with translations except the first two and the last. My references [*Op.*] are to Alciati's *Opera Omnia*, 4 vols., Basel (Guarinus), 1582.

[3] *A.P.* 5.94.3–4, 302.17–8; 9.85, 387, 441, 502; 10.26, 44, 48; 11.76, 176, 181, 275, 312.4, 330, 373, 376.11–2, 398, 425; 16.18, 19.

[4] *A.P.* 9.75; 10.43, 108, 119; 11.154.5–6, 376 in the section *De verborum et rerum significatione*, and a translation of *A.P.* 11.356 in *De liberis et posthumis*. Some very slight references I have passed over.

[5] *M. Accii Plauti . . . Comoediae*, Basel (Hervagen), 1568, pp. 77 and 88 respectively.

quotes his translation of *A.P.* 16.32*;[1] and in his epistle *Contra Vitam Monasticam* quotes *A.P.* 7.314 and 10.44.[2] Several of these quotations consist of only one line; but most of them are complete and accompanied by translations.[3] The translations are mainly the same as those printed in Cornarius' *Selecta Epigrammata*, but there are some that do not appear in that book, namely translations of *A.P.* 7.314; 9.85, 441, 502; 10.26, 44, 108, 119; 11.154.5–6, 176, 181, 275, 312.4, 330, 355.2, 373, 398, 425, 16.18 (prose).[4] These nineteen versions all appear in books published long after the date of Amerbach's excerpts from Alciati's manuscripts.

One occasional use of an epigram merits more attention. When Alciati at last secured his professorship at Pavia, and fortune seemed to smile upon him, he delivered an inaugural oration in which he alludes to his past vicissitudes, and bears witness to the support he had always received from his legal studies:[5]

Tradunt Zenonem philosophum, cum naufragium fecisset, dixisse, se nunquam felicius navigasse, quam cum rebus amissis vacare philosophiae deinde coepisset. Idem ut usurpare ego possum, qui cum in patria otio quondam nimiaque tranquillitate fere marcescerem, atrocitate bellorum demum excitatus peregrinari coepi, et ad hanc disciplinam confugi, quae mihi plane fuit, quod proverbio Graeco dicitur, *Myrtili clypeus*. Fuit is ingentis animi miles, scuto pugnare solitus, qui cum ad maritimam expeditionem navigasset, submersa forte navi eidem clypeo innixus in tutum portum delatus est. De quo hunc in sensum Leonidas poeta scripsit:

> Bina pericla unis effugi Myrtilis armis,
>   Cum premererque solo, cum premererque salo.
> Incolumem ex acie clypeus me praestitit, idem
>   Navifragem apprensus littus adusque tulit.

Sic mihi haec egregia professio omni in tempore, omni in fortuna auxilio fuit, quod ceu senectuti vestrae viaticum, ut et vos comparetis, hortor suadeoque.

The epigram here made to illustrate Alciati's whole life is *A.P.* 9.42. Alciati's translation had already been printed by Cornarius in 1529, and had appeared among the Emblems in

---

[1] Graevius, *Thesaurus Antiquitatum et Historiarum Italiae* (Leyden, 1704), 2.47 (first published at Milan in 1625).

[2] Ed. by Antonius Matthaeus, Leyden, 1695.

[3] The Register will make clear the nature of the quotation in each case.

[4] A translation by Alciati of *A.P.* 10.26 is given by Cornarius, but differs from that in *Parerga*.

[5] *Opera* 4.1035; also quoted in Comment. of the 1621 *Emblemata*, p. 685.

1531. In the Emblem the device shows a man in armor swimming on his shield, and behind him, on shore, a military camp.[1] The motto is: *Auxilium nunquam deficiens*.

BARTOLOMMEO SIMONETTA

(*fl.* 1510)

Simonetta was a son of a noble and learned Milanese, Giovanni Simonetta, and was one of several brothers who became men of note. Little is known of his life, which seems to have been a quiet one devoted to letters. He was a friend of Alciati and of Nicolaus Pacedianus. He is buried in S. Maria della Grazie.[2] Simonetta's poems seem mostly to have perished, save for one or two commendatory pieces on his friends' books. Argelati mentions a six-line epigram by him in the manuscript of Alciati's *Epigrammata* preserved in the Visconti Library. Probably this is the translation of *A.P.* 9.148 printed by Cornarius in 1529 (below, p. 284); it would have been taken, along with Alciati's translations, by Amerbach from Alciati's manuscript about 1520 (above, p. 196):[3]

> Defle hominum vitam plus quam, Heraclite, solebas,
> In lachrymas totos solve age nunc oculos.
> Concute maiori splenem, Democrite, risu,
> Et toto resonans ore cachinnus hiet.
> Vita fuit nunquam post condita saecula mundi
> Et risu pariter dignior et lachrymis.

VENTURINO VASOLLI

(*fl.* 1540)

Vasolli, a native of Fivizzano, appears to have been a teacher of literature at Pavia. He was married, his wife's name being Peregrina. In 1540 he published at Pavia a small book of epigrams, *Epigrammatum Sylva*, dedicated to the Imperial Legate, Alfonso Davalo.[4] At

---

[1] This was the device after 1534; the first edition merely shows a warrior standing beside his shield. The epigram, when turned to the uses of an emblem, is generalized by the substitution of *'sedulus'* for *'Myrtilus'* in the first line.

[2] Argelati, *Bibl. Med.* 2.1394.

[3] In Cornarius (p. 20) it is followed by Alciati's version of the same epigram; see Register.

[4] *Venturini Vasolli Fivizanen. Epigrammatum Sylva. Ad Illustriss. Alphonsum Davalum, Vasti Principem, Excellentiss. in Italia pro Caesare. In alma civitate Papien. Studiorum hospitio.* anno M.D. XXXX. Ff. 1–40ʳᵒ. On f. 4ʳᵒ is a laudatory poem addressed to Vasolli by Hieronymus Quercens, who calls him 'bonus grammaticus, bonus poeta.'

the same place in 1553 appeared his *Amoenissimum Musarum Viridarium*, dedicated to the Doge of Venice, Francesco Donato.[1]

The *Epigrammatum Sylva* mainly consists of occasional, or more exactly, laudatory epigrams addressed to the great persons of Vasolli's day—Andrea Doria, Pietro Aretino, Paul III, and many others. He appears to favor the nobility of Genoa. Among these verses, most of which are at least written in a tolerable style, are several wretched *facetiae*, and some few epigrams of a general application. These last include nine that come from the Anthology, though their Greek origin is not acknowledged: *A.P.* 5.78; 9.126; 10.84; 11.273 (3 versions), 384, and 430 (2 versions). Worse than Vasolli's failure to acknowledge a Greek source, is his suppression of the fact that hardly any of these translations are entirely his own. The first (5.78) may be his work—it is not a direct translation. The second (9.126) is doubtful; it appeared in the following year among the verses of Scaphenatus (below, p. 210), whose translations are more numerous than those of Vasolli, and otherwise arouse no suspicion. The version of 10.84 seems to be Vasolli's own. But of the versions of 11.273 the first is Alciati's, the second mainly Sleidan's, only the third being by Vasolli. The coupling of Alciati and Sleidan shows that he was copying from the *Selecta Epigrammata* of Cornarius (below, p. 283). From the same source he took Bergius' version of 11.384, adding to it an amplifying couplet; and finally, for 11.430, he borrows from Cornarius the translations by Sir Thomas More and Luscinius. These stolen articles are variously treated. The last two are taken over without change. Sleidan's version of 11.273 is corrected. Originally it read:

> Ut pes, sic animus tibi claudicat indicioque
> Pes fuerit, quali praeditus es animo.

In the second line ēs is only not quite impossible; Vasolli writes: quali es praeditus ingenio, and makes the translation his own. He follows it with an inferior version wholly by himself:

> Pectore ceu gressu certum est te vivere claudo:
> Effigies animum porrigit ipsa tuum.

---

[1] *Venturini Vasolli Fivizanensis Poetae Amoenissimum Musarum Viridarium. Ad Illustrissimum Franciscum Donatum, Venetiarum Ducem Sereniss.* Papiae. Apud Franciscum Moschenium. M.D. LIII. Ff. 1-52ᵛᵒ. On f. 27ʳᵒ is an epigram addressed to the poet's wife. Copies of both Vasolli's books are in the writer's possession.

Vasolli's second book, aside from favoring the nobility of Venice rather than that of Genoa, is of the same character as the first; indeed some of the contents of the earlier volume are here reprinted, including the verses drawn from *A.P.* 5.78; 9.126; 11.384, and 430. An improvement has been introduced into the last line of the version of 9.126; otherwise there are no changes. In addition to these, the *Musarum Viridarium* contains epigrams by Vasolli recalling *A.P.* 5.95 and 9.440 (f. 23ro).

JOANNES BAPTISTA SCAPHENATUS
(*fl.* 1541)

Virtually nothing is known of Scaphenatus. He published a book of Latin verse at Venice in 1541 [at the end: 1542] entitled *Elegiae et Epigrammata*. On the title-page he is announced as 'a citizen of Milan.' Argelati (*Biblioth. Script. Mediol.*) gives his name as Sclafenatus, his father's name as Thomas and his mother's as Catherina Zerba. Among the members of his family was a cardinal, Joannes Jacobus Sclafenatus. This information he gained from the tombs of the Sclafenati, among which was that of Joannes Baptista, in the church of S. Maria della Passione at Milan.

Scaphenatus' epigrams include 16 translations from the Greek Anthology: *A.P.* 5.180; 7.149, 216; 9.72, 126,[1] 166, 293, 331, 749; 11.193, 214; 12.235; 16.129, 130, 174, 276. The following are his versions of 16.130 and 276:

> Aspice quam vere Niobes lachrymatur imago
> Saxea, natorum tristia fata dolens,
> Spirantem aspiceres etiam, sed denegat illi
> Ars animam, similis marmoreae est Niobi.

> Haec simulacra tibi posuit Periander, Arion,
> Delphino haec qui te per vada falsa tulit.
> Et factum admirans exclamat protinus: 'Ergo
> Nos servant pisces, nos perimunt homines?'

COUNT NICCOLÒ D'ARCO (ARCHIUS)
(1479–1546)

Archius was born at Arco near the north end of Lake Garda, Arco being a fief of his family. As the younger son he was sent to be educated as page in the court of the Emperor Ferdinand III. Later he saw service in Flanders under Fürstenberg. The death of his elder

---

[1] On this version see above, p. 209.

brother putting him at the head of his family, he returned to Arco, and devoted the remainder of his life to literary pursuits. His death is believed to have occurred in the year in which his Latin poems were published. These were entitled *Numerorum libri iv*, and appeared at Mantua in 1546.[1]

The last couplet of the following epigram by Archius shows that he had *A.P.* 7.174 in mind:

AD DAPHNIN

Nec posthac coryli grata deiectus in umbra
    Mulcebis pecudes carmine, Daphni, tuas;
Nec patriis posthac texes umbracula Nymphis;
    Populea sternes nec tibi fronde torum.
Iuppiter afflavit te fulmine: vespere sero
    Ad stabula attonitae vix rediere boves.

The edition of 1762 also gives to Archius an imitation of *A.P.* 9.627, taken, says a note, from the Aldine *Carminum collectio* of 1533. This proves to be the version printed—for the first time, Baehrens believed—in 1882 in the *Poetae Latini Minores* (4.438), from *Cod. Riccard*, 2939, a fifteenth-century MS. The epigram is given above, p. 26. It cannot be certainly claimed for Archius.[2]

PIER VETTORI

(1499–1585)

Vettori's reputation is that of the foremost classical scholar of his time in Italy. He belonged to a noble Florentine family. In Greek he had for teachers Andrea Dazzi, Marcello Hadriano, and Giorgio Riescio of Poggibonsi; he studied mathematics with Giuliano Ristori of Prato; and jurisprudence for a time at Pisa. In 1517 he married; in 1522 he went to Spain with the escort that was to fetch the new pope Adrian VI to Italy. Most of his life, save for one or two short periods in Rome, was passed in Florence. In 1538 Duke Cosimo named him public professor of Greek and Latin, a position he held with great honor till his death. His best works are his edition of Cicero (1537), his Commentaries on Aristotle's *Rhetoric* (1548), *Poetics* (1560), *Politics* (1576), and *Nicomachean Ethics* (1584), and his *Variae Lectiones*, of which twenty-five books were published in 1553, and thirteen more in 1569. His *Epistolae et Orationes* appeared in 1586, edited by his grandson, Francesco Vettori. There are monographs on Vettori by

---

[1] My references are to the edition published at Verona in 1762.

[2] I find no further notice of an Aldine *Carminum collectio* of 1533. Archius has (*Num.*, p. 234) a version of the Anacreontic that appears in part as *A.P.* 11.48; but does not follow the form given in the Anthology.

W. Rüdiger, *Petrus Victorius aus Florenz*, Halle, 1896, and by Francesco Niccolai, *Pier Vettori (1499–1585)*, Florence, 1912.

The Anthology was not, apparently, a book that Vettori turned to with any frequency; an examination of his chief works hardly yields a quotation. Some interest in it on his part is, however, betrayed by a manuscript miscellany written out by him, and now preserved in the Staatsbibliothek at Munich (*Cod. Gr.* 235); it contains (ff. 234–7) epigrams by Anyte, Leonidas, Nicarchus, Palladas, Archias, Bianor, Phanias, etc.[1]

A brief chapter in Vettori's *Variae Lectiones* (20.17) touches on the Platonic epigrams *A.P.* 7.669–70, which he quotes from Diogenes Laertius, and *A.P.* 5.78, taken from Gellius; but is chiefly interesting for containing the Anacreontic Λέγουσιν αἱ γυναῖκες, which had been given to him by Henri Estienne in his passage through Florence. Of the epigrams Vettori merely says that he thinks *A.P.* 7.669 should be separated from 770.[2]

FAUSTO SABEO (SABAEUS)

(*c.* 1478–*c.* 1558)

Sabeo's translations from the Anthology remained till late in the eighteenth century the most extensive made by any Italian. They form by far the greater part of his large book of Latin verse (872 pages), in which they are sown on an average of three to a page.

Of Sabeo not much is known beyond what may be gathered from his book: *Epigrammatum Fausti Sabaei Brixiani Custodis Bibliothecae Vaticanae Libri Quinque ad Henricum Regem Galliae: Primus de Diis; Secundus de Heroibus; Tertius de Amicis; Quartus de Amoribus; Quintus de Miscellaneis*, Romae apud Valerium et Aloisium Doricum fratres Brixien. M.D.LVI. He was born at Brescia, and was *custos* of the Vatican Library. This post, it seems, he held under seven popes—from Leo X to Paul IV. He was sent by Leo, we learn from one of his poems, to the North (perhaps to England and Ireland) in search of ancient manuscripts. When setting out on this journey he left three books of *Amores* in the keeping of a supposed friend, who on his return denied the trust (*Epig.*, p. 840). After the sack of Rome (1527) Sabeo addressed a poem to Clement VII urging him to repair the losses of the library (p. 846). He was the first editor of Arnobius, *Adversus Gentes*

---

[1] Ignaz Hardt, *Elect. Bibl. Monac. Codd. Graeci Msc.* in Aretin's *Beyträge zur Geschichte und Literatur* 4 (1805). 580. Vettori's collection of MSS., more than 250 in number, after his death was taken first to Rome, then to Mannheim, and finally to Munich (Maillot in Aretin's *Beyträge* I (1803).75.).

[2] G. J. Voss (*De Veterum Poetarum Temporibus*, Amsterdam, 1696, p. 227) says that Vettori praises the epigrammatist Palladas in *Var. Lect.* 16.15; but I can find no reference to Palladas in Vettori's book.

(1542), and possibly of Aithicus' *Cosmographia* (1513). He claimed the acquaintance of many of the scholars and great persons of his day; and his poems abound in epigrams addressed to them—to Janus Lascaris (p. 542), Aleander (p. 483), Francis I of France (p. 865), Calcagnini (p. 754), Cardinal Pole (p. 583), Angelo Colocci (p. 562), Bembo (p. 544), Cardinal Jean du Bellay (*passim*), and many others. A set of verses on human life (p. 722) is addressed to a brother Pietro Sabeo. Perhaps the most interesting of these personal addresses is that to Michelangelo (p. 472), in which Sabeo imagines a novel kind of collaboration between himself and the painter. It is sufficiently naïve.

> Quod te amo, te et veneror, turba admiratur, et haeret,
> Quis nam sit tantae nodus amicitiae.
> Nescit enim, studio simili quod iungimur; ambo
> Fingimus, ingenio namque ego, tuque manu.
> Ipse ego et electis verbis, tuque ille colore,
> Utraque pictura ars atque poesis inest.
> Sed tua muta silet, fatur mea garrula ut Echo,
> Si retices reticet, si loqueris loquitur.
> Quod si nostra forent iuncta, ut nos iungimur, essent
> Viva, dares corpus, verba ego et ingenium.

There is a notice of Sabeo in A. M. Quirini, *Specimen Variae Litteraturae, quae in Brixia florebat* (Brescia, 1739) 2.167, and in Roscoe, *Leo X* (1846) 2.279–280; but neither has gone beyond what may be gathered from the *Epigrammata*.

Even the lines to Michelangelo, just quoted, depend on the Anthology, for the fourth couplet is virtually identical with Sabeo's translation of *A.P.* 9.27, on Echo. His book is dedicated to Henry II of France, to whom he applies a translation of *A.P.* 9.219; the original is an epigram written by Diodorus of Sardis in praise of Nero (probably the son of Germanicus). Sabeo's *Epigrammata* are almost wholly translations from the Anthology. His original epigrams were scattered among these; but most of what profess to be original are obviously modeled on the Greek. He commonly makes more than one version of a single Greek epigram, and often places different versions in various parts of his volume. The headings of Sabeo's four books, as given in his title, do not give an exact account of their contents; the attempt, however, at grouping is modeled on the Anthology. As a translator he aims, in general, to be literal, and to put his version into the same number of lines as the original. That, to be sure, is one of the canons that few translators of the Greek epigrams would venture to break.

The following examples of Sabeo's skill are taken, respectively, from the amatory, votary, sepulchral, epideictic, and satirical epigrams, and epigrams on works of art.

> Non magnum si ridet Amor, ferit, urit et una:
> Huic sunt adfines spicula, flamma, mare.
> Vulcanus coniunx, Gradivus matris amator;
> Nata mari est genitrix dulcis amara Venus.
> Dat mare saevitiam, Mars tela intincta cruore,
> Blanditias genitrix, Mulciber ipse faces.
>
> (*A.P.* 5.180)

The original of the next is given above on p. 191. It will be observed that Sabeo does not allow the name of the dedicant—Eudemus in the Greek—to disturb the metre of his first line. *Blandior*, in his second line, must be an anticipation of J. G. Schneider's conjecture: πρηυτάτῳ; it can hardly be a misunderstanding of πιοτάτῳ, the universal reading in Sabeo's day.—

> Excitat hoc templum Zephyro Budemus in agris,
> Solus enim est ventis blandior ipse aliis:
> Affuit oranti spirans ocyssime ab imis,
> Leniret fructum caulibus ut peponum.
>
> (*A.P.* 6.53)

Sabeo's translations from the sepulchral epigrams are very numerous. The following, however, though among the epitaphs, cannot strictly be called one:

> Fune petram Bocus serpens conscenderat altam,
> Forte boum pastor, cerea regna petens,
> Cum canis armenti custos, dominumque secutus,
> Corrosit funem mellis amore gravem:
> Corruit et praeceps pastor miserabilis, et mel
> Dulce aliis, illi funera amara dedit.
>
> (*A.P.* 7.622)

Here Sabeo makes a point such as one might expect—a commonplace which the original author, Antiphilus, avoids:

> τὸ δ' ἀτρυγὲς ἀνδράσιν ἄλλοις
> κεῖνο μέλι ψυχῆς ὤνιον εἰρύσατο

[That honey, which other men could not gather, he still grasped at the cost of his life.]

A.P. 9.627 is the original of Shakespeare's last two sonnets; the following is Sabeo's version of that epigram:

> Sub platano viridi apposita iam lampade Nymphis,
> Victus erat somno nequitiosus Amor.

Inter se haec dicunt, 'Nitamus lampada, Nymphae,
  Suffocare, hominum quae male corda cremat.'
Dumque volunt flammas extinguere, lympha calescit;
  A Nymphis calidae sic oriuntur aquae.

Like Valeriano, Sabeo exercises his pen in composing Replies and Allusions to the epigrams he translates, and also in
turning the same epigram in more than one way. Once he
makes as many as thirteen versions of the same epigram. His
skill may be sufficiently seen in two versions of *A.P.* 9.346 (cf.
above, p. 134):

Quae terram totam et pontum, Philomela, volasti,
  Suspendes nidum Colchidos ad statuam?
Sperasti servare tuos num Colchida pullos,
  Quae propriis natis parcere non voluit?

Quae terram atque salum, Pandione nata, secasti,
  Elegis Aeeae nidificare sinu.
Stulta quidem credis servari a Colchide natos;
  Servabitne tuos, perdere sueta suos?

From the satirical epigrams we may be content with his version of *A.P.* 11.237:

Vipera Cappadocem iam saeva momordit, et hausto
  Sanguine pestifero est mortua Cappadocis.

A.P. 16.276 is on a statue of Arion and the Dolphin, supposed to have been erected by Periander:

Erexit statuam Periander Arionis et qui
  Aequora sulcanti tegora curva dedit;
Delphini monstrat placidi pia fabula, quantum
  Exuperent homines impietate feras.

The following are the epigrams employed by Sabeo:[1]

A.P. 2.414; 5.2, 3, 4 (version and *allusio*), 7 (2 versions), 8, 10, 11
(2 versions and reply), 12, 13.1–6, 16, 20, 21, 22, 24, 25, 26, 30, 36,
39, 41, 64, 65, 66, 68, 69, 80 (4 versions), 81, 82, 83+4, 87, 89, 90,
92–95, 97, 101, 103, 106, 107, 110–3, 115, 117, 119, 124, 127, 130, 133,
139 (2 versions), 140, 141, 143–5, 147–8, 151 (2 versions), 155 (2 versions), 168, 171, 176–7, 179, 180 (6 versions), 187, 189–90, 194, 196–7,
210, 212, 215–6, 217 (2 versions), 221–2, 223 (2 versions), 225, 228–9,
231–2, 234, 236–7, 239, 241, 254, 256, 258.5–6, 261–3, 266–70, 273–4,
279–81, 282 (2 versions), 286–8, 292–3, 295 (9 versions), 298, 300, 306,
308;

---

[1] In the Register I have not distinguished the 'allusions' from the translations; save
that they are always listed last among Sabeo's versions of a given epigram.

6.1 (3 versions), 5, 9, 11, 13–6, 18–22, 23 (2 versions), 24, 26 (2 versions), 27–8, 30, 32–3, 35–6, 38–9, 41, 42 (2 versions), 43–4, 46–7, 50–6, 58–62, 65, 67, 69–73, 76, 77 (7 versions), 79–81, 83, 86–9, 97, 102, 104–5, 117, 120, 124–5, 129–31, 134, 154 (7 versions), 155–7, 160–1, 164, 166, 169 (2 versions), 171, 172, 174–5, 180, 183, 190, 196, 198, 208, 218–9, 221, 228, 236, 241 (2 versions), 243, 246–7, 249, 259, 283 (2 versions), 285–7, 291–2, 302–3, 306, 309, 312, 324–6, 328, 331, 333, 340.3–6;

7.1, 3 (3 versions), 4–6, 8 (2 versions), 9, 11 (2 versions), 13, 15 (3 versions), 16 (3 versions), 17–20, 22 (version and *allusio*), 23.1–6, 23.7–8 (4 versions), 25, 27–30, 32 (2 versions), 33 (2 versions), 36, 43–4, 46 (3 versions), 47, 49–53, 55, 57 (3 versions), 58–60, 61 (2 versions), 62 (3 versions), 63, 66–75, 76 (4 versions), 78, 80, 83 (2 versions), 84–5, 89–92, 99, 108–9, 110 (2 versions), 114, 119–21, 123–6, 127 (2 versions and *allusio*), 128–30, 134, 135 (2 versions), 136–43, 145–51, 152 (2 versions), 153, 156–7, 160–62, 166, 170–4, 178–80, 182, 184–6, 190 (2 versions), 191, 195–7, 201 (2 versions), 204, 207 (2 versions), 208–9, 212–3, 216, 217 (7 versions), 218–9, 221–3, 224 (3 versions), 225–7, 229, 230 (2 versions), 231–8, 239 (4 versions), 240 (2 versions), 241–3, 245, 249, 250–1, 254, 257, 261, 264, 265 (3 versions), 266, 268–75, 279–80, 282, 284–9, 291, 294–5, 298, 300–1, 304–5, 307–8, 310, 311 (2 versions), 312, 313 (3 versions), 314–7, 321, 323 (2 versions), 326–30, 333, 338, 340, 342 (2 versions), 344.1–2, 344.3–4, 346, 348–50, 351.1–6, 351.7–10 (2 versions), 352 (2 versions), 354–5, 359, 369, 376, 378, 381, 383, 387, 396, 398, 400, 403–4, 408, 412–14, 417, 421, 431–2, 433 (2 versions), 434, 437–9, 442, 444–5, 451–2, 455–6, 459, 461 (2 versions), 465–8, 470–1, 477–80, 483, 485–90, 492–3, 499–500, 505 (2 versions), 507.1–2, 512, 515 (2 versions), 522, 526, 528–9, 530 (version and reply), 532, 534.1–2 (5 versions), 535–6, 540–1, 546–7, 549, 551–2, 554, 556, 558–9, 560.3–8, 562, 564, 565 (3 versions), 566, 567 (2 versions), 568–9, 573, 575, 578, 580+581, 582, 588–91, 593–5, 597–8, 601, 604–8, 610–3, 615, (2 versions), 616 (3 versions), 617 (7 versions), 621–3, 628–9, 632, 634, 637 (3 versions), 641, 643, 646–7, 649 (2 versions), 655 (2 versions), 656–7, 662.1–4, 666, 667 (version and *allusio*), 668, 669+670 (2 versions), 674, 676 (4 versions), 680, 684, 687–8, 691, 696, 702, 714–5, 740–1, 745 (2 versions,) 747 (2 versions), 748;

9.1 (2 versions), 2–3, 4 (2 versions), 5, 7–8, 9.1–4, 9.5–6, 10 (2 versions), 12 (5 versions), 13.1–2 (3 versions), 13.3–8 (2 versions), 14–7, 18 (2 versions), 19–24, 26–9, 30 (2 versions), 31 (2 versions), 32, 37 (?), 38 (2 versions), 39 (2 versions), 40–1, 43, 44 (4 versions), 46 (2 versions), 47, 48 (2 versions), 49, 51, 52 (2 versions), 53 (2 versions), 54 (2 versions), 55 (2 versions), 56 (13 versions), 57–9, 61–2, 64, 66, 67 (3 versions), 68 (2 versions and *allusio*), 69 (2 versions), 70–2, 74–6, 78–9, 82–3, 85, 87–8, 89 (2 versions), 92–5, 97, 99, 103.1–6, 104–7, 108 (4 versions), 109, 111 (2 versions and *allusio*), 112, 114–7, 118 (3 versions), 120 (2 versions), 122–3, 124 (3 versions and *allusio*), 125, 126 (5 versions), 128+129, 130 (2 versions), 132, 133 (3 versions), 134

(2 versions), 136–8, 141 (3 versions), 142–3, 146 (3 versions), 148, 150–4, 156–8, 160–1, 162 (2 versions), 163 (4 versions), 165–7, 171 (2 versions), 172, 173 (version and *allusio*), 175–6, 178, 179 (2 versions and *allusio*), 183, 185 (version and *allusio*), 186–92, 197, 199, 204, 206–8, 211–3, 218–9, 222–4, 226, 228, 231, 233 (2 versions), 236, 238, 241 (2 versions), 244, 245 (2 versions), 246, 247 (2 versions), 248–9, 252–3, 254 (2 versions), 255, 257–8, 259 (2 versions), 260 (2 versions), 261, 265, 269–70, 274 (2 versions), 275, 278 (2 versions), 279–80, 283, 285 (version and *allusio*), 286–7, 289, 292 (2 versions), 293–4, 295 (version and *allusio*), 298 (version and *allusio*), 299, 301, 302 (2 versions), 303, 304 (version and *allusio*), 305–9, 310 (version and *allusio*), 311–4, 316, 321, 322 (2 versions), 323, 324 (4 versions), 327 (3 versions), 331–3, 335, 339, 341, 346 (2 versions), 347 (2 versions and *allusio*), 351 (4 versions), 354, 356, 357 (3 versions), 358–60, 362.1–11, 363, 365–6, 368, 370–4, 378–80, 382 (version and *allusio*), 383–4, 386, 387 (2 versions), 391 (3 versions), 394 (2 versions), 395–6, 398, 401–2, 404, 406, 407 (2 versions), 410 (2 versions), 412–3, 417 (2 versions and *allusio*), 420 (2 versions), 422 (2 versions), 431, 438 (version and *allusio*), 439, 440 (version and *allusio*, p. 130), 441, 442 (3 versions), 443, 444 (2 versions), 447–9, 451–2, 453 (3 versions), 455 (2 versions), 456 (2 versions), 457–9, 461, 462 (version and *allusio*), 468, 474–5, 481, 484, 488 (version and *allusio*), 489, 491, 497 (2 versions), 498 (2 versions), 505–6, 515, 517, 518 (3 versions), 519, 523 (2 versions), 526 (version and *allusio*), 527.2, 529 (3 versions), 530 (2 versions), 536–7, 540, 541 (version and *allusio*), 545, 548, 549 (3 versions), 557, 561–3, 564 (version and *allusio*), 568–9, 571, 573, 575–7, 580–1, 583, 585–6, 589 (2 versions), 590, 591 (2 versions), 592–3, 595, 597, 606 (version and *allusio*), 607 (2 versions), 608–13, 616–25, 627, 630–1, 633 (2 versions), 634, 637–9, 644–5, 647 (3 versions), 648 (2 versions), 649, 651–4, 657–9, 661, 663–5, 667, 669, 677, 683–4, 699, 701, 707 (3 versions), 708, 710, 713–5, 717 (2 versions), 718, 719 (3 versions), 720, 721 (2 versions), 722–7, 730 (version and *allusio*), 731–4, 736–7, 739–41, 747–9, 752, 754–7, 759, 762–3, 765, 767, 769, 771, 774–6, 779–83, 784 (2 versions), 788, 793, 796–7, 799–800, 805, 807 (2 versions), 809, 822–7;

10.1–5, 8, 13, 21, 28, 30 (5 versions), 31, 32 (2 versions), 34, 35 (version and *allusio*), 36, 38–9, 41–2, 44 (3 versions), 45 (2 versions), 46–7, 50–1, 55, 57, 59 (2 versions), 60–9, 71–4, 76, 78, 80 (2 versions), 84, 88, 93, 97–9, 102, 104, 106, 107.1 (2 versions), 108, 111, 112 (version and reply), 113, 116, 118 (2 versions), 119, 121 (2 versions), 123, 124 (2 versions), 125;

11.1, 3, 7, 8 (2 versions), 9, 14–5, 19, 22–5, 26 (2 versions), 28, 31 (2 versions), 32–3, 39, 43 (3 versions), 49–54, 55 (3 versions), 56, 58 (2 versions), 59, 60, 61 (3 versions), 62 (3 versions), 63–4, 67, 70–2, 75 (2 versions), 76–7, 79, 82 (2 versions), 83, 85–6, 92, 95, 103–4, 106, 110–1, 113, 116, 119–22, 124–5, 131, 133–4, 136, 138–41, 145 (4 versions), 148, 151, 153 (2 versions), 154, 156, 159–60, 162–3, 165–7, 168 (2 versions), 169, 171, 178, 186–7, 189, 191, 192 (2 versions), 193 (3 versions), 194, 200–1, 202 (3 versions), 203–4, 207–9, 211, 213, 216–7, 225, 229, 234, 237, 239–41, 244–5, 246 (2 versions), 247–9, 250–7, 259, 265, 268, 270–1, 272 (version and *allusio*), 273, 275–6, 278, 282–3, 287 (3 versions), 288, 292, 294, 297 (2 versions and *allusio*), 298, 299–303 (+341; see Register), 305–6, 309, 311–3, 315–8, 323 (2 versions), 324–5, 331, 334–5, 341–3, 348–9, 356 (3 versions), 357, 365–6, 368–70, 373, 375, 377, 378 (2 versions), 379, 381 (3 versions), 385 (version and *allusio*), 386, 388–90, 391 (2 versions), 393 (2 versions), 395, 397.2–4, 398, 401, 404–6, 408, 410, 413, 414 (2 versions and *allusio*), 416, 418 (2 versions), 419–21, 423 (2 versions), 425, 427, 428 (2 versions), 429, 430 (4 versions), 431, 432 (2 versions), 436, 442;

12.113, 234–5; 13.29; 14.2, 7, 74; 15.51; 16.1, 3–5, 7, 11–2, 13 (2 versions), 14 (2 versions), 16 (2 versions), 17–8, 19 (3 versions), 20, 23 (2 versions), 27, 29–30, 31 (2 versions), 32 (2 versions), 33–4, 37–8, 40–2, 54+54*, 57 (3 versions), 58, 59 (2 versions), 61, 64, 68, 75 (2 versions), 77–8, 80–1, 87–92, 99–102, 104–6, 107 (2 versions), 108 (2 versions), 109, 111–5, 116 (4 versions), 117–22, 125, 127–8, 129 (7 versions and 4 *allusiones*), 130, 131.1–6, 131.7–10, 132–3, 135 (3 versions), 136–7, 138 (2 versions), 139, 141–6, 148–51, 154 (2 versions), 155 (2 versions), 156–7, 159–62, 164–73, 176–81, 183–4, 185 (2 versions), 186–91, 193, 194 (2 versions), 196–9, 200 (3 versions), 201 (2 versions), 202–5, 207 (2 versions and *allusio*), 208–17, 220–1, 222 (2 versions), 223, 224 (2 versions), 225–30, 232–43, 245, 246 (2 versions), 247–54, 256, 260–2, 267–8, 270 (2 versions), 271–2, 274, 275 (2 versions), 276–8, 281, 284, 286–8, 291 (2 versions), 292–4, 295 (2 versions), 297, 299, 303, 305, 309–11, 313–5, 318 (3 versions), 321, 324–5, 326 (2 versions), 327–9, 331 (2 versions), 333.

FRANCESCO MARIA MOLZA

(1489–1544)

Molza was born at Modena of noble parents. His early passion for learning was insatiable, and he quickly mastered Latin, Greek, and Hebrew. His father took him to Rome about 1505. Here, it is said, the irregularities that were to stain his life had their beginning. He returned, however, at his father's bidding, to Modena in 1512 to marry Masina Sartorio, with whom he lived for four years. He then abandoned her and their children, and returned to Rome, where he remained —save for two years (1523–5) at Bologna—till near the end of his life. It was not only, or perhaps mainly, to pursue his discreditable amours that Molza betook himself to Rome; the society of the learned men there gathered was an irresistible attraction. He was highly esteemed by Bembo, Sadoleto, the younger Beroaldo, Tebaldeo, Colocci, Longolius, Lampridio, Tolomei, Annibale Caro, Pier Vettori—in a word, by all the literary world. From 1529 to 1535 he waited on the Cardinal Ippolito de' Medici, and, after Ippolito's death, entered the service of the Cardinal Alessandro Farnese. He died at Modena. The celebrated poetess Tarquinia Molza was the daughter of his eldest son, Camillo.

Molza wrote with equal success in Latin and in Italian, but his reputation, as a Latin poet at least, though good, is not what it would probably have been if more of his poems had been published at a time when the personal memory of the poet was still fresh. Most of them remained in MS. until the eighteenth century, only a small selection having appeared in the miscellanies.[1]

Molza's Latin epigrams are formed on the Anthology. Like Navagero and others of his contemporaries he takes a marked delight in the dedicatory form; but, as we have noticed in other cases, it is usually impossible to convict him of borrowing the content of any particular epigram. Apparently he finds it best suited to this style to imagine dedications to Ceres and the country gods. The following is fairly close to *A.P.* 6.36:

AD CEREREM

Haec tibi, magna Ceres, Daphnis iam messe peracta
    Affixit foribus spicea dona tuis.
Tu, Dea, fac illi iacto de semine rursus
    Falcem hebetent valida gramina secta manu.

When, however, Molza turns to make strict translations, again in common with his contemporaries, he prefers the anecdotal epigrams. The following is his version of the epigram (*A.P.* 9.561) on a vine that produced sour grapes:

Solis inaccessam radiis quis cautibus horrens
    Vitem aluit dira sub regione locus?
Ten Scythia, aut nivibus densis insessa Pyrene,
    Aut tulit Hispani ferrea gleba soli?
Immites turpi fundens quae palmite succos,
    Tentantem miris inficis ora modis.
Digna, Lycurge, tua tandem haec quae sola bipenni
    Ad terram prono vertice caesa cadat.

Twenty-three epigrams are more or less directly translated by Molza into Latin: *A.P.* 5.168; 6.26, 36, 67, 171, 236; 7.196,

---

[1] Molza's editor was Serassi: *Delle Poesie Volgari e Latine di Fr. Maria Molza . . . colla Vita scritta da Pierantonio Serassi.* 3 vols. Bergamo, 1747-1754. I mostly refer to this edition; but on occasion to the selection in *Carm. Illust. Poet. Ital.*, vol. 6. The translations from the Anthology in vol. 3 of Serassi's ed. were taken, the editor says, from a MS. written for the most part in Molza's own hand. On the general character of Molza's Latin verse may be consulted Ellinger, *op. cit.* 1.215ff. For his Italian imitation of *A.P.* 16.200 see below, p. 302.

209, 216, 348, 635; 9.31, 67, 77, 240, 346, 387, 561, 826; 11.365;
16.160, 234, 274.[1]

THE EDITION OF THE NICOLINI
(1550)

An edition of the Anthology was put out at Venice in 1550,
shortly before the third Aldine appeared, by Pietro and Giovan Maria Nicolini da Sabbio.[2] It is an almost literal reprint
of the second (1521) Aldine.[3] The title-page promises a number
of 'newly discovered epigrams,' but these prove to be Sappho's
Hymn to Aphrodite, and Anacreon, *frg.* 70 (πῶλε Θρηκίη). The
chief value of the edition lay in the Indices, the first to be made
for the Anthology, which, because of its miscellaneous character, absolutely demands such apparatus. Although no new manuscripts were consulted for the epigrams, the edition was carefully gone over, apparently with a copy of the 1494 edition,
since in *A.P.* 7.647 (*Plan.* 3.23.14),[4] where the first two Aldines
and later Stephanus have the misprint Ποργώ, the Nicolini, together with Lascaris, have the right form Γοργώ. On the whole,
the Nicolini's edition was superior to all previous editions, and
shows evidence of having been revised by a good scholar.[5]

---

[1] *A.P.* 6.236 is given by Landi, below, p. 243, n. 1.

[2] The Nicolini were a family of printers whose press functioned at Venice from
c. 1520 to *c.* 1551. The printers of the Anthology represent the last generation. They
printed a number of devotional works. (See Ester Pastorello, *Tipografi, Editori, Librai
a Venezia nel secolo xvi*, Florence, Olschki, 1924, p. 59.)
Copies of this edition are apparently rarer than copies of the first Aldine.
Fr. Jacobs had failed to see one when he published his edition (1796). There is a copy
in the Harvard College Library.

[3] The contents of each page, lines, indentations, etc., are the same. The title is:
Ἀνθολογία Διαφόρων Ἐπιγραμμάτων ἀρχαίοις συντεθειμένων σοφοῖς ἐπὶ διαφόροις
ὑποθέσεσιν, εἰς ἑπτὰ τμήματα διῃρημένη. *Florilegium diversorum epigrammatum in septem libros distinctum, diligenti castigatione emendatum, cui nonnulla nuper inventa epigrammata in fine adiecta sunt, una cum indice tam rerum quam auctorum copiosissimo.*
[device] Venetiis. At the end: Venetiis apud Petrum et Joan. Mariam Nicolinos Sabienses, impensa Melchioris Sessae. Anno Domini M.D.L.
It is made up of ff. 1–288+11 unnumbered folios containing the new matter and
the Indices. Like the Aldines it is a small octavo.

[4] Since the Nicolini's edition and the third Aldine follow the second Aldine in
omitting *A.P.* 7.560 (*Plan.* 3.23.3) and inserting *A.P.* 7.184 as *Plan.* 3.23.18 and not,
like other editions, as *Plan.* 3.23.11, the epigram here in question is No. 3.23.12 in
those three editions.

[5] For example, all editions of *Plan.* except this one and the third Aldine omit the
first distich of *A.P.* 6.340 (*Plan.* 1.28.2); the Nicolini's editor filled it in from Theocritus.
For the relations between this edition and the third Aldine see below, p. 230.

PIETRO CORDATO (CORAULO)
(1532–1550)

Pietro Cordato, or rather Coraulo, was a nephew of Pierio Valeriano (above, p. 175), and like him a native of Belluno. His father's name was Niccolò Coraulo, and a brother of that name is addressed by their uncle in a miniature ode.[1] Pietro learned Latin and Greek from his uncle. At his death at the age of eighteen he left enough literary compositions to form a small volume, which was published in 1553 at Florence: *Petri Cordati Adolescentis Bellunensis Praeludia*. The volume contains orations, epistles, a dialogue, and two books of poems. These last, to which the title *Praeludia* principally refers, are dedicated to the author's father in a letter written on a journey to Venice.[2]

Like his uncle, Cordato devotes a section of his poems to translations from the Anthology. He has versions of *A.P.* 9.108 (3 versions), 369; 10.108 (2 versions), 124*; 11.208, 369; 16.165, 175. In each instance the initial words of the Greek original accompany his Latin translation. I give two examples:

> In stadium Eutichides piger est, ad prandia velox,
> Usque adeo, ut possis dicere ad haec volitat.
> *(A.P.* 11.208)
> Praxiteles Venerem Pario de marmore fecit.
> Quam simul aspexit Cyprogenia Venus,
> Gavisa est, tollensque ad coelum lumina dixit:
> 'O ego clausa in eo marmore viva forem!'
> *(A.P.* 16.175)[3]

ACHILLE BOCCHI
(1488–1562)

Bocchi, a member of a noble Bolognese family, was at twenty famous for his learning. He attached himself to Alberto Pio of Carpi, and like Alberto became himself Imperial Orator at the Papal Court. He received honors from Julius III and also from the city of Bologna, where he was at one time lecturer in Greek, rhetoric, poetry, and humanity. In his palace at Bologna he founded the *Accademia Bocchiana* (1546). Among his friends were the Flaminii, Sadoleto,

---

[1] *Pierii Valeriani Hexametri, Odae, et Epigrammata*, Venice, 1550, f.113.

[2] A brief notice of Cordato occurs in Augusto Buzzati's *Bibliografia Bellunese* (Venice, 1890), p. 14, but adds little that may not be learned from Cordato's book.

[3] Cordato usually keeps more closely to his model. The original here is by Antipater and, according to the lemma in the Planudean Anthology, refers to the Armed Aphrodite at Sparta, not to the Aphrodite of Praxiteles:

> Καὶ λίθος ὡς Παφίη θωρήξατο, ἢ τάχα μᾶλλον
> εἶδε λίθον Παφίη καὶ ὤμοσεν· "Ἠθελον εἶναι."

Giovan Battista Pio, and Lilio Giraldi. Like them he produced Latin verse. His poems, though highly praised by Giraldi, have never been completely printed.[1] Bocchi had a press in his Academy from which he issued in 1555 the only book for which he is now remembered: *Symbolicarum Quaestionum de Universo Genere quas serio ludebat libri quinque*.[2]

Bocchi's *Symbolicae Quaestiones* are *emblemata*. One of them, entitled *Tumulus Cleombroti* (p. 31), is a *responsum* to *A.P.* 7.471, the Greek of which is quoted with Gaurico's translation. On another page (27) we have a picture lettered ΛΙΜΟΣ and ΧΡΟΝΟΣ, and exhibiting a gallows with the legend: *Spes Ultima*; below it is a version of *A.P.* 9.497:

> Fames amorem sedat atra; sin minus,
> Tempus; nisi hoc, laqueus . . .

FRANCESCO FRANCHINI
(1495–1554)

Franchini was a native of Cosenza. The early part of his life was that of a man of action; he followed Charles V in several campaigns. But he died Bishop of Massa and Piombino. At all times he was a poet, and associated with the first Latin poets of his day—Flaminio, Fracastoro, Valeriano, and others. His poems were published at Rome in the year of his death, and reprinted at Basel in 1558.[3] In 1564 they were placed on the Index.[4]

The epigram plays a conspicuous part in Franchini's verse, his epigrams occupying a greater part of his book than all the rest of his poems; and he has directly borrowed enough from the Anthology to show that he was fully conscious of Greek models in forming his epigrammatic style. His sources are never acknowledged.

Franchini is one of the first modern imitators of Meleager's prettiest epigrams on Zenophila and Heliodora; he combines the first part of *A.P.* 5.147 with the 'point' of 144:

---

[1] *Lusuum Libellus ad Divum Leonem X*. The MS. is in the Laurentian Library at Florence (33, 42). Bandini says that the best part of it is that printed in *Carm. Illust. Poet. Ital.* 2.333–360. Other works, in prose, by Bocchi are listed by Mazzuchelli.

[2] References in the Register are to this edition. The book was republished at Bologna in 1574.

[3] References are to the first edition: *Poemata*, Rome, 1554. The *poemata* (pp. 3–125) are followed by *Epigrammatum libri v* in a separate pagination (pp. 1–139). Page-references are to this part [*Epig.*].

[4] Reusch, *Die Indices Librorum Prohibitorum*, Tübingen, 1886, p. 262.

AD LEUCIAM

Floribus intextam variis tibi mitto corollam,
  Quos avida legi picta per arva manu.
Sunt nigrae violae, sunt lilia candida, sunt et
  Purpureae gelido non sine rore rosae.
Sperne tamen cuncta haec, mea Leucia, scinde coronam:
  Lilia tu terris, tu rosa, tu viola es.

In a different vein he translates *A.P.* 11.104:

Tanquam elephante Coton formica vectus ad imam
  Parvus humum praeceps concidit et periit:
Ac moriens, cui nondum animi vocesque superbae
  Conciderant, dixit: 'Sic periit Phaëton.'

The following verses show Franchini writing in the manner of
the Greek epigrammatists without a special model:

Ut Cypriam vidit pictam, nomenque tabellae
  Inscriptum, dixit diva repente Venus:
'Picturae quid pictor opus fuit addere nomen?
  Non mea me notam sola facit facies?'

Franchini employs the following: *A.P.* 5.36, 69, 94.3–4 (2 versions), 144 (147), 168; 7.59, 323; 9.322, 489, 749; 11.104, 127,
165, 199, 203, 214, 278, 427; 16.159, 160, 165, 169.1–2, 213.

RANUCCIO FARNESE

(†1565)

Calderini notices, as existing in the Ambrosian Library at
Milan, a copy of the first Aldine Anthology with the inscription:
'Hunc librum emit Ranutius Farnetius MDXLV die XXIII Au-
gusti.'[1] It contains manuscript notes that exhibit learning and
judgment; for example, on the first epigram of *Plan.*, Book I:
'Vide scholia in Pindarum,' and, on the first epigrams of Book
IV: 'Satis ineptum, satis bonum, ineptum, insulsum, frigidum,
non omnino malum,' etc. The notes are most copious on the
first three books.

The owner of the volume was no doubt, as Calderini suggests,
Cardinal Ranuccio Farnese, second son of Alessandro Farnese
(Paul III), and known as Cardinal Sant' Angelo to distinguish
him from his brother Alessandro who was called Cardinal

---

[1] *Mem. del R. Ist. Lomb.* 22.228 n. 1.

Farnese. Both were patrons of learning. From 1558 to 1565 Fulvio Orsini acted as Ranuccio's librarian and secretary.[1]

FRANCESCO GIUSTINIANI

A copy of the 1494 Anthology, now in the Vatican Library (*Inc.* 813d), but once in the possession of the editor, Lascaris, and annotated by him, bears the mutilated signature of its next owner: . . . κίσκου τοῦ 'Ιουστινιανοῦ καὶ τῶν φίλων.[2] It also contains notes in the hand of this person. No scholar named Francesco Giustiniani is known.[3] The book passed into the hands of Orsini, and thence to the Vatican.

FRANCESCO FLORIDO SABINO
(*c.* 1500–*c.* 1550)

Florido, known as a champion of Erasmus against Étienne Dolet, was born at Donadeo in the region of the Sabines; and hence his cognomen. He studied at Bologna, and probably taught there; and seems on various occasions to have corrected for Paulus Manutius in Venice. He spent two years at Rome and four in Paris as private secretary to Alberto Pio of Carpi. His works are: *In M. A. Plauti aliorumque Scriptorum Calumniatores Apologia*, Lyons, 1537 and Basel, 1540; *Lectiones Subcisivae*, Basel, 1540; *Homeri Odysseae libri viii*, Paris, 1545; and a translation of Callimachus' Hymn to Diana (Paris, 1549) which he says he executed in four days.[4] The *Lectiones* contain observations on various authors, in the course of which Florido quotes *A.P.* 7.471.[5]

MARCANTONIO FLAMINIO
(1498–1550)

Flaminio's first book of Latin poetry was published when he was seventeen years old (*Carmina*, Fano, 1515); and from that day all learned circles were open to him. He was born at Saravalla, and his education was carefully directed by his father, Giovan Antonio.

---

[1] Nolhac, *Fulvio Orsini*, pp. 8–11; Litta, *Fam. Celeb.* 12 (Farnesi, Tav. x).
[2] Nolhac, *Fulvio Orsini*, p. 159.
[3] The name Francesco was fairly common in the Venetian family of the Giustiniani; best-known perhaps is that Francesco Giustiniani (1507–1554) who was resident at the court of Francis I in 1537 (Litta, *Fam. Celeb.*, Giustiniani di Venezia, Tav. III).
[4] See R. Sabbadini in *Giorn. Stor.* 8 (1886) 333–63.
[5] Gruter, *Lampas* (in which the *Lectiones* are reprinted) 1.1194.

After the publication of his book, the young poet was taken to Rome, where he won the immediate favor of Leo X. He visited Naples for the purpose of meeting Sannazaro, and was invited to Urbino by Castiglione. For a time he studied philosophy at Bologna; but his permanent residence was Rome. Among the humanists of his generation Flaminio has the distinction of being a thoroughly good man. His father is said to have taken pains to check in him an early vein of amatory poetry; and it is remarkable that a great part of Flaminio's verse bears a religious character.[1]

The central position occupied by Flaminio in Italian Latin verse makes any influence the Anthology may have had on him of some interest. Though mostly indirect, that influence existed, and was pervasive and formative in his work. The third and fourth books of his poems contain his *Lusus Pastorales*—certainly his most characteristic and pleasing compositions, and hence sometimes printed separately. In these poems he constantly had his eye on the Anthology, especially on the votive inscriptions; and, while he never directly translates any epigram, he often follows closely on his models. The first poem in the third book is a fair sample of the whole:

> Pan pater et Silvane senex Faunique bicornes,
> Tuque pharetratae candida turba deae,
> Si mea vos dulci delectat fistula cantu,
> Si semper vobis annua dona fero,
> Parcite purpureos, quaeso, violare racemos,
> Neu tangant avidae lutea pruna manus.
> Hunc agrum dat habere mihi Farnesius heros:
> Gratus ego haec illi munera prima dico.

Once he uses the well-worn conceit of *A.P.* 5.83, and again the theme of 5.168. In his earliest book of verses he has a translation of *A.P.* 7.526:

DE OTHRYADE, EX GRAECO

> Ecquem Othryade unquam, maxime,
> Praestantiorem, Iuppiter,
> Vidisti? Iniquo ex Thyreae agro
> Solus reverti noluit
> In patriam, sed fortiter

---

[1] *Marci Antonii, Joannis Antonii, et Gabrielis Flaminiorum . . . Carmina.* Padua (Cominus), 1743, with Memoir by F. M. Mancurtius. Marcantonio's epigrams were translated into French by Anne des Marquets, Paris, 1569. There is in English, *Fifty Select Poems of Marc-Antonio Flaminio, imitated by the late Rev. Edward William Barnard of Trinity College, Cambridge, with a short Memoir of the Author*, ed. by Archdeacon Wrangham (limited to 50 copies), Chester, 1829.

Adegit intra pectora
Ferrum, trophaeo ex proprio
Tibi dicato sanguine.

ANDREAS RAPITIUS

(*fl.* 1550)

Rapitius (Rapizzi?) published his Latin poems at Venice in
1552: *Facilioris Musae Carminum libri duo, quorum prior Epigrammata quaedam continet.* All that is known of him is on
his title-page—he was born at Trieste of a noble family. Among
his poems are translations of *A.P.* 9.39, 56, 331, 339, 592;
11.251. His version of *A.P.* 9.331 will serve as an example:

Fertur ab Aoniis nymphis, cum fulmine Bacchus
Flagraret, mediis praecipitatus aquis;
Hinc sobriis nymphis fuerat pergratus, at ignem
Incautus capies, hic nisi mixtus erit.

BENEDETTO ACCOLTI

(1497–1549)

Accolti belonged to a celebrated family, the Accolti of Arezzo, but
was himself born at Florence. He studied at Pisa. Entering the
ecclesiastical career, he was successively a papal secretary, Bishop of
Cadiz, Archbishop of Cremona, Archbishop of Ravenna, Cardinal
(May 3, 1527), and Governor of the March of Ancona. He fell into
disgrace under Paul III, and, after some months of imprisonment, retired to Ferrara, then to Venice, and finally returned to Florence.
Accolti was in correspondence with many of the humanists of his
generation, among whom may be mentioned Calcagnini.

The Latin poems of Accolti were published together with
those of four other Tuscan poets at Florence in 1562 in a collection called: *Carmina Quinque Hetruscorum Poetarum* (pp. 129–
136).[1] The most pleasing of Accolti's poems, as is the case with
so many of his contemporaries, are his dedicatory epigrams, of
which he has a notable group.[2] Like other modern practisers of
this style, he is conscious of the Anthology as his model, but
rarely approaches the substance of any epigram. Accolti has
dedications to Ceres, to the Nymphs, to Fistula, to Invidia, to
Pan, to the Muses, to Faunus, to Neptune, to Innocence, and to
Sleep. Some of these involve ideas unnatural to the Greeks, but

[1] Below, p. 229.
[2] These are reprinted in the *Carm. Illust. Poet. Ital.* 1.1–7.

others may be paralleled over and over in the sixth book of the Anthology. Yet Accolti generally succeeds in throwing over his Greek themes a Roman coloring. The following is a dedicatory epigram to Ceres:[1]

> Et surgunt laetis pulventia gramina campis,
>   Et favet optato pulvere mitis hiems,
> Et tibi, magna Ceres, segetem lustramus et agros,
>   Et tingunt sanctos bucula sacra focos.
> Tu face ne vanis messis nos ludat aristas,
>   Sed rumpat victis horrea limitibus.

GIAMBATTISTA GIRALDI CINTIO
(1504–1573)

Giambattista Giraldi, a relation of Lilio Gregorio, was like him a native of Ferrara. He received his education at the *Studio* of his native city, and had Celio Calcagnini for one of his teachers. In 1525 Giraldi, though hardly twenty-one, began to profess medicine and philosophy in the *Studio*; in 1537 he succeeded Calcagnini in the chair of literature. Later he became secretary to Duke Hercules II, and afterwards to Alfonso II. But in 1560, in the course of a literary dispute between him and G. B. Pigna, it was made plain that Pigna and not Giraldi had the Duke's favor. He retired to Mondovi, where he taught for several years until it became a question of transferring the *Studio* of that place to Turin. Giraldi was then invited by the Senate of Milan to become professor of eloquence at Pavia. Here he was admitted to the Academy of the *Affidati* under the name of *Cintio*. He was so tormented by the gout that he was soon forced to resign his professorship. He went back to Ferrara, and died there within three months of his return.

[On a use of the Anthology in Giraldi's vernacular works, see below, p. 315.]

Giraldi's reputation rests on his Italian tragedies and especially on his collection of stories, *Gli Hecatommithi* (Monte-Regale, 1565). One of these stories we must recur to on a later page. His Latin poems, *Poematia*, were first published at Ferrara in 1537, and were reprinted at Basel in 1540.[2] They consist of the types commonly cultivated by the humanist poets, and are in a good style. Among the epigrams are fourteen drawn from the Greek Anthology: *A.P.* 5.95, 180; 7.229; 9.24, 42, 61, 108, 420, 440 (p. 178); 11.76, 228; 16.129, 171, 175.

---

[1] *Carm. Hetrusc. Poet.*, p. 129; *Carm. Illust. Poet. Ital.* I.I. Some such epigram as *A.P.* 6.258 may be compared.

[2] My references are to the Basel edition.

Giraldi's treatment of his borrowings recalls Sannazaro, save that, where Sannazaro sometimes substituted a different point for the point of his original, Giraldi in at least one instance has a point directly the reverse of the Greek.[1] *A.P.* 5.95, on the three Graces made four by the existence of Dercylis, had to be already well-known in order to give point to Giraldi's couplet *Ad Vesbiam:*[2]

> Tres habuit Furias quondam; sed Vesbia manes
> Ut petiit, Furias quatuor Orcus habet.

His lines *In Lycum*, on the other hand, are a fairly close translation of *A.P.* 11.76:

> Narcissus liquidis dum se spectabat in undis
> Ipse sui (hei misero!) victus amore perit.
> Nunc tua forte tibi si occurrat turpis imago,
> Infelix, odio sic moriare tui.

He addresses to his teacher Calcagnini the praises that Leonidas of Tarentum had thought appropriate to Homer (*A.P.* 9.24):

AD CAELIUM CALCAGNINUM

> Ut sol cum toto radios diffundit Olympo,
> Sidera fulgenti lumine cuncta fugat,
> Sic Caeli promit sese cum daedala Musa,
> Carminibusque novum spargit in orbe iubar,
> Sola micat, cunctosque premit, qui luce corusca
> Flagrabant vates, lampadis igne suae.

ELIO GIULIO CROTTI (AELIUS JULIUS CROTTUS)
(*c.* 1500–1564)

Crotti was a well-known poet in his day, a friend of Lilio and Giovan Battista Giraldi, of Pigna, and other notable Ferrarese. He was born at Cremona, spent some years at the Court of Cesare Gonzaga at Mantua, and finally settled for the remainder of his life at Ferrara in the circle of Alfonso II. His Latin poems were published at Mantua in 1545, and at Ferrara in the year of his death.[3]

---

[1] He sometimes appears to have Sannazaro in mind—compare the beginnings of their respective imitations of *A.P.* 16.171 below in the Register. Their versions of *A.P.* 108 have points of resemblance.

[2] The verses I put down as imitated from *A.P.* 7.229 might be regarded as a reversal of *A.P.* 9.61.

[3] *Aelii Julii Crotti Hermione, eiusdem Floraliorum Spicilegia.* Mantua, 1545. *Opuscula.* Ferrara, 1564.

While relatively untouched by the influence of the Anthology, Crotti nevertheless has possible reminiscences of *A.P.* 5.78 and 7.311, and an exercise on the theme of Venus in Armor (cf. *A.P.* 16.174). This last he could have taken at second hand from any one of several modern poets:

IN VENEREM ARMATAM

Quid facies duro Calybe et duro Aegide pectus,
   Quid forti armatur, Diva, manus iaculo?
Arma hastam et clypeum forti concede Minervae;
   Illa gerat tecta Martia bella manu.
Nuda manus, nuda haec facies, haec nuda papilla,
   Visum hostem dulces attrahit in laqueos.

FABIO SEGNI (SEGNIUS)
(*fl. c.* 1550)

Segni was a Florentine, and belonged to the literary circle of Francesco Vinta and Benedetto Varchi. His Latin poems were published in the *Carmina Quinque Hetruscorum Poetarum*, Florence, 1562.[1] This volume was the monument of Segni's literary circle, and contains the poems of Vinta, Segni, Berni, Accolti, and Varchi—in that order. Segni has some interesting epigrams on the Florentine artists—Michelangelo, Da Vinci, and Cellini— for which he may have remembered similar poems in the Anthology. At all events he knew the Anthology. He has a translation of *A.P.* 9.357, an imitation of 9.440, and two translations of 9.647.[2] The following is his version of *A.P.* 9.357:

Quatuor illustris certamina Graecia ponit.
   Sunt duo sacra deis, et duo sacra viris.
Prima Iovis, Phoebique, Palaemonis, Archemorique,
   Quorum apium, malus, pinus, oliva, decor.

DOMITIUS MARINUS
(*fl.* 1530)

Marinus, while not directly indebted to the Anthology, feels its influence much as does Navagero whom he admires. He was a Venetian. His Latin poems were edited by his son Pamphilus, and published at the Aldine Press in 1550.[3] They consist of

---

[1] Referred to in the Register as *C.Q.H.P.*
[2] See below, p. 334.
[3] *Carmina Domiti Marini Veneti.* Venice, 1550. He addresses poems to Navagero (f. 14ro), to Alvise Priuli (f. 13vo), and to Lazzaro Bonamico (f. 14vo).

eclogues and epigrams. The following dedicatory verses show him composing in the manner of the Greek epigrams (*Carm.*, f. 21ʳᵒ):

IN AUCTOREM NUMEROSAE STIRPIS

Hos calamos tibi, Glauce, tuus piscator Amyntas
Atque haec Adriaco retia nota mari
Dedicat: inque altas supplex nunc porricit undas
Iam senior tremula lacque merumque manu.
Tu tibi surgentem sobolem ne desere Amyntae:
Et senis emeriti suscipe dona libens.

PAOLO MANUZIO

(1512–1574)

Paolo, the youngest of Aldus' sons, was deprived of his father when barely three years of age, and was taken to Asola to live with his mother's family. Soon, however, he was returned to Venice for the better educational facilities of that place. His father's friends welcomed and assisted him. The ardor with which he threw himself into his studies ended in the physicians forbidding him the use of books for two years. The Aldine Press meanwhile had been carried on by his grandfather, Andrea d'Asola, and the latter's sons Francesco and Federico (above, p. 171). The death of Andrea in 1529 seems to have given rise to disputes as to the inheritance of the press; in 1533 books began to appear with the names of Paolo and his uncles together: *in aedibus heredum Aldi et Andreae Asulani soceri*. This association did not last long, disputes recommenced in 1537, and after 1540 Paolo managed his press alone.

Paolo Manuzio was a scholar comparable with his father and infinitely superior to the Asolani. He made a specialty of Cicero. Besides his printing and his scholarly work, he found time for teaching and frequenting the society of scholars. In 1535 he visited Rome. In 1538 he spent some time visiting libraries in various parts of Italy. From 1556 to 1560 he was engaged in publishing for the ill-fated *Accademia Veneziana*. In 1561 he accepted the proposal of Pius IV that he come to Rome and found a press for the printing of the writers of the Church. This project, though it went well at first, came into difficulties, and Manuzio left Rome in 1570. After a year of travel he returned to Venice. He died while on a visit to Rome in 1574. The press in Venice had been kept active in all these years, latterly by Paolo's eldest son Aldus, who carried it on after his father's death.[1]

The third Aldine edition of the Anthology was printed by Paolo in 1550/51. Save for the type-fount it is an exact replica

---

[1] Renouard, *Annales de l'Imprimerie des Aldes*, Paris, 1803, 2.70–106; Nolhac in *Mélanges d'Archéol. et d'Hist.* 3 (1883). 286.

of the edition published by the Nicolini a few months before.[1] The date on the title-page is 1550, but that in the colophon is 1551. The title-page makes precisely the same claim as that of the Nicolini and in the same words, which are only differently arranged on the page. After the title-page everything is exactly the same in the two editions—pages, lines, indentations, and corrections.[2] After f. 288 the third Aldine has 10 unnumbered folios containing the Hymn to Aphrodite, Anacreon, *frg.* 70., and the Indices, copied from the Nicolini's edition.[3] A peculiarity of the third Aldine is that these unnumbered folios copied from the edition of the Nicolini are printed in Paolo's new Greek type, which is larger than the regular Aldine type in which the rest of the volume is printed.

In the absence of any external information on the reasons for the thoroughgoing identity of these two editions published at Venice almost at the same time, the simplest explanation seems to me to be something like this. Paolo had a real interest in the Anthology, and had determined to reissue it, following, as was natural, the second Aldine in format. As he was on the point of doing this, the Nicolini brought out their edition, which, as it happened, likewise followed the second Aldine in format, but also had several new advantages. It was easy to run through the new Aldine edition, still in type, and incorporate the Nicolini's corrections, and an obvious advantage to appropriate their two new poems and their Indices.[4] For this last material, on the unnumbered folios (sigg.* to **ii), Paolo used his new types as an experiment. Time was required to make these changes, so that the book which was intended to appear in 1550 did not actually come out until 1551. It, and not the Nicolini's edition, was now the latest; and the Nicolini's edition apparently suffered from the competition, since it did not circulate widely and copies are

[1] This fact appears to have been known to Stadtmüller, who employs every Planudean edition except the third Aldine in the critical notes of the Teubner edition.

[2] E.g., both have the correction Γοργώ for Ποργώ on f. 151ʳᵒ, as noted above (p. 220); both have the complete epigram in *Plan.* 1.28.2 (=*A.P.* 6.340); both omit *Plan.* 3.23.3 (*A.P.* 7.560), and place *Plan.* 3.23.11 as 3.23.18 (above, p. 220, notes 4 and 5).

[3] The Indices are crowded so as to make one unnumbered folio fewer than in the Nicolini's edition. The Aldine has its register with Aldine name and the date on *verso* of the last index-page, then blank folio, then the Aldine device on *verso* of a third folio. The Nicolini edition has its register on the *verso* of the last index-page, then colophon on *recto* of the next folio, and device on the *verso*.

[4] As Renouard (*Ann.* 1.68) observes, these Indices would serve for the first two Aldines as well, since all four editions correspond page for page.

now very rare, while the third Aldine is far from being a rare book.

Karl Preisendanz reports the presence, in the Marcian Library at Venice, of a paper MS. containing what appears to be a complete Latin prose translation of the Anthology, the work of Paolo Manuzio.[1] A note written on the first page records that the MS. once belonged to the library of the Colonna family, and that it was acquired by Mons. Angelini from a bookseller named Bestrucci. In the margin beside the first epigram is this note: Est mei/ francisci/ Paparecti/ Romani/ Can/ pillani/ mi/ CXC Bñi B/ Camilli/ Prin/ cipis/ Pam/ philij.

The translation is literal, and is accompanied by a commentary which is full but elementary, as the treatment of the first epigram (*A.P.* 9.357) will show:[2]

'Archie in Quatuor certamina: Quatuor sunt certamina per greciam (quatuor .s. certamina), sacra duo quidem mortalium (isthmia .s. et nemea), duo vero imortalium (olympia .s. et pythia), Iovis Latonide palemonis Archemori. Premia autem horum oleaster poma apia pinus.' On *certamina* he notes: 'ponitur et pro loco certaminis.' Then: 'Dicta est tota grecia ab Elleno Deucalionis filio, cum prius civitas una hoc nomine apellaretur. Ponitur et prefato opheltes: lycurgi nemee regionis fuit filius qui espeditionem parentibus Argivis contra Thebanos perijt morsus a Serpente. Poma intelligit que addebantur Corone captae et templo Apollinis.'

ANTONIO SEBASTIANO MINTURNO

(†1574)

The name Minturno, by which alone Sebastiano is remembered, is said to have been taken from an old city in the Kingdom of Naples named Minturna, which had existed near Traetto where he was born. He studied philosophy with Agostino Nifo in Naples, and followed him to Sessa and Pisa. Here Minturno's devotion to the amorous passion is said to have interrupted his studies for two years. In 1521 he went to Rome, where he was protected by the Colonnas. In their castle of Genazzano he learned Greek from a certain maestro Paolo, and made some progress in Hebrew. In order to escape the plague he left Rome in 1523 and returned to Sessa, where he studied mathematics, and thence to Naples. At this time he took up the composition of vernacular verse. The wars caused him to remove to Sicily, where the viceroy Monteleone welcomed him and granted him a pension of

---

[1] *Wochenschrift f. Klass. Philol.* for 1916, p. 1077. This MS. had not been catalogued in 1930.
[2] This is one of several extracts printed by Preisendanz.

200 ducats. In 1559 Minturno became Bishop of Uggento, and in that capacity attended the Council of Trent. In 1565 he was transferred to the bishopric of Cotrone, where he died.

Minturno is remembered for his books on the theory of poetry—his *De Poeta* (1559) and its Italian form (1564). His *Rime* appeared in 1559; and his Latin poems, *Epigrammata et Elegiae* at Venice in 1564.[1]

[On Minturno's vernacular poetry see below, p. 321]

Minturno's Latin epigrams are divided between personal and occasional themes and themes drawn from classical mythology. Of the latter the Anthology supplies its share. Minturno employs *A.P.* 7.152, 234, 433; 9.10, 183; 16.140, 159, 174, 331. These are mostly close translations; his version of *A.P.* 16.174 shows how close:

> Armatam Venerem aspiceret cum caesia Pallas,
>   'Vis, Cypri, iudicium sic subeamus?' ait.
> Quae tenerum ridens: 'Clypeos attollere contra
>   Audes? Si vici nuda, quid arma ferens?'

Attention to the Anthology on the part of a modern epigrammatist is part of the doctrine of Minturno's poetical theory. This has already been discussed (above, pp. 62–3). In his *De Poeta* Minturno takes for an example of the epigram the epitaph of Midas (*A.P.* 7.153), giving it in a verse-translation. He cites the epigram of Cyrillus (*A.P.* 9.369) and that of Parmenion (*A.P.* 9.342) on the nature of the epigram, and gives a verse-translation of the second:

> A Musis procul est multos Epigrammate versus
>   Complecti, an quaeras in stadio dolichon?
> In dolicho cursus crebro torquetur, acuta
>   Pectoris in stadio concita vis rapitur.

As epigrammatists he mentions Simonides, Alcaeus, Archias, Athenaeus, Agathias, Antipater, Palladas, Philippus, Antiphilus, Leonidas, Lucian, Bianor, and Lucilius.

SCIPIONE CAPECE

(†c. 1562)

Capece was a professor of law in Naples, where his family was one of some note. He is best known as the author of a Lucretian poem entitled *De Principiis Rerum libri ii* (Venice, 1546). His *Elegiae et Epigrammata* only saw the light in 1594 at Naples. All his poems were

---

[1] My references (*Epig.*) are to this volume.

edited, under the title *Opere Poetiche*, by Francesco Maria Ricci at
Venice in 1754.[1] Capece is said to have procured the first publication
of Donatus on Virgil. Among his friends are mentioned Bernardo
Tasso and Garcilasso de la Vega.

The epigrams of Capece include translations of *A.P.* 9.346
and 16.129, the first accompanied by the translations of Politian, Alciati, Nicolas Bourbon, and Marullus, the second by
those of Ausonius, More, Lily, and Alciati. Politian's version of
A.P. 9.346 is given above, p. 134, and that of Marullus on p.
113; Capece's follows:

> Orbe alio advolitans tandem hic consedit hirundo,
>   Medeae ut nidum figerit in gremio.
> Heu volucrem incautam! Num illi tua pignora credas,
>   Quae potuit natos dilacerare suos?

Both Marullus' version and Capece's require a *lemma* to make
clear that the epigram refers to a statue or painting of Medea.

BERARDINO ROTA
(1509–1575)

Rota was a Neapolitan, and owes his fame—not yet altogether ex-
tinct—mainly to a form of poetry that belongs peculiarly to Naples,
the piscatory eclogue. This form, which his countryman Sannazaro
had invented and practised in Latin, Rota transferred to the vernacular. He was a leading figure in the literary life of the middle of the
sixteenth century, and numbered among his friends Annibale Caro,
Pier Vettori, and Paolo Manuzio, not to mention those who belonged
to Naples, as Paterno and Minturno. He was a knight of the Order of
St. James, and held the position of Secretary to the city of Naples.

Besides being a follower of Sannazaro, Rota was a Petrarchist, and
composed sonnets to his lady *in vita* and *in morte;* that his lady was
also his wife gives these verses a peculiar interest She was Porzia
Capece, and died in 1559. Rota's poems possess genuine feeling. These
Sonetti et Canzoni were published with the poet's *Ecloghe Pescatorie*
(separate title and pagination) at Naples in 1560.[2]

[See below, p. 312 for Rota's vernacular verse]

Rota's Latin verse is singularly like his vernacular verse in
character, and shows the same preoccupations. It consists of
Elegies, Epigrams, and *Sylvae*, the last poem of the *Sylvae* being
a lament for his wife. These poems were published in 1567.[3]

---

[1] My references are to this volume.
[2] My references (below, p. 312) are to this edition. They were reprinted with Rota's
Latin poems at Naples in 1572 and again at the same place in 1726.
[3] *Berardini Rotae equitis Neapolitani Poemata: Elegiarum lib. iii; Epigrammatum*

In form Rota's Latin epigrams belong to the Greek tradition;
yet it is usually impossible to assign them to definite originals. He has, for instance, several pieces *De Amore Dormiente*
that recall *A.P.* 16.211 only by the general theme.[1] An epigram
Ad Nisam needs only to be put into Greek to be at least worthy
of Rufinus, the writer of *A.P.* 5.74, which Rota's epigram resembles in substance as well as style:[2]

> Quas bona Flora rosas Paphiis modo legerat hortis,
>   Excoluit tenera quas Cytherea manu,
> Uberibus madidas lacrymis tibi mittit Amyntas,
>   Ac simul his animam floribus implicitam.
> Nisa cape. His poteris niveas ornare papillas,
>   His poteris nitidas nectere Nisa comas.
> Floris honos brevis est: brevis est quoque gratia formae,
>   Dum licet, ah verno tempore disce frui.

That Rota knew the Anthology at first hand is demonstrated
by his close translation of *A.P.* 9.130:[3]

DE PALLADE ET BACCHO

> Undique saeptam oleam vidit pendentibus uvis
>   Et risum simulans talia Pallas ait:
> 'Nulla, Lyaee, tibi ratio cum Pallade, nam tu
>   Ebrius, incestus; sobria, casta, soror.'

LUIGI ANNIBALE DELLA CROCE (CRUCEIUS)
(1509–1577)

Della Croce was born at Milan of a noble family, and was for many
years Secretary to the Senate of his native city. His principal literary
work was a Latin translation of Achilles Tatius, the first to be made
(Basel, 1554). He had earlier published the last four books under the
title: *Narrationis Fragmentum e Graeco Latine Conversum* (Lyons,
1544), from a manuscript communicated to him by Ottavio Ferrari,
but without knowing their authorship. He died in the plague that
visited Milan in the autumn of 1567, and was buried in the church
of the Padri Eremitani.[4]

Latin poems by Della Croce were included in the *Carmina*

---

*lib. iiii; Sylvarum, seu Metamorphoseon lib. i; Naenia, quae nuncupatur Portia. Ad
Peraphanum Riberam Proregem Neapolitanum.* Venice (Giolito), 1567 (referred to as
Poem.).
  [1] Cf. the verses of Gravina, above, p. 114, n. 3.
  [2] Rota, *Poem.*, p. 71.
  [3] *Poem.*, p. 117. Cf. also the epigram, *Myrtus loquitur*, in *Poem.*, p. 65.
  [4] Crasso, *Istoria di Poeti Greci* (Naples, 1678), p. 38.

Poetarum Nobilium of G. P. Ubaldini, Milan, 1563. Among them is an imitation of *A.P.* 7.669:

PLATONICA IMITATIO

Te quoties claro spectantem sidera coelo,
Stella, tuor, toties coelum aveo fieri,
Pluribus ut quo oculis te specto, hoc plura meum cor
Hauriat, ardori pausa sit unde suo.

BENEDETTO EGIO (AEGIUS)

(†1567)

Benedetto Egio of Spoleto was a Roman humanist of the circle frequented in youth by Fulvio Orsini. He may have taught in Paris. A Latin translation of Apollodorus' *Bibliotheca* was published by him in 1555 at Rome, and an Italian version of Paulus Diaconus, *De Gestis Longobardorum* several years earlier (1547). After Egio's death Orsini acquired several books from his library as mementos of him, among them a copy of the first Aldine Anthology. This volume is now in the Vatican Library (*Vat. A.* 16. 8ᵛᵒ), and bears the signature: B. Αἰγίου.[1]

FRANCESCO ROBORTELLO

(1516–1567)

Robortello refers to the Greek epigrams in his treatise on the Epigram (above, pp. 60–2), and specifically to *A.P.* 6.130 (p. 35); 7.145 (p. 39); 9.12 (p. 40), 113 (p. 40).

LORENZO GAMBARA

(1496–1586)

Gambara was born at Brescia. He entered an ecclesiastical career, and after some years of travel settled in Rome. He once visited Germany. At Rome he frequented the society of Fulvio Orsini, whom he assisted in several publications. His own literary reputation rests on his Latin narrative poems, *Gigantomachia*, *Daphnis et Chloe*, and especially *De Navigatione Christophori Colombi*. His smaller pieces are said to have given their author so little satisfaction that he regretted the time spent in their composition, and committed them, to the number of ten thousand verses, to the fire. A certain number survive in the *Carmina Illustrium Poetarum Italorum* (vol. 5); and among them an imitation of *A.P.* 9.258:

---

[1] Nolhac, *Fulvio Orsini*, p. 175.

Hos latices ne accede meos, nec tange, viator,
   Sanguine foedata est si tua dextra manus.
Nostrae etenim lymphae Bacchi gratissima miscent
   Munera; non saevi pocula Martis amant.

In 1568 Orsini published the poems of the nine Greek poetesses together with the lyric and elegiac poets and Bion and
Moschus. Gambara supplied a Latin verse translation of the
bucolic poems.[1] This of necessity included *A.P.* 9.440 (p. 384)
and 16.200.

GIOVAN MATTEO TOSCANO

(*c.* 1500–*c.* 1578)

Toscano was a native of Milan, but spent the greater part of his
life in France. He died at Paris. He is chiefly known for his two-
volume collection of Italian Latin poets, *Carmina Illustrium Poetarum
Italorum*, Paris, 1576, 1577, the best collection made up to that time,
and the basis of those which followed.[2] His own verse is included in the
first volume. Most valuable is his biographical work, *Peplus Italiae*,
published at Paris in 1578. As a friend of Jean Dorat, he was doubtless
known to Ronsard and the rest of the Pléiade; Dorat addresses him
him in several poems.[3] Toscano for his part declares himself to be a
pupil of Dorat.

Among Toscano's epigrams are imitations of *A.P.* 5.268;
11.151; and 16.14. He thus treats 5.268:[4]

AD AMANTES

Nullus amans posthac vereare Cupidinis arma,
   Ne fodiant pectus ignea tela tuum.
In nos exhausit totam ferus ille pharetram;
   In vulnus superest nulla sagitta novum.
Iamque illi volucres, alio ne transeat, alas
   Pectoris exussit fervida flamma mei.

[1] *Carmina Novem Illustrium Feminarum . . . et Lyricorum . . . Elegiae . . . Bucolica,
Bionis et Moschi, Latino versu a Laurentio Gambara expressa . . . ex Bibliotheca Fulvi
Orsini Romani.* Antwerp (Plantin), 1568. Only the *Bucolica* have translations. The
epigram of Antipater (*A.P.* 9.26) on the nine, and others also from the Anthology on
the individual poetesses, are quoted without translation.

[2] This book must not be confused with the collection, frequently referred to in the
present work, having the same title, but edited by Bottari and published at Florence
(1719–1726) in 11 vols. Nor is G. M. Toscano to be confused with M. Toscano of Rome
(below, p. 257).

[3] Dorat, *Poematia* (Paris, 1586), pp. 89, 93, 113.

[4] Toscano's poems were reprinted in vol. 9 of Bottari's collection, from which I
quote them.

GIROLAMO CARDANO

(1501–c. 1576)

Cardano was born at Pavia, perhaps not in wedlock, but was educated at the house of his father, the jurist and physician Fazio Cardano, at Milan. In 1521 he went to Pavia to study, and two years later was lecturer on Euclid there. In 1524 his father died, and Girolamo went to Padua. In the next year he was Rector of the Paduan *Studio;* but 1526 found him at Sacco. He married in 1531. After 1534 he was professor of mathematics, and then medicine, at Milan. In 1554 he traveled to Paris, Edinburgh, and London. He returned to teach at Pavia. In 1560 his eldest son was put to death for poisoning his wife. This and further distresses made Pavia intolerable to Cardano; he was forbidden to teach at Milan; and so he accepted an invitation to Bologna. In 1570 he was suddenly thrown into prison, probably on a charge of impiety. Cardinals Borromeo and Morone rescued him, secured for him a pension from Pius V, and took him to Rome. His latest work was the composition of his autobiography *De Vita Propria.*

Cardano has three translations from the Anthology introduced incidentally into his works, two in his *De Consolatione* and one in his *De Sapientia.*[1] Two of these are in prose, and the third is Filelfo's translation of *A.P.* 7.433.

This last occurs in Cardano's *De Consolatione* (*Op.* 1.614). In the same work he finds a place for *A.P.* 10.84. Life, he says, is so full of distress, that it is well to reckon up the sources of consolation. 'As I think it over from the beginning, many considerations occur to me, any one of which carefully contemplated will show you how needlessly one is tormented in adversity, and . . . how empty this life is . . . and how continually to be bewailed in the manner of Heraclitus, just as Palladas says. [Here he quotes the epigram, and supplies the following translation]: "Lachrymans natus sum, et lachrymans morior; inveni autem vitam totam in multis lachrymis. O genus hominum lachrymabile, infirmum, miserabile, tractum super terram, et dissolutum."'[2]

In *De Sapientia* he makes use of *A.P.* 11.193, which he translates: 'Invidia est res pessima; verum hunc solum bonum habet in se: absumet enim invidentium oculos et cor.'[3]

---

[1] *Opera Omnia,* ed. by C. Spon, 10 vols. Lyons, 1663.
[2] *Op.* 1.590.
[3] *Op.* 1.521.

IPPOLITO CAPILUPI

(1512–1580)

Ippolito Capilupi was Bishop of Fano. He, his brothers Lelio and Giulio, and their nephew Giulio, all made reputations for themselves as Latin poets. Their Virgilian centos—especially those of Lelio—have been much admired. Among Ippolito's shorter pieces one, *Amorem Auro non Precibus Flecti*, rests on *A.P.* 9.420; another, *In Cupidinis Statuam Dormientis*, possibly echoes *A.P.* 16.210. The first follows:[1]

> Cur toties Lalagen crudelem dicis, Amynta?
> Cur miser assiduis fletibus ora rigas?
> Pone modum lacrymis, iam tandem pone querellis,
> Non prece, non lacrymis, ianua victa patet;
> Victa patet gemmis, patet auri pondere victa,
> Plus prece, plus lacrymis, dona in amore valent.
> Pro prece da gemmas igitur, pro fletibus aurum,
> Hoc Danaës quondam est turris aperta Iovi.

NATALE CONTI (COMES)

(†1582)

Though born at Milan, where his parents happened at that time to be, Conti was a Venetian. He became professor of rhetoric at Padua, having among his pupils Francesco Panigarola who was later famous as a religious writer (Argelati, *Scr. Med.* 2.1030). From the insertion among Conti's poems of a number of pieces by Milanese writers, Tiraboschi conjectured that he was not only born at Milan, but lived much in that city. He is known for a history of his own times: *Universae Historiae sui Temporis libri xxx* (Venice, 1581), for his poem on hunting: *De Venatione libri iiii* (Venice, 1551), but mainly for his work on mythology: *Mythologiae libri x* (Venice, 1568). He published Latin translations of Athenaeus, Hermogenes, Aphthonius, and other Greek authors; and himself wrote in Greek a poem on the twenty-four hours of the day, dedicated to Cosimo de' Medici (Venice, 1550). His *Carmina* appeared at Venice in 1560.

Conti's Latin poems show no influence from the Anthology. His best-known work, however, the *Mythologia*, is amply illustrated from the Greek epigrams, which are mainly given in the author's own metrical versions.[2] For example, when he treats

---

[1] *Capiluporum Carmina*, ed. by J. Castalio, Rome, 1590.
[2] My references are to the Geneva edition of 1651: *Mythologiae, sive Explicationis Fabularum, libri x, in quibus omnia prope Naturalis et Moralis Philosophiae Dogmata in Veterum Fabulis Contenta fuisse demonstratur.* This volume also contains *Mythologia*

of Venus and her birth from the sea (*Myth.* 4.13), he mentions Apelles' picture and Antipater's epigram on it:

Cum nuper nata fuisset Venus, hanc ex undis maris egredientem ambobus manibus e capillis et e facie aquam marinam expressisse inquiunt. Quare omnium pictorum facile princeps Apelles Cous celeberrimam illam Venerem emergentem, quae divinum prope opus creditum fuit, pinxit; cuius mirabilitatem et praestantiam ita expressit Sidonius Antipater. [Here he quotes *A.P.* 16.178, and translates:]

> Egressam nuper Venerem de marmoris undis
>   Aspice, praeclari nobile Apellis opus.
> Exprimit aequoream manibus de crinibus undam,
>   E longis spumas exprimit illa comis.
> Hac visa Pallas, sic cum Iunone locuta est:
>   'De forma Veneri cedere iure decet.'

In some such way as this Conti makes use of the following epigrams: *A.P.* 5.65, 217; 6.36, 44, 51, 59, 105, 164; 7.8, 412, 617; 9.16.1, 72, 75, 100, 142, 157, 266, 327, 331, 345, 357, 405.1–2, 577, 647, 724, 790, 823, 827; 10.3, 8, 27, 29, 57, 62, 69, 80, 112; 11.343.1–2; 16.3, 17, 87, 89, 92 (Ausonius), 93, 131, 144, 154, 171, 173, 178, 185.1–2, 185.3–6, 207, 215, 221.7–8, 229.3–4, 232, 233, 235, 253, 263.

PIETRO ANGELIO (PETRUS ANGELIUS BARGAEUS)

(1517–1596)

A native of Barga, Angelio studied law and the humanities in Bologna. A love-affair was the cause of his quitting that city, and he went to Venice. Then he undertook a journey to Constantinople, made another journey to France, and finally returned to Italy, where he was professor at Reggio in 1546. He was next professor at Pisa, and at the same time adviser on matters of learning to Cardinal Ferdinando de' Medici, first at Rome and later at Florence. His acquaintance was very wide among the literary men of his time, and his name is often encountered in their works. He was one of the five principal critics to whom Tasso's *Gerusalemme* was submitted. He died at Pisa.

Angelio attempted many kinds of poetry. Perhaps his best-known poem—in the sense of being oftenest mentioned—is his long work on hunting: *Cynegeticon libri vi* (1561). Epigrams make up only one book of Angelio's *Poemata*, but are numerous enough to show that he preferred the Greeks as models in this

---

Musarum by Geoffroy Linocier, at the end of which is quoted *A.P.* 16.220. Other editions of Conti's book, after the first, are: Venice, 1581; Frankfort, 1581; Paris, 1588; Lyons, 1602; Geneva, 1612; *ibid.*, 1653.

form. His themes commonly recall this or that Greek epigram, even when his treatment of them is, perhaps intentionally, different. Then he has a number of direct translations. This is his version of *A.P.* 9.561:[1]

> Quae nam autem infelix regio, quae nam invia soli
>   In Scythicis vitem hanc educat ora iugis?
> An Celtarum alpes glacie nivibusque rigentes
>   Fertilis an ferri nutrit Iberus ager?
> Quae tam immaturos progignere sueta racemos
>   Commendat miseris tristia vina cadis.
> At tu quid cessas illuc properare, Lycurge,
>   Et stirpem invisam deiicere ultor humi?

Angelio carries on the tradition of the dedicatory epigram. In the following he probably depends on *A.P.* 6.154:[2]

PRIMITIAE

> Et Pani et Cereri et Baccho dat rusticus Aegon
>   Primitias ruris munera parva sui.
> Lac Pani, Cereri spicas, Bacchoque racemos:
>   Ut vitem, ut segetes, ut tueantur oves.
> Quod si nec grando, mala nec rubigo luesque,
>   Nec fures poterunt, nec nocuisse lupi:
> Debita tum vestras felix cadet hostia ad aras
>   Pani haedus, Cereri sus, tibi, Bacche, caper.

In all, Angelio employs *A.P.* 5.94; 6.154; 7.173, 242, 434; 9.61, 391, 561; 11.194; 16.151.

In a dissertation on the destruction of the buildings of ancient Rome, Angelio finds a place for *A.P.* 9.606 and 620, which he quotes and puts into Latin verse.[3] The second he says he translated in his youth; both are imaginary inscriptions for baths; the first (*A.P.* 9.606) follows:

> Quam prius ardebas Venerem, Mars, aspice divam,
>   Hic se dum puro flumine nuda lavat;
> Aspice nantem illam: nec iam vereare futurum, ut
>   Intactam aspicias Pallada, Tiresias.

---

[1] References are to *Poemata Omnia . . . item Marii Columnae Quaedam Carmina.* Florence (Giunti), 1568, and to *Petri Angelii Bargaei Poemata Omnia diligenter ab ipso recognita*, Rome 1585. The Italian poems of Angelio were also published with those of his friend Mario Colonna: *Poesie Toscane dell' Illustriss. Sign. Mario Colonna et di M. Pietro Angelio, con l'Edipo Tiranno Tragedia di Sofocle tradotta dal medesimo Angelio*, Florence, 1589. They consist of forty sonnets and a *canzone;* no traces of the Greek epigrams appear in them.

[2] See also above, p. 190, n. 1.

[3] *De Privatorum Publicorumque Aedificiorum Urbis Romae Eversoribus Epistola ad Petrum Usembardum* [Secretary to Duke Ferdinand], in Graevius, *Thesaurus Antiquitatum Romanorum* 4 (Venice, 1732). 1869–92. The essay was first published at Florence in 1589.

COSTANZO LANDI

(1521–64)

Landi, Count of Compiano, is best known for his work on numismatics. He was born at Piacenza, and was accounted a prodigy for a Latin elegy written by him at the age of twelve. He studied at Bologna under Romolo Amaseo, and at Ferrara and Pavia under Alciati, and became doctor of laws at Piacenza in 1548. In 1551 he went to Pavia to study philosophy and medicine, but was hindered in this plan by his uncle, Count Frederico Scotti, who thought he was now too old to frequent the schools. When Scotti died soon after, Landi was able to carry out his intention. As he became more and more attached to the study of numismatics he finally fixed on Rome as the place most rich in the materials of his subject. He died there untimely at the age of forty-three. He published many minor writings, of which may be mentioned: *Lusuum Puerilium Libellus*, Ferrara, 1545; *Carmina*, Piacenza, 1549; and *In Epithalamium Catulli Annotationes*, Pavia, 1550. His best work was: *In Veterum Numismatum Romanorum Miscellanea Explicationes*, Pavia, 1559, republished at Leyden in 1695 as *Selectorum Numismatum Praecipue Romanorum Expositiones*. I have had access only to the works mentioned below.

Among Landi's minor pieces is the following: *Lettera . . . sopra una Impresa d'un Pino, con i Motti Postovi, e con la Dechiaratione di Tutta la Natura del Pino*, Milan, 1560. The body of the work is dated from Piacenza, November 2, 1557. It is addressed to Count Prospero Tedesco, whose device (given on the title-page) was a pine-tree, with the motto: MITH ZAIHT. This motto puzzles Landi, who thinks it must have been corrupted from the Greek! The letter is followed by an additional note written after Landi had gone to Pavia in 1558. Here he adds to his quotations from antiquity on the pine three epigrams from the Anthology: 'Sottogiongerò due epigrammi greci bellissimi, quali son nel primo libro delli epigrammi, tradotti dal Greco, dove il Pino si lamenta con quelli artefici che volevano farlo nave per navicar per il mare, e dice, che non è atta da essere fatta nave, perchè apporta seco mal'augurio, essendo soggetta quando è in terra a Borea, perchè tanto più nel mare sarà combattuta da venti.' He then quotes, evidently from Soter, the translations of *A.P.* 9.376 by More and Sleidan, Sleidan's translation of *A.P.* 9.31, and More's of *A.P.* 9.30. Finally he remarks that one of the Duke's lancers had informed him that Tedesco's motto was in German, and meant simply 'col tempo.'

In Landi's *Numismata* fourteen Greek epigrams are given either in Greek with a translation or in translation only. The versions are mostly drawn from Soter or from the *Emblemata* of the author's teacher, Alciati.[1] In discussing a coin bearing the name C. Postumius and figures connected with Diana, he introduces *A.P.* 9.581, and provides his own translation. He says:[2] 'In the first book of the Greek Epigrams, which Bartholomaeus Moyranus—a man abundantly skilled in Greek literature and adorned with philosophical knowledge—has recently been explaining to me privately at home—the following truly elegant poem by Leo the Philosopher occurs on the first page.'[3] Here we see the Anthology actually in use. Of Moyranus I have been unable to learn anything further. Landi's translation follows:

> Phoebe, procul iaculans, idemque sagittifer, ora
> Ut Diana feras e sylvis excitet acres
> Caesaris in laudem, populi plausumque potentis.
> Quae tamen haud feriant iaculantis corpus inultae,
> Nam Deus in terris facit haec spectacula Caesar.

GIAMBATTISTA AMALTEO
(AMALTHEUS)
(1525+1573)

Two generations of the Amaltei were famous for their Latin poets —in each case three brothers. Giambattista belongs to the younger and more famous generation. Although he has no single poem so well-known as his brother Girolamo's epigram on Acon and Leonilla, his poems as a whole merit higher praise for sincerity of tone than those of either Girolamo or the third brother, Camillo. The family was of Oderzo. Giovanni like Girolamo studied at Padua. He then acted as tutor in the family of a Venetian noble; and in 1554 visited England in the suite of the Venetian ambassador. Later he was secretary to the Republic of Ragusa, and still later secretary to Pius IV.

The poems of the three brothers were published at Venice in 1627 in a volume entitled: *Trium Fratrum Amaltheorum . . . Carmina; Accesere Hieronymi Aleandri Junioris Amaltheorum Cognati Poematia.* Up to this time they had led a precarious existence in the miscellanies; some of Giambattista's verses, for example, are in Lampridio's *Carmina* (1550).

---

[1] *A.P.* 5.79 ('Laert. Int.' and Bentinus), 80 ('Laert. Int.'); 6.236 (Molza. 'Ex Graecis desumptum, ut puto.'); 7.145 (Alciati), 353 (?Landi, 2 lines); 9.17 (no trans.), 18 (Ausonius), 163 (Marullus, Velius, Alciati), 283 (prose-paraphrase, after Obsopoeus), 581 (Landi); 11.38 (Velius), 43 (Velius), 210 (prose). References in the Register are to the edition of 1695.

[2] *Num.*, p. 134.

[3] *A.P.* 9.581=*Plan.* 1.1.4.

The epigrams of Giambattista alone show traces of the Anthology. He has two poems on the theme of *A.P.* 5.83–84 (and 15.35), translations of 6.26 and 7.381, and unmistakable reminiscences of 9.19 and 585. The following is his version of *A.P.* 7.381:

> Vecta levi pinus sinuosa per aequora remo,
> Dum legit Aegeum, dum legit Oceanum,
> Consenuit, nigrisque rogis incensa Lycarbae
> Est dominum ad Stygios una sequuta lacus.

FULVIO ORSINI[1]

(1529–1600)

Fulvio Orsini was by birth an illegitimate scion of the great Roman family whose name he bore. At first he was reared in all the pomp of his father's establishment; then suddenly a rupture between his parents reduced his mother and her child to the support of public charity. The young Orsini became a choir-boy at St. John Lateran, where the learned Canon Gentile Delfini noticed him and undertook his education. He also received encouragement from the Bishop of Nocera, Angelo Colocci (above, p. 167), and became known to Basilio Zanchi, Latino Latini, Lelio Capilupi, and their friends. Orsini became a canon of St. John Lateran in 1554. In 1559 Delfini died, recommending Orsini to the protection of the Cardinals Alessandro and Ranuccio Farnese (above, p. 223). He acted first as Ranuccio's librarian, and on the latter's death in 1565 joined the household of Alessandro. For a quarter of a century he tended and increased the Cardinal's magnificent collections of antiquities. Alessandro died in 1589, but his heir, Odoardo Farnese, made Cardinal in 1591, retained the confidence and the services of Orsini. The latter had long been one of the most distinguished scholars of the age, and his acquaintance was sought by men of learning from every part of Europe. He outlived all his friends of his own generation, and died in 1600. Orsini's chief works are *Virgilius Illustratus*, Antwerp, 1567; *Carmina Novem Illustrium Feminarum*, etc. (above, p. 237); *Imagines et Elogia Virorum Illustrium*, etc., Rome, 1570; *Familiae Romanae*, Rome, 1577; *Festi de Verborum Significatione Fragmentum*, Rome, 1581; Polybius, *De Legationibus*, Antwerp, 1582. The book by which he is best known is his *Imagines*.

Several of Orsini's publications have on their title-pages the words, '*Ex bibliotheca Fulvi Orsini*,' having been printed from

[1] Virtually all that is here said of Orsini comes from the admirable work of Pierre de Nolhac, which must be constantly in the hands of any person who interests himself in the intellectual life of the Italian Renaissance—*La Bibliothèque de Fulvio Orsini, Contributions à l'Histoire des Collections d'Italie et à l'Étude de la Renaissance*. Paris (Bibliothèque de l'École des Hautes Études), 1887.

MSS. in his own library, which was one of the richest private collections of classical books ever assembled. He was specially interested in acquiring the libraries, particularly the autographed volumes, of the great scholars of the earlier Renaissance. He bequeathed his books to the Vatican, where they may still be seen. The inventory of these books, made by Orsini himself, still exists (*Vat. Lat.* 7205), and by tracing out its entries in the Vatican Library Nolhac has been able to show just what books and MSS. were once in the possession of certain of the early humanists. Use has been made of this information, so far as concerns the Anthology, in earlier pages of the present book. Here it does not seem amiss to summarize the evidence of Orsini's own interest in the Greek epigrams.

Orsini possessed one complete MS. of the Planudean Anthology,[1] and seven smaller ones. It is not known who owned the complete MS. before him. Of the smaller MSS., one is the selection already mentioned made by Politian for private use (above, p. 124); a second is attached to a MS. of Porphyry's *Isagoge* (*Vat. Graec.* 1386, ff. 34–94) and once belonged to Carteromaco (above, p. 153); a third is a small collection supplementary to Planudes inserted in a copy of the 1494 edition that has notes in the hand of Lascaris (above, p. 120); and a fourth is a similar supplement copied into a first Aldine.[2] Fifth, the 'notebook' of Lascaris (above, p. 115) contains some epigrams. Sixth, a MS. of various emendations made by Musurus together with epigrams still unpublished in the time of Orsini (above, p. 157). A seventh MS., written in the hand of Orsini himself and now *Barberinus Gr.* I 123, was used by Sternbach for his study of the 'Appendix' to Planudes.[3]

Orsini's library contained eleven printed copies of the Anthology—five of the *editio princeps* and six of the first Aldine. One copy of the first edition came from the library of his early friend Colocci (above, p. 167); another Orsini wrongly believed to have belonged to Bishop Andrea di Bussi of Aleria (above, p. 92); while the remaining three had notes or additions in the hand of Janus Lascaris. The copies of the first Aldine were

---

[1] No. 53 in Orsini's list: 'Epigrammatario Graeco in carta pergamena'; *Vat. Graec.* 1372, 336ff. (above, p. 30). Nolhac briefly describes it, *op. cit.*, p. 339 n.

[2] No. 65 in Orsini's list (Nolhac, p. 355).

[3] Above, p. 32. This seems not to coincide with any entry in Orsini's Inventory.

also autographed. One came from the library of Carteromaco, and bore his notes (above, p. 153); one Orsini wrongly thought had notes by Antonio Urceo Codro (above, p. 123); a third contained emendations by Leonico (above, p. 154); a fourth had belonged to Benedetto Egio (above, p. 236); and a fifth contained supplementary epigrams in an unknown hand.[1] A sixth contained various corrections by Orsini himself.[2]

The testimony of Orsini has been invoked to prove the existence at one time in the library of Colocci of a MS. ampler in content than any copy of the *Planudea* (above, pp. 32-3 and 167).

Whatever mention there may be of the Anthology in the unpublished correspondence of Orsini does not concern the present study.[3] Among his published works the edition of the Greek poetesses, of course, contains epigrams; indeed the book may have been suggested by *A.P.* 9.26 (above, p. 133). Among the parallels to Virgil cited in his *Virgilius Illustratus*, he gives *A.P.* 6.177 (on *Ecl.* 1.2); 7.173 (on *Ecl.* 5.24), 627 (on *Ecl.* 1.70); 9.341 (on *Ecl.* 5.13), 507 (on *Ecl.* 1.70);[4] and 16.151 (on *Aen.* 4.36).

JOANNES MARIA BAGNAUS

(?1570)

This writer, otherwise unknown, was a native of Borgo in Tuscany (*Burgensis*). Among the few poems ascribed to him in the *Carmina Illustrium Poetarum* is one addressed to the Grand Duke Cosimo, in whose time I have therefore assumed him to have lived. The following couplet in the same collection is a translation of *A.P.* 9.394:

IN PECUNIAM, EX GRAECO

Numme, pater colacum, peperit te cura dolorque:
Te tenuisse, metus, te caruisse, dolor.

---

[1] This and one of the copies of the 1494 edition that contains additions by Lascaris I have already counted among the MSS.

[2] Now *Vat.* A. 18ᵇ 8ᵛᵒ. According to Nolhac it is beautifully bound in a mosaic binding, and bears the inscription: Φουλβίου τοῦ Οὐρσίνου κτῆμα καὶ πόνος. He gives no specimen of Orsini's corrections.

[3] He sent a copy of *A.P.* 7.6, in its inscriptional form, to Antonio Agustín in a letter published by Crawford, *Publications of the Modern Language Association* 28 (1913). 588.

[4] *A.P.* 9.507, absent from the *Planudea*, was here first edited by Orsini from the Life of Aratus. Cf. also Stadtmüller's crit. not. on *A.P.* 6.164 and 352.

GIAMBATTISTA PIGNA (NICOLUCCI)

(1530–1575)

Pigna was probably born at Ferrara. His family name was Nicolucci, but his father, who was an apothecary, was called Pigna from his shop-sign which chanced to be a pine-cone. The young Giambattista early showed a passion for study, and had the best masters of the time: L. G. Giraldi, Giraldi Cintio, Alessandro Guarini, Francesco Porto, and Vincenzo Maggi. Beginning at the age of twenty, Pigna was professor of Greek and Latin eloquence at the *Studio*. Three years later he published his Latin poems. He won the favor of Alfonso while the latter was only heir to the Ferrarese dukedom, and rose to great importance in the State when Alfonso succeeded; but was cut off in the prime of life, dying November 4, 1575. Pigna's greatest work is doubtless his *Istoria de' Principi di Este* (Ferrara, 1570); his best-known work is *I Romanzi* (Venice, 1554), which occasioned the famous quarrel, with mutual charges of plagiarism, between him and Giraldi Cintio. Pigna's Latin poems, the work of his youth, do him great credit.

Pigna joined to his own Latin poems those of Calcagnini and Lodovico Ariosto. It was the first appearance in print of Ariosto's Latin verse, which had been turned over to Pigna by the poet's son Virginio. The volume is dedicated to Alfonso II: *Io. Baptistae Pignae Carminum lib. quatuor. . . . His adiunximus Caelii Calcagnini Carm. lib. iii; Ludovici Areosti Carm. lib. ii.* Venice, 1553. Pigna's poems are good, always smooth and intelligible; his *Satyrae* have also a certain interest from their narrative form. Giraldi has accorded his pupil a distinguished place in the second of his dialogues on the poets of the time.

Pigna does not find so much use for the Greek epigrams as do Calcagnini and Ariosto; yet the style of his shorter pieces is epigrammatic in the Greek rather than in the Roman sense. On occasion he constructs figure-poems—the *Fistula* (*Carm.*, pp. 97–99) being evidently imitated from *A.P.* 15.21. Again, he produces dedicatory epigrams, for example, to Pan and Cybele (*Carm.*, p. 33). Once only, however, does he make a translation directly from the Anthology; it is a version of one of the Platonic epigrams (*A.P.* 5.78):

EX GRAECO

Dum ne deficiam quaero legere oscula labris,
    Colligit ore puer deficientem animam.
Dum mox ut redeat quaero rapere oscula labris,
    Surripit ore puer non redeuntem animam.

FRANCESCO DENALIO

(*fl.* 1550)

Denalio, a native of Reggio in Lombardy, was a jurist and a poet of some note. His Latin *Poemata* appeared at Bologna in 1563, his *Rime* at the same place in 1580. The latter I have not seen. Quadrio mentions also *Centones Laudesque Domini Nostri Jesu Christi* as published in 1610, and says that Denalio received the laural crown from the Emperor Charles V.

The Anthology is reflected, but not directly, in the third book of Denalio's *Poemata*, a large section of which consists of votive epigrams under the title *Lusus Pastorales*. The same book contains an epigram, *De Venere*, that goes back ultimately to *A.P.* 16.160, but with developments of Denalio's own invention:

> Cum bene se Cypris fictam vidisset in aere,
>   Sic dixit Phidiae: 'Num tibi nuda fui?'
> 'Nuda nec ante meos oculos, fas hoc mihi nec sit,
>   Tam bene sed ferrum te, Dea, finxit, ait.
> Nec mirum, quando ferrum sub Marte feroci est,
>   Te similem ferrum si tibi perpoliit.'

PUBLIUS FRANCISCUS SPINULA

(*fl.* 1563)

The little known of Spinula's life is gathered from his poems.[1] His father's name was Gabriele, and Francesco was born in Milan. There he studied, and for a time taught; but most of his life he spent away from Milan, teaching at Brescia, Verona, Padua, and Venice. His *Epigrammata* are dedicated to Stefano Maria Ugonio of Brescia, who appears to have succored Spinula in a time of distress. Spinula was living in Venice when his *Opera* appeared; in the Epistle placed before his Epodes he says his poems were composed at Milan, Venice, and Padua, and that the second epode was written at the house of Leonardo Mocenigo overlooking the Adriatic.

Traces of the Anthology are, as is natural, to be found mainly in Spinula's epigrams. Yet the circumstance that he is imitating Catullus and Horace in the metres and style of his other books

---

[1] *Opera: Poematon libri iii; Carminum libri iv; Epodon liber; Carminum Secularium liber; Elegorum libri x; Hendecasyllaborum liber; Epigrammaton libri iii.* Venice (Ziletti), 1563. Each part has a separate pagination;my references are to *Epig.* or *Epod.* Argelati, *Bibliotheca Scriptorum Mediolan.*, Milan, 1745, adds nothing to our knowledge of Spinula. There is an estimate of his verse by Ellinger, *op. cit.*, 1.289. Spinula has verses addressed to Ippolito Capilupi (*Poem.*, p. 33) and to G. B. Pigna (*Carm. Saec.*, p. 28).

is no guaranty of their contents. Among his Epodes, indeed, is
a version of *A.P.* 9.111:

> Nec Thracia ipsa gaudet ortu infantium,
> Nec morte, sic ut nos, dolet.
> Lugubris infans quod sit hic passurus et
> Mala atque fata tristia,
> Tristatur ortu: morte gaudet illius,
> Quod is puer, qui nudus, ut
> Proiecti ab undis navitae, miserrimus
> Humi iacebat, indigus
> Vitali ope omni, quem parentis nixibus
> Et ventre in oras luminis
> Profuderat Natura, vagitu omnia
> Ingente complentem loca,
> Quantum sibi in vita hac malorum fleverat
> Restare, tandem evaserit.

Among his *Epigrammata* Spinula has nine derived from the
Anthology. At one point (pp. 49–50) he presents six translations
'ex epigrammatis Graecis.'[1] To *A.P.* 7.669, which he translates,
he supplies a *responsum*. The verses are addressed to *Lippa;* but
if any *double entente* underlies the name, the point is hard to
detect.

AD LIPPAM

> Lux mea, quid coelum spectas? Fiam ut tibi Olympus,
> Innumeris quo te luminibus videam.

LIPPAE RESPONSUM

> O utinam faciant oculos me numina totam:
> Ut pulchrum intento lumine te videam.

The following is from *A.P.* 9.379:

> Vel murem, quod ait populus, mordere nocentes,
> Verbum sic falsum est, ut secus eveniat:
> Vel mus innocuos lacerat, letumque minantes
> Ecce draco sontes horridus ipse fugit.

In all, Spinula translates or imitates *A.P.* 5.95; 7.669 (with
responsum); 9.13, 111, 369, 379; 11.381, 430; 16.174.

ANTONIO RICCOBONI

(1541–1599)

Riccoboni's name is remembered for his Latin translation of Aristotle's *Poetics*. He was born at Rovigo, and studied at Venice and

---

[1] Of these, the fourth and sixth are not from the Anthology.

Padua under Paolo Manuzio, Sigonio, and Muret. He taught literature at Rovigo, and in 1571 succeeded to the chair of rhetoric at
Padua, a position which he held until his death. He published many
editions of ancient rhetorical writers, and composed a useful history
of the University of Padua (1598).

At the end of Garzoni's *Piazza*, noticed below, is printed a
Latin epigram by Lorenzo Massa followed by commendatory
verses from several scholars. Riccoboni is represented by a
letter, in which, while expressing admiration for Massa's poem,
he nevertheless finds it not to be an epigram. As examples of
proper epigrams he quotes *A.P.* 9.379 and 676, giving Latin
translations in prose. *A.P.* 9.676: 'Prusae nymphis cedimus.
Verum et ipsae meliores nobis valete Pythiades. Aliae vero
omnes, post Pythia et Prusam, nostris nymphis cedite Naiades.'
It is an inscription for a fountain on Mount Olympus in Mysia.

TOMMASO GARZONI

(1549–1589)

Garzoni was born at Bagnacavallo in the Romagna. On completing
his literary studies in his native city, he was sent in 1563 to Ferrara
and later to Siena, to study law. At Siena, however, he shifted his
interest to the Church, and in 1566 took the vows of a canon regular.
Thereafter he gave himself up to a literary career. His chief works,
though deficient in taste and judgment, were often reprinted and
translated into foreign languages; they are: *Il Teatro di Varii e
Diversi Cervelli Mondani* (Venice, 1583), *La Piazza Universale* (Venice,
1585), and *L'Hospidale de' Pazzi* (Ferrara, 1586).

The seventy-fourth chapter of *La Piazza Universale* is entitled, 'Delle Meretrici'; it contains versions of *A.P.* 7.217 and
16.204.1–2.[1] The second is:

> Praxiteles pinxit prius est quem passus Amorem,
> Deprompsit proprio pectore qui archetypum.

GIOVANNI GIOVANE (JUVENIS)

(*fl.* 1575)

Giovane, a secular priest of Taranto, is known for a tract,
De Schismate (Louvain, 1573), and for a volume on the history
of Taranto, *De Antiquitate et varia Tarentinorum Fortuna*

---

[1] I use the fourth edition: *La Piazza Universale di tutte le Professioni del Mondo*,
Venice, 1589, p. 594. The other works of Garzoni contain nothing from the Anthology.

(Naples, 1589). The latter book was reprinted in Graevius' *Thesaurus Antiquitatum et Historiarum Italiae*, tome 9, part 5 (Leyden, 1723).[1] In this treatise the third chapter of Book 3 relates to certain famous men connected with Taranto. Here Giovane quotes *A.P.* 7.122, on Pythagoras, with the translation of Bentinus, obviously taken from Laertius; and in the same chapter quotes from the Anthology, with his own translations, a selection of eight epigrams by Leonidas of Tarentum. Of Leonidas he has himself nothing to say. The epigrams are *A.P.* 6.188; 7.295, 715; 9.24, 99, 106; 16.182, and 306. His verse translations are not very well done, and for the last three epigrams he quotes (*A.P.* 6.188; 16.182, 306), he subsides into prose. His version of Leonidas' epitaph made by the Greek poet for himself (*A.P.* 7.715) here follows:

> Sat procul Italica terra, patriaque Tarento
>   Et iaceo et mortem vicerat iste dolor.
> Erronum vita haec non vita est: ipse sororum
>   Musarum coetu diligor atque choro.
> Atque Leonida haud periit, sed vivet in aevum,
>   Plures spero dies nomen habere meum.

ANTONIO POSSEVINO

(1534–1611)

Born at Mantua and educated at Rome, Possevino began life in the service of Cardinal Ercole Gonzaga. In 1559 he joined the Society of Jesus; and, beginning with a mission to the Duke of Savoy in 1560, was constantly employed by the Court of Rome in important negotiations in every part of Europe where it seemed possible to do something to stem the tide of Protestantism. The most remarkable of his missions was undertaken in 1581 to convert the Tsar of Russia, Ivan IV, to the Roman religion. About 1586 Possevino relaxed his political activity sufficiently to take up again the literary interests of his youth. Among his numerous productions chief places are accorded to his *Bibliotheca Selecta* (2 vols, Rome, 1593), his *Apparatus Sacer* (3 vols, Venice, 1603–6), and his *Muscovia* (Vilna, 1586). Antonio was a younger brother of Giambattista Possevino mentioned below, p. 319.

Among the lesser works of Possevino is one entitled *Tractatio de Poësi et Pictura ethica, humana, et fabulosa collata cum vera, honesta, et sacra*, Lyons, 1595.[2] As noticed above (p. 66), it

---

[1] I quote from this edition. There is a notice of Giovane in Toppi.
[2] I have been unable to consult any other of Possevino's works.

contains a chapter on the epigram, comprising a brief theory of the form, and, following that, some remarks on the Anthology. Possevino's aim, of course, is to bring profane learning into line with a sacred ideal. His observations on the Anthology are introduced with the words: 'Cautio in librum Epigrammatum Graecorum':

Ex libro . . . Epigrammatum seligi possent, quae tum ad sacra, tum ad moralia pertinent. At quoniam saepe loco Dei unius, plures Dii more ethnico ponuntur, idcirco eorum loco Deus esset inserendus; atque ita corrigenda epigrammata. Quale exempli causa illud esset ex Luciano [*A.P.* 10.27]:

> Ἀνθρώπους μὲν ἴσως λήσεις, ἄτοπόν τι ποιήσας.
> οὐ λήσεις δὲ θεούς, οὐδὲ λογιζόμενος.

Igitur loco illius θεούς dicendum esset θεόν. Ut vero constaret versus sic forsan scribi posset:

> οὐ λήσεις δὲ θεόν, μηδὲ λογιζόμενος.

Quo disticho monemur, quantumlibet improbe agendo fefellimus homines, Deum tamen ne cogitatione quidem fallere nos posse.

Reliqua, quae olent obscenitatem aut idolatriam, facile eradi possent, sicque tutior esset libri Epigrammatum Graecorum usus.

At tamen quae falsos illos Deos arguunt adulterii, avaritiae, ac similium vitiorum, relinquendi essent, ut iacent, quale illud [*A.P.* 9.48]:

> Ζεὺς κύκνος, ταῦρος, σάτυρος, χρυσὸς δι' ἔρωτα
> Λήδης, Εὐρώπης, Ἀντιόπης, Δανάης.

Ob Laeden, Danaën, Europen, Antiopenque
Iuppiter est aurum, taurus, olor, satyrum.

He further cautions readers against the Commentary of Obsopoeus, which (besides the fact that the author was a heretic) contains much that calls for expurgation; and similar care must also be taken with the Commentary of Brodaeus.

GIAMBATTISTA EVANGELISTA

Of Evangelista nothing appears to be known. A writer of this name, from Rimini, appears with ten sonnets in the *Rime di Diversi et Eccellenti Autori* (Venice, 1556), pp. 291–6; some of his pieces are addressed to Bembo, and he was probably a member of the circle of Domenico Veniero. Conceivably it was the same person who published *Poematum . . . Lusus*, [Venice], 1589, and *Orationes*, Venice, 1596.[1] The Latin poet is represented in the

---

[1] A copy of the *Lusus* is in St. Mark's Library; and the British Museum has a copy of the *Orationes*.

fourth volume of *Carm. Illust. Poet. Ital.* Evangelista's Latin poems appeared at a time when the Greek epigrams were likely to have little direct influence on them. They contain distant echoes. In the *Lusus* are poems recalling *A.P.* 7.308 and 12.235; two epigrams possibly echo *A.P.* 5.98. None is close enough to merit quotation; they are noted in the Register.

GIAMBATTISTA PINELLI
(1594)

Pinelli is a typical Latin poet of the counter-reform period. He was a Genoese, and seems to have passed his life in his native city. Among his friends was Pietro Angelio of Barga. Pinelli issued his poems in 1594, addressing them to the Accademia della Crusca, of which he was a member. A new edition was published in 1605.[1]

Only in an exceptional Italian Latin poet of Pinelli's time do we expect to find traces of any real knowledge of the Greek epigrams. Pinelli is not an exception. The only possible echo of the Anthology in his verse is a distant one, relayed to him through a well-known Latin translation. The original epigram is *A.P.* 9.49, on Hope and Fortune. Pinelli echoes the translation given above, p. 165, but his lines occur in a poem entitled *Ad Deliam*, a dream of his mistress!—

> Ite procul, larvae, procul ite, insomnia vana;
> Sat me lusistis: ludite nunc alios.

EMILIO PORTO
(c. 1550–1610)

Emilio was the son of Francesco Porto, who informed Scaliger on the Anthology once in the hands of Sophianus (above, p. 31); indeed it has been conjectured that Emilio himself later possessed this manuscript. He was born during his father's sojourn at Ferrara, was taken by him to Geneva, and left that place after his father's death in 1581. From that year till 1591 he professed Greek at Lausanne. In 1592 he was called to Heidelberg, where the remainder of his life was spent. He produced editions and translations of Greek authors, but is best known for his lexicographical works: *Dictionarium Ionicum Graeco-Latinum* (Frankfort, 1603); *Dictionarium Doricum* (Frankfort, 1604); *Pindaricum Lexicon* (Hanau, 1604).

Among the manuscripts collected by D'Orville and now in the

[1] *Carminum liber primus [—tertius]*, Florence (Giunti), 1594; Genoa, 1605.

Bodleian Library is one described as follows:[1] '"Æmilij Porti, Fr. P. C. F., Graecorum Epigrammatum Interpretatio Latina, cum brevissimis notis. O[pus] c[oeptum] die Martis 6 non. 1604." These notes may be in the author's hand.' An examination of this manuscript would provide fairly good evidence whether Emilio did or did not know the Palatine MS. before its discovery by Salmasius.[2]

GIAMBATTISTA BRACCIESCHI
(† 1612)

Braccieschi was a Dominican of the convent of San Marco in Florence. He is said to have had an exact knowledge of Latin, Greek, and Hebrew, and to have been respected as an orator, poet, mathematician, astronomer, and theologian. Most of his works have remained in manuscript—among them *Rime; Serie delli Duchi di Spoleto*, etc. (MS. of 1590); *Commedia della Conversione di Sant' Agostino* (MS. in Riccardiana); and *Aenigmatum Liber* (Cod. 192 of S. Marco).[3] The one work published by Braccieschi seems to have been *Discorsi* (Camerino, 1586).

Mazzuchelli says of Braccieschi's *Aenigmatum liber:* 'È scritto in versi Latini, e sta unito a diversi Epigrammi Greci composti in lode di soggetti santi e illustri.' The model for these Greek epigrams must have been the Anthology, of which Braccieschi possessed a copy—probably in an Aldine edition.[4] A manuscript of Braccieschi in the Magliabecchi collection contains Greek epigrams by him, and also Italian versions of *A.P.* 9.359–60.[5]

CRISTOFORO FINOTTI
(*c*.1570–*c*.1640)

Finotti, a Venetian, was a member of the religious order of the Somaschi. His life was passed as a teacher of rhetoric; in the volume of his *Orationes*, published at Venice in 1647, are introductory lectures on the *Poetics* and the *Rhetoric* of Aristotle, neither of which is above the general level of Italian school-exercises of the day. As a funeral

---

[1] Ms. D'Orville 277, ff. 1–107; Madan, *Summary Catalogue of Western Manuscripts in the Bodleian Library* 4.101 (No. 17155).

[2] The father, Francesco Porto, is said by Weiss to have left notes on the Anthology (see his article on Francesco in the *Biographie Universelle*). See also above, p. 43.

[3] Mazzuchelli.

[4] 'Epigrammatum Graecorum libri septem in-8' according to the catalogue of Braccieschi's books given by Léon Dorez in *Rev. des Biblioth.* 7 (1897). 100. Braccieschi had in charge the sale of the library of Pier Leoni.

[5] Olivieri in *Stud. Ital. Filol. Class.* 5.418 (No. 57 = *Conventi* J. IX. 29).

orator he enjoyed no small reputation, and was chosen to deliver orations over three Doges, Marino Grimani, Niccolò Donato, and
Giovanni Cornaro. Besides his Orations, Finotti published two books
of Latin verse, one entitled *Sertum Poeticum seu Carminum libri
quatuor* (Venice, 1606), the other *Parnassi Violae* (Venice, 1617).

Finotti's poems are almost entirely of a religious character,
and hence will owe little in substance to the Anthology. Their
titles, especially *Sertum Poeticum*, may be thought to echo that
of the *Florilegium*. The *Sertum Poeticum* contains two books of
Emblemata, among which *Emb.* 109—*Myrtilus cum Clypeo*—is
a manipulation of *A.P.* 9.42; Finotti probably took his notion
from Alciati. In the same volume he has five versions of *A.P.*
9.12, of which the first follows:

DE CLAUDO ET COECO

Loripedes incedit dum gressu ad moenia coeci,
  Coecus loripedis lumine pergit iter;
Munere non simili sibi munera pensat uterque,
  Quod facit ille oculis, efficit iste pede.

SELECTA EPIGRAMMATA, 1608

*Selecta Epigrammata ex Florilegio et alia quaedam ex Veteribus
Poetis Comicis potissimum Latino carmine conversa*. Rome,
1608. Pp. 363+[5].

The selection of epigrams from the Anthology made by
Joannes Soter of Cologne has often been referred to in the preceding pages, and is somewhat particularly described below in
an Appendix. It formed the basis of several later selections,
among which was the book here under notice. The *Selecta
Epigrammata* of 1608 was founded on the third (1544) edition
of Soter's book. It differs from its original in the following respects: (1) In containing (pp. 288–363) passages and fragments
from the comic poets; (2) in containing (pp. 255–271) a translation of the epigrams of Archias by Daniel Alsworth;[1] (3) in
somewhat changing the order of Soter, though the Planudean
division into seven books is retained; (4) in the suppression of
the names of certain translators; and (5) by the addition of 62
new translations.

The book is a Jesuit publication, and is pedagogical in aim.

---

[1] The discussion of these translations is reserved for a study of the Anthology in
English writers.

Soter's book, so deeply tinged with the German Reform, had therefore to be somewhat modified. The name of Sleidan appears with his translations on almost every page of Soter; here it is abolished, but his translations, being good in themselves, are retained. Soter's own versions also appear without his name, as do those of Jordanus, Beatus Rhenanus, Obsopoeus, and Venatorius. The names of Luscinius, Jausserandus, Bucoldus, Bentinus, and Hermannus a Nova Aquila, since the Church had nothing to complain of in them, are not blotted out. Erasmus holds an equivocal position under the initials 'E.R.'

The new translations here added to Soter's collection—besides Alsworth's Archias—mostly fall into two groups. In the first place there are 20 translations, without name of translator, which have been taken from the edition of the Anthology published in 1600 by the house of Wechel at Frankfort; these are by Obsopoeus and Venatorius (below, p. 286). In the second place there are 37 translations under the initials 'B. Gu.' These are the work of Bandino Gualfreducci (below, p. 258), who was probably the editor of the volume. Besides these there are four anonymous versions (*A.P.* 7.647; 9.31, 247, 704), and one (*A.P.* 9.592) under the initials 'H.B.,' which I have been unable to trace beyond this book.

Tables given below (pp. 278–83) state the full contents of Soter's third edition, and therefore, with the following additions, the contents of the present book (Alsworth's Archias is, of course, omitted):

A.P. 6.256 (B. Gu., p. 6), 334 (B. Gu., p. 251); 7.323 (B. Gu., p. 285), 371 (B. Gu., p. 287), 373 (B. Gu., p. 283), 447 (B. Gu., p. 284), 545 (B. Gu., p. 283), 551 (B. Gu., p. 285), 570 (B. Gu., p. 282), 590 (B. Gu., p. 281), 673 (B. Gu., p. 282), 674 (anon., p. 97); 8.1 (B. Gu., p. 284);

9.13 (B. Gu., p. 12), 13.3–8 (B. Gu., p. 12), 23 ([Obsopoeus], p. 84), 24 ([Venatorius], p. 90), 62 ([Obsopoeus], p. 99), 66 ([Venatorius], p. 96), 85 ([Obsopoeus], p. 84), 109 ([Obsopoeus], p. 82), 137 (B. Gu., p. 12), 148 ([Venatorius], p. 26), 161 ([Obsopoeus], p. 98), 186 ([Venatorius], p. 98), 192 ([Venatorius], p. 90), 230 ([Obsopoeus], p. 21), 247 (anon., p. 85), 279 ([Venatorius], p. 18), 298 (B. Gu., p. 16), 322 (B. Gu., p. 14), 323 (B. Gu., p. 15), 327 (B. Gu., p. 13), 354 ([Venatorius], p. 18), 357 (B. Gu., p. 4), 375 (B. Gu., p. 10), 391 (B. Gu., p. 5), 557 (B. Gu., p. 5), 575 ([Venatorius], p. 95), 581 (B. Gu., p. 6), 592 (H. B., p. 130), 704 (anon., p. 185);

10.3 (B. Gu., p. 286), 34 ([Obsopoeus], p. 117), 39 ([Obsopoeus], p. 110), 40 ([Obsopoeus], p. 110), 54 (B. Gu., p. 287), 74 ([Obsopoeus], p. 22), 75 ([Obsopoeus], p. 107), 88 (B. Gu., p. 285), 102 ([Obsopoeus], p. 79), 105 (B. Gu., p. 286);

11.13 (B. Gu., p. 286), 110 (B. Gu., p. 281), 281 (B. Gu., p. 288);
16.1 (B. Gu., p. 7), 2 (B. Gu., p. 7), 3 (B. Gu., p. 7), 23 (B. Gu., p. 8),
24 (B. Gu., p. 8), 25 (B. Gu., p. 8).

AGESILAO MARESCOTTI
(1577–1618)

Marescotti, a noble Bolognese, was chamberlain to Pope
Paul V. He published a learned and curious work on masks, at
Bologna in 1610: *De Personis et Larvis . . . Syntagmation.*[1] In
this book the author, properly enough, finds a place for *A.P.*
11.408, of which he presents the following translation:

> Saepe caput tingis, nunquam tinctura senectam,
>   Nunquam rugosas explicitura genas.
> Desine iam faciem stibio depingere totam,
>   Persona est etenim tunc tibi, non facies.
> Nil habes hinc lucri; quae est haec dementia? Fucus
> Et color haud Hecubam fecerit unquam Helenam.

The translation is not entirely the work of Marescotti; rather
he has only retouched the old version by Sir Thomas More, but
he has much improved it in ease and point—it was already close
enough to the Greek original. More had written:

> Saepe caput tinguis, nunquam tinctura senectam,
>   Aut tonsura genis quae tibi ruga tuis.
> Desine iam faciem stibio perfundere totam,
>   Ne persona tibi haec sit modo, non facies.
> Quum nihil assequeris fuco stibioque, quid amens
>   Vis tibi? nunquam Hecuben haec facient Helenen.

MATTEO TOSCANO
(†1624)

Toscano was a Roman by birth, but appears to have spent his
life in France. He is not to be confused with the better-known
Giovan Matteo Toscano (above, p. 237). All that is known
of the present Toscano is that he died at Condom in 1624,
having published in 1620 at Bordeaux a volume of epigrams
entitled *Anthologia Epigrammatum.* The title is intended to refer the reader at once to the Greek Anthology, and the initial
impression is carried forward within the book by a considerable
number of translations. Toscano is always an imitator, and

---

[1] I use the second edition, Rome, 1639.

when not translating from the Anthology is paraphrasing the Latin poets. His chosen themes are God, the soul, virtue, and kindred subjects. No doubt he was an ecclesiastic.

The *Anthologia* contains twenty-three versions from the Greek epigrams: *A.P.* 5.68; 9.15, 39, 108, 179, 221, 339, 367, 420, 443, 497, 627, 749 (2 versions); 10.29, 74; 11.170, 171, 264, 294, 309, 419; 16.14. He thus renders *A.P.* 10.29:

> Nullos laedit Amor mortales; desidiosae
> Sed sibi praetexunt hunc animae iuvenum.

The following version of the theme of *A.P.* 9.627, if really by Toscano, gives a better impression of his skill:[1]

> Dum Baiis dormiret Amor prope littus in umbra,
> Murmure detentus lene fluentis aquae,
> Conspexere illum Nymphae multo igne coruscum,
> Et raptas lymphis supposuere faces.
> Quis gelidam credat subito exarsisse liquorem
> Atque inde aeternos emicuisse focos?
> Nec mirum, his flammis, toties quibus arserat aether,
> Vos quoque perpetuum si caluistis aquae.

ALEXANDER SINCLITICUS

(*fl.* 1620)

Sincliticus was by birth a Cretan. He is known to have been teaching at the University of Padua in 1620. A copy of the first (1503) Aldine Anthology, once in his possession, and containing notes in his hand, was in the Pinelli library, and, when that collection was dispersed in 1790, came into the hands of Chardon de la Rochette.[2] Many of Chardon's books passed to the Bibliothèque Nationale, but this one seems not to have been among them.

BANDINO GUALFREDUCCI

(1565–1627)

Gualfreducci was born at Pistoia, joined the Jesuits, and for a time taught rhetoric in his Order at Rome. Later he became Latin Secretary to the General of the Order, and finally, near the end of his life, retired to the Jesuits' house in Rome, where he died. He wrote a considerable amount of Latin verse, principally dramas. His miscellane-

---

[1] It is ascribed to Matthaeus Faetanus of Naples in the *Carm. Illust. Poet. Ital.* 4.182.

[2] Chardon, *Mélanges de Critique et de Philologie* (Paris, 1812) 1.235–6.

ous verse was collected in the following volume: *Variorum Carminum libri sex. Sophoclis Oedipus Tyrannus eodem interprete.* Rome (apud heredem Barth. Zannetti), 1622.

Gualfreducci took an unusual interest in the Greek Anthology; and it may well be that it was owing to his interest that it came to play a part in Jesuit education. The sixth book of his *Carmina* is wholly made up of translations from the Greek epigrams arranged roughly in the order of the Planudean collection. The section is headed: 'E Graeco libro Anthologiae.'

These translations in many instances are the same as those published in the *Selecta Epigrammata* of 1608 under the initials 'B. Gu.,' and it seems probable that Gualfreducci was the editor of that Selection.[1] In the intervening fourteen years he had added to his translations, and in some cases had improved the old ones. There are twenty-six new translations in the *Carmina*.[2] The following is Gualfreducci's version of *A.P.* 7.346:

> Hoc erit (heu!) marmor nostrae, mihi rapte Sabine,
>   Exiguum eximiae pignus amicitiae.
> Te quaeram assiduus: tu, si potes, actus ad umbras,
>   Me super haud Lethes pocula dira bibas.

A.P. 9.298 is an epigram by Antiphilus on a miracle wrought upon a blind man in the mysteries of Demeter at Eleusis. This Gualfreducci renders in the following manner.[3]

> Templum adii baculo nixus privatus honore
>   Sacrorum et radiis, auree Phoebe, tuis.
> Participem fecere Deae solisque sacrique;
>   Nocte sacrum aspexi, nocte mihi orta dies.
> Orgia nunc celebrans posito vagor urbe bacillo.
>   Clarior et lingua lux mihi testis erit.

In all, Gualfreducci translates *A.P.* 6.256, 334; 7.66.3-4, 323 (2 versions; only 1 in *Sel. Epig.*), 346, 371, 373, 447, 545, 551, 570, 590 (different version in *Sel. Epig.*), 673; 8.1; 9.10, 11, 12, 13 (different version in *Sel. Epig.*), 13B (only in *Sel. Epig.*), 53,

---

[1] Above, p. 256. Both books were published by Zannetti.

[2] *A.P.* 7.66.3, 323, 346, 590; 9.10, 11, 12, 13, 53, 61, 110, 204, 248, 283, 291, 304, 354, 369, 397, 447, 517, 561; 10.69; 11.282; 16.107, 129. Two translations (*A.P.* 9.13.3-8 and 581) which occur in *Sel. Epig.* are omitted from the *Carmina*.

[3] I give a literal translation of the Greek: 'My staff brought me to the temple, for I was not only not a participant in the mysteries, but not even in the sunlight. Yet the goddesses made me an initiate of both, and I know that on that night I was purged even of the darkness of my eyes [i.e., as well the darkness of his soul]. Without a staff I returned to the city heralding the mysteries of Demeter with my eyes more clearly than with my tongue.'

61, 110, 137, 204, 248, 283, 291, 298, 304, 322, 323, 327, 354, 357, 369, 375, 391, 397, 447, 517, 557, 561, 581 (only in *Sel. Epig.*); 10.3, 54, 69, 88, 105; 11.13, 110, 281, 282; 16.1, 2, 3, 23, 24, 25, 107, 129.

GIROLAMO ALEANDRO THE YOUNGER
(1574–1629)

The younger Aleander belonged to the same family as his more famous namesake, and like him was born at Motta. He was also a relation of the Amaltei. As secretary to Cardinal Bandini, Aleander passed his later years in Rome.

The *Poematia* of Aleander were published at Venice in 1627. together with the poems of the brothers Amaltei, in the volume mentioned above, p. 243. He has an epigram in imitation of *A.P.* 11.198, on a man with a long nose, or of 11.203, on the same subject, and a translation of 16.185. The last (on Heracles and Dionysus) follows:[1]

> Ex Thebis ambo, Iove nati, proelia amantes:
> Hunc thyrsi, hunc clavae pondera ferre iuvat;
> Parque columnarum positus, par cultus in armis;
> Hic cervi exuvias, ille leonis habet.
> Utrique aera crepant; Iuno grave numen utrique;
> E terra ad superos ignis utrumque tulit.

This version first appeared, with the Greek text, in Aleander's dissertation on an ancient marble, *Antiquae Tabulae Marmoreae Solis Effigie Simbolisque Exculptae Explicatio.*[2] In the same work he gives the text, with prose versions, of *A.P.* 9.316 and parts of 16.254 and 256.

OTTAVIO TRONSARELLI
(*fl.* 1630)

Tronsarelli was the author of two epic poems, one on the Emperor Constantine, *Il Constantino* (Rome, 1629), the other on the battle of Lepanto, *La Vittoria Navale* (Rome, 1633), of more than thirty melodramas (Rome, 1632), and of numerous other pieces in prose and verse. He was a native of Rome, and a member of the *Accademia degli Ordinati* in that city.

[1] A set of verses by Aleander, quoted by Allacci (below, p. 265, n. 4), turns the conceit of *A.P.* 16.295–296—that heaven, and no Greek city, was the birthplace of Homer —to the praise of Antonio Querenghi. (Gronovius, *Thesaurus* 10.1730).

[2] Graevius, *Thesaurus Ant. Rom.* 5 (Venice, 1732). 717. The work was first published at Rome in 1616, and was reprinted at Paris in 1617.

A small book of Latin verse by Tronsarelli, *Janus Quadri-frons, in amatoria, heroica, varia et sacra distinctus* (Rome, 1639), contains two vague and distant echoes of the Anthology —one, *De Niobe Myronis* (*sic*), depending on *A.P.* 16.129, the other a couplet on Venus in armor (cf. *A.P.* 16.176):

> Belligeram tractat Venus hastam: Martis amantem
> Non vult imbellem fortis habere Lacon.

ANTONIO GERMANO

(*fl.* 1630)

Germano, a professor of *litterae humaniores* presumably at Rome, published at Rome, and dedicated to Urban VIII, in 1630, a book of proverbs entitled: *Giardino di Sentenze Volgari e Latine di Diversi Auttori Antichi e Moderni*. The book is introduced by a commendatory Epistle in the name of the pope himself. The proverbs are given each in an Italian couplet, which is followed by numerous quotations from the ancients and moderns. Greek parallels are put into Latin.

The Anthology contributes to Germano's collection both directly, when he gives the epigrams in a prose version, seemingly his own, and indirectly, when he quotes what happens to be a translation from the works of Alciati or another Latin writer.[1] The use to which he puts his illustrations is exemplified by his proverb on Ingratitude:

> Tal volta all'huom ingiuria far si vede,
> Da chi haver ne sperò gloria e mercede.

Two illustrations of this proverb are from the Anthology:

> Lupum ex propriis mammis nutrio invita,
> Sed me cogit pastoris stultitia;
> Auctus enim a me contra me rursus fera erit.
> Beneficium mutare non potest.
> (*A.P.* 9.47)

> Malus vir dolium est perforatum in quod omnes
> Immittens gratias in vanum effudisti.
> (*A.P.* 9.120)

---

[1] The prose-translations are noted in the Register. As they differ from those of Lubinus (above, p. 38), the only complete prose-rendering of the Anthology Germano could have known, I assume that they are his own work. They are from *A.P.* 7.71.5-6; 9.47, 120; 10.27, 30, 42, 46, 74, 95, 108. The verse-translations are from *A.P.* 9.47 (p. 172, Alciati), 111 (p. 403, Alciati), 231 (p. 15, Alciati); 10.26 (p. 308, W. Lily), 31 (p. 399, anon.), 36 (p. 17, Obsopoeus; p. 172, Ausonius), 43 (p. 239, Volaterranus), 84 (pp. 398 and 403, Luscinius); 11.166 (p. 308, Th. More).

POPE URBAN VIII (MAFFEO BARBERINI)
(1568–1644)

Barberini was a Florentine of noble family. At the age of three he lost his father; his mother had him carefully educated, and finally sent him to Rome to study with the Jesuits. He attained the doctorate at Pisa in 1588. He began his ecclesiastical career under Sixtus V, was made governor of Fano and protonotary apostolic by Gregory XIV, and was sent by Clement VIII to congratulate Henry IV of France on the birth of the Dauphin (1601). In 1604 he was made titular archbishop of Nazareth, and sent as nuncio to France. Paul V created him cardinal in 1606, and made him archbishop of Spoleto two years later. Largely by French influence he was elected successor to Gregory XV, August 6, 1623. As chief pontiff he augmented the domains of the Church, in particular by the Duchy of Urbino; founded the College of the Propaganda; and condemned the books of Jansen. He was an encourager of arts and letters, being himself a man of taste and learning. His Latin poems were published in 1631, and his Italian *Rime* in 1640, both at Rome.

In his Latin verse there is an epigram, 'On the statue of Niobe in the Medicean Gardens,' evidently modeled on *A.P.* 16.129:[1]

> Bis septem Niobe natis orbataque caro
>   Coniuge sum, ducto facta rigore lapis.
> Ecce tamen spiro: nec enim de marmore finxit
>   Me faber, at vitae reddidit arte nova.
> Lumina non fundunt lacrymas; non marmoris hic est
>   Candor; habent tristi pallida membra metu.
> Omnis inest sensus, nec linguae deficit usus;
>   Sed taceo, timeo nam mage cauta loqui.

VINCENZO ALSARIO DELLA CROCE
(1576–c. 1631)

Alsario was a Genoese physician of considerable note in his day. He was a student of Latin and Greek; and his first published work was *De Invidia et Fascino Veterum* (Lucca, 1595), printed when he was nineteen. A list of his numerous books, almost wholly of a medical character, may be found in Michaud's *Biographie Universelle*. He introduces *A.P.* 10.51 into his *De Invidia*, giving a translation in prose.[2]

---

[1] *Maphaei S. R. E. Card. Barberini nunc Urbani PP. VIII Poemata*, Rome, 1631, p. 165.

[2] Graevius, *Thesaurus Antiquitatum Romanarum* 12 (Venice, 1737). 892.

LEONE ALLACCI

(1586–1669)

Allacci was a Greek, born in the island of Chios. He was taken by his maternal uncle Michael Nauridis to Italy to be educated, first to Calabria, and later (1599) to Rome. There he was admitted to the College of St. Athanasius. Finishing his course in 1610, he was for four years secretary to the Bishop of Anglona. About this time he made a journey to Smyrna and Chios, returning, however, to Rome, where he took the degree of Doctor of Medicine in 1616. Paul V made him professor of Greek at the Vatican; and Gregory XV employed him in several honorable capacities, sending him in 1623 to Germany to conduct the Palatine Library to Rome. Allacci was a voluminous writer on the theological points at issue between Rome and the Orthodox Church. In 1661 he became librarian of the Vatican.[1]

As has been noted above (p. 31), it was in the library of the Counts Palatine at Heidelberg that Salmasius in 1606/7 discovered what we know as the Palatine MS. of the Anthology. It had since remained there.[2] In 1622 Heidelberg was captured by Tilly; the Palatine Library was given to Maximilian of Bavaria as his share of the booty, and by him was presented to the pope. In this way the Vatican Library was enriched by a large number of valuable MSS., the greater part of which it still retains. The Anthology, however, was removed to Paris in 1797 by order of the French Directory; and, with the exception of some leaves at the end, was restored to Heidelberg at the close of the Napoleonic wars.

Of the last days of the MS. in Italy an account has been preserved by Chardon de la Rochette, a contemporary of the event. 'The Pope' (Pius VI), he says, 'was so jealous of retaining the MS. that he had it carried to Terracina with his most precious jewels; but our Commissioners had it brought back again, and observing that it had been newly bound and that the Anacreon had been removed, they had the Anacreon brought back too, and the two parts were counted as only one MS.'[3]

The Palatine MS. was in Rome for the better part of two

---

[1] On Allacci see Legrand, *Bibl. Hell.* (xviie siècle), pp. 435–471. Allacci's *Breve Relatione del Viaggio fatto in Germania* was published by Chr. Baehr in the *Heidel. Jahrb. der Literatur* for 1872. It contains no reference to the Anthology. I have not seen Curzio Mazzi, *Leone Allacci e la Palatina di Heidelberg*, Bologna, 1893.

[2] Save that in 1615 it was sent to Paris and Dijon for the use of Salmasius. The librarian at Heidelberg from 1602 to 1622 was Janus Gruter.

[3] Chardon, *Mélanges* 1.289.

centuries; and, it must be confessed, this was one of the causes
of its not being edited at all till near the end of the eighteenth
century, and not adequately then. If it had been at Heidelberg
in the seventeenth century, we may be certain that a scholar
would have been found to edit it. In Rome it was comparatively neglected. Allacci himself knew its value, and paid it
some attention.[1] After his return from Germany he was appointed librarian to Cardinal Francesco Barberini. In the Barberini Library, since become a part of the Vatican, are several
MSS. containing excerpts from the Anthology. The description
of one of these provides evidence of Allacci's interest in the epigrams: 'No. 50. Graeca epigrammata varia (cum emenda-
tionibus manu Allatii scriptu).'[2]

After Allacci, I can name only Spalletti, Zenobetti, and Cardinal Quirini (below, pp. 414, 403, and 391) who, among Italians, studied the MS. Lucas Holstein, Lucas Langermann, and
Philippe d'Orville may be mentioned among foreigners who examined it in Rome.

Among the original writings of Allacci that are of a secular
character is a treatise on the birthplace of Homer: *De Patria
Homeri*, Lyons, 1640. He treated the same subject in a long
Greek poem called *Homeri Natales*.[3] His purpose in both works
is to put forward the claim of his native Chios to be the birthplace of Homer. In the prose treatise he properly therefore
quotes the epigrams that bear on his subject; each epigram is
provided with a translation. These are usually borrowed—*A.P.*
9.97 is accompanied by the version of Venatorius, *A.P.* 16.295
by that of Sabeo, etc. In a few instances he employs translations

---

[1] In his *De Patria Homeri*, chap. 14 (Gronovius, *Thes.* 10.1831), Allacci quotes the
authority of the *Palatinus* on the authorship of *A.P.* 7.5: 'In Manuscripto antiquissimo,
quod e Palatina in Vaticanam Bibliothecam allatum est, in quo Corona Meleagri,
Philippi, et Agathiae Sylloge Epigrammatum Graecorum a Constantio [sic] Cephala
in capita secundum materiam reducta hoc Silentiarii epigramma sub nomine ἀδήλου, vel
Alcaei Mitylenaei legitur. . . . Quod si verum est, et verum esse tanti Codicis fide mihi
persuadeo, auctor, qui Chiis Homerum vindicat, multo, Paulo Silentiario, qui sub aetate
Justiniani scribebat, longeque antiquior est, ideoque et gravior.' Again in an epistle to
Gabriel Naudé, printed in Liceto's *Responsa de Quaesitis per Epistolas* (Bologna, 1640),
he describes the state of preservation in which he found the MS. (quoted by Preisendanz,
Praef. to Sijthoff's phototype ed. of *Pal.* 23, col. xi).

[2] Seymour de Ricci, 'Manuscrits Grecs de la Bibliotheca Barberina' in *Revue des
Bibliothèques* 17 (1907). 81ff. Cf. Nos. 69, 123 (above, p. 30), and 185; the last is from
the Palatine MS., but is not, seemingly, in the hand of Allacci.

[3] Both works are reprinted in vol. 10 of Gronovius' *Thesaurus Graecarum Antiquitatum*, Venice, 1735; my references are to this volume.

by his friends. *A.P.* 11.442 is translated by Francesco Lucido:[1]

> Quem ter Cecropidae quondam eiecere tyrannum,
>   Et totidem scitis restituere suis,
> Collegi ingenio Pisistratus acer Homeri
>   Quae sparsim fuerant carmina sueta cani;
> Noster erat civis vates, namque aureus ille,
>   Mopsopidae Smyrnam si coluistis avi.

Another friend of Allacci was Andrea Baiano, a Spaniard born at Goa in the East Indies. He taught grammar at Rome, was known as a theologian, and published orations, epistles, and poems, including a translation of the *Aeneid* into Greek.[2] Baiano thus renders *A.P.* 16.320:

> Lis ab Aristida periit, quae ingentis Homeri
>   De patria Ioniis urbibus ante fuit.
> Namque omnes perhibent Smyrnam peperisse Poetam,
>   Quae quoque Aristidem rhetora digna tulit.

A third friend from whom Allacci borrows a translation is Sabiro Angrisani, otherwise unknown. He translates *A.P.* 7.1:

> Abstulit heroum cantorem griphus Homerum
>   Mire intortus, Ios qua iacet in pelago.
> Nectare perfusum Nereïdes inde marina
>   Texerunt corpus littoreo lapide.
> Ille etiam Thetim et natum heroumque labores
>   Concinit atque Ithaci facta operosa ducis.
> Parva licet, pelagi felix Ios insula, namque
>   Musarum sidus continet et Charitum.

The translations of eight epigrams are by Allacci himself; for example, *A.P.* 7.7:[3]

> Hellada divinum qui totam cantat Homerum
>   Theba tulit, centum quae patuit foribus.

In all, *De Patria Homeri* contains translations of the following:[4] *A.P.* 7.1 (Angrisani), 2 (Lucido), 3 (Allacci), 4 (Allacci),

---

[1] I have failed to identify this person.

[2] The Latin version of Allacci's *Homeri Natales* was made by Baiano.

[3] Of this anonymous epigram Allacci says (Gronov. 10.1739): 'In nonnullis codicibus MSS. Antipatro Sidonio tribuitur.' No such attribution is known to the critical notes of Stadtmüller. To be sure, in both *Plan.* and *Pal.* the epigram stands between two which are assigned to Antipater of Sidon. In the MS. of Constantine Lascaris (above, p. 108) it is attached to the preceding one, but Allacci would hardly know this.

[4] Add to these a number of modern exercises on the theme of the rivalry of the seven cities—one by the French writer Martialis Monerius, one by the Portuguese Jeronimo Cerera (Gronov. 10.1724), and those of Sannazaro, Marullus (=16.295), M. A. Casanova, Ciriaco, Filelfo, and the younger Aleander.

5 (Sabeo), 7 (Allacci); 9.97 (Venatorius), 192 (Allacci), 213 (Sabeo), 455 ([Obsopoeus]); 11.442 (Lucido); 14.66 (Allacci); 15.36 (Argoli), 37 (Argoli), 38 (Argoli), 40N (Argoli); 16.292 (Xylander), 293 (Allacci), 294 (Sabeo), 295 (Sabeo), 296 (Xylander; Allacci), 297 ([Gaza]; Sabeo), 298 (H. Stephanus), 320 (Baiano).

Allacci promised to publish several of the unedited epigrams of Nossis, Moero, Anyte, Philippus of Thessalonica, and Leonidas of Tarentum in a new edition of his Σύμμικτα; but of this edition all that appeared was the Table of Contents, published as a prospectus at Rome in 1668.[1] He did, however, print a number of the epigrams of Simonides, some of them hitherto unpublished, in his *De Symeonum Scriptis* (Paris, 1664).[2]

A copy of Stephanus' edition of the Anthology, once owned by Allacci, is now in the British Museum, and has notes in Allacci's hand.

VINCENZO GUINISI
(1588–1653)

Guinisi was born at Lucca; joined the Jesuits in his thirteenth year; and in later life taught rhetoric in the Roman College. He was destined to continue the history of the Society begun by Sacchini, but gave this over to become secretary to Vitelleschi, General of the Order. His publications include: *Allocutiones Gymnasticae*, Rome, 1626, etc.; *Poesis Vario Carminum Genere*, Rome, 1627, Antwerp, 1633, *ibid.*, 1637, etc.; and a number of sermons.

In Guinisi's *Poesis* (ed. 1637, p. 257) there is an exercise by him on the theme of *A.P.* 6.54 in 27 lines, beginning:

Pulsabat digitis lyram lyristes,
Cum fides, male passa verberantem
Nervo dissiliente dissecatur.
At cicadula, mens canora silvae,
Aestatis Melopaea garrientis,
Iacturam fidis ambitu fideli
Et dulcis vice vocis implet ultro.
Nam, lyram superinsidens disertam,
Pro cassa fide sufficit locatque
Vocem dulciloquae necessitati:

---

[1] Reprinted by Fabricius (Harles), *Bibl. Graec.* 14.1 ff. The excerpts from the Anthology were to be in Book 7, articles 130, 132, and 133.

[2] *De Sym.*, p. 212–6. In all, he here quotes *A.P* 6.144, 197, 212–7; 7.77, 254–5, 258, 270, 296, 348, 443, 496, 509, 511, 514; 13.11, 14, 19–20, 26, 30–1; but *A.P.* 7.254–5, 258, 348, and 270 are in *Plan.*, and several of the others were known in some form from Thucydides, Plutarch, etc. Allacci gives prose translations of *A.P.* 7.348 and 13.31.

Sic se temperat ad canentis usum,
Ut quidquid digitis canit lyristes,
Illud ore cicada prosequatur. . . .

GIAMBATTISTA BARGIOCCHI

(1589–1662)

Bargiocchi, a distinguished Jesuit preacher, was born at Novara, and entered the Order when sixteen. Most of his life seems to have been passed at Rome; and he died there in 1662. A poem in his praise by Palmotta was published at Ancona in 1663. Bargiocchi's only publication was his volume of Latin epigrams: *Epigrammata Sacra, Moralia, et Demonstrativa*. Rome, 1644. A second, augmented, edition appeared at Rome in 1660.

Among his 'moral' epigrams he has four that are modeled on well-known originals from the Anthology: *A.P.* 7.623; 9.44, 114 (or 351); 16.174 (*In feminam armatam*).[1] The verses I take to be an imitation of *A.P.* 7.623 localize the incident described, as the Greek epigram does not; the comparison at the end also has no source in the Greek.

Diruta terrae motu Antiochia, reperta est
    mulier mortua lactans infantem vivum.

Cum cecidit magno terrae concussa fragore
    Clara per Argolicas Antiochia plagas,
Inventa est genitrix praebens lac mortua nato,
    Qui de materno funere vivus erat.
O mirum! Solymaea parens crudelior urso,
    Ne pereat, nati membra tenella vorat:
Haec perit, ut sugat maternos filius annos,
    Illa feris peior, mater at ista fuit.

GIACOMO FILIPPO TOMASINI

(1597–1654)

Tomasini was a Paduan, but died at Città Nuova in Istria, where he was bishop. The bishopric is said to have been presented to him by Urban VIII in recognition of his *Petrarca Redivivus* (Padua, 1650). Tomasini is also known for his *Elogia* of famous Paduans (Padua, 1630; 1632), an edition of the letters of Cassandra Fedele (1636), and several works on archaeology, among which is *De Donariis Veterum* (Udine, 1639). In this last work he makes some use of the Greek epigrams, though

[1] I have used the second edition.

far less than the matter would seem to call for.[1] He confines himself, however, mainly to the Roman side of his subject. In treating of offerings to Venus (Chap. 16) he refers to *A.P.* 6.1 and 80, giving Ausonius' version of the first; and when speaking of the offerings of vine-dressers (Chap. 27) refers to *A.P.* 6.36, 56, 74; 9.331. He quotes none of these; only of the last giving a partial prose rendering: 'Iunctum Nymphi est Bacchus gratus, et ignem ardentem capies, hunc nisi miscueris.'

VINCENZO GALLO

(*fl.* 1626–60)

[See above, p. 67]

JOANNES COTTUNIUS

(*c.* 1600 – *c.* 1657)

Cottunius was a Greek, born at Veria (ancient Beroea) near Salonika. He early came to Italy, where he received most of his education, becoming Doctor of Medicine, Philosophy, and Theology. In 1632 he was professor of philosophy at Padua, having perhaps before that been at Bologna. In Padua he established a seminary for young Greeks. He was a correspondent of his countryman Leone Allacci.[2] Besides his epigrams and his book on the epigram, Cottunius published two psychological works: *De Triplici Statu Animae Rationalis* (Bologna, 1628; Padua, 1653) and a Commentary on the *De Anima* of Aristotle (Padua, 1657).

Cottonius' Greek epigrams were published at Padua in 1653: Ἑλληνικῶν Ἐπιγραμμάτων βιβλία δύο. *Graecorum Epigrammatum libri duo.* Probably he was pleased to regard himself as a successor of the ancient, or at least the Byzantine, epigrammatists. Apart from some such general influence, however, the rôle played by the Anthology in Cottunius' book is slight; he alludes (p. 1) to *A.P.* 9.64 (on Hesiod), and imitates 9.65 and 523. His

---

[1] References to *De Don.* are to the edition of Graevius, *Thesaurus Ant. Rom.* 12 (Venice, 1737). A second edition had appeared at Padua in 1654.

[2] Five letters from Cottunius to Allacci and one from Allacci to him are in the Biblioteca Vallicelliana at Rome (*Rivista delle Biblioteche* 2, 1889, 106); the latest is dated 1657; Cottunius writes from Padua. As his book on the epigram was published at Bologna in 1632, and the first of these letters from Padua was written in 1639, his removal to Padua seems to have occurred between those dates.

imitation of 9.65 is made in praise of a citizen of Venice named Civrano:[1]

Γαίη κόσμος ἔαρ, δελφὶν ἅλι, ἄστρα δ' Ὀλύμπῳ,
Ἰταλίη Ἕνετοι, τοῖς δὲ Κιβρανός ἐστι.

Cottunius' book on the writing of epigrams has been spoken of above (p. 68). It was published more than twenty years before his own epigrams appeared, having been printed at Bologna in 1632: *De Conficiendo Epigrammate liber unus*. Thirteen illustrations are taken from the Anthology, each provided with a Latin verse-translation. These translations, however, are mostly, if not all, borrowed, though Cottunius gives no indication that they are not his own.[2] They are as follows: *A.P.* 7.153 (p. 5, Minturno); 9.48 (Cottunius?), 163 (p. 83, Alciati), 342 (p. 56, Minturno), 346 (Cottunius?), 369 (p. 56, Soter), 448 (Cottunius?), 455 (p. 51, Allacci); 10.32 (p. 57, Gellius), 44 (p. 407, Sabeo), 106 (Cottunius?), 111 (p. 57, Soter); 16.1 (p. 78, Gualfreducci).

The version of *A.P.* 9.346 may be given with caution as possibly the work of Cottunius:

> Per mare, per terras volitando vagaris, hirundo,
>   Medeae picta nidificas tabula?
> An tibi custodem pullorum Colchida fidam
> Speras, quae partus sustulit ipsa suos?

OTTAVIO FERRARI

(1607–1682)

Ferrari was educated in Milan, his native city; and began teaching there at the Ambrosian College in 1628. After 1634 he was professor of rhetoric and Greek at Padua, where he died on March 7, 1682. He composed three dissertations: *De Pantomimis et Mimis; De Balneis;* and *De Gladiatoribus*.[3] The first of these contains two epigrams from the Anthology (*A.P.* 7.563 and 11.254), with Latin translations in prose.

---

[1] A Pietro Civrano was *bailo* at Constantinople in 1682 (Barozzi and Berchet, *Relazioni*, ser. 5, 1856); a Girolamo Civrano was a person of consequence in Friuli in 1626 (Soranzo, *Bibliografia Veneziana*, Venice, 1885, p. 351).

[2] He refers to the following without translation: *A.P.* 9.53, 108, 502; 16.387.*

[3] *De Pant.* is in Sallengre, *Novus Thesaurus Antiquitatum Romanarum* 2 (Venice, 1735). 677 ff; the other two are in Poleni, *Utriusque Thesauri Antiquitatum Romanarum Graecarumque Nova Supplementa* 3 (Venice, 1737), 298 ff and 317 ff, respectively. An edition of two of them had been given by Fabricius, with a sketch of Ferrari's life: *Dissertationes Duae*, Helmstedt, 1728.

GIOVANNI ARGOLI
(*c.* 1609–*c.* 1660)

Giovanni was the son of a well-known mathematician, Andrea Argoli, and was born at Tagliacozzo in the Abruzzi. At the age of fifteen he published a poem on the silkworm, *Bombace e Seta* (Rome, 1624). Two years later, emulous of the reputation Marino had just gained with his *Adone*, the young Argoli is said to have shut himself in an apartment, where he was visited only by servants bringing his food, and in seven months, at the age of seventeen, produced his *Endimione* (Rome, 1626). It met with a success apparently at least equal to the author's hopes. In 1632 he followed his father to Padua (where the latter was professor of mathematics), taking the doctorate in law. Yet he returned to literature, which he taught with success at Bologna until about 1640. Thereafter he again turned to the law, and held office in the government of Cervia and Lugo. In addition to his Italian verse, Argoli produced a number of poems in Latin, and several works on archaeology and philology.[1]

Among these last are notes on the *De Ludis Circensibus* of Onofrio Panvinio (Padua 1642).[2] Here Argoli finds occasion to refer to the Anthology eight times; he gives verse-translations of five epigrams (*A.P.* 6.259; 9.221; 11.75, 259; 16.186), quotes in part two others (*A.P.* 16.338.3 and 351.5), and refers to *A.P.* 16.42. I give his translation of *A.P.* 9.221:

> Adspicio saevum sub marmore robur Amoris,
> Cui dat torva fero colla sub axe leo:
> Una manus flagrum supra caput, altera frenum
> Substinet, et floret plurima in arte charis:
> Horreo sanguineum; nam si vexare leonem
> Audet, difficile est parcat ut ille viris.

In Allacci's *De Patria Homeri* (above, p. 264) *A.P.* 15.36, 37, 38, and 40N, were printed for the first time, being drawn from the Palatine MS. They are accompanied by Latin translations from the pen of Argoli.[3]

OTTAVIO FALCONIERI
(1646–1676)

Issued from an ancient Florentine family, Falconieri attained distinction in an ecclesiastical career and as an anti-

---

[1] A list of Argoli's works will be found in Mazzuchelli.
[2] Reprinted with Panvinio's treatise in Graevius' *Thesaurus Ant. Rom.* 9 (Venice, 1735). 62ff, which I use.
[3] Cf. Dübner, in Didot Anthology 2.525, on *A.P.* 15.36: 'Graece eademque versibus latinis expressa, non optime, profert Allatius De Patria Homeri.' *A.P.* 40N is printed in Dübner's notes.

quarian. He died at Rome. A number of archaeological works by him may be seen in Gronovius' *Thesaurus;* among them his *Inscriptiones Athleticae* (Rome, 1668), into which he has introduced a verse translation of *A.P.* 16.52.

NICCOLÒ PINELLI
(*fl.* 1690?)

Pinelli, a Florentine, has an *Additamentum* to Panvinio's dissertation mentioned in the last article but one, in which he quotes *A.P.* 9.221 and 16.350, giving Latin prose versions, and makes other more general references to the Greek epigrams.[1]

PIETRO ALOÏS
(†1667)

Aloïs was a Jesuit, and taught in Jesuit colleges at Naples and Lucca (see Mazzuchelli). His Latin epigrams were first published at Lyons in 1635; and again at Naples in 1646: *Epigrammatum Centuriae vi.* In the Naples edition (p. 482) is an epigram that seems to be modeled on *A.P.* 16.326; it is entitled: *De Pythagorae Statua a gallo artifice plastico opere affabre elaborata, in amici museo.*

> Praxiteles Gallus per corpora plura vagantem
> Cogit Pythagoran hoc animare lutum.
> Posse reor Samium facundas edere voces,
> Et sophiae eloquio promere dona suo;
> At suadere silens cum prisca silentia vellet,
> Hinc tacitus nullos exprimit ore sonos.

The sense of the Greek epigram is: 'The painter has portrayed Pythagoras himself, and you would have seen him with his voice, if Pythagoras had wished to speak.' The epigram preceding (*A.P.* 16.325) is on a statue of Pythagoras, and makes almost the same point; Aloïs may have had both in mind.

NICOLAUS PESSINUS
(before 1720)

Save that Pessinus was a native of Lucca, there seems to be no information obtainable on him. A few poems are given as his

---

[1] Graevius, *Thes.* 9.489.

in the *Carmina Illustrium Poetarum*, and among them the following version of *A.P.* 9.616:

DE GRATIIS

Coelestes Charitum quondam dum forte lavantur,
Subripuit vestes abiitque Amor, hasque reliquit
In foribus nudas, castoque pudore rubentes.

GUGLIELMO MODIZIO[1]

Virgilius a Calumniis Vindicatus autore Gulielmo Modicio Monteferratensi, Eiusdem autoris Epigrammata et in sacrum annum M.D.LXXV. Carmen. Perugia, 1575. Among the epigrams in this volume are nine borrowed from the Anthology, namely from *A.P.* 7.309 (f. 95[vo]); 9.18 (f. 82[vo]), 61 (2 versions, f. 82[vo]), 391 (3 versions, ff. 81–2),[2] 557 (f. 82[ro]); 16.81 (f. 84[vo]). A number of inscriptions for fountains also bear a general resemblance to similar pieces in the Greek collection.

[1] Modizio's book came to hand too late to be noticed in its proper place; nor could his translations be listed in the Register.

Little is known of Modizio save what can be gleaned from his books; he published *Carmen de Victoria Christianae Classis*, Naples, 1572. Morano, *Catalogo scritt. di Casale*, says he was a native of Montemagno, and gives his name as Modizio or Moizio. Epigrams addressed to the author at the end of his *Virgilius* speak of his age and the failure of his sight. He himself has epigrams addressed to a number of well-known persons.

[2] 'E Graeco post Politianum et alios.'

APPENDIX TO PART I

An attempt is here made to describe the very important books of select epigrams, with Latin translations, got out by two German scholars, Joannes Soter and Janus Cornarius, and to give an account of the translations included by a third German scholar, Vincent Obsopoeus, in his Commentary on the Anthology. All three books were widely used in every part of Europe.

The *Epigrammata Graeca* compiled by Soter was printed at Cologne in 1525 by the compiler, and was enlarged by him and reissued in 1528. A third edition, again somewhat enlarged, was published by Stephanus Melechus Gravius at Freiburg in 1544. Meanwhile, in 1529, Cornarius had taken Soter's 1528 edition as the basis of his own *Selecta Epigrammata*, published at Basel, reprinting almost everything that concerns the Anthology, and adding over 500 new translations. This book has already been spoken of above, pp. 196–201.

In preparing his book of select translations in 1570 Henri Estienne followed Soter and Cornarius as models, and drew on their contents. His book in turn was taken over and increased by the Englishman John Stockwood in 1597. The collections of Soter and Cornarius also formed the basis of a book of French translations by Tamisier (1589). As we have already seen, the 1544 edition of Soter was reprinted with significant changes at Rome in 1608 (above, p. 255). In 1602 Hieronymus Megiser published at Frankfort *Anthologia seu Florilegium Graecolatinum*, a book of 1095 pages, containing most of the Soter-Cornarius collection, and the work of some 25 translators unknown to them. His book was reprinted in 1614 as *Omnium Horarum Opsonia*. In 1618–9 at Görlitz, Elias Cüchler began publishing an edition of the whole Anthology, accompanying each epigram with translations drawn from these standard collections; he desisted after issuing five *centuriae*. Finally, Andreas Rivinus (Bachmann) published a collection under almost the same title as Megiser's first publication: *Florilegium Graecolatinum . . . Epigrammatum . . . in trium chiliadum centurias distributorum* (Gotha and Leipzig, 1651); this was reissued after

273

his death as *Florilegium Diversorum Epigrammatum Veterum Graecorum* (Leipzig, 1657).[1]

The importance of Obsopoeus' *Annotationes* is sufficiently indicated below.

JOANNES SOTER

Soter's book, as just said, appeared in three editions: (1) at Cologne in 1525, (2) at Cologne in 1528, and (3) at Freiburg in Breisgau in 1544. It is entitled: *Epigrammata aliquot Graeca Veterum Elegantissima, eademque Latine ab utriusque linguae viris doctissimis versa, atque nuper in rem studiosorum e diversis autoribus per Joannem Soterem collecta, nuncque primum edita.*[2]

Like its successors, this small book of selections follows the Planudean order, with excerpts from each of the seven books.[3] There is more from the first three books than from the last four. The Greek text is that of the first (1503) Aldine. Each Greek epigram is followed by one or more Latin versions, gathered, as the title-page announces, from a variety of sources. A few epigrams are without translations. The second and third editions are enlarged from the first, not only by additional Greek epigrams and translations, but also by generous quotations from Homer, Theocritus, and other poets, suggested by the themes of certain epigrams.[4]

The first two editions were printed by the collector himself. Soter was a learned printer of Cologne, originally named Johann Heyl. He was among the earliest in that city to employ Greek types; indeed he not only had a Greek fount, but could print Hebrew and Ethiopic as well, as his tetraglot Psalter (1518) shows.[5] The editor of this Psalter,

---

[1] See Rubensohn, *Griechische Epigramme . . . in Deutschen Übersetzungen*, Weimar, 1897. Translations from the Anthology made by individual German scholars played their part on both sides of the Alps. A few may be mentioned. I have failed to find *Epigrammata quaedam lepidiora* mentioned by Fabricius-Harles as published by Curio at Basel in 1521; but note Camerarius and Micyllus, *Epigrammata Veterum Poetarum* (Basel, 1538), and Rudolph Walther, *Selectorum e Graecis Scriptoribus Epigrammatum Centuriae duae* (Zürich, 1548); see also Velius and Luscinius in the ensuing notice of Soter. The *Florilegium* (Rostock, 1600) of Eilhard Lubinus was important—there is a copy in the Riccardiana at Florence; it is a verse-translation of the entire first book of *Plan.* Of more importance was Lubinus' prose-version of the whole Anthology (above, p. 38).

[2] The title-pages of the second and third editions omit *aliquot* and *nuper*, and make the appropriate changes of *primum*.

[3] The first edition, however, has nothing from Book 7 (= *A.P.* 5), except *A.P.* 5.302.

[4] These passages are disregarded in the tables given below. The 1525 edition already contained Callimachus' *Bath of Pallas* with the translation by Politian.

[5] His device, at the end of *Epig.*[2], has mottoes in Hebrew, Greek, Ethiopic, and Latin, all in praise of *health*.

Johann Potken, is said to have been related to him. Soter had also a press at Solingen, where he might print books that could not appear at Cologne. Besides the Psalter and the *Epigrammata*, Soter's editions include a Macrobius (1524), mentioned in his *Epigrammata* (1528, p. 178), and a Nicander (1530). After his death (*c.* 1536) Soter's publishing business was carried on by his two sons Melchior and Jacob until 1562.

Soter was a scholar, and his own translations are not the least competent in his book; at one point (1528, p. 175) he gives a Greek epigram of his own composition. His reason for making his book was a fresh delight in the Anthology, which, it seems, he had but recently chanced upon. In his Preface of 1525 he writes of it: 'Cum forte fortuna nuper in Epigrammatum Graecorum opus incidissem, verissimum mihi Horatianum hoc visum est, "Graiis ingenium, Graiis dedit ore rotundo Musa loqui." Tanta enim in eo eruditionis est varietas, tantum artificium, ut Musas universas suas dotes certatim eo contulisse verissime dixeris.' This first edition was soon exhausted, and a second called for.

The second edition, not so carefully printed as the first, is much larger, containing, Soter says, about 200 new epigrams. A third edition was not needed until 1544, probably because Cornarius' book, appearing about the time of Soter's second edition, helped to occupy the field. The third edition of Soter, by Gravius at Freiburg in Breisgau, is based on the second, with some few additions.

As the first edition was swallowed up in the second, and as the third adds very little, the second (1528) edition is here made the basis of reference; new material introduced into the third edition is given at the end. Here follows a list of the translators in the second edition, with notice of any differences between this edition and the first. Then follows a table of the epigrams translated in the second edition; material not in the first edition being printed in italics.

AEDITUUS (above, p. 10). AEGIDIUS, Petrus: tr. of *A.P.* 7.745 is from Erasmus' *Adagia*. ALCIATUS, Andreas (above, p. 197). ALEANDER, Hieronymus (above, p. 185). ANDRELINUS, Faustus: the verses quoted by Soter from Andrelinus are merely analogous to *A.P.* 9.504; none of the books of Latin poetry by Andrelinus that I have seen owes anything to the Anthology. ARCHITHRENIUS (Joannes de Altavilla. *fl.* 1184): Soter includes verses from 'Archithrenius' on the Seven

Sages as equivalent to *A.P.* 7.81; they may be seen in Wright's *Satirical Poets of the Twelfth Century* 1.349. ARNOLDUS VESALIENSIS (1484–1534) was born at Wesel, and went to Cologne in 1501. There he spent his life, latterly as professor at the university. He was canon of the Cathedral in 1531. AUSONIUS (above, p. 23). BEATUS RHENANUS (Bilde von Rheinau, 1485–1547): the well-known humanist. BENTINUS, Michael (above, p. 89): in his first edition Soter assigns Bentinus' translations to Curio; making the change in 1528. BERGIUS: I have failed to identify this translator. BRIXIUS (Germain Brice or De Brie): to be discussed among French translators. BUCOLDUS, Gerard (Bucholds or Bucholtz): he is said to have been in Cologne in 1529; later he was *physicus regius* in Paris (Eckstein, *Nomenclator*). Probably he was in Cologne also in 1528, and known to Soter; the few epigrams (*A.P.* 11.19, etc.) translated by him, all of a convivial character, first appear in the 1528 edition. CALCATERRA, Antonius: not identified. CATULUS (above, pp. 10–1). Soter prints 'Catullus.' CRINITUS (above, p. 145). ERASMUS: the translations by E. are taken from his *Adagia*. That of *A.P.* 11.141 alone is in the first edition of Soter. FILELFO (above, p. 95). GAURICUS (above, p. 186). GAZA (above, p. 96). GELLIUS (see Gaza). GEORGIUS ANONYMUS (? Hermonymus, below). GERMANICUS (above, p. 19). GUARINO (above, p. 91). HAMERUS, Nicolaus: I cannot identify this translator, who first appears in the second edition. HERMONYMUS, Georgius (*fl.* 1476): originally from Sparta, H. taught Greek and copied MSS. in Paris, where Reuchlin and Budé were among his pupils (See Omont: 'Georges Hermonyme de Sparte' in *Mém. de la Soc. de l' Hist. de Paris* 12.65.). LABERIUS: the lines ascribed to Laberius under *A.P.* 11.47 seem to be modern. LAERT. INTERP. (above, p. 89): in the edition of 1525 these versions were assigned to 'Ambrosius' (Traversari). LANDINO (above, p. 109). LASCARIS, Janus: not in the 1525 edition. (Above, p. 114.) LILY, W.: the English humanist. LUSCINIUS, Ottomarus (Ottmar Nachtigall 1487–1535): a musician and humanist, born at Strassburg; studied at Paris, Louvain, Padua, and Vienna. At Paris he learned Greek from Aleander, and studied Latin literature with Andrelinus. Later his travels extended to Greece and Asia Minor. Returning to Germany he became organist at Augsburg; then (1526) retired to Basel, until the progress of the Reform drove him to Freiburg in Breisgau (end of 1528). Here he quarreled with Erasmus. Apparently he died in his native city. Luscinius is one of the more considerable German translators of the Greek epigrams; his versions appeared in his book *Seria Jocique*, dedicated to his patron Anton Fugger, and published at Strassburg in 1529.[1] The book consists of (1) Plutarch, *De Profectu Morum* (pp. 1–19) and (2) *Epigrammatum Graecorum Veterum Centuriae duae Latinitate Donatae* (pp. 19–136). No earlier publication of these versions seems to have occurred; such as Soter prints in his first and second editions doubtless reached him through private channels. Cornarius (below, p. 284) probably drew on the

---

[1] The Preface is dated 'ex Academia Friburgensi. id. Januar. 1529.'

Seria Jocique. In the following lines Luscinius translates *A.P.* 9.446:

Dulcia cuncta homini fors praebuit. Urbe repostum
  Hinc decus, hinc socii; grata domique quies;
Agris deliciae; lucrum mari; et extera tellus
  Rara docet; concors coniugioque domus;
Exors est curis coelebs; nati addere robur
  Norunt, at orbos non tenet usque timor.
Flore iuventutis vires, sapientia canis
  Parta. Igitur vive, et si sapis auge genus.

In each case Luscinius prints first the Greek, then a Latin prose-summary, then his verse. MARA, Guillaume de: to be treated with French writers. MARTIAL (above, p. 21). MARULLUS (above, p. 112). MELANCHTHON, Philip (1497–1560): Soter may have taken Melanchthon's version of *A.P.* 16.388 from the latter's *Farrago aliquot Epigrammatum*, Hagenau, 1528. In his *Epigrammatum libri sex*, Wittenberg, 1563, are translations of *A.P.* 5.93 and 7.249 (but the second is Cicero's version). All are in *Opera*, ed. by Bretschneider, Halle, 1842, vol. 10. MORE, Sir T.: the English humanist. Soter takes the versions of More and Lily from their *Progymnasmata* (1518). HERM. a NOVA AQUILA Co. (Hermann Graf von Neuenaar, *c.* 1491–1530): Nauenaar studied at Cologne (1504); in 1509–10 he accompanied Caesarius to Italy. In 1524 he was Chancellor of the University of Cologne. He died at the Diet of Augsburg. He is known as a historical writer and as a supporter of Reuchlin; letters between him and Melanchthon may be seen in the latter's *Opera* (*ed. cit.*). OVID (above, p. 18). PHILOSTRATI INTERPRES, i.e., Alamanno Rinuccini ('Raynutius Alemanus' in Cornarius; above, p. 106). PIUS, i.e. Giovanni Battista Pio (above, p. 144). POLITIAN (above, p. 124). SANNAZARO (above, p. 141). SLEIDAN, Johann (*c.* 1506–1556): the celebrated historian. Sleidan was born in the Electorate of Cologne (at Schleiden), and studied in the city. The appearance of a few translations by him in Soter's first edition adds to the importance of the collection, since they are among the earliest things printed by the future historian of the Reformation; but they are anonymous in the 1525 Soter, Sleidan's name being added in 1528. He revised his translations for the edition of 1544 (see below). STRABONIS INTERPRES, i.e., Guarino da Verona (for *A.P.* 7.249) and Gregorio Tifernas (for *A.P.* 16.27); see above, pp. 91–2. SUETONIUS (above, p. 19). VALLA, Lorenzo (above, p. 98). VELIUS, Caspar Ursinus (Caspar Bernhardi of Schweidnitz near Breslau, *c.* 1493–1539): Velius studied at Cracow and Leipzig, and then learned Greek at Bologna. He taught Greek at Vienna, where he was appointed to the chair of rhetoric in 1524; later he became historian to Ferdinand and tutor to his children. In 1539 he was drowned in the Danube.[1]

---

[1] It is usually hinted that Velius may have committed suicide. The testimony of Obsopoeus, writing immediately after the event, is against this: 'Ursinus, qui nuper magna cum bonarum literarum iactura et ingenti totius aulae regiae moerore et luctu apud Viennam Pannoniae, dum animi gratia in littore Istri deambulat, parte ripae avulsus et undis absorptus est' (*Annot.*, p. 52).

Velius' translations from the Anthology (94 in number) form the fifth
book of his *Poemata*, published by Froben at Basel in 1522. The Greek
text accompanies each translation. Velius probably learned to esteem
Michael Bentinus at this time; he has an epigram addressed to Bentinus and full of praise. Of these 94 translations, Soter took only a
very few for his first edition—perhaps not at first hand—and printed
them without Velius' name; in the second edition the greater number
of them (84) appear, assigned to their author. VIRGIL: the lines on the
Muses, given by Soter as parallel to *A.P.* 9.504, and those on the
labors of Hercules parallel to 16.91–92, are in the Latin Anthology
(above, pp. 25–6). VITUS WINTZ: this presumably designates Vitus
Winshemius (Veit Oertel), 1501–1570, professor of Greek at Wittenberg; so at least Megiser understood it when reprinting these translations in 1602. Vitus translates *A.P.* 7.3, 153 and 9.448, with some
other pieces not from the Anthology. VOLATERRANUS, i.e. Raffaello
Maffei (above, p. 142).

The following table gives the epigrams translated in the first
two editions of Soter's book. Italics indicate material added in
the second edition. In parentheses are given the names of the
translators of each epigram, together with the page on which the
epigram (text) occurs in the second (1528) edition; the translations often run over to the next page.[1]

A.P. 2.92 (Pius, p. 306); 5.7 (*More*, p. 316), *20* (*Velius*, p. 318), *28*
(*Velius*, p. 319), *34* (*Sleidan*, p. 320), *69* (*Velius*, p. 317), 78 (Gellius =
Gaza, Crinitus, Marullus, Catulus, pp. 216–9), 79 (*Laert. Int., Ben-
tinus*, p. 314), *80* (*Laert. Int., Bentinus*, p. 314), *93* (*Velius*, p. 317),
94 (*Velius*, p. 317), *113* (*Velius*, p. 315), *125* (*Velius*, p. 318), *176*
(*Velius*, p. 315), *180* (*Velius*, p. 316), *216* (*Velius*, p. 312), *217* (*Slei-
dan*, p. 319), *224* (*Sleidan*, p. 319), *225* (*Velius*, p. 312), *234* (*Velius,
Luscinius*, p. 313), *258.5* (*Velius*, p. 313), 302 (no tr., p. 27);

6.1 (More, p. 308), *12* (*Velius*, p. 310), 18–20 (Ausonius, p. 309),
26 (*Sleidan*, p. 307), 76 (*Sleidan*, p. 307), 77 (*Velius, Sleidan*, p. 311),
158 (*Velius*, p. 308), *164* (*Velius*, p. 311), *181* (*Velius*, p. 310), *187*
(*Velius*, p. 311), *314* (*Soter*, p. 86), *315–8, 320* (no tr., pp. 85–6), *331*
(*Sleidan*, p. 308);

7.3 (*Guarino, Vitus Wintz.*, p. 232), 8 (*Sleidan*, p. 233), *32* (*incert.*,
p. 233), 57 (Laert. Int., Bentinus, p. 228[2]), 60 (Guarino, Laert. Int.,
Bentinus, Sleidan, p. 206), 61 (Guarino, Laert. Int., Bentinus,
pp. 235–6), 62 (Laert. Int., Bentinus, p. 236), 64 (Ausonius, p. 228[2]),
72 (More, p. 208), 80 (Laert. Int., Bentinus, p. 240), 81 (*Archithrenius*,
p. 137), 83 (Laert. Int., Bentinus, p. 228[2]), 84 (Laert. Int., p. 229[2]),
85 (Laert. Int., p. 229[2]), 89 (Laert. Int., Bentinus, p. 229[2]), 90 (Laert.

---

[1] In the second edition the pagination is badly confused; to pass over minor errors,
at p. 237 there is a relapse to p. 227, which is not corrected, so that we get two sets of
pp. 227–237. I have marked the second set with a superior 2.
In the Register references are to the second edition (Soter[2]).

Int., Bentinus, p. 231²), 91 (Laert. Int., Bentinus, p. 231²), 92 (Laert. Int., Bentinus, p. 232²), 99 (Bentinus, p. 232²), 100 (Laert. Int., Bentinus, p. 241), 108 (Laert. Int., Bentinus, p. 227²), 109 (Laert. Int., Bentinus, p. 227²), 110 (Laert. Int., Bentinus, Erasmus, p. 233²), 112 (Laert. Int., p. 214), 114 (Laert. Int., Bentinus, p. 234²), 119 (Bentinus, p. 138), 120 (Bentinus, p. 138), 121 (Laert. Int., Bentinus, p. 234²), 122 (Laert. Int., Bentinus, p. 235²), 123 (Laert. Int., Bentinus p. 235²), 124 (Laert. Int., Bentinus, p. 236²), 125 (Laert. Int., Bentinus, p. 236), 126 (Laert. Int., Bentinus, More, p. 237), 127 (Laert. Int., Bentinus, p. 237), 128 (Laert. Int., Bentinus, p. 238), 129 (Laert. Int., Bentinus, p. 238), 130 (Laert. Int., Bentinus, p. 239), 135 (More, p. 229), 143 (Sleidan, p. 228), *145 (Velius*, p. 228), *151 (Erasmus*, p. 228), *152 (Erasmus*, p. 228), 153 (Laert. Int., Bentinus, Vitus Wintz., p. 222), *159 (Sleidan*, p. 223), 160 (More, Sleidan, p. 207), *161 (Velius*, p. 208), 217 (Politian, Laert. Int., Bentinus, p. 225), *220 (Sleidan*, p. 224), 224 (Ausonius, p. 224), *225 (Sleidan*, p. 227), 229 (Ausonius, Filelfo, Crinitus, p. 209), 230 (no tr., p. 213), *238 (Velius*, p. 214), 248 (Valla, p. 211), 249 (Valla, Strab. Int., p. 211), 250 (no tr., p. 211), 253 (Soter, p. 212), 256 (Philost. Int., p. 212), 259 (Laert, Int., Bentinus, p. 212), 265 (More, p. 230), *288 (Velius*, p. 231), 290 (More, p. 231), *308 (Velius*, p. 223), *310 (Sleidan*, p. 214), 311 (Ausonius, Politian, Velius, p. 220), 313 (Volaterranus, Sleidan, p. 221), *317 (Sleidan*, p. 221), 323 (Lily, More, p. 207), 326 (Bentinus, p. 240), 348 (Volaterranus, p. 219), *353 (Sleidan*, p. 230), *356 (Sleidan*, p. 214), 357 (Alciati, Sleidan, p. 215), 396 (Ausonius, p. 227), 433 (Filelfo, p. 212), 489 (Politian, p. 224), 508 (Laert. Int., Bentinus, p. 229), *519 (Sleidan*, p. 219), 538 (More, Sleidan, p. 226), 542 (see *A.P.* 9.56), 553 (More, p. 226), 615 (Laert. Int., *Bentinus*, De Mara, p. 234), 616 (Laert. Int., p. 234), 617 (Laert. Int., Landino, Bentinus, Marullus, p. 235), 666 (De Mara, p. 221), *668 (Sleidan*, p. 232), 669 (Guarino, Laert. Int., Bentinus, p. 215), 670 (Ausonius, Guarino, Bentinus, Laert. Int., Marullus, p. 215), 676 (Gaza, Volaterranus, p. 240), *684 (Soter, Sleidan*, p. 196), 688.3 (Luscinius, p. 33), *695 (Velius*, p. 226), 704 (Alciati, p. 219), 745 (Aegidius, p. 233);

9.*1 (Velius*, p. 76), *10 (Sleidan*, p. 93), 11–13 (Ausonius, Politian, More, pp. 3–5), 14 (no tr., p. 93), 15 (Bergius, p. 48), 17 (no tr., p. 77), 18 (Velius, p. 77), 30 (More, p. 104), *31 (Sleidan*, p. 104), 39 (Bentinus, p. 10), *42 (Sleidan*, p. 103), 44–5 (Laert. Int., Bentinus, Ausonius, Aleander, p. 134), 47 (Erasmus, Velius, p. 75), 48 (More, Lily, Velius, p. 81), 49 (More, Lily, p. 125), *50 (More*, p. 146), 51 (Sleidan, p. 146), *52 (Velius*, p. 74), *53 (Soter*, p. 85), *55 (Soter*, p. 39), 56 (Germanicus, Politian, p. 46), *58 (Martial*, p. 102), 61 (More, Lily, Velius, Marullus, Politian, p. 6), 67 (Erasmus, More, Luscinius, *Velius, Sleidan*, Soter, Crinitus, p. 100), 68 (More, *Sleidan*, p. 102), *69 (Sleidan*, p. 102), 74 (Lily, More, Velius, p. 126), 75 (Ovid, Suetonius, p. 9), 99 (Soter, p. 9), 105 (More, p. 104), 106 (More, p. 105),[1] *108 (Sannazaro*, p. 10), *109 (Sleidan*, p. 103), 110 (More, p. 19), 111

---

[1] More's verses are rather a translation of *A.P.* 9.398, as Cornarius saw.

(Luscinius, p. 22), 125 (Pius, *Calcaterra,* p. 98), 126 (More, p. 76), 132 (More, p. 125), 133 (Erasmus, More, p. 37), 137 (Politian, Soter, p. 5), 138 (Velius, Luscinius, p. 110), 145 (Ausonius, p. 20), 146 (Marullus, p. 48), 148 (Luscinius, Velius, p. 23), *160 (Sleidan, Soter,* p. 120), 163 (Marullus, Velius, p. 138), 168 (Luscinius, Ausonius, p. 42), *170 (Sleidan,* p. 125), *172 (Soter,* p. 21), *173 (Soter,* p. 43), *212 (Sleidan,* p. 87), *213 (Sleidan,* p. 86), *222 (Sleidan,* p. 94), *247 (Sleidan,* p. 106), *291 (Sleidan, Herm. a Nov. Aq.,* p. 8), *305 (Sleidan,* p. 105), *331 (Erasmus,* p. 106), 339 (Erasmus, p. 44), 346 (Marullus, p. 145), *347 (Velius,* p. 77), 357 (Volaterranus, Pius, Alciati, Politian, p. 1), 359 (Luscinius, *Velius,* Erasmus, Ausonius, p. 23), 360 (Luscinius, *Velius,* Erasmus, p. 28), 366 (Hermonymus, Herm. a Nov. Aq., p. 136), 368 (Erasmus, p. 107), 369 (Soter, p. 99), 371 (Ausonius, p. 78), 376 (More, Sleidan, p. 105), 378 *(Velius,* Luscinius, p. 45), 379 (More, *Sleidan,* p. 121), 380 *(Velius, Sleidan,* p. 124), 387 (More, p. 121), 391 (Politian, p. 2), 394 (Soter, p. 111), [398] (More, p. 105), 440 (Politian, incertus, *Velius,* p. 50), 442 (More, p. 126), 444 (Arnold. Vesal., Soter, p. 37), 446 (Luscinius, p. 35), *448 (Soter, Vitus Wintz.,* p. 114), 456 *(Soter,* Marullus, p. 73), 469 (Bergius, p. 18), 489 (Soter, p. 80), 496 (Bentinus, Laert. Int., p. 17), 502 (Pius, p. 88), 503 (Erasmus, p. 88), 503* (Soter, p. 108), 504 ('Virgil,' Andrelinus, p. 119), 506 (Ausonius, More, Lily, *Herm. a Nov. Aq.,* p. 118), 530 (More, p. 127), 540 (Laert. Int., p. 137), *561 (Pius,* p. 3), 567 (Pius, p. 74), *569 (Bentinus,* p. 135), *575 (Sleidan, Velius,* p. 117), *576 (More,* p. 83), 577 (Volaterranus, p. 99), *591 (incertus,* p. 262), 606 (Arnold. Vesal., p. 290), 608 (Arnold. Vesal., p. 290), *618 (Velius, Sleidan,* p. 291), 639 (Soter, p. 291), *640* (no tr., p. 291), 647 (Soter, p. 302), 648 (Velius, Soter, p. 302), *701 (Sleidan,* p. 302), 702 (Herm. a Nov. Aq., Soter, p. 302), 713–5 (Ausonius. p. 245), 716–7 *(Velius,* p. 245), 718 *(Velius,* p. 245), 719 *(Velius,* p. 245), 720 *(Velius, Sleidan,* p. 246), 721 (Ausonius, *Sleidan,* p. 246), 722–3 (no tr., p. 246), 724 *(Velius,* p. 246), *725 (Velius,* p. 247), 726 *(Velius,* p. 247), 727 *(Velius,* p. 247), 728 (no tr., p. 246), 729 *(Velius,* p. 247), 730 (Ausonius, *Sleidan,* p. 248), 731–42 (no tr.; *Greek epig. by Lascaris* and 8 epigg. on the theme—Myron's Heifer—by Ausonius, pp. 249–52), *747 (Velius,* p. 289), *750 (Velius,* p. 289), 759 (Soter, Ausonius, Bergius, p. 290), 783 (Soter, p. 227), 784 *(Sleidan, Lascaris,* p. 300), 793–6 (no tr., p. 249), 797 (Velius, p. 249), 798 (no tr., p. 249);

10.26 (Ausonius, Lily, More, p. 21), 27 (Bergius, Soter, p. 81), 30 (Ausonius, p. 75), 31 (Luscinius, p. 31), 32 (Gellius, p. 78), 33 (Bergius, Soter, p. 48), *37 (Sleidan,* p. 145), *39 (Sleidan,* p. 134), *41 (More, Sleidan,* p. 112), 42 (Soter, p. 102), 43 (Volaterranus, p. 146), *44 (Soter,* p. 94), 45 (More, Velius, p. 129), 46 (More, incertus, p. 123), *50 (Sleidan,* p. 122), 51 (More, Erasmus, *Hamerus,* p. 130), 58 (Luscinius, Lily, More, p. 31), *59 (Sleidan,* p. 110), *60 (Sleidan,* p. 113), *62 (Sleidan,* p. 127), 63 (More, *Sleidan,* p. 122), 65 (Luscinius, p. 31), 69 (More, p. 79), 72 (Luscinius, p. 32), 73 (Luscinius, More, p. 32), *76 (Sleidan,* p. 124), 80 (incertus, *Sleidan,* p. 128), 84 (Lus-

cinius, p. 33), 85 (Bergius, p. 79), 88 (Bergius, *More*, p. 79), *95*
(*Erasmus*, p. 96), 106 (Erasmus, p. 18), 108 (More, p. 76), *111* (*Soter*,
p. 131), 112 (More, Lily, incertus, p. 81), 116 (More, p. 38), *117*
(*Sleidan*, p. 135), 119 (More, Lily, p. 22), 121 (More, Lily, *Velius*,
p. 95), *122* (*Sleidan*, p. 128), 123 (Luscinius, p. 35), 124 (Luscinius,
p. 36), 124* (Luscinius, p. 36);

  11.8 (More, p. 185), *9* (*Velius*, p. 185), *19* (*Bucoldus*, p. 186), *23*
(*Sleidan*, p. 194), *28* (*Velius*, p. 195), *31* (*Bucoldus*, p. 186), *32* (*Bucoldus*, p. 186), *38* (*Velius*, p. 195), 43 (More, *Velius*, *Sleidan*, p. 196),
45 (*Bucoldus*, p. 187), 46 (More, p. 187), *47* (*More, incertus, 'Laberius'*,
p. 188), *49* (*Velius*, p. 196), 50 (Erasmus, More, p. 37), *51* (*Sleidan*,
p. 146), *55* (*Bucoldus*, p. 192), *58* (*Bucoldus*, p. 193), *61* (*Velius*,
Sleidan, p. 193), 68 (More, p. 154), *69* (*Soter*, p. 154), 70 (Alciati,
Velius, p. 154), *76* (*Velius*, p. 157), 77 (More, *Velius*, p. 149), 95
(Luscinius, Herm. a Nov. Aq., Velius, Sleidan, p. 170), *97* (*Velius*,
p. 173), 103 (More, p. 171), 104 (Ausonius, p. 172), 111 (More,
Luscinius, Velius, Soter, p. 172), 113 (Ausonius, p. 164), 114 (Ausonius, p. 164), *117* (*Velius*, p. 165), 127 (More, Brixius, Sleidan,
p. 177), *132* (*Velius*, p. 178), 138 (More, p. 156), 141 (Erasmus, Martial, p. 182), 145 (More, Luscinius, Ausonius, p. 183), *146* (*More*,
p. 184), 149 (Luscinius, p. 184), 151 (Luscinius, p. 185), *156* (*Sleidan*,
p. 201), *159* (*More, Sleidan*, p. 150), 161 (More, p. 150), 163 (Ausonius, p. 151), *166* (*More*, p. 197), *168* (*Sleidan*, p. 197), 170 (More,
p. 198), *186* (*Sleidan*, p. 168), 187 (*Sleidan*, p. 168), *190* (*Soter*,
p. 169), *193* (*Soter*, p. 131), *198* (*Velius*, p. 158), 201 (More, p. 159),
203 (Luscinius, Velius, p. 158), *205* (*Sleidan*, p. 170), 208 (More,
p. 170), 209 (More, Sleidan, p. 182), 213 (More, Sleidan, p. 162), 214
(Luscinius, Velius, p. 163), *215* (*Sleidan*, p. 164), *226* (*Sleidan*,
p. 180), *227* (*Sleidan*, p. 180), *239* (*Pius, Herm. a Nov. Aq., Martial*,
p. 160), 244 (Alciati, p. 174), 251 (More,[1] Luscinius, p. 169), *253*
(*Velius*, p. 175), 254 (Ausonius, More, Herm. a Nov. Aq., p. 176),
255 (Ausonius, More, p. 177), 256 (Alciati, p. 155), 257 (Martial,
p. 165), *260* (no tr., p. 162), 264 (Luscinius, p. 200), 266 (More, p. 159),
268 (More, p. 159), 270 (More, p. 200), 273 (More, Lily, Sleidan,
p. 203), *277* (*Luscinius, Velius*, p. 175), *278* (*Soter*, p. 157), 279
(Ausonius, p. 156), 280 (Luscinius, p. 166), *282* (*Hamerus*, p. 86),
287 (More, p. 159), *292* (*Beatus Rhenanus*, p. 202), 294 (Lily, More,
p. 198), *297* (*Sleidan*, p. 173), *305* (*Velius*, p. 179), 307 (Marullus,
p. 204), 310 (More, Luscinius, p. 160), *315* (*Velius*, p. 169), *318*
(*Sleidan*, p. 153), *323* (*Soter*, p. 95), *337* (*Velius*, p. 162), 343 (Sleidan,
p. 173), 348 (Luscinius, p. 36), *349* (*Luscinius, Velius, Sleidan*, p. 151),
367 (*Soter*, p. 160), 369 (More, Luscinius, Velius, Sleidan, p. 153), 381
(Luscinius, p. 157), 384 (Bergius, Soter, p. 202), *385* (*Hamerus*,
p. 98), *390* (*Sleidan*, p. 162), 391 (More, Lily, Luscinius, p. 200), 395
(More, Lascaris, p. 181), *401* (*Soter, Sleidan, Georgius Anonymus*,

---

  [1] More's translation of this epigram was employed by the Jesuit Carlo Casalicchio
in his *Utile col Dolce overo quattro centurie di argutissimi detti e fatti di saviissimi huomini*,
Venice, 1723, pp. 305–6. The book first appeared at Naples in 1671.

p. 166), 408 (More, Velius, Sleidan, p. 155), 410 (More, p. 203), 412 (More, p. 181), 413 (Luscinius, p. 199), *414* (*Soter*, p. 204), *416* (*Sleidan*, p. 123), 418 (More, Luscinius, p. 160), 419 (Arnold. Vesal., p. 42), *428* (*Sleidan*, p. 149), 430 (More, p. 202), 432 (More, p. 150), *433* (*Sleidan*, p. 164), *437* (*Soter*, p. 178);

12.235 (Velius, p. 316); 13.29 (Volaterranus, Luscinius, Soter, p. 107);

16.3 (Alciati, p. 2), 4 (More, p. 7), *14* (*Lascaris*, p. 74), 16 (More, *Erasmus*, p. 100), 23 (Soter, p. 206), 27 (Strab. Int., p. 219), 31 (no tr., p. 236), *32* (*Sleidan*, p. 243), 32* (Alciati, p. 243), 68 (Alciati p. 243), *75* (*Sleidan*, p. 243), *81* (*Velius*, p. 244), *84* (*Sleidan*, p. 244), *89* (*Velius*, p. 252), *91–2* ('Virgil,' p. 252), 93 (Luscinius, Velius, p. 255), *97* (*Sleidan*, p. 255), *107* (*Sleidan*, p. 256), 120.3 (Budaeus, p. 256), 129 (More, Lily, Sleidan, Ausonius, p. 257), 135 (Gauricus, p. 257), 136 (Ausonius, p. 258), 137–8 (Ausonius, p. 258), 141 (no tr. p. 145), 151 (Sleidan, Ausonius, p. 259), 152 (no tr., p. 262), *155* (*Soter*, p. 261), 160 (Ausonius, Sleidan, p. 272), *168* (*Velius*, p. 273), 169 (*Velius*, *Sleidan*, p. 273), 174 (Ausonius, Politian, p. 273), 178 (Ausonius, Herm. a Nov. Aq., Sleidan, Politian, p. 274), *183* (*Sleidan*, p. 276), *185* (*Velius*, p. 276), 195 (Sleidan, p. 278), 200 (Politian, Marullus, p. 279), *207* (*Velius*, *Sleidan*, p. 280), 209 (Licinus, Aedituus, p. 49), *214* (*Sleidan*, p. 280), *215* (no tr., p. 281), 223 (Erasmus, p. 282), 224 (Erasmus, p. 282), 236 (Priap., p. 283), 246 (Lily, More, p. 283), 247 (Alciati, p. 284), *251* (*Velius*, p. 284), 263 (Ausonius, p. 284), 271 (Luscinius, Velius, p. 285), 275 (Erasmus, More, Ausonius, p. 285), *278* (*Velius*, p. 289), 292 (Guarino, p. 303), 296 (Guarino, Marullus, p. 303), 297–8 (Gellius=Gaza, p. 304), 304 (Politian, p. 305), *334* (*Bentinus*, p. 305), *388* (*Melanchthon*, p. 320).

So much for the first two editions. The third (1544) edition makes but few additions to the second. The new translators are Joannes ARTOPOEUS (Becker), 1520–c. 1580, a native of Worms, and professor of law at Freiburg; Lodovicus JAUSSERANDUS, otherwise unknown to me; Joannes JORDANUS, an editor of Theophrastus, *Hist. Plant.*, Lyons, 1552; and Thomas VENATORIUS (Gechauff), concerning whom see below, p. 287. Sleidan appears to have kept in touch with the collection, since in this third edition he has improved a number of his translations; see, for example, the Register under *A.P.* 9.31. The following are the translations added in the 1544 edition:[1]

A.P. 5.240 (Venatorius, p. 359), 247 (Jausserandus, p. 359); 7.66.1–2 (Jordanus, p. 263), 66.3–4 (Jausserandus, p. 263), 69 (Jordanus, p. 259), 136 (Jordanus, p. 253), 138 (Jordanus, p. 253), 152 (Alciati,

---

[1] Some of the new material is not from the Anthology, namely verses and translations on pp. 127, 131, 169, 183, and 206.

p. 253), 230 (Jordanus, p. 235), 327–8 (Jausserandus, p. 227), 433 (Erasmus, p. 234), 650 (Jordanus, p. 257); 9.17 (Jordanus, p. 91); 10.36 (Jordanus, p. 110), 39 (Jordanus, Luscinius, p. 149), 116 (Artopoeus, p. 45); 11.53 (Luscinius, Jordanus, p. 162); 16.14 (Jordanus, p. 57), 274 (Jausserandus, p. 326), 275 (Alciati, p. 328), 310 (Jordanus, p. 348).

JANUS CORNARIUS (HAGENBUT)
(1500–1558)

Selecta Epigrammata Graeca Latine Versa, ex septem epigrammatum graecorum libris. Accesserunt omnibus omnium prioribus editionibus ac versionibus plus quam quingenta epigrammata, recens versa ab Andrea Alciato, Ottomaro Luscinio, ac Jano Cornario Zuiccaviensi. Basel (Bebellius), Aug., 1529. 422 pp.+errata-sheet. [Corn.]

Cornarius was a physician. He studied the Humanities under Petrus Mosellanus, became *magister* (Wittenberg, 1521), and then turned to the study of medicine (*doctor*, 1523). He practised medicine at Rostock, in the pay of Henry IV, Duke of Mecklenburg, partly in the city and partly at Court, where he seems to have assisted the studies of Henry's son Magnus. It is to Duke Magnus that the collection of Greek epigrams is dedicated. Cornarius traveled in the Netherlands, England, and France, and spent a year (1529) in Basel with Jerome Froben. At Basel he began the study of the Greek medical writers; and this opened to him the sphere of his greatest usefulness. His translations into Latin of Hippocrates, Galen, Dioscorides, etc., were of prime importance to German, and indeed to European, medicine. Later he taught at Marburg, and finally at Jena, where he died.

The *Selecta Epigrammata*, edited by Cornarius, is simply an enlargement of the second edition of Soter's *Epigrammata Graeca* published the year before (1528) at Cologne. The compiler seems to assume that Soter's book is a standard collection and common property, for he nowhere refers to Soter unless vaguely in the words: 'accesserunt omnibus omnium prioribus editionibus ac versionibus.' The Dedication to Duke Magnus does nothing to explain the writer's relation to Soter; it merely recommends the epigram as a literary form, apologizes for the writer's having had to do with such trifles, and prays that the Muses may inspire Duke Magnus to similar exercises.

With few exceptions Cornarius' book contains all the epigrams that are in Soter's second edition, and in the same order; it also contains virtually all the translations (only occasionally Soter's own versions are excised in favor of Cornarius'); but the excerpts from Homer, Theocritus, etc., are omitted, their places being more than filled by 500 new epigrams from the Anthology. The translations of these new epigrams are the work of Cornarius himself, of Ottomarus Luscinius (Nachtigall), and of Alciati.

Alciati's part in the book has already been reviewed (above, p. 197). As for Luscinius, his translations had been published only seven months before in his own *Seria Iocique* (above, p. 276). Cornarius, or rather Bebellius, may have made an arrangement with him, since he was living in Basel at this time. An example of Cornarius' own skill has been given above (p. 199). These three are the principal new contributors to the collection.

Four other translators, unknown to Soter, are represented by a few translations in Cornarius' book. The most distinguished of them is Janus PANNONIUS (Johann Cesinge), 1434–1472, a pupil of Guarino da Verona at Ferrara, but by birth a Hungarian, and in 1460 made Bishop of Fünfkirchen at the request of King Matthew Corvinus. In his Dedication, Cornarius commends Pannonius as an example to Duke Magnus: 'Nuper apud Pannonas baro generosus Janus Quinqueecclesiensis Episcopus in hac re [composing epigrams] tantum praestitit, ut cum omni vetustate compari possit.' Pannonius doubtless studied the Greek epigrams in Italy; there was no printed edition during his lifetime. His *Sylva Panegyrica et Epigrammata quaedam* (Basel, Froben, 1518), contains no translations; these seem to have been drawn from his MSS. for later editions. I am unable to say where Cornarius got them. (See above, p. 165; also Carducci, *Gioventù di Ludovico Ariosto*, chap. 4). CANNIUS, Nicolaus (Cane), *c.* 1504–1555. A well-known *famulus* of Erasmus; he is introduced by Erasmus into the Colloquy *Cyclops*, first printed in 1529. Cane was rector of the Ursulines at Amsterdam about 1532, and, after joining the Reform, pastor of the New Church there. On Barptolomeus SIMONETA, translator of *A.P.* 9.148, see above, p. 208. M. APIARIUS, to whom is assigned a version of *A.P.* 16.168, is probably the music-printer Mathias Biener (*c.* 1500–*c.* 1553) of Strassburg and Bern. (See Eitner, *Quellen-Lexikon* 1.178.)

Cornarius' book is better printed than Soter's second edition, and corrects some of its errors.

In the following table is listed only matter that is added in Cornarius' book to the collection of Soter; the few omissions are also noted. By taking this table, therefore, with that on p. 278 ff., the entire contents of Cornarius' book may be arrived at.[1] (A) stands for Alciati, (C) for Cornarius, and (L) for Luscinius.

[1] In the Register references to all the translations in the Soter-Cornarius collection are to the pages of both Soter[2] and Cornarius, in so far as they appear in both.

A.P. 2.1.97 (C); 5.11 (C), 36 (L), 42 (C), 59 (C), 68 (C), 69 (A), 70 (C, A), 78 (omitted), 93 (L), 94 (A), 97 (C), 101 (C), 113 (L), 125 (L), 127 (A), 155 (C), 180 (L), 210 (L), 222 (A), 224 (C), 229 (C), 240 (L), 247 (L), 256 (C), 261 (C), 267 (L), 302 (A);

6.1 (L), 69 (C), 70 (C), 77 (L, A), 80 (A), 158 (A), 283 (A), 303 (A, C), 309 (A);

7.7 (C), 8 (C), 32 (C), 33 (C), 46 (C), 60 (C), 68 (C), 73 (A), 89 (A), 135 (C), 137 (C), 145 (C, A), 148 (C), 151 (C), 152 (A), 153 (omits Laert. Int.), 157 (C), 161 (A), 162 (C), 170 (C), 172 (A), 178 (C), 216 (A), 221 (C), 230 (C), 233–4 (A), 250 (C), 263 (C), 265 (C), 266 (A), 270 (C), 271 (C), 282 (C), 288 (A), 308 (L), 309 (C), 314 (C), 317 (C), 320 (C), 324 (C), 327 (C), 329 (C), 335 (A), 336 (C), 342 (C), 348 (C), 349 (C), 350 (C), 383 (A), 396 (A), 433 (C, A), 451 (L, C), 461 (C), 551 (C), 572 (C), 574 (A), 595 (C), 599 (C), 600 (C), 675 (C);

9.8 (L), 9.5 (C, L), 11–13B (A, L), 15 (A), 16 (C, A), 24 (C), 26 (A), 27 (C), 29 (C), 31 (A), 39 (A, C), 42 (A), 47 (A, Janus Pannonius), 51 (L, C), 52 (A), 53 (C, omits Soter), 54 (L, C), 55 (C), 74 (L, A), 77 (C), 80 (C), 85 (C), 86 (A), 94 (A), 95 (A), 106 (C), 108 (L), 111 (A), 114 (C, L), 115 (A), 117 (A), 118 (A), 119 (L, C), 120 (C, L), 122 (A), 127 (L), 132 (A, L), 133 (A, C), 138 (omits the 2nd trans. by L), 141 (A), 145 (L), 146 (A, 2 versions), 148 (Barptolomaeus Simoneta, A, omits L), 150 (A), 158 (A), 160 (omits Soter), 162 (A), 163 (L, C), 165–7 (A), 172 (C, omits Soter), 173 (A, omits Soter), 176 (C), 192 (C), 199 (C), 213 (C), 221 (A), 222 (A), 223 (A), 248 (A), 259 (A), 261 (C), 279 (A), 291 (A, omits H. a Nova Aq.), 308 (A), 339 (A), 345 (C, 2 versions), 379 (A, L), 391 (A), 394 (A, C), 410 (A), 420 (A), 431 (C), 440 (C, p. 58), 441 (C), 444 (A), 448 (omitted), 455 (C), 456 (C, A, omits Soter), 469 (omitted), 489 (Pius), 497 (A), 506 (omits H. a Nova Aq.), 515 (C, A), 523 (A), 530 (L), 535 (L, C), 540 (C), 548 (A), 557 (A, C), 590 (C), 595 (C), 608 (C), 647 (L), 648 (L), 652 (C), 654 (incertus),[1] 664 (A), 666 (C), 711 (C), 713–17, 720, 729–30 (A), 763 (C), 771 (C), 783 (C), 787 (L);

10.3 (C), 26 (A), 27 (A, L), 28 (L, C), 29 (C), 32 (omitted), 34 (C), 36 (C), 37 (L), 39 (L), 40 (L), 42 (L, omits Soter), 43 (A, L), 44 (L), 47 (C), 48 (A), 52 (L, C), 53 (C), 57 (C), 58 (A), 59 (C), 62 (L), 63 (C), 67 (A), 69 (L), 76 (C), 80 (L), 84 (A), 88 (A, omits More), 93 (A), 95 (omitted), 98 (A), 99 (C), 102 (L, C), 105 (L), 106 (omitted), 109 (C), 114 (C), 125 (L, C);

11.3 (C), 23 (N. Cannius), 31 (C), 45 (C), 46 (C), 47 (A), 49 (L), 50 (A, L), 51 (L), 54 (C), 61 (N. Cannius), 68 (C), 70 (L), 76 (L, A), 101 (C), 104 (C), 105 (C), 107 (A), 110 (L), 111 (omits Soter), 112 (C), 113 (C), 114 (C), 115 (C), 116 (C), 118 (C), 119 (C), 120 (C, A), 121 (C), 122 (C), 123 (C), 124 (C), 125 (C), 148 (C), 153 (L, A), 156 (C, N. Cannius), 159 (L), 162 (L), 163 (C), 167 (L), 169 (L), 171 (A), 172 (C), 173 (A), 174 (C), 179 (C, L), 181 (L, C), 184 (C), 186 (C), 187 (L), 188 (C), 190 (C, omits Soter's second trans.), 192 (L), 193 (L), 194 (C), 198 (A), 199 (C), 200 (A), 201 (C), 203 (A), 208 (C), 213

---

[1] It is Politian's translation.

(C), 214 (C), 216 (C), 226 (Martial, A), 227 (C), 228 (C), 235 (C),
237 (C), 239 (omits Martial), 245 (C), 250 (L, C), 251 (A), 254 (L),
257 (C), 259 (L), 260 (C), 263 (C), 266 (C), 267 (C), 268 A, C),
272 (A), 273 (A), 278 (C, A), 279 (C), 280 (C), 281 (L, C), 282 (C,
omits N. Hamerus), 287 (C), 288 (C), 292 (C), 294 (A), 305 (L), 306
(C), 307 (C, L), 312 (C), 323 (L, omits Soter), 324 (C), 330 (L), 331
(L), 333 (C), 340 (C), 364 (C), 365 (L), 366 (C), 367 (C, omits Soter),
369 (A), 376 (A), 378 (C), 381 (A), 382 (C), 384 (C, omits Soter),
385 (C, omits N. Hamerus), 387 (L, C), 389 (L), 390 (L), 391 (A),
392 (C), 393 (C), 395 (A), 398 (C, L), 401 (omits Soter and G. Anon.),
403 (L, A), 404 (C, A), 405 (A), 406 (A, C), 408 (C), 410 (A, L),
413 (A), 414 (C, L, omits Soter), 416 (C), 418 (A), 421 (A, C), 422
(C), 423 (C), 426 (L), 428 (A, C, L), 429 (C, 2 versions), 430 (L), 431
(A, C, L), 432 (L), 433 (C), 434 (C), 435 (C), 436 (C), 437 (C);
 12.235 (omits Velius' second trans.); 15.41 (C), 42 (C);
 16.4 (C, A), 9 (L), 18 (L, C), 19 (A), 24 (C), 28 (C), 57 (C), 58 (C),
60 (A), 107 (A), 108 (A), 115–6 (A), 120 (omits Budaeus, C), 129 (A),
141 (omitted), 143 (C), 145 (C, A), 146 (A), 152 (A), 154 (C), 155
(C), 157 (C), 159 (C), 160 (C), 161 (C), 163 (C), 164 (C), 165 (C),
166 (C), 167 (C), 168 (C, M. Apiarius), 169 (C), 170 (C), 171 (A, C),
172 (C), 173 (C), 174 (C, A), 175 (C), 178 (C), 179 (C), 180 (C),
181 (C), 194 (C), 197 (A), 201 (A), 207 (A), 209 (C, A),[1] 223 (C),
224 (C, A), 250 (A), 251 (A), 267 (C), 268 (C), 270 (C), 272 (C),
273 (C), 274 (C), 275 (C, A), 313 (C), 314 (C), 317 (C), 325 (C),
326 (C), 342 (C), 346 (C), 352 (C), 357 (C).

VINCENT OBSOPOEUS
(†1539)

THOMAS VENATORIUS
(c. 1488–1551)

Obsopoeus composed a Latin Commentary on the first, second, third, and seventh books of the Planudean Anthology, in-
troducing into it a considerable number of metrical translations,
most of which had been made by himself, and some few by his
friend Thomas Venatorius. In the last book, and to some degree
elsewhere, he availed himself of the translations published by
Cornarius. The Commentary was edited by Venatorius soon
after the death of Obsopoeus, and published at Basel in 1540
with the title: *In Graecorum Epigrammatum libros quatuor Annotationes longe doctissimae*.[2] It was the first commentary to be
published on the Anthology.

---

[1] Cornarius prints this epigram twice (pp. 53 and 362).
[2] Referred to in the Register as 'Obsop.' An extended account of the commentary is
given by Pierre Herbert, *Trav. Inéd.*

Obsopoeus' book was widely used during the sixteenth century; the translations in particular were often quoted and included in books of selections. The editors of the Wechel Anthology in 1600 reprinted the entire commentary of Obsopoeus together with that of Brodaeus and the Greek *scholia*. As theirs was the edition of the Anthology most used during the next two centuries, the translations of Obsopoeus and Venatorius take on a special importance for our subject.

Vincent Heydnecker, (called Obsopoeus, it is said, because he was the son of a cook), was born in Bavaria, and first appears as head of the choir-school at Salzburg. He entered the university of Leipzig in 1524 (April 23), and in the same year published a Latin translation of a treatise by Luther (*De Constituendis Scholis*, Hagenau). Other translations from Luther followed, especially a collection of letters (*Epistolarum Farrago*, Hagenau, 1525). About 1527 he settled in Nürnberg, where he published a translation of Lucian's *Hermotimus* and two books of the *Iliad* (1527). Here he became a member of the circle of Wilibald Pirckheimer. In 1529 he was made rector of the Latin school at Ansbach, a position in which he seems to have remained for the rest of his life. Known as a good critic, he served his age well as an editor of classical authors. To him are due the *edd. pr.* of Polybius (Hagenau, 1530), Heliodorus (Basel, 1534), and of Diodorus Siculus 16–20 (Basel, 1539), and editions of the *Epistles* of St. Basil and the *Symposium* of Xenophon. Besides his notes on the Anthology, he produced *Castigationes ac Diversae Lectiones* on the orations of Demosthenes (Nürnberg, 1534), and is credited with a treatise on rhetoric. As a Latin poet, he is remembered for his *De Arte Bibendi libri iii* (Nürnberg, 1536). Letters by him may be read in the collection of those of Pirckheimer; and some are preserved in MS. in the Bamberg Kreisarchiv. He possessed a remarkable library, a part of which is now at Erlangen.[1]

Venatorius (Gechauff) was also a member of Pirckheimer's circle. He is said to have played a determining rôle in the formation of Protestant theology. A native of Nürnberg, he was trained as a mathematician by Johann Schoner. Later he studied at various universities. Entering the Dominican order, he returned to Nürnberg in 1520, probably at the suggestion of Pirckheimer, and from 1523 to 1532 preached in the Dominican church. After joining the Reform he was pastor of the Church of St. James. In 1544 he went for six months to Rothenburg to spread the Reformation. Most of his published works are of a theological character; but the *ed. pr.* of Archimedes, published by him in 1544, and his metrical version of Aristophanes' *Plutus* (1531), as well as his interest in the Anthology, mark his humanist side.

[1] Allen, *Erasmi Epistolae* 7.401.

As an example of Obsopoeus' translations we may take his version of *A.P.* 10.34; I give his note as well: 'Epigramma venustum et elegans, quod cum Euangelica doctrina plane consentit, Nolite soliciti esse, etc. Hoc sic transtulimus:

> Si quid cura potest, sit sollicito tibi cura;
> At si diis curae es, quid tua cura potest?
> Sollicitus nec eris sine daemone, nec sine cura,
> Ut sit cura tibi, cura sit illa dei.'

He finds in *A.P.* 7.401 a model for a satirical epitaph on Clement VII. The following translations of *A.P.* 11.54 he had introduced into his *Ars Bibendi*:

> Decrepitum ridet matrum me turba, iubetque
> In speculo aetatis cernere relliquias.
> Ast ego, num nivei mihi sint nigrive capilli,
> Nil moror, ad finem cum mea vita ruat.
> Laetus odoratis unguentis atque coronis,
> Et vino curas denique pello meas.

The translation of *A.P.* 9.575 that follows is by Venatorius:

> Destituent prius astra polum, citiusque profundae
> Sol faciem noctis splendidus induerit,
> Ante sapor salsi pelagi dulcescit amarus,
> Restituet vitam mortuus ante sibi,
> Gloria quam pereat sublime aut nomen Homeri,
> Cuius apud doctos Musa perennis erit.

[In the table of translations, epigrams marked (V) are translated by Venatorius, those not marked are rendered by Obsopoeus. References in the Register are both to the *Annotationes* of 1540 and to the Wechel Anthology of 1600.]

A.P. 7.8, 18, 23, 32, 61 (Bentinus), 62 (Bentinus), 69, 71, 108 (Bentinus), 109 (Bentinus), 138, 146, 168, 173, 174, 230, 241, 294, 308, 309, 310, 315, 320, 328, 339, 346, 348, 350, 353, 356, 357, 358, 359, 360, 398, 401 (1 trans. and 1 imit.), 412, 518, 559, 572, 605, 650, 656, 668, 673, 674, 703;

9.23, 24 (V), 33, 35, 42, 43, 48 (V), 50, 52, 62, 66 (V), 67, 68 (V), 69 (V), 75 (V), 77, 80, 85, 96, 97 (V), 105, 108, 109, 133 (V, 2 versions), 136, 148 (V), 151, 161, 165, 166, 185, 186 (V), 192 (V), 230, 278, 279 (V), 305, 322 (V), 324 (V), 331, 341, 354 (V, 2 versions), 357 (V), 363, 376, 387, 424, 453, 455 (V and O), 506 (V, 2 versions), 575 (V, 2 versions), 583;

10.26 (V), 29 (V), 31 (V), 34, 36, 39, 40 (2 versions), 42, 43, 47, 53, 58 (1 version by V and 2 by O), 59, 63, 65 (V), 69, 74, 75, 85, 100, 102, 113, 117, 121, 124;

11.3, 8, 9, 10, 19, 20, 23, 24, 25, 45, 51, 54, 55, 56, 57, 61, 62, 63, 103, 106, 110, 111, 131, 166, 192, 193, 208, 214, 226, 227, 251, 264, 265, 268, 273, 276, 277, 282, 294, 297, 340, 365, 372, 382, 389, 391, 392, 395, 397;

16.1 (V), 4 (V and O), 16.

PART II

VERNACULAR WRITERS OF THE SIXTEENTH CENTURY[1]

MARIO EQUICOLA

(c. 1470–1525)

In his youth Equicola was associated with the Academy of Pontano in Naples; in later life he was an honored member of the literary circle of Ferrara. He had been a pupil of Pomponio Leto in Rome and of Janus Lascaris in Florence. He was born of good family at Alvito in the Terra di Lavoro; and his fortunes were bound up with those of the Cantelmi, the ducal family of Sora and Alvito. The Cantelmi were driven from their domains in 1487, and Equicola followed them into exile. It was probably at this period that he pursued his studies in Rome and Florence. Sigismondo Cantelmo had taken refuge with the Duke of Ferrara, his wife being Margherita Maroscelli of that city, and Equicola went to Ferrara to be Margherita's secretary. In 1503 he went with Sigismondo to join the French, who were supposed to be willing to restore the Cantelmi, and again he accompanied Sigismondo to Blois in 1505; in 1506 he performed a mission for Ippolito d'Este to the king of Naples; but for the most part between 1496 and 1508 he lived in Ferrara. There he enjoyed the society of Ariosto, Calcagnini, Lilio Giraldi, and their friends. He also knew Niccolò d'Arco. He appears between Alessandro Guarini and Pietro Aretino in Ariosto's *Orlando* (46.14).

In 1508 Equicola transferred his allegiance from the Cantelmi to the Gonzaghi, and went to Mantua to become the preceptor of Isabella. Here he made new literary friends, and during this period— he remained at the Mantuan Court for the rest of his life—his principal works were composed. He became secretary to Isabella and to her son the young Duke Federigo, fulfilling several diplomatic missions for them to Rome, Urbino, and Naples. He died in 1525.[2]

---

[1] There are two or three possible traces of the Anthology in the vernacular literature of the end of the fifteenth century, but they are quite ambiguous. I have discussed them in the Introduction (above, p. 48). The likeliest are in the poems of Politian, among which may be specially noticed his *Pan e Eco*; this poem he himself couples in regard to form with *A.P.* 16.152 (above, p. 125).

[2] On Equicola see Domenico Santoro, *Della Vita e delle Opere di Mario Equicola*, Chieti, 1906.

Most of Equicola's Latin and Italian works are historical. His *Chronica de Mantua* was published in 1521; his *Pro Gallis Apologia* (1509) was dedicated to Lascaris.[1] But the book which keeps his name alive is *Il libro di Natura d'Amore*, published at Venice only a month before the author's death.[2] It had, however, long been written, first in Latin, the Latin version being completed between 1495 and 1496, and then in Italian in 1509. The Italian version seems not to have been made by Equicola, but was corrected and enlarged by him.[3]

The treatise deals with the nature of love: 'Plato and Dionysius the Areopagite hold the tiller, Aristotle and St. Augustine tend the sails, while Cicero, assisted by the historians and poets, pulls the oars.' It is divided into six books, of which the first resumes earlier theories on the subject; the second describes love as the source of all desires, and divides it into several kinds, as divine or human; the third discusses love under these categories; in the fourth are treated sensual love and the influence of the stars; in the fifth is set forth the sort of education that will make a person truly amiable; finally, the sixth book is a 'cabalistic' or metaphysical treatment of love, whose end is found to be God himself.

The fifth book, on how to make oneself amiable, concludes with a section in which the would-be poetical lover is instructed 'how the Latin and Greek poets, Provençal jongleurs, French rhymers, Tuscan singers, and Spanish trovatori have praised their mistresses and described their own passions.' The summary that follows fills nearly forty pages, and is a truly remarkable performance. Immediately after the conceits of the Latin poets, Equicola comes to the Greek Anthology. One can hardly refrain from supposing that for this he received the direct assistance of Janus Lascaris. His summary of the amatory epigrams is here given in full, with indications of the epigrams

[1] Here Equicola acknowledges the instruction he had received from the first editor of the Anthology: 'Quae tunc tumultuarie scripseram recognoscenda putavi, tibique dicare, cum, si qua in me est, tibi praesertim debeam litterarum' (Santoro, p. 26, note 1). Equicola mentions Lascaris' pleasure in a Greek comedy by Demetrios Moschus in a letter written to Aldus from Mantua, June 15, 1510 (*Lettere di Scrittori Italiani del Secolo xvi*, ed. by Giuseppi Campori, Bologna, 1877, in 'Scelta di Curiosità Letterarie,' No. 157, p. 139).

[2] My references are to the edition printed by the Nicolini at Venice in 1536: *Libro di Natura d'Amore . . . novamente stampato et con somma diligentia correto*. Santoro, p. 167, lists 14 editions before 1607, and notices one Spanish and two French translations.

[3] Santoro, p. 173.

Equicola has in mind. He arranges them by authors, and begins with Meleager, not because of the merits of that writer, but because several of his epigrams open the seventh book of the Planudean collection:[1]

Così parimente percorreremo li epigrammatisti greci tra' quali primo me occorre Meleagro. Questo non ha luogo dove fuggire perchè amore sempre è seco, ne mai il lascia respirare [*A.P.* 5.139]. Ammonisce le zenzale che cessino da molestar le membra dell' amata, mordendola, con rompergli il sonno, se non vogliono provare la forza d'uno geloso [*A.P.* 5.151]; desia che una di loro vada alle orecchie di quella, e li immurmure essere da lui aspettata [*A.P.* 5.152]. Eshorta l'amica consentire a' suoi voti, il che deve fare perciò che, se la bellezza se invecchia, è giusto prima si parta che ne faccia ad altrui parte; se dura, diane volontieri, chè non si deve essere avara di quel che è permanente in lei senza suo detrimento [*A.P.* 12.235, by Strato in *Pal.*; in *Plan.* assigned to Meleager]. Prega Amore, che acquiete lo suo disiderio, altrimente morirà, e lasciarà scritta con sua infamia la causa dell'homicidio [*A.P.* 5.125]. Sentendosi Amore chiamare crudele, se ride, e piglia piacere delle ingiurie dettegli da' mortali, perchè del nostro mal dire si pasce [*A.P.* 5.176]. Se maraviglia il poeta, che Venere nata in mare dalle onde parturisca fuoco [*A.P.* 5.176]. Vuole più tosto odire la voce della amata, che la cithara di Apollo [*A.P.* 5.141]. Fugge Amore, et esso il vede nascosto nelli occhi di Zenophila [*A.P.* 5.177]; laquale vede haver havuta d'Amore le bellezze, da Venere lo accarezzare, dalle Gratie la gratia [*A.P.* 5.196]. Gigli, rose, narcisi, et ogni altro fiore sono inferiori a questa, tra' fiori fiore amabilissimo [*A.P.* 5.144]; Cupido e le Muse li han dato lo scettro delli amori [*A.P.* 5.140]. Nè conosce se la bellezza, o la gratia, o il cantare dell' amica più il cruccia; ma sente apertamente tutto brusciarse [*A.P.* 5.139.5–6].

Paulo Silentiario si lamenta esserli state ligate le mani con un capello del che se rise, persuadendose poterse sciogliere a suo arbitrio, ma poi che conobbe il vinculo esser indissolubile, suspirò, per star attaccata la sua vita da si fragile vinculo, e che l'amata con quello dovunque vuole il mena [*A.P.* 5.230]. Scrive esser maggior sua pena che quella di Tantalo, perciò che colui non si cruccia per disiderio di bellezza non vedendola, e se teme quel sasso che li pende sopra 'l capo, sa certo che non può morire due volte; ma esso amante se sente struggere vivo, e vivere con la morte propinqua [*A.P.* 5.236]. Sentese già mancare non altrimente ch' el fuoco suole nelli altari, poi che li è mancato quello che li dava nutrimento, così è mancato il calore, e 'l luogo restato freddo [*A.P.* 5.239]. Havendo ingiuriosamente chiusali in faccia la porta Galathea, crede il proverbio esser falso: 'la ingiuria scioglie l'amore,' perchè vede in lui la ingiuria concitare e commovere più il furore; giurò stare un anno longi da lei, e la mattina subito corse a quella [*A.P.* 5.256]. Dicesi che chi è morso di can rabbioso

---

[1] *Natura d'Amore* (1536), ff. 179ro ff. I have repunctuated the selection.

vede imagine nell' acqua; dubita che amore non l'habbia fatto devenire rabbioso, ch' el mare, il fiume, il vino li representa sempre la imagine dell' amata [*A.P.* 5.266]. Non sia chi tema più hormai delle saette di Cupido, che in me, dice 'l poeta, ha vacuata tutta la pharetra, e per non abbandonarme mai se ha nel mio cuore troncate le ali [*A.P.* 5.268]. Si lamenta delli occhi suoi stessi che troppo fissamente risguardano la bellezza di chi ama, però meritamente son bagnati spesso da fredde lagrime, et è ben degno, che per lei suspira l'alma come prima causa di tanto fuoco [*A.P.* 5.226].

Macedonio per più longamente possere contemplare l'amata, prega 'l sole che voglia fermarse come solea in vedere Phetonte, e tarde come è sua usanza nelli Cimmerij [*A.P.* 5.223]. Supplica Amore che cesse ferire il suo cuore, e suo fegato; ma piacciagli ferire qualche altro membro [*A.P.* 5.224]. Ha una gran ferita, donde continuamente escono lagrime, e le altre sue ferite dubita non haverse mai a consolidare, ne Machaon essere sufficiente a sanarle; sola l'amata le può ridurre in cicatrici, e serà a lui qual fu Achille a Thelepho [*A.P.* 5.225].

Agato [*sic*, for Agatia] Scolastico si duole che tutta la notte piange, et in l'aurora adormentato le rendene lo svegliano, e lo remetteno in lagrime [*A.P.* 5.237]. L'absentia dell'amata gli è notte oscurissima, la presentia gli è luce et giorno chiaro [*A.P.* 12.60]. Bevendo donde quella beve, piglia basci e gratia [*A.P.* 5.261]. Qualunque dice 'so innamorato, e so savio,' dice bugia, perchè amor non concorda con sapientia, e lo animo in pazzia non può ben discorrere [*A.P.* 5.267]. Si duole non haver li piaceri che gullano li altri giovani, e non poter vedere luce stando ascoso in casa, dove li pensieri occulti lo consumano [*A.P.* 5.297: incorrect interpretation]. Si ricorda di quel savio che disse: 'Niuna cosa troppo,' che persuadendosi esser amato se insuperbio; mutossi la amica che così da alto roinato si buttò alli piedi di quella, cridando: 'Perdoname, chè errò la gioventù' [*A.P.* 5.299].

Philodemo sentiva ch' el suo animo l'eshortava a fugire amor di Heliodora, ma non haver forza, chè l'animo admonendolo non meno amava [*A.P.* 5.24]. Vuol amar sempre Philenio, ben che picciola et brunetta sia, più crispa ch' el appio, più tenere che agnello, fin che trovarà cosa più perfetta [*A.P.* 5.121].

Pallas [*sic*, for Pallada] accusa Giove che non si trasmuta come suole per non essere la sua inferiore ad alcuna [*A.P.* 5.257].

Lucilio prega Cupido che, o li lieve l'amore, o li aggiunga l'essere amato [*A.P.* 5.68].

Quell'altro e di fuoco e di neve le percosse non teme, ch'el fulmine di Giove non paventa qualunque è da Amore domato [*A.P.* 5.168].

Rufino dice la sua amata haver la bellezza di Venere, parlare di Calliope, la persona fiorita di primavera, la castità et prudentia di Themis, le mani di Pallade [*A.P.* 5.70]. Afferma le Gratie esser quattro, Venere due, le Muse dieci, perciò che in tutte loro Dorcali è Musa, Gratia, e Venere [*A.P.* 5.95]. Melita ha li occhi di Giunone, di Minerva le mani, di Venere le mammelle, di Thetide li piedi: felice chi la vede, felicissimo chi la ode, semideo chi l'ama, immortal dio chi

usa con lei; costei come li superi merita templi [*A.P.* 5.94]. Trovò sola
l'amica, et abbracciando li piedi disse: 'Salva questo huomo perduto,
e donali lo spirito, che già fugge.' Dicendo questo piangea, et ella li
asciucava le lagrime [*A.P.* 5.66]. Pur che l'amata andasse per la piazza
col petto senza velamento desia esser vento [*A.P.* 5.83].

Juliano prega Venere che se favorische chi pate pericoli in mare,
voglia aiutar lui naufragio in terra [*A.P.* 5.11:anon., but Julianus in
Plan.].

Le più selette sententie de' Greci Epigrammi circa amor mi paion
queste.

NICCOLÒ MACHIAVELLI
(1469–1527)

Machiavelli belonged to an ancient Florentine family, many members of which had taken part in the administration of the Republic.
His father, Bernardo, was a jurist. Little is known of Niccolò's early
life; he probably did not receive a humanistic education, and seems
to have known no Greek. In 1498 he was chosen secretary to the
Signoria, in which capacity he served till the return of the Medici in
1512. During this period he fulfilled several missions of state, being
sent to Catherine Sforza at Forlì in 1499, on several occasions to
Louis XII in France, to Urbino in 1502 to treat with Cesare Borgia,
and to Maximilian I in Germany. He became convinced that Florence
should cease to employ mercenaries, and instead intrust her safety to
a citizen army. Much of his life was devoted to realizing this idea.
The restoration of the Medici cost him his employments; and, on
suspicion of conspiracy, he was thrown into prison and tortured, but
released under the amnesty of the new Medici pope, Leo X. He retired to his small estate near San Casciano, and, in the years of leisure
that followed, produced his best literary works: *Il Principe* (1513;
publ. 1531), *I Discorsi sopra la Prima Deca di T. Livio* (1531), *L'Arte
della Guerra* (1521), and his comedy *Mandragola* (written *c.* 1513).
Though ready to serve the Medici, he was neglected by them till
1519. In 1520 the Cardinal Giulio de' Medici commissioned him to
write the history of Florence, his last great book (1525). Thereafter
he was occasionally employed in State affairs. In 1526 he was entrusted with the fortification of the city against the oncoming imperial army, whose attack, however, fell upon Rome. This belated
attention of the Medici reacted to his prejudice when they were
driven out for the second time in 1527. He died on June 22 of that
year, leaving his wife and five children in straitened and uncertain
circumstances. He was buried in Santa Croce.

Machiavelli's *Capitolo dell' Occasione*, best-known of his
verses, is taken from Ausonius' handling of the theme of *A.P.*
16.275. That Ausonius rather than the Greek itself was before
him, is easily shown; for example, Occasion, a god in Greek, is

a goddess to Ausonius and Machiavelli; her companion, Repentance, who appears in both the Latin and the Italian, is absent from the Greek poem. Save for the first two lines, which are more generalized, Machiavelli's poem is a close translation of Ausonius. This generalization, amounting to the omission of the sculptor's name and indeed of any indication that a statue is in question, may reflect the remarks of Politian on the two ancient poems (above, p. 126). The poem was addressed to Filippo de' Nerli.[1]

> Chi sei tu, che non par donna mortale?
>   Di tanta grazia il ciel t'adorna e dota!
>   Perchè non posi? e perchè a' piedi hai l'ale?—
> 'Io son l'Occasïon, a pochi nota;
>   E la cagion che sempre mi travagli
>   È perchè io tengo un piè sopra una ruota.
> Volar non è ch' al mio correr s'agguagli;
>   E però l'ale a' piedi mi mantengo,
>   Acciò nel corso mio ciascuno abbagli.
> Gli sparsi miei capei dinanzi io tengo;
>   Con essi mi ricopro il petto e 'l volto,
>   Perch' un non mi conosca quando io vengo.
> Dietro dal capo ogni capel m'è tolto,
>   Onde in van si affatica un, se gli avviene
>   Ch' io l'abbia trapassato, o s'io mi volto.'
> 'Dimmi: chi è colei che teco viene?'
>   'È Penitenza; e però nota e intendi:
>   Chi non sa prender me, costei ritiene.
> E tu, mentre parlando il tempo spendi,
>   Occupato da molti pensier vani,
>   Già non t'avvedi, lasso! e non comprendi
> Com' io ti son fuggita tra le mani!'

BERNARDO ACCOLTI

(†c. 1535)

Bernardo was a son of the celebrated historian Benedetto Accolti of Arezzo; it is not known how old he was when his father died in

---

[1] Machiavelli, *Opere*, Milan, 1805, 8.374. A good example of a modern writer independently hitting upon the same figure as an ancient one, may be seen in Machiavelli's *Canzone* (*ibid.*, p. 415) beginning:

> Se avessi l'arco e l'ale,
>   Giovanetto Giulio,
>   Tu saresti lo Dio, che ogni uomo assale.

Compare Asclepiades, *A.P.* 12.75, (not in *Plan.*):

> Εἰ πτερά σοι προσέκειτο, καὶ ἐν χερὶ τόξα καὶ ἰοί,
>   οὐκ ἂν Ἔρως ἐγράφη Κύπριδος, ἀλλὰ σύ, παῖς.

1466. He frequented the Court of Urbino, where he is mentioned by Castiglione as attending the Duchess's literary *soirées*. Later he removed to Rome, and became an Apostolic Scribe and *Abbreviatore*, winning the favor of Leo X. Whether from the pope or by his own wealth, he secured the lordship of Nepi, which at one time he lost, but regained under Paul III. He was still alive in 1534, as is proved by a letter of his to Paul III, who became pope in that year; but probably died soon after. He left two illegitimate children, a son Alfonso, who succeeded him as lord of Nepi, and a daughter, Virginia, whom he had married to Count Giambattista Malatesta with a dowry of ten thousand *scudi*.[1]

He was known as *l'Unico Aretino*. Varchi regarded him as the equal of Tebaldeo and superior to Sasso and the Altissimo; his powers of improvisation were especially remarkable. Pietro Aretino reports how the people thronged to his recitations. Ariosto celebrates him (*Or. Fur.* (46.10)):

<blockquote>Il gran lume aretin, l'Unico Accolti.</blockquote>

Unfortunately he left but little published work to support his name. Besides two letters in the collection of Pietro Aretino, and some complimentary verses in various books, we have from him only a slight comedy, *Verginia*, a dozen sonnets, some *strambotti*, and a poem in terza rima on the Madonna. The comedy was recited at the marriage of Antonio Spanocchi in Siena, and was printed with the *strambotti* and other poems at Florence in 1513. The book went through a great number of editions.[2]

Only the *strambotti* here concern us. They are 31 in number. In these Accolti's style shows what the style of the sixteenth century was going to be; his subjects are drawn from classical or neo-Latin sources, and he was probably conscious that his pieces correspond to the classical epigram.[3] Francesco Redi says that among them there are 'molti acutissimi e sull' andare de' buoni epigrammi de' Greci e de' Latini.'[4] The first ten *strambotti* are on classical subjects, the remainder are amatory lyrics, mostly addressed to 'Giulia.' Three are derived from the Anthology (*A.P.* 9.126, 346; and 16.162), two others are epitaphs that have parallels, at least, in the Greek epigrams,[5] and a

---

[1] Mazzuchelli. Little is to be learned from Francesco Gavagni, *L'Unico Aretino* ... *e la Corte dei Duchi d'Urbino*, Arezzo, 1906, but the book contains some hitherto unedited poems.

[2] My references are to the seventh: *Verginia, Comedia ... con un Capitolo della Madonna, nuovamente corretta, & con somma diligentia ristampata*. Venice (Zoppino), 1535.

[3] In the 1535 edition they are recommended for their 'argutie,' and introduced as 'strambotti acutissimi.'

[4] Annot. on his *Bacco in Toscana*, quoted by Mazzuchelli.

[5] *Niobe* (f. 48vo); *Alessandro* (f. 49ro).

fifth is from *The Honey-Stealer* ascribed to Theocritus. The three drawn from the Anthology are so freely treated as to suggest that they do not come directly from the Greek.

ORESTE

Da'l morto padre, a l'agitato Oreste,
Che del sangue materno el terren tinse,
L'esterrefatta madre aprì la veste
Che già le membra infortunate cinse,
E disse al figlio con parole meste,
Quando per darli morte el ferro strinse:
Qual prima o 'l petto o 'l ventre ferirai?
L'un ti nutrì, ne l'altro ti portai.
(*A.P.* 9.126)

Accolti's substitution of an eagle for the swallow of the original seems quite unparalleled:

AQUILA

Veder perir tuo parto, e tua semenza,
Regal Aquila diva, assai mi dole.
Che ti giova haver fatto esperienza
Del interrita vista emula al sole,
Dapoi c'hai posto con mala sentenza
Sotto a piè di Medea tuo nido et prole?
Chè mal perdonerà a' figliuol tuoi,
Quella che perdonar non seppe a' suoi.
(*A.P.* 9.346)

The third owes only the first couplet to the Greek:

GIULIA

Giulia, vedendosi in marmo scolpita,
Disse: O scultor, dove m' hai vista ignuda?
Rispose lui: Ne la fronte smarrita
D'un che t'ama e vuoi morte in terra el chiuda.
Onde lei: Se a chi m'ama tolgo vita,
Perchè m'hai fatta pia, essendo cruda?
—Perchè esprimer sol può lo scultore
Che mostra el volto e non che pensa el core.
(*A.P.* 16.162)

ROMOLO AMASEO

(1489–1552)

Romolo was a son of Gregorio Amaseo, professor of the Latin language in Venice. He was born at Udine, and studied first with his father and later at Padua, where he began to teach in 1508. The war of the League of Cambrai led to his removing to Bologna, where he taught till 1543, when Paul III called him to Rome. Thereafter he was employed by Paul and his successor on diplomatic missions, some of these taking him to the Court of the Emperor and to several German princes. He had married in Bologna, and had several children; his wife seems to have died about 1550. In that year Julius III made him a papal secretary, a post which he only lived two years to enjoy. Among his works are translations of Xenophon's *Anabasis* (Bologna, 1533) and of Pausanias (Rome, 1547), and *Orationes* (Bologna, 1580). He was highly regarded by the leading literary men of his time.

In the second part of the *Lettere facete di diversi* there are three letters from Amaseo to Giovan Antonio Serrone.[1] The first is written by an amanuensis, Amaseo being ill at the time, and, as it is of a private nature, is couched in 'parabole.' Seemingly some intrigue in which the writer was interested was turning out ill; he says: 'Io vorrei . . . finir quest' ultimo atto della mia comedia, over più presto tragedia, con l'esser riputato o il poeta o l'attore, e non del popol tutto . . . favola. Tanto è, che *Non prece, non pretio potuit victoria vinci.* Con mutar una sola parola del Greco le ho mandati intagliati, i due suoi alberi, con un motto, che dice: ἐλπὶς καὶ νίκη, μέγα χαίρετε, χαίρετε ἄμφω.' The Greek is from *A.P.* 9.134 (νίκη for τύχη). It does not seem possible to tell to whom Amaseo's letter refers.

CLAUDIO TOLOMEI

(*c.* 1492–1555)

No one can study Italian literature of the Cinquecento long without realizing the influence of Tolomei on his contemporaries. Something has already been said of his place in the history of the Italian epigram (above, pp. 49 and 58). His epigrams and those of his friends, however, being inextricably connected with their metrical experiments, as has been remarked, lie slightly off the highway of literature. Hence, though coming later, Alamanni, and not Tolomei, must be accepted as the originator of the Italian epigram.

A sketch of Tolomei's life is given by Tiraboschi (*Storia* 7.3.76–7), who calls him 'uno de' più benemeriti scrittori della lingua Italiana, che avesse il secolo.' Tolomei belonged to a noble family of Siena, but after 1516 mainly resided in Rome, where he was received at the papal Court. He was in the service of Cardinal Ippolito de' Medici (1529–35), and later in that of Pier Luigi Farnese, Duke of Parma,

---

[1] *Delle Lettere Facete et Piacevoli di Diversi Grandi Huomini* . . . raccolte per M. Francesco Turchi, libro secondo, Venice, 1575, p. 53.

with whom he spent the years 1543–47 at Piacenza. After Parma's tragic death, Tolomei returned to Rome, and was named Bishop of Corsolo, a small island in the Adriatic. In 1552 he was in Siena, and was appointed one of the sixteen citizens to form an embassy to the King of France. This mission consumed two years. Tolomei returned to Rome at the end of 1554, and there died on the twenty-third of the March following.

Tolomei surrounded himself in Rome with a group of men all inspired with the thought of making an Italian verse-literature based on rules of quantity. Their experiments in this form were published in their *Versi et Regole* at Rome in 1539.[1] As they were mainly interested in the verse-form, and less in trying to write poetry, they looked about for ready-made materials, and naturally went often to the Latin poets, ancient and modern, whose metres they aimed to reproduce. The brevity of the epigram made it suitable to their purpose; and in translating the epigrams of the Latin poets they inevitably took several that originate in the Anthology.

Tolomei himself has a set of verses resembling *A.P.* 5.147, and a second recalling, through Navagero, *A.P.* 9.374.[2] The first is:

> Questi soavi fiori, queste herbe, et queste novelle
>   Rose, pur hor colte da 'nnamorata mano,
> E 'n ghirlande poi dolcissimamente legate
>   La 've natura vedi d'un pari et arte gire,
> Al crin biondo sopra Lice candida ponle, et adorna
>   Lor di vaghezza tua, te di vaghezza loro.
> Et mostra, in sembianza pari, come poco ti possa
>   L'alma natura mai vincere, et arte meno.

Dionigi Atanagi da Cagli (*fl.* 1539–1545) has reminiscences of *A.P.* 5.78 and 95.

Antonio Renieri da Colle has verses resembling *A.P.* 5.147. Gabriello Zerbo has the conceit of *A.P.* 5.230.

The 'Versioni di Anonomi,' however, in the section, 'Epi-

---

[1] An extended study of Tolomei and his friends would be welcome. Their book. *Versi et Regole de la Nuova Poesia Toscana*, was largely reprinted, with selections from similar experiments, by Carducci in his *Poesia Barbara in Italia nei Secoli xv e xvi*, Bologna, 1881; but he made no historical study of them. The *regoletti*, be it remarked, are not concerned with general questions, but merely are rules for the length of syllables in Italian.

[2] The first is reproduced by De-Mauri, *Ep. It.*, p. 40. An Italian version by Tolomei of an epigram of Marcantonio Flaminio, in its turn recalling *A.P.* 5.168, may be found in *Flaminiorum Carmina* (1743), p. 93; and a sonnet taken from *Anacr.* 4 or *A.P.* 11.48 occurs in Atanagi's collection: *Rime di diversi nobili poeti toscani*, Venice, 1565; cf. Ferrari in *Giorn. Stor.* 20 (1892). 404.

grammi di Autori Latini,' have more echoes—*A.P.* 6.53 (Navagero), 258 (Statius Romanus);[1] 9.16 (*idem.*), 36 (*idem.*), 56
(Germanicus),[2] 108 (Sannazaro), 440 (*idem.* sig. Mii), 627
(Statius Romanus); 12.73 (Catulus); 16.209 (Statius Romanus), 297 (M. A. Casanova). Sannazaro's imitation of *A.P.*
9.108 has been given above (p. 141); the anonymous Italian
version of this follows:

> Molto d'Amor fiero con Giove si dolse Diana,
> Che di ferir gli altri troppo era sempre vago.
> Allor, chiamatolo, disse il padre sommo ad Amore:
> 'Spezzerà esto mio folgore i dardi tui.'—
> Il lascivo dio soggiunse, le penne movendo:
> 'Che fia s'or anco, reso il folgore, cigno sei?'

AGOSTINO BEAZZANO

(*c.* 1490–*c.* 1571)

Beazzano was born at Treviso of a Venetian family. At an early age
he went to Rome, and, between 1513 and 1515, was received at the
Court of Leo X. He was on terms of intimacy with Cardinal Bembo,
from whose correspondence most of what is known of him is drawn.
Ill-health compelled him to withdraw to Verona, and finally to return
to Treviso, where the last eighteen years of his long life were passed.
A list of his works is given by Mazzuchelli.

The following *stanza* was probably written by Beazzano with
A.P. 16.120 in mind:[3]

> Chi è costui che nel metallo spira,
> E mostra più che umano esser nel volto?—
> Alessandro è, che così morto aspira
> A quel che morte importuna gli ha tolto.—
> Ma perchè sta pien di disdegno e d'ira
> Col generoso aspetto al ciel rivolto?—
> A Giove dice: 'Aspetta la mia guerra,
> Se 'l ciel tu non mi dai, come la terra.'

Beazzano has changed, and blunted, the point of the Greek. I
give a translation of the original ascribed to Archelaus or
Asclepiades: 'The boldness of Alexander and his whole form

---

[1] I have not identified Statius Romanus.
[2] 'Da C. Caesare'; see above, p. 19.
[3] *Raccolta di Lirici e Satirici Italiani*, Florence, 1835, p. 780. No trace of the Greek
epigrams appears in Beazzano's *Delle Cose Volgari e Latine*, Venice, 1538 (2nd ed.,
Rime Volgari e Latine, Venice, 1551); but a group of 40 Italian epitaphs, beginning on
sig. F iiii, shows the influence of the Greek and Latin form, even to the indentation of
every second line to produce the effect of the distich. See also above, p. 59, n. 2.

were modeled by Lysippus. What power this bronze possesses! Gazing up to Zeus the brazen figure seems about to say: "I have set the Earth under my feet; do you, O Zeus, for your part, keep Olympus."'

FRANCESCO MARIA MOLZA
(1489–1544)

[On Molza's career and his Latin poems, see above, p. 218.]

In this sonnet Molza uses the conceit of *A.P.* 16.200:[1]

> Torna Amore a l'aratro, e i sette colli,
>   Ove era dianzi il seggio tuo maggiore,
>   Spogliato, e nudo del sovran suo onore,
>   Fuggi con gli occhi di duol gravi e molli.
> O speranze fallaci, O pensier folli!
>   Morta è colei sul bel giovanil fiore,
>   Che ad alta speme apriva ogni umil core;
>   Taccio di me, che sole altro non volli.
> Dunque, miser, la stiva in vece d' arco
>   Usar potrai, e in panni vili avvolto
>   Fender co' buoi le campagne intorno,
> Ch' ella giungendo a l' ultimo suo varco
>   Ogni atto vago estinse; e a te fu tolto
>   L' usato ardire: O benedetto giorno!

LUIGI ALAMANNI
(1495–1556)

Alamanni came of a noble Florentine family distinguished for its devotion to the cause of the Medici. His father, Piero di Francesco Alamanni, had been Gonfaloniere and ambassador, and in 1497 was confined to one of his own villas on suspicion of desiring the return of the Medici to Florence. Luigi, however, though favored by Giulio de' Medici when the latter became head of the State, had imbibed a love of liberty from his literary studies and associates which put him into the opposition. He belonged to the circle of young men who met in the famous gardens of the Rucellai family, the Orti Oricellari, and, besides the sons of Bernardo Rucellai, included Alamanni, Antonio Bruccioli, Zanobi Buondelmonte, and others. Machiavelli often was there, and Francesco da Diacceto the Platonist who had been Alamanni's teacher at the *Studio*.

Alamanni married in 1516, and began life as a peaceful citizen. He was discovered, however, in 1522 to be one of a conspiracy to take the life of Giulio de' Medici. Bruccioli and Buondelmonte were also

---

[1] *Poesie*, Milan, 1808, p. 172. The sonnet was first printed in Domenichi's *Rime Diverse* (1545) I.119.

implicated. The conspirators fled to Venice, and eventually made their way to France, where they were welcomed at the Court of Francis I.

A part of the year 1524 was spent by Alamanni in Provence awaiting the result of a French expedition into Italy. He was still in France when his protector Francis I was made captive at Pavia in 1525. Two years later hope arose from another quarter. The Imperial army took Rome, and besieged Clement VII (Giulio de' Medici) in the Castle of St. Angelo. This was a signal for the Florentines to shake off the yoke; the Medici were again expelled, and political exiles, including Alamanni, were recalled.

The poet's life was now filled with affairs of State—negotiations with France, public business in Genoa, a mission as 'under-ambassador' to Charles V (1529). But by the treaty of Barcelona Florence was restored to the pope. Alamanni, who happened to be in Genoa, was forced to remain there, and finally found it necessary to retire once more to France.

From this time forward Alamanni was established at the French Court. In 1539 he made an extended journey into Italy in the train of Cardinal Ippolito d'Este, visiting Rome, Padua, and Ferrara, and conversing with Benedetto Varchi, Annibale Caro, Pietro Aretino, Cellini, Vittoria Colonna, and other celebrated persons. In 1541 he was Francis I's ambassador to Venice; in 1543 he was ambassador to Genoa. His first wife died about this time, and he married Elena Bonaiuti, one of the ladies of Catherine de' Medici. Catherine made him her *maître d'hôtel*. Alamanni's new security bore fruit in literary work. His *Coltivazione* was published in 1546, and in January of the same year he dedicated his epigrams to the Princess Marguerite. After the death of Francis, Alamanni continued in the favor of Catherine, now Queen of France. He died in 1556 at Amboise, where the Court happened to be at that time.

While Alamanni is not a poet of the first rank, he obtains a certain importance from his position—a representative of the best of Italian literary culture, but domiciled in France at the dawn of modern French literature—and from the kind of thing he did—he is the first poet of any power to give himself up to the imitation of ancient forms in the vernacular. He exerted a real influence on the Pléiade. The contents of Alamanni's book of poems may profitably be compared with those of Ronsard and Baïf. In particular we may here observe that these two writers are prolific in epigrams just as Alamanni is, and like him they seek their models not in Marot, but in the Greek Anthology.[1] Marot seemingly deserves the title of first epigram-

---

[1] Alamanni is cited by Du Bellay in the *Deffence*. See further Henri Hauvette, *Luigi Alamanni, sa Vie et son Œuvre*, Paris, 1903, pp. 444–5, and J. Vianey in *Revue des Langues Romanes* 43 (1900). 433–6.

matist in the modern languages, but had no influence on Alamanni, who went directly to the ancients. 'For Alamanni,' says
Hauvette, 'the word "epigram" preserved its etymological
sense, and the form remained what it originally was to the
Greeks—an inscription.'[1]

Alamanni's epigrams were composed with the encouragement of Marguerite of Savoy, the daughter of Francis I, and were
dedicated to her at the beginning of January, 1546. They
mostly remained unprinted until 1587.[2] Meanwhile they circulated in manuscript, and became well-known in Italy.

Alamanni has in all some 129 epigrams.[3] Of these, 38 are
translated or imitated from the Greek, and 33 from the Anthology. To these must be added two echoes in Alamanni's
elegies, so that we have altogether 35 borrowings on the part of
Alamanni from the Greek Anthology.[4] Hauvette rightly finds
that Alamanni's epigrams 'correspond perfectly with the poet's
most characteristic tendencies, with the constant pains he took
to introduce classical traditions into Italian poetry.'

Alamanni's imitation of the Greek epigrams in the matter of
form has already received attention in the Introduction (p.
59). Our attention here is confined to his substantial borrowings. As a rule he follows his models somewhat closely, as may
be seen in his treatment of the two celebrated epigrams on human life (*A.P.* 9.359–360):

MISERIE DELLA VITA

Qual vita è da cercar? in corte hai doglie
  E invidie; alti pensier fra le tue soglie;
Pena in villa, in mar tema, in altrui tetto
  Povero hai dispiacer, ricco sospetto;
Prender moglie è travaglio: vive solo
  Chi non l'ha in tutto; gran peso è il figliuolo:

---

[1] *Op. cit.*, p. 262. Hauvette finds it hard to understand why Alamanni included a
translation of the *Amor Fugitivus* of Moschus among his epigrams. He evidently did so
because he had the Anthology before him (see above, p. 3).

[2] *Epigrammi con Alcuni Epitaffi* (Paris). Thirteen only had been inserted in the
Libro v delle Rime di Diversi Illustri Signori, Venice, 1555. Hauvette, *op. cit.*, p. 557.

[3] The best edition of Alamanni's works is *Versi e Prose*, ed. by Pietro Raffaelli,
2 vols. Florence, 1859. This contains 114 epigrams; to which 15 are added in Frati's
Rime Inedite del Cinquecento, Bologna, 1918.

[4] *A.P.* 5. *81*, *83*, 91 (or 143); 6.1 (twice used); 7.33 (?), 46, 184, 249, 396; 9.13, 39,
44, *49*, *56*, 74, 138, 293, 304, 359, 360, 394, 440 (2.137), 442, 495 (?), 497; 10.72;
11. *193*, 252, 294, 392; 16.9, 14, 174, *388*. Italic numerals indicate translations or imitations found in Frati's *Rime Inedite* and not in Raffaelle; in the Register, these books
are referred to as *Rim. Ined.* and *Versi* respectively.

Il non averne è duol; la giovinezza
  È senza senno, frale è la vecchiezza.
Dunque o non nascer mai bramar si deve,
  O nato, men durar, che al foco neve.

CONDIZIONI DELLA VITA

Ogni sorte di vita al saggio piace:
  In corte è somma gloria, in casa pace,
Diporto in villa, in mar guadagno; fuore
Della sua patria il ricco porta onore,
Il povero più si cela; quel che ha moglie,
  Ha più conforto: chi non l'ha, men doglie.
Son sostegno i figliuoli: queta è l'orbezza;
  Robusta è gioventù, saggia è vecchiezza.
Brami dunque ciascun non morir mai,
  O di Nestor i dì vincer d'assai.

Alamanni may have seen in his own life a commentary on thes e poems.

King Francis I himself made a version of *A.P.* 9.56. Teocreno, who was then at the French Court, has an epigram on the king's performance (above, p. 182). It is impossible to say whether Alamanni's translation of the same epigram has any connection with that incident:

Sopra l'Hebro indurato il fanciul Thrace
  Scherzando, sotto i piedi il giel si sface,
Cade fra l'onde rapide, e la testa
  Risecata dal ghiaccio in alto resta;
La qual la madre ardendo, 'Di me nacque,
  Questo, disse, alle fiamme, il resto all' acque.'

ANTON FRANCESCO RAINERIO (RINIERI)
(*fl.* 1550)

Rainerio was a native of Milan. He served as secretary to Cardinal Verulano, papal legate at Piacenza, and later became secretary to the infamous Duke of Parma and Piacenza, Pier Luigi Farnese, to whom he addressed many of his sonnets. He appears to have acted as ambassador from Pier Luigi to the pope. When Farnese was assassinated in 1547, Rainerio was received at the Court of Urbino, the Duke of Urbino being a son-in-law of his late protector. He soon passed, however, into the service of Duke Ottavio Farnese and his duchess, the celebrated Margaret of Parma. The favor he enjoyed at their Court is said to have aroused the jealousy of his fellow courtiers to such a degree that he gladly accepted the invitation of Julius III to come to Rome and attend on the pope's nephews Balduino and Fabiano del

Monte.[1] Rainerio was a friend of Giovanni della Casa, Annibale Caro, Molza, and Lodovico Dolce.

Rainerio published a comedy entitled *Altilia* (Mantua, 1550), a book of poems, *Cento Sonetti* and *Le Pompe* (Milan, 1553-4, and again Venice, 1554),[2] and *Carmina* (Rome, 1555). The *Cento Sonetti* is dedicated to Fabiano del Monte, and is provided with a brief commentary by Girolamo Rainerio. Among these sonnets are three which the commentator says are imitations of epigrams in the Anthology; perhaps one other should be added. The following is Sonnet 9 with its commentary:[3]

> Le prime nevi e i gigli ancor non colti,
>   Vince quell' una bella ignuda mano;
>   L'or puro e terso, al sol fiammeggia invano
>   Al par de be capegli, hor cinti, hor sciolti.
> Son da voi le vaghezze e gli honor tolti
>   A'i più be poggi, al più bel verde piano;
>   Se co 'l tenero piè, gite pian piano
>   Per entro i fior, sott' a le piante accolti.
> Rari e celesti doni in voi son giunti:
>   *Beltà, ch' a se mi trahe, com' esca pesce;*
>   *Gratia poi, che com' hamo il cor mi prende.*
> Quindi è, che i pensier miei da voi disgiunti
>   Non fien, se morte in me l'arco non tende,
>   Morte, che nel mel nostro il tosco mesce.

'[Sonetto] amoroso et facilissimo; con imitatione d' un' epigramma Greco sovra la beltà e la gratia, assimigliando la beltà a l'esca che alletta, ma non prende senza l'hamo, che è la gratia.'[4]

---

[1] Argelati, *Bibl. Script. Mediolan.* 2.1186; Quadrio, *Storia* (1741) 2.242; Bongi, *Annali di Gabriel Giolito* 1.450.

[2] See the following note. The book was again reprinted at Bologna in 1712.

[3] References are to the 1553-4 edition: *Cento Sonetti di M. Antonfrancesco Rainerio, gentilhuomo milanese, con brevissima espositione dei soggetti loro,* [Milan], 1553. The title-page of the *Espositione* is dated 1554. At the end: Impressi in Milano per Gio. Antonio Borgia. I have not seen the edition printed by Giolito at Venice in 1554, nor yet the edition of 1712. A good many of the sonnets had previously appeared at Venice in 1547 in a miscellany published by Giolito: *Rime di Diversi nobili huomini et eccelenti poeti nella lingua thoscana, libro secondo.* Again in Lodovico Dolce's *Rime di Diversi et Eccelenti Autori* (*Rime Scelte*, vol. 1)—I use the edition of 1556—sixty-nine poems are printed under Rinieri's name (so spelled in the miscellanies). Of these, however, 21 are not in the *Cento Sonetti*, and I owe to Professor Walter L. Bullock the information that at least 18 of these, and possibly all 21, belong to Benedetto Varchi, and appear elsewhere under his name, 18 in his *Rime* and three in later editions of Dolce's book. The text of the sonnets as printed in the miscellanies frequently differs from that of the *Cento Sonetti.*

[4] The epigram (*A.P.* 5.67) is by Capito:

> Κάλλος ἄνευ χαρίτων τέρπει μόνον. οὐ κατέχει δέ,
>   ὡς ἄτερ ἀγκίστρου νηχόμενον δέλεαρ.

Sonnet 37 is said in the *Espositione* to be an imitation of a Greek epigram which declares it to be impossible to escape Love whether on land, in the sea, or in the sky, for he overtakes one with the bow on land, by swimming in the sea, and by flying in the sky. No epigram in the Anthology has exactly that sense; *A.P.* 5.59 and 16.213 may be compared. Sonnet 22 is based on *A.P.* 16.104. Probably also Sonnet 13 (*Su 'l vespro, allhor*) contains a reminiscence of *A.P.* 5.225. The last three lines are:

> Sol que' begli occhi, ond' io son hor disgiunto
> Et la man micidial, che i colpi feo,
> Puon saldar le mie fere alte ferute.

The Greek says similarly: 'I am Telephus, maiden; do thou be faithful Achilles: with thy beauty heal my desire, even as you smote me.'

A selection of Rainerio's Latin poems appears in the *Carmina Illustrium Poetarum* (vol. 8), but shows no influence from the Anthology; yet in Abraham Wright's *Delitiae Delitiarum* (Oxford, 1637), p. 106, may be read the following version of *A.P.* 16.326 ascribed to 'Franciscus Rainerius':[1]

> Pythagoram pictor poterat pinxisse loquentem,
> Verum Pythagoram conticuisse iuvat.

ANTON FRANCESCO DONI
(*c.* 1503–1574)

Doni, a Florentine, entered the Servite order early in life, but left it to become a secular priest and live by his pen—that is, by patronage. He left Florence about 1540 to travel through Italy in search of a patron. From 1545 to 1547 he was again in Florence, but finally removed to Venice, where most of his books were published. He retired to Arqua in 1564, and died at the neighboring village of Monselice in September, 1574. His works, of a pleasant, sometimes satirical, character, were once widely read. At one time he was a friend of Pietro Aretino, to whose class as a writer he belongs, though he wanted Aretino's power; they later became implacable enemies.

In Doni's *Pistoletti Amorosi* (Venice, 1552, p. 9) there is an echo of *A.P.* 7.669; the conceit was by this time a commonplace:

> Quando io vi veggio
> Senz' atti fieri e rei,
> Mille occhi haver vorrei,
> Nè dal cielo altra gratia e favor chieggio.

[1] I have not succeeded in finding Rainerio's *Carmina* of 1555.

VINCENZO CARTARI

(fl. 1550)

Cartari is known only from his works. He was a native of Reggio. In 1551 (Venice) he published a translation of the *Fasti* of Ovid, and in 1562 (Venice) *Il Compendio dell' Istoria di Mons. Paolo Giovio.* He is remembered, however, for his *Immagini degli Dei degli Antichi*, first published at Venice in 1556, and thereafter reissued many times to the end of the seventeenth century. At first the book consisted only of verbal descriptions of the gods, with references to authorities; but beginning with the fourth edition (1571) pictures were added. There are Latin, French, and English translations of it.

The picture of Καιρός (Opportunity) shows a youth, with long hair over his forehead, poised on a sphere, and carrying a razor in his hand. Cartari's authorities appear to be mainly Politian and Giraldi (above, pp. 126 and 184): 'Fu dunque il dio Cero dei Greci, il medesimo che era la Occasione dei Latini, del quale Posidippo fece un epigramma [*A.P.* 16.275] descrivendo la sua imagine, onde Ausonio tolse forse l'argumento del suo quando depinse la Occasione.'[1] He proceeds, in the manner of Politian, to notice the differences between Ausonius and Posidippus.[2]

GIROLAMO RUSCELLI

(c. 1500–1566)

Ruscelli is better known as an editor of Italian poets than as an original writer. He was born at Viterbo, lived for a time at Rome under Paul III, and finally removed to Venice, where he corrected for the press of Valgrisi. At the same time Lodovico Dolce was correcting for the nearby press of Giolito, and Ruscelli and he were soon involved in a bitter controversy over the editions of Boccaccio put out by their respective houses. Ruscelli appears in an ironical light in Tasso's *Minturno*. He died in Venice, after a long and painful illness, and was buried in the Church of St. Luke at the side of Dolce and Atanagi. Besides composing a number of original works of a miscellaneous character, he was editor of a *Decameron* (1552), of *Il Sesto Libro delle Rime di Diversi Eccellenti Autori* (1553), a Petrarch (1554), and many other books.[3] His *Commentarii della Lingua Italiana libri sette* came out posthumously at Venice in 1581.

---

[1] *Immagini*, Venice, 1580, p. 480; Padua, 1615, p. 426.
[2] Argelati, *Bibl. degli Volgar.* (1767) 1.63 says that Cartari translates an anonymous Greek epigram on Echo. This seems not to be true; Cartari translates an epigram by Ausonius on Echo, and at the point where he treats of this deity gives a long Italian example of the type of verse known as 'Echo.'
[3] List in the *Biographie Universelle.*

In 1558 appeared Ruscelli's anthology of lyric poems called *I Fiori delle Rime de' Poeti Illustri*.[1] In compiling and naming his collection he had in mind the Greek Anthology; he says in his Dedicatory Epistle: 'Ho fatta scelta non solamente de gli autori, ma ancora ne gli autori, per fare un libro in questo genere, che sia per esser gratissimo et utilissimo ad ogni bello ingegno, et per consequente per vivere eternamente. Et si come alcuni dotti et giudiciosi nel far' una tale sceglitura ne gli autori Greci, diedero a tal libro il nome di Raccolta di Fiori di Epigrammi, cosi è paruto a me col giudicio di molti di chiamar lietamente questo nostro Fiori di Rime de i Poeti Illustri.' He makes no attempt to arrange the sonnets otherwise than by authors.

GIOVAN LUIGI RICCIO

(*fl.* 1550)

Riccio belonged to the circle of Angelo di Costanzo, Ferrante Caraffa, and Lodovico Paterno, and was evidently a Neapolitan. Five sonnets by him are printed by Ruscelli in the *Sesto Libro delle Rime* mentioned in the preceding article, one being accompanied by a *risposta* by Costanzo, another by one by Caraffa. The first of the five sonnets is an imitation of *A.P.* 9.523 turned by Riccio into a glorification of the Neapolitan general Acquaviva.[2]

> Mandate, O Muse, in terra un' altro Omero,
>   Poi che d' un' altro Achille ha il Ciel ornato
>   Il secol nostro, ond' io lieto e beato
>   Veder' ancora il mio Sebeto spero.
> Questi del ceppo d' Acquaviva altero
>   A ristorar d' Italia i danni nato,
>   Con l'invitto valor nel primo stato,
>   Ritornerà l' antico e giusto Impero.
> Da la costui virtute ardente e viva,
>   Con cui suole adoprar l' ingegno e l' arme,
>   Sarà lo Scita e 'l Gallo in fuga messo.
> Ma già vedere il vostro intento parme;
>   Perchè volete, ch' ei medesmo scriva,
>   Sendo Achille e Omero egli a se stesso.

---

[1] Reprinted at Venice in 1569, 1579, and 1586. I use the 1586 edition.
[2] It is uncertain on what warrior the original was composed:

Καλλιόπη πολύμυθε μελισσοβότου Ἑλικῶνος,
    τίκτε μοι ἄλλον Ὅμηρον, ἐπεὶ μόλεν ἄλλος Ἀχιλλεύς.

'Eloquent Calliope of Helicon, where feed the bees, bear me another Homer, since another Achilles has appeared.'

DOMENICO VENIERO

(*c*. 1517–1582)

Veniero, a noble Venetian, was one of the more esteemed sonneteers in the generation next after Bembo's; indeed Bembo was his early encourager. In 1549 a nervous disorder deprived Veniero of the use of his limbs; but he became the centre of a numerous literary society, and is accounted after Badoaro the founder of the Venetian Academy (1558). To him among others Tasso submitted his *Gerusalemme*. Veniero's own poems have been justly praised, though the decay of taste is already apparent in them. They remained scattered in the collections of Dolce and Ruscelli until 1751, when they were brought together and edited by Serassi at Bergamo.

It has not seemed proper to omit from the present study the following sonnet of Veniero, although it is mainly a version of Horace, *Carm*. 4.10. The similarity of Horace's poem to *A.P.* 6.1 has already been noticed (above, p. 14, n. 1); Veniero must have had that similarity more or less clearly in mind when he added to his sonnet a last line echoing the last line of the Greek epigram (above, p. 23, n. 3) by a similar play on 'can' and 'will.'[1]

> O più ch' altra giamai cruda e rubella
> D'Amor', a cui ben fu largo e cortese
> D'ogni suo dono il ciel, ch' a farvi intese
> La più vaga del mondo, e la più bella,
> Quando i crin biondi, e l'una e l'altra stella
> Fian senza l'oro, e le faville accese,
> E mille rughe havran le guancie offese,
> Ch'avorio terso fa l'età novella,
> E ne lo specchio quasi in poco d'hora
> Vedrete un' altra, invan con gli occhi molli
> Direte: 'Hor qual pensier meco soggiorna?
> Perchè tal non l'hebb' io giovane ancora?
> O con questa mia mente il bel non torna?
> *Oggi, lassa, non posso, allor non volli.*'

GIAMBATTISTA STROZZI

(1504–1571)

So many prominent members of the Florentine family of the Strozzi bore the name of the patron of Florence, that it is not altogether

---

[1] Ruscelli, *Libro Sesto*, (Venice, 1553) f. 130ro. Three lines of a second sonnet (*ibid.* f. 133ro) possibly echo *A.P.* 5.94:
> Ma ben può certo in costei sola dirsi,
> Ch'a la bellezza, a l'honestate, al senno,
> E Ciprigna, e Diana, e Palla unirsi.

certain which is the author of a book of madrigals published in 1593. Researches by Luigi Sorrento, however, seem to vindicate the *Madrigali* for that Giambattista Strozzi who was Consul of the Florentine Academy in 1540.[1] He is referred to as 'il Vecchio' to distinguish him from a younger namesake, and lived through the central years of the sixteenth century. For a Strozzi he spent a peaceful life. He was a student at Padua in 1530 when the Medici gained final control of Florence; and he seems to have early won the regard of Cosimo I. In 1542 he married Maria di Bindo Altoviti, by whom he had two sons, Lorenzo and Filippo. His life was passed in literary pursuits, although he published little, and his madrigals were left in manuscript until published by his sons at Florence more than twenty years after his death.

Strozzi's book of madrigals was one of the earliest collections of this kind of verse to be made, even though it did not appear in print until many others were in the field. As Strozzi wrote it, and as the madrigal became a popular form of verse or song in the second half of the sixteenth century, it differs widely from the madrigal composed by Petrarch. The difference lies mainly in an assimilation of the later madrigal to the epigram, and represents in a subtle manner the modification of mediaeval forms by a new consciousness of the forms of antiquity.

Strozzi's contact with the Anthology does not appear to have been at first hand. One of his madrigals ultimately comes from *A.P.* 9.346, but there is probably a Latin version intervening.

> Non perdonò quest' empia a' figli suoi;
> E tu folle oggi in grembo le t'annidi,
> E tu stolta le fidi
> Quest' infelici tuoi:
> Fuggi 'l marmo spietato, e i dolci nidi
> Appendi in qualche selva;
> Non ha tale orca il mar, la terra belva.

Strozzi omits to let the reader know that *quest' empia* is Medea.[2]

To this same Strozzi is attributed an epigram on Michelangelo's *Night*, which forms the subject of a famous anecdote in Vasari.[3] That Sorrento has not been able to trace the epigram

---

[1] Strozzi, *Madrigali*, ed. by Luigi Sorrento, Strassburg (Bibliotheca Romanica), 1909.

[2] Another of Strozzi's madrigals echoes *A.P.* 7.669:
> Beato il Ciel, che mille e mille luci
> Ha da quest' una Luce
> Mirar . . . .

[3] *Vita di Michelagnolo*. The epigram is ascribed to Strozzi by editors of Vasari on the authority of the *Notizie degli Uomini Illustri dell' Accademia Fiorentina*, chap. 112.

in manuscript argues nothing against Strozzi's authorship;
which, however, remains uncertain. Vasari says that when the
Night was first exhibited these verses were written upon it:

> La Notte che tu vedi in sì dolci atti
> Dormire, fu da un Angelo scolpita
> In questo sasso, e perchè dorme ha vita:
> Destala se no 'l credi, e parleratti.

When the sculptor, who was a poet, read these perfect lines, he
replied in the person of his statue:

> Grato m' è 'l sonno, e più l'esser di sasso,
> Mentre che 'l danno e la vergogna dura;
> Non veder, non sentir m' è gran ventura;
> Però non mi destar, deh! parla basso.

Possibly, as Grimm has asserted, the first quatrain was suggested by *A.P.* 16.248, an epigram that was fairly well known.[1]
It is by Plato the Younger:

> Τὸν Σάτυρον Διόδωρος ἐκοίμισεν, οὐκ ἐτόρευσεν.
>   ἢν νύξῃς, ἐγερεῖς· ἄργυρος ὕπνον ἔχει.

[The Satyr was put to sleep, not sculptured, by Diodorus. If you prod
him, you will waken him; the silver is asleep.]

BERARDINO ROTA
(1509–1575)
[On Rota and his Latin poetry see above, p. 234.]

In his vernacular poems Rota, as has already been indicated,
was a Petrarchist. We shall not, therefore, expect to find many
explicit borrowings from the Anthology in his *Sonetti et Canzoni*. There are, nevertheless, one or two echoes, the following
lines, for instance, being possibly a manipulation of *A.P.*
16.388:[2]

> Mentre con gli occhi il verde prato ardea
>   Madonna, et hor di questo, hor quel fioretto
>   Tessea ghirlanda a l' aurea testa intorno,
> Amor trovò, che fra' be' fior giacea,
>   Et lo strinse nel crin vago et negletto.
> Quando egli accorto di sì bel soggiorno,
>   Gridò prigion sotto il beato velo:
> 'Habbiasi il ciel chi vuol, questo è il mio cielo.'

---

[1] Hermann Grimm, *Life of Michael Angelo* (Eng. Trans.) 2.498. Grimm's further
assertion that Philostratus, *Imag.* 1.22, was required for the sculptor's reply has less to
recommend it.

[2] Above, p. 146. References are to the 1560 edition of Rota's poems (above, p. 234.)

As one of the interlocutors in Minturno's Italian *Poetica*, Rota is made to suggest the equivalence of the Italian sonnet and 'what the Greeks and Latins call *epigramma*' (above, p. 57). Some of Rota's own sonnets recall the epigrams. There are votive sonnets, as, for example, one addressed to the breezes.[1] Another sonnet closes on an echo of *A.P.* 9.49:[2]

> Qual huom, che in varie guise attende in scena
> Uscir hor l'uno hor l'altro, et meraviglia
> Et exempio ne prende, et si consiglia
> Con gli accidenti altrui, che 'l tempo mena;
> Tal in questa di froda et d'error piena
> Vita mortal. . . .
> Et dico: 'O quanto è ben per chi primo esce
> Dal terreno theatro! . . .
> Dir pò: Speranza a Dio, Fortuna a Dio.'[3]

LODOVICO PATERNO
(*fl.* 1560)

Many histories of Italian literature make some reference to Paterno's poems, but virtually nothing seems to be known of him personally. A very little may be gleaned from his books. He was a Neapolitan. He exchanged sonnets with several well-known poets— Rota, Angelo di Costanzo, Benedetto Varchi, Ferrante Caraffa, Antonio Terminio, and Luigi Tansillo. As a poet he is most often mentioned for his *Satire* (published with those of Ariosto and others by Valvassori, Venice, 1565); but his most serious work was his imitation of Petrarch. In 1560 was published at Venice a book entitled: *Nuovo Petrarca di M. Lodovico Paterno, distinto in quattro parti; la prima e seconda, in Vita e in Morte di M. Mirtia; la terza de' Varij soggetti, e la quarta de' Trionfi.*[4] This attempt at close imitation of Petrarch

---

[1] *Son.*, f. 53ᵛᵒ; *A.P.* 6.53 may be compared.

[2] Above, p. 27. The prevailing figure, however, is that of *A.P.* 10.72.

[3] Possibly the following expressions at the beginning of Rota's third Piscatory Eclogue ought to be compared with *A.P.* 6.26 (*Eglog.*, f. 6ᵛᵒ):

> Da la man mia
> Nel cavernoso et liquido soggiorno
> Staran securi i pesci.

> Ἰχθύες ἀλλὰ νέμοισθε γεγηθότες, ὅττι θαλάσσῃ
> δῶκεν ἔχειν Κινύρου γῆρας ἐλευθερίην.

[Ye fishes, feed joyfully, for Cinyras' old age has granted the sea its freedom].
In *Eglog.*, f. 45ʳᵒ, the line, *Decima del mar Gratia et quarta Musa*, contains a curious transformation: cf. *A.P.* 5.95.

[4] The title, *Nuovo Petrarca* (not given by Paterno), was resented, and changed in the remaining copies of this edition to *Rime*. In a second edition, Naples, 1564, the title is, *La Mirzia*. A third part, *La Mirzia parte terza*, was published at Palermo in 1568. The first edition, to which I shall refer as *Nuov. Pet.*, was edited by Lelio Fortunato, in whose dedication to Philip II Paterno is referred to as 'quel gentile e modesto giovane.' The change of title is explained, from Paterno's own letters, by Crescimbeni, *Volg. Poes.*, Venice, 1730, 2.422.

possibly bears some relation to the similar attempt of Rota (above, p. 234).

Among his sonnets Paterno has at least two echoes of the Anthology. His knowledge may be at second hand. Thus he begins a sonnet with the conceit of *A.P.* 9.523:

> A cantar di Filippo, anzi d'Achille
> Cercate, O sacre Muse, un' altro Homero:
> Chè sotto 'l giusto suo possente impero
> Veggio Oriente pien d'arme e faville.

Again, in the second quatrain of a later sonnet, he repeats the familiar strain:

> O Mandi 'l giusto cielo in questa parte
> Novello Homero a voi, ch' Achille hor siete,
> Il qual, pensando pareggiar, vincete
> D' ardir, di forza, di giudicio, e d' arte.

This Greek epigram evidently was admired in Paterno's coterie inasmuch as it had already done service with his friend Riccio for the praises of Acquaviva.[1]

A year later (1561), also at Venice, was published Paterno's *Nuove Fiamme*, a book of miscellaneous verse.[2] The Anthology is again among his sources. One octave is taken, perhaps by way of Ausonius' Latin, from *A.P.* 16.129:[3]

> Vissi, ma poi mi fer di viva un sasso
> Gl' invitti, audaci figli di Latona:
> Niobe io son, che par si mova il passo,
> Che tocchi e giunga ove 'l desio mi sprona.
> Se tu nol sai, di marmo privo e casso
> D' aura vital, Prassitele mi dona
> Vita, e di pietra mi fà viva e vera:
> Tanto può l'arte, e ch' i' non mai più pera.

Most interesting of Paterno's derivatives from the Anthology is the following sonnet fashioned out of Navagero's imitation of *A.P.* 6.53.[4]

---

[1] Above, p. 309. In *Nuov. Pet.*, p. 459, is a sonnet addressed by Paterno to Riccio, and *ibid.*, p. 618, is Riccio's *risposta*.

[2] *Le Nuove Fiamme di M. Lodovico Paterno, partite in cinque libri: il primo di Sonetti e Canzoni pastorali, il secondo di Stanze, il terzo di Elegie, il quarto di Nenie e Tumuli, et l'ultimo di Egloghe marittime, amorose, lugubre, illustri, e varie.* This is also dedicated by Lelio Fortunato, this time to Don Carlos.

[3] The original is given above, p. 146.

[4] Above, p. 191. A second sonnet of Paterno is also reminiscent of *A.P.* 6.53 (*Nuov. Fiam.*, f. 7ro).

Aure, O Aure, che 'l ciel nudo e sereno
  Cingete con le piume inamorate:
  Et fra le selve dolce mormorate,
  Spargendo i sonni a le fresch' ombre in seno:
Queste ghirlande et questo vaso pieno
  D' amomo et croco, et questi d'odorate
  Viole ampi canestri, a voi sacrate
  Vi dona Alceo, ch' al mezo dì vien meno.
Voi l'arsura temprate homai, che l'onde,
  Et l'aria, e i campi d'ogn' intorno incende,
  Et mostra le sue forze in ogni parte;
E in mentre a ventilar le biade attende,
  Et rocamente al suono Echo risponde,
  Scacciate voi le paglie a parte a parte.

Paterno has echoes of *A.P.* 5.78 (twice), 83; 6.53 (twice); 9.523 (twice); and 16.129. They probably all come to him through Latin versions. From a similar source, probably from Pontano, comes his concept of *Tumuli* (epitaphs), a type of poem that has its roots in the Anthology.

GIAMBATTISTA GIRALDI CINTIO

[Cf. above, p. 227.]

Giraldi's *Hecatommithi*, or hundred novels, is one of the more successful Renaissance imitations of the *Decameron* of Boccaccio. It was first published at Monte Regale in 1565. The stories are drawn from the most diverse sources; and one, the eighth novel of the ninth decade, from the Anthology, *A.P.* 44 or 45. I give 9.44, which has been ascribed to Plato:

$$\text{Χρυσὸν ἀνὴρ εὑρὼν ἔλιπε βρόχον· αὐτὰρ ὁ χρυσόν}$$
$$\text{ὃν λίπεν οὐχ εὑρὼν ἦψεν ὃν εὗρε βρόχον.}$$

[A man finding gold, left his rope; but the one who left the gold, not finding it, hanged himself by the rope which he found.]

This *tour de force* of brevity is expanded by Giraldi into a novel of some 5400 words. His story is lively, and is provided with a happy ending.[1] The following is a summary of the novel, which is supposed to be told by a lady named Virginia:

When Scipio was besieging Carthage, Chera, a rich Carthaginian

---

[1] The argument reads as follows: 'Chera nasconde un thesoro, Elisa è per impiccarsi per la gola: e nel annodare un capestro ad una trave, ritrova il nascosto thesoro; et toltolo vi lascia il capestro; Filene, figliuola di Chera, va per pigliare il thesoro e ritrovatovi il laccio, si vuole con esso impiccare; è aitata da Elisa, et ristorata in parte del danno vive felice.'

widow, concealed at the end of a rafter in her house a treasure consisting of gold and jewels. The city falling, she was compelled to make
a hasty escape to Sicily with her little daughter Filene; and her house
passed into the hands of a Roman soldier. The soldier had a daughter
named Elisa.

On her deathbed Chera told Filene how to recover the treasure, and
gave her a paper with writing on it to correspond with a paper attached to the gold. As Filene was in love with a powerful Sicilian, who
disdained her because of her poverty, she determined to go to Carthage after her inheritance.

Meantime at Carthage Elisa was in the same predicament; she
was in love with a rich man, who disdained the poor soldier's daughter.
In despair she took a rope and went to an empty room in her father's
house prepared to hang herself. In fastening the halter to a beam she
dislodged the treasure. Concealing the rope where the treasure had
been, she carried the gold to her father; and soon after was married
to the man she desired. Father and daughter took care to conceal the
origin of their riches.

Filene now arrives in Carthage disguised as a youth, and takes
service in the soldier's neighborhood. She becomes familiar with his
house, and finds an opportunity to visit the room where the treasure
was left. To her dismay she finds there only the rope abandoned by
Elisa; with this she prepares to hang herself. But her half-stifled
lament is heard by Elisa, who comes, learns her story, and brings
her to her father and husband. The latter, a Carthaginian, will do
nothing to help Filene, but the Roman soldier, reverencing Fortune,
offers to restore her treasure. As he has already doubled it by invest-
ment, his daughter will not be deprived of her dowry. This Filene refuses to accept. Finally a solution is hit on by Elisa, whereby Filene
is to be regarded as her sister. The haughty Sicilian, too, is induced to
come to Carthage and marry Filene.

'Great was the amazement that arose in the minds of those who
heard this tale, . . . but, seeing the fortunes of both parties brought into
such felicity, they all remained exceedingly content.'

LODOVICO CASTELVETRO

(1505–1571)

Castelvetro was born into a noble family of Modena. He was carefully educated, attended the universities of Bologna, Ferrara, Padua,
and Siena—in that order—and to please his father took the degree of
Doctor of Laws at Siena. Poor health compelled him to retire to
Modena, where he became an active encourager of literature. In 1553
began his bitter quarrel with Annibale Caro, arising out of Castelvetro's criticism of Caro's *canzone: Venite a l'ombra de' gran gigli
d'oro;* in the course of this controversy each was charged with attempting to get the other murdered. Already in 1542 Castelvetro,
with the rest of the Academy of Modena, had been obliged to sign a

formulary protesting orthodoxy in matters of faith. In 1557 the persecution was renewed. Castelvetro is thought to have taken refuge in Ferrarese territory. At any rate he soon appeared at Rome for the purpose of clearing himself. He was specifically charged with having translated a work of Melanchthon. After several examinations, learning that the decision was likely not to favor him, he made his escape from detention, and by night fled from Rome. He found a haven at Chiavenna. Together with his brother Giovanni Maria, who thus suffered for aiding his escape, Castelvetro was condemned and excommunicated as a hardened heretic (1561). Later he applied for permission to present himself to the Council of Trent for justification; the pope required him to come to Rome. Instead Castelvetro withdrew to Lyons. He was now busy with his Commentary on Aristotle's *Poetics*. At Lyons he was persecuted; his house was set on fire, on which occasion the scholar was only heard to cry: 'Save my *Poetics*!' He was obliged to leave Lyons. He went to Geneva, and then followed his brother to the Court of Maximilian II. His *Poetics* is dedicated to Maximilian. The plague soon drove him from Vienna; and he returned to Chiavenna, where he died. The charge of heresy is said to have been quite unfounded.

After Castelvetro's *Poetics* (Vienna, 1570) his best-known work is a commentary on the Italian poems of Petrarch: *Le Rime del Petrarca brevemente sposte*, Basel, 1582.[1] The numerous similarities of thought and imagery that exist between the love-poems of the Anthology and the sonnets of Petrarch, and the commonplace of criticism whereby the sonnet of the Italians was regarded as the counterpart of the epigram of the Greeks, might easily have suggested to a commentator on Petrarch the notion of illustrating his poems by quotations from Meleager, Paulus Silentiarius, and their like. Yet Castelvetro is the only commentator on Petrarch to do anything of the sort. He quotes more from the Anthology than from any other Greek book. For example, he illustrates the imagery of two lines in *Son.* 3 by a couplet of Meleager (*A.P.* 12.113):[2]

> Quand' io fui preso, e non me ne guardai
> Che i be' vostri occhi, Donna, mi legaro.

> Καὐτὸς Ἔρως ὁ πτανὸς ἐν αἰθέρι δέσμιος ἧλω
> τοῖς σοῖς ἀγρευθεὶς ὄμμασι, Τιμάριον.

With Sonnet 5 Castelvetro prints *A.P.* 5.292 entire, adding

---

[1] A second edition, 2 vols, fol., was printed by Zatta, Venice, 1756.

[2] Long before this, in his criticism of Caro, he had quoted this epigram for an example of a well-formed metaphor (*Ragioni d'alcune cose segnate nella Canzone di Messer Annibal Caro*, Venice, 1560, f. 73ro). He there translated it: 'Et esso Amore alato in aere fu fatto prigione essendo stato co tuoi occhi irrietito, Timaria.'

no comment. The parallel is not without interest, though the similarities are, of course, only general. With two exceptions Castelvetro's quotations from the Anthology are confined to the first part of the *Rime*. He finds no parallels between the Greek epigrams and the poems on the death of Laura. If this represents a preconception on his part, he misjudged the Anthology; for it would be easy to illustrate the second part of the *Rime* from the epigrams with at least as good parallels as those he hits on for the first part.[1] He finds two illustrations in the Anthology for passages in the *Trionfi*.[2]

In a list of books once owned by Castelvetro, drawn from the archives of Modena by Sandonnini, a volume entitled '*Epigrammata Graeca*' duly appears. There are no means of telling what edition it was.[3]

The following imitation of *A.P.* 16.174 was printed in 1781 by Tiraboschi from a manuscript of sixteenth-century epigrams by Modenese writers, belonging to Giambattista Vicini (below, p. 396).[4]

EX GRAECO

Spartanam ut vidit Venerem Bellona: 'Quid, inquit,
    Arma haec imbelli corpore, Cypri, geris?'
Cui Venus: 'Armipotens tu scilicet una Dearum?
    Sunt etiam Paphiae, sunt sua bella Deae.'

FRANCESCO BECCUTI (IL COPPETTA)

(1509–1553)

Francesco Beccuti, known as Il Coppetta, came from an ancient and noble family of Perugia. After the usual course in *litterae humaniores*, he studied law, in which he attained the doctorate and a professorship. He was soon drawn into the service of the State, and in 1548 fulfilled a mission on behalf of Perugia to the Cardinal of Urbino. Besides his diplomatic services, he acted as governor successively of Casa Castalda, Sassoferrato, and Norcia, and had been elected governor of Foligno at the time of his death. He was buried at Perugia in

---

[1] E.g., compare *Son.* 242 and Meleager's epigram on the death of Heliodora (*A.P.* 7.476).

[2] Castelvetro's quotations are as follows (page-numbers refer to the 1582 edition): *A.P.* 5.210 (*Canz.* 20, p. 359), 223 (*Sest.* 7, p. 406), 225 (*Canz.* 3, p. 69), 229 (*Son.* 138, p. 314), 268 (*Giud. del. Trion. della Cast.*, pt. 2, p. 248), 292 (*Son.* 10, p. 27), 297 (*Son.* 211, p. 421); 7.15 (*Trion. d'Amor.* 3, pt. 2, p. 231), 243 (*Canz.* 2, p. 67), 262 (*Son.* 186, p. 384), 344.3 (*Canz.* 2, p. 66), 383 (*Sest.* 1, p. 40); 11.81 (*Canz.* 3, p. 69); 12.113 (*Son.* 3, p. 17); 16.81 (*Son.* 57, p. 159), 135 (*Son.* 144, p. 320), 221 (*Canz.* 2, p. 66).

[3] Tommaso Sandonnini, *Lodovico Castelvetro e la sua Famiglia*, Bologna, 1882, p. 320.

[4] Tiraboschi, *Biblioteca Modenese* 1.481.

S. Francesco de' Conventuali. The first collective edition of Il Coppetta's *Rime* was printed at Venice in 1580.[1]

A sonnet written by Beccuti in the last year of his life 'On the Death of Francesco Colombo, called Plato,' is composed of the Platonic epigrams on Aster (*A.P.* 7.669–70):[2]

> Stella gentil, ch' a la tua stella unita
>   Lei vagheggi e te stessa e l'altre erranti,
>   Fossi cielo io, che con tanti occhi e tanti
>   Vedrei la chiara tua luce infinita.
> Eri fra noi la stella alma e gradita
>   Ch' in oriente al sol fiammeggia innanti;
>   Espero or sei, ch'i tuoi bei raggi santi
>   Nascondi a questa e scopri a l'altra vita.
> O divin Plato! io non mille occhi e mille
>   Chieggio, ma d' esser talpa, acciò non miri
>   La fiera stella che m'è data in sorte;
> La quale, o poggi in alto o in basso giri,
>   Par ch' irata ver' me sempre sfaville,
>   Quasi nuovo Orione, e guerra e morte.

In the first quatrain he employs the conceit of *A.P.* 7.669, in the second that of 7.670; in the sestet he returns to 7.669 in order to revoke the wish expressed in the first quatrain.

GIAMBATTISTA POSSEVINO

(1520–1549)

The questions in moral philosophy raised by the practice of dueling long engaged the attention of Italian writers in the sixteenth century. Among the numerous treatises on the subject, special interest has attached to the *Dialogo dell' Honore* of Giambattista Possevino, elder brother of the well-known writer Antonio Possevino. The Possevini were natives of Mantua, and were protected by Cardinal Ercole di Gonzaga. As a page in the family of this great man, Giovanni Battista received an excellent education; thence he passed as secretary into the service first of Cardinal Cortese and later of Cardinal Ippolito d'Este. A letter from Bernardino Maffei to Paolo Giovio, September 14, 1545 (quoted by Tiraboschi, *Stor.* 7.2.67), when Possevino was in Rome in the house of Cardinal Cortese, gives evidence of the young man's remarkable learning in languages and archaeology, but speaks of

---

[1] My references are to *G. Giudiccione e F. Coppetta Beccuti, Rime*, ed. by Ezio Chiorboli, Bari, 1912. Beccuti imitates Ausonius' version of *A.P.* 7.311.

[2] Francesco Colombo of Perugia was a philosopher and physician. He attempted to imitate Plato in his lectures and writings, and received the name 'Plato' from Cardinal Marcello Cervio (later Pope Marcellus II), who admired him. The name was kept in his family long after his death. He died in 1553, leaving many philosophical works and a *De Re Medica*.

him as 'figliuolo della melancolia.' He died at Rome at the age of twenty-nine. His only book was edited by his brother.

The *Dialogo dell' Honore* first appeared at Venice in 1553.[1] The speakers are Possevino himself and Giberto di Correggio. Antonio Bernardi, author of a Latin work against dueling printed only in 1562, asserted that he had lent his manuscript, already completed, to Possevino, who had made undue use of it in his Dialogue. There appear to be grounds for the charge; but it must not be forgotten that Possevino did not himself publish his work.[2]

The argument of the Dialogue is pointed from time to time with citations from the ancient poets. In Book IV the question is raised: In what does the nobility of cities consist? and answered: In the excellent men they produce. Then follow citations of the ancients, among which is a version of *A.P.* 7.139, an anonymous epigram. 'Et quel Poeta Greco dice:

> Troia con Hettor cadde, ne difesa
> Alcuna contra Greci mai più fece.
> Pella con Alessandro; il che ben mostra
> Che i cittadin danno alla patria fama,
> Non la cittade pregio a i cittadini.'

COSTANZO LANDI
[Cf. above, p. 242]

LUCA ANTONIO RIDOLFI
(*fl.* 1550)

Ridolfi was a merchant and literary man, resident for the greater part of his life in Lyons. He edited the *Decameron*, with a life of Boccaccio, Lyons, 1555; the *Canzoniere* of Petrarch, *ibid.*, 1574; and published a *Ragionamento* on passages of the *Cento Novelle* (1557), a similar work on passages of Dante and Petrarch (1560), and a dialogue entitled *Aretefila* (1560), all at Lyons. Campori records a conjecture of Moreni that he was the son of Giovan Francesco Ridolfi, born in 1510, and elected senator in 1570.[3] He was a friend of Varchi.

The *Aretefila* of Ridolfi is addressed to Francesco d'Alessandro Nasi of Venice. In the Dialogue, as the title-page

---

[1] Other editions: 1556, 1558, 1564; I employ the 1553 edition.
[2] Tiraboschi, *loc. cit.* note (a).
[3] *Lettere di Scrittori Italiani del Secolo xvi*, ed. by Giuseppe Campori ('Scelta di Curiosità Letterarie' 157), Bologna, 1877, p. 308. Campori published five letters by Ridolfi, and refers to others in the collection of Paolo Manuzio.

announces, 'reasons are adduced, on the one hand to prove that the love of corporeal beauty may reach the heart by means of the sense of hearing, and on the other to prove that its entrance is only through the eyes; at the end a decision is pronounced on the question.' Towards the close, the discussion turns on the means of putting an end to love, and mention is made of various remedies proposed by the poets, and finally that of Luigi Alamanni in an epigram till then unpublished.[1] On this epigram the following comment is made: 'L'epigramma è bellissimo, disse Aretefila, si come sono tutte le composizioni di quel gentilissimo autore, e i remedij sono in maggior parte quegli che Crate Tebano dava a gl' innamorati, dicendo loro, che la fame e il tempo giovava a cacciare tal passione, ma che non potendo usare tali cose, ricorressero al laccio per finire in un tratto tal malattia.'[2]

ANTONIO SEBASTIANO MINTURNO
[Cf. above, p. 232.]

Minturno's *Panegirico in Laude d'Amore* is a prose work interspersed with poems; it is included in his *Rime* of 1559.[3] Among these verses are four imitations of the Greek epigrams— *A.P.* 5.64, 89, 131; and 10.29. The following lines are made in imitation, as he says of 'l'ingegnoso Asclepiade' (*A.P.* 5.64):

Folgora, tona pur, nevica, piovi,
Mostra ciel quanto puoi per l'aria oscura,
E tutto il mondo sotto sopra movi,
Ch' io già non ho del tuo Signor paura:
Chi vince me, vinse anco tutti i Giovi.
E se m' ancidi, non però non dura
L'alto furor, che mai non sarà fine
A l'amorose mie fiamme divine.

In his *Rime* proper Minturno employs *A.P.* 5.95, 180, 225, 268, and 9.357. *A.P.* 5.180 he treats as follows:

Qual cosa nova o strana
S' Amor piagne e s'adira,
E coi begli occhi lega, incende, e tira?

---

[1] The epigram (Raffaelle 2.140) is listed in the Register as an imitation of *A.P.* 9.497.

[2] Crates, *A.P.* 9.497: 'Hunger causes love to cease—if not hunger, time; but if these fail to quench the flame, then the only cure you have left is to hang yourself.'

[3] *Rime et Prose . . . nuovamente mandate in luce* [ed. by G. Ruscelli]. Venice, 1559.

Non nacque la costui vezzosa madre
Ne l'onde? non è padre
Di lei l'ardente cielo, e caro amico
Marte, e già sposo antico
Vulcano? Or le catene e' il cieco ardore
Ha di Vulcano Amore,
Le saette e'l furore
Di Marte, e 'l pianto, e l'ira
Del mare, e la celeste fiamma spira.

The *De Poeta* of Minturno was issued by him in an Italian form as *L'Arte Poetica* in 1563. The references to the Anthology remain virtually as they were in the Latin version; *A.P.* 7.153 is put into Italian verse, but the epigram of Parmenio is not given at all. In the Italian *Poetics* Minturno introduces his discussion of the differences between the sonnet and the epigram, which naturally found no place in the Latin treatise.[1] As he had advised the modern Latin epigrammatist to imitate the Greeks rather than the Romans, so he advises the Italian epigrammatist.[2]

In a letter addressed to the Marchesana della Padula, written at Naples, August 2, 1536, Minturno compliments his correspondent on her study of Greek, borrowing terms from *A.P.* 5.95:[3] 'Ella è fra noi un' altra Pallade, un' altra Venere, e la quarta Gratia; così sia la decima Musa.'

LODOVICO GUICCIARDINI

(1521–1589)

Lodovico was a nephew of the Florentine historian Francesco Guicciardini. He was variously employed by Alessandro de' Medici and his successor Cosimo. Then, for reasons unknown, he left Florence, and ended a period of travel by settling in Antwerp. Here he at first enjoyed the favor of the Duke of Alva, but a criticism of Alva's administration, expressed in one of his books, caused his imprisonment, from which he was only released upon the intercession of the Grand Duke of Tuscany. Thereafter apparently he continued to reside quietly in Antwerp. His *Commentarii* (1560) dealt with contemporary Dutch history; his *Memorie* (1565) were in part a continuation of his uncle's *History;* his *Descrizione* (1567) again dealt with the Netherlands, and was translated into French, German, and Latin. A

[1] See above, pp. 57, and 62–3. References to the Italian version are to *L'Arte Poetica del Signor Antonio Minturno*, Naples, 1725.
[2] Above, p. 63, n. 2.
[3] *Lettere di Messer Antonio Minturno*, Venice, 1549, f. 178.

volume of a lighter character was published in Venice in 1565, entitled: *Detti et Fatti Piacevoli et Gravi di Diversi Principi, Filosofi, et Cortigiani;* and was reissued with slight changes at Antwerp in 1568 under a new title: *Hore di Recreatione.*[1] In the new book some sections of the earlier are omitted, and there are other slight differences, but in the bulk of contents the two are identical.

The book consists of short anecdotes or sentences drawn from history, literature, or the author's experience; they have chiefly a moral significance. Some of these instances are drawn from the Anthology, but not always at first hand. *A.P.* 9.148 comes to Guicciardini from Alciati:[2]

L'humane operationi da una banda esser degne di riso, dall' altra di pianto.

Heraclito et Democrito erano due filosofi famosissimi. Questo considerando le pazzie de gli huomini, sempre rideva, quello, considerando le lor miserie, sempre piangeva. Or a questo proposito volendo l'Alciato dimostrare, che la vita humana, se ne va sempre di male in peggio, fece sopra ciò questi piacevoli versi:

> Più dell' usato, Heraclito, ti veggio
> Pianger gli affanni dell' humana vita;
> Perchè ella se ne va di mal in peggio,
> Et la miseria homai fatta è infinita.
> Te, Democrito, ancor più rider veggio,
> Che non solevi, et la tua man m'addita,
> Che le pazzie son maggiori intanto,
> Che non è pari il riso et meno il pianto.

Guicciardini has translated the verses of *Emblem* 152 (above, p. 204).

Guicciardini's *Detti et Fatti* appeared in the same year as Giraldi Cintio's *Hecatommithi*, a book not altogether dissimilar in kind. Giraldi, as we have seen, there makes a long story out of *A.P.* 9.44 or 45. Guicciardini has the following anecdote on the same theme:[3]

Marcantonio Battistei havendo perduti cinquecento scudi sopra una nave sommersa, se n'andava come disperato per impiccarsi. Ma volendo attaccare la corda ad una trave, vi trovò dentro per sorte mille scudi riposti; onde tutto rasserenato et lieto se gli prese et in quel cambio lasciato il capestro andò via. Or ecco non molto dipoi il padrone de' danari, ilquale per vedergli, et maneggiargli alquanto

---

[1] I use the *Detti et Fatti* of 1565 and the *Hore* of 1598. Though virtually identical the two books went through many editions side by side; see the catalogues of the British Museum and the Bibliothèque Nationale. A French translation of the *Hore* appeared in 1571, and was three times reprinted; an English translation by James Sandford was printed in 1576: *Houres of Recreation or Afterdinners.*

[2] *Detti* (1565), f. 106ro; *Hore* (1598), p. 168.

[3] *Detti* (1565), f. 3ro; cf. Giraldi, above, p. 315.

veniva. Imperò non gli trovando, et in luogo loro veggendo il capestro, fu vinto da tanto dolore, che senza più oltre, s'appiccò con esso.

Giraldi's story and this one have a detail in common which is not from the Greek, namely the rafter where the treasure was hidden. As Guicciardini makes no pretense of originality, and could have written the anecdote on very short notice, he may have taken the hint from Giraldi. The anecdote has disappeared from the *Hore di Recreatione*.

If Guicciardini did not know the Anthology at first hand, he probably knew one of the collections like that of Soter. For an account of misers he borrows three epigrams:[1]

Hermone fu tanto avaro (secondo attesta Lucilio) che sognando egli di havere spesi certi danari, si strangolò per eccessivo dolore da se medesimo [*A.P.* 11.264]. Dinarco Fidone [*sic*] fu similmente sì avaro, che essendosi egli disperato, per certa perdita ricevuta, lasciò d'impiccarsi, per non spendere sei quattrini in un pezzo di corda, cercando la morte a miglior mercato [*A.P.* 11.169]. Et Hermocrate fu per istrema avaritia, accompagnata di tanta stoltitia, che morendosi lasciò herede di tutti i suoi beni sè medesimo [*A.P.* 11.171]. Onde saggiamente disse Biante, che la avaritia è Metropoli della pazzia, et della malvagità de gli huomini.[2]

STEFANO GUAZZO

(1530–1593)

Guazzo was born at Casale, the capital of Monferrato; his father Giovanni had been treasurer to the Dukes of Mantua. Stefano received a legal training; and on several occasions acted as ambassador for Duke Guglielmo Gonzaga of Monferrato—once to Spain, and once to Pius V. He early retired, however, from official duties, devoting himself instead to literary pursuits, and in particular to the re-establishment at Casale of the Academy of the *Illustrati*, of which under the name of *l'Elevato* he was himself the chief ornament. He was twice happily married. For the purpose of advancing the legal studies of his son Antonio, he removed to Pavia in 1589. He was welcomed in that city, and made a member of the Academy of the *Affidati*, whose president he later became. He died at Pavia.

The writings of Guazzo were admired in his time all over Europe as models of style and courtliness. Here we have to speak of three of them, two of which were among his most

---

[1] *Detti* (1565), f. 105[vo]; *Hore* (1598), p. 168.
[2] In all, Guicciardini employs the following epigrams (in the Register *Detti* is referred to in the 1565 ed. and *Hore* in the 1598): *A.P.* 9.44 (or 45), 111, 130, 148, 331, 497; 11.169, 171, 264.

famous works; these are *La Civil Conversazione* (Brescia, 1574) and *Dialoghi Piacevoli* (Venice, 1586). The third was posthumous: *La Ghirlanda della Contessa Angela Bianca Beccaria* (Genoa, 1595).

Most of Guazzo's translations from the Anthology are in the *Dialoghi* and the *Ghirlanda*. The second is described as a 'contesta di madrigali di diversi autori, raccolti e dichiarati dal sig. Stefano Guazzi ... ove s'introducono diverse persone a ragionare nella prima giornata delle frondi, nella seconda de' fiori, e nella terza de' frutti intrecciati in essa Ghirlanda.' The very name *Ghirlanda* could have been suggested by the Anthology (*Florilegium*); and in turn probably gave the hint for the more celebrated *Guirlande de Julie*.[1] At all events Guazzo has woven into his garland translations of six of our epigrams: *A.P.* 9.331; 11.23, 237, 398; 16.68, and 171. In citing *A.P.* 11.23 he gives the sense of the first line in his introductory words, and translates lines 5–6: 'Un Greco scrittore, poichè dall' astrologo gli fù annonciata la brevità della vita, disse:[2]

> Poi che m'appresso al fin, vò darmi al bere,
> Et così Baccho a me farà il destriere,
> Per portarmi a Pluton veloce e presto,
> U' fora il gir a piè troppo molesto.

In the *Dialoghi* Guazzo employs *A.P.* 5.95; 7.23; 9.44; 10.112; 11.193, 294 (Alamanni).[3] For 11.193 he writes:

> Giustissima è l'invidia, che l'autore
> Tosto punisce, e li consuma il core.

In Guazzo's best-known work, his *Civil Conversazione*, there are three quotations from the Anthology: *A.P.* 7.314; 9.13 (after Alamanni); and 11.408.6. Each is given in translation. Only the first is complete, the last being only a single line—yet even this single line served to transmit the thought of the epigram to the English annalist Stow.[4]

---

[1] Guazzo could not have known about the *Stephanos* of Meleager.
[2] The poet is Antipater of Sidon:

> Ὠκύμορόν με λέγουσι δαήμονες ἀνέρες ἄστρων·
>   εἰμὶ μέν, ἀλλ' οὔ μοι τοῦτο, Σέλευκε, μέλει.
> εἰς ἀΐδην μία πᾶσι καταίβασις· εἰ δὲ ταχίων
>   ἡμετέρη, Μίνω θᾶσσον ἐποψόμεθα.
> πίνωμεν· καὶ δὴ γὰρ ἐτήτυμον, εἰς ὁδὸν ἵππος
>   οἶνος, ἐπεὶ πεζοῖς ἀτραπὸς εἰς ἀΐδην.

[3] The version of 9.44 is founded on Alamanni's translation of the same epigram.
[4] There were two French translations of the *Civil Conversazione* published in 1579—one by Gabriel Chappuys at Lyons, and the other, independently, by François de Belle-

GIAMBATTISTA GUARINI
(1538–1612)

The author of the *Pastor Fido* belonged to the family established
in Ferrara by his ancestor Guarino da Verona. He studied law at
Padua; but in 1557 became professor of rhetoric and poetry at
Ferrara. About this time he married. In 1564 he went to Padua, where
he was elected to the *Accademia degli Eterei*, and became a friend of
Tasso. Three years later he returned to Ferrara to the Court of Alfonso
II; he performed a number of diplomatic missions. After the death of
Pigna (above, p. 247) and the restraint of Tasso, Guarini enjoyed un-
divided honor at the ducal Court, but seems to have grown tired of it,
retiring to his villa *La Guarina*. In 1585 Alfonso recalled him to become his secretary. In the same year the *Pastor Fido* was represented
for the first time at Milan. Soon Guarini again abandoned Ferrara,
and lived successively at Venice, Florence, and Turin, returning to
La Guarina in 1589. The following year his wife died; and the next
fourteen years saw him a wanderer in various parts of Italy. He was
unfortunate in his domestic life mostly as a result of his irascibility
(below, p. 359); and his frequent removals reflect this. Even in 1504
his return to Ferrara was not final; he later went to Rome, where he
was president of the *Umoristi* in 1611; and he died in 1612 at Venice.

Guarini shows no direct knowledge of the Anthology; but he
was plunged in the stream of the literary tradition of his age
too completely to miss its influence altogether. In the *Pastor
Fido* (first printed in 1590), one or two conceits, by this time
well-worn, ultimately go back to Greek epigrams. The conceit
of the Platonic epigram *A.P.* 5.78 is reproduced in the following words spoken by Mirtillo:[1]

> Su queste labbra, Ergasto,
> Tutta sen venne allor l'anima mia;
> E la mia vita, chiusa
> In così breve spazio,
> Non era altro che un bacio.

forest at Paris. Chappuys' version was reprinted at Lyons in 1580, and again in 1592;
Belleforest's at Paris in 1590, and again at Geneva in 1598. The translations from the
Anthology are given in verse. A Latin version by George Salmuth, printed opposite
the Italian text, appeared at Strassburg in 1614; *De Civili Conversatione Domini
Stephani Guazzi libri quatuor.* Here the verse-translations (pp. 12, 30, 420) are turned
into prose. What seems to be a second Latin translation was printed at Leyden in 1650:
Stephani Guazzi de Civili Conversatione Dissertationes Politicae . . . ab Elia Reusnero.
This I have not seen. There is a Dutch translation by Gomes van Triere: *Van den
Heuschen Burgerlycken Ommegangh,* Alckmaer, 1603. The English version was by George
Pettie (after the French of Chappuys): *The Civile Conversation of M. Steeven Guazzo,*
London, 1581 (three books only, the fourth, translated by Bartholomew Young, being
added in the second edition, 1586; the whole is reprinted in the 'Tudor Translations,'
2 vols. London, 1925).

[1] Act 2, sc. 1. *Il Pastor Fido e il Compendio della Poesia Tragicomica,* ed. by Gioa-
chino Brognoligo, Bari, 1914, p. 52.

The same conceit recurs in the chorus at the end of the second act. The long passage with the responses of Echo (Act 4, sc. 8) is an elaborate example of the device introduced into vernacular verse by Politian, probably with a Greek epigram for model (above, p. 77).[1]

Guarini's *Rime* appeared at Venice in 1598, and consists of two parts—106 sonnets and 150 madrigals, with the addition of two short sets of octaves. Here, again, few of the poems are imitative, but most of them are made up of well-turned commonplaces. Among the poems that are imitations, three come from Theocritus, one is translated from a couplet of Ausonius on Dido, and one—Madrigal 53—is ultimately derived from *A.P.* 5.94.2–3.[2]

> Felice chi vi mira,
> Ma più felice chi per voi sospira,
> Felicissimo poi
> Chi sospirando fa sospirar voi.
> Ben hebbe amica stella
> Chi per donna si bella
> Può far contento in un' l'occhio e 'l desio,
> E sicuro può dir, 'Quel core è mio.'

GIOVAN TOMMASO CAVAZZA

(1540–1611)

In the *Galatina Letterata* of Alessandro Tommaso Arcudi (Genoa, 1709, p. 47) is a notice of Cavazza, whose papers had come into the hands of the author. He gives a list of the unpublished works of Cavazza, among which he mentions 'Gli Epigrammi Greci Tradotti in Verso Italiano.'[3]

---

[1] The words of Dorinda (Act 2, sc. 2):

> Giugni agli omeri l'ali
> Sarai novo Cupido,

recall *A.P.* 12.75–78; but these epigrams were not known in Guarini's day; cf. Machiavelli, above, p. 296, n. 1.

[2] The theme of *Mad.* 105 may be compared with *A.P.* 5.68, and that of *Mad.* 79 with *A.P.* 5.81.

[3] My information is entirely derived from the notice of Arcudi's book given in the *Giornale de' Letterati d'Italia* 18.287–288 (Venice, 1714). Cavazza was a native of Galatina, and was buried there, in the convent of the Predicatori, Santa Maria delle Grazie. He knew Latin, Greek, and Hebrew, and was versed in philosophy and theology. Of his numerous writings in Latin and Italian the only one published was a letter at the end of Giammichele Marziano's translation of Antonio Galateo's history of the taking of Otranto.

LUIGI GROTO (CIECO D'ADRIA)

(1541–1585)

In his day Groto enjoyed a European reputation. He was born of a noble family at Adria in Venetia, and, he tells us, became blind when eight days old. Unluckily we know little of his early life or of his education; but he must have been remarkably precocious, with his handicap, since he was chosen by the Venetians in 1556, when he was fourteen, to deliver the address of welcome to the Queen of Poland, and again in the same year to make an address at the installation of the Doge Lorenzo Priuli.[1] In 1565 when the Academy of the *Illustrati* was formed at Adria, Groto became its first president. In 1570 he lectured at Bologna. Himself the author of tragedies, he took the part of Oedipus in the version of Sophocles' *Oedipus Rex* prepared by Orsatto Giustiniani and presented at the carnival of 1585 at Vicenza. In September of that year he died.

Groto's verse already shows many of the vices of style that later insured the success of Marino and his school. In the early seventeenth century his work was known in England. Lady Politic Would-be in *Volpone* had read him:

> Which of your poets? Petrarch or Tasso or Dante?
> Guarini? Ariosto? Aretine?
> Cieco di Hadria? I have read them all.

Groto's *Adriana* was the first tragedy to be composed on the theme of Bandello's novel of Romeo and Juliet, and it has been suggested that Shakespeare had read it.[2] *Volpone* was performed in 1605 or 1606. Francis Davison's *Poetical Rhapsody* (1602) contains a section of Inscriptions, translated (without acknowledgment) from Groto.[3] One of these comes ultimately from the Anthology. Drummond of Hawthornden also borrows from him.[4]

The Greek epigrams play an important rôle in Groto's *Rime*.[5] It is, in fact, in his and the succeeding generation of vernacular poets that they are most in evidence, enjoying an influence such as they had only enjoyed among the Latin poets of the time of Leo X. Even when Groto does not imitate any given epigram,

---

[1] These facts are all well-attested, coming from the orations in question. See Tiraboschi, *Storia* 7.3.3.58. Groto's teachers were Scipione Gesualdo de' Belligni of Naples and Celio Calcagnini—the latter, as Tiraboschi notes, not the Ferrarese scholar (above, p. 178), who died in the year of Groto's birth.

[2] Chiarini, *Studi Shakespeariani*, Leghorn, 1893, p. 243.

[3] Noticed by J. M. Thomson in Bullen's edition.

[4] See *Poetical Works*, ed. by Kastner, 1913, 1.167.

[5] The first volume of Groto's *Rime*, published in 1577, was reprinted in 1587. My references are to this edition, Venice, 1587, and to *Rime, parte terza*, ibid. 1610. I have not seen the *Rime* of 1592. Besides these lyrical poems he wrote several plays and pastorals. In 1570 he published a translation of the first Iliad; his *Orazioni* appeared in 1585 (reprinted 1602); and his *Lettere* were published in 1601.

his manner and theme often recall the Greek. Many of his epigrams are imagined to be for works of sculpture, recalling the
fourth book of the Planudean Anthology, and looking forward to
the *Galleria* of Marino. Among these he introduces a version of
A.P. 16.129:

> Fui Niobbe, indi in sasso mi cangiai.
> Poi da man di scoltor dotto scolpita
> Quasi tornando a vita,
> Niobbe un' altra volta diventai.
> E i' ho questo di più, che sendo sasso,
> Del mio dolor primiero ho il petto casso.

The blind poet translates two epigrams that refer to the blind—
A.P. 9.11 and 46. The sonnet-form is new for the well-worn
theme of the first of these; it is a triumph of repetition:

CIECO E ZOPPO

> Su gli homeri d'un cieco un zoppo ascende,
> Così 'l cieco camina, il zoppo vede.
> Il zoppo presta l'occhio, il cieco il piede;
> Ciascun quel ch' ei non ha da l'altro prende.
> Ciascun l' ufficio ben prestato rende;
> L'un mira e insegna, l'altro rege e incede.
> La fatica del premio a par procede;
> Quel che un non ha riceve, e quel che ha, spende.
> Fan duo corpi imperfetti un corpo intero,
> Poichè un col passo altrui qual cervo corre,
> Vede un con l'occhio altrui come cervero;
> Ciascun soccorso vien, mentre socorre.
> Il zoppo mostra, il cieco fa il sentero.
> Così per seminar ciascun può corre.

It will be noticed in the ensuing list of Groto's borrowings
that the amatory epigrams begin with him to excite more attention. Most of his translations are in the form of madrigals, as is
the following version of *A.P.* 5.97:

> Amor, se pur sei Dio,
> Dei esser giusto parimente e pio:
> Se giusto, perchè sol contra me scocchi,
> E madonna non tocchi?
> Se pio, perchè perdoni
> A lei, e a me ti apponi?
> Hor sù, se nome vuoi fra i veri Dei,
> Lei meco impiaga, o me sana con lei.

In all, he employs *A.P.* 5.68, 69, 83+84, 94 (?), 95, 97, 230, 236;

7.*64*, *311*, *396*, 669; 9.11, *17* (cf. *18*), 30, 34, *44*, 46, 56, 109, 126 (2 versions), 152, 397, 442, 591 (?), 727+734; 16.*14*, 81, 107, 129, 151 (?), *160*, 174, *178*, *196*, *222*, 295 (cf. 296).[1]

TORQUATO TASSO
(1544–1595)

When Tasso was seven years old, he was taken by his mother from Sorrento, where he was born, to Naples. His father, the poet Bernardo Tasso, had been obliged to follow the Prince of Salerno, his patron, into exile in France. Torquato's first teachers were the Jesuits of Naples. In 1552 the elder Tasso, venturing to return as far as Rome, summoned his son to him; and in Rome the boy began the serious study of Latin and Greek. In 1561 he was sent to study at Padua, but migrated to Bologna the year following, just after the publication of his *Rinaldo*. In consequence of a lampoon, which he seems to have written, he fled in 1564 to Mantua, where his father now served the Gonzaghi; and ultimately took his degree at Padua. He immediately (1565) entered the service of Cardinal Luigi d'Este, to whom he had dedicated his *Rinaldo*, and went to Ferrara.

As the Cardinal's client, Tasso became a member of the Court of Alfonso II. His literary work went forward. When, in 1570, he accompanied his patron to Paris, he left behind in the keeping of friends the completed first draft of his *Gerusalemme Liberata* and a great part of his lyrical poems. In 1573 he composed his pastoral drama *Aminta*. In 1575, on the death of Pigna, he was appointed his successor as historiographer of Ferrara.

The change that now passed over his life has been variously and romantically explained. That he suffered from some form of insanity, however, no one probably would now deny; and it is likewise without question that the Duke treated him as well as he knew how. In 1579, while the poet was confined in the Hospital of St. Anna, pirated editions of the *Gerusalemme* began to appear, followed by better ones corrected by his friends. The poem was received with acclaim, and soon became the centre of critical controversy. In 1586 Vincenzo Gonzaga gained the consent of Alfonso to take Tasso to Mantua; but, after a year there, the poet made his way to Rome and Naples. Afterwards he spent some time with the Grand Duke of Tuscany; and in 1592, on an invitation secured for him by a young admirer, G. B. Manso, he visited the Prince of Conca at Capua, and made the acquaintance of the Prince's secretary, the poet Marino. In May, Tasso went to Rome to be the guest of the Cardinals Cinzio Passeri and Pietro Aldobrandini. After another visit to Naples, he returned to the Cardinals near the end of 1594, with his last sickness already in his veins. He died in the monastery of San Onofrio on the

---

[1] Italic numerals indicate that the translation only appeared in Groto's *Rime* of 1610; one version of 9.126 should be added to these (cf. Register).

Janiculum, April 21, 1595; having recently finished his literary career with the *Gerusalemme Conquistata*, a revision of his great poem.

Tasso was a man of learning, and the themes of Greek poetry easily found a place in his works. Nor were the Greek epigrams neglected. One will not expect to find traces of them in his narrative poems. The *Gerusalemme*, however, contains two echoes of the Platonic epigram *A.P.* 5.78; but this theme was a commonplace, and the *Gerusalemme* is without further influence from the epigrams. One of these echoes occurs in the scene in the gardens of Armida (16.19), in a passage describing the passion of Armida for Rinaldo:

> S'inchina, e i dolci baci ella sovente
> Liba or dagli occhi e dalle labbra or sugge;
> Ed in quel punto ei sospirar si sente
> Profondo sì, che pensi: *or l'alma fugge,*
> *E in lei trapassa peregrina.*

The original is given above, p. 22. The same figure occurs again to Tasso's mind later in the poem, and he makes Erminia give expression to it over the wounded Tancredi (19.108); but here it is rather more than a conceit:

> Lecito sia ch'ora ti stringa, e poi
> Versi lo spirto mio fra i labbri tuoi.

Tasso's *Aminta* contains his *Amor Fuggitivo*, an imitation of Moschus (=*A.P.* 9.440); and one of his sonnets is built on the same theme.[1]

In his lyrical poems, however, Tasso shows unmistakable interest in the epigrams. The style of his madrigals constantly recalls the Anthology; and in particular some of them are translations.[2] The point of the following, from *A.P.* 16.200, is very different from that of the Greek:

[1] See *Amer. Journ. of Philol.* 49.115–6. Otherwise the *Aminta*, though in many passages a mosaic of classical imitiations, appears to owe nothing directly to the Anthology. The following parallels are given for what they may be worth; page-references are to Solerti's edition of Tasso's *Teatro*, Bologna, 1895. *Am.*, Prl. 45 (p. 7): Deposto ho l'ale, la faretra, e l'arco (cf. *A.P.* 16.200 and Tasso's madrigal given below). *Am.* 1.1.177 (p. 20): Allor che fuggirai le fonti, solo Per tema di vederti crespa e brutta (cf. *A.P.* 11.76). *Am.* 2.2.151 (p. 59): E che giova fuggir da lui c'ha l'ale? (cf. *A.P.* 5.59).

[2] *Rime*, ed. by Angelo Solerti, 4 vols. Bologna, 1898–1902; Augusto Sainati, *La Lirica di Torquato Tasso*, Pisa, 1912. Sainati says (1.83): 'Abbiamo rilevato una caratteristica, accenniamo ad una somiglianza: i madrigali migliori del Tasso ricordano spesso, molto da vicino gli epigrammi dell' Antologia Greca, anzi si potrebbe affermar quasi che non pochi di essi sono veri e propri epigrammi in lingua italiana, epigrammi per lo spirito animatore, non per le qualità esteriori, s'intende.' This he qualifies in a note: 'Con questo non intendiamo di fare un' affermazione avente un valore assoluto; chè i madrigali del Tasso . . . risentono molteplici influssi, di poeti classici e di volgari e altresì dei lirici del nostro Rinascimento.'

Amor l'arco e la face
Depose, e i buoi congiunse
E con sua verga stimulolli e punse.
Ben conobbe Ciprigna il suo bifolco
Segnare il duro solco;
Ond' ella disse a lui: 'Che spargi, Amore?'
Rispose: 'Gioie—e mieterò dolore!'

Λαμπάδα θεὶς καὶ τόξα, βοηλάτιν εἵλετο ῥάβδον
οὖλος Ἔρως, πήρην δ' εἶχε κατωμαδίην·
καὶ ζεύξας ταλαεργὸν ὑπὸ ζυγὸν αὐχένα ταύρων
ἔσπειρεν Δηοῦς αὔλακα πυροφόρον.
εἶπε δ' ἄνω βλέψας αὐτῷ Διΐ· Πλῆσον ἀρούρας,
μή σε τὸν Εὐρώπης βοῦν ὑπ' ἄροτρα βάλω.

[Having laid aside his torch and his bow, cruel Love took up a goad for driving oxen, and carried a scrip slung from his shoulder; and yoking the patient oxen, he sowed the wheat-bearing furrow of Demeter. Then looking up to Zeus himself he said: 'Fill my fields with crops, if you don't want me to put you to the plough—Europa's bull.']

This theme of Moschus—for the epigram is ascribed to him—was borrowed again by Tasso for a sonnet.[1]

Tasso's best imitation of a Greek epigram is a madrigal on the theme of *A.P.* 7.669, the well-known Platonic epigram. It is addressed to the poetess Tarquinia Molza, granddaughter of Francesco Maria Molza: 'A la signora Tarquinia Molza, la qual studiando la sfera andava la sera a contemplar le stelle':

Tarquinia, se rimiri
I bei celesti giri,
Il cielo esser vorrei;
Perchè ne gli occhi miei
Fisso tu rivolgessi
Le tue dolci faville,
Io vagheggiar potessi
Mille bellezze tue con luci mille.

This became one of the most popular of Tasso's madrigals, repeatedly appearing, with musical setting, in the madrigal-collections of the time.[2]

---

[1] *Sotto il giogo*, etc., Solerti 3.75.
[2] Solerti 1.403, 406, 416. Graziani, *Il Primo Libro de' Madrigali* (Venice, 1588), Mayone, *Il Primo Libro de' Madrigali* (Naples, 1604), E. G. Gagliano, *Il Terzo Libro de' Madrigali* (Venice, 1605). In these collections the first line is regularly generalized as *Mentre, mia stella, miri*, which is also nearer the Greek:

Ἀστέρας εἰσαθρεῖς ἀστὴρ ἐμός· εἴθε γενοίμην
οὐρανός, ὡς πολλοῖς ὄμμασιν εἰς σὲ βλέπω.

Tasso's admiration for the Platonic epigrams finds expression in his *Lezione sopra un Sonetto di Monsignor della Casa*. It is a question of conceits and of simplicity in poetic diction:[1]

Ma non voglio che per ora mi vaglia l'autorità del Petrarca, non quella di Omero, di Pindaro, di Alceo; . . . vagliami almeno quella di Platone, padre e dio (se così dire è lecito) de' filosofi. Leggansi i suoi Epigrammi amorosi, che salvi da l'ingiuria de' tempi ci sono restati; che non si vedrà in loro nè il carro del suo Fedro, nè le cose che dice Socrate aver da Diotima apparate; ma sì ben concetti puri, candidi, gravi ed arguti, e tali, quali egli giudicò a quella maniera di poesia convenirsi: chè già non si può dubitare che egli per difetti degli altri filosofici, questi così fatti usasse. E per esempio, uno ne voglio addurre che egli scrisse ad un fanciullo, nomato Stella, il quale era intento a lo studio della sfera; e con tutto ciò, nè la qualità di quel giovane erudito, nè la materia il persuase, che più tosto dotto volesse parere in quella scienza, che arguto nel commune uso di parlare.' [Here he quotes the Greek of *A.P.* 7.669].

Two other poems of Tasso are inspired by the Platonic epigrams, one a sonnet on the death of Sisto Medici, a member of the Order of the Predicatori, that recalls *A.P.* 7.670 (Solerti 3.11), the other a madrigal on the theme of *A.P.* 5.78, the same theme that we have found in the *Gerusalemme* (Solerti 2.368).[2] We have, indeed, no direct evidence that Tasso knew the Greek Anthology at all. The Platonic epigrams, which are his favorites, might have come to him from any of several sources—for example, from Diogenes Laertius; while *Amor Fugitivus* and *A.P.* 16.200 (ascribed to Moschus) may both have come from an edition of the Bucolic poets.[3]

Solerti (3.79) quotes an 'anonymous' Latin version of the same epigram, which turns out, however, to be the translation by Annibale della Croce (above, p. 236)—with *tacito* for *claro* in the first line. On p. 531 of the same volume Solerti gives the following imitation found by him in *Cod. Marcian. Ital.* ix, 112:

Mentre, O mia vaga Stella,
Baldanzosa rimiri
Gli alti celesti giri,
Del ciel foss' io in sì beata e bella
Parte, e l'eterno Giove
Non consentisse che mirassi altrove.

[1] Tasso, *Prose Diverse*, ed. by Cesare Guasti, Florence, 1875, 2.123.
[2] See the Register under these epigrams.
[3] The following seems only to be a coincidence. Dioscorides has the following epigram, that appears (*A.P.* 5.138) in the Palatine MS., but was not in the *Planudea*, and hence could not have been known to Tasso:

Ἵππον Ἀθήνιον ᾖσεν ἐμοὶ κακόν· ἐν πυρὶ πᾶσα
Ἴλιος ἦν. κἀγὼ κείνῃ ἅμ' ἐφλεγόμαν.
οὐ δείσας Δαναῶν δεκέτη πόνον· ἐν δ' ἐνὶ φέγγει
τῷ τότε καὶ Τρῶες κἀγὼ ἀπωλόμεθα.

ANTONIO QUERENGHI

(1546–1633)

Querenghi was a Paduan, a pupil of Sperone Speroni, and lived long in great estimation at Rome as secretary to the College of Cardinals. He is said to have been chosen, before Famiano Strada, to write the history of Alessandro Farnese and the Netherland wars, and by Henry IV to write the history of his reign. Nothing of this kind seems ever to have been published by him; and most of his works are of a miscellaneous character. The younger Aleandro lauds him in an epigram already noticed in these pages (above, p. 260, note), and Tassoni introduces him with high praise into his *Secchia Rapita* (5.26).[1] Querenghi's *Poesie* appeared at Rome in 1621.

Querenghi, under the name of *l'Intricato*, was a member of the *Occulti* of Brescia. In their *Rime* he quotes *A.P.* 9.647, gives a paraphrase in prose, and adds 'a fine quatrain of M. Fabio Segni' (above, p. 229):[2]

> Fulmine disiectas quod habet Victoria pennas,
> 　　Quae Tyberim impendens despicit Arce super;
> Roma metu parcas: placidi haec sunt signa Tonantis,
> 　　Ne possit volucres inde movere gradus.

[*The Horse* was Athenion's song—an evil horse to me: all Troy was on fire, and with it I was burning. Though I had not feared the Danaans' ten years' labor; yet in the fire that burned then, both the Trojans and I were consumed.]
Compare Tasso (Solerti 4.111):

> Fu già favola antica
> Troia ed Argo e Micene
> E 'l Ciclope e Caribdi e le Sirene;
> Ma già quel foco è spento . . .
> Or quella vecchia fama
> Ringiovenisce quasi in dolci rime
> Con un suo stil sublime
> Il mio signor, ch' amante io dir non oso
> Se ben m'onora ed ama,
> E 'l mio foco amoroso
> Con l'incendio di Troia anco raccende
> E con le fiamme sue la mia risplende.

An imitation of Dioscorides by Crinagoras (*A.P.* 9.429) is equally absent from the Planudean Anthology.

　　Sainati, *op. cit.*, 1.102 note, suggests *A.P.* 5.144 as a parallel to the following lines beginning *Mad.* 307 (Solerti 2.367):

> Non sono in queste rive
> Fiori così vermigli
> Come le labbra de la donna mia.

[1] Quoted by Tiraboschi:
> Questi era in varie lingue uom principale,
> Poeta singolar, tosco, e latino,
> Grand' orator, filosofo morale,
> E tutto a mente avea Sant' Agostino.

[2] *Rime degli Academici Occulti con le loro Imprese et Discorsi.* Brescia, 1568 p. 47

This version of the Greek epigram is then rendered into Italian by Querenghi:

> Perchè fuoco dal Cielo a la Vittoria,
> Che da la Rocca mira 'l Tebro altero,
>   Hor habbia spennacchiate ambedue l'ale.
> Non temer Roma; chè di Giove amico
> Questi son segni; perchè non possa indi
> Stender' altrove i suoi volanti passi.

GIROLAMO BORNATI

(*fl.* 1568)

In the *Rime* of the *Occulti* of Brescia, just mentioned, Bornati, whose academical name was *l'Abstruso*, has a madrigal on the theme of *A.P.* 5.78.

> Baci, che le colombe già imitaste,
>   Mentre fra bei rubini
>   Di Lidia pastorella
>   Amorosetta et bella
>   Suggendo andai licori almi et divini,
> L' alma, che su le labbra mi furaste,
> Farà ritorno in me; s'avvien, che quella
> Infinita dolcezza un'altra volta,
> Mercè di grato Amor, da me fia colta.

FILIPPO ALBERTI

(1548–1612) ⏺

Alberti was a friend and literary adviser of Tasso. He was born at Perugia, and in 1580 published a history of his native city. His *Rime* appeared at Rome in 1602; but many of his poems had long been known from the miscellanies, particularly the *Rime Piacevoli di Cesare Caporali, del Mauro, et d'altri auttori*.[1]

Among Alberti's poems are four madrigals taken from the following four epigrams: *A.P.* 5.124, 237, 266; and 11.54. The first follows:

> Pomo acerbetto sei,
>   Vaga fanciulla, e da begli occhi fuora
>   Sol verginelle Gratie spiri ancora;
>   Ma già Cupido aguzza i dardi rei,

---

[1] My references [*Rime*] are to the fourth impression of this book, Venice, 1587. It was first printed at Parma, 1582, as *Raccolta di Alcune Rime Piacevoli*. I have not seen Alberti's own *Rime*.

Già in man la face ha tolto
Per accenderla poi nel tuo bel volto.
Fuggiam, fuggiamo, amanti,
Mentre nel cener giace il foco occolto;
Mentre non è nel duro nervo il telo!
Ah! quai minaccia il Cielo incendi, e quanti!
Ben è presagio il core,
Che fia brev' esca il mondo a tant' ardore.

Alberti's version of *A.P.* 5.266 was translated into English by
Drummond of Hawthornden; the Italian follows:[1]

Huom che ferito sia
Da saetta di can rabido e stolto
Scorge di cane ogn' hor ne l'acque il volto;
Forse rabbioso Amore,
Cangiato in voi col velenoso dente,
A me trafitto ha 'l core;
E m' ha rapito con furor la mente;
E non è fonte o rio,
Ove non miri anch' io, fida mia stella,
L' imagin vostra desiata e bella.

JACOPO MAZZONI

(1548–1598)

For learning, and especially for unusual powers of memory, Mazzoni was one of the prodigies of his age. He is said not to have been
worsted in a contest with the 'admirable' Crichton. Unlike his rival
Mazzoni has, by his work on Dante, really deserved the attention of
posterity. He was born at Cesena. In 1577 he published at Bologna
five thousand one hundred and ninety-seven 'Questions' embracing
every known department of knowledge. He became professor of
philosophy at Cesena, and then successively at Macerata, Pisa, and
Rome. He died at Cesena when only 49 years old. His *Difesa di Dante*
was published at Cesena in 1587; and in 1597 at Venice he published
an attempt to reconcile Plato and Aristotle: *In Universam Platonis et
Aristotelis Philosophiam Praeludia.*

The *Difesa di Dante* remains an ample testimony of Mazzoni's
vast, though hardly critical, erudition.[2] The Anthology is one of
a host of books ancient and modern from which illustrations are
drawn. He quotes, entire or in part, some 37 epigrams, taken

---

[1] Alberti's and not Moro's as stated by Kastner in his edition of Drummond
(1.227). Has Drummond, perhaps, other debts to Alberti?
[2] *Della Difesa della Comedia di Dante*, Cesena, 1587. This comprises three books; a
new edition was published at Cesena in 1688 in two volumes, the second of which contained Books 4–7, which had not before seen the light.

from nearly every part of the collection, and accompanies them
with translations either by himself (in Italian) or by others (in
Latin and mostly without acknowledgment). The *Difesa* often
aspires to be a sort of *Poetics*, and often has little directly to do
with the text of the *Commedia*. And hence it happens that his
quotations from the Anthology never are in direct illustration of
Dante; he does not, for example, quote *A.P.* 7.396, which might
have been a proper illustration of *Inf.* 26.52.[1] A fair example of
his practice occurs in Book 3, Chap. 13. The subject is: That the
Poets have altered History. Among his instances he cites Virgil's treatment of Dido, quoting *A.P.* 16.151 (with Ausonius'
Latin version), in which Dido is made to protest that she was
not at all as Virgil represents her. To this finally is subjoined
Dante's echo of Virgil in *Inf.* 5.61–2.

Mazzoni appears to have employed Brodaeus' edition of the
Anthology, since Brodaeus proves to be the 'scholiaste latino'
once referred to (p. 82). Where he does not make his own Italian
versions, he draws on the third (1544) edition of Soter's *Epigrammata Graeca*.[2] He makes acknowledgment of his borrowing
only in the case of Ausonius, Volaterranus, and Alciati. Mazzoni's Italian versions are in prose.

A table of citations follows; it will be seen that Mazzoni occasionally gives no translation at all. The epigrams marked
(M.) appear in his own translation:

A.P. 6.33.6 (p. 82); 7.57 (p. 431, M.), 218.3 (p. 464), 492 (p. 726),
524.3–4 (p. 575), 669 (p. 429, Laert. Int.[3]); 9.18 (p. 27), 30 (p. 424,
More), 31 (p. 424, Sleidan), 39 (p. 455, Bentinus), 53 (p. 110, Soter),
105 (p. 424, More), 110 (*Som.* 81, M.), 112 (p. 41, M.), 125 (p. 84,
Pius), 160 (p. 27), 173 (p. 112, Soter), 357 (p. 440, Volaterranus), 371
(p. 27, Ausonius), 376 (p. 424, More), 502 (p. 114, M.), 540 (p. 28);
10.43 (p. 48, Volaterranus), 50 (p. 600, Sleidan); 11.104 (p. 408, Ausonius), 140 (p. 276), 198 (p. 59, Velius), 376 (p. 132, Alciati), 405
(p. 48), 418 (p. 48, More); 16.29 (p. 689), 95.3–4 (p. 458), 151 (p. 456,
Ausonius).

The last four books of Mazzoni's treatise, first printed in
1688, are altogether hardly more than half the length of the
first three. Only three epigrams are employed in these new

---

[1] Above, p. 21, n. 1.
[2] That he employs the third edition is proved, for example, by his quotation (p. 424)
of the revised version of Sleidan's translation of *A.P.* 9.31, which appears only in this
edition (above, p. 282). His quotation of Alciati's version of *A.P.* 11.376 is not from
Soter.
[3] See above, p. 276.

books—*A.P.* 9.39 (p. 323), 75 (p. 53), and 378 (p. 198). Of these the first is not translated, the second has an Italian version by Mazzoni, and the third is accompanied by the Latin of 'un scrittore moderno' who proves to be Luscinius (from Soter).

LEONARDO ORLANDINI (DAL GRECO)
(1552–1618)

Orlandini was a native of Trapani. He studied theology and law at Palermo, and later held several ecclesiastical offices there, being abbot of San Giovanni degli Eremiti. He is the author of *Variarum Imaginum libri tres* (according to Jöcher). As a member of the *Accesi* of Palermo, he contributed to their *Rime*, first published in 1571.[1]

Among the poems of the *Accesi*, Orlandini has an imitation of *A.P.* 16.171 and a sonnet compounded of *A.P.* 7.669 and 670; the sonnet follows:[2]

> Vedi fra l'altre stelle, O Stella mia,
>   Com' io bramando i tuoi lucidi rai
>   Qui sol rimaso, ogn' hor piango i miei guai,
>   E la mia sorte invidiosa e ria.
> Se mi conceda il Ciel, che 'l Cielo io sia
>   Per poterti mirar quando tu vai
>   Con mille raggi, e non oscuri mai,
>   Segnando al ver' onor dritta la via.
> Mentre vivevi in questo Mondo ingrato,
>   Mondo infelice, eri la vaga Stella,
>   Ch' a noi mena sereno e nuovo il giorno.
> Or morta, e su nel cerchio almo e beato
>   D' eterni lumi, sempre chiara e bella,
>   Espero sei, ch' allumi d'ogn' intorno.

LEONARDO SPINOSA
(*fl.* 1590)

In the *Discorsi et Annotationi* of Giulio Guastavini on the *Gerusalemme* of Tasso (Pavia, 1592), the editor quotes, in illustration of Canto 16, Stanza 19, Lines 6–7 (above, p. 331), the Platonic epigram, *A.P.* 5.78, with the Latin imitation found in Gellius; and adds a more literal version in Italian by Spinosa:

---

[1] I have not been able to find any copy of the first edition, but use the second: *Rime degli Accademici Accesi di Palermo*, Palermo and Venice, 1726. Compare Carducci, *Poesia Barbara*, p. 352.

[2] The imitation of *A.P.* 16.171 is in 'quantitative' verse, and is given by Carducci, *op. cit.*, p. 357.

'Ma più da vicino assai, e senza giunta di concetto alcuno, e quasi parola per parola, come che molto leggiadramente in volgare, dal mio gentilissimo Sig. Leonardo Spinosa del Signor Stefano in questo modo:[1]

> Mentre dolci porgea
> Al mio Agatone i baci,
> L'anima in cima delle labbra avea,
> Che di dolcezza vinta
> Ne trasse quasi al trapassar accinta.'

BERNARDINO BALDI

(1553–1617)

Baldi was born at Urbino, June 5, 1553, of a noble family originally from Perugia. His early studies were directed by Giovan Andrea Palazzi of Fano and Giovan Antonio Turonei of Urbino. Later he devoted himself to mathematics under Federigo Commandino, and still later (1573) was sent by his father to study philosophy at Padua. The plague caused him to quit Padua in 1575; he returned home, studied mathematics with Guidobaldo del Monte, and began to make a name for himself. The Duke of Guastalla, Ferdinando Gonzaga, succeeded in attaching Baldi to himself, and in 1586 presented him with the Abbey of Guastalla. Baldi then took orders, and thereafter gave much attention to ecclesiastical scholarship. He visited Rome, and was made Protonotarius Apostolicus. In 1609 he retired from his benefice, returned to Urbino, and attached himself to the Duke. The latter sent him to Venice to congratulate Antonio Memmo in 1612, when Memmo became Doge. Baldi died on October 10, 1617. He was a universal scholar and a pleasing writer. Besides his own language he is said to have had a knowledge of Hebrew, Syriac, Arabic, Greek, Latin, Slavonic, Hungarian, Persian, Provençal, French, German, and Spanish (Mazzuchelli). His reputation was first made as a mathematician, but he became expert also in history, geography, archaeology, philosophy, and theology. Among his numerous works may be mentioned: *Il Lauro, scherzo giovanile* (1580); *La Corona dell' Anno* (Vicenza, 1589); *Versi e Prose* (Venice, 1590); *Il Diluvio Universale* (Pavia, 1604); *Carmina Latina* (Parma, 1609); *De Verborum Vitruvianorum Significatione* (Augsburg, 1612); *In Mechanica Aristotelis Problemata Exercitationes* (Mainz, 1621).[2]

Since the publication of Baldi's epigrams by Ciàmpoli, the Abbot of Guastalla at length takes his place with Alamanni and

---

[1] *Opere di Torquato Tasso*, Pisa, 1821–31, 26. 65.
[2] More complete lists may be found in Mazzuchelli and in Ciàmpoli's edition of Baldi's poems mentioned below.

Pensa as one of the principal Italian epigrammatists.[1] His epigrams number 1155. The collection of them was begun probably in 1605, and was finally put in shape, doubtless for printing, in 1614, Baldi's clean copy being dated August 25 of that year. Their author calls them *Epigrammi Volgari, secondo l'uso latino e greco*, and divides them into five books: 1. *Morali*, 2. *Gravi*, 3. *Arguti*, 4. *Ridicoli*, 5. *Varii*, a division that recalls the Greek Anthology.[2]

Besides his own observation of contemporary manners, Baldi has a number of literary sources; Martial is not disdained by him as by some of his immediate predecessors; Ausonius is occasionally used; and a decisive portion of his themes come from the Greek. Fifty-four of his pieces are imitations of epigrams in the Anthology. He favors the satirical type. His imitations range from fairly strict reproduction of the original to the utmost freedom of treatment.[3] As an example of close imitation we may take his versions of *A.P.* 9.223 and 11.264.[4]

> Drizzò perito arcier suo dardo al cielo,
> E a l'aquila di Giove alto pervenne,
> Tal che l'augel ferito a terra venne
> Seco traendo sanguinoso il telo.
> Ma nel cader, mira del ciel vendetta,
> Su l'arcier cadde e ginne il dardo al core;
> Onde il ferito e 'l feritor si more,
> E tinta è di due sangui una saetta.

> Sognando Ermon che spesa facea grave,
> S'appiccò per l'affanno ad una trave.

---

[1] *Gli Epigrammi Inediti, gli Apologhi, e le Ecloghe*, ed. by Domenico Ciàmpoli, 2 vols, Lanciano (Carabba), 1914. See also the study by Luigi Ruberto in *Propugnatore* 15 (1882). 1.118–38, 380–98; 2.136–78 (separately printed as *Studi su Bernardino Baldi*, Bologna, 1883). The epigrams exist in two autograph MSS. in the National Library at Naples: *Codd.* XIII, D, 31 and XIII, D, 52.

[2] *Cod.* XIII, D, 31, also contains Baldi's Latin and Greek epigrams, not yet wholly published (cf. Ciàmpoli 1.5). I have not seen the *Carmina* of 1609.

[3] *A.P.* 5.125; 7.209, 305, 319; 9.1, 5, 30, 32, 34, 44, 49, 74, 85, 110, 170, 182, 223, 231, 257, 261, 374, 517, 826; 10.44, 60, 63, 72 (2 imit.), 98, 116; 11.3, 50, 53, 76, 103, 105, 151, 166 (2 imit.), 179, 198, 237, 264, 343, 365, 390, 391, 394, 408, 414, 429, 431; 16.14, 326. References in the Register are to the numbers of Ciàmpoli's edition.

[4] The Greek of *A.P.* 9.223 may be literally rendered as follows: 'When the eagle that circles aloft, of birds the only one that visits heaven, was bearing a message from Zeus, he did not escape the observation of a Cretan. The archer stretched his swift bowstring; and the winged creature was slain by the winged shaft. Yet the justice of Zeus failed not to mark that man alone: the bird fell on him, and he paid the penalty for aiming his arrow well, the bird pierced his neck with the dart that had lodged in its own heart; and one bolt drank the blood of two victims.' *A.P.* 11.264: 'Having spent money in a dream, the miser Hermon, out of vexation, hanged himself.'

His freer manner may be illustrated by the following, in which he takes only part of the first line of *A.P.* 9.517, and develops it for a contemporary allusion:[1]

AL P. FRANCESCO RASI ARETINO MUSICO

Se voi d'Orfeo maggior, Francesco, dico,
Son le parole mie reali e vere:
Che se trasse col canto il grande antico
E col suon di sue corde arbori e fere,
Voi rapireste lui, sì son possenti
Quei che mischiate al suon musici accenti.

Recognizable imitations do not exhaust Baldi's debt to the Anthology. A very considerable number of the rest of his epigrams are formed on themes that he knew were treated by the Greeks—epitaphs on heroes and warriors,[2] epitaphs on animals,[3] epigrams on works of art,[4] and many others. It is not too much to say that his whole collection owes its character to the Greek epigram. For an example of similarity of theme we may take No. 1056, which may be compared generally with *A.P.* 11.159–64, on astrologers:

L' astrologo Caron, mentre la morte
Esser vicina a Temison dicea,
Subitano morì; ah, strana sorte,
Predir il suo, non l'altrui fin dovea!
Dunque mostrò che vanità fu madre
A l'arte incerta, e folle ardire il padre.

The name Temison is intended to give a Greek flavor.

Apart from his epigrams Baldi's Italian poems, so far as I have seen them, show no indebtedness to the Anthology.[5] No. 56 of his prose *Apologhi*, however, recalls *A.P.* 9.31: 'Un pino, di cui era fatto un albero di nave, trovandosi rotto in una tempesta, diceva: "Ben son io infelicissomo, poi che il mutar paese non m'ha cambiato ventura." '

---

[1] Ὀρφεὺς ϑῆρας ἔπειϑε, σὺ δ' Ὀρφέα.

[2] E.g., No. 273 on Alexander the Great, and No. 415 on a statue of Antaeus and Hercules on a fountain.

[3] E.g., No. 275: Epitafio di Leone, Cane de Caccia.

[4] E.g., No. 381: Sopra un Cupido di Bronzo.

[5] Besides Ciàmpoli's edition I have seen the *Versi e Prose* of 1590 and the *Eclogues* in the Milan Classics.

CELSO CITTADINI

(1553–1627)

Cittadini occupies a place of honor in the long line of scholars who have worked on the Italian language. His *Trattato della Vera Origine e del Processo e Nome della Nostra Lingua*, and his *Origini della Toscana Favella*, were published during his lifetime; but several treatises on related subjects remained to be printed in his *Opere*, which appeared, with a biography by Girolamo Gigli, at Rome in 1721. He also wrote on Heraldry, and is said to have had 'an exact knowledge of medals.' Cittadini was born at Rome, though his family came from Siena, and, after spending many years in Rome, he returned to the paternal city, where he taught. He died there. He left a considerable number of manuscripts, which Pope Alexander VII, who had been his pupil, sought to procure; but it was known that the Grand Duke of Tuscany also coveted them, and the pope yielded to him (Tiraboschi, *Stor.* 8.3.5). These papers were the basis of the *Opere* of 1721.

Cittadini composed a certain amount of verse, of which he published *Rime Platoniche* at Venice in 1585, but much more was left scattered in manuscript or printed in ephemeral form. The following sonnet is said to come from a collection of the verses of the Siena Academy.[1] It is a rather pleasant imitation of *A.P.* 7.669:

Mentre di notte al bel seren si stava
 Fileto intento a rimirar le stelle,
 Com' egli suole, e le più ardenti, e belle
 A' begli occhi di Pirra assimigliava;
Rapto per man d' Amor così cantava:
 'Tu, che 'n cerchio girando volgi or quelle,
 Onde pendea il mio ben, dolci fiammelle,
 Ed or forse il gran duol, che sì m'aggrava:
Se 'l mio fiero destin, lasso, m' ha tolta
 La speme d' arrivar là dove aspira
 Quest' alma, acciò che in pianto io mi consumi,
Trasformassim' io 'n te solo una volta,
 Per poterla veder, quando ti mira,
 Come fai tu, con tanti e sì bei lumi.'

GIROLAMO CASONE

(*fl.* 1598)

Casone seems to have been a native of Oderzo, but beyond that nothing appears to be known of him. His *Rime* were pub-

[1] Gobbi, *Scelta di Sonetti e Canzoni*, 2nd ed., Bologna, 1718, 2.226. I have been unable to find the poems of the Siena Academy referred to by Gobbi.

lished at Venice in 1598.[1] The poems mostly consist of madrigals on real or supposed works of art. One has the theme of *A.P.* 6.1:

> Questa dipinta imago,
>   Che con l'imago ne lo specchio mio
>   Contese del mio bel volto natio,
>   Questa imago gentile,
>   A te sola simile,
>   Hor che invecchio, hor che men bella sono,
>   Madre d'Amor, io ti consacro e dono.

[1] The copy of Casone's poems in the Bibliothèque Nationale in Paris is bound with the *Rime* of Angelo Grillo (Venice, 1599) and the *Madrigali* of G. B. Leoni (*ibid.*, 1598).

PART III

THE SEVENTEENTH AND EIGHTEENTH CENTURIES

MAURIZIO MORO

(*fl.* 1600)

Moro was a Venetian priest. As a member of the Academy of the *Cospiranti*, he published some of his books under the academic name of 'Il Costante.' His works include: *Sonetti Varii*, Vicenza, 1589; *Rime Spirituali et Funerali*, Treviso, 1590; *Il Giardino de' Madrigali*, Venice, 1593; *I Tre Giardini de' Madrigali . . . con il Ghiaccio et il Fuoco d'Amore, le Furie Ultrici, e il Ritratto delle Cortigiane*, Venice, 1602; *Rappresentatione del Figliuolo Prodigo*, Venice, 1585 and 1606; *Cronica delle Cose Notabili di Verona*, Verona, 1611; *La Passione di Giesù Christo d'Alberto Durero*, Venice, 1612; *Pomposi Fregi di Verona*, Verona, 1611; and *Le Dogliose Lagrime nella Morte del Celebre Pittore Sig. Carlo Saraceni*, Venice, 1620.[1] Moro also had a hand in the *Gareggiamento Poetico*, published at Venice in 1611 (below, p. 355).

We are concerned only with the *Tre Giardini de' Madrigali* of 1602. Twelve madrigals are from the Anthology.[2] Inasmuch as these poems were known beyond the borders of Italy, Moro takes on some importance as a transmitter of the Greek themes; several of his pieces, and among them imitations of the Anthology, were translated by Drummond of Hawthornden.[3] Moro himself, one is inclined to suspect, picked them up from a neo-Latin source. He is not averse to employing the same theme over again for more than one madrigal, and in two instances has made the same Greek epigram serve for three separate poems.

The following is Moro's version of *A.P.* 5.266 by Paulus Silentiarius, an epigram which, though noticed by Equicola, had found few translators among Italian writers:

---

[1] Copies of the first three books mentioned are in St. Mark's Library at Venice; the others, except the last, are to be found in the British Museum; the last I take from Cicogna, *Saggio di Bibliografia Veneziana*, p. 670.

[2] *A.P.* 5.163, 168, 210, 266; 9.346 (3 versions); 16.129, 171, 174 (3 versions).

[3] *Works*, ed. by Kastner, 1.100 and 2.176; but see above, p. 336, n. 1.

345

> Huom, che rabbioso cane habbia ferito,
>   In chiaro fiume, in fonte,
>   Scorge del feritor l'irata fronte;
>   Così 'l tiranno ardito
>   D'Amor fero e possente,
>   Che nel mio core afflitto impresse il dente,
>   In fiume, in limpid' acque,
>   Mostra 'l mio Feritore, e chi mi piacque.

The next is a version of an epigram that attracted more notice surely than its intrinsic merits warrant; Moro himself used it three times. The original is *A.P.* 9.346:

> Garrula Rondinella,
>   Quest' è Medea crudele, e ancor nol vedi?
>   Se l'empia ai figli suoi fu fiera e fella,
>   Che farà a'tuoi c' ha in seno?
>   Sciocca, da lei che chiedi?
>   Foco, ferro, o veleno?
>   Mira al tuo scampo, mira,
>   Ch' il suo petto crudele avvampa d'ira.

GIAMBATTISTA MANSO
(1561–1645)

Manso was a Neapolitan nobleman, Marchese di Villa, who served his age well in the capacity of a Maecenas. He was the founder of the Academy of the *Oziosi* in Naples, and of the College of Nobles to which he left his property. He published a Life of Tasso (Rome, 1634), *Dialoghi dell' Amore* (Milan, 1608), and *Poesie Nomiche* (Venice, 1635). He is best known, however, for his kindness to Tasso and Marino, and later his hospitality to the young Milton. Doubtless many other literary men were assisted by him, as, for example, Giuseppe Battista (below, p. 365), who was his literary executor.[1]

Manso's verse is hardly of the sort that owes much to the Greek epigrams; yet he has a sonnet on the theme of *A.P.* 7.669:

> Gli Occhi della S. D. volti al cielo gli
>   accendono desiderio d'esser un cielo
>   per rimirargli.

> Mentre, donna, ne gli alti eterni giri
>   Volgi lo sguardo a contemplar le stelle,
>   E 'l tuo splendor, che 'n te non pregi, in quelle
>   Vagamente cosparto, intenta ammiri,

---

[1] On Manso see Michele Manfredi, *G. B. Manso nella Vita e nelle Opere*, Naples 1919.

O come par che 'l cielo amante giri
   De gli occhi suoi ver' te l'auree facelle;
   E da te apprenda ardenti i raggi, ond' elle
   Raccendano 'l lor lume e i miei desiri!
Io di questi sol ardo e vivo e splendo:
   Deh! se converso in lucide faville
   Novo ciel divenendo al ciel m'ergessi,
Avveria pur ch' in me talor volgendo
   Tuoi vaghi lumi, io vagheggiar potessi
   Mille bellezze tue con luci mille.

There is probably no direct relation between this sonnet and the madrigal by Tasso on the same theme.

GASPARE MURTOLA
(c. 1560–c. 1624)

Murtola was a Genoese, and studied literature and law in his native place. He went to Rome as secretary to Giovanni Serra, who became Cardinal and was ambassador of the Pope to the Emperor. Murtola accompanied him on this journey to Vienna. Afterwards, being in Turin, Murtola attracted the attention of Carlo Emmanuele of Savoy, and was made his secretary. While at the Court of Savoy, he published his poem on the creation: *Della Creazione del Mondo, Poema Sacro, Giorni Sette, Canti Sedici* (Venice, 1608). Marino, who was then also in Milan, ridiculed the new poem in a satirical sonnet. A violent quarrel arose between the two poets. Marino followed up his first attack with a whole volley of sonnets which he called the *Murtoleide;* Murtola replied with a *Marineide.* Finally, when Marino appeared to be getting the better of the affair, Murtola waited for his enemy one day in a street of Turin with an arquebus. He missed Marino, but wounded Marino's companion, a favorite of the Duke. For this attempt he was imprisoned, but Marino generously secured his release. Murtola nevertheless is said to have intrigued to drive Marino from Turin, and to have succeeded. He himself left soon after, and passed the remainder of his life in Rome. It is related that Paul V once questioned him on his attack on Marino, and received from the poet the ambiguous reply: 'È vero, ho fallito.'

Prior to the publication of his *Creazione* Murtola had been known as a Latin poet for his *Nutriciarum sive Naeniarum libri tres* (Venice, 1602), and as a lyric poet for his *Rime* (Venice, 1604). The *Rime* is divided into several books entitled: *Gli Amori, Gli Occhi, Le Venere.* The verses are mostly madrigals, and in taste and subject often recall the writer's rival, Marino. Like Marino, Murtola has madrigals on works of art, which he wrote doubtless with the fourth book of the Planudean Anthology more or less clearly in mind.

In addition to such stylistic influence, the Anthology supplied
the substance of nineteen pieces in Murtola's *Rime*.[1] The following is from *A.P.* 5.11:

> Bella madre d'Amore,
> Se per te da l'infido
> Oceano altri è scorto
> Sicuramente in porto,
> Hor che naufragio il core
> Misero in terra pate
> Per terreno beltate,
> Porgigli aita ancor con le tue belle
> Lucidissime stelle.

One of Murtola's versions of *A.P.* 16.171 will show him ad-
hering more closely than usual to the original:

> Perchè l'armi di Marte,
> Madre d' Amore, apprendi,
> E le altrui piaghe attendi?
> Poni, poni in disparte
> L' hasta e lo scudo, armata;
> A che vincerlo vuoi
> Se nuda vincer puoi?

TOMMASO STIGLIANI
(*fl.* 1600)

Stigliani is known as a severe, but defeated, critic of Marino (Tiraboschi, *Stor.* 8.3.3.5). He was born at Matera in Basilicata; and in
1603 entered the service of the Duke of Parma. Later he appears to
have been in the Court of Cardinal Scipione Borghesi; and finally in
that of Giannantonio Orsini, Duke of Bracciano, in whose service he
died some time after 1625 at the age of eighty. He published *Rime* at
Venice in 1601, and again in 1605; an epic poem called *Il Mondo
Nuovo* in 1617; and *L'Occhiale* in 1625. It was in the last that he
launched his heaviest attack on Marino; and it drew upon its author
the fire of all the friends of Marino—the author of the *Adone* himself
died just at this time.

Stigliani's *Rime* of 1605 is divided into eight books, a division
that may well owe something to the Anthology: 1. *Amori Civili*;
2. *Pastorali*; 3. *Marinareschi*; 4. *Giocosi*; 5. *Soggetti Eroici*; 6.
Morali; 7. *Funebri*; 8. *Famigliari*. He has four translations—
A.P. 5.42, 94; 6.1; 9.346.[2] The last of these is thus rendered:

---

[1] References in the Register are to the 1604 edition. The epigrams imitated by Murtola are: *A.P.* 5.11, 59, 274; 7.311, 669; 9.589, 591; 11.428 (2 versions); 12.235; 16.129
(3 versions), 171 (3 versions).

[2] In the Register, references are to *Rime*, Venice, 1605. There is a handful of

Sai quale statua è quella,
Ov' hai tu 'l nido posto,
Semplice Rondinella?
De la cruda Medea. Mutalo tosto,
Mutalo, ne fidare i figli tuoi
A chi già uccise i suoi.

HIERONIMO VIDA

(1563-1591)

Vida published some poems together with a dialogue entitled *Il Sileno* at Venice in 1589. A second book, *De' Cento Dubbi Amorosi* was published at Padua in 1621 by a relation, Agostino Vida. The family was from Capo d'Istria, and according to Agostino was of some note.[1] This book is dedicated to Girolamo Lando, Venetian ambassador to England. According to the Dedication, Vida merited the titles of philosopher and poet, and belonged to the *Accademia degli Olimpici*. The Olympians were an academy of Vicenza. Agostino professed to have many other works of Hieronimo's in manuscript, which he intended to publish, an intention he apparently never carried out. In fact the *Cento Dubbi* itself was not completed, there being only ten pieces in it.

Among the questions discussed, the third is: 'Chi sia più degno d'esser amato, o l'armigero o il litterato.' At the end of this discussion is placed a madrigal that reflects *A.P.* 16.171, but probably only through the imitation by Ausonius (above, p. 105):

Canta la tromba generosa al Cielo
Di vittoria e valore,
Che ottien amando il Cavallier d'Amore.
Splende Venere armata,
Che in tal sembiante ne fà mostra a Marte,
E sdegna libri e carte,
Donde la guancia altrui divien men grata.
Stia con Saturno il grave,
Non con Amor' affabile e suave.

GIAMBATTISTA MARINO

(1569-1625)

Marino's father, a Neapolitan lawyer, wished his son to enter his own profession; but the life of poetry and pleasure, so alluring in the

---

Stigliani's poems in Croce's *Lirici Marinisti*, Bari, 1910. Stigliani's versions of *A.P.* 6.1 and 9.346 are given without their author's name in the Commentary to the 1621 ed. of Alciati's *Emblemata*, pp. 331 and 259 respectively.

[1] Agostino Vida was secretary to a gentleman of Padua named Capitanio.

Naples of that day, soon distracted the young man from legal studies. He plunged into a course of excesses that finally obliged his father to drive him from the house. Marino had already made known his poetical talents; and the Maecenas of Naples, G. B. Manso, at first received him in his home, and then prevailed upon the Grand Admiral of Naples, the Prince of Conca, to take him as secretary. In the house of this prince Marino made the acquaintance of Tasso, who encouraged his poetical ambitions. Apparently his irregularities did not cease. Having aided one of his friends in the abduction of a young girl, he was thrown into prison; and when Manso secured his release, he was again arrested for forging a letter to prove that his friend was a priest and not subject to the law. This time he escaped to Rome. Here he arrived in 1599. He secured the patronage of Cardinal Pietro Aldobrandini, found time to collect his poems, and repaired to Venice to print them. Returning to Rome, he followed the Cardinal to Ravenna and later to Turin, where he was well treated by the Duke of Savoy. He was now engaged on his great poem, the *Adone*.

He attached himself to the Court of Savoy; but in 1608 or 1609 the intrigues attendant on his quarrel with Murtola (above, p. 347) seem to have lost him the favor of Carlo Immanuele. He returned to Rome in 1612. Three years later he accepted the invitation of Marie de Médicis and her minister Concini to join the Court of France. In Paris he finished his *Adone*, published there in 1623. He was much made of in Paris, and was an honored frequenter of the Hôtel de Rambouillet; but after the fall of Concini he felt less secure, and, upon completing his poem, returned first to Turin, then to Rome, and finally to Naples. He entered his native city under an arch of triumph, and was made president of Manso's *Accademia degli Oziosi*. The duties of this office, however, (including a weekly lecture), were too onerous for his weakened physical strength, and he died shortly after his return, on March 26, 1625.

To a reader of Marino's lyric poetry, nothing is more evident than his dependence on classical writers. His style takes its pitch from them. Here is no countryman of Dante and Petrarch, but of Propertius and Ovid, perhaps of Philodemus and Meleager. In a long letter written to Claudio Achillini from Paris, Marino makes the defence of his borrowed glories:[1] 'Il tradurre (quando però non sia secondo l'usanza pedantesca) merita anzi loda che riprensione. . . . Tradurre intendo, non già vulgarizzare da parola a parola, ma con modo parafrastico, mutando le circostanze della ipotesi, ed alternando gli accidenti senza guastar la sostanza del sentimento originale. Ho tradotto senza dubbio anch'io talora per proprio passatempo e talora per compiacerne altrui; ma *le mie traduzioni sono state solo dal latino, o*

---

[1] *Opere*, ed. by Zirardini, Naples, 1861, p. xii.

pur dai greco passato nella latinità e non da altro idioma, e
sempre con le mentovate condizioni.' In view of the definite
statement, we may assume that any imitations of the Greek
epigrams we find in Marino's works came to him by way of
Latin translations.

The manner and often the matter of Marino's lyric poems
suggest the Greek epigram. The degree to which the spirit of
Meleager or of Philodemus has been transmitted to him can be
shown at once by the following madrigal:[1]

AMOR SECRETO

Ardi contento e taci,
  O di secreto amore
  Secretario, mio core.
  E voi, sospiri, testimoni ascosi
  De' miei furti amorosi,
  Che per uscire ad or ad or m'aprite
  Le labbra, ah! non uscite!
  Ch' ai saggi, oimè! de l'amorosa scola
  Il sospiro è parola.

Meleager and Philodemus address their lamps in much the same
terms as Marino here addresses his heart and sighs—συνίστορα
τῶν ἀλαλήτων.[2]

Marino's first book of lyrical poems was *La Lira* (Venice,
1602), in two parts, to which a third part was added in 1608.
In the volume of 1602 are several poems on works of art, one
of which is derived from *A.P.* 16.162:[3]

La dea, che 'n Cipro e 'n Amatunta impera,
  Quando, o dove a te, Fidia, ignuda apparse?
  Forse quando l' Egeo, che d'amor n'arse,
  Solcò nascente in su la conca altera?
O pure allor che de la terza sfera
  Al troiano pastor venne a mostrarse?
  O lei vedesti i bei membri lavarse
  Là ne' fonti di Pafo e di Citera?
Forse—e ben esser può—scolpisti lei,
  Mentre che, 'n braccio al fèro dio de l'armi,
  Era vago spettacolo agli dèi?

---

[1] *La Lira*, pt. 3 (1630), p. 341.
[2] *A.P.* 5.4.1.; cf. 5.5 and 8.
[3] *Lira* 1.205. Note that Phidias is substituted for Praxiteles of the original. The
1602 *Lira* likewise contains a madrigal on the theme of *A.P.* 9.440 (above, p. 3, n. 3);
another, *Amor di Marmo in Fontana*, may come from *A.P.* 16.14; and a second sonnet,
on a *Venus* of Apelles, recalls *A.P.* 16.178. The third part of *La Lira* (for which I use
the edition published at Venice in 1630) contains a sonnet reminiscent of *A.P.* 5.210,
and a religious poem modeled on *A.P.* 9.440 (above, p. 3, n. 3).

Così pens' io, nè meraviglia parmi;
  Chè, s'ogni dio vi fu, tu pur dio sei,
  Ch' uomo non è chi può dar vita a' marmi.

Marino's predecessor, possibly his model, in this sort of subject, Luigi Groto, found materials in the Anthology. Conceivably Marino also, while not directly translating from the Greek,
nevertheless was conscious that a portion of the Anthology com-
prised verses of this sort, and even that the sonnet just quoted
came ultimately from that source. At all events, the notion of
these little poems on works of art evidently pleased him, for in
1620 at Venice he issued a whole collection of them in two parts:
La Galleria . . . distinta in Pitture e Sculture. Most of these
pieces were written on actual works of art then existing, as the
Calisto of Guido Reni and the like. Others were for imaginary
works or for ancient works no longer extant. The verses on
similar subjects that had appeared in the *Lira* were here reprinted. In the *Galleria* it must be admitted that Marino had
his eye on the Anthology. In all, twelve poems are from that
source.[1] One of these is announced as 'from the Greek,' but, as
we shall see, this only means that Marino's immediate Latin
model was similarly labeled 'e Graeco.' The epigram in question
appears under the heading *Capricci* in the first part (*Pitture*) of
the volume, and is from *A.P.* 11.214:

DI PINTURA GOFFA. DAL GRECO.

Due tavole dipinse
  Sciocco pittor—Deucalione in quella,
  Fetonte in questa finse.
  Fornita opra sì bella,
Chiedea qual fusse del suo bel disegno
  Prezzo conforme e degno.—
Gli rispose l'Oracolo per gioco:
'L' una merita l'acqua, e l'altra il fuoco.'

In the second part (*Sculture*) Marino translates five epigrams
on the *Heifer* of Myron, and two or three others; and repeats
from the *Lira* of 1602 the imitations of the Anthology he had
given there. The following is one of the epigrams on Myron's
Heifer (*A.P.* 9.732):

----

[1] *A.P.* 7.311; 9.721, 727, 732, 733, 737, 756; 11.214; 16.14 (?), 107, 162, 178. There is
also in the *Galleria* an epigram entitled *Statua d'Amore Fulminata* (*Gal.* 2.41) that could
have been suggested by a version of *A.P.* 16.250.

O tu, che passi, il passo
Arresta a questo sasso;
S'incontri a caso il mio pastore tra via,
Digli, ch' uopo non fia,
O per valli, o per monti ire a cercarmi,
Ne trovar funi, o lacci da legarmi,
Ch' io qui per opra di Scultor perfetto
Immobili l'aspetto.

Many of Marino's earlier epigrams on painting and sculpture
were, he says, written while he was still at Naples, and inspired by the gallery of the Prince of Conca.[1]

What Latin translations Marino may have fastened upon for
the Greek epigrams I cannot in every case pretend to say. Perhaps the epigrams on Myron's *Heifer* are from Calcagnini
(above, p. 180). The possibilities may be consulted in the Register. The paraphrastic manner of translation, which he advocated, makes identification difficult. However, his version of
A.P. 11.214, given as 'from the Greek,' is from the translation
by Dazzi (above, p. 163), as the mention of the Oracle, unknown to the Greek, plainly indicates; Dazzi labels his verses
'e Graeco.'

Marino's other books of lyrical or pastoral verse—*Epitalami*
(1616), *La Murtoleide* (1619), *La Sampogna* (1620), *Egloghe*
(1620)—show no influence from the Anthology. Nor have I detected any allusion to it in his published correspondence.

The *Adone*, crammed as it is with classical mythology, might
be supposed to have caught in its elaborate web some themes
from the Greek epigrams. It contains, however, no direct borrowing. The following may be remote echoes, and are here
given for what they may be worth:[2] *A.P.* 5.78 (*Ad.* 8.130, 132),
95 (*Ad.* 11.65), 210 (*Ad.* 15.29.6); 7.182 (*Ad.* 4.56 and 14.299.5),
669 (*Ad.* 2.132.5); 9.440 (*Ad.* 1 *passim*), 455 (*Ad.* 20.515);
16.174 (*Ad.* 2.156.7), 180 (*Ad.* 7.137), 275 (*Ad.* 6.193). In *Ad.*
2.132, for example, Marino falls into the theme of *A.P.* 7.669
as into a commonplace:

Fossi la notte, o fossi il ciel sereno, . . .
Per poter rimirar cose sì belle,
Con tante viste, quante son le stelle.

[1] *Poes. Var.*, ed. by Croce, p. 412.
[2] In the Register, references are to Marino's *Opere* in Zirardini's edition mentioned
above.

On the other hand, *A.P.* 7.182 is no more than an analogue to *Ad.* 4.56:

> In esequie funebri inique stelle
> Cangian le nozze tue liete e festanti?
> Le chiare tede in torbide facelle?
> Le tibie in squille e l'allegrezze in pianti?

The epigram is by Meleager, for a girl who died on her wedding-night: 'But in the morning they raised the death-wail, and the wedding-song was stilled and changed to a sound of lament; and the same torches that then shed their light by her marriage-couch now lighted her dead on her way down to Hades.'[1]

Marino is commonly said to represent the culmination in Italian poetry of the overwrought and luscious style. Much of his boldness, particularly in amatory themes, it may be suggested, results from his having, more than others, transferred to the vernacular a style of imagery that had long been favored among neo-Latin poets. Marino's debt to these writers derveses investigation. Certainly on reading his sonnets one frequently gropes in one's memory for neo-Latin epigrams that one feels sure lie behind the Italian.[2]

---

[1] The same theme appears in other epigrams, notably in *A.P.* 7.712.

The theme of *A.P.* 12.75 (not in *Plan.*) is almost identical with that of *Ad.* 16.220. Marino may depend on Machiavelli or on Guarini; see above, p. 296, n. 1 and p. 327, n. 1. But he uses it for the purposes of satire:

> Se l'arco avesse in man, la benda in fronte,
> L'ali sul tergo e il piè non fusse torto,
> Ei mi parrebbe alle fattezze estrane,
> Lo Dio d'Amor de' topi e delle rane.

Similarly compare *Ad.* 19.65.5 with *A.P.* 12.76 (also wanting in *Plan.*):

> Se non andasse ignudo e fosse inerme,
> Potria rassomigliarlo il tuo figliolo.
> S'egli non avea gli occhi ed avea l'ale,
> Potea parer Amor nato mortale.

[2] In this respect Marino strikes one as a belated follower of the French Pléïade. Like Du Bellay—possibly with him in mind—he has a poem based on Navagero's imitation of *A.P.* 6.53 (*Poesie Varie*, ed. by Croce, p. 82):

ALLE AURE

> Questo vaso d'amomo e questi acanti,
>   Primo pregio d'april, queste odorate
>   Rose ad un parto con l'aurora nate,
>   Questo cesto di gigli e d'amaranti,
> A voi, de l'aria peregrine erranti,
>   Fien sacri, aure felici, aure beate,
>   Se, mentre per lo ciel l'ali spiegate,
>   Vosco trarrete i preghi miei volanti;
> Sì che questi, ch' io spargo, amari accenti
>   Oda di là, dove n'andate or voi,
>   Elpinia, e 'l flebil suon de' miei lamenti.

IL GAREGGIAMENTO POETICO
(1611)

Il Gareggiamento Poetico del Confuso Accademico Ordito: Madrigali Amorosi, Gravi, e Piacevoli, ne' quali si vede il Bello, il Leggiadro, e il Vivace dei più Illustri Poeti d'Italia. . . . Venice (Barezzo Barezzi), 1611. This collection is dedicated to Giulio Cesare di Capova, Prince of Conca. It consists of nine parts, each with a separate title-page, and, in all, of 413 folios of madrigals. The dedications are dated from Padua at the end of 1610 and the beginning of 1611 by the secretary of the *Orditi* under the name 'Ammassato.' 'Il Confuso' is said by Quadrio to have been the academic name of Carlo Fiamma.[1] The madrigals are mainly from writers of the last part of the sixteenth and the beginning of the seventeenth century.

The Anthology contributes the themes of twenty-four pieces: *A.P.* 5.78 (Michelangelo Angelico), 95 (M. A. Virtuani), 124 (F. Alberti); 6.1 (G. Casone; Stigliani); 7.669 (Groto; Tasso; G. B. Maurizio); 9.346 (G. B. Strozzi; 2 by M. Moro; C. Fiamma; A. Nardi; C. Simonetti; P. Petracci; 4 by V. Belli), 440 (Isabella Andreini; G. B. Marino); 16.129 (C. Fagagna), 200 (P. Torelli), 295 (Groto). Some of these imitations have already been mentioned, namely those by Alberti, Casone, Groto, Moro, Stigliani, G. B. Strozzi, and Tasso (on imitations of *A.P.* 9.440 see above, p. 3, n. 3).

Of the remaining, those of Michelangelo Angelico and Marcantonio Virtuani present but faint traces of well-worn themes.[2]

> Ben avrete de l'opra il premio poi:
> Forza e vigor da' miei sospiri ardenti,
> Grazia ed odor da' dolci fiati suoi.

A second sonnet, *Dono di Pesci*, (*ibid.*, p. 96), likewise a dedicatory poem, may also have a neo-Latin source. Two madrigals (*Lira*, pt. 3, 1630, p. 319) are inscribed: 'Traportato del Pontano.'

[1] Quadrio 1 (1742). 109. A number of books by Fiamma, who is said to have been a Venetian, appeared about this time (cf. the catalogues of the British Museum and the Bibliothèque Nationale); 'L' Ammassato' writes as though the compiler were no longer living. Indeed sonnets by Carlo Fiamma are included by Ruscelli in the *Sesto Libro delle Rime* published in 1553. The little that is known of the *Orditi* of Padua is given by Maylender, *Storia delle Accademie d'Italia* 4.141.

Of the verses in the *Gareggiamento* signed only with initials, those by 'M.M.' are most numerous, and are evidently the work of Maurizio Moro.

[2] Angelico came from Vicenza, was a member of the Academy of the *Olimpici*, and published a translation from Galen: *L'Antidotario*, Vicenza, 1613. His *Poesie* were collected and published at Venice in 1665 (Mazzuchelli). Virtuani is only known as the author of a poem in *terza rima* entitled *Viaggio di Montagna*, the manuscript of which was noticed by Quadrio in the Ambrosian Library

Giovanni Battista Maurizio seems to be totally unknown; Quadrio notes verses by him in the *Tempio* dedicated to Cardinal Cintio Aldobrandini, Bologna, 1600. His version of *A.P.* 7.669 has little merit. Carlo Coquinato Fagagna gives a very loose treatment of the theme of *A.P.* 16.129 on Niobe.[1] The version of *A.P.* 16.200 by Pomponio Torelli merits quoting:[2]

> Havea deposto e la faretra e l'arco,
> E d'insoliti panni
> Rustici e vili sostenea l'incarco,
> Già pronto a le fatiche et a gli affanni,
> Amor crudele, a un grave
> Giogo, scherzando, i tardi buoi giongea.
> Già sparso il seme havea,
> E frutto n'attendea dolce e soave,
> Onde a Giove rivolto: 'Queste amiche
> Piagge a Clori orna tu di bionde spiche,
> Tu, disse, le feconda, e se nol fai,
> Sotto altra Europa novo Toro andrai.'

Eleven versions of *A.P.* 9.346 form a true *gareggiamento*. Carlo Fiamma, we have seen, may have been the compiler of the collection. Agostino Nardi was a native of Fano; his *Rime* appeared in 1613. Late in life he joined the Franciscan Order. Cesare Simonetti was likewise from Fano, but of an earlier generation; his *Rime* appeared at Padua in 1579, and again, enlarged, in 1586. A modern edition was made at Fano in 1831: *Rime Scelte*, etc.[3] Pietro Petracci was a Venetian; he published (? at Venice) *Rime Diverse*, composed a volume of madrigals, and two anthologies: *Le Muse Sacre* (Venice, 1608) and *La Celeste Lira* (*ibid.*, 1612). Valerio Belli was better known. His reputation as a poet was respectable, and as an orator he was deemed worthy to pronounce the funeral oration over Andrea Palladio, the architect, at Vicenza in 1580. Belli was himself a

---

[1] Fagagna was born at Treviso, became doctor of laws, but died young; he is said to have left a volume of madrigals, but his verses are known only from such anthologies as the *Gareggiamento*. See Quadrio 2 (1741). 461.

[2] Torelli (1539–1608) was a nobleman, descended from the counts of Guastalla. He studied at Padua, then traveled in France. His wife was a niece of Pius V. Ottavio Farnese and the famous Alessandro employed him in persuading Philip II to restore the citadel of Piacenza. The heir of the Farnesi was put in his charge. He died at Parma, where he had lived and published his writings. The principal of these are: *Rime Amorose* (Parma, 1575); *Trattato del Debito del Cavaliero* (*ibid.*, 1596); *Carminum libri sex* (*ibid.*, 1600); and five tragedies: *Tancredi* (1579), *Merope* (1598), *Galatea* (1603), *Vittoria* (1603), and *Polidoro* (1605). Of these I have seen the *Rime Amorose*, in which I note a free treatment of the theme of *A.P.* 7.669.

[3] Flamini, *Cinquecento*, p. 575.

native of that city. His *Madrigali* appeared at Venice in 1599, his *Testamento Amoroso* at Vicenza in 1619. The imitations of *A.P.* 9.346 by these five writers here follow:[1]

CARLO FIAMMA

Fuggi il marmo spietato,
Garruletta loquace;
Non miri il volto irato
De la crudel, che negò a' figli pace?
Troppo semplice affidi
In grembo di Medea la prole, e i nidi:
Che se di marmor è, ben a mille a mille
Percosso manda fuor fiamme e faville.

AGOSTINO NARDI

Rondinella loquace,
A che semplice affidi
A la crudel Medea la prole, e i nidi?
Non è non è con l'altrui sangue pia,
Chi verso il suo fu ria.

CESARE SIMONETTI

Semplice Rondinella,
E mal' accorta poi,
Che fidi i figli tuoi
Cari, a Medea d'ogni pietà rubella?
Sarà al tuo sangue pia
Quella che al suo fu si malvagia e ria?

PIETRO PETRACCI

Incauta Rondinella,
Se tu fabrichi 'l nido
De la crudel Medea nel seno infido,
Io t'arreco novella,
Ch' in un loco, in un tempo avranno poi
E la culla e la tomba i figli tuoi.

VALERIO BELLI

Di Medea cruda è quella
Statua, dov' hai tu 'l nido,
Misera Rondinella:
O consiglio mal fido
Credere i figli tuoi
A lei, ch' uccise i suoi!

[1] For the original see above, p. 134.

RISPOSTA

Uccise il figlio anch' ella,
    Quest' empia Rondinella,
    Se già mostrosi ignuda
    D'Amor, fia sempre cruda:
    Lì sta ben che s'annide,
    Son due madri homicide.

Progne il suo figlio uccise,
    Nè humanità, nè affetto
    Materno raffrenò l'irato petto;
    Che meraviglia fie,
    Ch' ora che è fatto uccello i figli oblie?

MEDEA RAGIONA

Qual empia, qual rubella
    Lingua di me favella?
    Qual destra scrive, ch'io
    Mort' habbia il sangue mio?
    Morto ah! s'io nel mio petto
    Annido uccelli, a fiere dò ricetto?
    Pio cor, giudice sei,
    S'io tengo altrui, spent' havrò i figli miei?

GIOVAN FRANCESCO MAIA MATERDONA
(fl. 1625)

Materdona was a native of Misagna in the Terra d'Otranto, near Brindisi. His *Rime* were published at Venice in 1629 and reprinted in 1630 at Milan.[1] He is known as a follower of Marino.

One of Materdona's poems is a translation of *A.P.* 9.44, beginning:

Huom, che moria di fame,
    Sol di viver satollo,
    Per morir s'havea misso un laccio al collo.
    Indi a poco un tesoro
    Trovò. . . .

Very likely he did not take it directly from the Greek. Another of his poems, *Alla sua Lucerna*, recalls *A.P.* 5.8; and a third, *A una Zanzara*, is based on a theme that was a great commonplace in amatory verse to the sixteenth and seventeenth centuries, and that probably goes back to the Anthology (*A.P.* 5.152).[2]

---

[1] References are to the first edition.
[2] See above, p. 129.

ALESSANDRO GUARINI
(*c.* 1565–1636)

Alessandro was the eldest of the four sons of G. B. Guarini, author of the *Pastor Fido;* the date of his birth is uncertain.[1] Sent at an early age to study at the *Sapienza* of Perugia, he promptly returned to Ferrara, complaining of poor health and bad treatment at the hands of his fellow students. His father commanded him to go back to Perugia. He respectfully declined (as he says), and had finally to take refuge from his angry parent at the home of an uncle at Parma. A reconciliation was effected in 1584. Two years later his father married him to a wealthy heiress, Virginia Palmiroli, whose father was recently dead, and himself took over the management of her property. Soon the young couple found courage to dispute this arrangement, and were driven from the house. They resorted to the law; but Duke Alfonso, in order to avoid scandal, appointed an arbiter. Seemingly his decision was too favorable to the son, for the old poet soon after gave up his offices at Court and retired from Ferrara.[2] In 1593 father and son once more were reconciled in a meeting at the Court of the Gonzaghi at Mantua. Alessandro soon after began to reside in Padua. Trouble again broke out in 1601. This time Alessandro left Italy, accompanying Bentivoglio to Brussels; but he was compelled to hasten back to meet the lawsuit his father had set in motion against him in his absence. In 1610 the elder published a pamphlet attacking his son. Alessandro had won the suit.

The younger Guarini seems at one time to have been professor of *litterae humaniores* in Ferrara, and Secretary to the Duke. Besides minor verses, which appear never to have been collected, he published a comedy, *Bradamante Gelosa* (Ferrara, 1616), and two prose works: an *Apologia di Cesare* (*ibid.*, 1632), and *Il Farnetico Savio* (*ibid.*, 1610), on the madness of Tasso, whom he had undoubtedly known. Alessandro died on August 14, 1636.

Among the scattered verses of Alessandro is the following imitation of *A.P.* 6.1:[3]

> Ruppe lo specchio, e disse,
> Piangendo la fuggita età novella,
> Donna che fu già bella:
> 'Specchio incostante, omai
> Morta la mia beltà tu non vivrai;
> Chè mirar questo volto
> Qual è non voglio, e qual già fu m'è tolto.

---

[1] My notice of Alessandro is mainly from Vittorio Rossi, *Battista Guarini ed Il Pastor Fido*, Turin, 1886, pp. 31, 89 ff., and 109. The account of the disputes between father and son is quoted by Rossi from Alessandro's manuscript *Apologia* (*Cod. Ferrar.* 156. t. II); though naturally colored by the impulse of self-defence, it seems to contain no statement that can be proved false.

[2] He had had worse domestic troubles; his daughter Anna had been murdered by her husband, Count Ercole Trotti, with the connivance of her brother Girolamo.

[3] *Rime Oneste de' Migliori Poeti*, Bergamo, 1750, 2.395.

ANSALDO CEBÀ

(1565–1623)

Cebà, a member of a noble Genoese family connected with the Grimaldi, received his education, first in Genoa, probably from the Jesuits, and then at the University of Padua, where his teachers in poetics and moral philosophy were Sperone Speroni and Giasone de Nores. He also acquired a good knowledge of Greek. Returning in 1591 to Genoa, he was made a member of the Academy of the *Addormentati*, and soon distinguished himself by his academic lectures. His first book of verse, *Rime*, appeared in 1596 at Padua and Antwerp. The love-poetry of a Petrarchan stamp which it contained—celebrating a Genoese lady, Aurelia Spinola—gave way in a second volume of *Rime* (Rome, 1611) to religious and moral themes. At Genoa in 1615 he published an epic poem entitled *Ester;* in 1617 his *Cittadino di Repubblica;*[1] in 1620 his translation of Theophrastus' *Characters*. In 1621, also at Genoa, appeared *Esercizii Accademici;* a dialogue, *Il Gonzaga over del Poema Heroico;* a tragedy, *La Principessa Silandra;* and *Il Principio dell' Historia Romana*. A second epic poem, *Il Furio Camillo*, a second tragedy, *Alcippo Spartano*, and two volumes of *Lettere*, came out in 1623, the year of Cebà's death. A third tragedy, *Le Gemelle Capovane*, was printed for the first time in Maffei's *Teatro Italiano* (vol. 2), Verona, 1723.[2]

Cebà's version of Theophrastus, *I Charatteri Morali di Theophrasto*, is followed by a commentary in which the translator several times has recourse to the Greek epigrams to illustrate his original. For example, on the character of the Parsimonious Man (*Char.* 10), in illustration of the words, ἑστιῶν τοὺς δημότας μικρὰ τὰ κρέα κόψας παραθεῖναι, (invitando a desinare suoi popolani, taglia piccoli pezzi di carne e ponli loro davanti), he cites several examples of miserliness, and adds: 'E poco diverse ancora son quelle [miserie], che dice, proverbiando, Ammiano [*A.P.* 11.413] di certo Apelle, ch' invitava gli amici a soli messi d'herbe, pur com' essi fossono pecore; e che tocca Automedonte [*A.P.* 11.325] d'un altro, cui dice, gabbando, non voler nominare, perchè essendo colui stizzoso, havea gran paura, non per vendetta l'invitasse da capo.'[3] Though he takes both these epigrams from Stobaeus,[4] elsewhere he quotes directly from the

---

[1] Eng. trans. by C. E. Lester, New York, 1845.
[2] On Cebà see Belloni, *Il Seicento*, in Vallardi's *Storia Letteraria d'Italia*. I regret not having seen G. Bertolotto's *Liguri Ellenisti: Ansaldo Cebà*, in the *Giornale Ligustico* for 1890, mentioned by Belloni.
[3] *Char.* (1620), p. 119.
[4] Cf. above, p. 6, n. 2.

Anthology. In all, he cites *A.P.* 9.11, 13B; 10.95; 11.172, 325, 413.

BENEDETTO FIORETTI
(1579–1642)

Fioretti was born at Mercatale in the diocese of Pistoia, October 18, 1579. It appears that he turned to letters only in his thirtieth year. His first attempts at poetry meeting with no success, he devoted himself to compiling a mammoth work about poetry. The result is almost indescribable. Fioretti brings together not only all that prolonged study could discover on the subject of poetry and the various branches of poetry, but also a great part of what has been said on particular poets and on their poems. His lists of authorities are imposing, and the minutiae with which he is mainly concerned give his pages a forbidding aspect. There is almost no attempt at arrangement. The book is called *Proginnasmi Poetici*, and was published under Fioretti's academic name, Udeno Nisiely, at Florence in 1620, in two volumes; later editions were increased to four and finally to five volumes. This encyclopedia apparently had readers, for it was reprinted after the author's death.[1] Its best justification is as a sort of forerunner of Quadrio.

Fioretti belonged to the Florentine Academy of the *Apatisti*—for he made his home in Florence—and, after the founder Coltellini, was its most enthusiastic promoter. His fellow academicians included Carlo Dati and Benedetto Buommattei. He may have conversed with Milton. Towards the end of his life he turned to religious and ethical themes. His *Esercizi Morali* began to appear in 1633; his *Osservazioni di Creanze* only came out in 1675.

In the first volume of Fioretti's *Proginnasmi* he boasts of having used 367 authorities; but he exceeds this in later volumes. It would be surprising not to find the Anthology in so great a number. As a matter of fact, he often refers to it, sometimes with a prose version in Latin of the epigram in question, sometimes with merely a bare reference, and sometimes with a quotation from the notes of Brodaeus or Obsopoeus, showing that he used the Wechel edition of 1600. He quotes the prose versions of Eilhardus Lubinus.

Proginnasmo 119 of vol. 3 is entitled: *Pindaro esaltato sopra tutti i Lirici*. In it he quotes and explains *A.P.* 7.34: 'Negli Epigrammi Greci trovansi registrate molte fedi onoratissime di vari poeti sopra il merito d'un tanto lirico. Quivi Antipatro, l.3, cap. 25, il nomina *Piericam Cytharam*, *et sacrorum gravesonantium*

---

[1] All my references are to the edition published at Florence in 1695.

hymnorum conditorem. Nobilissima allegoria. *Piericam Cytha-ram:* per antonomasia Poeta Lirico è solo Pindaro sopra gli altri. *Sacrorum hymnorum:* non ode poetiche, ma composizioni divine sono le sue. *Gravesonantium:* piene e ornate di suon numeroso, e di magnificenza elocutoria.' In this section Fioretti makes four further quotations from the Anthology, besides quoting more than a dozen other authorities, and the whole extends to little more than two pages.[1]

When Fioretti discusses the sonnet, he does not fail to mention the comparison of that form with the Greek epigram:[2]

> Si contrasta se il nostro sonetto è l'epigramma de' Greci e de' Latini. . . . Quanto sia differente il nostro sonetto dall' epigramma, te ne accerterai dal considerare le condizioni appartenenti all' uno e all' altro. Perocchè vedrai l'epigramma esser talora infin d'un verso, e non più, e alle volte lungo, e finalmente instabile di grandezza, e applicativo ad ogni materia o nobile o vile. Ma il sonetto vero è sempre di 14 versi, e sopra cose non abiette secondo l'uso generale. Molto più stretta conformità con l'epigramma tiene il madrigale che il sonetto.

At the end of Fioretti's third volume is a selection of the poetry of the *Apatisti*. No authors' names are given, and doubtless Crescimbeni was right in assuming that the verses are Fioretti's own. The following sonnet is said to be composed 'Ad imitazione dell' Idillio *Dum semihiulco suavio* di Platone appo Agellio, e negli Epigrammi Greci' (*A.P.* 5.78). It is inscribed to Pietro Bardi, Count of Vernio.[3]

> Mentre mi lassa la mia Dea d'amore
> Le sue labra sposar co' baci in sorte,
> L'alma alle nozze vien, seco a la corte
> Di tutti i sensi, e resta morto il core.
> Giunta al convito, in un sospir si more,
> Sepolta di due labra entro le porte.
> Ma poi ravviva, e bea l'alma sua morte
> Fra le delizie sue, pietoso Amore.
> Giuro che in ciel non an tal mensa i dei;
> Non a in suo regno Amor si dolci frutti
> Pari a questo amoroso mio ristoro.

---

[1] Besides merely general references, and references to whole chapters of *Anth. Plan.* (as Bk. 1, chap. 46; Bk. 1, chap. 59; and Bk. 2, chap. 47 in *Progin.* 5.181), Fioretti cites the following epigrams—figures in parentheses refer to volume and page of the 1695 edition: *A.P.* 2.23 (1.125) 414; (2.120); 5.132 (2.13), 237 (3.140), 262 (5.237); 7.1 (3.204), 6 (*ibid*), 34 (3.310), 35 (*ibid.*), 39 (4.164), 196 (5.64), 419 (3.371); 9.11 ff. (5.100), 184 (3.310), 188 (3.283), 401 (5.215), 469 (1.35), 583 (3.406); 11.148 (3.371); 16.147 (2.13), 151 (1.33), 305 (3.310).

[2] *Progin.* 4.232.

[3] Fioretti's birthplace was in the county of Vernio.

O labra, O bocca, ove gli spirti miei,
Suggendo il mel d'Amor, trionfan tutti,
Io direi più, ma di dolcezza moro.

GIOVAN FRANCESCO LOREDANO

(1606–1661)

PIETRO MICHIELE

(1603–?)

Giovan Francesco Loredano, the younger, was a member of the celebrated Venetian family which gave several doges to the Republic. His abilities made themselves evident at an early age, and the ordinary restrictions were set aside to allow him to sit in the Senate, and to hold the office of Treasurer at the castle of Palma Nuova, an important post, while still a youth. He was afterwards Procuratore di Peschiera. Loredano is said to have been well trained in Greek and Latin literature. He took a leading part in the literary life of Venice, founding in 1630 the Academy of the *Incogniti*, which met in his palace. Of his numerous works none is much esteemed, though most of them went through five or six editions in the seventeenth century, and several of them were translated into other languages. Among them may be mentioned *Gli Scherzi Geniali* (Venice, 1635), *Novelle Amorose* (*ibid.*, 1643), *Il Cimiterio* (*ibid.*, 1645), *Lettere* (*ibid.*, 1653). Loredano died on August 13, 1661.

Pietro Michiele was also a member of an old Venetian family. He was a member of Loredano's Academy, and known as a literary man in his day. He married a Ferrarese lady in 1643. His works include *La Benda di Cupido* (Venice, 1634), *Rime* (*ibid.*, 1642), and *Il Licida* (Venice, 1644). His name also appears on the title-page of the *Cimiterio* with that of Loredano.

The *Cimiterio* or *Epitafi Giocosi* consists of four Centuries of humorous epitaphs.[1] The fact of their being literary exercises, and not real epitaphs, brings these sepulchral epigrams at once into comparison with the Anthology. Humorous epitaphs are not unknown to the Greek (cf. *A.P.* 7.605; 11.226). The same subjects occupy the ancient and the modern versifiers, for example: famous men (*Cim.* 1.15 and *A.P.* 7.239–40), misers (*Cim.* 1.1 and *A.P.* 11.170), literary characters (*Cim.* 1.16, 20 and *A.P.* 7.136, etc.), drunkards (*Cim.* 1.48 and *A.P.* 7.24), animals (*Cim.* 1.36; 2.35 and *A.P.* 7.189–216).

[1] References are to the edition of 1658; the fourth Century was added in the edition of 1654.

The first epitaph in the *Cimiterio* is written precisely on the theme of *A.P.* 11.170:[1]

> Sen giace qui tra questi marmi unita
> D'un Avaro crudel l'alma meschina,
> Che pianse quando morte hebbe vicina
> La spesa del sepolcro e non la vita.

The following epigrams may have inspired particular epitaphs in the *Cimiterio: A.P.* 7.120, 209, 220, 308, 311, 325, 455, 456, 572; 11.170, 401; 16.294.

ANTON GIULIO BRIGNOLE SALE
(1605–1665)

Brignole was a Genoese nobleman, Marchese di Groppo, and son of Giovan Francesco Brignole Sale, Doge of Genoa. Little is recorded of his early years, though he certainly knew Chiabrera and Ansaldo Cebà, and was influenced by them. He was a member of the Academy of the *Addormentati*, and lived a literary and political life until 1652. In that year (his wife having died in 1648), he joined the Jesuits, leaving his unmarried children in the care of his mother. His principal works are: *Le Instabilità dell' Ingegno* (Bologna, 1635); *La Colonna per l' Anime del Purgatorio; Maria Maddelena Peccatrice e Convertita* (Genoa, 1636); *Tacito Abburattato* (Genoa, 1643); *Il Santissimo Rosario Meditato* (Genoa, 1647); *Della Storia Spagnuola* (Genoa, 1640); *Il Carnovale* (Venice, 1663); *Gli Due Anelli Simili* (Macerata, 1671); *Il Satirico Innocente* (Genoa, 1648); *La Vita di S. Alessio* (Genoa, 1648). The last two are said to be the best, representing the tendency to simplicity which appeared in reaction against Marinism in the middle of the seventeenth century.[2]

Brignole published his epigrams under the title: *Il Satirico Innocente, Epigrammi trasportati dal Greco all' Italiano e commentati dal Marchese Anton Giulio Brignole Sale*. He pretends to have discovered an ancient manuscript containing Greek epigrams, which were then translated into Latin by Paolo Domenico Chiesa, a Genoese lawyer. Needless to say the epigrams are Brignole's own. The implication of his title, however, is not without significance. The style of the Greek epigram is, as it were, held up as the model of simplicity for the poets of the new school. It is indeed only the style of the Greek epigram that Brignole would imitate; he draws no matter from the

---

[1] Cf.: Δακρύει Φείδων ὁ φιλάργυρος, οὐχ ὅτι θνῄσκει,
ἀλλ' ὅτι πέντε μνῶν τὴν σορὸν ἐπρίατο.

[2] Michele de Marinis, *Anton Giulio Brignole Sale e i suoi Tempi*. Genoa, 1914.

Anthology.[1] For simplicity and purity of diction he has been highly praised; without the words of his title-page, however, few readers of his epigrams would suspect that he had the Greek epigram in mind. The following is an example of his style:

> È morto Rubicone, e al capezzale
> Fino all' estremo spirto ebbe il boccale;
> Sì che il suo corpo vile
> È, assai più che cadavero, barile.
> A smaltir tanto vin, s'io ben discerno,
> D'uopo era un sonno eterno.

MICHELANGELO TORCIGLIANO
(†1679)

Torcigliano was a native of Lucca, where he died, November 25, 1679. After his death his works appeared under the title *Eco Cortese*, at Lucca, published by the Marescandoli, in three parts, the first in 1680, the second in 1681, and the third in 1683. Quadrio mentions among the contents of this book translations into Italian verse of the *Song of Songs* (in the second vol.), of the *Attis* of Catullus, of a certain number of *Anacreontea*, and of several Greek epigrams. Since I have been unable to find a copy of Torcigliano's book, I can only quote Quadrio's words:[2] 'Oltre alla versione d'Anacreonte vi si trovano pur varie altre di altri Greci, che lavorarono sul gusto d'Anacreonte, e sono Giuliano Imperadore d'Egitto, Teocrito, Eugene, Leonida Tarentino, Tiberio Erone [*sic*], Antipatro Sidonio, Leonida, Simonide, ed alcuni Incerti, i quali tutti si leggono nell'*Anthologia*.' The only Greek epigram ascribed to Eugenes is *A.P.* 16.308.

GIUSEPPE BATTISTA
(*c.* 1615–1675)

Battista was born in the Grottaglie, between Brindisi and Taranto. When very young he lost his parents; but he was able to study both at

---

[1] Harles in Fabricius' *Bibliotheca Graeca* 4.449 wrongly gives Brignole's book as a translation from the Anthology; the error was noticed by Chardon de la Rochette (*Mélanges* 1.225).

[2] *Stor.* 7 (1752). 107; cf. *Stor.* 2 (1741). 331 and 7.142, 243. Two slight works of Torcigliano, not mentioned by Quadrio, are in St. Mark's Library at Venice: *Aurora fra le Nereide* (without place or date of publication) and *Gryphius Purpureus*, Venice, 1637. Neither owes anything to the Greek epigrams. Torcigliano's translations from the Anthology are also mentioned by Argelati and Paitoni (below, p. 404) and by Carcani, *Raccolta* 1.xvi (below, p. 426). Paitoni, in Argelati's *Bibl. Volg.* 1.50, says that Torcigliano lived in Venice.

his native place and later with the Jesuits in Naples. Here he came to the notice of G. B. Manso, who apparently took him to live at his own house. He became a member of the *Oziosi;* and was Manso's literary executor. After the death of Manso (1645) Battista spent some time with the Prince of Avellino, and then withdrew to his native village, where he lived a simple literary life. Though greatly troubled by physical ailments, he made frequent journeys in southern Italy. He died at Naples, March 6, 1675. Battista's poems were once admired; they fitted the taste of their day. Tiraboschi finds Battista 'a bad poet, who united in himself all the faults of his age,' but admits that his treatise on Poetry (1676) was influential.[1] Battista appears to have been on friendly terms with Pietro Aloïs, Lorenzo Crasso, Pietro Michiele, and Giovan Francesco Loredano.

In the Latin *Epigrammata* of Battista there is no specific debt to the Anthology.[2] Yet his Italian poems comprise a fair number of translations. This circumstance marks Battista's kinship with the poets of Marino's generation. They read little Greek themselves, but in their vernacular poems often borrowed from the Latin poets of the early sixteenth century. Hence their vernacular poems are more likely to bear traces of the Anthology than are their Latin poems, in which they shunned direct copying of their predecessors. Battista never gives any sign of knowing that his Italian verses have behind them Greek originals.[3] The following example is typical of his relation to the Greek epigrams. The original is *A.P.* 9.148:

Τὸν βίον, Ἡράκλειτε, πολὺ πλέον ἤπερ ὅτ' ἔζης,
δάκρυε· νῦν ὁ βίος ἐστ' ἐλεεινότερος.
τὸν βίον ἄρτι γέλα, Δημόκριτε, τὸ πλέον ἢ πρίν·
νῦν ὁ βίος πάντων ἐστὶ γελοιότερος.
εἰς ὑμέας δὲ καὶ αὐτὸς ὁρῶν τὸ μεταξὺ μεριμνῶ,
πῶς ἅμα σοὶ κλαύσω, πῶς ἅμα σοὶ γελάσω.

These verses were thus imitated by the French Latinist, Étienne Pasquier (1529–1615), somewhat freely, as is his wont:[4]

---

[1] Mazzuchelli gives a catalogue of Battista's works. There is a brief monograph on the poet by Emidio Ursoleo (Pescara, 1922). The account of him given by his friend Lorenzo Crasso, *Elogii d'Huomini Letterati*, Venice, 1666, p. 334, is accompanied by a portrait.

[2] *Epigrammatum Centuria Prima*, Venice, 1646; *Epigrammatum Centuriae Tres*, *ibid.*, 1653; 1659. An epitaph for Niobe (*Epig.*, 1646, p. 82) ends with a conceit similar to that of *A.P.* 7.311:
Sum mihimet tumulus, sum tumulata simul.

[3] I have employed a volume of Battista's poetry made up of two parts: *Delle Poesie Meliche*, Venice, 1666 (part 1), 1665 (part 2); and also Croce's *Lirici Marinisti*. There seem, in all, to be five parts of the *Poesie Meliche*, the fifth published at Bologna, 1670; hence I have not a complete control of his poems. The first part originally appeared at Venice in 1653.

[4] *Delitiae Poetarum Gallorum*, ed. by Janus Gruter, Frankfort, 1609, 2.852.

Heraclite, gemis, rides, Democrite, semper;
    Omnia convexi vana sub axe poli
Ut risum, ut gemitum diffunditis. En ego vestrum
    Lugeo sic risum, rideo sic gemitum.
Scilicet in vanis cum sit spes nulla medendi,
    Vanior est risus, vanior est gemitus.

The point of the original has been modified. The Greek epigrammatist hints that both philosophers were right: 'I am at a
loss as to how I am to weep with the one of you and laugh with
the other.' Pasquier concludes that, since all is vanity, both
laughter and weeping are also vain. So Battista:

Democrito, tu ridi, e col tuo riso
    Tutte le umane cose a scherno prendi,
    E, sia del fato o mesto o lieto il viso,
    Con lieto viso ogni accidente attendi.
E tu, col mento in sulla destra assiso,
    Piangi, Eraclito, e sempre al pianto intendi;
    Forse che quanto è fra di noi diviso,
    Lacrimosa tragedia esser comprendi.
Ma siate pure al pianto o al riso intenti,
    Chè 'l riso e 'l pianto a me rassembra intanto
    Vano delirio delle vostre menti.
I mali di quaggiù gravi son tanto
    Che, per guarir le travagliate genti,
    È vano il riso ed è più vano il pianto.

On other occasions Battista draws closer to the Greek. The
next two examples, which illustrate this, are versions of *A.P.*
6.331 (Alcon the Archer) and of *A.P.* 9.359, the first of the
ever-popular pair of epigrams on human life. That he does not
also have the companion piece (*A.P.* 9.360) suggests that he
has not gone directly to the Anthology, for translators regularly take both of these epigrams together. This is one circumstance whereby it can be shown that Battista is really translating the Latin version by Gaurico (above, p. 187). The translation of *A.P.* 6.331 is from the Latin of Politian:

IL FATTO D'ALCONE

Fanciul nudrito in su l'oasse algente,
Mentre i sensi sopisce in grembo a un prato,
Sovra il tenero petto arrota il dente,
E la vita gli beve, angue squamato.
Lo mira Alcone, il genitor dolente,
E dall' arco Sarmatico lunato,

Poichè licenziò canna stridente,
Salva, l'aspe ferito, il figlio amato.
Del gran colubro poi le spoglie opime
Col dardo volator, d'un pino altero
Trionfante sospende in su le cime.
E d'innalzar colà mostra pensiero
Un vivo segno et un trofeo sublime
Di padre amante, e di perito arciero.[1]

Like most of Battista's poems that go back to the Anthology, his version of *A.P.* 9.359 (after Gaurico) is in the form of a sonnet:

INFELICITÀ DELLE COSE UMANE

Delusa umanità! La vita urbana
　　Mille soffre litigi in mezzo al foro,
　　E, se 'l umore guidi appresso un toro.
　　È madre di fatiche arte villana.
Se fidar voglio un pino all' onda insana,
　　Invece d'arrichir, la morte imploro.
　　Provoca mille spade un sol tesoro,
　　E spiace altrui la povertà profana.
Letto, dove è consorte, ha sempre lite,
　　E dove ella non è, l'huom' esser suole
　　Come l'olmo esser suol senza la vite.
Hai dolore, s'hai figli, e senza prole
　　Misero sei. Beato sol s'addite
　　Chi morì nato, o mai non vide il sole.

While confident that there is an intermediary between the Greek and every one of Battista's versions from the Anthology, I have not in most cases succeeded in finding it. He has versions of the following: *A.P.* 6.331 (after Politian); 7.66; 9.77, 148 (after Pasquier), 359 (after Gaurico), 376, 449, 456, 721, 727; 10.65. The themes of *A.P.* 9.721 and 727 (on Myron's *Heifer*) occur in a single sonnet (*Mel.* 2.80); as Pasiphae is linked with the subject by Battista but not by the Greek writer, I assume he is following Ausonius (*Daedale, cur vana*), who makes the same association.

CAROLUS ACONITANUS
(*fl.* 1651)

This writer, known only from his *De Arte Epigrammate* (above, p. 68), was a cleric regular of the Order *della Madre di*

---

[1] The sentiment of the first part of the last line is not in the Greek epigram, but is in the third couplet of Politian's translation: *Sed numquam pius errat amor.*

Dio delle Scuole Pie, and was connected with the Church of Sant' Antonio in Padua.[1] Presumably he taught rhetoric in his Order. His book contains four translations from the Anthology, by Bentinus and More, taken from Soter or one of Soter's derivatives. The translations are marked 'e Graeco': *A.P.* 7.121 (Bentinus, p. 236); 9.48 (More, p. 28), 133 (More, p. 212); 11.251 (More, p. 213).

CARLO RUBERTO DATI
(1619–1676)

Dati belonged to a noble Florentine family, several members of which had already made their name honorably known in literature. Carlo had for teachers Romolo Bertini, the younger Pier Vettori and G. B. Doni; from the last two he learned Greek. He joined with eagerness in the passion for physical experiments which is characteristic of his age, was a member of the *Accademia del Cimento*, and yet like his friend Redi, who had similar interests, was devoted to literature. He was a Della Cruscan, under the name of 'lo Smarrito,' and helped with their Dictionary. With these studies he combined the profession of banker, and was something of a goldsmith. He was librarian to Cardinal Giovan Carlo de' Medici. He succeeded G. B. Doni as professor of Latin and Greek in the Florentine *Studio* (1648). After 1666 he received a pension from Louis XIV; but neither that monarch nor the Queen of Sweden was able to draw him from his native city, where he finished his life. Dati was one of Milton's Italian friends; he composed an address that stands at the beginning of Milton's Latin poems; and is referred to by Milton in *Epitaphium Damonis* 136–8. There is a letter to him from Milton under the date, April 21, 1647 (*Prose Works*, ed. by St. John, 3.500).

Among Dati's works the first place is held by his *Vite de' Pittori Antichi*, published at Florence in 1667. Naturally the Anthology affords many illustrations for a work of this sort, and Dati on occasion availed himself of them, though not to the same extent as Junius, who, in his *De Pictura Veterum* (1637) had used some 66 epigrams. Dati's work is in any case far less elaborate; he has written only the lives of Zeuxis, Protogenes, Parrhasius, and Apelles; and refers to only 10 epigrams.[2]

---

[1] The *Catalogue* of the British Museum suggests that his name may have been Carolus Marzeus.

[2] *Vite*. Milan ('Classici Italiani'), 1806. The epigrams are *A.P.* 9.595 (p. 167), 761 (p. 34), 776 (p. 5); 16.111 (p. 95), 178–182 (p. 228), 204 (p. 197). Only *A.P.* 9.595, 761; and 16.111 are translated.

In his life of Parrhasius, when speaking of the *Philoctetes* of that painter, Dati gives a translation of *A.P.* 16.111: 'É mentovato anche il *Filottete*, i travagli del quale rappresentò col pennello stupendamente. E sopra questa pittura si legge un bellissimo epigramma di Glauco da me largamente tradotto:

> Vide Parrasio gl' infiniti affanni
> Di Filottete, e colorirgli elesse.
> Sorde lagrime fan lunga dimora
> Nell' asciutte palpebre, e dentro chiusa
> Aspra cura mordace il cuor gli rode.
> Saggio Pittore, e perchè fare eterno
> Il duol di questo eroe, che ben dovea
> Dopo tanti travagli aver quiete?'

FRANCESCO REDI
(1626–1698)

Redi was born at Arezzo. He attained the doctorate in philosophy and medicine at Pisa. In 1648 he was invited to Rome by the Colonnas, and for five years taught rhetoric in their family. Then he became physician to Ferdinand II, Grand Duke of Tuscany; when Ferdinand died he was continued in his position by Cosimo III. He was one of the founders of the *Accademia del Cimento* (1657); and as a member of that society performed important experiments in natural science. The letters that embody his observations are said to be models of the expository style. Yet Redi is chiefly remembered as a poet, one of the best the seventeenth century produced; and his chief poem, the dithyramb, *Bacco in Toscana* (Florence, 1685), can never be read without pleasure. He knew Latin, Greek, and Arabic, as well as something of the chief modern languages. He was a member of the *Accademia della Crusca*, and worked on their Dictionary; as one of the first Arcadians he assumed the name *Anicio Traustio*. In 1666 he was public lecturer on the Italian language in the Florentine *Studio*. His last years were spent at Pisa, where his health was better than at Florence.

Redi worked on his *Bacco in Toscana* from 1673 to 1685. It consists of about one thousand irregular lines, and for grace and propriety of rhythm is unsurpassed by any similar poem in modern literature.[1] Bacchus, returning from his conquest of the East, is seated with Ariadne in a Tuscan meadow. He sings to her the praises of wine, and particularly of the Italian wines to

---

[1] The English version by Leigh Hunt is well-known (*Poetical Works*, ed. by Milford, p. 468).

the disparagement of all other national drinks. As the poem nears an end, broken rhythms and incoherent sentences produce the effect of drunken frenzy, and, this subsiding, Bacchus, who has already passed judgment on most of the Italian wines, calls for the king of them all—Montepulciano. In the course of the poem Redi finds opportunities for graceful compliments to the Grand Duke, and to his literary friends, Salvini, Menzini, Filicaia, Lemene, the Abbé Regnier, and others.

It is not the poem itself, however, with which we are concerned. Redi was an academician. His poem fills thirty pages in the Milan edition, while the annotations with which he previded it fill roughly three hundred.[1] The display of learning is unmistakable, but Redi had learning to display. An enormous number of illustrations are gathered about his poem from the literatures of many languages—not excluding the Turkish; and naturally, both from the nature of his subject and because of his literary form, he often turns to the Greek. Here no authority is more often appealed to than the Anthology.

The dithyramb begins with these lines:

> Dell' Indico Oriente
> Domator glorioso il Dio del vino.

This description of Bacchus Redi illustrates from $A.P.$ 9.524, where (10) the word Ἰνδολέτην (slayer of Indians) is applied to the god.[2]

His note on lines 41–2 suggests a possible source for his interest in the Anthology at this time—it was a favorite book of his friend Salvini. The lines are:

> Arianna, mio nume, a te consacro
> Il tino, il fiasco, il botticin, la pevera.

The note is as follows: 'In un epigramma di Eratostene nel lib.6. dell' Antologia [$A.P.$ 6.77] Senofonte consacra un doglio voto a

---

[1] *Opere di Francesco Redi*, Milan ('Classici Italiani'), 1809, vol. 1.

[2] $A.P.$ 9.524 is a hymn made up entirely of epithets applied to Dionysus, which are arranged, four to a line, alphabetically as follows:

> Ἀβροκόμην, ἀγροῖκον, ἀοίδιμον, ἀγλαόμορφον,
> Βοιωτόν, Βρόμιον, Βακχεύτορα, βοτρυοχαίτην.

It continues through omega. Redi quotes all of iota:

> Ἰνδολέτην, ἱμερτόν, ἰοπλόκον ἰραφιώτην.

As his texts gave him εἰραφιώτην for the last word, he was led to write a page on the pronunciation of Greek, and hence on the possible date of the hymn.

Bacco, pregandolo ad accettarlo volentieri; poichè non ha altro da offerirgli:

> Οἰνοπότας Ξενοφῶν κένεον πίθον ἄνθετο Βάκχῳ.
> δέχνυσο δ' εὐμενέως, ἄλλο γὰρ οὐδὲν ἔχει.

Debbo questo luogo alla cortesia dell' eruditissimo Sig. Antonmaria Salvini, che nella seguente maniera lo portò nell' idioma latino:

> Quod vacuum Xenophon tibi vas dicat, accipe, Bacche;
> Namque aliud, quod det, non habet ille tibi.'

Redi's references to the Anthology are given by book only (as here), and he seems likely therefore to have used one of the current Selections; that this was Soter's, or one of the Selections based on Soter's, is suggested by his employment of the translation by 'Geraldo Buchold' for *A.P.* 9.58.[1] In all, he refers to fourteen epigrams.[2]

BARTOLOMMEO BEVERINI
(1629–1686)

Beverini was born at Lucca. He is said to have been a finished scholar at fifteen; and at Rome, in his sixteenth year, he joined the Order of the Mother of God, taking vows in 1647. He taught theology in Rome, and later, rhetoric at Lucca. His numerous works are listed by Mazzuchelli. Beverini was one of the chief correspondents of Francesco Redi (see the latter's *Lettere*, ed. Milan, 1809, 4.324 ff.).

The Latin poems of Beverini were published at Lucca in 1674: *Carminum libri septem*. These typical academic exercises include three translations from the Anthology—*A.P.* 7.294, 381; and 16. 200.[3] Beverini acknowledges his sources, for example: 'Nauta navi propria crematus, ex Graeco Messenii' (*A. P.* 7. 381):

> Una tulit vivum, morientem vexit et una,
> Cum domino pariter nata perire ratis.
> Ipsa aluit vivum, defuncti corpus adussit,
> Una undis, flammis utilis una fuit.
> Felix, qui propria secuit maris aequora cymba
> Et propria infernum puppe peregit iter.

---

[1] *Opere* 1.202; see above, p. 276.

[2] The figures within parentheses refer to the pages of vol. 1 of Redi's *Opere*, Milan, 1809: *A.P.* 6.77 (p. 49), 158 (p. 42); 7.669 (p. 200); 9.298 (p. 271), 368 (p. 97), 524 (p. 35), 645 (p. 43); 10.118 (p. 229); 11.34 (p. 48), 58 (p. 202), 59 (p. 275), 60 (pp. 46 and 281); 13.29 (p. 222); 16.248 (p. 329).

[3] The last must be in Beverini's *Carmina*, but I have missed it there; it is, as indeed are also the other two, in the *Carm. Illust. Poet. Ital.* vol. 2.

DOMENICO GISBERTI

(*fl.* 1672)

Gisberti was secretary to the Duke of Bavaria. In 1670 he published at Munich a volume of poems, *Poesie Liriche*, and two years later at the same place, a work entitled: *Le Nove Muse*. In this second book he gives the attributes of each of the Muses with remarks on the kind of poetry presided over by them. In a list of works consulted he names 'Gli epigrammi greci di Giovanni Brodeo.' This probably refers to the Wechel edition of the Anthology (Frankfort, 1600) rather than to the original publication of Brodaeus' commentary in the Basel edition (Froben), 1549. Within his book Gisberti finds occasion to quote *A.P.* 9.504 (p. 131) in the Latin translation of L. G. Giraldi.

LORENZO CRASSO

(† *c.* 1683)

Lorenzo Crasso, Barone di Pianura, was a Neapolitan, a doctor of laws, and an active lawyer. He was a man of wealth, and possessed a notable library. Other than these meagre details, and his books, nothing appears to be known of him. He had many friends among the literary men of his time, and one frequently meets with poems addressed to him in their books—Giuseppe Battista belonged to this circle.[1] Crasso published *Epistole Heroiche*, Venice, 1655 (imitations of Ovid); *Elogi d' Huomini Letterati*, Venice, 1656 (each notice being preceded by a portrait); *Istoria de' Poeti Greci e di que' che'n Greca Lingua han poetato*, Naples, 1678; and *Elogi di Capitani Illustri*, Venice, 1683. As only the first part of the last book was published, it has been conjectured that Crasso died at this time or just before.

Crasso's *Istoria de' Poeti Greci* professes to supersede the similar works of Patrizi and Voss; and, while far from exhaustive, it is in many ways a creditable performance, and contains some information even to-day not easily found elsewhere. This applies, of course, particularly to the writers of Greek verse nearly contemporary with the author; for he includes not only the Greeks of the Renaissance, and such others as write in Greek as Alessandra Scala, Turnèbe, and Dorat, but comes down to Urban VIII and Leone Allacci. His notices of the ancient poets are usually too perfunctory. Bernardo di Cristoforo, who writes

[1] Above, p. 365.

the Address to the Reader, says that Crasso while composing this work was so tormented by the gout as to be scarcely able to hold his pen.

The articles of the *Istoria* are alphabetically arranged. Since an attempt is made to include all the Greek epigrammatists, these form a conspicuous part of the work. Crasso's remarks on them are made at second hand, all apparently from the Wechel edition of the Anthology, since Obsopoeus and Brodaeus are his authorities. The epigrams are commonly quoted in the Latin prose version of Lubinus (above, p. 38); but on occasion a verse translation is borrowed from the Wechel Anthology (e.g., *A.P.* 7.80: *Ist.*, p. 190), or, more often, from a version of Diogenes Laertius (the verse-translations by Bentinus). The following is a typical entry (*Ist.*, p. 139):

DEMOCARI [DAMOCHARIS]

Questo poeta va nominato ora Damocari, ora Democari, ora Damocaride. Fu poeta lirico, anche insigne grammatico. Nell' Antologia vi sono alcuni suoi epigrammi, e alla di lui morte leggesi di Paolo Silenziario il seguente epigramma [*A.P.* 7.588]:

Democharis fati ultimam subiit terram.
 Hei, pulchrum Musae barbiton silet.
Periit Grammaticae sacra basis. Circumflua Cos,
 Et rursus luctum habes qualem super Hippocratem.

Vincenzo Ossopeo chiosa così: 'In Damocharim, qui fuit poeta lyricus et insignis grammaticus, cuius mentionem Athenaeus facit; cuius obitum Coum insulam non minore dolore, quam Hippocratis deflevisse dicit' [Wechel Anthol., p. 310].

Crasso's quotations from the Anthology are not confined to his notices of the epigrammatists. In his articles on other Greek poets he finds numerous opportunities to quote the epigrams and epitaphs; in some instances his only source of knowledge is a Greek epigram, as for the poet Joannes lauded in *A.P.* 7.697; and he goes so far as to include the names of poetasters held up to ridicule in several satirical epigrams (as *A.P.* 11.133, 188, and 312), though it is hardly doubtful that these are fictitious.

A place among the Greek poets is found for Maximus Planudes (*Ist.*, p. 327), but without mention on Crasso's part of his work on the Anthology. This work is dealt with by Volaterranus and Voss in the extracts Crasso quotes from them.[1]

---

[1] Volaterranus: 'Epigrammata Veterum Graecorum, resectis lascivioribus, in unum iam vulgo sparsum volumen coegit.'

Besides a large number of less definite references to the Anthology, impossible here to control, Crasso has translations of the following:[1] *A.P.* 2.111–6, 219–23, 291–6, 354–6, 357–60, 361–6, 392; 5.78 (Gaza); 7.4, 6, 8–11, 13, 17–20, 22, 25, 30,34, 35, 39, 41, 42, 45 (Giraldi), 46, 54 (Sanchez), 55, 69, 71, 75, 80 (Bentinus), 89, 92 (Bentinus), 104 (from Laert.), 107 (from Laert.), 114 (Bentinus), 116 (from Laert.), 122 (Bentinus), 125, 126 (Bentinus), 127 (Bentinus), 142, 313 (Aretinus or Volaterranus; from Giraldi), 348 (Crasso?), 355, 370, 412, 414, 416–7, 558, 576, 588–9, 593, 595, 617, 620 (Bentinus), 629, 674 (L. G. Giraldi), 697, 706, 714–6, 745 (Aegidius); 9.25–6, 66, 118, 145, 184.1, 186–90, 211, 213, 250, 283, 308, 342, 390, 545, 565, 571.4, 581; 10.46, 97; 11.131, 133, 158, 188, 312; 13.29; 14.101 (Bentinus); 16.61, 91, 276, 296, 311, 334 (Bentinus).

GIUSEPPE BARBERIO

(fl. 1675)

What is known of Barberio comes from his own brief sketch of his life in his *Miseries of the Greek Poets.* He was born at Sant'Elia, Diocese of Casini, in the Kingdom of Naples. Writing in 1685, he says he has been twenty years away from his native place; presumably, however, he did not leave the Kingdom of Naples, since his books were published in that city. Mazzuchelli says he was a parish priest. He was at any rate a teacher, for he names among his 'miseries' ungrateful pupils: 'Paupertate dira, domestico bello, discipulis ingratis, lite maximo cum potentioribus maximo cum periculo.' He was a man of learning, with a bent for poetry: 'Natus ad poesim; Thuscam, Latinam frequentavi, Graecam attigi.' Besides his *De Miseria Poetarum Graecorum liber* (Naples, 1685), Barberio lists thirty other works which he says he has published. They include treatises on poetry and poets and on theological questions in Latin, and, in the vernacular, *Nottole Poetiche, Versi e Prose,* three comedies: *Accortezza all 'Improviso, Amoroso Fallo, Le Frenesie;* and other dramatic pieces.[2]

Barberio's *De Miseria* was written in imitation of Valeriano's *De Infelicitate.* Each notice includes an epigram on the poet concerned, usually of Barberio's own composition, but often borrowed from L. G. Giraldi (above, p. 183) or others. In this way he has some eleven translations from the Anthology: *A.P.* 7.3 (Giraldi), 24 (Calcagnini), 39.3–4 (from a translation of Plutarch), 54 (Giraldi), 92 (Bentinus), 313 (Aretinus *ap.*

---

[1] Where the number is not followed by a name in parentheses the translation is usually in the prose of Lubinus—marked 'L-prose' in the Register.

[2] The *De Miseria* was reprinted with Alcionio's *Medices legatus de Exsilio,* Leipzig, 1707, and in Gronovius' *Thesaurus Antiq. Graec.* 10.797–851, which last I employ. Barberio's other works are difficult to find; Mazzuchelli only vouches for *Atlas Fidei* and *Romani Imperii Triumphus,* both published at Naples in 1686.

Giraldi), 348 (Giraldi), 615 (Giraldi), 616 (Giraldi), 617 (?) 674 (Giraldi). He does not always give the translator credit; and shows no evidence of knowing that the verses he borrows had Greek originals.

Yet he knew the Anthology. Among the Greek poets he includes Maximus Planudes, who, he vaguely says, 'suas etiam passus est miserias,' adding these verses in the person of Planudes:[1]

> Hoc mihi pro meritis? Musarum Florida Graium
> Digessi. Vatum gloria vivit adhuc.
> Hoc ego iam merui, quoniam non casta recidi,
> Impiaque, ut sancte Floridus esset ager.

CARLO MARIA MAGGI
(1630–1699)

Maggi, a native of Milan, was secretary to the Senate of that city, and professor of Greek in the Palatine School. He was a close friend of Muratori, who edited his *Rime Varie* in 4 vols. at Milan in 1700. A larger edition was published in 1708 at Venice in 6 vols., entitled *Poesie Varie*. Maggi had already published a single volume with the title *Rime Varie* at Turin and Florence in 1688. Finally there appeared a volume entitled *Rime e Prose* at Venice in 1719.

In a review of this last book, published in the *Giornale de' Letterati d'Italia* 32 (Venice, 1719). 213, the writer quotes Scipione Maffei for the following remarks on Maggi: 'Per confermar parimente di quanto pregiudicio fosse al Maggi la sua vaghezza di pensieri, e di sentenze, si fa avvertire, come avendo lui tradotti del greco alcuni epigrammi dell' Antologia, quasi essi fossero imperfetti o rozzi, aggiunse a ciascheduno la chiusa, cioè una sentenza nel fine, con che vengono i più di que' componimenti a deformarsi, e a perdere ogni bellezza.'

Paitoni says that Maggi in his *Rime Varie* has turned an epigram by Philippus into a sonnet.[2] Argelati takes from Scipione Maffei's list of translators the statement that Maggi translated two epigrams as madrigals in his *Rime Varie*, and others in his *'Opere*, vol. 1.'[3] These translations I have failed to find. They

---

[1] Gronovius, *Thes. Graec.* 10.846. In the third line he echoes Volaterranus' words given above, p. 374, n. 1.

[2] Paitoni, *Biblioteca degli Autori . . . Volgarizzati*, Venice, 1766–74, 2.69.

[3] Argelati, *Biblioteca degli Volgarizzatori*, ed. by Villa, Milan, 1767, 1.63. Compare Maffei, *Opere*, Venice, 1790, 19.337.

are not in Maggi's *Rime Varie* of 1688. I believe they are not in his *Rime Varie* of 1700. Unfortunately I have been unable to consult his *Poesie Varie* of 1708 or the *Rime e Prose* of 1719.

Muratori himself, in his life of Maggi, gives the following account of the poet's translations from Greek writers:[1]

Recò molti loro componimenti in versi Italiani, e massimamente una gran parte degli Epigrammi, che leggonsi nell' Antologia, o sia Florilegio de' Greci. Alcuni di questi sono già pubblicati, ed altri ancora godranno ora il medesimo beneficio, essendosi per disavventura smarrito il rimanente d'essi. A ciò posso aggiungere, ch' egli leggiadramente componeva versi in quella favella, un saggio de' quali eccovi a me una volta trasmesso in lode del dottissimo e celebre Signor Antonio Magliabechi, Bibliotecario di S.A.R. il Gran Duca di Toscana:

> Μνημοσύνη Μούσων μητήρ σοι δῖα πάρεστι·
> υἱὸς Μνημοσύνης Μαλιαβηκὶ πέλεις.
> ταύτῃ θαυμαστός συ μαθήματα πάντα φυλάττεις,
> κτήματα Πιερίδων ὥσπερ ἀδελφὸς ἔχεις.

Io mi presi ardire di trasportarli così in Latino:

> Te Dea Mnemosyne genuit, tibi semper adhaeret
> Mnemosyne Aonidum, Maliabeche, parens.
> Hac duce, doctrinas solide complecteris omnes,
> Suntque tuae, ut fratris, divitiae Aonidum.

BENEDETTO AVERANI

(1645–1707)

Averani was born in Florence of a good family. His brother Giuseppe, who survived to edit Benedetto's works, was a celebrated jurist and philosopher, and a second brother, Niccolò, was known as a lawyer and mathematician. As a child, Benedetto gave evidence of a good mind, and in the early stages of mathematics and Latin was self-taught. In rhetoric he had for teacher a Jesuit named Vincenzo Glaria. He was sent by his father to Pisa to study law; in his spare time he kept up his literary and mathematical interests. The fame of his learning got abroad, and Cardinal Leopold de' Medici promised him the chair of literature at Pisa. Averani redoubled his efforts. One of his exercises was to turn Sallust and Celsus into Greek. He was made professor of Greek at Pisa in 1676. In that capacity he lectured on the Anthology, Euripides, and Thucydides. His audience was usually large, composed of professors and visitors as well as students. Among his pupils at Pisa was the afterwards famous Anton Maria Salvini (below, p. 382). A few years later he advanced to the professorship of

[1] *Vita di Carlo Maria Maggi*, Naples, 1757, p. 32.

litterae humaniores, lecturing now on Livy, Virgil, and Cicero's *De Oratore*. His lectures, which were published after his death, contain little in the way of philological discovery; but Averani was endowed with a remarkable memory, and it is still possible to profit from the wealth of parallel passages he has drawn together from the whole range of ancient literature. He did not give up his interest in Greek, but continued to teach it privately. He composed in addition to his lectures an Italian dissertation on the fourth sonnet of Petrarch, and was himself a writer of vernacular poetry.[1] He was always at work, and gained a great reputation. The University of Padua and Pope Innocent XI both tried in vain to induce him to leave Pisa. His health was never good; in August, 1707, he suffered an apoplectic stroke, and died in the last days of December. He is buried in the Campo Santo.

Ten years after Benedetto's death his brother Giuseppe brought out, in three large folio volumes, his *Opera Latina* to which he prefixed a Life. The first two volumes contain the Dissertations on several classical authors mentioned above, and the third his thirty Orations, one delivered each year on the first of November for the opening of the University, together with Familiar Epistles, Latin Poems, and a most elaborate Index (494 pages, double columns) for the Dissertations alone, since there is, preceding, a separate Index to the Orations and Epistles.[2]

Averani began to be professor of Greek literature at Pisa in 1676. His first lectures were on the Greek Anthology, and were continued on the same subject into the following year. The *Dissertationes in Anthologiam* are eighty-six in number, and fill 226 pages, double columns, in his Works.

It must be remembered that these dissertations were presented to students, and are designed for that purpose; they make no pretention of furnishing the world of scholarship with new interpretations or other matter of research. Averani says he will give a grammatical interpretation of each epigram, explaining all obscure words and usages, and providing a literal translation of each poem. He actually does this, and further explains the material contents of the epigrams with considerable fullness. In eighty-six dissertations he discusses only thirty-five epigrams. He begins at the beginning of the Planudean Anthology, but, after following the order of that collection for a time, sees that he cannot manage the whole, and thereafter selects. Elementary as his explanations are, they are designed

---

[1] A ms. in the Bibl. Nazionale Centrale at Florence (Cl. 7. 1, No. 867) contains verses by him (Mazzatinti, *Inventari* 13.181).

[2] *Opera Latina, regiae celsitudini Cosmi III, Magni Etruriae Ducis, dicata.* 3 vols. fol., Florence, 1717.

to display the wealth of the professor's reading; for example, in
the second dissertation he seeks illustrations in Cicero, Plato,
Thucydides, Demetrius Phalereus, Arrian, Aristotle, Clement
of Alexandria, Homer, Horace, Virgil, Eustathius, Apollodorus,
Pausanias, Ovid, Pindar, Statius, Lycophron, Strabo, Aristophanes, *scholia* on Aristophanes' *Plutus*, Seneca (*Her. Fur.*),
Suetonius, Plutarch, Livy, Sallust, Galen, Hippocrates, Lucian,
and Apuleius. In an addendum (*Op.* 2.381) a dozen more are
added. The one source from which he never draws illustrations
is the Anthology itself!

In the first dissertation he is chiefly interested in developing
the notion, contained in the title of the Anthology, of flower-
gathering. He states briefly that the Anthology was collected
by Maximus Planudes. One would have expected better of the
professor of Greek at Pisa in the third quarter of the seventeenth century.

In the second dissertation he begins with the first epigram of
the *Planudea* (*A.P.* 9.357). His method here is his method
throughout. He identifies the epigrammatist, Archias, with
Cicero's client, remarks on the importance of the Greek games,
quotes the epigram, and translates:

> Quattuor instituit certamina Graecia, quorum
>   Sunt duo sacra homini, sunt duo sacra deo.
> Iupiter, Archemorus, Phoebus, Melicerta coluntur.
>   Sunt apium, malum, pinus, oliva, decus.

He then takes up individual words—e.g., ἀγῶνες means *certamina*, and has several related words, as ἀγωνόθεται, etc. Next
he gives an account of the first-mentioned games, the Olympic.
In the third dissertation he is still occupied with the same epigram, giving an account of the Pythian games and the Pythian
oracle. In this way his discussion of the first epigram occupies
him through his sixth lecture. On other occasions he finds less
to explain.[1]

The twenty-first Dissertation is Averani's introductory lecture to the second year of his course. He hints that his hearers
need not fear being wearied by monotony, first because of the

---

[1] The epigrams commented on by Averani in his first year are: *Diss.* 2-6 (*A.P.*
9.357); *Diss.* 7-9 (*A.P.* 9.391); *Diss.* 10 (*A.P.* 9.557); *Diss.* 11-12 (*A.P.* 6.256); *Diss.*
13-14 (*A.P.* 9.375); *Diss.* 15 (*A.P.* 9.165); *Diss.* 16-18 (*A.P.* 9.248); *Diss.* 19-20 (*A.P.*
16.178).

varied contents of the Anthology, and secondly, because he in-
tends to set no bounds to his illustrations. 'For what is not to
be found in that great treasury of Greek elegance? How many
things may here be read on the gods of antiquity, on their worship, and their cults, how many things about famous generals,
illustrious philosophers, good poets, astronomers, mathema-
ticians! Here is much on distinguished orators, and others eminent in art and in science. Many also are the excellent things
said about peace and war, on the inconstancy of Fortune, on the
ruin of powerful cities. Jests of the banquet-table are not wanting, nor valuable moral precepts, nor amatory themes, censure
of the wicked, praise of the great and famous; much learning is
here, many a fact concerning antiquity; and frequent mention
of the games of the theatre and Circus, of athletes, and of all
manner of monuments, is to be found in this varied, this mani-
fold work.'[1]

In the second year, it will be seen, he evidently gave a more
complete course than in the first. The last of his dissertations
on the Anthology, moreover, does not give any indication that
it is the final lecture of his series. It may be that he actually delivered more lectures than were afterwards polished for publication. As an example of his translations in the second year,
we may take that of his final dissertation (*A.P.* 9.291):

> Si totum spatiosa bibat Germania Rhenum,
>   Oceanusque omnes invehat altus aquas,
> Caesaris intrepidi dum vis invicta manebit,
>   Nil robur laedet, Roma superba, tuum.
> Sacra Iovi quercus sic stat radicibus imis,
>   At folia excutiunt arida facta Noti.

Averani seldom recurs to the Anthology in his later lectures.
In his sixteenth dissertation on Thucydides he repeats his
translation of *A.P.* 16.1, and in his twenty-second dissertation
on Cicero, quotes and translates *A.P.* 9.247; elsewhere he has a

---

[1] In the second year Averani discussed the following: *Diss.* 22–3 (*A.P.* 9.453); *Diss.*
24–5 (*A.P.* 9.307); *Diss.* 26 (*A.P.* 9.287); *Diss.* 27–8 (*A.P.* 7.146); *Diss.* 29–32 (*A.P.*
7.73); *Diss.* 33–5 (*A.P.* 11.3); *Diss.* 36–9 (*A.P.* 9.298); *Diss.* 40 (*A.P.* 7.669–670); *Diss.*
41 (*A.P.* 10.108); *Diss.* 42 (*A.P.* 10.19); *Diss.* 43 (*A.P.* 7.461); *Diss.* 44–8 (*A.P.* 16.183);
Diss. 49–54 (*A.P.* 16.1; 9.61); *Diss.* 55–8 (*A.P.* 9.39); *Diss.* 59–63 (*A.P.* 9.266); *Diss.*
64 (*A.P.* 9.54, 127); *Diss.* 65 (*A.P.* 11.31); *Diss.* 66–8 (*A.P.* 7.275); *Diss.* 69–72 (*A.P.*
7.162); *Diss.* 73–5 (*A.P.* 7.9); *Diss.* 76 (*A.P.* 9.29); *Diss.* 77 (*A.P.* 9.408); *Diss.* 78–81
(*A.P.* 10.66, 122); *Diss.* 82–4 (*A.P.* 7.68; 16.200); *Diss.* 85–86 (*A.P.* 9.291).

bare half-dozen references.[1] He used a Wechel Anthology of 1600.

In all, Averani translates the following: *A.P.* 6.256;7.9, 68, 73, 146, 162, 275, 461, 465, 670; 9.29, 39, 54, 61, 127, 165, 247, 248, 266, 287, 291, 298, 307, 357, 375, 453, 557; 10.19, 66, 108, 122; 11.3, 31; 16.1, 2, 151.9–10, 183, 200.

ANDREA PERRUCCI
(1651–1704)

Perrucci was born at Palermo, and made his home in Naples. He is chiefly known as a writer of plays and melodramas. In 1695 he published his lyrical poems at Naples under the title: *Idee delle Muse.* One sonnet in this collection is constructed on the theme of *A.P.* 9.148—Democritus and Heraclitus—but is far from being a direct imitation of the Greek.[2]

MICHELE CAPPELLARI
(1630–1717)

Cappellari was born at Belluno. He studied at Padua. An early poem won him the attention of the Venetian senator Basadonna, who took him to Rome when he went as ambassador to Alexander VII. Here Cappellari won favor; the pope granted him the decanate of Belluno. He returned, however, with Basadonna to Venice, where his fame as a poet continued to increase. When Basadonna became cardinal, Cappellari returned to Rome with him. After the cardinal's death other friends secured for Cappellari a professorship at Padua, but he soon left it to become Latin Secretary to the Queen of Sweden. He now began a Latin epic poem in her honor. When Christina died in 1689, he received a pension, and finally left Rome for Venice, between which city, Belluno, and Padua, he passed the rest of his life. In 1700 at Venice appeared his *Christina Lustrata;* for which Clement XI granted him a second pension. After 1714 he retired to his country house near Belluno, and there died, February 19, 1717. Besides his early works and his poem on Christina, he published *Naufragium Felix* (Venice, 1668); *Poematum tomus primus, in quo Epigrammatum pars prior* (Padua, 1697); and *Poematum tomus ii, Sylvarum et Epigrammatum pars posterior* (1702).[3]

---

[1] In *Diss.* 5 on Euripides he cites *A.P.* 9.148 and 10.72, and in *Diss.* 19 refers to *A.P.* 9.378; in *Diss.* 30 on Thucydides he cites *A.P.* 7.182, and in *Diss.* 34 cites *A.P.* 9.101; finally in *Diss.* 15 on Livy he translates two lines of *A.P.* 16.151.

[2] It is reprinted in Croce's *Lirici Marinisti*, p. 518.

[3] Bernardi in *Biog. degli Ital. Illust.* 10 (Venice, 1845). 216–20.

In his epigrams of 1697 Cappellari finds use for *A.P.* 9.49, 61, and 106. The first of these he employs in a poem deploring his inability to get away from Rome, probably after the death of the Queen of Sweden:

ROMA ADHUC MORARI CONQUERITUR.

'Quid mihi cum Roma? Quid cum septemplice monte?
Quid mihi cum nymphis, Tibridis unda, tuis?
Ἐλπὶς καὶ ἡ Τύχη, μέγα χαίρετε· τὸν λίμεν' εὖρον·
οὐδὲν ἐμοί χ' ὑμῖν· παίζετε τοὺς μετ' ἐμέ.

sive: Iam prope finis adest: Spes et Fortuna, valete;
Ludite nunc alios. Iam prope finis adest.'
Saepius haec iacto; iactanti saepius et iam
Accincto effugium vis inimica vetat.
Ut mihi permittant iam tandem fata recursus;
Trivimus in lucta iam prope lustra duo.
Egressum Latiis ex quo conamur ab oris:
Currere ter potui solis utramque domum.
Par labor ingressus Teucris si forte fuisset,
Roma, caput mundi, nunc quoque nulla foret.

ANTON MARIA SALVINI
(1653–1729)

Salvini, a Florentine, was one of the most distinguished scholars of his time. His university education was received at Pisa under Benedetto Averani, to whom he refers as 'amantissimo mio maestro e delle lettere eloquentissimo mantenitore.'[1] At the age of twenty-three he succeeded Carlo Dati (above, p. 369) in the chair of Greek literature at the Florentine *Studio;* and he filled that position for fifty-three years. He was a member of the *Apatisti*, a Della Cruscan, and one of the first Arcadians.

It is impossible to estimate Salvini's use of the Anthology; the epigrams turn up in almost everything he wrote; many, perhaps all of them, are translated in the manuscripts he left; and he would on occasion supply illustrations from the Anthology for the works of his friends (cf. above, p. 372). Doubtless Salvini's interest in the collection is to be traced to the lectures delivered by Averani at Pisa in 1676–77.

Much of Salvini's scholarly activity was consumed in composing illustrative notes for new editions of various Italian writers. The Anthology was always at hand. It has to be con-

---

[1] *Discorsi* (1786) 3.35; cf. Salvini's oration, *Delle Lodi di Benedetto Averani*, Florence, 1709.

fessed at times that he seems to quote more from a love of the Anthology than for the light his quotation throws on the author before him. By way of examples may be mentioned his edition of Giusto de' Conti's *Bella Mano* (Florence, 1715), wherein *A.P.* 7.670 is made to illustrate the second *canzone;* his notes on Lippi's *Malmantile;* and those on Muratori's *Perfetta Poesia* (Venice, 1724, 1.283). In the last-mentioned he gives a Latin verse-translation of *A.P.* 16.14.

Salvini supplied notes for Antonio Francesco Gori's *Monumentum, sive Columbarium Libertorum et Servorum Liviae Augustae* (Florence, 1727), among which he quotes *A.P.* 10.43 with a translation into Latin verse. Similarly in Gori's *Inscriptiones Antiquae Graecae et Latinae* (3 vols, Florence, 1727, 1734, 1744) he has a translation of *A.P.* 16.103 in the second volume. In the first volume Gori himself quotes *A.P.* 10.43 and gives a prose version.[1]

In 1717 at Venice Salvini published a translation of Theocritus into Italian verse, including, of course, the pieces common to the *Bucolica* and the Anthology.[2] He has also a translation of the sixth book of Diogenes Laertius, and in this necessarily translates four epigrams.[3]

In his academical discourses Salvini refers to the Greek epigrams with a certain frequency.[4] These short lectures on miscellaneous subjects were presented before the *Apatisti.* Salvini could not fail to quote the Anthology when discussing the following question: 'Qual fusse più ragionevole, o il riso di Democrito o il pianto d' Eraclito?' Very likely the question was itself suggested by the epigram (*A.P.* 9.148). Salvini gives a Latin version:

> Heraclite, magis iam nunc quam feceris olim,
> Nos defle—vita est nunc lacrimabilior.
> Democrite, et ride mage nunc quam feceris olim,
> Nam vita est risu nunc mage digna tuo.

[1] I have not attempted to canvass all Salvini's editions for possible translations. Doni's *Inscriptions* (8.91) contains a version by him of *A.P.* 7.15 (copied by Bonada and the *Anitchità di Ercolano*). Redi (*Opere*, 1809, 1.97) refers to a translation of *A.P.* 9.368 in Salvini's *Discorsi*, but I have been unable to find it.
[2] Above, p. 3, n. 2. These translations are listed in the Register from the second edition: *Teocrito Volgarizzato.* Arezzo, 1754 (with notes by Regnier Desmarais): *A.P.* 6.177, 336–340; 7.659–661, 663, 664; 9.338, 432–435, 437, 440 (p. 114) 598–600; 16.200.
[3] *Discorsi Accademici*, Florence, 1733. *A.P.* 7.115, 116, 326; 9.497.
[4] The *Discorsi Accademici* were published in Florence in three parts: in 1712, in 1725, and in 1733. Except for the translation of Laertius, I refer to the edition of the *Discorsi* published at Naples (6 vols. in 3), 1786.

Aspiciens ego vos, incerta mente laboro
Quomodo vobiscum rideam, et usque fleam.

Salvini's *Discorsi* contain translations of, or references to, *A.P.*
9.39, 148; 10.30; 38; 11.78, and 398. Of these, 9.39 and 148 are
translated into Latin verse; 10.30 into Italian verse; and the
others are merely quoted in part.

His labors with the Anthology were, however, far more extensive than his published works might indicate. He left an
Italian verse translation of the whole—or almost the whole—
collection. This manuscript, never printed, is—or was—preserved in the Biblioteca Marucelliana at Florence. Bandini, who
was librarian of the Marucelliana before he went to the Laurentian, drew upon this manuscript when he wanted some translations to compare with those of Carcani in a review of the latter's
Anthology (below, p. 426). He refers to the translation of Salvini as 'quasichè completa.' Carcani protests that, had he
known about Salvini's version, he would not have made a new
one.[1]

Bandini gives the first four epigrams of the Planudean Anthology (*A.P.* 9.357, 391, 557, 581) in Salvini's translation as
examples of his skill. The first two follow:

> Quattro son ludi in Grecia; quattro sacri.
>   Due di mortali, e d'immortali due.
>   Di Giove, Apollo, Palemone, Archemoro:
>   Premj—oliastro, mele, ed apio, e pino.
>   (*A.P.* 9.357)

> S'esercitar di forte lotta ai premj,
>   L'un di Nettun, l'altro di Giove stirpe.
>   Per lebete di rame essi non giuocano,
>   Ma chi riporteranno o vita o morte.
>   Cade Anteo: ben convien ch'Ercol di Giove
>   Vinca; d'Argivi, e non di Libj è lotta.
>   (*A.P.* 9.391)

Carcani admits that Salvini is very exact in his translations, especially in reproducing expressions natural to Greek, but somewhat unusual in Italian. His own translations, he hints, cannot
lay claim to this questionable virtue.

---

[1] Bandini's review, from the *Novelle Letterarie*, Florence, 1789, No. 49, is given by
Carcani at the front of the second part of his Anthology. The notice of Salvini's death,
in the *Novelle della Repubblica delle Lettere*, June 11, 1729, p. 191, mentions among his
unpublished works translations of 'un gran numero d'epigrammi greci'; cf. G. Poggiali,
Testi di Lingua 2.65.

Salvini's Latin translations from the Anthology seem also to have been numerous. They too remain mostly in manuscript. Two manuscripts in the D'Orville collection at Oxford (D'Orville 239 and 243) contain selections from them; and No. 243 also has notes by Salvini on the epigrams.[1] Further notes by Salvini on the Anthology are contained in a manuscript that once belonged to Brunck and is now at Paris (*Cod. Graec. suppl.* 392). Among Salvini's manuscripts in Florence at least one (*Cod. Marucell.* A 148) contains a group of Greek epigrams.[2]

Latin translations of certain of the epigrams of St. Gregory (*A.P.*, Book 8, consists entirely of his epigrams) were made by Salvini, and printed by Bandini in *S. Joannis Chrysostomi in Ninivitarum Poenitentiam Homilia*, Florence, 1763, pp. 113–23.[3] The following is a version of *A.P.* 8.138 (p. 119):

> Melliti Amphilochi tumulus, qui mente loquendoque
> Omnes Cappadoces vincere iam potuit.

CARLO D'AQUINO
(1654–1737)

Aquino was born at Naples, entered the Jesuit Order in 1669, and taught rhetoric in their college in Rome. He published three volumes of Latin poems: *Carminum tomi tres* [1. *Epigrammatum libri iv; Miscellaneorum liber; Anacreon Recantatus.* 2. *Heroicorum libri ii; Elegiarum libri iii; Lyricorum liber.* 3. *Satyrae xii;* Notes and Indices], Rome, 1701–3. His first book of heroic poems is dedicated to James II of England, then an exile in Rome.

Only one of Aquino's poems has its origin in the Anthology; and it must be owned that it does not prove him to have known our collection, since the epigram on Cleombrotus (*A.P.* 7.471) may be found more easily in other places.

> Desilit, aeternae captus dulcidine vitae,
>   E turri praeceps Ambrociota puer.
> Sic Plato perpetuum populos transmittis in aevum?
>   Ne pereant, homines atque perire doces?
> Assertor vitae qui debuit esse perennis,
>   Phaedon carnificem se stupet esse tuus.

---

[1] Six of Salvini's translations were printed by Wellesley from *Cod.* 243, namely those of *A.P.* 7.15; 9.66, 455, 773, 809; 11.237 (*Anthologia Polyglotta*, London, 1849). D'Orville visited Salvini in Florence about 1726.

[2] Vitelli in *Stud. Ital. Filol. Class.* 2.561.

[3] These are not listed in my Register. Salvini's manuscript, from which presumably Bandini took them, is now in the Riccardian Library. An anonymous manuscript of the eighteenth century, in the same library, may here be mentioned (N.I. xxii. 162, f.34ro–46vo); it contains prose versions of one hundred epigrams from the Anthology.

GIOVAN VINCENZO GRAVINA

(1664–1718)

Gravina, in his day a leading authority on law, was born at Roggiano near Cosenza, and was early sent to study with his cousin, Gregorio Caloprese, at Scalea. Later he pursued legal studies under Serafino Biscardi in Naples, at the same time perfecting himself in Greek at the school of Gregorio Messere. In 1689 he went to Rome, where he lived at first with a member of the papal Court, Paolo Coardo. His first work, *De Corrupta Morali Doctrina*, was published at Naples in 1691; his *Opuscula*, Rome, 1696, mainly dealt with educational questions. Innocent XII made him professor of civil law at the Roman *Sapienza* in 1699; and in 1703 he passed to the chair of canon law. His best work was on legal subjects, and brought him into many controversies. His principal work, *De Origine Iuris*, was published at Leipzig in 1708. The years 1714–16 he spent in Calabria resting and attending to the inheritance bequeathed him by Caloprese. He died two years later in Rome, survived by his mother, to whom he left his property in Calabria. His Roman possessions were left to the poet Metastasio, who had been his protégé. Other famous pupils of Gravina were Lorenzo Gori and Orazio Bianchi. He was a member of Arcadia and of numerous other academies in Italy and Germany.

The work of Gravina that is best remembered is his discourse on poetry, first published in 1708: *Della Ragion Poetica libri due, e Della Tragedia libro uno*.[1] In the *Ragion Poetica*, wishing to mention the Greek female poets, he quotes Antipater's epigram on them (*A.P.* 9.26) and translates it into *versi sciolti*:

> Queste Elicona ed il Pierio scoglio
> Alme donne nudrì d'inni divini,
> Presilla, Miro, Anita a Omero eguale,
> Saffo splendor delle fanciulle Lesbie,
> Erinna, Telesilla, e te, Corinna,
> Che cantasti di Pallade lo scudo,
> Nosside, e Mirti di soave suono,
> Tutte d'eterni fogli produttrici.
> Ha dato il cielo nove Muse, e nove
> Per letizia immortale a noi la terra.

---

[1] I have not seen the first edition; in the edition of 1731 (Venice) the epigram from the Anthology appears on p. 33; in the *Opere Scelte* (Milan, 1819) on p. 55. In the last-mentioned volume is a *Vita* of Gravina by his pupil Giovanni Battista Passeri. There is an authoritative study of him by Francesco Moffa in *Studi di Letteratura Italiana* 7 (1907). 165–349.

GIAMBATTISTA FELICE ZAPPI
(1667–1719)

Zappi is designated 'the younger,' since his great-grandfather, Giambattista Zappi, was also known as a poet. He was born at Imola; was educated at the college of Montalto in Bologna; and went to Rome to study law. There he came to the attention of Innocent XII, who presented him in course of time with several civil offices. The emoluments therefrom, added to a considerable private fortune, made Zappi a wealthy man. He was much occupied with learned academies, being a member of the *Infecondi*, a founder of the Arcadians of Rome, etc. His wife was Faustina Maratti, daughter of the painter Carlo Maratti, and herself a poet and academician. Among the Arcadians they were called Tirsi Leucasio and Aglauro Cidonia. Their poems (usually published together) were first printed in 1723 at Venice.

Zappi has a madrigal taken from *A.P.* 9.108:[1]

> Disse Giove a Cupido:
> 'Che sì, fanciullo infido,
> Ch' io ti spennacchio l'ali,
> E ti spezzo quell' arco, e quegli strali?'—
> 'Eh Padre altitonante,
> Tante minacce e tante?
> A quel ch' ascolto, hai voglia di tornare
> A far due solchi in mare
> Colle corna da bove,'
> Disse Cupido a Giove.

ANSELMO BANDURI
(1671–1743)

Banduri, a Benedictine of the congregation of Meleda, was born at Ragusa, and was reputed to be a son of the Grand Duke of Tuscany. He went to France at the expense of the Grand Duke in 1702. In Paris he soon gained a reputation for learning, fully justified in 1711 by the publication of his work on the Eastern Empire. In 1715 he was made a member of the Académie des Inscriptions. His second great work, *Numismata Imperatorum Romanorum*, was published at Paris in 1718. In 1724 the Duke of Orleans appointed him his librarian.

Imperium Orientale sive Antiquitates CPolitanae in quatuor partes distributae. 2 vols. Paris, 1711. Book Seven of this work consists of 'varia epigrammata' having to do with the history and antiquities of Constantinople, and drawn from the third, fourth, and fifth books of the Planudean Anthology. The

---

[1] *Rime dell' Avvocato Gio: Battista Felice Zappi e di Faustina Maratti*, 2nd ed., Venice, 1725, p. 110.

epigrams are faced by Latin verse translations acknowledged to be the work of Alciati, Cornarius, Septimius Florens Christianus, Paul Estienne, Franchini, Grotius, Frédéric Morel, Sleidan, Velius, Pierre Menard, and Theobaldus. Only one epigram is translated by Banduri himself. He evidently drew largely on the *Selecta Epigrammata* of Cornarius; but most of his translations come from the literary tradition of his adopted country, and must be reserved for a study of the Anthology in France. The greater number of the translations are by Menard, and these were taken by Banduri from the *Historia Byzantina* of Du Cange, first published in 1680. Theobaldus may be Theobald of Constance, a Capuchin, who preached in the Austrian Forelands in the early years of the eighteenth century, and died in 1723; he is known mainly as a theological writer. Theobaldus' translations are confined to the fifth book of Planudes (=*A.P.* Book 2)—Christodorus' description of the statues in the gymnasium of the Zeuxippus. Indeed, this book supplies the bulk of Banduri's excerpts from the Anthology; but owing to their nature these epigrams scarcely concern the literary influence of the Anthology. Banduri gives, in all, 246 epigrams.[1] His own translation is from *A.P.* 9.668:

> Dulcis Amoris adest lucus; qua blanda Favoni
> Leniter arboreas ventilat aura comas:
> Roscidaque innumeris splendescunt floribus arva,
> Ac laeto violae germine dulce nitent.
> Ac dulci effusas e gurgite, terna papilla
> Una aliam superans, eiaculatur aquas.
> Inde senex Iris, medio subiecta diei
> Frondea pulchrarum regna secat Dryadum.
> Pampineas inter stirpes quoque pinguis oliva
> Floret et aprico largius uva loco.
> Undique lusciniae resonant, quaeque aemula cantu
> Occinit argutum parva cicada melos.
> Neve domum hanc, hospes, praeterlabare patentem,
> Excipias facili sed bonus aure preces.

FRANCESCO FORZONI ACCOLTI
(1674-1708)

Francesco was a son of the celebrated Pier Andrea Forzoni Accolti, one of the chief editors of the *Vocabolario della Crusca*. Francesco

---

[1] It has not seemed necessary to list these translations here or in the Register. In *Imp. Or.* they are in vol. 1 (pt. 3, pp. 135-75); Banduri's version of *A.P.* 9.668 is on p. 151.

received his literary education in his native Florence, and then studied law for five years at Pisa, taking the doctorate. Meantime he became known as a Latin and Italian poet, and was invited to join the *Accademia de' Remoti* at Pisa. After he returned to Florence he lived in the midst of the literary world, and became a member of all the leading societies. His Arcadian name was Aristile Pentelio. While constantly occupied in literary pursuits, he did not neglect the law, becoming *avvocato*. His untimely death was mourned by the best men of the time.[1]

In Crescimbeni's *Istoria della Volgar Poesia* (1714),[2] there is quoted an epigram of Musicius (*A.P.* 9.39) with a translation by Accolti:[3]

> Disse alle Muse un dì la Cipria dea:
> 'Fate a Dione, O Verginelle, onore,
> O v' armo contro Amore.'—
> E le Muse alla vaga Citerea:
> 'Queste belle parole
> Serba al tuo Marte amato;
> Chè intorno a noi mai non avvien, che vole
> Quel garzoncello alato.'

ANTONMARIA BISCIONI
(1674–1756)

Biscioni was a Florentine. His early education completed, he was compelled to gain a livelihood as a private teacher. In 1697 he entered the priesthood, and was enabled to pursue his studies at the University, where he took the doctorate in theology. In 1708 he was made a custodian of the Laurentian Library. He now resolved to re-establish his education, and studied Hebrew and Greek, the second under Antonmaria Salvini. He later received a benefice, and was made Royal Librarian of the Laurentian in 1741, and canon of S. Lorenzo in 1745. He belonged to most of the literary academies of Florence and to the Arcadians of Rome. He is buried in the crypt of S. Lorenzo, his epitaph being composed by his close friend Giovan Andrea Giulianelli (below, p. 403). In his early teaching period he had (c. 1695)

---

[1] Crescimbeni, *Istoria* (1730) 3.242. In A. M. Salvini's oration for the elder Forzoni Accolti the son's gifts and purity of character are lauded (Dati, *Raccolti di Prose Fiorentine*, pt. 5, vol. 1, p. 3). There is a sonnet on the death of Francesco by Salvinio Salvini in the supplement to Gobbi, *Rime d'Alcuni Autori Viventi*, Venice, 1727, pt. 4, p. 611. The same volume (pp. 261–2) contains four sonnets by Francesco; while a selection from his Latin verse was included by Bottari in the *Carm. Illus. Poet. Ital.* 4.443–53. According to Crescimbeni, many of his manuscripts were preserved in the archives of Arcadia.

[2] Not in the first edition (1698).

[3] *Istor.*, Venice, 1731, 1.396. Crescimbeni does not elsewhere show any knowledge of the Anthology. Becelli (below, p. 394) complains of his not considering the relations of the Greek epigram and the short Italian poem in dialogue form.

among his pupils Giovanni Bottari, later a distinguished scholar, and editor of the great collection of Italian Latin poets—*Carmina Illus- trium Poetarum Italorum* (below, p. 443).

The works of Biscioni are mainly in the form of commen- taries or short annotations on various Italian writers. Among them are notes on the *Malmantile Racquistato* of Lorenzo Lippi.[1] Here he finds occasion to translate *A.P.* 11.78. The epigram has nothing to do with the passage of the *Malmantile* in question (9.13); Biscioni has had reason to refer to the verb τύπτειν from which the modern word 'tipo,' i.e., 'stampa,' comes: 'Ma in proposito delle stampe, fatte sul mostaccio d'un antico giuoca- tore di pugna, evvi un faceto epigramma del greco Lucilio, che in nostra lingua voltato, dice così:[2]

> È un vaglio, Apollofane, il tuo capo,
> O qual fu mai più traforato arnese,
> Son tane di formiche, or dritte, or torte,
> E par, che con bizzarre e varie note
> Un lirico eccellente il Lidio v'abbia
> Intavolato sopra, o il Frigio canto.
> Or franco vibra il minaccevol pugno
> E combatti pur lieto in duro arringo:
> Chè se colpo novello a te discende
> Quel ch' hai riscosso, avrai, ma non già nuova
> Capir nel capo tuo potrà ferita.'

DOMENICO REGOLOTTI
(*c.* 1675–1735)

Regolotti, a Roman by birth, on completing his studies received a minor post in the Vatican Library. In 1712 he was admitted to the bar, and for several years practised his profession. In 1720 King Vit- torio Amedeo, who had just re-established the University of Turin, called him thither to be Professor of Greek. In 1724 the professorship of poetry was added. The opening lecture of his course on poetry, *De Poeseos Utilitate*, was published after his death in *Miscellanea di Varie Operette* (Venice, *c.* 1740). His chief work was a translation of Theocritus (1729), which, however, was so unfavorably received that he attempted to give up his position at Turin. He remained, not being able to find another place. He also published an *Oratio de Die Natali Caroli-Emmanuelis*, Turin, 1733.

---

[1] These notes first appeared in the second volume of the *Malmantile* published at Florence in 1731, and were reprinted in several later editions. I use *Il Malmantile ... colle note di Puccio Lamone e d'altri* [i.e., A. M. Salvini and Biscioni], 4 vols, Prato, 1815.

[2] Sebastiano Pauli, *Modi di Dire Toscani* (Venice, 1761), p. 232, quotes Biscioni's translation as illustrating the locution: *Fare delle spalle altrui una chittera.*

Regolotti is here mentioned for his translation of Theocritus: *Teocrito Volgarizzato*, Turin, 1729, which contains versions of 24 epigrams.[1] The poems are rendered in Italian *versi sciolti;* and on the whole the renderings deserve the rough handling they got from the critics of the time. The version of *A.P.* 9.434 follows:

> Evvi un altro Teocrito di Scio:
> Ma io, che queste cose
> A scrivere m'accinsi,
> Teocrito pur sono,
> Uno de' molti, che produsse e nutre
> Di Siracusa la cittade eletta;
> Di Prassagora figlio,
> E di Filina conta.
> Fra tutti gli altri pregi
> Primier m' arroga quel, se giusto sei,
> Che mai li carmi altrui spacciai per miei.

GIROLAMO (*alias* ANGELO MARIA) QUIRINI
(1680–1757)

Cardinal Quirini was a Venetian of good family. At seven years of age he was sent with his elder brother to the college of the Jesuits at Brescia. He determined to take orders, and, against the wishes of his family, joined the Benedictines in Florence in 1696. Two years later he took the vows, and changed his name to Angelo Maria. In Florence he cultivated the society of scholars. In 1710, with a view to visiting scholars and libraries beyond the Alps, he set out to travel. In Holland he gained the friendship of Le Clerc, Cardinal Polignac, and others; in England he visited Newton, Bentley, and Burnet. After two years in Paris he returned to Italy in 1714. Clement XI took notice of him; Innocent XIII made him Archbishop of Corfu; Benedict XIII made him Bishop of Brescia and Cardinal; Clement XII chose him as librarian of the Vatican. He belonged to the chief academies of Europe; his obliging manner pleased all; even Voltaire sang his praises. He published a great number of works on ecclesiastical and literary history, some of which, as his *Specimen Variae Literaturae quae in Brixia florebat* (Brescia, 1739), must still be consulted. He died at Brescia.

At the request of the German scholar Reimerus, Quirini undertook in 1753 to study the (then) Vatican and Barberini MSS. of the Anthology for Johann Jacob Reiske, who was about to bring out his *Anthologia* (cf. above, p. 38). Quirini agreed in

[1] *A.P.* 6.177, 336–340; 7.534, 658–61, 663, 664; 9.338, 432–4, 437, 440 (p. 271), 598–600; 13.3; 16.200.

March to do this, and Reimerus told Reiske to write to him his directions; but Reiske delayed, and on May 4 Reimerus wrote to urge him on, quoting a part of the Cardinal's letter, as follows:[1]

L'Antologia Greca ha fatto la delizia de' miei studi giovenili, e dovendomi in quest' anno trasferire a Roma, vi prometto, che farò uno studio particolare su i due codici Vaticano e Barberiniano da voi indicatimi, ma fa d'uopo, che il vostro dotto amico e molto da me stimato Sr. Rescio mi faccia avere un foglio in cui mi esprima qual ricerca debba farsi in detti codici, per render compito il suo desiderio, il quale per essere il vostro ancora, impegna le mie maggiori premure. [At the end of the letter he added:] Per farvi conoscere di non essermi dimenticato delle vostre premure di compiacere l'amico vostro dottissimo Rescio, vi presento la notizia, che da Roma mi è stata mandata: Il codice che contiene tutta l'Antologia Greca è Palatino Vaticano segnato n. 33, in pergameno in 4to grande, in pag. 710, ossia fogli 355.[2] Il carattere greco dimostra esser stato scritto nel sec. xi.

The next letter of Reimerus to Reiske, dated May 19, 1753, shows that Reiske had meantime declined to wait for the study to be made:[3] 'Non possum improbare consilium tuum, Vir Doctissime, de edenda quamprimum Anthologia Lipsiensi, antequam tibi lectiones eius Vaticanae suppeditentur. Urgere enim te iubet propositum iminens forte mutatio loci et conditionis; et praestat habere nos epigrammata isthaec ex uno saltem codice, quam carere iisdem in saecula. Forte et postea paucis paginis collationes Vaticanae possent adiungi. Scribam id hodie Viro Eminentissimo, ut ne frustra mittendum sibi codicem expectet.'

Reiske's book came out in 1754 without any collations from Quirini.[4] Apparently Reiske wanted to get it out of his hands before his ardor cooled; but there seems also to have been another reason for his not getting the collations. Exactly what this was escapes me. When the obliging disposition already shown by Quirini is recalled, and his position in Rome, and

---

[1] J. J. Reiske, *Von ihm selbst Aufgesetzte Lebensbeschreibung*, Leipzig, 1783, p. 695 (among the correspondence).

[2] If this information is exact, it suggests that the division of the ms. into two parts had not yet taken place in 1753. Waltz (*Anthol. Grec.* l.xxxix) has no real grounds for suspecting that the division was made when the ms. was first removed to the Vatican in 1623. The new bindings seen by the French commissioners in 1797 (above, p. 263) also suggest that the division and rebinding had then but recently taken place. Cf. Preisendanz, *Praef.* to the photographic reproduction, coll. viii–ix.

[3] Reiske, *op. cit.*, p. 697.

[4] *Anthologiae Graecae a Constantino Cephala conditae libri tres.* Leipzig, 1754.

further the expressions of Reimerus' last letter, the following explanation in Reiske's Preface (p. xxxii) is completely baffling: 'Per eminentissimum Cardinalem Quirinum . . . litterarum et amplissimi ordinis sui immortale decus . . . non stetit, quin promissa in humanissimis ad me litteris collatione codicis Vaticani potirer. Sed intercessit quorundam religio, quam spes est etiam expugnandam aliquando esse.'[1]

In Quirini's notice of Fausto Sabeo (above, p. 212) in his *Specimen* of the literature of Brescia (2.191), published in 1739, he has in mind a different side of the Anthology from that which was the delight of his youth. It is a question of Sabeo's lubricity: 'Ea Sabaei in obscoenis argumentis tractandis licentia clarius se prodit in iis epigrammatis, quae sive ex Graecae Anthologiae sive ex Ovidianae Metamorphoseos turbidis fontibus in libros suos derivavit.'

GIULIO CESARE BECELLI

(1685–1750)

Becelli, a native of Verona, studied with the Jesuits and finally joined their Society. In 1710, however, with the proper authorization, he left them, married, and became a teacher. He wrote much and with more facility than taste; yet he was a member of several academies, at Bologna, Modena, Padua, and Verona where in particular his talents were admired. Although anything but a wealthy man, he is said to have printed all his works at his own expense. After his death his memory was honored with a volume of verse entitled: *Rime e Versi in Morte di Giulio Cesare Becelli*, Verona, 1750. In addition to his book on poetry here to be noticed, Becelli published *Esame della Rettorica Antica* (Verona, 1735–6; 1739); *Se Oggidì Scrivendo si debba Usare la Lingua Italiana del Buon Secolo* (*ibid.*, 1737); *Trattato Nuovo della Divisione degli Ingegni e Studi* (*ibid.*, 1738); *De Ratione Puerilium Studiorum* (*ibid.*, 1741); *De Bibliotheca Instituenda* (*ibid.*, 1747); *Erodoto Alicarnasseo* [first three books] (*ibid.*, 1733); *Il Gonnella canti 12* (*ibid.*, 1739); and numerous other poems and treatises.

Becelli's discourse on poetry appeared in 1732 at Verona: *Della Novella Poesia, cioè del Vero Genere e Particolari Bellezze della Poesia Italiana, libri tre;* it is addressed to the *Accademia de'Filarmonici* of Verona.[2] Becelli finds that the Italian epigram

---

[1] In his *Lebensbeschr.* (p. 106) Reiske places Cardinal Quirini in a list of his friends and correspondents.

[2] Scipione Maffei was an honorary, and Girolamo Pompei (below, p. 421) an active, member of this society.

and epitaph are literary forms derived from the Greek (p. 40):
'Gli epigrammi ancora ed epitaffi sono di forma greca, o seri o
giocosi che sieno.'[1] On the question of the Greek epigram and
the sonnet, he subscribes to Fioretti's opinion that the difference is great, and that the madrigal is more like the epigram.
Of the epigram in dialogue form he says: 'Delle brievi poesie a
dialogo fatte, il Crescimbeni vanamente pur cerca se agl'Italiani o a' Provenzali si debba l'origine concedere, posciachè di
tal sorte epigrammi sonovi nella Greca Antologia' (p. 41).

FRANCESCO SAVERIO QUADRIO
(1695–1756)

Quadrio was born at Ponte in the Valtelline. Having finished his
literary studies early, he somewhat impulsively abandoned an intention to study law at Pavia, and joined the Society of Jesus instead.
He was about twenty years old when he began to teach Latin in their
school at Padua. After five successful years he was sent to Bologna
to study theology, and to teach at the same time in the College of S.
Saverio. Later he preached in Venice and Modena, and again took up
teaching at Padua. In 1734 he published an essay *Della Poesia Italiana*
in two books, and about that time conceived the notion of a great
work on all kinds of poetry. For this he made long researches in the
libraries of Venice, Milan, and Bologna. He was received in Rome by
Benedict XIV in 1743. He finally settled in Milan for the printing of
his book. He had long suffered from attacks of melancholy, which at
this time took the form of resentment against his Order. One day in
1744 he left Milan, and on the way to Como stripped off his habit,
which he left on the highroad. He then made his way into Switzerland,
and finally to Paris, where he was well received by the scholarly
world, in particular, it is said, by Voltaire. He returned to Italy in
1747; and was excused by the pope from wearing the garb of a Jesuit.
Benedict also provided him with a livelihood. In the following year
Count Pallavicini, the Governor of Milan, made him his librarian;
and five years later, on the retirement of Pallavicini, Quadrio entered
a convent of the Barnabite Brethren, where he died, November 21,
1756.

Quadrio's great work, *Della Storia e della Ragione d'Ogni
Poesia*, appeared in seven volumes, the first printed at Venice in
1736, and the last at Milan in 1759. His method is to give at once
the theory of the forms of poetry and their history. Vol. 1 treats
the nature of poetry in general, its forms, its matter, its

---

[1] He has just mentioned the versified enigmas that may be found in the Anthology.

language; vols. 2 and 3 are on lyric poetry, with an attempt to catalogue the lyric poets of all nations; vols. 4 and 5 similarly treat the drama; vol. 6 deals with epic and didactic poems; vol. 7 contains *addenda* and an Index. The completed work, though bristling with errors, is even yet indispensable to the student of Italian literary history. It is not very successful in its treatment of foreign poetry.

The Epigram is discussed in Volume 3; and the treatment accorded it is good for the time. Quadrio's sketch of the history of the Anthology is all that one could ask for.[1] He begins with a history of the form, that is, its growth from inscriptions, then speaks of the metre proper to the epigram, the proper length, and the character of the form, and gives a catalogue of Greek epigrammatists, followed by a notice of the collections of Meleager, Philippus, Agathias, and Planudes. He is not aware of Cephalas.

In speaking of the character of the epigram and the madrigal he says (*Stor.* 3.367): 'Il vero carattere di questi componimenti lo dobbiamo noi trarre da' Greci. Questi soli ne hanno compresa la vera idea, e chi piglia per le mani l'Antologia, vi trova cose da rimanerne incantato. Non è, che in quel libro molte fredde e scipite cose ancor non si leggano; ma ogni nazione ebbe sempre i suoi buoni e cattivi secoli, e in ogni lingua vi furono ognora de' buoni e de' cattivi poeti.'

GIACOMO MARTORELLI

(1699–1777)

Martorelli, a Neapolitan, studied at the archiepiscopal seminary in Naples (1710), and became (1723) a teacher of the ancient languages in that institution. In 1738 he was made professor of Greek at the University. (Eckstein, *Nomenclator.*)

In 1756 at Naples, Martorelli published a dissertation entitled *De Regia Theca Calamaria*, in the course of which he discusses *A.P.* 6.62. He proposes (p. 209) to read γραμμῆς in line 1, and ἰθύτατον in line 3; and suggests that one distich has been lost. This last suggestion had the approval of Jacobs.[2]

---

[1] The third vol. was published at Milan in 1742; the Epigram is dealt with on pp. 361–79. Certain remarks are repeated from his *Poes. Ital.* of 1734, p. 399.

[2] Jacobs, *Anth. Graec.* (1817) 3.136. I have not myself seen Martorelli's work.

FRANCESCO MARIA BONADA

(1706–1755)

Bonada was a native of Terra della Trinità (diocese of Mondovi). In 1725 he took the vows of the Order of the *Scuole Pie*. He taught rhetoric in several schools in Rome. From 1750 to 1753 he acted as Assistant-Provincial of his Order. He died at Rome.

Bonada's principal literary work was a collection of metrical inscriptions: *Carmina ex Antiquis Lapidibus*, 2 vols. Rome, 1751, 1753. He illustrates the inscriptions with a considerable number of epigrams from the Anthology, and to these he adds versions by well-known translators—'Ambrogio,' Ricolvi, Salvini, Joshua Barnes, Jan van Meurs, Antonio Rivautella, and others.[1]

GIAMBATTISTA VICINI

(1709–1782)

Vicini was a son of a judge at Finale near Modena; and in his day a well-known man of letters, an Arcadian, and historiographer of Correggio. Tiraboschi (*Scritt. Moden.*) lists 40 works by him; many of these are poetical works, as *Poemetti Filosofici* (Modena, 1772) and *Stanze e Capitoli* (Venice, 1777). None of his original verse, however, so far as I have examined it, shows any traces of the Greek epigrams. Only in his translation of the Greek bucolic poets has he anything from the Anthology: *Gl' Idillj di Teocrito, di Mosco, e di Bione . . . traslati*. Venice, 1781.

Here follows Vicini's version of *A.P.* 7.658:[2]

> Or fia ch'i' riconosca di leggiero
> Se a' buoni e a' rei tu fai lo stesso onore,
> Quando questo sepolcro, O passeggiero,
> Avverrà che tu sì dicendo onore:
> Pace a la tomba che d' Eurimedonte
> Lieve sta sopra a la sacrata fronte.

---

[1] Bonada usually refers to the source of his translations. Salvini is represented by a translation of *A.P.* 7.15 taken from Doni's Dorian Inscriptions 8.91 (Bonada 1.410). Barnes' translations are from his *Vita Euripidis*, pp. 32, 34; and are from *A.P.* 7.44–47. No reference is given for Van Meurs; his collected works were printed in 12 volumes, Florence, 1741–63. On Ricolvi and Rivautella see below, p. 398.

[2] In all, he translates *A.P.* 6.177, 336–40; 7.534, 658, 660, 661, 663, 664; 9.338, 432–34, 437, 440 (p. 106), 598–600; 16.200.

ANONYMOUS

(1746)

'Επικαὶ καὶ ἐλεγειακαὶ γνῶμαι. *Epicae et Elegiacae Sententiae Minorum Poetarum Graecorum, Pythagorae, . . . Addita Monosticha Incertorum a Grotio Collecta, et Nonnulla Epigrammata Moralia Excerpta ex Anthologia, Graece et Latine. In usum scholarum.* Venice, 1746.

This schoolbook, published by Simeone Occhi, contains, as indicated in the title, a section from the Anthology: 'Epigrammata Moralia ex Anthologia selecta, a variis auctoribus Latine reddita' (pp. 187–224). Many of the translations are taken from Soter, or one of his derivatives (above, p. 274); four translations from Lucian are by Joannes Benedictus; while the prose versions prove to be those of Lubinus (above, p. 38). Benedictus was a friend of Casaubon and professor of Greek at Saumur; his translations were taken from his *Lucian,* Saumur, 1619 (or Amsterdam, 1687).

The epigrams contained in the volume are the following:[1]

A.P. 9.61 (More); 9.231 (prose); 9.527 (prose); 9.39 (Bentinus); 10.74 (prose); 10.106 (Erasmus); 9.43 (prose); 9.110 (More); 9.145 (Ausonius); 9.172 (Soter); 10.31 (Benedictus); 9.573 (prose); 10.93 (prose); 10.115 (prose); 9.111 (Luscinius); 10.26 (Venatorius); 9.148 (Luscinius); 9.54 (prose); 9.127 (prose); 10.28 (Benedictus); 9.261 (prose); 11.419 (Arnold. Vesaliensis); 9.8 (prose); 9.47 (prose); 10.30 (Luscinius); 9.373 (prose); 10.69 (More); 9.120 (Luscinius); 7.342 (prose); 10.112 (More); 9.72 (prose); 9.119 (prose); 10.121 (Lily); 10.102 (prose); 9.138 (Velius); 10.41 (More); 10.27 (Benedictus); 10.60 (Sleidan); 10.63 (More); 10.76 (Sleidan); 10.80 (Sleidan); 11.193 (Soter); 10.39 (Sleidan); 10.117 (Sleidan); 9.163 (Marullus); 10.36 (Obsopoeus); 9.51 (Sleidan); 10.79 (prose); 10.42 (Obsopoeus); 11.53 (prose); 10.41 (Sleidan); 11.390 (Sleidan); 10.35 (Vitus Apermachius); 11.299 (prose); 11.300 (prose); 11.301 (prose); 11.302 (prose); 11.303 (prose); 11.341 (prose); 10.37 (Sleidan); 11.166 (More); 11.294 (More); 10.43 (Volaterranus); 7.73 (prose); 16.201 (prose); 11.431 (Benedictus); 9.767 (prose); 9.768 (prose); 9.769 (prose); 11.428 (Sleidan); 10.122 (Sleidan); 16.331 (prose); 7.308 (Velius); 16.89 (De la Monnoye).

---

[1] For once I depart from my practice in these tables of listing the epigrams in the order of the Palatine Anthology; here I list them in the order of their appearance in the book in question, so as to give an idea of its arrangement.

GIOVAN PAOLO RICOLVI
(1712–1748)

ANTONIO RIVAUTELLA
(1708–1753)

Ricolvi was an archaeologist and translator. He made an Italian version of Pope's poems, edited a collection of Italian poets, and, with Rivautella, produced *Marmora Taurinensia* (2 vols., Turin, 1743, 1747). His *Opuscoli Postumi* appeared at Turin in 1762, preceded by a Memoir of the author. Like Ricolvi, Rivautella was all his life connected with Turin. From 1735 he was librarian of the University, and from 1751 till his death curator of the Museum. Besides his work with Ricolvi on the Turin marbles, he was part-author of *Codices Manuscripti Bibliothecae Regii Taurinensis Athenaei* (2 vols., Turin, 1749).

In the *Marmora Taurinensia*—a series of dissertations on archaeological treasures of Turin—the Anthology is brought into use for illustration, seventeen epigrams being quoted and regularly provided with Latin translations in verse. Which of these versions are the work of Ricolvi and which of Rivautella, or whether all are the work of one, cannot be determined. I incline to ascribe them all to Ricolvi, since, as presently to be noticed, he is otherwise a notable translator from the Anthology; but in the two or three instances where Ricolvi, in his acknowledged translations, turns the same verses that are translated in the *Marmora Taurinensia*, his versions are quite different; and—though this fact carries but little weight—one version from the *Marmora* is quoted by Bonada (above, p. 396) as being by Rivautella.

One example of their use of the Anthology may be given. The subject for illustration is a relief picturing four Bacchantes:[1]

Non omittendum tamen est hoc loco quoddam Anacreontis, ut creditur, tetrastichon [*A.P.* 6.134], alicui profecto subscriptum olim anaglyptico operi Bacchas exhibenti tres cultu non multum a nostris dissimiles, ut ex ipso epigrammate paene cernitur. Hem illud. [Greek] Ita latine reddi utcumque potest:

> Quae thyrsum gerit est Heliconias, altera vero
> Leucippe, Glauce tertia pone venit.
> Monte simul redeunt, Dionyso dona ferentes
> Maturam uvam, hederes, anniculumque caprum.

---

[1] Reinach, *Répertoire des Reliefs*, 3 (1912). 424, No. 3 (Ménades).

Verba primi versus certo argumento sunt ex hisce tribus feminis unam tantum habuisse thyrsum, quandoquidem ex thyrso illam distinguit, inquiens, *quae thyrsum gerit est Heliconias*, quae verba inania essent, si ceterae una forent armatae thyrsis. [Etc.]

The writer then passes to a similar discussion of *A.P.* 16.59.

The following appear in *Marmora Taurinensia: A.P.* 2.361; 6.134; 7.6, 8–10, 370, 617; 9.75 (1.64: Ovid), 187, 316; 10.36; 11.310, 343; 16.59, 275 (2.5: Grotius, Ausonius), 301 (1.181: no trans.).[1]

On Ricolvi's death in 1748 he left a number of unpublished papers, which saw the light fourteen years later under the title, *Opuscoli Postumi*. These papers include one entitled: *Dissertazione sull' Antologia osia Raccolta d' Epigrammi Greci* (pp. 51–94). After a brief introduction on the nature of the Anthology, Ricolvi presents a goodly number of epigrams illustrating the various types, and adds translations into Latin or Italian or into both languages, together with brief comments. Occasionally, instead of making a new translation, he employs one of the well-known Renaissance versions.[2] For these, in part, he made use of Soter's selections. The following will serve as examples of Ricolvi's translations:

> Multa vorans et multa bibens multisque lacessens
> Scommatibus, iacet hic Timocreon Rhodius.
>
> (*A.P.* 7.348)

> Invidia nil peius; habet tamen utile quiddam,
> Invidiosorum lumina corque premens.
>
> (*A.P.* 11.193)

> Illa ego Graeca charis ridens nequam, agmen amantum
> Tot iuvenum, Lais, cui stetit ante fores,
> Hoc speculum dono Paphiae; me namque videre
> Qualis sum, nolo, qualis eram, nequeo.

---

[1] *A.P.* 7.6 is given (1.181) without trans., a version of the inscriptional form (= Kaibel 1084a) having just been presented; it is this version that Bonada ascribes to Rivautella.

The well-known Turin relief of 'Kairos,' illustrated in *Mar.* by *A.P.* 16.275, is reproduced in the 'Loeb' Anthology under that epigram.

[2] On p. 75 he quotes the following without translation: *A.P.* 9.53, 524; 16.107, 271, 387. On p. 71 attention is drawn to a parallel between Petrarch, *Son.* 83 (L'aspettata vertù) and *A.P.* 7.225; both poems declare that a name enshrined in verse outlives one inscribed in stone.

Io Laide, che ridea
Cotanto baldanzosa
Di tutta Grecia, e avea
Già frotta numerosa
Alla mia porta avanti
Di giovanotti amanti,
Or di Paffo alla dea
Questo mio specchio dono.
A me questo che vale?
Vecchierella infelice,
A cui già più non cale
Di mirarmi, qual sono,
E qual fui, più non lice.
                                (A.P. 6.1)

The following are translated into Latin in Ricolvi's *Dissertazione:*[1]
A.P. 6.1, 306; 7.225, 308, 311, 348, 353, 549, 666, 688.3, 695 (2 versions); 9.13 (More, p. 61), 39, 47, 48, 56 (Germanicus, p. 67), 61, 67, 108 (1 version by Ricolvi, 1 by Sannazaro, p. 108), 110, 148, 162, 163 (2 versions), 166, 316, 369, 541, 629, 713, 717, 720; 10.31 (2 versions), 33, 36, 39, 98 (2 versions), 113; 11.61,[2] 95, 104, 192, 193, 198, 268, 277, 394, 418 (More, p. 79), 430; 13.29 (2 versions); 16.3, 97, 200, 214, 275.
    The following are also accompanied by Italian translations: *A.P.* 6.1, 306; 7.308, 348, 688.3, 695; 9.13, 39, 56, 48, 61, 75, 108 (1 version by Ricolvi, 1 by Zappi, p. 88), 110, 148, 162, 163, 541; 10.31, 33, 36, 39, 98, 113; 11.61, 95, 193, 268, 277, 394, 430; 16.3, 200, 214, 275.

ANTONIO BONGIOVANNI
(1712–1760?)
GIROLAMO FRANCESCO ZANETTI
(1713–1782)

Bongiovanni was born in the vicinity of Verona, and received his early education from his brother, archpriest of Lunigo. He finished his education at Padua, acquiring an excellent knowledge of Latin, Greek, Hebrew, theology, and civil and canon law. He established himself in Venice, and was intimately allied with Girolamo and Antonmaria Zanetti in his literary studies. Antonmaria was Keeper of Manuscripts in St. Mark's Library, and with him Bongiovanni published the catalogue of that rich collection: *Graeca D. Marci Bibliotheca Codicum Manuscriptorum per titulos digesta*, Venice, 1740 (above, p. 30), and *Latina et Italica D. Marci*, etc., Venice, 1741. For this

---

[1] Where no name is added in parentheses the translation is Ricolvi's.
[2] At this point (p. 85) Ricolvi had before him Soter's *Epigrammata*, taking from it, and translating, an epigram by Sir Thomas More, given by Soter as a remote parallel to *A.P.* 11.61.

work the Senate awarded to each author a gold medal of great weight. In 1740 Bongiovanni also published the *Scholia* on Homer from *Cod. Marc.* 453; in 1752, *Leontii Monachi Hierosolymitani quaedam ad Historiam Ecclesiasticam Spectantia;* in 1754, *Libanii Sophistae Orationes xvii;* and in 1759, *Theodoreti Opuscula duo.* The date of his death is not known, but it may have occurred, prematurely, about 1760.

Bongiovanni had collaborated with Antonmaria Zanetti in compiling the Catalogue of St. Mark's Library. It was with the elder brother of Antonmaria, Girolamo Francesco Zanetti, that he produced the translations from the Anthology here in question. Girolamo was a Venetian by birth. He early acquired a mastery of Greek and Latin; and devoted himself to archaeology. His earliest work, *Ragionamento dell' Origine e dell' Antichità della Moneta Veneziana*, Venice, 1750, established his reputation. In 1764 he won a prize awarded by the French Académie des Inscriptions, for his work on the early civilization of Egypt, and a second time in 1769 for a monograph on the worship of Saturn and Rhea. After an unsuccessful attempt to be made his brother's successor as *custos* of St. Mark's library in 1778, the year in which Antonmaria died, he was asked to become professor of law at Padua. There he died December 16, 1782. Besides the works already mentioned, Zanetti produced a number of treatises on various archaeological matters.[1]

It has been the custom in Italy for scholars and poets, wishing to honor the marriage of some prominent person, to print a set of verses to be presented as a marriage-gift. Translations are particularly suited to this purpose, and no translations better suited perhaps than some chosen from the Anthology. Such a book of translations was presented by Bongiovanni and Zanetti to a noble friend Tommaso Mocenigo-Soranzo, on the occasion of his marriage to Elena Contarini, September 16, 1752: *Varj Epigrammi della Greca Antologia Recati in Lingua Volgare*, Venice (Ant. Zatta).[2]

In their address to the reader the translators describe their book as a brief essay towards a larger book of translations which they had almost ready; this, however, seems never to have appeared. They mention earlier Italian writers, notably Tasso and Alamanni, who had mingled translations from the Anthology

---

[1] A list of these is given in the *Biogr. Univ.* 45.379.

[2] The translators' names do not appear on the title-page, but at the end of the address to Mocenigo-Soranzo. There is a copy in St. Mark's Library.

A similar use of the Greek epigrams was made by Bettinelli (below, p. 416). The practice continued into the nineteenth century; for example: *Epigrammi Greci Tradotti da Francesco Negri* [per nozze di Giovanni Papadopoli], Venice, 1835 [29 epigrams in 2+29 pp.]; of which an enlarged edition (xiii+110 pp.) appeared at Venice in 1843. Copies of both editions are in St. Mark's Library.

with their own verses; and risk the suggestion that, if all such Italian translations were gathered together, the resulting collection would form a new Tuscan Anthology of no mean bulk. Finally, they defend their method of translation, its varying degrees of freedom, and present their 131 versions.[1] These are written in *versi sciolti*, and appear to have been rapidly if not hastily done. The following is their version of *A.P.* 7.668 (a sailor speaks):

> Nè lo spirar di Zeffiro nè lieta
> Ridente calma faran sì ch'io solchi
> Su lieve pin l'onde tranquille e chete;
> Chè i passati perigli e le procelle,
> Tutte ho nel cor, e gli rammento e tremo.

A list of their translations follows: *A.P.* 5.70, 113; 6.331; 7.33, 73, 112, 148, 186, 216, 224, 265, 294, 308, 313, 314, 353, 590, 600, 608, 668, 669–70;

9.3, 17, 18, 47, 52, 54, 56, 62, 72, 74, 87, 106, 110, 120, 126, 127, 143, 162, 166, 167, 221, 247, 303, 305, 378, 386, 444, 489, 497, 515, 526, 530, 647, 826;

10.26, 27, 28, 30, 36, 39, 46, 59, 63, 65, 69, 76, 105, 112, 116;

11.50, 95, 103, 104, 117, 118 (2 versions), 120, 122, 127, 159, 163, 166, 170, 171, 179, 184, 194, 199, 200, 201, 208, 209, 214, 227, 228, 251, 259, 264, 266, 268, 276, 277, 281, 311, 315, 330, 390, 401, 408, 418, 421, 429, 432;

16.14, 50, 58, 107, 119, 120, 168, 169, 174, 181, 195, 200, 207, 215, 216, 293.

In the Catalogue of the Greek MSS. compiled by Bongiovanni and the younger Zanetti, Planudes' autograph (*Cod.* 481) is in the main well described.[2] The following are a few passages from their description:

Codex 481. in 4°. membranaceus. foliorum 123. saeculi xiv. Anthologia Epigrammatum in sectiones vii distributa. Codex conlatus est cum editione Eilhardi Lubini 1604. Sectionum tituli nonnumquam ab editis differunt, et aliquando plures, aliquando pauciores sunt. [They notice 4 epigrams not in the printed editions, only one of which —*A.P.* 9.813—is counted in the Anthology to-day, the other three not being in the Palatine MS.] Post Sectionem vii, a fol. nempe 77 ad 80 epigrammata plura habentur in diversa argumenta sine ulla generali inscriptione. Sequuntur folio 80. ver. et seqq. Pauli Silentiarii in Thermas Pythias, [etc.—being the material Aldus drew from this MS. to add to his edition of 1503 (above, p. 149)]. AMMONII Philosophi

---

[1] No clue is given as to which epigrams either of the translators is responsible for.
[2] *Graeca D. Marci Bibliotheca*, pp. 252–3.

et Rhetoris Metaphrasis epica Evangelii S. Joannis edita sub nomine Nonni Panopletae. Nota sequitur: Ἐγράφη ἡ μετάφρασις αὕτη τοῦ κατὰ Ἰωάννην ἁγίου Εὐαγγελίου, χερὶ Μαξίμου μοναχοῦ τοῦ Πλανούδη, ἐντὸς Κωνσταντινουπόλεως, κατὰ τὴν μονὴν τοῦ Ἀκαταλείπτου ἐπονομαζομένην, μηνὶ Σεπτεμβρίῳ, ἔτους ϛω΄ δεκάτου. Scripta est haec Metaphrasis Evangelii S. Joannis manu Maximi Planudis monachi, Constantinopoli, in Monasterio cognomento Τοῦ Ἀκαταλείπτου mense Septembri, anno 6810 (Christi 1302).

The year should be 1301, the cataloguers having failed to reckon on the Byzantine year beginning with September.[1]

GIAMBATTISTA ZENOBETTI

(fl. 1750)

Zenobetti appears to have been a Florentine, and to have received his education in the *Studio* of his native city, where he learned Greek from Giovan Andrea Giulianelli. Nothing further seems to be known of him, save his publication of the two books mentioned below.

Anthologia Selecta ad Usum Studiosae Italicae Juventutis. Leghorn, 1753. Pp. [8]+64. This small schoolbook is arranged, like the Westminster Collection used in England, in distichs (pp. 1–27) and quatrains (pp. 29–64). There are notices on the epigrammatists. In his Preface Zenobetti says: 'Ex illis . . . temporibus, dum ab Jo. Andrea Julianellio . . . in Seminario Florentino Graecis incumbebam literis, pulcherrimorum Graecorum Epigrammatum amore quodam correptus sum. . . . Nunc quae vobis offero sint satis, et epigrammatum horum lepore et venustate illecti Graeca persequimini studia, ut avia Pieridum peragrantes loca ad integrorum sacrorumque Homeri et Pindari fontium haustus adcedere non expalleatis.'

Μελεάγρου Γαδαρήνου εἰς τὸ ἔαρ εἰδύλλιον. *Meleagri Gadareni in Ver Idyllion.* Rome, 1759. Pp. 32. In this edition of Meleager's poem on Spring (*A.P.* 9.363) Zenobetti gives, along with the Greek text, a translation into Latin prose, and illustrates the poem with many other Greek epigrams, which he also provides with prose translations. There is an index of these (p. 28). Zenobetti took his text directly from the Palatine MS., then in the Vatican Library, and seems to have believed that his edition

---

[1] Cf. K. Radinger in *Rhein. Mus.* 58 (1903).303, who gives a better transcription of the note: κατὰ τὴν μονὴν τοῦ Σωτῆρος χριστοῦ τὴν τοῦ Ἀκ. ἐπ. μ. Σεπτ. ἰνδικτιῶνος ιγ΄. ἔτους ϛω΄ δεκάτου: ϛ̄: ϛ̄. The indiction, as Radinger observes, is of the year preceding (1300).

was the first. The poem is, however, in the Planudean Anthology (1.91.16).[1]

FILIPPO ARGELATI

(1685–1755)

JACOPO MARIA PAITONI

(c. 1710–1774)

After completing his studies at Bologna, his birthplace, Argelati removed to Florence to benefit by the scholarly society to be found there. He later contemplated migrating to France, but the affairs of his family recalled him to Bologna. He finally settled in Milan, choosing this place as most fit for carrying out the great work which, together with Muratori, he was then planning—the collection of historical materials now known under the title of *Scriptores Rerum Italicarum*. He performed many similar services to scholarship, the most useful of the books he composed unassisted being his *Bibliotheca Scriptorum Mediolanensium* (2 vols., Milan, 1745), and the posthumous *Biblioteca degli Volgarizzatori Italiani* (5 vols., Milan, 1767). He died at Milan.

Paitoni was a Venetian. He joined the order of the Somaschi, and became librarian of their house. His minor publications, aside from some translations, are mainly based on the rich collection of fifteenth-century books which they possessed. Argelati's *Biblioteca degli Volgarizzatori* had not yet been given to the public when the similar but better work of Paitoni began to appear: *Biblioteca degli Autori Antichi Greci e Latini Volgarizzati* (5 vols., Venice, 1766–74). Argelati's editor hastened to bring out his work, making some additions, and declaring that Paitoni had determined not to go on. Fortunately, however, Paitoni resumed his task.

However useful in general, neither Argelati's work nor Paitoni's nor the less elaborate work of Scipione Maffei which had suggested theirs (above, p. 376) is of much value on the translations of the Greek epigrams. Argelati mentions as translators of certain epigrams: Vincenzo Cartari,[2] Francesco Forzoni Accolti,[3] Carlo Maria Maggi,[4] Mazzoni,[5] Francesco Antonio Cappone,[6] Michelangelo Torcigliano,[7] Girolamo Garimberto,[8]

---

[1] Cf. Didot Anthol. 2.207.
[2] Above, p. 308.
[3] Above, p. 388.   [4] Above, p. 376.   [5] Above, p. 366.
[6] *Liriche Parafrasi*, Venice, 1670. Argelati's statement (*Bibl.* 1.63), that Cappone has in this book a translation of Antipater, seems to be an error. Cappone has (*Lir.*, p. 265) a version of the *Amor Fugitivus* of Moschus (*A.P.* 9.440).
[7] See above, p. 365.
[8] Argelati (*Bibl.* 1.63) is mistaken in saying that Garimberto's *Concetti* (Venice, 1565) contains several conceits from Antipater.

and Bongiovanni and Zanetti. Many of these references may be by Argelati's editor, Angelo Teodoro Villa. Paitoni mentions Maggi,[1] Brignole Sale,[2] Bongiovanni and Zanetti,[3] and Salvini.[4]

CESARE GAETANI DELLA TORRE
(1718–1808)

Count Cesare Gaetani della Torre, discoverer of the inscription of Queen Philistis, deserves to be remembered as a good scholar and archaeologist. He was born at Syracuse, and studied with the Jesuits. On completing his education he repaired to Naples and to Rome, where he frequented the society of the learned. Returning to his native city, he devoted himself to archaeological and historical studies. He published many valuable papers, but never completed the history of Syracuse which was his ultimate aim. On the suppression of the Jesuits, he received the chair of moral philosophy at the University of Syracuse. Besides his historical studies he published eclogues and other works of *belles lettres* in prose and verse.

Della Torre is mentioned in this place for his translation of Anacreon and the bucolic poets: *Odi di Anacreonte e gli Idillj ed Epigrammi di Teocrito, Bione, e Mosco, Poeti Greci, Tradotti in Rime Italiane*. Rome, 1775.[5] This contains versions of the following epigrams: *A.P.* 6.177, 336–340; 7.534.1–2, 658–61, 663–4; 9.108 (after Longepierre), 338, 432–4, 437, 440 (p. 49²), 598, 599, 600; 13.3; 16.200. His version of *A.P.* 7.658 follows:

> Mi avvedrò, viatore,
> Se agli uomini dabbene
> Dai tu qualche vantaggio, o pari onore
> L'empio da te si ottiene.
> Dirai: 'Dà grazia e pace
> Il ciel benigno a questa
> Tomba, che lieve giace
> Di Eurimedonte sulla sacra testa.

RAIMONDO CUNICH
(1719–1794)

Cunich was a Jesuit professor. Born at Ragusa, he early lost his father, and was sent at the age of fifteen to study with the Jesuits in

---

[1] Paitoni (*Bibl.* 2.69) says that Maggi has made an epigram by Philippus into a sonnet in his *Rime Varie* (cf. above, p. 376).
[2] Above, p. 364.   [3] Above, p. 400.   [4] Above, p. 382.
[5] Referred to in the Register as *Odi*. There are two systems of pagination, the second of which I have referred to with a superior 2.

Rome. Here his principal teacher in Greek and Latin literature was
Carlo Roti. After completing the philosophical course, he taught
grammar for a year at Fermo, and then, for six years, humanity at
Città di Castello and at Florence. Returning to Rome to take up
theology, he was set to teaching at Sant' Andrea on the Quirinal, and
for fifteen years taught there with notable success. The epigrapher
Morcelli was one of his pupils. Thence he went to the Roman College,
and taught there for the last thirty years of his life. He had a great
reputation not only as a teacher, but also as an orator and Latin poet;
and was a member of the Academies of the *Infecondi*, and the *Occulti*,
and of the Arcadians of Rome, among whom he assumed the name
Perelao Megaride. A man of great modesty, he could hardly be per-
suaded to publish his writings, but yielded to the request of Baldassarre Odescalchi that he print his translations from the Anthology and
from Homer. The translations from the Anthology are to be discussed
below; the Latin version of the *Iliad* appeared at Rome in 1776. Apart
from these, Cunich's only notable book is his *Epigrammatum libri v*
(Parma, 1803; with additions, Reggio, 1827). These original epigrams
show no specific influence from the Anthology, though possibly their
arrangement is based on Planudes. Cunich died November 22, 1794,
and was buried in the Church of the SS. Apostoli.[1]

When editing Zamagna's *Eco* in 1764, Cunich joined there-
with 45 Latin translations from the Anthology: *Selecta Carmina
Graecorum versa Latine*. Five years later he issued an entire book
of translations, dedicated to Odescalchi, and entitled *Anthologica sive Epigrammata Anthologiae Graecorum Selecta latinis
versibus reddita et animadversionibus illustrata* (Rome, 1771.
xii+191 pp.). This book was reprinted without changes at
Venice in 1784, together with a new edition of Cunich's *Iliad*.[2]

The *Anthologica* is divided into eight sections: 1. *Encomias-
tica;* 2. *Satyrica;* 3. *Moralia;* 4. *Votiva;* 5. *Sepulchralia;* 6. *Lugu-
bria;* 7. *Ludicra;* 8. *Varia*. The epigrams are well-chosen, and
are representative, save that no section of *Amatoria* is included.
A very few epigrams are taken which are not in the Anthology,
and at the end Cunich gives Callimachus' *Bath of Pallas*. In this
he may have been influenced by Soter. His illustrative notes,
mainly parallels from Greek and Latin authors, are brief and
interesting. He does not print the Greek originals of his epigrams, but gives references to the Planudean Anthology.

Cunich's translations were widely used, frequently referred to,
and apparently the only form in which many of his countrymen

---

[1] Vaccolini in Tipaldo's *Biografia degli Italiani Illustri* 1.55.
[2] References, '*Anth.*,' in the Register are to the edition of 1771.

knew the Greek epigrams. The Italian poet Passeroni owes a whole volume of his works to Cunich, while Felici and Pagnini at least kept an eye on Cunich's translations when making their own.[1]

The following is Cunich's version of *A.P.* 11.391:

> Mus Asclepiadae tecta intra visus avaro est,
> Qui metuens damnum, 'Quid tibi quaeris?' ait.
> Cui mus subridens: 'Parce, o bone, parce timori:
> Non victum quaero te penes at latebram.'

A list of all Cunich's translations follows:[2]

A.P. 5.74, 230; 6.1 (2 versions), 9, 36, 44, 46, 52, 53, 62, 73, 77, 84, 86, 97, 115, 130, 134, 152, 158, 161, 164, 177, 198, 236, 256, 309, 331, 334, 336;

7.4, 8, 9, 10, 12, 13, 15, 16, 22, 39, 40, 55, 58, 66, 69, 70, 71, 73, 80, 109, 128, 136, 139, 140, 145, 146, 150, 153, 157, 159, 160, 161, 173, 174, 187, 196, 204, 205, 226, 227, 228, 229, 231, 235, 238, 242, 251, 257, 258, 265, 274, 280, 282 (2 versions), 285, 293, 302, 308, 310, 317, 318, 320, 321, 346, 350, 351, 353, 355, 408, 432, 434, 447, 451, 453, 461, 464, 487, 489, 492, 510, 512, 518, 519, 521, 522, 524, 525, 528, 530, 534, 538, 540, 553, 555.5, 565, 593, 605, 649, 674, 688.3, 703, 740, 741; 8.126, 137;

9.3, 12, 18 (2 versions), 19, 20, 23, 24, 25, 26, 27, 29, 32, 36, 37, 39, 40, 47, 49, 50, 55, 58, 59, 61, 62, 64, 66, 67, 68, 72, 74, 77, 80, 84, 85, 87, 93, 96, 97, 99, 100, 101, 102, 105, 107, 108, 110, 111, 114, 115, 117, 120, 127, 130, 131, 133, 136, 138, 141, 144, 146, 147, 148, 151, 152, 153, 154, 162, 163, 165, 166, 172, 176, 177, 178, 179, 183, 189, 192, 204, 215, 218, 221, 224, 231, 236, 242, 246, 248, 254, 259, 262, 266, 267, 271, 277, 279, 283, 285, 288, 289, 291, 292, 293, 295, 302, 304, 306, 307, 316, 320, 322+323, 324, 327, 331, 341, 344, 346, 347, 359, 360, 367, 369, 372, 375, 376, 387, 391, 405, 408, 413, 432, 441, 447, 484, 489, 497, 506, 518, 523, 526, 530, 541, 549, 550, 557, 561, 562, 566, 575, 576, 577, 588, 664, 669, 679, 701, 702, 704, 715, 717, 718, 719, 721, 724, 749, 768;

10.1, 3, 8, 13, 26, 27, 28, 29, 30, 31, 37, 39, 46, 47, 51, 55, 60, 64, 65, 66, 69, 72 (2 versions), 73, 74, 80, 93, 98, 102, 105 (2 versions), 108, 112, 119, 122, 123, 125;

11.9, 13, 50, 53, 68, 71, 72, 75, 76, 77, 80, 81, 103, 104, 115, 122, 124, 125, 127, 131, 133, 135, 138, 141, 145, 146, 147, 151, 152, 153,

[1] Below, pp. 408, 423, and 430. For instance, Passeroni, Felici, and Pagnini all employ Cunich's *Nice* for *Niconoe* of the original in *A.P.* 11.71; and in *A.P.* 11.184 translate his *templo*, a word not represented in the Greek. These and similar correspondences may be noted in the Register.

[2] Of these translations, the following had been printed in Zamanga's *Eco* (Rome, 1674): 6.158, 164, 177, 334, 336; 7.66, 69, 109, 145, 317, 318, 447, 519, 522, 524; 9.39, 49, 55, 66–7, 107, 133, 148, 177, 204, 266, 322+323, 327, 346, 359, 360, 391, 530, 557, 701, 702; 10.26, 65, 119; 11.186, 190; 16.107, 129, 142.

154, 159, 160, 162, 176, 178, 184, 186, 187, 190, 192, 193, 194, 198,
208, 209, 210, 211, 213, 214, 237, 249, 250, 251, 253, 254, 255, 257,
258, 259, 265, 266, 268, 270, 274, 277, 281, 293, 294, 304, 305, 310,
313, 315, 324, 325, 331, 335, 340, 365, 374, 375, 378, 386, 387, 390,
391, 392, 394, 397, 399, 406, 408, 410, 413, 419, 428, 429, 430, 431,
435;

13.3, 29; 14.2; 15.51; 16.1, 2, 4, 5, 7, 8, 11, 12, 14, 17, 53, 54, 58,
59, 60, 68, 74, 81, 97, 100, 103, 107, 114, 119, 120, 129, 142, 165,
169+170, 174, 176, 183, 185, 186, 190, 192, 193, 198, 200, 207, 211,
223, 227, 238, 247, 295, 324, 326.

GIAN CARLO PASSERONI

(1713–1802)

Passeroni was a satirical poet of ability. Born near Nice, he received his education mostly at Milan. The papal nuncio Lucino took
him into his service, and thus gave him an opportunity to spend some
time in Rome and in Cologne. Retiring to Milan, Passeroni there
spent most of his life in real poverty as a simple priest. Meanwhile his
satires, in particular his enormous poem, *Il Cicerone*, were being read
by every one. They brought him great fame, but no money, so that
Sterne, who visited him, was distressed to find so famous an author
living in so mean a condition. Sterne is said to have studied Passeroni's works with care.

The poetical works of Passeroni, *Rime*, are in ten volumes,
published at Milan from 1775 to 1802. The third volume, Milan,
1789, is almost wholly given up to translations from the Anthology.[1] These are dedicated to Francesco Fontana, who, we
learn, had urged Passeroni to publish them.[2] In his Address to
the Reader the translator explains that he is not translating from
the Greek, but from the Latin versions of Cunich; had he been
translating the originals, he would have felt obliged to be more
literal; as it is, he has made somewhat free with his sources:

> Io di nuovo in volgar gli ho trasportati,
> O rimpastati, per non dir corrotti:
> Forse un altro diría parafrasati.

Since explanatory notes are needed for an understanding of
these Greek epigrams, and since it is the weakness of readers to
pass over notes at the foot of the page, he has incorporated all
such necessary comments into the poems themselves. The reason

---

[1] *Rime: Tomo iii, Che contiene la Traduzione di alcuni Epigrammi Greci.*
[2] Fontana was the friend and biographer of Girolamo Pompei (below, p. 421).

is that of the satirical poet. Many of these translations, he says, were made on restless nights between sleeping and waking, so that the reader need not wonder if they put him to sleep also. The author's sleep, he adds, was at least productive of something. He ends in a full vein of satire; he hopes that a better translator may follow him; but challenges the reader who is disposed to be critical to attempt a like exercise.

Cunich, more economical than the Greek, had put *A.P.* 6.1 into a single couplet:

> Hoc Venere speculum suspendit Lyda: nequiret
> Iam se quod iuvenem cernere; nolet anum.

Passeroni gives full vent to his moralizing impulse, and produces the following paraphrase (note that he retains Cunich's 'Lyda' for the 'Laïs' of the Greek):

> Lida a Ciprigna questo specchio offerse;
> Chè di vedersi giovane concesso
> A lei non era; e di vedersi in esso
> Vecchia, e rugosa, il cor non le sofferse:
> Oh quante, oh quante potrien dir lo stesso!
> Ma quella verità che gli occhi aperse
> A Lida, oggi li chiude a tante e tante,
> Che grinzo più di Lida hanno il sembiante.
> Lo stesso si può dir di me, che attendo
> A compor versi nell' età cadente,
> Etate in cui manca la lena e 'l foco,
> E in cui ciascun cantor diventa roco;
> E la cetra, che al collo ancora appendo,
> Dovrei già avere appesa a un salce, o a un chiodo;
> Ma l'amor proprio inganna in più d'un modo.

While it is easily possible to identify Passeroni's originals, twice removed as they are, he has dealt with the themes in a manner so unlike the Greek that there is no point in criticizing them as one might translations. How far from the style of the original is his exercise on the theme of *A.P.* 9.372!—

IL ROSIGNUOLO

> Incappato in una rete
> Era un povero usignuolo,
> Che col canto tenea liete
> Le persone per lo addietro;
> E sfogando in flebil metro

Giva allor l'acerbo duolo.
In udir le sue querele
Io non volli esser crudele.
I miei passi ver lui volsi,
E a que' vincoli lo tolsi.
'Serbar, dissi, que' si denno
Cui natura ed il ciel dienno
Di tenere in gioja e in festa
Color, che hanno orecchi in testa;
Quando a que' non sieno uguali
Di Re Mida, o d'altri tali,
Che non san che cosa sia
Estro, musica, harmonia.'

The Latin version by Cunich, upon which Passeroni's was based, is as follows:

Haesit araneoli rara intra texta cicada,
Pendens aeriis cassibus implicita.
Hanc ego sub pedicis audivi triste canentem,
Nec spretam captus carmine praeterii:
Exemi at laqueis, dixi et 'servare, Camenae
Cui dant argutis dulce sonare modis.'

The original is anonymous:[1]

Λεπτὸν ὑφηναμένα ῥαδινοῖς ὑπὸ ποσσὶν ἀράχνα
τέττιγα σκολιαῖς ἔνδετον εἶχε πάγαις.
ἀλλ' οὐ μὰν λεπταῖσιν ἐπαιάζοντα ποδίστραις
τὸν φιλαοιδὸν ἰδὼν παῖδα παρετρόχασα·
λύσας δ' ἐκ βροχίδων ἀπεκούφισα, καὶ τόδ' ἔλεξα·
'Σώζου μουσείῳ φθεγγόμενος κελάδῳ.'

As Passeroni does not reproduce Cunich in every instance, it has seemed best to give the full list of his translations in this place.

A.P. 5.74, 230; 6.1 (2 versions), 9, 36, 46, 52, 62, 73, 77, 84, 158, 161, 164, 177, 198, 336;

7.4, 10, 12 (2 versions), 15, 16, 39, 66, 70, 71, 80, 109, 128, 136 (2 versions), 145, 157, 161, 196, 204, 205, 228, 229, 235, 242, 257, 265, 280, 282 (2 versions), 285, 293, 302, 308, 317, 318, 320, 321, 346, 350, 351, 353, 355, 408, 432, 434, 447, 451, 453, 461, 487, 489, 521, 525, 528, 530, 538, 553, 565, 593, 660, 674, 688.3, 703, 740; 8.126, 137;

---

[1] 'Having woven a delicate web under its slender feet, a spider held imprisoned therein a cicada, with its twisted fetters. When I saw the little singer lamenting in the delicate snares, I did not run by, but loosed him from the nooses, and consoled him, saying: "Be thou saved, thou utterer of the Muses' song." '

9.12, 18, 23, 24, 25, 26, 27, 36, 37, 39, 40, 47, 49, 55, 61, 62, 64, 66, 72, 74, 85, 87, 93, 96, 99, 100, 101, 108, 114, 115, 120, 127, 130, 133, 136, 138, 141, 144, 146, 148, 151, 152, 154, 162, 163, 166, 172, 189, 204, 224, 236, 254, 259, 271, 277, 279, 283, 291, 293, 295, 304, 331, 344, 346, 359, 360, 372, 376, 387, 391, 405, 413, 447, 484, 489, 506 (2 versions), 523, 526, 530 (2 versions), 549, 557, 575, 576, 577, 664, 669, 701, 702, 715, 717, 718, 719, 721, 724, 749, 768;

10.13, 26, 28, 30, 31, 37, 39, 46, 47, 51, 55, 60, 64, 66, 74, 93, 102, 105, 108, 119, 122, 125;

11.50, 53, 68, 71, 75, 76, 77, 81, 122, 125, 145, 151, 152, 159, 162, 178, 186, 187, 190, 192, 193, 198, 208, 209, 211, 213, 214, 237, 250, 255, 258, 265, 266, 268, 270, 274, 277, 281, 294, 304, 313, 315, 325, 331, 340, 365, 387, 390, 394, 397, 399, 406, 408, 413, 419+420, 429, 430, 431, 435; 12.60; 13.3, 29; 15.51;

16.1, 2, 4, 8, 12, 14, 53 (2 versions), 54, 58 (2 versions), 59, 60, 68, 74, 81 (2 versions), 97, 100, 103, 114, 119, 120, 142, 165 (2 versions), 169, 174, 176, 183, 185, 192, 198, 200, 207, 211, 223, 227, 295, 324, 326.

PASQUALE CARCANI

(1721–1783)

Pasquale Carcani was a Neapolitan lawyer and archaeologist. He learned Greek without a master, but gained great proficiency in it. After acting for some time as secretary to the minister Tanucci, he was made secretary of the commission appointed by Carlo III for the purpose of publishing the antiquities of Herculaneum. The Illustrative Notes of the first five, and in part also of the last three volumes of the *Antichità di Ercolano* are Carcani's work, though printed anonymously. The *Antichità di Ercolano* is a magnificent work, still consulted, in eight volumes, containing reproductions of the paintings, statuary, and lamps, recovered at Herculaneum in the great excavations carried on under King Carlo; the figures are accompanied by a descriptive text, and copious illustrative notes. The volumes were printed at the Royal Press in the following order: Vol. 1, pt. 1 (Catologo), 1755; Vol. 1, pt. 2 (Pitture 1), 1757; Vol. 2 (Pitture 2), 1760; Vol. 3 (Pitture 3), 1762; Vol. 4 (Pitture 4), 1765; Vol. 5 (Bronzi 1), 1767; Vol. 6 (Bronzi 2), 1771; Vol. 7 (Pitture 5), 1779; Vol. 8 (Lucerne), 1792.

In his notes Carcani makes no little use of the Greek epigrams. In fact, he often introduces them more for their intrinsic interest than because they explain anything in the work of art he happens to be dealing with. Occasionally, of course, they really throw light on it, but more often they are suggested by a previous quotation of Carcani's own. He quotes the Greek text, and translates the epigrams into *versi sciolti*, in this way rendering about 55 pieces.[1]

A strong generic likeness exists between much Campanian wall-painting and the Alexandrian epigrams (cf. above, p. 13), so that Carcani's constant reference to the Anthology is far from being out of place. He did well, for instance, to illustrate a painting which represents two *amorini* riding on goats that they have bridled, by quoting *A.P.* 6.312, translated by him as follows:

> I ragazzi, O capron, purpuree briglie
> Mettendoti, e 'l capestro nella bocca,
> I giuochi equestri celebran del dio
> Vicino al tempio, affinchè dolcemente
> Rallegrati da te sieno portati.

Once only, Carcani departs from his rule and translates an epigram (*A.P.* 11.154) into rhyme:

> Chi povero e ignorante oggi vi sia,
> Non va più, come pria,
> Le macine a rivolger del mulino,
> E più non fa per vivere il facchino;
> Ma nutrisce un barbone,
> Ed alzando il bastone
> Va per le cantonate, e grida audace:
> 'Io son della virtù primo seguace;
> Questo è del savio Ermodoto il precetto:
> Chi quattrini non ha,
> Più fame non avrà, tolto il farsetto.'

Carcani, we learn from his step-son, contemplated a complete edition of the Greek Epigrams accompanied by blank-verse translations; and it was he who interested Gaetano in the Anthology (below, p. 427).

[1] *A.P.* 5.29, 34, 93, 94.1–2, 125, 260, 279; 6.72, 74, 87, 134, 148 (2 versions), 172, 173, 207, 220, 281, 293, 311, 312; 7.15 (with Salvini's Latin), 156, 222, 223, 357, 413, 424, 425, 669; 9.39, 312, 357, 530, 543, 557, 647, 824.6–8, 826, 827; 10.80; 11.115, 154, 434; 12.239; 13.29; 16.99, 120, 171, 173, 185, 204, 207 (2 versions), 214, 215, 278, 281, 286, 310. Besides these, he quotes phrases from a good many others that need not here be specified. In the foregoing list, *A.P.* 6.148, 173, 207, 220, 281; 7.424, 425; and 9.543, are not in *Plan.*, but were taken by Carcani from Reiske's *Anthologia* or Küster's Suidas, to which he refers.

When Carcani's step-son published his edition of the Anthology (below, p. 426), he employed some of Pasquale's translations, marking them with an asterisk; others which he filled out from his father's versions he marked with a dagger. Altogether these number eighteen: *A.P.* 6.134; 7.156, 357, 413, 669; 9.16, 39, 312 (†), 357; 11.112, 115; 16.99, 120, 185, 207, 214 (†), 215, 281. On the other hand, some of the translations in the *Antichità di Ercolano* (especially in the last volume) may be by the younger Carcani, since several of them are reprinted in the latter's Anthology unmarked by asterisk or dagger. These are the versions of *A.P.* 6.172; 7.222, 223, 10.80.

AVERARDO DE' MEDICI
(†1808)

De' Medici was a Florentine, belonging to a collateral branch of the Ducal house. His relationship may be found in Litta.[1] He married Livia Guadagni, by whom he had several children. As an Arcadian under the name of *Cinisbo* he published some ephemeral works. His death took place October 26, 1808.

In 1772 De' Medici published at Leghorn a selection of translations from the Anthology into Latin and Italian verse. In 1780 at Pescia he reissued the translations with 10 additions in a volume entitled *Saggio di Prose e Versi Toscani e Latini*. Finally, in a third edition, Florence, 1790, 10 further additions were made, and the book returned to its original title: *Scelta di Epigrammi Greci Tradotti in Versi Latini e Toscani*.[2] The third edition is dedicated to Giovanni Domenico Stratico, professor of sacred history at Pisa.

On each page is printed a Greek epigram followed by the Latin and Italian versions, and, at the bottom, brief notes. De' Medici's Latin is good, and invariably as compact as the original, whereas his Italian is frankly looser. Here follow his translations of *A.P.* 7.669.

> O utinam caelum, spectas dum sidera, fiam,
> Inspiciam ut multis te, mea Stella, oculis.

> Vezzosissima Stella,
> Mentre tue luci ardenti
> Fissi agli astri lucenti,
> Allor fra me disio
> Di farmi un Cielo anch' io;
> Onde tua faccia bella
> Possa mirar contento
> Con cento lumi e cento.

In this way he gives double translations of each of these epigrams:

A.P. 5.28, 74, 101, 130, 146, 168, 234, 262, 268, 282; 6.83, 97, 158, 301, 336; 7.73, 76, 146, 160, 161, 225, 229, 234, 272, 391, 599, 669; 9.23, 29, 39, 47, 61, 97, 126, 157, 163, 221, 283, 391, 453, 577; 10.65, 74, 122; 11.349; 16.1, 14, 77, 200, 207.

[1] Pomponio Litta, *Famiglie Celebri Italiane*, vol. 2, *Medici*, Tav. xviii.
[2] My references are to the third edition.

GIUSEPPE SPALLETTI

(†c. 1792)

When Friederich Jacobs undertook to edit the Anthology, the Palatine manuscript was still in Rome. Through his friends he engaged the interest of Wilhelm Uhden, who was in Rome as agent of the King of Prussia. Uhden made many notes for him, and had begun a complete collation of the manuscript, when a piece of good fortune befell that rendered this work unnecessary.

The Abate Giuseppe Spalletti had been Greek Scholar at the Vatican Library, and had given particular attention to the Palatine manuscripts.[1] In 1781 he printed a literal reproduction of the *Anacreontea* contained in the Palatine MS. of the Anthology. So great had been his interest in this particular MS. that he had made a complete copy of it in his own hand. This work he finished March 30, 1776, and in September of the same year he collated his apograph with the original throughout. Again in March, 1791, he repeated the collation. He reproduced every detail; no one has ever been able to show that he made a single error. He set great store by his apograph, and after his death his heirs put a high price upon it.

When Uhden learned that this MS. was for sale, he communicated the information to Jacobs and Schlichtegroll, Jacobs' colleague at Gotha. The price named seemed at first an obstacle, until Schlichtegroll interested Duke Ludwig Ernst of Gotha and Altenburg in the MS. The Duke directed Uhden to purchase it for the public library of Gotha. Uhden then acquired it at a price lower than that first named; and, before sending it to Germany, once more collated it with the original. Jacobs was probably justified in believing that, so far as text was concerned, it was of equal authority with the Palatine MS.[2]

The Anacreon published at his own expense by Spalletti in 1781 is a beautiful folio volume of sixty pages.[3] In his Address to

[1] *Cod. Vat. Lat.* 10262 is an inventory in Spalletti's hand of the Greek MSS. in the Palatine-Vatican collection; he there styles himself 'Bibliothecae Vaticanae Graecus Scholastes.'

[2] Jacobs, *Praefatio*, pp. xvi–xvii. Jacobs mistakenly gives Spalletti's Christian name as Joannes.

Spalletti had some correspondence with Chardon de la Rochette concerning the Anthology; this is preserved in Paris (*Cod. Paris. Suppl. Graec.* 448, I, 1, 2).

[3] Ἀνακρέοντος . . . Συμποσιακὰ Ἡμιάμβια, *Anacreontis Convivialia Semiambia*. Romae, in aedibus J. Spalletti.

the Reader he describes his transcript of the Palatine MS., and expresses surprise at the little attention paid to the MS. since the time of Allacci. The text of the *Anacreontea* is printed in a type especially made for the occasion; and each poem is illustrated by a drawing made by Michel Angelo Ricciolini and engraved by Camillo Tinti and Petro Bombelli. In the margins is printed the Latin translation by Joshua Barnes. Preceding the odes Spalletti gives a facsimile of pp. 676–91 of the MS., engraved by Filippo Piale. Spalletti believed the MS. to be of the tenth century.

SAVERIO BETTINELLI

(1718–1808)

The second half of the eighteenth century had no more characteristic figure than Bettinelli—a witty and gallant abate, an Arcadian, cosmopolitan in his views, and in everything an admirer of Voltaire. He was born at Mantua. After studying with the Jesuits he entered their Order in 1736, and taught literature at Brescia, Bologna, and Venice, and at Parma where he was director of the College of Nobles (1759). He traveled in Germany and France as tutor to the sons of the Prince of Hohenlohe; and, being in Lorraine, was sent by King Stanislaus on a mission to Voltaire, with whom he thereafter continued in correspondence. Returning to Italy, after a residence in Verona, he became professor of Italian eloquence at Modena, and when the Jesuits were suppressed in 1773 was in charge of the schools of that place. He retired to Mantua and collected his works (8 vols., Venice, 1780). During the French invasion he lived at Verona, but was able to return to Mantua in 1793 to prepare a more complete edition of his writings (*Opere edite e inedite, in prosa ed in versi.* 24 vols., Venice, 1799–1802). In his last years he was loaded with honors, and when he died was buried in the Panteon of Mantua. He is best known for his attack on Dante in *Lettere Virgiliane* (1757), and for his historical work in the manner of Voltaire: *Il Risorgimento d'Italia negli Studj, nelle Arti, e nei Costumi dopo il Mille* (1773).

The epigram was of more than ordinary interest to Bettinelli. He was eager to see the type flourish in Italy, especially the epigram as written in France. Yet he admired the Anthology too, and sought models therein. His influence is surely to be detected in the new growth of epigram-writing that sprang up at the end of the century; several of the well-known epigrammatists were his friends. In 1787 he published *Lettere a Lesbia Cidonia sopra*

gli Epigrammi [reprinted in 1792; in *Op.*, vols. 21–2]. In these 25
letters the elaborate divisions of previous writers on the subject
are entirely discarded; we have only Bettinelli's own impressions gathered from a wide acquaintance with the modern epigram. His main purpose is to hold up the French as models of
epigrammatic style; his few versions from the Anthology are
suggested by Voltaire. More translations from the Anthology
occur in *Lettere di una Dama ad una sua Amica su le Belle Arti*
(1793) [*Op.* 13.81]. Of these epigrams he says: 'I più son tratti
dall' Antologia, . . . son tradotti, o imitati, da un Arcade, . . . il
qual contro l'uso d'Arcadia odia a morte in sì piccoli e brevi
componimenti le parole e le rime parasite sì care a tutti i tradu-
tori, o traditori.' He takes still more from the Anthology in his
Epigrammi [*Op.* 22. 68–113]. The first group of epigrams was
composed in honor of the marriage of Maximilian Strozzi and
Adelaide Pallavicino. Another, 'per le nozze Cacciapiatti di
Novara,' is entitled *Epigrammi di Maniera Greca*. None of
these last owes its substance to the Anthology; the success with
which the manner is imitated may be judged from the following
specimen (compare, however, *A.P.* 5.268):

> O Cupido, ove son l'ali,
> Che incostante, infido, ingrato
> Fan chiamarti? Ohimè! per quali
> Brave man sei spennacchiato,
> E senz' arco e face e strali
> Lieto insieme e imprigionato?
> Ah sì, tronchi i vanni tuoi,
> Più partir di qua non vuoi.

Serving an occasional purpose, Bettinelli's translations or
imitations are made with some freedom, not always with
great spirit; the following verses from his *Lettere di una Dama*
will serve as an example of his better manner; they render
A.P. 16.170:

> Venere Gnidia al Portico chi mira,
> Paridi loda d'un giudicio raro;
> Ma chi nel tempio suo Pallade ammira,
> Oh, Pari, grida, oh pastorello ignaro!

Bettinelli, as one might expect of a student of the Renaissance, knows the Italian translations of the sixteenth century;

he is fond of comparing them. The following is a typical page from the *Lettere a Lesbia Cidonia*:[1]

Il miglior disinganno che possa ottenersi del cattivo gusto, che regna negli epigrammi, è quello de' paragoni. Io ve ne porrò qui alcuno più degno del vostro fino discernimento. Sia quello dell' Antologia sopra la Venere Armata degli Spartani [*A.P.* 16.174]:

> Armatam vidit Venerem Lacedaemone Pallas;
>   'Nunc certemus, ait, iudice vel Paride.'
> Cui Venus: 'Armatam cur me, temeraria, temnis,
>   Quae quo te vici tempore inermis eram?'

> Armata a Sparta Venere
> Palla vide: 'A duello
> Or veniam, disse, e giudice
> Sia pure il pastorello.'
> A cui Ciprigna: 'In armi
> Perchè sì temeraria
> Ardisci disprezzarmi?
> Tu non hai più memoria,
> Che inerme ebbi vittoria?'

Non mi fa scrupolo il numero de' versi, chè corti essendo poco più spazio tengono de' quattro esametri. Ma qualch' altro scrupolo mi sento avere. Voi l'indovinate facilmente. Ora leggete quello del Subleyras:

> Pallade vide armata Citerea,
>   E disse: 'Vuoi combatter meco, O Dea?'
> Rispose questa: 'E come osi sfidarmi?
> Nuda io ti vinsi— or che farei con l'armi?'

Venga appresso l'Alamanni sì colto e stimato, e stupite che sia peggior dell' altro:

> Vide Vener armata Palla, e disse:
>   'Combattiam ora, e giudichi Parisse;'
> A cui Vener: 'Tu stolta armata spregi,
> Chi già nuda ti vinse, e porta pregi?'

Anche questo ha il difetto di far dubitare se sia Venere o Palla la dea armata. Ma è il minor difetto. In verità que' cinquecentisti abusavano del lor credito, o noi siam troppo facili ad ammirarne l'eleganza. Eccone un altro:

> Vide Minerva un dì di piastra e maglia
> Vener armata gir pel mondo, a cui
> 'Or, disse, entriamo a singolar battaglia
> Con Paride anco giudice tra nui.'
> Cui Citerea rispose: 'Adunque vui

[1] *Let.* 9 in *Op.* 21.75–6.

> Credete, ch'io per vincervi non sia
> Armata, se vi vinsi ignuda pria?'

Questo è del cieco d'Adria [above, p. 328], Luigi Groto, che in quel secolo gareggiò coll' Alamanni in epigrammi, avendone ciascun d'essi più di cento nelle lor opere. Ma l'uno e l'altro o furono assai dispregiatori di questo genere, poco studio applicandovi, o non ebbero altro gusto che quel di scrivergli.

In all, Bettinelli employs the following:

A.P. 5.155; 6.1 (2 versions),[1] 130; 7.71, 109, 310, 455, 464, 605; 9.49, 108, 166, 221, 408, 515, 702; 10.69; 11.53, 76, 255; 16.81, 103, 129 (after Voltaire), 168 (after Voltaire), 170, 174,[2] 181, 198, 211.

ANGELO MARIA BANDINI
(1726–1800)

Bandini was born in Florence. He was educated by the Jesuits, and early showed an aptitude for scholarly pursuits. In 1747 he visited Vienna as secretary to the Bishop of Volterra, and was presented to the Emperor, who agreed to receive the dedication of his *Specimen Litteraturae Florentinae*. Later Bandini went to Rome and took orders. His health necessitated a return to Florence, and there in 1750 he took charge of the celebrated library of Alessandro Marucelli. Six years later the Emperor made him librarian of the Laurentian, a position which he filled until his death. Of his many works by far the most serviceable are his Catalogues of the Laurentian manuscripts.

Bandini's treatment of the Florentine MSS. of the Anthology is thorough. On Chalcondyles' MS. (*Plut.* 31, *cod.* 28; cf. above, p. 30) he writes in part as follows:[3] 'Continet hic codex Anthologiam sive Florilegium variorum Epigrammatum, in VII libros divisum, et a Maximo Planude collectum, ut ex primi libri titulo paene evanido eruitur. Singulis autem libris Index Capitum praecedit, rubrica conscriptus; itemque uniuscuiusque epigrammatis titulum auctorisque nomen rubrae litterae distinguunt. Nec desunt quandoque in margine parva quaedam scholia ab eadem manu exarata [cf. above, p. 158]. Hunc itaque

---

[1] The version printed in *Lettere di una Dama* is accompanied by the Latin of Ausonius and the French translation by Voltaire.

[2] Accompanied (as above) with the Latin of Ausonius and the Italian versions of Alamanni, Groto, and Subleyras.

[3] *Catalogus Codicum Graecorum Bibliothecae Laurentianae.* 3 vols. Florence, 1764, 1768, 1770. Notices of the Anthology are in vols. 2 and 3; that of 31, 28 is in vol. 2, col. 99.

codicem maxima diligentia conscriptum, praecipua quadam recensione dignum existimavimus; ac propterea singula epigrammata in ipso contenta, cum Florilegio edito in corpore Poetarum Graecorum Veterum Iac. Lectii ita contulimus, ut eorum initium ac finem in utroque exemplari inter se componentes, quae vel deesse, vel abundare in alterutro comperimus, ea omnia lectori significare operae pretium duxerimus.' He gives his collation. About half-way through he realized the disadvantages of using Lect's *Corpus* and turned (col. 102) to the Wechel *Anthologia*.

In the same volume (col. 105) he describes Lascaris' *editio princeps*. He quotes the Epistle to Piero de' Medici entire (coll. 106–112).[1]

His notices of the smaller MSS. are collected in his Index (Vol. 3, coll. 468–9).

In Bandini's *De Florentina Juntarum Typographia* (Lucca, 1791) 2.144 he observes that there are 2568 epigrams in the Juntine edition of the Anthology (above, p. 169).

Bandini reviewed the earlier volumes of Carcani's edition of the Anthology in the *Novelle Letterarie* No. 49, for 1789, comparing Carcani's versions with those of Salvini.[2]

GIUSEPPE PARINI

(1729–1799)

Parini, reckoned as one of the restorers of taste in Italy, was born at Bosisio, and educated at the school of S. Alessandro directed by the Barnabites at Milan. He published his first poems in 1752, and was immediately elected to several academies. In 1754 he entered the priesthood; and in the same year became tutor in the ducal family of the Serbelloni. A quarrel with the Duchess led to his leaving them in 1762. In 1767 he received a small bequest, and two years later made his livelihood secure by accepting the chair of eloquence at the Palatine school. When the Jesuits were suppressed (1773), he passed to the Accademia di Brera. His life thereafter was uneventful save for

---

[1] There is a notice of the 1494 edition also in F. J. B. Audiffredi, *Specimen Historico-Criticum Editionum Italic. Saec. XV* (Rome, 1794), p. 342.

[2] Above, p. 348; below, p. 428. The edition of Callimachus, with translation, published by Bandini in 1763 at Florence, contains Latin versions of the epigrams, which are, however, taken by Bandini from the Leyden edition of 1761; they are by J. A. Ernesti. ([Greek title] *Callimachi Cyrenaei Hymni cum Lat. Int. a ... A.M. Salvinio ... necnon eiusdem Callimachi Graeca Epigrammata adiecit A. M. Bandinius....* Florence, 1763.)

the publication of his poems, and the troubles attendant on the French Revolution.

Parini left a few translations to attest his attention to the ancient poets. Among these is a version of *A.P.* 16.200, for which, to be sure, he hardly needs to have gone directly to the Anthology:[1]

DA MOSCO

Deposta un giorno l'orrida facella
 È quell' arco crudel che i petti schiaccia,
 Prese Amore in ispalla una bisaccia
 E un pugnitoio in cambio di quadrella;
E posta sotto il giogo una vitella
 O un giovenco che fosse o due, li caccia
 Per lo incolto terren con una faccia
 D'un villan che si stizza ed arrovella.
Quasi 'l bellico a' Numi si sconficca,
 D'Amor ridendo che l'aratro muove,
 E la semenza per le zolle ficca.
Quand' e' rivolto al ciel grida: 'Ser Giove,
 O fa' di mèsse questa terra ricca,
 O ch' io di nuovo ti converto in bove.'

In a list of books drawn up by Parini, probably as a basis for an ideal scheme of education, the Greek Anthology duly appears.[2]

GUGLIELMO DELLA VALLE

(*c.* 1730–1794)

Della Valle came from Siena. He entered the Franciscan Order at an early age, and was sent to Bologna. There he made the acquaintance of the celebrated musician G. B. Martini, an *Elogium* of whom he published after the latter's death (Bologna, 1784). In 1785, being at the cloister of the Franciscans in Naples, he published in that city a more extensive work on Martini under the title of *Memorie Istoriche*. He made a name for himself by his works on painting, in which his persistent endeavor was to show that the development of the art in Italy was continuous, at least in Pisa and Siena, and that the imitation of antiquity, practised by some Florentine artists, had no real effect on the tradition. These views were mostly set forth in his *Lettere Sanesi sopra le Belle Arti*, 3 vols., Venice, 1782, Rome, 1785, *ibid.*, 1786. He published an edition of Vasari, Siena, 1791. He was secretary-general of his Order.

---

[1] *Versi e Prose . . . con un Discorso di Giuseppe Giusti*, Florence, 1860, p. 297.
[2] The list is printed by Mazzoni, *Tutte le Opere di Giuseppe Parini*, Florence, 1925, p. 1038.

Della Valle supplied a *proemio* to each of Dati's lives of the painters (above, p. 369). In these he finds occasion to translate two Greek epigrams—*A.P.* 9.776 and 16.178[1]—the second as follows:

> Ecco Ciprigna dai materni flutti
> Ora emergente, opra immortal di Apelle.
> Oh qual molcendo il crin nel mare immerso
> La bianca man ne spreme il salso flutto!
> Non di bellezza più moveran lite,
> Se la vedran Minerva e l'alma Giuno.

GIROLAMO POMPEI

(1731–1780)

Count Girolamo Pompei is a poet of some reputation. He was born at Verona, and studied with the Jesuits. In particular he perfected himself in the knowledge of Greek literature and of the Italian poetry of the early Renaissance, seeking to draw from both principles on which to found his own style. After some not unsuccessful essays in the drama, he returned to the pastoral, which had early been his favorite form, and to the kind of poetry represented by the Anthology. Yet his translation of Plutarch gained him most honor.

Pompei's *Raccolta Greca* (Verona, 1781), containing 100 translations from the Anthology, was dedicated to Brunck.[2] As a translator he is more skilful than Bongiovanni and Zanetti and more faithful than Felici or Passeroni. He regularly uses a six- or nine-line stanza, though often, of course, he is content to give in three lines the substance of the Greek. His version of *A.P.* 9.39 is a typical example:

> A le Muse Ciprigna: 'Fate onore,
>   O giovincelle, a Venere; od armato
>   Farò che contra voi ne venga Amore.'
> E a Ciprigna le Muse: 'Questi tuoi
>   Ciarlari a Marte. Non ispiega il volo
>   Cotesto fanciulluzzo inverso noi.'

The following epigrams are translated by Pompei in his *Raccolta:*

A.P. 5.15, 21, 62, 67, 69, 70, 74, 76, 92–5, 141, 144, 151, 152, 155, 163, 177, 178, 266; 6.1, 19, 283; 7.142, 160, 195, 217, 218, 309, 565, 593, 603, 669, 670; 9.39, 51, 61, 62, 72, 74, 76, 127, 145, 148, 163, 231,

---

[1] Dati, *Vite*, Milan ('Classici Italiani'), 1806, pp. 30 and 136.

[2] I use vol. 2 of Pompei's *Opere*, published in 6 vols at Verona (Moroni), 1790–1. In the *Parnaso Italiano* 53.36 (Venice, 1791) is a sonnet by Pompei on the theme of *A.P.* 5.83+4+*A.P.* 15.35.

322, 323, 394, 401, 515, 526, 530, 719–21, 724, 729–32, 737, 738, 794;
10.27, 28, 30, 37, 58, 65, 66, 79, 80, 93, 122; 11.75, 76, 186, 211, 226,
229, 237, 250, 266, 268, 294, 381; 12.60; 16.77, 78, 81, 129, 165, 166,
168, 178, 204, 211, 324.

FRANCESCO SAVERIO DE' ROGATI

(1745–1827)

Rogati is known as the author of a drama for music entitled
Armida Abbandonata, and as a translator of Anacreon and
Sappho: *Le Odi di Anacreonte e di Saffo, recati in versi Italiani*,
2 vols., Colle, 1782; 1783; 1818; Paris (Didot), 1835.[1] Necessarily
he translates *A.P.* 11.47, 48, and 16.388, the last as follows:[2]

Nel fare un serto   Invan le piume
  Di rose belle,   Scuote il tiranno,
  Colgo fra quelle   Io lo tracanno
  Nascosto Amor.   Fra il buon liquor.

Per l'ali il prendo,   Per questo avviene,
  Che porta al tergo,   Che ognora io provo
  Nel vino immergo   Un grato, un nuovo
  Quel traditor.   Palpito al cor.

CARLO FELICI

(*fl.* 1785)

Of the Abate Carlo Felici nothing seemingly is known save
what appears on the title-page of his books: 'Professore di belle
lettere nel seminario vescovile Toscolano.' He was a protonotary apostolic. He published *Epigrammi Tratti dal Greco* at
Frascati in 1787;[3] and also at Frascati, in 1795, a new selection
entitled *Epigrammi Tratti dal Greco, umiliati a S.A.R. Eminen-
tissima il signor Cardinale denominato Duca di York . . . in
occasione di una pubblica accademia.*[4] None of the translations

---

[1] There is an account of Rogati in Tipaldo's *Biog. Ital. Illus.* 4.387. Born at Bagnolo,
he studied in Naples and in Rome, and, entering the legal profession, settled in Naples,
where he held a number of civil offices.

[2] *A.P.* 16.388 is also translated from the *Anacreontea* by the Abate Antonio Conti,
in his *Prose e Poesie* (Venice, 1739) 1.273.

[3] Referred to in the Register as *Epig*[1].

[4] Referred to as *Epig*[2]. (the pagination is in Roman numerals). Henry, younger
brother of Charles Edward Stuart ('Prince Charlie'), was made Bishop of Ostia, Velletri,
and Frascati soon after 1745, was created Cardinal in 1747, and made Archbishop of
Tusculum in 1761. The Villa Muti at Frascati was his favorite residence.

of the first book were repeated in the second. Felici's versions are always competent, and often the best in Italian. He is one of the more considerable translators of the epigrams in the eighteenth century. It is evidently implied that the Anthology found a place in the instruction given at the Episcopal Seminary at Frascati. Occasionally at least Felici's versions are dependent on those of Cunich (above, p. 407).

The following translation of *A.P.* 11.391 is taken from Felici's first book:

> Vide un topo entro il suo tetto
> Asclepiade, e paventando
> D'alcun danno: 'Ah maledetto,
> Che, diss' egli, vai cercando?'
> Quegli a lui dolce ridendo:
> 'Non temer danno o periglio;
> Chè appo te non cibo intendo
> Ritrovar, ma un nascondiglio.'

His translation of *A.P.* 16.12 is in the same volume:

> Vieni, riposati,
> O peregrino,
> All' ombra placida
> Di questo pino,
> Che al dolce sibilo
> D'aura leggiera
> Risponde, ed agita
> La cima altera.
> Limpido e garrulo
> Tra sponda e sponda,
> Il rio, che mormora,
> Increspa l'onda;
> E Pan capripede
> Del luogo donno,
> Con rozza fistola
> Invita al sonno.

From the volume of 1795 I take his version of *A.P.* 9.108:

> 'Arco e freccie io ti torrò'
> Ad Amor Giove dicea.—
> Ed Amor gli rispondea:
> 'E se Cigno io ti farò?'

Felici's *Epigrammi* of 1787 contains translations of *A.P.* 5.74, 142, 147; 6.1, 9, 26, 36, 53, 73, 84, 158, 164; 7.4, 8, 13, 16, 23, 59, 71, 139, 146, 153, 160, 174, 204, 205, 206, 210, 216, 265, 285, 293, 308, 310, 452, 500, 586, 593, 605, 616, 646, 703;

9.18, 36, 39, 47, 49, 61, 64, 66, 67, 85, 87, 95, 99, 109, 116, 118, 130, 138, 153, 158, 162, 163, 204, 221, 271, 293, 307, 320, 323, 324, 346, 359, 360, 378, 410, 438, 441, 523, 526, 562, 572, 577, 664, 720, 721, 725;

10.13, 26, 27, 30, 37, 60, 65, 69, 74, 79, 81, 84, 112, 116, 123;

11.68, 71, 104, 190, 193, 194, 203, 301, 302, 307, 340, 356, 391, 397, 408, 428, 429, 430, 435; 14.7; 15.51;

16.4, 12, 58, 107, 120, 129, 151, 170, 174, 178, 183, 193, 198, 200, 201, 207, 211, 214, 245, 247, 324.

In the volume of 1795 the following are translated: *A.P.* 6.77, 86, 161, 236, 331; 7.136, 280, 323, 434, 530, 555.5; 9.3, 4, 72, 77, 108, 154, 224, 236, 240, 259, 265, 267, 277, 285, 312, 316, 339, 387, 405, 530, 576, 654; 10.1, 28, 31, 66, 122; 11.76, 184; 16.1, 90, 99, 104, 114, 125, 132, 165, 248, 388.

CARLO RONCALLI-PAROLINO

(1732–1811)

Count Carlo Roncalli was a son of the celebrated archaeologist and physician, Francesco Roncalli of Brescia. After studying in his native place at the Jesuits' college, Carlo was sent to Bologna, but, giving too little attention there to his studies, was summoned home. In Brescia he made the acquaintance of several young poets; and some of his early verses are contained in a volume published by them: *Rime di Vari Autori Bresciani Viventi* (Brescia, 1761). Roncalli now traveled in Italy and in France; he was in Paris in 1769. After his return, a personal quarrel led to the writing of the first of his epigrams. In this way he found his true vein, and remains one of the best Italian epigrammatists. The remainder of his life seems to have been passed in Brescia without incident.

Roncalli's first published epigrams were translations from the French: *Epigrammi*, Brescia, 1783. They were in part reprinted by Bodoni at Parma in 1786. Then followed *Epigrammi Libretto Secondo*, Parma, 1792, Latin epigrams translated into Italian. A collective edition appeared at Florence in 1796: *Epigrammi e Madrigali Italiani*. The first complete edition was that of 1801: *Epigrammi* (Venice).[1] Roncalli's original epigrams mostly belong to his last period.

The bulk of Roncalli's epigrams are translations; many from the French and from the Latin, and a very considerable number from the Anthology. Strictly, however, these are also from the Latin, for Roncalli employs not the Greek, but the translations

---

[1] My references are to this edition and to that of 1792.

of Ausonius, Cunich, and others, as the basis of his own. In the edition of 1792, for example, the Latin—mostly Cunich's—is printed on the left-hand page, with the Italian opposite.

Roncalli was specially pleased with *A.P.* 11.76, and made two versions of it, of which the one here given is the later and better:

> Un giorno il bel Narciso
> Specchiandosi nell' acque,
> Tanto a se stesso piacque,
> Che ne morì d'amor.
> Tu, con quel brutto viso
> Sempre allo specchio stai,
> Nè quel sembiante mai
> Ti fa morir d'orror.

The edition of 1801 contains translations representing the following epigrams; an asterisk indicates that the translation had appeared in the *Epigrammi* of 1792: *A.P.* 5.69, 83+4+ 15.35, 97; 6.1*; 7.308*, 320, 353*; 9.12*, 20*, 23*, 75, 106, 346*, 721*; 10.58; 11.68*, 76* (2 versions; the one printed above is not in the edition of 1792), 169, 170, 250*, 264, 397*, 408* (2 versions; only one in the edition of 1792; see Register), 431*; 12.235; 16.14*, 32, 120*, 185*. The following translations appearing in the edition of 1792 were not reprinted in 1801:[1] *A.P.* 7.293, 318, 688.3; 9.36, 99.[2]

MAFFEO PINELLI

(1736–1785)

For several generations Pinelli's family had been directors of the Ducal Press at Venice, and Maffeo succeeded his father in that capacity. The cares of the press and the collection of books, pictures, and antiquities formed the occupation of his life. He was only moderately wealthy, yet assembled one of the finest libraries of the century. His only literary work was a translation of Harwood's *View of the Various Editions of the Greek and Roman Classics*—*Prospetto di Varie Edizioni degli Autori Classici Greci e Latini* (Venice, 1780); to this he contributed valuable notes. His closest friend was Jacopo Morelli (1745–1819), the celebrated librarian of St. Mark's, who undertook the task of cataloguing Pinelli's treasures with a view to sale after the latter's death. He issued a catalogue of the pictures in 1785, and in 1787 a catalogue of the books in six volumes: *Bibliotheca Maphaei Pinelli*

---

[1] These versions and those in the preceding list marked with asterisks (i.e., all the translations in the 1792 edition) were taken from Cunich, except those of *A.P.* 9.12 and 9.721, which are from Ausonius.

[2] Imitations of *A.P.* 5.256 and 7.455 are in the *Epig. di Mod. Aut.* (Faenza, 1819), and an imitation of 9.749 in De-Mauri's *L'Epig. Ital.* (Milan, 1918). These I have failed to note in going through Roncalli's *Epigrammi*.

Veneti magna cum studio collecta (Venice). The library was purchased in 1789 by the London booksellers Robson and Edwards, who issued an abstract of Morelli's catalogue (*Bibliotheca Pinelliana*, London, 1789), and sold the books in 1790. They received 9356 pounds sterling, 6786 pounds for the Greek and Latin books and 2570 pounds for the rest.

Pinelli's Anthologies are listed in vol. 2 of Morelli's catalogue (1787), pp. 256–9. They included two copies of the *editio princeps*, one on vellum, with the Epistle to Piero de' Medici copied in manuscript,[1] and one on paper with the Epistle; a copy of the first Aldine with 'sixteenth-century manuscript notes';[2] a copy of the edition of the Giunti; a second (1521) Aldine; Badius' (1531) edition; the 1549 edition with Commentary by Brodaeus; the third Aldine; Stephanus' edition; the Wechel (1600) edition; that of Lubinus (1604); the *Poetae Graeci Veteres*, vol. 2 (Cologne 1614); Reiske's *Anthol. Graec. lib. iii* (1754), with Warton's reprint (1766); and two copies of Brunck's *Analecta* (1772–76).[3] Of selections he had: the second and third editions of Soter, but not the first; Melanchthon and Micyllus' *Epigrammata* (Hagenau, 1528); the *Epigrammata Selecta* of Micyllus and Camerarius (Basel, 1538); Stephanus' translations (1570); Leich's *Carmina Sepulchralia* (1745); Klotz's *Stratonis Epigrammata* (1764); Zenobetti's edition of Meleager's poem on Spring; and Wolf's *Poetriarum octo . . . Fragmenta* (Hamburg, 1734).[4]

GAETANO RINFORZO CARCANI

(*fl.* 1785)

Gaetano Rinforzo was the step-son of Pasquale Carcani (above, p. 411). He was director of the Royal Press at Naples. From this press he issued an edition of the Planudean Anthology with an Italian translation in *versi sciolti:* Ἀνθολογία Διαφόρων Ἐπιγραμμάτων εἰς ἑπτὰ βιβλία διῃρημένη. *Raccolta di*

---

[1] The printed Epistle is wanting in all copies on vellum.

[2] See above, p. 258.

[3] Morelli mistakenly lists among the Anthologies the *Anthologicon* of Michael Neander (Basel, 1556), which is not an edition of the Greek Anthology.

[4] Here may be mentioned a copy of the first Aldine Anthology used by Friedrich Jacobs in the Public Library of Gotha. Jacobs reports that the title-page bore, 'literis fere evanescentibus,' the following inscription: 'De figli et Eredi di n. Marco Maffei.' It had come to Gotha from the library of the Swedish Orientalist, Karl Aurivillius (1717–1786); see Jacobs, *Proleg.*, p. xcvi.

Varj Epigrammi divisa in sette libri. Naples, 1788–96 (large quarto, four volumes in six). In part it was intended to display the fine work that could be done by the Royal Press; and the question remains whether this or the Anthology published about the same time by De Bosch at Utrecht is the more magnificent. Carcani reproduces the Planudean Anthology, adding the proems of Meleager, Philippus, and Agathias at the front. The Greek text is on the left-hand pages, faced by the translation. Preceding the Anthology is a Preface of thirty-one pages.

Carcani planned to make an edition of the entire Anthology as follows: Vols. 1–4, the Planudean Anthology; adding at the end of the fourth volume illustrations of ancient mythology customs, games, and the like, drawn from the epigrams; also, under a separate heading, the *variae lectiones* and *scholia* from a copy of the 1494 edition. To this he meant to add an Index of Authors, an Index of First Lines, and an Index of Words and Subjects; all this to be preceded by a tractate on the writers of the Anthology. Finally, he would add the epigrams given by Brunck not in the *Planudea*, together with other epigrams not then edited at all. He could hardly expect to get all this into four volumes. As a separate work in two volumes, yet uniform with this, he aimed to publish what he calls the *Antologia Minore*, that is the *Anthologia* of Reiske (above, p. 391).

Evidently Carcani did not clearly realize what the bounds of his task were, when he proposed this programme.[1] Actually he only accomplished the seven books of Planudes with the translation (adding the proems as aforesaid). He asserts that every epigram has been confronted with the text of Brunck.

Virtually the only new matter in Carcani's edition is, then, the translation. It is the first complete translation to be printed in any modern language. The idea of such an edition of the Anthology had been a cherished dream of the elder Carcani:[2]

Pasquale Carcani, di sempre acerba e sempre onorata ricordanza per me suo figliuolo . . . pensava di dare una perfetta edizione di quest' opera; poichè avendo tradotto in versi sciolti gran quantità di Epigrammi Greci, e questi inseriti nell' opera delle Illustrazioni delle *Antichità di Ercolano*, avea idea di tradurre il resto all' istesso modo, e così perfezionare questa bella impresa. Ma distratto dal grave peso

---

[1] For example, Reiske's *Anthologia* would have already been printed in the first part since it was digested by Brunck in his *Analecta*.

[2] Pref., p. xvii.

degli affari politici, che non gli permettevano un momento libero, ed
oppresso dall' enorme fatica delle Illustrazioni delle *Antichità Erco-
lanesi*, avea cercato più volte d'infiammare la mia giovanile mente per
siffatta opera, che oh! avessi potuto compirla sotto la sua direzione,
che allora sarebbe parsa per avventura di quelli pregi adorna, che da
me solo non ha potuto ricevere.[1]

The following may serve as examples of Gaetano's translations:

> Un platano son io, che da una vite
> Cinto e coverto, delle chiome altrui
> M'adorno e infioro. Ma co' verdi rami
> Pria l'uve sue nutrii; di frondi or privo
> Quale allor essa fu, son io del pari.
> Deh! possa alcun negli anni appresso a gara
> Tale amica nudrir, che seppe sola
> Negli estremi miei dì darmi mercede.
>
> (*A.P.* 9.231)

> Dolce è in estate a un sitibondo il bere
> La neve; dolc' è a' marinai d'inverno
> Veder ghirlande di fiorito aprile;
> Ma più dolc' è, quando una coltre insieme
> Due amanti ricopre, e da tal coppia
> Vien del pari Ciprigna celebrata.
>
> (*A.P.* 5.169)

CARLO GASTONE, CONTE DELLA TORRE DI REZZONICO

(1742–1796)

Della Torre, a well-known literary figure of the settecento, was
educated under Bettinelli at Parma, where his father was in the
Duke's service. His best work, *I Giornali de' Viaggi*, was the result of
travels in England, Holland, and Germany during 1786–90. He became brigadier of the Duke of Parma's guards, but lost his offices
when accused by Cagliostro of being one of his followers, even though
the charge was unfounded. He died at Naples. His *Opere* appeared at
Como, 1815–30, in ten volumes, edited by Francesco Mocchetti.

---

[1] Inasmuch as the younger Carcani gives a translation of the entire Planudean
collection, except a few epigrams of unusual lubricity, and in view of his edition's appearing very near the end of the period embraced in the present study, I have not deemed
it necessary to list his versions in the Register.

Among contemporary reviews of Carcani's Anthology may be mentioned that of
Bandini (above, p. 419), discussed by Carcani himself at the beginning of Libro II;
and a still more favorable notice in the *Giornale de' Letterati* (Pisa) 1791, pp. 220–34.

In a *Dissertazione sugli Amori d'Ero e di Leandro* (*Op.* 2.341), Della Torre criticizes a translation by Froelich of *A.P.* 7.666 (on Hero and Leander), and quotes the epigram.

LUIGI SUBLEYRAS
(1743–1814)

Subleyras was a native of Rome. His mother, born Maria Felice Tibaldi, was a well-known miniaturist; and, his father, Pietro Subleyras, having died young, Luigi owed to her efforts the careful education he received. Some assistance was given her by Benedict XIV. Early poetical efforts of Subleyras won him a reputation, and he was soon a member of Arcadia and other academies. He became secretary to Monsignor Angelo Maria Durini, whom he accompanied to Poland when Durini was papal nuncio. In Vienna he made the acquaintance of Metastasio. On his return to Rome in 1773, Subleyras secured a place as *minutante* in the secretariat of state under Pius VI. About 1783, however, through the devices of enemies, he fell under a suspicion of disloyalty and was forced to retire. He became a prey to melancholy, which increased when Italy was invaded by the French, so that he lost all heart for poetical composition, and never realized his early promise. He lived till 1814, in July of which year he died in the Hospital of Santo Spirito, and was buried in the cemetery of that institution, without the honor of a stone to mark the place. His most esteemed work is his translation of Catullus (Rome, 1774; reprinted 1812). He has verses in the *Rime* of the Arcadians, vol. 12 (Rome, 1759); in *Triplice Omaggio degli Arcadi a Pio VI* (Rome, 1775); in *Rime degli Aborigini*, pt. 2 (Rome, 1781); in *Prose e Versi degli Accademici Infecondi*, vol. 1 (*ibid.*, 1764); and in the *Giornale delle Belli Arti* (*ibid.*, 1784).[1]

At the time of Subleyras' first poetical successes and his election to Arcadia, he is said to have devoted himself to the translation of the Greek epigrams: 'Volle . . . dedicarsi alla versione di greci epigrammi, la quale, per l'amore che vi pose, riescì ottima: egli la mandava alle stampe del 1759.'[2] Bozoli, who says this, gives no further indications. Possibly the translations comprise his contributions to the Arcadian *Rime* of 1759, a book which I have been unable to consult. One of his versions (*A.P.* 16.174) is quoted by Bettinelli, and has been given above (p. 417). Bettinelli evidently did not think highly of Subleyras as translator; perhaps it is to him that he refers in his criticism of Arcadian translations (above, p. 416).

[1] G. M. Bozoli in Tipaldo's *Biografia degli Italiani Illustri* 5.483.
[2] Bozoli, p. 484.

LUCA ANTONIO (*alias* GIUSEPPE MARIA) PAGNINI

(1737–1814)

Pagnini was born at Pistoia. His abilities and the good training he received from Cesare Franchini attracted attention to him, and the Carmelites invited him to join their chapter in Florence. On going to them, he changed his name to Giuseppe Maria. Later he was sent to Parma, where he taught, first, philosophy in his Order, then rhetoric and Greek at the Academy. While at Parma he published most of his verse. Still later (1806) he became professor of Greek, and afterwards of Latin literature, at Pisa. He was reputed to be one of the most learned men of the time, and had many distinguished friends, among them Bettinelli, Condillac, and Alfieri. He is reported never to have passed a day without reading something in Cicero and translating a piece of Latin or Greek. His translations are his chief claim to remembrance, especially his Horace (1814).

Among Pagnini's translations is a version of the Greek bucolic poets; *Poesie Bucoliche Italiane, Latine, e Greche*, Parma, 1780.[1] This, of course, includes some versions from the Anthology. Later he published a volume devoted to the epigrams alone: *Epigrammi Volgarizzati del Greco . . . libri tre*. Parma, 1800 [*Epig.*]. The contents of this book are mainly from the Anthology, although certain epigrams are from other sources, and a few are not from the Greek at all. They are divided into three books of about 150 epigrams each (179 pages in all). The translator appears to have employed Brunck's *Analecta*, which he describes in his Preface; and he translates several pieces included by Brunck but not belonging to the Anthology. Certain of his translations, however, show that at times he had Cunich's Latin versions before him rather than the Greek (see above, p. 407). In the Preface mention is made of seven of his predecessors in turning Greek epigrams into Italian, namely Averardo de' Medici, Bettinelli, Pompei, Roncalli, Passeroni, Vargas, and Gargallo.[2] He discusses the types of verse suitable for such translations; and himself actually employs a variety of metres.

---

[1] My references are to *I Poeti Greci*, ed. by Silvestro Centofanti, Florence, 1841 [*Poet. Gr.*].

[2] The published work of Tommaso Gargallo (*c.* 1764–1844) mostly lies beyond the downward limit set for the present study. See his *Opere Edite ed Inedite*, published by Marchese Filippo Francesco di Castel Lentini, 4 vols. [Florence], 1923–5. He has (*Op.* 2.587) from the Anthology only the following parody of the epitaph of Midas (*A.P.* 7.153):

EPITAPH OF A SLAVE

Io servo fui. Tu, donna mia Timata,
A me tuo balio ergesti urna onorata.
Vivi felice; e quando al fin verrai
Quaggiù, me servo anche tra l'ombre avrai.

(A.P.7.178)

THE NUT-TREE

Io noce appresso il comun calle posto
Son di turba insolente a' sassi esposto,
Che fe' tutti i miei rami a mano a mano
Cader con mille colpi infranti al piano.
Che giova a me di frutta essere adorno?
Altro non ne ho che maggior danno e scorno.

(A.P. 9.3)

The following are translated by Pagnini in his *Epigrammi:*[1]

A.P. 5.6, 34, 36, 50, 59, 66, 67, 74, 89, 94, 95, 101, 146, 176, 210, 224, 268, 288; 6.1, 12, 19, 76, 121, 134, 146, 154, 283, 301, 352;
7.6, 15, 54, 58, 62, 66.3–4, 69, 71, 72, 80 ,89, 108, 136, 139, 140, 142, 146, 148, 150, 151, 160, 161, 173, 178, 205, 226, 229, 235, 236, 238, 239, 249, 259, 264, 265, 266, 267, 268, 269, 271, 272, 274, 277, 279, 280, 284, 288, 308 (1 trans. and 1 imit.), 309, 310, 313, 317, 323, 325, 336, 346, 348 (2 versions), 356, 387, 408, 415, 451, 454, 461, 464, 471, 489, 505, 521, 525, 532, 538, 553, 557, 565, 580, 582, 593, 599, 608, 611, 667, 669, 670, 674, 712, 713;

> Io, Magnanimità, vergin metallica,
>   Qui sto d'Alfio ad ornar la sepoltura,
>   Gran marescial d'una coorte gallica.
> Come l'oste appressavasi alle mura,
>   Morì costui, chiuso tre dì 'n cantina,
>   Fra la puzza, la fame, e la paura.
> E qui starò, sinchè la peperina
>   Al coniglio, alla mosca il mel gradisca,
>   Il lardo a' gatti, i polli alla faina;
> Sinchè beli l'agnel, l'oca garrisca,
>   Latri 'l can, mugga il bue, ringhi 'l destriere,
>   L'asino ragghi, ed il porcel grugnisca,
> Immobile ammonendo il passeggiere,
>   Che d'Alfio presso al mausoleo cammini,
>   A recitargli qualche *Miserere;*
> Salvo che qua non vengan gli assassini
>   De' creditori a tormi . . . E allora appunto
>   La trasportaro in zecca a far quattrini,
> Pe' debiti pagarne del defunto.

The celebrated Count Angelo d'Elci (1764–1824) must be omitted for the same reason; his *Poesie Italiane e Latine* appeared at Florence in 1827. Wellesley, *Anthologia Polyglotta*, p. 454, gives his version of *A.P.* 9.455:

Cantava Apollo: l'udì Omero, e scrisse.

[1] His original epigrams, *Epigrammi Morali Cento*, Parma, 1799, owe nothing in substance to the Anthology.

9.1, 3, 13, 18, 19, 24, 31, 34 (?), 37, 39, 42, 44 or 45, 47, 48, 52, 54,
55, 61, 66 (2 versions), 67, 68, 72, 74, 78, 97, 106, 108, 110, 111, 118,
120, 126, 127, 130, 131, 133, 138, 141, 146, 147, 148, 154, 157, 160,
162, 166, 167, 175, 176, 221, 245, 259, 269, 271, 295, 299, 303, 304,
310, 322, 346 (2 versions), 391, 394, 398, 420, 448, 453, 456, 488, 489,
497, 498, 506, 523, 526, 530, 549, 577, 608, 616, 618, 622, 627, 636,
637, 639, 647, 648, 652, 654, 701, 702, 715, 716, 718, 719 (2 versions),
720, 721, 723, 724, 727, 729, 731, 732, 738, 742, 749, 781, 795; 10.26,
27, 29, 30, 36, 42, 51, 58, 72, 73, 80 (?), 95, 105, 108, 112, 116, 119;
11.46, 50, 53, 68, 71, 76, 80, 118, 125, 131, 138, 143, 145, 152, 159,
172, 176, 178, 184, 187, 188 (2 versions), 190, 192, 193, 201, 208, 213,
214, 215, 226 (2 versions), 228, 229, 232, 237 (?), 240, 250, 255, 264,
266, 268, 270, 273, 274, 276, 278, 281, 294, 303 (?), 310, 315, 334, 340,
349, 369, 375, 385, 395, 397, 408, 413, 414, 419, 429, 430, 431 (2 versions), 432, 435, 436; 12.51, 60, 67, 71, 78, 89, 102, 103, 118, 140, 150,
234; 13.7, 24, 25, 28; 14.1, 2, 3, 5, 7, 12, 13, 14, 42, 48, 56, 57, 59, 60,
64, 101, 127, 130, 145, 146, 147;
16.1, 3, 5, 14, 28, 53, 68, 81, 89, 103, 107, 108, 114, 119, 120, 122,
129, 135, 138, 140, 145, 150 (?), 152, 158, 159 (2 versions), 161, (2 versions), 162, 163, 164, 165, 166, 168, 169, 194, 198, 200, 207, 211, 222,
223, 238, 248, 293, 298, 299, 304, 312, 319, 325, 326 (2 versions), 331.

Among his translations of the bucolic poets Pagnini has versions of
the following epigrams: *A.P.* 6.177, 336–40; 7.534.1–2, 658, 659–61,
663, 664; 9.338, 432–34, 437, 440 (p. 872), 598–600; 13.3; 16.200.

FRANCESCO FONTANI

(1748–1818)

Fontani was librarian of the Riccardiana in Florence, his native
city. He had been educated in the religious order of the Eugeniani,
had become a priest, and taught for a time at the Bandinellian College in Rome. He never gave up his parochial duties. Returning to
Florence, he was instrumental in inducing the commune to purchase
the Riccardian Library and save it from dispersal. He suffered some
distress in his later years from the part he had taken during the French
invasion. His tomb is in Santa Maria Novella. Among his numerous
works may be mentioned: *Florilegium ex Graecis Scriptoribus*, Rome,
1778; *Novae Eruditorum Deliciae*, 3 vols., Florence, 1785, 1788, 1793;
and *Viaggio Pittorico della Toscana*, 3 vols., Florence, 1801–5.[1]

According to Harles (Fabricius, *Bibl. Graec.* 4.456) Fontani
promised to publish a supplement to the Anthology, consisting
of about 900 new pieces which he had found. Obviously he
never did so; and what he meant is hard to determine. Harles
does not give the source of his information.

[1] Full list by L. Ciampolini in *Biog. degli Ital. Illus.* 3.484.

PIETRO ANTONIO CREVENNA
(†1792)

Crevenna, a man of wealth and learning, was a native of Milan, but established himself as a merchant in Amsterdam. From his step-father, Jacopo Filippo Bolongaro, he had inherited a large fortune; and he generally went under the name of Bolongaro-Crevenna. The library he collected was one of the finest private collections of its time. In 1776 at Amsterdam he published a catalogue made by himself, in 6 vols.: *Catalogue Raisonné de la Collection de Livres de M. Pierre-Antoine Crevenna;* and in 1789, wishing to sell most of his books, he issued a second catalogue in 5 vols.: *Catalogue des Livres de la Bibliothèque de M. Pierre-Antoine Bolongaro-Crevenna.* The remainder were sold in 1793 after his death, on which occasion a third catalogue was issued. Crevenna died on a visit to Rome in 1792. He left unfinished a history of the printing-press. Among his friends was Hieronymus de Bosch, the editor of the Anthology.

The sale-catalogue of 1789 lists the following Anthologies (Nos. 3430–42): the *editio princeps* of 1494 (a complete copy); the first, second, and third Aldines; Stephanus' edition (1566); the Wechel edition (1600); Lubinus' ed. with trans. (1604); Reiske's *Anthol. Graec.* (1754); the third (1544) edition of Soter's *Epigrammata;* Stephanus' translations (1570); Leich's *Carmina Sepulcralia* (1745); and Klotz's *Strato* (1764); as well as Vavasseur's *De Epigrammate* (No. 4333), and the like. The sale took place in the owner's house at Amsterdam, April 26 to June 15, 1790. All the Anthologies were sold except the copy of the 1494 edition, which was withheld. Presumably it was sold in 1793.

GIAMBATTISTA MUTINELLI
(1747–1825)

Mutinelli was a lawyer. He was born at Verona and educated at Padua; his life was passed at Venice, where he held several public offices. He took an interest in neo-Latin poetry, and published some Italian translations from it. A number of his verses appeared in the *Anno Poetico ossia Raccolta Annuale* (vol. 1), Venice, 1793; among them poems founded on *A.P.* 5.144; 12.114; 16.14, 77, 200. These themes may have come to him through the Latin poets of the sixteenth century.[1] At all events

---

[1] In the same miscellany he has a version of Sannazaro's famous epigram on the city of Venice.

it will be seen that the following version of *A.P.* 16.77 handles
the theme more freely than is usual in a translator who has his
eye immediately on the Greek:[1]

Chi pinger può la rubiconda aurora,
Del sole i raggi ardenti,
E gli astri rilucenti,
Potrà, Clori gentil, pingere ancora
La tua guancia vermiglia,
Gli occhi sereni, e le stellanti ciglia;
Altra immagin migliore
Tenta indarno adombrar mortal pittore.

AURELIO DE' GIORGI-BERTÒLA
(1753–1798)

Bertòla was born at Rimini. In his sixteenth year, unwillingly as it
seems, he entered the Olivetan brotherhood. He promptly ran away
to Hungary and became a soldier, but soon tired of the life, returned,
and re-entered his Order. Later he was sent as reader to the house of
the Olivetans in Siena. His first work, called *Notti Clementine*, on the
death of Clement XIV, appeared at Arezzo in 1775. For about ten
years he held the chair of geography and history in the *Accademia di
Marina* at Naples. He published his *Lezioni* at Naples in 1782. He
now removed to Vienna, again abandoned his habit, and played the
rôle of gallant *abate* so familiar in that age. Giving his attention to
German literature, he made a name for himself as the first to introduce the German poets into Italy, by his translations of Goethe,
Wieland, Kleist, and especially Gessner, whose acquaintance he made
in 1787 at Zürich. In 1797, having returned to Italy, he was a member of the 'Central Administration' of Emilia and editor of the *Giornale Patriottico*. But he was already the victim of a consumption. He
retired to his native place, and died there on June 30, 1798, in his
forty-fifth year.[2]

Among Bertòla's epigrams, of which in 1788 he published
about 60, are a few *imitazioni*; seven of these are imitations of
Greek epigrams.[3] Bertòla prefers the satirical sort. In the

---

[1] The original, by Paulus Silentiarius, may be translated as follows: 'The pencil has
scarcely portrayed the girl's eyes; it has not portrayed her hair nor the excellent bright-
ness of her complexion. If any one can paint the flashing light of the sun, he will paint
also the flashing light of Theodora.' This was the Empress Theodora.

[2] This account of Bertòla is mainly taken from De-Mauri's *L'Epigramma Italiano*,
pp. 146–8, where there is a list of Bertòla's works, and of works on him. My references
to Bertòla's poems are to *Poesie Edite ed Inedite*, 2 vols. Ancona, 1815. His epigrams
first appeared at Pavia in 1788: *Saggio sull' Idillio e Saggio sopra la Favola, con Raccolta di Favole e di Epigrammi*. This book was reprinted in the following year at Bassano.

[3] *A.P.* 6.1; 11.68, 76, 254, 310; 16.121, 129.

following imitation of *A.P.* 11.254 the substitution of Cato for Canace of the original renders the point more immediately intelligible:

> Ruggi, muggi, urli, non canti:
> Pur d'esprimere ti vanti
> Degli eroi la storia vera;
> E Caton forse tal era.
> Ma i nostri occhi a ferir viene
> Un difetto capitale,
> Ch' esci vivo dalle scene—
> E la storia non è tale.

CLEMENTINO VANNETTI
(1754–1795)

Vannetti was born at Rovereto. Both his parents took an interest in literature, which they communicated to their son. He wrote at the age of fourteen a Latin comedy entitled *Lampadaria*, and at fifteen a Latin life of St. Gothard. In 1792 he published *Observationes* on Horace, in three volumes. He was a corresponding member of the *Accademia della Crusca*. Among his friends were Pompei and Bettinelli. A belated celebration of Vannetti's centenary was observed in the Trentino in 1908.

Among the still unpublished works of Vannetti is a volume of *Epigrammi Toscani*. Some of these pieces, however, saw the light in 1806: *Epigrammi del Cav. Clementino Vannetti*, Rovereto, . . . *per nozze della nobile donzella Elisabetta Cobelli col Conte Gasparo Fioravanti Zannelli*.[1]

These published epigrams include a translation of *A.P.* 12.235, formerly ascribed to Meleager, but in Vannetti's time known to be by Strato:

> Se la bellezza a perdersi è sì presta,
> Fatene dono intanto che l'avete;
> O s' ella dura, certo non dovete
> Temer di darmi un bene che vi resta.

GIOVAN GHERARDO DE' ROSSI
(1754–1827)

De' Rossi was born in Rome. His father destined him for the bar, but pecuniary reverses brought his legal studies to a premature end;

---

[1] De-Mauri, *L'Epigramma Italiano*, p. 165. A useful list of Vannetti's works as well as of studies on him is given by De-Mauri on pp. 166–8. The translation about to be mentioned is taken from De-Mauri; I have not been able to find it in Vannetti's *Opere*, Venice, 1826–31.

and the young De' Rossi, who had always preferred literature, was free to try his fortunes in a literary career. His first publications in verse and prose brought him to the notice of the senator Rezzonico, who gave him a part in the *Memorie per le Belle Arti* (Rome, 1785–88). Here De' Rossi's success drew the attention of Cardinal Buoncompagni; and partly through the Cardinal's influence he was made director of the Academy of Fine Arts established in Rome by the Portuguese government. He was made Cavaliere of the Order of St. James. Under the short-lived Roman Republic he acted as Minister of Finance; but this did not hinder his continuance as Director of the Academy upon the re-establishment of the pope. Besides numerous works on the fine arts, De' Rossi was the author of several comedies.[1]

De' Rossi's interests in poetry and in the graphic arts united to produce what is perhaps his finest work, his *Scherzi Poetici e Pittorici*. This was first published in Rome in 1794, and was republished by the Bodoni Press at Parma in 1795. It is a sort of emblem-book, consisting of 41 epigrams, each accompanied by an excellent engraving executed by Francesco Rosaspina after originals by the Portuguese Tekeira.[2]

The twenty-eighth engraving represents Eros holding a plough, to which are yoked doves in place of oxen; a man, at his left, addresses him. The accompanying verses show that the conceit is based on *A.P.* 16.200, but with a reference to Tasso's imitation of this epigram:[3]

> Univa al giogo due colombe Amore,
> Novello agricoltore:
> Era vomero il dardo, e del terreno
> Fendea col dardo il seno.
> 'Amor, gli dissi, ne' lavori tuoi
> Per compagno mi vuoi?'
> 'Sì, mi rispose il fanciulletto infido,
> I semi che alla terra ora confido,
> Tu, venendomi a canto,
> Innaffiar puoi col pianto.'

EDVARD ROMEO AF VARGAS BEDEMAR
(1770–1847)

Edvard Romeo, Count of Vargas, was born at Kiel, and belonged to the junior line of a well-known Spanish family. While he was a

---

[1] There is a partial list of his works in the *Biographie Universelle*.
[2] According to De-Mauri, *op. cit.*, p. 172, there are copies of the Bodoni edition having the engravings colored in bistre and others painted in the Etruscan manner, as well as those in which the figures are merely engraved in black and white.
[3] Above p. 332.

student in Germany his parents died; he went to Spain, became lieu-
tenant in the Spanish artillery, and served in the siege of Ceuta.
There he killed his chief, Lieutenant-Colonel Lerma, in a duel; after
which he escaped to Marseilles in a Danish ship, and accepted the
advice of the Danish Consul to vanish for a time in Corsica. At the
end of three years, in consequence of an affair of gallantry, he left
Corsica for Siena. Here his literary career began with the publication
in Italian of the Essay on the Greek Epigram that is our present concern. In the following year (1797) he published a companion essay,
Dell' Anacreontica Greca, at Rome. On the founding of the *Accademia
Italiana* at Siena in 1798, Vargas was chosen president. The next year
found him aide-de-camp to Field-marshal Froelich at the siege of
Ancona. Accident threw him in the way of the Queen of Naples, who
invited him to her kingdom, and made him Lieutenant-Colonel of her
artillery, an instructor in the Military Academy, and a director of the
munitions-factory. His favor came to an end, and he retired in the
autumn of 1805. After a year in Sardinia as Controller of Mines, he
returned to Siena, but made enemies there by an attempt to reform
the Academy. The French, moreover, suspected him of political intrigues. He was thrown into prison, and was saved from execution
only by the intercession of Baron Schubart with the authorities in
Paris. He was released on condition that he remove to Denmark.

Schubart having paved the way, he was warmly received at the
Danish Court. This was in 1809; before the year was out he had received from the king a stipend to enable him to study the minerals of
Norway. His travels took him to the North Cape, Lapland, and East
Sweden (1810–12). In 1813 he earned Frederick's displeasure by
swearing allegiance to the new king of Norway, but his disgrace was
short, and he was presently restored to his post as Chamberlain. In
1814 he wrote, in French, an account of his recent travels; but the
state of affairs in Paris hindered its publication. The author therefore
turned it into German, and his *Reise nach dem Hohen Norden* (Frankfort, 1819) proved to be the work for which he was longest remembered. He made a number of later journeys to Scotland, the Faroe
Islands, Russia, Austria, Switzerland, and France, collecting mineral
specimens, in which he was very expert. His greatest journey, financed
as usual by the Danish government, lasted from 1835 to 1839, and
included the Canary Islands, Madeira, and Portugal. He published
Resumo de Observacoes Geologicas, Lisbon, 1837. On the accession of
Charles VIII to the throne of Denmark, Vargas was made head of the
Natural History Museum. He died March 15, 1847, unmarried; but
left a son, whom he had legitimated in 1817, and who later rose to a
high position in Russia.[1]

Vargas was twenty-six years old when his essay on the Greek
epigram appeared: *Dell' Epigramma Greco, Saggio di Ed. R.
Conte di Vargas*. Siena, 1796. The book is dedicated to Count

[1] C. F. Bricka, *Dansk Biografisk Lexikon* 18 (1904). 260–3.

Bernstorff. Vargas' method is the simple one of dividing his subject into what seem to him to be its logical sections, stating each topic, and then at once illustrating his divisions with appropriate epigrams, which he translates. The book, then, is little more than a 'reasoned' set of translations from the Anthology. The logical divisions are mainly the conventional ones given in modern treatises on the epigram, as already described above (pp. 60–72). The following is a résumé of Vargas' essay, with a list of the epigrams translated in each section.[1]

Chapter I. Origin of the Epigram among the Greeks [*A.P.* 11.42].
Chapter II. Classification of the Epigrams.
    1. Epigrams that set forth the subject simply [*A.P.* 6.22, 158, 164, 336; 7.249 (2 versions), 489, 505; 9.110, 322, 327].
    2. Epigrams in which the application is expressly made [*A.P.* 7.62; 9.37, 47, 52, 74, 130, 221, 720; 16.210, 214, 275].
    3. Epigrams that set forth the subject from a unique and striking ['sensibile'] point of view [*A.P.* 2.1 (69), 1 (78), 1 (99), 1 (288); 5.14, 15, 51, 66, 94, 102, 139, 144, 239, 270; 7.22, 23; 9.214, 386, 517, 586, 623, 668, 715, 721, 823; 16.12, 68, 113, 128, 129, 135, 150, 159, 168, 204, 248, 324].
    4. Epigrams that unite different subjects [*A.P.* 5.36, 125, 163, 288; 7.72, 348, 525; 9.39, 48, 108, 122, 167, 346, 488, 627; 10.58; 11.3, 68, 125, 138, 214, 255, 403, 414; 16.14, 152].
Chapter III. History of the Greek Epigram.
    1. Vicissitudes of the Anthology.
    2. Nature of the Epigram [originally an inscription].
    3. Its essential qualities ['brevità, eleganza, acume o punta'].
    4. Differences between the Epigram and other types of poetry.
    5. The Prerogatives of the Epigram.
    [Chap. III contains *A.P.* 5.74, 83+4+15.35; 6.189; 9.369; 10.31, 39, 73; 11.53; 16.388].

The treatise ends with a recommendation of the Anthology as a source of models for all who would imitate the Greeks in the epigram.[2]

Vargas always gives the Greek text along with his translations. He evidently used an edition of the Planudean Anthology.

The prime requisite of brevity is recognized in his translations; witness his two attempts to render the Spartan's Epitaph (*A.P.* 7.249):

[1] On the reverse of his title-page he translates *A.P.* 7.713, an epigram by Antipater of Sidon on Erinna and on the 'numberless myriads of later poets' who are claimed by oblivion.
[2] Above, p. 72.

Va, passagiero; a Sparta di', che noi
Qui cademmo fedeli ai cenni suoi.

IN ALTERA MANIERA

Va, passagiero; che noi
Sol per serbar sue leggi
Siam qui sepolti, a Sparta dir tu puoi.

I give also his versions of two other much-translated epigrams:

Rondinella,
Che varcasti tanti lidi,
A Medea tuo nido or fidi?
Speri tu che guardi i tuoi
Chi diè morte ai figli suoi?

(*A.P.* 9.346)

Menestrato, hai dipinto
Deucalione e Faetonte, e chiedi
Quale dei due dell' altro sia migliore;
Dell' interno valore
Se noi prendiam per giudicarne il segno,
Del fuoco l'un, l'altro dell' acqua è degno.

(*A.P.* 11.214)

LUIGI CERRETTI

(1738–1808)

Cerretti was born at Modena, and became professor of Eloquence there. Because of his political sentiments he found it best to withdraw to France in 1799; but under the Cisalpine Republic he returned and became professor in the University of Pisa. His name is honorably linked with the revival of taste in Italy, in which his *Istituzione di Eloquenza* (Milan, 1811) is said to have played its part.

Cerretti's *Epigrammi* appeared at Pisa in 1797. His model is rather Catullus than Martial on the one hand, or the Anthology on the other; but one of his distichs is taken from the Greek (*A.P.* 9.530):[1]

Fortuna t'innalzò, perchè credea
Non esser senza ciò tenuta dea.

---

[1] *Poesie*, Pisa, 1813, p. 103; *Poesie Scelte*, Milan, 1822, p. 202. The original is:
Οὐκ ἐθέλουσα Τύχη σε προήγαγεν, ἀλλ' ἵνα δείξῃ,
ὡς ὅτι καὶ μέχρι σοῦ πάντα ποιεῖν δύναται.

FULVIO MARIO MARIANI

(1779–1828)

Mariani received his elementary education at his birthplace,
Soncino, province of Cremona. Later he studied law at Milan, and in
that city also attended the lectures of Parini. He held various ad-
ministrative offices, the last being that of *Commissario Direttoriale* at
Romano in the province of Bergamo, where he died. He was a member
of the Academies of Savignano and Cesena, and published the later
editions of his *Epigrammi* under his academic name of *Ofelio Cimelio*
(Forlì, 1808 and 1812); the first edition was published without the
author's name at Milan in 1797.[1]

Among Mariani's epigrams are imitations of *A.P.* 7.160, 451,
461 (2 versions); and 11.257. The first of these follows:

DAL GRECO

Prode di Marte impavido seguace
    Timocrito qui giace:
Dio, che sol guerra agogni, e strage, e morte,
Perchè risparmi il vile, e perdi il forte?

FILIPPO PANANTI

(1769–1837)

Pananti, a native of Ronta nel Mugello in Tuscany, studied at
Pistoia and at Pisa, attaining the doctorate of Laws at the second of
these places (1789). He established himself in Florence, but made no
effort to practise the legal profession. He sided with the French during
their rule in Tuscany, and consequently, when the old order was re-
established in 1803, had to take refuge in France. After teaching for a
time in southern France, he visited Spain and the Netherlands, and
settled in London as a teacher of Italian. Here he composed a successful drama for music: *Il Poeta di Teatro* (1808), said to be partly auto-
biographical and partly indebted to Passeroni and Sterne. Attempting
to return to Italy in 1813, he was taken by the Algerian pirates. Rescued by the English resident in Algiers, he finally reached Florence.
Here for the last twenty years of his life he resided in the house of a
friend, dying of an apoplectic stroke in 1837. His *Avventure e Osservazioni sopra le Coste di Barberia* (2 vols., Florence, 1817) is his best-
known work, being translated into several foreign languages. His
Epigrammi first appeared at Milan in 1799.

---

[1] De-Mauri's *Epigramma Italiano*, the source of my information on Mariani, contains (p. 180) a list of his writings. The *Epigrammi di Moderni Autori* (Faenza, 1819),
pp. 55–66, under the name, Ofelia Cimilèo, gives a selection from the *Epigrammi* of
1808. I have seen nothing of Mariani's except these two selections.

As an epigrammatist Pananti is probably unsurpassed in Italian. Very few of his epigrams are translations, and those which are, generally come from the French. This is but natural at the end of the eighteenth century. Three only are derived from the Anthology, and those indirectly; two are founded upon the Latin of Ausonius,[1] the third probably upon the French of Voltaire.[2]

LO SPECCHIO DI NIOBE [*sic*] DA AUSONIO

Lo specchio mio ti dono,
O Diva del piacere;
Qual fui non posso, e come fatta sono
Non mi voglio vedere.
(*A.P.* 6.1)

DEL RITRATTO D' UN CATTIVO ORATORE

Che bel ritratto! è proprio somigliante!
Ha un sol difetto—d'essere parlante.
(*A.P.* 11.145)

Una vipera a Luca s'avventò,
Che cosa vi credete che seguisse,
Che Luca ne morisse?
La vipera crepò.
(*A.P.* 11.237)

PIETRO GIORDANI
(1774–1848)

Giordani was born at Piacenza. In 1797, perhaps from disappointment in love, he entered the Benedictine Order. Three years later, however, he left the reglious life, and secured a minor civil office in Milan. Then he taught natural history in the *liceo* of Como. Next he held a subordinate position in the library and University of Bologna. This he lost through an attempt to supplement his salary by secretarial work. After some wanderings he became *segretario comunale* at Cesena; and in 1808, as a reward for his *Panegirico* on Napoleon, was made pro-secretary of the *Accademia di Belle Arti* of Bologna. In 1815 he had to leave this position, and went to Milan. He was already esteemed the best prose-writer in Italy. In 1817 he received his paternal inheritance; but pecuniary difficulties only gave way to political persecution. He had returned to Piacenza, but was exiled; he went to Florence, but new troubles sent him to Parma. He was twice arrested, and often came under suspicion of the authorities. This only increased

---

[1] *Opere in Versi e in Prosa*, 3 vols., Florence, 1824–5, 2.109, 136.
[2] *Epigrammi di Mod. Aut.*, Faenza, 1819, p. 30.

his fame among the lovers of liberty, and every page he wrote was eagerly scanned. 'Giordani,' says Minghetti, 'was a name that made our hearts throb.'[1] To-day he is chiefly remembered as the champion of Monti and encourager of Leopardi. His works, the best of which were concerned with the fine arts, were not of a permanent nature, unless his *Iscrizioni*, epitaphs of great dignity and taste, should be taken as an exception. He died at Parma.

Most of Giordani's literary work lies outside the limits set for the present study; but a passage in one of his youthful letters, written in 1798, about two years before he left the monastery, falls within our scope. Pietro, from the monastery of San Sisto at Piacenza writes to his brother Ilario in the monastery of San Giovanni at Parma:[2] 'Oh il mio Ilario! quando vedrai le cose greche, gli epigrammi spezialmente! Oh che bellezze! Oh che mirabile espression di natura! Io mi figuro Venere sorgente dal mare. (Oh perdona, per carità, questo pensiero, veramente non troppo monacale!)'

This outburst on the part of the young Giordani may be accepted as evidence that the Anthology, with its 'marvelous expression of Nature,' was going to be beloved in the romantic age that followed, no less than it had been admired in the four centuries that were past.

---

[1] Quoted by Mazzoni, *L'Ottocento*, 1.509.
[2] Quoted by Stefano Grosso in a letter to Carducci (above, p. 160 n.). Ilario was the monastic name of Giordani's eldest brother, Antonio.

REGISTER

Here are enumerated, under the divisions of the Palatine Anthology (with 'Book 16'): (1) cross-references to epigrams of similar theme; (2) occurrences of the epigrams in ancient books other than the epigram-collections; (3) all translations, imitations, and allusions noticed in the present volume, except the complete translation of the Anthology by Gaetano Carcani (above, p. 426), and the less interesting quotations of Banduri and of Bonada (above, pp. 387 and 396). I have likewise omitted references to the *Selecta Epigrammata* of 1608 (above, p. 255), when the translations have already been referred to Soter and Cornarius. Each translation or imitation is listed by its initial words; and all entries are as strictly as possible in chronological order.

Where there is any slight disagreement in the numeration of the epigrams between the various editions of the Palatine Anthology, I have followed Dübner's edition (Paris, Didot, 1864, 1888). Notice is given in each case where an epigram here listed does not appear in the Planudean Anthology.

The abbreviations of book-titles may in every case be resolved by reference to the article, above, devoted to the author in question. For convenience, however, there follows a list of abbreviations for the books, especially miscellanies, most often referred to.

A List of Abbreviations

Ant. Ercol.   Reale Accademia Ercolanese di Archeologia. *Le Antichità di Ercolano*. 8 vols. Naples, 1755–92.

Buecheler.   *Anthologia Latina sive Poesis Latinae Supplementa.* Ed. by F. Buecheler and A. Riese. Second ed. 2 vols in 4. Leipzig, 1893–7; vol. 3, ed. by E. Lommatzsch, Leipzig, 1926.

C.I.G.   *Corpus Inscriptionum Graecarum.* Berlin, 1828–

C.I.L.   *Corpus Inscriptionum Latinarum.* Berlin, 1863–

Corn.   *Selecta Epigrammata Graeca ... versa ab Andrea Alciato, Ottomaro Luscinio, ac Jano Cornario.* Basel, 1529.

C.P.It.   *Carmina Illustrium Poetarum Italorum.* [Ed. by Giovanni Bottari]. 11 vols. Florence, 1719–26.

C.P.N.   [Joannes Paulus Ubaldinus] *Carmina Poetarum Nobilium J.P.U. studio conquisita.* Milan, 1563.

C.Q.H.P.   *Carmina Quinque Hetruscorum Poetarum.* Florence, 1562.

C.Q.P.   *Carminum Quinque Illustrium Poetarum.* Florence, 1553.

Didot Anthol.   *Epigrammatum Anthologia Palatina cum Planudeis et Appendice Nova.* 3 vols. Paris (Didot), 1864–90.

The first two vols. were edited by Fr. Dübner; the
third, containing epigrams omitted from *Pal.* and
Plan., by E. Cougny.

Ἐπ. καὶ Ἐλ. Ἐπικαὶ καὶ Ἐλεγειακαὶ Γνῶμαι. Venice, 1746 [above,
p. 379].

Gareg.   *Il Gareggiamento Poetico.* Venice, 1611 [above, p.
355].

Geffcken.   *Griechische Epigramme.* Ed. by Johannes Geffcken.
Heidelberg, 1916.

Graev., *Thes.*   J. G. Graevius. *Thesaurus Antiquitatum Romanarum.* Second ed. 12 vols. Venice, 1732–37.

Gronov, *Thes.*   J. Gronov. *Thesaurus Graecarum Antiquitatum.*
Second ed. 13 vols. Venice, 1732–37.

Kaibel.   *Epigrammata Graeca ex Lapidibus Conlecta.* Ed. by
G. Kaibel. Berlin, 1878.

L-Prose.   The prose version of the Planudean Anthology made
by Eilhardus Lubinus. *Florilegii Variorum Epigrammatum in septem libros distributi primus [—septimus].*
[Heidelberg, 1604].

Obsop.   Vincent Obsopoeus. *In Graecorum Epigrammatum
libros Annotationes.* Basel, 1540.

Pal.   The Palatine Anthology.

Piaz. Univ.   Tommaso Garzoni, *La Piazza Universale.* Venice,
1587.

Pigna.   *Io. Baptistae Pignae Carminum libri quatuor.* Venice,
1553.

Plan.   The Planudean Anthology.

PLM   *Poetae Latini Minores.* Ed. by E. Baehrens. 5 vols.
Leipzig, 1879–83.

Preger.   *Inscriptiones Graecae Metricae ex Scriptoribus praeter Anthologiam collectae.* Ed. by Th. Preger. Leipzig,
1891.

Rim. Onest.   [Angelo Mazzoleni]. *Rime Oneste de' Migliori Poeti
Antichi e Moderni.* 2 vols. Bergamo, 1750.

Sallengre, *Thes.* Albert Henri de Sallengre. *Novus Thesaurus Antiquitatum Romanarum.* 3 vols. Venice, 1735.

Sel. Epig.   *Selecta Epigrammata ex Florilegio.* Rome, 1608.

Soter.²,³   [See above, pp. 274–83].

Stadtmüller. *Anthologia Graeca Epigrammatum Palatina cum
Planudea.* Ed. by H. Stadtmüller. Vols. 1, 2.1, and
3.1. Leipzig, 1894–1906.

Versi et Reg. *Versi et Regole de la Nuova Poesia Toscana.* Rome,
1539.

Wech.   *Epigrammatum Graecorum . . . libri vii.* Frankfort
(Heredes Andreae Wecheli), 1600.

Wellesley.   Henry Wellesley. *Anthologia Polyglotta. A Selection
of Versions in Various Languages, chiefly from the
Greek Anthology.* London, 1849.

Palatine Anthology, Book II[1]

2.23.   Fioretti. Paeaniensium concionator [L-prose]. *Prog.* 1. 125.
2.69.   Vargas. Saffo di Lesbo. *Sag.*, p. 64.
2.78.   Vargas. Sfolgorò Citera. *Sag.*, p. 59.
2.92.   Pio. Julius insignis. *Lamp.* 1. 432; Soter², p. 306; Corn., p. 389.
2.97.   Cornarius. Adstat at huic. Corn., p. 389.
2.99.   Vargas. Una Venere bennata. *Sag.*, p. 58.
2.111. Crasso. Neque relinquas [L-prose]. *Ist.*, p. 510.
2.219. Crasso. Pudenti vero [L-prose]. *Ist.*, p. 403.
2.288. Vargas. Pieno di maraviglia. *Sag.*, p. 60.
2.291. Crasso. Bellator intonsus [L-prose]. *Ist.*, p. 6.
2.354. Crasso. Et sapiens Heracletus [L-prose]. *Ist.*, p. 190.
2.357. Crasso. Et imago gravis [L-prose]. *Ist.*, p. 130.
2.361. Crasso. Stabat Menander [L-prose]. *Ist.*, p. 338.
        Rivautella-Ricolvi. In bene turritis. *Mar.* 1. 184.
2.372. In *Vita Thucyd.* (West., p. 203n).
2.392. Crasso. Stabat et Alcmaeon (L-prose]. *Ist.*, p. 21.
2.414. Sabeo. Quem tu Roma potens. *Epig.*, p. 381.
        Fioretti. Amicus Ausoniis [L-prose]. *Prog.* 2. 120.

Book V

5.2.   Sabeo. Multa reposcentem tum. *Epig.*, p. 662.
5.3.   Cf. Ovid. Nunc etiam somni. *Am.* 1. 13. 7f.
        Cf. Ovid. Illum dum refugis. *Am.* 1. 13. 37f.
        Nicetas Eugen. Τιθωνέ, γῆρας. *Dros.* 6. 620.
        Sabeo. O Crysilla, diu. *Epig.*, p. 685.
5.4.   Cf. Propertius. O me felicem, o nox. *Eleg.* 2. 15. 1–2.
        Navagero. Hanc praeter tu sancta. *C.Q.P.*, p. 32.
        Sabeo. Aebria palladio quum. *Epig.*, p. 650.
        Sabeo. Fida lucerna mihi. *Epig.*, p. 863.
5.5.   [Not in *Plan.*]. Lines 3–4 in Stobaeus, *Flor.* 3. 28. 9 (Wach.
        and Hense).
5.6.   Tibullus. Nec iurare time. *Eleg.* 1. 4. 21–2.
        Pagnini. Callignoto giurò. *Epig.*, p. 134.
5.7.   Cf. *A.P.* 5. 165.
        More (Sir T.). Lychne reversuram ter. Soter², p. 316; Corn.,
        p. 414.
        Sabeo. Eraclia ad me iurata. *Epig.*, p. 656.
        Sabeo. Dulcia quae spectas. *Epig.*, p. 656.
5.8.   Cf. Propertius. Hoc perdit miseras. *Eleg.* 2. 28. 7–8.
        Sabeo. Vos tantum nobis testis. *Epig.*, p. 651.
        Cf. Materdona. O ne le mie vigilie. *Rime*, p. 6.
5.10.   Cf. Tibullus. Quid tibi, saeve, rei. *Eleg.* 1. 6. 3–4.
        Cf. Tibullus. Nec pecudes, velut ante. *Eleg.* 2. 1. 71–2.
        Sabeo. Odi et Amorem ipsum. *Epig.*, p. 671.

---

[1] Book I, Christian Epigrams, not being represented in the Planudean collection, is virtually without influence. This statement also applies to Books III and IV.

5.11. Cornarius. Si in pelago servas. Corn., p. 422.
Paraphrased by Equicola, above, p. 295.
Sabeo. Suppetias praebens. *Epig.*, p. 119.
Sabeo. Per te iuravit praesens. *Epig.*, p. 863.
Sabeo. Quid mihi cum terra? (a reply). *Epig.*, p. 119.
Murtola. Bella madre d'Amore. *Rime*, p. 45.

5.12. Sabeo. Lota coronemus, Prodice. *Epig.*, p. 665.

5.13. 1–6. Sabeo. Praeterit autumnus iam. *Epig.*, p. 654.

5.14. With v. 14 cf. *A.P.* 5. 78 and 12. 73.
Anselmo. Suavia, mi Ina, nimis. *Epig.*, hiiii.
Vargas. D'Europa un bacio. *Sag.*, p. 52.

5.15. Angeriano. Nunc ubi Praxiteles? 'Ερωτ. biiii; *C.P.It.* 1. 269.
Pompei. Prassitele or dov'è? *Op.* 2. 159.
Vargas. Ov'è Prassitel. *Sag.*, p. 50.

5.16. Sabeo. Crinibus auratis luna. *Epig.*, p. 670.

5.18. [Not in *Plan.*] Cf. Horace. Ne sit ancillae. *Carm.* 2. 4.

5.20. Velius. Non ego ut vetulae. Soter², p. 318; Corn., p. 418.
Costanzi (G.). Nec me virgo capit. *Epig.* Oiiii.
Sabeo. Nulla puella mihi. *Epig.*, p. 672.

5.21. Ausonius. Dicebam tibi, 'Galla. *Opus.* 19. 34.
Sabeo. Nonne tibi, o Prodice. *Epig.*, p. 665.
Pompei. Invecchiam noi, non te. *Op.* 2. 156.

5.22. Sabeo. Me tibi mancipium. *Epig.*, p. 692.

5.23. Cf. *A.P.* 5.164.
Cf. Propertius. At te celatis aetas. *Eleg.* 3. 25. 11f.

5.24. Paraphrased by Equicola, above, p. 294.
Sabeo. Ignem anima experta. *Epig.*, p. 660.

5.25. Cf. Propertius, *Eleg.* 3. 16.
Sabeo. Cydilla quotiens sub sole. *Epig.*, p. 654.

5.26. Cf. Ovid. Seu pendet nivea pulli. *Am.* 2. 4. 41–4.
Sabeo. Si te caeruleis. *Epig.*, p. 675.

5.28. Velius. Nunc tua cum periit. Soter², p. 319; Corn., p. 419.
Medici (A. de'). Nunc mihi, cum facies. *Scelt.*, p. vii.
Medici (A. de'). Or sì mi dici addio. *Scelt.*, p. vii.

5.29. [Not in *Plan.*]
Carcani (P.). Dolce è il giacer. *Ant. Herc.* 4. 12.

5.30. Cf. Tibullus. Hinc clavim ianua. *Eleg.* 2. 4. 31f.
Sabeo. Omnia quam eximie. *Epig.*, p. 684.

5.34. Cf. *A.P.* 5. 217.
Sleidan. Iuppiter ut Danaën. Soter², p. 320; Corn., p. 420.
Carcani (P.). Oro diè Giove a Danae. *Ant. Herc.* 6. 131.
Pagnini. Giove con l'oro vinse. *Epig.*, p. 165.

5.36. Luscinius. Contendere simul Rhodope. Corn., p. 417.
Sabeo. Certabant una Rhodope. *Epig.*, p. 652.
Franchini. De forma certamen. *Epig.*, p. 85.
Vargas. Un dì qual delle tre. *Sag.*, p. 81.
Pagnini. Per vanto di beltà. *Epig.*, p. 117.

5.39. Sabeo. Emoriendum inquam. *Epig.*, p. 674.

5.41. Sabeo. Quis te sic nudam. *Epig.*, p. 622.
5.42. Cf. *A.P.* 12. 200.
       Martial. Qualem, Flacce, velim. *Epig.* 1. 57.
       Cf. Ausonius. Hanc volo, quae non. *Opus.* 19. 56.
       Costanzi (G.). Larga mihi nimium mulier. *Epig.* Oiiii.
       Cornarius. Simplicem ego nolo. Corn., p. 421.
       Stigliani. Se con lunga fierezza. *Lir. Mar.*, p. 18.
5.50. [Not in *Plan.*].
       Claudian. Paupertas me saeva domat. Ed. Jeep 2. 146.
       Claudian. Esuriens pauper telis. Ed. Jeep 2. 146.
       Bianchi. La dura povertade. Wellesley, p. 71.
       Pagnini. Son povertate e amor due. *Epig.*, p. 94.
5.51. Vargas. Era amato, baciava. *Sag.*, p. 55.
5.53. [Not in *Plan.*] Cf. *A.P.* 5. 193.
5.54. [Not in *Plan.*] Cf. *A.P.* 5. 116.
5.57. [Not in *Plan.*] Cf. Ovid, *Am.* 2. 9.
5.58. [Not in *Plan.*] Cf. *A.P.* 5. 98, 224, and 268.
5.59. Nicetas Eugen. ὃν πτηνὸν οὐδείς. *Dros.* 8. 100.
       Costanzi (G.) Irritus aligerum fugere. *Epig.* Oiiii.
       Cornarius. Irritus ille labor, fugere. Corn., p. 422.
       Cf. Rainerio. Dai gemelli di Leda. *Cent. Son.* xxxvii.
       Murtola. Folle e ben sciocco sei. *Rime*, p. 204.
       Pagnini. Fuggire Amor che vale? *Epig.*, p. 69.
5.62. [Not in *Plan.*] Cf. *A.P.* 5. 282.
       Pompei. Non per anche dal tempo. *Op.* 2. 158.
5.64. Cf. *A.P.* 5. 168.
       Sabeo. Me nive, me tenebris. *Epig.*, p. 663.
       Minturno. Folgora, tona pur, nevica. *Rime*, p. 142.
5.65. Sabeo. Ad Ganimedam aquila. *Epig.*, p. 686.
       Conti. Ipse aquila ad pulchrum. *Myth.* 9. 13.
5.66. Paraphrased by Equicola, above, p. 295.
       Sabeo. Oravi genua amplectens. *Epig.*, p. 679.
       Vargas. In un buon punto. *Sag.*, p. 54.
       Pagnini. Sola in buon punto. *Epig.*, p. 124.
5.67. Nicetas Eugen. Ἄχαρι τέρπει κάλλος. *Dros.* 8. 102–3.
       Rainerio. Le prime nevi, e i gigli. *Cent. Son.* ix.
       Pompei. Beltà che non ha grazie. *Op.* 2. 212.
       Pagnini. Bellezza, che di grazie *Epig.*, p. 162.
5.68. Cf. *A.P.* 5. 88 and 97.
       Ausonius. Hoc, quod amare vocant. *Opus.* 19. 90.
       Cornarius. Fac ut amer rursus. Corn., p. 417.
       Paraphrased by Equicola, above, p. 294.
       Sabeo. Aut moderare meam. *Epig.*, p. 858.
       Groto. Aure . . . Portate i miei. *Rime* (1587), p. 71.
       Cf. Guarini (G.B.). Amor, poichè non giova. *Rime*, f. 110ᵛᵒ
          [*Mad.* cv].
       Toscano (Mat.). Vel ne prorsus amem. *Anth.*, p. 145.
5.69. Cf. Propertius. Cedite iam, divae. *Eleg.* 2. 2. 13–4.

Nicetas Eugen. Ἥρα δέ σε βλέπουσα. *Dros.* 8. 104.
Velius. Maeonin intuitae fors. Soter[2], p. 317; Corn., p. 415.
Alciati. Flava oculos Pallas. Soter[2], p. 317; Corn., p. 415.
Sabeo. Pallas ut inspexit. *Epig.*, p. 664.
Franchini. Pectora nuda meae. *Epig.*, p. 93; *C.P.It.* 5. 123.
Groto. Se stata fosse la mia. *Rime* (1587), p. 23.
Pompei. Come Palla e Giunon. *Op.* 2. 153.
Roncalli. Quando viste ebber. *Epig.* (1801), p. 72.

5.70.   Cf. *A.P.* 5. 140.
Angeriano. Tres quondam nudas vidit. Ἐρωτ. Biiii.
Cornarius. Forma tibi est Veneris. Corn., p. 415.
Alciati. Forma tibi Veneris. Corn., p. 415.
Paraphrased by Equicola, above, p. 294.
Bongiovanni and Zanetti. Hai la beltà di Venere. *Epig.*, p. 8.
Pompei. La beltà de la diva. *Op.* 2. 135.

5.74.   Cf. Propertius. Ac veluti folia arentis. *Eleg.* 2. 15. 51–4.
Angeriano. Floribus intextam diversis. Ἐρωτ. Ciiii; *C.P.It.* 1.
           279.
Anselmo. Accipe diverso contextam. *Epig.* Ii.
Anisio. In Pyrrhae serto ut. *Poem.*, f. 90vo.
Rota. Quas bona Flora rosas. *Poem.* (1567), p. 71.
Cunich. Hanc, Rhodoclea, tibi. *Anth.*, p. 88.
Medici (A. de'). Mitto tibi hanc, Rhodocle. *Scelt.*, p. viii.
Medici (A. de'). Questo serto gentil. *Scelt.*, p. viii.
Pompei. A te, O Rodocléa, ne mando. *Op.* 2. 154.
Felici. Questo di varii fior serto. *Epig.*[1], p. 88.
Passeroni. Filli mia, questa ghirlanda. *Rime* 3. 167.
Vargas. Questa di fior, ch'io. *Sag.*, p. 103.
Pagnini. Questa da me si manda. *Epig.*, p. 82.

5.76.   Pompei. Pria d'amabil color. *Op.* 2. 160.
5.77.   [Not in *Plan.*]
        Cf. Propertius. Et cupere optatis animam. *Eleg.* 1. 13. 17.
5.78.   [Not in *Plan. codd.*, but in Stephanus' ed. (1566), p. 562]. Cf.
        A.P. 5. 14 and *A.P.* 12. 73. The epig. is quoted by Diogenes
        Laertius, 3. 32.
Cf. Petronius. Et transfudimus hinc. *Sat.* 79.
Anon. in Aulus Gellius. Dum semihiulco savio. *N.A.* 19. 11.
Marcus Aurelius. At ego ubi animus sit. [prose]. *Epist.*, p. 4
        (Naber).
Gaza. Savia dans Agathoni. Gellius (1489), Riiii[vo]. Soter[2],
        p. 216.
Brugnolo gives Gaza's tr. Laert. 3.
Beroaldo (F.), the elder, quotes Gaza's tr., from Brugnolo's
        Laert. *Orat.* f. vi.
Marullus. Suaviolum invitae rapio. Soter[2], p. 218.
Crinitus. Dum te Neaera suavior. *H.D.*, p. 582; Soter[2], p. 217.
Bentinus retains Gaza's tr. *Laert.* (1524), p. 105.
Anselmo. Mirari mea Nyssa soles. *Epig.* Iii.

Anisio. Perna Catosso animam. *Poem.*, f. 31ro

Atanagi. A me l'alma beve. Carducci, *Poes. Barb.*, p. 168.

Vasolli. Da mihi suaviolum. *Epig.*, f. 16ro; *Virid.*, f. 20ro.

P. Vettori mentions this ep., *Var. Lect.* 20. 17.

Pigna. Dum ne deficiam quaero. *Carm.*, p. 106.

Scaliger. Hoc mihi restabat. *Poem.* 1. 123.

Paterno. Qualhor giunge mia bocca. *Nuov. Fiam.*, f. 52ro.

Paterno. I tuo' bei lumi. *Nuov. Fiam.*, f. 49ro.

Tasso. Lecito sia ch'ora. *Gerus.* 19. 108. 7–8.

Tasso. Or l'alma fugge. *Gerus.* 16. 19. 6–7.

Guarini (G. B). Su queste labbra. *Past. Fid.* 2. 1(Brognoligo, p. 52).

Guarini (G. B.). Se non la bocca. *Past. Fid.* 2. 6 (Brognoligo, p. 80).

Crotti. Ut primum in me. *Flor. Spic.*, f. 82ro.

Bornati. Baci che le columbe. *Rim. Occult.*, p. 5.

Spinosa. Mentre dolci porgea. Tasso, *Op.* 26. 65.

Marino. Sì profondo piacer. *Adone* 8. 130. (p. 140).

Angelico (M. A.) In un sospiro. *Gareg.* 2. 62vo.

Fioretti. Mentre mi lassa. *Prog.* 3. 504.

Crasso quotes Gaza's version. *Ist.*, p. 13.

5.79. Diogenes Laertius 3. 32.

Brugnolo? Malo ego te ferio. Laert. 3; Soter^2, p. 314; Corn., p. 410.

Bentinus. Malo ego te ferio. *Laert.*, p. 105; Soter^2, p. 314; Corn., p. 411.

Quoted by Landi, *Num.*, p. 158.

5.80. Diogenes Laertius 3.32.

Brugnolo? Malum ego: me mittit. Laert. 3; Soter^2, p. 314; Corn., p. 410.

Bentinus. Malum ego: me. *Laert.*, p. 105; Soter^2; Corn.

Angeriano. Flos ego qui venio. 'Ερωτ. Diiii; *C.P.It.* 1. 286.

Valeriano. Pomum ego; quique tibi. *Poem.*, p. 114; *C.P.It.* 10. 162.

Sabeo. Sum malum, tu pulchra. *Epig.*, p. 650.

Sabeo. Mittit amans malum. *Epig.*, p. 651.

Sabeo. Malum ego, me misit. *Epig.*, p. 653.

Sabeo. Annue, Xantippe. *Epig.*, p. 655.

Quoted by Landi, *Num.*, p. 158.

5.81. Ariosto. Hasne rosas, an te. Polidori 1. 356.

Ariosto. Vendere velle rosas. Polidori. 1. 356.

Valeriano. Es Rosa fersque rosam. *Poem.*, p. 118; *C.P.It.* 10. 172.

Alamanni. Vendi, Rosa, la rosa. *Rim. Ined.* (Frati), p. 36.

Sabeo. Sive rosas roseamque. *Epig.*, p. 666.

Cf. Guarini (G. B.). Dono Licori a Batto. *Rime*, p. 97.

5.82. Sabeo. Cur me blanda lavas. *Epig.*, p. 661.

5.83. [*A.P.* 5. 83, 5. 84, and 15. 35 form but one epigram in *Plan.*

(7. 153); all treatments of the theme are therefore gathered
in this place.]
Cf. Ovid. *Am.* 2. 15.
Cf. *Anacreontea* 22 (Preisendanz).
The epigram (*A.P.* 5. 83–4) is quoted in *Schol.* on Dio of Prusa
2, p. 556 (Reich).
Nicetas Eugen. Εἰ δὲ ζέφυρος. *Dros.* 8. 107–9.
Paraphrased by Equicola, above, p. 295.
Alamanni. Per farti una ghirlanda. *Rim. Ined.* (Frati), p. 36.
Flaminio. Hos tibi purpureos. *Carm.*, p. 95; *C.P.It.* 4. 394.
Sabeo. Esse velim ventus. *Epig.*, p. 666.
Amalteo (G. B.). O ego dum nitidos. *Tr. Frat.*, p. 134.
Amalteo (G. B.). Dum te rura tenent. *Tr. Frat.*, p. 138.
Giraldi (L. G.). Aura levis nostrae quae. *Op.* 2. 629.
Paterno. Fuggendo; ah ah foss'. *Nuov. Fiam.*, f. 50ᵛᵒ.
Tasso. Perchè, diceva, anch'io. Solerti 2. 373.
Groto. Un di quei fior foss'io. *Rime*, p. 112.
Pompei. Qual Dafne là su. *Parn. Ital.* 53. 36.
Vargas. Ah! fossi un' aura. *Sag.*, p. 100.
Roncalli. Fosse, mentr' io ti. *Epig.* (1801), p. 48.
5.87. Sabeo. Spernit Amorem ipsum. *Epig.*, p. 667.
5.88. Cf. *A.P.* 5. 68, 97 and 6. 80. 6.
Ausonius. Aut restingue ignem. *Opus.* 19. 91.
5.89. Sabeo. Non amor est quum quis. *Epig.*, p. 667.
Minturno. Non è già egli Amor. *Rime*, p. 139.
Pagnini. No, quello Amor non è. *Epig.*, p. 164.
5.90. Sabeo. Mirrha ut te placem. *Epig.*, p. 677.
5.91. Philostratus. Πέπομφά σοι στέφανον. *Epist.* 30 (Didot 2).
Beroaldo (the younger). Ad te mittimus. *Carm.* sig. Niiii.
Alamanni. Lucidissime gemme. *Versi* 2. 124.
5.92. Angeriano. Ecce tumet forma. Ἔρωτ. D; *C.P.It.* 1. 279.
Sabeo. Se Rhodope extollit. *Epig.*, p. 664.
Pompei. Di sue bellezze va. *Op.* 2. 161.
5.93. Cf. *A.P.* 12. 120.
Velius. Exanimo armatus ratione. Soter², p. 317; Corn, p. 416.
Luscinius. Dum ratione potens. Soter², p. 317; Corn., p. 416.
Melanchthon. Sum satis illecebras. *Op.* 10. 662.
Sabeo. Armavi ratione animos. *Epig.*, p. 664.
Carcani (P.). Di ragion contro Amor. *Ant. Herc.* 2. 156.
Pompei. D'armatura di senno. *Op.* 2. 155.
5.94. Cf. Propertius. Immortalis ero, si. *Eleg.* 2. 14. 10.
Cf. Propertius. Si dabit haec multas. *Eleg.* 2. 15. 39.
Costanzi (G.). Iuno oculos, Thetis. *Epig.* Oiiii.
Calenzio. Foelix qui teneros. *Opus.* A5.
Equicola paraphrases this epigram, above, p. 295.
Velius. Lumina Iunonis Melite. Soter², p. 317; Corn., p. 416.
Alciati. Quae dignos Iunone oculos. Corn., p. 417.
Alciati quotes vv. 3–4, *Op.* 4.387.

Veniero. Ne la madre, onde nacque. *Lib. Sest.* f. 133ro.

Veniero. Ne la madre, onde nacque. *Lib. Sest.* f. 133ro.

Sabeo. Iuno oculis Melete es. *Epig.*, p. 665.
Franchini. Pulchra manus Hebe, Iuno. *Epig.*, p. 5.
Franchini. Te quicunque videt. *Epig.*, p. 71.
Angelio. Invidet hos oculos. *Poem.*, p. 388.
Cf. Groto. Quel che la sposa. *Rime*, p. 23.
Guarini (G. B.). Felice chi vi mira. *Rime*, f. 84ro.
Stigliani. Felice chi ti vede. Croce, *Lir. Mar.*, p. 18.
Carcani (P.). Hai gli occhi di Giunone. *Ant. Ercol.* 3. 59.
Pompei. Le mani hai tu. *Op.* 2, 157.
Vargas. Le pupille di Giuno. *Sag.*, p. 53.
Pagnini. Tu, Melite, mia Dea. *Epig.*, p. 109.

5.95. Cf. *A.P.* 5. 146 and 9. 515.
Angeriano. Sunt geminae Veneres. Ἔρωτ. Aiii.
Sannazaro. Quarta Charis, decima es. *Poem.*, p. 220.
Cf. Sannazaro. Exultat palma Venus. *Poem.*, p. 165.
Equicola paraphrases this epigram, above, p. 294.
Ariosto. O rarum formae decus. Polidori 1. 354.
Anselmo. Graecia tres Charites. *Epig.* Dii; *C.P.It.* 1. 300.
Minturno. Acciochè si come ella. [prose]. *Let.*, f. 178ro.
Atanagi. Mentre che lo spirto. Carducci, *Poes. Barb.*, p. 168.
Giraldi Cintio. Tres habuit furias. *Poem.*, p. 174.
Vasolli. Tres Charites coelum. *Virid.*, f. 22vo.
Vasolli. Tres nunc syderea Charites. *Virid.*, f. 35ro.
Sabeo. Gratiae et his crescunt. *Epig.*, p. 864.
Minturno. Eran le Gratie tre. *Rime*, p. 207.
Spinula. Quot Veneres? Binae. *Epig.*, p. 40.
Guazzo. Tu due Ciprigne, Hilaria. *Dial.*, f. 147ro.
Groto. Due sono hoggi le Dee. *Rime*, p. 23.
Virtuani. A gli atti, al viso. *Gareg.* 1. 39vo.
Cf. Marino. Le Grazie, che son tre. *Ad.* 11. 65 (p. 191).
Pompei. Quattro le Grazie son. *Op.* 2. 226.
Pagnini. Due le Venere or son. *Epig.*, p. 154.

5.97. Cf. *A.P.* 5. 68 and 88.
Cf. Tibullus. Nec tu sis iniusta Venus. *Eleg.* 3. 11. 13–4.
Angeriano. Es Deus, ambobus si. Ἔρωτ. Aiiii; *C.P.It.* 1. 258.
Angeriano. Fallitur esse deum. Ἔρωτ. Ciiii.
Cornarius. Saeve puer, credere deus. Corn., p. 418.
Sabeo. Certe Amor aequales. *Epig.*, p. 651.
Groto. Amor, se pur sei Dio. *Rime* (1587), p. 63.
Roncalli. Amor, se un Dio tu sei. *Epig.* (1801), p. 54.

5.98. Cf. 5. 58, 224, and 268.
Cf. Propertius. Quid tibi iucundum est. *Eleg.* 2. 12. 18.
Angeriano. Postquam picta fuit. Ἔρωτ. Eiii; *C.P.It.* 1. 290.
Cf. Tebaldeo. Non più saetti. Above, p. 47, n. 1.
Cf. Evangelista. Quid lacerum laceras. *C.P.It.* 4. 124.
Cf. Evangelista. En! morior, torquere. *C.P.It.* 4. 123.

5.101. Cornarius. Salve, virgo. Et tu. Corn., p. 419.

Sabeo. Salve, virgo. Et tu. *Epig.*, p. 686.
Medici (A. de'). Salve, virgo. Salve et tu. *Scelt.*, p. xlii.
Medici (A. de'). Salve. Tu ancor. *Scelt.*, p. xlii.
Pagnini. P. Ti saluto, donzella. *Epig.*, p. 163.

5.102. Vargas. La gracil Dioclea. *Sag.*, p. 53.
5.103. Sabeo. Quamdiu ego, o Prodice. *Epig.*, p. 666.
5.106. Sabeo. Foemina, quid latrans. *Epig.*, p. 676.
5.107. Sabeo. Non ignarus amo. *Epig.*, p. 682.
5.110. Sabeo. Formosae Euphrantes unum. *Epig.*, p. 673.
5.111. Sabeo. Predixi quum parva. *Epig.*, p. 663.
5.112. Sabeo. Exarsi comum, quis. *Epig.*, p. 654.
5.113. Velius. Dives ambaris, modo. Soter[2], p. 315; Corn., p. 411.
Luscinius. Dira fames quid non. Corn., p. 412.
Sabeo. Qualem habet esuries. *Epig.*, p. 655.
Bongiovanni and Zanetti. Mentre ricco tu. *Epig.*, p. 8.
5.115. Sabeo. Dilexi Demo Paphiam. *Epig.*, p. 622.
5.116. [Not in *Plan*.] Cf. *A.P.* 5. 54.
5.117. Sabeo. Me formose foves. *Epig.*, p. 673.
5.118. Cf. *Idyl. de Rosa.* Quam modo nascentem. *Anth. Lat.* (Reiske) 646.
5.119. Sabeo. Te licet evolvas dextrum. *Epig.*, p. 675.
5.121. Equicola paraphrases this epigram, above, p. 294.
5.123. [Not in *Plan*].
Nicetas Eugen. Σὺ γοῦν, Σελήνη. *Dros.* 8. 110–2.
5.124. Sabeo. Nondum folliculis. *Epig.*, p. 655.
Alberti. Pomo acerbetto sei. *Rime*, p. 206.
5.125. Velius. Non aurum in pluvium. Soter[2], p. 318; Corn., p. 418.
Luscinius. Esto alius pluvium. Corn., p. 419.
Equicola paraphrases this epigram, above, p. 293.
Cf. Baldi. Cangiossi Giove per Europa. *Epig.* 620.
Carcani (P.). Esser oro io non voglio. *Ant. Ercol.* 6. 131.
Vargas. Mai vò scorrer qual rio. *Sag.*, p. 90.
5.127. Alciati. Persuasam eloquio nostra. Corn., p. 422.
Sabeo. Exarsi Alcippen. *Epig.*, p. 674.
5.129. [Not in *Plan*.]
Cf. Ovid. Illa placet gestu. *Am.* 2. 4. 29–30.
5.130. Sabeo. Quid moeres? incompta. *Epig.*, p. 669.
Medici (A. de'). Quid moeres, laniasque. *Scelt.*, p. xlv.
Medici (A. de'). Che t'ange, o bella. *Scelt.*, p. xlv.
5.131. Cf. *A.P.* 5. 139.
Cf. Propertius. Nec causam, nec apertos. *Eleg.* 2. 4. 9–10.
Minturno. Gli occhi amorosi. *Rime*, p. 139.
5.132. Horace. O crus, o bracchia! *Sat.* 1. 2. 92.
Cf. Ovid. Quos umeros, quales. *Am.* 1. 5. 19f.
Cf. Ovid. Candida si non sum. *Her.* 15. 35.
Fioretti. Et licet opica [L-prose]. *Prog.* 2. 13.
5.133. Cf. Tibullus. Asper eram et bene. *Eleg.* 1. 5. 1–2.
Sabeo. Stultus abesse duas. *Epig.*, p. 667.

5.135. Cf. *A.P.* 9. 229.
5.138. [Not in *Plan.*] Cf. *A.P.* 9. 429.
  Cf. Tasso. Fu già favola antica. Solerti 4. 111.
5.139. Cf. *A.P.* 5. 131.
  Equicola paraphrases this epigram, above, p. 293.
  Sabeo. Eliodora melos ridenti. *Epig.*, p. 599.
  Sabeo. Dulce melos, per Pana. *Epig.*, p. 642.
  Vargas. E' pur dolce il tuo. *Sag.*, p. 55.
5.140. Cf. *A.P.* 5. 70.
  Equicola paraphrases this epigram, above, p. 293.
  Sabeo. Suada sedens labiis. *Epig.*, p. 661.
5.141. Cf. *A.P.* 5. 292. 7–8.
  Equicola paraphrases this epigram, above, p. 293.
  Sabeo. Heliodora meas tua. *Epig.*, p. 647.
  Pompei. Ne gli orecchi la voce, *Op.* 2. 168.
5.142. Cf. *A.P.* 143.
  Cf. Angelo Grillo. Quand' io miro. *Rime*, f. 131ᵛᵒ.
  Felici. Dalle trecce inanellate. *Epig.*¹, p. 83.
5.143. Cf. 142.
  Cf. Philostratus. Περιϑήση δὲ οὐ σύ. *Epist.* 29, *fin.* (Didot 1).
  Calcagnini. Texta corona rosa. Pigna, p. 213; *C.P.It.* 3. 81.
  Sabeo. Marcescit sertum circa. *Epig.*, p. 649.
5.144. Angeriano. Iam crescent albi flores, Ἔρωτ. Ciiii.
  Equicola paraphrases this epigram, above, p. 293.
  Sabeo. Candida iam viola. *Epig.*, p. 647.
  Franchini. Floribus intextam variis. *Epig.*, p. 2; *C.P.It.* 5.
    116.
  Cf. Tasso. Non sono in queste rive. Solerti. 2. 367.
  Pompei. Già s'apron le viole. *Op.* 2. 164.
  Mutinelli. Torna il maggio odorato. *An Poet.* 1. 174.
  Vargas. Fiorisce la ridente. *Sag.*, p. 56.
5.145. Cf. Propertius. Et mihi non desunt. *Eleg.* 1. 16. 7.
  Cf. Ovid. At tu, non laetis. *Am.* 1. 6. 67f.
  Angeriano. Ante fores madidae. Ἔρωτ. Diiii; *C.P.It.* 1. 286.
  Sabeo. Illic ante fores. *Epig.*, p. 860.
5.146. [Not in *Plan.*] Cf. *A.P.* 5. 95 and 9. 515.
  Medici (A. de'). Nuper Acidalius Charis. *Scelt.*, p. xxxii.
  Medici (A. de'). Tre più non son. *Scelt.*, p. xxxii.
  Pagnini. Quattro le Grazie or. *Epig.*, p. 139.
5.147. Cf. Tolomei. Questi soavi flori. Carducci, *Poes. Barb.*, p. 37.
  Cf. Renieri. Deh, prendi tu questi. Carducci, *Poes. Barb.*, p.60.
  Franchini. Floribus intextam variis. *Epig.*, p. 2; *C.P.It.* 5. 116.
  Sabeo. Texo albam violam. *Epig*,. p. 634.
  Felici. Colgo la candida. *Epig.*¹, p. 63.
5.148. Sabeo. Heliodora sua ut visum. *Epig.*, p. 648.
5.151. Cf. *A.P.* 5. 152.
  Scala (B.). Congressum petis sic. Above, p. 130.
  Cf. Politian. Τοὺς κώνωπας ἐρᾶν. Del Lungo, p. 223.

Equicola paraphrases this epigram, above, p. 293.
Gravina (P.). Ite mali culices. *Poem.*, f. 30ᵛᵒ.
Sabeo. Clarisoni o culices. *Epig.*, p. 633.
Sabeo. Vocales o vos culices. *Epig.*, p. 648.
Pompei. O voi zanzare stridule. *Op.* 2. 165.

5.152. Cf. *A.P.* 5. 151.
Equicola paraphrases this epigram, above, p. 293.
Cf. Materdona. Animato rumor, tromba. *Rime*, p. 5; *Lir. Mar.*, p. 107.
Pompei. Vola, o zanzara; va. *Op.* 2. 166.

5.155. Cf. Angeriano. Quid speculum spectas? Ἔρωτ. Eiiii.
Cf. Angeriano. Se nudam aurato dum spectat. Ἔρωτ. Biiii.
Cornarius. Pectore fixa sedet nostro. *Corn.*, p. 402.
Sabeo. Cordis Amor nostri. *Epig.*, p. 653.
Sabeo. Cordis in imo animam. *Epig.*, p. 857.
Pompei. Amore stesso dentro. *Op.* 2. 162.
Bettinelli. Vide Silvia, e disse. *Op.* 13. 86.

5.158. [Not in *Plan.*]
Ausonius. Punica turgentes. *Opus.* 19. 96.

5.163. Cf. *A.P.* 12. 249.
Cf. Moro. Al viso tuo vid'io. *Giar.* 1. 2. 12 (1. 79).
Pompei. Ape, che pasci i fior. *Op.* 2. 163.
Vargas. Tu che di fior ti pasci. *Sag.*, p. 78.

5.164. [Not in *Plan.*] Cf. *A.P.* 5. 23.
5.165. [Not in *Plan.*] Cf. *A.P.* 5. 7.
5.168. Cf. *A.P.* 5. 64.
Cf. Angeriano. Non ego turbati. Ἔρωτ. Aii; *C.P.It.* 1. 253.
Equicola paraphrases this epigram, above, p. 294.
Molza. Ignibus ure meum saevis. *Poes.* 3. 205.
Flaminio. Et tonat et vento. *Carm.*, p. 93; *C.P.It.* 4. 393.
Tolomei. Tuona e soffiano. Flaminio, *Carm.*, p. 93.
Franchini. Me iaculis pete, me. *Epig.*, p. 3.
Sabeo. Imbre, fame, et flamma. *Epig.*, p. 652.
Cf. Moro. Fulmina Giove irato. *Giar.* 1. 2. 13 (1. 79).
Medici (A. de'). Me nive, me flammis. *Scelt.*, p. xlix.
Medici (A. de'). Ponmi fra il gelo. *Scelt.*, p. xlix.

5.171. Cf. *A.P.* 5. 261 and 295.
Sabeo. Hic scyphus exultat. *Epig.*, p. 634.

5.176. Velius. Saevus Amor, quid tum. *Soter*², p. 315; *Corn.*, p. 413.
Equicola paraphrases this epigram, above, p. 293.
Sabeo. Saevus Amor, saevus, quid. *Epig.*, p. 857.
Mignault. Saevus Amor, saevus. Quid. Alciati, *Emb.* 113.
Pagnini. Crudele Amor, crudel. *Epig.*, p. 163.

5.177. Equicola paraphrases this epigram, above, p. 293.
Cf. Lampridio. Cui tantas Cytherea. *C. P. It.* 6. 29.
Sabeo. Agrestem et rigidum. *Epig.*, p. 634.
Pompei. Io chiamo Amore, l'aspro. *Op.* 2. 169.

5.178. Pompei. Si venda pur, benchè. *Op.* 2. 170.

5.179. Sabeo. Certe ego succendam. *Epig.*, p. 661.
5.180. Velius. Tela nihil mirum. Soter[2], p. 316; Corn., p. 413.
Luscinius. Quid mirum crudelis. Corn., p. 414.
Giraldi Cintio. Quid mirum exultet si. *Poem.*, p. 175; *C.P.It.* 5. 396.
Scaphenatus. Arridens oculis, arcu. *Eleg.* Biiii.
Sabeo. Ignea quid mirum. *Epig.*, pp. 155, 862.
Sabeo. Non magnum si ridet. *Epig.*, pp. 155, 863; *C.P.It.* 8. 200.
Sabeo. Iram, tela, faces. *Epig.*, p. 156.
Sabeo. Quid mirum arcitenens. *Epig.*, p. 862.
Sabeo. Si iaculatur Amor. *Epig.*, pp. 155, 862.
Sabeo. Iram, tela, faces. *Epig.*, p. 863.
Minturno. Qual cosa nova o strana. *Rime*, p. 203.
5.186. [Not in *Plan.*]
Cf. Tibullus. Iam Delia furtim. *Eleg.* 1. 6. 5–8.
5.187. Sabeo. Ecce aliena leae, Dorcas. *Epig.*, p. 652.
5.189. Sabeo. Imbre madens hyemis. *Epig.*, p. 635.
5.190. Sabeo. Spirantes zeli insomnes. *Epig.*, p. 658.
5.193. [Not in *Plan.*] Cf. *A.P.* 5. 53.
5.194. Sabeo. Molliculam et lepidam. *Epig.*, p. 645.
5.196. Equicola paraphrases this epigram, above, p. 293.
Sabeo. Formam, Amor, ipsa Venus. *Epig.*, p. 693.
5.197. Sabeo. Per crines pulchros. *Epig.*, p. 646.
5.210. Luscinius. Heu Didyme totum rapuit. Corn., p. 408.
Sabeo. Hei mihi, me eripuit. *Epig.*, p. 646.
Castelvetro quotes this epigram. *Petr.*, p. 359.
Cf. Moro. Se' bruna e si mi piaci. *Giar.* 1. 1. 35 (1. 42).
Cf. Marino. Nera sì, ma se' bella. *Lira* (1630), p. 336.
Cf. Marino. Brunetta sì, ma sovr'. *Ad.* 15. 29 (p. 290).
Pagnini. La bella Nice me a me. *Epig.*, p. 153.
5.212. Cf. Propertius. Sed certe pennas. *Eleg.* 2. 12. 15.
Sabeo. Usque sonant strepitu. *Epig.*, p. 659.
5.215. Sabeo. Supplico Amor facias. *Epig.*, p. 646.
5.216. Velius. Si quis amas ne sis. Soter[2], p. 312; Corn., p. 302.
Sabeo. Ne submitte animum. *Epig.*, p. 653.
5.217. Cf. *A.P.* 5. 34.
Cf. Horace. Inclusam Danaen turris. *Carm.* 3. 16.
Sleidan. Iuppiter illapsus per. Soter[2], p. 319; Corn., p. 420.
Conti. Aureum in caecas. *Myth.* 7. 18.
Sabeo. Viderat inclusam. *Epig.*, p. 22.
Sabeo. Iuppiter intactae perfregit *Epig.*, p. 650.
5.221. Sabeo. Quam diu in accenso. *Epig.*, p. 629.
5.222. Alciati. Si citharam tractas. Corn., p. 403.
Sabeo. Si citharam plectro. *Epig.*, p. 629.
5.223. Equicola paraphrases this epigram, above, p. 294.
Sabeo. Abiunges charos tu ne. *Epig.*, p. 34.
Sabeo. Ne violente meum cogas. *Epig.*, p. 630.

Castelvetro quotes this epigram. *Petr.*, p. 406.
5.224. Cf. *A.P.* 5. 58, 98, and 268.
Nicetas Eugen. Εἰ δ'οὐκ ἀρεστόν. *Dros.* 3. 253–4.
Sleidan. Arripe Amor quodvis. Soter[2], p. 319; Corn., p. 404.
Cornarius. Cor mihi linque heparque. Corn., p. 404.
Equicola paraphrases this epigram, above, p. 294.
Pagnini. Fiedimi pur, salvo. *Epig.*, p. 144.
5.225. Nicetas Eugen. Σὺ νῦν 'Αχιλλεύς. *Dros.* 3. 251–2.
Anselmo. Plaga Amor est misero. *Epig.*, Hiiii; *C.P.It.* 1. 305.
Velius. Hulcus amor nostrum. Soter[2], p. 312; Corn., p. 406.
Equicola paraphrases this epigram, above, p. 294.
Cf. Rainerio. Su 'l vespro, allhor. *Cent. Son.* xiii.
Sabeo. Vulnus amorem habeo. *Epig.*, p. 631.
Minturno. Donna da' vostri lumi. *Rime*, p. 200.
Castelvetro quotes this epigram. *Petr.*, p. 69.
5.226. Cf. Philostratus, *Epist.* 51 (Didot 12).
Equicola paraphrases this epigram, above, p. 294.
5.228. Cf. Tibullus. Quid tibi nunc molles. *Eleg.*, 1. 8. 9f.
Sabeo. Cui Calamistrato te. *Epig.*, p. 631.
5.229. Nicetas Eugen. Τὴν Νιόβην κλαίουσαν. *Dros.* 6. 574.
Cornarius. Plorantem pastor Nioben. Corn., p. 406.
Sabeo. Plorantem inspiciens Nioben. *Epig.*, p. 633.
Castelvetro quotes this epigram. *Petr.*, p. 314.
5.230. Equicola paraphrases this epigram, above, p. 293.
Cf. Zerbo. Nè sì amica face. Carducci, *Poes. Barb.*, p. 195.
Cf. Groto. Quand' io vagheggio. *Rime* (1587), p. 57.
Cf. Manso. Sul collo d'alabastro. *Poes.*, p. 18.
Cf. Manso. Crespe chiome dorate. *Poes.*, p. 19.
Cunich. Aureolum vellens flavo. *Anth.*, p. 85.
Passeroni. Nice dal capo un biondo. *Rime* 3. 206.
5.231. Sabeo. Os numero Charitum. *Epig.*, p. 688.
5.232. Sabeo. Dilexi Hippomanem animum. *Epig.*, p. 692.
5.234. Cf. Tibullus. Vidi ego qui iuvenum. *Eleg.* 1. 2. 89–90.
Velius. Acer eram et primis. Soter[2], p. 313; Corn., p. 407.
Luscinius. Qui potui iuvenis. Soter[2], p. 313; Corn., p. 407.
Alciati. Immersus studiis. *Emb.* 109.
Sabeo. Ante fui invictus. *Epig.*, p. 689.
Mignault. Quum prius in duris. Alciati, *Emb.* 108 (109).
Medici (A. de'). Ille ego qui Veneris. *Scelt.*, p. xxxix.
Medici (A. de'). Quell'io che già degli. *Scelt.*, p. xxxix.
5.236. Cf. Politian. Iam iam ego vel sortem. Del Lungo, p. 145.
Cf. Gravina (P.). Cervus ut ardenti. *Poem.*, f. 9ᵛᵒ.
Equicola paraphrases this epigram, above, p. 293.
Sabeo. Est levior nostris. *Epig.*, p. 683.
Cf. Groto. Tra vaghi pomi. *Rime* (1587), p. 55.
5.237. Cf. *Anacreon.* 10 (Preisendanz).
Nicetas Eugen. Πᾶσαν μὲν ἤδη. *Dros.* 6. 609–19.
Anisio. In te quid tantum. *Poem.* f. 94ʳᵒ.

Equicola paraphrases this epigram, above, p. 294.
Alciati. Quid matutinos Progne. *Emb.* 70.
Sabeo. Tota nocte gemo. *Epig.*, p. 688.
Alberti. Perch' io pianga. *Rime*, p. 213–5.
Fioretti cites this epigram. *Prog.* 3. 140.

5.239. Equicola paraphrases this epigram, above, p. 293.
Sabeo. Vis flammae extincta. *Epig.*, p. 690.
Vargas Spento è l'ardor. *Sag.*, p. 51.

5.240. Luscinius. Mollis amor fulvo. Corn., p. 410.
Venatorius. Auro adeundus amor. Soter³, p. 359.

5.241. Sabeo. Dum dicturus eram. *Epig.*, p. 691.

5.246. [Not in *Plan.*]
Nicetas Eugen. Σοὶ μαλθακὸν φίλημα. *Dros.* 6. 584–9.

5.247. Cf. Theocritus. Καὶ φεύγει φιλέοντα. Theoc. 6. 17.
Luscinius. Nomen habes praedulce. Corn., p. 410.
Jausserandus. Parmenis es falso. Soter³, p. 359.

5.248. [Not in *Plan.*] Cf. Ovid, *Am.* 1. 7.

5.252. [Not in *Plan.*] Cf. *A.P.* 5. 128.
Nicetas Eugen. Ἀλλ' ἐκδυθείης. *Dros.* 6. 598–601.

5.253. [Not in *Plan.*]
Nicetas Eugen. Νεύεις κάτω, ποθοῦσα. *Dros.* 3. 163–172.

5.254. Sabeo. Hei mihi, bis senis. *Epig.*, p. 686.

5.255. [Not in *Plan.*]
Cf. Propertius. Non ego complexus. *Eleg.* 1. 13. 19f.

5.256. Cornarius. Ante meos Galatea. Corn., p. 408.
Equicola paraphrases this epigram, above, p. 293.
Sabeo. Vesper erat, Galatea. *Epig.*, p. 633.
Cf. Roncalli. Pien di livor. *Epig. Mod. Aut.*, p. 4.

5.257. Cf. Propertius. Cur haec in terris. *Eleg.* 2. 2. 3–4.
Nicetas Eugen. Καὶ τοῦ Διός. *Dros.* 6. 589.
Equicola paraphrases this epigram, above, p. 294.

5.258. [Plan. omits vv. 1–4.]
Nicetas Eugen. Σοὶ καὶ ῥυτίς. *Dros.* 6. 593.
Velius. Nae tuus alterius [vv. 5–6]. Soter², p. 313; Corn., p. 408.
Sabeo. Si tua adhuc veri. *Epig.*, p. 860.

5.259. [Not in *Plan.*]
Nicetas Eugen. Βαρύνεται σὸν ὄμμα. *Dros.* 3. 243–50.

5.260. Cf. Tibullus. Illam, quidquid agit. *Eleg.* 4. 2. 4f.
Carcani (P.). Stringi in rete il tuo. *Ant. Ercol.* 5. 225.

5.261. Cf. *A.P.* 5. 171 and 295.
Cf. Philostratus. Εἰ δὲ βούλει, τὸν μέν. *Epist.* 24 (Didot 33).
Cf. Aristaenetus. Τοῦτον δὴ τὸν τρόπον. Arist. 1. 25. 9.
Cornarius. Non ego pocula amo. Corn., p. 412.
Equicola paraphrases this epigram, above, p. 294.
Sabeo. Vini avidus non sum. *Epig.*, p. 690.

5.262. Sabeo. Heu et dulci loqui. *Epig.*, p. 623.
Fioretti cites this epigram. *Prog.* 5. 237. 11.
Medici (A. de'). Heu! me fata tuis. *Scelt.*, p. xix.

Medici (A. de'). A! ch'io non posso. *Scelt.*, p. xix.
5.263. Sabeo. Ne fungum emittas. *Epig.*, p. 684.
5.266. Carteromaco. Percussum rabiente. Ciampi, *Mem.*, p. 110.
Equicola paraphrases this epigram, above, p. 294.
Sabeo. Ore venenato si vir. *Epig.*, p. 625.
Alberti. Huom che ferito sia. *Rime.*, p. 205.
Moro. Huom che rabbioso. *Giar.* 1. 1. 39 (1. 44).
Pompei. Uomo, che sia da. *Op.* 2. 203.
5.267. Cf. Propertius. In me tela manent. *Eleg.* 2. 12. 13–4.
Luscinius. Quid gemis? Aeger amo. Corn., p. 409.
Equicola paraphrases this epigram, above, p. 294.
Sabeo. Cur lachrymaris? Amo. *Epig.*, p. 693.
5.268. Cf. *A.P.* 5. 58, 98, and 224.
Cf. Propertius. Et caput impositis. *Eleg.* 1. 1. 4.
Cf. Propertius. Sed certe pennas. *Eleg.* 2. 12. 14.
Cf. Angeriano. Non procul hinc. 'Ερωτ. Ciii; *C.P.It.* 1. 274.
Equicola paraphrases this epigram, above, p. 294.
Sabeo. Ne timeat quisquam. *Epig.*, p. 689.
Minturno. Più non si teme. *Rime*, p. 68.
Toscano (G. M.). Nullus amans posthac. *C.P.It.* 9. 373.
Castelvetro quotes this epigram. *Petr.*, p. 248.
Medici (A. de'). Nemo pharetrati formidet. *Scelt.*, p. xlviii.
Medici (A. de'). Nessun più tema Amore. *Scelt.*, p. xlviii.
Pagnini. Nessun paventi più. *Epig.*, p. 78.
5.269. Sabeo. Sedi unus medio nuruum. *Epig.*, p. 606.
5.270. Cf. Propertius, *Eleg.* 1. 2.
Sabeo. Non rosae opus. *Epig.*, p. 624.
Vargas. Nè di fregi la rosa. *Sag.*, p. 50.
5.273. Nicetas Eugen. 'Αρωγός ἐστι τῆς Κύπ. *Dros.* 3. 176–88.
Sabeo. Quae splendore prius. *Epig.*, p. 626.
5.274. Sabeo. Pectoris in calido. *Epig.*, p. 625.
Murtola. La vostra bella imago. *Rime*, f. 186ᵛᵒ.
5.275. [Not in *Plan.*] Cf. Propert. 1. 3; Ovid, *Am.* 1. 13 and *Her.* 1. 140.
5.279. Sabeo. Eertia iam coepit. *Epig.*, p. 680.
Carcani (P.). Cleofantide ritarda. *Ant. Ercol.* 8. 94.
5.280. Sabeo. Tu ne etiam languens. *Epig.*, p. 627.
5.281. Sabeo. Post choreas laeta. *Epig.*, p. 680.
5.282. Cf. *A.P.* 5. 62.
With v. 4 cf. Anon. Παίσατε. τῶν δ'ἐτέων. Hephaestion, *Ench.*
15. 8.
Sabeo. Usque sui ad limen. *Epig.*, p. 626.
Sabeo. Et licet ad senium. *Epig.*, p. 859.
Medici (A. de'). Dum, Melite, squalles. *Scelt.*, p. xliii.
Medici (A. de'). Dove, O Melitta, andò. *Scelt.*, p. xliii.
5.286. Sabeo. Dic Cleopfanti, charis. *Epig.*, p. 687.
Cf. Angeriano. Pectore sub nostro. 'Ερωτ. C iii; *C.P.It.* 1. 274.
5.287. Sabeo. Discere conatus si me. *Epig.*, p. 628.
5.288. Sabeo. Tempore quo fuerat. *Epig.*, p. 624.

Vargas. Dal dì che Cariclea. *Sag.*, p. 80.
Pagnini. Dal dì che Cariclea. *Epig.*, p. 108.
5.292. Cf. *A.P.* 5. 141.
Sabeo. Hic terra arridet. *Epig.*, p. 856.
Castelvetro quotes this epigram. *Petr.*, p. 27.
5.293. Sabeo. Nescit Amor pugnax. *Epig.*, p. 860.
5.295. Cf. *A.P.* 5. 171 and 261.
Sabeo. Nectar olent, tangas. *Epig.*, p. 625.
Sabeo. Tange, invenisti, mulce. *Epig.*, p. 626.
Sabeo. O patera unde fluit. *Epig.*, p. 631.
Sabeo. Suavia habes crater. *Epig.*, p. 665.
Sabeo. Tange labella calix. *Epig.*, p. 670.
Sabeo. Ori haere et gusta. *Epig.*, p. 672.
Sabeo. Dulci ore invento crater. *Epig.*, p. 811.
Sabeo. Fortunate calix. *Epig.*, p. 811.
Sabeo. In tot conversus. *Epig.*, p. 811.
5.297. Equicola paraphrases this epigram, above, p. 294.
Castelvetro quotes this epigram. *Petr.*, p. 421.
5.298. Sabeo. Se Maria extollit dilecta. *Epig.*, p. 627.
5.299. Equicola paraphrases this epigram, above, p. 294.
5.300. Sabeo. Elata cervice tumens. *Epig.*, p. 605.
5.301. Cf. Propertius. Quo fugis a demens? *Eleg.* 2. 30. 1–2.
5.302. Cf. *A.P.* 9. 359.
Quoted without translation in Soter[2], p. 27.
Alciati. Quis Veneris mihi callis. Corn., p. 405.
Alciati quotes vv. 17–8, with tr., *Op.* 4.477.
5.306. Sabeo. Suspiras, loqueris miseranda. *Epig.*, p. 628.
5.308. Sabeo. Siste superba gradum. *Epig.*, p. 656.

Book VI

6.1. Cf. *A.P.* 6.18, 19, 20, and 9. 260.
Cf. Horace. Dices heu, quoties. *Carm.* 4. 10.
Propertius. Non ita complebant. *Eleg.* 2. 6. 1–2.
Cf. Ovid. Tempus erit, quo vos. *Med. Fac.* 47–8.
Ausonius. Lais anus Veneri. *Opus.* 19. 65.
Claudian. Haud aliter iuvenum. *In Eutrop.* 1. 90.
Olympiodorus quotes this epigram, *in Plat. Alc. I.* 31 (Creu-
zer).
More (Sir T.). Nequiter arrisi tibi. Soter[2], p. 308; Corn.,
p. 395.
Luscinius. Pro foribus Graios. Corn., p. 395.
Anisio. Qua non in Latio forma. *Poem.*, f. 90[v].
Alciati. . . . illam iam carpserat. *Emb.* 74.
Alamanni. Flora, il sommo valor. *Versi* 1. 95.
Cf. Alamanni. Me speglio antico. *Versi* 1. 95.
Bonamico. Iam domita ingratae. *Carm.*, p. 56.
Sabeo. Iam turbam elusi. *Epig.*, p. 628.

Sabeo. Quae turbam irrisi. *Epig.*, p. 630.
Sabeo. Hellada quae tumidam. *Epig.*, p. 123.
Cf. Veniero. O più ch'altra. *Lib. Sest.*, f. 130ro.
Anon. *ap.* Mignault. Lais anus speculo. Alciati, *Emb.* 74.
Casone. Questa depinta imago. *Rime* f. 4ro.
Cf. Casone. Io Lico agricoltore. *Gareg.* 8. 208vo.
Guarini (A.). Ruppe lo specchio. *Rim. Onest.* 2. 395.
Stigliani. Vistasi Nicolosa. *Rime*, p. 269.
Tomasini refers to Gr. and quotes Ausonius' tr. Graev., *Thes.*
12. 814.
Ricolvi. Ille ego Graeca Charis. *Op.*, p. 87.
Ricolvi. Io Laide, che ridea. *Op.*, p. 87.
Cunich. Hoc Veneri speculum. *Anth.*, p. 99.
Cunich. Lyda hoc do Veneri. *Anth.*, p. 99.
Pompei. Quella io, che deridea. *Op.* 2. 187.
Felici. Sospendo a Venere. *Epig.*[1], p. 86.
Bertòla. Io reco a te questo. *Poes.* 1. 177.
Passeroni. Questo specchio a te. *Rime* 3. 232.
Passeroni. Lida a Ciprigna. *Rime* 3. 54.
Bettinelli. Il suo speglio. [Quotes the tr. of Ausonius and Voltaire]. *Op.* 21. 81.
Bettinelli. Venere, a te sacrò. *Op.* 22. 98.
Roncalli. Venere, a te la tua. *Epig.* (1792), p. 83; (1801), p. 61.
Pananti. Lo specchio mio ti. *Op.* 2. 136.
Pagnini. Io che mille veggendo. *Epig.*, p. 25.

6.5.　Cf. *A.P.* 6. 27, 28, 29, and 90.
Sabeo. Tela cruenta hamos. *Epig.*, p. 69.

6.6.　[Not in *Plan.*] Quoted by Herodotus (5. 59); and by *Schol. Vat.* on Dion. Thrax (Hilgard, p. 185).
Valla. Optulit Amphitryon me. Herod., f. 136vo.

6.7.　[Not in *Plan.*] Quoted by Herodotus (5. 60).
Valla. Scaeus in assueto. Herod., f. 136vo.

6.8.　[Not in *Plan.*] Quoted by Herodotus (5. 61).
Valla. Laodamus ipsum tripodem. Herod., f. 137ro.

6.9.　Cf. *A.P.* 6. 302 and 303.
Sabeo. Arcus incurvi, tum tincta. *Epig.*, p. 114.
Cunich. Hunc arcum et pharetram. *Anth.*, p. 98.
Felici. Questa faretra e questo. *Epig.*[1], p. 67.
Passeroni. Promaco vincitore. *Rime* 3. 100.

6.11.　Cf. *A.P.* 6. 12–16, 179–87.
Sabeo. Longa offert Pani. *Epig.*, p. 84.

6.12.　[See under *A.P.* 6. 11].
Velius. Accipe tergemini triplicis. Soter[2], p. 310; Corn., p. 397.
Pagnini. Tre reti accogli. *Epig.*, p. 43.

6.13.　[See under *A.P.* 6. 11]. Kaibel, *Carm. Epigr.* 1104.
Sabeo. Haec tres germani. *Epig.*, p. 80.

6.14. [See under *A.P.* 6. 11].
Sabeo. Instrumenta artis ponunt. *Epig.*, p. 81.
6.15. [See under *A.P.* 6. 11].
Sabeo. Tres tibi, Pan, fratres. *Epig.*, p. 153.
6.16. [See under *A.P.* 6. 11].
Sabeo. Tres haec germani. *Epig.*, p. 83.
6.18. Cf. *A.P.* 6. 1, 19, 20 and 9. 260.
Soter² (p. 309) and Cornarius (p. 395) quote without tr.
Sabeo. Formosam speciem. *Epig.*, p. 24.
6.19. Cf. *A.P.* 6. 1, 18, 20, and 9. 260.
Quoted without tr. by Soter² (p. 309) and by Cornarius (p. 395).
Sabeo. Cypria largiris speciem. *Epig.*, p. 123.
Pompei. Ben, Venere, tu doni. *Op.* 2. 192.
Pagnini. La bellezza è tuo don. *Epig.*, p. 45.
6.20. Cf. *A.P.* 6. 1, 18, 19, and 9. 260.
Quoted without tr. by Soter² (p. 309) and by Cornarius (p. 395).
Sabeo. Medorum Graii validas. *Epig.*, p. 29.
6.21. Sabeo. Irrigui fossorem horti. *Epig.*, p. 536.
6.22. Sabeo. Quae potuit collecta. *Epig.*, p. 87.
Vargas. Una matura melagrana. *Sag.*, p. 31.
6.23. Sabeo. Qui colis horrisonum. *Epig.*, p. 70; p. 136.
6.24. Sabeo. Attritum frustra rate. *Epig.*, p. 104.
6.25. Cf. *A.P.* 6. 26.
6.26. Cf. *A.P.* 6. 25.
Sleidan. Hoc Cinyras nymphis. Soter², p. 307; Corn., p. 393.
Molza. Humida suspendit nymphis. *Poes.* 3. 207.
Amalteo (G. B.). Cui calamos, nassasque. *Tr. Frat.*, p. 145.
Sabeo. Obtulit haec nymphis. *Epig.*, p. 74.
Sabeo. Rete istud Cyneres. *Epig.*, p. 809.
Felici. Sospende a voi Nereide. *Epig.*¹, p. 127.
6.27. Cf. *A.P.* 6. 5, 28, 29, 90.
Sabeo. Plenum oculis linum. *Epig.*, p. 28.
6.28. Cf. *A.P.* 6. 5, 27, 29, and 90.
Sabeo. Perplexos calamos, remum. *Epig.*, p. 74.
6.29. [Not in *Plan.*] Cf. *A.P.* 6. 5, 27, 28, and 90.
6.30. Cf. *A.P.* 6. 38.
Sabeo. Rete ubi coniunxit. *Epig.*, p. 93.
6.32. Sabeo. Cruribus hirsutis. *Epig.*, p. 39.
6.33. Sabeo. Haec piscatores habitas. *Epig.*, p. 75.
Mazzoni quotes line 6 without tr. *Difesa*, p. 82.
6.35. Cf. *A.P.* 6. 106.
Sabeo. Capripedi Valeson Divo. *Epig.*, p. 105.
6.36. Molza. Haec tibi, magna Ceres. *C.P.It.* 6. 361.
Conti. Alma Ceres parvo. *Myth.* 1. 17.
Sabeo. Haec tibi rura colens. *Epig.*, p. 58.
Tomasini refers to this epigram, *De Don.* 27. Graev. 12. 856.

Cunich. Hos tibi, flava Ceres. *Anth.*, p. 98.
Felici. Questi manipoli. *Epig.*[1], p. 39.
Passeroni. A te questi non piccioli. *Rime* 3. 55.

6.38. Cf. *A.P.* 6. 30.
Sabeo. Rete coronatum plumbo. *Epig.*, p. 75.
Cf. Priuli. Haec, Neptune, tibi. *C.P.It.* 7. 525.

6.39. Cf. *A.P.* 6. 174.
Sabeo. Eraclia, Ephron, satyre. *Epig.*, p. 87.

6.41. Sabeo. Lora boum, stivam. *Epig.*, p. 29.

6.42. Alciati quotes v. 4, *Op.* 3.592.
Sabeo. Exigui Alcimenes cultor. *Epig.*, pp. 47 and 97.

6.43. Sabeo. Nympharum servam pluvias. *Epig.*, p. 14.

6.44. Conti. Heronax Satyris. *Myth.* 5. 7.
Sabeo. Musti avidis Satyris. *Epig.*, p. 91.
Cunich. Heronax munus Satyris. *Anth.*, p. 96.

6.45. Cf. *A.P.* 6. 169.
6.46. Cf. *A.P.* 6. 159.
Sabeo. Quae Mavortis erat prius. *Epig.*, p. 111.
Cunich. Hanc belloque bonam. *Anth.*, p. 91.
Passeroni. Questa tromba di rame. *Rime* 3. 97.

6.47. Cf. *A.P.* 6. 48.
Sabeo. Stridentem atque cavum. *Epig.*, p. 94.

6.48. Cf. *A.P.* 6. 47.
Cf. Navagero. Iam telas, calathosque. *C.Q.P.*, p. 28.

6.49. Quoted by Athenaeus 232C, and by Eustath. on *Il.* 23. 510.

6.50. Quoted by Plutarch, *Aristides* 19. 6 and *Moralia* 873B.
Sabeo. Iam Graeci unanimes. *Epig.*, p.147.

6.51. Cf. *A.P.* 6. 94 and 234.
Conti. Alma parens Tellus. *Myth.* 9.5.
Sabeo. Mater terra mihi. *Epig.*, p. 698.

6.52. Sabeo. Sic iacuisti olim. *Epig.*, p. 45.
Cunich. Sacra, Panomphaei munus. *Anth.*, p. 99.
Passeroni. Asta mia, sacra a Giove. *Rime* 3. 56.

6.53. Navagero. Aurae, quae levibus. *C.Q.P.*, p. 23.
Anon. Fresche aurette, voi. [after Navagero] *Versi et Reg.* Mi;
Carducci, *Poes. Barb.*, p. 265.
Sabeo. Excitat hoc templum. *Epig.*, p. 59.
Paterno. Aure leggiadre, che. *Nuov. Fiam.*, f. 7[ro].
Paterno. Aure, O aure, che 'l ciel. *Nuov. Fiam.*, f. 36[ro]; *Rim.
Onest.* 1. 269.
Angelio (?). Aure, che tra le frondi. Navagero, *Op.* (1718),
p. 284.
Cf. Marino. Questo vaso d'amomo. *Poes. Var.*, p. 82.
Cunich. Eudemus viridi parvum. *Anth.*, p. 92.
Felici. Eudemo un piccol tempio. *Epig.*[1], p. 25.

6.54. Cf. *A.P.* 9. 584. The same story is related by Strabo (VI,
p. 260); and by Clemens Alex., *Protrept.*, p. 2.
Alciati. Locrensis posuit tibi. *Emb.* 185.

Sabeo. Suspendit Locrus Musis. *Epig.*, p. 80.
Guinisi. Pulsabat digitis lyram. *Poes.*, p. 257.

6.55. Sabeo. Pytho et acidaliae. *Epig.*, p. 40.
6.56. Sabeo Viticomo satyrum Bromio. *Epig.*, p. 94.
Tomasini refers to this epigram. Graev. 12. 856.
6.57. Navagero. Ille tuus Pan montivage. *C.Q.P.*, p. 23.
6.58. Sabeo. Fulcra tori frustra. *Epig.*, p. 36.
6.59. Conti. Minervae crines posuit. *Myth.* 3. 18.
Sabeo. Nacta procum impubem. *Epig.*, p. 15.
6.60. Sabeo. Pamphilion crines formosos. *Epig.*, p. 96.
6.61. Sabeo. O felix vere. *Epig.*, p. 471.
6.62. Sabeo. Ferrum quo calami. *Epig.*, p. 833.
Martorelli discusses this ep. *De Theca Cal.*, p. 209.
Cunich. Et teres hoc plumbum. *Anth.*, p. 99.
Passeroni. E riga e piombo atto. *Rime* 3. 55.
6.65. Sabeo. Sculptorem plumbum. *Epig.*, p. 159.
6.67. Molza. Hos cultros atque haec. *Poes.* 3. 208.
Sabeo. Hoc plumbum, hunc canorem. *Epig.*, p. 104.
6.69. Cf. *A.P.* 6. 70.
Cornarius. Navem Neptuno Crantus Corn., p. 399.
Sabeo. Neptuno navem sacravit. *Epig.*, p. 49.
6.70. Cf. *A.P.* 6. 69.
Cornarius. Rex maris et solidae. Corn., p. 400.
Sabeo. Rex maris et terrae. *Epig.*, p. 99.
6.71. Sabeo. Pinguia serta tibi. *Epig.*, p. 124.
6.72. Sabeo. Sidentem inspexi leporem. *Epig.*, p. 121.
Carcani (P.). Presso una vite sacra. *Ant. Ercol.* 8. 106.
6.73. Sabeo. Debilis ob senium. *Epig.*, p. 89.
Cunich. Hanc Daphnis Pani. *Anth.*, p. 97.
Felici. Offre a Pan Dafnide. *Epig.*[1], p. 60.
Passeroni. Giunto all' età senile. *Rime* 3. 97.
6.74. Tomasini refers to this epigram. Graev. 12. 856.
Carcani (P.). La bassaride Eurinome. *Ant. Ercol.* 7. 66.
6.76. Sleidan. Vir tuus Anchises hic. Soter[2], p. 307; Corn., p. 393.
Sabeo. Vir tuus Anchises. *Epig.*, p. 125.
Pagnini. Il tuo consorte Anchise. *Epig.*, p. 21.
6.77. Velius. Bacche, cadum tibi. Soter[2], p. 311: Corn., p. 399.
Sleidan. Quem Xenophon tibi. Soter[2], p. 311; Corn., p. 399.
Alciati. Bacche, bibax Xenophon. Corn., p. 399.
Sabeo. Vinosus Zenophon, placide. *Epig.*, p. 98.
Sabeo. Dolium habe Zenophon. *Epig.*, p. 98.
Sabeo. Dolium habe placidus. *Epig.*, p. 98.
Sabeo. Id quod habet Zenophon. *Epig.*, p. 99.
Sabeo. Fronte hilari cape. *Epig.*, p. 149.
Sabeo. Quum nil optineat. *Epig.*, p. 150.
Sabeo. Suspice, Bacche, tuus. *Epig.*, p. 150.
Redi quotes this epigram. *Op.* 1. 49.
Salvini. Quod vacuum Xenophon. Redi, *Op.* 1. 49.

Cunich. Huncce cadum Xenophon. *Anth.*, p. 92.
Felici. Poichè il vin bevve. *Epig.*[2], p. xvi.
Passeroni. Senofonte, da tutti. *Rime* 3. 98.

6.78. [Not in *Plan.*] Cf. *A.P.* 6. 177.
6.79. Sabeo. Non vertenda magis. *Epig.*, p. 91.
6.80. With line 6 cf. *A.P.* 5. 88.
      Alciati. Delitiae hic vates. Corn., p. 397.
      Sabeo. Daphniacis Agathi e libris. *Epig.*, p. 26.
      Tomasini refers to this epigram, Graev. 12. 813.
6.81. Sabeo. Contectum tauro clypeum. *Epig.*, p. 62.
6.83. Sabeo. Ad tripodem Phoebi. *Epig.*, p. 79.
      Medici (A. de'). Ad tripodem Eumolpus. *Scelt.*, p. l.
      Medici (A. de'). Questo che il suono. *Scelt.*, p. l.
6.84. Cunich. Hocce Iovi clypei. *Anth.*, p. 98.
      Felici. Questo di forte clipeo. *Epig.*[1], p. 82.
      Passeroni. Questo avanzo di scudo. *Rime* 3. 52.
6.85. Cf. *A.P.* 6. 86.
6.86. Cf. 85.
      Sabeo. Hastam, ocreas, galeam. *Epig.*, p. 507.
      Cunich. Ensis, scutum, ocreae. *Anth.*, p. 92.
      Felici. Rufo sospende a Pallade. *Epig.*[2], p. xvi.
6.87. Sabeo. Nebridas et tyrsum noster. *Epig.*, p. 129.
      Carcani (P.). Il nostro Pan. [3 lines]. *Ant. Ercol.* 2. 176.
6.88. Sabeo. Aurea lascivis Cypri. *Epig.*, p. 28.
6.89. Sabeo Circa securos lapides. *Epig.*, p. 76.
6.90. [Not in *Plan.*] Cf. *A.P.* 6.5, 27, 28, 29.
6.94. [Not in *Plan.*] Cf. *A.P.* 6. 51 and 234.
6.96. [Not in *Plan.*] Cf. Virgil. Arcades ambo. *Ecl.* 7. 4.
6.97. Sabeo Cuspidem Alexandri. *Epig.*, p. 389.
      Cunich. Cuspis Alexandri. *Anth.*, p. 91.
      Medici (A. de'). Inclyta, Pellaeus quam. *Scelt.*, p. xxviii.
      Medici (A. de'). Asta, che il Duce. *Scelt.*, p. xxviii.
6.102. Sabeo. Uvae immaturae rosae. *Epig.*, p. 85.
6.103. Cf. *A.P.* 6. 205.
6.104. Sabeo. Incurvas messis falces. *Epig.*, p. 102.
6.105. Conti. E pruna dono. *Myth.* 3. 18.
      Sabeo. Stagnicola, anguillam. *Epig.*, p. 78.
6.106. Cf. *A.P.* 6. 35.
6.114. Cf. *A.P.* 6. 115 and 116.
6.115. Cf. 114 and 116.
      Cunich. Mugitu Orbeli saltus. *Anth.*, p. 90.
6.116. Cf. 114, 115.
6.117. Sabeo. Ex violento igni. *Epig.*, p. 106.
6.120. Sabeo. Non solum nove residens. *Epig.*, p. 81.
6.121. Pagnini. Or sì secure e liete. *Epig.*, p. 136.
6.124. Sabeo. Scutum hominum ex hum. *Epig.*, p. 111.
6.125. Sabeo. Saepe meo tutata fui. *Epig.*, p. 111.
6.129. Sabeo. Octo arcus, octo galeas. *Epig.*, p. 78.

6.130. Quoted by Diodorus, *exc. Vat.* 22. 3 (p. 52 Dind.); Plutarch,
 Pyrrh. 26; Pausanias 1. 13. 2.
 Robortello refers to this epigram. *Scr. Ep.*, p. 35.
 Giraldi (L. G.). Haec tibi dona refert. *Op.* 1. 337.
 Sabeo. Suspendit Pyrrhus tibi. *Epig.*, p. 111.
 Cunich. Scuta Molloseus rex. *Anth.*, p. 94.
 Bettinelli. Io Pirro l'Epiro. *Op.* 22. 98.
6.131. Sabeo. Scuta ab Lucanis. *Epig.*, p. 112.
6.134. Sabeo. Quae nam est tyrson. *Epig.*, p. 120.
 Rivautella-Ricolvi. Quae thyrsum gerit. *Mar.* 1. 43.
 Carcani (P.). Quella, che tiene. *Ant. Ercol.* 6. 141; *Rac.* 4. 33.
 Cunich. Haec thyrsum gestans. *Anth.*, p. 168.
 Pagnini. Eliconia quella è. *Epig.*, p. 125.
6.138. [Not in *Plan.*] Kaibel 758.
6.144. [Not in *Plan.*] Geffcken 63.
 Published by Allacci, *De Sym.*, p. 214.
6.146. [Not in *Plan.*]
 Pagnini. Riede, Lucina, ov'ora. *Epig.*, p. 143.
6.148. [Not in *Plan.*]
 Carcani (P.). La figliuola di Crizia. *Ant. Ercol.* 4. 278.
 Carcani (P.). Callistia, figlia a Cr. *Ant. Ercol.* 8. 98.
6.151. Cf. *A.P.* 6. 195.
6.152. Cunich. Furcillasque, pedumque. *Anth.*, p. 90.
6.154. Cf. *A.P.* 6. 158.
 Sabeo. Agresti haec Pani. *Epig.*, p. 90.
 Sabeo. Pan quod amas animal. *Epig.*, p. 162.
 Sabeo. Dona, Biton, Pani. *Epig.*, p. 162.
 Sabeo. Sacravit Bromio. *Epig.*, p. 162.
 Sabeo. Naiades, haec vobis. *Epig.*, p. 162.
 Sabeo. Pani hircum. *Epig.*, p. 161.
 Sabeo. Serta, caprum, thyrsos. *Epig.*, p. 161.
 Angelio. Et Pani et Cereri. *Poem.*, p. 395.
 Pagnini. Biton pastore a Pane. *Epig.*, p. 138.
6.155. Sabeo. Crovilos atque comae. *Epig.*, p. 110.
6.156. Sabeo. Vernantem crinem ipse. *Epig.*, p. 24.
6.157. Sabeo. Quae Gorgi es custos. *Epig.*, p. 540.
6.158. Cf. *A.P.* 6. 154.
 Velius. Pani caprum nymphisque. Soter[2], p. 308; Corn., p. 394.
 Alciati. Pani capram nymphisque. Corn., p. 394.
 Cf. Navagero. Dat Cereri Telison. [The name 'Telison' comes
 from *A.P.* 6.35]. *C.Q.P.*, p. 26.
 Redi refers to this epigram, *Op.* 1. 42.
 Cunich. Pani haedum, atque rosas. *Anth.*, p. 99.
 Medici (A. de'). Pani haedum Nymphisque. *Scelt.*, p. xvi.
 Medici (A. de'). A Pane a Bacco ed alle N. *Scelt.*, p. xvi.
 Felici. In questo verde sito. *Epig.*, p. 89.
 Passeroni. Al Dio Pan questo. *Rime* 3. 232.
 Vargas. Triplice dono offre Biton. *Sag.*, p. 30.

6.159. [Not in *Plan*.] Cf. *A.P.* 6. 46.
6.160. Cf. *A.P.* 6. 247.
    Sabeo. Matutinarum recinentem. *Epig.*, p. 15.
6.161. Sabeo. Hesperiis rediens victor, *Epig.*, p. 26.
    Cunich. Hesperio rediens Marcel. *Anth.*, p. 28.
    Passeroni. Tornando dalla Spagna. *Rime* 3. 183.
    Felici. Marcello dall' Esperia. *Epig.*², p. xiv.
6.163. Cf. *A.P.* 9. 322, 323.
    Dazzi. Quis male grata meis. *Poem.*, p. 128.
6.164. Cf. Virgil. Glauco et Panopeae et. *Geor.* 1. 437.
    Velius. Glauce, tibi et Nereo. Soter², p. 311; Corn., p. 400.
    Conti. Inoque Glaucoque. *Myth.* 8. 4.
    Sabeo. Hos, Melicerta, tibi. *Epig.*, p. 140.
    Cunich. O Glauce, o Nereu pater. *Anth.*, p. 96.
    Felici. A Melicerta, a Nereo. *Epig.*¹, p. 55.
    Passeroni. O Glauco, O Nereo, ed Ino. *Rime* 3. 51.
    Vargas. A Glauco, a Nereo. *Sag.*, p. 29.
6.166. Sabeo. Quadraginta mari ex nautis. *Epig.*, p. 110.
6.169. Cf. *A.P.* 6. 45.
    Sabeo. Cuspidibus multis. *Epig.*, p. 30.
    Sabeo. Dorsa super portantem. *Epig.*, p. 30.
6.171. Molza. Sol pater, eductum. *Poes.* 3. 204.
    Sabeo. Sydera pulsantem. *Epig.*, p. 27.
6.172. Sabeo. Pulchra velut murex. *Epig.*, p. 91.
    Carcani (G.?). Porfiride di Cnido. *Ant. Ercol.* 6. 401.
6.173. [Not in *Plan*.] Reiske, p. 19.
    Carcani (P.). La Frigia Archilli. *Ant. Ercol.* 8. 72.
6.174. Cf. *A.P.* 6. 39, 288, and 289.
    Sabeo. Aequevae aequales tibi. *Epig.*, p. 97.
6.175. Sabeo. Venandi arte canem. *Epig.*, p. 104.
6.177. [Not in *Plan*.] Cf. 6. 78. The epig. occurs in MSS. of Theo-
    critus; and is in the Juntine Theoc. of 1515. Theoc. *Inscr.* 2.
    Orsini (F.) quotes this epig. on Virgil, *Ecl.* 1. 2. *Virg. Ill.*, p. 6.
    Salvini. Il bianco Dafni, che colla. *Teoc.*, p. 184.
    Regolotti. Dafni, quel che sì. *Teoc.*, p. 258.
    Cunich. Candidus agresti pulcre. *Anth.* p. 100.
    Della Torre. Dafni, quel' bianco. *Ode*, p. 365.
    Vicini. Quei che fu la sampogna. *Gl'Id.*, p. 184.
    Passeroni. Il candido Filen, dotto. *Rime* 3. 57.
    Pagnini. Il bianco Dafni. *Poet. Gr.* p. 870.
6.179. Cf. *A.P.* 6. 11–16, and 179–87.
    Alciati quotes vv. 1–2, *Op.* 3.602.
6.180. Sabeo. Si iaculatur Amor. *Epig.*, p. 155.
6.181. Velius. Tergemini fratres, vario. Soter², p. 310; Corn., p. 398.
6.183. Sabeo. Aeris, undae, et humi. *Epig.*, p. 98.
6.187. Velius. Pani sacer fratrum. Soter², p. 311; Corn., p. 398.
6.188. Giovane. Cres Therimachus [prose]. *Ant. Tar.* 3. 3.
6.189. Anon. Nymphae, fonticolae. Burmann, *Anth. Lat.* 2. 470.

Vargas. Vaghe Ninfe del rio. *Sag.*, p. 108.
6.190. Cf. *A.P.* 6. 191 and 300.
    Sabeo. Nominis eximii et laudis. *Epig.*, p. 90.
6.191. Cf. 190 and 300.
6.195. [Not in *Plan.*] Cf. *A.P.* 6. 151.
6.196. Sabeo. Octopedem pagurum. *Epig.*, p. 76.
6.197. [Not in *Plan.*] Quoted by Thucydides (1. 132. 2); by Demos-
    thenes (59. 97); Aristodemus (Mueller, *F.H.G.* 5. 1. 7);
    Plutarch (*Moral.* 873C); Suidas (*s.v.* Παυσανίας); and
    Arsenios (*Paroem.*, p. 397).
    Nepos. Suo ductu barbaros [prose]. *Pausan.* 1.
    Allacci published this ep., *De Sym.*, p. 214.
6.198. Sabeo. Vernantem sub temporibus. *Epig.*, p. 127.
    Cunich. Hunc flavae tondens. *Anth.*, p. 89.
    Passeroni. Questa bionda lanugine. *Rime* 3. 232.
6.205. [Not in *Plan.*] Cf. *A.P.* 6. 103.
6.206. Cf. 207.
6.207. [Not in *Plan.*] Cf. 206.
    Carcani (P.). Questi calzari di Bitinia. *Ant. Ercol.* 4. 298.
6.208. Sabeo. Quae haec talaria. *Epig.*, p. 33.
6.212-17. [Not in *Plan.*] Published by Allacci, *De Sym.*, p. 214.
6.213. [Not in *Plan.*]
    Cf. Tzetzes. Ἐξ ἐπὶ πεντήκοντα. *Chil.* 1. 636.
6.214. [Not in *Plan.*] Quoted by *schol.* on Pindar, *Pyth.* 1. 155.
6.215. [Not in *Plan.*] Quoted by Plutarch, *Moral.* 870F.
6.217. [Not in *Plan.*] Cf. *A.P.* 6. 218-221 and 237.
6.218. Cf. *A.P.* 6. 217, 219-21, and 237.
    Sabeo. Testibus excisis Cybeles. *Epig.*, p. 283 (285).
6.219. Cf. *A.P.* 6. 217-8, 220-21, and 237.
    Sabeo. Splectro ex horribili. *Epig.*, p. 57.
6.220. [Not in *Plan.*] Cf. *A.P.* 6. 217-19, 221, and 237.
    Carcani (P.). Da Tessinunte a Sardi. *Ant. Ercol.* 8. 71.
6.221. Cf. *A.P.* 6. 217-20 and 237.
    Sabeo. Grandine, tum tonitru. *Epig.*, p. 730.
6.222. [Not in *Plan.*] Cf. 223.
6.223. Cf. 222.
6.228. Sabeo. Attritum sulcis, confectum. *Epig.*, p. 22.
6.234. [Not in *Plan.*] Cf. *A.P.* 6. 51 and 94.
6.236. Cf. Colocci, Cum ratis Antoni. *C.P.It.* 3. 430.
    Molza. Ferrea rostra olim. Landi, *Num.*, p. 86.
    Sabeo. Actiacum Martem testantia. *Epig.*, p. 56.
    Cunich. Aerea nostra, vagis olim. *Anth.*, p. 38.
    Felici. Noi, che quì vedi pendere. *Epig.*[2], p. xix.
6.237. [Not in *Plan.*] Cf. *A.P.* 6. 217-21.
6.239. [Not in *Plan.*] Quoted by Suidas, *s.v.* σμήνη.
6.241. Sabeo. Gratiam utranque. *Epig.*, p. 209.
    Sabeo. Cassis utranque habuit. *Epig.*, p. 704.
6.243. Sabeo. Imbracon atque Samum. *Epig.*, p. 44.

6.246. Sabeo. Pectoris ornatum cursu. *Epig.*, p. 69.
6.247. Cf. *A.P.* 6. 160.
Sabeo. Carmine arundineo. *Epig.*, p. 144.
6.248. [Not in *Plan.*] Quoted by Suidas, *s.v.* Λάγυνος.
6.249. Sabeo. Extinctam assuetum. *Epig.*, p. 158.
6.253. Cf. *A.P.* 6. 334.
6.256. Gualfreducci. Promissa torvi colla. *Var.*, p. 281; *Sel. Epig.*, p. 6.
Averani. Robusta tauri colla. *Op.* 1. 32.
Cunich. Taurinaeque toros. *Anth.*, p. 15.
6.257. [Not in *Plan.*] Quoted by Suidas, *s.v.* ἀμφιφορῆα.
6.258. [Not in *Plan.*] Quoted by Suidas, *s.v.* ὄγμος.
Cf. Accolti (Ben.). Et surgunt laetis. *C.P.It.* 1. 1.
Cf. Anon. Titiro sparso pria. *Versi et Reg.* Ni; Carducci, *Poes. Barb.*, p. 262.
6.259. Sabeo. Carcere quis nam. *Epig.*, p. 33.
Argoli. Hermes carceribus. Graev., 9. 67.
6.260. Cf. *A.P.* 16. 205.
6.261. [Not in *Plan.*] Quoted by Suidas, *s.v.* ὄλπη.
6.281. [Not in *Plan.*]
Carcani (P.). Madre, tu che di. *Ant. Ercol.* 8. 73.
6.283. Cf. Tibullus. At quae fida fuit. *Eleg.* 1. 6. 77–80.
Alciati. Praecellens opibus. Corn., p. 116.
Sabeo. Numosi fuerant cui. *Epig.*, p. 86.
Sabeo. Quae prius extiterat. *Epig.*, p. 681.
Pompei. Costei che fu da pria. *Op.* 2. 219.
Pagnini. Lei che sì ricca. *Epig.*, p. 26.
6.285. Sabeo. Quae coluit radiis. *Epig.*, p. 22.
6.286. Sabeo. Fimbriae ad extremum. *Epig.*, p. 85.
6.287. Sabeo. Diva tibi hanc. *Epig.*, p. 143.
6.288. [Not in *Plan.*] Cf. *A.P.* 6. 39, 174, and 289.
6.289. [Not in *Plan.*] Cf. *A.P.* 6. 39, 174, and 288.
6.291. Sabeo. Bacchi anus exsiccans. *Epig.*, p. 779.
6.292. Sabeo. Purpuream vestem. *Epig.*, p. 85.
6.293. [Not in *Plan.*]
Carcani (P.). Dedicati quì sono. *Ant. Ercol.* 7. 235.
6.300. [Not in *Plan.*] Cf. *A.P.* 6. 190 and 191.
6.301. [Not in *Plan.*]
Medici (A. de'). Hanc navem Eudemus. *Scelt.*, p. xxix.
Medici (A. de'). Disse Eudemo ai Traci. *Scelt.*, p. xxix.
Pagnini. Lieve barchetta. *Epig.*, p. 131.
6.302. Cf. *A.P.* 303.
Sabeo. Noctivagi a tegete. *Epig.*, p. 171.
6.303. Cf. *A.P.* 6. 302.
Alciati. Si panem petitis, mures. Corn., p. 70.
Cornarius. Si petitis panem, mures. Corn., p. 70.
Sabeo. Si cupitis Cererem, mures. *Epig.*, p. 283 (285).
6.306. Sabeo. Olla haec ad caenes. *Epig.*, p. 822.

Ricolvi. Ollam, fuscinam, et hunc. *Op.*, p. 77.
Ricolvi. Questa pentola e questa. *Op.* p. 77.
6.307. [Not in *Plan.*]
Cf. Martial. Qui tonsor tota. *Epig.* 7. 64.
6.309. Lines 1–2 quoted by Rhodiginus, *Lect.* 19. 4.
Alciati. Hanc sphaeram in sese. Corn., p. 401.
Sabeo. Saltantem e buxo rumbum. *Epig.*, p. 110.
Cunich. Laudatamque pilam. *Anth.*, p. 95.
6.311. [Not in *Plan.*]
Carcani (P.). Di, forestier, che. *Ant. Ercol.* 8. 11.
6.312. Sabeo. Puniceas chorus ecce. *Epig.*, p. 737.
Carcani (P.). I ragazzi, O capron. *Ant. Ercol.* 2. 244.
6.314. Soter. Hanc tibi Penelope. Soter², p. 86.
Sanchez. Penelope, tibi has. *Op.* 2. 494.
6.315–8, 320. Quoted without tr. in Soter², pp. 85–6.
6.324. Sabeo. Eversori orbis posuit. *Epig.*, p. 158.
6.325. Sabeo. Ille ab humo, alter. *Epig.*, p. 87.
6.326. Sabeo. Lybs tibi Lysimachi. *Epig.*, p. 97.
6.328. Sabeo. Ista genethliacis. *Epig.*, p. 97.
6.331. Politian. Vidit ut implicitum. Del Lungo, p. 545.
Pio. Quin etiam ille pater. *Lamp.* 1. 412.
Sleidan. Cum pater aspiceret. Soter², p. 308; Corn., p. 396.
Sabeo. Tela manu rapuit trepida. *Epig.*, p. 27.
Battista. Fanciul nudrito in sù. *Poes. Mel.* 1. 3.
Bongiovanni and Zanetti. Vede Alcone il figl. *Epig.*, p. 3.
Cunich. Ut pater immanem. *Anth.*, p. 93.
Felici. Alcon del figlio misero. *Epig.*², p. xix.
6.333. Sabeo. Iam scintillasti ter. *Epig.*, p. 678.
6.334. Cf. *A.P.* 6. 253.
Anselmo. Antra, domus Nympharum. *Epig.*, Kii.
Gualfreducci. Antra, et Nympharum. *Var.*, p. 285; *Sel. Epig.*,
    p. 251.
Cunich. O caules, o rupes. *Anth.*, p. 95.
6.336. [Not in *Plan.*] Theocritus, *Inscr.* 1.
Salvini. Le rose rugiadose. *Teoc.*, p. 184.
Regolotti. Quelle che miri. *Teoc.*, p. 257.
Cunich. Hoc ego serpullum. *Anth.*, p. 100.
Medici (A. de'). Serpillum Aoniis. *Scelt.*, p. xxx.
Medici (A. de'). Sermollino eletto. *Scelt.*, p. xxx.
Della Torre. Quelle rose. *Ode*, p. 363.
Vicini. E quel serpillo. *Gl'Id.*, p. 184.
Passeroni. Questo folto serpillo. *Rime* 3. 233.
Vargas. Il cupo sermollin. *Sag.*, p. 31.
Pagnini. Le rugiadose rose. *Poet. Gr.*, p. 870.
6.337. [Not in *Plan.*] Theocritus, *Inscr.* 8.
Salvini. A Mileto anco il figlio. *Teoc.*, p. 186.
Regolotti. Il figlio di Peone. *Teoc.*, p. 262.
Della Torre. Venne a Mileto. *Ode*, p. 369.

Vicini. Venne a Mileto. *Gl'Id.*, p. 186.
Pagnini. Venne in Mileto. *Poet. Gr.*, p. 870.
6.338.   [Not in *Plan.*] Theocritus, *Inscr.* 10.
Salvini. Questo a voi, Dee. *Teoc.*, p. 186.
Regolotto. Questo di terso e ben. *Teoc.*, p. 264.
Della Torre. Dive, che nove siete. *Ode*, p. 369.
Vicini. A te, de la Dee. *Gl'Id.*, p. 189.
Pagnini. Questo a voi tutte. *Poet. Gr.*, p. 871.
6.339.   [Not in *Plan.*] Theocritus, *Inscr.* 12.
Salvini. Provveditor di cori. *Teoc.*, p. 187.
Regolotti. Demotele, quel conte. *Teoc.*, p. 265.
Della Torre. Di bande danzatrici. *Ode*, p. 370.
Vicini. Il reggitor Demotele. *Gl'Id.*, p. 187.
Pagnini. Questo tripode, O Bacco. *Poet. Gr.*, p. 871.
6.340.   Theocritus, *Inscr.* 13.
Sabeo. Prospera res fuit [vv. 3–6]. *Epig.*, p. 119.
Giraldi (L.G.) quotes the epig. and gives prose tr. *Op.* 1. 374.
Salvini. Venere, ma non la volgar. *Teoc.*, p. 187.
Regolotti. La Venere che miri. *Teoc.*, p. 265.
Della Torre. Non è già questa. *Ode*, p. 371.
Vicini. Questa Vener è ben. *Gl'Id.*, p. 187.
Pagnini. Questa Vener non è. *Poet. Gr.*, p. 871.
6.341.   [Not in *Plan.*] Quoted by Herodotus (4. 88); and in *Chron. Simeonis* (Mueller, *G. G. Min.* 2. 43).
Valla. Qui rati pistosum coniunxit. Herod., f. 108vo.
6.343.   [Not in *Plan.*] Quoted by Herodotus (5. 77), and by Diodorus (10. 24); and a *frg.* found as an inscription (Kaibel 748).
Valla. Attica perdomitis aeri. Herod., f. 160[ro].
6.352.   Pagnini. Questo egregio lavor. *Epig.*, p. 123.

Book VII

7.1.   Anselmo. Implicito, heroum vatem. *Epig.*, p. Biiii.
Sabeo. Cantorem heroum. *Epig.*, p. 364.
Angrisani. Abstulit heroum cantorem. Gronov., *Thes.* 10. 1800.
Fioretti. Heroum cantorem [L-prose]. *Prog.* 3. 204.
7.2.   Lucido. Flexanimum, Musisque. Gronov., *Thes.* 10. 1801.
7.3·   Occurs in *Contest of Homer and Hesiod* 326; quoted by Suidas, *s.v.* Ὅμηρος ὁ ποιητής; in *Vita Homeri* (West., p. 31; cf. Preger, p. 24); quoted by Tzetzes, *Exeg. in Iliad.* (Herm., p. 37).
Guarino da Verona. Conditur hoc tumulo. Soter[2], p. 232; Corn., p. 291.
Codro Urceo quotes the epig, without tr. *Op.*, p. 177.
Winshemius. Hic sacrum terra caput. Soter[2], p. 232; Corn., p. 291.
Sabeo. Terra caput sacrum. *Epig.*, p. 367.
Sabeo. Sacrati capitis. *Epig.*, p. 348.

Sabeo. Nominis aeterno vatem. *Epig.*, p. 232.
Giraldi (L.G.). Sacrum hic terra caput. *Op.* 2. 69.
Allacci. Condit humus caput. Gronov., *Thes.* 10. 1798.
Barberio. Quotes Giraldi and Allacci. Gronov., *Thes.* 10. 819.

7.4.   Sabeo. Pieridum os sacrum. *Epig.*, p. 202.
Allacci. Hic os Pieridum, divus. Gronov., *Thes.* 10. 1801.
Crasso. Hic Pieridum sapiens [L-prose]. *Ist.*, p. 378.
Cunich. Pieridum sacer interpres. *Anth.*, p. 126.
Felici. Qui, saggio interprete. *Epig.*[1], p. 80.
Passeroni. Il sacerdote delle Muse. *Rime* 3. 251.

7.5.   Known to Ciriaco and to Filelfo (above, pp. 94 and 96).
Sabeo. Non si me ex auro. *Epig.*, p. 203.
Allacci quotes the epig. with Sabeo's tr. Gronov., *Thes.* 10.
1831.

7.6.   Cf. Kaibel 1084a.
Sabeo. Qui tuba virtuti. *Epig.*, p. 202.
Orsini sends a copy of inscr. to Agustín (above, p. 246, n. 3).
Fioretti refers to this epig., *Prog.* 3. 204.
Crasso. Heroum praeconem virtutis [L-prose]. *Ist.*, p. 378.
Rivautella-Ricolvi. Praeconem heroum. *Mar.* 1. 180.
Pagnini. Il banditor de' valorosi. *Epig.*, p. 93.

7.7.   Cornarius. Hic situs est divus. Corn., p. 291.
Allacci. Hellada divinum, qui. Gronov., *Thes.* 10. 1739.

7.8.   Cf. Ovid Quid pater Ismario. *Am.* 3. 9. 21–2.
Sleidan. Non quercus, non saxa. Soter[2], p. 233; Corn., p. 291.
Cornarius. Demulsas quercus non. Corn., p. 292.
Obsopoeus. Non ultra quercus. Obsop., p. 448; Wech., p. 389.
Conti. Non quercus, non saxa *Myth.* 7. 14.
Sabeo. Non mage saxa trahes. *Epig.*, p. 203.
Sabeo. Robora, nec petras. *Epig.*, p. 202; *C.P.It.* 8. 202.
Crasso. Non adhuc delinitas [L-prose]. *Ist.*, p. 385.
Rivautella-Ricolvi. Iam neque tu plantas. *Mar.* 1. 117.
Cunich. Orpheu, non silvas. *Anth.*, p. 136.
Felici. Non più selve, e sassi. *Epig.*[1], p. 14.

7.9.   Giraldi (L.G.). Quique sacros ritus. [lines 5–6]. *Op.* 2. 54.
Sabeo. Orphea Thraicii. *Epig.*, p. 390.
Crasso. Orphea Thraciis in iugis [L-prose]. *Ist.*, p. 383.
Averani. Orphea Threiicii tumulatum. *Op.* 1. 186.
Rivautella-Ricolvi. Calliope natum musa. *Mar.* 1. 117.
Cunich. Orphea Threicii nemoroso. *Anth.*, p. 101.

7.10. Crasso. Calliopes Orphea [L-prose]. *Ist.*, p. 385.
Rivautella-Ricolvi. Calliopes atque Œagri. *Mar.* 1. 118.
Cunich. Calliopes prolem atque. *Anth.*, p. 129.
Passeroni. D'Orfeo la morte. *Rime* 3. 86.

7.11. Sabeo. Dulce opus Erinae. *Epig.*, p. 358.
Sabeo. Dulcior Erines labor. *Epig.*, p. 339.
Crasso. Dulcis Erinnae hic labor [L-prose]. *Ist.*, p. 194.

7.12. Cunich. Nuper, suavidico vernos. *Anth.*, p. 130.

Passeroni. Qui giace Erinna. *Rime* 3. 116.
Passeroni. Mentre in Pindo tu cogli. *Rime* 3. 217.

7.13.   Sabeo. Virgo recens vates. *Epig.*, p. 362.
Crasso. Virginem iuvenem [L-prose] *Ist.*, p. 194.
Cunich. More apis eximios. *Anth.*, p. 143.
Felici. Erinna tenera. *Epig.*[1], p. 49.

7.15.   Anon. Blandus Amor docuit. See above, p. 94.
Ciriaco. Tanto ego carminibus. See above, p. 94.
Sabeo. Cantantes tam vinco. *Epig.*, p. 757.
Sabeo. Nomine sum Sapho. *Epig.*, p. 204.
Sabeo. Sic ego foemineum. *Epig.*, p. 204.
Castelvetro quotes this epigram. *Petr.*, p. 231.
Salvini. Femineos cantus superavi. Doni, *Inscr.* 8. 91; Bonada
    1. 410; *Ant. Ercol.* 5. 132.
Carcani (P.). Saffo è il mio nome. *Ant. Ercol.* 5. 132.
Cunich. Sappho ego foemineum. *Anth.*, p. 9.
Passeroni. Cede ogni donna a me. *Rime* 3. 32.
Pagnini. Saffo è il mio nome. *Epig.*, p. 126.

7.16.   Sabeo. Ossa tenes Sapho. *Epig.*, p. 373.
Sabeo. Muta es sub tumulo. *Epig.*, p. 362.
Sabeo. Muta et surda iaces. *Epig.*, p. 340.
Cunich. Ossa quidem et nomen. *Anth.*, p. 124.
Felici. Questa marmorea. *Epig.*[1], p. 84.
Passeroni. Di Saffo chiuse qui son. *Rime* 3. 246.

7.17.   Sabeo. Iuxta urnam Aeoliam. *Epig.*, p. 340.
Crasso. Æolicum ad tumulum [L-prose]. *Ist.*, p. 449.

7.18.   Obsopoeus. Marmore ne pensato. Wech., p. 398.
Sabeo. Non hominem in saxo. *Epig.*, p. 390.
Crasso. Virum non ex lapide. [L-prose]. *Ist.*, p. 20.

7.19.   Sabeo. Elandum Hymenaee tuum. *Epig.*, p. 225.
Crasso. Gratiosum Alcmanem. [L-prose]. *Ist.*, p. 20.

7.20.   Sabeo. Flos extincte iaces. *Epig.*, p. 248.
Crasso. Extinctus es senex. [L-prose]. *Ist.*, p. 472.

7.22.   Sabeo. Sensim hedera adserpas. *Epig.*, p. 248.
Sabeo. Quis ne Sophocleum. *Epig.*, p. 248.
Crasso. Tacite super tumulum. [L-prose]. *Ist.*, p. 472.
Cunich. Ite Sophocleum placide. *Anth.*, p. 126.
Vargas. Tacita sulla tomba. *Sag.*, p. 64.

7.23.   Obsopoeus. Florescant hederae, Anacreon. Obsop., p. 458;
    Wech., p. 399.
Sabeo. Floreat asserpens tumulo. *Epig.*, p. 226.
Cf. Guazzo. Nè rose, nè amaranti. *Dial.* f. 124ro.
Felici. Di bei corimbi carica. *Epig.*[1], p. 16.
Vargas. Mista ai corimbi intorno. *Sag.*, p. 63.

7.23.7–8. [Sometimes taken as a separate epig.]
Sabeo. Quod dilecta fuit. *Epig.*, p. 453.
Sabeo. Quod tibi dulcis. *Epig.*, p. 360.
Sabeo. Et recinens et amans. *Epig.*, p. 234.

Sabeo. Tu cantu et sonitu. *Epig.*, p. 234.

7.24. Cf. Calcagnini. At te, sancte senex. Giraldi, *Op.* 2. 341; *C.P.It.* 3. 105.
Barberio quotes Calcagnini's imitation. Gronov., *Thes.* 10. 837.

7.25. Sabeo. Marmor amatorem puerorum. *Epig.*, p. 233.
Crasso. Hic Anacreontem [L-prose]. *Ist.*, p. 30.

7.27. Sabeo. Cum superis sis gloria. *Epig.*, p. 257.

7.28. Sabeo. Hospes, in hoc tumulo. *Epig.*, p. 367.

7.29. Sabeo. Gesseris ut bene te. *Epig.*, p. 338.

7.30. Sabeo. Talis olor saxo tumulatur. *Epig.*, p. 322.
Crasso. Tumulus Anacreontis [L-prose]. *Ist.*, p. 30.

7.32. Anon. Saepius hoc dixi. Soter[2], p. 233; Corn., p. 293.
Cornarius. Saepe quidem cecini. Corn., p. 293.
Obsopoeus. Saepius hoc monui. Obsop., p. 462; Wech., p. 402.
Sabeo. Saepe quidem dixi. *Epig.*, p. 220.
Sabeo. Si prius hoc dixi. *Epig.*, p. 338.

7.33. Cornarius. Plurima quum potasset. Corn., p. 294.
Cf. Alamanni. Disse l'ebro Azerol. *Versi* 2. 136.
Sabeo. Potu es Anacreon. *Epig.*, p. 356.
Sabeo. Multa bibens te. *Epig.*, p. 368.
Bongiovanni and Zanetti. Poichè tanto beesti. *Epig.*, p. 1.

7.34. Fioretti. Piericam cytharam [L-prose]. *Prog.* 3. 310.
Crasso. Piericam citharam [L-prose]. *Ist.*, p. 415.

7.35. Fioretti. Pindarus benesonantium [L-prose]. *Prog.* 3. 310.
Crasso. Benevolus fuit hospitibus [L-prose]. *Ist.*, p. 415.

7.36. Sabeo. Scaenales hederae. *Epig.*, p. 233.

7.39. Plutarch quotes lines 3–4. *Moral.* 604E.
Fioretti. Qui tragicum cantum [prose]. *Prog.* 4. 164.
Crasso. Qui tragicam et super [L-prose]. *Ist.*, p. 200.
Crasso [from Plut.]. Æschylus Euphor. *Ist.*, p. 200.
Barberio [from Plut.]. Æschylus Euphor. Gronov., *Thes.* 10. 834.
Cunich. Eximio tragicam primus. *Anth.*, p. 111.
Passeroni. Eschilo, che innalzo. *Rime* 3. 78.

7.40. Cunich. Æschylon hoc marmor. *Anth.*, p. 103.

7.41. Crasso. O beate ambrosiis. [L-prose]. *Ist.*, p. 98.

7.42. Crasso. O magnum Battiadae [L-prose]. *Ist.*, p. 98.

7.43. Sabeo. Valle vale, Euripides. *Epig.*, p. 330.

7.44. Sabeo. Te licet, Euripides. *Epig.*, p. 306.
Barnes (J.). Dira licet tibi mors. Bonada 1. 412.

7.45. Quoted in *Vita Euripidis* (West., pp. 135, 140).
Giraldi (L.G.). Est momumentum Graecia. *Op.* 2. 268.
Crasso quotes Giraldi's version. *Ist.*, p. 218.
Barnes (J.). Graecia tota quidem. Bonada 1. 413.

7.46. Costanzi (A.). Euripidis tua non. *Epig.* Bii[vo].
Cornarius. Non monumenta tibi. *Corn.*, p. 294.
Cf. Alamanni. Questo marmo, Luisa. *Versi* 2. 143.

Sabeo. Non est, Euripidi. *Epig.*, p. 376.
Sabeo. Non humus Euripiden. *Epig.*, p. 313.
Sabeo. Non haec urna tua. *Epig.*, p. 330; *C.P.It.* 8. 209.
Crasso. Non tuum hoc [L-prose]. *Ist.*, p. 218.
Barnes (J.). Hoc tibi non monumentum. Bonada 1. 413.

7.47. Sabeo. Non ignota iaces. *Epig.*, p. 355.
Barnes (J.). Graecia tota tuum. Bonada 1. 413.

7.49. Sabeo. Terra tegit tumulum. *Epig.*, p. 370.
7.50. Sabeo. Euripidis tentans vates. *Epig.*, p. 339.
7.51. Sabeo. Non muliebre oestrum. *Epig.*, p. 370.
7.52. Sabeo. Hellados ingentis sertum. *Epig.*, p. 337.
7.53. Quoted by Dio of Prusa 2. 11 (Arnim); in the *Contest of Hom. and Hes.* 322; Gellius refers to this epigram, *N.A.* 3. 11. 3; quoted by Proclus, *Vita Hom.* 26. 50 (West., p. 25).
Known to Ciriaco d'Ancona; see above, p. 93.
Codro Urceo. Hesiodus Musis [prose]. *Op.*, p. 207.
Cf. Politian. Ergo et chalcidico. *Nut.* 388; Del Lungo, p. 392.
Giraldi (L.G.). Hesiodus posuit Musis. *Op.* 2. 73.
Sabeo. Hesiodus vobis, Musae. *Epig.*, p. 364.

7.54. Quoted by Pausanias 9. 38. 4; quoted in *Contest of Hom. and Hes.* 323; by Tzetzes, *Vita Hesiod.* (West., p. 49).
Codro Urceo. Hesiodum tuli Ascra. *Op.*, p. 207.
Politian. Ossaque fatali tellus. *Nut.* 395; Del Lungo, p. 393.
Giraldi (L.G.). Fertilis Ascra quidem. *Op.* 2. 75.
Sanchez. Hesiodi patria est. *Op.* 2. 459.
Crasso quotes Sanchez' version. *Ist.*, p. 204.
Barberio quotes Giraldi's version. Gronov., *Thes.* 10. 820.
Pagnini. Tra quanti prova. *Epig.*, p. 91.

7.55. Sabeo. Locridos umbroso. *Epig.*, p. 365.
Crasso. Locridis in nemore [L-prose]. *Ist.*, p. 204.
Cunich. Locridos in nemore. *Anth.*, p. 108.

7.57. Diogenes Laertius, 9.7.
Brugnolo? Dixit opus sapiens. Laert. 9.7; Soter[2], p. 228[2]; Corn., p. 299.
Bentinus. Quisnam tam sapiens. *Laert.*, p. 322; Soter[2], p. 228[2]; Corn., p. 299.
Sabeo. Ecquis eris sapiens. *Epig.*, p. 378.
Sabeo. Ecquis tanta sciens. *Epig.*, p. 320.
Sabeo. Ecquis tam prudens. *Epig.*, p. 306.
Mazzoni. Chi fu mai tanto. *Difesa*, p. 431.

7.58. Sabeo. Contineas quamvis regnum. *Epig.*, p. 242.
Cunich. Persephone, expertes. *Anth.*, p. 165.
Pagnini. Benchè sotterra hai. *Epig.*, p. 87.

7.59. Sabeo. Rex hominum felix. *Epig.*, p. 449.
Cf. Franchini. Asper et immitis. *Epig.*, p. 81.
Felici. Varca Democrito. *Epig.*[1], p. 120.

7.60. Diogenes Laertius 3.43.
Guarino da Verona. Ante alios castus. Soter[2], p. 206.

Brugnolo? Mortales cunctos. Laert.; Soter², p. 206; Corn., p. 246.

Ficino. Temperantia iustitiaque [prose]. *Op.* 1. 770.

Bentinus. Iusticia cunctis. *Laert.*, p. 108; Soter², p. 206; Corn., p. 246.

Sleidan. Hic iacet ille Plato. Soter², p. 206; Corn., p. 246.

Cornarius. Omnes exuperans. Corn., p. 247.

Sabeo. Divus Aristocles. *Epig.*, p. 211.

7.61. Cf. *A.P.* 16.31. Diogenes Laertius 3. 44.

Guarino da Verona. Tellus memora sinu. Soter², p. 235; Corn., p. 296.

Brugnolo? Occulit hic corpus. Laert.; Soter², p. 236; Corn., p. 296.

Ficino. Plato in deorum numerum [prose]. *Op.* 1. 770.

Bentinus. Corpus habet gremio. *Laert.*, p. 108; Soter², p. 236; Corn., p. 296.

Obsopoeus quotes the version of Bentinus. Obsop., p. 486; Wech., p. 417.

Sabeo. Terra suo gremio. *Epig.*, p. 361.

Sabeo. Terra sinu condit. *Epig.*, p. 452.

7.62. Diogenes Laertius 3.44.

Brugnolo? Quid monumenta super. Laert.; Soter², p. 236.

Bentinus. Quid monumenta super. *Laert.*, p. 109; Soter², p. 236.

Obsopoeus quotes Bentinus' version. Obsop., p. 486; Wech., p. 418.

Sabeo. Cur tumulo insistis. *Epig.*, p. 452.

Sabeo. Cur coelum aspiciens. *Epig.*, p. 290 (274).

Sabeo. Cur tumulum et cuius. *Epig.*, p. 308.

Mignault. Cur aquila ad tumulum. Alciati, *Emb.*, 33.

Vargas. Perchè su questa tomba. *Sag.*, p. 38.

Pagnini. Perchè su questa tomba. *Epig.*, p. 115.

7.63. Sabeo. Excipe Diogenem. *Epig.*, p. 314.

7.64. Ausonius. Dic, canis, hic cuius. *Opus.* 6. 28.

Cornarius (p. 299) and Soter² (p. 228) give Ausonius' tr.

Groto. Can, di quel cane. *Rime* (1610), f. 80.

7.66. [In *Plan*, this ep. is divided, each distich forming an ep.]

Ausonius. Pera, polenta, tribon. *Opus.* 6. 29.

Jordanus. Diogenis vitae sap. [vv. 1–2]. Soter³, p. 265.

Jausserandus. Omnia nauclero porto. [vv. 3–4]. Soter³, p. 265.

Sabeo. Quam leve onus vitae. [vv. 1–2]. *Epig.*, p. 487.

Sabeo. Nulla mea in terra. [vv. 3–4]. *Epig.*, p. 345.

Gualfreducci. Cuncta fero ad Styg. [vv. 3–4]. *Var.*, p. 293.

Battista. Scendi al varco. [vv. 3–4]. *Poes. Mel.* 1. 78.

Cunich. Vivitur et parvo *Anth.*, p. 79.

Passeroni. Anche con poco si può. *Rime* 3. 196.

Pagnini. Tutto porto a Caronte [vv. 3–4]. *Epig.*, p. 18.

7.67. Sabeo. Qui ferruginea subvectas. *Epig.*, p. 198.

7.68.   Cornarius. Umbrarum vector lachrymas. *Corn.*, p. 300.
      Sabeo. Umbrarum adventu tu. *Epig.*, p. 349 (351).
      Averani. Qui lacrymis gaudes. *Op.* 1. 213.
7.69.   Cf. Alciati. Archilochi tumulo. *Emb.* 51.
      Jordanus. Cerbere, qui timidis. Soter[3], p. 259.
      Obsopoeus. Cerbere, qui trepidas. Obsop., p. 450; Wech.,
        p. 391.
      Sabeo. Cerbere, terribili qui. *Epig.*, p. 366.
      Crasso. Cerbere, horrendum [L-prose]. *Ist.*, p. 60.
      Cunich. Cerbere, qui magnis. *Anth.*, p. 175.
      Pagnini. Cerbero, che spaventi. *Epig.*, p. 19.
7.70.   Sabeo. Nunc mage quam prius. *Epig.*, p. 348.
      Cunich. Ostia Tartarei, si. *Anth.*, p. 167.
      Passeroni. Cerbero, tu che co'. *Rime* 3. 69.
7.71.   Obsopoeus. Archilochus iacet hoc. Obsop., p. 451; Wech.,
        p. 392.
      Sabeo. Haec urna Archilochi. *Epig.*, p. 366.
      Mignault. Littoreum Archilochi. Alciati, *Emb.* 51.
      Germano. Ne fors crabones [prose, vv. 5–6]. *Giard.*, p. 297.
      Crasso. Archilochi hic tumulus [L-prose]. *Ist.*, p. 60.
      Cunich. Archilochi hoc bustum. *Anth.*, p. 103.
      Felici. Quest' avello al mar. *Epig.*[1], p. 119.
      Passeroni. Giace Archiloco qui. *Rime* 3. 155.
      Bettinelli. Passegero, qui sen giace. *Op.* 22. 98.
      Pagnini. Questa vicina al mar. *Epig.*, p. 20.
7.72.   More (Sir T.). Ista Neoclidae gnatos. Soter[2], p. 208; Corn.,
        p. 251.
      Sabeo. Prole Neoclidae gemina. *Epig.*, p. 383.
      Vargas. Figli di Neocle entrambi. *Sag.*, p. 78.
      Pagnini. Salve, O gemina prole. *Epig.*, p. 121.
7.73.   Alciati. Pro tumulo pone Italiam. Corn., p. 254; *Emb.*, 133.
      Sabeo. Simplice pro tumulo pone. *Epig.*, p. 268.
      Mignault. Marmareo in tumulo. Alciati, *Emb.* 133.
      Sanchez. Pro tumulo exiguo. *Op.* 3. 259 (*Emb.* 133).
      Averani. Pone sepulcrali pro. *Op.* 1. 80.
      Bongiovanni and Zanetti. Di augusto avello. *Epig.*, p. 10.
      'L-prose.' Pro sepulcri lapide. Ἐπ. καὶ Ἐλεγ. No. 64.
      Cunich. Victrix pro tumulo. *Anth.*, p. 117.
      Medici (A. de'). Graecia funereo pro. *Scelt.*, p. 1.
      Medici (A. de'). Poni grecia per urna. *Scelt.*, p. 1.
7.74.   Sabeo. Turba Themistocli. *Epig.*, p. 267.
7.75.   Sabeo. Stersicorum [*sic*] eximium. *Epig.*, p. 343.
      Crasso. Stesichorum valde [L-prose]. *Ist.*, p. 488.
7.76.   Sabeo. Extrema includis tu. *Epig.*, p. 217.
      Sabeo. Naufragium metuens. *Epig.*, p. 217.
      Sabeo. Infidum expertus pontum. *Epig.*, p. 723.
      Sabeo. Qui mare velivolum. *Epig.*, p. 797.
      Medici (A. de'). Olim mercator, patrii. *Scelt.*, p. xl.

Medici (A. de'). Stanco del mar Timocrito. *Scelt.*, p. xl.

7.77. [Not in *Plan.*] Quoted by *schol.* on Aristides, *Milt.* 265C (p. 201 Frommel); Tzetzes, *Chil.* 1. 632–3.
Published from *Cod. Pal.* by Allacci, *De Sym.*, p. 214.

7.78. Sabeo. Non te ater morbus. *Epig.*, p. 345.

7.80. Given by Diogenes Laertius 9. 1 (Heraclitus); with lines 5–6 cf. Kaibel 618a, 9–10.
Cf. Virgil. Cantando puerum memini. *Eclog.* 9. 52.
Cf. Ovid. Utque solebamus consumere. *Trist.* 5. 13. 17.
Cf. Persius. Tecum etiam longos memini. *Sat.* 5. 41
Brugnolo? Heraclite mihi quidam Laert.; Soter², p. 240; Corn., p. 314.
Bentinus. Heraclite mihi quidam. *Laert.*, p. 313: Soter², p. 240; Corn., p. 314.
Sabeo. Detulit, Heraclete, tuum. *Epig.*, p. 199.
Giraldi (L. G.). Dixerat, Heraclete, mihi. *Op.* 2. 127.
Crasso. Quotes Bentinus' tr. *Ist.*, p. 190.
Cunich. Heraclite, tua est mihi. *Anth.*, p. 141.
Passeroni. Eraclito mio sorzio. *Rime* 3. 87.
Pagnini. Quando di te narrato. *Epig.*, p. 169.

7.81. Cf. Archithrenius. Cleobolus Lycios. Soter², p. 137.

7.83. Given by Diogenes Laertius 1. 1 (Thales).
Brugnolo? Hunc quae nutrivit. Laert.; Soter², p. 228²; Corn., p. 300.
Bentinus. Hunc quae nutrivit. *Laert.*, p. 12; Soter², p. 228²; Corn., p. 300.
Sabeo. Terra Thaletem habuit. *Epig.*, p. 346.
Sabeo. Tempore qui astrologos. *Epig.*, p. 355.

7.84. Given by Diogenes Laertius 1. 1 (Thales).
Brugnolo? Nempe hic exiguus. Laert.; Soter², p. 229²; Corn., p. 301.
Bentinus. Nempe hic exiguus. *Laert.*, p. 14.
Sabeo. Terra humili tectum. *Epig.*, p. 497.

7.85. Given by Diogenes Laertius 1. 1 (Thales).
Brugnolo? Gymnicon aspiceret cum. Laert.; Soter², p. 229²; Corn., p. 301.
Beroaldo (elder) quotes tr. from Brugnolo. *Var. Op.* f. xiivᵒ.
Bentinus. Gymnicon aspiceret cum. *Laert.*, p. 13.
Sabeo. Iuppiter e stadio. *Epig.*, p. 273.

7.86. [Not in *Plan.*] Given by Diogenes Laertius 1. 2 (Solon).
Brugnolo? Quae dudum rabidas. Laert.
Arsenios quotes this epigram. *Paroem.*, p. 446.
Beroaldo (elder) quotes tr. from Brugnolo. *Var. Op.*, f. xiirᵒ.
Bentinus. Quae dudum insanas. *Laert.*, p. 22.

7.87. [Not in *Plan.*] Given by Diogenes Laertius 1. 2 (Solon).
Brugnolo? Cypria defunctum cremavit. Laert.
Beroaldo (elder) quotes tr. from Brugnolo. *Var. Op.*, f. xiirᵒ.
Bentinus. Cypria defunctum substraxit. *Laert.*, p. 21.

7.88. [Not in *Plan.*] Diogenes Laertius 1. 4 (Chilon).
Brugnolo? Phosfore reddatur polux. Laert.
Beroaldo (elder) quotes tr. from Brugnolo. *Var. Op.*, f. xii^{vo}.
Bentinus. Phosphore reddatur Pollux. *Laert.*, p. 26.

7.89. Given by Diogenes Laertius 1. 4 (Pittacus).
Brugnolo? Hospes Atarnites rogitavit. Laert.; Soter^2, p. 229^2;
Corn., p. 302.
Arsenios quotes this epigram. *Paroem.*, p. 675.
Bentinus. Nuper Atarnaeus rogitavit. *Laert.*, p. 29; Soter^2,
p. 229^2; Corn., p. 302.
Alciati. Pittace me vinclis. Corn., p. 303.
Sabeo. His Mithyleneus. *Epig.*, p. 273.
Crasso. Hospes Atarnita [L-prose]. *Ist.*, p. 418.
Pagnini. Un giovine Atarneo. *Epig.*, p. 114.

7.90. Given by Diogenes Laertius 1. 5 (Bias); by 'Eudocia', *Viol.* 94.
Brugnolo? Petra Prienaeum tegit. Laert.; Soter^2, p. 231^2;
Corn., p. 303.
Beroaldo (elder) quotes tr. from Brugnolo. *Var. Op.*, f. xii^{vo}.
Bentinus. Petra Prienaeum tegit. *Laert.*, p. 31; Soter^2, p. 231^2;
Corn., p. 304.
Sabeo. Terra Prienaeum tegit. *Epig.*, pp. 273, 376.

7.91. Given by Diogenes Laertius 1. 5 (Bias).
Brugnolo? Petra Bianta tegit. Laert.; Soter^2, p. 231^2; Corn.,
Corn., p. 304.
Beroaldo (elder) quotes tr. from Brugnolo. *Var. Op.*, f. xii^{vo}.
Bentinus. Hic situs est Bias. *Laert.*, p. 32; Soter^2, p. 231^2;
Corn., p. 304.
Sabeo. Quae sensim infernas. *Epig.*, p. 314.

7.92. Given by Diogenes Laertius 1. 8 (Anacharsis).
Brugnolo? Suadebat Scythicas errans. Laert.; Soter^2, p. 232^2;
Corn., p. 305.
Bentinus. In Scythiam patrias. *Laert.*, p. 39; Soter^2, p. 232^2;
Corn., p. 305.
Sabeo. Venit ut in Scythian. *Epig.*, p. 272.
Barberio quotes Bentinus' tr. Gronov., *Thes.* 10. 822.
Crasso quotes Bentinus' tr. *Ist.*, p. 28.

7.93. [Not in *Plan.*] Diogenes Laertius 1. 11 (Pherecydes).
Bentinus. Desinit in me omnis. *Laert.*, p. 45.

7.94. [Not in *Plan.*] Diogenes Laertius 2. 3 (Anaxagoras); Aelian,
V.H. 8. 19.

7.95. [Not in *Plan.*] Diogenes Laertius 2. 3 (Anaxagoras); Cedrenus,
Hist. 1. 278 (Bekker).

7.96. [Not in *Plan.*] Diogenes Laertius 2. 5 (Socrates).
Brugnolo? Nunc bibe nam vere. Laert.
Bentinus. Nunc bibe apud superos. *Laert.*, p. 62.

7.97. [Not in *Plan.*] Diogenes Laertius 2. 6 (Xenophon).
Brugnolo? Non solum ad Persas. Laert.
Bentinus. Non tantum ad Persas. *Laert.*, p. 66.

7.98. [Not in *Plan*.] Diogenes Laertius 2. 6 (Xenophon).

7.99. Diogenes Laertius 3. 30; v. 6 is quoted by Apuleius, *Apol.* 10.
Apuleius. Civibus ingenti. *Apol.* 10.
Bentinus. Et lachrymas Hecubae. *Laert.*, p. 104; Soter[2],
p. 233[2]; Corn., p. 305.
Sabeo. Laomedontiadis nuribus. *Epig.*, p. 272.

7.100. Diogenes Laertius 3. 31.
Cf. Ovid. Et merito. Quid enim. *Am.* 3. 12. 9.
Apuleius quotes this epig. *Apol.* 10.
Apuleius? Dixerit hic tantum. *Apol.* 10.
Brugnolo? Nunc quoniam nihil. Laert.; Soter[2], p. 241; Corn.,
p. 315.
Bentinus. Nunc quoniam nihil est. *Laert.*, p. 104; Soter[2],
p. 241; Corn., p. 315.

7.101. [Not in *Plan*.] Diogenes Laertius 4. 1 (Speusippus).

7.102. [Not in *Plan*.] Diogenes Laertius 4. 2 (Xenocrates).
Brugnolo? Vas ubi Xenocrates non. Laert.
Bentinus. In pelvim quondam lapsus. *Laert.*, p. 132.

7.103. [Not in *Plan*.] Diogenes Laertius 4. 4 (Crates).
Bentinus. Noc Polemona situm. *Laert.*, p. 135.

7.104. [Not in *Plan*.] Diogenes Laertius 4. 6 (Arcesilaus).
Arsenios quotes this epig. *Viol.*, p. 119.
Crasso? Arcesilae meri. *Ist.*, p. 55.

7.105. [Not in *Plan*.] Diogenes Laertius 4. 8 (Lacydes).
Brugnolo? Fama tui, Lacyde. Laert.
Bentinus. Fama est, Lacyde. *Laert.*, p. 149.

7.106. [Not in *Plan*.] Diogenes Laertius 10. 16 (Epicurus); Hesy-
chius Mil. (Mueller, *F.H.G.* 4. 164).
Brugnolo? Hoc moriens caris. Laert.
Bentinus. Hoc moriens charis. *Laert.*, p. 351.

7.107. [Not in *Plan*.] Given, with slight changes, by Diogenes Laert.
5. 1 (Aristotle).
Crasso? Nuper Aristotelem. *Ist.*, p. 74.

7.108. Cf. *A.P.* 7. 109. Diogenes Laertius 3. 45.
Brugnolo? En animas hominum. Laert.; Soter[2], p. 227[2]; Corn.,
p. 297.
Ficino. Phoebus Aesculapium [prose]. *Op.* 1. 770.
Bentinus. Ni doctum Graecis. *Laert.*, p. 109; Soter[2], p. 227[2];
Corn., p. 297.
Sabeo. Arte animas hominum. *Epig.*, p. 346.
Obsopoeus quotes Bentinus' tr. Obsop., p. 486; Wech., p. 418.
Pagnini. A te, Esculapio. *Epig.*, p. 47.

7.109. Cf. 108. Diogenes Laertius 3. 45. cf. Olympiodorus, *Vita
Plat.* (Westermann, p. 388).
Quoted by Bessarion. *In Cal Plat.* 4. 2.
Bessarion? Sol genuit terris. *In Cal. Plat.* 4. 2.
Brugnolo? Accidit ut Titan. Laert.; Soter[2], p. 227[2]; Corn.,
p. 298.

Bentinus. Produxit nobis Ascelpion. *Laert.*, p. 109; Soter[2], p. 227[2]; Corn., p. 298.

Valeriano. Produxit Aesculapium. *Poem.*, p. 115; *C.P. It.* 10. 165.

Obsopoeus quotes Bentinus' tr. Obsop., p. 487; Wech., p. 418.

Sabeo. Immisit terris. *Epig.*, p. 305.

Cunich. Phoebus te, Asclepi. *Anth.*, p. 33.

Passeroni. Febo fu d'Esculapio. *Rime* 3. 255.

Bettinelli. Da Febo fu Esculapio. *Op.* 22. 97.

7.110. Diogenes Laertius 5. 2 (Theophrastus).

Brugnolo? Non arcum frangi. Laert.; Soter[2], p. 233[2]; Corn., p. 306.

Bentinus. Haud vane quidam. *Laert.*, p. 166; Soter[2], p. 233[2]; Corn., p. 306.

Erasmus. Ni foret intentus. Soter[2], p. 233[2]; Corn., p. 306.

Sabeo. Ille, ut ait, verum. *Epig.*, p. 290 (274).

Sabeo. Non igitur vanum. *Epig.*, p. 368.

7.111. [Not in *Plan.*] Diogenes Laertius 5. 3 (Strato.).

Brugnolo? Corpus erat tenuis. Laert.

Bentinus. Corpus erat tenuis. *Laert.*, p. 174.

7.112. Diogenes Laertius 5. 4 (Lyco).

Brugnolo? Praetereunda mihi non sunt. Laert.; Soter[2], p. 214; Corn., p. 260.

Bentinus. Praetereunda mihi non sunt. *Laert.*, p. 175.

Bongiovanni and Zanetti. Nè già Licon. *Epig.*, p. 36.

7.113. [Not in *Plan.*] Diogenes Laertius 5. 5 (Demetrius).

7.114. Diogenes Laertius 5. 6 (Heraclides).

Brugnolo? Clarus Heraclide voluisti. Laert.; Soter[2], p. 234[2]; Corn., p. 306.

Bentinus. Mirum Heraclides quid. *Laert.*, p. 181; Soter[2], p. 234[2]; Corn., p. 307.

Sabeo. Famam, Heraclide, tentasti. *Epig.*, p. 303.

Crasso quotes Bentinus' tr. *Ist.*, p. 188.

7.115. [Not in *Plan.*] Diogenes Laertius 6. 1 (Antisthenes); Hesychius Mil. (Mueller, *F.G.H.* 4. 158).

Brugnolo? Est tibi vita canis. Laert.

Bentinus. In vita canis acer. *Laert.*, p. 188.

Salvini. Antistene, in tua vita. *Disc.* (1733), p. 187.

7.116. [Not in *Plan.*] Diogenes Laertius 6. 2 (Diogenes); Zonares, *s.v.* ἄγε (ed. Tittmann 1. 35); Suidas, *s.v.* ἄγε.

Brugnolo? Diogenes age loquere. Laert.

Bentinus. Diogenes age loquere. *Laert.*, p. 206.

Crasso. Diogenes, age [prose]. *Ist.*, p. 159.

Salvini. Via dite, Diogene. *Disc.* (1733), p. 214.

7.117. Given by Diogenes Laertius 7. 1 (Zeno).

7.118. [Not in *Plan.*] Diogenes Laertius 7. 1 (Zeno).

Bentinus. Cittensem varie extinctum. *Laert.*, p. 226.

7.119. Quoted by Plutarch, *Moral.* 1094B; Athenaeus 10. 418F;
Diogenes Laertius 8. 1 (Pythag.).
Bentinus. Pythagoras quondam diis. *Laert.*, p. 281; Soter[2],
p. 138; Corn., p. 136.
Sabeo. Litteram ut e coelo. *Epig.*, p. 387.

7.120. Diogenes Laertius 8. 1 (Pythagoras); Suidas, *s.v.* Ξενοφάνης.
Bentinus. Qui catulum duro miseratus. *Laert.*, p. 288; Soter[2],
p. 138.
Sabeo. Praeterit utque canem. *Epig.*, p. 387.
Cf. Loredano. Pitagora quì giaccio. *Cimit.* 3. 26.

7.121. Diogenes Laertius 8. 1 (Pythagoras).
Brugnolo? Non refugis solus. Laert.; Soter[2], p. 234[2]; Corn.,
p. 307.
Bentinus. Haud quaquam solus. *Laert.*, p. 291; Soter[2], p. 234[2];
Corn., p. 307.
Sabeo. Non animata unus. *Epig.*, p. 303.
Patavinus gives Bentinus' tr. *De Art.*, p. 236.

7.122. Diogenes Laertius 8. 1 (Pythag.).
Brugnolo? Heu, Heu, quid. Laert.; Soter[2], p. 235[2]; Corn.,
p. 308.
Bentinus. Heu, Heu, Pythagoras. *Laert.*, p. 291; Soter[2],
p. 235[2]; Corn., p. 308.
Giovane quotes Bentinus' tr. *Ant. Tar.* 3. 3.
Crasso quotes Bentinus' tr. *Ist.*, p. 423.

7.123. Diogenes Laertius 8.2 (Empedocles).
Brugnolo? Empedocles rapida purgasti. Laert.; Soter[2],
p. 235[2]; Corn., p. 308.
Bentinus. Empedocles rapida purgasti. *Laert.*, p. 301; Soter[2],
p. 235[2]; Corn., p. 308.
Sabeo. Tu quoque iam, Empedocles. *Epig.*, p. 271.

7.124. Diogenes Laertius. 8. 2 (Empedocles).
Brugnolo? Cruribus Empedocles confractis. Laert.; Soter[2],
p. 236[2]; Corn., p. 309.
Bentinus. Cruribus Empedocles collisis. *Laert.*, p. 301; Soter[2],
p. 236[2]; Corn., p. 309.
Sabeo. Empedoclem curru fama. *Epig.*, p. 272.

7.125. Diogenes Laertius 8. 3 (Epicharmus).
Brugnolo? Quam superat Phaeton. Laert.; Soter[2], p. 236[2];
Corn., p. 309.
Bentinus. Quantum sol vincit. *Laert.*, p. 302; Soter[2], p. 236[2];
Corn., p. 310.
Sabeo. Quam Phaetontis equi. *Epig.*, p. 200.
Crasso. Quantum superat [L-prose]. *Ist.*, p. 185.

7.126. Diogenes Laertius 8. 7 (Philolaus); Suidas, *s.v.* ὑπόνοια.
Brugnolo? Suspitio dico cuncti. Laert.; Soter[2], p. 237[2]; Corn.,
p. 310.
Bentinus. Suspitio haud res est. *Laert.*, p. 305; Soter[2], p. 237[2];
Corn., p. 310.

More (Sir T.). Magnam habet in rebus. Soter², p. 237²; Corn.,
p. 310.
Sabeo. Credulitas cura est. *Epig.*, p. 199.
Crasso quotes Bentinus' tr. *Ist.*, p. 238.

7.127. Diogenes Laertius 9. 1 (Heraclitus); Hesychius Mil. (Mueller,
F.H.G. 4. 165).
Brugnolo? Saepe ego miratus. Laert.; Soter², p. 238; Corn.,
p. 311.
Bentinus. Mecum ego Heraclitum. *Laert.*, p. 309; Soter²,
p. 238; Corn., p. 311.
Sabeo. Heraclete, tuos quum. *Epig.*, p. 315.
Sabeo. Heraclete, miser sic. *Epig.*, p. 287 (275).
Sabeo. Heraclete, tuum quum. *Epig.*, p. 315.
Crasso quotes Bentinus' tr. *Ist.*, p. 190.

7.128. Cf. Cicero. εἰς ἐμοὶ μύριοι. ad *Att.* 16. 11. 1.
Diogenes Laertius 9. 1 (Heraclitus); Hesychius Mil. (Mueller,
F.H.G. 4. 166).
Brugnolo? Heracletus ego, quid. Laert.; Soter², p. 238; Corn.,
p. 311.
Bentinus. Sum Heraclitus ego. *Laert.*, p. 311; Soter², p. 238;
Corn., p. 311.
Sabeo. Heracletus ego. *Epig.*, p. 393.
Cunich. Heraclitus ego, quid me. *Anth.*, p. 10.
Passeroni. Sono Eraclito, ignavi. *Rime* 3. 158.

7.129. Diogenes Laertius 9. 5 (Zeno Eleat.).
Brugnolo? Tu bona quaesisti. Laert.; Soter², p. 239; Corn.,
p. 312.
Bentinus. Fortiter extincto. *Laert.*, p. 317; Soter², p. 239;
Corn., p. 312.
Sabeo. Tentasti, o Zeno. *Epig.*, p. 450.

7.130. Diogenes Laertius 9. 8 (Protagoras).
Brugnolo? Te quoque Protagoram. Laert.; Soter², p. 239;
Corn., p. 312.
Bentinus. Te quoque Protagoram. *Laert.*, p. 327; Soter²,
p. 239; Corn., p. 313.
Sabeo. Protagora, et de te. *Epig.*, p. 304.

7.133. [Not in *Plan.*] Diogenes Laertius 9. 8 (Anaxarchus).
Brugnolo? Tundite, Necrocreon, caella. Laert.
Bentinus. Contrahite in rugas. *Laert.*, p. 328.

7.134. Sabeo. Gorgiae Cynici. *Epig.*, p. 304.

7.135. More (Sir T.). Thessalus Hippocrates. Soter², p. 229; Corn.,
p. 281.
Cornarius. Hic iacet Hippocrates. Corn., p. 281.
Sabeo. Qui tot perdomuit. *Epig.*, p. 201.
Sabeo. Thessalus Hippocrates. *Epig.*, p. 243.

7.136. Costanzi (A.). Herois Priami tumulus. *Epig.*, Biiᵛᵒ.
Jordanus. Tumba brevis Priami. Soter³, p. 253.
Sabeo. Non quod si parva. *Epig.*, p. 167.

Cunich. Hic Priami tumulus. *Anth.*, p. 111.
Passeroni. Di Priamo per disgrazie. *Rime* 3. 140.
Passeroni. Di Priamo ecco il sepolcro. *Rime* 3. 78.
Felici. Vedi quel tumolo. *Epig.*[2], p. viii.
Pagnini. Questa, non quale. *Epig.*, p. 143.
7.137. Cornarius. Hectora quid tumulo. Corn., p. 281.
Sabeo. Hectora ne confer. *Epig.*, p. 255.
Scaliger (J. C.). Ne tenui ingentem. *Poem.* 1. 289.
7.138. Jordanus. Semper Homeri. Soter[3], p. 253.
Obsopoeus. Hector Maeoniis semper. Obsop., p. 398; Wech., p. 346.
Sabeo. Hector Homeriaco semper. *Epig.*, p. 346.
7.139. Ausonius. Hectoris hic tumulus. *Opus.* 6. 14.
Possevini (G. B.). Troia con Hettor. *Honor.*, p. 213.
Sabeo. Hectore cum forti. *Epig.*, p. 252.
Cunich. Hectore cum magno. *Anth.*, p. 22.
Felici. Cadde al suol la rocca. *Epig.*[1], p. 117.
Pagnini. Con Ettore fini di Troja. *Epig.*, p. 8.
7.140. Sabeo. Istius patrem nomenque. *Epig.*, p. 242.
Cunich. Dic nomen, patrem. *Anth.*, p. 112.
Pagnini. Mio nome, il genitor. *Epig.*, p. 156.
7.141. Sabeo. Thessale, te extollent. *Epig.*, p. 260.
7.142. Sabeo. Magnanimo Aeacidae. *Epig.*, p. 169.
Mignault. Hic positus Graiis. Alciati, *Emb.* 35.
Crasso. Tumulus Achillis [L-prose]. *Ist.*, p. 6.
Pompei. La tomba è questo. *Op.* 2. 219.
Pagnini. Questa è la tomba. *Epig.*, p. 21.
7.143. Sleidan. Insignes pietate, simul. Soter[2], p. 228; Corn., p. 278.
Sabeo. O vos praestantes. *Epig.*, p. 260.
7.144. [Not in *Plan.*]
Ausonius. Hoc tegor in tumulo. *Opus.* 6. 8.
7.145. Cf. 146. In 'Aristotle', *Peplus* 7; Athenaeus, 4.163A, quotes a manipulation of this epigram; Eustathius, *ad. Il.* B 557.
Ausonius. Aiacis tumulo pariter. *Opus.* 6. 3.
Velius. Dilaniata comas, visu. Soter[2], p. 228; Corn., p. 278.
Cornarius. En misera hic Virtus. Corn., p. 278.
Alciati. Aiacis tumulum lachrymis. Corn., p. 279; *Emb.* 48.
Sabeo. Hic ego scissa. *Epig.*, p. 258.
Quoted by Landi, *Num.*, p. 126.
Robortello refers to this epig. *Scrip. Epig.*, p. 39.
Mignault. Ad tumulum sedeo. Alciati, *Emb.* 48.
Cunich. Aiacis busto assideo. *Anth.*, p. 112.
Passeroni. In questo lido, ove è. *Rime* 3. 59.
7.146. Cf. 145.
Obsopoeus. Ad tumulum Aiacis. Obsop., p. 395; Wech., p. 345.
Sabeo. Ad tumulum Aiacis. *Epig.*, p. 251.
Sanchez. Aiacis propter Rhoeteo. *Op.* 3. 130; Alciati, *Emb.* 49.
Averani. Aiacis tumulo Rhoetheo. *Op.* 1. 75.

Cunich. Aiacis tumulum Rhoeteo. *Anth.*, p. 110.
Medici (A. de'). Hic ubi Rhoeteis. *Scelt.*, p. iii.
Medici (A. de'). Sulla tomba d'Aiace. *Scelt.*, p. iii.
Felici. Io qui sul Retèo. *Epig.*[1], p. 13.
Pagnini. Su la tomba d'Ajace. *Epig.*, p. 153.
7.147. Sabeo. Navibus amissis. *Epig.*, p. 258.
7.148. Cornarius. Aiacis tumba haec. Corn., p. 280.
Sabeo. Hoc tumulo est Aiax. *Epig.*, p. 306.
Bongiovanni and Zanetti. Questo è l'avel. *Epig.*, p. 54.
Pagnini. In questa tomba giace. *Epig.*, p. 9.
7.149. Scaphenatus. Cum non alterius posset. *Eleg.*, Ci.
Sabeo. Conditus in Troia. *Epig.*, p. 363.
7.150. Quoted in *schol.* on Aristides, *Panath.* 218A (p. 52 Frommel).
Costanzi (A.). Aiax strage virum nimia. *Epig.*, Bii[vo].
Sabeo. Post palmam multi *Epig.*, p. 363.
Cunich. Aiax ad Troiam, post. *Anth.*, p. 123.
Pagnini. Per mille imprese Ajace. *Epig.*, p. 89.
7.151. Cf. 152.
Erasmus. Aiaci datus ensis. Soter[2], p. 228; Corn., p. 279.
Cornarius. Baltheus et gladius. Corn., p. 279.
Sabeo. Quam male succedant. *Epig.*, p. 349.
Pagnini. Ettore un brando diè. *Epig.*, p. 89.
7.152. Cf. 151.
Erasmus, Atque ita ab hoste [vv. 7–8]. Soter[2], p. 228; Corn.,
p. 280.
Alciati. Bellorum coepisse ferunt. Corn., p. 280; *Emb.* 168.
Soter[3], p. 253.
Sabeo. Munera amara Hector. *Epig.*, p. 349.
Sabeo. Quam male sortiti. *Epig.*, p. 299 (287).
Minturno. Priamides ferro Aiacem. *Epig.*, f. 2[vo].
Mignault. Exitiale inter se Hector. Alciati, *Emb.* 167.
7.153. Appears as No. 3 among the Homeric Epigrams; criticized by
Plato, *Phaedrus* 264D; cf. 'Longinus,' *De Subl.* 36. 2;
quoted by 'Dio of Prusa' 37. 38; with differences, in *Contest
of Hom. and Hes.* 324; Diogenes Laertius 1. 6 (Cleobolus);
Ps.-Herodotus, *Vita Homeri* (West., p. 5).
Brugnolo? Aenea virgo Midae. Laert.; Soter[2], p. 222.
Ficino. Aenea virgo sum [prose]. Tr. *Phaedr.* 264D.
Bentinus. Aenea sum virgo Midae. *Laert.*, p. 33; Soter[2],
p. 222; Corn., p. 267.
Winshemius. Virginis ora gero. Soter[2], p. 222; Corn., p. 267.
Anisio. Aenea sum virgo custos. *Poem.*, f. 62[ro].
Sabeo. Aenea sum virgo. *Epig.*, p. 352.
Minturno. Aenea sum virgo. Regis. *De Poet.*, p. 411.
Minturno. Vergine io son. *L'Art. Poet.*, p. 279.
Cottunius quotes Minturno's Latin version. *De Confic.*, p. 5.
Cunich. Aenea virgo Midae. *Anth.*, p. 120.
Felici. Di Mida al tumolo. *Epig.*[1], p. 70.

Gargallo. Io, Magnanimità. *Op.* 2. 587.

7.155. 'Eudocia' quotes lines 1–2. *Viol.* 427.

7.156. Sabeo. Et visco et calamis. *Epig.*, p. 366.
Carcani (P.). Col vischio e colle. *Ant. Ercol.* 7. 158; *Rac.* 3. 157.

7.157. Cf. *A.P.* 9. 112.
Cornarius. Me annorum decadas. *Corn.*, p. 71.
Sabeo. Tres decades et sex. *Epig.*, p. 802.
Cunich. Ter denos tribuunt. *Anth.*, p. 70.
Passeroni. Ho settant' anni e trenta. *Rime.* 3. 210.

7.159. Sleidan. Orpheae cytharae celebratur. Soter[2], p. 223; Corn., p. 268.
Cunich. Quam citharae blandum. *Anth.*, p. 104.

7.160. More (Sir T.). Fortis erat bello. Soter[2], p. 207; Corn., p. 250.
Sleidan. Conditur hoc saxo. Soter[2], p. 207; Corn., p. 250.
Sabeo. Strenuus in bello. *Epig.*, p. 811.
Cunich. Armipotens iacet heic. *Anth.*, p. 109.
Medici (A. de'). Conditur in tumulo. *Scelt.*, p. xiv.
Medici (A. de'). Quì Timocrito è sotterra. *Scelt.*, p. xiv.
Pompei. Ben in mezzo ai conflitti. *Op.* 2. 196.
Felici. Chiudon Timocrito. *Epig.*[1], p. 11.
Pagnini. Quest' è del forte. *Epig.*, p. 122.
Mariani. Prode di Marte. *Ep. Mod. Aut.*, p. 58.

7.161. Marullus. Nuncia magnanimi volucris. Alciati, *Emb.* 33 (ed. 1621).
Velius. Nuntia fare Iovis. Soter[2], p. 208; Corn., p. 250.
Alciati. Quae te causa movet. Corn., p. 250; *Emb.* 33.
Sabeo. Nuntia dic Iovis alti. *Epig.*, p. 796.
Mignault. Fare age quid sedeas. Alciati, *Emb.* 33.
Cunich. Alituum regina. *Anth.*, p. 110.
Medici (A. de'). Nuncia fida Iovis. *Scelt.*, p. iv.
Medici (A. de'). Messagiero di Giove. *Scelt.*, p. iv.
Passeroni. Regina degli augei. *Rime* 3. 77.
Pagnini. P. O del gran Giove. *Epig.*, p. 85.

7.162. Cornarius. Euphratem ne impone. Corn., p. 276.
Sabeo. Eufratem tu ne combure. *Epig.*, p. 818.
Averani. Euphratem flammis ne. *Op.* 1. 178, 180.

7.164. [Not in *Plan.*] Found on a stone in Phrygia (Kaibel 248).

7.166. Sabeo. Extremo expirans. *Epig.*, p. 802.

7.168. Obsopoeus. Optet, si qua volet. Obsop., p. 386; Wech., p. 337.

7.169. Quoted by Hesychius Milet. (Mueller, *F.H.G.* 4. 152); Dionysius Byzant. (Wesch, p. 36); Constantinus Porphyrog. *De Themat.* 2. 12 (p. 64B); Codinus, *De Orig. Const.* (Bekker, p. 10).
Cornarius. Tres annos natum, iuxta. Corn., p. 269.

7.170. Sabeo. Ludentem circa puteum. *Epig.*, p. 803.

7.171. Sabeo. Sacra avis hic celeres. *Epig.*, p. 820.

7.172. Alciati. Dum turdos visco. Corn., p. 283; *Emb.* 105.
Sabeo. Arcebam longe sturnos. *Epig.*, p. 845.
Mignault. Qui sturnum iactis. Alciati, *Emb.* 104.
Sanchez (Fer.). Qui prius et sturnum. Alciati, *Emb.* 104.

7.173. Obsopoeus. Sponte sua repetunt. Obsop., p. 475; Wech.,
p. 409.
Sabeo. Sponte sua ad caulum. *Epig.*, p. 205.
Angelio. Iniussae rediere et oves. *Poem.* (1585), p. 349.
Orsini quotes this epig. on Virgil, *Eclog.* 5. 24.
Cunich. Septa petunt pavidae. *Anth.*, p. 142.
Pagnini. Sparso di neve e pavido. *Epig.*, p. 54.

7.174. Obsopoeus. Therimache, haud ultra, Obsop., p. 475; Wech.,
p. 409.
D'Arco. Nec posthac coryli. *Num.*, p. 159.
Sabeo. Non mage decurres. *Epig.*, p. 367.
Cunich. Heu, heu, infelix. *Anth.*, p. 142.
Felici. Ahi misero Terìmaco! *Epig.*[1], p. 32.

7.178. Cornarius. Servus ego. servus sane. Corn., p. 275
Sabeo. Me domine altorem. *Epig.*, p. 620.
Pagnini. Io servo fui. *Epig.*, p. 48.

7.179. Sabeo. Nunc domine et sub humo. *Epig.*, p. 643.

7.180. Sabeo. Est dolor eversus mortis. *Epig.*, p. 644.

7.182. Cf. *A.P.* 7. 712.
Sabeo. Non Hymenaeus erat praesens. *Epig.*, p. 749.
Cf. Marino. In esequie funebri inique. *Ad.* 4. 56 (p. 56).
Cf. Marino. Invece d'Imeneo ti fia. *Ad.* 14. 299. 5 (p. 277).
Averani cites this epig. *Op.* 1. 305.

7.184. Cf. *A.P.* 7. 490 and 611.
Alamanni. Della vergin Elisa è qui. *Versi* 2. 143.
Sabeo. Virginis urna Helenae sum. *Epig.*, p. 638.

7.185. With v. 5 cf. Ovid. Et face pro thalami. *Her.* 20. 172.
Sabeo. Terra habet Italia. *Epig.*, p. 640.

7.186. Sabeo. Nuper enim in thalamo. *Epig.*, p. 793.
Bongiovanni and Zanetti. A lei, che bella. *Epig.*, p. 18.

7.187. Cunich. Nico anus innuptae. *Anth.*, p. 79.

7.188. [Not in *Plan.*]
Cf. Ovid. At mihi nec Iuno. *Her.* 6. 45.

7.190. Cf. *A.P.* 7. 364.
Probably referred to by the elder Pliny. *H.N.* 34. 57.
Sabeo. Mulcenti locustae agros. *Epig.*, p. 766.
Sabeo. Sub tumulo tristis. *Epig.*, p. 767.

7.191. Sabeo. Ante ego pastores. *Epig.*, p. 641.

7.195. Sabeo. Votorum fallax. *Epig.*, p. 807.
Pompei. Locusta, che lusinghi. *Op.* 2. 167.

7.196. Sabeo. Quae sylvas facis. *Epig.*, p. 57.
Molza. Ebria cui studium. *Poes.* 3. 201.
Fioretti refers to this epig. *Prog.* 5. 64.
Cunich. O quae dulce sonans. *Anth.*, p. 177.

Passeroni. O cicaletta, ch'ebbra. *Rime* 3. 146.
7.197. Sabeo. Dum locusta lyram. *Epig.*, p. 806.
7.201. Sabeo. Non mage laticoma. *Epig.*, p. 765.
Sabeo. Non plus dulcisonam. *Epig.*, p. 798.
7.203. Cf. with line 4, Catullus 3. 11–12: Qui nunc it per iter.
7.204. Cf. *A.P.* 7. 205–6.
Sabeo. Non mage eris scopulis. *Epig.,*. p. 764.
Cunich. Aeriis, perdix, deducta. *Anth.*, p. 150.
Felici. Tolta da rupi aeree. *Epig.*[1], p. 4.
Passeroni. Starna gentil, venuta. *Rime* 3. 63.
7.205. Cf. 204 and 206.
Cunich. Perdicem feles avido. *Anth.*, p. 150.
Felici. Quella gatta ingorda. *Epig.*[1], p. 6.
Passeroni. Quel gatto, che con. *Rime* 3. 64.
Pagnini. Un gatto, che schempiata. *Epig.*, p. 29.
7.206. Cf. 204–5.
Felici. Te, gatto rio, produssero. *Epig.*[1], p. 31.
7.207. Sabeo. Nuper adhuc tenerum. *Epig.*, p. 733.
Sabeo. Si superest nobis. *Epig.*, p. 733.
7.208. Sabeo. Sacravit tumulum hunc. *Epig.*, p. 811.
7.209. Molza. Formicae aeternum pereat. *Poes.* 3. 191.
Sabeo. Hic tibi, formica. *Epig.*, p. 276.
Cf. Baldi. Quel sassolino, O viator. *Epig.* 1091.
Cf. Loredano. Morij nel far un dì. *Cimit.* 3. 56.
7.210. Felici. Già fatta era una. *Epig.*[1], p. 118.
7.212. Sabeo. Ventipedis mergi hunc. *Epig.*, p. 733.
7.213. Sabeo. In viridi ramo pini. *Epig.*, p. 766.
7.214. [Not in *Plan.*] Cf. *A.P.* 7. 215–6.
7.215. [Not in *Plan.*] Cf. *A.P.* 7. 214, 216.
7.216. Cf. *A.P.* 7. 214–5.
Alciati. Delphinem invitum me. Corn., p. 283; *Emb.* 167.
Scaphenatus. Me gravis in siccum. *Eleg.*, Diiii.
Molza. Delphinum ingentem curvi. *Poes.* 3. 207.
Sabeo. Ad terram tractus. *Epig.*, p. 800.
Sanchez. Delphinum me fluctus. *Op.* 3. 306; *Emb.* 166.
Mignault. Delphinem pelagi rapidus. Alciati, *Emb.* 166.
Bongiovanni and Zanetti. Me dolfin le onde. *Epig.*, p. 18.
Felici. Me delfino in terra. *Epig.*[1], p. 117.
7.217. Athenaeus quotes a slightly different version. *Deip.* 13. 589C.
Diogenes Laertius gives this epigram (3. 31).
Brugnolo? Archeanassa iacet. Laert.; Soter[2], p. 225; Corn.,
p. 273.
Politian. Archeanassa mihi meretrix. Del Lungo, p. 543; Soter[2],
p. 225; Corn., p. 273.
Bentinus. Archeanassa mihi est. *Laert.*, p. 104; Soter[2], p. 225;
Corn., p. 274.
Sabeo. Igne gravi et gemino. *Epig.*, p. 614.
Sabeo. Dulce etiam in senio. *Epig.*, p. 620.

Sabeo. Ex Colophone fui. *Epig.*, p. 659.
Sabeo. Ex Colophone iacet. *Epig.*, p. 639.
Sabeo. Fax Colophonis obit. *Epig.*, p. 647.
Sabeo. Archeanassa, iacet. *Epig.*, p. 676.
Sabeo. Archeanassa iacet pellex. *Epig.*, p. 677.
Calcagnini. Dum tenera et vernis. Pigna, p. 199.
Garzoni. Archenassam ego teneo. *Piaz. Univ.*, p. 594.
Pompei. Archeanassa, quell' amica. *Op.* 2. 190.

7.218. Sabeo. Et cum auro. *Epig.*, p. 618.
Mazzoni quotes line 3. *Difesa*, p. 464.
Pompei. Quella che fra le porpore. *Op.* 2. 178.

7.219. Sabeo. Floribus in cunctis. *Epig.*, p. 683.

7.220. Sleidan. Laïdos antiquae vidi. Soter², p. 224; Corn., p. 27.
Cf. Loredano. Laide sen giace. *Cimit.* 2. 23.

7.221. Cornarius. Iam matura viro. Corn., p. 272.
Sabeo. Ad Veneris lusus. *Epig.*, p. 618.

7.222. Cf. Sabeo. Molle sub hoc duro. *Epig.*, p. 601.
Carcani (G.?). Qui le tenere membra. *Ant. Ercol.* 8. 74.

7.223. Sabeo. Quae circum Cybelen. *Epig.*, p. 619.
Carcani (G.?). La ballerina Aristia. *Ant. Ercol.* 8. 74.

7.224. Cf. *A.P.* 7. 743.
Ausonius? Viginti atque novem. *Opus.* 23. 34.
Soter² (p. 224) and Cornarius (p. 272) give the version ascribed to Ausonius.
Sabeo. Viginti atque novem. *Epig.*, p. 256.
Sabeo. Viginti enixa atque novem. *Epig.*, p. 750.
Sabeo. Viginti atque novem natos. *Epig.*, p. 750.
Bongiovanni and Zanetti. Callicratea i mi. *Epig.*, p. 19.

7.225. Apostolios gives the substance in prose. *Paroem.* 16. 44.
Sleidan. Saxa cavat tempus. Soter², p. 227; Corn., p. 277.
Alciati. Aeacidae tumulum Rhaeto. *Emb.* 136.
Sabeo. Longa dies lapidem. *Epig.*, p. 260.
Mignault. Longa dies saxumque. Alciati, *Emb.* 135.
Ricolvi. Saxa vel ipsa friat. *Op.*, p. 70.
Ricolvi compares Petrarch, *Son.* 83. *Op.*, p. 71.
Medici (A. de'). Ferrum longa dies. *Scelt.*, p. xxxviii.
Medici (A. de'). Tutto passa fra noi. *Scelt.*, p. xxxviii.

7.226. Sabeo. Pro Abderis moriens. *Epig.*, p. 756.
Cunich. Abdera impositum flammis. *Anth.*, p. 109.
Pagnini. Sul rogo d'Agaton. *Epig.*, p. 118.

7.227. Sabeo. Non Leo sic ferus est. *Epig.*, p. 261.
Cunich. Tale nec in silvis. *Anth.*, p. 117.

7.228. Ausonius. Me sibi et uxori. *Opus.* 6. 34.
Cunich. Me sibi et uxori. *Anth.*, p. 107.
Passeroni. Per se, per la moglier. *Rime* 3. 58.

7.229. Quoted by Plutarch, *Moral.* 235A.
Ausonius. Excipis adverso quod. *Opus.* 19. 43.
Filelfo. Exanimis Pitanen clypeo. *Orat.*, Ỹv.

Crinitus. Traiectus hasta pectus. *H.D.*, p. 568.

Soter[2] (pp. 209–11) and Cornarius (pp. 251–4) give the three preceding imitations and related, but not derivative, pieces by Marullus and Politian.

Arsenios quotes this epigram, *Viol.*, p. 454.

Sabeo. Quum super exanimis clypeo. *Epig.*, p. 263.

Giraldi Cintio. Ut clypeo impositum. *Poem.*, p. 169.

Cunich. Extinctus Pitanae clypeo. *Anth.*, p. 31.

Medici (A. de'). Exanimis super arma. *Scelt.*, p. ii.

Medici (A. de'). Da sette colpi orribilmente. *Scelt.*, p. ii.

Passeroni. Portato a casa sopra. *Rime* 3. 178.

Pagnini. Con sette piaghe. *Epig.*, p. 137.

7.230. Cf. *A.P.* 7. 433, 531; 9. 61, 397, 447.

Quoted without tr. in Soter[2], p. 213.

Cornarius. Ex bello quum te fugitivum. Corn., p. 258.

Jordanus. Quum bello exciperet. Soter[3], p. 235.

Obsopoeus. Quum profugum e bello. Obsop., p. 324; Wech., p. 289.

Sabeo. Quum timidum e bello. *Epig.*, p. 216.

Sabeo. Mater ut e bello. *Epig.*, p. 217.

7.231. Sabeo. Ambraciae in cursu. *Epig.*, p. 264.

Cunich. Sic clypeum Ambraciae. *Anth.*, p. 29.

7.232. Sabeo. Lydia Amintor humus. *Epig.*, p. 499.

7.233. Cf. *A.P.* 7. 234; 9. 354.

Anselmo. Quem non hostiles. *Epig.*, Eii.

Alciati. Aelius Ausoniis audax. Corn., p. 259.

Sabeo. Elius Ausonio miles. *Epig.*, p. 335.

7.234. Cf. *A.P.* 7. 233 and 9. 354.

Alciati. [See under 233].

Sabeo. Bellica serta ferens. *Epig.*, p. 267.

Minturno. Palladis Ausoniae cum. *Epig.*, f. 2[ro].

Medici (A. de'). Strenuus Argorum dux. *Scelt.*, p. xii.

Medici (A. de'). Elio il duce possente. *Scelt.*, p. xii.

7.235. Sabeo. Qualem mentem. *Epig.*, p. 335.

Cunich. Ne metire virum. *Anth.*, p. 116.

Passeroni. Temistocle qui giace. *Rime* 3. 80.

Pagnini. Non della tomba. *Epig.*, p. 50.

7.236. Sabeo. Urna Themistoclis non. *Epig.*, p. 331.

Pagnini. Del patrio suol desire. *Epig.*, p. 130.

7.237. Sabeo. Sculpe meum supra. *Epig.*, p. 333.

7.238. Velius. Primus ego Æmathiam. Soter[2], p. 214; Corn., p. 259.

Sabeo. Æmathiam primus qui. *Epig.*, p. 191.

Cf. Scaliger (J. C.). Materiam superavi. *Poem.* 1. 288.

Cunich. Æmathiam incendi. *Anth.*, p. 105.

Pagnini. Me che primiero. *Epig.*, p. 49.

7.239. Quoted by Suidas, *s.v.* φάτις.

Sabeo. Falsa in Alexandro mors. *Epig.*, p. 486.

Sabeo. Falsus Alexandrum est. *Epig.*, p. 201.

Sabeo. Magnus Alexander. *Epig.*, p. 201.
Sabeo. Mortuum Alexandrum. *Epig.*, p. 200.
Pagnini. Chi vuol morto Alessandro. *Epig.*, p. 150.
7.240. Sabeo. Tantalus iste cinis. *Epig.*, p. 337.
Sabeo. Si quis Alexandri. *Epig.*, p. 337.
7.241. Obsopoesus. Multum te, Ptolomaee. Obsop., p. 363; Wech., p. 319.
Sabeo. Multa tibi, Ptolomee. *Epig.*, p. 260.
7.242. Cf. *A.P.* 7. 251.
Sabeo. Hic ne iugo. *Epig.*, p. 299 (287.)
Angelio. Qui propriae quondam. *Poem.*, p. 393.
Cunich. Hos, patriae qui colla. *Anth.*, p. 123.
Passeroni. Degli Eroi, che alla. *Rime* 3. 247.
7.243. Sabeo. Phocensi in saxo quae. *Epig.*, p. 261.
Castelvetro quotes this epig. *Petr.*, p. 67.
7.245. Cf. Kaibel 27.
Sabeo. Cunctorum tempus custos. *Epig.*, p. 757.
7.247. Quoted by Plutarch, *Flaminius* 9. 2.
7.248. Quoted by Herodotus (7. 228); by Diodorus (11. 33); by Aristides (49. 380); and by Suidas, *s.v.* Λεωνίδης.
Valla. Terdecies centum hic. *Herod.*, f. 209ᵛᵒ; Soter², p. 211; Corn., p. 255.
7.249. Quoted by Herodotus (7.228); by Lycurgus (*In Leocr.* 109); by Strabo (9. 429); by Diodorus (11. 33); and by Suidas, *s.v.* Λεωνίδης.
Cicero. Dic hospes Spartae. *Tusc. Dis.* 1. 101.
Guarino da Verona. Dic Lacedaemoniis hac. Strabo, f. xxxiiᵛᵒ.
Valla. Nos Lacedaemoniis refer. *Herod.*, f. 209ᵛᵒ.
Soter² (p. 211) and Cornarius (p. 255) give the tr. of Valla and Guarino.
Arsenios quotes this epigram. *Viol.*, p. 118.
Alamanni. Da poi ch' in Termopile. *Versi* 2. 126.
Sabeo. Hospes, dic Spartae. *Epig.*, p. 265.
Vargas. Và, Passagiero, a Sparta. *Sag.*, p. 28.
Vargas. Và, Passagiero, che voi. *Sag.*, p. 28.
Pagnini. Nunzio a Sparta ne va. *Epig.*, p. 108.
7.250. Quoted by Plutarch (*Moral.* 870F); by Aristides (49.380).
Soter² (p. 211) quotes the Gr., but gives no tr.
Cornarius. Merserat in summo. Corn., p. 255.
Sabeo. Stantem in praecipiti. *Epig.*, p. 266.
7.251. Cf. *A.P.* 7. 242.
Sabeo. Gloriam inextinctam. *Epig.*, p. 352.
Cunich. Hos, patriae decus. *Anth.*, p. 109.
7.253. Quoted by *schol.* on Aristides, *Panath.* 229A (p. 58 Frommel).
Soter. Maxima si virtus. Soter², p. 212; Corn., p. 256.
7.254. Sabeo. Gaudete, o fortes, *Epig.*, p. 336.
7.254–5. Edited by Allacci, *De Sym.*, p. 212.
7.256. Quoted by Philostratus, *Life of Apollonius* 1. 24.

Rinuccini. Qui quondam Aegaei. Soter[2], p. 212; Corn., p. 256.
7.257. Quoted by *schol.* on Aristides, *Panath.* 229A, B (pp. 58–9, Frommel).
    Sabeo. Cecropiae nati. *Epig.*, p. 263.
    Cunich. Cecropidae Persas bello. *Anth.*, p. 7.
    Passeroni. L'Attica fulminante. *Rime* 3. 31.
7.258. Edited by Allacci, *De Sym.*, p. 212.
    Cunich. Graia manus iuvenum. *Anth.*, p. 102.
7.259. Diogenes Laertius 3. 33; *schol.* on Hermogenes, Τέχνη 'Ρητ. (Waltz 7. 1, p. 193); Suidas, *s.v.* Ἱππίας.
    Brugnolo? Eubee nunc gens. Laert.; Soter[2], p. 212; Corn., p. 256.
    Bentinus. Euboeae fuimus Eretrum. *Laert.*, p. 105; Soter[2], p. 212; Corn., p. 256.
    Pagnini. Quel, ch' Eretria spedì. *Epig.*, p. 71.
7.261. Sabeo. Quid parere? et partus. *Epig.*, p. 499.
7.262. Theocritus, *Inscr.* 23.
    Quoted by Castelvetro on Petrarch, *Son.* 186. *Petr.*, p. 384.
7.263. Cornarius. Te quoque, Clenorida. Corn., p. 285.
7.264. Cf. Propertius. Ut quotiens Paeti. *Eleg.* 3. 7. 27.
    Sabeo. Sit mare sulcanti. *Epig.*, p. 326.
    Pagnini. Spiri secondo alla tua. *Epig.*, p. 11.
7.265. More (Sir T.). Naufragus hac situs est. Soter[2], p. 231; Corn., p. 285.
    Cornarius. Naufragi ego tumulus. Corn., p. 285.
    Sabeo. Naufragio perii. *Epig.*, p. 326.
    Sabeo. Naufragus hic situs. *Epig.*, p. 326.
    Sabeo. Rusticus hoc, nauta. *Epig.*, p. 819.
    Bongiovanni and Zanetti. Di tal, che in mar. *Epig.*, p. 9.
    Cunich. Naufragus heic iaceo. *Anth.*, p. 125.
    Felici. Quì giaccio naufrago. *Epig.*[1], p. 85.
    Passeroni. Io naufrago quì giaccio. *Rime* 3. 83.
    Pagnini. Un naufrago sotterra. *Epig.*, p. 10.
7.266. Alciati. Naufragi ab tumulo. Corn., p. 286.
    Sabeo. Urna Diocleos immersi. *Epig.*, p. 792.
    Pagnini. Il naufrago Diocle è qui. *Epig.*, p. 10.
7.267. Pagnini. Perchè sì presso al mare. *Epig.*, p. 9.
7.268. Sabeo. Vidisti, quod naufragio. *Epig.*, p. 765.
    Pagnini. A me naufrago il mar. *Epig.*, p. 88.
7.269. Sabeo. Inque mari atque solo. *Epig.*, p. 224.
    Pagnini. A te, nocchier, più che. *Epig.*, p. 88.
7.270. Cornarius. Primitias frugum Spartani. Corn., p. 287.
    Sabeo. Primitias frugum. *Epig.*, p. 227.
    Edited by Allacci, *De Sym.*, p. 215.
7.271. Cornarius. Quam nollem celeres naves. Corn., p. 287.
    Sabeo. Quam cuperem celeres. *Epig.*, p. 227.
    Pagnini. Ah! se fosser le nave. *Epig.*, p. 148.
7.272. Sabeo. Naxius haud periit. *Epig.*, p. 226.

Medici (A. de'). Naxius haud tumulum. *Scelt.*, p. xxxiii.
Medici (A. de'). In terra nò, ma in mar. *Scelt.*, p. xxxiii.
Pagnini. In terra nò, ma in mar. *Epig.*, p. 134.

7.273. Sabeo. Summa procella Euri. *Epig.*, p. 227.

7.274. Sabeo. Timoclis nomen. *Epig.*, p. 334.
Cunich. Timoclis nomen clamo. *Anth.*, p. 124.
Pagnini. Io Timocle pur chiamo. *Epig.*, p. 75.

7.275. Sabeo. Iam Peloponessus Cretensem. *Epig.*, p. 760.
Calcagnini. Me Peloponnesus, me. Pigna, p. 215.
Averani. Te Peloponnesus Creteque. *Op.* 1. 171.

7.277. [Not in *Plan.*]
Pagnini. V. Chi mai, naufraga salma. *Epig.*, p. 166.

7.279. Sabeo. Desine remigium semper. *Epig.*, p. 327.
Pagnini. E pinta e rostri a che. *Epig.*, p. 10.

7.280. Sabeo. Hic cumulus terrae est. *Epig.*, p. 328.
Cunich. Bustum est hic tumulus. *Anth.*, p. 120.
Passeroni. Qui dove di terren quel. *Rime* 3. 215.
Felici. Arresta i validi. *Epig.*[2], p. xxi.
Pagnini. Un tumolo quì sta. *Epig.*, p. 50.

7.282. Cf. *A.P.* 7. 350 and 675.
Costanzi (A.). Sum nautae tumulus. *Epig.*, Bii[vo].
Cornarius. Naufragi ego tumulus, quid. Corn., p. 289.
Sabeo. Sum tumulus mersi. *Epig.*, p. 821.
Cunich. Naufragus heic iaceo, quid. *Anth.*, p. 109.
Cunich. Naufragus heic iaceo, tu. *Anth.*, p. 109.
Passeroni. Io naufrago qui giaccio. *Rime* 3. 59.
Passeroni. Un naufrago qui giace. *Rime* 3. 158.

7.284. Sabeo. Esto a me cubitis. *Epig.*, p. 394.
Pagnini. Otto cubiti, O mar, ti. *Epig.*, p. 68.

7.285. Cf. Propertius. Sed tua nunc volucres. *Eleg.* 3. 7. 11.
Cf. Ovid. Ossa superstabunt. *Her.* 10. 123.
Cf. Ovid. Quantum in te, Theseu. *A.A.* 3. 35.
Sabeo. Non pulvis nec onus. *Epig.*, p. 333.
Cunich. Non pulvus parvusque. *Anth.*, p. 118.
Felici. Non un sasso in breve. *Epig.*[1], p. 45.
Passeroni. Non sasso angusto. *Rime* 3. 81.

7.286. Sabeo. Exagitate miser Nicanor. *Epig.*, p. 330.

7.287. Sabeo. Defunctum cruciabit. *Epig.*, p. 821.

7.288. Velius. Neutra habet integrum. Soter[2], p. 231; Corn., p. 286.
Alciati. Integer ullius non sum. Corn., p. 286.
Sabeo. Emoriens totus nullius. *Epig.*, p. 327.
Pagnini. Nè mar nè terra intero. *Epig.*, p. 12.

7.289. Cf. *A.P.* 7. 550.
Sabeo. Antea submersum Penei. *Epig.*, p. 760.

7.290. More (Sir T.). Aequoris insanas evasit. Soter[2], p. 231; Corn.,
p. 287.

7.291. Sabeo. Et coma stillat adhuc. *Epig.*, p. 644.

7.293. Cunich. Non hiems gravis. *Anth.*, p. 143.

Felici. Non tempestoso turbine. *Epig.*[1], p. 46.
Passeroni, Non crudo verno irato. *Rime* 3. 236.
Roncalli. Non spento in mar. *Epig.* (1792), p. 57.

7.294. Obsopoeus. Longaevum aequorea. Obsop., p. 414; Wech., p. 359.
Sabeo. Grinea pontivagum. *Epig.*, p. 329.
Beverini. Rimosa Gryneus dum. *Carm.*, p. 153; *C.P.It.* 2. 213.
Bongiovanni and Zanetti. Quel vecchierel Grineo. *Epig.*, p. 9.

7.295. Sabeo. Viventem e nassis. *Epig.*, p. 761.
Giovane. Therina Nestoreum. *Ant. Tar.* 3. 3.

7.296. [Not in *Plan.*] Quoted by Diodorus (11.62); by Aristides (49. 380); and by *schol.* on Aristides, *Panath.*, p. 263C (p. 70 Frommel).
Quoted by Arsenios, *Paroem.*, p. 409; *Viol.*, p. 329.
Edited by Allacci, *De Sym.*, p. 215.

7.298. Sabeo. Durum est quum sponsa. *Epig.*, p. 640.

7.300. Sabeo. Contexit tellus haec. *Epig.*, p. 344.

7.301. Sabeo. Rex Spartane Leo. *Epig.*, p. 497.

7.302. Cunich. Quemque sua extinctum. *Anth.*, p. 125.
Passeroni. Ha 'l suo morto ogni. *Rime* 3. 250.

7.304. 'Dio of Prusa' (37. 39) and Pollux (5. 47) quote lines 1–2.
'Eudocia' quotes lines 1–2 (Pollux). *Viol.* 96.
Sabeo. Vir fuit Ippemon. *Epig.*, p. 757.

7.305. Cf. *A.P.* 7. 381, 585, 635; and 9. 242.
Sabeo. Quum cymbam in ponto. *Epig.*, p. 330.
Cf. Baldi. Morto il vecchio Mirson. *Epig.* 328.

7.306. [Not in *Plan.*] Quoted by Plutarch (*Themistocles* 1.1); by Athenaeus (13.576C).

7.307. Sabeo. Nomen mi, quid enim? *Epig.*, p. 249.

7.308. Velius. Quinquennem rapuit puerum. Soter[2], p. 223; Corn., p. 269.
Sleidan. Callimachus quinquennis. Soter[2], p. 223; Corn., p. 270.
Luscinius. Saeva rapit manibus. Corn., p. 270.
Obsopoeus. Quinquennum Pluto. Obsop., p. 367; Wech., p. 322.
Dazzi. Me puerum nullis. *Poem.*, p. 118.
Sabeo. Curarum immunem crudelis. *Epig.*, p. 256.
Cf. Evangelista. Fortunate puer, teneris. *Poem.*, f. 84vo.
Cf. Loredano. Qui sepolto è un fanciul. *Cimit.* 2. 94.
The tr. of Velius is given in Ἐπ. καὶ Ἐλ. No. 73.
Bongiovanni and Zanetti. Me fanciul di cinque. *Epig.*, p. 41.
Ricolvi. Callimachum, puerum quin. *Op.*, p. 69.
Ricolvi. Callimaco son io. *Op.*, p. 70.
Cunich. Quinquennis puer, et. *Anth.*, p. 123.
Felici. Un busto compio appena. *Epig.*[1], p. 54.
Passeroni. Calimaco qui giace. *Rime* 3. 115.

Roncalli. A cinqu'anni le. *Epig.* (1792), p. 93; (1801), p. 65.
Pagnini. Garzon d' un lustro. *Epig.*, p. 29.
Pagnini. Colsemi in frasca età. *Epig.*, p. 148.
7.309. Cornarius. Sexaginta annos vixi. Corn., p. 270.
Valeriano. Si cubat hic, quisnam. *Poem.*, p. 113; *C.P.It.* 10.
159.
Obsopoeus. Pauperie et senio. Obsop., p. 370; Wech., p. 324.
Pompei. Dionigi Tarsio giaccio. *Op.* 2. 223.
Pagnini. Io senza prender moglie. *Epig.*, p. 94.
7.310. Cf. *A.P.* 7. 356–60, 516, 580–1.
Sleidan. Abdidit hac tellura. Soter[2], p. 214; Corn., p. 260.
Obsopoeus. Condidi hic latro. Obsop., p .340; Wech. p. 301.
Sabeo. Qui me interfecit. *Epig.*, p. 759.
Cunich. Abdidit huc me latro. *Anth.*, p. 108.
Felici. M'uccise, e chiusemi. *Epig.*[1], p. 116.
Cf. Bettinelli. Qui morto m'ha. *Op.* 22. 99.
Pagnini. Chi me dal mondo. *Epig.*, p. 7.
7.311. Quoted by Eustathius (on Il. Ω 614); by Triclinius (on Soph.,
Elec., 150); and by Eumathius, p. 209 (Hilberg).
Ausonius? Habet sepulcrum non id. *Opus.* 23. 27.
Politian. Hoc est sepulcrum intus. Del Lungo, p. 545; Soter[2],
p. 220; Corn., p. 265.
Velius. Hoc in sepulchro mortuus. Soter[2], p. 220; Corn.,
p. 265.
Alciati. En statuae statua. *Emb.* 67.
Sabeo. Intus habet nullum. *Epig.*, p. 489.
Sabeo. Non opus inferiis. *Epig.*, p. 206.
Scaliger (J. C.) Intus sepulchrum non. *Poem.* 1. 151.
Cf. Crotti. Bis septem infelix Niobe. *Opusc.*, p. 132.
Beccuti. Dido, chi giace [from Auson.]. *Rime*, p. 252.
Groto. A morto questo avel non. *Rime* (1610), f. 79.
Murtola. Non mi curo di tomba. *Rime*, f. 225[ro].
Marino. Ecco a se stessa. *Poes. Var.*, p. 239.
Loredano. Stupido, O peregrin. *Cimit.* 2. 97.
Battista. Sum Niobe infelix. *Epig.* (1646), p. 82.
Ricolvi. Non habet hic tumulus. *Op.*, p. 74.
7.312. Sabeo. Romulidum quos atra. *Epig.*, p. 758.
7.313. Quoted by Plutarch (*Antonius* 60.4); and in *Platonis Vita* 2
(West., p. 393).
Aretinus. Hic sum post vitam. L. G. Giraldi, *Op.* 2. 97.
Volaterranus [=Aretinus. Cf. above, p. 142]. *Com. Urb.*,
p. 460; Soter[2], p. 221; Corn., p. 266.
Sleidan. Hic iaceo postquam. Soter[2], p. 221; Corn., p. 266.
Sabeo. Hic iaceo abrumpens. *Epig.*, p. 253.
Sabeo. Fortunae gravis obtruncans. *Epig.*, p. 253.
Sabeo. Hinc animam effundens. *Epig.*, p. 253.
Giraldi (L. G.) quotes Gr. and Aretinus' tr. *Op.* 2. 97.
Barberio quotes Aretinus' tr. from Giraldi. Gronov. 10. 822.

Crasso quotes Aretinus' tr. from Giraldi. *Ist.*, p. 518.
Bongiovanni and Zanetti. Spirai l'anima tetra. *Epig.*, p. 49.
Pagnini. Qui dove il varco all'egro. *Epig.*, p. 115.
7.314. Cornarius. Unde ego, vel nomen. Corn., p. 266.
Alciati. Ne patriam nomenque. *Vit. Mon.*, p. 47.
Sabeo. Ne discas patriam. *Epig.*, p. 254.
Guazzo. Qui giaccio e non son. *Civ. Con.* (1574), f. 5ro.
Bongiovanni and Zanetti. Non chieder il mio. *Epig.*, p. 50.
7.315. Obsopoeus. Undique spinosis me. Obsop., p. 364; Wech., p. 318.
Sabeo. Ramnum utinam tenuis. *Epig.*, p. 813.
7.316. Lines 1–2 are quoted in *Vita Platon.* 2 (West., p. 393).
Sabeo. Vade super tumulum. *Epig.*, p. 271.
7.317. Sleidan. Ten' magis oblectant. Soter[2], p. 221; Corn., p. 266.
Cornarius. Quid magis ingratum est. Corn., p. 267.
Sabeo. Timon, non magis hos. *Epig.*, p. 255.
Cunich. Luxne magis, Timon. *Anth.*, p. 114.
Passeroni. Dimmi il vero, Timone. *Rime* 3.79.
Pagnini. V. Timone, or che se'. *Epig.*, p. 112.
7.318. Cunich. Hoc hominum ille osor. *Anth.*, p. 119.
Passeroni. Io Timone degli uomini. *Rime* 3.81.
Roncalli. Gli uomini odiai. *Epig.* (1792), p. 23.
7.319. Cf. Baldi. Va' piano, O peregrin. *Epig.* 1092.
7.320. Cf. Propertius. Terra tuum spinis. *Eleg.* 4. 5. 1–2.
Lines 3–4 are quoted by Plutarch (*Antonius* 70.4).
Cornarius. Ingentes circum tumulum. Corn., p. 267.
Obsopoeus. Et spinae atque pali. Obsop., p. 363; Wech., p. 318.
Cunich. Hunc circa tumulum. *Anth.*, p. 119.
Passeroni. Io Timone degli uomini. *Rime* 3. 82.
Roncalli. Gli uomini odiai. Il mio. *Epig.* (1801), p. 42.
7.321. Sabeo. Suscipe terra senem. *Epig.*, p. 141.
Cunich. Terra sinu Eucratiden. *Anth.*, p. 106.
Passeroni. Eucratide benevola ricevi. *Rime* 3.234.
7.322. [Not in *Plan.*, but appears in Stephanus' ed., 1566, p. 499.]
Included in the *Peplus* of 'Aristotle' (No. 15); and quoted by Diodorus (5. 79).
7.323. Cf. *A.P.* 7. 551.
More (Sir T.). Quattuor hic tumulus fratres. Soter[2], p. 207; Corn., p. 248.
More (Sir T.). Quattuor hic tumulus. *ibid.*
Lily. Quattuor hic tumulus. *ibid.*
Franchini. Fratres hoc tumulo duo. *Epig.*, p. 125.
Sabeo. Continet una duos. *Epig.*, p. 316.
Sabeo. Bis duo habent unum. *Epig.*, p. 641.
Gualfreducci. Fratres unus habet. *Var.*, p. 292; *Sel. Epig.*, p. 285.
Gualfreducci. Bis fratres duo sunt. *Var.*, p. 292.

Felici. Di due fratelli giacciono. *Epig.*[2], p. iv.

Pagnini. Quest' urna ha duo. *Epig.*, p. 178.

7.324. Cf. Propertius. In lapide hoc uni nupta. *Eleg.* 4. 11. 36.

Cornarius. Hic iaceo fama cunctis. Corn., p. 272.

7.325. Cf. *A.P.* 16. 27. Quoted by Strabo (14, p. 672); Diodorus (2. 23); Dio of Prusa (4. 135); Athenaeus (8, p. 336A); Stephanus Byz., *s.v.* Ἀγχιάλη; *schol.* in Arist. *Av.* 1021; Tzetzes, *Chil.* 3. 456; prose par. in Georgius Hamart., *Chron*, p. 9; 'Eudocia,' *Viol.*, p. 372; phrases in numerous writers (see A. Nauck in *Bull. de l'Acad. des Sc. de St. Petersbourg* 8 (1865). 398, and Preger, p. 184).

Cicero. Haec habeo quae edi. *Tusc.* 5. 101; cf. *Fin.* 2. 32.

Cf. Rabirius. Hoc habeo quodcumque dedi. Seneca, *Ben.* 6. 3. 1.

Anon. Dum vixi, vixi quomodo. *Carm. Epig.* 187 (Buech.).

Anon. Quod edi bibi mecum habeo. *C.I.L.* 6. 18131.

Cf. Loredano. Senza havere o di sesso. *Cimit.* 2. 26.

Cf. Pagnini. Le laute mense e l'orgoglioso. *Epig.*, p. 66.

7.326. Quoted by Diogenes Laertius 6. 86.

Bentinus. Tantum habeo quantum. *Laert.*, p. 209; Soter[2], p. 240; Corn., p. 313.

Sabeo. Tanta habeo quanta. *Epig.*, p. 315.

Salvini. Ciò, che di bel studiai. *Disc.* (1733), p. 219.

7.327. Cornarius. Mortalis quum sis, quid. Corn., p. 248.

Jausserandus. Cum sis mortalis. Soter[3], p. 227.

Sabeo. Quum sis mortalis. *Epig.*, p. 183.

7.328. Obsopoeus. Quod saxum lachrymas. Obsop., p. 311; Wech., p. 280.

Jausserandus. Qui non te absumpto. Soter[3], p. 227.

Sabeo. Quae te defunctum. *Epig.*, p. 183.

7.329. Cf. *A.P.* 7. 353 and 455.

Cornarius. Boscia ego sacra ad Lenaei. Corn., p. 284.

Sabeo. Mortida apud Bacchi. *Epig.*, p. 371.

7.330. Sabeo. Quod cernis marmor. *Epig.*, p. 497.

7.333. Sabeo. Ad Stygios nostri. *Epig.*, p. 219.

7.335. Alciati. Politta, gemitu parce. Corn., p. 264.

7.336. Cornarius. Pauperie atque annis. Corn., p. 270.

Pagnini. Io vinto da vecchiezza. *Epig.*, p. 7.

7.338. Sabeo. Archiae o fili, tibi. *Epig.*, p. 223.

7.339. Obsopoeus. Nullo errore meo venio. Obsop., p. 290; Wech., p. 260.

7.340. Sabeo. Luctibus humectans. *Epig.*, p. 621.

7.341. [Not in *Plan.*] Quoted by Marinus, *Proclus* 36.

7.342. Cf. *A.P.* 10. 105.

Cornarius. Mortuus expecto te. Corn., p. 75.

Sabeo. Occubui, sed te. *Epig*, p. 213.

Sabeo. Ipse hodie perii. *Epig.*, p. 213.

'L-prose.' Mortuus sum. Ἐπ. καὶ Ἐλεγ. No. 29.

7.344. 1–2. Found in an inscription at Mytilene [*C.I.G.* 2168 (5–6)].
  Sabeo. Optimus iste hominum. *Epig.*, p. 247.
7.344. 3–4. Sabeo. Ni foret iste animo. *Epig.*, p. 758.
  Castelvetro quotes this epig. on Petr., *Canz.* 2. *Petr.*, p. 66.
7.345. Cf. *A.P.* 7. 450. Quoted by Athenaeus 8. 335C.
  Giraldi (L.G.) quotes Gr. and gives prose paraphrase. *Op.* 2.
  125.
7.346. With lines 2–3 cf. *Carm. Epig.* 179 (Buecheler): Bene adqui-
  escas.
  Obsopoeus. Parvulus iste lapis. Obsop., p. 316; Wech., p. 283.
  Sabeo. Optimae eris nostrae. *Epig.*, p. 316.
  Gualfreducci. Hoc erit heu! marmor. *Var.*, p. 289.
  Cunich. Sit lapis hic nostrae. *Anth.*, p. 106.
  Passeroni. Fede, dolce Sabin. *Rime* 3. 166.
  Pagnini. Sia questa pietra. *Epig.*, p. 50.
7.347. [Not in *Plan.*] Quoted by 'Dio of Prusa' (37.19 Arnim); by
  Plutarch (*Moral.* 870F).
7.348. Quoted by Athenaeus (10.415F).
  Volaterranus. Multa bibens tum multa vorans. *Com. Urb.*,
  p. 758; Soter², p. 219; Corn., p. 263.
  Quoted by Rhodiginus, *Lect.* 7. 11.
  Cornarius. Multa vorans, et multa. Corn., p. 263.
  Obsopoeus. Multa vorans, et multa. Obsop., p. 349; Wech.,
  p. 308.
  Molza. Multa vorans, et multa. *Poes.* 3. 205.
  Sabeo. Multa vorans, et multa. *Epig.*, p. 812.
  Giraldi. (L.G.). Multa bibens, et multa. *Op.* 2. 259.
  Crasso. Multa vorans, et multa. *Ist.*, p. 517.
  Allacci. Cum multa comederim [prose]. *De Sym.*, p. 213.
  Barberio quotes Giraldi's tr. Gronov., *Thes.* 10. 836.
  Ricolvi. Multa vorans, et multa. *Op.*, p. 69.
  Ricolvi. Di Rodi è quì sepolto. *Op.*, p. 69.
  Vargas. Timocreonte io fui. *Sag.*, p. 91.
  Pagnini. Timoleon natio. *Epig.*, p. 139.
  Pagnini. Dopo molto mangiar. *Epig.*, p. 124.
7.349. Cornarius. Pauca vorans, et pauca. Corn., p. 263.
  Sabeo. Parva vorans, et parva. *Epig.*, p. 812.
7.350. Cf. *A.P.* 7. 282 and 675.
  Cornarius. Nauita ne quaeras. Corn., p. 289.
  Obsopoeus. Heus bone, ne quaeras. Obsop., p. 423; Wech.,
  p. 367.
  Sabeo. Ne quaeras cui nam. *Epig.*, p. 823.
  Cunich. Cuius sim tumulus. *Anth.*, p. 107.
  Passeroni. Non cercar chi mi sia. *Rime* 3. 244.
7.351. Cf. 352.
  (1–6) Sabeo. Per Stygis horrendum. *Epig.*, p. 794.
  (7–10) Sabeo. Per Superos Manesque. *Epig.*, p. 263.
  (7–10) Sabeo. Per Superos Manesque. *Epig.*, p. 794.

Cunich. Iuramus quidquid. *Anth.*, p. 142.
Passeroni. Noi, di Licambe onesta. *Rime* 3. 86.
7. 352. Cf. 351.
Sabeo. Per Iovis inferni dextram. *Epig.*, p. 259.
Sabeo. Per dextram inferni. *Epig.*, p. 774.
7.353. Cf. *A.P.* 7. 329 and 455.
Cf. Propertius. Et canis, in nostros. *Eleg.* 4. 5. 73.
Sleidan. Haec vetulae sunt busta. Soter[2], p. 230; Corn., p. 284.
Obsopoeus. Haec est annosae. Obsop., p. 408; Wech., p. 353.
Quoted by Landi, *Num.*, p. 31.
Bongiovanni and Zanetti. Questa è la tomba. *Epig.*, p. 36.
Ricolvi. Hoc subter saxo. *Op.*, p. 73.
Cunich. Haec vetulae sunt busta. *Anth.*, p. 111.
Passeroni. Di Marenide il corpo. *Rime* 3. 245.
Roncalli. In questo marmo. *Epig.* (1792), p. 81; (1801) p. 62.
7.354. Sabeo. Medeae haec tumulus. *Epig.*, p. 354.
7.355. Sabeo. Voce viatores hilari. *Epig.*, p. 318.
Crasso. Hilaram vocem [L-prose]. *Ist.*, p. 432.
Cunich. Haec hilares ad busta. *Anth.*, p. 106.
Passeroni. Salutate quest' urna. *Rime* 3. 233.
7.356–60 have the same theme; cf. *A.P.* 7. 310, 516, 580, and 581.
7.356. Sleidan. Occultas modo, non sepelis. Soter[2], p. 215; Corn.,
p. 260.
Obsopoeus. Occisum sepelis. Obsop., p. 340; Wech., p. 301.
Pagnini. M'ascondi perchè. *Epig.*, p. 7.
7.357. Alciati. Me sepelis tantum. Soter[2], p. 215; Corn., p. 260; *Op.*
4. 269.
Sleidan. Me licet occultes. Soter[2], p. 215; Corn., p. 261.
Obsopoeus. Quamvis me condas. Obsop., p. 340; Wech.,
p. 301.
Carcani (P.). Benchè da alcun non. *Ant. Ercol.* 8. 12; *Rac.* 3.
53.
7.358. Obsopoeus. Occidis, dextra condis. Obsop., p. 340; Wech.,
p. 301.
7.359. (1–2) Obsopoeus. Me exanimem miti. Obsop., p. 340; Wech.,
p. 301.
(3–4) Obsopoeus. Nunc quum me tumulo. Obsop., p. 340;
Wech., p. 301.
Sabeo. Si prius inspiciens. *Epig.*, p. 720.
7.360. Obsopoeus. Occiso manibus tumulum. Obsop., p. 340; Wech.,
p. 301.
7.364. [Not in *Plan.*] Cf. *A.P.* 7. 190.
7.369. Sabeo. Rhetoris Antipatri tumulus. *Epig.*, p. 198.
7.370. Crasso. Qui Baccho et Musis [L-prose]. *Ist.*, p. 339.
Meursius. Hic ego Cecropiden. Bonada 1.408.
Rivautella-Ricolvi. Acceptus Baccho et Musis. *Mar.* 1. 184.
7.371. Gualfreducci. Terra fuit genitrix. *Var.*, p. 290; *Sel. Epig.*,
p. 287.

7.373. Gualfreducci. Fulgebant Milete tuae. *Var.*, p. 288; *Sel. Epig.*, p. 283.
7.376. Sabeo. Quid miseri errantes. *Epig.*, p. 251.
7.378. Sabeo. Eliodorus obit. *Epig.*, p. 218.
7.379. [Not in *Plan.*] Cf. *A.P.* 9. 708.
7.381. Cf. *A.P.* 7. 305, 585, 635; and 9. 242.
Sabeo. Iam maris et senii. *Epig.*, p. 239.
Amalteo (G.B.). Vecta levi pinus. *Tr. Frat.*, p. 144.
Beverini. Una tulit vivum. *Carm.*, p. 158; *C.P.It.* 2. 214.
7.382. Cf. 393.
7.383. Alciati. Hic homines miseri. Corn., p. 288.
Sabeo. Urnam hominis penitus. *Epig.*, p. 228.
Castelvetro quotes this epig. on Petr. *Sest.* 1. *Petr.*, p. 40.
7.385. [Not in *Plan.*] Cf. Quintus Smyrn. 7. 409.
7.387. Sabeo. Thionoes hymenaea. *Epig.*, p. 639.
Pagnini. Io della cara sposa. *Epig.*, p. 16.
7.391. [Not in *Plan.*]
Medici (A. de'). Clavigeri, infernos. *Scelt.*, p. xli.
Medici (A. de'). Dall' imo infernal. *Scelt.*, p. xli.
7.393. [Not in *Plan.*] Cf. 382.
7.396. Cf. 399.
Ausonius? Nec Stygiis lacis. *Opus.* 23. 25; Soter[2], p. 227; Corn., p. 277.
Alciati. Oedipode infoelix genitos. Corn., p. 278.
Cf. Alamanni. Dei dui frati Eteocle. *Versi* 2. 129.
Sabeo. Natorum Oedipedis Thebas. *Epig.*, p. 190.
Groto. Nel rogo de fratelli. *Rime* 3 (1610). f.82.
7.398. Cf. 533.
Obsopoeus. Haud scio num. Obsop., p. 409; Wech., p. 354.
Sabeo. An si foedem. *Epig.*, p. 224.
7.399. [Not in *Plan.*] Cf. 396.
7.400. Sabeo. Testa hominis duri. *Epig.*, p. 249.
7.401. Obsopoeus. Clemens, quo nunquam. Obsop., p. 479; Wech., p. 411.
Obsopoeus. Hospes cede procul. Obsop., p. 478; Wech., p. 411.
7.403. Cf. Propertius. Si tumulus lenae. *Eleg.* 4. 5. 75–8.
Sabeo. Ducebam ad iuvenum. *Epig.*, p. 816.
7.404. Sabeo. Aggere arenoso gelidum. *Epig.*, p. 763.
7.405. Cf. 408.
7.408. Cf. 405.
Sabeo. Pertransite quiete. *Epig.*, p. 312.
Cunich. Hunc tacitus tumulum. *Anth.*, p. 122.
Passeroni. O tu, chiunque sii. *Rime* 3. 84.
Pagnini. Va innanzi, O viator. *Epig.*, p. 51.
7.412. Obsopoeus. Tota tua, Pylade. Obsop., p. 473; Wech., p. 409.
Conti. Extinctum luget, Pylades. *Myth.* 1. 13.
Sabeo. Te Pylade, enectum. *Epig.*, p. 377.
Crasso. Omnis tibi mortuo [L-prose]. *Ist.*, p. 413.

7.413. Sabeo. Non opus elegi muliebre. *Epig.*, p. 817.
Carcani (P.). Non scelsi già delle ben. *Ant. Ercol.* 7. 240; *Rac.* 3. 137.
7.414. Politian refers to this epig. *Epist.* 11. 10 (p. 417).
Sabeo. Iucundum ridens transi. *Epig.*, p. 191.
Crasso. Et vehementer ridens [L-prose]. *Ist.*, p. 445.
7.415. [Not in *Plan.*]
Pagnini. Di Batto il figlio. *Epig.*, p. 179.
7.416. [Not in *Plan.*]
Crasso. Eucratis filius Meleager [prose]. *Ist.*, p. 333.
7.417. Sabeo. Insula mi nutrix Tyrus. *Epig.*, p. 249.
Crasso. Insula mea nutrix [L-prose]. *Ist.*, p. 333.
7.419. Fioretti. Si tu Syrus es, Salam [L-prose]. *Prog.* 3. 371.
7.421. Sabeo. Quid tibi apri spolium? *Epig.*, p. 369.
7.424. [Not in *Plan.*]
Carcani (P.). Dimmi, che pensò mai. *Ant. Ercol.* 8. 64.
7.425. [Not in *Plan.*]
Carcani (P.). Non ti fia di stupor. *Ant. Ercol.* 8. 142.
7.429. Janus Lascaris alludes to this epig. Above, p. 116, n. 1.
7.430. [Not in *Plan.*] Cf. 431 and 526.
7.431. Cf. 430 and 526.
Sabeo. Tercenti e patria. *Epig.*, p. 388.
7.432. Sabeo. O Lacedemonii, vobis. *Epig.*, p. 263.
Cunich. O Lacedaemonii, clarum. *Anth.*, p. 115.
Passeroni. Qui giace, O Lacedemoni. *Rime* 3. 79.
7.433. Cf. *A.P.* 7. 230, 531; 9. 61, 397, and 447.
Quoted by Plutarch (*Moral.* 240E), and again, lines 5–8, (*Moral.* 241A); lines 1–2 are given by Tzetzes (Cramer, *Anecd. Ox.* 4. 43).
Filelfo. Hunc timidum mater. *Orat.*, Zii (also sig. Ivi.); Soter[2], p. 212; Corn., p. 258.
Alciati. Materno caesus fugiens. Corn., p. 257.
Cornarius. Peccantem in leges. Corn., p. 257.
Erasmus. Transgressum leges mater. Soter[3], p. 234.
Sabeo. Transgressum leges Demetrion. *Epig.*, p. 268.
Sabeo. Ignavum a bello. *Epig.*, p. 268.
Minturno. Transgressum leges, Demetri. *Epig.*, f.2ro.
Cardano quotes Filelfo's tr., *Op.* 1. 614.
7.434. Sabeo. Hostium ad insidias. *Epig.*, p. 336.
Angelio. Octo olim natos bello. *Poem.*, p. 388.
Cunich. Quos misit gnatos. *Anth.*, p. 32.
Passeroni. Mandò otto figli. *Rime* 3. 184.
Felici. Otto figliuoli in guerra. *Epig.*[2], p. xv.
7.437. Sabeo. Optime ad Eurotam. *Epig.*, p. 331.
7.438. Sabeo. Tu quoque in Aetholos. *Epig.*, p. 262.
7.439. Sabeo. Sic Pylium imberbem. *Epig.*, p. 254.
7.442. Sabeo. Illorum est tumulus. *Epig.*, p. 307.
7.443. [Not in *Plan.*] Published by Allacci, *De Sym.*, p. 215.

7.444. Sabeo. Aedes Andragorae somno. *Epig.*, p. 218.
7.445. Sabeo. Contegimur sylva. *Epig.*, p. 489.
7.447. Gualfreducci. Hospes erat brevior. *Var.*, p. 289; *Sel. Epig.*, p. 284.
      Cunich. Sum brevis, et tumulus. *Anth.*, p. 113.
      Passeroni. Picciolo io son. *Rime* 3. 143.
7.450. [Not in *Plan.*] Cf. 345.
7.451. Cf. *C.I.G.* 6276 (7–8), found at Rome.
      Luscinius. Ecce Saon sacro concessit. Corn., p. 247.
      Cornarius. Dormit et imposita requiescit. Corn., p. 247.
      Sabeo. Somne Saona Diconis. *Epig.*, p. 141.
      Cunich. Haec habet urna Saona. *Anth.*, p. 115.
      Passeroni. Qui dorme il buon Saone. *Rime* 3. 71.
      Pagnini. Chiuso ha qui dentro. *Epig.*, p. 129.
      Mariani. Compiuto alfine. *Ep. Mod. Aut.*, p. 58.
7.452. Sabeo. Hospes ad Eubuli. *Epig.*, p. 250.
      Felici. Al freddo cenere. *Epig.*[1], p. 48.
7.453. Cunich. Implentem vitae nondum. *Anth.*, p. 115.
      Passeroni. Di Nicotele suo d'ingegno. *Rime* 3. 79.
7.454. [Not in *Plan.*] Quoted by Athenaeus (10. 436E).
      Pagnini. Due volte tracannato. *Epig.*, p. 132.
7.455. Cf. 329 and 353.
      Sabeo. Urna Maronidis vetulae. *Epig.*, p. 799.
      Cf. Loredano. Parca crudel, che i. *Cimit.* 1. 48.
      Cf. Bettinelli. Qui si sta il bon. *Op.* 22. 99.
      Cf. Roncalli. In questo marmo. *Epig. Mod. Aut.*, p. 10.
7.456. Sabeo. Nutricem ipse Hieron. *Epig.*, p. 799.
      Cf. Loredano. Io, che vivendo già. *Cimit.* 1. 35.
7.459. Sabeo. Crethida verbosam. *Epig.*, p. 806.
7.461. Cf. Martial. Mollia non rigidus. *Epig.* 5. 34. 9–10.
      Cf. *Carm. Epig.* 1313. 3 (Buecheler): Terraque quae mater.
      Cornarius. Omniparens tellus, nunquam. Corn., p. 247.
      Sabeo. Non gravis Antigenes. *Epig.*, p. 351.
      Sabeo. Terra parens, gaude. *Epig.*, p. 506.
      Averani. Omniparens, tibi quando. *Op.* 1. 112.
      Cunich. Omniparens tellus. *Anth.*, p. 123.
      Passeroni. Conosciuto non ho fanciul. *Rime* 3. 144.
      Pagnini. Terra, nessun d'Aussigene. *Epig.*, p. 36.
      Mariani. Sii leggiero. *Ep. Mod. Aut.*, p. 58.
      Cf. Mariani. Gianni architetto. De-Mauri, p. 182.
7.464. With lines 7–8 cf. *Carm. Epig.* 2080. 7–8 (Buecheler-Lommatzch): Pignora dividimus; comitatur. [Found in Jersey.]
      Cunich. Infernam puppim linquens. *Anth.*, p. 135.
      Cf. Bettinelli. Di due gemelli madre. *Op.* 22. 101.
      Pagnini. Di due gemelli madre. *Epig.*, p. 145.
7.465. With lines 7–8 cf. Kaibel 675 [found at Bordeaux].
      Sabeo. Pulvis defossus nunc. *Epig.*, p. 818.
      Averani. Defossus nuper cinis. *Op.* 1. 86.

7.466. Sabeo. Ah miser Anticles. *Epig.*, p. 393.
7.467. Sabeo. Artimidore, super tumulo. *Epig.*, p. 347.
7.468. Sabeo. Munere ter misero. *Epig.*, p. 454.
7.470. Sabeo. Dic percuntancti [*sic*]. *Epig.*, p. 805.
7.471. Cicero paraphrases this epig. *Tusc. Disp.* 1. 84.
      Quoted by Sextus Empiricus, *Adv. Math.* 48, ed. Bekker,
        p. 609; David, *Prol. et in Porphyr. Isag. Comm.*, ed. Busse,
        p. 31; Elias, *In Porphyr. Isag. Comm.*, ed. Busse, p. 14;
        Ammonius, *In Porphyr. Isag. Prooem.* 20, ed. Busse, p. 4;
        Schol. Vat. on Dio Thrax (Hilgard, p. 160).
      Gaurico (P.). Vita vale, muro praeceps. Bocchi, *Sym.*, p. 31.
      Quoted by Sabino. Gruter, *Lamp.* 1. 1194.
      Bocchi. Ambraciota mare situs [prose]. *Sym.*, p. 31.
      Sabeo. Sol valeas dicendo. *Epig.*, p. 305.
      Aquino. Desilit, aeternae captus. *Carm.* 1. 115.
      Pagnini. Addio, Sol, disse. *Epig.*, p. 132.
7.477. Sabeo. Istud ne fiat nimium. *Epig.*, p. 345.
7.478. Sabeo. Ecquis es? et cuius. *Epig.*, p. 254.
      Giraldi (L.G.) quotes this epigram. *Op.* 1. 738.
7.479. Cf. 480.
      Sabeo. Petra rotunda ego. *Epig.*, p. 239.
7.480. Cf. 479.
      Sabeo. Os mihi iam tritum. *Epig.*, p. 804.
7.483. Sabeo. Orce prece et pretio. *Epig.*, pp. 255, 802.
7.485. Sabeo. Spargite cana super. *Epig.*, p. 253.
7.486. Sabeo. Saepe super tumulo. *Epig.*, p. 362.
7.487. Sabeo. Ante faces absumpta. *Epig.*, p. 328.
      Cunich. Heu miseranda iaces. *Anth.*, p. 124.
      Passeroni. La misera Filenia. *Rime* 3. 84.
7.488. Sabeo. Eheu! mortua Aristocratea. *Epig.*, p. 347.
7.489. Politian. Timados hic pulvis. Del Lungo, p. 544; Soter[2],
        p. 224; Corn., p. 273.
      Sabeo. Timadis hoc saxum. *Epig.*, p. 800.
      Cunich. Timadis hic cinis. *Anth.*, p. 125.
      Passeroni. Qui di Timade son. *Rime* 3. 115.
      Vargas. Timade è qui sepolta. *Sag.*, p. 27.
      Pagnini. Di Timade ecco il fral. *Epig.*, p. 123.
7.490. Cf. 184 and 611.
      Sabeo. Lugeo parthenicem. *Epig.*, p. 673.
7.492. Sabeo. Nos ignominiam. *Epig.*, p. 641.
      Mazzoni quotes this epig. *Difesa*, p. 726.
      Cunich. O patrium Milete solum. *Anth.*, p. 8.
7.493. Sabeo. Non morbo Rhodope. *Epig.*, p. 643.
7.496. [Not in *Plan.*] Published by Allacci, *De Sym.*, p. 215.
7.499. Sabeo. Qui mare sulcatis. *Epig.*, p. 229.
7.500. Sabeo. Marmor inane meum. *Epig.*, p. 231.
      Felici. O tu, che i passi. *Epig.*[1], p. 24.
7.504. Cf. *A.P.* 7.702.

7.505. Sabeo. Nassa tui et remus. *Epig.*, p. 489.
Sabeo. A patre piscator. *Epig.*, p. 439.
Vargas. Menisco genitore. *Sag.*, p. 26.
Pagnini. Menisco il genitore. *Epig.*, p. 119.
7.507. 1–2. Sabeo. Inspicis haud Croesi. *Epig.*, p. 250.
7.508. Diogenes Laertius 8. 2 (Empedocles).
Brugnolo? Pausaniae medico Anchito. Laert.; Soter², p. 230;
Corn., p. 281.
Bentinus. Pausaniam Anchiti natum. *Laert.*, p. 296; Soter²,
p. 230; Corn., p. 281.
7.509. [Not in *Plan.*] Published by Allacci, *De Sym* , p. 215.
7.510. Cunich. Ossa peregrinus pulvis. *Anth.*, p. 125.
7.511. [Not in *Plan.*] Published by Allacci, *De Sym.*, p. 215.
7.512. Sabeo. Horum hominum tellus. *Epig.*, p. 247.
Cunich. Horum ob virtutem. *Anth.*, p. 102.
7.514. [Not in *Plan.*] Published by Allacci, *De Sym.*, p. 215.
7.515. Sabeo. Eheu morbe atrox. *Epig.*, p. 318.
Sabeo. Eheu morbe atrox animis. *Epig.*, p. 638.
7.516. Cf. *A.P.* 7. 310, 356–60, 580–1.
7.518. Obsopoeus. Pastorem Astacidem rapuit. Obsop., p. 476;
Wech., p. 409.
Cunich. Cretaeum Astaciden. *Anth.*, p. 27.
7.519. Sleidan. Visus heri nobis longo. Soter², p. 219; Corn., p. 263.
Cunich. Cui nota est vitae sors. *Anth.*, p. 141.
7.521. Cunich. Cyzicon adveniens. *Anth.*, p. 114.
Passeroni. O passeggier, se a. *Rime* 3. 82.
Pagnini. A te lieve opra sia. *Epig.*, p. 167.
7.522. Sabeo. Timonoe, quae nam es? *Epig.*, p. 801.
Cunich. Timonoe, quaenam es? *Anth.*, p. 113.
7.524. Beroaldo (younger). Sexte, quid est. *Carm.* Niii; Wech.,
p. 305.
Mazzoni quotes this epig. *Difesa*, p. 575.
Cunich. Dic, lapis, anne. *Anth.*, p. 114.
7.525. Cunich. Qui tumulum hunc praeter. *Anth.*, p. 113.
Passeroni. Tu, che passi vicino. *Rime* 3. 70.
Vargas. O tu, che a questo. *Sag.*, p. 77.
Pagnini. Di Callimaco e figlio. *Epig.*, p. 168.
7.526. Cf. *A.P.* 7. 430–1.
Flaminio. Ecquam, Othryade, unquam. *Carm.*, p. 82.
Sabeo. Iuppiter Otriadem. *Epig.*, p. 238.
7.528. Sabeo. Phanaretes latum ad tum. *Epig.*, p. 343.
Cunich. Tristia Phaenaretes olim. *Anth.*, p. 128.
Passeroni Su questa tomba. *Rime* 3. 252.
7.529. Sabeo. Ad coelum et Manes. *Epig.*, p. 759.
7.530. Sabeo. Excipe me solam. *Epig.*, p. 376.
Sabeo. Cymba mea haec rimosa. *Epig.*, p. 377.
Cunich. Accipe cum gnatis me. *Anth.*, p. 135.
Passeroni. Caron, me sola co' miei. *Rime* 3. 85.

Felici. O tu, che l'ombre pallide. *Epig.*², p. vii.
7.531. [Not in *Plan.*] Cf. *A.P.* 7. 230, 433; 9. 61, 397, and 447.
7.532. Sabeo. A cultu agrorum. *Epig.*, p. 764.
    Pagnini. Me da' campi tiro. *Epig.*, p. 18.
7.533. [Not in *Plan.*] Cf. 398.
7.534. [Only lines 1–2 are in *Plan.*] Cf. 650.
    Sabeo. Ipsa parum vivens. *Epig.*, p. 329.
    Sabeo. Temporis exigui. *Epig.*, p. 762.
    Sabeo. Nec te hora inspiciat. *Epig.*, p. 762.
    Sabeo. Ultra horam ne nauta. *Epig.*, p. 763.
    Sabeo. Solum hora sulcato. *Epig.*, p. 764.
    Regolotti. Perdona, deh perdona. *Teoc.*, p. 263.
    Cunich. Vitae parce, ratem. *Anth.*, p. 127.
    Della Torre. Uom, risparmia. *Odi*, p. 369.
    Vicini. Ben sia che a la. *Gl'Id.*, p. 189.
    Pagnini. Uom, risparmia la vita. *Poet. Gr.*, p. 871.
7.535. Sabeo. Non mage cum capris. *Epig.*, p. 617.
7.536. Sabeo. Nondum erat extinctus. *Epig.*, p. 337.
7.538. More (Sir T.). Hic servus dum vixit. Soter², p. 226; Corn.,
    p. 275.
    Sleidan. Vivus erat miser hic. Soter², p. 226; Corn., p. 276.
    Cunich. Servus eram vivus. *Anth.*, p. 108.
    Passeroni. Servo vissi io, ma morte. *Rime* 3. 157.
    Pagnini. Vil servo, finch' ebb'io. *Epig.*, p. 46.
7.540. Sabeo. Per superum regem. *Epig.*, p. 250.
    Cunich. O bone, sic faveat. *Anth.*, p. 116.
7.541. Sabeo. Hostibus oppositus. *Epig.*, p. 262.
7.542. Cf. *A.P.* 9. 56, under which all imitations of this theme are
    listed.
7.545. Gualfreducci. Dextrum iter est Erebi. *Var.*, p. 289; *Sel. Epig.*,
    p. 283.
7.546. Sabeo. Spiculum egestatis. *Epig.*, p. 800.
7.547. Sabeo. Non patris inscripsit. *Epig.*, p. 304.
7.549. Sabeo. In Sypilo petra. *Epig.*, p. 317.
    Ricolvi. Bis septem Niobe natorum. *Op.*, p. 74.
7.550. Cf. *A.P.* 7. 289.
7.551. Cf. *A.P.* 7. 323.
    Cornarius. Lutius et Paulus fratres. Corn., p. 249.
    Sabeo. Loetius et Paulus. *Epig.*, p. 616.
    Gualfreducci. Letoeus Paulo geminus. *Var.*, p. 292; *Sel. Epig.*,
    p. 285.
7.552. Sabeo. Hospes, quid ploras? *Epig.*, p. 801.
7.553. [The sentiment of this epigram—slave in body, not in mind—
    is of frequent occurrence in ancient writers; see the parallels
    collected by Boissonade in the Didot Anthology 1. 486.]
    More (Sir T.) Ante fuit solo Sosime. Soter², p. 226; Corn.,
    p. 275.
    Cunich. Serva prius fueram. *Anth.*, p. 116.

Passeroni. Zosima io son, il di. *Rime* 3. 80.
Pagnini. Viva fui serva sol. *Epig.*, p. 27.
7.554. Sabeo. Hanc super Architeles. *Epig.*, p. 327.
7.555.5. Cunich. Attulit hoc virtus. *Anth.*, p. 106.
Felici. La tua virtute, O Nosto. *Epig.*², p. xx.
7.556. Sabeo. Te moriente Orcus. *Epig.*, p. 259.
7.557. Pagnini. Il terzo oltra. *Epig.*, p. 69.
7.558. Sabeo. Furtim surripuit fructum. *Epig.*, p. 635.
Crasso. Mors quidem depopulata [L-prose]. *Ist.*, p. 446.
7.559. Obsopoeus. Vidit tres luctus. Wech., p. 348.
Sabeo. Ars medica inspexit. *Epig.*, p. 200.
7.560. 3–8. Sabeo. Quot tibi inferias. *Epig.*, p. 645.
7.561. Cf. 562.
7.562. Cf. 561.
Sabeo. Quid tibi vis Crateri. *Epig.*, p. 276.
7.563. Ferrari. Taces, Chrysomale, instar. Sallengre 2.689.
7.564. Sabeo. Olim absque inferiis. *Epig.*, p. 342.
7.565. Sabeo. Quam bene pinxisti. *Epig.*, p. 299 (287).
Sabeo. O utinam errasset pictor. *Epig.*, p. 266.
Sabeo. Pingens Theodetim. *Epig.*, p. 266.
Cunich. Ipsam Theodoten pictor. *Anth.*, p. 33.
Pompei. Ben il pittor, quale. *Op.* 2. 191.
Passeroni. Quale era Teodote. *Rime* 3. 181.
Pagnini. Egregio dipintore. *Epig.*, p. 90.
7.566. Sabeo. Prima parens Lucina. *Epig.*, p. 256.
7.567. Sabeo. Urna haec Candaulis. *Epig.*, p. 331.
Sabeo. Peccavere omnes, uxor magis. *Epig.*, p. 332.
7.568. Sabeo. Bis sex annorum. *Epig.*, p. 56.
7.569. Sabeo. Thessaliam si tu. *Epig.*, p. 620.
7.570. Gualfreducci. Dulcitium, dum vixit. *Var.*, p. 288; *Sel. Epig.*,
p. 282.
7.572. Cornarius. Illicitos quum forte. Corn., p. 285.
Obsopoeus. Probrosis thalamis. Obsop., p. 410; Wech., 355.
Cf. Loredano. Sono due amanti in questi. *Cimit.* 1. 92.
7.573. Sabeo. Rhetoricae antiquae. *Epig.*, p. 198.
7.574. Alciati. Dum meditare Agatho. Corn., p. 290.
7.575. Sabeo. Urna Rhodes, mulier. *Epig.*, p. 267.
7.576. Crasso. Mortuus es, o Pyrro? [L-prose]. *Ist.*, p. 416.
7.578. Sabeo. Venari validum hirsutos. *Epig.*, p. 820.
7.580. Cf. 7. 310, 356–60, 516, 581.
Sabeo. Non me occultabis, tellus. *Epig.*, p. 218.
Pagnini. A me sepolcro diè. *Epig.*, p. 8.
7.582. Sabeo. Naufrage, plaude mihi. *Epig.*, p. 380.
Pagnini. Naufrago, salve. Infra. *Epig.*, p. 12.
7.585. Cf. *A.P.* 7. 305, 381, 635; and 9. 242.
7.586. Cf. Propertius 3. 7.
Felici. Perchè accusi il mare. *Epig.*¹, p. 42.
7.588. Sabeo. Damocaris subit. *Epig.*, p. 326.

Crasso. Democharis fati [L-prose]. *Ist.*, p. 139.
7.589. Sabeo. Quisquis es hac gradiens. *Epig.*, p. 360.
Crasso. Nihil annuncies [L-prose] *Ist.*, p. 219.
7.590. Sabeo. Inclyte Ioannes reginae. *Epig.*, p. 438.
Gualfreducci. Clarus Ioannes. Mortalis. *Sel. Epig.*, p. 281.
Gualfreducci. Clarus eram; mortalis. *Var.*, p. 288.
Bongiovanni and Zanetti. A. Generoso Giovanni. *Epig.*, p. 51.
7.591. Sabeo. Sum statio Hyparci. *Epig.*, p. 353.
7.593. Sabeo. Quae fuerat primum. *Epig.*, p. 127.
Crasso. Prius florentem [L-prose]. *Ist.*, p. 214.
Cunich. Florentem roseisque genis. *Anth.*, p. 108.
Pompei. Quella che in mente. *Op.* 2. 186.
Felici. Giace in quest' urna. *Epig.*[1], p. 4.
Passeroni. Sepolta Eugenia è qui. *Rime* 3. 243.
Pagnini. Eugenia, a cui la rosa. *Epig.*, p. 32.
7.594. Sabeo. Conderis in nullo. *Epig.*, p. 343.
7.595. Cornarius. Heliodorus ubi moritur. *Corn.*, p. 261.
Sabeo. Turba poetarum veterum. *Epig.*, p. 397; *C.P.It.* 8.212.
Crasso. Mortuus est Theodorus [L-prose]. *Ist.*, p. 502.
7.597. Sabeo. Dulce canens. *Epig.*, p. 219.
7.598. Sabeo. Ingenium invalidum. *Epig.*, p. 344.
7.599. Cornarius. Hic Formosa iacet. *Corn.*, p. 273.
Medici (A. de'). Nomine dicta Καλή. *Scelt.*, p. xlvi.
Medici (A. de'). Bella di nome. *Scelt.*, p. xlvi.
Pagnini. Bella di nome. *Epig.*, p. 87.
7.600. Cf. 601.
Cornarius. Maturo es thalamo. *Corn.*, p. 291.
Bongiovanni and Zanetti. Te 'n sua stagion. *Epig.*, p. 28.
7.601. Cf. 600.
Sabeo. Eheu! magnarum charitum. *Epig.*, p. 636.
7.603. Anon. Vicisti priscos longaeva. *Carm. Epig.* (Buecheler) 1388.
5–6.
Pompei. Crudo è Caronte. *Op.* 2. 191.
7.604. Sabeo. Flebilibus palmis lectum. *Epig.*, p. 639.
7.605. Obsopoeus. Haec tibi busta Rhodo. Obsop., p. 384; Wech.,
p. 335.
Sabeo. Ex praestante Rhode saxo. *Epig.*, p. 269.
Cunich. Hunc tumulum pulcro. *Anth.*, p. 52.
Bettinelli, Sì nobil mausoleo. *Op.* 22. 97.
Felici. Tomba marmorea. *Epig.*[1], p. 41.
7.606. Sabeo. Qui prius et liber. *Epig.*, p. 351.
7.607. Sabeo. Invida anus propriis. *Epig.*, p. 808.
7.608. Sabeo. Deplorans genetrix nati. *Epig.*, p. 266.
7.608. Bongiovanni and Zanetti. Dell'estinto figliuol. *Epig.*, p. 40.
Pagnini. Piagnea Menippa il caro. *Epig.*, p. 149.
7.610. Sabeo. Qui rapuit sponsam. *Epig.*, p. 819.
7.611. Cf. *A.P.* 7. 184 and 490.
Sabeo. Inviolatum Helenen. *Epig.*, p. 636.

Pagnini. Dopo morto il figliuol. *Epig.*, p. 14.

7.612. Sabeo. Eheu! quae Romae. *Epig.*, p. 221.

7.613. Sabeo. Phryx pater ista tibi. *Epig.*, p. 231.

7.615. Quoted by Diogenes Laertius (*Prooem.*).
Quoted in the 1494 Musaeus (Aldus).
Brugnolo? Eumolpi exanimem. Laert.; Soter², p. 234; Corn., p. 294.
Bentinus. Eumolpi exanimem. *Laert.*, p. 2; Soter², p. 234; Corn., p. 294.
Mara (Gul. de), Eumolphi charum nunc. Soter², p. 234; Corn., p. 295.
Sabeo. Dilectum Eumolphi pignus. *Epig.*, p. 341.
Sabeo. Musaeum Eumolphi. *Epig.*, p. 341.
Giraldi (L.G.). Eumolphi charum tenet. *Op.* 2. 58.
Barberio quotes Giraldi's tr. Gronov., *Thes.* 10. 815.

7.616. Quoted by Diogenes Laertius (*Prooem.* 4).
Brugnolo? Candida purpureis redimitum. Laert., Soter², p. 234; Corn., p. 295.
Volaterranus gives the tr. printed by Brugnolo. *Com. Urb.*, p. 382.
Bentinus. Candida purpureis redimitum. *Laert.*, p. 2.
Sabeo. Thebanum tenet urna. *Epig.*, p. 342.
Sabeo. Uraniae peperit. *Epig.*, p. 342.
Sabeo. Cui caput ornarunt. *Epig.*, p. 360.
Giraldi (L.G.). Thebanum ista Linum. *Op.* 2. 47.
Barberio quotes Giraldi's tr. Gronov., *Thes.* 10. 813.
Felici. Del Teban Lino le ceneri. *Epig.*¹, p. 15.

7.617. Quoted by Diogenes Laertius (*Prooem.* 5); cf. Didot Anthol., vol. 3, 2. 99 (p. 106).
Landino. Orphea chrysolyram. Soter², p. 235; Corn., p. 295.
Brugnolo? Orphea candenti transfixum. Laert.; Soter², p. 235; Corn., p. 295.
Quoted by C. Lascaris, *Mar. Taur.* 1. 96.
Marullus. Orphea dum miseranda. Soter², p. 235; Corn., p. 295.
Bentinus. Orphea candenti traiectum. *Laert.*, p. 3; Soter², 235; Corn., p. 295.
Conti. Conditus a Musis tumulo. *Myth.*, 7. 13.
Sabeo. Quem trifida exussit. *Epig.*, p. 325.
Sabeo. Iuppiter altitonans. *Epig.*, p. 341.
Sabeo. Aurati vates plectri. *Epig.*, p. 341.
Sabeo. Hic situs a Musis. *Epig.*, p. 343.
Sabeo. Igne Iovis victum. *Epig.*, p. 362.
Sabeo. Aonidum manus hoc. *Epig.*, p. 369.
Sabeo. Orphea Castalides. *Epig.*, p. 454.
Giraldi (L.G.). Orpheus hic positus. *Op.* 2. 54.
Barberio. Orphea Musarum famulum. Gronov., *Thes.* 10. 815.
Crasso. Thracem cum aurea [L-prose]. *Ist.*, p. 386.

Rivautella-Ricolvi. Insignem fidibus. *Mar.* 1. 96.
7.618. [Not in *Plan.*] Diogenes Laertius 1.6 (Cleobulus).
7.619. [Not in *Plan.*] Diogenes Laertius 1.7 (Periander).
 Brugnolo? Et sophia et nummis. Laert.
 Beroaldo (F.), the elder, quotes Brugnolo. *Var. Op.* f. xii^{vo}.
 Bentinus. Et sophia et nummis. *Laert.*, p. 36.
7.620. [Not in *Plan*]. Diogenes Laertius 1.7 (Periander); Suidas, *s.v.*
 Περίανδρος.
 Brugnolo? Ne tibi iam doleat. Laert.
 Beroaldo (F.), the elder, quotes from Brugnolo. *Var. Op.* f.
 xii^{vo}.
 Bentinus. Ne tibi iam doleat. *Laert.*, p. 36.
 Crasso quotes Bentinus' tr. *Ist.*, p. 408.
7.621. Sabeo. Non ego regna. *Epig.*, p. 248.
7.622. Sabeo. Fune petram Bochus. *Epig.*, p. 418; *C.P.It.* 8. 218.
7.623. Sabeo. A genetrice trahas. *Epig.*, p. 270.
 Cf. Bargiocchi. Cum cecidit magno. *Epig.*, p. 122.
7.627. Orsini quotes this epig. on Virgil, *Ecl.* 1. 70. *Virg.*, p. 14.
7.628. Sabeo. Plurima et ante suum. *Epig.*, p. 763.
7.629. Sabeo. Tantus humum hanc. *Epig.*, p. 361.
 Crasso. An terreum subiisti [L-prose]. *Ist.*, p. 469.
7.632. Sabeo. Ex modicis parvus scalis. *Epig.*, p. 803.
7.634. Sabeo. Defunctos capulum. *Epig.*, p. 256.
7.635. Cf. *A.P.* 7. 305, 381, 585; and 9. 242.
 Molza Communis Fati consors. *Poes.* 3. 207.
7.637. Sabeo. Exiguos pisces. *Epig.*, p. 495.
 Sabeo. Solus nave senex. *Epig.*, p. 495.
 Sabeo. Solus lyntre hami. *Epig.*, p. 496.
7.641. Sabeo. Bis senis signum. *Epig.*, p. 371.
7.643. Cf. 671.
 Sabeo. Evandri recitare hymnos. *Epig.*, p. 809.
7.646. Cf. 647.
 Sabeo. Haec circumpositis. *Epig.*, p. 453.
 Felici. Calda di lagrime. *Epig.*[1], p. 10.
7.647. Cf. 646.
 Sabeo. Sic Gorgo est charam. *Epig.*, p. 637.
7.649. Sabeo. Pro thalamo illustri. *Epig.*, p. 640.
 Sabeo. Splendentem ob thalami. *Epig.*, p. 642.
 Cunich. Hanc tibi pro thalamo. *Anth.*, p. 168.
7.650. Cf. 534.
 Obsopoeus. Aequora, vela, rates. Obsop., p. 422; Wech.,
 p. 365.
 Jordanus. Undosum pelagus fugito. Soter[3], p. 257.
7.652. Cf. Propertius. Sed tua nunc volucres. *Eleg.* 3. 7. 11.
7.655. Sabeo. Parva licet me condat. *Epig.*, p. 671.
 Sabeo. Sufficit exiguus pulvis. *Epig.*, p. 251.
7.656. Obsopoeus. Huic modicae glebae. Obsop., p. 332; Wech.,
 p. 295.

Sabeo. Gleba licet modica. *Epig.*, p. 337.
7.657. Sabeo. Qui montem hunc colitis. *Épig.*, p. 319.
7.658. [Not in *Plan.*] Theocritus, *Inscr.* 15.
Regolotti. Un argomento certo. *Teoc.*, p. 267.
Della Torre. Mi avvedro, viatore. *Odi*, p. 372.
Vicini. Or fia ch' i' riconosca. *Gl'Id.*, p. 187.
Pagnini. Vedrò, se i buon. *Poet. Gr.*, p. 871.
7.659. [Not in *Plan.*] Theocritus, *Inscr.* 7.
Salvini. Un pargoletto figlio. *Teoc.*, p. 186.
Regolotti. Un pargoletto figlio. *Teoc.*, p. 266.
Della Torre. Un pargoletto figlio. *Odi*, p. 372.
Pagnini. Lasciasti un picciol. *Poet. Gr.*, p. 871.
7.660. [Not in *Plan.*] Theocritus, *Inscr.* 9.
Martial. A Sinuessanis conviva. *Épig.* 11. 82.
Salvini. Forestier, questo un. *Teoc.*, p. 186.
Regolotti. Un uom di Siracusa. *Teoc.*, p. 263.
Della Torre. Ospite, l'uom. *Odi*, p. 369.
Vicini. Orton di Siracusa. *Gl'Id.*, p. 186.
Passeroni. Odi due motti: Orton. *Rime* 3. 249.
Pagnini. O forestiero, il Siracusio. *Poet. Gr.*, p. 870.
7.661. [Not in *Plan.*] Theocritus, *Inscr.* 11.
Salvini. Tomba d' Eustene. *Teoc.*, p. 187.
Regolotti. D' Eustene è questa. *Teoc.*, p. 264.
Della Torre. Questa tombe è. *Odi*, p. 370.
Vicini. Del fisonomo Eustene. *Gl'Id.*, p. 187.
Pagnini. Del fisonomo saggio. *Poet. Gr.*, p. 871.
7.662. Theocritus, *Inscr.* 16.
Sabeo. Multarum virgo comitum. *Epig.*, p. 637.
7.663. [Not in *Plan.*] Theocritus, *Inscr.* 20.
Salvini. Alla Treessa il piccolo. *Teoc.*, p. 188.
Regolotti. Il piccolo Medio. *Teoc.*, p. 268.
Della Torre. Alla Treessa il piccolo. *Odi*, p. 374.
Vicini. Qui ne la strada questo. *Gl'Id.*, p. 188.
Pagnini. A Tracia donna il pargolo. *Poet. Gr.*, p. 871.
7.664. [Not in *Plan.*] Theocritus, *Inscr.* 21.
Salvini. Fermati, e guarda l'antico. *Teoc.*, p. 188.
Regolotti. Fermati, passagero. *Teoc.*, p. 269.
Della Torre. Ferma, e Archiloco. *Odi*, p. 375.
Vicini. Il piè sofferma. *Gl'Id.*, p. 188.
Pagnini. T'arresta, e il prisco. *Poet. Gr.*, p. 871.
7.666. Mara (G. de). Hic est tranatus. Soter[2], p. 221; Corn., p. 265.
Anselmo. Haec freta Abdenus nabat. *Epig.*, D.
Sabeo. Hac tranabat aquas. *Epig.*, p. 358.
Ricolvi. Ista Leandri aedes. *Op.*, p. 74.
Rezzonico discusses this epig. *Op.* 2. 341.
7.667. Sabeo. Quid nostrae vanis. *Epig.*, p. 809.
Sabeo. Heu nihil intactum. *Epig.*, p. 809.
Pagnini. Perchè voi tutti da. *Epig.*, p. 150.

7.668. Sleidan. Non ego, si placidum. Soter[2], p. 232; Corn., p. 288.
Obsopoeus. Non ego, vel tumidas. Obsop., p. 422; Wech.,
p. 366.
Sabeo. Ne mihi, ridentes si. *Epig.*, p. 762.
Bongiovanni and Zanetti. Nè lo spirar. *Epig.*, p. 9.

7.669. Quoted by Apuleius (?) *Apology* 10; Diogenes Laertius 3. 29.
Apuleius? Astra vides: utinam fiam. *Apol.* 10.
Guarino da Verona. Ardentes stellas. Soter[2], p. 215; Corn.,
p. 261.
Brugnolo? O utinam caelum. Laert.; Soter[2], p. 215; Corn.,
p. 261.
Constanzi (A.). Stella meus stellas dum. *Epig.*, Bii[vo].
Arsenios quotes this epig., *Paroem.*, p. 312.
Bentinus. O utinam coelum. *Laert.*, p. 104; Soter[2], p. 216.
Valeriano. Astra inter colis. *Poem.*, p. 114; *C.P.It.* 10. 159.
Valeriano. Stella meus stellis. *Poem.*, p. 114; *C.P.It.* 10. 159.
Bonamico. Stella meus stellas nunc. *Carm.*, p. 56.
Doni (A. F.). Quando io vi veggio. *Pist.*, p. 9.
Sabeo. Stella mea, inspicias.[1] *Epig.*, p. 59.
Sabeo. Inspice clara meum.[1] *Epig.*, p. 59.
Muret. Stella meus, stellas. Averani, *Op.* 1. 103.
P. Vettori remarks on this ep., *Var. Lect.* 20. 17.
Della Croce. Te quoties claro spectantem. *C.P.N.*, f.12[vo].
Spinula. Lux mea, quid spectas. *Epig.*, p. 41.
Spinula. O utinam faciant. *Epig.*, p. 41.
Mazzoni quotes the tr. of Brugnolo-Bentinus. *Difesa*, p. 429.
Beccuti. Stella gentil, ch' a la.[2] *Rime*, p. 247.
Tasso. Mentre, mia stella, miri. Solerti 3.79.
Anon. Mentre, O mia vaga Stella. *Ibid.* 3. 531.
Tasso quotes and comments on this epig., *Prose Div.* 2. 123.
Torelli. Qualhor pien d'ineffabile. *Rime*, f. 23[vo].
Groto. Mentre tu, la cui vista. *Rime* (1587), p. 171.
Orlandini. Vedi fra l'altre stelle. *Accesi* 1. 296.
Strozzi (G. B.). Beato il Ciel, che mille. *Mad.*, p. 56.
Murtola. Haver, Donna, occhi mille. *Rime*, f. 40[vo].
Marino. Fossi la notte, o fosse. *Ad.* 2. 132. 5 (p. 31).
Cittadini. Mentre di notte. *Scelt. di Son.* 2. 226.
Manso (G. B.). Mentre, Donna, ne gli. *Poes.*, p. 15.
Maurizio. Quando sei volta. *Gareg.* 3. 32[ro].
Redi refers to this epig. *Op.* 1. 200.
Bongiovanni and Zanetti. O dolce Stella mio.[2] *Epig.*, p. 2.
Carcani (P.). Stella, le stelle miri? *Ant. Ercol.* 8. 12; *Rac.* 3. 63.
Medici (A. de'). O utinam Coelum, spectas. *Scelt.*, p. xxxv.
Medici (A. de'). Vezzosissima Stella. *Scelt.*, p. xxxv.
Pompei. Gli astri rimiri tu. *Op.* 2. 188.
Pagnini. Mia cara Stella, or c'hai. *Epig.*, p. 15.

---

[1] Sabeo combines *A.P.*7.669–670 in one epigram, as in *Plan.*
[2] *A.P.*7.669 is here combined with 670.

7.670. Cf. Kaibel 568 (*C.I.G.* 6249) found at Rome. The epig. is quoted by Apuleius, *Apol.* 10; and by Diogenes Laert. 3. 29.

Apuleius? Lucifer ante meus. *Apol.* 10.

Cf. Ausonius. Βάκχος ἐνὶ ζωοῖσιν. *Opus.* 19. 49. 2.

Ausonius? Stella prius superis. *Opus.* 23. 12.

Guarino da Verona. Stella prius fulgebas. Soter², p. 216; Corn. p. 262.

Brugnolo? Iam dudum vivis fulgebas. Laert.; Soter², p. 216; Corn., p. 262.

Brugnolo? Iam dudum sydus lucebas. Laert.; Soter², p. 216; Corn., p. 262.

Chalcondyles (D.). Ἡ ἀτρεκὴς σοφίη. Above, p. 102.

Cf. Pontano. Nostra die quod Stella. *Carm.* (1518), p. 107.

Marullus. Lucebas superis, mea. Soter², p. 215; Corn., p. 262.

Arsenios quotes this epig., *Paroem.*, p. 312.

Bentinus. Iamdudum vivis lucebas. *Laert.*, p. 104; Soter², p. 215; Corn., p. 262.

Valeriano. Olim inter vivos fulgebas. *Poem.*, p. 114; *C.P.It.* 10. 159.

Sabeo. Nam vivis vivens lucebas.[1] *Epig.*, p. 59.

Sabeo. Tu prius in terra.[1] *Epig.*, p. 59.

P. Vettori remarks on this ep., *Var. Lect.* 20. 17.

Beccuti. Eri fra noi la stella.[1] *Rime*, p. 247.

Cf. Tasso. Come in turbato ciel. Solerti 3. 11.

Orlandini. Mentre vivevi.[1] *Accesi* 1. 296.

Averani. Inter viventes fulgebas. *Op.* 1. 103.

Salvini quotes this epig. on Conti, *Bella Mano*, canz. 2.

Bongiovanni and Zanetti. In fra viventi.[1] *Epig.*, p. 2.

Pompei. Ben tu da pria. *Op.* 2. 189.

Pagnini Quest' urna chiude. *Epig.*, p. 151.

7.671. Cf. 643.

7.673. Obsopoeus. Ne mea praeteriens. Obsop., p. 311; Wech., p. 280.

Gualfreducci. Si genus innocuum vivit. *Var.*, p. 228; *Sel. Epig.*, p. 282.

7.674. Obsopoeus. Naec urna Archilochi. Wech., p. 392.

Sabeo. Moenide Musa. *Epig.*, p. 487.

Giraldi (L. G.). Archilochi hic tumulus. *Op.* 2. 327.

Anon. Hi sunt Archilochi. *Sel. Epig.*, p. 97.

Barberio quotes Giraldi's tr. Gronov., *Thes.* 10. 840.

Crasso quotes Giraldi's tr. *Ist.*, p. 60.

Cunich. Archilochus iacet heic. *Anth.*, p. 121.

Passeroni. Giace Archiloco qui. *Rime* 3. 253.

Pagnini. Archiloco qui giace. *Epig.*, p. 54.

7.675. Cf. *A.P.* 7. 350 and 282.

Cornarius. Naufragi trepidus dubitas. Corn., p. 289.

[1] *A.P.* 7.670 is combined in this version with 669.

7.676. For the substance cf. Joannes Chrysost. Migne 60. 111.
Macrobius quotes this epig., *Sat.* 1. 11. 14.
Gaza. Servus Epictetus fueram. Gellius (1489), Dvi[vo]; Soter[2], p. 240; Corn., p. 313.
Volaterranus. Servus Epictetus genitus. *Com. Urb.*, p. 350; Soter[2], p. 240; Corn., p. 313.
Sabeo. Servus eram et pauper. *Epig.*, p. 287 (275).
Sabeo. Irus egestate. *Epig.*, p. 287 (275).
Sabeo. Irus inops servusque. *Epig.*, p. 361.
Sabeo. Servus eram et pauper. *Epig.*, p. 450.
Sanchez quotes Gaza's tr. *Op.* 3. 508.

7.677. [Not in *Plan.*] Quoted by Herodotus 7.228.
Valla. Nobilis hoc bustum. Herod. f. 209[vo].
Giraldi (L. G.) gives Valla's tr. *Op.* 2. 335.

7.680. Sabeo. Pastor Ioannes phariae. *Epig.*, p. 335.

7.681–688 are on the same theme.

7.684. Soter. Non sibi divinus mortalis. Soter[2], p. 197.
Sleidan. Quilibet humana contentus. Soter[2], p. 197; Corn., p. 230.
Sabeo. E numero divum. *Epig.*, p. 494.

7.687. Sabeo. Fraudem ammoniacam. *Epig.*, p. 746.

7.688. Sabeo. Iurabant duo Chaldei. *Epig.*, p. 437.

7.688. 3–4. Luscinius. O quam vana tenet. Soter[2], p. 34; Corn., p. 30.
Ricolvi. Quam vesanus homo. *Op.*, p. 59.
Ricolvi. Ben pazzo è l'uom. *Op.*, p. 59.
Cunich. O homines, vanum genus. *Anth.*, p. 83.
Passeroni. O stoltezza degli uomini. *Rime* 3. 205.
Roncalli. Oh dell' uom trista. *Epig.* (1792), p. 19.

7.691. Sabeo. Alcestis nova sum. *Epig.*, p. 271.

7.695. Velius. Nunquid pudicae Cassiae. Soter[2], p. 226; Corn., p. 174.
Velius. An ora cernis haec. Soter[2], p. 226; Corn., p. 175.
Ricolvi. Pulchrae ac pudicae. *Op.*, p. 70.
Ricolvi. Quam cernis sculptam. *Op.* p. 70.
Ricolvi. Vedi qui 'l volto pinto. *Op.*, p. 70.

7.696. Cf. *A.P.* 16. 8.
Sabeo. Corpore foedato et lacero. *Epig.*, p. 138.

7.697. Cf. 698.
Crasso. Hoc Ioannem abscondit [L-prose]. *Ist.*, p. 264.

7.698. [Not in *Plan.*] Cf. 697.

7.702. Cf. 504.
Sabeo. Praeda expiscantem. *Epig.*, p. 792.

7.703. Obsopoeus. Thyrsis oves pingui. Obsop., p. 476; Wech., p. 411.
Cunich. Thrysis oves solitus. *Anth.*, p. 178.
Felici. Tirsi, che delle Ninfe. *Epig.*[1], p. 65.
Passeroni. Tirsi, che a Pan non. *Rime* 3. 74.

7.704. Referred to by Cicero, *De Fin.* 3. 64; paraphrased by Seneca,

De Clem. 2. 2; quoted by Suetonius, *Nero* 38; by Dio Cassius 58. 23; the Emp. Julian quotes v. 2, *Orat.* 8 (242B); quoted by Stobaeus, *Ecl.* 2. 252 (Wach.-Hense, vol. 2, p. 121); by Suidas, *s.v.* Τιβέριος.

Alciati. Me terra functo. Soter[2], p. 219; Corn., p. 262; *Op.* 3. 600.

7.706. [Not in *Plan.*] Diogenes Laertius 7. 7 (Chrysippus).
Crasso. Vertigo capit [prose]. *Ist.*, p. 133.

7.708. [Not in *Plan.*] Athenaeus 6. 241F.

7.709. [Not in *Plan.*] Plutarch, *Moral.* 599E.
Barbato. Sardiaci patres vestro. Plut. (1572), *Moral.* 2. 272.

7.712. [Not in *Plan.*] Cf. *A.P.* 7. 182.
Pagnini. Tomba di Bauci son. *Epig.*, p. 137.

7.713. With lines 8–9 cf. Lucretius. Parvus ut est cygni. *De Rer.* 4. 181.
Vargas. Stringe il suo canto. *Sag.* verso of tit. -p.
Pagnini. In brevi note chiude. *Epig.*, p. 116.

7.714. Cf. Politian. Ibyce, quique marem. *Nut.* 615f.; Del Lungo, p. 412.
Sabeo. Rhegyon Italiae. *Epig.*, p. 339.
Giraldi (L. G.) refers to this epig. *Op.* 2. 341.
Crasso. Regium Italiae luculentae [L-prose]. *Ist.*, p. 297.

7.715. Sabeo. Quam iaceo a terra. *Epig.*, p. 486.
Crasso. Procul ab Italiae [L-prose]. *Ist.*, p. 308.

7.716. Crasso. Maturior, sed [L-prose]. *Ist.*, p. 227.

7.725. [Not in *Plan.*]
Cf. Virgil. Quis deus, Octavi. *Catal.* 11 (14).

7.735. Cf. Tibullus. Te spectem, suprema. *Eleg.* 1. 1. 59–60.

7.740. Cf. Kaibel 298.
Sabeo. Critonem supra lapis. *Epig.*, p. 804.
Cunich. Scriptus ego Crethona. *Anth.*, p. 121.
Passeroni. Un pezzo è già, che. *Rime* 3. 314.

7.741. Teocreno. Othriaden, Spartae rarum. *Poem.* Ciii; Stephanus, *Epig. Gr.*, p. 24.
Baldus (Vido). Semianimis miles trans. Teocreno and Steph., *locc. citt.*
Colin (Jac.). O brutus innumera. Teocreno and Steph., *locc. citt.*
Sabeo. Othriyadem taceat. *Epig.*, p. 290 (274).
Cunich. Quis nunc Othryadem. *Anth.*, p. 27.

7.743. [Not in *Plan.*] Cf. *A.P.* 7. 224.
Cf. Martial. Marmora parva quidem. *Epig.* 10. 63.

7.744. Given by Diogenes Laertius 8. 91 (Pythagoras).

7.745. Cf. Politian. Ibyce, quique marem, *Nut.* 615; Del Lungo, p. 412.
Aegidius. Quondam ad desertum. Soter[2], p. 233; Corn., p. 293.
Sabeo. Littore deserto iam te. *Epig.*, p. 338.

Sabeo. E nemore eggressi. *Epig.*, p. 354.
Giraldi (L. G.) quotes Aegidius' tr. *Op.* 2. 342.
Crasso quotes Aegidius' tr. from Giraldi. *Ist.*, p. 293.

7.746. Quoted by Porphyr., *Vit. Pythag.* 17; Cyril., *Contr. Iulian.*
342C; cf. Preger, p. 179.

7.747. Quoted by Zosimus (3. 34).
Sabeo. Iulianus iacet hic. *Epig.*, p. 319.
Sabeo. Sub Styge Iulianus. *Epig.*, p. 319.

7.748. Sabeo. Quis molem hanc. *Epig.*, p. 136.

Book VIII

8.1. Gualfreducci. Hic tegit egregios. *Var.*, p. 289; *Sel. Epig.*,
p. 284.

8.126. [Not in *Plan.*]
Cunich. Quis iacet heic? *Anth.*, p. 119.
Passeroni. Qui d'Antiloco uom. *Rime* 3. 83.

8.137. [Not in *Plan.*]
Cunich. Heus oratores, fari. *Anth.*, p. 118.
Passeroni. Or favellar potete. *Rime* 3. 81.

8.138. [Not in *Plan.*]
Salvini. Melliti Amphilochi tumulus. *Epig. S. Greg.*, p. 119.

Book IX

9.1. Cf. *A.P.* 9. 2.
Velius. Ubera vix posito. Soter[2], p. 77; Corn., p. 67.
Sabeo. Ubera dum caprae. *Epig.*, p. 722.
Sabeo. Dorcadis enixae. *Epig.*, p. 727.
Baldi. Ferì serpe crudel. *Epig.* 292.
Pagnini. Alla poppa di cerva. *Epig.*, p. 106.

9.2. Cf. *A.P.* 9. 1.
Sabeo. Hydra necem intentans. *Epig.*, p. 734.

9.3. Cf., for substance, Babrius 151.
Ovid. Nux ego iuncta viae. *Nux* (*PLM* 1. 88).
Alciati. Ludibrium pueris. *Emb.* 193.
Sabeo. Sum plantata viam. *Epig.*, p. 713.
Bongiovanni and Zanetti. O sventurata noce. *Epig.*, p. 23.
Cunich. Nux ego iuncta viae. *Anth.*, p. 134.
Felici. Presso la via piantarono. *Epig.*[2], p. viii.
Pagnini. Io noce appresso. *Epig.*, p. 14.

9.4. *A.P.* 9. 4–6 are on the same subject.
Sabeo. Quae prius in sylvis. *Epig.*, p. 832.
Sabeo. Usque nothi fructus. *Epig.*, p. 715.
Felici. Io, che giacea dimentico. *Epig.*[2], p. xii.

9.5. On the same subject as 4 and 6.
Sabeo. O pire iucundo. *Epig.*, p. 727.
Cf. Baldi. Tu che portar. *Epig.* 291.

9.6. [Not in *Plan.*] On same subject as 4–5.

9.7. Sabeo. A prece si vacat. *Epig.*, p. 132.

9.8. Costanzi (A.). Multum venturi spes. *Epig.*, Biii.
Luscinius. Praecipitat mentem. Corn., p. 50.
Sabeo. Semper enim vitae. *Epig.*, p. 116.
'L-prose.' Semper futurae vitae. Ἐπ. καὶ Ἐλεγ. No. 233.

9.9.1–4. Sabeo. Usque meis precibus. *Epig.*, p. 18.

9.9.5–6. Costanzi (G.). Et domus et patria est. *Epig.*, Oiiii.
Luscinius. Cui domus est victusque. Corn., p. 92.
Cornarius. Et patria atque domus. Corn., p. 92.
Sabeo. Et patria atque domus. *Epig.*, p. 413.

9.10. Aelian relates the same anecdote. *N.A.* 7. 11.
Sleidan. Extendit polypus bibula. Soter², p. 93; Corn., p. 81.
Valeriano. Polypus aequorea porrectus. *Poem.*, p. 112; *C.P.It.* 10. 154.
Sabeo. Frigus amans solemque. *Epig.*, p. 738.
Sabeo. Multipedem ut vidit. *Epig.*, p. 738.
Minturno. Polypus aranti late. *Epig.*, f. 5ʳᵒ.
Gualfreducci. Corpus in aequorea. *Var.*, p. 288.

9.11. [*A.P.* 9. 11–13 are on the same subject; it has not always been possible to distinguish exactly the imitations of these epigrams.]
Cf. St. Augustine. Iste non potest ambulare. *Enarr. in Psal.* 125, 12 (ed. Ben. 4. 1426).
Ausonius. [See under *A.P.* 9. 12.]
More (Sir T.). Claudipedem gestat caecus. Soter², p. 4; Corn., p. 6.
More (Sir T.). Caecus claudipedem gestat. Soter; Corn. *ibid.*
More (Sir T.). Caecus fert claudum. Soter; Corn. *ibid.*
More (Sir T.). Claudum caecus onus. Soter; Corn. *ibid.*
More (Sir T.). Tristis erat nimium. Soter; Corn. *ibid.*
More (Sir T.). Utilius nihil esse. Soter; Corn. *ibid.*
More (Sir T.). Cum claudo caecus. Soter; Corn. *ibid.*
Luscinius. Coniunxit fortuna duos. Corn., p. 7.
Groto. Su gli homeri d'un cieco. *Rime* (1587), p. 155.
Fioretti cites these epigrams. *Prog.* 5. 100.
Gualfreducci. Hic oculos est, ille. *Var.*, p. 283.
Cebà refers to *A.P.* 9. 11 and 13. 3–6. *Theofr.*, p. 36.

9.12. [See note under *A.P.* 9. 11.]
Ausonius? Insidens caeco graditur. *Opus.* 23. 5.
Ausonius? Ambulat insidens caeco. *Opus.* 23. 6.
Alciati. Loripedem sublatum humeris. Corn., p. 7; *Emb.* 161.
Robortello refers to this epig. *Scrip. Epig.*, p. 40.
Sabeo. Mendicum caecus. *Epig.*, p. 230; *C.P.It.* 8. 206.
Sabeo. Caecus enim et claudus. *Epig.*, p. 697.
Sabeo. Cui grassum natura. *Epig.*, p. 697.
Sabeo. Luce carens fuit hic. *Epig.*, p. 698.
Sabeo. Pro gressu hic lumen. *Epig.*, p. 698.
Mignault. Caecus ut errabat. Alciati, *Emb.* 160.
Finotti. Loripes incedit dum. *Sert.*, p. 387.

Finotti. Ducitur et ducit. *Sert.*, p. 387.
Finotti. Fortes loripedi coecus. *Sert.*, p. 387.
Finotti. Qui laesus pedibus. *Sert.*, p. 387.
Finotti. Quis ducit, coecus. *Sert.*, p. 388.
Gualfreducci. Circumfert scapulis. *Var.*, p. 283.
Gallo quotes the versions ascribed to Auson. *Opusc. cap.* 5.
Cunich. Fert caecus claudum. *Anth.*, p. 176.
Passeroni. Un poverello, ch'era. *Rime* 3. 241.
Roncalli. Per concorde bisogno. *Epig.* (1792), p. 39; (1801), p. 47.

9.13.1–2. [See note on *A.P.* 9. 11. In *Plan.* (1. 4. 3) this couplet is correctly detached from lines 3–8; see below.]
Politian. Τυφλὸς ἄπους τ'ἤτην. Del Lungo, p. 209; Soter[2], p. 4; Corn., p. 6.
Valeriano. Quaerens edaci corpori. *Poem.*, p. 113; *C.P.It.* 10. 159.
Alamanni. Porta il cieco il rattratto. *Versi* 2. 140.
Sabeo. Lumen erat coeci. *Epig.*, p. 697.
Sabeo. Huic gressum. *Epig.*, p. 229.
Sabeo. Hunc claudum, hunc caecum. *Epig.*, p. 230.
Guazzo quotes the second couplet of Alamanni. *Civ. Con.*, f. 17[ro].
Calcagnini. Non potis est caecus. Pigna, p. 210: *C.P.It.* 3. 79.
Spinula. Infelix humero captus. *Epig.*, p. 49.
Mignault. Ut tradant operas. Alciati, *Emb.* 160.
Gualfreducci. Caecus homo claudum. *Sel. Epig.*, p. 12.
Gualfreducci. Mendici duo sunt. *Var.*, p. 283.
Ricolvi quotes More: Caecus fert claudum, for this epig.— see under *A.P.* 9. 11. *Op.*, p. 61.
Ricolvi. Un cieco e un zoppo. *Op.*, p. 61.
Pagnini. Mentre un cieco sul. *Epig.*, p. 18.

9.13.3–8. [See note on *A.P.* 9. 11 and on *A.P.* 9. 12. These lines are printed as *A.P.* 9. 13B in some editions.]
Sabeo. Errabant ambo coecus. *Epig.*, p. 699.
Sabeo. Hic mutilus plantis. *Epig.*, p. 230.
Mignault. Mutili et errones ambo. Alciati, *Emb.* 160.
Gualfreducci. Manci ambo, mendici. *Sel. Epig.*, p. 12.
Cebà. [See under *A.P.* 9. 11.]

9.14.   Cf. *A.P.* 9. 94 and 227.
Sabeo. Per vada dum ponti. *Epig.*, p. 748.

9.15.   Cf. *A.P.* 16. 209.
Cf. Porcius Licinus. Custodes ovium. Gellius, *N.A.* 19. 9.
Cf. Valerius Aedituus. Quid faculam praefers. *Ibid.*
Cf. Pontano. Exhausit pharetra. *Op.* 4. 3572.
Bergius. Huc properate omnes. Soter[2], p. 49; Corn., p. 52.
Alciati. Qui cineres et ligna. Corn., p. 52.
Sabeo. Qui cupit ignem ipsum. *Epig.*, p. 116.
Toscano (M.). Tu, caeca qui nocte. *Anth.*, p. 144.

9.16. Alciati. Tres Charites, tres. Corn., p. 52.
Cornarius. Sunt Charites ternae. Corn., p. 52.
Anon. Me solo tre donne, *Vers. et Reg.*, Miiii[v°].
Conti. Sunt triplices. *Myth.* 4. 15.
Sabeo. Tres Charites dulci. *Epig.*, p. 117; *C.P.It.* 8. 197.
Carcani (P.). Tre son le Grazie. *Rac.* 1. 133.

9.17. Cf. *A.P.* 9. 18 and 371.
Jordanus. Monte lepus summo. Soter[3], p. 91.
Sabeo. In mare praecipitem. *Epig.*, p. 723.
Quoted by Landi, *Num.*, p. 43.
Groto. Non satio, non contento. *Rime* (1610), f. 79.
Bongiovanni and Zanetti. Mentre tenta involarsi. *Epig.*, p. 16.

9.18. Cf. *A.P.* 9. 17 and 371.
Ausonius. Trinacrii quondam currentem. *Opus.* 19. 35.
Velius. A cane venanti profugum. Soter[2], p. 77; Corn., p. 68.
Sabeo. A cane me elapsum. *Epig.*, p. 724.
Sabeo. Quo fugiam? Canibus. *Epig.*, p. 724.
Quoted by Landi, *Num.*, p. 43.
Mazzoni quotes and paraphrases this epig. *Difesa*, p. 27.
Bongiovanni and Zanetti. Un cane i' fuggo. *Epig.*, p. 16.
Cunich. Terrestris fugi ora canis. *Anth.*, p. 154.
Cunich. Terrestris fugi . . . lepus. *Anth.*, p. 154.
Felici. A sorte io lepre timida. *Epig.*[1], p. 40.
Passeroni. Mentre fuggo un can. *Rime* 3. 116.
Pagnini. Fuggendo un can terrestre. *Epig.*, p. 54.

9.19. Cf. *A.P.* 9. 20–1. For the substance cf. Aesop, *Fabb.* 174,
174b (Halm); and Babrius 29.
Amalteo (G. B.). Mollibus insignem phaleris. *Tr. Frat.*, p. 146.
Sabeo. Qui celeres transmisit. *Epig.*, p. 736.
Cunich. Alipedum toties fulsit. *Anth.*, p. 152.
Pagnini. Questo d'Aquila il nome. *Epig.*, p. 97.

9.20. Cf. 19 and 21.
Sabeo. Victor ad Alpheum. *Epig.*, p. 282 (284).
Cunich. Ille ego Pisae merui. *Anth.*, p. 143.
Roncalli. Io che l'onor della. *Epig.* (1792), p. 37; (1801), p. 47.

9.21. Cf. 19–20.
Sabeo. Pegasus incuso ingratam. *Epig.*, p. 742.

9.22. Sabeo. Praegnantem Diana tibi. *Epig.*, p. 120.

9.23. Obsopoeus. Quum foret Archippus. Obsop., p. 126; Wech., p. 109.
Sabeo. Agricola Archippus morbo. *Epig.*, p. 417.
Cunich. Tristi deficiens morbo. *Anth.*, p. 76.
Medici (A. de'). Agricola Archippus crudeli. *Scelt.*, p. xxxi.
Medici (A. de'). Già presso a valicar. *Scelt.*, p. xxxi.
Passeroni. Archippo a' figli suoi. *Rime* 3. 198.
Roncalli. Da morbo oppresso. *Epig.* (1792), p. 11; (1801), p. 38.

9.24.   Cf. Politian. Etenim ut stellas. *Nut.* 339; Del Lungo, p. 389.
         Cf. Lascaris (J). Πάντ' ἀνέφαιν' εἰδώς. *Epig.*, f. 8ʳº.
         Aleander (G.), the elder, quotes from this epig. Above, p. 186.
         Cornarius. Obfuscat splendore suo. Corn., p. 108.
         Giraldi Cintio. Ut sol cum toto. *Poem.*, p. 166; *C.P.It.* 5. 394.
         Venatorius. Omnia vi lucis superat. Obsop., p. 149; Wech.,
              p. 132.
         Sabeo. Sydera ut obscurat. *Epig.*, p. 196; *C.P.It.* 8. 201.
         Giovane. Astra quis ignorat? *Ant. Tar.* 3. 3.
         Cunich. Solis ut exortu primo. *Anth.*, p. 34.
         Passeroni. Come, quando tra noi. *Rime* 3. 110.
         Pagnini. Come spuntando il Sol. *Epig.*, p. 46.
9.25.   Crasso. Scriptum hoc [L-prose]. *Ist.*, p. 54.
         Cunich. Hic liber est Arati. *Anth.*, p. 17.
         Passeroni. D'Arato il libro. *Rime* 3. 75.
9.26.   Politian. Non illi Praxilla. *Nut.* 633–6; Del Lungo, p. 414.
         Alciati. Suaviloquas hymnis. Corn., p. 109.
         Sabeo. Sacriloquas Helicon. *Epig.*, p. 192.
         Giraldi (L. G.) alludes to this epig. *Op.* 2. 123. 28, 41.
         Sanchez. Has Helicon hymnis. *Op.* 2. 485.
         Crasso. Has divinis [L-prose]. *Ist.*, pp. 38, 369, 432.
         Gravina (G. V.). Queste Elicona, ed il. *Rag. Poet.*, p. 33.
         Cunich. Florifer has Helicon. *Anth.*, p. 19.
         Passeroni. Queste sono le illustri. *Rime* 3. 76.
9.27.   Cornarius. Echo vocalem et mutam. *Corn.*, p. 71.
         Sabeo. Pertransi bona lingua. *Epig.*, p. 767.
         Cf. Calcagnini. Responsant valles. Pigna, p. 203.
         Cunich. Echo ego, muta modo. *Anth.*, p. 170.
         Passeroni. Donna son io, che or. *Rime* 3. 240.
9.28.   Cf. 101–3.
         Sabeo. Etsi sum sparsa hic. *Epig.*, p. 754.
9.29.   Cornarius. Nautarum o princeps. Corn., p. 97.
         Sabeo. Pontum attentasti. *Epig.*, p. 496.
         Averani. Nautarum ductrix audacia. *Op.* 1. 193.
         Cunich. Dux iuvenum invenit. *Anth.*, p. 77.
         Medici (A. de'). Mittere, dux iuvenum. *Scelt.*, p. xxvii.
         Medici (A. de'). Ardir, che in giovin petto. *Scelt.*, p. xxvii.
9.30.   Cf. *A.P.* 9. 31, 33, 105, 131, and 376.
         More (Sir T.). Ventis pinus humo. Soter², p. 104; Corn., p.98.
         Sabeo. Pro rate naufragium. *Epig.*, p. 418, 753.
         Sabeo. Fracta ego sum pinus. *Epig.*, p. 747.
         Landi quotes More's version, *Let.*, f. 22ʳº.
         Mazzoni quotes Gr. with More's tr. *Difesa*, p. 424.
         Groto. Fui pianta in alto. *Rime* (1587), p. 159.
         Baldi. Sprezzommi il vento. *Epig.* 310.
9.31.   Cf. *A.P.* 9. 30, 33, 105, 131, and 376.
         Sleidan. Quid pinus a vobis. Soter², p. 104; Corn., p. 98.
         Sleidan. Pinus ego a vobis. Soter³, p. 117.

Alciati. Ventoso nautae cur. Corn., p. 98.
Valeriano. Quorsum me a ventis. *Poem.*, p. 112; *C.P.It.* 10.
155.
Molza. Eversam agricolae. *Poes.* 3. 208.
Sabeo. Montibus ex longis. *Epig.*, p. 413.
Sabeo. Quid fabri primum. *Epig.*, p. 770.
Landi quotes Sleidan's first version, *Let.*, f. 22ʳᵒ.
Mazzoni quotes Gr. and Sleidan's second tr. *Difesa*, p. 424
Cf. Baldi. Un Pin, di cui [prose]. *Versi e Pr.*, p. 584.
Pagnini. Me su i materni monti. *Epig.*, p. 100.

9.32. Cf. 35.
Sabeo. Littoribus fueram violentis. *Epig.*, p. 747.
Baldi. Sul lido mi sedea. *Epig.* 311.
Cunich. Constructam nuper me. *Anth.*, p. 131.

9.33. Cf. *A.P.* 9. 30, 31, 105, 131, and 376.
Obsopoeus. Nondum facta ratis perii. Obsop., p. 151; Wech.,
p. 114.

9.34. Cf. *A.P.* 36, 106, and 398.
Groto. Questa misera nave. *Rime* (1587), p. 165.
Baldi. Io che dieci e dieci. *Epig.* 314.
Pagnini. Me spento si confonda. *Epig.*, p. 154.

9.35. Cf. 32.
Obsopoeus. Proxima vix factum. Obsop., p. 151; Wech.,
p. 114.

9.36. Cf. *A.P.* 9. 34, 106, and 398.
Anon. Lungi da flutti rei. *Vers. et Reg.* Miiiiᵛᵒ; Carducci, *Poes.
Barb.*, p. 261.
Cunich. Tot longos pelagi. *Anth.*, p. 183.
Felici. Io, ch' l'oceano. *Epig.*[1], p. 91.
Passeroni. Io nave altera, che. *Rime* 3. 240.
Roncalli. Io, che tra il flutto. *Epig.* (1792), p. 95.

9.37. Cf. Sabeo. Fons ego difficilis. *Epig.*, p. 776.
Cunich. Hauri, sed tacitus. *Anth.*, p. 183.
Passeroni. Bei, ma taci.—Olà. *Rime* 3. 257.
Vargas. Tacito bei.—Per quel. *Sag.*, p. 38.
Pagnini. N. Tacito attingi. *Epig.*, p. 11.

9.38. Sabeo. Ex hoc fonte bibas. *Epig.*, p. 732.
Sabeo. Hospes ad hunc fontem. *Epig.*, p. 745.

9.39. Quoted by Diogenes Laertius 3. 33.
Brugnolo? Pieridas Cypris Cyprim. Laert.
Ficino. Cum Venus Musis [prose]. *Op.* 1. 499.
Cantalicio. Haec Cypris ad Musas. Above, p. 123.
Bentinus. Haec Venus ad Musas. *Laert.*, p. 105; Soter[2], p. 10;
Corn., p. 13.
Alciati. Haec Venus ad Musas. Corn., p. 13; *Op.* 4. 643.
Cornarius. Sic Venus ad Musas. Corn., p. 13.
Anisio. Sic Musis Venus: Ergo. *Poem.*, f. 92ʳᵒ.
Alamanni. Vener disse alle Muse. *Versi* 2. 140.

Rapitius. Spreta Venus Musis. *Facil.*, f. 6ro.
Sabeo. Haec Venus ad Musas. *Epig.*, p. 13.
Sabeo. Cypria ait Musis. *Epig.*, p. 48.
Mignault. Sic Venus ad Musas: Venerem. Alciati, *Emb.* 115.
Mazzoni quotes the Gr. with Bentinus' tr. *Difesa*, p. 455.
Toscano (M.). Cypria sic Musis. *Anth.*, p. 141.
Averani. Me colite, Aonides. *Op.* 1. 139, 140.
Forzoni-Accolti (F.). Disse alle Muse. Crescimbeni, *Ist.* 1.
　397.
Salvini. Musis pulchra Venus. *Disc.* 4. 229.
The tr. by Bentinus is given in 'Επ. καὶ 'Ελ. (No. 4).
Carcani (P.). Così Venere un dì. *Ant. Ercol.* 2. 10; *Rac.* 1. 41.
Ricolvi. Alma Venus Musis: Et. *Op.*, p. 86.
Ricolvi. Disse Venere alle Muse. *Op.*, p. 86.
Cunich. Cypris ait Musis. *Anth.*, p. 86.
Medici (A. de'). Me colite, Aonides. *Scelt.*, p. xv.
Medici (A. de'). Disse all' Aonie. *Scelt.*, p. xv.
Pompei. A le Muse Ciprigna. *Op.* 2. 188.
Felici. Disse alle Muse Venere. *Epig.*[1], p. 69.
Passeroni. A Venere ubbidite. *Rime* 3. 205.
Vargas. Alle Muse Ciprigna. *Sag.*, p. 82.
Pagnini. Disse Ciprigna alle. *Epig.*, p. 80.

9.40. Cf. *A.P.* 9. 41–2 and 109.
Sabeo. Non tantum, quum. *Epig.*, p. 221.
Cunich. Non inter pugnas tantum. *Anth.*, p. 42.
Passeroni. Io fido scudo e saldo. *Rime* 3. 130.

9.41. Cf. *A.P.* 9. 40, 42, and 109.
Sabeo. In me tela tuli. *Epig.*, p. 745.

9.42. Cf. *A.P.* 9. 40–1 and 109.
Sleidan. Unum bina mihi. Soter[2], p. 103; Corn., p. 96.
Alciati. Bina pericla unis. Corn., p. 96; *Emb.* 162.
Giraldi Cintio. Offert Neptuno clypeum. *Poem.*, p. 175.
Obsopoeus. Effugi geminum clypeo. Obsop., p. 122; Wech.,
　p. 106.
Mignault. Unis damna duo. Alciati, *Emb.* 161.
Finotti. Obvia districtis quae. *Sert.*, p. 223.
Corsonius quotes Obsopoeus' tr. Finotti, *Sert.*, p.223.
Pagnini. Mercè d'un sol arma. *Epig.*, p. 75.

9.43. Obsopoeus. Vestitus tenuis contentus. Obsop., p. 28; Wech.,
　p. 26.
Sabeo. Laena mihi simplex. *Epig.*, p. 118.
'L-prose.' Sufficit mihi laenae. 'Επ. καὶ 'Ελ. No. 7.

9.44. Cf. 45. Diogenes Laertius 3. 33. Cf. Aesop, *Fab.* 53 (Halm).
Ausonius. Qui laqueum collo. *Opus.* 19. 14.
Ausonius? Thesauro invento qui. *Opus.* 23. 11.
Brugnolo? Deposuit laqueos; aurum. Laert.; Soter[2], p. 134;
　Corn., p. 131.
Aleander (G.), elder. Aurum qui reperit. Soter[2], p. 134.

Bentinus. Aurum qui reperit. *Laert.*, p. 105; Soter[2], p. 134;
   Corn., p. 131.
Alamanni. Un che impiccarsi. *Versi* 2. 136.
Sabeo. Auro hic invento. *Epig.*, p. 775.
Sabeo. Hic aurum inveniens. *Epig.*, p. 775.
Sabeo. A trabe qui laqueo. *Epig.*, p. 414.
Sabeo. Fune trabi annexa. *Epig.*, p. 544.
Giraldi Cintio bases a novel on this epig. *Hecat.* 9. 8.
Cf. Guicciardini (L.). Marcantonio Batistei [prose]. *Det.*
   (1565), f. 3ro.
Guazzo quotes the version of Alamanni. *Dial.*, f. 35ro.
Groto. Quel, che havea il laccio. *Rime* (1610), f. 80.
Baldi. Se 'n già per appiccarsi. *Epig.* 887.
Materdona. Huom, che moria di fame. *Rime*, p. 75.
Bargiocchi. Dum cubat umbrosae. *Epig.*, p. 112.
Pagnini. Chi strozzar si volea. *Epig.*, p. 5.

9.45. [Translations of this epig. cannot be distinguished from translations of 44; accordingly all versions of the theme have
   been assigned to that epigram; 45 is quoted in old edd. of
   Stobaeus, *Flor.* 10.]

9.46. Sabeo. Et caeca et sterilis. *Epig.*, p. 61.
Sabeo. Orba erat et natis. *Epig.*, p. 8.
Groto. Io, che 'l ventre. *Rime* (1587), p. 148.

9.47. Cf. Aesop, *Fab.* 373 (Halm).
Pannonius. Agna lupum pasco. Corn., p. 65.
Erasmus. Lacto lupum uberibus. Soter[2], p. 75; Corn., p. 64.
Velius. Admoveo nolens catulo. Soter[2], p. 75; Corn., p. 64.
Alciati. Capra lupum non sponte. Corn., p. 65; *Emb.* 64.
Ariosto. Foetum invita lupae. Pigna, p. 296; Polidori 1. 356.
Teocreno. Lacto lupum uberibus. *Poem.*, Ciii.
Sabeo. Quod mea parvus adhuc. *Epig.*, p. 727.
Mignault. Capra lupum lacto. Alciati, *Emb.* 64.
Mignault. Lacto lupi catulum. Alciati, *Emb.* 64.
Germano. Lupum ex propriis [prose]. *Giard.*, p. 170.
Germano quotes Alciati's version. *Giard.*, p. 172.
'L-prose.' Lupum ex propriis. Ἐπ. καὶ Ἐλ. No. 24.
Bongiovanni and Zanetti. Colle proprie mie. *Epig.*, p. 37.
Ricolvi. Huncce lupum ipse. *Op.*, p. 64.
Cunich. Cogor ovis lactare. *Anth.*, p. 72.
Medici (A. de'). Invitam me lacte. *Scelt.*, p. xxi.
Medici (A. de'). Dall' inuman desio. *Scelt.*, p. xxi.
Felici. Son costretta io. *Epig.*[1], p. 106.
Passeroni. Son costretta a lattar. *Rime* 3. 94.
Vargas. Allatto un lupo io. *Sag.*, p. 34.
Pagnini. M'allevo a mio dispetto. *Epig.*, p. 67.

9.48. Costanzi (A.). Hic taurus, cygnus. *Epig.*, Biivo.
Lippi (L.). Fit cycnus, taurus. *Dist.*, p. 65; *C.P.It.* 6. 132.
Cf. Lippi (L.). Gradivus Bacchus Leneus. *Dist.*, p. 65.

Arsenios quotes this epig. *Paroem.*, p. 435.
Angeriano. Fit cycnus, taurus. Ἔρωτ., Ei.
More (Sir T.). Taurus, olor, satyrus. Soter², p. 81; Corn., p. 76.
Lily (W.). Taurus, olor, satyrus. Soter², p. 81; Corn., p. 76.
Velius. Iuppiter Europam nivei. Soter², p. 81; Corn., p. 76.
Venatorius. Ob Leden, Danaen. Obsop., p. 91; Wech., p. 79.
Sabeo. Taurus, olor, satyrus. *Epig.*, p. 4.
Sabeo. Bos, volucris, satyrus. *Epig.*, p. 108.
Possevino (A.). Ob Laeden, Danaen. *Poes. et Pict.*, c. 19.
Cottunius. Fit cycnus, taurus. *Confic.*, p. 103.
Patavinus quotes More's tr. *De Art.*, p. 28.
Ricolvi. Taurus, olor, satyrus, fitque. *Op.*, p. 69.
Ricolvi. Giove prese il sembiante. *Op.*, p. 69.
Vargas. Leda, Europa, Antiope. *Sag.*, p. 82.
Pagnini. Per Leda, Europa, Antiope. *Epig.*, p. 69.
9.49. Cf. *A.P.* 9. 134–5 and 172.
Cf. Virgil. Nam mihi parta quies. *Aen.* 7. 598.
Anon. Actumst, excessi, Spes. *Carm. Epig.* (Buecheler), 409. 8.
Anon. Cura, labor, meritum. *PLM* (Baehr.) 5. 386.
Anon. Effugi tumidam vitam. *Carm. Epig.* (Buech.) 434. 13.
Anon. Evasi, effugi. Spes. *Carm. Epig.* (Buech.) 1498.
Anon. Ha, evasi, effugi. *Carm. Epig.* (Buech.-Lommatzsch) 2139.
Anon. Gloria divitiae. De Rossi, *Inscr. Chr.* 2. 267, 20.
Pannonius. Inveni portum. Spes. *Poem.* (1784). 1. 531; above, p. 165.
More (Sir T.). Iam portum inveni. Soter², p. 125; Corn., p. 123.
Lily (W.). Inveni portum. Spes. Soter², p. 125; Corn., p. 123.
Alamanni. Speme e fortuna addio. *Rim. Ined.* (Frati), p. 33.
Sabeo. Vitrea spes et tu, fallax. *Epig.*, p. 530.
Rota. Qual huom, che in varie. *Son.* (1560), f. 52ᵛᵒ.
Cf. Baldi. Chi vi conduca a me. *Epig.* 36.
Pinelli (G. B.). Ite procul, larvae. *C.P.It.* 7. 247.
Cappellari. Quid mihi cum Roma? *Poem.*, p. 131.
Cunich. O Spes, o Fortuna, valete. *Anth.*, p. 71.
Felici. Addio, speranza. *Epig.*[1], p. 110.
Passeroni. Sorte, speranze, addio. *Rime* 3. 210.
Bettinelli. Addio, speranze, addio. *Op.* 22. 108.
9.50. Cf. Theognis 795–6.
More (Sir T.). Tu teipsum oblectes. Soter², p. 146; Corn., p. 140.
Valeriano. Tute animim exhilara. *Poem.* p. 113; *C.P. It.* 10. 158.
Obsopoeus. Oblectans animum. Obsop., p. 197; Wech., p. 174.
Cunich. Fac quod opus. *Anth.*, p. 82.

Pagnini. Ben adempi i dover tui. *Epig.*, p. 165.

9.51. Sleidan. Omnia fert aetas. Soter[2], p. 146; Corn., p. 141.
Luscinius. Omnia fert aetas, quid. Corn., p. 141.
Cornarius. Omnia fert aetas, fortunaque. Corn., p. 141.
Sabeo. Omnia fert aetas, vafer. *Epig.*, p. 17.
The version of Sleidan is given in 'Επ. καὶ 'Ελ. (No. 47).
Pompei. Tutto avvien che l'età. *Op.* 2. 189.

9.52. Velius. Capturo pisces hamata. Soter[2], p. 74; Corn., p. 62.
Alciati. Quum curvos piscator aquis. Corn., p. 63.
Obsopoeus. Quidam squamosos. Obsop., p. 63; Wech., p. 57.
Sabeo. Littore in Ionio. *Epig.*, p. 317.
Sabeo. Piscibus insidias limo. *Epig.*, p. 527.
Pontanus (Spanmüller) quotes Sleidan's tr. *Poet. Inst.*, p. 50.
Bongiovanni and Zanetti. Stava cert' uom. *Epig.*, p. 13.
Vargas. Gittando l'amo. *Sag.*, p. 40.
Pagnini. Mentre dal lido un pescator. *Epig.*, p. 17.

9.53. [This epig. may be read in reverse; where there are two trans-
lations, the second is from the reverse form.]
Lascaris (J.) alludes to this epig. Above, p. 116, n. 1.
Soter. Hippocrates decus est. Soter[2], p. 85.
Soter. Ingluviem premere hic. Soter[2], p. 85.
Cornarius. Hippocrates hominum lux. Corn., p. 78.
Sabeo. Exuviae Stygis et mortis. *Epig.*, p. 185.
Sabeo. Hippocrates erat hic. *Epig.*, p. 185.
Mazzoni quotes the Gr. and both Soter's trr. *Difesa*, p. 110.
Gualfreducci. Hippocrates erat Orbi. *Var.*, p. 287.
Cottunius quotes the Gr. without tr. *Confic.* cap. 27.
Ricolvi quotes the Gr. without tr. *Op.*, p. 75.

9.54. Cf. *A.P.* 9. 55 and 118. Quoted by Stobaeus, *Flor.* 116. 27
(Meineke).
Quoted by Arsenios, *Paroem.*, p. 344.
Cornarius. Absens expetimus, veniens. Corn., p. 37.
Luscinius. Dum procul est, speras. Corn., p. 37.
Valeriano. Dum senium absistit. *Poem.*, p. 113; *C.P.It.* 10. 156.
Sabeo. Absens quisquis optat. *Epig.*, p. 517.
Sabeo. Quisquis senectam. *Epig.*, p. 719.
Averani. Quisquis senectutem cupit. *Op.* 1. 160.
Bongiovanni and Zanetti. Fin che vecchiezza. *Epig.*, p. 33.
'L-prose.' Senectus cum abest 'Επ. καὶ 'Ελ. No. 18.
Pagnini. Qual grave mal vecchiezza. *Epig.*, p. 43.

9.55. Cf. 54 and 118.
Costanzi (A.). Stulte senescentes optant. *Epig.*, Biii[ro]
Soter. Dii dent Nestoreos. Soter[2], p. 39; Corn., p. 36.
Cornarius. Qui senio pressus vult. Corn., p. 36.
Sabeo. Si cupis ulterius. *Epig.*, p. 576.
Sabeo. Vivere qui senium. *Epig* , p. 711.
Cunich. Qui postquam senuit. *Anth.*, p. 81.
Passeroni. A chi è già vecchio. *Rime* 3. 129.

Pagnini. A chi già d'anni. *Epig.*, p. 61.

9.56.　　Cf. *A.P.* 7. 542.

Germanicus. Thrax puer adstricto. *PLM* 4. 103.

Cf. Martial. Qua vicina pluit. *Epig.* 4. 18.

Paulus Diaconus quotes Germanicus' version. Neff, p. 68.

Politian. Παῖς ''Εβρῳ ἐπέθρωσκε. Del Lungo, p. 210.

Soter[2] (p. 47) and Cornarius (p. 47) quote *A.P.* 7. 542 and
　　9. 56, giving the tr. of Germanicus and Politian's imitation;
　　Soter also quotes Martial.

Anon. Fanciullo ardito nel. Carducci. *Poes. Barb.*, p. 256.

Teocreno. Thrax puer, oppressit. *Poem.*, Fi.

Teocreno. Non ut ais peperit. *Poem.*, Fi.

Alamanni. Sopra l'Hebro indurato. *Rim. Ined.* (Frati), p. 33.

Sabeo. Frigus ob hybernum. *Epig.*, p. 836.

Sabeo. Non bene frigus adhuc. *Epig.*, p. 837.

Sabeo. Duratum ventis divulsum. *Epig.*, p. 837.

Sabeo. Dum puer adducto Thrax. *Epig.*, p. 837.

Sabeo. Rupit onus gelidas. *Epig.*, p. 837.

Sabeo. Quum puer astrictum. *Epig.*, p. 838.

Sabeo. Factus iners glacie. *Epig.*, p. 838.

Sabeo. Frigore bruma rigens. *Epig.*, p. 838.

Sabeo. Dum nati intumulat. *Epig.*, p. 838.

Sabeo. Strymonium hybernus. *Epig.*, p. 839.

Sabeo. In geminas partes. *Epig.*, p. 839.

Sabeo. Tentabat puer obductum. *Epig.*, p. 839.

Sabeo. Thraicii glacies Hebri. *Epig.*, p. 171.

Rapitius. Dum puer in glacie. *Facil.*, f. 6ro.

Giraldi quotes the version of Germanicus. *Op.* 2. 195.

Groto. Mentre sù 'l fiume. *Rime* (1587), p. 158.

Pontanus (Spanmüller) quotes Germanicus. *Poet. Inst.*, p. 50.

Gallo quotes Germanicus' version. *Opusc.* c. 7.

Bongiovanni and Zanetti. Su le gelate onde. *Epig.*, p. 14.

Ricolvi quotes Germanicus' version. *Op.*, p. 67.

Ricolvi. In su l'Ebro agghiacciato. *Op.*, p. 67.

9.57.　　Cf. 70.

Sabeo. Ecquid continuum infelix. *Epig.*, p. 744.

9.58.　　Cf. Martial. Barbara pyramidum sileat. *Epig.* 1.

Soter[2] (p. 103) and Cornarius (p. 95) quote the Gr. with Mar-
　　tial as illustration.

Sabeo. Pervia iam plaustris. *Epig.*, p. 747.

Cunich. Crebris trita rotis. *Anth.*, p. 16.

9.59.　　Sabeo. Palmae quadruplices humeris. *Epig.*, p. 51.

Cunich. O Cai, Romae columen. *Anth.*, p. 18.

9.61.　　Cf. *A.P.* 7. 230, 433, 531; 9. 397, and 447.

Marullus. Mater Lacaena conspicata. *Epig.* 2, p. 19; Soter[2],
　　p. 7; Corn., p. 8.

Politian. 'Εκπροφυγόντα μάχας τόν. Del Lungo, p. 208; Soter[2];
　　Corn., *ibid.*

Anselmo. Ut bello agnovit natum. *Epig.*, D.

Casanova. Dum se et dum patria. *C.P.N.*, f. 92ro; *C.P.It.3.* 293.

More (Sir T.). In patriam amissis. Soter^2, p. 6; Corn., p. 8.

Lily (W.). Quum nudum e bello. Soter^2, p. 6; Corn., p. 8.

Velius. In patriam amissis refugum. Soter^2, p. 7; Corn., p. 8.

Soter and Cornarius also give the verses of Marullus and Politian.

Giraldi Cintio. Antilochus socios medio. *Poem.*, p. 176.

Sabeo. In natum imbellem. *Epig.*, p. 236.

Angelio. Effugit exanimis nudato. *Poem.*, p. 383.

Pontanus (Spanmüller) quotes Marullus' imit. *Poet. Ints.*, p. 50.

Gualfreducci. Viderat exutum spoliis. *Var.*, p. 286.

Cappellari. Saeva Lacon clypeo. *Poem.*, p. 149.

Averani. Vidit ut abiecta fugientem. *Op.* 1. 131.

The version of More is given in Ἐπ. καὶ Ἐλ. (No. 1).

Ricolvi. Cum gnatum e pugna. *Op.*, p. 67.

Ricolvi. Vide madre Spartana. *Op.*, p. 68.

Cunich. Ut mater gnatum vidit. *Anth.*, p. 8.

Medici (A. de'). Ut videt ex acie. *Scelt.*, p. vi.

Medici (A. de'). Visto madre Spartana. *Scelt.*, p. vi.

Pompei. Visto madre Spartana. *Op.* 2. 221.

Felici. Allor che il figlio. *Epig.*^{1}, p. 97.

Passeroni. Vedendo il figlio suo. *Rime* 3. 33.

Pagnini. Spartana donna il figlio. *Epig.*, p. 60.

9.62. Obsopoeus. Hospes turritus quondam. Obsop., p. 165; Wech., p. 144.

Sabeo. Troiam urbem sacram. *Epig.*, p. 310.

Bongiovanni and Zanetti. Me, grande inclita. *Epig.*, p. 22.

Cunich. Hospes, me, celsis. *Anth.*, p. 32.

Pompei. Quell' Ilio sacro. *Op.* 2. 198.

Passeroni. O passeggier, me. *Rime* 3. 109.

9.63. [Not in *Plan.*]

Cf. Horace. Donec non alia. *Carm.* 3. 9. 5.

9.64. Cf. Hesiod, *Theog.* 21f.

Cf. Ovid. Nec mihi sunt visae. *A.A.* 1. 27.

Politian. Scilicet huic, patriis. *Nut.* 382f; Del Lungo, p. 392.

Sabeo. Pastor eras, Musae. *Epig.*, p. 382.

Cottunius alludes to this epig. Ἐλλ. Ἐπ., p. 1.

Cunich. Te, dum pascis oves. *Anth.*, p. 23.

Felici. Serto di lode intessere. *Epig.*^{1}, p. viii.

Passeroni. Mentre pascavi il gregge. *Rime* 3. 174.

9.65. Angeriano. Veris honor flos est. Ἔρωτ. f. ii.

Cottunius. Γαίη κόσμος ἔαρ, δελφίν. Ἐλλ. Ἐπ., p. 8.

9.66. Costanzi (A.). Mnemosyne obstupuit. *Epig.*, Bii.

Politian. Mnemosyne audito. Del Lungo, p. 126.

Feretrius. Audito obstipuit. Del Lungo, p. 126n.

Venatorius. Mnemosyne admirans. Obsop., p. 152; Wech., p. 134.
Sabeo. Mnemosine expavit. *Epig.*, p. 225.
Crasso. Mnemosynem cepit [L-prose]. *Ist.*, p. 451.
Salvini. Mnemosyne audivit. Wellesley, p. 151.
Cunich. Mnemosine audivit Sappho. *Anth.*, p. 18.
Felici. Mnemosine udì, Saffo. *Epig.*[1], p. 15.
Passeroni. Calliope udì di Saffo. *Rime* 3. 39.
Pagnini. Mnemosine udì Saffo. *Epig.*, p. 63.
Pagnini. Melpomene gridò da stupor. *Epig.*, p. 55.

9.67. Cf. Crinitus. Marmoream effigiem. *H.D.*, p. 580; Soter[2], p. 101.
Soter. Forte redimibat privignus. Soter[2], p. 101.
More (Sir T.). Flore novercalem cingis. Soter[2], p. 100; Corn., p. 92.
Erasmus. Exiguo lapidi puer. Soter[2], p. 100; Corn., p. 92.
Luscinius. Privignus tentat statuam. Soter[2], p. 101; Corn., p. 92.
Velius. Dat puer exiguo monumento. Soter[2], p. 101; Corn., p. 93.
Sleidan. Busta coronavit prignus [*sic*]. Soter[2], p. 101; Corn., p. 93.
Molza. Ornabat tumulum sertis. *Poes.* 3. 204.
Obsopoeus. Serta novercali dederat. Obsop., p. 118; Wech., p. 102.
Sabeo. Serta novercali tumulo. *Epig.*, pp. 413, 775.
Sabeo. Morte putans vitae. *Epig.*, p. 495.
Ricolvi. Privignus, nimia ductus. *Op.*, p. 76.
Cunich. Forte puer cippo dum. *Anth.*, p. 51.
Felici. Mentre di funebri. *Epig.*[1], p. 25.
Pagnini. Breve colonna su l'avello. *Epig.*, p. 135.

9.68. Cf. 69.
More (Sir T.). Privigno vel amans. Soter[2], p. 102; Corn., p. 94.
Sleidan. Privignos etiam perdunt. Soter[2], p. 102; Corn., p. 94.
Venatorius. Triste malum semper. Obsop., p. 118; Wech., p. 102.
Sabeo. Etsi amat usque. *Epig.*, pp. 495, 776.
Sabeo. Fac fugias, privigne. *Epig.*, p. 776.
Cunich. Triste noverca malum. *Anth.*, p. 74.
Pagnini. La matrigna a' figliastri. *Epig.*, p. 88.

9.69. Cf. 68.
Sleidan. Ira novercarum quid non. Soter[2], p. 102; Corn., p. 94.
Venatorius. Privigno vel amantis. Obsop., p. 118; Wech., p. 102.
Sabeo. Ira novercalis gravis. *Epig.*, p. 413.
Sabeo. Pernitiosa etiam. *Epig.*, p. 416.

9.70. Cf. 57.
Sabeo. Tristi blesa sono. *Epig.*, p. 730.

9.71. Sabeo. Suspensi o quercus. *Epig.*, p. 717.

9.72. Scaphenatus. Mercurius bonus est. *Eleg.*, Diii.
Conti. Mercurius facilis. *Myth.* 7. 1.
Sabeo. Hermes est facilis. *Epig.*, p. 51.
Bongiovanni and Zanetti. Cortese è il buon. *Epig.*, p. 56.
'L-prose.' Non fastidiosus. Ἐπ. καὶ Ἐλ. No. 31.
Cunich. Herma ego, pastores. *Anth.*, p. 151.
Pompei. Mite è Mercurio. *Op.* 2. 182.
Passeroni. Facile nume io sono. *Rime* 3. 125.
Felici. Pastori, io son Mercurio. *Epig.*², p. vii.
Pagnini. Dono a Mercurio ben. *Epig.*, p. 4.

9.74. Cf. Horace. Nunc ager Umbreni. *Sat.* 2. 2. 133–35.
Cf. Lucian, *Nigrinus* 26.
Cf. St. Basil. Σήμερον τοῦδε ἀγρός. *Com. in Ps.* 62 (p. 304).
More (Sir T.). Nuper Achaemenidae. Soter², p. 126; Corn., p. 123.
Lily (W.). Nuper Achaemenidae. Soter², p. 126; Corn., p. 123.
Velius. Fundus Achaemenidae. Soter², p. 126; Corn., p. 123.
Alciati. Fundus Aristagorae. Corn., p. 124.
Luscinius. Nuper Achaemenidae. Corn., p. 124.
Valeriano. Fundus Achaemenidae. *Poem.*, p. 112; *C.P.It.* 10. 154.
Alamanni. Casa di Menalippo. *Versi* 2. 141.
Sabeo. Villula Achemenidae. *Epig.*, p. 739.
Baldi. Campo fui Filon. *Epig.* 82.
Bongiovanni and Zanetti. Di Achemenide già. *Epig.*, p. 42.
Cunich. Fundus Achaemenidae. *Anth.*, p. 80.
Pompei. D'Achemenide un dì. *Op.* 2. 228.
Passeroni. D'Archemenide un tempo. *Rime* 3. 201.
Vargas. D'Archemenide fui prima. *Sag.*, p. 37.
Pagnini. D'Archemenide un tempo. *Epig.*, p. 13.

9.75. Cf. 99. Appears in an inscription, Kaibel 1106 (above, p. 13).
Ovid. Rode, caper vitem. *Fast.* 1. 357.
Ovid. Vite caper morsa. *Met.* 15. 114.
Babrius. Τράγος * εὐθαλοῦς. *Fab.* 181 (Crusius).
Suetonius quotes the epig., *Domit.* 14.
Quoted in *schol.* on Aristophanes, *Plut.* 1129.
Quoted by Suidas, *s.v.* ἀσκὸς Κτησιφῶντος.
Cf. Aesop. *Fabb.* 404, 404ᵇ (Halm).
Politian quotes this epigram, *Misc.* 26; *Op.* 1. 518.
Soter² (p. 9) and Cornarius (p. 12) give Ovid's tr.; Soter also quotes from Suetonius.
Venatorius. Me rodes licet. Obsop., p. 22; Wech., p. 18.
Alciati quotes Gr. and Ovid, *Op.* 2.1090.
Conti. Rodas me licet. *Myth.* 5. 13.
Sabeo. Me licet absumas. *Epig.*, p. 716.
Liceto quotes Conti's tr., *De Lucern.* (1653), col. 761.
Mazzoni. Anchor che tu mi [prose]. *Difesa* (1688) 2. 53.

Quoted by Rivautella-Ricolvi. *Mar.* 1. 183.
Ricolvi. Rodi pur, capro. *Op.*, p. 61.
Roncalli. Mordimi pur, dicea. *Epig.* (1801), p. 50.

9.76. Cf. *A.P.* 9. 343 and 396.
Sabeo. Saepe fugam merulae. *Epig.*, p. 772.
Pompei. Allor che giuso. *Op.* 2. 184.

9.77. Cornarius. Iliaci pueri forma. *Corn.*, p. 130.
Molza. Acta odiis rapti. *Poes.* 3. 206.
Obsopoeus. Puncta Phrygis rapti. Obsop., p. 190; Wech.,
   p. 168.
Battista. Mille di gelosia. *Mel.* 2. 24.
Cunich. Saeva Iovis coniunx. *Anth.*, p. 172.
Felici. Quando all' etere soglie. *Epig.*[2], p. x.

9.78. Sabeo. Tu ne me incuses. *Epig.*, p. 716.
Pagnini. Mia colpa, O viator. *Epig.*, p. 13.

9.79. Sabeo. Nativo fructu spolior. *Epig.*, p. 715.

9.80. Cornarius. Tu levis astrorum. *Corn.*, p. 91.
Obsopoeus. Vatum sidereos quisquis. Wech., p. 96.
Cunich. At male sit vobis. *Anth.*, p. 52.

9.82. Sabeo. Anchorae in aequoreo. *Epig.*, p. 741.

9.83. Sabeo. Delphinum nati. *Epig.*, p. 728.

9.84. Cunich. Eversam pelago puppim. *Anth.*, p. 138.

9.85. Cornarius. Quam fera tempestas. *Corn.*, p. 97.
Alciati. Obruta navis erat. *Op.* 4.540.
Obsopoeus. Fregerat undisono. Obsop., p. 123; Wech., p. 107.
Sabeo. A sale disiecta navi. *Epig.*, p. 414.
Baldi. Mentre rotta la nave. *Epig.* 309.
Cunich. Fracta ratis ponto. *Anth.*, p. 39.
Felici. Era tra scogli. *Epig.*[1], p. 36.
Passeroni. Ruppe il mio legno. *Rime* 3. 113.

9.86. Del Tuppo. Ostrea servabat clausa. *Fab. Aes.*, Oiii[vo].
Alciati. Regnator penus et mensae. Corn., p. 69; *Emb.* 95.
Mignault. Helluo et omnivorans. Alciati, *Emb.* 95.

9.87. Cf. Dio of Prusa 12.7 and 72. 14, and Aesop, *Fab.* 105ff (Halm).
Sabeo. Frondibus extremis quercus. *Epig.*, p. 751.
Bongiovanni and Zanetti. Lascia d'ir, merlo. *Epig.*, p. 6.
Cunich. Quercum linque istam. *Anth.*, p. 171.
Felici. Non più la lingua. *Epig.*[1], p. 23.
Passeroni. Lascia cotesta quercia. *Rime* 3. 243.

9.88. Sanchez. Praepetibus pennis vento. *Op.* 3. 187.
Sabeo. Incusans Boream super. *Epig.*, p. 739.

9.89. Sabeo. Filiole atque pater. *Epig.*, p. 856.
Sabeo. Legerat, extremas spicas. *Epig.*, p. 417.

9.92. Sabeo. Aebriae ubi fuerint. *Epig.*, p. 423.

9.93. Sabeo. Pisoni Antipater genialem. *Epig.*, p. 38.
Cunich. Pisoni magno, munera. *Anth.*, p. 169.
Passeroni. Antipatro a Pison. *Rime* 3. 149.

9.94. Cf. *A.P.* 9. 14 and 227.

Alciati. Polypedem venatus Acron. Corn., p. 83.
Valeriano. Gynnichus ut cepit. *Poem.*, p. 112; *C.P.It.* 10. 154.
Sabeo. Polypon expiscans iam. *Epig.*, p. 743.

9.95. Alciati. Ante diem vernam. Corn., p. 138; *Emb.* 194.
Sabeo. A nive candenti madidas. *Epig.*, p. 606.
Mignault. Sparsa nive hyberno. Alciati, *Emb.* 193.
Sanchez (Fer.). Canus December. *Op.* 3. 349.
Sanchez (Fer.). Bruma fremebat. *Op.* 3. 349.
Nunius. Gallina hyberis. Sanchez, *Op.* 3. 348.
Felici. Gallina mansuetissima. *Epig.*[1], p. 8.

9.96. Obsopoeus. Antigenes Siculus. Obsop., p. 180; Wech., p. 160.
Cunich. Antigenes gnatae civis. *Anth.*, p. 76.
Passeroni. Vicino a morte Antigene. *Rime* 3. 197.

9.97. Venatorius. Andromaches etiam num. Obsop., p. 150; Wech.,
p. 132.
Sabeo. Andromachae sentimus. *Epig.*, p. 223.
Allacci quotes this epig. with Venatorius' tr. Gronov., *Thes.*
10. 1724.
Cunich. Andromachae audimus fletum. *Anth.*, p. 13.
Medici (A. de'). Et nunc Andromache. *Scelt.*, p. xi.
Medici (A. de'). D'Andromaca odo ancor. *Scelt.*, p. xi.
Pagnini. D'Andromaca odo ancor. *Epig.*, p. 72.

9.99. Cf. 75.
Soter. Barbatus caper alta. Soter[2], p. 10; Corn., p. 12.
Sabeo. Dum petit alta hircus. *Epig.*, p. 702.
Giovane. Insiliens hircus. *Ant. Tar.* 3. 3.
Cunich. Dente malo aggressus. *Anth.*, p. 79.
Felici. Con gl' ingordi acuti. *Epig.*[1], p. 50.
Passeroni. I germogli, le frondi. *Rime* 3. 197.
Roncalli. Mordimi pur. *Epig.* (1792), p. 47.

9.100. Cf. *A.P.* 9. 408.
Conti. Latonae partus nutrix. *Myth.* 9. 6.
Cunich. Sancta o Latoidum. *Anth.*, p. 13.
Passeroni. Errò chi disse Delo. *Rime* 3. 46.

9.101. Cf. *A.P.* 9. 28, 102-3.
Averani cites this epig. *Op.* 1. 315.
Cunich. Heroum patriae nusquam. *Anth.*, p .137.
Passeroni. Non sol mojon gli. *Rime* 3. 216.

9.102. Cf. *A.P.* 9. 28, 101, and 103.
Cf. Propertius. O Veii veteres et vos. *Eleg.* 4. 10. 27-30.
Cunich. Argos caelestis quondam. *Anth.*, p. 139.

9.103. Cf. *A.P.* 9. 28, 101-2.
Sabeo. Auri dives eram. *Epig.*, p. 773.

9.104. Sabeo. Fabula Homero Argos. *Epig.*, p. 777.

9.105. Cf. *A.P.* 9. 30, 31, 33, 131, 376.
More (Sir T.). Ventis pinus humo. Soter[2], p. 104; Corn., p.98.
Obsopoeus. Cur ventis fractam. Obsop., p. 151; Wech., p. 114.
Sabeo. Nondum facta ratis. *Epig.*, p. 756.

Mazzoni quotes More's tr. *Difesa*, p. 424.
Cunich. Fracta Notis iaceo. *Anth.*, p. 167.
9.106. Cf. *A.P.* 9. 34, 36, and 398.
More (Sir T.). Iam ratis aequoreas. Soter[2], p. 105.
Cornarius. En navis ponti tantas. Corn., p. 99.
Sabeo. Quae scapha effugi. *Epig.*, p. 753.
Giovane. Ignis me exussit. *Ant. Tar.* 3. 3.
Cf. Cappellari. Arbor eram, nuda. *Poem.*, p. 18.
Bongiovanni and Zanetti. Nave io mi son. *Epig.*, p. 55.
Pagnini. Arsa dal foco dopo. *Epig.*, p. 155.
Roncalli. Io, che tra il Putto. *Epig.* (1801), p. 66.
9.107. Sabeo. Parvula inaequalis tumidum. *Epig.*, p. 752.
Cunich. Dicor parva ratis. *Anth.*, p. 77.
9.108. Sannazaro. De Veneris nato. *Poem.*, p. 197.
Marullus. Lascivum iratus pater. *Epig.* 2, p. 21.
Anisio. Iupiter haec in Amorem. *Poem.*, f. 92[ro].
Soter[2] (p. 10) and Cornarius quote Sannazaro's imitation.
Luscinius. Iupiter ad puerum Veneris. Corn., p. 12.
Anon. Molto d'Amor fiero. *Ver. et Reg.*, Miii; Carducci, *Poes.*
    Barb., p. 258.
Giraldi Cintio. Iupiter ut sensit. *Poem.*, p. 157.
Obsopoeus. Tela tibi eripiam. Obsop., p. 24; Wech., p. 20.
Calcagnini. Perfringit, penetrat. Pigna, p. 212.
Cordato. Olim minatus Iuppiter. *Prael.*, p. 110.
Cordato. Amori altitonans ait. *Ibid.*
Cordato. Iuppiter his dictis. *Ibid.*
Sabeo. Iuppiter audaci puero. *Epig.*, p. 7.
Sabeo. Non credis, lascive. *Epig.*, p. 63.
Sabeo. Iuppiter arma tibi. *Epig.*, p. 72.
Sabeo. Omnia tela Tonans. *Epig.*, p. 72.
Toscano (M.). Tela Cupido tua. *Anth.*, p. 141.
Cottunius quotes this epig. *Confic.* cap. 26.
Zappi (G. B. Felice). Disse Giove a Cupido. *Rime*, p. 110.
Ricolvi. Iupiter Idalio puero. *Op.*, p. 88.
Ricolvi. Che mi tien, fanciul. *Op.*, p. 88.
Ricolvi also gives Sannazaro's imit. *Op.*, p. 88.
Cunich. Tela adimam tibi. *Anth.*, p. 149.
Della Torre. Giove ad Amor dicea. *Odi*, p. 131.[2]
Passeroni. Disse Giove ad Amor. *Rime* 3. 123.
Bettinelli. G. Che sì che d'arco. *Op.* 13. 85.
Felici. Arco e freccie io. *Epig.*[2], p. xxviii.
Vargas. Giove ad Amor: Toglierti. *Sag.*, p. 82.
Pagnini. Il re degl' immortali. *Epig.*, p. 66.
9.109. Cf. *A.P.* 9. 40–2.
Sleidan. Nescio te scuti. Soter[2], p. 104; Corn., p. 96.
Obsopoeus. Nescio num clypeum. Obsop., p. 122; Wech.,
    p. 106.
Sabeo. Nescio si clypeum. *Epig.*, p. 414.

Groto. Scudo non sò, se più. *Rime* (1587), p. 156.
Felici. Dovrò fidissimo. *Épig.*[1], p. 44.

9.110. Cf. Archilochus 22 (Diehl).
More (Sir T.). Agros ego haud. Soter[2], p. 19; Corn., p. 15.
Gaurico. Non campos cupio. Epig. [4].
Scaliger (J. C.). Ne Gygae mihi, ne. *Poem.* 1. 158.
Mazzoni. Non bramo già [prose]. *Difesa*, Som. 81.
Gualfreducci. Non ingentia rura divis. *Var.*, p. 287.
Cf. Baldi. Io non domando a Dio. *Epig.* 64.
Bongiovanni and Zanetti. Colme di bionda. *Epig.*, p. 39.
More's tr. is given in 'Επ. καὶ 'Eλ. (No. 8).
Ricolvi. Non vastos peto. *Op.*, p. 62.
Ricolvi. Campi ubertosi e vasti. *Op.*, p. 62.
Cunich. Non amo segetes. *Anth.*, p. 75.
Vargas. Fertili campi io non. *Sag.*, p. 33.
Pagnini. Non io di campi spazio. *Epig.*, p. 73.

9.111. Luscinius. Laudantur Thraces, natos. Soter[2], p. 22; Corn.,
p. 19.
Alciati. Ecquis non laudet Thracas? Corn., p. 19.
Sabeo. Laudantur Thraces natos. *Epig.*, p. 512.
Sabeo. Thracia laudetur. *Epig.*, p. 74.
Sabeo. Barbara terra licet. *Epig.*, p. 74.
Spinula. Nec Tracia ipsa gaudet. *Epod.*, p. 21.
Guicciardini (L.). I popoli di Tracia [prose]. *Det.*, f. 12[vo].
Germano quotes Alciati's version. *Giard.*, p. 403.
Luscinius' version is given in 'Επ. καὶ 'Eλ. (No. 15).
Cunich. Et merito Thraces. *Anth.*, p. 78.
Pagnini. Danno i Traci a ragion. *Epig.*, p. 46.

9.112. Cf. *A.P.* 7. 157.
Sabeo. Bis tres terque. *Epig.*, p. 214.
Mazzoni. Trent' anni e sei [prose]. *Difesa*, p. 41.

9.113. Robortello refers to this epig. *Scr. Epig.*, p. 40.

9.114. Cf. *A.P.* 9. 351.
Luscinius. Infans praecipiti casu. Corn., p. 139.
Cornarius. A tegulis summis terram. Corn., p. 139.
Sabeo. Errantem puerum per. *Epig.*, p. 612.
Bargiocchi. Dum genetrix flores capit. *Epig.*, p. 109.
Cunich. Reptabat, iam iam. *Anth.*, p. 18.
Passeroni. Barcollando un bambino. *Rime* 3. 45.

9.115. Cf. 116.
Alciati. Aeacidae Hectoreo perfusum. Corn., p. 43; *Emb.* 28.
Sabeo. Hectore conspersum. *Epig.*, p. 238.
Mignault. Quem clypeum Laertiades. Alciati, *Emb.* 28.
Sanchez. Hectoreo clypeum. *Op.* 3. 85.
Cunich. Pelidae clypeum. *Anth.*, p. 72.
Passeroni. Di Pelide lo scudo. *Rime* 3. 95.

9.116. Sabeo. Iustior ipse fuit. *Epig.*, p. 142.
Mignault. Aequior est iudex. Alciati, *Emb.* 28.

Sanchez. Iudicio pulchro. *Op.* 3. 85.
Felici. Palla, di te fu giudice. *Epig.*[1], p. 103.

9.117. Alciati. Cum patrio Pyrrhus. Corn., p. 67.
Sabeo. Extructum ad patris. *Epig.*, p. 204.
Cunich. Caede Polyxenia tristes. *Anth.*, p. 146.

9.118. Cf. *A.P.* 9. 54–5; cf. Theognis 527–8; quoted by Stobaeus
Flor. 116. 11 (Meineke).
Costanzi (G.). Hei mihi quam senium. *Epig.*, Oiiii[ro].
Alciati. Hei mihi pubertas. Corn., p. 37.
Sabeo. Hei mihi pubertas. *Epig.*, p. 237.
Sabeo. Ob pubertatem doleo. *Epig.*, p. 714.
Sabeo. Tam me pubertas. *Epig.*, p. 581.
Crasso. Hei mihi ob [L-prose]. *Ist.*, p. 507.
Felici. Argomento di mie pene. *Epig.*[1], p. 95.
Pagnini. Vecchiezza tiemmi. *Epig.*, p. 140.

9.119. Luscinius. Blandiloqui placeant. Corn., p. 85.
Cornarius. Si quis adulantes. Corn., p. 85.
'L-prose.' Si quis vir imperans. Ἐπ. καὶ Ἐλεγ. No. 32.

9.120. Cf. Theophrastus. τοὺς φίλους αὑτοῦ. *Char.* 20. 9.
Luscinius. Rimarum plenus perdit. Corn., p. 65.
Cornarius. Pertusum vas est ingratus. Corn., p. 65.
Sabeo. Dolium inane est vir. *Epig.*, p. 733.
Sabeo. Urna foraminibus plena. *Epig.*, p. 722.
Germano. Malus vir dolium [prose]. *Giard.*, p. 170.
Bongiovanni and Zanetti. Una botte forata è. *Epig.*, p. 38.
Luscinius' tr. is given in Ἐπ. καὶ Ἐλ. (No. 28).
Cunich. Vir malus urna carens. *Anth.*, p. 80.
Passeroni. Un vaso senza fondo. *Rime* 3. 160.
Pagnini. Orcio forato è l'uomo. *Epig.*, p. 13.

9.122. Alciati. Quid rapis hei, Progne. Corn., p. 103; *Emb.* 180.
Sabeo. Attica natorum esuriens. *Epig.*, p. 732.
Mignault. Cur agedum in praedam. Alciati, *Emb.* 178.
Vargas. Tu d'Atene in grembo. *Sag.*, p. 76.

9.123. Sabeo. Summa piri tondes. *Epig.*, p. 720.

9.124. Politian. Cum Mars Daphne se. Del Lungo, p. 547.
Sabeo. Phoebe timende arcu. *Epig.*, p. 6.
Sabeo. Quum Mars coniunctus. *Epig.*, p. 79.
Sabeo. Phoebus ubi fuerat. *Epig.*, p. 79.
Sabeo. Quam non ventorum domuit. *Epig.*, p. 79.

9.125. Cf. Claudian. Et quos nascentes exploras. *In Ruf.* 2. 112.
Pio. Audaces rapido Celtae. *Ann. Post.* 23; *Lamp.* 1. 420.
Soter[2], p. 99; Corn., p. 88.
Calcaterra. Audaces rapido dubios. Soter[2], p. 99; Corn., p. 88.
Sabeo. Zelotypi audaces Celtae. *Epig.*, p. 409.
Mazzoni quotes the tr. of Pio. *Difesa*, p. 84.

9.126. Accolti (Bern.) Da 'l morto padre. *Verg.*, f.48[ro].
More (Sir T.). Qua gladium intrudes. Soter[2], p. 76; Corn.,
p. 66.

Valeriano. Quo, quo machaeram. *Poem.*, p. 113; *C.P.It.* 10.
158.

Vasolli. Impius in matrem gladium. *Epig.*, f.14ro; *Virid.*, f.
11ro.

Scaphenatus. Impius in matrem. *Eleg.*, Ci.

Cf. Calcagnini. Quom Nero in exitium. Pigna, p. 208.

Sabeo. Stringentem ferrum. *Epig.*, p. 546.

Sabeo. Contra uterum. *Epig.*, p. 471.

Sabeo. Ut natum inspexit. *Epig.*, p. 349 (351).

Sabeo. In ventrem an mammas. *Epig.*, p. 310.

Sabeo. Irruere in seipsam. *Epig.*, p. 270.

Groto. Perchè col padre dolce. *Rime* (1587), p. 145.

Groto. O tristo guiderdon. *Rime*, pt. 3 (1610), p. 76.

Bongiovanni and Zanetti. Su, su: a quel parte. *Epig.*, p. 50.

Medici (A. de'). Perfide, quo gladium? *Scelt.*, p. xxiv.

Medici (A. de'). Dove quel ferro. *Scelt.*, p. xxiv.

Pagnini. Empio, dov' hai diretto. *Epig.*, p. 66.

9.127. Cf. Antiphanes in Stobaeus, *Flor.* 116. 13 (Meineke).

Luscinius. Dolia si fundum gustu. *Corn.*, p. 37.

Averani. Accipiunt acidum vina. *Op.* 1. 161.

Bongiovanni and Zanetti. Se quel dolce licor. *Epig.*, p. 23.

'L-prose.' Si relictum sit. 'Επ. καὶ 'Eλ. No. 19.

Cunich. Vasis ut in fundo. *Anth.*, p. 70.

Pompei. Se poco di vin dolce. *Op.* 2. 222.

Passeroni. Come quel po' di vin. *Rime* 3. 94.

Pagnini. Quando entro a' vasi. *Epig.*, p. 58.

9.128–9. Sabeo. Hac illac serpebat. *Epig.*, p. 298 (282).

9.130. Politian. Quid me implicatis. Del Lungo, p. 547.

Ariosto. Hicne rosas inter. Pigna, p. 293; Polidori 1. 352.

Beroaldo (younger). Quid me racemis. *Carm.*, Nv.

Alciati. Quid me vexatis, rami? *Emb.* 24.

Sabeo. Ecquid palladiam plantam. *Epig.*, p. 45.

Sabeo. Palladis arbor ego. *Epig.*, p. 143.

Rota. Undique septem oleam. *Poem.* (1567), p. 117.

Cf. Rota. Amplexam Paphia. *Poem.* (1567), p. 65.

Mignault. Quid me palmitibus. Alciati, *Emb.* 24.

Guicciardini. Perchè mi fai [prose]. *Det.*, f.57vo.

Cunich. Arbor ego castae. *Anth.*, p. 73.

Felici. Sono di Pallade. *Epig.*[1], p. 101.

Passeroni. Alla casta Dea d'Atene. *Rime* 3. 161.

Vargas. Arbor di Palla io son. *Sag.*, p. 36.

Pagnini. Arbor di Palla io son. *Epig.*, p. 109.

9.131. Cf. *A.P.* 9. 30, 31, 33, 105, and 376.

Cunich. Quae solis iacui. *Anth.*, p. 167.

Pagnini. Me pin su i monti. *Epig.*, p. 52.

9.132. More (Sir T.). Hi duo detraxere. *Soter*[2], p. 125; Corn., p. 120.

Alciati. Quum tam dissideant. Corn., p. 120.

Luscinius. Iuncta simul Veneri. Corn., p. 120.

Sabeo. Caecus Amor castusque. *Epig.*, p. 855.
9.133. Costanzi (G.). Qui semel uxorem duxit. *Epig.*, Oiiii[ro].
Erasmus. Altera connubium. Soter[2], p. 37; Corn., p. 33.
More (Sir T.) Qui capit uxorem. Soter[2], p. 37; Corn., p. 33.
Rhodiginus. Si quis ducta [prose]. *Lect.* 28. 14.
Alciati. Coniunx cui periit. Corn., p. 33.
Venatorius. Qui repetit thalamos. Obsop., p. 34; Wech., p. 31.
Venatorius. Qui sequitur rursus. Obsop., p. 34; Wech., p. 31.
Sabeo. Si quis erit cupiens. *Epig.*, p. 177.
Sabeo. Nubere qui tentat. *Epig.*, p. 320.
Sabeo. Si quis erit, nuptam. *Epig.*, p. 170.
Patavinus quotes More's tr. *De Art.*, p. 212.
Cunich. Uxorem ducit qui. *Anth.*, p. 73.
Passeroni. Chi la seconda volta. *Rime* 3. 213.
Pagnini. Chi, la primiera moglie. *Epig.*, p. 15.
9.134. Cf. *A.P.* 9. 49, 135, and 172.
Cf. Amaseo. Ἐλπὶς καὶ Νίκη. *Lett.*, p. 54.
Sabeo. Ipse viam inveni. *Epig.*, p. 55.
Sabeo. Vitrea spes, et tu. *Epig.*, p. 135.
9.135. [Not in *Plan.*] Cf. *A.P.* 9. 49, 134, and 172.
9.136. Cf. Nonnus, *Dion.* 20. 372.
Obsopoeus. Pascere oves utinam. Obsop., p. 184; Wech.,
p. 162.
Sabeo. O si me genitor. *Epig.*, p. 175.
Cunich. Me pater o utinam. *Anth.*, p. 130.
Passeroni. Volesse il ciel, che. *Rime* 3. 121.
9.137. Quoted by David, *Prol. et in Porphyr. Isag. Comm.*, p. 33
(Busse).
Politian. Οὐδετέρους ἀδικῶ τὸ γάρ. Del Lungo, p. 211; Soter[2],
p. 5.
Soter. Mortuus heu medius. Soter[2], p. 6.
Soter. Phoebum quod videas. Soter[2], p. 6.
Soter. Ditem non lacero [from Polit.]. Soter[2], p. 6.
Sabeo. Una fame elanguet. *Epig.*, p. 700.
Gualfreducci. Dimidium periit nostri. *Var.*, p. 284; *Sel. Epig.*,
p. 12.
9.138. Velius. Pauper eram iuvenis. Soter[2], p. 111; Corn., p. 105.
Luscinius. Pauper eram ... modo. Soter[2], p. 111; Corn., p. 105.
Luscinius. Pauper eram ... nunc. Soter[2], p. 111.
Dazzi. Pauper eram iuvenis senior. *Poem.*, p. 118.
Alamanni. Povero giovin fui, ricco. *Versi* 2. 137.
Sabeo. Pauper eram iuvenis. *Epig.*, p. 460.
The tr. by Velius is given in Ἐπ. καὶ Ἑλ. (No. 35).
Cunich. Pauper eram iuvenis. *Anth.*, p. 71.
Felici. Già di lanugine. *Epig.*[1], p. 109.
Passeroni. Povero fui da giovine. *Rime* 3. 141.
Pagnini. Fui giovane mendico. *Epig.*, p. 52.
9.141. Alciati. Qui phreniti pressus. Corn., p. 90.

Sabeo. Hic phrenesi fuerat. *Epig.*, p. 853.
Sabeo. Excubat hic frenesi. *Epig.*, p. 852.
Sabeo. Hic nimis, iste nihil. *Epig.*, p. 466.
Cunich. Lethargo hic pressus. *Anth.*, p. 147.
Passeroni. Giacean due Sozj. *Rime* 3. 124.
Pagnini. Un vinto da letargo. *Epig.*, p. 94.
9.142. Conti. Montivagum colimus. *Myth.* 5. 6.
Sabeo. Ductor Amadryadum. *Epig.*, p. 464.
9.143. Sabeo. Mi domus est simplex. *Epig.*, p. 48.
Bongiovanni and Zanetti. Lieve è l'albergo. *Epig.*, p. 49.
9.144. Cunich. Cypridos hic locus est. *Anth.*, p. 14.
Passeroni. E' sacro questo luogo. *Rime* 3. 141.
9.145. Ausonius. Effigiem, rex Croese. *Opus.* 6. 30.
Ausonius? Effigiem, rex Croese. *Opus.* 23. 35.
Soter[2] (p. 20) and Cornarius (p. 16) give the second version
   ascribed to Ausonius.
Gaurico. Diogenem Pluto venientem. *Epig.* [6]; *C.P.It.* 5. 276.
Luscinius. Perfecta ut manes vidit. Corn., p. 16.
Gallo quotes Ausonius' version. *Opusc.* c. 5.
Crasso. Veniens in [L-prose]. *Ist.*, p. 159.
Ausonius' version is given in Ἐπ. καὶ Ἐλ. (No. 9.).
Pompei. Com' Diogene, il cane. *Op.* 2. 223.
9.146. Marullus. Quaenam haec tam. *Epig.*, 3, p. 40; Soter[2], p. 48;
   Corn., p. 50.
Politian. Spes simul et Nemesin. Del Lungo, p. 547.
Anselmo. Spem Nemesimque una. *Epig.*, Biiii.
Alciati. Spes simul et Nemesis. Corn., p. 50; *Emb.* 46.
Alciati. Quae dea tam laeto. Corn., p. 50.
Luscinius. Dum quereris sperasque. Corn., p. 50.
Sabeo. Spem posui ante aram. *Epig.*, p. 113.
Sabeo. Haec spes, haec Nemesis. *Epig.*, p. 113.
Sabeo. Spes Nemesi iuncta est. *Epig.*, p. 116.
Cunich. Dedicat heic una Nemesin. *Anth.*, p. 73.
Passeroni. A nemesi offro incenso. *Rime* 3. 195.
Pagnini. Un' ara stessa a Nemesi. *Epig.*, p. 179.
9.147. Cunich. Ite sacri Cereris celsa. *Anth.*, p. 41.
Pagnini. Di Cerere a ministri. *Epig.*, p. 49.
9.148. Luscinius. Tempore vix credas. Soter[2], p. 23.
Velius. Tristius atque olim. Soter[2], p. 23; Corn., p. 20.
Simonetta (B.). Defle hominum vitam. Corn., p. 20.
Alciati. Plus solito humanae. Corn., p. 20; *Emb.* 152.
Venatorius. Haec magis, Heraclete. Obsop., p. 30; Wech.,
   p. 27.
Sabeo. Heraclete, fleas plus. *Epig.*, p. 190.
Guicciardini. Più dell' usato [after Alciati]. *Det.*, f. 106ro.
Battista. Democrito, tu ridi. *Lir. Mar.*, p. 421.
Perrucci. Se Democrito stempra. *Lir. Mar.*, p. 518.
Averani cites this epig. *Op.* 1. 402.

Salvini. Heraclite, magis. *Disc.* I. 109.
Luscinius' tr. is given in 'Επ. καὶ 'Ελ. (No. 17.)
Ricolvi. Heraclite, fleas mage. *Op.*, p. 63.
Ricolvi. Piangi, Eraclito, adesso. *Op.*, p. 63.
Cunich. Nunc vitam fleto multo. *Anth.*, p. 69.
Pompei. La vita piangi, Eraclito. *Op.* 2. 220.
Passeroni. Piangi, Eraclito, il mondo. *Rime* 3. 209.
Pagnini. Eraclito, or vie più. *Epig.*, p. 47.

9.149. Cf. *A.P.* 9. 150 and 255.
9.150. Cf. *A.P.* 9. 149 and 255.
      Alciati. Pauper Aristides armenta. Corn., p. 48.
      Sabeo. Census Aristidis. *Epig.*, p. 402.
9.151. Cf. *A.P.* 16. 317.
      Obsopoeus. Dorica dic ubi sit. Obsop., p. 170; Wech., p. 148.
      Sabeo. Forma, Corinthe, tua. *Epig.*, p. 302 (286).
      Cunich. Illa ubi nunc abiit. *Anth.*, p. 137.
      Passeroni. Ove, Corinto, andò. *Rime* 3. 217.
9.152. Sabeo. Ilios haec quondam. *Epig.*, p. 753.
      Cf. Groto. Scorgonsi del mio incendio. *Rime* (1587), p. 142.
      Cunich. Anni furta vide decimi. *Anth.*, p. 50.
      Passeroni. Qualora io leggo. *Rime* 3. 108.
9.153. Sabeo. Urbs ubi muri illi. *Epig.*, p. 731.
      Cunich. Troia, ubi nam tua. *Anth.*, p. 132.
      Felici. Dove, O Troja, i muri. *Epig.*[1], p. 3.
9.154. Sabeo. Quae colis hanc urbem. *Epig.*, p. 71.
      Cunich. Salve, urbis praeses. *Anth.*, p. 132.
      Passeroni. Salve, O Palla, mia. *Rime* 3. 144.
      Felici. Salve, O Tritonia. *Epig.*[2], p. iii.
      Pagnini. Diva, che in guardia. *Epig.*, p. 102.
9.156. Sabeo. Cerne decem annorum. *Epig.*, p. 739.
9.157. Cf. Anisio. Quam fuit impius ille. *Poem.*, f.137[vo].
      Conti. Quis prior esse deum. *Myth.* 4.14.
      Sabeo. Si nocuisse dei non est. *Epig.*, p. 116.
      Medici (A. de'). Quis fuit ille, deum. *Scelt.*, p. xliv.
      Medici (A. de'). Chi primo fu che pose. *Scelt.*, p. xliv.
      Pagnini. Chi fe' d'Amore un nume? *Epig.*, p. 77.
9.158. Alciati. Ludebant parili tres. Corn., p. 49; *Emb.* 130.
      Anisio. Tres quondam dubias. *Poem.*, f.109[vo].
      Sabeo. Tres quondam inter se. *Epig.*, p. 403.
      Mignault. Tres quondam simul. Alciati, *Emb.* 129.
      Felici. Tre semplicette vergini. *Epig.*[1], p. 105.
9.159. Ausonius. Abiecta in triviis. *Opus.* 19. 23.
9.160. Cf. Choricius, *Op.*, p. 378 (Foerster).
      Sleidan. Herodotus cum se Musis. Soter[2], p. 120; Corn.,
          p. 112.
      Soter. Dona olim Herodoto. Soter[2], p. 120.
      Soter. Hospitio Herodotus. Soter[2], p. 120.
      Sabeo. Hospitio Herodotus. *Epig.*, p. 235.

Mazzoni quotes the Gr. without tr. *Difesa*, p. 27.

Pagnini. Erodoto alle Muse. *Epig.*, p. 53.

9.161. Obsopoeus. Hesiodi quondam manibus. Obsop., p. 160; Wech., p. 141.

Sabeo. Quum manibus. *Epig.*, p. 205.

9.162. Alciati. Vilis canna prius. Corn., p. 40.

Calcagnini. Agrestis fueram calamus. Pigna, p. 206.

Calcagnini. Candida succisis qui. Pigna, p. 212; *C.P.It.* 3. 81.

Sabeo. Qui modo sum calamus. *Epig.*, p. 65.

Sabeo. Planta fui sterilis. *Epig.*, p. 815.

Bongiovanni and Zanetti. Canna era i' già. *Epig.*, p. 48.

Ricolvi. Planta fui calamus. *Op.*, p. 66.

Ricolvi. Pianta già fui. *Op.*, p. 66.

Cunich. Nuper canna fui. *Anth.*, p. 11.

Felici. Io fui già canna. *Epig.*[1], p. 100.

Passeroni. Canna sterile io fui. *Rime* 3. 43.

Pagnini. Già canna un tempo. *Epig.*, p. 59.

9.163. Marullus. Cum ferret medios. *Epig.* 3, p. 36; Soter[2], p. 138; Corn., p. 137.

Anselmo. Confectum aetate Aeneas. *Epig.*, Aii; *C.P.It.* 1. 306.

Velius. Iliaco Aeneas igni. Soter[2], p. 139; Corn., p. 137.

Luscinius. Iliaca e flammis rapuit. Corn., p. 137.

Cornarius. Flamma volans totam. Corn., p. 137.

Alciati. Per medios hostes. *Emb.* 195.

Valeriano. Igne ex Iliaco telisqus. *Poem.*, p. 113; *C.P.It.* 10. 156.

Sabeo. Ex igne Iliaco. *Epig.*, pp. 264, 391.

Sabeo. Ereptum flammis. *Epig.*, p. 402.

Sabeo. Clamabat pius Aeneas. *Epig.*, p. 509.

Sabeo. Flammarum e medio. *Epig.*, p. 610.

Quoted by Landi. *Num.*, p. 8.

Mignault. Sustulit Aeneas Graium. Alciati, *Emb.* 194.

Cottunius quotes Alciati's version. *Confic.*, p. 83.

Marullus' tr. is given in 'Επ. καὶ 'Ελ. (No. 45.)

Ricolvi. Iliaca e flamma rapiens. *Op.*, p. 63.

Ricolvi. Iliacas inter flammas. *Op.*, p. 63.

Ricolvi. Tra le fiamme, onde. *Op.*, p. 63.

Cunich. Iliaco ex igni media. *Anth.*, p. 7.

Medici (A. de'). Ex igne Iliaco. *Scelt.*, p. xxvi.

Medici (A. de'). Dal fuoco d'Ilio. *Scelt.*, p. xxvi.

Pompei. Enea, l'eroe, del. *Op.* 2. 225.

Felici. Fuor della fiamma. *Epig.*[1], p. 111.

Passeroni. Carico Enea dell' onorato. *Rime* 3. 32.

9.165. Cf. 167.

[Cornarius quotes *A.P.* 9. 165–167, and gives a poem by Alciati as combining all three:]

Alciati. Foemina nos tacitis urit. Corn., p. 42.

Obsopoeus. Est mulier Iovis ira. Obsop., p. 41; Wech., p. 37.

Sabeo. Ira tonantis inest. *Epig.*, p. 73.
Averani. Ira Iovis magni. *Op.* 1. 42.
Cunich. Ira Iovis mulier. *Anth.*, p. 65.
9.166. Costanzi (A.). Castam atque incestam. *Epig.*, Bii^{vo}.
Alciati. [See under *A.P.* 9. 165.]
Anisio. Seu casta est mulier. *Poem.*, f. 128ro.
Scaphenatus. Tyndaris exitium sacer. *Eleg.*, Diii.
Obsopoeus. Nulla Melesigeni non. Obsop., p. 41; Wech., p. 37.
Sabeo. Quaeque mala. *Epig.*, p. 308.
Bongiovanni and Zanetti. Demostra Omero, che. *Epig.*, p. 7.
Ricolvi. Quaelibet exitiale malum. *Op.*, p. 81.
Cunich. Qualiscunque nocet. *Anth.*, p. 163.
Passeroni. Sien di buoni, o rei. *Rime* 3. 235.
Bettinelli. Elena druda il Frige. *Op.* 22. 103.
Pagnini. Secondo Omero è. *Epig.*, p. 57.
9.167. Cf. *A.P.* 9. 165.
Costanzi (G.). Ignem alium similem. *Epig.*, Oiiii^{vo}.
Alciati. [Cf. under *A.P.* 9. 165.]
Sabeo. Foeminam ob ignem. *Epig.*, p. 714.
Bongiovanni and Zanetti. Giove del foco in vece. *Epig.*, p. 12.
Vargas. Per un fuoco diè Giove. *Sag.*, p. 83.
Pagnini. Pel foco a lui rapito. *Epig.*, p. 79.
9.168. Cf. the epigram given in the Didot Anthol., vol. 3 (3. 145),
which is the original of the version ascribed to Ausonius,
'Arma virumque' docens, etc. (*Opus.* 23. 3), which Soter
(p. 42) and Cornarius (p. 38) refer to *A.P.* 9. 168.
Luscinius. Grammatico ducta est. Soter², p. 42; Corn., p. 38.
9.170. Sleidan. Quemquam ventres erat. Soter², p. 125; Corn., p. 120.
Cf. Baldi. S' il cervel sopra. *Epig.* 74.
9.171. Cf. 175.
Sabeo. Organa Pieridum. *Epig.*, p. 712.
Sabeo. Tristia castarum vendo. *Epig.*, p. 559.
9.172. Cf. *A.P.* 9. 49, 134–5.
Soter. Non spes, non fortuna. Soter², p. 21.
Cornarius. Non ego fortunam nec spem. Corn., p. 17.
Sabeo. Non mage spes curae. *Epig.*, p. 706.
Soter's version is given in 'Επ. καὶ 'Ελ. (No. 10.).
Cunich. Non fortuna ultra. *Anth.*, p. 82.
Passeroni. Della fortuna io non. *Rime* 3. 204.
9.173. Soter. Grammaticae auspicium. Soter², p. 43.
Alciati. Si magni inspicias. Corn., p. 39.
Sabeo. Carmina grammatices. *Epig.*, p. 823.
Sabeo. Grammatices inter casus. *Epig.*, p. 824.
Mazzoni gives Soter's version. *Difesa*, p. 112.
9.175. Cf. 171.
Sabeo. Postquam Dorotheus. *Epig.*, p. 386.
Pagnini. Io Callimaco e Pindaro. *Epig.*, p. 71.
9.176. Cornarius. Rhetora me dicis, quamvis. Corn., p. 122.

Sabeo. A te invitatus. *Epig.*, p. 175.
Cunich. Ad coenam invitas. *Anth.*, p. 179.
Pagnini. Dell' invitarmi a cena. *Epig.*, p. 33.
9.177. The anecdote is told by Philostratus, *Heroic.* 681 (Didot, p. 279).
Cunich. Aiacis tumulo superadstitit. *Anth.*, p. 148.
9.178. Sabeo. Primum solis eram. *Epig.*, p. 196.
Cunich. Quae solis fueram. *Anth.*, p. 20.
9.179. Sabeo. Ex thure invictum. *Epig.*, p. 64.
Sabeo. Thure sagittiferum. *Epig.*, p. 117.
Sabeo. Quis thure arsuro. *Epig.*, p. 117.
Toscano (M.). Ture sagitti ferum. *Anth.*, p. 144.
Cunich. Ture sagittiferum. *Anth.*, p. 157.
9.180. Cf. *A.P.* 9. 181–3.
9.182. Cf. Baldi. Sfortunata Fortuna. *Epig.* 321.
9.183. Cf. 180–2.
Sabeo. In reliquum mutata. *Epig.*, p. 107.
Minturno. Tu quoque, Fortuna. *Epig.*, f.5ro.
Cunich. Tu quoque versa iocus. *Anth.*, p. 180.
9.184. Valeriano. Praeter rotundi vim. *Poem.*, p. 112; *C.P.It.* 10. 155.
Sanchez. Primos scirem novem. *Op.* 2. 474.
Fioretti. Musarum sacrum [from L-prose]. *Prog.* 3. 310.
Crasso. Pindare Mus. [line 1, L-prose]. *Ist.*, p. 82.
9.185. Obsopoeus. Hi sunt Archilochi. Obsop., p. 154; Wech., p. 137.
Sabeo. Haec metra Archilochi. *Epig.*, p. 181.
Sabeo. Archilochi hi non sunt. *Epig.*, p. 181.
9.186. Quoted in the 1498 Aristophanes (Aldus).
Venatorius. Carmina Aristophanis. Obsop., p. 155; Wech. p. 137.
Sabeo. Paginae Aristophanis. *Epig.*, p. 181.
Crasso. Libri Aristophanis [L-prose]. *Ist.*, p. 70.
9.187. Sabeo. Excerpsere tibi mellito. *Epig.*, p. 180.
Crasso. Ipsa tibi in os [L-prose]. *Ist.*, p. 337.
Rivautella-Ricolvi. Pieridum varios. *Mar.* 1. 183.
9.188. Sabeo. Eloquii os Graeci. *Epig.*, p. 213.
Fioretti. Atticae facundae [L-prose]. *Prog.* 3. 283.
Crasso. Atticae facundae [L-prose]. *Ist.*, p. 427.
9.189. Sabeo. Ite ad Iunonis. *Epig.*, p. 231.
Crasso. Venite ad [L-prose]. *Ist.*, p. 449.
Cunich. Iunonis magnae in lucum. *Anth.*, p. 9.
Passeroni. O voi di Lesbio candide. *Rime* 3. 36.
9.190. Quoted by Eustathius on *Il.* B 711.
Cf. Politian. Castalio ceu melle. *Nut.* 633–4; Del Lungo. p. 414.
Rhodiginus. Quanto Erinna [lines 7–8; prose]. *Lect.* 14.1.
Giraldi (L.G.). Erinna melior [lines 7–8]. *Op.* 2. 124.
Sabeo. Lesbius Erinnes favus. *Epig.*, p. 197.

Crasso. Lesbus Erinnae [L-prose]. *Ist.*, p. 194.
9.191. Sabeo. Haud facile bis nostris. *Epig.*, p. 232.
9.192. Cf. Politian. Ἥδε βίβλος τίνος ἐστί. Del Lungo, p. 216.
Anselmo. Cuius et his inest. *Epig.*, Niiii.
Cornarius. Cuius vos libri? *Corn.*, p. 108.
Venatorius. Quid nam estis libri? Obsop., p. 150; Wech.,
p. 133.
Sabeo. Quid tegitis libri? *Epig.*, p. 179.
Allacci. Libri cuius estis? Gronov., *Thes.* 10. 1810.
Cunich. Dicite, quaenam estis? *Anth.*, p. 19.
9.197. Sabeo. Oque tui capitis. *Epig.*, p. 214.
9.198. Giraldi (L.G.) quotes the Gr. *Op.* 2. 214.
9.199. Cornarius. Immortalem artem verita. Corn., p. 78.
Valeriano. Qui liber hic auro. *Poem.*, p. 113; *C.P.It.* 10. 157.
Sabeo. Aenthei Oribasii. *Epig.*, p. 184.
9.204. Sabeo. Ne me ne Aiacis. *Epig.*, p. 701.
Gualfreducci. Aiacis lapidem ne me. *Var.*, p. 291.
Cunich. Me magni Aiacis lapidem. *Anth.*, p. 47.
Felici. Non ardire, O passegero. *Epig.*[1], p. 1.
Passeroni. No, scagliarmi non. *Rime* 3. 106.
9.205. [Not in *Plan.*] Appears at head of Theocritus-MSS. (Ahrens,
Bouc. 2. 21).
9.206. Sabeo. Verborum o quantum messem. *Epig.*, p. 541.
9.207. Sabeo. Altivolentem animum. *Epig.*, p. 286 (288).
9.208. Sabeo. Ductus Epicteti sapientis. *Epig.*, pp. 246, 350.
9.211. Sabeo. Poeonem, Chirona. *Epig.*, p. 185.
Crasso. Paeon et Chiron [L-prose]. *Ist.*, p. 358.
9.212. Sleidan. Multa quidem retulit. Soter[2], p. 87; Corn., p. 79.
Sabeo. Pharmaca multa bona. *Epig.*, p. 185.
9.213. Quoted in the 1499 Dioscorides-Nicander (Aldus).
Sleidan. Inter praecipuas Colophon. Soter[2], p. 87; Corn.,
p. 79.
Cornarius. Insignis Colophon urbes. Corn., p. 79.
Sabeo. Et Colophon urbes. *Epig.*, p. 184.
Allacci gives Sabeo's tr. and the Gr. Gronov., *Thes.* 10. 1788.
Crasso. Et Colophon [L-prose]. *Ist.*, p. 358.
9.214. Vargas. Porfirio, coi color sai. *Sag.*, p. 66.
9.215. Cunich. Foemineo generi semper. *Anth.*, p. 136.
9.216. Cf. *A.P.* 9. 250 and 253.
9.218. Sabeo. Heu, vellem hybernis. *Epig.*, p. 418.
Cunich. O utinam tristi vesani. *Anth.*, p. 131.
9.219. Sabeo. Ex Ithaca sterili. *Epig.*, p. 457.
9.221. Chalcondyles (B.) paraphrases this epig. Gudius, *Epist.*,
p. 137.
Alciati. Aspice ut invictus veris. Corn., p. 62; *Emb.* 106.
Mignault. Quid video in gemma. Alciati, *Emb.* 105.
Mignault. Indomitum specto. Alciati, *Emb.* 105.
Sanchez. Conspicor invictum. *Op.* 3. 214.

Toscano (M.). Annulus insculptum gemmae. *Anth.*, p. 144.
Argoli. Adspicio saevum sub marmore. Graev., *Thes.* 9. 62.
Pinelli (N.). Contemplor inevitabilem [prose]. Graev., *Thes.* 9. 489.
Bongiovanni and Zanetti. Amor maravigliando. *Epig.*, p. 39.
Cunich. In gemma Libyci vidi. *Anth.*, p. 172.
Medici (A. de'). Ecce Amor indomitus. *Scelt.*, p. xxxiv.
Medici (A. de'). Miro qui sculto Amore. *Scelt.*, p. xxxiv.
Felici. In gemma lucida. *Epig.*[1], p. 21.
Bettinelli. Ecco il fanciullo. *Op.* 13. 82.
Vargas. In questa gemma Amor. *Sag.*, p. 41.
Pagnini. Invitto domatore. *Epig.*, p. 76.

9.222. Sleidan. Orbum luce verum. Soter[2], p. 94; Corn., p. 82.
Alciati. Aspiciens puerum immanes. Corn., p. 82.
Gravina (P.). Humanum mediis fluitare. *Poem.*, f.26ro.
Sabeo. Terreno exanimi per. *Epig.*, p. 743.

9.223. Cf. 265.
Alciati. Regia quae puerum volucris. *Corn.*, p. 43.
Sabeo. Dum volucrum regina. *Epig.*, p. 734.
Baldi. Drizzò perito arcier. *Epig.* 295.

9.224. Sabeo. Sum pulchra uberibus. *Epig.*, p. 184.
Cunich. Me pingui ante alias. *Anth.*, p. 28.
Passeroni. Cedano a me quante son. *Rime* 3. 173.
Felici. Fra quante capre pascono. *Epig.*[2], p. xiii.

9.226. Sabeo. Eia agite, o flavae. *Epig.*, p. 744.

9.227. [Not in *Plan.*] Cf. *A.P.* 9. 14 and 94.

9.228. Sabeo. Natum inopina suum. *Epig.*, p. 425.

9.229. Cf. *A.P.* 5. 135.

9.230. Obsopoeus. Fessus es ascendens. Obsop., p. 25; Wech., p. 21.

9.231. Ariosto. Arida sum, vireoque. Pigna, p. 293; Polidori 1. 352.
Alciati. Arentem senio, nudam. *Emb.* 160.
Teocreno. Arverim quanvis, amplexu. *Poem.*, Cii.
Colin. Arida serpenti platanus. Teocreno, *Poem.*, Cii.
Dazzi. Arentem inserpens platanum. *Poem.*, p. 128.
Giraldi (L.G.). Extemploque monet tales [vv. 5–6]. *Op.* 1. 52.
Sabeo. Me platanum arentem. *Epig.*, p. 703.
Mignault. Me siccam platanum. Alciati, *Emb.* 159.
Sanchez. Me platanum siccam. *Op.* 3. 298.
Baldi. Stringea con braccia. *Epig.* 290.
Germano gives Alciati's version. *Giard.*, p. 15.
'L-prose.' Mortuam me platanum. Ἐπ. καὶ Ἐλεγ. No. 2.
Cunich. Me platanum aridulam. *Anth.*, p. 76.
Pompei. Me inaridito platano. *Op.* 2. 183.

9.233. Sabeo. Nunquam infelicem. *Epig.*, p. 700.
Sabeo. Infelix Midon dum. *Epig.*, p. 700.

9.236. Sabeo. Sacramenta trium extrema. *Epig.*, p. 753.
Cunich. Parcarum leges regali. *Anth.*, p. 25.

Passeroni. Col real sangue la caduta. *Rime* 3. 179.
Felici. La Parca inesorabile. *Epig.*[2], p. xi.
9.238. Sabeo. Phoebus hic impubes. *Epig.*, p. 120.
9.240. Molza. Errantem oblita peteret. *Poes.* 3. 209.
Felici. Cozzava un grande ariete. *Epig.*[2], p. xvii.
9.241. Sabeo. Egit Apollo boves. *Epig.*, p. 5.
Sabeo. Phoebe, bubulcus eras. *Epig.*, p. 109.
9.242. Cf. *A.P.* 7. 305, 381, 585, 635.
Cunich. Glaucus Nessaeae fauces. *Anth.*, p. 170.
9.244. Sabeo. Undique quum tegeret. *Epig.*, p. 721.
9.245. Sabeo. Affluit infaustis. *Epig.*, p. 602.
Sabeo. Concubitus primos. *Epig.*, p. 602.
Pagnini. Da Petale infelice. *Epig.*, p. 99.
9.246. Sabeo. Iuxta convivas iocus. *Epig.*, p. 416.
Cunich. Potoris inter vini. *Anth.*, p. 153.
9.247. Sleidan. Austro nuper humi. Soter[2], p. 106; Corn., p. 101.
Sabeo. Iam platanum evulsit. *Epig.*, p. 415.
Sabeo. Iam platanum evulsit. *Epig.*, p. 772.
Anon. Nuper me platanum. *Sel. Epig.*, p. 85.
Averani. Frondentem late platanum. *Op.* 2. 245.
Bongiovanni and Zanetti. Me frondeggiante. *Epig.*, p. 4.
9.248. Alciati. Si talis sacrum venisset. Corn., p. 15.
Sabeo. Si Bacchus talis sacrum. *Epig.*, p. 32.
Giraldi (L.G.) refers to this epig. *Op.* 2. 168. 12.
Gualfreducci. Aetherium Liber si talis. *Var.*, p. 291.
Averani. Si talis quondam. *Op.* 1. 49.
Cunich. Si talis sacri ad culmen. *Anth.*, p. 26.
9.249. Anon. Heic stans vertice. Burmann, *A.L.* 2. 471.
Sabeo. Ramosam arbustum. *Epig.*, p. 153.
9.250. Cf. *A.P.* 9. 216 and 253.
Crasso. Surrexi cum cithara [L-prose]. *Ist.*, p. 38.
9.252. Sabeo. Vir turbam inspiciens. *Epig.*, p. 295 (283)
9.253. Cf. 216 and 250.
Sabeo. Inclytus in Thebis Cadmi. *Epig.*, p. 777.
9.254. Sabeo. Si pia progenies. *Epig.*, p. 373.
Sabeo. Pignora parturiens misera. *Epig.*, p. 405.
Cunich. Funereo tantum foecunda. *Anth.*, p. 145.
Passeroni. Tre figlie partorii. *Rime* 3. 62.
9.255. Cf. 149–50.
Sabeo. Pauper Aristides sed felix. *Epig.*, p. 554.
9.257. Cf. 258.
Sabeo. Fons fueram purus. *Epig.*, p. 106.
Baldi. Tien da me lunge. *Epig.* 1053.
9.258. Cf. 257.
Cf. Anisio. Abstine ab Eurota. *Poem.*, f.160[ro].
Sabeo. Qui prius unda fuit. *Epig.*, p. 133.
Gambara (L.). Hos latices ne accede. *C.P.It.* 5. 296.
9.259. Alciati. Corruit a summo domus. Corn., p. 33.

Sabeo. Quum super infantem. *Epig.*, p. 177.
Sabeo. Quum domus alta. *Epig.*, p. 557.
Cunich. Corruit ad terram. *Anth.*, p. 26.
Passeroni. Crollò da' fondamenti. *Rime* 3. 168.
Felici. Dal più sublime vertice. *Epig.*[2], p. xi.
Pagnini. Di cima a fondo rovinò. *Epig.*, p. 61.

9.260. Cf. *A.P.* 6. 1, 18–20.
Sabeo. Omnium eram iaculum. *Epig.*, p. 605.
Sabeo. Graeciae eram iaculum. *Epig.*, p. 856.

9.261. Cornarius. Oenanthas inter vigui. *Corn.*, p. 38.
Sabeo. Quae fueram soliis. *Epig.*, p. 711.
Baldi. Questi rami che miri. *Epig.* 289.
'L-prose.' Quae antea foliis. Ἐπ. καὶ Ἐλεγ. No. 21.

9.262. Cunich. Clara fuit matrum in coetu. *Anth.*, p. 145.

9.264. [Not in *Plan.*] Cf. 273.

9.265. Cf. 223.
Sabeo. Fixa aquila a iaculo. *Epig.*, p. 110.
Felici. Mentre a tornar sull' etere. *Epig.*[2], p. ix.

9.266. Cf. 340.
Politian refers to this epig. *Epist.* 11. 10.
Conti. Fabula de lotis. *Myth.* 6. 15.
Averani. Multiforem inspirat dum. *Op.* 1. 148.
Cunich. Multiforam arguto. *Anth.*, p. 39.

9.267. Cunich. Nicerati proles Damis. *Anth.*, p. 144.
Felici. Navigando il mare Icario. *Epig.*[2], p. xvii.

9.268. [Not in *Plan.*]
Cf. Martial. Icta gravi telo. *Epig. Lib.* 13, 14.
The anecdote is related by Aelian, *N.A.* 7. 12.

9.269. Cf. Cicero, *De Offic.* 3. 90.
Sabeo. Puppe mari infracta. *Epig.*, p. 415.
Pagnini. Rotta una nave in mar. *Epig.*, p. 95.

9.270. Sabeo. Aureum ad usque. *Epig.*, p. 411.

9.271. Cunich. Dic, marem qua non sis. *Anth.*, p. 140.
Felici. In quel dì non sei. *Epig.*[1], p. 19.
Passeroni. O mare, O mare, e qual. *Rime* 3. 61.
Pagnini. E quando, O mare, a non. *Epig.*, p. 28.

9.272. [Not in *Plan.*] A similar story is related by Plutarch, *Moral.*
967A; by Pliny, *H.N.* 10. 60; and by Aelian, *N.A.* 2. 48. As
a fable it appears in Avianus, *Fab.* 27; and in his imitators,
Anon. of Asti (Hervieux 2. 443), and two other anonymous
writers (Hervieux 2. 468 and 497).

9.273. [Not in *Plan.*] Cf. 264.

9.274. Cf. *A.P.* 10. 101.
Sabeo. Et terram in teretes. *Epig.*, p. 734.
Sabeo. Cogor inequales sulcos. *Epig.*, p. 725.

9.275. Sabeo. Codrus aprum sternens. *Epig.*, p. 422.

9.276. Cf. 308.

9.277. Cf. Ovid. Quid mecum, foriose. *Am.* 3. 6. 87–96.

Cunich. Quid torrens tam dira. *Anth.*, p. 169.
Passeroni. Orgoglioso torrente. *Rime* 3. 147.
Felici. Torrente, che precipiti. *Epig.*², p.v.
9.278. Obsopoeus. Urna non magna vidit. Obsop., p. 177; Wech.,
p. 155.
Sabeo. Amne trahi rapido iuvenis. *Epig.*, p. 843.
Sabeo. Quae defunctorum. *Epig.*, p. 417.
9.279. Alciati. Et ferventem animis. Corn., p. 11.
Venatorius. Cum tercentenos mavortia. Obsop., p. 19;
Wech., p. 16.
Sabeo. Magnanima ut vidit. *Epig.*, p. 139.
Cunich. Ire iterum in Stygia. *Anth.*, p. 24.
Passeroni. Allorchè vide con serena. *Rime* 3. 225.
9.280. Sabeo. Vidit ut Eurotam Spartae. *Epig.*, p. 777.
9.283. Sabeo. Pyrenea iuga atque. *Epig.*, p. 68.
Quoted by Landi., *Num.*, p. 43.
Gualfreducci. Vos iuga Pirenes. *Var.*, p. 292.
Crasso. Montes Pyrenaei [L-prose]. *Ist.*, p. 252.
Cunich. Alpini saltus atque. *Anth.*, p. 24.
Medici (A. de'). Vos Pyrenaei montes. *Scelt.*, p. x.
Medici (A. de'). Il nevoso Appennin. *Scelt.*, p. x.
Passeroni. Le Alpi scoscese. *Rime* 3. 175.
9.285. Alciati. Turrigeris humeris. *Emb.* 177.
Sabeo. Non mage pugnabis. *Epig.*, p. 182.
Sabeo. Et licet intrepidi. *Epig.*, p. 182.
Mignault. Non iam turritus. Alciati, *Emb.* 176.
Cunich. Non fert in media. *Anth.*, p. 38.
Felici. Non più turriti aggiransi. *Epig.*², p. xviii.
9.286. Sabeo Astiterat Pyrrhae mihi. *Epig.*, p. 722.
9.287. Sabeo. Non egressa prius. *Epig.*, p. 220.
Averani. Quae claram volucris. *Op.* 1. 73.
9.288. Cunich. Hospes, Cecropidum. *Anth.*, p. 92.
9.289. Sabeo. E Troia in reditu. *Epig.*, p. 236.
Cunich. Puppibus o malefida. *Anth.*, p. 140.
9.291. Hermann a Nov. Aq. En ego quae rerum. Soter², p. 8.
Sleidan. Oceanus moveat licet. Soter², p. 8; Corn., p. 10.
Alciati. Oceanus quavis fluctus. Corn., p. 10; *Emb.* 42.
Mignault. Oceanus quanquam ipse. Alciati, *Emb.* 42.
Gualfreducci. Non, pater Oceanus si. *Var.*, p. 286.
Averani. Si totum spatiosa. *Op.* 1. 223.
Cunich. Oceanus non si fluctus. *Anth.*, p. 28.
Passeroni. Si scanteni lo Inferno. *Rime* 3. 181.
9.292. Sabeo. Una dolore parens. *Epig.*, p. 420.
Sabeo. Iam cinis unus erat. *Epig.*, p. 405.
Cf. Beccuti. L'un figlio ardeva. *Rime*, p. 251.
Cunich. Hoc flammae imposito. *Anth.*, p. 144.
9.293. Anselmo. Inventa Xerxes iam. *Epig.*, Fiiii.
Alamanni. Di Leonida il corpo. *Versi* 2. 126.

Scaphenatus. Purpureo insigni Xerxes. *Eleg.*, Biiii.
Sabeo. Spartanum horribili. *Epig.*, p. 350.
Cunich. Ipse suo cecidit. *Anth.*, p. 37.
Felici. Quando immortal Leonida. *Epig.*[1], p. 34.
Passeroni. Morto che fu Leonida. *Rime* 3. 89.

9.294. Sabeo. Dux Spartane, tibi. *Epig.*, p. 179.

9.295. Sabeo. Ne mireris equum. *Epig.*, p. 737.
Sabeo. Si gemo, si indignor. *Epig.*, p. 737.
Cunich. Adsuetus campis non. *Anth.*, p. 25.
Passeroni. Sopra una nave strascinato. *Rime* 3. 175.
Pagnini. Questo puledio che pe' campi. *Epig.*, p. 99.

9.296. For the anecdote cf. Pausanias 10.19.

9.298. Sabeo. Duxerat ad templum. *Epig.*, p. 19.
Sabeo. Alma Ceres, nata et. *Epig.*, p. 19.
Gualfreducci. Templum adii baculo nixus. *Var.*, p. 285; *Sel.*
Epig., p. 16.
Averani. Quum sacris foret. *Op.* 1. 94.
Redi refers to line 7 [il vino chiamato lagrime]. *Op.* 1. 271.

9.299. Cf. 347.
Sabeo. Qui placidi fuimus. *Epig.*, p. 721.
Pagnini. Non pure i solchi aprir. *Epig.*, p. 100.

9.301. Sabeo. Tardipedem inter equas. *Epig.*, p. 795.

9.302. Cf. 548.
Sabeo. Morsibus infantem. *Epig.*, p. 735.
Sabeo. Dilaniastis apes. *Epig.*, p. 735.
Mignault. Repentem per humum. Alciati, *Emb.*, 111.
Cunich. Hermonacta malae puerem. *Anth.*, p. 136.

9.303. Sabeo. Luna laboranti Latonae. *Epig.*, p. 735.
Bongiovanni and Zanetti. Alle gentil Calatina. *Epig.*, p. 53.
Pagnini. A Calatina dalle doglie. *Epig.*, p. 100.

9.304. Cf. Alamanni. Per monstrar pari al ciel. *Versi* 2. 126.
Sabeo. Iam maris et terrae. *Epig.*, p. 212.
Sabeo. Iam mare transmissum. *Epig.*, p. 212.
Gualfreducci. Terrarum pontique olim. *Var.*, p. 291.
Cunich. Per mare qui pedibus. *Anth.*, p. 36.
Passeroni. A colui, che di ponti. *Rime* 3. 180.
Pagnini. Quei, che con novo. *Epig.*, p. 48.

9.305. Sleidan. Hesterno mihi forte. Soter[2], p. 106; Corn., p. 100.
Obsopoeus. Plenus heri fueram. Obsop., p. 136; Wech., p. 120.
Sabeo. Simplicibus lymphis. *Epig.*, p. 33.
Bongiovanni and Zanetti. A me satollo di pura. *Epig.*, p. 4.

9.306. Sabeo. Amplius, o fabri, sylvas. *Epig.*, p. 771.
Cunich. Lignator, silvas ratibus. *Anth.*, p. 21.

9.307. Sabeo. Caesaris ex ara peperit. *Epig.*, p. 89.
Averani. Quae renuit Phoebum. *Op.* 1. 68.
Cunich. Daphne Phoebum olim. *Anth.*, p. 37.
Felici. Dafne fuggì sollecita. *Epig.*[1], p. 35.

9.308. Cf. 276.

Alciati. Delphini insidens vada. Corn., p. 83; *Emb.* 90.
Sabeo. Aequorei fueras ubi. *Epig.*, p. 748.
Mignault. Praecipitem e navi. Alciati, *Emb.* 89.
Crasso. Latrones cum [L-prose]. *Ist.*, p. 65.
9.309. Sabeo. Accendens prunas hyemis. *Epig.*, p. 713.
9.310. Sabeo. Dentibus attritum. *Epig.*, p. 279 (281).
Sabeo. Dentibus intrito mus. *Epig.*, p. 279 (281).
Pagnini. Tritato un topo avea. *Epig.*, p. 16.·
9.311. Sabeo. Per cervae alipedi. *Epig.*, p. 121.
9.312. Sabeo. Glandiferam matrem. *Epig.*, p. 726.
Carcani (P.). Cessa, deh! cessa. *Ant. Ercol.* 8. 90; *Rac.* 1. 97.
Felici. Tronca il corbezzolo. *Epig.*[2], p. xxvii.
9.313. Cf. *A.P.* 16. 228.
Sabeo. Hic sedeas hilaris. *Epig.*, p. 279 (281).
9.314. Sabeo. Hic ego Mercurius. *Epig.*, p. 146.
9.316. Sabeo. Qui callem hunc teritis. *Epig.*, p. 38.
Aleander (G.), younger. Qui hanc properatis [prose]. Graev.,
    Thes. 5. 725.
Rivautella-Ricolvi. Hac quisquis properas. *Mar.* 1. 126.
Ricolvi. Hac quicunque venis. *Op.*, p. 72.
Cunich. Audi, quisquis iter. *Anth.*, p. 156.
Felici. O passeggier, che. *Epig.*[2], p. xxii.
9.320. Rhodiginus quotes without tr., *Lect.* 29. 18.
Cunich. Eurotas dixit Veneri. *Anth.*, p. 157.
Felici. Disse l'Eurota a Venere. *Epig.*[1], p. 47.
9.321. Anselmo. Terribilem cristis galeam. *Epig.*, Cii.
Sabeo. Cypri quid hasta tibi. *Epig.*, p. 157.
9.322. Cf. *A.P.* 6. 163; and 9. 323.
Teocreno. Non mea sunt spolia. *Poem.*, Ciii.
Baldus (V.). Talia quis nostris. Teocreno, *ibid.*
Colin. Non sunt belligeri. *Ibid.*
Venatorius. Quis Marti posuit. Obsop., p. 8; Wech., p. 7.
Sabeo. Non mea sunt spolia. *Epig.*, p. 146.
Sabeo. Non mea sunt spolia . . . inquam. *Epig.*, p. 68.
Franchini. Quae spolia haec? haec arma. *Epig.*, p. 92.
Gualfreducci. Non mea sunt; quis dona. *Var.*, p. 284; *Sel.*
    Epig., p. 14.
Cunich. Unde, malum, spolia haec? *Anth.*, p. 175.
Pompei. Mie non son queste. *Op.* 2. 194.
Vargas. No, mio non è questo. *Sag.*, p. 34.
Pagnini. No, mie non son tai. *Epig.*, p. 111.
9.323. Cf. *A.P.* 6. 163; and 9.322.
Anselmo. Quis clypeos Martis. *Epig.*, Biiii.
Sabeo. Ardentes clypeos, quis. *Epig.*, p. 13.
Gualfreducci. Scuta quis affixit. *Var.*, p. 284; *Sel. Epig.*, p. 15.
Cunich. Unde, malum, spolia. *Anth.*, p. 175.
Pompei. Chi quest' aste incruente. *Op.* 2. 181.
Felici. Chi qui l'intatta lancia. *Epig.*[1], p. 12.

9.324. Venatorius. Hic quid agis Gnidiae. Obsop., p. 9; Wech., p. 7.
Sabeo. Rustica arundo audes. *Epig.*, p. 62.
Sabeo. Quid tibi cum Paphia. *Epig.*, p. 86.
Sabeo. Ad Venerem irrumpis. *Epig.*, p. 86.
Sabeo. Deseris incultas rupes. *Epig.*, p. 87.
Cunich. Fistula, qui Veneris. *Anth.*, p. 97.
Felici. Che dalle rozze labbia. *Epig.*[1], p. 66.
9.327. Conti. Munera Ephydriades. *Myth.* 5. 12.
Sabeo. Naiades haec vobis. *Epig.*, p. 66.
Sabeo. Sacrat Ephytriades. *Epig.*, p. 25.
Sabeo. Naiades, Hermocreon. *Epig.*, p. 69.
Gualfreducci. Numina Ephydriadum. *Var.*, p. 285; *Sel. Epig.*, p. 13.
Cunich. Nymphae, Naiades Nymphae. *Anth.*, p. 94.
Vargas. Addio, Ninfe del fonte. *Sag.*, p. 32.
9.331. Anon. Infantem Nymphae Bacchum. *PLM* (Baehr.) 5. 406.
Erasmus. Bacchus ut e flammis. Soter[2], p. 106; Corn., p. 101.
Alciati. Cum Semeles de ventre. *Emb.* 25.
Scaphenatus. Excipiunt Bacchum simulac. *Eleg.*, Diiii.
Obsopoeus. Ignivomo Bacchus saliens. Obsop., p. 136; Wech., p. 121. (*Cf. De Art. Bib.* 2, *ad. fin.*)
Calcagnini. Ardentis Semeles audens. Pigna, p. 204; *C.P.It.* 3. 75.
Valeriano. Ardentem ex utero Semeles. *Poem.*, p. 113; *C.P.It.* 10. 156.
Conti. E cinere ut Bacchum. *Myth.*, 5. 13.
Rapitius. Fertur ab Aoniis Nymphis. *Facil.*, f.6[vo].
Fracastoro gives the first tr. noted above. *Op. Om.* (1555) p. 234.
Sabeo. Dum salit igne infans. *Epig.*, p. 61.
Mignault. Prosiliit rapido cum Bacchus. Alciati, *Emb.* 25.
Guicciardini. Bacco fanciullo uscendo. *Det.*, f.51[ro].
Guazzo. Lavar le Ninfe Baccho. *Ghirl.*, p. 442.
Tomasini. Iunctum Nymphi est Bacchus [prose]. Grave., *Thes.* 12. 856.
Cunich. Sortentem cinere ex atro. *Anth.*, p. 81.
Passeroni. Di cenere e fuligine. *Rime* 3. 202.
9.332. Sabeo. Pergamus Paphiae ad fanum. *Epig.*, p. 652.
9.333. Sabeo. Ponti humilem ad terram. *Epig.*, p. 106.
9.335. Sabeo. Ligna, viator, inest. *Epig.* p. 205.
9.337. [Not in *Plan.*] Cf. *A.P.* 9. 824; and 10.11.
Propertius. Et leporem, quicumque. *Eleg.* 3. 13. 43–6
9.338. [Not in *Plan.*] Theocritus, *Inscr.* 3.
Salvini. Tu dormi al suol di foglie. *Teoc.*, p. 184.
Regolotti. Dafni, tu che le membra. *Teoc.*, p. 258.
Della Torre. In un letto di foglie. *Odi*, p. 365.
Vicini. Tu dormi, e te sparso. *Gl'Id.*, p. 185.

Pagnini. Dafni, tu dormi, e su. *Poet. Gr.*, p. 870.

9.339. Erasmus. Scorpius e terra. Soter[2], p. 45; Corn., p. 44.
Alciati. Raptabat volucres captum. Corn., p. 44; *Emb.* 173.
Rapitius. Scorpius e terra. *Facil.*, f. 13[vo].
Sabeo. E liquido volitans. *Epig.*, p. 403.
Mignault. Quondam conspicuo se. Alciati, *Emb.* 172.
Toscano (M.). Dum niger involitat. *Anth.*, p. 65.
Felici. Corbo famelico. *Epig.*[2], p. ix.

9.340. [Not in *Plan.*] Cf. 266.

9.341. Obsopoeus. Vera mihi Nymphae. Obsop., p. 161; Wech.,
p. 142.
Sabeo. Dicite quaerenti Nymphae. *Epig.*, p. 121.
Orsini quotes this epig. on Virgil, *Ecl.* 5. 13.
Cunich. Dicite mi, Nymphae, Daphnisne. *Anth.*, p. 173.

9.342. Cf. Calcagnini. Malim elegos, malim. Pigna, p. 200.
Minturno. A Musis procul est. *De Poet.*, p. 412.
Cottunius quotes Minturno's tr. *Confic.*, p. 56.
Crasso. Dico versuum [L-prose]. *Ist.*, p. 405.

9.343. Cf. *A.P.* 9. 76 and 396.

9.344. Cunich. Lineolis olim fallebam, *Anth.*, p. 176.
Passeroni. Finchè le stelle. *Rime* 3. 145.

9.345. Cornarius. Non Athamas furiis. Corn., p. 138.
Cornarius. Natum Athamas perimit. Corn., p. 139.
Conti. Non furor in miserum. *Myth.* 6. 7.

9.346. Cf. *A.P.* 16. 141.
Marullus. Quid vaga tot terras. *Epig.* 3., p. 42; Soter[2], p. 145;
Corn., p. 140.
Politian. Medeae statua est. Del Lungo, p. 546.
Pio. Terram omnem cum [prose]. *Val. Flac. Comm.*, f. xiiii.
Accolti (Bern.) Veder perir tuo parto. *Verg.*, f. 49[ro].
Beroaldo (younger). Quid me immerentem [v. 10]. *Carm.*,
N ii.
Alciati. Colchidis in gremio. *Emb.* 54.
Molza. Sub truce quid nidum. *Poes.* 3. 205.
Sabeo. Quae terram atque salum. *Epig.*, p. 611.
Sabeo. Quae terram totam et. *Epig.*, p. 609.
Capece. Orbe alio advolitans. *Op. Poet.*, p. 275.
Capece quotes the Gr. and tr. by Marullus, Politian, Nico-
las Bourbon, and Alciati.
Mignault. Tot saltus, undasque. Alciati, *Emb.* 54.
Strozzi (G.B.). Non perdonò quest'empia. *Mad.*, p. 40.
Moro. Garrula Rondinella. *Giar.* 1. 3. 8 (1. 125).
Moro. Progne loquace, fia. *Giar.* 1. 3. 9 (1. 125).
Moro. Barbara Progne, non. *Giar.* 1. 2. 54 (1. 100).
Stigliani. Sai quale statua è. *Rime*, p. 326.
Fiamma. Fuggi il marmo spietato. *Gareg.* 3. 40vo.
Nardi. Rondinella loquace. *Gareg.* 3. 40ro.
Simonetti. Semplice rondinella. *Gareg.* 3. 40ro.

Petracci. Incauta rondinella. *Gareg.* 3. 41.ᵗᵒ
Belli. Di Medea cruda è quella. *Gareg.* 3. 40ᵛᵒ.
Belli. Uccise il figlio anch' ella. *Gareg.* 3. 40ᵛᵒ.
Belli. Progne il suo figlio. *Gareg.* 3. 41ᵗᵒ.
Belli. Qual empia, qual rubella. *Gareg.* 3. 41ᵗᵒ.
Cottunius. Per mare, per terras. *Confic.*, p. 77.
Cunich. Medea haec, nidum cui. *Anth.*, p. 171.
Felici. Cittadina rondinella. *Epig.*[1], p. 20.
Passeroni. Medea barbara è costui. *Rime* 3. 248.
Roncalli. In questo quadro infido. *Epig.* (1792), p. 79; (1801), p. 61.
Vargas. Rondinella. *Sag.*, p. 75.
Pagnini. Rondinella, che scorso. *Epig.*, p. 118.
Pagnini. Questa è Medea. Che fai. *Epig.*, p. 38.

9.347. Cf. 299.
Velius. Non solum humectas. Soter[2], p. 77; Corn., p. 68.
Sabeo. Qui soliti sulcos. *Epig.*, p. 724.
Sabeo. Novimus haud solum. *Epig.*, p. 728.
Sabeo. De terra ad naves. *Epig.*, p. 728.
Cunich. Non terram sulcare. *Anth.*, p. 170.

9.351. Cf. 114.
Sabeo. Praecipiti in tecto. *Epig.*, p. 834.
Sabeo. Tecta super serpens. *Epig.*, p. 358.
Sabeo. Praecipiti impluvio. *Epig.*, p. 313.
Sabeo. Nuper tecta errans. *Epig.*, p. 178.

9.354. Cf. *A.P.* 7. 233–4.
Venatorius. Omnia quem perdens. Obsop., p. 15; Wech., p. 13.
Venatorius. Quem non perdiderat. Obsop., p. 15; Wech., p. 13.
Sabeo. Quem non absumpsit. *Epig.*, p. 552.
Gualfreducci. Quem veritus Mavors. *Var.*, p. 286.

9.356. Sabeo. Ex alio reclusa damus. *Epig.*, p. 409.

9.357. [This is the initial epigram of *Plan.*]
Ausonius. Quattuor antiquos celebravit. *Opus.* 7. 20.
The Gr. is quoted in a ms. of Plato (*Paris*, 1807).
Merula. Quattuor exercet certamina. *Comm. in Juv.*, *Sat.* 8
Politian. Ζηνὸς 'Ολύμπια νικῶντες. Del Lungo, p. 209; Soter[2], p. 1.
Costanzi (G.). Quattuor Hellas habet. *Epig.*, Oiiii.
Volaterranus. Graecia concelebrat duo. *Com. Urb.*, p. 690; Soter[2], p. 1; Corn., p. 1.
Pio. Quatuor insignis certamina. *Lamp.* 1. 384; Soter[2], p. 1; Corn., p. 1.
Alciati. Sacra per Argivas. Soter[2], p. 1; Corn., p. 1; *Op.* 3. 572.
Venatorius. Bis geminos celebrat. Obsop., p. 2; Wech., p. 2.
Segni. Quattuor illustris certamina. *C.Q.H.P.*, p. 112; *C.P.It.* 9. 26.

Conti. Quattuor in Graecis. *Myth.* 5. 4.
Sabeo. Bis duo apud Danaos. *Epig.*, p. 11.
Sabeo. Graecia sacravit ludos. *Epig.*, p. 11.
Sabeo. Insunt Argivas certamina. *Epig.*, p. 139.
Manuzio (P.). Quatuor sunt certamina [prose]. Above,
    p. 232.
Minturno. Quattro famose feste. *Rime*, p. 182.
Mazzoni gives Gr. and Volaterranus' tr. *Difesa*, p. 440.
Gualfreducci. Bis duo sunt Graecis. *Var.*, p. 280; *Sel. Epig.*,
    p. 4.
Averani. Quattuor instituit. *Op.* 1. 3.
Salvini. Quattro son ludi. Carcani, *Rac.* 2. v.
Carcani (P.). Quattro giochi ha la Grecia. *Ant. Ercol.* 7. 279;
    Rac. 1. 5.

9.358. Appears in MSS. of Plato (*Paris.* 1808; *Vind. theol.* 203).
    Quoted by Elias on *Categor. Arist.* (ed. Busse, p. 133).
    Lascaris (J.) alludes to this epig. Above. p. 116, n. 1.
    Sabeo. Si Plato non me. *Epig.*, p. 410.

9.359. Cf. *A.P.* 5. 302; 9. 360, 446. With line 10 cf. Theognis 425–
    8; Sophocles, *O.C.* 1225; Alexis, *frg.* 141, 14 (Kock); Aris-
    totle, *frg.* 40 (Rose), i.e. Plutarch, *Cons. ad Apoll.* 27;
    Contest of Hom. and Hes. 315; Cicero, *Tusc.* 1. 114. The
    epig. is quoted in numerous MSS.; see Stadtmüller *ad loc.*
    It is given by Stobaeus, *Flor.* 98, 57 (Meineke).
    Ausonius. Quod vitae sectabor iter. *Opus.* 7. 2; Soter[2],
        p. 25; Corn., p. 24.
    Erasmus. Quod nam iter humanae. Soter[2], p. 24; Corn., p. 23.
    Luscinius. Quem teneas vitae callem. Soter[2], p. 24; Corn.,
        p. 22.
    Velius. Nam quod iter vitae. Soter[2], p. 24; Corn., p. 22.
    Gaurico. Quis queat humanae. *Epig.* [5]; *C.P. It.* 5. 277.
    Alamanni. Qual vita è da cercar? *Versi* 2. 140.
    Sabeo. Quem vitae incedes callem? *Epig.*, p. 704.
    Braccieschi. Italian version. Cf. above, p. 254.
    Battista. Delusa umanità. La vita. *Mel.* 2. 79.
    Cunich. Quod mihi iam vitae. *Anth.*, p. 87.
    Felici. E quel forma di vivere. *Epig.*[1], p. 27.
    Passeroni. E perchè tanto ho. *Rime* 3. 152.

9.360. Cf. 359 and 446.
    Erasmus. Quamlibet immo viam. Soter[2], p. 29; Corn., p. 26.
    Luscinius. Quam libeat vitae callem. Soter[2], p. 28; Corn.,
        p. 25.
    Velius. Omne iter insistas vitae. Soter[2], p. 28; Corn., p. 26.
    Alamanni. Ogni sorte di vita. *Versi* 2. 141.
    Sabeo. Vitae omnis callem. *Epig.*, p. 704.
    Braccieschi. Italian version. Cf. above, p. 254.
    Cunich. Quod mihi non vitae. *Anth.*, p. 87.
    Felici. Qual mai di vita genere. *Epig.*[1], p. 29.

Passeroni. E perchè da bramar. *Rime* 3. 154.

9.362. Sabeo. Unda Alphaee Iovis. [1–11]. *Epig.*, p. 49.

9.363. Cf. Horace, *Carm.* 1. 4; and an anon. Greek epig. in Didot
Anthol. vol. 3, 3. 189 (p. 322).

Obsopoeus. Nubila ventosae tandem. Obsop., p. 200; Wech.,
p. 180.

Cf. Sannazaro. Già per li boschi. *Arcad.*, ed. Scherillo, p. 11.

Sabeo. Quum glacialis hyems. *Epig.*, p. 784.

Zenobetti. Ventosa hyeme [prose]. *Mel. Gad.*, p. 2.

9.365. Politian. Χάλκειον δονάκων ὁρόω. Del Lungo, p. 215.

Lascaris (J.). Λαινέους δόνακας. *Epig.*, f. 10ʳᵒ.

Sabeo. Mutata est calamis. *Epig.*, p. 782.

9.366. Quoted in *Cod. Paris.* 1808; cf. Didot Anthol., vol. 3, 4. 48
(p. 403).

Ausonius? Septem patriam sapientum. *Opus.* 22. 8.

Cf. Hyginus. Optimum est, Cleobulus. *Fab.* 221.

Apostolios quotes several lines (see L. and Schn. Index, under
Anthol. Pal.).

Cf. Guarino da Verona. Nomina septenum *Wien. Stud.* 19.
128.

Hermonymus (G.). Verba loquor septem. Soter², p. 136;
Corn., p. 135.

Hermann a Nov. Aq. Nomina, dicta, urbes. Soter, *ibid.;*
Corn., *ibid.*

Alciati. Haec habeas, septem. *Emb.* 187.

Sabeo. Dicta cano septem. *Epig.*, p. 187.

Sanchez. Verba canam septem. *Op.* 3. 336.

9.367. Toscano (M.). Divitias Theron proles. *Anth.*, p. 123.

Cunich. Rem patriam Theron. *Anth.*, p. 52.

9.368. Erasmus. Bacche quis? Verum. Soter², p. 107; Corn., p. 102.

Sabeo. Tu quis et unde venis. *Epig.*, p. 751.

Redi refers to this epig., *Op.* 1. 97.

9.369. Costanzi (A.). Perpulchrum est epigramma. *Epig.*, Biiiʳᵒ.

Costanzi (G.). Scribere me brevibus. *Epig.*, Niiiʳᵒ.

Soter. Omne epigramma venustum. Soter², p. 99; Corn.,
p. 89.

Cf. Calcagnini. Malim elegos, malim. Pigna, p. 200.

Cordato. Versibus omne bonum. *Prael.*, p. 111.

Minturno cites this epig., *De Poet.*, p. 413.

Spinula. Distichon est epigramma. *Epig.*, p. 49.

Gualfreducci. Distichon est praeclarum. *Var.*, p. 293.

Cottunius quotes Soter's version. *Confic.*, p. 56.

Ricolvi. Ut plausum referant. *Op.*, p. 57.

Cunich. Versiculos epigramma. *Anth.*, p. 175.

Vargas. Sono due versi belli. *Sag.*, p. 96.

9.370. Sabeo. Fallere lina, canes, nec. *Epig.*, p. 723.

9.371. Cf. 17–8.

Ausonius. [Cf. under *A.P.* 9. 18.] Soter², p. 78; Corn., p. 69.

Sabeo. Veloci pedibus veluti. *Epig.*, p. 735.
Mazzoni quotes this epig. with Ausonius' tr., *Difesa*, p. 27.

9.372. Sabeo. Sub pedibus tenuem. *Epig.*, p. 282 (284).
Cunich. Haesit araneoli rara. *Anth.*, p. 74.
Passeroni. Incappato in una rete. *Rime* 3. 162.

9.373. Sabeo. Me pastor deserta. *Epig.*, p. 295 (283).
'L-prose.' Quid me solitudine. 'Επ. καὶ 'Ελ. No. 26.

9.374. Cf. Navagero. Et gelidus fons est. *C.𝒬.P.*, p. 25.
Sabeo. Illimen emittit tibi. *Epig.*, p. 182.
Cf. Tolomei. Ecco 'l chiaro rio. Carducci, *Poes. Barb.*. p. 48.
Tansillo. E freddo è il fonte [Navagero]. *Poes. Lir.*, ed. Fioren-
tino, p. 27.
Riccoboni. Semper fluentem [prose]. *Piazz. Univ.* sub. fin.
Cf. Baldi. O passeggier che polveroso. *Epig.* 404.

9.375. Valeriano. Quae feritas? quisquis. *Poem.*, p. 115; *C.P.It.* 10.
165.
Mignault. Quis temere hanc uvam. Alciati, *Emb.* 25.
Gualfreducci. Quis temere incoctum. *Var.*, p. 283; *Sel. Epig.*,
p. 10.
Averani. Quis carpsit nondum. *Op.* 1. 37.
Cunich. Quis temere hunc pulcra. *Anth.*, p. 166.

9.376. Cf. *A.P.* 9. 30, 31, 33, 105, 131.
More (Sir T.). Pinus ego ventis. Soter[2], p. 105; Corn., p. 99.
Sleidan. Ut mare perlustrem. Soter[2], p. 105; Corn., p. 99.
Obsopoeus. Vincibilem ventis faber. Wech., p. 115.
Landi quotes the tr. of More and Sleidan. *Let.*, f. 22[ro].
Mazzoni quotes the Gr. and More's tr. *Difesa*, p. 424.
Battista. Con ferro pertinace. *Mel.* 2. 43.
Cunich. Stulte faber, quid me. *Anth.*, p. 184.
Passeroni. A che tanta fatica. *Rime* 3. 71.

9.378. Velius. Pone ruinosas homicida. Soter[2], p. 45; Corn., p. 45.
Luscinius. Dum caperet somnos murum. Soter[2], p. 46; Corn.,
p. 45.
Sabeo. In somnis homicidae. *Epig.*, p. 29.
Mazzoni quotes the Gr. with Luscinius' tr. *Difesa* (1688) 2. 198.
Referred to by Averani, *Op.* 1. 448.
Bongiovanni and Zanetti. Appiè di un vecchio. *Epig.*, p. 54.
Felici. Sotto vetusto portico. *Epig.*[1], p. 103.

9.379. Cf. *A.P.* 11. 237.
More (Sir T.). Ausus erit mordere. Soter[2], p. 121; Corn.,
p. 113.
Sleidan. Increbuit vulgo, vel murem. Soter[2], p. 121; Corn.,
p. 113.
Alciati. Vel murem mordere malos. Corn., p. 114.
Luscinius. Mordeat exiguus mihi. Corn., p. 114.
Sabeo. Morderetque virum mus. *Epig.*, p. 731.
Spinula. Vel murem, quod ait. *Epig.*, p. 50.
Riccoboni. [Prose trans.] Garzoni, *Piaz.* sub. fin.

9.380. Velius. Si corydus cantu queat. Soter², p. 124; Corn., p. 120.
Sleidan. Si corydus cygni vocem. Soter², p. 125; Corn., p. 120.
Sabeo. Si parilis cycno decantat. *Epig.*, p. 423.
9.382. Sabeo. Dilecti heroes Danai. *Epig.*, p. 383.
Sabeo. Me miseram, quo me. *Epig.*, p. 384.
9.383. Cf. 384 and 580.
Pio quotes this epig. without trans. *Lamp.* 1. 473.
Giraldi (L. G.). Primus Thoth docuit. *Op.* 2. 575.
Sabeo. Incidit primum September. *Epig.*, p. 782.
9.384. Cf. 383 and 580.
Sabeo. Ex me stellatis. *Epig.*, p. 783.
9.386. Sabeo. Viderat in Nilo nudam. *Epig.*, p. 140.
Bongiovanni and Zanetti. Te Venere mirò. *Epig.*, p. 31.
Vargas. Dianzi veggendo Venere. *Sag.*, p. 48.
9.387. Germanicus. Martia progenies, Hector. *PLM* (Baehr.) 4. 102.
The epig is quoted in *Schol. Venet.* on Iliad. (cf. Stadtm.), and
in *scholia* on Tzetzes, *Chil.* (Cramer, *Anec. Ox.* 2. 254).
More (Sir T.). Gradivi genus Hector. Soter², p. 121; Corn.,
p. 113.
Alciati quotes More's tr. *Op.* 4.429.
Molza. Nostra tuas si forte. *Poes.* 3. 205.
Obsopoeus. Martia stirps Hector. Obsop., p. 167; Wech.,
p. 145.
Sabeo. Martia progenies Hector. *Epig.*, p. 177.
Sabeo. Si sub humo haec. *Epig.*, p. 345.
Cunich. Armipotens Hector, terra. *Anth.*, p. 33.
Passeroni. Ettore illustre formidabil. *Rime* 3. 180.
Felici. Ettore, se nell' erebo. *Epig.*², p. v.
9.390. Crasso. Pueris e prioribus. [L-prose]. *Ist.*, p. 339.
9.391. Politian. Incaluere animis dura. Del Lungo, p. 545; Soter²,
p. 2; Corn., p. 2.
Beroaldo (younger). Ad durum exercere. *Carm.*, N iiii.
Alciati. Conservere manus validae. Corn., p. 2; *Op.* 4. 623.
Sabeo. Neptuni atque Iovis. *Epig.*, p. 168.
Sabeo. Progenies, Neptune, tua. *Epig.*, p. 168.
Sabeo. Aequoris et coeli. *Epig.*, p. 168.
Angelio. Anne hoc Alcides. *Poem.* (1585), p. 355.
Gualfreducci. Pugnae avidi valida. *Var.*, p. 280; *Sel. Epig.*,
p. 5.
Averani quotes Gr. and Politian's tr. *Op.* 1.17.
Salvini. S'esercitar di forte. Carcani, *Rac.* 2. vi.
Cunich. Exarsere truces dura. *Anth.*, p. 31.
Medici (A. de'). Adsueti in lucta validam. *Scelt.*, p. xlvii.
Medici (A. de'). Usi a sudar nella palestra. *Scelt.*, p. xlvii.
Passeroni. Venner, come leoni. *Rime* 3. 177.
Pagnini. Mossero in giostra. *Epig.*, p. 77.
9.394. Choricius. Χρυσέ, κακῶν ἀρχηγέ. [prose]. *Frg.* 2 (Foerster,
p. 544).

Costanzi (G.). Palponum pater es. *Epig.*, Oiiii.

Soter. Palpantum pater aes. Soter[2], p. 111.

Alciati. Aurum blanditiae pater. Corn., p. 105.

Cornarius. Assentatorum pater aurum. Corn., p. 105.

Valeriano. Gnathonum pater es, aurum. *Poem.*, p. 113; *C.P. It.* 10. 156.

Cf. Valeriano. Si procul ergo dolor. *Poem.*, p. 113; *C.P.It.* 10. 156.

Alamanni. L'oro è padre d'error. *Versi* 2. 137.

Bagnaus. Numme, pater colacum. *C.P.It.* 2. 7.

Sabeo. Scurrae aurum genitor. *Epig.*, p. 23.

Sabeo. Tu scurris genitor. *Epig.*, p. 23.

Pompei. O de le cure e dei dolor. *Op.* 2. 177.

Pagnini. L'oro è di mali. *Epig.*, p. 164.

9.395. Sabeo. Dulce magis patria. *Epig.*, p. 179.

9.396. Cf. 76 and 343.

Sabeo. Incidit ante diem. *Epig.*, p. 776.

9.397. Cf. *A.P.* 7. 230, 433, 531; 9. 61, and 447.

Groto. Odi tal patria, e di tal. *Rime* (1587), p. 153.

Gualfreducci. Fugerat arma Lacon. *Var.*, p. 286.

9.398. Cf. *A.P.* 9. 34, 36, and 106.

More (Sir T.). Iam ratis aequoreas. Soter[2], p. 105; Corn., p. 100.

Sabeo. Quae maris undisoni. *Epig.*, p. 744.

Pagnini. Nave campata dal furor. *Epig.*, p. 155.

9.401. Sabeo. Foedera amicitiae mater. *Epig.*, p. 402.

Fioretti. Natura invenit [L-prose]. *Prog.* 5. 215.

Pompei. La Natura, che suol. *Op.* 2. 176.

9.402. Quoted by Appain, *Bell. Civ.* 2. 86.

Quoted by Xiphilinus in *Exc. Dion. Cass.* 69. 11. 1.

Giraldi (L. G.). Ossa viri magni, tenui. *Op.* 2. 203.

Sabeo. Quam male tectus. *Epig.*, p. 394.

9.404. Sabeo. Sponte laborati flaventia. *Epig.*, p. 721.

9.405. Conti. Adrastea utinam. [lines 1–2]. *Myth.* 9. 19.

Cunich. Adrastea, puer, te. *Anth.*, p. 30.

Passeroni. Così l'invida Nemesi. *Rime* 3. 177.

Felici. Te salvi Nemesi. *Epig.*[2], p. xv.

9.406. Sabeo. Me prope adhuc ranam. *Epig.*, p. 752.

9.407. Sabeo. Quum maris ad latum. *Epig.*, p. 709.

Sabeo. Non pudet, o monstrum. *Epig.*, p. 709.

9.408. Cf. 100.

Averani. [Space is left in *Op.* 1. 199 for a missing tr.]

Cunich. O utinam instabili ventis. *Anth.*, p. 134.

Bettinelli. Alla prole Latonia. *Op.* 22. 102.

9.410. Alciati. Muscipulam haud metuens. Corn., p. 46.

Valeriano. Improbus omnivorusque sorex. *Poem.*, p. 112; *C.P. It.* 10. 155.

Sabeo. Mus avidus ganeae. *Epig.*, p. 720.

Sabeo. Cuncta vorans serpensque. *Epig.*, p. 742.
Felici. Un topo che coll' avido. *Epig.*[1], p. 96.
9.412. Sabeo. Iam florens cicer est. *Epig.*, p. 214.
9.413. Sabeo. Vitis parva tenet. *Epig.*, p. 794.
Cunich. Parva, ferax pulcris. *Anth.*, p. 20.
Passeroni. Isola angusta io son. *Rime* 3. 48.
9.415. Cf. 416.
9.416. Cf. 415.
9.417. Sabeo. Multa laborantem. *Epig.*, p. 278 (280).
Sabeo. Venantem Lampona Mydae. *Epig.*, p. 736.
Sabeo. Emoriens Lampon peperit. *Epig.*, p. 736.
9.420. Alciati. Quid fles? an validum. Corn., p. 60.
Giraldi Cintio. Quid tentas undis. *Poem.*, p. 174.
Capilupi (Ipp.). Cur toties Lalagen. *Carm.*, p. 125.
Sabeo. Ne fletu mulcere putes. *Epig.*, p. 117.
Sabeo. Flectere ne credas. *Epig.*, p. 64.
Toscano (M.). Nemo unquam lacrimis. *Anth.*, p. 144.
Pagnini. Vincere invan tu speri. *Epig.*, p. 95.
9.422. Sabeo. Supplico per natos. *Epig.*, p. 709.
Sabeo. Oravit charum moritura. *Epig.*, p. 814.
9.424. Obsopoeus. Aeriae nubes, ubi. Obsop., p. 175; Wech., p. 150.
9.429. [Not in *Plan.*] Cf. *A.P.* 5. 138.
9.431. Cf. Aesop, *Fab.* 67 (Halm).
Cornarius. Aurum amo, sed Martis. Corn., p. 107.
Sabeo. Aurum amo, sed metuens. [S. has 10 versions of this one-line epig; all are on the same page of his book.] *Epig.*, p. 422.
9.432. [Not in *Plan.*] Theocritus, *Inscr.* 6.
Salvini. Ah Tirsi poverel! *Teoc.*, p. 186.
Regolotti. Ahi Tirsi meschinello. *Teoc.*, p. 262.
Cunich. Thyrsi, abiit (tristes. *Anth.*, p. 146.
Della Torre. Struggi a stille a stille. *Odi*, p. 367.
Vicini. Tirsi infelice, e che. *Gl'Id.*, p. 186.
Pagnini. Misero Tirsi, e che. *Poet. Gr.*, p. 870.
9.433. [Not in *Plan.*] Theocritus, *Inscr.* 5.
Salvini. Vuoi per le Ninfe. *Teoc.*, p. 185.
Regolotti. Se t'aitan le Ninfe. *Teoc.*, p. 261.
Della Torre. Se ti aiutin le Ninfe. *Odi*, p. 367.
Vicini. Per le Ninfe mi dì. *Gl'Id.*, p. 186.
Pagnini. Vuoi tu dolce sonarmi. *Poet. Gr.*, p. 870.
9.434. [Not in *Plan.*] In several MSS. of Theocritus (cf. *Schol.* ed. Wendel, p. 6); in the Aldine and Juntine edd.
Giraldi (L. G.). Non ego Chius qui. *Op.* 2. 110.
Anon. Haec ego composui. Theoc. ed. Commelin. (*ap.* Della Torre, p. 376).
Salvini. Altro di Scio è Teoc. *Teoc.*, p. 189.
Regolotti. Evvi un altro Teocrito. *Teoc.*, p. 270.
Della Torre. Tutt' altro è quel. *Odi*, p. 376.

Vicini. Un Teocrito v'ha. *Gl'Id.*, p. 189.
Pagnini. Altro v'ebbe Teocrito. *Poet. Gr.*, p. 872.

9.435. Theocritus, *Inscr.* 14.
Salvini. Conoscerò, se fai qualche. *Teoc.*, p. 187.

9.436. [Not in *Plan.*] Theocritus, *Inscr.* 24.

9.437. Theocritus, *Inscr.* 4.
Salvini. Caprar, la via voltando. *Teoc.*, p. 185.
Regolotto. Dal camin tuo piegando. *Teoc.*, p. 259.
Della Torre. Delle querce. *Odi*, p. 366.
Vicini. Caprar, dal tuo camin. *Gl'Id.*, p. 185.
Pagnini. Capraio, da quel vicolo. *Poet. Gr.*, p. 870.

9.438. Sabeo. Quae terram evertunt. *Epig.*, p. 295 (283).
Sabeo. Oci inimica. *Epig.*, p. 282 (284).
Felici. Infra spinetti e frutici. *Epig.*[1], p. 106.

9.439. Sabeo. Crinibus ornatum fueram. *Epig.*, p. 359.

9.440. [See above, p. 3, note 3.]

9.441. Cornarius. In triviis vidi Vulcanum. Corn., p. 77.
Alciati. Herculis in trivo. *Op.* 4.518.
Sabeo., Qui prius astabat. *Epig.*, p. 132.
Cunich. Alcidem in trivio nuper. *Anth.*, p. 83.
Felici. Teste vidi in un trivio. *Epig.*[1], p. 73.

9.442. More (Sir T.). Pisces dum captat. Soter[2], p. 127; Corn., p. 124.
More (Sir T.). Mars erat iste meus. Soter[2], p. 127; Corn., p. 124.
Alamanni. Una donna richissima. *Versi* 2. 142.
Sabeo. Dum piscaretur iuvenis. *Epig.*, p. 854.
Sabeo. Virgo opulenta virum. *Epig.*, p. 5.
Sabeo. Dum piscatorem tendentem. *Epig.*, p. 106.
Groto. Ama vil piscator ricca. *Rime* (1587), p. 157.

9.443. Sabeo. Tu ne unquam Veneri. *Epig.*, p. 124.
Toscano (M.). Claude animum Veneri. *Anth.*, p. 153.

9.444. Arnold. Vesalien. Virginitas pulchris. Soter[2], p. 37; Corn., p. 34.
Soter. Optima virginitas homini. Soter[2], p. 37; Corn., p. 34.
Alciati. Ad Venerem properate. Corn., p. 35.
Sabeo. Virginitatis opes. *Epig.*, p. 710.
Sabeo. Virginitas laudanda. *Epig.*, p. 719.
Bongiovanni and Zanetti. Bello e ricco giojello. *Epig.*, p. 46.

9.446. Cf. 359–60.
Luscinius. Dulcia cuncta homini. Soter[2], p. 35; Corn., p. 31.

9.447. Cf. *A.P.* 7. 230, 433, 531; 9. 61, and 397.
Anselmo. Spartana post sodalium. *Epig.*, M.
Sabeo. Signe relinquentem. *Epig.*, p. 701.
Gualfreducci. Civibus extinctis. *Var.*, p. 286.
Cunich. Torva tuens gnatum. *Anth.*, p. 33.
Passeroni. Il figlio, che fuggia. *Rime* 3. 182.

9.448. Homeric Epigrams, 17; occurs in an inscr. (Kaibel 1105);

quoted by Proclus, *Chrestom.*, in Gaisford's *Hephaest.* (1855)
I. 446; in *Contest of Hom. and Hes.* 326; by Tzetzes, *Exeg.
Iliad.* 37. 18 (Hermann); in the *Vitae* of Homer (West., pp.
25, 28, 30).
Boccaccio. Homines de Arcadia [prose]. Above, p. 83.
Codro Urceo quotes the epig. without tr. *Op.*, p. 177.
Soter and Winshemius. Num quid Arcadii. Soter², p. 114.
Sabeo. Vos piscatores. *Epig.*, p. 225.
Giraldi (L. G.). gives Gr. with Lat. paraphrase. *Op.* 2. 448.
Cottunius. Num quicquam Arcadii. *Confic.*, p. 57.
Pagnini. O. Voi che festosi. *Epig.*, p. 141.

9.449. Sabeo. Quis domat igne ignem? *Epig.*, p. 119.
Battista. Son fatto amante io. *Mel.* 2. 16.

9.450. Quoted in *Vita Euripidea* (West., pp. 137, 140).

9.451. Cf. 452.
Sabeo. Vir tuus occultum. *Epig.*, p. 195.

9.452. Cf. 451.
Sabeo. Hanc soror, o Progne. *Epig.*, p. 350.

9.453. Obsopoeus. Ipse tibi supplex. Obsop., p. 54; Wech., p. 50.
Sabeo. Extollit vultus ad te. *Epig.*, p. 64.
Sabeo. Iuppiter aetherie. *Epig.*, p. 112.
Sabeo. Bos ipse ante aras. *Epig.*, p. 147.
Averani. Ecce tuam taurus supplex. *Op.* I. 64, 66.
Medici (A. de'). Ecce tuam supplex taurus. *Scelt.*, p. xvii.
Medici (A. de'). Questo presso al morir. *Scelt.*, p. xvii.
Pagnini. Questo presso l'altar. *Epig.*, p. 74.

9.455. Cf. *A.P.* 16. 268 and 293.4.
Cf. Philostratus. Ἀπόλλων αὐτὰ ποήσας. *Heroic.* 16 (Didot,
p. 726).
Synesius refers to the point made in this epig. *De Dione*,
p. 59B.
Cantalicio. Quidquid grandiloquo. *C.P.It.* 3. 133.
Politian. Obstupuit prorsusque. *Nut.* 345; Del Lungo, p. 389.
Anisio. Aureus aurata cithara. *Poem.*, f. 95ʳᵒ.
Cornarius. Ipse quidem cecini. Corn., p. 109.
Obsopoeus. Haec modulabar ego. Obsop., p. 151; Wech.,
p. 133.
Venatorius. Ipse quidem cecini. Obsop., p. 151; Wech., p. 133.
Sabeo. Quaeque ego cantabam. *Epig.*, p. 323.
Sabeo. Ipse ego quum. *Epig.*, p. 223.
Allacci gives Obsopoeus' tr., Gronov., *Thes.*, 10. 1729.
Cf. Marino. Qui tacque Apollo. *Ad.* 20. 515 (p. 448).
Cottunius gives Allacci's version. *Confic.*, p. 51.
Salvini. Omero scrisse: dettò. Wellesley, *Anth.*, p. 454.
D'Elci. Cantava Apollo. *Ibid.*

9.456. Marullus. Cum male formosum. *Hymn.* (1504), B12; Soter²,
p. 73²; Corn., p. 61.
Soter. Si libitum ut sequerer. Soter², p. 73².

Soter. Me sequi si placuit. Soter[2], p. 73[2].
Alciati. Quum male formosum. Corn., p. 61.
Cornarius. Qui insano tauri. Corn., p. 60.
Sabeo. Me mugire doce. *Epig.*, p. 142.
Sabeo. Pasiphae infelix. *Epig.*, p. 308.
Battista. Mira quel toro. *Mel.* 2. 23.
Pagnini. Se m'insegnasti. *Epig.*, p. 92.

9.457. Sabeo. Nunc mea nota tibi. *Epig.*, p. 233.
9.458. Sabeo. Salve, Ithace, post. *Epig.*, p. 215.
9.459. Sabeo. Inter mortales scelerum. *Epig.*, p. 372.
9.461. Sabeo. Fine mei patris. *Epig.*, p. 311.
9.462. Sabeo. Tu mihi saevum. *Epig.*, p. 269.
Sabeo. Aeterni o cineres. *Epig.*, p. 269.
9.468. Sabeo. Sudasti, virtute tuus. *Epig.*, p. 19.
9.469. Bergius. Sudor et assidui. Soter[2], p. 18.
Fioretti. Tibi gratiam [L-prose]. *Prog.* 1. 35.
9.474. Sabeo. Sum miserata tuam. *Epig.*, p. 61.
9.475. Sabeo. Europae atque Asiae. *Epig.*, p. 137.
9.476. Cf. Politian. Μὴ μέμφοισθ' ἐπὶ δυρί. Del Lungo, p. 212.
9.478. Giraldi (L. G.) refers to this epig. *Op.* (1696) 1. 738.
9.481. Sabeo. Perdidit Eusthephius. *Epig.*, p. 412.
9.483. Sanchez. Ex mortiferis Persis. *Op.* 3. 274.
9.484. Sabeo. Utrem ventorum coepit. *Epig.*, p. 458.
Cunich. Utrem ventorum, donum. *Anth.*, p. 164.
Passeroni. Giunto il Campione. *Rime* 3. 65.
9.485. [Not in *Plan.*] Cf. Heliodorus, *Aeth.* 3. 2.
9.488. Sabeo. In schiade occubuit. *Epig.*, p. 406.
Sabeo. Qui potuit mulcere. *Epig.*, p. 406.
Vargas. Terpi, cantor di Schia. *Sag.*, p. 84.
Pagnini. Terpi di Schia ceterator. *Epig.*, p. 126.
9.489. Ausonius. Rufus vocatus rhetor. *Opus.* 19. 61; Soter[2], p. 80;
Corn., p. 73.
Soter. Filia Grammatici peperit. Soter[2], p. 80; Corn., p. 73.
Pio. Filia grammatici peperit. Corn., p. 73.
Valeriano. Prognata grammatico. *Poem.*, p.113; *C.P.It.* 10. 158.
Sabeo. Dilecto coniuncta viro. *Epig.*, p. 770.
Franchini. Tres nati sunt, Gaure. *Epig.*, p. 16.
Bongiovanni and Zanetti. La figlia di un. *Epig.*, p. 14.
Cunich. Grammatico muliebre genus. *Anth.*, p. 164.
Passeroni. Sendo nato a un grammatico. *Rime* 3. 238.
Pagnini. La figlia d'un grammatico. *Epig.*, p. 59.
9.490. Cf. Heliodorus, *Aeth.* 8. 11.
9.491. Cf. Stobaeus 1. 5. 14 (Wach. and Hense. 1. 77).
Sabeo. Luna, Venus, Mars, Sol. *Epig.*, p. 52.
9.492–4. [These are all alike; and are not in *Plan.*]
9.495. Cf. Alamanni. Come fortuna sia. *Versi* 2. 128.
9.496. Quoted by Diogenes Laertius 6. 1 (Antisthenes), and again in
7. 1 (Zeno).

Brugnolo? Stoicidae menti solum. Laert.; Soter[2], p. 17; Corn., p. 14.

Bentinus. Stoicidae spectata. *Laert.*, p. 187; Soter[2], p. 17; Corn., p. 14.

Bentinus. O Stoicae gnari sectae. *Laert.*, p. 226; Soter[2], p. 17; Corn., p. 14.

9.497. Cf. Ovid. Non habet unde suum. *Rem. Am.* 749.

The epig. is referred to by Clement of Alex., *Strom.* 2. 20. 121.

Quoted by Diogenes Laertius 6. 86 (Crates).

Quoted by Suidas, *s.v.* Κράτης 'Ασκώνδου.

Angeriano. Consule quid faciam. 'Ερωτ. Bi.

Alciati. Amorem egena sedat. Corn., p. 62.

Anisio. Pauperies saepe et tempus. *Poem.*, f. 89[ro].

Alamanni. Chi spegner brama. *Versi* 2. 140.

Valeriano. Fames amorem sedat. *Poem.*, p. 115.

Bocchi. Fames amorem sedat. *Sym.*, p. 27.

Sabeo. Lascivum domat ipsa. *Epig.*, p. 65.

Sabeo. Longa dies audaxque. *Epig.*, p. 48.

Giraldi (L. G.) quotes without tr. *Op.* 2. 255.

Ridolfi. La fame e il tempo [prose]. *Aret.*, p. 153.

Guicciardini. Cratete Tebano [prose]. *Det.*, f. 97[ro].

Toscano (M.). Medela amoris est. *Anth.*, p. 141.

Salvini. La fame posa Amore. *Disc.* (1733), p. 219.

Bongiovanni and Zanetti. La fame al mal. *Epig.*, p. 37.

Cunich. Dura fames aliis. *Anth.*, p. 148.

Pagnini. La dura fame in altri. *Epig.*, p. 30.

9.498. Quoted by Agathias, *Hist.* 2. 31.

Sabeo. Esca canum iaceat. *Epig.*, p. 236.

Sabeo. Ne sepeli, intectum. *Epig.*, p. 706.

Pagnini. Restisi pur qual merta. *Epig.*, p. 27.

9.502. Pio. Condito mihi opus. *Lamp.* 1. 565; Soter[2], p. 89; Corn., p. 81.

Alciati. Condito indigeo. *Op.* 4.507.

Mazzoni. Del condito ho bisogno [prose]. *Difesa*, p. 114.

Cottunius quotes this epig. without tr. *Confic.* cap. 11.

9.503. Pio quotes this epig. without tr. *Lamp.* 1. 442.

Erasmus. Divinum quiddam vimque. Soter[2], p. 88; Corn., p. 80.

9.503.* This monostich = Nicander, *Theriac.* 741.

Soter. E tauro nascuntur apes. Soter[2], p. 108; Corn., p. 422.

9.504. Cf. Andrelinus. Namque meas variis. Soter[2], p. 119; Corn., p. 110.

Giraldi (L. G.). Calliope heroi monstravit. *Op.* 1. 253.

Gisberti quotes Giraldi's tr. *Nov. Mus.*, p. 131.

9.505. Sabeo. Terpsicorem haud vidit. *Epig.*, p. 133.

9.506. Ausonius. Lesbia Pieriis Sappho. *Opus.* 19. 51; Soter[2], p. 118; Corn., p. 110.

Marullus. Quod Sappho Aoniis. *Epig.* 1, p. 7.

Cf. Politian. Illam etiam decimo. *Nut.* 637; Del Lungo, p. 414.

More (Sir T.). Musas esse novem. Soter[2], p. 118; Corn., p. 110.

Lily (W.). Quam temere dixere. Soter[2], p. 118; Corn., p. 110.

Hermann a Nov. Aq. Esse novem falso. Soter[2], p. 118.

Venatorius. Esse novem quidam. Obsop., p. 153; Wech., p. 136.

Venatorius. Esse novem Musas. Obsop.; Wech. *ibid.*

Sabeo. Ignari esse novem. *Epig.*, p. 206.

Cunich. Esse novem perhibent. *Anth.*, p. 40.

Passeroni. Nove le Muse fur. *Rime* 3. 186.

Passeroni. Errò colui che disse. *Rime* 3. 135.

Pagnini. Con poco senno alcuni. *Epig.*, p. 55.

9.507. [Not in *Plan.*] Quoted in *Vita Arati* (West., p. 54). Published by Orsini on Virgil, *Ecl.* 1. 70. *Virg.*, p. 14.

9.509. [Not in *Plan.*] Quoted by Herodotus (8. 96), by Strabo (9. 398), and by Eustathius on Dionys. Perieg. 591.

Guarino. Coliades sane mulieres. *Strabo* (1494), f. 76[vo].

Valla. Horrebunt remis mulieres. *Herod.*, f. 224.

9.515. Cf. *A.P.* 5. 95 and 146.

Cf. Ausonius? Tres fuerant Charites. *Opus.* 23. 13.

Costanzi (A.). Tres dicunt Charites. *Epig.*, Biii[ro].

Angeriano. Tres Charites, tribus. Ἐρωτ. Ciii; *C.P.It.* 1. 274.

Anselmo. Gratiae erant tres. *Epig.*, Bii; *C.P.It.* 1. 299.

Alciati. Quattuor hac Charites. Corn., p. 84.

Cornarius. Tres Charites tantum. Corn.,p. 84.

Anisio. Tres Charites sunt. *Poem.*, f. 138[vo].

Valeriano. Sunt Gratiae tres. *Poem.*, p. 114; *C.P.It.* 10. 162.

Valeriano. Tres prisci Charites. *Poem.*, p. 114; *C.P.It.* 10. 162.

Sabeo. Gratiae erant ternae. *Epig.*, p. 122.

Bongiovanni and Zanetti. Tre son le Grazie. *Epig.*, p. 31.

Pompei. Tre son le Grazie. *Op.* 2. 221.

Bettinelli. Le Grazie sono tre. *Op.* 13. 90.

9.517. Politian refers to this epig. *Epist.* 11. 10.

Sabeo. Orphea ducentem. *Epig.*, p. 386.

Gualfreducci. Vicit apros Orpheus. *Var.*, p. 291.

Baldi. Se voi d'Orfeo. *Epig.* 286.

Vargas. Rapia le fere Orfeo. *Sag.*, p. 65.

9.518. Cf. 526.

Sabeo. Moenia Rex coeli produc. *Epig.*, p. 101.

Sabeo. Claude Deum aeratas. *Epig.*, p. 101.

Sabeo. Posse peti coelum. *Epig.*, p. 139.

Cunich. Macyni effracta stat. [?]. *Anth.*, p. 12.

9.519. Sabeo. Bacche, bibam, vincamque. *Epig.*, p. 479.

9.523. Alciati. Maeoniden alium parias. Corn., p. 11.

Riccio (G. L.). Mandate, O Muse Ruscelli, *Lib. Sest.*, f. 201[ro].

Sabeo. Da mihi Homerum alium. *Epig.*, p. 303.

Sabeo. Calliope pascentis. *Epig.*, p. 139.
Paterno. A cantar di Filippo. *Nuov. Petr.*, p. 345.
Paterno. O mandi 'l giusto cielo. *Nuov. Petr.*, p. 473.
Cottunius. Μοῦσά μοι ἄλλον "Ομηρον. Ἑλλ. Ἐπ., p. 22.
Cunich. Musa, alium caeli vitales. *Anth.*, p. 31.
Felici. Or tu, Calliope fervida. *Epig.*[1], p. 32.
Passeroni. Torni un Omero omai. *Rime* 3. 183.
Pagnini. Musa, a te un altro. *Epig.*, p. 124.

9.524. Lines 1–3, 5, 15 occur in an inscr. (*C.I.G.* 38); 'Eudocia' quotes this epig. *Viol.* p. 123.
Redi quotes from this epig. *Op.* 1. 35.
Ricolvi quotes the epig. without tr. *Op.*, p. 75.

9.525. Giraldi (L. G.) quotes the whole epig., but tr. only line 1: Ingentem Paeana cano. *Op.* 1. 242.

9.526. Cf. 518.
Sabeo. Claude, Deus, magni. *Epig.*, p. 144.
Sabeo. Quid iuvat aeternas. *Epig.*, p. 145.
Bongiovanni and Zanetti. Su chiudi omai. *Epig.*, p. 47.
Cunich. Caeli claude fores. *Anth.*, p. 14.
Pompei. Del grande Olimpo. *Op.* 2. 210.
Felici. D'inespugnabili. *Epig.*[1], p. 7.
Passeroni. Chiudi del ciel. *Rime* 3. 140.
Pagnini. Chiudi d'Olimpo. *Epig.*, p. 62.

9.527. Quoted by Herodotus (5. 56).
Valla. Intoleranda, leo, tolera. *Herod.*, f. 136[vo].
Sabeo. Supplicium nemo poterit. *Epig.*, pp. 708, 794.
Giraldi (L. G.) quotes Valla's version. *Op.* 2. 459.
'L-prose.' Perfer leo intoleranda. Ἐπ. καὶ Ἑλ. No. 3.

9.529. Politian. Unius effugi torum. Del Lungo, p. 547.
Sabeo. Unius effugiens Phoebi. *Epig.*, p. 66.
Sabeo. Plurima nanciscor, unum. *Epig.*, p. 89.
Sabeo. Unum exosa torum. *Epig.*, p. 89.

9.530. More (Sir T.). Non tibi quod faveat. Soter[2], p. 127; Corn., p. 125.
Luscinius. Non fortuna favens. Corn., p. 125.
Sabeo. Haud fortuna volens. *Epig.*, p. 60.
Sabeo. Non merito ipsa tuo. *Epig.*, p. 60.
Bongiovanni and Zanetti. Te volentier non. *Epig.*, p. 44.
Carcani. Nò, la Fortuna te. *Ant. Ercol.* 5. 152.
Cunich. Fors invita istuc te. *Anth.*, p. 46.
Pompei. Ti alzò Fortuna. *Op.* 2.227.
Passeroni. A questa eccelsa. *Rime* 3. 186.
Passeroni. La Fortuna gran cose. *Rime* 3. 187.
Felici. Sollevotti fortuna a suo. *Epig.*[2], p. xxviii.
Pagnini. Contro sua voglia alzato. *Epig.*, p. 142.
Cerretti. Fortuna t'inalzo, poichè. *Poes.* (1813), p. 103.

9.535. Luscinius. Bacchus iners hedera. Corn., p. 133.
Cornarius. Bacchus amat hederas. Corn., p. 133.

9.536. Sabeo. Nabat aqua in pelagus. *Epig.*, p. 40
9.537. Sabeo. Quid rapis obtundens. *Epig.*, p. 421.
9.540. Quoted by Hesychius Mil. (Mueller, *F.H.G.* 4. 166); by Diogenes Laertius 9. 1 (Heraclitus).
Brugnolo? Noli Heraclitum rapido. Laert.; Soter[2], p. 138; Corn., p. 136.
Lascaris (J.) alludes to this epig. Above, p. 116, n. 1.
Bentinus. Noli Heraclitum rapido. *Laert.*, p. 313.
Cornarius. Nec tu, Heraclite, celer. Corn., p. 136.
Rhodiginus. Non esse festinanter [prose]. *Lect.* 15. 20.
Sabeo. Ne celer attenta. *Epig.*, p. 188.
Mazzoni quotes the Gr., *Difesa*, p. 28.
9.541. Sabeo. Arte laborata haec. *Epig.*, p. 740.
Sabeo. Grandia utrunque polum. *Epig.*, p. 741.
Ricolvi. Nos tibi Diogenes. *Op.*, p. 82.
Ricolvi. Noi due coppe lavorate. *Op.*, p. 82.
Cunich. Haec duo Theogenes. *Anth.*, p. 152.
9.543. [Not in *Plan.*] Reiske 728.
Carcani (P.). Il Tessalo drappel. *Ant. Ercol.* 8. 57.
9.545. Sabeo. Callimachi est opus. *Epig.*, p. 193.
Crasso. Callimachi limatur [L-prose]. *Ist.*, p. 97.
9.548. Cf. 302.
Alciati. Matre procul licata. Corn., p. 74; *Emb.* 112.
Sabeo. Errantem lactentemque. *Epig.*, p. 738.
Mignault. Errantem in trivio. Alciati, *Emb.* 111.
9.549. Anisio. Nymphae fontanae quo. *Poem.*, f. 94[ro].
Sabeo. Quae vos solis aquas. *Epig.*, p. 173.
Sabeo. Fontium amoenae undae. *Epig.*, p. 213.
Sabeo. Undae ubi nam tantae? *Epig.*, p. 407.
Cunich. Fons, tua quo fugiens. *Anth.*, p. 139.
Passeroni. O Fonte, le onde tue. *Rime* 3. 60.
Pagnini. V. Fonte, ove mai quel. *Epig.*, p. 30.
9.550. Cunich. Non ego te claram inficior. *Anth.*, p. 49.
9.557. Alciati. Ecce Meneclides Arias. Corn., p. 3.
Cornarius. Ecce Menecliden Arian. Corn., p. 3.
Sabeo. Tarse, tuum authorem. *Epig.*, p. 195.
Gualfreducci. Progenies Arias Meneclis. *Var.*, p. 281; *Sel. Epig.*, p. 5.
Averani. Non stadii cursorem. *Op.* 1. 25.
Salvini. Aria di Menecleo. Carcani, *Rac.* 2. vi.
Carcani. Il figlio di Menecleo. *Ant. Ercol.* 6. 132.
Cunich. Tarse, Arias Menecli. *Anth.*, p. 15.
Passeroni. Aria, figlio di Menaclo. *Rime* 3. 35.
9.561. Pio. Agrestem vitem te nunquid. Soter[2], p. 3; Corn., p. 4.
Molza. Solis inaccessam radiis. *Poes.* 3. 203.
Sabeo. Quae nam te glacies. *Epig.*, p. 708.
Angelio. Quae nam autem infelix. *Poem.*, p. 379.
Gualfreducci. Quis male te cultus. *Var.*, p. 282.

Cunich. Nam quae te agrestem. *Anth.*, p. 181.
9.562. Cf. Martial. Psittacus a vobis. *Epig.* 14. 73.
Sabeo. Psitacus humanas. *Epig.*, p. 831.
Cunich. Psittacus e cavea. *Anth.*, p. 181.
Felici. Dal suo dorato carcere. *Epig.*[1], p. 37.
9.563. Sabeo. Sicubi comperies fructus. *Epig.*, p. 237.
9.564. Sabeo. Quae circum auricomos. *Epig.*, p. 729.
Sabeo. Sedula apis veris. *Epig.*, p. 729.
9.565. Crasso. Venit Theaetetus [L-prose]. *Ist.*, p. 495.
9.566. Cunich. Vox brevis est, cessit. *Anth.*, p. 173.
9.567. Pio. Cum Veneris puero. *Lamp.* 1. 504; Soter[2], p. 75; Corn.,
p. 64.
Scaliger (J. C.). Quae segmentatis pressisset. *Poem.* 1. 151.
9.568. Sabeo. Nile, via erranti. *Epig.*, p. 417.
9.569. Quoted by Diogenes Laertius 8. 2 (Empedocles).
Chalcidius. Namque ego iamdudum. *PLM* (Baehr.) 6. 409.
Bentinus. Nam, memini, fueram. *Laert.*, p. 302; Soter[2], p. 135;
Corn., p. 133.
Sabeo. Iam fueram quandoque. *Epig.*, p. 210.
Giraldi (L. G.). Non ego mortalis. *Op.* 2. 99.
9.571. Cf. Politian. Nec vulgare canit. *Nut.* 618–9; Del Lungo,
p. 412.
Sabeo. Pindarus ex Thebis. *Epig.*, p. 193.
Crasso. Grata vero [line 4, L-prose]. *Ist.*, p. 82.
9.572. Felici. O Vergini Castilie. *Epig.*[1], p. viii.
9.573. Sabeo. Alterius mensae ne. *Epig.*, p. 707.
'L-prose.' Ne tu alienis. Ἐπ. καὶ Ἐλ. No. 12.
9.575. Velius. Sed prius Alcisae. Soter[2], p. 117.
Velius. Cum tria sint passim. Soter[2], p. 118.
Sleidan. Astra prius caelo deerunt. Soter[2], p. 117; Corn.,
p. 110.
Anisio. Luminaque extingui poterunt. *Poem.*, f. 90[vo].
Venatorius. Ipsa suos mundo. Obsop., p. 151; Wech., p. 133.
Venatorius. Destituent prius astra. Obsop., p. 151; Wech.,
p. 133.
Sabeo. Extinguet coelum potius. *Epig.*, p. 197.
Cunich. Ante polum linquent. *Anth.*, p. 40.
Passeroni. Pria dal ciel si vedran. *Rime* 3. 114.
9.576. More (Sir T.). Cur ita me laedis. Soter[2], p. 83; Corn., p. 77.
Sabeo. Quid Paphiam excrucians. *Epig.*, p. 140.
Cunich. Cur Venerem irritas. *Anth.*, p. 179.
Passeroni. Palla, non m'irritar. *Rime* 3. 104.
Felici. Che vai destando. *Epig.*[2], p. xxvi.
9.577. Synesius quotes this epig. *De Don. Ast.* 1585B (Migne).
Volaterranus. Mortales quamvis norim. Soter[2], p. 100; Corn.,
p. 90; Wech., p. 97.
Bonamico. Mortalem me nosco breves. *Carm.*, p. 55.
Conti. Novi ego mortalis quod. *Myth.* 9. 13.

Sabeo. Mortalem novi meque. *Epig.*, p. 238.
Cunich. Mortalisque brevisque. *Anth.*, p. 182.
Medici (A. de'). Vivo diem moriarque. *Scelt.*, p. xxii.
Medici (A. de'). Lo so, mortale io sono. *Scelt.*, p. xxii.
Felici. So che mortal son io. *Epig.*[1], p. 87.
Passeroni. Mortale io sono e breve. *Rime* 3. 242.
Pagnini. Mortal io son, mel so. *Epig.*, p. 34.

9.580. Cf. 383–4.
    Sabeo. Consulibus primus mensis. *Epig.*, p. 726.

9.581. Sabeo. Phoebe potens arcu. *Epig.*, p. 67.
    Landi. Phoebe, procul iaculans. *Num.*, p. 134.
    Gualfreducci. Pieridum rex arcitenens. *Sel. Epig.*, p. 6.
    Crasso. Sagittarie, Musarum [L-prose]. *Ist.*, p. 307.
    Salvini. Arcier sulle Pieridi. Carcani, *Rac.* 2. vii.

9.583. Obsopoeus. Si sapis, o lector. Wech., p. 95.
    Sabeo. Me cape si sapis. *Epig.*, p. 373.
    Fioretti. O amice, si sapiens [L-prose]. *Prog.* 3. 406.

9.584. Cf. *A.P.* 6. 54.
    Mignault. Eunomus hic ego. Alciati, *Emb.* 184.
    Sanchez. Eunomus ut Parthin. *Op.* 3. 331.

9.585. Cf. Amalteo (G. B.). Captivos ut forte senex. *Tr. Frat.*,
    p. 146.
    Sabeo. Bis duo sunt. *Epig.*, p. 148.

9.586. Sabeo. Dic, pastor, cuius. *Epig.*, p. 806.
    Vargas. Questi filar di piante. *Sag.*, p. 70.

9.588. Cunich. Qualis in aerata vim. *Anth.*, p. 2.

9.589. Sabeo. Iunonem effigiens Plastes. *Epig.*, p. 73.
    Sabeo. Iunonem effingens. *Epig.*, p. 476.
    Murtola. Perchè, scultor, Giunone. *Rime*, f. 201vo.

9.590. Cornarius. Quae natura nequit. Corn., p. 343.
    Sabeo. Quae natura nequit. *Epig.*, p. 469.

9.591. Anon. Artifici fuerant mutuis. Soter[2], p. 262; Corn., p. 343.
    Sabeo. Sol videt e clara Paphiam. *Epig.*, p. 39.
    Sabeo. Certantes dulci Paphiam. *Epig.*, p. 127.
    Cf. Groto. Vulcan mira il ritratto. *Rime* (1587), p. 160.
    Murtola. Di Venere e di Marte. *Rime*, f. 158[ro].

9.592. Sabeo. O quam stultus. *Epig.*, p. 813.
    Rapitius. Quo clypeum malenata. *Facil.*, f. 8[vo].
    H.B. Caelator stultus, regem. *Sel. Epig.*, p. 130.

9.593. Cf. *A.P.* 16. 142.
    Anisio. Commistam furiis pietatem. *Poem.*, f. 88[vo].
    Sabeo. Impiam esse piam. *Epig.*, p. 477.

9.595. Cornarius. Optimus expressit seipsum. Corn., p. 318.
    Sabeo. Optimus in tabula semet. *Epig.*, p. 382.
    Dati. Ritrasse il volto suo. *Vite*, p. 167.

9.596. Quoted by Diogenes Laertius 1. 3 (Chilon).
    Bentinus. Hic sapiens forti natus. *Laert.*, p. 27.

9.597. Sabeo. Mancus eram ad summos. *Epig.*, p. 769.

9.598. [Not in *Plan*.] Theocritus, *Inscr.* 22.
Salvini. Il figliuolo di Giove. *Teoc.*, p. 189.
Regolotti. Quest' uomo da Camerio. *Teoc.*, p. 269.
Della Torre. Quel Pisandro Camirese. *Odi*, p. 375.
Vicini. Pisandro di Camir tra. *Gl'Id.*, p. 189.
Pagnini. Pisandro di Camiro. *Poet. Gr.*, p. 871.

9.599. [Not in *Plan*.] Theocritus, *Inscr.* 17.
Salvini. Rimira, O forestiero. *Teoc.*, p. 188.
Regolotti. Riguarda attentamente. *Teoc.*, p. 267.
Della Torre. Forestier, che qui. *Odi*, p. 373.
Vicini. O forestiero, con attenti. *Gl'Id.*, p. 188.
Pagnini. Tu questo simulacro. *Poet. Gr.*, p. 871.

9.600. [Not in *Plan*.] Theocritus, *Inscr.* 18.
Salvini. Dorico è il suono. *Teoc.*, p. 188.
Regolotti. De la fabella Dorica. *Teoc.*, p. 267.
Della Torre. Dorico il suon. *Odi*, p. 374.
Vicini. E Dorico è lo stile. *Gl'Id.*, p. 188.
Pagnini. Già fu in Dorico. *Poet. Gr.*, p. 871.

9.606. Arnold. Vesal. Quam prius arsisti. Soter[2], p. 290; Corn., p. 379.
Sabeo. Quam prius arsisti. *Epig.*, p. 154; *C.P.It.*, 8. 199.
Sabeo. Pone ensem galeamque. *Epig.*, p. 154.
Angelio. Quam prius ardebas. Graev., *Thes.* 4. 1890.

9.607. Sabeo. Lotae hic sunt Charites. *Epig.*, p. 441.
Sabeo. Lotae hic sunt Charites. *Epig.*, p. 152.

9.608. Arnold. Vesal. Nimirum Venerem talis. Soter[2], p. 290; Corn., p. 379.
Cornarius. Aut Venus ex illis. Corn., p. 379.
Sabeo. Cyprim aqua aut talis. *Epig.*, p. 622.
Pagnini. O d'acqua tal nacque. *Epig.*, p. 35.

9.609. Cf. 609* and 638.
Sabeo. Deliciae hoc Charitum. *Epig.*, pp. 152, 683.

9.609.* Cf. 609 and 638.
Sabeo. Balneum inest Charitum. *Epig.*, p. 152.

9.610. Imitated in an inscr. *C.I.G.* 3. 5875 (Kaibel 1118).
Sabeo Parvum opus est. *Epig.*, p. 433.

9.611. Sabeo. Balneo in hoc parvo. *Epig.*, p. 812.

9.612. Sabeo. Arbor ut exiguo folio. *Epig.*, p. 799.

9.613. Sabeo. Momus ait lacrymans. *Epig.*, p. 812.

9.616. Soter[2] (p. 245) quotes without tr.
Sabeo. Hic se nudarunt. *Epig.*, p. 153; *C.P.It.* 8. 199.
Pessinus (N.). Coelestes Charitum. *C.P.It.* 7. 156.
Pagnini. Bagnandosi le Grazie. *Epig.*, p. 156.

9.617. Sabeo. Dic tu, haec qui. *Epig.*, p. 137.

9.618. Velius. Nil degustata mentita. Soter[2], p. 291; Corn., p. 379.
Sleidan. Fabula, Lotophagos quae. Soter[2], p. 291; Corn., p. 380.
Sabeo. Lotophagum haud mendax. *Epig.*, p. 808.

Pagnini. Ciò che del Loto antica. *Epig.*, p. 152.
9.619. Sabeo. Viceris unde Venus. *Epig.*, p. 151.
9.620. Sabeo. Proxima amori est spes. *Epig.*, p. 833.
Angelio. Spes prope amoris adest. Graev., *Thes.* 4. 1890.
9.621. Sabeo. Si desyderii vis. *Epig.*, p. 657.
9.622. Sabeo. Aut trahit uxoris. *Epig.*, p. 662.
Pagnini. S'entro a quest' acque. *Epig.*, p. 152.
9.623. Sabeo. Cypria in auratis. *Epig.*, p. 153.
Vargas. Con le Grazie e il figlio. *Sag.*, p. 70.
9.624. Sabeo. Erexit quidam quasi me. *Epig.*, p. 442.
9.625. Sabeo. Quis mihi sidus erit. *Epig.*, p. 152.
9.626. Cf. Regianus. Ante bonam Venerem. *PLM* (Baehr.) 4. 359.
9.627. Cf. Anon. Baiarum dum forte capit. *PLM* (Baehr.) 4. 438.
Cf. Angeriano. Quum dormiret Amor. Ἐρωτ. Bii; *C.P.It.* 1.
263.
Cf. Angeriano. Inclyta laudatas peteret. Ἐρωτ. Ciiii.
Cf. Arco (N. d'). Baiarum dum forte capit. *Num.*, p. 159.
Cf. Anon. Al lido gia di Baia. *Versi et Reg.*, Miiii; Carducci,
Poes. Bar., p. 260.
Sabeo. Sub platano viridi. *Epig.*, p. 791.
Cf. Toscano (M.). Dum Baiis dormiret Amor. *Anth.*, p. 145.
Vargas Appiè di questi platani. *Sag.*, p. 79.
Pagnini. Sopita in dolce sonno. *Epig.*, p. 121.
9.629. Ricolvi. Vellem dixisses, aqua. *Op.*, p. 76.
9.630. Sabeo. Conveniunt regi. *Epig.*, p. 374.
9.631. Sabeo. In pretio Danais. *Epig.*, p. 140.
9.633. Cf. 637.
Sabeo. Non minus hoc Iuno. *Epig.*, p. 152.
Sabeo. Auratum ut placuit. *Epig.*, p. 425.
9.634. Sabeo. Iurarunt Charites habitare. *Epig.*, p. 660.
9.636. Pagnini. Se avesse il saggio. *Epig.*, p. 156.
9.637. Cf. 633.
Sabeo. Postquam se hic lavit. *Epig.*, p. 659.
Pagnini. Poscia che Vener qui. *Epig.*, p. 101.
9.638. Cf. 609 and 609*.
Sabeo. Tres Orchomeni hoc. *Epig.*, p. 603.
9.639. Soter. Cypris, Amor, Charites. Soter², p. 291; Corn., p. 380.
Sabeo. Cypria, Amor, Charites. *Epig.*, p. 446.
Pagnini. Ciprigna con le Grazie. *Epig.*, p. 107.
9.640. Soter² (p. 291) has this epig. without tr.
9.641. Quoted by Zonares, *Ann.* 14.7, and by Constantine Porph. 1.
5. (Bekker, p. 27).
9.642. Cf. 643–4.
9.644. Cf. 642–3.
Sabeo. Agricola o utinam. *Epig.*, p. 481.
9.645. Sabeo. Sub Tmolo egelido. *Epig.*, p. 473.
Redi quotes and paraphrases line 8. *Op.* 1. 43.
9.647. Soter. Aeterna est tibi. Soter², p. 302; Corn., p. 381.

Luscinius. Roma caput mundi. Corn., p. 381.
Conti. Roma potens alis. *Myth.* 4. 14.
Calcagnini. Amisit volucres praepes. Pigna, p. 214; *C.P.It.* 3. 82.
Calcagnini. Nescia perpetuas victoria. Pigna, p. 214; *C.P.It.* 3. 82.
Segni (F.). Amissis nunquam poterit. *C.Q.H.P.*, p. 107.
Segni (F.). Fulmine disiectas quod. *C.Q.H.P.*, p. 106.
Sabeo. Roma caput rerum. *Epig.*, p. 166.
Sabeo. Martia, perpetuos. *Epig.*, p. 166.
Sabeo. Laus tua Roma orbis. *Epig.*, p. 169.
Scaliger (J. C.) quotes this epig. *Poet.* 3. 125.
Querenghi. Perchè fuoco dal ciel. *Rim. Occult.*, p. 47.
Bongiovanni and Zanetti. O reina del mondo. *Epig.*, p. 1.
Carcani (P.) gives one line. *Ant. Ercol.* 2. 225.
Pagnini. Roma, donna del mondo. *Epig.*, p. 20.
9.648. Costanzi (G.). Civis et externus charus. *Epig.*, Oiiii.
Velius. Civis et hospes eris. Soter², p. 303; Corn., p. 382.
Soter. Charus erit mihi hospes. Soter², p. 303; Corn., p. 382
Luscinius. Hospes amicus eris mihi. Corn., p. 382.
Sabeo. Aeque hospes civisque. *Epig.*, p. 432.
Sabeo. Idem hospes civisque. *Epig.*, p. 436.
Pagnini. Comune ospizio son. *Epig.*, p. 149.
9.649. Sabeo. A summo usque imum. *Epig.*, p. 503.
9.651. Sabeo. Iucundum ternis prospecto. *Epig.*, p. 436.
9.652. Cornarius. Frigus in aestate. Corn., p. 383.
Sabeo. Aestate atque hyeme. *Epig.*, p. 137.
Pagnini. L'estate fresca. *Epig.*, p. 171.
9.653. Quoted in *Flor. Monac.* 105 (Meineke, *Stob.* 4. 275).
Sabeo. Virtutem ante ipsam. *Epig.*, p. 224.
9.654. Politian. Ite alio, fures; nulla. Del Lungo, p. 546; Corn., p. 383.
Costanzi (G.). Ite domos alias lucrosas. *Epig.*, Oiiii^vo.
Sabeo. Quaere domos alias. *Epig.*, p. 773.
Felici. Ladri, da questa sede. *Epig.*², p. xx.
Pagnini. Ingordi ladri, altre. *Epig.*, p. 116.
9.657. Quoted by Zonares, *Ann.* 14. 10.
Sabeo. Hic ubi terra aperit. *Epig.*, p. 824.
9.658. Sabeo. Virginis Astreae squallebant. *Epig.*, p. 808.
9.659. Sabeo. Quam bonus in senio. *Epig.*, p. 731.
9.661. Sabeo. Felix arbor ego. *Epig.*, p. 696.
9.663. Sabeo. Purgat humi sedem pontus. *Epig.*, p. 428.
9.664. Alciati. Cuius sit locus hic. Corn., p. 377.
Sabeo. Naiades hic certant. *Epig.*, p. 600.
Cunich. Quarum sit locus hic. *Anth.*, p. 41.
Felici. Or fra le najade. *Epig.*¹, p. 81.
Passeroni. Fra le ninfe del mare. *Rime* 3. 129.
9.665. Sabeo. Cede nemus sacrum Daphnes. *Epig.*, p. 750.

9.666. Cf. 784.
Cornarius. Non Amor est magnus. Corn., p. 376.
9.667. Sabeo. Ipse hortis et aquis. *Epig.*, p. 150.
9.668. Banduri. Dulcis Amoris adest. *Imp. Or.* 1. 3. 151.
Vargas. Bello è il giardin. *Sag.*, p. 69.
9.669. Sabeo. Ad nemora approperans. *Epig.*, p. 150; *C.P.It.* 8. 199
Cunich. Huc ades, huic languens. *Anth.*, p. 35.
Passeroni. Arresta, O stanco. *Rime* 3. 105.
9.676. Riccoboni. Prusae nymphis [prose]. *Piaz. Univ.*, sub fin.
9.677. Sabeo. Me multo extruxit. *Epig.*, p. 457.
9.679. Cunich. Omnes Axiocho certatim. *Anth.*, p. 10.
9.683. Sabeo. Mascula aqua Alpheus. *Epig.*, p. 134.
9.684. Quoted in *Schol. Vat.* on Dion. Thrac. (Hilgard, p. 185).
Sabeo. Sum nata Oceani. *Epig.*, p. 807.
9.685. Line 1 cited in *Orac. Sibyl.* 3. 736; also in Zenobius 5. 18;
by Greg. Cyp. 4. 41; by Lactantius, *Div. Inst.* 7. 20. 1; and
by Apostolios 11. 49.
9.687. Cf. Martial. Haec mihi quae colitur. *Epig.*, 10. 32.
9.699. Sabeo. Hausit Alexander Macedo. *Epig.*, p. 728.
9.700. [Not in *Plan.*] Quoted by Plutarch, *Moral.* 436B; by Pausanias (10. 27); and *Schol.* on Plato, *Gorg.* 448B.
9.701. Cf. 702.
Sleidan. Ista quidem digna. Soter², p. 302; Corn., p. 381.
Sabeo. Haec Iove digna domus. *Epig.*, p. 808.
Cunich. Haec domus est Iove. *Anth.*, p. 3.
Passeroni. Casa da Giove è questa. *Rime* 3. 27.
Pagnini. Non fia che a sdegno. *Epig.*, p. 145.
9.702. Cf. 701.
Hermann a Nov. Aquil. Hanc tibi Cecropidae. Soter², p. 302;
Corn., p. 381.
Hermann a Nov. Aquil. Cecropidae hanc posuere. Soter²,
p. 302; Corn., p. 381.
Soter. Cecropidae excelsam hanc. Soter², p. 302; Corn.,
p. 381.
Cunich. Thesidae magno templum. *Anth.*, p. 89.
Passeroni. Questo tempio al padre. *Rime* 3. 231.
Bettinelli. Dà un tempio a Giove. *Op.* 22. 98.
Pagnini. Questo gran tempio. *Epig.*, p. 63.
9.703. [Extract from Herodotus 4. 91.]
9.704. A surviving inscr. (Kaibel 889b).
Anon. Saxa cavat tempus. *Sel. Epig.*, p. 185.
Cunich. Ipsum longa dies. *Anth.*, p. 11.
9.707. Sabeo. Sum similis pelago. *Epig.*, p. 819.
Sabeo. Gurgite par pelago. *Epig.*, p. 25.
Sabeo. Nomine sum fluvius. *Epig.*, p. 40.
9.708. Cf. *A.P.* 7. 397.
Sabeo. Barbarus insano. *Epig.*, p. 538.
9.709. [Not in *Plan.*]

Cf. Pliny. Eutychides [fecit] Eurotam. *N.H.* 34. 78.
9.710. Sabeo. Montibus impositos montes. *Epig.*, p. 147.
9.711. Cornarius. Ipsam grammaticam quum. Corn., p. 386.
9.713. *A.P.* 9. 713–42 and 793–8 are all on Myron's *Heifer.*
Cf. Propertius. Atque aram circum steterant. *Eleg.* 2. 31. 7–8.
Cf. Pliny, *N.H.* 34–57.
Cf. Ausonius. Unam iuvencam pastor. *Opus.* 19. 75.
Quoted in Soter² (p. 245) without tr.
Alciati. Vacca Myronis opus. Corn., p. 319.
Cf. Calcagnini. Ecce homines perdit. Pigna, p. 211; *C.P.It.* 3.
80.
Sabeo. Vacca Myronis ego. *Epig.*, p. 108.
Ricolvi. Bucula sum ipsa Myronis. *Op.*, p. 75.
9.714. Quoted without tr. in Soter², p. 245.
Alciati. At tu sacra Myron. Corn., p. 319.
Sabeo. Qua ratione Myron. *Epig.*, p. 108.
9.715. Cf. *A.P.* 11. 178.
Ausonius? Pasce greges procul. *Opus.* 23. 29; Soter², p. 245;
Corn., p. 320.
Alciati. Pastor age armentum. Corn., p. 320.
Sabeo. Pasce, bubulce, boves. *Epig.*, p. 108.
Cunich. Pasce, bubulce, boves. *Anth.*, p. 14.
Passeroni. Va via con que' tuoi. *Rime* 3. 40.
Vargas. Guardiano, ai paschi. *Sag.*, p. 73.
Pagnini. Storna di qua, O pastor. *Epig.*, p. 122.
9.716. Alciati. Haud ego cocta focis. Corn., p. 320.
Pagnini. Non artefice cura. *Epig.*, p. 122.
9.717. Velius. Aut pecudem hanc. Soter², p. 245; Corn., p. 320.
Alciati. Ferrea tota bovi huic. Corn., p. 320.
Sabeo. Aera Myron sapiens. *Epig.*, p. 803.
Sabeo. Aenea vel cutis est. *Epig.*, p. 108.
Scaliger (J. C.). Aut extra aerato est. *Poem.* I. 151.
Ricolvi. Aenea forte fuit Vaccae. *Op.*, p. 75.
Cunich. Aerea vel pellis vaccam. *Anth.*, p. 32.
Passeroni. Di bronzo questa vacca. *Rime* 3. 184.
9.718. Velius. Ipse Myron dicet. Soter², p. 245; Corn., p. 320.
Sabeo. Forte Myron dicet. *Epig.*, p. 108.
Scaliger (J. C.). Est ubi, ait Myron. *Poem.* I. 151.
Cunich. Ipse Myro attonitus. *Anth.*, p. 32.
Passeroni. Questa, disse Mirone. *Rime* 3. 185.
Pagnini. Forse dirà Miron. *Epig.*, p. 117.
9.719. Velius. Non ego mendaci. Soter², p. 246; Corn., p. 321.
Sabeo. Mentitur, si se dicit. *Epig.*, p. 108.
Sabeo. Falsa Myron dicit. *Epig.*, p. 724.
Sabeo. Repperit errantem ipse. *Epig.*, p. 737.
Cunich. Me non aere Myron. *Anth.*, p. 34.
Pompei. Mentì Mirone; ne mi ha. *Op.* 2. 213.
Passeroni. Di Miron non son fattura. *Rime* 3. 111.

Pagnini. Me già non fuse, ma. *Epig.*, p. 142.
Pagnini. Me non foggio Miron. *Epig.*, p. 45.
9.720. Velius. Ne mea membra. Soter², p. 246; Corn., p. 321.
Sleidan. Isti fixa petrae. Soter², p. 246; Corn., p. 321.
Alciati. Huic nisi me aptasset. Corn., p. 321.
Sabeo. Cum reliquis bubus. *Epig.*, p. 768.
Ricolvi. Pasceret una aliis bos. *Op.*, p. 76.
Pompei. Se Miron non mi avesse. *Op.* 2. 215.
Felici. Vaccarella, insiem con voi. *Epig.*¹, p. 17.
Vargas. Se Mirone col marmo. *Sag.*, p. 36.
Pagnini. Se a questa pietra. *Epig.*, p. 22.
9.721. Ausonius. Ubera quid pulsas. *Opus.* 19. 69.
Ausonius? Errasti attendens haec. *Opus.* 23. 28; Soter², p. 246;
Corn., p. 321.
Sleidan. Qua spe sic properas. Soter², p. 246; Corn., p. 321.
Calcagnini. En vitulus frustra. Pigna, p. 211; *C.P.It.* 3. 79.
Sabeo. Cur vitula accedis. *Epig.*, p. 772.
Sabeo. Ad vaccam accessit. *Epig.*, p. 726.
Marino. Giovenco semplicetto. *Gal.* 2. 20.
Battista. Fatica di Mirone. *Mel.* 2. 80.
Cunich. Quid mugis? mammas. *Anth.*, p. 18.
Pompei. O vitello, perchè. *Op.* 2. 216.
Felici. A che muggisci e per. *Epig.*¹, p. 17.
Passeroni. A che ti lagni e gemi? *Rime* 3. 40.
Roncalli. Invano a me le poppe. *Epig.* (1792), p. 9; (1801),
p. 37.
Vargas. Perchè all mio seno. *Sag.*, p. 73.
Pagnini. Perchè accostando vai. *Epig.*, p. 23.
9.722. Given without tr. in Soter², p. 246; Corn., p. 321.
Sabeo. Praetereas procul hinc. *Epig.*, p. 730.
9.723. Given without tr. in Soter², p. 246; Corn., p. 321.
Calcagnini. Vacca Myronis agros adiens. Pigna, p. 211; *C.P.*
It. 3. 79.
Sabeo. Me plumbum marmorque. *Epig.*, p. 774.
Pagnini. Se piombo e pietra non. *Epig.*, p. 86.
9.724. Velius. Bucula, opinor. Soter², p. 247.
Conti. Mugiet ipsa, puto. *Myth.* 4. 6.
Sabeo. Bos puto clamabit. *Epig.*, p. 758.
Cunich. Mugiet haec tua bos. *Anth.*, p. 18.
Pompei. Muggirà questa vacca. *Op.* 2. 215.
Passeroni. Muggirà la tua vacca. *Rime* 3. 40.
Pagnini. Che voglia pur mugghiare. *Epig.*, p. 142.
9.725. Velius. Mista gregi reliquo. Soter², p. 247; Corn., p. 322.
Sabeo. Immixtam bubus quaerens. *Epig.*, p. 779.
Felici. Da più vacche intorno. *Epig.*¹, p. 121.
9.726. Ausonius. Bucula sum, caelo. *Opus.* 19. 68. 1–2; Soter²,
p. 250; Corn., p. 327.
Velius. Aut hanc forda sua. Soter², p. 247; Corn., p. 323.

Calcagnini. Ventre boves pariunt. Pigna, p. 211; *C.P.It.* 3. 79.

Sabeo. Quae vitulum enixa. *Epig.*, p. 787.

9.727. Velius. Mugiret, quis sit. Soter[2], p. 247; Corn., p. 323.

Sabeo. Aenea sit quamvis. *Epig.*, p. 787.

Groto. Questa vacca è si ben. *Rime* (1587), p. 157.

Cf. Marino. A quel bel marmor. *Gal.* 2. 20.

Cf. Battista. Fatica di Mirone. *Mel.* 2. 80.

Pagnini. Questa, benchè di rame. *Epig.*, p. 117.

9.728. Given without tr. in Soter[2], p. 246; Corn., p. 321.

Calcagnini. Mugio sed quod non. Pigna, p. 211; *C.P.It.* 3. 80.

9.729. Velius. Et iuga et huic aliquis. Soter[2], p. 247; Corn., p. 323.

Alciati. Si quis aratra ferens. Corn., p. 323.

Pompei. Il saldo aratro e il. *Op.* 2. 216.

Pagnini. Se l'aratro sul collo. *Epig.*, p. 86.

9.730. Cf. Choricius. Εἴ με δάμαλις ἴδοι. *Op.* (Foerster), p. 383.

Ausonius. Sic me taurus init. *Opus.* 19. 68. 3–6; Soter[2], p. 251; Corn., p. 327.

Ausonius? Me vitulus cernens. *Opus.* 23. 30; Soter[2], p. 248; Corn., p. 323.

Sleidan. Si videat vitulus. Soter[2], p. 248; Corn., p. 323.

Alciati. Mugiet aspiciens vitulus. Corn., p. 324.

Calcagnini. Quod non sit vivae. Pigna, p. 211; *C.P.It.* 3. 80.

Sabeo. Mugiet inspiciens vitulus. *Epig.*, p. 760.

Sabeo. Taurus init, vitula. *Epig.*, p. 760.

Pompei. Darà muggiti, se il. *Op.* 2. 217.

9.731. Ausonius. Necdum caduco sole. *Opus.* 19. 74; Soter[2], p. 251; Corn., p. 328.

Sabeo. Stare Myron iussit. *Epig.*, p. 790.

Pompei. Qui me vacca Miron. *Op.* 2. 217.

Pagnini. Me qui locò Miron. *Epig.*, p. 23.

9.732. Quoted without tr. in Soter[2], p. 248 and in Corn., p. 324.

Calcagnini. Si me quaerentem. Pigna, p. 211; *C.P.It.* 3. 80.

Sabeo. Si intueare meo rogo. *Epig.*, p. 756.

Marino. O tu, che passi il passo. *Gal.* 2. 19.

Pompei. O pellegrin, se t' addiviene. *Op.* 2. 218.

Pagnini. Se il mio bifolco. *Epig.*, p. 86.

9.733. Quoted without tr. in Soter[2], p. 248 and in Corn., p. 324.

Sabeo. Bucculam amice Myron. *Epig.*, p. 761.

Marino. Tu pur latte mi chiedi. *Gal.* 2. 20.

9.734. Ausonius. Quid me, taure, paras. *Opus.* 19. 73.

Quoted without tr. on Soter[2], p. 248 and in Corn., p. 324.

Sabeo. Ad vaccam frustra. *Epig.*, p. 762.

Groto. Questa vacca è si ben. *Rime* (1587), p. 157.

9.735. Quoted by Soter and Cornarius as above (733).

Calcagnini. Stulte, quid exuggis. Pigna, p. 212.

9.736. Quoted by Soter and Cornarius as above (733).

Sabeo. Non praevenisti formans. *Epig.*, p. 46.

9.737. Quoted by Soter and Cornarius as above (733).
Anselmo. Ut vivam, licet exagitet. *Epig.*, Hii.
Sabeo. Quo properare facis. *Epig.*, p. 298 (282).
Marino. La giovenca un bifolco. *Gal.* 2. 21.
Pompei. Giovenca di metallo è. *Op.* 2. 213.

9.738. Strozzi (T. V.). Naturam atque Artem. *Pat. et. Fil.*, f. 147.
Cf. Lascaris (J.). Σεῖο Μύρων δάμαλιν. *Epig.*, f. 7ʳᵒ; Soter²,
p. 250; Corn., p. 326.
Quoted by Soter and Cornarius as above (733).
Calcagnini. Quod fieri arte potest. Pigna, p. 211.
Baldi. Chi le schiere del mar. *Epig.* 440.
Pompei. Sopra questa giovenca. *Op.* 2. 214.
Pagnini. Arte e Natura oprar. *Epig.*, p. 23.

9.739. Quoted without tr. in Soter², p. 249 and Corn., p. 326.
Sabeo. Teque, myopa, Myron. *Epig.*, p. 770.

9.740. Quoted without tr. in Soter², p. 250 and Corn., p. 326.
Calcagnini. Plumbea vincla Myron. Pigna, p. 210; *C.P.It.* 3.
79.
Sabeo. Petra basis retinet. *Epig.*, p. 815.

9.741. Quoted by Soter and Cornarius as above (740).
Sabeo. Ex aere es tibi. *Epig.*, p. 47.

9.742. Quoted without tr. by Soter and Cornarius as above (740).
Pagnini. Perchè, O bifolco. *Epig.*, p. 105.

9.746. Cf. 747.

9.747. Cf. 746.
Velius. Quinque boum effigies. Soter², p. 289; Corn., p. 378.
Sabeo. Formam quinque bovum. *Epig.*, p. 45.

9.748. Cf. 752.
Sabeo. Sobria vel fias amathisti. *Epig.*, p. 138.

9.749. Scaphenatus. Cur Amor in cyatho? *Eleg.*, Diiii.
Sabeo. In cyatho puerum. *Epig.*, p. 657.
Franchini. In patera cur pictus. *Epig.*, p. 65.
Toscano (M.). In cyatho quid Amor? Sat. *Anth.*, p. 145.
Toscano (M.). In cyatho quid Amor? Cur. *Anth.*, p. 145.
Cunich. Quorsum Amor in cyatho? *Anth.*, p. 179.
Passeroni. Dunque anche nel bicchiere. *Rime* 3. 127.
Roncalli. Perchè scolpisti. De-Mauri, p. 119.
Pagnini. Perchè in un nappo Amore? *Epig.*, p. 33.

9.750. Velius. Bubus in articulo. Soter², p. 290; Corn., p. 378.

9.751. Costanzi (G.). Signum hiacynthus. *Epig.*, Oiiiivᵒ.

9.752. Cf. 748.
Sabeo. Docta manus fecit. *Epig.*, p. 212.

9.753. Claudian. Lymphae, quae tegitis. *Op.* (Jeep) 2. 169.

9.754. Sabeo. Cur crystallus aquam. *Epig.*, p. 440.

9.755. Sabeo. Arte opus hoc tanta. *Epig.*, p. 410.

9.756. Sabeo. Praxiteles salit arte. *Epig.*, p. 707.
Cf. Marino. Reggetelo reggete. *Gal.* 2. 42.

9.757. Sabeo. Pinxerat Iphion quondam. *Epig.*, p. 714.

9.759. Cf. 760.
Cf. Ausonius. Αἴξ, χίμαρος, πήρη. *Opus.* 19. 50; Soter², p. 290.
Soter. Saxum unum auriga. Soter², p. 290; Corn., p. 378.
Bergius. Pastor, capra, pedum [from Auson.]. Soter², p. 290.
Sabeo. Saxum, rheda, auriga. *Epig.*, p. 154.

9.760. Cf. 759.

9.761. Dati. . . . da colori ingannato. *Vite*, p. 34.

9.762. Sabeo. Me faber ignipotens. *Epig.*, p. 302 (286).

9.763. Cornarius. Praevaricans leges me. *Corn.*, p. 387.
Sabeo. Non bene agens oculis. *Epig.*, p. 732.

9.764. Cf. 765–6.

9.765. Cf. 764 and 766.
Sabeo. Obtendor lecto sponsae. *Epig.*, p. 805.

9.766. Cf. 764–5.

9.767. Cf. 768–9.
Sabeo. Huic residens mensae. *Epig.*, p. 325.
'L-prose.' Sedens hic apud pulchris. 'Επ. καὶ 'Ελ. No. 67.

9.768. Cf. 767 and 769.
'L-prose.' Ludicra quidem omnia. 'Επ. καὶ 'Ελ. No. 68.
Cunich. Cuncta vide ut vario. *Anth.*, p. 70.
Passeroni. Vedi, come fortuna. *Rime* 3. 103.

9.769. Cf. 767–8.
Sabeo. Ludicra sunt placidis. *Epig.*, p. 696.
'L-prose.' Placidis quidem haec. 'Επ. καὶ 'Ελ. No. 69.

9.771. Cornarius. Sic Bromium ipsa. Corn., p. 387.
Sabeo. It Thetis excoepit. *Epig.*, p. 846.

9.773. Cf. *A.P.* 16. 194.
Costanzi (G.). Transtulit in formam. *Epig.*, Oiiii.
Salvini. Sartago facta est. Wellesley, *Anth. Pol.*, p. 156.

9.774. Cf. *A.P.* 16. 60.
Sabeo. Baccha quidem e pario. *Epig.*, p. 367.

9.775. Sabeo. Baccha Iovem satyrum. *Epig.*, p. 792.

9.776. Sabeo. Christallo in parvo. *Epig.*, p. 668.
Dati refers to this epig., *Vite*, p. 5.
Della Valle. Le Grazie ed il color. Dati, *Vite*, p. 30.

9.779. Sabeo. Aspice Iustini. *Epig.*, p. 375.

7.780. Sabeo Qui nidum amplectens. *Epig.*, p. 846.

9.781. Sabeo. Recludor si me claudis. *Epig.*, p. 438.
Pagnini. Se tu mi serri. *Epig.*, p. 162.

9.782. Sabeo. Artifices resecant bis. *Epig.*, p. 156.

9.783. Cf. Ausonius. Mercurio genitore satus. *Opus.* 19. 102; Soter²,
p. 277; Corn., p. 357.
Soter. Me vir Mercurium. Soter², p. 277; Corn., p. 357.
Cornarius. Mas me Mercurium. Corn., p. 357.
Sabeo. Hermes sum maribus. *Epig.*, p. 41.

9.784. Cf. 666.
  Lascaris (J.). Parvula ne temnas. *Epig.*, f.14vo; Soter², p. 300;
    Corn., p. 380.
  Carteromaco alludes to this epig. Above, p. 153.
  Sleidan. Parvula ne contemnito. Soter², p. 300; Corn., p. 380.
  Sabeo. Gratia in exiguis. *Epig.*, p. 144.
  Sabeo. Gratia inest parvis. *Epig.*, p. 152.
9.786. [Not in *Plan.*] Quoted by Demosthenes 7. 40. (*De Haloneso*).
9.787. Luscinius. Qui prius errabas tota. Corn., p. 382.
9.788. Sabeo. Immortale aevum. *Epig.*, p. 126.
9.790. Conti. Quis tulit e caelo. *Myth.* 3. 18.
9.793. *A.P.* 793–8 are on Myron's Heifer; cf. 713–42.
  Soter and Cornarius quote this epig, without tr. Soter², p. 249;
    Corn., p. 325.
  Sabeo. Hanc vitulam inspiciens. *Epig.*, p. 768.
9.794. Soter and Cornarius quote this epig, without tr. Soter²,
    p. 249; Corn., p. 325.
  Pompei. A quel parte, O pastor. *Op.* 2. 214.
9.795. Soter and Cornarius quote this epig. without tr. Soter², p. 249;
    Corn., p. 325.
  Pagnini. O a questa vacca diè. *Epig.*, p. 86.
9.796. Soter and Cornarius quote this epig. without tr. Soter², p. 249;
    Corn., p. 325.
  Sabeo. Plastes, plasma tuum. *Epig.*, p. 814.
9.797. Velius. Me leo conspiciens. Soter², p. 249; Corn., p. 325
  Sabeo. Me leo hiat cernens. *Epig.*, p. 471.
9.798. Soter and Cornarius quote this epig. without tr. Soter², p. 249;
    Corn., p. 325.
9.799. Sabeo. Iucundus regi Muselius. *Epig.*, p. 432.
9.800. Sabeo. Haec opera adiunxit. *Epig.*, p. 813.
9.805. Sabeo. Bellipotens dum Mars. *Epig.*, p. 468.
9.807. Sabeo. Venari nam solis iter. *Epig.*, p. 845.
  Sabeo. Venari Phaetontis iter. *Epig.*, p. 467.
9.809. Sabeo. Optimam aquam dixit. *Epig.*, p. 334.
  Salvini. Quod citharam pulsans. Wellesley, *Anth. Pol.*, p. 142.
9.813. [Not in edd. of *Plan.;* quoted from *Marc.* 481 by Bongiovanni
    and Zanetti (above, p. 402).]
9.822. Sabeo. Coelum ex argento. *Epig.*, p. 302 (286).
9.823. Conti. Conticeant Dryadum. *Myth.* 5. 6.
  Sabeo. Umbrosi colles sileant. *Epig.*, p. 50.
  Vargas. Taccia in vetta delle rupe. *Sag.*, p. 67.
9.824. Cf. *A.P.* 9. 337; and 10.11.
  Sabeo. Prospera tum felix. *Epig.*, p. 54.
  Carcani (P.). E alcun di voi [lines 6–8]. *Ant. Ercol.* 6. 146.
9.825. Sabeo. Quam male amo infelix. *Epig.*, p. 96.
9.826. Cf. Colocci? Huius Nympha loci. Burmann, *Anth. Lat.* 1. 62.
  Cf. Molza. E Bacchi mensis furto. *Poes.* 3. 186.
  Sabeo. Hunc satyrum Bacchi. *Epig.*, p. 194.

Cf. Baldi. Se di Bacco sei servo. *Epig.* 403.
Bongiovanni and Zanetti. Esperta man, che sola. *Epig.*, p. 2.
Carcani (P.). Ma Satiro di Bacco. *Ant. Ercol.* 6. 165.
9.827. Conti. Nam sum ego cornuti. *Myth.* 5. 7.
Sabeo. Cornigeri existo famulus. *Epig.*, p. 375.
Carcani (P.). Son del cornuto Bacco. *Ant. Ercol.* 6. 165.

Book X

10.1. Cf. 2, 4–6, 14–6.
Sabeo. Nunc placidum est pelagus. *Epig.*, p. 746.
Cunich. Hora mari facilem dat. *Anth.*, p. 34.
Felici. Le rondinelle riedono. *Epig.*[2], p. xxiii.
10.2. Cf. 1, 4–6, 14–6.
Sabeo. Opportunus adest cursus. *Epig.*, p. 749.
10.3. Cornarius. Qui petis hinc orcum. *Corn.*, p. 74.
Conti. Undique recta ibis. *Myth.* 3. 4.
Sabeo. Ad manes est recta. *Epig.*, p. 496.
Gualfreducci. Tartaream ad sedem. *Var.*, p. 290; *Sel. Epig.*,
p. 286.
Cunich. Pronum iter est Orci. *Anth.*, p. 71.
10.4. Cf. 1, 2, 5, 6, 14–6.
Sabeo. Navibus extendas iam. *Epig.*, p. 770.
10.5. Cf. 1, 2, 4, 6, 14–6.
Sabeo. Iam Philomela trahi nidum. *Epig.*, p. 105.
10.6. Cf. 1, 2, 4, 5, 14–6.
10.8. Conti. Littora parvus ego. *Myth.* 5. 15.
Sabeo. Montem habito ad littus. *Epig.*, p. 109.
Cunich. Parvus ego in speciem. *Anth.*, p. 22.
10.11. Cf. *A.P.* 9. 337 and 824.
10.13. Sabeo. O pulchram laurum. *Epig.*, p. 730.
Cunich. Heic lauri virides. *Anth.*, p. 41.
Felici. Qui lauri ombreggiano. *Epig.*[1], p. 90.
Passeroni. Qui l'allora verdeggia. *Rime* 3. 128.
10.14. Cf. 1, 2, 4–6, 15–6.
10.15. Cf. 1, 2, 4–6, 14, 16.
10.16. Cf. 1, 2, 4–6, 14–5.
10.19. Averani. Hac tu luce genis. *Op.* 1. 108.
10.21. Sabeo. Cypria pacis amans. *Epig.*, p. 151.
10.26. Ausonius? Re fruere, ut natus. *Opus.* 23. 18; Soter[2], p. 21;
Corn., p. 17.
More (Sir T.). Tanquam iam moriturus. Soter[2], p. 21; Corn.,
p. 17.
Lily (W.). Divitiis utare tuis. Soter[2], p. 21; Corn., p. 17.
Alciati. Utere divitiis ut morti. Corn., p. 18.
Alciati. Re fruere, exitio. *Op.* 4.328.
Venatorius. Utere divitiis veluti. Obsop., p. 29; Wech., p. 26.
Germano quotes Lily's version. *Giard.*, p. 308.
Bongiovanni and Zanetti. Usa dell'aver tuo. *Epig.*, p. 38.

Venatorius' version is given in Ἐπ. καὶ Ἐλ. (No. 16).
Cunich. Disce frui partis rebus. *Anth.*, p. 79.
Felici. Dei morir? de' beni. *Epig.*[1], p. 52.
Passeroni. Pensa, che hai da morire. *Rime* 3. 199.
Pagnini. Godi de' beni tuoi. *Epig.*, p. 27.

10.27. Cf. Theon. οἷον Πιττακὸς ὁ Μιτυληναῖος. *Progym.* 5 (Spengel, *Rh. Gr.*, vol. 2.).
Costanzi (A.). Forte homines lateant. *Epig.*, Biii[ro].
Bergius. Improbe mortales quamvis. Soter[2], p. 81; Corn., p. 75.
Soter. Impostor licet usque. Soter[2], p. 81; Corn., p. 75.
Alciati. Forte viros quae tu. Corn., p. 75.
Luscinius. Ut celes hominum. Corn., p. 75.
Conti. Si quid turpe facis. *Myth.* 2. 6.
Possevino (A.) remarks on this ep., *Poes. et Pict.*, cap. 19.
Germano. Homines quidem fortasse [prose]. *Giard.*, p. 261.
Bongiovanni and Zanetti. Mentre a mal far. *Epig.*, p. 52.
A translation by Benedictus (above, p. 397) is in Ἐπ. καὶ Ἐλεγ. (No. 37).
Cunich. Impia facta latent. *Anth.*, p. 80.
Pompei. Oprando cosa rea. *Op.* 2. 199.
Felici. Sovvente agli uomini. *Epig.*[1], p. 53.
Pagnini. Il tuo malvagio oprare. *Epig.*, p. 6.

10.28. Costanzi (A.). Omnis vita quidem brevis. *Epig.*, Biii[ro].
Luscinius. Vita brevis tota est. Corn., p. 49.
Cornarius. Qui bene semper agunt. Corn., p. 50.
Valeriano. Tota brevis vita est. *Poem.*, p. 113; *C.P.It.* 10. 156.
Sabeo. Qui bene agunt. *Epig.*, p. 34.
Bongiovanni and Zanetti. Breve è la vita. *Epig.*, p. 53.
Tr. by Benedictus (above, p. 397) in Ἐπ. καὶ Ἐλ. (No. 20).
Cunich. Tota brevis vita est. *Anth.*, p. 81.
Pompei. A chi felice sia. *Op.* 2. 200.
Passeroni. Breve è la vita. *Rime* 3. 202.
Felici. A quei che vivono. *Epig.*[2], p. xxiv.

10.29. Costanzi (G.). Non amor humanum. *Epig.*, Oiiii[vo].
Cornarius. Immeritum incusant mortalia. Corn., p. 61.
Venatorius. Non amor innodat. Obsop., p. 62; Wech., p. 56.
Conti. Nullum Amor offendit. *Myth.* 4. 14.
Minturno. Non è cagion di male. *Rime*, p. 137.
Toscano (M.). Nullos laedit Amor. *Anth.*, p. 153.
Cunich. Non Amor humanum. *Anth.*, p. 80.
Pagnini. Non nuoce al mondo. *Epig.*, p. 53.

10.30. Cf. Euripides. Τὰς χάριτας ὅστις. *Erech.*, frg. 1 (17).
Ausonius. Gratia, quae tarda est. *Opus.* 19. 16; Soter[2], p. 75; Corn., p. 64.
Cf. Ausonius. Si bene quid facias. *Opus.* 19. 17; Soter[2], p. 75; Corn., p. 64.

Costanzi (G.). Gratior est quaecunque. *Epig.*, Oiiii[v]º.

Gaurico. Gratia sit semper. *Epig.* [5].

Gaurico. Gratia iam praesto. *Epig.* [5].

Sabeo. Gratia quae praesto. *Epig.*, p. 607.

Sabeo. Parva inquam. *Epig.*, p. 610.

Sabeo. Grata vel ingrata est. *Epig.*, p. 638.

Sabeo. Prompta charis charitum. *Epig.*, p. 650.

Sabeo. Gratia quae pigra. *Epig.*, p. 652.

Giraldi (L.G.) refers to Gr. and quotes Auson. *Op.* 2. 533.

Germano. Celeres gratiae [prose]. *Giard.*, p. 119.

Salvini. Le grazie, che si fan. *Disc.* 1. 235.

Bongiovanni and Zanetti. Quanto più tosto. *Epig.*, p. 43.

A tr. by Luscinius is given in Ἐπ. καὶ Ἐλ. (No. 25).

Cunich. Gratior est celerat. *Anth.*, p. 80.

Pompei. Sono le grazie più. *Op.* 2. 228.

Felici. Quella grazia, che presto. *Epig.*[1], p. 52.

Passeroni. Se vuoi farmi un favor. *Rime* 3. 200.

Pagnini. Grazia pronta è ben grata. *Epig.*, p. 8.

10.31. Luscinius. Mortales fugiunt nos. Soter[2], p. 31; Corn., p. 27.

Venatorius. Omnia nos fugiunt. Obsop., p. 31; Wech., p. 28.

Sabeo. Praetereunt homines. *Epig.*, p. 45.

Germano? Omnia mortales fugiunt. *Giard.*, p. 399.

A tr. by Benedictus (above, p. 397) is given in Ἐπ. καὶ Ἐλ. (No. 11).

Ricolvi. Divitiae aut abeunt. *Op.*, p. 59.

Ricolvi. Fluxa hominum bona. *Op.*, p. 59.

Ricolvi. Ogni ben di quaggiù. *Op.*, p. 59.

Cunich. Mortale est quod habes. *Anth.*, p. 81.

Passeroni. Caduchi sono i beni. *Rime* 3. 201.

Felici. Se tutto è labile. *Epig.*[2], p. xxiii.

Vargas. Mortali son dell' uom. *Sag.*, p. 102.

10.32. The numerous occurrences of this proverb in Greek writers are collected in Leutsch and Schneidewin, *Paroem. Graec.* 1. 148.

Cf. Gellius. Inter os et offam multa. *N.A.* 13. 17; Soter[2], p. 78.

Given by Apostolios (14.46) and Arsenios (43.75).

Sabeo. Multa cadunt inter calices. *Epig.*, p. 725.

Sabeo. Multa cadunt inter pendentia. *Epig.*, p. 801.

Cottunius gives Gellius' version. *Confic.*, p. 57.

10.33. Bergius. Dicere de cunctis bona. Soter[2], p. 48; Corn., p. 51.

Soter. Est de omnibus fari. Soter[2], p. 48.

Ricolvi. Laudare volupe est. *Op.*, p. 59.

Ricolvi. Niun vuol esser ripreso. *Op.*, p. 59.

10.34. Quoted by Arsenios, *Paroem.* p.381.

Cornarius. Si quid cura potest, ut. Corn., p. 141.

Obsopoeus. Si quid cura potest, sit. Obsop., p. 197; Wech., p. 174.

Sabeo. Si curae esse potest. *Epig.*, p. 60.

10.35. Cf. Petronius. Nomen amicitiae sic. *Sat.* 80.
Sabeo. Gratus es haud peccans. *Epig.*, p. 125.
Sabeo. Inculpatus homo cum. *Epig.*, p. 125.
A tr. by 'Apermachius' is included in 'Επ. καὶ 'Ελ. (No. 53).
10.36. Cf. Theognis. "Η με φίλει καθαρόν. *Eleg.* 89–92.
Cornarius. Nil peius natura. Corn., p. 85.
Obsopoeus. Nil homine invenit. Obsop., p. 102; Wech., p. 91.
Jordanus. Provida mortales inter. Soter[3], p. 110.
Sabeo. Inter mortales nihil. *Epig.*, p. 406.
Germano quotes Obsopoeus' version. *Giard.*, p.17.
Rivautella-Ricolvi. Nemo homines inter. *Mar.*, *Praef.* [6].
Bongiovanni and Zanetti. Cosa peggior natura. *Epig.*, p. 45.
The version of Obsopoeus is given in 'Επ. καὶ 'Ελ. (No. 46).
Ricolvi. Nil reperire licet. *Op.* p. 62.
Ricolvi. Nel mondo altro non. *Op.*, p. 62.
Pagnini. Tra gli uomini non v'ha. *Epig.*, p. 6.
10.37. Sleidan. Sit mora consiliis. Soter[2], p. 145; Corn., p. 140.
Luscinius. Sanius efficiet mora. Corn., p. 140.
Valeriano. Consilium utilius lento. *Poem.*, p. 113; *C.P.It.* 10.
158.
Sleidan's version is given in 'Επ. καὶ 'Ελ. (No. 60).
Cunich. Consilium lauda quod. *Anth.*, p. 80.
Pompei. Miglior consiglio è. *Op.* 2. 199.
Felici. È miglior quant' è. *Epig.*[1], p. 53.
Passeroni. Esaminalo ben, pesalo. *Rime* 3. 200.
10.38. Quoted by Athenaeus 7.281E.
Sabeo. Tempora habent Amor. *Epig.*, p. 743.
Salvini. Tempo è d'amare. *Disc.* 6. 51.
10.39. Costanzi (A.). Thesauri instar habet. *Epig.*, Biii[vo].
Sleidan. Si quis amicitiae. Soter[2], p. 134; Corn., p. 132.
Luscinius. Ingens thesaurus bonus. Corn., p.132; Soter[3], p. 150.
Obsopoeus. Heliodore, bonus thesauri. Obsop., p. 191; Wech.,
p. 168.
Jordanus. Est ingens homini. Soter[3], p. 149.
Sabeo. Hunc, qui fidus amat. *Epig.*, p. 426.
Bongiovanni and Zanetti. Cui serbarselo seppe. *Epig.*, p. 52.
The tr. of Sleidan is given in 'Επ. καὶ 'Ελ. (No. 43).
Ricolvi. Foedus amicitiae si. *Op.*, p. 60.
Ricolvi. Un amico se avrai. *Op.*, p. 60.
Cunich. Thesaurum reperit. *Anth.*, p. 71.
Passeroni. Un gran tesoro trovano. *Rime* 3. 211.
Vargas. Per chi lo sa serbar. *Sag.*, p. 102.
10.40. The same lines occur as Theognis 1151–2.
Luscinius. Commutes nolim praesentem. Corn., p. 133.
Obsopoeus. Ne quaeras alium praes. Obsop., p. 191; Wech.,
p. 168.
Obsopoeus. Ne quaeras alium veteris. Obsop., p. 191; Wech.,
p. 168.

10.41. More (Sir T.). Divitiis animi solas. Soter[2], p. 113; Corn., p. 106.
Sleidan. Nobilis est animi. Soter[2], p. 113; Corn., p. 106.
Anisio. Non sunt divitiae. *Poem.*, f.95[ro].
Sabeo. Impediunt animum. *Epig.*, p. 459.
In 'Επ. καὶ 'Ελεγ. are given the tr. of More (No. 36) and Sleidan (No. 51).

10.42. Soter. Sermoni occulto linguam. Soter[2], p. 102.
Luscinius. Profuit arcanis posuisse. Corn., p. 95.
Obsopoeus. Fac arcana premat. Obsop., p. 118; Wech., p. 103.
Sabeo. Ora sigillato, arcanum. *Epig.*, p. 421.
Sanchez. In verbo linguae. *Op.* 3. 39.
Germano. Arcanorum verborum [prose]. *Giard.*, p. 322.
The tr. by Obsopoeus is given in 'Επ. καὶ 'Ελ. (No. 49).
Pagnini. Tien chiuso con sugello. *Epig.*, p. 5.

10.43. Appears as an inscr. (Kaibel 1122); quoted by Eustathius on *Iliad* 7. 282.
Volaterranus. Sex horae tantum rebus. *Com. Urb.*, p. 734; Soter[2], p. 146; Corn., p. 142.
Alciati. In sextam labor. Corn., p. 142; *Op.* 2. 1031.
Luscinius. In sex procedat. Corn., p. 142.
Obsopoeus. Sex horas iusto. Obsop., p. 198; Wech., p. 177.
Valeriano. Horae severis quattuor. *Poem.*, p. 114; *C.P.It.* 10. 161.
Giraldi (L.G.). Sufficit in sextam. *Op.* 2. 605.
Mazzoni quotes the tr. by Volaterranus. *Difesa*, p. 48.
Germano quotes Volaterranus' tr. *Giard.*, p. 239.
Gori. Sex horae negotiis [prose]. *Inscr.* 1.93.
Salvini. Sufficiunt tantum sex. Gori, *Monument.*, p. 213.
Volaterranus' tr. is given in 'Επ. καὶ 'Ελ. (No. 63).

10.44. Eustathius quotes line 4 on *Iliad* 19. 138 (p. 1176).
Soter. Munere te accepto. Soter[2], p. 94; Corn., p. 84.
Luscinius. Et domino et fratri. Corn., p. 84.
Alciati. Munera qui dederit. *Op.* 4.329, 1085.
Alciati. Cum quicquam dederim. *Con. Vit. Mon.*, p. 20.
Sabeo. Te dominum fratrem. *Epig.*, p. 407.
Sabeo. Vis scribi frater. *Epig.*, p. 407.
Sabeo. Si nil largiris. *Epig.*, p. 411.
Baldi. S' io ti dono. *Epig.* 58.
Cottunius quotes Sabeo's first tr. *Confic.*, p. 407.

10.45. More (Sir T.). Heus homo si memor. Soter[2], p. 129; Corn., p. 127.
Velius. Quid pater egit, homo. Soter[2], p. 130; Corn., p. 128.
Sabeo. Si memor es. *Epig.*, pp. 176, 484.

10.46. More (Sir T.). Rebus in humanis. Soter[2], p. 123; Corn., p. 118.
Anon. Non mediocre bonum. Soter[2], p. 123; Corn., p. 118.
Sabeo. Doctrinam haud parvam. *Epig.*, p. 174.
Germano. Magna eruditio [prose]. *Giard.*, p. 349.

Crasso. Magna doctrina [L-prose]. *Ist.*, p. 423.
Bongiovanni and Zanetti. Salutevol precetto. *Epig.*, p. 7.
Cunich. Posse loqui magnum. *Anth.*, p. 84.
Passeroni. Il saper parlare è. *Rime* 3. 229.
10.47. Cornarius. Ede, bibe, et luctus. Corn., p. 104.
Obsopoeus. Indulge genio, luctum. Obsop., p. 144; Wech.,
p. 128.
Sabeo. Ebibe, ede abscondens. *Epig.*, p. 196.
Cunich. Huc epulas, huc vina. *Anth.*, p. 84.
Passeroni. Quà del vin, ragazzo. *Rime* 3. 229.
10.48. Alciati. Imperium quae serva. Corn., p. 89; *Op.* 4. 582.
10.50. Sleidan. Non ut Homerus ait. Soter[2], p. 122; Corn., p. 115.
Alciati. Sole satae Circes. *Emb.* 76.
Sabeo. Immutasse viros. *Epig.*, p. 349.
Mignault. Non credam Circen. Alciati, *Emb.* 76.
Mazzoni quotes Sleidan's tr. *Difesa*, p. 600.
10.51. More (Sir T.). Invidia est peior. Soter[2], p. 130; Corn., p. 128.
Erasmus. Peior livore est. Soter[2], p. 131; Corn., p. 129.
Hamerus. Multa est quam miseri. Soter[2], p. 131.
Sabeo. Peior enim invidia. *Epig.*, p. 435.
Alsario. Invidia ex sententia [prose]. Graev., *Thes.* 12. 892.
* Cunich. Invidia est melior. *Anth.*, p. 85.
Passeroni. La invidia, dice Pindaro. *Rime* 3. 208.
Pagnini. Che l'invidia migliore. *Epig.*, p. 72.
10.52. Luscinius. Euge tibi deus est. Corn., p. 126.
Cornarius. Rite deus docto est. Corn., p. 126.
10.53. Cornarius. Vivere quid mirum. Corn., p. 114.
Obsopoeus. Si parricidas felices. Obsop., p. 174; Wech., p. 153.
10.54. Gualfreducci. Exitium non sola. *Var.*, p. 290; *Sel. Epig.*,
p. 287.
10.55. Sabeo. Etsi te iactas. *Epig.*, p.158.
Cunich. Uxori servire negas. *Anth.*, p. 180.
Passeroni. Pamfilo, dici spesso. *Rime* 3. 67.
10.57. Cornarius. Et ventrem et quae. Corn., p. 122.
Conti. Iure invisa deis. *Myth.* 4. 14.
Sabeo. Solvitur ob ventrem. *Epig.*, p. 128.
10.58. Cf. Job 1. 21. Quoted by S. Maximus (Migne, *P.G.* 91. 800);
and by Georgios Gnomolog. (Boissonade, *Anec.* 1. 22).
Costanzi (A.). Nudus terram inii. *Epig.*, Biii[ro].
Arsenios quotes this epig. *Paroem.*, p. 344.
More (Sir T.). Nudus ut in terram. Soter[2], p. 31; Corn.,
p. 27.
Lily (W.). Ingredior nudus terram. Soter[2], p. 31; Corn., p. 27.
Luscinius. Conscendi terram nudus. Soter[2], p. 31; Corn., p. 27.
Alciati. Nudus humo exilii. Corn., p. 27.
Venatorius. Nudus eram veniens. Obsop., p. 32; Wech., p. 28.
Obsopoeus. Natus ut in terram. Obsop., p. 32; Wech., p. 28.
Obsopoeus. Nudus humum intravi. Obsop., p. 32; Wech., p. 28.

Pompei. Nudo sopra il suol. *Op.* 2. 173.
Vargas. Nudo v'entrai, nudo. *Sag.*, p.83.
Pagnini. Ignudo venni in terra. *Epig.*, p. 61.
Roncalli. Nudo sopra la terra. *Epig.* (1801), p. 20.

10.59. Cf. 69.
Sleidan. Expectare necem, res. Soter[2], p. 110; Corn., p. 104.
Cornarius. Instantis fati sunt. Corn., p. 104.
Obsopoeus. Est gravis anxietas. Obsop., p. 145; Wech., p. 128.
Sabeo. Expectare necem dolor. *Epig.*, p. 172.
Sabeo. Continua instantes mors. *Epig.*, p. 415.
Bongiovanni and Zanetti. Attender morte è. *Epig.*, p. 35.

10.60. Sleidan. Quo tibi divitiae. Soter[2], p. 113; Corn., p. 107.
Sabeo. Ditescis, sed quid. *Epig.*, p. 425.
Baldi. Sei ricco? e che fia. *Epig.* 68.
Sleidan's tr. is included in 'Επ. καὶ 'Ελ. (No. 38).
Cunich. Ditescis. Quid tum? *Anth.*, p. 84.
Felici. Se' ricco, e immagini. *Epig.*[1], p. 74.
Passeroni. Sei ricco, ed arricchisci. *Rime* 3. 228.

10.61. Sabeo. Effuge divitiis tumidos. *Epig.*, pp. 173, 425.

10.62. Sleidan. Iudicio fortuna carens. Soter[2], p. 127; Corn., p. 125.
Luscinius. Lege caret certa. Corn., p. 125.
Conti. Improba non novit. *Myth.* 4. 9.
Sabeo. Legibus haud ullis. *Epig.*, p. 126.

10.63. More (Sir T.). Nunquam vixisti. Soter[2], p. 122; Corn., p. 116.
Sleidan. Parcunt fata viro. Soter[2], p. 123; Corn., p. 116.
Cornarius. Qui nunquam vixit. Corn., p. 116.
Obsopoeus. Nunquam vixit egens. Obsop., p. 178; Wech., p. 157.
Sabeo. Hic qui vixit inops. *Epig.*, p. 174.
Baldi. Non vive il poverel. *Epig.* 71.
Bongiovanni and Zanetti. Non visse il poveruom. *Epig.*, p. 35.
More's tr. is given in 'Επ. καὶ 'Ελ. (No. 39).

10.64. Sabeo. Herage [*sic*], abi tantus. *Epig.*, p. 426.
Cunich. Ille tuus quonam fatus? *Anth.*, p. 47.
Passeroni. Quel tuo fasto ove. *Rime* 3. 187.

10.65. Costanzi (A.). Vita quasi cursus. *Epig.*, Bii[vo].
Luscinius. Vita rapit miseros. Soter[2], p. 32; Corn., p. 28.
Venatorius. Vita hominum rapidis. Obsop., p. 32; Wech., p. 28.
Sabeo. Lubrica vita hominum. *Epig.*, p. 167.
Battista. Nave è la vita. *Mel.* 2. 36.
Bongiovanni and Zanetti. Periglioso varcar. *Epig.*, p. 47.
Cunich. Vita mare est, nautae. *Anth.*, p. 83.
Medici (A. de'). Vita mare est, anceps. *Scelt.*, p. xxxvi.
Medici (A. de'). Mare è la vita. *Scelt.*, p. xxxvi.
Pompei. Un navigar pien. *Op.* 2. 174.
Felici. La vita è mar. *Epig.*[1], p. 72.

10.66. Sabeo. Quum quis opes pauper. *Epig.*, p. 483.

Averani. Quum quis inops est. *Op.* 1. 204.
Cunich. Magnas nactus opes. *Anth.*, p. 47.
Pompei. Tal che da l'esser. *Op.* 2. 185.
Passeroni. Carmi di beni. *Rime* 3. 107.
Felici. In oro e in titoli. *Epig.*², p. iii.
10.67. Costanzi (G.). Rebus in adversis. *Epig.*, Oiiii^vo.
Alciati. Mnemosyne felix. Corn., p. 94.
Sabeo. Mnemosyne, salve longum. *Epig.*, p. 52.
10.68. Sabeo. Consulo quod fugias. *Epig.*, p. 855.
10.69. Cf. 59.
More (Sir T.). Num stultum est. Soter², p. 79; Corn., p. 72.
Luscinius. Mortem cur timeas. Corn., p. 72.
Obsopoeus. Mortem quid prodest. Obsop., p. 85; Wech., p. 74.
Conti. Cur timor est vobis. *Myth.* 3. 13.
Sabeo. Curantem morbos. *Epig.*, p. 404.
Gualfreducci. Mortem quis metuat? *Var.*, p. 287.
Bongiovanni and Zanetti. Fonte è morte. *Epig.*, p. 17.
More's tr. is given in Ἐπ. καὶ Ἐλ. (No. 27).
Cunich. Quid mortem horretis? *Anth.*, p. 74.
Felici. A che in orrore. *Epig.*¹, p. 2.
Bettinelli. No, non temete. *Op.* 22. 102.
10.71. Sabeo. Doliolum aspiciens. *Epig.*, p. 115.
10.72. Luscinius. Disce iocos, scena. Soter², p. 32; Corn., p. 29.
Cf. Alamanni. Son gli Dei spettator. *Versi* 2. 141.
Sabeo. Vita omnis scaena. *Epig.*, p. 705.
Baldi. È nostra vita una verace. *Epig.* 25.
Baldi. La vita nostra è. *Epig.* 222, 492.
Averani cites this epig. *Op.* 1. 402.
Cunich. Vita hominum est. *Anth.*, p. 84.
Cunich. Ludus et est hominum. *Anth.*, p. 84.
Pagnini. Scena e scherzo è. *Epig.*, p. 58.
10.73. Cf. Anon. Ὡς ἐθέλει τὸ φέρον. Boissonade, *Anec.* 2. 475.
Cf. ep. in S. Maximus (Migne, *P.G.* 91. 829).
More (Sir T.). Si ferris ferre et. Soter², p. 32; Corn., p. 29.
Luscinius. Si ducunt te fata. Soter², p. 32; Corn., p. 29.
Sabeo. Si quod fert, te fert. *Epig.*, p. 157.
Cunich. Fata ferunt te. *Anth.*, p. 83.
Vargas. Se tu il fato hai. *Sag.*, p. 102.
Pagnini. Dove il fato ti. *Epig.*, p. 108.
10.74. Obsopoeus. Nec fortuna favens. Obsop., p. 25; Wech., p. 21.
Sabeo. Fac ne te extollat. *Epig.*, p. 93.
Toscano (M.) Nec fortuna opulenta. *Anth.*, p. 22.
Germano. Omnia enim [prose; lines 3–7]. *Giard.*, p. 388.
Germano. Virtus autem [prose; lines 5–7]. *Giard.*, p. 138.
'L-prose.' Neque opulentae. Ἐπ. καὶ Ἐλ. No. 5.
Cunich. Nec tibi fortunae. *Anth.*, p. 86.
Medici (A. de'). Haud extollaris. *Scelt.*, p.v.
Medici (A. de'). L'impeto del desio. *Scelt.*, p.v.

Felici. Non ti sollevi. *Epig.*[1], p. 79.

Passeroni. Aura d'ambizion. *Rime* 3. 230.

10.75. Obsopoeus. Spirantes tenuem vivi. Obsop., p. 189; Wech., 166.

10.76. Sleidan. Ni quis ab immodicis. Soter[2], p. 124; Corn., p. 119.

Cornarius. Vivere cui gratum. Corn., p. 119.

Sabeo. Vivere non gratum est. *Epig.*, p. 424.

Bongiovanni and Zanetti. Cara non è per sè. *Epig.*, p. 42.

Sleidan's version is given in 'Επ. καὶ 'Ελ. (No. 40).

10.78. Sabeo. Ante tuum quam tu. *Epig.*, p. 421.

10.79. 'L-prose.' Nocte recedente. 'Επ. καὶ 'Ελ. No. 48.

Pompei. Di giorno in giorno. *Op.* 2. 175.

Felici. Fugge il tempo. *Epig.*[1], p. 75.

10.80. Costanzi (G.). Vita hominum ludus. *Epig.*, Oiiii[ro].

Anon. Sola hominum vitam. Soter[2], p. 128; Corn., p. 126.

Sleidan. Ludit in humanis rebus. Soter[2], p. 128; Corn., p. 126.

Luscinius. Ludus Fortunae vita. Corn., p. 126.

Conti. Vita hominum ludus. *Myth.* 4. 9.

Sabeo. Vita hominum infelix. *Epig.*, p. 176.

Sabeo. Vita hominum infelix. *Epig.*, p. 482.

Sleidan's tr. is given in 'Επ. καὶ 'Ελ. (No. 41).

Carcani (G.?). Scherzo della Fortuna. *Ant. Ercol.* 6. 92; *Rac.* 1. 415.

Cunich. Vita hominum est ludus. *Anth.*, p. 82.

Pompei. Di guai l'umana vita. *Op.* 2. 173.

Cf. Pagnini. Molte all' uman parere. *Epig.*, p. 56.

10.81. Felici. Vidi in piaggia dilettosa. *Epig.*[1], p. 112.

10.84. Angeriano. Flens veni in terris. 'Ερωτ., Biiii; *C.P.It.* 1. 269.

Rhodiginus. Lachrymans sum natus [prose]. *Lect.* 20. 2.

Alciati. Flens ego sum genitus. Corn., p. 30.

Luscinius. Fundebam lachrymis. Soter[2], p. 33; Corn., p. 30.

Vasolli. Nascentem lachrymae. *Epig.*, f. 10[ro].

Sabeo. Huc lachrymans veni. *Epig.*, p. 705.

Cardano. Lachrymans natus [prose]. *Op.* 1. 590.

Germano quotes the version by Luscinius. *Giard.*, pp. 398, 403.

Felici. Molli d'amare lagrime. *Epig.*[1], p. 73.

10.85. Angeriano. Ut grex porcorum morti. 'Ερωτ., Aiiii.

Bergius. Vivimus heu morti. Soter[2], p. 79; Corn., p. 72.

Obsopoeus. Servamur morti. Obsop., p. 85; Wech., p. 74.

10.88. Bergius. Carcer et infernus. Soter[2], p. 79; Corn., p. 72.

Cf. More. Damnati ac morituri. Soter[2], p. 80.

Alciati. Vita hominum infelix. Corn., p. 73.

Sabeo. Affectus animae corpus. *Epig.*, p. 405.

Gualfreducci. Corpus, crux animi, carcer. *Var.*, p. 287; *Sel. Epig.*, p. 285.

10.90. Cf. 91.

10.91. Cf. 90.

10.93.   Alciati. Fortunam urgentem melius. Corn., p. 18.
Sabeo. Fortunam urgentem est. *Epig.*, p. 32.
'L-prose.' Melius est fortunam. 'Επ. καὶ 'Ελ. No. 13.
Cunich. Praestat fortunae pondus. *Anth.*, p. 65.
Pompei. Meglio è Fortuna. *Op.* 2. 177.
Passeroni. Della sorte soffrir. *Rime* 3. 226.

10.95.   Quoted by Arsenios, *Paroem.*, p. 533.
Erasmus. Equidem virum odi. Soter[2], p. 96.
Valeriano. Nil movet, absenti. *Poem.*, p. 114; *C.P.It.* 10. 161.
Cebà quotes the first two lines, *Theo.*, p. 32.
Germano. Odi virum duplicem [prose]. *Giard.*, p. 333.
Pagnini. L'uom doppio ho in odio. *Epig.*, p. 150.

10.97.   Sabeo. Quum me grammatice. *Epig.*, p. 712.
Crasso. Libram annorum [L-prose]. *Ist.*, p. 397.

10.98.   Alciati. Quum tacet, haud. Corn., p. 118; *Emb.* 11.
Sabeo. Si tacet imprudens. *Epig.*, p. 525.
Mignault. Dum tacet indoctus. Alciati, *Emb.* 11.
Sanchez. Cum tacet indoctus. *Op.* 3. 39.
Cf. Baldi. Taci, chè parrai. *Epig.* 67.
Ricolvi. Indoctus taceat. *Op.*, p. 59.
Ricolvi. Si sileat rudis. *Op.*, p. 60.
Ricolvi. Da saggio fa colui. *Op.*, p. 60.
Cunich. Stultus nil distat. *Anth.*, p. 85.

10.99.   Cornarius. Pondero saepe tuum. Corn., p. 122.
Sabeo. Saepe tuum obprobrium. *Epig.*, p. 424.

10.100.   Obsopoeus. Exigua est omnis. Obsop., p. 291; Wech., p. 261.

10.101.   Cf. *A.P.* 9. 274.

10.102.   Cf. Martialis. Nec volo me summis. *PLM* (Baehr.) 4. 117.
Luscinius. Non me tempestas. Corn., p. 91.
Cornarius. Non mihi saeva maris. Corn., p. 92.
Obsopoeus. Nec nimium saevus me. Obsop., p. 117; Wech., p. 101.
Sabeo. Non mare me exagitet. *Epig.*, p. 412.
'L-prose.' Nec me hyeme pontus. 'Επ. καὶ 'Ελ. No. 34.
Cunich. Nolo mihi nimio. *Anth.*, p. 78.
Passeroni. Non vo', che a suo. *Rime* 3. 165.

10.104.   Sabeo. Salve hera Diva. *Epig.*, p. 118.

10.105.   Cf. *A.P.* 7. 342.
Cf. Horace. Debemur morti nos. *Ars Poet.* 63.
Gaurico. Omnia debentur morti. *Epig.* [2].
Luscinius. Morte mea quidam. Corn., p. 75.
Gualfreducci. Quod iaceo Theodorus. *Var.*, p. 290; *Sel. Epig.*, p. 286.
Bongiovanni and Zanetti. Gode un certo Teodoro. *Epig.*, p. 53.
Cunich. Heic iaceo Theodorus. *Anth.*, p. 107.
Cunich. Mortuus heic Theodorus. *Anth.*, p. 107.
Passeroni. Io Teodoro giaccio qui. *Rime* 3. 244.

Pagnini. Veggio un lieto. *Epig.*, p. 58.

10.106. Cf. Plato, *Phaedo* 69C. [For other occurrences of this proverb see Leutsch and Schneidewin, *Paroem. Graec.* 1. 151.]

Ficino. Narthecophori quidem [prose]. Tr. of *Phaedo.*

Erasmus. Plures thyrsigeros. Soter[2], p. 18.

Sabeo. Tyrsigeri plures, rari. *Epig.*, p. 107.

Cottunius. Multos thyrsigeros. *Confic.*, p. 57.

Erasmus' version is given in 'Επ. καὶ 'Ελ. (No. 6).

10.107. [= Euripides, *frg.* 684 and 1025.]

Quoted by Joannes Lydus, *De Mens.* (Jan.), ed. Wünsch, p. 71.

Sabeo. Fortunatus erit. *Epig.*, p. 126.

Sabeo. Absque Deo nullus. *Epig.*, p. 126.

10.108. Quoted by Plato, *Alcibiades II* (142E); Proclus *in Rem. Pub.*, p. 402; Orion, *Anth.* 5. 17 (Meineke, *Stob.* 4. 257).

Ficino. Juppiter, rex, optima [prose]. tr. of Plato.

More (Sir T.). Da bona, sive rogere. Soter[2], p. 76; Corn., p. 66.

Valeriano. Bonum omne do. *Poem.*, p. 113; *C.P.It.* 10. 157.

Alciati. Sive velint homines. *Op.* 2.1098.

Cordato. Da bona poscenti. *Prael.*, p. 110

Cordato. Precor roganti ac non. *Ibid.*

Sabeo. Da bona supplicibus. *Epig.*, p. 132.

Germano. Rex Iuppiter [prose]. *Giard.*, p. 240.

Averani. Quae bona sunt, nobis. *Op.* 1. 106.

Cunich. Sive rogem, seu non. *Anth.*, p. 74.

Passeroni. Giove, ten prieghi. *Rime* 3. 213.

Pagnini. O ch' io tel chieggia. *Epig.*, p. 89.

10.109. Cornarius. Sermo omnis vanus. Corn., p. 89.

10.110. [= Aristophanes, *Frogs* 1431–3.] Quoted by Plutarch, *Alcib.* 16.2.

Valeriano. Catulum leonis alere. *Poem.*, p. 114; *C.P.It.* 10. 160.

Mignault. Catulum leonis alere. *Emb.* (1621), p. lii.

10.111. Reproduced in an inscr. (Kaibel 1116).

Soter. Lividus ipse domat. Soter[2], p. 133; Corn., p. 130.

Sabeo. Livorem livor. *Epig.*, p. 782.

Cottunius employs Soter's version. *Confic.*, p. 57.

10.112. Cf. the inscr. Balnea vina Venus cor. Buecheler 1499; Soter,[2] p. 81.

Cf. the inscr. Balnea vina Venus fac. Engstrom 148.

Costanzi. (A.). Ah miser inferni. *Epig.*, Biii.

More (Sir T.). Si quis ad infernos. Soter[2], p. 81; Corn., p. 75.

Lily (W.). Nos caligantis rapiunt. Soter[2], p. 81; Corn., p. 75.

Rhodiginus quotes without tr., *Lect.* 28. 35.

Conti. Vina lavacra Venus. *Myth.* 4. 13.

Sabeo. Balnea vina Venus prae. *Epig.*, pp. 43, 405.

Cf. Sabeo. Mortem etiam fraenant. *Epig.*, pp. 43, 405.

Guazzo. Io fui già ricco. *Dial.*, f. 162ᵛᵒ.

Bongiovanni and Zanetti. Il vino, i bagni. *Epig.*, p. 15.

The version by More is given in 'Επ. καὶ 'Ελ. (No. 30).

Cunich. Qui florente aevo. *Anth.*, p. 73.

Felici. Vuoi nella florida. *Epig.*[1], p. 107.

Pagnini. Il vino, i bagni. *Epig.*, p. 4.

10.113. Obsopoeus. Non volo divitias. Obsop., p. 29; Wech., p. 26.

Sabeo. Nolo ego nec precibus. *Epig.*, p. 236.

Ricolvi. Non precor a superis. *Op.*, p. 61.

Ricolvi. Oro da' Dei non chieggo. *Op.*, p. 61.

10.114. Cornarius. Iudicium est Orco. Corn., p. 117.

10.115. 'L-prose.' Vive cum ratione. 'Επ. καὶ 'Ελ. No. 14.

10.116. More (Sir T.). Hoc quisque dicet. Soter[2], p. 38; Corn., p. 36.

Valeriano. Quotquot mariti sunt. *Poem.*, p. 113; *C.P.It.* 10. 156.

Artopoeus. Coniugis infaustos. Soter[3], p. 45.

Sabeo. Quisquis suos patitur. *Epig.*, p. 578.

Baldi. Certo è dire naufragio. *Epig.* 20.

Bongiovanni and Zanetti. Niun di color. *Epig.*, p. 31.

Felici. Se pensi a prendere. *Epig.*[1], p. 100.

Pagnini. Non sa che cosa è. *Epig.*, p. 48.

10.117. Sleidan. Ipsa ego, qui fidum. Soter[2], p. 135; Corn., p. 132.

Obsopoeus. Sum syncerus. Obsop., p. 192; Wech., p. 169.

Sleidan's tr. is given in 'Επ. καὶ 'Ελ. (No. 44).

10.118. Sabeo. Ex his nil peccans. *Epig.*, p. 494.

Sabeo. Qualiter, unde orior. *Epig.*, p. 769.

Redi quotes from this epig., *Op.* 1. 229.

10.119. Costanzi (G.). Corpora multa alere. *Epig.*, Oiiii.

More (Sir T.). Multas aedificare. Soter[2], p. 22; Corn., p. 18.

Lily (W.). Corpora multa alere. Soter[2], p. 22; Corn., p. 19.

Alciati. Aedificare domos. *Op.* 2.1199.

Sabeo. Pascere tot servos. *Epig.*, p. 707.

Cunich. Conde domos multas. *Anth.*, p. 45.

Passeroni. Banchetta, gioca, ama. *Rime* 3. 185.

Pagnini. Far molti pranzi. *Epig.*, p. 79.

10.120. [=Nonnos, *Dionys.* 42.209–10.] *Flor. Monac.* 120 (Meineke, *Stob.* 4. 276).

10.121. Cf. *A.P.* 11. 390.

More (Sir T.). Non aeque nocet hic. Soter[2], p. 96; Corn., p. 86.

Lily (W.). Non is tam laedit. Soter[2], p. 96; Corn., p. 86.

Velius. Non aeque damno est. Soter[2], p. 96; Corn., p. 87.

Obsopoeus. Non sic ille nocet. Obsop., p. 103; Wech., p. 92.

Sabeo. Non tantum nocet hic. *Epig.*, p. 172.

Sabeo. Ille minus laedit. *Epig.*, p. 408.

Lily's tr. is given in 'Επ. καὶ 'Ελ. (No. 33).

10.122. Cf. Claudian. Incubuit nunquam coelestis. Jeep 2. 138; *Carm. Min.* 5. 38.

Sleidan. Multa potest Fortuna. Soter², p. 128; Corn., p. 127.
Averani. Multa potest numen. *Op.* 1. 210.
Sleidan's tr. is given in 'Επ. καὶ 'Ελ. (No. 71).
Cunich. Multa, putes fieri. *Anth.*, p. 53.
Medici (A. de') Multa potest, absurda. *Scelt.*, p. xxiii.
Medici (A. de'). Opra tutto la Sorte. *Scelt.*, p. xxiii.
Pompei. Cose molte, benchè. *Op.* 2. 209.
Passeroni. Può la sorte assai. *Rime* 3. 191.
Felici. Tu fidi a sorte. *Epig.*², p. xxiv.

10.123. Luscinius. Non mihi vita patet. Soter², p. 35; Corn., p. 32.
Sabeo. Quis mortem, o vita. *Epig.*, p. 170.
Cunich. Quirem utinam sine morte. *Anth*, p. 69.
Felici. Oh senza estinguermi. *Epig.*¹, p. 98.

10.124. Luscinius. Sanum nil, pulvis. Soter², p. 36; Corn., p. 32.
Obsopoeus. Omnia sunt risus. Obsop., p. 33; Wech., p. 30.
Valeriano. Omnia sunt risus. *Poem.*, p. 113; *C.P.It.* 10. 157.
Sabeo. Omnia sunt risus. *Epig.*, p. 171.
Sabeo. Pulvere, tum risu. *Epig.*, p. 321.

10.124.* Luscinius. Cura patris niti. Soter², p. 36; Corn., p. 32.
Cordato. Immensi angores. *Prael.*, p. 111.

10.125. Luscinius. Difficilis res est. Corn., p. 133.
Cornarius. Sunt multi, quamvis. Corn., p. 133.
Sabeo. Usque salutatum. *Epig.*, pp. 210, 426.
Cunich. Perfacile est quiddam. *Anth.*, p. 72.
Passeroni. Si trovano gli amici. *Rime* 3. 227.

Book XI

11.1. Sabeo. Sex vini sextas portans. *Epig.*, p. 768.
11.3. Angeriano. Optarem fieri dives. 'Ερωτ., Biiii; *C.P.It.* 1. 268.
Cornarius. Divitias cupii quondam. Corn., p. 218.
Obsopoeus. Sicut erat quondam. Obsop., p. 278; Wech., p. 250.
Sabeo. Dives opum fieri. *Epig.*, p. 787.
Cf. Baldi. Quando io penso fra me. *Epig.* 105.
Averani. Olim opibus volui. *Op.* 1. 88.
Vargas. Ricco qual Creso esser. *Sag.*, p. 74.
11.4. [Not in *Plan.*]
Cf. Ovid. Et cole, quos dederit. *Am.* 3. 4. 45–8.
11.5. Costanzi (G.). Frumentum quicunque domi. *Epig.*, Oiiiiᵛᵒ.
11.7. Sabeo. Nulla potest mulier. *Epig.*, p. 612.
11.8. Found also on a tomb near Rome (Kaibel 646b); cf. inscr. from Cos (Geffcken 209).
More (Sir T.). Serta, unguenta, meo. Soter², p. 185; Corn., 216.
Obsopoeus. Marmoreas statuas. Obsop., p. 279; Wech. p. 251.
Sabeo. Ne date marmoreis. *Epig.*, p. 463.
Sabeo. Si donare cupis. *Epig.*, p. 463.

11.9.   Velius. Ne cum fastidit. Soter², p. 185; Corn., p. 217.
        Obsopoeus. Nam neque demissis. Obsop., p. 279; Wech.,
            p. 251.
        Sabeo. Ne mi iterum. *Epig.*, p. 244.
        Cunich. Pinguis ne saturo. *Anth.*, p. 157.
11.10. Obsopoeus. Prandioli nostri leges. Obsop., p. 292; Wech.,
            p. 262.
11.11. [Not in *Plan.*]
        Cf. Martial. Omnia cum retro pueris. *Epig.* 3. 23.
11.13. Gualfreducci. Aurora Aurorae succedit. *Var.*, p. 290; *Sel.
        Epig.*, p. 286.
        Cunich. Lux lucem trudit. *Anth.*, p. 75.
11.14. Sabeo. Ductus heri ad coenam. *Epig.*, p. 789.
11.15. Sabeo. Si lacerare omnem. *Epig.*, p. 404.
11.17. Cf. 358.
11.19. Bucoldus. Sis laetus, bibe. Soter², p. 186; Corn., p. 217.
        Obsopoeus. Et bibe, Democrates. Obsop., p. 280; Wech.,
            p. 253.
        Dazzi. Oblectare, bibe, fugit. *Poem.*, p. 118.
        Sabeo. Ebibe et exulta. *Epig.*, p. 789.
11.20. Obsopoeus. Quae canis et loccas. Obsop., p. 280; Wech.,
            p. 253.
11.22. Sabeo. Est draco formosus. *Epig.*, p. 419.
11.23. Sleidan. Me brevis esse ferunt. Soter², p. 194; Corn., p. 225.
        Cannius. Me cita fata manent. Corn., p. 226.
        Obsopoeus. Victurum astrologi modico. Obsop., p. 292;
            Wech., p. 263.
        Sabeo. Mi breve vivendi. *Epig.*, p. 245.
        Guazzo. Poi che m'appresso. *Ghirl.*, p. 433.
11.24. Obsopoeus. Saepius o Helicon. Obsop., p. 281; Wech., p. 253.
        Sabeo. Quondam Helicon dederas. *Epig.*, p. 244.
11.25. Obsopoeus. Stertis, amice? vocet. Obsop., p. 281; Wech.,
            p. 253.
        Sabeo. Te vocat et dormis. *Epig.*, p. 789.
11.26. Sabeo. Exagitata mero quis. *Epig.*, p. 53.
        Sabeo. Sum madidus varii. *Epig.*, p. 53.
11.28. Velius. Quinque pedes spatium. Soter², p. 195; Corn, p. 226.
        Sabeo. Quinque pedum terrae. *Epig.*, p. 616.
11.30. [Not in *Plan.*]
        Cf. Ovid. Quae mihi ventura est. *Am.* 3. 7. 17–8.
11.31. Bucoldus. Haud ita Pleïadum. Soter², p. 186; Corn., p. 218.
        Cornarius. Pleïadum occasum, saevas. Corn., p. 218.
        Sabeo. Non tam Pleïadum. *Epig.*, p. 136.
        Sabeo. Pleïadum haud adeo. *Epig.*, p. 479.
        Averani. Non me Pleïadum. *Op.* 1. 163.
11.32. Bucoldus. Musarum memores laetarum. Soter², p. 186; Corn.,
            p. 228.
        Sabeo. Invenit Musam Bacchus. *Epig.*, p. 479.

11.33. Sabeo. Furtim hedera obliquo. *Epig.*, p. 479.
11.34. [Not in *Plan.*]
        Cf. Horace, *Carm.* 1. 38.
        Redi. Annaffia il polmone [line 7]. *Op.* 1. 48.
11.38. Lines 5–6 occur on a gem (*C.I.G.* 7298).
        Velius. Pauperies haec grata. Soter², p. 195; Corn., p. 227.
        Quoted by Landi, *Num.*, p. 31.
11.39. Cf. Martial. Hoc quoque non nihil. *Epig.* 12. 74. 9–10.
        Sabeo. Foemina heri mecum. *Epig.*, p. 685.
11.42. Vargas. Benchè ognor stabil. *Sag.*, p. 19.
11.43. More (Sir T.). E terra genitus, sub. Soter², p. 196; Corn.,
           p. 227.
        Velius. Fictile vas terra. Soter², p. 196; Corn., p. 227.
        Sleidan. Pocula da vini. Soter², p. 196; Corn., p. 227.
        Sabeo. Me genuit tellus. *Epig.*, p. 245.
        Sabeo. Trade laboratum. *Epig.*, p. 754.
        Sabeo. Confectum e terra. *Epig.*, p. 769.
        Landi gives Velius' tr., *Num.*, p. 31.
11.45. Bucoldus. Quem cupis, hic potus. Soter², p. 187; Corn., p. 229.
        Cornarius. Quantum quisque velit. Corn., p. 229.
        Obsopoeus. Sunt sponte exhausti. Obsop., p. 283; Wech.,
           p. 254.
11.46. More (Sir T.). Vespere cum bibimus. Soter², p. 187; Corn.,
           p. 219.
        Cornarius. Est homo blandum animal. Corn., p. 219.
        Pagnini. Siam uomini la sera. *Epig.*, p. 31.
11.47. Cf. 58. Plutarch (*Moral.* 470C) gives v.1; cf. *Anacreont.* 8
           (Preisendanz). In edd. of the Anthol. down to that of
           Estienne (1566) *A.P.* 11.47 formed one piece with 11.48.
        Cf. 'Laberius.' Non mi cupio aurum. Soter², p. 190; Corn.,
           p. 222.
        More (Sir. T.). Non est curae mihi. Soter², p. 188; Corn.,
           p. 220.
        Anon. Non cura magnificentum. Soter², p. 189; Corn., p. 221.
        Alciati. Haud curo Gygis aurum. Corn., p. 223.
        Scaliger (J.C.). Tecum mihi quid, o Mars. *Poem.* 1. 150.
        Rogati. Gige, un dì signor. *Odes d'An.*, p. 27.
11.48. [=*Anacr.* 4 (Preisendanz)]. Quoted by Gellius, *N.A.* 19. 9. 6.
        Gaza. Argentum tornans, fabrica. *Gellius* (1489), Rii^vo.
        Arco (N. d'). Ne mihi Pleiades pingas. *Num.*, p. 234.
        Tolomei. Non mi far, O Vulcan. *Giorn. Stor.* 20 (1892). 404.
        Raius. Nunc torno facili. *C.P.It.* 8. 52.
        Rogati. Tu, che in argento. *Odes d'An.*, p. 29.
11.49. Velius. Sumere nec nimium. Soter², p. 196; Corn., p. 227.
        Luscinius. Vina nocent, nimium. Corn., p. 228.
        Sabeo. Optima mensura est. *Epig.*, p. 53.
        Mignault. Nec minor esto modus. Alciati, *Emb.* 25.
        Mignault. Nec nimio sed nec. Alciati, *Emb.* 25.

11.50. Costanzi (A.). Apprime is felix qui. *Epig.*, Biii[ro].
More (Sir T.). Qui capit uxorem. Soter[2], p. 37.
More (Sir T.). Res gravis est uxor. Corn., p. 35.
Erasmus. Altera connubium experto. Soter[2], p. 37; Corn., p. 35.
Alciati. Est felix qui non. Corn., p. 35.
Luscinius. Ille mihi felix primo. Corn., p. 35.
Rhodiginus. Felix primum quidem [prose]. *Lect.* 28. 14.
Sabeo. Cui tria contingunt. *Epig.*, p. 710.
Baldi. È felice primier. *Epig.* 16.
Bongiovanni and Zanetti. Primieramente beato. *Epig.*, p. 17.
Cunich. Ante alios felix. *Anth.*, p. 154.
Passeroni. Una gran contentezza. *Rime* 3. 171.
Pagnini. Felice chi da' debiti. *Epig.*, p. 28.

11.51. Sleidan. Aestas una potest haedum. Soter[2], p. 146; Corn., p. 141.
Luscinius. Horis perge frui. Corn., p. 141.
Obsopoeus. Utere temporibus. Obsop., p. 198; Wech., p. 176.
Valeriano. Utendum est aetate. *Poem.*, p. 113; *C.P.It.* 10. 158.
Sabeo. Cuncta cito florem. *Epig.*, p. 611.

11.52. Anisio. Inache, virgineo puer. *Poem.*, f.91[ro].
Sabeo. Virgineo captus laqueo. *Epig.*, p. 143.

11.53. Angeriano. I, lege nunc florem. 'Ερωτ., Diiii; *C.P.It.* 1. 282.
Luscinius. Arridet rosa quum. Soter[3], p. 162.
Jordanus. Exiguo rutilans. Soter[3], p. 162.
Sabeo. Forma rosas brevis. *Epig.*, p. 663.
Baldi. Passai, fioria la rosa. *Epig.* 95.
'L-prose.' Rosa senescit brevi. 'Επ. καὶ 'Ελ. No. 50.
Cunich. Mane rosam vidi. *Anth.*, p. 71.
Passeroni. Bella sull'alba. *Rime* 3. 220.
Cf. Bettinelli. Vaga fanciulla, O Rosa. *Op.* 22. 102.
Vargas. La rosa ha corta vita. *Sag.*, p. 103.
Pagnini. In verde siepe all'. *Epig.*, p. 178.

11.54. Cf. *Anacr.* 7 (Preisendanz).
Cornarius. Illudat cano liceat. Corn., p. 219.
Obsopoeus. Decrepitum ridet matrum. Obsop., p. 284; Wech., p. 256.
Sabeo. Despicit antiquum. *Epig.*, p. 788.
Alberti. Nisa mi dice, e Clori. *Rim. Piac.*, p. 206.

11.55. Bucoldus. Da potum, ut curas. Soter[2], p. 192; Corn., p. 224.
Obsopoeus. Funde Falerna mihi. Obsop., p. 285; Wech., p. 256.
Sabeo. Vitrea porge mihi. *Epig.*, p. 244.
Sabeo. Ex vitro cyathos. *Epig.*, p. 788.
Sabeo. Inger formosum. *Epig.*, p. 790.

11.56. Obsopoeus. Indulge Baccho, sorbens. Obsop., p. 285; Wech., p. 256.
Sabeo. Quid tu te excrucias. *Epig.*, p. 574.

11.57. Obsopoeus. Canus odorifero. Obsop., p. 286; Wech., p. 256.
11.58. Cf. 47.
        Bucoldus. Non aurum optavi. Soter², p. 193; Corn., p. 224.
        Sabeo. Non aurum, terrae. *Epig.*, pp. 245, 790.
        Sabeo. Non aurum, vestes. *Epig.*, p. 514.
        Redi refers to Bucoldus' tr. *Op.* 1. 202.
11.59. Sabeo. Compotatores hilari. *Epig.*, p. 148.
        Redi quotes from this epig., *Op.* 1. 275.
11.60. Sabeo. Heus servi mensam. *Epig.*, p. 669.
        Redi refers to this epig., *Op.* 1. 281.
        Redi. Scacciamo co' bicchier [line 2]. *Op.* 1. 46.
11.61. Sleidan. Astitit aegroto medicus. Soter², p. 193; Corn., p. 224.
        Velius. Visit heri inclemens. Soter², p. 193; Corn., p. 224.
        Cannius. Venit ad aegrotum. Corn., p. 225.
        Obsopoeus. Hesterna mihi luce. Obsop., p. 288; Wech., p. 258.
        Sabeo. Dirus heri medicus. *Epig.*, p. 208.
        Sabeo. Astitit hesterna. *Epig.*, p. 226.
        Sabeo. Hostilis medicus me. *Epig.*, p. 313.
        Ricolvi. Languenti medicus mihi. *Op.*, p. 84.
        Ricolvi. Jer giacqui infermo. *Op.*, p. 84.
11.62. Cf. Euripides. βροτοῖς ἅπασι κατθανεῖν. *Alcest.* 782.
        Cf. Horace, *Carm.* 1. 11.
        Obsopoeus. Debita fata manent. Obsop., p. 288; Wech.,
           p. 258.
        Sabeo. Debemus morti nos. *Epig.*, p. 478.
        Sabeo. Mors instat cunctis. *Epig.*, p. 505.
        Sabeo. Omnes emorimur. *Epig.*, p. 575.
11.63. Obsopoeus. Vos quibus innocui. Obsop., p. 288; Wech., p. 259.
        Sabeo. Vos quibus innocui. *Epig.*, p. 489.
11.64. Sabeo. Immensos fluctus. *Epig.*, p. 615.
11.66. Cf. Martial. Cum sis ipsa domi. *Epig.* 9. 37.
11.67. Cf. 69.
        Martial. Mammas atque tatas. *Epig.* 1. 100.
        Sabeo. Bis quadringentas messes. *Epig.*, p. 436.
11.68. Martial. Iurat capillos esse. *Epig.* 6. 12.
        More (Sir T.). Tinguis capillos foemina. Soter², p. 154; Corn.,
           p. 154.
        Cornarius. Inficis, o Nicylla. Corn., p. 155.
        Cunich. Te, Nicylla, comas. *Anth.*, p. 55.
        Felici. Sopra il calvi io. *Epig.*¹, p. 56.
        Passeroni. Tinge il crin. *Rime* 3. 218.
        Bertòla. Dicon che il crin. *Poes.* 1. 178.
        Roncalli. Che Cloe si tinga. *Epig.* (1792), p. 17; (1801), p. 40.
        Vargas. V'ha chi dice. *Sag.*, p. 88.
        Pagnini. Che tu tingi le chiome. *Epig.*, p. 57.
11.69. Cf. 67.
        Soter. Canos tinxisset postquam. Soter², p. 154; Corn., p. 155.

11.70. Alciati. Nupsit anus iuveni. Soter[2], p. 154; Corn., p. 155; *Op.* 3. 589.
Velius. Duxit anum iuvenis. Soter[2], p. 154; Corn., p. 155.
Luscinius. Duxit anum iuvenis. Corn., p. 155.
Sabeo. Duxit anum uxorem. *Epig.*, p. 440.

11.71. Sabeo. Nicanoe viguit. *Epig.*, p. 444.
Cunich. Florebat Nice, sed. *Anth.*, p. 43.
Felici. Fioriva il roseo. *Epig.*[1], p. 113.
Passeroni. Fu Nice in fior. *Rime* 3. 190.
Pagnini. Nice fioria; ma. *Epig.*, p. 62.

11.72. Sabeo. Garrula, cana, procax. *Epig.*, p. 441.
Cunich. Cana comam, linguam. *Anth.*, p. 64.

11.75. Sabeo. Quondam habuit bonus. *Epig.*, p. 187.
Sabeo. Optimus hic quondam. *Epig.*, p. 194.
Argoli. Hic in Olympiaca. Graev., *Thes.* p. 322.
Cunich. Clarus Olympiaco. *Anth.*, p. 53.
Pompei. Costui che per Olimpico. *Op.* 2. 206.
Passeroni. Da Giovine avea gli. *Rime* 3. 190.

11.76. Velius. Rostro adeo cum sis. Soter[2], p. 157; Corn., p. 160.
Anselmo. Cum tu sis facie. *Epig.*, Iiiii; *C.P.It.* 1. 306.
Luscinius. Quum foedet vultum. Corn., p. 160.
Alciati. Grype cave ad speculum. Corn., p. 161; *Op.* 4. 399.
Giraldi Cintio. Narcissus liquidis. *Poem.*, p. 195; *C.P.It.* 5. 393.
Sabeo. Tale tenens rostrum. *Epig.*, p. 448.
Baldi. Se tu non vuoi. *Epig.* 662.
Cunich. Insignis rostro ingenti. *Anth.*, p. 58.
Pompei. Avendo ceffo tu. *Op.* 2. 207.
Passeroni. Piramo, O tu, che hai. *Rime* 3. 139.
Roncalli. Se ami te stesso. *Epig.* (1792), p. 7; (1801), p. 37.
Roncalli. Un giorno il bel Narciso. *Epig.* (1801), p. 8.
Bertòla. Tremo, se il guardo. *Poes.* 1. 179.
Felici. Con quella tua piramide. *Epig.*[2], p. xxv.
Bettinelli. Fuggi, fuggi quel ruscello. *Op.* 22. 108.
Pagnini. Fuggi, Piramo, il fonte. *Epig.*, p. 138.

11.77. More (Sir T.). Dux Ithacus, patria. Soter[2], p. 149; Corn., p. 143.
Velius. Iam Laertiadae bis. Soter[2], p. 149; Corn., p. 143.
Valeriano. Post viginti annos. *Poem.*, p. 114; *C.P.It.* 10. 161.
Dazzi. Quattuor incolumem. *Poem.*, p. 119.
Sabeo. Vidit ut in patria. *Epig.*, p. 186.
Cunich. Quatuor errasset lustris. *Anth.*, p. 53.
Passeroni. Tornato a casa Ulisse. *Rime* 3. 192.

11.78. Biscioni. È un vaglio, Apollofana. *Mal. Raq.* (1815) 4. 16.
Salvini quotes this epig., *Disc.* 6. 214.

11.79. Sabeo. Emeritus nupsi pugil. *Epig.*, p. 192.

11.80. Cunich. Hunc pugiles Apin. *Anth.*, p. 158.
Pagnini. Grati locaro i giostrator. *Epig.*, p. 31.

11.81. Castelvetro quotes this epig. on Petr., *Canz.* 3. *Petr.*, p. 69.
Cunich. Quotquot sunt pugilum. *Anth.*, p. 54.
Passeroni. Ho combattuto in molte. *Rime* 3. 191.

11.82. Sabeo. Cadmus in Arcadia. *Epig.*, p. 186.
Sabeo. Ille ego certavi. *Epig.*, p. 427.

11.83. Sabeo. Cursorem iam terra. *Epig.*, p. 180.

11.85. Sabeo. Armatus media Marcus. *Epig.*, p. 185.

11.86. Sabeo. Currat enim aut sedeat. *Epig.*, p. 429.

11.92. Sabeo. Caius heri extremum. *Epig.*, p. 493.

11.95. Luscinius. Dormierat nanus dum. Soter[2], p. 171; Corn., p. 192.
Hermann a Nov. Aq. Exiguum Macrona videns. Soter[2],
p. 171; Corn., p. 192.
Velius. Parvulus aestivo dormivit. Soter[2], p. 171; Corn.,
p. 192.
Sleidan. Pumilio quum forte Macron. Soter[2], p. 171; Corn.,
p. 192.
Sabeo. Sole sub aestivo. *Epig.*, p. 493.
Bongiovanni and Zanetti. Mentre il picciol. *Epig.*, p. 40.
Ricolvi. Mus forte aestivo. *Op.*, p. 79.
Ricolvi. Mentre dormia Macron. *Op.*, p. 79.

11.97. Velius. Urbem aliam Stratoniceo. Soter[2], p. 173; Corn., p. 197.

11.101. Cornarius. In somnis ventum. Corn., p. 197.

11.102. Cf. 308.

11.103. More (Sir T.). Ex atomis Epicurus. Soter[2], p. 172; Corn.,
p. 193.
Obsopoeus. Ex atomis Epicurus. Obsop., p. 250; Wech.,
p. 229.
Sabeo. Concretum ex atomis. *Epig.*, p. 493.
Cf. Baldi. Berenice il figliuol. *Epig.* 892.
Bongiovanni and Zanetti. Scritto lasciò Epicuro. *Epig.*, p. 26.
Cunich. Ex atomis rerum hanc. *Anth.*, p. 158.

11.104. Cf. 392.
Ausonius? Faustulus insidens formicae. *Opus.* 23. 20; Soter[2],
p. 172; Corn., p. 194.
Cornarius. Formicae e tergo. Corn., p. 194.
Sabeo. Deiecit miserum. *Epig.*, p. 188.
Franchini. Tanquam elephante Coton. *Epig.*, p. 64.
Mazzoni quotes the tr. ascribed to Auson. *Difesa*, p. 408.
Bongiovanni and Zanetti. Cavalcando una secca. *Epig.*, p. 32.
Ricolvi. Forte vehebatur formica. *Op.*, p. 80.
Cunich. Formicae impositus. *Anth.*, p. 159.
Felici. Sul tergo asceso. *Epig.*[1], p. 58.

11.105. Cornarius. Eumecum magnum quaerebam. Corn., p. 191.
Cf. Baldi. Tutin che con gli occhiali. *Epig.* 893.

11.106. Obsopoeus. Cheremon tenui. Obsop., p. 251; Wech., p. 230.
Sabeo. Aera sulcabat tenui. *Epig.*, p. 188.

11.107. Alciati. Quum spaciaretur non. Corn., p. 195.

11.110. Cf. Martial. Thaida tam tenuem. *Epig.* 11. 101.

Luscinius. Certarunt quondam minimi. Corn., p. 196.
Obsopoeus. Tres graciles ineunt. Obsop., p. 251; Wech., p. 230.
Sabeo. Tres tenues quondam. *Epig.*, p. 191.
Gualfreducci. Tres dudum exigui. *Var.*, p. 292; *Sel. Epig.*, p. 281.

11.111. More (Sir T.). Ut fugeret miserae. Soter², p. 172; Corn., p. 195.
Luscinius. Pygmaeo est laqueus. Soter², p. 172; Corn., p. 195.
Velius. Quum macer optaret. Soter², p. 172; Corn., p. 195.
Soter. Pendulus esse volens. Soter², p. 173.
Obsopoeus. Invisam Diophon quaerens. Obsop., p. 251; Wech., p. 321.
Sabeo. Frangere colla volens. *Epig.*, p. 350 (352).

11.112. Cornarius. Ipse diem et iubeas. Corn., p. 179.
Carcani. Pria d'ungerti. *Rac.* 2. 71.

11.113. Ausonius. Alcon histerno signum. *Opus.* 19. 81; Soter², p. 164; Corn., p. 175.
Cornarius. Marce, Iovem saxum. Corn., p. 175.
Sabeo. Marcus heri demisit. *Epig.*, p. 456.

11.114. Ausonius. Languenti Marco dixit. *Opus.* 19. 80; Soter², p. 164; Corn., p. 176.
Cornarius. Hermogeni medico astrologus. Corn., p. 176.

11.115. Cornarius. Devovere velis si hostem. Corn., p. 177.
Cunich. Si quis erit, Dionysi. *Anth.*, p. 160.
Carcani (P.). Se un nemico hai. *Ant. Ercol.* 7. 219; *Rac.* 2. 71.

11.116. Cornarius. Amphitrioniaden quondam. Corn., p. 177.
Sabeo. Ad Styga demisit. *Epig.*, p. 456.

11.117. Velius. Ungebat Chrysen Capito. Soter², p. 165; Corn., p. 183.
Valeriano. Curabat Capito vitiatum. *Poem.*, p. 113; *C.P.It.* 10. 567.
Bongiovanni and Zanetti. Il prode Capiton. *Epig.*, p. 11.

11.118. Cornarius. Non lavit Philon medicus. Corn., p. 177.
Bongiovanni and Zanetti. Fedon non mi toccò. *Epig.*, p. 40.
Bongiovanni and Zanetti. Non mi cacciò. *Epig.*, p. 54.
Pagnini. Fidon non m'applicò. *Epig.*, p. 64.

11.119. Cornarius. Strangulet an lavet. Corn., p. 178.
Sabeo. Quam celer est. *Epig.*, p. 459.

11.120. Cornarius. Tendere gibbosum spondet. Corn., p. 178.
Alciati. Quum gibbum cuperet. Corn., p. 178.
Sabeo. Pollicitus quidam. *Epig.*, p. 778.
Bongiovanni and Zanetti. Socle promise un giorno. *Epig.*, p. 51.

11.121. Cornarius. Perdit Acestoriden. Corn., p. 178.
Sabeo. Perdit Acestoridem. *Epig.*, p. 459.

11.122. Cornarius. Quinque lavat, totidem. Corn., p. 179.
Sabeo. Una quinque lavat. *Epig.*, p. 457.
Bongiovanni and Zanetti. Venti malati Alesside. *Epig.*, p. 44.

Cunich. Aegros quinque simul. *Anth.*, p. 64.
Passeroni. Alessi visitò cinque. *Rime* 3. 221.
11.123. Cornarius. Agis Aristagoram lavit. Corn., p. 181.
11.124. Cornarius. Quaeris qui fuimus. Corn., p. 180.
Sabeo. Hospes forte petis. *Epig.*, p. 471.
Cunich. Hospes, quae tumulos. *Anth.*, p. 64.
11.125. Cornarius. Damon vespillo, medicus. Corn., p. 80.
Sabeo. Humani in generis. *Epig.*, p. 492.
Cunich. Fraternum egregii. *Anth.*, p. 44.
Passeroni. Crate chirurgo. *Rime* 3. 132.
Vargas. Il medico Cratea. *Sag.*, p. 88.
Pagnini. Col becchino Damon. *Epig.*, p. 105.
11.127. More (Sir T.). Sunt etiam in Musis. Soter[2], p. 177; Corn., p. 203.
Brixius. Sunt furiae et Musis. Soter[2], p. 177; Corn., p. 203.
Sleidan. Carmina multa facis. Soter[2], p. 177; Corn., p. 203.
Franchini. Sunt etiam in Musis. *Epig.*, p. 26.
Bongiovanni and Zanetti. Sì fra le Muse. *Epig.*, p. 19.
Cunich. Est etiam in Musis. *Anth.*, p. 68.
11.131. Obsopoeus. Deucalioneis non tot. Obsop., p. 261; Wech., p. 237.
Dazzi. Deucalionaeis non tot. *Poem.*, p. 117.
Sabeo. Deucalionis aquis. *Epig.*, p. 207.
Crasso. Neque Deucalionis [L-prose]. *Ist.*, p. 432.
Cunich. Deucalionei non tot. *Anth.*, p. 58.
Pagnini. Non quella che già. *Epig.*, p. 65.
11.132. Velius. Hos odi, quîs nemo. Soter[2], p. 178; Corn., p. 204.
Velius. Odi maxime, Caesar. Soter[2], p. 178; Corn., p. 204.
11.133. Sabeo. Mortuus Eutichides. *Epig.*, p. 207.
Crasso. Mortuus est [L-prose]. *Ist.*, p. 219.
Cunich. Occidit Eutychides. *Anth.*, p. 59.
11.134. Sabeo. Coepimus inter nos. *Epig.*, p. 541.
11.135. Cunich. Ne puerum plora. *Anth.*, p. 59.
11.136. Sabeo. Non sic vulnificum. *Epig.*, p. 183.
11.138. More (Sir T.). Quum mihi grammaticus. Soter[2], p. 156; Corn., p. 158.
Sabeo. Ore solicismum facio. *Epig.*, p. 444.
Cunich. Grammaticum modo si. *Anth.*, p. 56.
Vargas. L'immagin del grammatico. *Sag.*, p. 90.
Pagnini. Quando la mente. *Epig.*, p. 130.
11.139. Sabeo. Grammaticus Zeno. *Epig.*, p. 434.
11.140. Sabeo. Vatibus in coena. *Epig.*, p. 755.
Mazzoni quotes the Gr. *Difesa*, p. 276.
11.141. Martial. Non de vi neque caeda. *Epig.* 6. 19; Soter[2], p. 183; Corn., p. 212.
Cf. Lucian, *Rhet. Praec.* 18.
Erasmus. Succula, bos, et capra. Soter[2], p. 183; Corn., p. 212.
Sabeo. Ipse suem patruum. *Epig.*, p. 391.

Cunich. Sus mihi sublatus. *Anth.*, p. 60.
11.143. Pagnini. Pluto ricusa il passo. *Epig.*, p. 104.
11.145. Cf. *A.P.* 11. 149, 151; 16. 317 and 318.
Ausonius. Rhetoris haec Rufi. *Opus.* 19. 9; Soter[2], p. 184; Corn., p. 213.
Ausonius. Ore pulcro et ore. *Opus.* 19. 10; Soter[2], p. 184; Corn., p. 213.
More (Sir T.). Ipse tacet Sextus. Soter[2], p. 183; Corn., p. 213.
Luscinius. Ecce silet rhetor. Soter[2], p. 183; Corn., p. 213.
Sabeo. Sextus non loquitur. *Epig.*, p. 474.
Sabeo. Marmoris est Sexti. *Epig.*, p. 475.
Sabeo. Icon declamat Sexti. *Epig.*, p. 494.
Sabeo. Sexte, taces, tua. *Epig.*, p. 504.
Cunich. Haec Sexti vivit. *Anth.*, p. 44.
Passeroni. Di Flacco statua. *Rime* 3. 189.
Pananti (F.). Che bel ritratto. *Op.* 2. 109.
Pagnini. Questo è Filonda. *Epig.*, p. 147.
11.146. More (Sir T.). Quinque soloecismis. Soter[2], p. 184; Corn., p. 214.
Cunich. Quinque soloecismos. *Anth.*, p. 48.
11.147. Cunich. Rhetor tam subito. *Anth.*, p. 48.
11.148. Cornarius. Ipse soloecissat. Corn., p. 214.
Sabeo. Ante solycismum fecit. *Epig.*, p. 241.
Fioretti quotes this epig. *Prog.* 3. 371.
11.149. Cf. *A.P.* 11. 145, 151; 16. 317, and 318.
Luscinius. Picte Medon rhetor. Soter[2], p. 184; Corn., p. 216.
11.151. Cf. *A.P.* 11. 145, 149; 16. 317, and 318.
Luscinius. Rhetoris est statua. Soter[2], p. 185; Corn., p. 216.
Valeriano. Haec est imago. *Poem.*, p. 112; *C.P.It.* 10. 153.
Sabeo. Rhetoris haec statua. *Epig.*, p. 243.
Baldi. L'imago di Sigeo. *Epig.* 638.
Cf. Toscano (G.M.). Perspicuos latices. *C.P.It.* 9. 353.
Cunich. Rhetoris es Flacci. *Anth.*, p. 48.
Passeroni. Questa effigie. *Rime* 3. 91.
11.152. Cunich. Paulle, tuum fieri. *Anth.*, p. 48.
Passeroni. Se vuoi, che faccia. *Rime* 3. 189.
Pagnini. Vuoi che a' nostri. *Epig.*, p. 147.
11.153. Cf. Martial. Hunc, quem saepe. *Epig.* 4. 53.
Luscinius. Sis liceat Cynicus. Corn., p. 239.
Alciati. Esse quidem Cynicum. Corn., p. 239.
Sabeo. Te penitus cynicum. *Epig.*, p. 246.
Sabeo. Obque pedes nudos. *Epig.*, p. 792.
Cunich. Te fateor cynicum. *Anth.*, p. 57.
11.154. Alciati. Hermodoti hoc dogma [vv. 5–6]. *Op.* 2.1219.
Sabeo. Qui sine litterulis. *Epig.*, p. 208.
Carcani (P.). Chi povero e ignorante. *Ant. Ercol.* 7. 234.
Cunich. Qui rudis est pauperque. *Anth.*, p. 56.
11.155. Cf. Martial. Cum depilatos. Chreste. *Epig.* 9. 27.

11.156. Sleidan. Credis, quod barba. Soter[2], p. 201; Corn., p. 240.
Cornarius. Quum barbam credas. Corn., p. 240.
Cannius. Unde malum, credis. Corn., p. 240.
Sabeo. Artificem mentis barbam. *Epig.*, p. 438.

11.158. Crasso. Luget pera et [L-prose]. *Ist.*, p. 158.

11.159. More (Sir T.). Saepe patri frater. Soter[2], p. 150; Corn., p. 148.
Sleidan. Vitalem fore dixerunt. Soter[2], p. 150; Corn., p. 149.
Luscinius. Ore patri vates. Corn., p. 149.
Dazzi. Uno omnes fratrem. *Poem.*, p. 125.
Sabeo. Ore uno astrologi. *Epig.*, p. 431.
Bongiovanni and Zanetti. Predisser gl'indovini. *Epig.*, p. 20.
Cunich. Patri saepe meo. *Anth.*, p. 55.
Passeroni. Quanti Astrologhi celebri. *Rime* 3. 166.
Pagnini. Al mio germano una. *Epig.*, p. 158.

11.160. Sabeo. Disponunt quicunque. *Epig.*, p. 386.
Cunich. Quid Mars, quidve. *Anth.*, p. 55.

11.161. More (Sir T.). Nesimus ecce pugil. Soter[2], p. 150; Corn., p. 149.

11.162. Luscinius. A vate explorat quidam. Corn., p. 152.
Sabeo. An peteret Rhodon. *Epig.*, p. 436.
Cunich. Anne Rhodum tuto. *Anth.*, p. 65.
Passeroni. Un nocchier, che. *Rime* 3. 224.

11.163. Ausonius. Doctus Hylas caestu. *Opus.* 19. 95; Soter[2], p. 151; Corn., p. 149.
Cornarius. Nesimus arte pugil. Corn., p. 150.
Sabeo. Ad vatem luctator. *Epig.*, p. 499.
Bongiovanni and Zanetti. Giro ad Olimpo. *Epig.*, p. 33.

11.164. Cf. Beroaldo (younger). In caput astrologus. *Carm.*, R ii.

11.165. [In old edd. of Stobaeus, *Flor.* 10.]
Sabeo. Argentum atque aurum. *Epig.*, p. 482.
Franchini. Endymion stomacho dum. *Epig.*, p. 20.

11.166. Cf. 294. [In old edd. of Stobaeus, *Flor.* 10.]
More (Sir T.). Te ditem appellant. Soter[2], p. 197; Corn., p. 230.
Obsopoeus. Dives opum cunctis. Obsop., p. 297; Wech., p. 268.
Dazzi. Sis dives licet. *Poem.*, p. 121.
Sabeo. Dives es, ut dicunt. *Epig.*, p. 482.
Baldi. Molti te dicon ricco. *Epig.* 107.
Cf. Baldi. Per lasciar ricchi. *Epig.* 91.
Germano quotes More's version. *Giard.*, p. 308.
Bongiovanni and Zanetti. Che tu sia ricco. *Epig.*, p. 32.
More's version is included in 'Επ. καὶ 'Ελ. (No. 61).
Rolli. Ha ricchezze! E che. *Poet. Comp.* 2. 177.

11.167. Cf. 173. [In old edd. of Stobaeus, *Flor.* 10.]
Luscinius. Ampla tibi res est. Corn., p. 231.
Valeriano. Tam dives auri, disce. *Poem.*, p. 114; *C.P.It.* 10. 162.

Sabeo. Aes retinens cur. *Epig.*, p. 437.
11.168. [In old edd. of Stobaeus, *Flor.* 10.]
Sleidan. Tempore crescit usura. Soter², p. 198; Corn., p. 231.
Sabeo. Tempus et usuram. *Epig.*, p. 485.
Sabeo. Quid velut aes. *Epig.*, p. 487.
11.169. [In old edd. of Stobaeus, *Flor.* 10.]
Luscinius. Dinarchus laqueo vitam. Corn., p. 231.
Dazzi. Guttur heri laqueo. *Poem.*, p. 121.
Sabeo. Se voluit Demarchus. *Epig.*, p. 491.
Guicciardini. Dinarco Fidone [prose]. *Det.*, f. 105ᵛº.
Roncalli. Rosmondo, a cui. *Epig.* (1801), p. 10.
11.170. [In old edd. of Stobaeus, *Flor.* 10.]
More (Sir T.). Chrysalus heu moritur. Soter², p. 198; Corn.,
p. 233.
Toscano (M.). Flet Phidon iamiam. *Anth.*, p. 106.
Cf. Loredano. Sen giace qui tra. *Cimit.* 1. 1 (p. 7).
Bongiovanni and Zanetti. Non già perchè. *Epig.*, p. 56.
Roncalli. Sta chiusa qui. *Epig.* (1801), p. 54.
11.171. Cf. Martial. Quadrantem Crispus. *Epig.* 5. 32.
[In old edd. of Stobaeus, *Flor.* 10.]
Alciati. Hermocrates moriens tabulas. Corn., p. 237.
Sabeo. Hermocrates moriens. *Epig.*, p. 246.
Cf. Scaliger (J.C.). Illuvie, diraque fame. *Poem.* 1. 151.
Guicciardini. Et Hermocrate fu [prose]. *Det.*, f. 105ᵛº.
Toscano (M.). Hermocrates moriens heredem. *Anth.*, p. 107.
Bongiovanni and Zanetti. Già vicino a spirar. *Epig.*, p. 25.
11.172. [In old edd. of Stobaeus, *Flor.* 10.]
Cornarius. Immersit pelago natum. Corn., p. 238.
Cebà. Cert'Aulo, che [prose]. *Theo.*, p. 157.
Pagnini. Aulo spilorcio in mare. *Epig.*, p. 152.
11.173. Cf. 167. [In old edd. of Stobaeus, *Flor.* 10.]
Cornarius. Tradis ad usuram. Corn., p. 238.
11.174. Cornarius. Egressa ex ponto Venus. Corn., p. 188.
11.176. Cicero quotes the proverb in line 5. *Ad Fam.* 9. 7.
Cf. Martial. Fur notae nimium. *Epig.* 6. 72.
Alciati. Alas ferentem Hermem. *Op.* 4.477.
Cunich. Hermam, pennipedem. *Anth.*, p. 62.
Pagnini. Un bel Mercurio. *Epig.*, p. 35.
11.178. Cf. *A.P.* 9. 715.
Sabeo. Longe hinc pasce boves. *Epig.*, p. 691.
Cunich. Pasce, bubulce, boves. *Anth.*, p. 61.
Passeroni. Va via di quà, bifolco. *Rime* 3. 93.
Pagnini. Su via di qua lontano. *Epig.*, p. 36.
11.179. Cf. *A.P.* 12. 75.
Cornarius. Si pedibus quantum. Corn., p. 188.
Luscinius. Interpres superum cedet. Corn., p. 188.
Baldi. S' avesse presto il pie'. *Epig.* 676.
Bongiovanni and Zanetti. Se i piei Dion. *Epig.*, p. 34.

11.181. Luscinius. Vidimus in bello te. Corn., p. 189.
Cornarius. Notus eras inter. Corn., p. 189.
Alciati. In bellis qui notus. *Op.* 4.473.
11.184. Cornarius. Ex horto Hesperidum. Corn., p. 189.
Bongiovanni and Zanetti. Menisco già tre. *Epig.*, p. 34.
Cunich. Hesperidum e templo. *Anth.*, p. 61.
Felici. Nel tempio delle Esperidi. *Epig.*², p. xxv.
Pagnini. Dell' Esperidi al tempio. *Epig.*, p. 36.
11.186. Prodromus quotes this ep., *Not. et Extr. Bibl. Nat.* 6. 552.
Sleidan. Nycticorax mortem cantu. Soter², p. 168; Corn., p.186.
Cornarius. Infaustum et lethale. Corn., p. 186.
Dazzi. Nycticorax laethale canit. *Poem.*, p. 117.
Sabeo. Noctua triste canens. *Epig.*, p. 492.
Cunich. Nycticorax ferale canit. *Anth.*, p. 59.
Pompei. La notturna civetta. *Op.* 2. 193.
Passeroni. La morte annunzia. *Rime* 3. 150.
11.187. Sleidan. Nocte canens tota. Soter², p. 168; Corn., p. 187.
Luscinius. Simylus insomnes vicinos. Corn., p. 187.
Dazzi. Nocte canens tota. *Poem.*, p. 117.
Sabeo. Occidit cantor vicinos. *Epig.*, p. 461.
Cunich. Tota nocte canens. *Anth.*, p. 59.
Passeroni. Macrino fortunato. *Rime* 3. 150.
Pagnini. Similo ha tutto ucciso. *Epig.*, p. 84.
11.188. Cornarius. Nicetas si quando. Corn., p. 187.
Crasso. Nicetas canens [L-prose]. *Ist.*, p. 362.
Pagnini. Niceta un vero Apollo. *Epig.*, p. 103.
Pagnini. Tu d'Apollo pareggi. *Epig.*, p. 17.
11.189. Sabeo. Stabant ante Iovem. *Epig.*, p. 472.
11.190. Soter. Hermogenem frustra. Soter², p. 169; Corn., p. 189.
Soter. Hermogenem tonsor. Soter², p. 169.
Cornarius. Hermogeni tonsor caput. Corn., p. 189.
Cunich. Tonderi Hermogenes. *Anth.*, p. 58.
Felici. Il capo Ermogene. *Epig.*¹, p. 59.
Passeroni. Rader dovendo a Ermogene. *Rime* 3. 137.
Pagnini. Cerca il barbiere invan. *Epig.*, p. 164.
11.191. Cf. Martial. Qui nondum Stygias. *Epig.* 11. 84.
Sabeo. O Mars, Mars, et non. *Epig.*, p. 839.
11.192. Luscinius. Pendere ut socium. Corn., p. 239.
Obsopoeus. Cum magis excelsa. Obsop., p. 309; Wech., p. 272.
Sabeo. Pendentem maiore. *Epig.*, p. 784.
Sabeo. Longior alterius quod. *Epig.*, p. 807.
Ricolvi. Alterius Diophon moriturus. *Op.*, p. 60.
Cunich. In cruce maiori. *Anth.*, p. 63.
Passeroni. Vedendo eretta Titiro. *Rime* 3. 219.
Pagnini. Diofon mirando un altro. *Epig.*, p. 68.
11.193. Cf. Isocrates. Τούτων αἴτιος ὁ φϑόνος. *Evag.* 190B; and Philemon,*frg.* 131 (Kock). The epig. occurs in an inscr. (Kaibel 1115).

Anon. *ap*. S. Jerome. Iustius invidia nihil. *PLM* (Baehr.)
  3. 169.
Filelfo. Invidia est quod [prose]. *Epist. Fam.* (above, p. 96).
Costanzi (A.). Haud expers, Mancine. *Epig.*, Biii^vo.
Soter. Pessima res livor. Soter², p. 131; Corn., p. 129.
Luscinius. Invidia quum sit. Corn., p. 129.
Obsopoeus. Grande malum livor. Obsop., p. 190; Wech.,
  p. 168.
Scaphenatus. Pessimus est certe. *Epig.*, Diii.
Alamanni. Invidia ha questo. *Rim. Ined.*, p. 34.
Sabeo. Res bona, tum mala. *Epig.*, p. 210.
Sabeo. Pessimum enim invidia. *Epig.*, p. 210.
Sabeo. Lividulis male cor. *Epig.*, p. 211.
Cardano. Invidia est res [prose]. *Op.* 1. 521.
Guazzo. Giustissima è l'invidia. *Dial.*, f. 161vo.
Soter's version is given in 'Επ. καὶ 'Ελεγ. (No. 42).
Ricolvi. Invidia nil peius. *Op.*, p. 60.
Ricolvi. Pessima cosa è invidia. *Op.*, p. 60.
Cunich. Hoc boni habet. *Anth.*, p. 73.
Felici. De' mali è il massimo. *Epig.*¹, p. 110.
Passeroni. La invidia, che una. *Rime* 3. 212.
Pagnini. Questo solo ha di buono. *Epig.*, p. 83.
11.194. Cornarius. Qui specubus gaudet. Corn., p. 190.
Sabeo. Quae colitis montes. *Epig.*, p. 141.
Angelio. Semicapri Panes et. *Poem.*, p. 387.
Bongiovanni and Zanetti. A Pane abitator. *Epig.*, p. 22.
Cunich. O Pan speluncis. *Anth.*, p. 97.
Felici. O Pan, O Fauni. *Epig.*¹, p. 57.
11.198. Velius. Hermocrates nasi. Soter², p. 159; Corn., p. 162.
Cf. Alciati. Grypi (si nescis). Corn., p. 162.
Dazzi. Castoris haud nasum. *Poem.*, p. 128.
Mazzoni quotes the Gr. and Velius' tr. *Difesa*, p. 59.
Aleander (G.), the younger. Non Diphilus nasum. *Tr. Frat.*,
  p. 278.
Baldi. A te sì vasto è. *Epig.* 845.
Ricolvi. Dic nasi Hermocritem. *Op.*, p. 78.
Cunich. Hermocrates nasi; nam. *Anth.*, p. 68.
Passeroni. Per parlar rettamente. *Rime* 3. 101.
11.199. Cornarius. Cur nunquam Grypus. Corn., p. 163.
Franchini. Mirabar tibi non. *Epig.*, p. 42.
Bongiovanni and Zanetti. L'adunco Sosittolide. *Epig.*, p. 24.
11.200. Alciati. Vicini ardebant aedes. Corn., p. 163.
Sabeo. Quum domus arderet. *Epig.*, p. 449.
Bongiovanni and Zanetti. Ardea per fuoco. *Epig.*, p. 24.
11.201. More (Sir T.). Fugerit ad Parthos. Soter², p. 159; Corn.,
  p. 164.
Cornarius. Si quis apud Parthos. Corn., p. 164.
Sabeo. Si quis apud Parthos. *Epig.*, p. 613.

Bongiovanni and Zanetti. Se a' Parti ignuda. *Epig.*, p. 30.
Pagnini. S'io nuda a Parti. *Epig.*, p. 129.
11.202. Sabeo. Perdidit antiquam Moschus. *Epig.*, p. 433.
Sabeo. Extulit uxorem antiquam. *Epig.*, p. 442.
Cf. Sabeo. Sustuli anum uxorem. *Epig.*, p. 480.
11.203. Velius. Cum fodit, esse solet. Soter[2], p. 158; Corn., p. 161.
Luscinius. Castoris est nasus. Soter[2], p. 158; Corn., p. 161.
Alciati. Anchora navigiis, valido. Corn., p. 162.
Sabeo. Castoris est nasus. *Epig.*, p. 464.
Franchini. Egregius forma Sabii. *Epig.*, p. 60.
Felici. Castore, il naso vostro. *Epig.*[1], p. 114.
11.204. Cf. *A.P.* 16. 20.
Sabeo. Rhetora funestam. *Epig.*, p. 454.
11.205. Sleidan. Eutychides Aulo semper. Soter[2], p. 170; Corn., p. 192.
11.207. Sabeo. Quinque lupi quod edunt. *Epig.*, p. 474.
11.208. Cf. 431.
More (Sir T.). Stare puer stadio. Soter[2], p. 170; Corn., p. 192.
Cornarius. Eutychides tardus cursor. Corn., p. 192.
Obsopoeus. Eutychides tardus cursu. Obsop., p. 247; Wech., p. 226.
Cordato. In stadium Eutichides. *Prael.*, p. 111.
Sabeo. Lentus erat stadium. *Epig.*, p. 474.
Bongiovanni and Zanetti. Lenti Eutichide. *Epig.*, p. 15.
Cunich. In stadio Eutychides. *Anth.*, p. 161.
Passeroni. Se corre al palio. *Rime* 3. 237.
Pagnini. Pigro alla lizza è. *Epig.*, p. 30.
11.209. More (Sir T.). Victor ad Herculeas. Soter[2], p. 182; Corn., p. 211.
Sleidan. Quamvis ad Herculeas. Soter[2], p. 182; Corn., p. 211.
Sabeo. Usque licet Calpen. *Epig.*, p. 798.
Bongiovanni and Zanetti. Se togliendo. *Epig.*, p. 20.
Cunich. Profer agros longe. *Anth.*, p. 75.
Passeroni. Stendi pure i campi. *Rime* 3. 164.
11.210. Quoted by Landi, *Num.*, p. 100.
Cunich. Laurum horret pavido. *Anth.*, p. 57.
11.211. Sabeo. Vidit ut in muro. *Epig.*, p. 447.
Cunich. Navalem miles carbone. *Anth.*, p. 57.
Pompei. Poichè dipinta su. *Op.* 2. 208.
Passeroni. Vedendo un dì dipinta. *Rime* 3. 134.
11.213. More (Sir T.). Haec tua quam nuper. Soter[2], p. 163; Corn., p. 173.
More (Sir T.). Sic te totum isthac. Soter[2], p. 163; Corn., p. 173.
Sleidan. Menodoti effigiem. Soter[2], p. 163; Corn., p. 173.
Cornarius. Menodoti effigiem. Corn., p. 173.
Sabeo. Menodotum pingens. *Epig.*, p. 458.
Cunich. Menodotum pinxit. *Anth.*, p. 155.
Passeroni. Di Menodoto già. *Rime* 3. 73.

Pagnini. Pinse Alcon di Menodoto. *Epig.*, p. 118.

11.214. Cf. Martial. Colchida quid scribis. *Epig.* 5. 53; Soter[2], p. 163.
Luscinius. Quaeris Deucalion. Soter[2], p. 163; Corn., p. 173.
Velius. Deucalione tibi et. Soter[2], p. 163; Corn., p. 174.
Cornarius. Pinxisti Phaethonta. Corn., p. 174.
Obsopoeus. Deucalion per te. Obsop., p. 234; Wech., p. 212.
Scaphenatus. Deucaliona tibi et. *Eleg.*, Diiii.
Dazzi. Deucaliona meus pinxit. *Poem.*, p. 116.
Franchini. Ponere conveniat qua. *Epig.*, p. 15.
Marino. Due tavole dipinse. *Gal.* 1. 311.
Bongiovanni and Zanetti. O Menestrato mio. *Epig.*, p. 21.
Cunich. Est tibi Deucalion. *Anth.*, p. 155.
Passeroni. Un per nome Menestrato. *Rime* 3. 72.
Vargas. Menestrato hai dipinto. *Sag.*, p. 89.
Pagnini. Deucalione e Faeton. *Epig.*, p. 32.

11.215. Sleidan. Proles viginti dedit. Soter[2], p. 164; Corn., p. 174.
Pagnini. Un pittor generato ha. *Epig.*, p. 132.

11.216. Cornarius. Qui blandus pueris. Corn., p. 147.
Sabeo. Sectantem pueros. *Epig.*, p. 239.

11.217. Sabeo. Suspitionem ipsam. *Epig.*, p. 429.

11.225. Cf. *A.P.* 12. 210.
Ausonius. Tris uno in lecto. *Opus.* 19. 59.
Sabeo. Lectus habet binos. *Epig.*, p. 755.

11.226. Cf. Martial. Sit tibi terra levis. *Epig.* 9. 29. 11; Corn., p. 207.
Sleidan. Te pulvis tegat. Soter[2], p. 180; Corn., p. 208.
Alciati. Sit tibi terra levis. Corn., p. 207.
Obsopoeus. Sit tibi terra levis. Obsop., p. 269; Wech., p. 242.
Pompei. Lieve la polve sia. *Op.* 2. 204.
Pagnini. Sia lieve a te la terra. *Epig.*, p. 38.
Pagnini. Lieve polve ti copra. *Epig.*, p. 93.

11.227. Sleidan. Lacte culex et melle. Soter[2], p. 180; Corn., p. 208.
Cornarius. Ante culex mihi lac. Corn., p. 208.
Obsopoeus. Lac dabit ante culex. Obsop., p. 269; Wech.,
p. 243.
Bongiovanni and Zanetti. Pria miele il calabron. *Epig.*, p. 34.

11.228. Cornarius. Matrem hic, patrem. Corn., p. 209.
Cf. Giraldi Cintio. Nam quid te mirer. *Poem.*, p. 174.
Bongiovanni and Zanetti. Tal il fratel. *Epig.*, p. 35.
Pagnini. Chi la madre, chi. *Epig.*, p. 165.

11.229. Sabeo. Dignum habuit podagra. *Epig.*, p. 834.
Pompei. Tardi avvien pur. *Op.* 2. 205.
Pagnini. Tardi alfin la podagra. *Epig.*, p. 109.

11.230. Cf. 231.
More (Sir T.). Mastauron elementa tibi. Soter[2], p. 180; Corn.,
p. 208.
Luscinius. Mastauron elementa duo. Soter[2], p. 180; Corn.,
p. 208.

11.231. Cf. 230.

11.232. Pagnini. Semper fosti una bestia. *Epig.*, p. 103.
11.233. Alciati. Acta notans Phaedrus. Soter[2], p. 174; Corn., p. 199;
        Op. 4. 252.
11.234. Sabeo. Si validus plantis. *Epig.*, p. 778.
11.235. Cf. 236.
        Cf. Phocylides *ap.* Strabo 10. 484; (Diehl. 1).
        Cornarius. Demodocus, Chii pravi. Corn., p. 209.
        Valeriano. Hoc quoque Demodoci. *Poem.*, p.114; *C.P.It.* 10.
        160.
        Valeriano. Hoc quoque Phocylidae. *Ibid.*
        Scaliger (J.C.) refers to this epig. *Poet.* 3. 125.
11.236. Cf. 235.
11.237. Cf. *A.P.* 9. 379.
        Cf. C. Manasses. ἔχιδνα γάρ τοι. *Erot.* 4. 72.
        Constantine Porph. quotes this epig. *Themat.* 1. 11 (Bekker,
        p. 2).
        More (Sir T.). Vipera Cappadocen. Soter[2], p. 180; Corn.,
        p. 209.
        Cornarius. Cappadocem morsu confecit. Corn., p. 209.
        Sabeo. Vipera Capadocem iam. *Epig.*, p. 789.
        Scaliger (J.C.). Vipera Tartareum Ligurem. *Poem.* 1. 172.
        Guazzo. De la vipera morso. *Ghirl.*, p. 483.
        Baldi. Aspron, se ti pungesse. *Epig.* 637.
        Salvini. Vipera Cappadocem. Wellesley, *Anth. Pol.* p. 397.
        Cunich. Cappadocem pupugit. *Anth.*, p. 52.
        Pompei. A un Cappadoce un dì. *Op.* 2. 212.
        Passeroni. Morso fu già un Capadoce. *Rime* 3. 93.
        Cf. Pagnini. Tre *Ci* maledettissimi. *Epig.*, p. 92.
        Pananti. Una vipera a Luca. *Ep. Mod. Aut.*, p. 30.
11.238. Quoted by Joannes Lydus, *De Mag.* 3. 57; and by Constantine
        Porph., *Themat.* 1. 11 (Bekker, p. 21).
11.239. Cf. Martial. Tam male Thais olet. *Epig.* 6. 93; Soter[2], p. 161.
        Pio. Maeonides non tale. Soter[2], p. 161; Corn., p. 171.
        Hermann a Nov. Aq. Tale Chimaera malum. Soter[2], p. 161;
        Corn., p. 171.
        Sabeo. Non ita Meonides foedum. *Epig.*, p. 613.
11.240. Sabeo. Non solum male olet. *Epig.*, p. 613.
        Pagnini. Non sol fetente è. *Epig.*, p. 128.
11.241. Cf. 242 and 415. Cf. Catullus 97.
        Sabeo. Pessime oles anima. *Epig.*, p. 485.
11.242. Cf. 241 and 415.
11.244. Alciati. Aeratum emisti miliarion. Soter[2], p. 174; Corn.,
        p. 198; *Op.* 4. 257.
        Sabeo. Ex aere emisti miliarion. *Epig.*, p. 476.
11.245. Cornarius. En paries Diophante. Corn., p. 206.
        Sabeo. Suscipit omne latus. *Epig.*, p. 797.
11.246. Cf. 247.
        Sabeo. Ex quibus, o saxis. *Epig.*, p. 785.

Sabeo. Qui cupit absque. *Epig.*, p. 786.
11.247. Cf. 246.
Sabeo. Nos mare sulcamus. *Epig.*, p. 240.
11.248. Sabeo. Non absumpta salo. *Epig.*, p. 798.
11.249. Cf. Martial. Donasti, Lupe, rus. *Epig.* 11. 18.
Cf. Anon. Fundum Varro vocat. Burmann, *Anth. Lat.* 3. 56.
Sabeo. Agrum Menophanes. *Epig.*, p. 215.
Cunich. Menophanis tam parvus. *Anth.*, p. 159.
11.250. Luscinius. Erratur dum mole. Corn., p. 202.
Cornarius. Pinxisti pinguem bene. Corn., p. 202.
Sabeo. Effinxit pinguem. *Epig.*, p. 604.
Cunich. Tam bene qui Crassum. *Anth*, p. 44.
Pompei. Ben del pingue uomo. *Op.* 2. 225.
Passeroni. Pera il pittore. *Rime* 3. 133.
Roncalli. Pera il pittore. *Epig.* (1792), p. 69; (1801), p. 57.
Pagnini. Pera il pittor con. *Epig.*, p. 127.
11.251. Apostolios quotes part of line 1 (*Paroem.* 6. 39).
More (Sir T.). Lis agitur surdusque. Soter[2], p. 169; Corn.,
    p. 191.
Luscinius. In ius forte trahit. Soter[2], p. 170; Corn,. p. 191.
Alciati. Certabat surdo surdus. Corn., p. 191.
Obsopoeus. Accusans surdus surdo. Obsop., p. 246; Wech.,
    p. 225.
Rapitius. Aspice quas cieant. *Facil.*, f. 13ro.
Sabeo. Tres fuerant surdi. *Epig.*, p. 475.
Patavinus gives More's tr. *De Art.*, p. 275.
Casalicchio quotes and paraphrases More's tr. *Utile*, p. 305.
Bongiovanni and Zanetti. Quistionavan due. *Epig.*, p. 29.
Cunich. Intendit litem surdo. *Anth.*, p. 162.
11.252. Alamanni. Tu m'hai in odio. *Versi* 2. 137.
Sabeo. Oscula si mihi das. *Epig.*, p. 451.
11.253. Cf. 254–5.
Velius. Nam quo te genitor. Soter[2], p. 175; Corn., p. 200.
Sabeo. Qua pater e quercu. *Epig.*, p. 390.
Cunich. Quanam te genitor. *Anth.*, p. 61.
11.254. Cf. 253 and 255.
Ausonius. Deceptae, felix casus. *Opus.* 19. 18.
Ausonius? Deceptae felix casus. *Opus.* 23. 36; Soter[2], p. 176;
    Corn., p. 201.
More (Sir T.). Caetera ad historiam. Soter[2], p. 176; Corn.,
    p. 201.
Hermann a Nov. Aq. Omnia perbelle dum. Soter[2], p. 176;
    Corn., p. 201.
Luscinius. Prodieras apte in. Corn., p. 201.
Valeriano. Omnia, ut historia. *Poem.*, p. 114; *C.P.It.* 10. 161.
Sabeo. Omnia ad historiam. *Epig.*, p. 189.
Ferrari (O.). Omnia iuxta [prose]. Sallengre, *Thes.* 2. 686.
Cunich. Omnia ad historiam. *Anth.*, p. 60.

Bertòla. Ruggi, muggi, urli. *Poes.* 1. 180.
11.255. Cf. 253–4.
Ausonius? Daphnen et Nioben. *Opus.* 23. 31; Soter[2], p. 177; Corn., p. 202.
More (Sir T.). Saltavit Nioben. Soter[2], p. 177; Corn., p. 202.
Sabeo. Memphis enim simus. *Epig.*, p. 303.
Cunich. Daphnenque et Nioben. *Anth.*, p. 68.
Passeroni. Niobe e Dafni. *Rime* 3. 227.
Bettinelli. Niobe e Dafne mi. *Op.* 22. 97.
Vargas. Con quel viso rincagnato. *Sag.*, p. 89.
Pagnini. Tu Dafne e Niobe. *Epig.*, p. 95.
11.256. Alciati. Tempore te dicunt. Soter[2], p. 155; Corn., p. 156.
Sabeo. Centum anni tibi. *Epig.*, p. 480.
11.257. Cf. Martial. Lotus nobiscum est. *Epig.* 6. 53; Soter[2], p. 166; Corn. p. 184.
Cornarius. Hermogenem in somnis. Corn., p. 184.
Sabeo. Mecum hilaris lotus. *Epig.*, p. 468.
Cunich. Hermogeni medico dixit. *Anth.*, p. 62.
Cf. Mariani. Morì improvviso. De-Mauri, p. 184.
11.258. Cunich. Hunc pugil haec. *Anth.*, p. 97.
Passeroni. Giove Olimpio, Aulo. *Rime* 3. 143.
11.259. Luscinius. Est fateor tibi nunc. Corn., p. 186.
Sabeo. Aemonium tu pascis. *Epig.*, p. 472.
Argoli. Thessalus est tibi. Graev., *Thes.* 9. 262.
Bongiovanni and Zanetti. Erasistrato mio. *Epig.*, p. 3.
Cunich. Thessalus est equus. *Anth.*, p. 161.
11.260. Soter gives Gr. without tr. (Soter[2], p. 162).
Cornarius. Hoc tibi iam vetus. Corn., p. 173.
11.263. Cornarius. Comedo insomnis dixit. Corn., p. 190.
11.264. Cf. 366. [In old edd. of Stobaeus, *Flor.* 10.]
Luscinius. Apparat in somnis. Soter[2], p. 200; Corn., p. 236.
Obsopoeus. Sordidus in somnis. Obsop., p. 301; Wech., p. 271.
Guicciardini. Hermone fu tanto [prose]. *Det.* f. 105vo.
Toscano (M.). Tantillum sumptum. *Anth.*, p. 109.
Baldi. Sognando Ermon. *Epig.* 904.
Bongiovanni and Zanetti. Sognò l'avaro. *Epig.*, p. 32.
Pagnini. Sogna l'avara Egon. *Epig.*, p. 80.
Roncalli. Mentre l'avara Albino. *Epig.* (1801), p. 3.
11.265. Obsopoeus. Si contra brucos. Obsop., p. 253; Wech., p. 231.
Sabeo. Si bellum indictum. *Epig.*, p. 196.
Cunich. Si contra bruchos. *Anth.*, p. 44.
Passeroni. Se si trattasse mai. *Rime* 3. 90.
11.266. Ausonius? *De Demosthenide* [epig. missing]. *Opus.* 23. 26.
More (Sir T.). Te speculum fallit. Soter[2], p. 159; Corn., p. 164.
Anselmo. Maenia nimis mendax. *Epig.*, Giiii; *C.P.It.* 1. 304.
Cornarius. Mendaci speculo. Corn., p. 164.

Bongiovanni and Zanetti. Demostenide mia. *Epig.*, p. 30.
Cunich. Falsa videt Nice. *Anth.*, p. 58.
Pompei. Demostenide specchio. *Op.* 2. 207.
Passeroni. Nice lo specchio tuo. *Rime* 3. 135.
Pagnini. Se il cristallo. *Epig.*, p. 119.
11.267. Cornarius. Non opus est radio. Corn., p. 164.
11.268. More (Sir T.). Nunquam, Procle, manu. Soter², p. 159; Corn., p. 164.
Alciati. Non potis est Grypus. Corn., p. 165.
Cornarius. Posse Proclum manibus. Corn., p. 165.
Obsopoeus. Non dextra Proclus. Wech., p. 204.
Sabeo. Haud Procrus dextra. *Epig.*, p. 470.
Bongiovanni and Zanetti. Poi che ha del. *Epig.*, p. 25.
Ricolvi. Nec tu, Procle, potes. *Op.*, p. 79.
Ricolvi. Proclo, tanto il tuo. *Op.*, p. 79.
Cunich. Nec dextra Proclus. *Anth.*, p. 151.
Pompei. Il naso con la man. *Op.* 2. 204.
Passeroni. Non si può forbire. *Rime* 3 .163.
Pagnini. Proclo soffiarsi il naso. *Epig.*, p. 31.
11.269. Cf. inscr. from Pompei, Kaibel 1138.
11.270. Quoted by Joannes Lydus, *De Mag.* 3. 46.
More (Sir T.). Effigiem statuere tibi. Soter², p. 200; Corn., p. 236.
Sabeo. Ex ferro hanc statuam. *Epig.*, p. 207.
Cunich. Haec tibi, rex orbis. *Anth.*, p. 46.
Passeroni. Altri di bronzo. *Rime* 3. 186.
Pagnini. Questa, O re, ferrea. *Epig.*, p. 84.
11.271. Sabeo. Iuxta difficilem. *Epig.*, p. 208.
11.272. Alciati. Neutrius est sexus. Corn., p. 147.
Sabeo. Non mas est pathicus. *Epig.*, p. 810.
Sabeo. Immo est vir pathicus. *Epig.*, p. 810.
11.273. Costanzi (G.). Mente nihil minus es. *Epig.*, Oiiiiᵛᵒ.
More (Sir T.). Clauda tibi mens est. Soter², p. 203; Corn., p. 243.
Lily (W.). Tardus es ingenio. Soter², p. 203; Corn., p. 243.
Sleidan. Ut pes, sic animus. Soter², p. 203; Corn., p. 244.
Cf. Anselmo. Mens levis, Hele. *Epig.*, Niiii.
Alciati. Claudus es, atque immo. Corn., p. 243.
Vasolli. Claudus es atque immo. *Epig.*, f. 11ᵛᵒ (above, p. 209).
Vasolli. Ut pes, sic animus. *Ibid.* (above, p. 209).
Vasolli. Pectore ceu gressu certum. *Epig.*, f. 11ᵛᵒ.
Obsopoeus. Ut pede, sic animus. Wech., p. 276.
Sabeo. Clauda tibi mens est. *Epig.*, p. 502.
Pagnini. Torta hai la mente. *Epig.*, p. 14.
11.274. Cunich. Dic mihi, si fas. *Anth.*, p. 54.
Passeroni. Dimmi, Mercurio, il ver. *Rime* 3. 193.
Pagnini. Dì, se ti piace. *Epig.*, p. 147.

11.275. Lascaris (J.) alludes to this epig., Above, p. 116, n. 1.
Crinitus quotes this epig. Above, p. 146, n. 4.
Alciati. Callimachus lustri. *Op.* 4.526.
Sabeo. Callimachi crimen. *Epig.*, p. 193.
11.276. Obsopoeus. Dum piger obscuro. Obsop., p. 258; Wech., p. 234.
Sabeo. Carcere conclusum. *Epig.*, p. 782.
Bongiovanni and Zanetti. Marco, lo scioperato. *Epig.*, p. 27.
Pagnini. Marco, celebre poltrone. *Epig.*, p. 64.
11.277. Luscinius. In somnis currens. Soter², p. 175; Corn., p. 199.
Velius. Nocte fatigatus cursu. Soter², p. 175; Corn., p. 199
Obsopoeus. Non ultra dormit Marcus. Obsop., p. 258; Wech.,
p. 234.
Bongiovanni and Zanetti. Sognò di notte. *Epig.*, p. 27.
Ricolvi. Marce piger, ficto. *Op.*, 80.
Ricolvi. Marco sogna che corre. *Op.*, p. 80.
Cunich. Quod piger in somno. *Anth.*, p. 62.
Passeroni. Sognò Fabio di correre. *Rime* 3. 219.
11.278. Soter. Extra doces mala tu. Soter², p. 157.
Anselmo. Cur Paridis damnas. *Epig.* Iiiii.
Cornarius. Rufe, docet Paridis. Corn., p. 159.
Alciati. Extra Helenam Iliacique. Corn., p. 159.
Sabeo. Tu Paridis mala. *Epig.*, p. 488.
Franchini. Per fora facta doces. *Epig.*, p. 31.
Pagnini. Tu fuori esponi. *Epig.*, p. 158.
11.279. Ausonius? Felix grammaticus non. *Opus.* 23.15; Soter²,
p. 157; Corn., p. 159.
Cornarius. Grammaticus tandem. Corn., p. 158.
11.280. Luscinius. Iudicium melius fuerit. Soter², p. 166; Corn., p. 184.
Cornarius. Ipse velim potius. Corn., p. 184.
11.281. Luscinius. Quum Magnus Stygii. Corn., p. 80.
Cornarius. Orcum Magnus adit. Corn., p. 80.
Gualfreducci. Magnus ubi ad manes. *Var.*, p. 287; *Sel. Epig.*,
p. 288.
Bongiovanni and Zanetti. Quando Magno discese. *Epig.*,
p. 10.
Cunich. Ad Styga quum vidit. *Anth.*, p. 34.
Passeroni. Appena il re dell'. *Rime* 3. 182.
Pagnini. Quando Magno discese. *Epig.*, p. 6.
11.282. Hamerus. Non ego iam vitae. Soter², p. 86.
Cornarius. Non fleo vitale. Corn., p. 78.
Luscinius. Exutos dulci vita. Corn., p. 78.
Obsopoeus. Non ego defunctos. Obsop., p. 97; Wech., p. 87.
Sabeo. Plus ego non doleo. *Epig.*, p. 178.
Gualfreducci. Quid gemis e misera. *Var.*, p. 288.
11.283. Sabeo. Multi multa ferunt. *Epig.*, p. 481.
11.286. Vv. 1–2 = Menander, *Monost.* 413, 133 (Meineke).
11.287. More (Sir T.). Qui miser uxorem. Soter², p. 159; Corn.,
p. 165.

Cornarius. Deformem uxorem cupias. Corn., p. 165.
Sabeo. Informi nuptae. *Epig.*, p. 445.
Sabeo. Inspicit hic noctem. *Epig.*, p. 464.
Sabeo. Nocte sub illustri. *Epig.*, p. 481.
11.288. Cornarius. Certabant sutor. Corn., p. 190.
Sabeo. Cum sutore ingens. *Epig.*, p. 477.
11.289. Cf. 290. [In old edd. of Stobaeus, *Flor.* 10.]
11.290. Cf. 289.
11.292. Beatus Rhenanus. Coelestem super axem. Soter², p. 202; Corn., p. 240.
Cornarius. Coeli axem super. Corn., p. 241.
Sabeo. Quum sedeas curru. *Epig.*, p. 350 (352).
11.293. Cunich. Pactus equum caudam. *Anth.*, p. 161.
11.294. Cf. 166. [In old edd. of Stobaeus, *Flor.* 10.]
Cf. Anon., inscr. Qui dum vita datast. Buecheler 1106.
More (Sir T.). Divitias locupletis. Soter², p. 198; Corn., p. 233.
Lily (W.). Divitias locupletis. *Ibid.*
Alciati. Divitias opulentis. Corn., p. 233.
Obsopoeus. Ditis opes tibi. Wech., p. 269.
Alamanni. Lidio, che tanto aduni, *Versi* 2. 142.
Sabeo. Divitiae tibi sunt. *Epig.*, p. 488.
Guazzo quotes Alamanni's version. *Dial.*, f. 24ᵛᵒ.
Toscano (M.). Divitias opulentis [?Alciati]. *Anth.*, p. 102.
More's tr. is given in 'Επ. καὶ 'Ελ. (No. 62).
Cunich. Dives censu, animo pauper. *Anth.*, p. 45.
Pompei. Ben ricchezza di ricco. *Op.* 2. 208.
Passeroni. Di sostanza è ricco. *Rime* 3. 136.
Pagnini. Gran ricchezza tu. *Epig.*, p. 148.
11.295. Cf. 396.
11.296. Quoted by Diogenes Laertius 7. 170 (Timon).
11.297. Sleidan. Sicne tibi mater. Soter², p. 173; Corn., p. 198.
Obsopoeus. Cur maiore merum. Obsop., p. 254; Wech., p. 233.
Sabeo. Ante mihi dederas. *Epig.*, p. 240.
Sabeo. Quomodo amas natum. *Epig.*, p. 780.
Sabeo. Quondam plus vino. *Epig.*, p. 780.
11.298. Sabeo. Ut dextram extendit. *Epig.*, p. 786.
11.299. Sabeo. Quid mirum, quid. *Epig.*, p. 725.
[Sabeo joins *A.P.* 11. 299–303 and 341 to make one poem; here each couplet is listed under the appropriate original.]
'L-prose.' Iniurius es? quid. 'Επ. καὶ 'Ελ. No. 54.
11.300. Cf. *A.P.* 15. 20.
Sabeo. Plurima mortalis iactas. *Epig.* ,p. 725.
'L-prose.' Multa dicis homo. 'Επ. καὶ 'Ελ. No. 55.
11.301. Sabeo. Sol Deus est lucis. *Epig.*, p. 725.
'L-prose.' Sol hominibus splendoris. 'Επ. καὶ 'Ελ. No. 56
Felici. Cielo e Terra il Sole. *Epig.*¹, p. 76.

11.302. Sabeo. Pauperiem, non me. *Epig.*, p. 725.
'L-prose.' Non me, paupertatem. 'Επ. καὶ 'Ελ. No. 57.
Felici. Io non già; la sorte. *Epig.*[1], p. 76.
11.303. Sabeo. Quid culpae? si sum. *Epig.*, p. 725.
'L-prose.' Si mendico, quid patior? 'Επ. καὶ 'Ελ. No. 58.
Cf. Pagnini. Che d'oro ho le man. *Epig.*, p. 126.
11.304. Cunich. Morbos quisque suos. *Anth.*, p. 67.
Passeroni. Hanno gli uomini tutti. *Rime* 3. 222.
11.305. Cf. 355.
Velius. O cui stultitia est. Soter[2], p. 179; Corn., p. 207.
Luscinius. Frons perfricta tibi. Corn., p. 207.
Sabeo. Quid tu te iactas. *Epig.*, p. 477.
Cunich. Cur tanto incedis. *Anth.*, p. 67.
11.306. Cornarius. Aegyptus tibi visa. Corn., p. 148.
Sabeo. Omnem adversatus. *Epig.*, p. 431.
11.307. Costanzi (A.). Est uxor Cytherea. *Epig.*, Biii[vo].
Marullus. Et Venus est uxor. *Epig.* 2, p. 28; Soter[2], p. 204;
Corn., p. 244.
Cornarius. Filius extat Amor. Corn., p. 244.
Luscinius. Moecha tibi Venus. Corn., p. 244.
Valeriano. Filium habes, qui est. *Poem.*, p. 114; *C.P.It.* 10.
161.
Felici. Sembra a me Venere. *Epig.*[1], p. 77.
11.308. Cf. 102.
11.309. [In old edd. of Stobaeus, *Flor.* 10.]
Sabeo. Trasimache insidiis. *Epig.*, p. 491.
Toscano (M.). Exercens foenus. *Anth.*, p. 108.
11.310. Cf. Martial. Dentibus atque comis. *Epig.* 12. 23.
More (Sir T.). Quur emitur fucus. Soter[2], p. 160; Corn.,
p. 166.
Luscinius. Mel, fucum, ceram. Soter[2], p. 160; Corn., p. 166.
Rivautella-Ricolvi, Mel, fucum, ceram. *Mar.* 1. 87.
Cunich. Empta coma est. *Anth.*, p. 68.
Bertòla. Tutto comprando vai. *Poes.* 1. 179.
Pagnini. Compre hai le chiome. *Epig.*, p. 62.
11.311. Sabeo. Sic piger est Pantanetus. *Epig.*, p. 781.
Bongiovanni and Zanetti. Cotanto scioperato. *Epig.*, p. 29.
11.312. Cornarius. Quisquis es hinc transi. Corn., p. 205.
Alciati. Flete, his impubes [v. 4]. *Op.* 4. 545.
Sabeo. Marcus ut inscribat. *Epig.*, p. 392.
Crasso. Nemine hic [L-prose]. *Ist.*, p. 322.
11.313. Cf. 371. [In old edd. of Stobaeus, *Flor.* 10.]
Sabeo. Splendentem argento. *Epig.*, p. 437.
Cunich. Argento in solido. *Anth.*, p. 43.
Passeroni. Invitata un giorno. *Rime* 3. 131.
11.315. Velius. Lysimachi pateram. Soter[2], p. 169; Corn., p. 187.
Sabeo. Lysimachi Anthiocus. *Epig.*, p. 457.
Bongiovanni and Zanetti. La coltre di Lasimaco. *Epig.*, p. 5.

Cunich. Lysimachi Antiochus. *Anth.*, p. 61.
Passeroni. Vide Iro d'Ida. *Rime* 3. 185.
Pagnini. Di Licanio una coltre. *Epig.*, p. 106.
11.316. Sabeo. Solus agona Milon. *Epig.*, p. 186.
11.317. Sabeo. Longanimem claudum. *Epig.*, p. 778.
11.318. Sleidan. Anticrates, docto. Soter², p. 153; Corn., p. 152.
Sabeo. Noverat Anticrates. *Epig.*, p. 432.
11.323. Soter. Rho Lambdaque solum. Soter², p. 95.
Luscinius. Palpo colax Graiis. Corn., p. 86.
Sabeo. Scurra assentator. *Epig.*, p. 408.
Sabeo. Labda et ro colacas. *Epig.*, p. 408.
11.324. Cornarius. Hanc tibi, Phoebe. Corn., p. 146.
Sabeo. Defero, Apollo, tibi. *Epig.*, p. 537.
Cunich. Quas porto tibi, Phoebe. *Anth.*, p. 51.
11.325. [In old edd. of Stobaeus, *Flor.* 10.]
Sabeo. Pes hircinus heri. *Epig.*, p. 746.
Cebà. . . . non voler [prose paraphrase]. *Theo.*, p. 119.
Cunich. Moestus heri hircinumque. *Anth.*, p. 51.
Passeroni. Jer cenai da un Messere. *Rime* 3. 159.
11.330. Luscinius. Comis heri convivia. Corn., p. 200.
Alciati. Hesterna ad coenam. *Op.* 4. 391.
Bongiovanni and Zanetti. Jeri chiamato fui. *Epig.*, p. 27.
11.331. Luscinius. Est tibi cymba, Philon. Corn., p. 206.
Giraldi (L. G.). Lembus erat nautae. *Op.* 1. 623.
Sabeo. Cymba Philonis erat. *Epig.*, p. 786.
Cunich. Cinna salutari ponti. *Anth.*, p. 152.
Passeroni. Cinna valica il mar. *Rime* 3. 66.
11.333. Cornarius. Tollere pharmaciis. Corn., p. 180.
11.334. Sabeo. Demagorum et pestem. *Epig.*, p. 240.
Pagnini. Demagora e la peste. *Epig.*, p. 103.
11.335. Sabeo. O Cynagire miser. *Epig.*, p. 447.
Cunich. Infelix, Cynegire. *Anth.*, p. 149.
11.337. Velius. Βουλεύεις, Agathine. Soter², p. 162; Corn., p. 172.
11.340. Cornarius. Iuravi o quoties. Corn., p. 170.
Obsopoeus. Saepe ego iuravi. Obsop., p. 229; Wech., p. 207.
Cunich. Iuravi, nunquam scripturam. *Anth.*, p. 43.
Felici. Già satire giurai. *Epig.*¹, p. 115.
Passeroni. Giurai di più non fare. *Rime* 3. 133.
Pagnini. Io di non far più. *Epig.*, p. 73.
11.341. Sabeo. Principium est odii. *Epig.*, p. 725.
'L-prose.' Laudare quidem optimum. 'Επ. καὶ 'Ελ. No. 59.
11.342. Sabeo. Herniam labentis heri. *Epig.*, p. 446.
11.343. Sleidan. Silvano quum sint. Soter², p. 173; Corn., p. 197.
Conti. Ut vinum ac [lines 1–2]. *Myth.* 6. 10.
Sabeo. Quum duo sint nati. *Epig.*, p. 779.
Baldi. Due compagni ha Timante. *Epig.* 881.
Rivautella-Ricolvi. Silvanus comites vinum. *Mar.* 1. 128.
11.348. Cf. Aesop, *Fab.* 29 (De Furia), 160 (Corais).

Luscinius. O caput invisum. Soter[2], p. 36; Corn., p. 33.
Sabeo. Vir superans feritate. *Epig.*, p. 718.

11.349. Luscinius. Unde age tu coelum. Soter[2], p. 151; Corn., p. 150.
Velius. Fare age qui caelum. Soter[2], p. 152; Corn., p. 150.
Sleidan. Te modica finxit. Soter[2], p. 152; Corn., p. 150.
Sabeo. Unde soli fines. *Epig.*, p. 431.
Medici (A. de'). Fare, age, metiris. *Scelt.*, p. xviii.
Medici (A. de'). Dimmi, a che cerchi. *Scelt.*, p. xviii.
Pagnini. Tu stai ravvolto. *Epig.*, p. 1.

11.352. Lascaris (J.) alludes to this epig. Above, p. 116, n. 1.

11.355. Cf. 305.
Alciati. Omnia qui gustas [v. 2]. *Op.* 4. 1004.

11.356. Alciati. Vera refert in te. *Op.* 1. 584.
Sabeo. In te non fallens. *Epig.*, p. 211.
Sabeo. In te non fallit. *Epig.*, p. 427.
Sabeo. Inspexit dubiam. *Epig.*, p. 428.
Felici. Lieve è di mente. *Epig.*[1], p. 111.

11.357. Sabeo. Filius atque pater. *Epig.*, p. 461.

11.358. Cf. 17.

11.364. Cornarius. Hic nihil et simplex. Corn., p. 117.

11.365. Luscinius. Calligenes ruris cultor. Corn., p. 153.
Obsopoeus. Calligenes quum iam. Obsop., p. 213; Wech.,
p. 192.
Molza. Caligenes terris dum. *Poes.* 3. 206.
Sabeo. Calligenes terrae. *Epig.*, p. 439.
Baldi. L' agricoltor Ticon. *Epig.* 916.
Cunich. Calligenes nuper post. *Anth.*, p. 45.
Passeroni. Finita ch'ebbe la. *Rime* 3. 169.

11.366. Cf. 264. [In old edd. of Stobaeus, *Flor.* 10.]
Cornarius. Thesaurum in somnis. Corn., p. 238.
Sabeo. Thesaurum in somnis. *Epig.*, p. 791.

11.367. Soter. Passeri habes vultum. Soter[2], p. 160.
Cornarius. Finxit te strutho. Corn., p. 166.

11.368. Sabeo. In vultu densa. *Epig.*, p. 458.

11.369. More (Sir T.). Grus ne te rapiat. Soter[2], p. 153; Corn.,
p. 154.
Luscinius. Ne te conficiat. Soter[2], p. 153; Corn., p. 154.
Velius. Tutus in urbe mane. Soter[2], p. 154; Corn., p. 154.
Sleidan. Ne grus pygmaei. Soter[2], p. 154; Corn., p. 154.
Alciati. Urbem tuto habita. Corn., p. 154.
Cordato. Tutus in urbe habita. *Prael.*, p. 111.
Sabeo. Urbem habita in tuto. *Epig.*, p. 434.
Pagnini. T'assicura in città. *Epig.*, p. 116.

11.370. Sabeo. Fucantem formam. *Epig.*, p. 452.

11.371. Cf. 313.
Cf. Martial. Invita centum. *Epig.* 4. 68.
Cf. Anon. Ad cenam Varus me. *PLM* 5. 390.

11.372. Obsopoeus. Compositum vento. Obsop., p. 252; Wech., p. 231.

11.373. Alciati. Calliope studiis dea. *Op.* 4. 494.
Sabeo. Est Dea Calliope. *Epig.*, p. 38.
11.374. Cunich. Fuco tende genas. *Anth.*, p. 63.
11.375. Sabeo. Scire volens quae. *Epig.*, p. 476.
Cunich. Sternueram iuxta. *Anth.*, p. 161.
Pagnini. Quand' io presso una. *Epig.*, p. 34.
11.376. Alciati. Rhetora vir quondam. Corn., p. 215; *Op.* 2. 1062.
Alciati quotes Gr. and tr. of vv. 11–2, *Op.* 4. 382.
Mazzoni quotes Gr. and Alciati's tr. *Difesa*, p. 132.
11.377. Sabeo. Infelix volucris. *Epig.*, p. 462.
11.378. Cornarius. Non queo grammatices. Corn., p. 159.
Sabeo. Grammaticen nequeo. *Epig.*, p. 468.
Sabeo. Grammatica excrucior. *Epig.*, p. 510.
Cunich. Grammaticam uxoremque. *Anth.*, p. 163.
11.379. Sabeo. Multa fuit passus. *Epig.*, p. 189.
11.381. Cf. Hipponax *ap.* Stobaeus, *Flor.* 68.8.
Costanzi (G.). Bile tumet semper. *Epig.*, Oiiii^vo.
Luscinius. Omnia cum mala sit. Soter², p. 157; Corn., p. 160.
Alciati. Est mulier mera. Corn., p. 160.
Anisio. Est mera lis homini. *Poem.*, f. 104ro.
Valeriano. Femina est fors. *Poem.*, p. 113; *C.P.It.* 10. 159.
Valeriano. Femina tota odium. *Poem.*, p. 113; *C.P.It.*, 10.
159.
Sabeo. Ira licet mulier. *Epig.*, p. 444.
Sabeo. Ira omnis mulier. *Epig.*, p. 446.
Sabeo. Foemina quaeque bonas. *Epig.*, p. 448.
Spinula. Quaelibet est semper. *Epig.*, p. 49.
Pompei. Fiele è ogni donna. *Op.* 2. 175.
11.382. Cornarius. Hic iacet Alcimenes. Corn., p. 182.
Obsopoeus. Alcymenes misera. Obsop., p. 240; Wech., p. 218.
11.384. Bergius. Si monachi cur tanta. Soter², p. 202; Corn., p. 241.
Soter. Quid vestro inani. Soter², p. 202.
Cornarius. Si monachi, cur tanta. Corn., p. 241.
Vasolli. Si monachi, cur tanta. *Epig.*, f. 19vo; *Virid.*, f. 8vo;
above, p. 209.
11.385. Hamerus. In speciem firmi. Soter², p. 98.
Cornarius. Quam metus et turpis. Corn., p. 87.
Sabeo. Fictus amor tuus est. *Epig.*, p. 409.
Sabeo. Falsus amas. *Epig.*, p. 409.
Pagnini. Tu ami per bisogno. *Epig.*, p. 139.
11.386. Sabeo. Vidit heri ut. *Epig.*, p. 190.
Cunich. Tristis heri cuidam. *Anth.*, p. 66.
11.387. [In old edd. of Stobaeus, *Flor.* 10.]
Luscinius. Singula sunt aliis. Corn., p. 232.
Cornarius. Coenamus semel hic. Corn., p. 232.
Cunich. Quisquis semel coenat. *Anth.*, p. 63.
Passeroni. Una volta di dì. *Rime* 3. 139.
11.388. Sabeo. Donec eris coelebs. *Epig.*, p. 321.

11.389. [In old edd. of Stobaeus, *Flor.* 10.]
Luscinius. Cornicem cervumque. Corn., p. 232.
Obsopoeus. Si tua vivacem. Obsop., p. 302; Wech., p. 271.
Sabeo. Cornicis si tu. *Epig.*, p. 502.

11.390. Cf. *A.P.* 10. 121.
Sleidan. Officio mecum certes. Soter[2], p. 162; Corn., p. 171.
Luscinius. Blandus amor valeat. Corn., p. 172.
Sabeo. Dilige re vera si. *Epig.*, p. 453.
Baldi. Se m'ami, ama con l'opre. *Epig.* 99.
Bongiovanni and Zanetti. Se amor mi porti. *Epig.*, p. 28.
The version by Sleidan is given in Ἐπ. καὶ Ἐλ. (No. 52).
Cunich. Odisti me? odium ne. *Anth.*, p. 63.
Passeroni. M'odj, Egon? non celar. *Rime* 3. 185.

11.391. [In old edd. of Stobaeus, *Flor.* 10.]
More (Sir T.). Murem Asclepiades ut. Soter[2], p. 201; Corn., p. 236.
Lily (W.). Murem Asclepiades in. Soter[2], p. 201; Corn., p. 237.
Luscinius. Murem Asclepiades cum. Soter[2], p. 201; Corn., p. 237.
Alciati. Murem Asclepiades ut. Corn., p. 237.
Obsopoeus. Murem Asclepiades sic. Obsop., p. 302; Wech., p. 271.
Sabeo. Murem Asclepiades sub. *Epig.*, p. 754.
Sabeo. Quid tibi, amice, cupis. *Epig.*, p. 754.
Pontanus (Spanmueller) quotes Lucilius. *Poet. Inst.*, p. 64.
Baldi. Veduto un topolin. *Epig.* 903.
Cunich. Mus Asclepiadae tecta. *Anth.*, p. 55.
Felici. Vide un topo entro. *Epig.*[1], p. 59.

11.392. Cf. 104.
Cornarius. Formicae alatae tergo. Corn., p. 196.
Obsopoeus. Formicae alatae conscenso. Obsop., p. 252; Wech., p. 231.
Alamanni. Trovando una formica. *Versi.* 2. 143.
Cunich. Rhetor ut Adrastus. *Anth.*, p. 159.

11.393. Cornarius. Non gravius onus est. Corn., p. 175.
Sabeo. Sarcina nulla ulli. *Epig.*, p. 455.
Sabeo. Nulla magis gravis. *Epig.*, p. 611.

11.394. Cf. Baldi. Colui, dice Tripaldo. *Epig.* 888.
Ricolvi. Optimus ille poeta. *Op.*, p. 81.
Ricolvi. Quel poeta sol si. *Op.*, p. 81.
Cunich. Optimus est vatum. *Anth.*, p. 160.
Passeroni. Tu m'hai fatto. *Rime* 3. 172.

11.395. Lascaris (J.). Interemit crepitus. *Epig.*, f. 15[ro]; Soter[2], p. 181; Corn., p. 210.
More (Sir T.). Te crepitus perdit. Soter[2], p. 181; Corn., p. 201.
Alciati. Si crepitum teneas. Corn., p. 210.

Obsopoeus. Et crepitus multos. Obsop., p. 272; Wech.,
 p. 245.
Sabeo. Ventris enim crepitus. *Epig.*, p. 863.
Pagnini. Il peto fa crepare. *Epig.*, p. 171.
11.396. Cf. 295.
11.397. [In old edd. of Stobaeus, *Flor.* 10.]
 Alciati. Septimius populos inter. *Emb.* 86.
 Obsopoeus. Vivens ut muli. Obsop., p. 309; Wech., p. 272.
 Sabeo. Nobile saepe [lines 2–4]. *Epig.*, p. 807.
 Mignault. Vivens ut muli dum. Alciati, *Emb.* 85.
 Sanchez. Vivens ut muli dum. *Op.* 3. 181.
 Cunich. Magnum nummorum vim. *Anth.*, p. 45.
 Felici. Strugge sue brame. *Epig.*[1], p. 115.
 Passeroni. Sacchi e scrigni. *Rime* 3. 134.
 Roncalli. Per quanto il tuo. *Epig.* (1792), p. 99; (1801),
 p. 67.
 Pagnini. Molti milioni conta. *Epig.*, p. 83.
11.398. Cornarius. Dum tingit, perdit. Corn., p. 158.
 Luscinius. Forte senex canos. Corn., p. 158.
 Alciati. Caesariem tingens. *Op.* 4.573.
 Sabeo. Qui caput infecit. *Epig.*, p. 443.
 Guazzo. Un vecchio tinge. *Ghirl.*, p. 27.
 Salvini quotes this epig. *Disc.* 6. 214.
11.399. Cunich. Grammatico quondam. *Anth.*, p. 50.
 Passeroni. Ad un dotto Gramatico. *Rime* 3. 109.
11.401. Sleidan. In medica quidam. Soter[2], p. 167; Corn., p. 185.
 Soter. Consuevit medicus. Soter[2], p. 166.
 Cf. Georgius anon. Romanus quidam. Soter[2], p. 167.
 Sabeo. Dilectum medicus gnatum. *Epig.*, p. 500.
 Cf. Loredano. Mille hò mandati. *Cimit.* 4. 47.
 Bongiovanni and Zanetti. Mandommi certo medico. *Epig.*,
 p. 21.
11.403. Cf. Martial. Quare quam multis. *Epig.* 12. 17.
 Luscinius. Contemptrix inopum. Corn., p. 244.
 Alciati. Diva beatorum domitrix. Corn., p. 244.
 Vargas. O dea di povertà. *Sag.*, p. 86.
11.404. Cornarius. Hernia quam res. Corn., p. 168.
 Cf. Alciati. Flumina tentabat. Corn., p. 168.
 Sabeo. Herniam habens Diophon. *Epig.*, p. 469.
11.405. Alciati. Grypus olfacit merum. Corn., p. 167.
 Sabeo. Olfaciente mero Nicon. *Epig.*, p. 451.
 Mazzoni quotes this epig. without tr. *Difesa*, p. 48.
11.406. Alciati. Iamdudum expecto veniat. Corn., p. 167.
 Cornarius. Rhetoris hic Grypi. Corn., p. 167.
 Dazzi. Non per multa Lycon. *Poem.*, p. 128.
 Sabeo. Rhetoris incurvum. *Epig.*, p. 455.
 Cunich. Hermogenis video nasum. *Anth.*, p. 147.
 Passeroni. D'Ermogene apparire. *Rime* 3. 123.

11.408. Cf. Martial. Mentiris iuvenem tinctis. *Epig.* 3. 43.
       More (Sir T.). Saepe caput tinguis. Soter[2], p. 155; Corn., p. 156.
       Velius. Inficis ora, dies. Soter[2], p. 155; Corn., p. 156.
       Sleidan. Tu licet unguento. Soter[2], p. 156; Corn., p. 156.
       Cornarius. Ora licet tingas. Corn., p. 157.
       Sabeo. Si caput inficias. *Epig.*, p. 441.
       Marescotti. Saepe caput tingis. *Pers.*, p. 87.
       Guazzo. Il liscio non può [line 6]. *Civ. Con.*, f. 123vo.
       Baldi. Giovane e fresca vuoi. *Epig.* 633.
       Bongiovanni and Zanetti. Ben puoi tingerti. *Epig.*, p. 38.
       Cunich. Tinge comas, oris nec. *Anth.*, p. 56.
       Felici. Che tingi il crin. *Epig.*[1], p. 56.
       Passeroni. Tingi la chioma pur. *Rime* 3. 220.
       Roncalli. Lisciate quanto vuoi. *Epig.* (1792), p. 75; (1801), p. 58.
       Roncalli. Tu ognor ti sbarbi. *Epig.* (1801), p. 51.
       Pagnini. Il crin, quanto vuoi. *Epig.*, p. 110.
11.410. More (Sir T.). Barbati Cynici baculoque. Soter[2], p. 203; Corn., p. 242.
       Cf. Alciati. Antonii Malcus successor. Corn., p. 242.
       Luscinius. Barbati in coena. Corn., p. 243.
       Sabeo. Barbati Cynici Cererem. *Epig.*, p. 209.
       Cunich. Barbigeri ille ingens. *Anth.*, p. 67.
11.412. More (Sir T.). Pingere difficile est. Soter[2], p. 181; Corn., p. 210.
11.413. [In old edd. of Stobaeus, *Flor.* 10.]
       Luscinius. Coenam, quid coenam? Soter[2], p. 199; Corn., p. 234.
       Cf. Alciati. Plurima noscendo. Corn., p. 234.
       Sabeo. Tanquam hortum. *Epig.*, p. 504.
       Cebà. . . . di certo Apelle [prose paraphrase]. *Theo.*, p. 119.
       Cunich. Non secus ac si. *Anth.*, p. 49.
       Passeroni. Come se avesse. *Rime* 3. 138.
       Pagnini. Qual se immolato. *Epig.*, p. 140.
11.414. Soter. Membra humana Venus. Soter,[2] p. 204.
       Cornarius. Solvere membra Venus. Corn., p. 245.
       Luscinius. Enervens vires Bacchus. Corn., p. 245.
       Valeriano. Membrifrago e Baccho. *Poem.*, p. 114; *C.P.It.* 10. 162.
       Sabeo. Laedit membra merum. *Epig.*, p. 756.
       Sabeo. Ex Venere et Baccho. *Epig.*, p. 756.
       Sabeo. Ex patre tam suavi. *Epig.*, p. 756.
       Baldi. Venere dolce sembra. *Epig.* 1082.
       Vargas. Strugge Bacco e strugge. *Sag.*, p. 86.
       Pagnini. Di Bacco e Vener. *Epig.*, p. 155.
11.415. Cf. 241–2.
11.416. Sleidan. Aurum vile mihi. Soter[2], p. 123; Corn., p. 117.

Cornarius. Te quum scorta. Corn., p. 117.
Sabeo. Quod commune etiam. *Epig.*, p. 853.

11.418. More (Sir T.). Si tuus ad solem. Soter², p. 160; Corn., p. 166.
Luscinius. Oris hient rictus. Soter², p. 160; Corn., p. 166.
Alciati. Haud solariolum. Corn., p. 166.
Sabeo. Sit soli oppositus. *Epig.*, p. 457.
Sabeo. Os aperi et nasus. *Epig.*, p. 485.
Mazzoni quotes the Gr. with More's tr. *Difesa*, p. 48.
Bongiovanni and Zanetti. Quel tuo naso. *Epig.*, p. 30.
Ricolvi gives More's tr. *Op.*, p. 79.

11.419. Cf. 420.
Arnold. Vesal. Si mentem sociam. Soter², p. 42; Corn., p. 38.
Sabeo. Si cum canicie. *Epig.*, p. 548.
Toscano (M.). Turpius esse nihil. *Anth.*, p. 159.
The tr. of Arnoldus is given in 'Επ. καὶ 'Ελεγ. (No. 22).
Cunich. Qui sapit, huic decori. *Anth.*, p. 86.
Passeroni. A un uomo saggio. *Rime* 3. 231.
Pagnini. Canuto crin con senno. *Epig.*, p. 24.

11.420. Cf. 419.
Cf. Martial. Non est mentitus. *Epig.* 11. 102.
Sabeo. Res veneranda senis. *Epig.*, p. 712.

11.421. Alciati. Si clam probra. Corn., p. 172; *Op.* 4. 670.
Cornarius. Si male me tractas. Corn., p. 172.
Sabeo. Si absentem me. *Epig.*, p. 467.
Bongiovanni and Zanetti. Se tu dì mal. *Epig.*, p. 26.

11.422. Cornarius. Phemie si saperes. Corn., p. 145.
11.423. Cornarius. Inficis immutasque. Corn., p. 107.
Sabeo. Omnia quum ringas. *Epig.*, p. 423.
Sabeo. Cunctorum tinctor. *Epig.*, p. 235.

11.425. Alciati. Hoc certum te scire. *Op.* 4.392.
Sabeo. Hoc Placiane velim. *Epig.*, p. 446.

11.426. Luscinius. Littera prima tibi. Corn., p. 198.
11.427. Sabeo. Exorcista fugat. *Epig.*, p. 451.
Franchini. Daemonas infestos. *Epig.*, p. 116.

11.428. Cf. Lucian. Αἰθίοπα σμήχειν ἐπιχειρῶ. adv. *Indoct.* 28.
Cf. Aesop. *Fab.* 13 (Halm).
Sleidan. Aethiopem quid stulte. Soter², p. 149; Corn., p. 144.
Alciati. Abluis Aethiopem quid. Corn., p. 144; *Emb.* 59.
Cornarius. Aethiopem quid stulte. Corn., p. 144.
Luscinius. Indi parce lavare cutem. Corn., p. 144.
Sabeo. Vane quid attentas? *Epig.*, p. 428.
Sabeo. Aethiopis faciem quid. *Epig.*, p. 429.
Murtola. Perchè d'acqua le gote. *Rime*, f. 97ᵛᵒ, 222ᵛᵒ.
Murtola. Che fai, bella mia. *Rime*, f. 97ᵛᵒ.
Sleidan's tr. is given in 'Επ. καὶ 'Ελεγ. (No. 70).
Cunich. Cur frustra corpus. *Anth.*, p. 54.
Felici. Il bruno a tergere. *Epig.*¹, p. 54.

11.429. Cornarius. Inter potores qui solus. Corn., p. 145.

Cornarius. Pocula qui moderata. *Corn.*, p. 145.
Sabeo. Aebrii erant omnes. *Epig.*, p. 215; *C.P.It.* 8. 203.
Baldi. Tu non t'inebrii. *Epig.* 670.
Bongiovanni and Zanetti. In una ragunata. *Epig.*, p. 16.
Cunich. Vinosos inter sapit. *Anth.*, p. 72.
Felici. De' briachi in mezzo. *Epig.*[1], p. 112.
Passeroni. Fra tutti i Sozj. *Rime* 3. 122.
Pagnini. D'ubbriachi compagni. *Epig.*, p. 159.

11.430. Cf. Th. Prodromus. 'Αλλ' οὔτε τῷ πώγωνι. Boissonade, *Anec.*
4. 434.
More (Sir T.). Si promissa facit. Soter[2], p. 202; Corn.,
p. 241.
Luscinius. Si cui protensa. Corn., p. 241.
Vasolli. Si promissa facit. *Epig.*, f. 17ᵛᵒ; *Virid.*, f. 38ᵛᵒ;
(above, p. 209).
Vasolli. Si cui protensa. *Ibid.*
Sabeo. Si fore barbatum. *Epig.*, p. 209.
Sabeo. Si sophiam donat. *Epig.*, p. 209.
Sabeo. Postquam et enim. *Epig.*, p. 210.
Sabeo. Si barba inspirat. *Epig.*, p. 324.
Cf. Spinula. Disperiit Paulus. *Epig.*, p. 43.
Ricolvi. Si promissa Sophum. *Op.*, p. 80.
Ricolvi. Se un Filosofo. *Op.*, p. 80.
Cunich. Si posita in longa. *Anth.*, p. 67.
Felici. Se nulla lunga. *Epig.*[1], p. 77.
Passeroni. Se il saver filosofico. *Rime* 3. 221.
Pagnini. Se nella lunga barba. *Epig.*, p. 64.

11.431. Cf. 208.
Anselmo. Lentus inire fugam. *Epig.*, Kiiii; *C.P.It.* 1. 300.
Alciati. Vesci celer es, sed. Corn., p. 144.
Cornarius. Si velox coenas. Corn., p. 144.
Luscinius. Dum pedibus piger. Corn., p. 144.
Valeriano. Si properantur edis. *Poem.*, p. 114; *C.P.It.* 10.
160.
Sabeo. Si velox comedis. *Epig.*, p. 185.
Baldi. Presta hai bocca. *Epig.* 634.
A tr. by Benedictus is given in 'Επ. καὶ 'Ελ. (No. 66).
Cunich. Currere qui lentus. *Anth.*, p. 158.
Passeroni. O tu, che corri. *Rime* 3. 237.
Roncalli. Sa a mangiar voli. *Epig.* (1792), p. 47; (1801),
p. 50.
Pagnini. A correr lento. *Epig.*, p. 29.
Pagnini. Se presto mangi. *Epig.*, p. 131.

11.432. More (Sir T.). Quem mordent pulices. Soter[2], p. 150; Corn.,
p. 145.
Luscinius. Infestos pulices dum. Corn., p. 145.
Sabeo. Extinxit lucem fatuus. *Epig.*, p. 428.
Sabeo. Extinxit lumen fatuus. *Epig.*, p. 702.

Bongiovanni and Zanetti. Certe importune. *Epig.*, p. 15.
Pagnini. Da una turba di pulci. *Epig.*, p. 4.
11.433. Sleidan. Corpora nuda potes. Soter², p. 164; Corn., p. 174.
Cornarius. Ipse quidem formas. Corn., p. 175.
11.434. Cornarius. Si caput hoc nudum. Corn., p. 146.
Carcani (P.). Se vedi un, che abbia. *Ant. Ercol.* 6. 370.
11.435. Cornarius. Nomine quo tandem. Corn., p. 215.
Cunich. Mirificus rhetor Bytus. *Anth.*, p. 48.
Felici. Bito è Rettorico. *Epig.*¹, p. 9.
Passeroni. Bito è grande Orator. *Rime* 3. 189.
Pagnini. Come sofista sia. *Epig.*, p. 70.
11.436. Cornarius. Et testudo volens. Corn., p. 215.
Rhodiginus. Facilius multo [prose]. *Lect.* 17. 11.
Sabeo., Candescent potius. *Epig.*, p. 787.
Pagnini. Testuggini volanti. *Epig.*, p. 75.
11.437. Quoted by Macrobius. *Sat.* 5. 20. 7; by Stephanus Byzant. 5
    (*s. v.* Γάργαρα); by Eustathius on *Il.* 6. 292.
Quoted by Volaterranus. *Comm. Urb.*, p. 341.
Soter. Miseret in petris solus. Soter², p. 178.
Cornarius. O Diotime, miser, qui. Corn., p. 205.
Giraldi (L. G.) quotes from Steph. Byz. *Op.* 2. 115.
11.442. Quoted in *Schol. Vat.* on Dion. Thrac. (Hilgard, pp. 30, 179);
    in *Homeri Vita* (West., pp. 27, 29); by Tzetzes, *Exeg.*, p. 8
    (Hermann).
Quoted by Codro Urceo, *Op.*, p. 177.
Sabeo. Ter me regnantem. *Epig.*, p. 359.
Lucido. Quem ter Cecropidae. Gronov., *Thes.* 10. 1791.

Book XII

12.5. [Not in *Plan.*]
    Cf. Ovid. Candida me capiet. *Am.* 2. 4. 39.
12.20. [Not in *Plan.*] Cf. *A.P.* 5. 93.
    Cf. Petronius. Quid factum est, quod. *Sat.* c. 20.
12.28–33. Cf. Horace, *Carm.* 4. 10.
12.43. [Not in *Plan.*]
    Cf. Propertius. Cui fuit indocti. *Eleg.* 2. 23. 1–2.
12.44. [Not in *Plan.*]
    Cf. Tibullus. Heu male nunc artes. *Eleg.* 1. 4. 57–8.
12.45. [Not in *Plan.*]
    Cf. Propertius. Nunc, quoniam ista. *Eleg.* 2. 9. 37–40.
12.46. [Not in *Plan.*]
    Cf. Propertius. Quam si perdideris. *Eleg.* 2. 12. 21.
12.51. [Not in *Plan.*]
    Pagnini. Mesci quel buon. *Epig.*, p. 129.
12.60. Equicola paraphrases this epig., above, p. 294.
    Anselmo. Cuncta simul video. *Epig.*, Giiii.
    Dazzi. Si te habeo, Telesino. *Poem.*, p. 126.
    Pompei. I' tutto veggio se. *Op.* 2. 165.

Passeroni. Tutto ho, Tirsi dicea. *Rime* 3. 170.
Pagnini. Allor ch'io sto. *Epig.*, p. 68.

12.65. [Not in *Plan.*]
Cf. Nicetas Eugen. Λήδας, Δάναης. *Dros.* 6. 592.

12.67. [Not in *Plan.*]
Cf. Martial. Aetherias aquila. *Epig.* 1. 6.
Pagnini. Il mio bel Dionisio. *Epig.*, p. 141.

12.69. [Not in *Plan.*]
Cf. Politian. Βλέψον μ' οὐρανόθεν. Del Lungo, p. 196.

12.71. [Not in *Plan.*]
Pagnini. Cleonico meschino. *Epig.*, p. 167.

12.73. [Not in *Plan.*] Cf. *A.P.* 5. 14 and 78.
Cf. Catulus. Aufugit mi animus. Gellius. *N.A.* 19. 9.
Anon. Fuggesi l'alma [from Catulus]. *Versi et Reg.*, Nii.

12.75. [Not in *Plan.*] Cf. *A.P.* 11. 179.
See above, pp. 296, n. 1; 327, n. 1; 354, n. 1.

12.78. [Not in *Plan.*]
Pagnini. Se Amor portasse. *Epig.*, p. 91.

12.89. Pagnini. Di tre vaghe donzelle. *Epig.*, p. 96.

12.101. [Not in *Plan.*]
Cf. Propertius. Tum mihi constantis. *Eleg.* 1. 1. 3–4.

12.102. [Not in *Plan.*]
Horace. Leporem venator ut alta. *Serm.* 1. 2. 105ff.
Cf. Ovid. Venator sequitur fugientia. *Am.* 2. 9. 9–10.
Pagnini. Il cacciator va su. *Epig.*, p. 127.

12.103. Pagnini. So rispondere in amore. *Epig.*, p. 145.

12.113. Sabeo. Ipse et Amor volucris. *Epig.*, p. 657.
Castelvetro compares Petr. *Son.* 3. *Petr.*, p. 17.

12.114. [Not in *Plan.*]
Cf. Mutinelli. Deh! per pietà. *An. Poet.* 1. 175.

12.118. [Not in *Plan.*] Cf. the inscr. (Kaibel 1111).
Cf. Ovid. Nox et Amor vinumque. *Am.* 1. 6. 59–60.
Pagnini. Se mossi di mia voglia. *Epig.*, p. 133.

12.119. [Not in *Plan.*] Cf. Pliny. Huc mihi vos largo. *PLM* 4. 103

12.131. [Not in *Plan.*]
Cf. Horace, *Carm.* 1. 30.

12.140. [Not in *Plan.*]
Pagnini. Quando Archestrato vidi. *Epig.*, p. 135.

12.147. [Not in *Plan.*]
Cf. Tibullus. Iussit Amor: contra quis. *Eleg.* 1. 6. 30.

12.150. [Not in *Plan.*]
Pagnini. Già Polifemo ritrovar. *Epig.*, p. 133.

12.175. [Not in *Plan.*]
Cf. Martial. Dantem vina tuum toties. *Epig.* 9. 25.

12.191. [Not in *Plan.*]
Cf. Martial. Cur here quod dederas. *Epig.* 4. 7.

12.194. [Not in *Plan.*]
Cf. Ovid. Talis eras, aquilamque. *Am.* 1. 10. 7–8.

12.200. [Not in *Plan*.] Cf. *A.P.* 5. 42.
12.208. [Not in *Plan*.]
        Cf. Ovid, *Am.* 2. 15.
12.210. [Not in *Plan*.] Cf. *A.P.* 11. 225.
12.234. Sabeo. Si tu te extollis. *Epig.*, p. 662.
        Pagnini. Se il tuo bel ti fa. *Epig.*, p. 53.
12.235. Cf. Didot Anthol., vol. 3, 4. 73 (p. 408).
        Cf. Ovid. Forma, nisi admittas. *Am.* 1. 8. 53.
        Equicola paraphrases this epig., above, p. 293.
        Velius. Si perit, impartire. Soter², p. 316; Corn., p. 414.
        Velius. Utere temporibus, variant. Soter², p. 316.
        Scaphenatus. Ante fugam si forma. *Eleg.*, Diiii.
        Cf. Evangelista. Vita fugit: celeri. *Poem.*, p. 72.
        Sabeo. Si tua forma fugit. *Epig.*, p. 622.
        Murtola. Se questa tua bellezza. *Rime* (1604), f. 222ᵛᵒ.
        Roncalli. Se la bellezza. *Epig.* (1801), p. 10.
        Vannetti. Se la bellezza. Above, p. 435.
12.239. Carcani (P.). Cinque chiedi? Io dò. *Ant. Ercol.* 6. 131.
12.249. [Not in *Plan*.] Cf. *A.P.* 5. 163.

Book XIII.

13.3. Theocritus, *Inscr.* 19.
       Regolotti. Ipponatte 'l poeta. *Teoc.*, p. 270.
       Cunich. Hipponax iacet heic. *Anth.*, p. 128.
       Della Torre. Il poeta Ipponace. *Odi*, p.376.
       Passeroni. Qui son le osse. *Rime* 3. 85.
       Pagnini. Il poeta Ipponatte. *Poet. Gr.*, p. 872.
13.7. [Not in *Plan*.]
       Pagnini. Meneta Lizio la faretra. *Epig.*, p. 130.
13.11. [Not in *Plan*.] Published by Allacci, *De Sym.*, p. 215.
13.14. [Not in *Plan*.] Published by Allacci, *ibid.*
13.16. [Not in *Plan*.] As an inscr. (Geffcken 129; Hiller 63; *I.G.* 5. 1.
       1564a).
13.19–20. [Not in *Plan*.] Published by Allacci, *De Sym.*, p. 215.
13.24. [Not in *Plan*.]
       Pagnini. In dono a Citerea. *Epig.*, p. 179.
13.25. [Not in *Plan*.]
       Pagnini. A Cerere Pilea. *Epig.*, p. 128.
13.26. [Not in *Plan*.] Published by Allacci, *De Sym.*, p. 215.
13.28. [Not in *Plan*.]
       Pagnini. Spesso la sacra a Bacco. *Epig.*, p. 157.
13.29. Quoted by Athenaeus (2. 39C); and vv. 1–2 by Zenobius
       (*Prov.* 6. 22). Cf. Horace, *Epist.* 1. 19. 3.
       Volaterranus. Dulce merum Musis [lines 1–2]. *Comm. Urb.*,
       p. 758; Soter², p. 108; Corn., p. 103.
       Luscinius. Praebet equum docto [1–2]. Soter², p. 108; Corn.,
       p. 103.
       Soter. Est sonipes vati [1–2]. Soter², p. 107; Corn., p. 102.

Rhodiginus. Vinum eleganti magnus [prose]. *Lect.* 28. 35.
Sabeo. Vinum equus est vati. *Epig.*, p. 750.
Sanchez. Iucundo sonipes vati. *Op.* 3. 68.
Crasso. Vinum sane gratioso [L-prose]. *Ist.*, p. 131.
Redi quotes from this epig., *Op.* 1. 222.
Ricolvi. Vini potor equeo. *Op.*, p. 83.
Ricolvi. Est alacer sonipes. *Op.*, p. 83.
Carcani (P.). Il vino a un buon. *Ant. Ercol.* 6. 166.
Cunich. Vinum est fortis equus. *Anth.*, p. 35.
Passeroni. Destriero ottimo è. *Rime* 3. 112.

13.30.   [Not in *Plan.*] Publ. by Allacci, *De Sym.*, p. 215.
13.31.   [Not in *Plan.*] Publ. by Allacci, *De Sym.*, p. 213, and tr. in
          prose: Ceia me incesset.

Book XIV

14.1.   [Not in *Plan.*]
          Pagnini. Pitagora sì disse. *Epig.*, p. 176.
14.2.   Sabeo. Sum Pallas conflata. *Epig.*, p. 740.
          Cunich. Pallas ego ex auri. *Anth.*, p. 182.
          Pagnini. Di giovani cantori. *Epig.*, p. 67.
14.3.   [Not in *Plan.*]
          Pagnini. Vener mirando Amor. *Epig.*, p. 174.
14.5.   [Not in *Plan.*]
          Pagnini. Di bianco genitor. *Epig.*, p. 159.
14.7.   Sabeo. Aeneus ipse leo. *Epig.*, p. 741.
          Felici. Qui, Leonida di bronzo. *Epig.*[1], p. 108.
          Pagnini. Leon di rame io son. *Epig.*, p. 177.
14.12.   [Not in *Plan.*]
          Pagnini. Sei vasi in peso. *Epig.*, p. 174.
14.13.   Pagnini. Far venti con due. *Epig.*, p. 175.
14.14.   [Not in *Plan.*]
          Pagnini. Un vento solo ir fa. *Epig.*, p. 161.
14.18.   [Not in *Plan*]. Cf. *A.P.* 16. 29.
14.34.   [Not in *Plan.*] Quoted by Achilles Tatius (2. 14).
14.40.   [Not in *Plan.*] Quoted by Athenaeus (10. 451F); a prose form
          occurs in Choeroboscus, Περὶ Τρόπων. (Walz 8. 816); cf.
          Tryphon, Περὶ Τρόπων (Walz 8. 734).
          Giraldi (L. G.). Una aliam gignit. *Op.* 2. 448.
14.42.   [Not in *Plan.*]
          Pagnini. Una Corona di sessanta. *Epig.*, p. 173.
14.48.   [Not in *Plan.*]
          Pagnini. Delle tre Grazie ognuna. *Epig.*, p. 172.
14.56.   [Not in *Plan.*, but in Stephanus' ed. (1566), p. 535.]
          Pagnini. Allorchè tu mi guardi. *Epig.*, p. 160.
14.57.   [Not in *Plan.*, but in Stephanus' ed. (1566), p. 535.]
          Pagnini. Di mia madre più. *Epig.*, p. 161.
14.59.   [Not in *Plan.*]
          Pagnini. Cinquanta figli meco. *Epig.*, p. 160.

14.60. [Not in *Plan.*, but in Stephanus' ed. (1566), p. 536.]
Pagnini. Con gran fatiche. *Epig.*, p. 161.
14.64. [Not in *Plan.*] Quoted by Athenaeus (10. 456B); *Schol.* on
Euripides, *Phoen.* 50 (Dindorf 3. 8, 51); Tzetzes on Lyco-
phr. 7; in *Laur.* 32, 9 (Soph., *Oe.R.*); in various MSS.
Cf. Ausonius. Illa etiam thalamos. *Opus.*, p. 202.
Erasmus. Est bipes in terris. Giraldi, *Op.* 2. 449.
Pagnini. Per movere ov' ei vuol. *Epig.*, p. 162.
14.65. [Not in *Plan.*] Quoted by Pausanias (10 24); Stephanus Byzant., *s.v.* "Ιος; Proclus, *Vita Homeri* (West., p. 24).
Giraldi (L. G.). Insula Ios patria. *Op.* 2. 69.
14.66. [Not in *Plan.*] Quoted by Ps.-Plutarch, *Vita Homeri* (West.,
p. 22); and by Eusebius, *Praep. Evang.* 5 (pp. 227, 229).
Giraldi (L. G.). Felix, infelix, nam. *Op.* 2. 68.
Allacci. Felix atque miser. Gronov., *Thes.*, 10. 1796.
14.67. [Not in *Plan.*] Quoted in *schol.* on Eurip., *Phoen.*, argu. (Dindorf 3.8); in *Laur.* 32, 9 (Soph., *Oe.R.*).
14.68. [Not in *Plan.*] Quoted by Eusebius, *Praep. Evang.* 6. 255.
14.69. [Not in *Plan.*] Quoted by Herodotus (1. 65); Diodorus, *Ex.
Vat.*, p. 1; Themistius, *Orat.* 19 (Dindorf, p. 275).
Valla. Ad mea venisti. *Herod.*, f. 11ᵛᵒ.
Ficino. Aethereo dilecte Jovi. *Op.* 1. 631.
14.73. [Not in *Plan.*] Quoted by Photius, *s.v.* 'Υμεῖς; *Schol.* on Theoc.
14. 48; Suidas, *s.v.* 'Υμεῖς; and by Arsenios, *Viol.*, p. 361.
14.74. Sabeo. Templa Deum reserata. *Epig.*, p. 848.
14.76. [Not in *Plan.*] Herodotus 1. 66; Diodorus, *Ex. Vat.*, p. 29
(Dind.).
Valla. Me petis Arcadiam. *Herod.*, f. 11ᵛᵒ.
14.78. [Not in *Plan.*] Herodotus 1. 67; Diodorus, *Ex. Vat.*, p. 29
(Dind.).
Valla. Est pars Arcadiae. *Herod.*, f. 12ʳᵒ.
14.79. [Not in *Plan.*] Herodotus 1. 85; Diodorus, *Ex. Vat.*, p. 28
(Dind.).
Valla. Lyde genus rex multorum. *Herod.*, f. 16ʳᵒ.
14.80. [Not in *Plan.*] Herodotus 1. 91.
14.81. [Not in *Plan.*] Herodotus 1. 174.
14.82. [Not in *Plan.*] Herodotus 3. 57.
Valla. Cum tamen in siphno. *Herod.*, f. 75ʳᵒ.
14.83. [Not in *Plan.*] Herodotus 4. 155; Diodorus, *Ex. Vat.*, p. 15
(Dind.).
Valla. Batte, venis vocis. *Herod.*, f. 118ᵛᵒ.
14.84. [Not in *Plan.*] Herodotus 4. 157.
Valla. Lanigerae Libyes scis. *Herod.*, f. 119ʳᵒ.
14.85. [Not in *Plan.*] Herodotus 4. 159.
Valla. Serior in Libyen. *Herod.*, f. 119ʳᵒ.
14.86. [Not in *Plan.*] Herodotus 5. 92.
Valla. Eetion te nemo licet. *Herod.*, f. 163ʳᵒ.
14.87. [Not in *Plan.*] Herodotus 5. 92.

Valla. Concepit in petris aquila. *Herod.*, f. 163ʳᵒ.

14.88. [Not in *Plan.*] Quoted by Herodotus (5.92); by Dio of Prusa
(37. 5); in *Contest of Hom. and Hes.* 322; by Proclus, *Vit.
Hes.* (West., p. 48).

Valla. Vir locuples nostras. *Herod.*, f. 163ᵛᵒ.

14.89. [Not in *Plan.*] Herodotus 6. 19.

Valla. Tunc quoque commentrix. *Herod.*, f. 172ʳᵒ.

14.90. [Not in *Plan.*] Herodotus 6. 77.

Valla. Verum quando marem. *Herod.*, f. 161ᵛᵒ.

Giraldi (L. G.). Quando marem victrix. *Op.* 2. 124.

14.91. [Not in *Plan.*] Herodotus 6. 86.

Valla. Glauce epycydides equidem. *Herod.*, f. 163ʳᵒ.

Quoted by Arsenios, *Viol.*, p. 172.

14.92. [Not in *Plan.*] Herodotus 7. 140.

Valla. Quid miserande sedes. *Herod.*, f. 196ᵛᵒ.

14.93. [Not in *Plan.*] Herodotus 7. 141.

Valla. Pallas Olympaicum multis. *Herod.*, f. 197ʳᵒ.

14.94. [Not in *Plan.*] Herodotus 7. 148.

Valla. Finitimis invise deis. *Herod.*, f. 195ᵛᵒ.

14.95. [Not in *Plan.*] Herodotus 7. 169.

14.96. [Not in *Plan.*] Herodotus 7. 220.

Valla. Vobis amplivagae colitis. *Herod.*, f. 208ᵛᵒ.

14.97. [Not in *Plan.*] Herodotus 8. 20.

Valla. Dum iuga barbaricus. *Herod.*, f. 213ᵛᵒ.

14.98. [Not in *Plan.*] Herodotus 8. 77.

Valla. Auricomae postquam. *Herod.*, f. 221ʳᵒ.

14.99. [Not in *Plan.*] Herodotus 9. 43.

Valla. Gramineis ripis Asopi. *Herod.*, f. 241ᵛᵒ.

14.101. [Not in *Plan.*] Quoted by Diogenes Laertius 1. 6 (Cleobulus);
and by Stobaeus 1. 8 (Wachs. and Hense 1. 99).

Brugnolo? Est unus genitor nati. Laert.

Bentinus. Est genitor proles. *Laert.*, p. 34.

Giraldi (L. G.). Est unus genitor, cuius. *Op.* 2. 123, 447.

Crasso gives Bentinus' tr. *Ist.*, p. 120.

Pagnini. Dodici figli ha un sol. *Epig.*, p. 1.

14.110. [Not in *Plan.*]

Cf. Symphosius. Sponte mea veniens. *PLM* (Baehr.) 4. 385.

14.112. [Not in *Plan.*] Herodotus 1. 55.

14.115. [Not in *Plan.*] Quoted by Stephanus Byzant., *s.v.* Βυζάντιον; and
by Codinus (p. 8).

14.127. [Not in *Plan.*]

Pagnini. Un quarto di sua vita. *Epig.*, p. 175.

14.130. [Not in *Plan.*]

Pagnini. Di quattro fonti. *Epig.*, p. 173.

14.145. [Not in *Plan.*]

Pagnini. Da' dieci scudi a me. *Epig.*, p. 176.

14.146. [Not in *Plan.*]

Pagnini. Se due scudi mi dai. *Epig.*, p. 175.

14.147.   [Not in *Plan.*] Given in *Contest of Hom. and Hes.* 319.
          Pagnini. Omero a chi richieselo. *Epig.*, p. 172.
14.148.   [Not in *Plan.*] Quoted by Suidas, *s.v.* 'Ιουλιανός.
14.150.   [Not in *Plan.*] Quoted by Plutarch, *Theseus* 3. 3.

Book XV

15.20.   [Not in *Plan.*] Cf. *A.P.* 11. 300.
15.21.   [Not in *Plan.*] Lines 1–2 are quoted by Melampus on Dion.
          Thrac. (Hilgard, p. 11).
          Cf. Pigna, *Carm.*, pp. 97–9.
15.27.   Imitated by Valeriano, *Poem.*, 1550, f. 134vo.
15.35.   See under *A.P.* 5. 83–4.
15.36.   [Not in *Plan.*] Gr. quoted by Allacci, Gronov., *Thes.* 10. 1766.
          Argoli. Utrosque ingeniosa tuos. Gronov 10. 1766.
15.37.   [Not in *Plan.*] Gr. quoted by Allacci, Gronov 10. 1766.
          Argoli. Hosce tuos geminos. Gronov 10. 1766.
15.38.   [Not in *Plan.*] Gr. quoted by Allacci, Gronov 10. 1766.
          Argoli. Cernens Cometas. Gronov 10. 1766.
15.40N.   [Not in *Plan.*] Gr. quoted by Allacci, Gronov 10. 1766.
          Argoli. Incompta vatis verba. *Ibid.*
15.41.   Cornarius. Constantine, tibi vivo. Corn., p. 392.
15.42.   Cf. *A.P.* 16. 365.
          Cornarius. Constantinus adit postquam. Corn., p. 391.
15.51.   Sabeo. Aeneus est, videas. *Epig.*, p. 501.
          Cunich. Aereus est quem cernis. *Anth.*, p. 7.
          Felici. Fuso in bronzo è quel. *Epig.*[1], p. 122.
          Passeroni. E' di bronzo il cignal. *Rime* 3. 119.

Book XVI.

16.1.   Anselmo. Non patria est Messana. *Epig.*, Kiiii.
          Venatorius. Non ego Messanae. Obsop., p. 5; Wech., p. 4.
          Sabeo. Non ego Messene. *Epig.*, p. 195.
          Gualfreducci. Haud ego Messene. *Var.*, p. 281; *Sel. Epig.*,
          p. 7.
          Cottunius employs Gualfreducci's tr. *Confic.*, p. 78.
          Averani. Non ego Messanae. *Op.* 1. 127, 268.
          Cunich. Non ego Messana. *Anth.*, p. 29.
          Medici (A. de'). Non ego Messanis. *Scelt.*, p. ix.
          Medici (A. de'). Non comune ai Messeni. *Scelt.*, p. ix.
          Passeroni. D'Argo a lottar non. *Rime* 3. 176.
          Felici. Non Argivo o Messenio. *Epig.*[2], p. xiv.
          Pagnini. Io giostrator non. *Epig.*, p. 70.
16.2.   Gualfreducci. Cerne Theodimum, qui. *Var.*, p. 282; *Sel. Epig.*,
          p. 7.
          Averani. Nosci Theocriti, qui. *Op.* 1. 15.
          Cunich. Cerne Theocritum, qui. *Anth.*, p. 42.
          Passeroni. Questo fiero garzon. *Rime* 3. 88.

16.3. Alciati. Isthmia Philonis. Soter², p. 2; Corn., p. 4; *Op.* 3. 572.
Conti. Isthmia devicit Diophon. *Myth.* 5. 1.
Sabeo. Saltu, ictu, iaculo. *Epig.*, p. 403.
Gualfreducci. Pythia Philonis Diophon. *Sel. Epig.*, p. 7.
Gualfreducci. Pythia Milonis Diophon. *Var.*, p. 282.
Ricolvi. Isthmiacis Diophon ludis. *Op.*, p. 69.
Ricolvi. Diofonte in lotta. *Op.*, p. 69.
Pagnini. Ne' ludi a Diofon. *Epig.*, p. 51.

16.4. More (Sir T.). Proiicitote meum. Soter², p. 7; Corn., p. 9.
Cornarius. Dehinc fato funitum. Corn., p. 9.
Alciati. Aeacidae moriens. Corn., p. 9; *Emb.* 154.
Obsopoeus. Post mortem Danai. Obsop., p. 17; Wech., p. 14.
Venatorius. Hectora post obitum. Obsop., p. 17; Wech., p. 14.
Sabeo. Nunc mea post fatum. *Epig.*, p. 323.
Cunich. Hectora Grajugenae. *Anth.*, p. 45.
Felici. Contra lo strenuo. *Epig.*¹, p. 98.
Passeroni. Ettore è morto. *Rime* 3. 225.

16.5. Sabeo. In Danaum Xerses. *Epig.*, p. 309.
Cunich. Huc tulit arma olim. *Anth.*, p. 12.
Pagnini. I Persi nemò Serse. *Epig.*, p. 35.

16.6.* Given by *schol.* on Aristides, *Panath.* 212B (Frommel, p. 48).

16.7. Sabeo. Mollibus inspirans. *Epig.*, p. 42.
Cunich. Qui, bonus argutam. *Anth.*, p. 90.

16.8. Cf. *A.P.* 7. 696.
Cunich. Iam neque piniferis. *Anth.*, p. 133.
Passeroni. Marsia infelice, ahi. *Rime* 3. 193.

16.9. Costanzi (G.). Musca canum est. *Epig.*, Oiiii^vo.
Luscinius. O venter cynomya. Corn., p. 18.
Alamanni. O ventre non saziabile. *Versi* 2. 142.

16.11. Sabeo. Umbrosae haec platano. *Epig.*, p. 142.
Cunich. Praeteriens platani. *Anth.*, p. 94.

16.12. Cf. 13.
Sabeo. Huc accede meam ad pinum. *Epig.*, p. 278 (280).
Cunich. Huc ades, hac subter. *Anth.*, p. 11.
Felici. Vieni; riposati. *Epig.*¹, p. 102.
Passeroni. T'arresta, O passeggier. *Rime* 3. 43.
Vargas. Vieni, e t'assidi. *Sag.*, p. 68.

16.13. Cf. 12.
Sabeo. Huc genialis ubi. *Epig.*, p. 535.
Sabeo. Alticomam iuxta hanc. *Epig.*, p. 719.

16.14. Lascaris (J.). Quis puerum Veneris. *Epig.*, f. 14vo; Soter²,
p. 74; Corn., p. 61.
Costanzi (A.). Qui te hinc pinxit. *Epig.*, Biii^ro.
Anisio. Heus tu qui ad fontem. *Poem.*, f. 90ro.
Valeriano. Exculptum ad fontes. *Poem.*, p. 113; *C.P.It.* 10.
157.
Cf. Valeriano. Propter aquas, flammae. *Poem.*, p. 113; *C.P.It.*
10. 157.

Calcagnini. Huic amor insedit. Pigna, p. 210; *C.P.It.* 3. 79.
Calcagnini. Qui puerum statuit. Pigna, p. 210; *C.P.It.* 3. 79.
Alamanni. Chi scolpio già. *Versi* 2. 142.
Jordanus. Fontibus apposuit. Soter³, p. 57.
Sabeo. Fontis ad hos latices. *Epig.*, p. 64.
Sabeo. Qui prope iam vitreos. *Epig.*, p. 124.
Toscano (G. M.). Adiectum fonti puerum. *C.P.It.* 9. 371.
Groto. Erri, sciocco pittor. *Rime*, pt. 3 (1610), f. 78.
Cf. Marino. Benchè di fredda pietra. *Lira* 2. 141.
Baldi. Chi ti pose del fonte. *Epig.* 296.
Toscano (M.). Marmoreum fonti quicumque. *Anth.*, p. 141.
Salvini. Sculptum a se quidam. Muratori, *Perf. Poes.* (1724) 1. 283.
Bongiovanni and Zanetti. Qual mai scultor. *Epig.*, p. 37.
Cunich. Imponis gelido cur. *Anth.*, p. 184.
Medici (A. de'). Qui primus tenerum. *Scelt.*, p. xxv.
Medici (A. de'). Scultor, perchè ti. *Scelt.*, p. xxv.
Passeroni. A che, pezzo scultore. *Rime* 3. 126.
Roncalli. In van scolpisti. *Epig.* (1792), p. 49; (1801), p. 50.
Mutinelli. Inesperto scultor. *Ann. Poet.* 1. 161.
Vargas. Chi pose appresso. *Sag.*, p. 84.
Pagnini. Chi di locare sculto. *Epig.*, p. 79.

16.16. More (Sir T.). Ingratum est quicquid. Soter², p. 100; Corn., p. 91.
Erasmus. Insuave est quicquid. Soter², p. 100; Corn., p. 91.
Obsopoeus. Omne supervacuum. Obsop., p. 117; Wech., p. 101.
Sabeo. Omne quod est nimium. *Epig.*, p. 412.
Sabeo. Importuna quidem sunt. *Epig.*, p. 412.

16.17. Conti. O Pan pascendis. *Myth.* 5. 6.
Sabeo. Carmina sacra canas. *Epig.*, p. 50.
Cunich. O Pan aureolas labro. *Anth.*, p. 168.

16.18. [In old edd. of Stobaeus, *Flor.* 10.]
Luscinius. Vive diu felix cui. Corn., p. 131.
Cornarius. Accipe tu laetus. Corn., p. 131.
Alciati. Gaude, accepta [prose]. *Op.* 4.390.
Sabeo. Mutuo habens mentem. *Epig.*, p. 235.

16.19. Alciati. Adveniens populo pacem. Corn., p. 148; *Op.* 4. 559.
Dazzi. Omnibus adveniens pax. *Poem.*, p. 125.
Sabeo. Adveniens populo pacem. *Epig.*, p. 434.
Sabeo. Accedens cunctis pax. *Epig.*, p. 434.
Sabeo. Altari assistens, Pax. *Epig.*, p. 435.

16.19.* Given by Athenaeus 5. 222A. Cf. *App. Verg.*, *Catal.* 2 (*PLM* 1. 130).

16.20. Cf. *A.P.* 11. 204.
Sabeo. Rhetora labrosum. *Epig.*, p. 242.

16.23. Soter. Dic quis, quo. Soter², p. 207; Corn., p. 248.
Soter. Casmylus hic iaceo. Soter², p. 207; Corn., p. 248.

Sabeo. Quis pater? Evagoras. *Epig.*, p. 333.

Sabeo. Dic quis es. *Epig.*, pp. 351, 470.

Gualfreducci. Quis? Cuius? patria. *Var.*, p. 282; *Sel. Epig.*, p. 8.

16.24. Cornarius. Milonis statua haec. Corn., p. 248.

Gualfreducci. Signum hoc Milonis. *Var.*, p. 282; *Sel. Epig.*, p. 8.

16.25. Gualfreducci. Cretum Sinope suspicis. *Var.*, p. 282; *Sel. Epig.*, p. 8.

16.26.* Quoted by Pausanias 7. 52.

16.26.** Quoted by Plutarch, *Flaminius* 9. 3.

16.27. Lines 4–5 = *A.P.* 7. 325.

Tifernas. Cum te mortalem. Strabo (1494), f. cxxiii; Soter², p. 220; Corn., p. 264.

Beroaldo (F.), the elder, quotes Tifernas' tr. *Var.*, A. iii.

Sabeo. Exple animum oblectans. *Epig.*, p. 332.

16.28. The first line is given by Dio of Prusa 7. 121.

Cornarius. Inter praecipuas evexit. Corn., p. 268.

Pagnini. Ne' flauti la Tebe. *Epig.*, p. 169.

16.29. Cf. *A.P.* 14. 18.

Sabeo. Si quem unquam. *Epig.*, p. 252.

Mazzoni quotes this epig. *Difesa*, p. 689.

16.30. Sabeo. Dextra Polycreti. *Epig.*, p. 200.

16.31. Cf. *A.P.* 7. 61.

Sabeo. Quod mortale tenet. *Epig.*, p. 305.

Sabeo. Corpus et ossa tenent. *Epig.*, p. 374.

16.32. Sleidan. Artificis Phaetonta. Soter², p. 243; Corn., p. 316.

Calcagnini. Exprimit in tabula. Pigna, p. 208.

Calcagnini. Parrasii arte potest. Pigna, p. 212.

Calcagnini. Exprimere arte potes. Pigna. p. 213.

Sabeo. Pingitur et Phaeton. *Epig.*, p. 216.

Sabeo. Et Phaeton pictus. *Epig.*, p. 306.

Cf. Roncalli. Se pinger osi i vivi. *Epig.* (1801), p. 50.

16.32.* Alciati. Iulianum Beroë. Soter², p. 243; Corn., p. 316; *Op.* 4. 200.

16.33. Sabeo. Tanta tui est animi. *Epig.*, p. 795.

16.34. Sabeo. Ista Philippe dicat. *Epig.*, p. 817.

16.37. Sabeo. Petron inaurata. *Epig.*, p. 796.

16.38. Sabeo. Non modo ad Ilissum. *Epig.*, p. 216.

16.40. Sabeo. Non modo fortunae. *Epig.*, p. 361.

16.41. Sabeo. Iuxta Reginam. *Epig.*, p. 228.

16.42. Sabeo. Regem Asiae hac. *Epig.*, p. 344.

Argoli refers to this epig. Graev., *Thes.* 9. 254.

16.50. Bongiovanni and Zanetti. Se con queste. *Epig.*, p. 2.

16.52. Falconieri. Fortasse me, hospes. Gronov. 8. 2319.

16.53. Cunich. Transiliat stadium. *Anth.*, p. 2.

Passeroni. Non si sa se voli. *Rime* 3. 27.

Passeroni. O salti, o voli. *Rime* 3. 27.

    Pagnini. Se la carriera. *Epig.*, p. 146.
16.54–54.* Sabeo. Extremum currens. *Epig.*, p. 265.
    Cunich. Qualis eras, Lada. *Anth.*, p. 2.
    Passeroni. Quale era Lada. *Rime* 3. 26.
16.57. Cornarius. Natura amentem. Corn., p. 317.
    Sabeo. Si Bacca insana. *Epig.*, p. 219.
    Sabeo. Si Baccha est amens. *Epig.*, p. 265.
    Sabeo. Quod Baccha est. *Epig.*, p. 265.
16.58. Cornarius. Contineas Baccham, quamvis. Corn., p. 317.
    Sabeo. Sit licet e saxo. *Epig.*, p. 345.
    Bongiovanni and Zanetti. Ferma quella Baccante. *Epig.*,
     p. 13.
    Cunich. Hanc cohibete, viri. *Anth.*, p. 6.
    Felici. Questa Baccante. *Epig.*[1], p. 121.
    Passeroni. Salda tien quella. *Rime* 3. 30.
    Cf. Passeroni. Risorto è Orfeo. *Rime* 3. 30.
16.59. Sabeo. Plangere forsan adhuc. *Epig.*, p. 307.
    Sabeo. Nondum forte aptam. *Epig.*, p. 380.
    Rivautella-Ricolvi. Quae pulsare manu. *Mar.* 1. 44.
    Cunich. Hanc sculptor Baccham. *Anth.*, p. 12.
    Passeroni. Ve' come pudibonda. *Rime* 3. 38.
16.60. Cf. *A.P.* 9. 774.
    Alciati. Quae haec Baccha? Corn., p. 317.
    Alciati quotes this ep., *Op.* 4. 253.
    Cunich. Quaenam ista? *Anth.*, p. 41.
    Passeroni. Che sei tu? *Rime* 3. 111.
16.61. Sabeo. Ortus et occasus. *Epig.*, p. 220.
    Crasso. Ortus, Occasus [L-prose]. *Ist.*, p. 356.
16.64. Sabeo. Hanc prope littus. *Epig.*, p. 307.
16.66. Quoted by Hesych. Mil. (Mueller *F.H.G.* 4. 152); Codinus,
     p. 12 (Bekker).
16.68. Alciati. Ambigo an haec. Soter[2], p. 243; Corn., p. 318; *Op.*
     4. 1092.
    Sabeo. Cypridis haec icon. *Epig.*, p. 360.
    Guazzo. Non so se questa. *Ghirl.*, p. 269.
    Cunich. Cypridis haec pulcrae. *Anth.*, p. 24.
    Passeroni. La immagine questa. *Rime* 3. 254.
    Vargas. Questa è l'immago. *Sag.*, p. 49.
    Pagnini. Di Berenice o di Ciprigna. *Epig.*, p. 107.
16.74. Cunich. Imperio miti paullum. *Anth.*, p. 73.
    Passeroni. Dolce e mite debbe. *Rime* 3. 195.
16.75. Sleidan. Cum Iove, cum Phoebo. Soter[2], p. 244; Corn., p. 318.
    Sabeo. Ad sua vota parens. *Epig.*, p. 6.
    Sabeo. Mavorti et Phoebo. *Epig.*, p. 71.
16.77. Sabeo. Vix oculos sed non. *Epig.*, p. 793.
    Medici (A. de'). Nulla potest oculos. *Scelt.*, p. xx.
    Medici (A. de'). Arte non v'è. *Scelt.*, p. xx.
    Pompei. Gli occhi a stento. *Op.* 2. 202.

Mutinelli. Che pinger può. *Ann. Poet.* 1. 158.

16.78. Sabeo. Invida pictura es. *Epig.*, p. 797.
Pompei. Pien se' d'astio. *Op.* 2. 229.

16.79. Synesius, *Epist.* 75.

16.80. Sabeo. Romulidas inter. *Epig.*, p. 124.

16.81. Velius. Aut deus e coelo. Soter[2], p. 244; Corn., p. 319.
Sabeo. Vel Deus e coeli. *Epig.*, p. 333.
Castelvetro quotes this epig. on Petr., *Son.* 57. *Petr.*, p. 159.
Groto. Mira Giunon la imagin. *Rime* (1587), p. 158.
Cunich. Iupiter ut fieri sic. *Anth.*, p. 3.
Pompei. O il Nume è in terra. *Op.* 2. 211.
Passeroni. O sali Fidia in ciel. *Rime* 3. 26.
Passeroni. Per ritrar Giove o Fidia. *Rime* 3. 26.
Bettinelli. Perchè fosse al vivo. *Op.* 22. 97.
Pagnini. Fidia, o Giove a te. *Epig.*, p. 5.

16.82. Quoted by Strabo 14. 2. 5; Cedrenus 1. 755 (Bekker); Constant. Porphyrog. 3. 99.

16.84. Sleidan. Est opere in nullo. Soter[2], p. 244; Corn., p. 319.

16.86. Cf. *Priap.* 10. Insulsissima. *PLM* (Baehr.) 1. 60.

16.87. Conti. Lumina sunt artis. *Myth.* 4. 6.
Sabeo. Artis, frugiferam. *Epig.*, p. 309.

16.88. Sabeo. Aes vocat indomitum. *Epig.*, p. 310.

16.89. Velius. Hic conviva prius. Soter[2], p. 252; Corn., p. 328.
Conti. Qui satis ante fuit. *Myth.* 6. 18.
Sabeo. Qui prius extiterat. *Epig.*, p. 451.
La Monnoye. Ille ego qui quondam. 'Επ. και 'Ελ. No. 74.
Pagnini. Chi a' celesti conviti. *Epig.*, p. 22.

16.90. Sabeo. Frange premens validis. *Epig.*, p. 77.
Felici. Stendi le braccia tenere. *Epig.*[2], p. xxix.

16.91-2. These epigrams are given in Soter[2] (p. 252) and Corn. (p. 329) with passages from 'Virgil' (=Ausonius) and Ovid on the same subject—the labors of Hercules.

16.91. Sabeo. Haec tua conspicias. *Epig.*, p. 122.
Crasso. Aspice mille [L-prose]. *Ist.*, p. 192.

16.92. Ausonius. Prima Cleonaei tolerata. *Opus.* 7. 25.
Lines 1-12 are given by Tzetzes, *Chil.* 2. 491-502; and in *Cod. Laur.* 32, 9 after the *Trachiniae* of Sophocles.
Conti gives Ausonius' version. *Myth.* 7. 1.
Sabeo. Compressit primum. *Epig.*, p. 77.

16.93. Luscinius. Perdomui Nemees monstrum. Soter[2], p. 255; Corn., p. 331.
Velius. Extinxi Nemeesque feram. Soter[2], p. 255; Corn., p. 332.
Velius. Infestum Nemees monstrum. Soter[2], p. 255; Corn., p. 332.
Conti. Dextra feram Nemeae. *Myth.* 7. 1.
Mignault. Extinxi Nemees monstrum. Alciati, *Emb.* 137.

16.95. Lines 3-4 are quoted by Mazzoni. *Difesa*, p. 458.

16.97. Sleidan. Quis vero lachrymas. Soter[2], p. 256; Corn., p. 332.

Ricolvi. Aes ululans quis. *Op.*, p. 73.
Cunich. Aera quis haec duxit. *Anth.*, p. 6.
Passeroni. Questo gruppo sembra. *Rime* 3. 120.
16.98. Costanzi (A.). Hic gravis et somno. *Epig.*, Bii[vo].
16.99. Sabeo. Terrarum atque Herebi. *Epig.*, p. 78.
Carcani (P.). Questo di tutti. *Ant. Ercol.* 6. 80; *Rac.* 4. 59.
Felici. Già chiaro dagli esperii. *Epig.*[2], p. xxix.
16.100. Sabeo. Quum videas clavam. *Epig.*, pp. 42, 356.
Cunich. Caesariem et clavae. *Anth.*, p. 1.
Passeroni. Se vedi pinto in tavola. *Rime* 3. 22.
16.101. Sabeo. Effinxit talem plastes. *Epig.*, p. 122.
16.102. Sabeo. Qualem te genuit. *Epig.*, p. 773.
16.103. Calcagnini. Hic Amor Herculea. Pigna, p. 206; *C.P.It.* 3. 76.
Salvini. Alcides, ubi clava. Gori, *Inscr.* 2. 136.
Cunich. Nunc ubi clava ingens. *Anth.*, p. 174.
Passeroni. Ove è la clava, Alcide. *Rime* 3. 68.
Bettinelli. Disarmato e umile. *Op.* 13. 87.
Pagnini. V. Ercole, ov'è la tua. *Epig.*, p. 74.
16.104. Cf. Rainerio. Quel, ch' apena fanciul. *Cent. Son.* xxii.
Sabeo. Hoc reliquum optabat. *Epig.*, p. 129.
Felici. E' pago di Saturnia. *Epig.*[2], p. xviii.
16.105. Sabeo. Mirum opus est. *Epig.*, p. 166.
16.106. Sabeo. Tam si insanisset. *Epig.*, p. 357.
16.107. Cf. 108.
Anselmo. Obruerat cera audaci. *Epig.*, Fiiii.
Sleidan. Cera tibi vitam. Soter[2], p. 256; Corn., p. 333.
Alciati. Icare, cera quidem. Corn., p. 333; *Emb.* 104.
Sabeo. Icare, demersit te. *Epig.*, p. 745.
Sabeo. Icare, cera olim. *Epig.*, p. 759.
Mignault. Icare, cera olim. Alciati, *Emb.* 103.
Sanchez. Icare cera quidem. *Op.* 3. 212.
Groto. Icaro (O come gira. *Rime* (1587), p. 158.
Marino. La cera, che fatale. *Gal.* 2. 35.
Gualfreducci. Icare, caera diem. *Var.*, p. 293.
Bongiovanni and Zanetti. Icaro, ti sovvenga. *Epig.*, p. 52.
Ricolvi quotes this epig. without tr. *Op.*, p. 75.
Cunich. Icare, cera olim te. *Anth.*, p. 155.
Felici. Già armato gli omeri. *Epig.*[1], p. 43.
Pagnini. La cera, Icaro. *Epig.*, p. 38.
16.108. Cf. 107.
Alciati. Icare Daedalides, cave. Corn., p. 334.
Sabeo. Aeneus existens. *Epig.*, p. 205.
Sabeo. Ex aere es, videas. *Epig.*, p. 759.
Pagnini. Icaro, tieni in mente. *Epig.*, p. 85.
16.109. Sabeo. Nescio quod verbum. *Epig.*, p. 254.
16.111. Sabeo. Urbe Philoctetem. *Epig.*, p. 235.
Dati. Vide Parrasio gl'. *Vite*, p. 95.
16.112. Sabeo. Ob Danaos plastes. *Epig.*, p. 378.

16.113. Sabeo. Nosco Philoctetem. *Epig.*, p. 287 (275).
Vargas. Sì Filottete è questo. *Sag.*, p. 46.

16.114. Sabeo. Pyrrhus ego ob patriam. *Epig.*, p. 444.
Cunich. Pyrrhus ego hunc. *Anth.*, p. 173.
Passeroni. Io Pirro al genitor. *Rime* 3. 74.
Felici. Pirro io son. *Epig.*², p. xiii.
Pagnini. Io Pirro al padre. *Epig.*, p. 32.

16.115. Cf. Tzetzes, *Chil.* 6. 964.
Alciati. Ex viro descendit. Corn., p. 335.
Cf. Alciati. Quid dicam? quonam. *Emb.* 5.
Sabeo. Hunc hominem. *Epig.*, p. 368.

16.116. Sabeo. Iunxit equo celeri. *Epig.*, p. 314.
Sabeo. Pars homo pars equus. *Epig.*, p. 368.
Sabeo. Vir defendit equum. *Epig.*, p. 368.
Sabeo. Vir pedibus, cervice. *Epig.*, p. 368.

16.117. Quoted by Choricius, *Op.*, p. 503 (Foerster).
Sabeo. Te, Cynagire, velut. *Epig.*, p. 445.

16.118. Sabeo. Interfectrices Med. *Epig.*, p. 114.

16.119. Sabeo. Vel tua dextra. *Epig.*, p. 228.
Bongiovanni and Zanetti. O Sicionio scultor. *Epig.*, p. 5.
Cunich. Mire opifex Lysippe. *Anth.*, p. 40.
Passeroni. Qual vivo foco. *Rime* 3. 127.
Pagnini. Del gran Pelleo. *Epig.*, p. 52.

16.120. Lines 3–4 are given by Plutarch (*Moral.* 331A; 335B); Tzetzes
Chil. 8. 425; 11. 107.
Budaeus. Aereus in coelum. Soter², p. 257.
Cornarius. Pectus Alexandri. Corn., p. 334.
Cf. Beazzano. Chi è costui che nel. *Rac. Lir.* (1835), p. 780.
Sabeo. Audaces animos. *Epig.*, p. 229.
Bongiovanni and Zanetti. Di Alessandro. *Epig.*, p. 5.
Carcani (P.). L'ardire di Alessandro. *Ant. Ercol.* 6. 236; *Rac.*
4.73.
Cunich. Quantus Alexander Lysippi. *Anth.*, p. 23.
Felici. Nel bronzo di Lisippo. *Epig.*¹, p. 20.
Passeroni. Oh qual grandezza. *Rime* 3. 259.
Roncalli. In questo bronzo. *Epig.* (1792), p. 23; (1801), p. 42.
Pagnini. D'Alessandro l'ardir. *Epig.*, p. 90.

16.121. Sabeo. Inspice Alexandrum. *Epig.*, p. 312.
Bertòla. Come Alessandro. *Poes.* 1. 179.

16.122. Sabeo. Pignus Alexandrum. *Epig.*, p. 372.
Pagnini. Mira Alessandro. *Epig.*, p. 146.

16.125. Sabeo. Lertiade, usque tibi. *Epig.*, p. 834.
Felici. Al greco Ulisse. *Epig.*², p. xxx.

16.127. Cf. Valeriano. Alciati, *Emb.* (1621), p. 149.
Sabeo. Hedorum regem. *Epig.*, p. 465.

16.128. Sabeo. Iphigenia furit. *Epig.*, p. 380.
Vargas. Delira Ifigenia. *Sag.*, p. 48.

16.129. Ausonius. Vivebam. Sum facta. *Opus.* 19. 63; Sabeo[2], p. 257;
 Corn., p. 335.
Marullus admired this epig. Above, p. 146.
Crinitus quotes Marullus. *Ibid.*
More (Sir T.). Dii ex viva lapidem. Soter[2], p. 257; Corn.,
 p. 335.
Lily (W.). Ex vita saxum Dii. Soter[2], p. 257; Corn., p. 335.
Sleidan. Ira deum violenta. Soter[2], p. 257; Corn., p. 335.
Alciati. Fecere ex viva marmor. Corn., p. 335.
Calcagnini. Qualis eram, me talem. Pigna. p. 215; *C.P.It.* 3.
 82.
Calcagnini. Vivam olim in lapidem. Pigna, p. 215; *C.P.It.* 3.
 83.
Giraldi Cintio. Me lapidem ex viva. *Poem.*, p. 171.
Scaphenatus. Me iussere Dei vivam. *Eleg.*, Biiii.
Capece (Sc.). Me superi in saxum. *Op.*, p. 277.
Sabeo. Me vivam in lapidem. *Epig.*, p. 385.
Sabeo. De viva in saxum. *Epig.*, p. 386.
Sabeo. Me e viva in marmor. *Epig.*, p. 387.
Sabeo. Iam lapidem e Niobe. *Epig.*, p. 388.
Sabeo. Divi et Praxiteles. *Epig.*, p. 388.
Sabeo. Me volvere Dei. *Epig.*, p. 389.
Sabeo. Illa fui Niobe. *Epig.*, p. 389.
Sabeo. Vivebam; in saxum. *Epig.*, p. 388.
Sabeo. Vixi, quam cernis. *Epig.*, p. 387.
Sabeo. Ne foret una satis. *Epig.*, p. 386.
Sabeo. Sum Niobe, quae viva. *Epig.*, p. 385; *C.P.It.* 8. 214.
Scaliger (J. C.). Ne quaeras Niobes. *Poem.* 1. 161.
Scaliger (J. C.). Ex viva Dii me. *Poem.* 1. 161.
Sanchez. Vivebam: fecere di. *Op.* 3. 154.
Paterno. Vissi, ma poi mi fer. *Nuov. Fiam.*, p. 25.
Groto. Fui Niobbe, indi. *Rime* (1587), p. 147.
Moro. Son Niobe in sasso. *Giard.* 3. 3. 90 (3. 182).
Cf. Murtola. Chi ti diè questa. *Rime*, f. 206ro.
Cf. Murtola. Scoltor sei troppo. *Rime*, f. 204vo.
Cf. Murtola. Non fù pietà, Scoltore, *Rime* f. 205vo.
Gualfreducci. Me Niobem divi. *Var.*, p. 293.
Cf. Fagagna. L'industre e saggio. *Gareg.*, p. 39ro.
Urban VIII. Bis septem Niobe. *Poem.*, p. 165.
Cf. Tronsarelli. Mater, quam divi. *Jan. Quad.*, p. 58.
Cunich. E viva saxum. *Anth.*, p. 6.
Pompei. Di viva, ch' era. *Op.* 2. 227.
Felici. Me viva Niobe. *Epig.*[1], p. 123.
Bertòla. In sasso un dì conversa. *Poes.* 1. 178.
Bettinelli. Di Niobe un sasso fece. *Op.* 21. 51.
Vargas. In pietra un dì. *Sag.*, p. 71.
Pagnini. Di donna viva un sasso. *Epig.*, p. 22.
16.130. Scaphenatus. Aspice quam vere. *Eleg.*, Biiii; *C.P.It.* 9. 5.

Sabeo. Forma infelicis Niobes. *Epig.*, p. 206.
16.131. Conti. Tantalis haec ipsa. *Myth.* 6. 13.
Sabeo. Tantalis haec [lines 1–6]. *Epig.*, p. 540.
Sabeo. Non matrem nati [lines 7–10]. *Epig.*, p. 353.
16.132. Sabeo. Sta prope, amice. *Epig.*, p. 206.
Felici. Il passo in questo. *Epig.*[2], p. xxvii.
16.133. Sabeo. Cur imprudentes. *Epig.*, p. 460.
16.135. Cf. 139. Cf. Choricius, *Op.*, p. 383 (Foerster).
Ausonius? Laude Timomachum. *Opus.* 23. 23.
Gaurico. Quod natos feritura. Soter[2], p. 257; Corn., p. 336;
C.P.It. 5. 276.
Sabeo. Nati infelices. *Epig.*, p. 348.
Sabeo. Ficta ab Timomacho. *Epig.*, p. 348.
Cf. Sabeo. Nudatum stringens. *Epig.*, p. 869.
Castelvetro quotes this epig. on Petr., *Son.* 144. *Petr.*, p. 320.
Vargas. Nel volto di Medea. *Sag.*, p. 44.
Pagnini. Di Timomacho l'arte. *Epig.*, p. 107.
16.136. Ausonius? Medea, vellet cum. *Opus.* 23. 21; Soter[2], p. 258;
Corn., p. 336.
Sabeo. Dextera Timomachi. *Epig.*, p. 365.
16.137. Ausonius? Quis te pictorum. *Opus.* 23. 22; Soter[2], p. 259;
Corn., p. 337.
Sabeo. Impia quis nam te. *Epig.*, p. 243.
16.138. Given without tr. in Soter[2], p. 259.
Sabeo. Aspice res mira. *Epig.*, p. 502.
Cf. Sabeo. Saeva videbatur Colchis. *Epig.*, p. 502.
Pagnini. La divin' arte. *Epig.*, p. 143.
16.139. Cf. 135.
Sabeo. Non animata animas. *Epig.*, p. 466.
16.140. Minturno. Mirum opus: ut potuit. *Epig.*, f. 6ᵣₒ.
Pagnini. Mira Medea, ch' estolle. *Epig.*, p. 125.
16.141. Cf. *A.P.* 9. 346.
Quoted without tr. in Soter[2], p. 145.
Sabeo. Blesa quid in natos. *Epig.*, p. 484.
16.142. Cf. *A.P.* 9. 593.
Sabeo. Insanis, licet es. *Epig.*, p. 354.
Cunich. Flet, furit, odit. *Anth.*, p. 21.
Passeroni. Geme, smania, ama. *Rime* 3. 50.
16.143. Cornarius. En Medeae oculos. Corn., p. 338.
Sabeo. Medeae statua haec. *Epig.*, p. 489.
16.144. Conti. Non dotem, magis an. *Myth.* 7. 8.
Sabeo. Proiicis Hippomanes. *Epig.*, p. 434.
16.145. Cornarius. Non te sculpsit homo. Corn., p. 338.
Alciati. Non te vir sculpsit. Corn., p. 338.
Sabeo. Non te mortalis. *Epig.*, p. 488.
Pagnini. Non umana arte, no. *Epig.*, p. 146.
16.146. Alciati. Hospes marmoream. Corn., p. 338.
Sabeo. Tangere marmoream. *Epig.*, p. 538.

16.147. Fioretti refers to this epig. *Prog.* 2. 13.
16.148. Sabeo. Cepheus Andromedam. *Epig.*, p. 539.
16.149. Sabeo. Argivae haec Helenae. *Epig.*, p. 486.
16.150. Sabeo. Ista Polycreti est. *Epig.*, p. 538.
    Vargas. Ecco di Policleto. *Sag.*, p. 46.
    Pagnini. L'Argivo Policleto. *Epig.*, p. 178.
16.151. Ausonius? Illa ego sum Dido. *Opus.* 23. 2; Soter[2], p. 260; Corn.
    p. 339.
    Marullus. Tu qui me casusque. *Epig.* 1, p. 6; Soter[2], p. 261;
    Corn., p. 340.
    Sleidan. Olim talis eram. Soter[2], p. 260; Corn., p. 339.
    Gaurico (P.). Egregiae Didus, hospes. *Epig.* [6].
    Sabeo. Haec vera effigies. *Epig.*, p. 462.
    Mazzoni gives the Gr. and the imit. ascribed to Auson. *Difesa,*
    p. 456.
    Angelio. Quam cernis, vera. *Poem.*, p. 393.
    Orsini quotes this epig. on Virg., *Aen.* 4. 36.
    Cf. Groto. Per ir dietro a Sicheo. *Rime* (1587), p. 145.
    Fioretti refers to this epig. and to Auson. *Prog.* 1. 33.
    Averani. Musa quid armasti [lines 9–10]. *Op.* 2. 41.
    Felici. In questa viva. *Epig.*[1], p. 123.
16.152. Cf. Politian. Che fai tu, Eco. *Stanze* (1912), p. 563.
    Politian quotes this epigram, *Misc.* 22.
    Quoted without tr. in Soter[2], p. 262.
    Alciati. Amica nobis Echo. Corn., p. 342.
    Vargas. Non negarmi, Eco. *Sag.*, p. 87.
    Pagnini. Dolce Eco amica. *Epig.*, p. 106.
16.154. Cornarius. En Echo in petris. Corn., p. 341.
    Conti. Echo saxosum cernis. *Myth.* 5. 6.
    Sabeo. Saxosum audi, hospes. *Epig.*, p. 7.
    Sabeo. Intueare, hospes. *Epig.*, p. 448.
16.155. Soter. Sum sermonisequa. Soter[2], p. 261; Corn., p. 341.
    Cornarius. Fex vocis sum Echo. Corn., p. 341.
    Calcagnini. Incola rupis ego. Pigna, p. 213; *C.P.It.* 3. 81.
    Sabeo. Crine decens, sed sum. *Epig.*, p. 10.
    Sabeo. Verbisequa est Echo. *Epig.*, p. 850.
16.156. Sabeo. Sum dea ab Arcadia. *Epig.*, p. 500.
16.157. Cornarius. Arma quid in media. Corn., p. 343.
    Sabeo. Arma gerens media. *Epig.*, p. 18.
16.158. Pagnini. Me Cintia degna. *Epig.*, p. 80.
16.159. Cornarius. Quisnam animam lapidi. Corn., p. 344.
    Sabeo. Quis nam inspiravit. *Epig.*, p. 72.
    Franchini. Unde decus tantum. *Epig.*, p. 5; *C.P.It.* 5. 117.
    Minturno. Qui Gnidiam fecit. *Epig.*, f. 6ro; *C.P.It.* 6. 318.
    Vargas. Chi diede vita. *Sag.*, p. 72.
    Pagnini. Chi l'alma infuse. *Epig.*, p. 83.
    Pagnini. Chi la pietra animò? *Epig.*, p. 24.
16.160. Cf. 162 and 168. Ausonius. [See 162.]

Angeriano. Aspiciens pictam. Ἔρωτ., Aiiii.
Angeriano. Parthenopen quum laeta. Ἔρωτ., Biiii.
Sleidan. Cum propriam effigiem. Soter[2], p. 272; Corn., p. 345.
Cornarius. Ipsa Venus Cnidios. Corn., p. 345.
Molza. Spiranti ductum spectans. *C.P.It.* 6. 365.
Sabeo. Pulchra Gnidum ponti. *Epig.*, p. 72.
Cf. Franchini. Marmoream aspiciens. *Epig.*, p. 5.
Cf. Denalio. Cum bene se Cypris. *Poem.*, p. 199.
Groto. Vidi se stessa Citherea. *Rime*, pt. 3 (1610), f. 79.

16.161. Cornarius. Non te Praxiteles. Corn., p. 345.
Sabeo. Te neque Praxiteles. *Epig.*, p. 88.
Pagnini. Te non il ferro. *Epig.*, p. 115.
Pagnini. Non te scarpello. *Epig.*, p. 25.

16.162. Cf. 160 and 168.
Ausonius. Vera Venus Gnidiam. *Opus.* 19. 67.
Cf. Accolti (Ber.). Julia, vedendosi. *Verg.*, f. 49[v°].
Sabeo. In Gnido ait. *Epig.*, p. 93.
Marino. La dea, che 'n Cipro. *Lir.*, pt. 1, p. 205; *Gal.*, p. 4.
Pagnini. Vener mirando il suo. *Epig.*, p. 81.

16.163. Cornarius. Nemo unquam Venerem. Corn., p. 345.
Pagnini. O nessum vide ignude. *Epig.*, p. 25.

16.164. Cornarius. Ipse decus formae. Corn., p. 346.
Sabeo. Formosam posui effigiem. *Epig.*, p. 88.
Pagnini. Tua bella imago. *Epig.*, p. 26.

16.165. Cornarius. Quum Cnidiam Pallas. Corn., p. 346.
Cordato. Cum Venerem regina. *Prael.*, p. 112.
Sabeo. Pallas ut inspexit. *Epig.*, p. 88.
Franchini. Te Venus ut Iuno. *Epig.*, p. 5; *C.P.It.* 5. 117.
Cunich. Pallasque et Iuno. *Anth.*, p. 32.
Pompei. Palla e Giunone. *Op.* 2. 197.
Passeroni. Disser Pallade e Giuno. *Rime* 3. 106.
Passeroni. Visero Giuno e la. *Rime* 3. 184.
Felici. Giuno e Pallade. *Epig.*[2], p. xvi.
Pagnini. Palla e Giuno. *Epig.*, p. 105.

16.166. Cornarius. Antea in Idaeis. Corn., p. 355.
Sabeo. Vidit in Ideis. *Epig.*, p. 92.
Pompei. Il bifolco da pria. *Op.* 2. 197.
Pagnini. Primo su i monti. *Epig.*, p. 92.

16.167. Cornarius. Quum videas Venerem. Corn., p. 350.
Sabeo. Si Venerem cernes. *Epig.*, p. 608.

16.168. Cf. 160 and 162.
Velius. Me Paris Anchisesque. Soter[2], p. 273; Corn., p. 346.
Cornarius. Ipsa Paris, nudam. Corn., p. 346.
Apiarius. Hanc Cytherea tibi. Corn., p. 346.
Sabeo. Me nudam Paris, Anchises. *Epig.*, p. 88.
Bongiovanni and Zanetti. Pari, Adone, ed. *Epig.*, p. 23.
Pompei. Paride e Anchise e Adon. *Op.* 2. 226.
Bettinelli. Anchise e Adon, gli è. *Op.* 21. 52.

Vargas. Vider me nuda Adone. *Sag.*, p. 72.
Pagnini. Me nuda Anchise e Pari. *Epig.*, p. 81.
16.169. Cf. 170.
Velius. Spumigenae Veneris. Soter², p. 273; Corn., p. 347.
Sleidan. Spumigenae Veneris. Soter², p. 273; Corn., p. 347.
Cornarius. Divinam effigiem Veneris. Corn., p. 347.
Sabeo. Aequoreae Veneris. *Epig.*, p. 93.
Franchini. Egregiam pulchrae [lines 1–2]. *Epig.*, p. 5; *C.P.It.* 5. 117.
Bongiovanni and Zanetti. Se la celeste. *Epig.*, p. 12.
Cunich. Aequoream Cnidia Venerem. *Anth.*, p. 4.
Passeroni. Chi la Ciprigna Dea. *Rime* 3. 28.
Pagnini. Si di Venere Pafia. *Epig.*, p. 82.
16.170. Cf. 169.
Cornarius. Quam Cnidiam cernis. Corn., p. 348.
Sabeo. Forte istud dices. *Epig.*, p. 100.
Cunich. Idem Cecropia si. *Anth.*, p. 4.
Felici. Se di Gnido su gli. *Epig.*[1], p. 33.
Bettinelli. Venere Gnidia al portico. *Op.* 13. 90.
16.171. Cf. Politian. Εἰς τί σάκος κρατέεις. Del Lungo, p. 220.
Sannazaro. Induerat thoraca humeris. *Op.*, p. 93.
Ariosto. Arma, Venus, Martis. Pigna, p. 296; Polidori, 1. 356.
Cf. Angeriano.Ibat venatum in silva. Ἔρωτ.Aiiii; *C.P.It.* 1.257.
Alciati. Cur Venus armigeri. Corn., p. 348.
Cornarius. Arma Venus Marti. Corn., p. 348.
Giraldi Cintio. Induerat thoraca humeris. *Poem.*, p. 157.
Conti. Haec Martis sunt arma. *Myth.* 4. 13.
Cf. Sabeo. Num satis est Pallas. *Epig.*, p. 80.
Orlandini. Mentre de l'arme. *Accesi* 1. 320; Carducci, *Poes. Barb.*, p. 357.
Guazzo. Venere armata, disse. *Ghirl.*, p. 464.
Moro. Venere, che fiammeggia. *Giard.* 2. 3. 14 (1. 128).
Murtola. Lascia lo scudo. *Rime*, f. 157ʳᵒ.
Murtola. Non coprir, non coprire. *Rime*, f. 157ʳᵒ.
Murtola. Perchè l'armi. *Rime*, f. 157ᵛᵒ.
Vida (H.). Canta la tromba. *Dub.*, p. 48.
Carcani (P.). Venere, e perchè. *Ant. Ercol.* 1. 154.
16.172. Cornarius. Ipsam aiunt Venerem. Corn., p. 348.
Sabeo. Quam demiraris censurae. *Epig.*, p. 100.
16.173. Cornarius. Ipsa Venus didicit. Corn., p. 349.
Conti. Usque Venus plenam. *Myth.* 4. 13.
Sabeo. Edidicit Cypris semper. *Epig.*, p. 100.
Giraldi (L. G.). Vos vero in thalamis. *Op.* 1. 377.
Carcani (P.). Sempre a portar. *Ant. Ercol.* 3. 70.
16.174. Ausonius. Armatam vidit Venerem. *Opus.* 19. 64; Soter², p. 274; Corn., p. 349.
Ausonius? Armatam Pallas Venerem. *Opus.* 23. 7; Soter², p. 274; Corn., p. 349.

Politian. [See 171.]
Cf. Sannazaro. Tractabat clypeum. *Op.*, p. 193.
Cornarius. Armatam vidit Venerem. *Corn.*, p. 350.
Alciati. Armatam Venerem cernens. *Corn.*, p. 350.
Scaphenatus. Aemula conspiciens. *Eleg.*, Biiii.
Alamanni. Vide Vener armata Palla. *Versi* 2. 136.
Giraldi (L. G.) quotes Gr. and Auson. (1). *Op.* 1. 377.
Cf. Scaliger (J. C.). Imbelli imbellis. *Poem.* 1. 183.
Minturno. Armatam Venerem aspiceret. *Epig.*, f. 3ᵛᵒ; *C.P.It.*
    6. 318.
Spinula. Mars armat Cypriam. *Epig.*, p. 55.
Cf. Crotti. Quid facies duro. *Flor. Spic.*, f. 81ʳᵒ.
Cf. Castelvetro. Spartanam ut vidit. *Bibl. Mod.* 1. 481.
Groto. Vide Minerva un dì. *Rime* (1587), p. 147.
Moro. D'acciar Pallade armata. *Giard.* 1. 3. 7. (1. 124).
Moro. Lece a me sola, O bella. *Giard.* 2. 3. 13. (1. 127).
Cf. Moro. Cinte le spalle havea. *Giard.* 1. 3. 26. (1. 134).
Cf. Marino. E sì possenti Dee. *Ad.* 2. 156. 7 (p. 33).
Cf. Bargiocchi. Imbellis mulier, quae ferro. *Epig.*, p. 154.
Bongiovanni and Zanetti. Pallada, vide Citerea. *Epig.*, p. 49.
Cunich. Vidit ut armatam. *Anth*,. p. 149.
Felici. Pallade vide un dì. *Epig.*¹, p. 125.
Passeroni. Vista Venere armata. *Rime* 3. 188.
Subleyras. Pallade vide armata. Bettinelli, *Op.* 21. 76.
Bettinelli. Armata a Sparta Venere. *Op.* 21. 75.
16.175. Cf. 246.
Cornarius. Assimilem Veneri armatae. *Corn.*, p. 355.
Cf. Giraldi Cintio. Sic similem Veneri. *Poem.*, p. 157; *C.P.It.*
    5. 391.
Cordato. Praxiteles Venerem. *Prael.*, p. 111.
16.176. Ariosto. Arma deo sua sunt. Pigna, p. 294; Polidori 1. 352.
Sabeo. Non alibi est talis. *Epig.*, p. 133.
Cf. Tronsarelli. Belligeram tractat. *Jan. Quad.*, p. 28.
Cunich. Nec Venus heic Spartae. *Anth.*, p. 16.
Passeroni. In abito diverso. *Rime* 3. 49.
16.177. Sabeo. Alma Venus risu. *Epig.*, p. 82.
Cf. Navagero. Quid magis adversum. *C.Q.P.*, p. 56.
16.178. Cf. 179–82. Cf. Pliny, *N.H.* 35. 91.
Ausonius? Emersam pelagi nuper. *Opus.* 23. 8; Soter², p. 275;
    Corn., p. 352.
Cf. Politian. Giurar potresti. *Stanze* 1. 101.
Hermann a Nov. Aq. Cyprida materno. Soter², p. 275; Corn.,
    p. 352.
Sleidan. Aspice, ut emergit. Soter², p. 275; Corn., p. 352.
Cornarius. Egreditur pontum. Corn., p. 352.
Conti. Egressam nuper Venerem. *Myth.* 4. 13.
Sabeo. Mirum opus inspicias. *Epig.*, p. 43.
Groto. Vagheggia Vener, che. *Rime*, pt. 3 (1610), f. 80ʳᵒ.

Marino. Ben n'ha sovra tutt'. *Lir.* 1. 207; *Gal.*, p. 5.
Dati refers to *A.P.* 16. 178–82. *Vite*, p. 228.
Averani quotes Gr. and Ausonius. *Op.* 1. 57.
Della Valle (G.). Ecco Ciprigna. Dati, *Vite*, p. 136.
Pompei. Fuor de l'onde del mar. *Op.* 2. 180.
Felici. Dall' arenoso oceano. *Epig.*[1], p. 18.
Giordani (P.) refers to this and the foll. epig. Above, p. 442.

16.179. Cf. 178, 180–2.
Cornarius. Visa fuit ponto egrediens. Corn., p. 353.
Sabeo. Emergentem undis. *Epig.*, p. 101.

16.180. Cf. 178–9, 181–2.
Cf. Politian. Κύπριν Ἀπελλείας ἔργον. Del Lungo, p. 219.
Cornarius. Salsa maris toto. Corn., p. 354.
Sabeo. Albentem instillans. *Epig.*, p. 34.
Cf. Marino. E con l'eburnea man. *Ad.* 7. 137 (p. 130).

16.181. Cf. 178–80, 182.
Cornarius. Materno ex thalamo. Corn., p. 354.
Sabeo. Ex utero nuper Paphia. *Epig.*, p. 89.
Bongiovanni and Zanetti. Sorse teste dal mar. *Epig.*, p. 13.
Cf. Bettinelli. Non sarebbe Troja. *Op.* 13. 89.

16.182. Cf. 178–81.
Giovane. Effugientem matris [prose]. *Ant. Tar.* 3. 3.

16.183. Sleidan. Dicito, quid commune. Soter[2], p. 276; Corn., p. 355.
Alciati. Haec Bacchus pater. *Emb.* 23.
Sabeo. Quid commune tibi. *Epig.*, p.'82.
Sanchez. Quid tibi commune. *Op.* 3. 67.
Mignault. Quid commune tibi. Alciati, *Emb.* 23.
Averani. Quid commune tibi. *Op.* 1. 115.
Cunich. Nam quid, Bacche. *Anth.*, p. 5.
Felici. Bacco, alla dea. *Epig.*[1], p. 125.
Passeroni. Visto avendo il dio. *Rime* 3. 22.

16.184. Sabeo. Pisoni ausonio custos. *Epig.*, p. 21.

16.185. Velius. Ortus uterque Iove. Soter[2], p. 277; Corn., p. 356.
Cf. Alciati. Natus uterque Iovis. *Emb.* 100.
Conti. Ambo Thebani [lines 1–2]. *Myth.* 5. 13.
Conti. Amborum columnae [3–6]. *Myth.* 5. 13.
Giraldi (L. G.) quotes Alciati. *Op.* 1. 324.
Sabeo. Ambo orti Thebis. *Epig.*, p. 128.
Sabeo. Exorti hic Thebis. *Epig.*, p. 149.
Aleander (G.), younger. Ex Thebis ambo. *Tr. Frat.*, p. 276;
    Graev., *Thes.* 5. 717.
Carcani (P.). Ambi di Tebe; ambi. *Ant. Ercol.* 7. 65; *Rac.* 4.
    III.
Cunich. Thebis orti ambo. *Anth.*, p. 4.
Passeroni. Nacquero entrambi. *Rime* 3. 29.
Roncalli. Ambo figli di Giove. *Epig.* (1792), p. 77; (1801), p. 60.

16.186. Sabeo. Mercurius pernix ego. *Epig.*, p. 771.
Argoli. Dicor ego velox, validus. Graev., *Thes.* 9. 67.

Cunich. Herma ego sum pedibusque. *Anth.*, p. 184.
16.187. Cf. Aesop, *Fab.* 66 (Halm); Babrius 119.
Sabeo. Quidam Atlantiadem. *Epig.*, p. 82.
16.188. Sabeo. Sortitus gratum variis. *Epig.*, p. 81.
16.189. Sabeo. Pervigil aerei custos. *Epig.*, p. 83.
16.190. Sabeo. Caprarum pastor Monichus. *Epig.*, p. 740.
Cunich. Hunc Morichus pastor. *Anth.*, p. 96.
16.191. Sabeo. Me rota confinxit. *Epig.*, p. 46.
16.192. Cunich. Hunc, o viator, quem. *Anth.*, p. 6.
Passeroni. T'inganni, O passeggier. *Rime* 3. 29.
16.193. Sabeo. Attingam cramben Cylleni? *Epig.*, p. 83.
Cunich. Paullum oleris licet. *Anth.*, p. 165.
Felici. Toccar mi lice. *Epig.*[1], p. 38.
16.194. Cf. *A.P.* 9. 773.
Costanzi (G.). Urere suetus amor. *Epig.*, Oiiii.
Cornarius. Aereus extat Amor. Corn., p. 358.
Sabeo. Aeneum Amorem ecquis. *Epig.*, p. 100.
Sabeo. Quare Amor est factus. *Epig.*, p. 148.
Pagnini. Di rame un fonditore. *Epig.*, p. 98.
16.195. Cf. 196–9.
Sleidan. Pinnifero quis vincla. Soter[2], p. 278; Corn., p. 359.
Bongiovanni and Zanetti. Chi fu colui. *Epig.*, p. 42.
16.196. Cf. 195, 197–9.
Sabeo. Impie quis nam te. *Epig.*, p. 17.
Cf. Groto. Erri, pittor, se senza. *Rime*, pt. 3 (1610), f. 78ʳᵒ.
16.197. Cf. 195–6, 198–9.
Alciati. Quis palmas vinclis. Corn., p. 359.
Sabeo. Quis vinctum manibus. *Epig.*, p. 20.
16.198. Cf. 195–7, 199.
Anselmo. Funde diu vinctus. *Epig.*, Kiiii; *C.P.It.* 1. 304.
Sabeo. Perpetuo vinctus. *Epig.*, p. 21.
Cunich. Fle, miser, incessum. *Anth.*, p. 177.
Felici. Piangi, sì piangi. *Epig.*[1], p. 62.
Passeroni. Piangi, misero, piangi. *Rime* 3. 73.
Cf. Bettinelli. Piangi pur, piangi. *Op.* 13. 84.
Pagnini. Stretto in catene. *Epig.*, p. 76.
16.199. Cf. 195–8.
Sabeo. Fle, geme, quae. *Epig.*, p. 23.
16.200. Marullus. Spreverat Idaliam. Soter[2], p. 279; Corn., p. 360.
Politian. Peram humeris habilem. Del Lungo, p. 528; Soter;
Corn.
Molza (F. M.). Torna Amore a l'aratro. Domenichi 1. 119;
Poes., p. 172.
Sabeo. Arva Amor invertens. *Epig.*, p. 4.
Sabeo. Peram humeris aptat. *Epig.*, p. 61.
Sabeo. Lampada deposita. *Epig.*, p. 114.
Gambara (L.). Saevus Amor sumpsit. *Illust. Fem.*, p. 387.
Tasso. Amor l'arco e la face. Solerti 2. 498.

Cf. Tasso. Sotto il giogo, ove. Solerti 3. 75.
Torelli. Havea deposto e la faretra. *Gareg.* 9. 222vo.
Beverini. Exuit auratos arcus. *C.P.It.* 2. 212.
Averani. Peram humero, stimulum. *Op.* 1. 222.
Salvini. Posta giù la sua face. *Teoc.*, p. 183.
Regolotti. Montato in desir novo. *Teoc.*, p. 294.
Bongiovanni and Zanetti. Archi e facelle. *Epig.*, p. 48.
Ricolvi. Ruricolae peram, bobus. *Op.*, p. 87.
Ricolvi. Venne un dì voglia. *Op.*, p. 87.
Cunich. Atque facem atque arcum. *Anth.*, p. 178.
Medici (A. de'). Abiiciens taedam. *Scelt.*, p. xiii.
Medici (A. de'). Gitta il protervo. *Scelt.*, p. xiii.
Della Torre. Posto giù l'arco. *Odi*, p. 130.
Vicini. Al suol deposta. *Gl'Id.*, p. 184.
Felici. L'arco e la fiaccola. *Epig.*[1], p. 68.
Passeroni. Depose Amor l'arco. *Rime* 3. 70.
Parini. Deposta un giorno. Giusti, p. 297.
Rossi (G. G. de'). Univa al giogo. *Scherz.* 28.
Mutinelli. Gittando Amor la face. *Ann. Poet.* 1. 160.
Pagnini. Posto giù face e strali. *Epig.*, p. 70.
Pagnini. Posto giù face ed arco. *Poet. Gr.*, p. 880.

16.201. Alciati. Dic ubi sunt incurvi. Corn., p. 361; *Emb.* 110.
Sabeo. Mitis erat, nam. *Epig.*, p. 12.
Sabeo. Arcus ubi incurvus? *Epig.*, p. 598.
Mignault. Arcus ubi reflexus. Alciati, *Emb.* 109.
'L-prose.' Ubi tibi arcus ille. Ἐπ. καὶ Ἐλ. No. 65.
Felici. Dov' è l'arco. *Epig.*[1], p. 61.

16.202. Sabeo. Ne me hospes factum. *Epig.*, p. 115.

16.203. Sabeo. Qui fastus nostros. *Epig.*, p. 41.

16.204. Quoted by Athenaeus 13. 591A.
Telesio. Praxiteles, quem passus. *Carm.* (1808), p. 6.
Sabeo. Quem male sensit. *Epig*, p. 67.
Garzoni. Praxiteles pinxit [lines 1–2]. *Piaz. Univ.*, p. 594.
Dati refers to this epig., *Vite*, p. 197.
Carcani (P.). Prassitele l'Amor. *Ant. Ercol.* 5. 159.
Pompei. Qual Prassitele in sè. *Op.* 2. 172.
Vargas. Quell'amor, che. *Sag.*, p. 61.

16.205. Cf. *A.P.* 6. 260.
Sabeo. Praxiteles Phryne. *Epig.*, p. 54.

16.207. Velius. Nudus Amor blandis. Soter[2], p. 280; Corn., p. 361.
Sleidan. Nudus Amor cur sic. Soter[2], p. 280; Corn., p. 362.
Alciati. Nudus Amor viden' ut. Corn., p. 362; *Emb.* 107.
Conti. Nudus Amor ridet. *Myth.* 4. 14.
Sabeo. Quid rides hoc saxum. *Epig.*, p. 103.
Sabeo. Nudus et imbellis. *Epig.*, p. 119.
Sabeo. Improbe inermis Amor. *Epig.*, p. 119.
Mignault. Nudus Amor mitis. Alciati, *Emb.* 106.
Sanchez. Nudus Amor ridet. *Op.* 3. 216.

Bongiovanni and Zanetti. Non d'arco armato. *Epig.*, p. 41.
Carcani. (P.), Nudo Amor perciò. *Ant. Ercol.* 5. 275.
Carcani (P.). L'arco non ha. *Ant. Ercol.* 8. 65; *Rac.* 4. 123.
Cunich. Nudus Amor blandum. *Anth.*, p. 180.
Medici (A. de'). Nudus Amor, quaeris. *Scelt.*, p. xxxvii.
Medici (A. de'). Vè come ride placido. *Scelt.*, p. xxxvii.
Felici. Ecco Amor, che. *Epig.*[1], p. 78.
Passeroni. Ride Amor dolcemente. *Rime* 3. 66.
Pagnini. D'arco e di strali. *Epig.*, p. 12.

16.208. Sabeo. Sit licet ipse inter. *Epig.*, p. 93.
16.209. Cf. *A.P.* 9. 15.
Cf. Anon. Tu qui lucernam. Buecheler 48; *C.I.L.* 4. 1941.
Alciati. Heus torrem sufflans. Corn., p. 362.
Cornarius. Quid torrem insufflas. Corn., p. 362.
Anon. Se l'estinta face. Carducci, *Poes. Barb.*, p. 261.
Sabeo. Qui cupis insufflans. *Epig.*, p. 93.
16.210. Cf. Capilupi (Ip.). Herculis ex humeris. *Carm.*, p. 72.
Sabeo. Repperit in viridi. *Epig.*, p. 16.
Vargas. Nella cupa foresta. *Sag.*, p. 43.
16.211. Cf. Angeriano. Dormis, saeve puer. 'Ερωτ. Ciiii; *C.P.It.* 1.
276.
Cf. Gravina (P.). Ne dubita, non. *Poem.*, f. 39[ro].
Sabeo. Dormis et vigiles. *Epig.*, p. 84.
Cf. Rota. Captanti somnum. *Poem.* p. 38.
Cunich. Dormis, qui vigiles. *Anth.*, p. 88.
Pompei. Tu ch'aspre cure. *Op.* 2. 201.
Felici. Tu nel crudel. *Epig.*[1], p. 93.
Passeroni. Dormi, Amor, che. *Rime* 3. 207.
Cf. Bettinelli. Dorme Amore, e cielo. *Op.* 13. 83.
Pagnini. Tu che ne' cuor. *Epig.*, p. 81.
16.212. Sabeo. Pendentem ex humeris. *Epig.*, p. 84.
16.213. Sabeo. Sis licet extensus. *Epig.*, p. 92.
Cf. Franchini. Quo sine mente ruis. *Epig.*, p. 37.
16.214. Quoted by Pio, *Annot.* 153 (*Lampas* 1. 539).
Sleidan. Aspice, ut exuviis. Soter[2], p. 280; Corn., p. 363.
Sabeo. Carne ut onusti. *Epig.*, p. 95.
Ricolvi. Cernis ovans Divum. *Op.*, p. 72.
Ricolvi. Mira di quai trofei. *Op.*, p. 72.
Felici. Lieti di ricche. *Epig.*[1], p. 92.
Carcani (P.). Vedi carchi di spoglie. *Ant. Ercol.* 7. 33; *Rac.*
4. 127.
Vargas. Lieti dell' altrui. *Sag.*, p. 42.
16.215. Given in Soter[2] (p. 281) and Corn. (p. 363) with parallels
from *Priapea.*
Conti. Exuviis superum laeti. *Myth.* 4. 14.
Sabeo. Intueare polum ut. *Epig.*, p. 44.
Bongiovanni and Zanetti. Mira come l'Olimpo. *Epig.*, p. 45.

Carcani (P.). Vedi, come gli Amori. *Ant. Ercol.* 7. 33; *Rac.* 4. 127.

16.216. Sabeo. Iunonem solus Polycletus. *Epig.*, p. 73.
Bongiovanni and Zanetti. L'Argivo Policleto. *Epig.*, p. 6.
16.217. Sabeo. Calliope vocor. *Epig.*, p. 749.
16.218. Cf. 219.
16.219. Cf. 218.
16.220. Sabeo. Pierides cunctae sumus. *Epig.*, p. 32.
16.221. Cf. 222 and 263.
Conti. Misit Athenarum [lines 7–8]. *Myth.* 9. 19.
Sabeo. Artifici quidam ferro. *Epig.*, p. 31.
Giraldi (L.G.). Sum Victoria [lines 9–10]. *Op.* 1. 447.
Quoted by Castelvetro on Petr., *Canz.* 2. Petr., p. 66.
16.222. Cf. 221 and 263.
Sabeo. Dum sibi me Persae. *Epig.*, p. 31.
Sabeo. Hunc lapidem Arsacidae. *Epig.*, p. 134.
Groto. Fui piena, e i Persi. *Rime*, pt. 3 (1610), f. 82ʳᵒ.
Pagnini. Me pietra e Persi. *Epig.*, p. 144.
16.223. Cf. 224.
Lascaris (J.). Praedicit Nemesis. *Centralbl.* 1. 342.
Quoted by Arsenios, *Paroem.*, p. 447; *Viol.*, p. 277.
Erasmus. Innuit hoc Nemesis. Soter², p. 282; Corn., p. 365.
Cornarius. Admonet et cubito. Corn., p. 365.
Alciati. Assequitur Nemesisque. *Emb.* 27.
Valeriano. Una manus cubitum. *Poem.*, p. 114; *C.P.It.* 10. 160.
Calcagnini. Frena manu normamque. Pigna, p. 209.
Sabeo. Praedicit Nemesis fraeno. *Epig.*, p. 31.
Giraldi (L. G.). Praedico hac Nemesis. *Op.* 1. 447.
Cf. Scaliger (J. C.). Pro censu alere. *Poem.* 2. 179.
Mignault. Mensura fraenoque. Alciati, *Emb.* 27.
Cunich. Fraena gero et normam. *Anth.*, p. 73.
Passeroni. Da Dea Nemesi io. *Rime* 3. 96.
Pagnini. Nemesi il braccio. *Epig.*, p. 90.
16.224. Cf. 223.
Lascaris (J.). En cubitum Nemesis. *Centralbl.* 1. 342.
Quoted by Arsenios, *Paroem.*, p. 447; *Viol.*, p. 277.
Erasmus. Continuo Nemesis cubitum. Soter², p. 282; Corn., p. 365.
Cornarius. Scire placet cubitum. Corn., p. 365.
Alciati. Assequitur Nemesisque. Corn., p. 365; *Emb.* 27.
Calcagnini. Sum Nemesis, hominum. Pigna, p. 208.
Sabeo. Quare contineam frenum. *Epig.*, p. 31.
Sabeo. Quare ulnam Nemesis. *Epig.*, p. 212.
Mignault. Mensuram teneo Nemesis. Alciati, *Emb.* 27.
16.225. Sabeo. Forte audire Deum. *Epig.*, p. 96.
16.226. Sabeo. Dulcibus hic labiis. *Epig.*, p. 102.
16.227. Sabeo. Florenti in prato. *Epig.*, p. 95.

Cunich. Heic prato in viridi. *Anth.*, p. 11.
Passeroni. Su questo erboso. *Rime* 3. 42.

16.228. Cf. *A.P.* 9. 313.
Sabeo. Rupe sub umbrosa. *Epig.*, p. 101.

16.229. Conti. Mercurium peperit [lines 3–4]. *Myth.* 5. 5.
Sabeo. Iste nepos Iovis. *Epig.*, p. 113.

16.230. Sabeo. Ne tibi fex ovium. *Epig.*, p. 102.

16.232. Cf. 233.
Conti. Arcada capripedemque. *Myth.* 5. 6.
Sabeo. Archada Melciades. *Epig.*, p. 96.

16.233. Cf. 232.
Conti. Montivagus custos. *Myth.* 5. 6.
Sabeo. Sylvarum cultor. *Epig.*, p. 30.

16.234. Molza. Tres capit hoc divos. *Poes.* 3. 207.
Sabeo. Tres habet hoc. *Epig.*, p. 103.

16.235. Conti. Sum Deus agrestis. *Myth.* 5. 6.
Sabeo. Sum Deus agrestis. *Epig.* p. 804.

16.236. Cf. *Priap.* 23. Hic me custodem. *PLM* 1. 65; Soter[2],
p. 283; Corn., p. 366.
Sabeo. Sepibus his olerum. *Epig.*, p. 30.

16.237. Cf. *Priap.* 76. Deprensos ego. *PLM* 1. 85.
Sabeo. Omnia subicio sulcos. *Epig.*, p. 102.

16.238. Cf. Martial. Fur notae nimium. *Epig.* 6. 72.
Sabeo. Sit licet hoc frustra. *Epig.*, p. 16.
Cunich. Vinea, custodem cui. *Anth.*, p. 158.
Pagnini. Cotesta vigna, a cui. *Epig.*, p. 151.

16.239. Sabeo. Erectum non me. *Epig.*, p. 157.

16.240. Sabeo. Maturas ficus video. *Epig.*, p. 113.

16.241. Sabeo. Ficus matura est. *Epig.*, p. 46.

16.242. Sabeo. Magnum istud telum. *Epig.*, p. 138.

16.243. Sabeo. Sum positus culto. *Epig.*, p. 801.

16.245. Sabeo. Inspiciens satyrum. *Epig.*, p. 746.
Felici. Punto da doglia. *Epig.*[1], p. 51.

16.246. Cf. 175.
More (Sir T.). Prorsum admiranda. Soter[2], p. 283; Corn.,
p. 366.
More (Sir T.). Aut isti satyrus. Soter[2], p. 283; Corn., p. 366.
Lily (W.). Aut satyrus fusus. Soter[2], p. 283; Corn., p. 366.
Sabeo. Aera vel ingressus. *Epig.*, p. 10.
Sabeo. Aut aes intravit. *Epig.*, p. 138.

16.247. Alciati. Sunt Satyri salcique. Soter[2], p. 284; Corn., p. 367; *Op.*
3. 574.
Sabeo. Certe omnes satyri. *Epig.*, p. 309.
Cunich. Esse scio satyros. *Anth.*, p. 162.
Felici. Già sò, che tutt'. *Epig.*[1], p. 69.

16.248. Cf. Pliny. Qui Satyrum in phiala. *N.H.* 33. 156.
Sabeo. Hunc satyrum haud. *Epig.*, p. 423.
Cf. Strozzi (G.). La Notte che tu. Above, p. 312.

Redi paraphrases this epig., *Op.* 1. 329.
Felici. Un satiro son io. *Epig.*[2], p. xxvi.
Vargas. Diodoro il suo Satiro. *Sag.*, p. 71.
Pagnini. Quel Satiro lavoro. *Epig.*, p. 110.

16.249. Sabeo. Proximus accedens. *Epig.*, p. 614.

16.250. Alciati. Aligerum fulmen fregit. Corn., p. 368; *Emb.* 108.
Sabeo. Alata alatus cernens. *Epig.*, p. 599.
Mignault. Aliger alatum fulmen. Alciati, *Emb.*, 107.
Cf. Marino. Non è, non è Tifeo. *Gal.* 2. 41.

16.251. Cf. Politian. Πολλάκι τοξευθείς. Del Lungo, p. 217.
Velius. Pennatum volucri. Soter[2], p. 284; Corn., p. 367.
Alciati. Aligerum aligeroque. Corn., p. 367; *Emb.* 111.
Sabeo. Adversum volucrem. *Epig.*, p. 146.
Mignault. Pennato Nemesis. Alciati, *Emb.* 110.
Giraldi (L. G.). quotes Alciati's version. *Op.* 1. 395.

16.252. Sabeo. Atque ego Acidalias. *Epig.*, p. 146.

16.253. Conti. Arcus ubi Diana. *Myth.* 3. 18.
Sabeo. Arcus ubi Diana. *Epig.*, p. 148.

16.254. Sabeo. Turba viatorum. *Epig.*, p. 48.
Aleander (G.), younger. Sacram Mercurio. Graev., *Thes.* 5. 722.

16.256. Sabeo. Si teneo sedem. *Epig.*, p. 47.
Aleander (G.), younger. Non enim [v. 3; prose]. Graev., *Thes.* 5. 723.

16.260. Sabeo. Si tu olera ad nostra. *Epig.*, p. 153.

16.261. Sabeo. Semitae utrique. *Epig.*, p. 145.

16.262. Sabeo. Ridentes Nymphae. *Epig.*, p. 134.

16.263. Cf. 221–2.
Ausonius. Me lapidem quondam. *Opus.* 19. 42; Soter[2], p. 285; Corn., p. 368.
Giraldi (L. G.) quotes Ausonius' tr. *Op.* 1. 447.
Conti. Huc saxum Persae. *Myth.* 9. 19.

16.265–6. Referred to by L. G. Giraldi, *Op.* 1. 44.

16.267. Cornarius. Unde est qui posuit. Corn., p. 369.
Sabeo. Unde fuit, qui te. *Epig.*, p. 222.

16.268. Cf. *A.P.* 9. 455 and 16. 293. 4.
Cornarius. Hippocrates te dictante. Corn., p. 371.
Sabeo. Coe tuam vocem. *Epig.*, p. 222.

16.270. Cornarius. Tempus erat quum. Corn., p. 369.
Sabeo. Tempus erat quo. *Epig.*, p. 223.
Sabeo. Mortales quandoque. *Epig.*, p. 286 (288).

16.271. Luscinius. Hippocrates hominum. Soter[2], p. 285; Corn., p. 371.
Velius. Hippocrates hominum. Soter[2], p. 285; Corn., p. 371.
Sabeo. Hippocrates hominum. *Epig.*, p. 389.
Ricolvi quotes Gr.; no tr. *Op.* p. 75.

16.272. Cornarius. Sanctus Iamblichus. Corn., p. 369.
Sabeo. Ad senium suavis. *Epig.*, p. 286 (288).

16.273. Cornarius. Filius ipse tibi. Corn., p. 370.

16.274. Cornarius. Magnus Iuliani medicus. Corn., p. 371.
Jausserandus. Iuliani regis. Soter³, p. 326.
Sabeo. Regis Iuliani. *Epig.*, p. 222.
Molza. Hic est ille olim. *Poes.* 3. 185.

16.275. Cf. Callistratus, *Descr.* 6.
Ausonius. Cuius opus?—Phidiae. *Opus.* 19. 33; Soter²,
p. 287; Corn., p. 373.
Politian discusses this epig. *Misc.* 49.
Cf. Marullus. Quis puer hic? Soter², p. 288; Corn., p. 376.
More (Sir T.). Unde erat hic. Soter², p. 286; Corn., p. 373.
Erasmus. Quae patria artifici? Soter², p. 286; Corn., p. 372.
Machiavelli. Chi sei tu, che non. *Op.* 8. 374.
Cornarius. Unde erat qui finxit? Corn., p. 374.
Alciati. Lysippi hoc opus. Corn., p. 375; *Emb.* 122; Soter³,
p. 328.
Gaurico. Cuius opus?—Quondam. *Epig.* [2]; *C.P.It.* 5. 277.
Sabeo. Quae nam Virgo. *Epig.*, p. 160.
Sabeo. Dic rogo quis Divum. *Epig.*, p. 810.
Giraldi (L. G.). Unde hic est Plastes? *Op.* 1. 35.
Mignault. Quis finxit plastes? Alciati, *Emb.* 121.
Sanchez. Quis figulus? *Op.* 3. 240.
Cartari refers to this ep., *Imag.* (1580), p. 480.
Cf. Marino. L'Occasion, che è. *Ad.* 6. 193 (p. 106).
Quoted by Rivautella-Ricolvi., *Mar.* 2. 5.
Ricolvi. Quis? quem te sculpsit. *Op.*, p. 65.
Ricolvi. Dimmi, che fe? cosa. *Op.*, p. 65.
Vargas. Donde, e chi lo scultor. *Sag.*, p. 39.

16.276. Scaphenatus. Haec simulachra tibi. *Eleg.*, Biiii; *C.P.It.*, 9. 5.
Sabeo. Erexit statuam Periander. *Epig.*, p. 234.
Sanchez. Constituit Periander. *Op.* 3. 185.
Crasso. Statuit Periander [L-prose]. *Ist.*, p. 64.

16.277. Sabeo. Vix pictura tuam. *Epig.*, p. 657.

16.278. Politian. Plectron habet citharae. Del Lungo, p. 142.
Velius. Plectra movet cytharae. Soter², p. 289; Corn., p. 377.
Sabeo. Plectron habet cytharae. *Epig.*, p. 668.
Carcani (P.). Ha della lira, ed ha. *Ant. Ercol.* 5. 203.

16.281. Sabeo. Balneum erat nullum. *Epig.*, p. 821.
Carcani (P.). Ora è bagno, non. *Ant. Ercol.* 7. 391; *Rac.* 4. 195.

16.284. Sabeo. Helladia hic sum. *Epig.*, p. 659.

16.286. Sabeo. Evincunt saltando. *Epig.*, p. 662.
Carcani (P.). La donna nel ballar. *Ant. Ercol.* 2. 45.

16.287. Sabeo. Concinuit iam lege. *Epig.*, p. 623.

16.288. Sabeo. Nomen habes thuris. *Epig.*, p. 658.

16.291. Sabeo. Horricomo huic Pani. *Epig.*, p. 154.
Sabeo. Flavicomo Pani. *Epig.*, p. 159.

16.292. Quoted by Ps-Plutarch, *Vit. Homer.* (West., p. 23).

Guarino da Verona. Nate Melete decus. Soter[2], p. 303; Corn., p. 383.

Sabeo. Hellados omnis honor. *Epig.*, p. 241.

Xylander. Nate Meletis, Homere. *Ap.* Allacci, Gronov., *Thes.* 10. 1787.

16.293. With line 4 cf. *A.P.* 9. 455 and 16.268.

Sabeo. Praelia qui scripsit. *Epig.*, p. 465.

Allacci. Ecquis perpetuis. Gronov., *Thes.* 10. 1729.

Bongiovanni and Zanetti. Qual fu colui. *Epig.*, p. 46.

Pagnini. Chi d'Ilio i casi. *Epig.*, p. 154.

16.294. Sabeo. Ex qua nam patria. *Epig.*, p. 341.

Cf. Loredano. Homero son, che qui. *Cimit.* 4. 71.

Allacci quotes Gr. and Sabeo's tr. Gronov., *Thes.* 10. 1730.

16.295. Cf. 296.

Marullus. Vane quid affectas. *Epig.* 3, p. 32; Soter[2], p. 304; Corn., p. 384.

Sabeo. Non Smyrnaeus ager. *Epig.*, p. 257.

Sabeo. Vos Colophona, sacro. *Epig.*, p. 447.

Groto. A che tant' opra. *Rime* (1587), p. 155.

Aleander (G.), younger. Incertus Graiorum. Gronov., *Thes.* 10. 1730.

Allacci quotes the Gr. and Sabeo's first tr. Gronov., *Thes.* 10. 1729.

Cunich. Non Smyrna tellus. *Anth.*, p. 8.

Passeroni. Mainò, la patria. *Rime* 3. 34.

16.296. Cf. 295.

Quoted by Ps-Plutarch, *Vit. Homer.* (West., p. 22).

Guarino da Verona. Diceris a multis. Soter[2], p. 304; Corn., p. 384.

Codro Urceo quotes Guarino's tr. *Op.*, p. 176.

Anon. See above, p. 37.

Quoted by Politian. *Op.* (1537) 3. 66.

Cf. Carteromaco. De patria magni. Politian, *Epist.* 12. 25.

Xylander. Sunt, Colophona, tibi. *Ap.* Allacci, Gronov., *Thes.* 10. 1730.

Allacci. Quidam tui. Gronov., *Thes.* 10. 1787.

Crasso. Sunt Colophona [L-prose]. *Ist.*, p. 372.

16.297. Cf. 298. Referred to by Gellius, *N.A.* 3. 11.

Cf. Boccaccio. Septem litigant. Above, p. 83.

Gaza. Septem urbes certant. Gellius (1489), Eviii[vo]; Soter[2], p. 305; Corn., p. 385.

Codro Urceo quotes Gr. with Gaza's tr. *Op.* p. 176.

Cf. Politian. Nec iam supremi. Del Lungo, p. 297.

Cf. Lascaris (J.). Πέντε πόλεις δέκα. *Epig.*, f. 12ro.

Sannazaro. Smyrna, Rhodos. *Poem*, p. 191.

Cf. Casanova. An Smyrna est, quae. *C.P.N.*, f. 93ro; *C.P. It.* 3. 294.

Cf. Anon. Fu Smirna il nido [after Casanova]. Carducci, *Poes. Barb.*, p. 264.
Cf. Tansillo. Sette illustre città. *Poes.*, ed. Fiorentino, p. 44.
Cf. Groto. Prese in Ismirna [after Casanova]. *Rime* (1587), p. 155.
Sabeo. Patriam Homero uni. *Epig.*, p. 379.
Allacci quotes Gr. with tr. by Gaza and Sabeo. Gronov., *Thes.* 10. 1770.

16.298. Cf. 297.
Allacci quotes Gr. and tr. by H. Stephanus. Gronov. 10. 1770.
Pagnini. Sette città vegg'io. *Epig.*, p. 73.

16.299. Sabeo. Es Chius? haud dico. *Epig.*, p. 241.
Pagnini. V. Se' tu di Chio? *Epig.*, p. 168.

16.301. Quoted by Rivautella-Ricolvi, *Mar.* 1. 181.

16.303. Sabeo. Ecquis Homere tuam. *Epig.*, p. 355.

16.304. Politian. Troiam canens, Homere. Del Lungo, p. 544; Soter[2], p. 305; Corn., p. 385.
Pagnini. Per la Meonia Musa. *Epig.*, p. 97.

16.305. Quoted in Eustath., *Vita Pind.* (West., p. 92).
Cf. Politian. Aerios procul in tractus. *Nut.* 558–61; Del Lungo, p. 406.
Sabeo. Quam tuba terribili. *Epig.*, p. 334.
Fioretti. Osseas quantum [L-prosse]. *Prog.* 3. 310.

16.306–7. Referred to by L. G. Giraldi, *Op.* 2. 340.

16.306. Giovane. Senem Anacreonta [prose]. *Ant. Tar.* 3. 3.

16.307. Cf. Politian. Non ego te longo. *Nut.* 585f; Del Lungo, p. 409.

16.308. Torcigliano? Cf. above, p. 365.

16.309. Sabeo. Cerne senem quem non. *Epig.*, p. 818.

16.310. Jordanus. Hanc opifex Sapphus. Soter[3], p. 348.
Sabeo. Dat natura potens. *Epig.*, p. 440.
Carcani (P.). Resa artefice in te. *Ant. Ercol.* 5. 133.

16.311. Quoted in *Vita Oppiani* (West., p. 66).
Sabeo. Omnimoda Oppianus. *Epig.*, p. 759.
Crasso. Oppianus libris [L-prose]. *1st.*, p. 382.

16.312. Pagnini. Quando Calliope Giorgio. *Epig.*, p. 96.

16.313. Cornarius. Quis statuam hanc. Corn., p. 386.
Sabeo. Quis te icon statuit? *Epig.*, p. 324.

16.314. Cornarius. Longino auratam urbs. Corn., p. 386.
Sabeo. Auratam meruit statuam. *Epig.*, p. 381.

16.315. Quoted without tr. by G. B. Pio, *Lamp.* 1. 455.
Sabeo. Sydera rhethorices. *Epig.*, p. 199.

16.317. Cf. *A.P.* 9. 151.
Ausonius. Rhetoris haec Rufi. *Opus.* 19.11.
Cornarius. Mutua et hinc surdus. *Corn.*, p. 387.

16.318. Cf. *A.P.* 11. 145, 149.
Ausonius. Elinguem quis te. *Opus.* 19. 12.
Ausonius. Haec Rufi tabula *Opus.* 19. 13; Soter[2], p. 184; Corn., p. 214.

Sabeo. Rhetoris elinguis statua. *Epig.*, p. 324.
Sabeo. Rhetoris effinxit quis. *Epig.*, p. 350.
Sabeo. Rhetoris ipsi tacens. *Epig.*, p. 813.
16.319. Pagnini. A tutt' altri, O Marin. *Epig.*, p. 158.
16.320. Baiano. Lis ab Aristida periit. Gronov., *Thes.* 10. 1806.
16.321. Sabeo. Rhetoris haec statua. *Epig.*, p. 369.
16.324. Sabeo. Prodita ab igne fui. *Epig.*, p. 143.
Cunich. Ante stylus fueram. *Anth.*, p. 9.
Pompei. Stilo, onde scriver. *Op.* 2. 224.
Felici. Io, che dapprima fui. *Epig.*[1], p. 127.
Passeroni. Era d'argento, or d'oro. *Rime* 3. 37.
Vargas. Tratto dal fuoco io. *Sag.*, p. 57.
16.325. Cornarius. Plurimum inexplicitos. Corn., p. 388.
Cf. Navagero. Quem toties vixisse. *C.Q.P.*, p. 36.
Sabeo. Ecquid inexplicitos. *Epig.*, p. 321.
Cf. Pagnini. Vivo in questa si mostra. *Epig.*, p. 98.
16.326. Cornarius. Pythagoram certa. Corn., p. 388.
Rainerio. Pythagoram pictor. Above, p. 307.
Sabeo. Pithagoram pictor. *Epig.*, pp. 316, 469.
Sabeo. Et licet e saxo. *Epig.*, p. 368.
Scaliger (J. C.). Ipsa tacens species. *Poem.* 1. 292.
Cf. Baldi. Chi pinse te, Pitagora. *Epig.* 402.
Cf. Aloïs. Praxiteles Gallus. *Epig.*, p. 482.
Cunich. Ipsum Pythagoram pictor. *Anth.*, p. 10.
Passeroni. Al guardo, al crine. *Rime* 3. 75.
Pagnini. Pitagora quest' è. *Epig.*, p. 98.
Pagnini. Di Pitagora queste. *Epig.*, p. 140.
16.327. Sabeo. Quam sapiens plastes. *Epig.*, p. 322.
16.328. Sabeo. Ut mentem extollit. *Epig.*, p. 364.
16.329. Sabeo. Est hic Aristoteles. *Epig.*, p. 435.
16.331. Anon. Hanc statuam posuere. Plutarch (1519), *init.*
Sabeo. Cur sua Plutarcho. *Epig.*, p. 314.
Sabeo. Erexere tibi statuam. *Epig.*, p. 363.
Minturno. Conspicuam, Plutarche. *Epig.*, f. 2ʳᵒ.
'L-prose.' Tuam nobilem imaginem. Ἐπ. καὶ Ἑλ. No. 72.
Pagnini. Questa a te di lavoro. *Epig.*, p. 101.
16.333. Ausonius. Pera, polenta, tribon. *Opus.* 19. 29.
Sabeo. Pera una et vestis. *Epig.*, p. 312.
16.334. Quoted by Diogenes Laertius 6.2 (Diogenes); by Suidas,
s.v. Φιλίσκος Αἰγ. (2); and by 'Eudocia,' *Viol.* 142.
Bentinus. Aera quidem absunt. *Laert.*, p. 206; Soter[2], p. 305;
Corn., p. 388.
Crasso gives Bentinus' tr. *Ist.*, p. 159.
16.337. Cf. 357.
16.338. Argoli. Quae numerans [line 3]. Graev., *Thes.* 9. 115.
16.340. Appears as an inscr. (Kaibel 935).
16.342. Cornarius. Porphyrium expressit. Corn., p. 390.
16.346. Cornarius. Fortuna ipsa suos. Corn., p. 390.

16.350. Pinelli (N.). Aliis sane [prose]. Graev., *Thes.* p. 498.
16.351. Argoli. Atque ideo [line 5]. Graev., *Thes.* 9. 98.
16.352. Cornarius. Aurigam aere vides. Corn., p. 391.
16.357. Cf. 337.
Cornarius. Anchisae Paphie. Corn., p. 391.
16.365. Cf. *A.P.* 15. 42.
16.387. Alciati quotes vv. 1–2, *Op.* 3.591.
Ricolvi quotes this epig. without tr. *Op.*, p. 75.
16.387.* Quoted by Cottunius, *Confic.*, cap. 27.
16.387.** Appears as an inscr. (Kaibel 1124).
16.388. *Anacreont.* 6 (Preisendanz).
Cf. Nicetas Eugen. ὃν καὶ πεπωκώς. *Dros.* 3. 142–5.
Crinitus. Dum sacrum Paphiae. *H.D.*, p. 539.
Melanchthon. Cum necterem corollam. Soter², p. 320; Corn.,
p. 421.
Cf. Alamanni. Per farsi una ghirlanda. *Rim. Ined.*, p. 31.
Valeriano. Dum serta texo, nactus. *Poem.*, p. 114; *C.P. It.*
10. 160.
Cf. Rota. Mentre con gli occhi. *Son.*, f. 6ᵛ°.
Conti (A.). Nell' intessere corone. *Prose* 1. 273.
Felici. Tessea ghirlanda idalia. *Epig.*², p. xxi.
Rogati. Nel fare un serto. Wellesley, p. 406.
Vargas. Intrecciando una corona. *Sag.*, p. 101.
Vargas. Pur ti ritrovo. *Sag.*, p. 101.

INDEX

[The Index is primarily intended to be a link between the Register and the earlier parts of the book, but has not been limited to that purpose. References to the Register itself have in general not been included.]

Acciaiuoli 106, 139, *164*
Accolti, Ben. 39, 41, *226–7*, 229
Accolti, Ber. 49, 58, *296–8*
Accolti, Fr. Forzoni 53, *388–9*, 404
Aconitanus. See Patavinus.
Acquiviva 309
Actianus 188
Addaeus 187
Aedituus *10–1*, 275, 282
Aegidius. See Gilles.
Aelian *4*, 8
Aesop 4, *8*
Affò 57n.
Agathias 6, 9, 10n., 62, 117, 168, 187, 200, 233, 264n., 294, 395, 427
Alamanni 49, 54, 57, 59, 73, 75, 299, *302–5*, 325, 339, 401, 417–8
Alberti 50, *335–6*, 355
Albuzzi 195–6, 200
Alcaeus of Messene 11n., 62, 168, 187, 233
Alcaeus of Mitylene 264n.
Alciati 40–1, 43, 77n., 93n., 113n., 177, *195–209*, 234, 242–3, 261, 269, 275, 279–86, 323, 337, 349n., 388, 443
Aldobrandini, T. 86n.
Aldus 39–40, 42, 100, 105–6, 118, *148–50*, 152, 155, 163, 169, 171, 230, 292n., 426
Aleander, G., the elder 151, 178, *185–6*, 213, 243, 275, 279
Aleander, G., the younger 44–5, *260*, 265n., 334
Alexis 3
Allacci 33, 45, 52, 260n., *263–6*, 268, 270, 373, 415
Alois 44, *271*, 366
Alopa, Lorenzo d' 37, 117
Alpheius of Mitylene 13, 187
Alsario. See Della Croce, Vincenzo A.
Alsworth 255–6
Amalteo, Aurelio 203n.
Amalteo, G. 74, 243
Amalteo, G. B. 178n., *243–4*
Amaseo 242, *298–9*
Ambrogio. See Traversari.
Amerbach 96n., 196–8, 203, 207–8
Ammianus 360
Ammonius 8, 402
Anacreon 3, 10, 220, 263, 365, 414, 422
Anacreontea 6, 146, 212, 263, 414–5, 422, 437

Andrelinus 275, 280
Andreini, Isabella 4n., *355*
Aneau 203n.
Angelico 355
Angelini 232
Angelio 190n., *240–1*, 253
Angeriano 40, *169–70*, 194
Angrisani 265
Anisio 40, *174–5*
Anonymous 7n., 25n., 26–7, 37n., 60n., 86n., 256, 278, 280–2, 300–1
Anselmo 41, *173–4*
Anthology, The Latin 25
Antigonus 13
Antipater 62, 221n., 233, 404n.
Antipater of Sidon 11–2, 48, 187, 194, 240, 265n., 325n., 361, 365, 438n.
Antipater of Thessalonica 19, 126, 133, 187
Antiphanes 2, 13
Antiphilus 19, 62, 233, 259
Antistius 187
Antologia Romana 51
Anyte 133, 212, 266, 386
Apermachius 397
Apiarius 284, 286
Apollinaris, Sid. 55
Apollodorus 379
Apollonides 13
Apostolios 8, 31, 150–1
Appian 4
Apuleius *23*, 25, 379
Aquino, Carlo, d' 53, *385*
Arabius 187
Aratus 7, 246n.
Archias 11, 62, 187, 212, 233, 255–6, 379
Archilochus 2
Archithrenius 275, 278
Archius. See Arco.
Arco, Niccolò d' 26, *210–1*, 291
Arcudi 327
Aretino, Lionardo. See Bruni.
Aretino, P. 291, 297, 303, 328
Argelati 365n., 376, *404–5, passim*
Argoli, G. 45, 266, *270*
Argyropulos 36, 101, 107, 124
Ariosto, Gabriele 162n.
Ariosto, Lod. 14n., 40, 45, 47, 113n., *159–62*, 178, 247, 284, 291, 297, 313, 328
Ariosto, Virg. 161, 247
Aristaenetus 6

Aristides 4, 8n., 154
Aristophanes 2, 101, 287, 379
Aristotle 3, 8, 61, 68, 97–8, 112, 154, 211, 249, 254, 268, 292, 317, 336, 379
Arnoldus Vesaliensis 276, 280, 282, 397
Arrian 379
Arsenios 8, 39, 150–1, 157
Artopoeus 282–3
Asclepiades 73, 296n., 301, 321
Asola, Andrea Torresano d' 171, 230
Asola, Federigo d' 230
Asola, Gio. Francesco d' 149–50, 155n., 171–2, 230
Astolfi 86n.
Atanagi 300, 308
Athenaeus 5, 62, 374
Athenaeus (epigrammatist) 233
Audiffredi 419n.
Augurelli 177
Augustín 246n.
Augustine, Saint 25, 292
Augustus 12–3, 137
Aurispa 86n.
Aurivallius 426n.
Aurogallus 89n., 90
Ausonius 23–5, 43, 48, 62, 67, 69n., 76, 79, 85, 92, 103–4, 126, 134, 146, 184, 194, 234, 243n., 261n., 268, 276, 279–82, 295–6, 308, 314, 327, 337, 340, 349, 368, 397, 418n., 425, 441
Automedon 13, 360
Averani, B. 52–3, 377–82
Avianus 8

B., H. 256
Babrius 8
Bacchylides 190
Badius Ascensius 37, 426
Bagnaus 246
Baiano 265–6
Baïf 303
Baldi, Ber. 49, 59, 339–41
Baldus, V. 182
Balzac, Guez de 60n.
Bandini, A. M. 117n., 384–5, 418–9, 428n.
Bandini, Fr. 111
Banduri 53, 387–8, 443
Barbato 169
Barberini, Fr., Card. 30, 264
Barberini, Maffeo. See Urban VIII.
Barberio 52, 375
Bardi, Pietro 362
Bargiocchi 44, 267
Barnes 396, 415
Bassus 187
Batteux 60n.
Battista 50–1, 346, 365–8, 373
Beatus Rhenanus 256, 276, 281
Beazzano 190n., 301
Bebellius 197–8, 202, 284

Beccuti 50, 318–9
Becelli 57n., 389n., 393
Belleforest 325n.
Belli 355–8
Bellini 177
Bembo 40, 45–7, 56, 108, 158, 172, 189, 213, 218, 252, 301, 310
Benedictus 397
Bentinus 88n., 89–91, 243n., 251, 276, 278–80, 282, 288, 337, 369, 374–5, 397
Bentley 171n., 391
Bergius 209, 276, 279–81
Bernardi 320
Bernhardi. See Velius.
Berni 229
Bernstorff 438
Beroaldo, F., the elder 40, 143, 144, 158
Beroaldo, F., the younger 158, 218
Bertini 369
Bertòla 54, 434
Bessarion 30, 34, 36, 97–8, 108, 114
Bestrucci 232
Bettinelli 53–4, 60, 72, 401n., 415–8, 428–30, 435
Betussi 82n.
Beverini 53, 372
Bianchi 386, 447
Bianor 8, 62, 233
Bibbiena 158
Bienati 143
Bigi 109n.
Biscioni 53, 389–90
Bisticci, V. da 91n.
Blount 60n.
Boccaccio 35, 45, 81–5, 308, 315, 320
Bocchi 187n., 221–2
Bodoni Press 424, 436
Boethus 13, 187
Boiardo 47, 100
Boileau 60n.
Bolzani. See Valeriano.
Bonada 53, 396, 398, 399n., 443
Bonamico 34, 180–1, 229n.
Bongiovanni 30n., 53, 400–2, 405, 421
Bonifacio 77
Bontemps 205
Borgia, C. 74, 295
Bornati 335
Bottari 180, 237n., 390, 443
Botticelli 48, 77
Boulier 86n.
Bourbon, N. 234
Braccieschi 254
Bracciolini 4n.
Brice, Germain 119n., 276, 281
Brignole Sale 51, 364–5, 405
Brixius. See Brice.
Brodaeus 37, 252, 287, 337, 361, 373–4, 426
Brugière de Barante 69n.

Brugnolo 86n., 87, *88–9*, 91, 99n., 142n., 143, 175. See also Laert. Int.
Brunck 38, 157, 169n., 385, 421, 426–7, 430
Bruni, Lionardo 85, 142, 375
Bucoldus 256, *276*, 281, 372
Budé 118, 276, 282, 286
Buonacciolli 92n.
Burley 81n.
Bussi, G. A. di 92, 97, 245.

Cadamosto 203n.
Cailly, Jacques de 60n.
Calcagnini 37, 40, 44, 60, 62, 77, 121n., 159n., *178–80*, 181, 185, 212, 226–8, 247, 291, 328, 353, 375
Calcaterra *276*, 280
Calderini 95n., 96n., 156–8, 223
Calenzio 107
Callimachus 3, 11, 13–4, 18, 20–1, 81–2, 187, 224, 274n., 419n.
Callinichos 35n.
Callistos 124
Callistratus 5
Calopar 151n.
Calvi 195, 198, 202
Camerarius 274n., 426
Campanus 56
Cane 284–5
Cannius. See Cane.
Cantalicio 123
Capece, Ant. 143
Capece, Sc. 40, *233–4*
Capilupi, Ipp. 41, *239*, 248n.
Capito 306n.
Cappellari 53, *381–2*
Cappone 4n., 404
Caraffa 309, 313
Carbone 159
Carcani, G. Rinforzo 38, 54, 365n., 384, 412, 419, *426–8*, 443
Carcani, P. 53, *411–2*, 426–7
Cardano 41, *238*
Carducci 47n., 48, 159, 161, 338n.
Caro, 218, 234, 303, 306, 316, 317n.
Cartari 51, *308*, 404
Carteromaco 35n., 39, 43, 112, 125, 148–9, *151–4*, 156, 167, 245–6
Casalicchio 281n.
Casanova, M. A. 41, *163–4*, 265n., 301
Casone 50, *342–3*, 355
Cassola 50
Castelvetro 51, *316–8*
Castiglione, B. 121n., 225, 297
Castiglione, Fr. da 34n.
Cato 25n., 435
Catullus 11, 56, 61–2, 64–5, 70–1, 175, 189n., 248, 365, 429, 439
Catulus 10–1, 276, 278, 301
Cavalcanti 111

Cavallo 178
Cavazza 327
Cebà 52, *360*, 364
Cecca da Siena 132
Cedrenus 7
Cephalas 9–10, 32, 117, 395
Cerealius 187
Cerera 265n.
Cerretti 54, *439*
Cesinge. See Pannonius.
Chalcidius 25
Chalcondyles B., 101, *165–6*
Chalcondyles, D. 30, 36, 39, 41, 48, *100–2*, 108, 114, 120n., 124, 125n., 127, 139, 148n., 154, 168, 418
Chapelain 70
Chappuys 325n.
Chardon de la Rochette 258, 263, 365n., 414n.
Chariteo 59n.
Charles V 118, 189, 200, 222, 303
Charles VIII of France 39, 106, 117–8, 132
Chénier, A. 17
Chiabrera 51, 364
Choeroboschus 6
Choricius 6
Chrestien, Fl. 388
Christina of Sweden 33n., 369, 381–2
Chrysococceus 95, 98
Chrysoloras, J. *95–6*
Chrysoloras, M. (1) 85, (2) 91
Chrysoloras, Theodora 95
Chrysostom 5, 97, 385
Cibo, Alano 119
Cicero 3n., *10–1*, 14n., 88, 92, 147, 193, 202n., 211, 230, 277, 292, 378–80, 430
Cimeleo, Ofelio. See Mariani.
Ciriaco 35, *93–5*, 96, 265n.
Cittadini 50, *342*
Civrano 269
Claudian 24
Clement, John 31
Clement of Alexandria 5, 379
Clement VII 41, 118, 167, 175, 212, 288, 295, 302–3
Cleombrotus 11, 222, 385
Codinus 7
Codro. See Urceo.
Colin 182–3
Colletet 60n., 69
Colocci 33, 41, 59n., 107, 119, 153–4, *166*, 213, 218, 244–6
Colombo 319
Colonna, Mario 241n.
Colonna, Vittoria 174, 303
Coltellini 361
Comandi 110
Comaschi 60n.

Commandino 339
Comparini 31, *121*
Conca, Prince of 330, 350, 353, 355
Condillac 430
Constantine Manasses 7
Constantine Porphyrogenitus 7
Contarini, Elena 53, 401
Contest of Homer and Hesiod 3-4, 133n.
Conti, Giusto di 383
Conti, Natale 40, *239-40*
Contoleone 120n.
Coppeta. See Beccuti.
Cordato 221
Corinna 133, 168, 386
Cornarius 38, 45, 145n., 185, 196-9, 201, 204, 206-9, 273, 276-7, *283-6*, 388, 443
Corréa 6on., 65-6
Costanzi, Ant. 37, 41, *111*, 147
Costanzi, G. 37, 41, *147-8*
Costanzo, Angelo di 309, 313
Cottunius, 42n., 52, 6on., 68-9, *268-9*
Crasso 52, 366, *373-5*
Crates 187, 321
Crescimbeni 6on., 72, 313n., 362, 389, 394
Crevenna 433
Crichton, Admirable 336
Crinagoras 12, 200, 334n.
Crinitus 39, 113, *145-7*, 276, 278-9
Cristoforo, Ber. di 373
Crotti 40, *228-9*
Cruceius. See Della Croce, L. A.
Cüchler 273
Cunich 54, 76, *405-7*, 408-10, 423, 425, 430
Curio 86n., 89-91
Cyril of Alexandria 5
Cyrillus 55, 63, 179, 187, 233
Cyrillus, Salvator 34n.

Damocharis 374
Daniello 56, 61
Dante 21n., 45, 51, 81, 109, 320, 328, 336-7, 350, 415
Darmarios 156-8
Dati 52-3, 361, *369-70*, 382, 421
Davaris 119-20
David (commentator) 8
Davison, Francis 328
Dazzi 39, *163*, 211, 353
De Bosch 38, 427, 433
Decembrio 91
D'Elci 431n.
Della Casa, Giovanni 51, 306, 333
Della Croce, Luigi Annibale 41, *235-6*, 333n.
Della Croce, Vincenzo Alsario 45, *262*
Della Torre, Cesare Gaetani 54, *405*
Della Torre di Rezzonico, Carlo Gastone 428-9

Della Valle, Guglielmo 420-1
Del Monte, F. 306
Del Monte, G. 339
Del Tuppo 37, *121-2*
Demetrius of Phalerum 379
Demosthenes 3, 36, 116
Denalio 248
Desportes 191n.
Diacceto, Fr. da 302
Dio Cassius 4, 8n.
Dio of Prusa 4.
Diodorus of Sardis 13
Diodorus Siculus 4, 287
Diogenes Laertius *5*, 9n., 35, 40, 85-91, 98, 108, 110-1, 143, 146, 212, 251, 333, 374, 383
Diogenian 9
Dionysius the Areopagite 292
Dionysius Byzantinus 5
Dionysius Periegetes 8n.
Dionysius Thrax 8n.
Dioscorides 187, 334n.
Diotimus 187
Dolce 306, 308, 310
Dolet 224
Domitian 19
Donatus, Alexander 6on.
Donatus, Ti. Claudius 234
Doni, A. F. 307
Doni, G. B. 369, 383n., 396n.
Dorat 43, 237, 373
D'Orville 3on., 38, 253, 264, 385
Dossi 77, 179
Dousa, Th. 77n.
Drummond 328, 336, 345
Du Bellay, Jean 213
Du Bellay, Joachim 49, 190, 303n., 354n.
Du Cange 388

Egio 236, 246
Elias (commentator) 8
Emilio 186
Empedocles 25
Ennius 43
Enrico 125
Epicae et Elegiacae Sententiae 397, 444
Epigonus 187
Equicola 48-9, 75n., *291-3*, 345
Erasmus 8, 40, 118-9, 148n., 151, 184-5, 193, 199n., 204, 224, 256, 275, 276, 279-84, 397
Erinna 2on., 133, 168, 368, 438n.
Erizzi palace 35n.
Ernesti 419n.
Erycius 187
Este, Isabella d' 120
Estienne. See Stephanus.
Etymologicon Magnum 2n.
Eudocia 7n.
Eugenes 365

Eumathius Macrembolites 7
Euphemios 32n.
Euphorion 19
Euripides 2n., 7, 34, 112, 377, 381n.
Eusebius 5
Eustathius 8n., 379, 647
Evangelista, G. B. 252–3
Evenus 13, 187
Evodus 187

Faetanus 258n.
Fagagna 355–6
Falconieri 270
Fantini 176
Farnese, Ranuccio 223–4, 244
Fedele 133n., 267
Felici 54, 421–3, 407
Feretrius 165
Ferrari 235, 269
Fiamma 355–7
Ficino 109–11, 124, 164
Filelfo 34–5, 87, 94–6, 99, 102, 265n., 276, 279
Filicaia 371
Finotti 44, 254–5
Fioretti 52, 57n., 361–2, 394
Flaminio, M. A. 41, 144, 158, 222, 224–5
Florilegium Monacense 7
Florus 25n.
Fontana 408
Fontani 432
Fortiguerri. See Carteromaco.
Forzoni Accolti. See Accolti.
Fracastoro 26, 189, 192, 222
Franceschini, Ber. de'. See Parthenio.
Franchini, Cesare 430
Franchini, Fr. 41, 188, 222–3, 388
Francis I of France 31n., 42, 118, 150n., 168, 181–2, 185, 189, 213, 303–5
Freire 60n., 72n.
Froelich 429, 437
Fronto 22n.

Gagliano 332n.
Galen 144, 154, 379
Gallo 52, 60n., 67, 69, 268
Gambara, L. 41, 236–7.
Gareggiamento Poetico, Il 51, 355–8, 444
Gargallo 430
Garimberto 404
Garzoni 250, 444
Guaradas 125
Gaurico 40, 69n., 75n., 143, 186–8, 195, 222, 276, 282, 367–8
Gaza 88n., 92, 96–8, 101n., 102, 123, 266, 276, 278–9, 282, 375
Gechauff. See Venatorius.
Gellius 10, 14n., 15, 22, 68, 83–4, 93, 97, 123n., 212, 269, 276, 278, 280, 282, 338, 362

Georgius Anonymus 276, 281, 286
Germanicus 12, 19, 24, 66–7, 70, 147n., 152, 185, 187, 200, 276, 279, 301, 400
Germano 51, 261
Gersus (=Glaucus?) 187
Getulicus 187
Giacomini 34n.
Gilles 185, 275, 279, 375
Giocondo 9n., 94n., 193
Giordani 441–2
Giovane 250–1
Giovio 76, 100, 144, 182n., 188, 190, 319
Giraldi, G. B. ('Cintio') 40, 51, 178, 227–8, 247, 315, 323–4
Giraldi, L. G. 37, 40, 45, 52, 60, 62, 133n., 142n., 162, 178, 180n., 183–5, 188, 189n., 222, 227–8, 247, 291, 308, 373, 375–6
Gisberti 373
Giulianelli 39, 389, 403
Giunti (printers) 169, 426
Giustiniani 120n., 224
Gombauld 60n.
Gomes van Triere 326n.
Gori, A. Fr. 383
Gori, L. 386
Gradenigo 35n.
Gravina, G. V. 53, 386
Gravina, P. 37, 40, 143–4
Gravius 273, 275
Graziani 332n.
Gregorio da Spoleto 159–60
Gregory the Theologian 10n., 385
Gregory XV 262–3
Grillo 343n., 453
Grotius 38, 60n., 388, 399
Groto 50, 328–30, 352, 355, 418
Gruter 31, 180, 263n.
Gualfreducci 42, 44, 256–7, 258–9, 269
Guarini, Alessandro 50, 247, 359
Guarini, G. B. (the elder) 3n., 37, 91, 122, 147–8, 159, 183
Guarini, G. B. (the younger) 56, 77, 326–8, 354n., 359
Guarino da Verona 37, 91–2, 93n., 95, 99, 111, 123, 140n., 276–9, 282, 284, 326
Guastavini 338
Guazzo 50–1, 324–5
Guicciardini, Lod. 51, 322–4
Guinisi 44, 266

Hadrian 9, 19
Hadriano 211
Hamerus 276, 280–1, 286
Hegesippus 187
Heinsius, D. 38n., 42n., 94n., 120, 139
Heliodorus 5, 287
Henry II of France 31n., 150n., 213
Heresbach 89n.

Hermannus a Nova Aquila. See Neuenaar.
Hermes Trismegistus 110, 149
Hermodorus 187
Hermogenes 8n.
Hermonymus 276, 280
Herodotus *1-2*, 35, 88, 99, 106, 110-1,
   168, 187
Hesiod 4n., 7, 93, 123, 268
Hesychius of Miletus 6
Heydnecker. See Obsopoeus.
Heyl. See Soter.
Hippocrates 379
Hipponax 9
Holbein 204n.
Holstein 264
Homer 2, 5, 7, 37-8, 81, 100, 132, 264,
   274, 283, 379, 386
Honainus 28n.
Honestus 187
Horace *14-5*, 40, 109, 248, 310, 379, 430
Huet 169n.
Hunt 370n.
Hutten, Ulrich von 150n.

Ion 187
Isocrates 3, 38, 109

Jacobs 1, 10n., 21n., 35n., 38, 414, 395,
   426n.
Jausserandus 256, *282-3*
Jensius 38n.
Jenson 87-8, 148
Jerome 25
Jesuits 42-4, 59, 65
John of Ravenna 91
John of Salisbury 81n.
Jonson 5
Jordanus 256, *282-3*
Jucundus. See Giocondo.
Julian the Emperor 5, 121, 137
Julianus, Prefect of Egypt 294, 365
Julius Polyaenus 19
Junius 369

Klotz 38n., 426, 433
Krohn 35n.

'Laberius' 276, 281
Laert. Int. 276, 280, 285, 337, See also
   Brugnolo.
Laertius. See Diogenes Laertius.
Lampridio 178, 180, 218
Lancelot 69
Landi 45, 51, 220n., *242-3*, 320
Landino 105, *109*, 124, 276, 279
Langerman 264
Lasca 59
Lascaris, C. 34, 36, 41, 98, *107-8*, 114,
   265n.

Lascaris, J. 29-31, 36-7, 39-42, 53, 98, 101,
   107, *114-21*, 124n., 125, 127-8, 131n.,
   139, 148-51, 153n., 155, 157, 160,
   162n., 163, 166n., 167, 175-6, 180, 186,
   195, 213, 220, 224, 245, 276, 280-2,
   291-2, 419
Latini, Latino 244
Laurentius 30, 36, 101
Le Brun 60n.
Le Clerc 38, 391
Lect 419
Le Fèvre 203n.
Leich 38, 426, 433
Leo the Philosopher 243
Leo X 41, 43, 56, 58-9, 74, 118, 144, 158,
   164, 167, 175, 183, 185, 212, 222n.,
   225, 295, 301, 328.
Leoni, G. B. 343n.
Leoni, Pier 254
Leoniceno *112*, 153, 156
Leonico *154*, 246
Leonidas 212, 233
Leonidas of Alexandria 9n., 19, 134, 207,
   365
Leonidas of Tarentum 13, 16-7, 187, 251,
   266, 365
Leontius scholasticus 179
Le Sage 26
Lessing 60, 73
Leto, Pomponio 167, 291
Licinus 10-1, 282
Lily 27, 165n., 185, 234, 261n., *276-7*,
   279-82, 397
Lippi, Lorenzo *109*
Lippi, Lorenzo (author of the *Malman-
   tile*) 53, 383, 390
Lollius 187
Longepierre 405
Longolius 86n., 218
Loredano 51, *363*, 366
Lubinus 28, 274n., 361, 374, 397, 402,
   426, 433, 444
Lucian 3-4, 14n., 21n., 62, 66n., 112, 233,
   252, 287, 377, 379, 397
Lucido 265-6
Lucilius 19, 21-2, 62, 187, 233, 294, 390
Lucretius 11
Luna 96
Luscinius 198-9, 256, 261n., 274n., *276-
   82*, 284-6, 338, 397, 443
Luxorius 25n.
Lycurgus 3
Lydus, Joannes 6
Lygdamus 15n.

Macedonius Consul 187, 294
Machiavelli 59, 74, *295-6*, 327n., 354n.
Macrin 181
Macrobius 13-4, *25*, 142
Maecius 187

Maffei, Ant. 142n.
Maffei, Marco 426n.
Maffei, R. See Volaterranus.
Maffei, Sc. 360, 376, 393n., 403
Maggi, C. M. 51, 53, *376–7*, 404
Maggi, V. 247
Maggio, Giuniano 141
Magliabechi 377
Magnus, Duke of Mecklenburg 283
Manso 50–1, 330, *346–7*, 350, 366
Manuzio, Aldo. See Aldus.
Manuzio, Paolo 41, 171, 180, 224, *230–2*, 234, 250, 320n.
Mara, G. de *277*, 279
Marchetti 191n.
Marcus Aurelius 22n.
Marescotti 45, *257*
Marguerite of Savoy 303–4
Mariani 54, *440*
Marino, G. B. 4n., 50, 52, 58n., 163, 270, 328–30, 346–8, *349–55*, 358, 366
Marinus, Domitius 229
Marinus (epigrammatist) 187
Marinus (philosopher) 7
Marot 58, 62, 73, 303
Marquale 203n.,
Martial 15n., *20–2*, 43, 55–7, 61–2, 64–5, 67, 69, 71, 96n., 126n., 128, 189n., 277, 279, 281, 286, 340, 439
Martinière 69n.
Martorelli 395
Marullus 37, 43, 66, *112–3*, 116, 126–7, 132, 134, 142, 146, 162, 170n., 173, 234, 243n., 265n., *277–82*, 397
Massa 250
Matarazzo 123
Materdona 358
Matthew Corvinus 140n., 284
Maurizio 355–6
Maximus, Saint 7
Mayone 332n.
Mazzoleni 444
Mazzoni 51, *336–8*, 404–5
Medici, Averardo de' 54, *413*, 430
Medici, Catherine de' 30, 119, 303
Medici, Lorenzo de' 95, 105, 109–10, 112, 114–5, 118, 124, 129, 131, 142n., 152
Medici, Piero de' 39, 110, 117, 120, 164, 419, 426
Medici, Sisto 333
Megiser 39, 273, 278
Melampus 8n.
Melanchthon *277*, 282, 317, 426
Meleager 9, 10n., 17, 46–8, 50, 73, 75, 128, 130–1, 222, 264n., 293, 317–8, 325n., 350–1, 354, 395, 403, 427, 433
Ménage, 42n., 60n., 120, 193
Menander 2n., 3
Menard 388
Menecrates 187

Meninni 57n., 58n., 72n.
Mercier 60n., 69
Merula 24, 34, 37, 41, *102–5*, 126, 133
Messere 386
Metrodorus 187
Meurs, Jan van 396
Michelangelo 202, 213, 229, 311–2
Michiele 363, 366
Micyllus 274n., 426
Mignault 203n., *204–6*
Milton 346, 361, 369
Mimnermus 2n.
Minturno 45, 50, 57, 60n., 62–3, 67–9, 72, 75n., *232–3*, 234, 269, 313, *321–2*
Mocenigo-Soranzo 53, 401
Modizio 272
Molza, Francesco Maria 41, 50, 158, *218–9*, 243n., *302*, 306, 332
Molza, Tarquinia 219, 332
Monerius, Martialis 265n.
Monnoye, Bernard de la 397
Morcelli 406
More, 31, 40, 66, 184, 204, 209, 234, 257, 261n., *277–82*, 337, 369, 397, 400
Morel, Frédéric 388
Morelli, J. 425–6
Moro 50, 336n., *345–6*, 355
Moschos, D. 292n.
Moschus 3, 16, 106, 132, 134, 237, 304n., 331–3, 396, 404n., 405
Mosellanus 283
Moyranus 243
Muratori 376–7, 383, 404
Muret 250
Murr, Chr. von 120
Murtola 50, *347–8*, 350
Musaeus 42, 148
Musicius 187, 389
Musurus 39, 41–2, 112, 148n., 150, 153, *155–8*, 160, 162n., 172, 180, 189, 245
Mutinelli 433
Myrtis 133, 386

Nachtigall. See Luscinius.
Nardi 355–7
Nasi 320
Navagero 40, 148n., 162n., 173, *189–92*, 219, 229, 300–1, 314, 354n.
Neander 426n.
Negri 401n.
Nepos 12
Nerli, Filippo de' 296
Nero 19, 21
Nestor of Laranda 2n.
Neuenaar 256, 277, 280–2, 285
Nicarchus 212
Nicetas Eugenianus 7
Nicole 60n., 69–71
Nicolini da Sabbio (printers) 37, 220, 231, 292n.

Nicolucci. See Pigna.
Nifo 232
Nonnos 6
Nossis 126, 133, 266, 386
Nunius 205
Nurcisius 103

Obsopoeus 38n., 243n., 252, 256, 261n., 273–4, 277n., *286–9*, 361, 374, 397, 444
Occhi 39, 397
Odescalchi 406
Oertel. See Winshemius.
Olympiodorus 8n., 101n.
Opitz 60n.
Oppian 7, 109
Orion 6
Orlandini 50, *338*
Orsini 30, 33, 41, 120, 123n., 152–4, 167, 224, 236, *244–6*
Ovid *16–9*, 21n., 77, 94n., 125, 147n., 149, 279, 350, 379, 393
Owen 60n.

Pagnini 54, 407, *430–2*
Paitoni 365n., 376, *404–5*
Palazzi 339
Palladas 9n., 27, 62, 68, 168, 203, 212, 233, 238, 294
Pallavicini 416
Pananti 54, 75, *440–1*
Pancratius (=Pancrates) 187
Paniciatus 147
Pannonius, Joannes, 37, 91, 165, *284–5*
Panormita 106
Panvinio 270–1
Paparectus 232
Parini *419–20*, 440
Parmenion 13, 55, 63, 179, 233
Parrhasius, Janus 165–6, 195
Parthenio, Ber. 190n.
Parthenius 14n.
Pasquier 366, 368
Passeroni 54, 407, *408–10*, 421, 430, 440
Patavinus 52, 68–9, 72n., *368–9*
Paterno 50, 234, 309, *313–5*
Patrizi 52, 373
Pauli, Sebastiano 390n.
Paulus Diaconus 28
Paulus Silentiarius 16n., 47, 149, 169n., 293, 317, 345, 374, 402, 434n.
Pausanias 4, 21n., 61, 379
Peiper 24, 103–4
Pensa 59, 340
Perrucci 381
Persius 20
Pessinus 271
Petau 33n., 155n.
Petracci 355–7
Petrarch 45–7, 51, 56, 81, 85n., 308, 311, 313, 317, 320, 328, 350, 378, 399n.

Petronius 20, 26
Phanias 212
Philemon 3
Philippus of Thessalonica 9, 10n., 13, 62, 126, 233, 264n., 266, 376, 395, 427
Phillips 60n.
Philodemus 11, 14, 183, 294, 350–1
Philostratus 5, 105
Philostratus 'the Lemnian' 5, 312n.
Phocylides 2
Photius 7
Pico 139, 148
Pigna 40, 56, 77, 159n., 178, 180n., 227, *247*, 326, 330, 444
Pilatus 5, 81–2, 85
Pinelli, G. B. 41, *253*
Pinelli, Maffeo 34n., 258, *425–6*
Pinelli, Niccolò 271
Pio, Alberto of Carpi 35n., 148, 155, 159, 221, 224
Pio, G. B. 40, 45, 122, *144–5*, 222, 277–8, 280–1, 285, 337
Pithou 155n.
Pius. See Pio, G. B.
Pius VI 263, 429
Planudes 1, 10, 30, 32–3, 34n., 76, 108, 117, 122, 143n., 183, 245, 374, 376, 379, 395, 402–3, 406, 418, 427
Plato 2, 5, 7–8, 11, 23, 98, 101n., 106, 109–10, 292, 315, 336, 362, 379
Plato junior 187, 312
Pliny (elder) 8, 20
Pliny (younger) 20, 25, 67 (?)
Plutarch 3, *4*, 8–9, 35, 85, 92n., 96, 105, 142n., 146, 169, 172, 266n., 375, 379, 421
Politian 20n., 33, 36–7, 39, 42–3, 45, 47–8, 77, 100–2, 109, 112–6, 120, 122, *124–40*, 142, 144–6, 152, 163–4, 193, 234, 245, 272n., 274n., 277, 279–80, 282, 285n., 291, 296, 308, 327, 367–8
Pollux 4
Polybius 120n., 287
Pompei 54, 393n., *421*, 430, 435
Pontano, G. 37, 40, 92, *106*, 143, 166, 173–4, 291, 315, 355n.
Pontanus. See Spanmüller.
Porphyry 7–8
Porto, Emilio 31, *253–4*
Porto, Francesco 31, 43, 247, 253, 254n.
Posidippus 14, 26, 308
Possevino, Ant. 60n., 66, *251–2*, 319
Possevino, G. B. 51, 251, *319*
Praxilla 133, 286
Priapea 15, 56, 282
Priuli *195*, 229n.
Proclus (grammarian) 4, 84n.
Proclus (philosopher) 7, 8n., 168
Prodromus 7
Propertius 15n., *16–7*, 18n., 350

Pucci 164-5
Pulex 116

Quadrio 53, 57n., 6on., 72, 355-6, 361, 365, *394-5*
Querenghi 26on., *334-5*
Quintilian 20
Quintus Smyrnaeus 5
Quirini, A. M. 39, 53, 79, 213, 264, *391-3*

Rabirius 14n.
Raderus, 66-7, 68
Rainerio, Antonfrancesco 50, *305-7*
Rainerio, Girolamo 306
Raius 589
Rapin 6on.
Rapitius 41, *226*
Redi 52, 297, 369, *370-2*, 383n.
Regianus 25
Regio 96n.
Regnier Desmarais 371, 383n.
Regolotti 54, *390-1*
Reimerus 391-3
Reiske 38, 391-3, 412, 426-7
Renaldini 6on.
Renieri, Antonio 300
Rezzonico. See Della Torre.
Rhianus 19
Rhodiginus *168*, 178-9, 193
Riccio, Giovan Luigi 50, *309*, 314.
Riccio, Pietro. See Crinitus.
Ricciolini 415
Riccoboni 249-50
Ricolvi 53, 108n., 396, *398-400*
Ridolfi, Luca Antonio 51, *320*
Ridolfi, Niccolò Card. 30, 119-20
Rinieri. See Rainerio.
Rinuccini *105-6*, 277, 279
Riva, Luca 122, 147, 159
Rivautella 108n., 396, *398*
Rivinus 38, 87n., 104, 273
Robortello 6on., 61-3, 66-7, *236*
Rogati 422
Roncalli-Parolino 54, 6on., *424-5*, 430
Ronsard 237, 303
Rosaspina 436
Rossettini 86n.
Rossi, Giovan Gherardo de' 435-6
Rota 40, 57, *234-5*, *312-3*
Rousseau, J.-B. 6on.
Rubio 6on., 66n.
Rufinus 9n., 294
Ruscelli 51, *308*, 310, 355n.

Sabeo 41, 43, 54, 76, 78, 206, *212-8*, 264, 266, 269, 393
Sabino, Fr. Florido 224
Saint-Mard 6on.
Sale. See Brignole Sale.
Salmasius 1, 31, 38, 254, 263

Salmuth 326n.
Salutati 85n.
Salvini 53-4, 86n., 139n., 371-2, 377, *382-5*, 389, 390n., 396, 405, 419
Sanchez, Fernando 205
Sanchez, Francesco 133n., *204-6*, 375
Sandford 323n.
Sannazaro 37, 40, 45, 48, 69n., 74, 113, 128, *141*, 143, 160n., 225, 228, 234, 265n., 277, 279, 301, 400, 433n.
Santo Stefano, Count of 108
Sappho 3, 11, 94, 132-3, 220, 386, 422
Satyrus 187
Scala, Alessandra 37, 112, 115, *127*, 131n., 132, 163, 373
Scala, Bartolommeo 37, 126-7, *129-32*
Scaliger, Joseph Justus 31, 42n., 193, 253
Scaliger, Julius Caesar 42, 59, 6on., 63-72, 76, 88, 170, *193-4*
Scaphenatus 41, *210*
Scholiasts 8, 156-8
Scolastico, Basguno 156
Sebastiano. See Minturno.
Sebillet 56, 6on., 62
Secundus, Joannes 17on., 196
Segni, Fabio 39, *229*, 234
Segni, G. F. 34n.
Selecta Epigrammata 1608 38, 42, *255-6*, 443-4
Seneca (elder) 12
Seneca (younger) 14n., 19n., 25, 379
Senecé 6on.
Serafino 47
Serapio 187
Serrone 299
Sessa 22on.
Sextus Empiricus 5
Shakespeare 26, 57, 214, 328
Sigonio 250
Simmias 187
Simonetta, Bart. 195, *208*, 284-5
Simonetta, Cicco 96
Simonetti, C. 355-7
Simonides 14n., 62, 168, 187, 233, 266, 365
Sincliticus 258
Sirleto 35n.
Sleidan 42, 199, 209, 256, *277-82*, 337, 388, 397
Sophianus 31, 119, 253
Sophocles 3, 8n., 36, 116, 132, 259, 328
Soter 38, 42-3, 66, 77n., 85, 89-92, 96n., 106n., 113n., 120, 140n., 142-5, 186, 187n., 197-8, 205, 255-6, 269, *273-86*, 324, 337, 369, 372, 397, 399, 400n., 406, 426, 443-4
Spalletti 53, 264, *414—5*
Spanmüller 60, 65
Spinosa 338
Spinula 41, *248-9*
Spon, Jacob, 35n.

Stampa 15n.
Statius, P. Papinus 21n., 379
Statius, Achilles 33
Statius Romanus 301
Statyllius Flaccus 19, 187
Stephanus Byzantinus 6.
Stephanus, H. 3, 6, 31, 38, 44, 86n., 145n.,
    147, 155, 157–8, 169n., 182n., 212, 220,
    266, 273, 426, 433
Stephanus, P. 147, 388
Stigliani 50–1, *348–9*, 355
Stissus 115n.
Stobaeus *6*, 186n., 360
Stockwood 44, 273
Stow 325
Strab. Int. 279, 282. See also Guarino and
    Tifernas.
Strabo 2, *4*, 35, 91–2, 379
Stratico, 413
Strato 9, 10n., 293, 433
Strozzi, Ercole 100, 113n., 148
Strozzi, Giambattista *50*, 56, 310–2, 355
Strozzi, Maximilian 416
Strozzi, Pietro 30
Strozzi, Tito Vespasiano 37, 40, 91,
    99–100, 160, 162, 178
Subleyras 54, 417, 418n., *429*
Suetonius *19*, 126, 277, 279, 379
Suidas 2n., *7*, 19, 29, 92n., 120n., 140,
    412n.
Symphosius 25n.
Syncleticus 34n.
Synesius 5

Tagliacarne. See Teocreno.
Tamisier 273
Tansillo 191n., 313
Tasso, Bernardo 144, 234, 330
Tasso, Torquato 50–1, 56–7, 308, 310,
    326, 328, *330–3*, 334n., 335,346–7, 350,
    355, 359, 401, 436
Tatius, Achilles 6, 235
Tebaldeo 47, 119n., 218, 297
Tekeira 436
Telesilla 133, 386
Telesio 188–9
Teocreno 41, *181–2*, 305
Thallus 13
Themistius 5
Theobaldus 388
Theocritus *3*, 8n., 34n., 48, 54, 220n., 274,
    283, 298, 327, 365, 383, 390–1, 396, 405
Theognis 2–3, 120n.
Theon 149
Theon, Aelius 5
Theophrastus 3, 52, 282, 360
Thucydides 2, 7, 36, 116, 266n., 377, 380
Thuilius 206
Thussanus 140n.
Thyillus 11

Tiberius 11–2., 19, 147n, 187, 365
Tibullus 15, 16n.
Tifernas *91–2*, 102, 143n., 277
Tolomei Claudio 49, 58–9, 75, 191n., 218
    299–300
Tomasini 34n., 45, *267*
Torcigliano 51, *365*, 404
Torelli 355–6
Torresano d'Asola. See Asola.
Toscano, Gio. Matteo 41–2, 180, 195,
    237, 257
Toscano, Matteo 42, 44, 237n., *257–8*
Trapp 60n.
Traversari 5, 35, *85–91*, 95, 98, 143, 386,
    396
Triboles, Demetrius 30
Triclinius 8n.
Trissino 56, 100
Trivisanus 34n.
Tronsarelli 260–1
Tryphon 5
Tullius Geminus 187
Tullius Laureas 11, 24, 147
Turnèbe 373
Turonei 339
Tzetzes, 7, 8n.

Ubaldini 163, 180, 236, 443
Ugoleto 24n., 103
Uhden 164, 414
Urban VIII 44, *261–2*, 267, 373
Urceo Codro 37, 40, 93n., *122–3*, 135,
    138–9, 140n., 246
Usembardus 241n

Valeriano Bolzani 41, 43, 101n., 166n.,
    175–7, 178, 192n., 215, 221–2, 375
Valerius Maximus 13n., 81n.
Valla, Giorgio 175
Valla, Lorenzo *98–9*, 185, 277, 279
Vannetti 54, *435*
Varchi 39, 56, 229, 297, 303, 306n., 313,
    320
Vargas 54, 60n., 72, 430, *436–9*
Varro 12, 22, 202
Vasari 311–2
Vasolli 4n., 41 *208–9*
Vauquelin de la Fresnaye 60n.
Vavasseur 38n., 60n., 70–1, 73, 433
Velius 66, 180, 204, 243n., 274n., *277*,
    278–82, 286, 337, 388, 397
Venatorius 256, 264, 266, 282, *286–9*, 397
Veniero 252, *310*
Vettori, Pier (the elder) 163, *211–2*, 218,
    234
Vettori, Pier (the younger) 369
Vicini 54, 318, *396*
Vida, Girolamo 188
Vida, Hieronimo 349
Vidal 46n.

Villa, Agostino 147
Villa, Angelo Teodoro 405
Vincent of Beauvais 81n.
Vinta 229
Virgil *13*, 20, 48, 109, 132, 246, 272, 278, 280, 282, 337, 378–9
Virtuani 355
Visconti, Ambrogio 196, 210, 203
Visconti, Gian Galeazzo 201
Vittorino 91, 97
Volaterranus (Maffei) 41, 45, 112, *142*, 145, 261n., 278–80, 282, 337, 374–5, 376n., 397
Voltaire 60n., 391, 394, 415–6, 418, 441
Voss 60n., 212n., 373–4

Walther 274n.
Warton, J. 74
Warton, T. 38, 426
Wheler 35n.
Whitney, Geoffrey 203n.
Winshemius 278–80

Wolf, Johann Christian 426
Wolfe, Reginald, 204n.
Wright, 307

Xiphilinus 8n.
Xylander 92, 266

York, Cardinal-Duke of 54, 422
Young 326n.

Zamagna 406, 407n.
Zanetti, Antonmaria 30n., 400–2
Zanetti, Girolamo Francesco 53, *400–2*, 405, 421
Zappi 53, *387*, 400
Zeno, Antonio 139n.
Zenobetti 39, 53, 264, *403*, 426
Zenobius 8
Zerbo 300
Zonares 7
Zosimus 5
Zosimus Thasius 187

CORNELL STUDIES IN ENGLISH

I. A Bibliography of Thomas Gray. CLARK SUTHERLAND NORTHUP. $3.00.

II. The Influence of Horace on the Chief English Poets of the Nineteenth Century. MARY REBECCA THAYER, Ph.D. $1.00.

III. The Dramatic Records of Sir Henry Herbert, Master of the Revels. JOSEPH QUINCY ADAMS. $2.50.

IV. A Geographical Dictionary of Milton. ALLAN H. GILBERT, Ph.D. $3.50.

V. Italian Social Customs of the Sixteenth Century and their Influence on the Literatures of Europe. THOMAS FREDERICK CRANE. $6.00.

VI. The Jonson Allusion-Book, a Collection of Allusions to Ben Jonson from 1597 to 1700. JESSE FRANKLIN BRADLEY, Ph.D., and JOSEPH QUINCY ADAMS. $5.00.

VII. The Ecclesiastical Sonnets of William Wordsworth, a Critical Edition. ABBIE FINDLAY POTTS, Ph.D. $3.00.

VIII. Milton's Theory of Poetry and Fine Art; an Essay; with a Collection of Illustrative Passages from his Works. IDA LANGDON, Ph.D. $2.00.

IX. A Register of Bibliographies of the English Language and Literature. CLARK SUTHERLAND NORTHUP, with Contributions by JOSEPH QUINCY ADAMS and ANDREW KEOGH. $5.00.

X. Plays and Masques at Court during the Reigns of Elizabeth, James, and Charles. MARY SUSAN STEELE, Ph.D. $4.00.

XI. A Bibliography of the Poetics of Aristotle. LANE COOPER and ALFRED GUDEMAN. $2.00.

XII. Milton on Education; the Tractate of Education, edited with an Introduction and Notes, with Supplementary Extracts from Other Writings of Milton. OLIVER MORLEY AINSWORTH, Ph.D. $2.75.

XIII. A Dictionary of Actors and of Other Persons Associated with the Public Representation of Plays in England before 1642. EDWIN NUNGEZER, Ph.D. $5.00.

XIV. Elizabeth Gaskell. GERALD DeWITT SANDERS, Ph.D. $3.50.

XV. The Latin Poems of John Milton, edited with an Introduction, an English Translation, and Notes. WALTER MAC-KELLAR, Ph.D. $3.00.

XVI. Gianfrancesco Pico della Mirandola On the Imagination; the Latin Text, with an Introduction, an English Translation, and Notes. HARRY CAPLAN. $1.00.

XVII. The Poetics of Aristotle in England. MARVIN THEODORE HERRICK, Ph.D. $1.75.

XVIII. The Wits, or, Sport upon Sport. JOHN JAMES ELSON, Ph.D. $4.50.

XIX. The Lost Plays and Masques, 1500-1642. GERTRUDE MARIAN SIBLEY, Ph.D. $2.00.

XX. Goldsmith and His Booksellers. ELIZABETH EATON KENT. $1.25.

XXI. Wordsworth and Reed: The Poet's Correspondence with His American Editor, 1836-1850; and Henry Reed's Account of His Reception at Rydal Mount, London, and Elsewhere in 1854. LESLIE NATHAN BROUGHTON. $3.00.

XXII. Fielding's Theory of the Novel. FREDERICK OLDS BISSELL, Jr., Ph.D. $1.00.

XXIII. The Greek Anthology in Italy to the Year 1800. JAMES HUTTON. $3.00.

XXIV. Walt Whitman in England. HAROLD BLODGETT. $2.50.

XXV. Charles Kingsley. STANLEY E. BALDWIN. $2.50.